X

SHAKESPEARE SURVEY

65

A Midsummer Night's Dream

ADVISORY BOARD

(1) Shakespeare and his Stage
(2) Shakespearian Production
(3) The Man and the Writer
(4) Interpretation
(5) Textual Criticism
(6) The Histories
(7) Style and Language
(8) The Comedies
(9) *Hamlet*
(10) The Roman Plays
(11) The Last Plays (with an index to *Surveys 1–10*)
(12) The Elizabethan Theatre
(13) *King Lear*
(14) Shakespeare and his Contemporaries
(15) The Poems and Music
(16) Shakespeare in the Modern World
(17) Shakespeare in his Own Age
(18) Shakespeare Then Till Now
(19) *Macbeth*
(20) Shakespearian and Other Tragedy
(21) *Othello* (with an index to *Surveys 11–20*)
(22) Aspects of Shakespearian Comedy
(23) Shakespeare's Language
(24) Shakespeare : Theatre Poet
(25) Shakespeare's Problem Plays
(26) Shakespeare's Jacobean Tragedies
(27) Shakespeare's Early Tragedies
(28) Shakespeare and the Ideas of his Time
(29) Shakespeare's Last Plays
(30) *Henry IV* to *Hamlet*
(31) Shakespeare and the Classical World (with an index to *Surveys 21–30*)
(32) The Middle Comedies
(33) *King Lear*
(34) Characterization in Shakespeare

(35) Shakespeare in the Nineteenth Century
(36) Shakespeare in the Twentieth Century
(37) Shakespeare's Earlier Comedies
(38) Shakespeare and History
(39) Shakespeare on Film and Television
(40) Current Approaches to Shakespeare through Language, Text and Theatre
(41) Shakespearian Stages and Staging (with an index to *Surveys 31–40*)
(42) Shakespeare and the Elizabethans
(43) *The Tempest* and After
(44) Shakespeare and Politics
(45) *Hamlet* and its Afterlife
(46) Shakespeare and Sexuality
(47) Playing Places for Shakespeare
(48) Shakespeare and Cultural Exchange
(49) *Romeo and Juliet* and its Afterlife
(50) Shakespeare and Language
(51) Shakespeare in the Eighteenth Century (with an index to *Surveys 41–50*)
(52) Shakespeare and the Globe
(53) Shakespeare and Narrative
(54) Shakespeare and Religions
(55) *King Lear* and its Afterlife
(56) Shakespeare and Comedy
(57) *Macbeth* and its Afterlife
(58) Writing About Shakespeare
(59) Editing Shakespeare
(60) Theatres for Shakespeare
(61) Shakespeare, Sound and Screen
    Shakespeare Survey: A Sixty-Year Cumulative Index
(62) Close Encounters with Shakespeare's Text
(63) Shakespeare's English Histories and their Afterlives
(64) Shakespeare as Cultural Catalyst
(65) *A Midsummer Night's Dream*

Aspects of *Macbeth*
Aspects of *Othello*
Aspects of *Hamlet*
Aspects of *King Lear*
Aspects of Shakespeare's 'Problem Plays'

SHAKESPEARE SURVEY

65

A Midsummer Night's Dream

EDITED BY

PETER HOLLAND

CAMBRIDGE
UNIVERSITY PRESS

CAMBRIDGE UNIVERSITY PRESS
Cambridge, New York, Melbourne, Madrid, Cape Town,
Singapore, São Paulo, Delhi, Mexico City

Cambridge University Press
The Edinburgh Building, Cambridge CB2 8RU, UK

Published in the United States of America by Cambridge University Press, New York

www.cambridge.org
Information on this title: www.cambridge.org/9781107024519

First published 2012

Printed and bound in the United Kingdom by the MPG Books Group

A catalogue record for this publication is available from the British Library

ISBN 978-1-107-02451-9 Hardback

EDITOR'S NOTE

Volume 66, on 'Working with Shakespeare', will be at press by the time this volume appears. The theme of Volume 67 will be 'Shakespeare's Collaborative Plays'.

Submissions should be addressed to the Editor at The Shakespeare Institute, Church Street, Stratford-upon-Avon, Warwickshire CV37 6HP, to arrive at the latest by 1 September 2013 for Volume 67. Pressures on space are heavy and priority is given to articles related to the theme of a particular volume. Please send a copy you do not wish to be returned. Submissions may also be made as attachments to e-mail to pholland@nd.edu. All articles submitted are read by the Editor and at least one member of the Advisory Board, whose indispensable assistance the Editor gratefully acknowledges.

Unless otherwise indicated, Shakespeare quotations and references are keyed to *The Complete Works*, ed. Stanley Wells, Gary Taylor, John Jowett and William Montgomery, 2nd edition (Oxford, 2005).

Review copies should be addressed to the Editor as above. In attempting to survey the ever-increasing bulk of Shakespeare publications our reviewers inevitably have to exercise some selection. We are pleased to receive offprints of articles which help to draw our reviewers' attention to relevant material.

In the current volume, I co-edited the section on the volume's theme, *A Midsummer Night's Dream*, with Stanley Wells. Working with him was, as always, a pleasure and an inspiration and I am most grateful for his assistance.

P.D.H.

CONTRIBUTORS

PASCALE AEBISCHER, University of Exeter
K. E. ATTAR, University of London
LAURA AYDELOTTE, University of Chicago
HELEN BARR, University of Oxford
SIBYLLE BAUMBACH, University of Mainz
ROBERT BEARMAN, Shakespeare Birthplace Trust
JACQUELYN BESSELL, University of Birmingham
TODD BORLIK, Bloomsburg University
CHARLOTTE BREWER, University of Oxford
HENRY BUCHANAN, University of Glasgow
HAL COBB, Shakespeare Behind Bars
BRIAN CUMMINGS, University of York
PAUL EDMONDSON, Shakespeare Birthplace Trust
ANDREW JAMES HARTLEY, University of North Carolina at Charlotte
MICHAEL HATTAWAY, New York University in London
ANDREAS HÖFELE, University of Munich
RUSSELL JACKSON, University of Birmingham
MICHAEL P. JENSEN, Ashland, Oregon
JOHN JOWETT, University of Birmingham
MATT KOZUSKO, Ursinus College
JESSE M. LANDER, University of Notre Dame
LAURA LEVINE, New York University
TOBY MALONE, Toronto
RUSS MCDONALD, Goldsmiths, University of London
CAROL THOMAS NEELY, University of Illinois at Urbana-Champaign
ERIC RASMUSSEN, University of Nevada, Reno
CAROL CHILLINGTON RUTTER, University of Warwick
MICHAEL SAENGER, Southwestern University
CHARLOTTE SCOTT, Goldsmiths, University of London
JAMES SHAW, University of Oxford
MARGARET SHEWRING, University of Warwick
STUART SILLARS, University of Bergen
HOLGER SCHOTT SYME, University of Toronto

LIST OF CONTRIBUTORS

CURT L. TOFTELAND, Shakespeare Behind Bars
MARGARET TUDEAU-CLAYTON, University of Neuchâtel
ROGER WARREN, University of Leicester
ROBERT N. WATSON, University of California, Los Angeles
STANLEY WELLS, Shakespeare Birthplace Trust

CONTENTS

CONTENTS

ILLUSTRATIONS

'A LOCAL HABITATION AND A NAME': THE ORIGINS OF SHAKESPEARE'S OBERON

LAURA AYDELOTTE

'... but the way is so full of yᵉ fayrey & straunge thynges, that such as passe that way are lost, for in that wood abydyth a kynge of yᵉ fayrey namyd Oberon'.[1] So the French knight, Huon de Bordeaux, is warned as he continues his journey in quest of four teeth and a tuft of the beard of Babylon's ruler, Admiral Gaudys. Literary scholars looking at mortals lost in another wood full of fairy and strange things in Shakespeare's *A Midsummer Night's Dream* have long identified Sir John Bourchier, Lord Berners's 1534 English translation of the French romance *Huon de Bordeaux* as the source for two aspects of the fairy king in Shakespeare's play. *Huon* is generally recognized as the source for Oberon's 'local habitation'. That is, it provides the most likely precedent for his location, not only in terms of the wood he abides in when first introduced in both the play and the romance but also his original habitation in an eastern or 'Indian' region.[2] The other widely accepted contribution of *Huon* to *A Midsummer Night's Dream* is the name Oberon itself, which first began to become a popular name for the fairy king in the English tradition with the publication of Berners's translation. However, while these origins of Oberon's name and geographic origins have been cited and mentioned briefly,[3] there has been little space devoted to a serious exploration of the way previous representations of the fairy king Oberon have influenced or been altered by Shakespeare in *Dream*.

This article takes a closer look at the Oberon character in Berners's translation of *Huon de Bordeaux* and at the Oberon of Robert Greene's 1594 play *The Scottish Historie of James the Fourth* as a way of inquiring into the origins of Shakespeare's Oberon. The fairy king of the sources is an often contradictory character, at once a beneficent guide and a darkly powerful threat; a meddlesome trickster and a haughtily detached observer of human affairs. Understanding these mixed origins not only provides new insights into the ways in which Shakespeare's Oberon was shaped by his predecessors but also suggests that certain aspects of Puck's character and the relationship between Puck and Oberon are indebted to the single figure of the fairy king in previous texts. Though ample scholarship has demonstrated that a number of English sources contributed to the character of Puck, I suggest that continental sources are also important for understanding Oberon's assistant, in that Shakespeare shares between Puck and

---

[1] *The Boke of Duke Huon of Burdeux*, trans. Sir John Bourchier, Lord Berners (1534), ed. S. L. Lee (London, 1882–87), p. 62.

[2] Margo Hendricks, '"Obscured by dreams": Race, Empire and *A Midsummer Night's Dream*', *Shakespeare Quarterly*, 47 (1996), 37–60. Hendricks provides the longest critical account of *Huon* as a source for Oberon in a critical passage on his associations with India.

[3] For the more significant mentions of *Huon* as a source for *Dream* see: Lee, ed., *Boke of Duke Huon*, 'Introduction', pp. xlix–li; William Shakespeare, *A Midsummer Night's Dream*, ed. Harold F. Brooks (London, 2004, repr. 2006), pp. lix and lxxxiv; William Shakespeare, *A Midsummer Night's Dream*, ed. Peter Holland (Oxford, 1994, repr. 2008), p. 31; Thomas Moisan, 'Antique Fables, Fairy Toys: Elisions, Allusion, and Translation in *A Midsummer Night's Dream*', in *A Midsummer Night's Dream: Critical Essays*, ed. Dorothea Kehler (New York, 2001).

Oberon many of the features and actions that are assigned to the fairy king alone in earlier sources.

I begin by looking at the provenance of the name Oberon and the many facets of the character of the fairy king that precede his appearance in Shakespeare's play. I then turn to the ways in which Shakespeare adapts these conflicting aspects of the fairy king in the characters of Oberon and Puck. This exploration of Oberon's origins helps to shed light on the question of what 'sort' of spirits they may be. I conclude by looking to Oberon's 'local habitation', or rather his lack thereof, demonstrating that Shakespeare's Oberon, rather than being a fixedly 'Eastern' figure, has a global identity that he owes to the source texts, and that Oberon's mixed geographic origins and shifting location, like his mixed associations with dark and light, are also important for understanding his relationship with Puck and the status as 'wanderer' that the two characters share.

I. OBERON BEFORE *DREAM*

The name 'Oberon' derives from the French name for the fairy king, 'Auberon', which in turn comes directly from the name of the Germanic elf king, 'Alberich'.[4] The line from Alberich to Oberon can be traced, not only through the etymology of the name but through shared narratives, events and features associated with the fairy king as he developed from the medieval Alberich to the Elizabethan Oberon. One common thread between all three incarnations of the fairy king is his association with the East, which I will look at more closely at the end of this article. Another common thread is his position as a matchmaker who assists or interferes with the love matches of mortals. Though Alberich may now be most famous as the dwarf from the *Niebelungenlied* that inspired Wagner's opera cycle, he was also a prominent character in the early thirteenth-century romance, *Ortnit*, in which the diminutive elf king Alberich encounters the hero Ortnit in the woods, where various struggles and trickery ensue between the two of them before Alberich goes on to aid

Ortnit in journeying to Tyre in order to win the hand of the beautiful daughter of Machorel, King of Jerusalem. This basic plot is clearly related to the plotline in *Huon de Bordeaux* in which Auberon aides Huon, not only in retrieving the teeth and beard hairs[5] of the pagan ruler of Babylon, Admiral Gaudys, in order to return with them to Charlemagne and restore his tarnished reputation, but also in winning the Admiral's beautiful daughter, Esclarmonde. Though Shakespeare's Oberon does not provide assistance with the same sort of romantic quest, he nonetheless falls in with a tradition of fairy kings helping mortals to meet their match.

The observation that the fairy king acts as a matchmaker for the humans he encounters may not be very revealing in and of itself, but it does raise the more complex issue of how he interacts with and is viewed by members of the non-fairy world in these narratives. The fairy king is notably a variable character who is alternately represented as dark, threatening and potent and as a light, helpful character, fond of jests and jolly entertainment. Within the Germanic and French romances, this split between a friendly and harmless fairy king and a powerful and fearsome fairy king is most clearly located in his physical appearance. When Ortnit first meets Alberich, he mistakes him for a harmless child, but is quickly put in his place when the dwarf packs a very powerful punch that knocks him flat.[6] The Auberon ('Oberon' in the Berners translation) of *Huon de Bordeaux* is described as 'but of .iii. fote, and crokyd shulderyd, but yet he hathe an aungelyke vysage, so that there is no mortall man that seethe hym but that taketh grete pleasure

---

[4] Lee, ed., *Boke of Duke Huon*, 'Introduction', pp. xxix–xxxi. Lee provides a more extensive account of not only the Germanic but the possible Welsh and Celtic origins of both the name and figure of Oberon the fairy king.

[5] As has been noted elsewhere, this is the probable source for Benedick's reference to 'fetch you a hair off the Great Cham's beard', in *Much Ado About Nothing* (2.1.251), a thing he would rather do than exchange three words with Beatrice.

[6] *Ortnit and Wolfdietrich: Two Medieval Romances*, trans. J. W. Thomas (Columbia, SC, 1986), p. 8.

to beholde his fase'.[7] Later he is referred to as 'the fayrest creature that ever nature formed'.[8]

This seemingly contradictory state of being both a deformed hunchbacked dwarf and the fairest creature formed by nature extends to the contradictory nature of the fairy king's actions in relation to the humans he meets. The figure of Alberich, in *Ortnit* and elsewhere, is certainly the most playful incarnation of the fairy king and relates the most clearly to an impish folklore figure like the English Puck. In *Ortnit* he delights in playing tricks on the pagan emperor and others using his invisibility, and he is frequently a figure of humour and mirth. At the same time he is clearly a figure of great power. His woods have enough of a bad reputation that, when Ortnit returns to the court after spending a few days out in the woods meeting Alberich, everyone has practically given him up for dead. Not only does Alberich display unexpected physical strength but he is able to make whole armies materialize on a whim and aids in the slaughter of huge numbers of pagans in assisting Ortnit to win the woman he desires. There are also several moments when Alberich plays with the boundary between exercising his power or behaving benignly towards Ortnit, such as the occasion of their first meeting when he steals and puts on Ortnit's most prized possession, a magic ring from his mother, uses the ring to turn invisible and taunt and frighten the knight, but then quickly changes his mind and restores the ring to the knight once more along with an offer of friendship.

Shakespeare was unlikely to have known the Alberich of such Germanic legends, but many aspects of the Alberich in *Ortnit* crop up in the source Shakespeare was most likely familiar with in the character of Auberon in *Huon de Bordeaux*. Auberon is a decidedly less humorous character than Alberich, and it is with the Auberon of *Huon* that the fairy king acquires a greater air of gravitas and a noble classical and magical lineage as the child of Julius Caesar and the fairy of the 'privy isle'.[9] All the same, there are distinct traces of the merry trickster Alberich in Auberon, who causes castles and other objects to appear or disappear in the forest in order to trick the senses of the men passing

through and who delights in feasting and entertaining in high style. More importantly, the ambiguity as to whether the fairy king is friendly or fearsome is heightened in *Huon*. The old man who first warns Huon about Auberon first expresses fear of a terrifying magical being who will prevent them from ever leaving the woods again and 'wyll make meruelous tempestes with thonder and lyghtenynges so that it shall seme to you that all the worlde sholde pereshe'.[10] At the same time he indicates that the dwarf's charms are, in fact, impotent and insubstantial. Though Auberon can conjure up 'a grete rynnynge riuer, blacke and depe' before the travellers, still 'ye may passe it at your ease, and it shall not wete the fete of your horse for all is fantesey and enchauntmentes'.[11] Thus Auberon is a figure both potentially terrifying and completely harmless. The great black river suggests a dark and frightening side of the fairy king, while the insubstantiality of that river reduces the ominous dark threat to an almost laughable trick.

This dynamic of fearful threats mixed with harmless illusions continues in the scene when Huon first encounters Auberon. As predicted, angry that Huon and his company will not speak to him because they have been warned of the dangers of doing so,[12] the fairy king not only stirs up terrible storms but also the foreseen dark river before

---

[7] Lee, ed., *Boke of Duke Huon*, p. 63.

[8] Lee, ed., *Boke of Duke Huon*, p. 73. We learn that his short stature and disfigurement are attributable to the curse laid on him by a fairy who didn't receive an invitation to his birth, and that another made it up to him by ensuring that he would be considered the fairest creature on earth. There may or may not be some connection between the short stature of the Oberon figure and the sometimes diminutive descriptions of Shakespeare's fairies.

[9] Lee, ed., *Boke of Duke Huon*, p. 72.

[10] Lee, ed., *Boke of Duke Huon*, p. 64.

[11] Lee, ed., *Boke of Duke Huon*, p. 64.

[12] As Lee points out in his introduction to *Huon de Bordeaux*, p. xxxii, this prohibition of speaking to fairies is one that Shakespeare refers to in *The Merry Wives of Windsor* when Falstaff declares 'They are fairies. He that speaks to them shall die' (5.5.46). It is possible that this detail was inspired by *Huon*, though it was also a widespread folk belief according to Melchiori's note on the line in the Arden edition of *Merry Wives*.

the hapless travellers. Yet his attacks and threats on the knight and his company range from the entertaining, almost comic, when he blows his horn and as a result the men 'hadde no powr to ryde any ferther but they began all to synge', to a serious threat to life and limb when Auberon orders his minions to 'go after them and slee them all, let none escape'.[13] There is a fine line between bloodshed and song until Huon finally speaks to the fairy king and Auberon professes his love and friendship for the hero, placing the fairy king squarely on the side of right.

Indeed, it is worth noting that both the Alberich and Oberon incarnations of the fairy king not only play friendly roles towards humans but they also strongly take the side of right in ensuring that justice is fairly served. Alberich serves more than once to draw attention to wrongs committed in violation of a chivalric code of ethics, as in the instance when Ortnit's uncle kills innocent women in the storming of Tyre,[14] while Auberon confronts Charlemagne in order to prevent him from unjustly hanging Huon, whom the fairy king sets free using his magic powers.[15] Thus the character of the fairy king varies from a seemingly unstable and menacing one to a measured provider of justice.

Before looking at the way the multi-faceted Oberon of *Huon* emerges in Shakespeare's *Dream* it will be useful to look first at the way Oberon entered the English dramatic tradition prior to Shakespeare's play. Not only was Lord Berners's translation of the romance popular enough to have gone through three sixteenth-century editions, but Henslowe notes the performance of a play adaptation entitled *Hewen of Burdoche* in 1593, just a few years before the probable date of *Dream*.[16] That play has unfortunately been lost, but there are a few other significant references to Oberon in the literature immediately preceding *A Midsummer Night's Dream*. One of these is the mention of Oberon in Spenser's *Faerie Queene*, where the sort of noble lineage established for him in *Huon* is both emphasized and given a contemporary political valence when he appears at the end of a long list of the highest lineage in fairy land in the book 'that hight, *Antiquitee of Faery* lond'[17] which Guyon

peruses in Book Two. Oberon is listed as the penultimate figure and father of the fair queen Tanaquill or Glorian, and is a thinly veiled stand-in for Henry VIII.[18]

In addition to this rather lofty use of Oberon's name, the fairy king also appears as a character in a series of rather peculiar choruses or framing scenes in Robert Greene's play, *The Scottish History of James the Fourth* (1594). The Oberon of this play is first depicted in shadowy tones in a graveyard speaking with a man, Bohan, who has chosen to live among the tombs and shun the world of men. While the Oberon of *Huon de Bordeaux* professes that he loves the hero and will help him to make his way in the world by fulfilling his quest, the Oberon of Greene's play introduces himself as 'Oberon, King of Fairies, that loves thee because thou hatest the world'.[19] The theme of the play itself, which the conversations between Oberon and Bohan frame, is about faithless love in which the King of Scotland attempts to kill his wife in order to take another woman as his lover, and Oberon's role in the play, rather than one of helpful matchmaker, like that of the Oberon and his predecessor Alberich in the romances, is one of detached and wryly amused observer as he watches the story of lust and betrayal unfold.

Yet, despite the darker overtones of the graveyard setting and his approval of Bohan's hatred of the world in response to the story of love gone dangerously awry which Bohan presents to the fairy king, Greene's Oberon seems concerned that he make clear that 'Oberon is king / Of quiet,

---

[13] Lee, ed., *Boke of Duke Huon*, p. 70.

[14] *Ortnit*, p. 24.

[15] Lee, ed., *Boke of Duke Huon*, pp. 258–9.

[16] *Henslowe's Diary*, ed. Walter W. Greg (London, 1904), p. 16. For a succinct account of the many variations of the text of *Huon de Bordeaux* and its English publication, see Michael Murrin, 'Huon at the Castle of Adamant', *Modern Philology*, 100 (2003), 552–5.

[17] Edmund Spenser, *The Faerie Queene*, ed. A. C. Hamilton (London, 2003), II.ix.60.

[18] Spenser, *Faerie Queene*, II.x.75. Oberon is also mentioned in connection with Huon at II.i.6.

[19] Robert Greene, *The Scottish Historie of James the Fourth* (London, 1970), Induction, 76.

pleasure, profit, and content.'[20] Just as the Auberon of *Huon* saves the hero from an unjust hanging, so Greene's Oberon similarly saves the foolish clown, Slipper, from the noose, and thus functions to see that justice is served and the most blatantly comic character of the play does not meet a tragic end. He also harkens back to the humour and delight in trickery and illusion that we have already seen with Alberich and the Auberon of *Huon de Bordeaux*, but rather than making castles and rivers appear and disappear or entertaining knights with an elaborate banquet, as Auberon does in *Huon*, Greene's Oberon resorts frequently to putting on dances, 'jigs' and dumb shows intended to amaze and entertain both himself and his companion Bohan. In one notable moment Oberon turns from the main action of the play and comments 'Here see I good fond actions in thy jig, / And means to paint the world's inconstant ways; / But turn thine eyen, see which I command.'[21] What follows is a dumb enactment of Semiramis in battle, with some brief explanation of how she fought after the death of Ninus and how her overthrow depicts the vanity of 'worldly pompe'. This portrayal of classical tragedy is presented and viewed with the same sort of detachment as the amusing dancing of the comic relief character Slipper and his brother the dwarf earlier in the play, and there is a very distinct sense in this scene of yet another Oberon character for whom the line between song and bloodshed is a relatively thin one.

Oberon's presentation of a 'jig' or brief entertainment alluding to Ninus and Semiramis in Greene's play may remind readers of the mechanicals' attempts in *A Midsummer Night's Dream* to present their scene at 'Ninny's tomb' (3.1.91) and is certainly a similarly incongruous – though significantly less sophisticated – presentation of a traditionally tragic scene in an over the top context.[22] More notably, Oberon's expression of approval of and interest in the 'fond actions', the errors and foibles of love and politics presented in Greene's play, mirrors Puck's well-known utterance at the prospect of watching the errors and foibles of the four lovers in *Dream*: 'Shall we their fond pageant see? Lord, what fools these mortals be!' Thus, in

the earliest existing appearance of Oberon on the English stage, he is already associated with the position of a spectator of 'fond' mortals and a certain amusement or light attitude towards the potentially ruinous aspects of love and life among men and women.

2. PUCK AND OBERON

As we have seen, by the time Shakespeare began writing his own depiction of the fairy king in *Dream* the figure of Oberon had amassed a character of varied and even apparently conflicting facets – from his origins as a trickster dwarf to his more serious and noble but still changeful character in *Huon de Bordeaux*, to his role as detached observer in Greene's play. The fine line between malice and benevolence, between dark associations and a position as an arbiter of justice that has emerged from a close look at the precedents for Shakespeare's Oberon is readily apparent in the presentation of the fairy king in *Dream*. As Michael Taylor has suggested, this is an essential but sometimes overlooked dynamic in the play:

An awareness of the fairies' delightfulness, however, should not blind us to the suggestion of equivocation in their presentation. There seem to be fine lines drawn between fragile charm, impish mischief and trivial malice.[23]

Indeed, there is not a clear cut answer to the question of exactly how dark or shady the 'king of shadows' (3.2.348), as Puck terms Oberon, is meant to be.

---

[20] Greene, *Scottish Historie*, Chorus I, 4–5.

[21] Greene, *Scottish Historie*, Chorus VI, 1–3.

[22] Whether Greene's mention of Ninus could have had any influence on Shakespeare's mentions of Ninus's tomb would be a matter of conjecture; however, the connection of such a scene with the term 'jig' in Greene's play might be interesting in light of C. L. Barber's conjecture that the Pyramus and Thisbe play in *Dream* could be considered a developed jig, a suggestion which Peter Holland highlights for consideration in the Oxford Classics edition of the play. See C. L. Barber, *Shakespeare's Festive Comedy* (Princeton, 1959), p. 154, n. 25; Holland, 'Introduction', p. 92.

[23] Michael Taylor, 'The Darker Purpose of *A Midsummer Night's Dream*', *Studies in English Literature*, 9 (1969), 259–73.

Shakespeare's Oberon is a potent king of the fairies, and we learn during his first encounter with Titania that in his anger, like the angry Oberon of *Huon de Bordeaux*, he has the power to affect the weather, causing killing fogs to creep up over the land until 'The seasons alter: hoary-headed frosts / Fall in the fresh lap of the crimson rose' (2.1.107–8) and, as Brooks notes, Oberon's command to Puck, 'overcast the night; / The starry welkin cover thou anon / With drooping fog as black as Acheron' (3.2.356–8) is reminiscent of Oberon's power in *Huon* to conjure the black river in order to frustrate and control those wandering in his woods.[24]

So Shakespeare's Oberon shares a darker cast with previous depictions of the fairy king, and he also shares with them a mischievous edge that leads, among other things, to the trick he plays on Titania and Bottom. What is different, however, about Shakespeare's fairy king is that he works as a part of a team in which many of the darker or more mischievous motives and actions are delegated and attributed to Puck, even if some of them may originate as Oberon's own ideas. The two characters spend a considerable amount of time on-stage together, almost acting as one character at times. Puck's role, though it doubtless owes much to English origins, looks back to the roots of Oberon's character in the trickster dwarf Alberich, parts of which still lingered in the representations of the fairy king in *Huon de Bordeaux*. Puck serves as the character to whom Oberon can delegate the task of fooling his wife and having fun with the mortals, things he wishes to happen and is entertained by but does not do himself. Puck is also the character to whom Shakespeare as a dramatist can delegate the task of being the one to make the errors and the injudicious moves that engender much of the humour and the mishap in the play while Oberon the fairy king can come in as the reassuring figure of temperance and justice who straightens everything out in the end.

This dynamic between the two characters is most evident in the two speeches that address the issue of just what sort of shadows the fairies of the play really are. Puck first urges Oberon to make haste so that they can finish their work by daylight:

My fairy lord, this must be done with haste,
For night's swift dragons cut the clouds full fast,
And yonder shines Aurora's harbinger,
At whose approach ghosts, wand'ring here and there,
Troop home to churchyards; damnèd spirits all . . .
Already to their wormy beds are gone,

(3.2.379–85)

In an often quoted passage Oberon responds by claiming, as the Oberon of Huon and of Greene's *Scottish History* also do, that he is not an unsavoury sort of fairy tied up with night and black magic:

But we are spirits of another sort,
I with the morning's love have oft made sport,
And like a forester the groves may tread
Even till the eastern gate, all fiery red,
Opening on Neptune with fair blessèd beams
Turns into yellow gold his salt green streams.

(3.2.389–94)

Oberon's defence is that they are not bound by the night and he thus attempts to distance himself from any association with damned spirits.[25] Here Puck is the one who injects a darker tone, just as when we first meet him he introduces a mildly dark humour when he describes his enjoyment in playing tricks on people by pulling stools out from under a woman, or spilling a gossip's drink. Puck is also the one elsewhere in the play who, though surely not a 'damned spirit' like the ghosts 'wand'ring here and there', still acts as the 'merry wanderer of the night'. He is the one who creates the majority of the trouble and unrest in the play, frightening the mechanicals with Bottom's transformation and causing the misunderstanding that creates the argument between the lovers which has the potential to become dangerous when they come to fight. Oberon, in contrast, plays the role, as he does

---

[24] See note in the Arden edition, ed. Brooks.

[25] In addition to the association of the Oberon in Greene's *Scottish History* with tombs, Katharine M. Briggs found one mention of a name similar to Oberon before Berners's translation of *Huon de Bordeaux*, a magician who was supposed to have conjured a spirit named 'Oberion', indicating that it is possible that this speech is intended to dispel any such old associations. *The Anatomy of Puck* (London, 1959), p. 114 and Appendix IV, pp. 255–61.

in much of the play, of the fairy king correcting the darker impulses and descriptions of his servant while he himself supplies an image of a 'spirit of another sort' cavorting with the golden dawn and bringing order. David Bevington has commented on this dynamic, connecting it with potentially violent or darker tensions within the play as a whole: 'This debate between Oberon and Puck reflects a fundamental tension in the play between comic reassurance and the suggestion of something dark and threatening.'[26] What is revealing about viewing this 'debate' between Oberon and Puck in light of previous representations of Oberon is that it suggests the way many of the features that Shakespeare brings out in these two characters originated in the many characteristics of a single character, that of Oberon the fairy king. The multiple aspects of Oberon's character are still present in Shakespeare's Oberon but the addition of the Puck character allows a dialogue to open up between the two, which in turn enables Oberon to distance himself from traits he wants to downplay, such as his darker tendencies or his less dignified desires to play tricks on people or otherwise interfere with human affairs. It also enables him to indulge certain less justifiable desires, such as the desire to get the better of Titania in their quarrel, while allowing Puck to take the credit and the blame for the humour and the misfortune he occasions.

3. GLOBETROTTING FAIRIES

Though he makes much of being able to frolic with the dawn, Oberon does, in fact, seem to be a creature mostly tied to the night. After the four lovers have been arranged appropriately he and Titania agree that they will return the next night for the nuptials of Theseus and Hippolyta but that in the meantime they will now depart:

> Trip we after nightës shade.
> We the globe can compass soon,
> Swifter than the wand'ring moon.
>
> (4.1.95–7)

The implication is that they must go with the passing of this night and return with the next, following

the orbit of the moon's sphere. The comparative 'swifter' suggests something akin to Oberon's boast that he is able to stay and flirt with the dawn. It also nicely implies a hastening of time whereby Oberon and Titania can push the boundaries of the night itself just as the time of the play will move us into the following night swifter than the time it would really take the moon to travel back again.[27]

This implied hastening or collapse of time also indicates a collapse of space or a hastening through space to new lands. Oberon and his queen are not only following the night but they are going to compass the globe, presumably following wherever night falls. If this is the case, then Shakespeare's Oberon is not only a figure who originates in the East or in 'Inde' but he visits that clime regularly as he follows the night around the globe, and the association with the East is one that he shares with previous incarnations of the fairy king as well. The Oberon of *Huon de Bordeaux* clearly resides in the East in his city of Momure, not far from the spot where he meets the knight Huon a few days' ride from Jerusalem and claims to be the son of Caesar and to have close family ties to a king of Egypt and Alexander the Great.[28] The Oberon mentioned in Spenser's *Faerie Queene* is listed as the end of a line that begins with Elfin whom 'all India obeyed / And all that now America men call'.[29]

Margo Hendricks notes these eastern origins for the previous incarnations of Oberon and also suggests that the Oberon of Greene's *Scottish History of*

---

[26] David Bevington, '"But We Are Spirits of Another Sort": The Dark Side of Love and Magic in *A Midsummer Night's Dream*', *Medieval and Renaissance Studies*, 13 (1975), 80–92. One impetus for Bevington's article is a response to the dark and violent reading of the play by Jan Kott, which, I tend to agree with Bevington and others, is too extreme a view of the play's delicately handled darker threads. Jan Kott, *Shakespeare Our Contemporary*, trans. Boleslaw Taborski (New York, 1964).

[27] There are other echoes of this line in Hippolyta's opening speech, 1.1.7–11 and in the boast of the fairy who first speaks with Puck: 'I do wander everywhere / Swifter than the moonës sphere' (2.1.6–7).

[28] Lee, ed., *Boke of Duke Huon*, p. 74.

[29] Spenser, *Faerie Queene*, II.x.72.5–6.

James the Fourth is similarly tied to the East because he presents dumb shows depicting the Assyrian queen, Semiramis and other eastern figures, such as Cyrus of Persia. Hendricks claims that: 'Whether he appears in England, Scotland, or the outskirts of Jerusalem, Oberon enters each locale as an already "localised" (thus ethnic) entity.'[30] Though Hendricks is right in indicating that the East and India are important locations for each of these presentations of Oberon, her claim for Oberon as a consistently 'localized' figure misses the fact that he becomes increasingly less 'localized', less easy to pin down to a specific spot across the sources. The identity of an eastern other is still in play for the Oberon of Shakespeare's *Dream*, but in a very different way from that in play for the Auberon of *Huon*.

As noted above, the Oberon of *Huon de Bordeaux* has a specifically named eastern habitation in the city of Momure. He does travel, usually employing magic to go directly from one spot to another, whether from place to place in the Middle East, or from his homeland to France, in order to intervene directly in the affairs of mortal men. The narrative of the *Huon* romance is also very much one of the Western knight visiting the Eastern realm, with the visits from the Eastern Oberon being a result of that journey. However, even by the time Oberon is mentioned in Spenser, this dynamic has changed. Now, rather than Oberon being a fairy king clearly resident in the East, he is the descendent of Elfin who is ruler not only of India, but also of the Americas. Oberon himself is associated with the lineage of Spenser's Faerie Land, a realm that both places him in a literary and imaginary space, and allegorically connects him to the Tudor monarchy of England.[31] The Oberon of Greene's play, despite the fact that his choice of subject for his dumb show may indicate some tie to the East, in fact resists any regional label, declaring himself 'of all the world / Tied to no place, though all are tied to me'.[32] Nowhere in the play is any particular place of origin specified for Greene's Oberon, so there is no reason to question his self-definition as a citizen of the world, not localized in any way. The Oberon of Greene's play is additionally 'tied

to no place' even in terms of his location in the play. Within the play's setting Oberon and Bohan occupy the space of the graveyard separate from the action of the court, a nebulous place on the border between the living and the dead where they can philosophize about the tragic or foolish actions of the play's characters. Textually speaking, they also occupy the series of choruses that exist outside the main narrative, in a sense again 'tied to no place' and quite unlike the place of the Auberon in *Huon* who is located in a specified destination central to the narrative of the romance.

The fly-by-night compassing of the globe undertaken by Oberon and Titania in Shakespeare's *Dream* is also very unlike the Auberon of *Huon* and more like the Oberon of Greene's play, tied to no place in the world. Rather than having any clear 'habitation' in either India or the woods outside Athens, Oberon and his queen are travellers between and through these and perhaps other places as well. Like the graveyard in which the Oberon of *The Scottish History* appears, Oberon and his fellow fairies in *Dream* also inhabit the forest as a space separate, transitional and ill-defined – difficult to tie down but for its opposition to the world of Theseus's court.

This lack of 'local habitation' is a characteristic shared by other fairies in the play, and one which again ties Oberon and Puck closely together. Oberon's declaration in Act 4 that he and Titania will compass the globe 'swifter than the wand'ring moon' echoes lines from the first speech by an anonymous fairy in Act 2, scene 1:

> Over hill, over dale,
>   Thorough bush, thorough brier,
> Over park, over pale,

---

[30] Hendricks, 'Obscured by Dreams', 48.

[31] R. W. Desai, in his response to Hendricks, similarly points out that Oberon's ancestor is 'an ideal ruler who is the founder of England's royal line', and that this problematizes readings of the passage that seek to place it in an imperialist framework. 'England, the Indian Boy, and the Spice Trade in *A Midsummer Night's Dream*', in *India's Shakespeare* (Newark, 2005).

[32] Greene, *Scottish History*, Chorus I, lines 6–7.

Thorough flood, thorough fire:
I do wander everywhere
Swifter than the moonës sphere . . . (2.1.2–7)

Thus, from the very beginning, the fairy world is defined as one inhabited by moving creatures, unfixed, outpacing the moon in their global flight, and wandering 'everywhere' while belonging nowhere. The term 'wander', which the fairy repeats in applying it to himself when he answer's Puck's initial query 'Wither wander you?' appears again when Puck describes himself as 'that merry wanderer of the night'. In Oberon's description of himself travelling, ever tripping 'after nightës shade', he would seem to have a close connection with his assistant Puck as a fellow wanderer of the night, despite his protests being 'of another sort'. Indeed, in addition to its relation to 'Auberon' and 'Alberich', the name 'Oberon' has an alternative etymology in the Latin verb *oberrare*, 'to wander'.

Yet, despite its marked similarity to the first fairy's description of travelling faster than the moon, Oberon alters the description of his own travels so that it is not himself but the moon which is 'wand'ring', thus subtly suggesting that the fault lies not in himself but in the stars. Just as the errors of the fairy king – the tricks and slips and mistakes – are deflected onto Puck while Oberon emerges as the potent figure who sets everything right in the end, so the fairy king's errant ways are also deflected, making Puck and the other fairies the wanderers of the play; even the moon is a wanderer, while Oberon emphasizes his own power to circle the globe rather than his nightly position as wanderer.[33]

Oberon is able to use Puck as a proxy for the actions of his own darker or less regulated impulses, and also as the intermediary between the fairy and the human world. This allows him to maintain a distance and separation between himself and the non-fairy world he influences. At the same time it is unclear exactly where the alternative to the real world, the fairy land of the play is located. It seems to be a part of the wood in Athens, but also somewhere in India. It contains features like those of an English wood. One critic has suggested that the woods outside Athens in *Dream* can be viewed as a heterotopia in Foucault's sense of the term.[34] If the woods do function to some extent as a kind of through-the-looking-glass counterpart to the many different social sites of the play's Athens, or even to various sites in Shakespeare's historical world, they do so also as a heterotopia in the much simpler sense of representing many places at once. Shakespeare's Oberon, in his compassing of the globe and his multi-regional associations, exploits the power of being tied to no place suggested by the Oberon of *The Scottish History*.

This sense of Oberon's detachment from a particular place partly suggests what R. W. Desai, in his criticism of what he sees as Margo Hendricks' over-reliance on a post-imperialist view of India in *Dream,* calls an era 'when Elfin, king of the fairies, ruled three dominions – India, Britain, and America – with equal justice and impartiality'.[35] This is not to say that many of the issues that Hendricks raises – race, exoticism, otherness – play no part in the references to India in *Dream*, but that, rather than setting up a dynamic based on imperial power or a direct struggle between East and West, the play creates a realm in which both East and West exist within the same sphere. It is uncertain where the power over this global, overlapping realm lies. It is a place continually explored by the wandering fairies but never fully defined or controlled. Just as Oberon is from both every place and no place, he exerts his power over both every

---

[33] In light of the way he refuses to describe himself as a 'wanderer', Oberon's response to Puck defining them as 'spirits of another sort' could be read as partly a defensive distancing from the ghosts 'wand'ring here and there' that Puck describes (3.2.382–9).

[34] Laurel Moffatt, 'The Woods as Heterotopia in *A Midsummer Night's Dream*', *Studia Neophilologica*, 76 (2004), 182–7. Moffatt quotes Foucault's definition of heterotopias as real places that function 'like counter-sites, a kind of effectively enacted utopia in which the real sites, all the other real sites that can found within the culture, are simultaneously represented, contested, and inverted'.

[35] Desai, 'England, the Indian Boy', p. 142.

place in the shadows of the night and, with the rising of the sun, no place at all.

In comparing the fairy realm of Spenser's *Faerie Queene* with the *Huon de Bordeaux* romance and others, Michael Murrin has suggested that Spenser makes a break from the realm of story to that of allegory when he makes a break with previous romantic tradition by ceasing to make clear how fairyland exists continuously in our world with 'precise itineraries and geographical locations for Eastern adventures'. Time and space become vague and he 'drops the normal world from his plot'.[36] It is, according to Murrin, at least partly due to this vagueness of time and space and discontinuity with the geography of the real world that Spenser's poem can become an allegorical mirror for Spenser's England and the West and which led to Coleridge's equation of 'fairyland with mental space independent of all particular space and time'.[37] Shakespeare does not go quite so far as Spenser in dropping the 'normal world', which is still a marked part of the play in the world of the court at Athens, but he does isolate his fairy king from any direct interaction with the 'real' world of the play, placing him in a geographically indeterminate space constantly in flux between East and West, as he and Titania themselves seem to be in their nightly circling of the globe.

We have now seen the way Shakespeare shaped and altered his sources in *Huon de Bordeaux* and related texts with regard to both Oberon's character and his geographic location. In both cases Shakespeare has multiplied what was present in the original. The single character of the fairy king becomes a partnership between Oberon and Puck, while the single and readily identifiable habitation of that fairy king in the East becomes an amorphous amalgam of Athens, England, India and the hard-to-define fairy realm. However, these changes are each to different effect. The reattribution of some of Oberon's attributes in the source texts to Puck unbraids some of the complexity and contradictions of the earlier fairy kings and allocates Oberon's positions as merry trickster and potent authority to two different figures. The multiplying of places, on the other hand, creates

increased complexity. Shakespeare's changes create a more manageable, streamlined set of characters but a more uncontrolled sense of place.

Why did Shakespeare go to the trouble of unravelling and repositioning the different strands that made up the earlier Au/Oberon? Why would the playwright have chosen to increase the stability of Oberon as a character by assigning his mischievous parts to his sidekick Puck? Why would he transform his Oberon into a more unstable global figure perpetually on the go rather than simply assign him a home in an eastern city like the Auberon of the romance? There are many possible ways of answering these questions. One straightforward answer to the last question is that Shakespeare wanted *Dream* to be, at least in the fairy portion, an international play, one that encompassed a range of places and brought together all the various associations attending on those places. As such, there might be fruitful future avenues of inquiry into the way an international *Dream* could be compared with other plays, such as *The Tempest* in which the play's location also evokes a range of potential geographic locales, from the Americas to Africa to India.

Within *Dream* itself one potential way to read the decision to separate and distil the parts of Au/Oberon's character into the Oberon/Puck pair while at the same time emphasizing the global and wandering nature of the fairies is in terms of how this allows the play to make a subtle statement about worldly power. As we have seen, the deflection of the fairy king's trickster nature and less seemly and dignified characteristics onto the character Puck, allows the Oberon of *Dream* to maintain control over his self-presentation as both a noble and potent figure. The changes from the source texts allow Shakespeare to present an Oberon who can preserve a stable and firm presence as the mastermind who ensures that everything comes out right in the end while using a second character to stir things up and cause the mishaps that help propel the play's plot. The addition of the Puck character also lends

---

[36] Michael Murrin, 'Fairyland', in *The Spenser Encyclopedia*, ed. A. C. Hamilton (Toronto, 1990), pp. 296–8.

[37] Murrin, 'Fairyland', p. 298.

Oberon an air of increased authority by the very fact that he now has an assistant to order around.

At the same time, the control exerted by this seemingly potent fairy king figure is continually undermined by the shifting quality of his habitation. Rather than a king in possession of a particular kingdom in a definable location, Oberon is a wanderer from place to place who cannot choose to stay but apparently must move with the night and the moon. Thus, Shakespeare's changes to his sources serve to emphasize Oberon's authority and status with respect to his relationship with other characters, but then undercut this authority with respect to the status, or rather lack of status, of his habitation. The threat is always present that, as much as Oberon is able to assert his power as a character and to manipulate the outcome in the lives of other characters, the world in which he exerts this power is an unstable one. It is probably no accident that, in the light of the morning after the departure of the fairies, it is Theseus, Oberon's counterpart as male ruler and authority figure in the mortal world, who is concerned with the way a local habitation and a name is based on 'airy nothing'. The thesis of Theseus's speech is that he does not believe in the 'antique fables' or 'fairy toys' created out of this airy nothing. Yet, for the audience who has just experienced the transition from a dramatic world of Oberon and his fairies to the dramatic world of Theseus and his fellow mortals,

it may be abundantly clear that, despite the powerful and contained nature of Oberon's presence as a character, his world, and he along with it, vanished in the winking of an eye and became relegated to the status of a dream remembered on Bottom's waking. Theseus may scoff at the creation of a local habitation and a name out of airy nothing from a sense of insecurity that to recognize the possibility that the 'nothing' once contained a figure like himself with a name and a place in the world of the stage, might also be to recognize that, no matter how potent a character he may be, his own place must in time shift, alter and disappear.

In his adaptation of the Oberon figure Shakespeare creates a more consistent fairy king character (or at least one who can maintain the appearance of consistency by allowing Puck to make the slip-ups); he increases the mutability of this fairy king figure's location, and he then ties both of these to the passing night and the passing of time. The link between place and time in Oberon and Titania's wanderings of the globe produces a world that shifts and vanishes. The relocation of the instability from Oberon's character to Oberon's habitations allows Shakespeare to demonstrate the way in which even the most potent and seemingly stable figure ultimately has no permanent place in the world, no place that will not, along with himself and his powers, be transformed to something 'no more yielding than a dream' (Ep. 6).

'WRINKLED DEEP IN TIME': EMILY AND ARCITE IN *A MIDSUMMER NIGHT'S DREAM*

HELEN BARR

When Theseus is offered the show of a drunken mob of women tearing the poet Orpheus limb from limb for his nuptial celebrations he dismisses it thus:

> That is an old device, and it was played
> When I from Thebes came last a conqueror.
> (*A Midsummer Night's Dream*, 5.1.50–1)[1]

How old and when? Theseus's allusion to his own backstory presents a temporal puzzle. In Chaucer's *The Knight's Tale*, Theseus returns in triumph from his conquest of Thebes, *after* he has married his Amazonian bride Hippolyta. In *Two Noble Kinsmen*, he interrupts his wedding (at what point in the play it happens is unclear) to wage war against Thebes *before* he returns to Athens with the two knights Palamon and Arcite he has taken prisoner. How, in *A Midsummer Night's Dream*, can Theseus already have witnessed a worn celebration in honour of his last victory against Thebes when his marriage to Hippolyta is not yet a day old? This long since event ought not yet to have happened. In the 'past source' of *The Knight's Tale* and the 'play yet to be written' that is *Two Noble Kinsmen*, Theseus's conquest of Thebes, foretold as past in *A Midsummer Night's Dream*, is plot-crucially present, along with its catastrophic aftermath.[2]

Theseus's faux-casual dismissal of the frenzied Maenads is a 'wrinkle, or fold in time' in the story of *A Midsummer Night's Dream*. It is, as Paul Strohm says of Petrarch's sonnet in Chaucer's *Troilus and Criseyde*, 'a doubling back or superimposition; a nonsynchronous intimation of past and future at the heart of the present'.[3] It contains a prediction, a hint, of the not-yet thing that has already occurred. This article argues that *A Midsummer Night's Dream* contains the story that was *The Knight's Tale* and the story it will have been: *Two Noble Kinsmen*. It contains them in both senses, for it is imperative that *A Midsummer Night's Dream* does not fully tell the story to which it keeps alluding.[4]

If Theseus has already conquered Thebes in *A Midsummer Night's Dream*, then where are his prisoners, Palamon and Arcite? And where too,

---

I thank Emma Smith and Paul Strohm for reading earlier drafts of this work, and for their invaluable feedback.

[1] In *Two Noble Kinsmen* the Jailer's Daughter's fantasy about the sexual threat posed by Palamon's imagined four hundred children; '[t]hey must be all gelt for musicians / And sing the wars of Theseus' (4.1.131–2), is also out of sync with the time-scheme of the play.

[2] Chaucer's *Knight's Tale* provides the chief source for *Two Noble Kinsmen*, while it is one of the Chaucerian 'elements' in composite sources for *A Midsummer Night's Dream*: Shakespeare, *A Midsummer Night's Dream*, ed. Harold F. Brooks (London, 1979), p. lviii; Ann Thompson, *Shakespeare's Chaucer; A Study in Literary Origins* (Liverpool, 1978), pp. 88–92 and Helen Cooper, *Shakespeare and the Medieval World* (London, 2010), pp. 211–19. Both Thompson and Cooper note Chaucerian influences on *Dream* beyond *The Knight's Tale*.

[3] Paul Strohm, 'Chaucer's *Troilus* as Temporal Archive', in *Theory and the Premodern Text* (Minneapolis, 2000), p. 91.

[4] There are parallels here (though inflected with a different temporality) to ways in which *A Midsummer Night's Dream*, through the naming of Theseus, brings the whole baggage of his notorious classical history into the play: see Peter Holland, 'Theseus's Shadows in *Dream*', *Shakespeare Survey* 47 (Cambridge, 1994), pp. 139–52 and Laurie Maguire, *Shakespeare's Names* (Oxford, 2007), pp. 78–90.

is Emelye, Hippolyta's sister?[5] 'We are not here' says Quince/Prologue (5.1.115). But the craftsmen are 'here' at Theseus's court, both as 'themselves' and the parts that they 'present/disfigure' (3.1.56). Differently, and yet likewise, Palamon, Arcite and Emelye are 'here' in *A Midsummer Night's Dream*; their parts in *The Knight's Tale* and *Two Noble Kinsmen* enfolded between Theseus's first worded 'Now' and the 'amends' (Amen/ends) with which *A Midsummer Night's Dream* 'properly' concludes.[6] While previous studies of the relationships between *A Midsummer Night's Dream*, *The Knight's Tale* and *Two Noble Kinsmen* have produced some dizzying textual intercourse[7] which perforate their temporal boundaries, the sequence of their composition is left largely intact: *The Knight's Tale* begets *Dream* begets *Two Noble Kinsmen*.[8] What I propose here, chiefly by examining the roles of Emelye and Arcite, is an intervention into the relationships of these plays that disobeys linear chronology. If we disaggregate the temporalities of *Dream* we reveal its stories of Emelye and Arcite that are predicted in *Two Noble Kinsmen* by the story that *The Knight's Tale* itself contains. Emelye and Arcite are always already 'here' in *Dream*.

EMILY[9]

It is well known that time in *Dream* doesn't submit to arithmetic. References to the moon don't add up. At the start of the play it is waning four days off its end, and yet when Quince consults his almanac in the wood (3.1.43–54), he triumphantly tells the craftsmen that the moon will shine brightly enough on the night of their performance to illuminate their play through an open casement window. The 'four days' which Theseus wishes to hurry in order to consummate his marriage unaccountably shrink to a single night.[10] Theseus may be determined to tell the time: '[n]ow' is his first word, but the present is not his to determine. Hippolyta immediately contradicts his observation that the moon's time is 'slow'; her reiterated 'quickly' stages early opposition to Theseus's version of events.[11] Midsummer is the season of the year suggested by the play's title, but Theseus, on finding the lovers asleep

in the wood in Act 4 remarks, '[n]o doubt they rose up early to observe / The rite of May' (4.1.131–2). His quip at the expense of the lovers betrays the fragility of his own hold over time. His reference to May wrinkles the temporality of *The Knight's Tale* and *Two Noble Kinsmen* into *Dream*. In *The Knight's Tale*, May is the month when Palamon and Arcite

---

[5] What is not now clear is the extent to which Richard Edwards's *Palamon and Arcite* (premièred at Oxford 1566) and now lost, could have been used as source material for both *A Midsummer Night's Dream* and *Two Noble Kinsmen*. Also now lost is the 1594 *Palamon and Arcite*. See Thompson, *Shakespeare's Chaucer*, p. 17; Cooper, *Shakespeare and the Medieval World*, pp. 208–11.

[6] Nicolas Tredell, *Shakespeare: A Midsummer Night's Dream: A Reader's Guide to Essential Criticism* (London, 2010), draws attention to the framing of the play between 'now' and 'ends', p. 1. (The 'Amen' is my own.)

[7] Jeffrey Masten, *Textual Intercourse: Collaboration, Authorship and Sexualities in Renaissance Drama* (Cambridge, 1997), pp. 42–55.

[8] See, for example, E. Talbot Donaldson, *The Swan and the Well: Shakespeare Reading Chaucer* (New Haven and London, 1985); Susan Green, 'A mad woman? We are made boys! The Jailer's Daughter in *Two Noble Kinsmen*', in *Shakespeare, Fletcher and the Two Noble Kinsmen*, ed. Charles H. Frey (Columbia, 1989), pp. 121–32; Alan Sinfield, 'Cultural Materialism and Intertextuality: The Limits of Queer Reading in *A Midsummer Night's Dream* and *Two Noble Kinsmen*', *Shakespeare Survey 56* (Cambridge, 2003), pp. 67–78; Hugh Richmond, 'Performance as Criticism: *Two Noble Kinsmen*', in Frey, *Shakespeare, Fletcher*, pp. 163–85; Helen Cooper, 'Jacobean Chaucer: *Two Noble Kinsmen* and Other Chaucerian Plays', in Theresa M. Krier, ed., *Refiguring Chaucer in the Renaissance* (Gainsville, 1998), pp. 189–209; Glynne Wickham, '*Two Noble Kinsmen* or *A Midsummer Night's Dream*, Part II?', *The Elizabethan Theatre VII*, ed. G. R. Hibbard (Ontario, 1980), pp. 167–96, and James R. Andreas, 'Remythologising *The Knight's Tale*: *A Midsummer Night's Dream* and *Two Noble Kinsmen*', *Shakespeare Yearbook*, 2 (1991), 49–68.

[9] I use the name Emily when I refer both to Emelye in *The Knight's Tale* and Emilia in *Two Noble Kinsmen*. If referring to each character in their respective works, the difference of spelling distinguishes them.

[10] Helen Hackett, *William Shakespeare: A Midsummer Night's Dream* (Plymouth, 1997), pp. 10, 14. Richard Wilson, 'The Kindly Ones: The Death of the Author in Shakespearean Athens', in *A Midsummer Night's Dream*, ed. Richard Dutton (London, 1996), p. 208.

[11] Philip C. McGuire, *Speechless Dialect: Shakespeare's Open Silences* (Berkeley, 1985), pp. 2–4.

fall fatally in love with the same woman, and it is May when Palamon and Arcite are discovered by Theseus fighting in the grove. In *Two Noble Kinsmen*, the rites of May are dramatized on stage; with Emilia at the heart of their festivities and strife. May, according to Arcite:

> is a solemn rite
> . . . and the Athenians pay it
> To th' heart of ceremony. O, Queen Emilia,
> Fresher than May, sweeter
> Than her gold buttons on the boughs . . .   (3.1.2–6)

May is a metonym for Emily,[12] for violence between men, and for impediment to arranged marriage. Theseus's temporal slip folds the trouble of Emily into *Dream*: Hippolyta's sister becomes available to the play's temporal imagination. In *The Knight's Tale*, Emelye is inseparable from Hippolyta: where Hippolyta appears, 'and Emelye' is next in line.[13] As in *Two Noble Kinsmen*, Emelye and Hippolyta attend Theseus when he catches Arcite and Palamon fighting. With Emily present, the wood contains violence between two men over one woman, so when Theseus finds the four lovers asleep on the ground of the wood in *Dream*, their love-triangles straightened into two neat pairs; he presumptuously and hastily directs them into marriage.[14] For the normative – and dynastic – couplings in *Dream* to work, Emily must be prevented. That is, she must be both stopped and seen coming. Her presence is rendered impossible by the exigencies of the plot of *Dream*, but her absence is supplied by familiarity with the story of the *Knight's Tale*. Once known, a recollection of Emily presents her role in the plot of *Dream* in which she must not be seen. But Theseus's attempts to rule time in *Dream*, to speed over what prevents his purpose, are overridden by the play's polysynchronicity. Neither Theseus, nor *Dream*, can define the play's own moment; its variable 'now' unfolds future and past 'Emilys' inside its bounds.

Two Noble Kinsmen, *Dream* and *The Knight's Tale* are intratemporal; they contain each other's stories. Like Theseus, Chaucer's Knight prevents them. This is how he introduces the temple of Diana:

> Now to the temple of Dyane the chaste
> As shortly as I kan, I wol me haste,
> To telle yow al the descripsioun.   (2051–3)

> Ther saugh I many another wonder storie,
> The which me list nat drawen to memorie.
>   (2073–4)

His reluctance to tell us what he sees introduces a scenario absent from the *Teseida*, the story from which his narration is supposed to be drawn,[15] but present in the story of *Two Noble Kinsmen* and *Dream*. He tells us he sees Diana in the temple, seated high on a hart, dogs at her feet, and underneath them a moon: 'wexynge it was and sholde wanye soone' (2079). He sees a series of lovers forced into sex against their will, all metamorphosed into something else, including Daphne, following her ordeal with Apollo. And he sees Lucina, Diana's other self, the goddess of childbirth, protector of women in travail (2055–85). The Knight fills a silence in *Teseida* with the desire for chastity and with desire between women which excludes men; a desire stated emphatically in Emelye's prayer to the 'chaste goddess of the 'wodes greene' (2297):

> Desire to ben a mayden al my lyf,
> Ne nevere wol I be no love ne wyf.
> I am thow woost, yet of thy compaignye,
> A mayde, and love huntynge and venerye,
> And for to walken in the wodes wilde
> And noght to ben a wyf and be with childe.

---

[12] In *The Knight's Tale* the description of Emelye in the garden more resembles that of a literary May morning *descriptio* than the portrait of a human being. May is mentioned four times. *The Riverside Chaucer*, ed. L. D. Benson *et al.* (Oxford, 1988), A.1035–55 (all subsequent references are to this edition and cited in the text).

[13] Priscilla Martin, *Chaucer's Women* (Basingstoke, 1996), p. 42.

[14] *A Midsummer Night's Dream*, ed. Stanley Wells (London, 2005), introduction by Helen Hackett, p. lxiii.

[15] The 'derke ymaginyngs' of the temple of Diana in which Emelye prays are those of Chaucer's Knight. In Boccaccio the temple is simply clean and adorned with hangings: Giovanni Boccaccio, *Teseida*, ed. Salvatore Battaglia (Florence, 1938), 7.72.

Noght wol I knowe compaignye of man.

(2305–11)

And whil I lyve, a mayde I wol thee serve.

(2330)

Emelye is a votaress to Diana and her moon, devoted to the 'compaignye' not of men, but of a chaste goddess. Theseus wants none of her, 'the pale companion is not for our pomp' (1.1.15). But Emily keeps on turning up. As here:

Flying between the cold moon and the earth
Cupid, all armed. A certain aim he took
At a fair vestal thronèd by the west,
And loosed his love-shaft smartly from his bow
As it should pierce a hundred thousand hearts.
But I might see young Cupid's fiery shaft
Quenched in the chaste beams of the wat'ry moon,
And the imperial vot'ress passèd on,
In maiden meditation, fancy-free.
Yet marked I where the bolt of Cupid fell.
It fell upon a little western flower –
Before, milk-white; now, purple with love's wound.

(*A Midsummer Night's Dream*, 2.1.156–67)

Oberon's 'fair vestal', so often associated with Elizabeth I,[16] the absent, excluded woman upon whom *Dream* depends,[17] etches the memory of Emily. Emily is the woman the play needs to exclude in order to reach its dynastic end, but the labour of this erasure is indelible, especially in these lines. While she has no throne, Emily is literally, not metaphorically, a votaress of the Amazonian empire, devoted to Diana, goddess of the moon. Dedicated to chastity, she wishes no part of Cupid's fiery shaft to pierce her maiden heart. But Emily, like the milk-white flower, cannot escape becoming empurpled with the bloody wound of ruptured maidenhead.[18] Oberon's speech in *Dream* will have been Emily's prayer to Diana in her temple in *The Knight's Tale*:

Syn thou art mayde and kepere of us alle,
My maydenhede thou kepe and wel conserve,
And whil I lyve, a mayde, I wol thee serve.

(2328–30)

And Diana's inability to grant her request:

. . . sodeynly she saugh a sighte queynte,
For right anon oon of the fyres queynte,

And quyked agayn, and after that anon
That oother fyr was queynt and al agon;
And as it queynte, it made a whistelynge
As doon thise wete brondes in hir brennynge;
And at the brondes ende out ran anon
As it were blody dropes many oon.

(2333–40)

Emelye's desperate desire to remain chaste speaks 'mayde' three times in three lines, only to be answered by the assonance of three 'queyntes' in the vision. Glossing 'queynte' always grammatically (and chastely) as 'extinguished/curious', editors gloss over the sense of its dysphemism: cunt.[19] The translation of 'mayde' into 'queynte' batters home the impact of Emelye's 'enforcèd chastity', while Diana's moon, with every little flower 'looks with a wat'ry eye, / And . . . weeps' (*Dream*, 3.1.189–90).[20] The erotic burning of the wet brands dripping blood will have been Oberon's white flower, source of erotic mayhem, swollen red. The Knight's failed attempt at courteous narration is not less but more grotesque than the single rose (the bloodied flower) that falls in the temple when Emilia is discharged from Diana's service in *Two Noble Kinsmen*.[21]

---

16 The association between this passage and Elizabeth I is reviewed in Helen Hackett, *Shakespeare and Elizabeth: The Meeting of Two Myths* (Princeton, 2009), pp. 114–24.

17 Louis Adrian Montrose, '"Shaping Fantasies": Figurations of Gender and Power in Elizabethan Culture', *Representations*, 2 (1983), 81.

18 Hackett, *A Midsummer Night's Dream*, explores the sexual symbolism of the milk white flower, and its purpling as a sign of female bleeding: menstruation and ruptured maidenhead, pp. 17–31.

19 Larry D. Benson discusses this issue in 'The Queynte Puns of Chaucer's Critics', *Studies in the Age of Chaucer*, 1 (1984), 23–47.

20 Cf. the scenario imagined in Michael Hoffman's film of *A Midsummer Night's Dream* (Fox Searchlight Pictures, 1999) when Norma's aria to the chaste moon, 'Casta diva' from Bellini's opera *Norma*, is played during the coupling of Bottom and Titania.

21 Gordon McMullan emphasizes Emilia's misinterpretation of the symbolism in this scene, and the agony of recognition in being 'discharged' from Diana's service. He argues that the 'rose becomes a symbolic palimpsest: at once a symbol of virginity, menstruation and defloration, and thus a sign of the heterosexual path a woman is obliged to tread if she is to mature in Theseus's Athens': 'A Rose for Emilia: Collaborative Relations in *Two Noble Kinsmen*', in *Renaissance*

Emily's frustrated desire courses through *Dream*'s endemic splittings and metamorphoses. *Dream* contains, of course, not just one votaress but two: the mother of the Indian changeling boy was 'a vot'ress' of Titania's order (2.1.123); she will have been of the unnamed woman in Diana's temple:

> A womman travaillynge was hire biforn;
> But for hir child so longe was unborn
> Ful pitously Lucyna gan she calle,
> And seyde, 'Help, for thou mayst best of alle!'
>
> (2083–6)

Just as Diana cannot preserve Emelye's white flower, so she cannot prevent Titania's votaress from dying in childbirth. Diana's inability to protect women in her service will also have been the death of Emilia's beloved Flavina who 'took leave o'th' moon – / Which then looked pale at parting' (*Two Noble Kinsmen*, 1.3.52–3). Emilia's love for Flavina is Emelye's denied desire to cling to her maiden Amazon life and the future perfect of the childhood devotion between Helena and Hermia 'with two seeming bodies but one heart', who 'grew together, / Like to a double cherry: seeming parted, / But yet an union in partition' (*Dream*, 3.2.209–213).[22] The strength of all these gynocentric bonds will have impeded the heteronormative conclusion that is so vital to Theseus's dynastic plans.[23] It has been argued that these female attachments must be placed in the past, so that they can be succeeded, got over.[24] Viewed within linear time, that is correct. But in the wrinkled time of these non-synchronous stories this powerful female block is never succeeded. Female–female attachment might be 'got over' at the level of diachronic plot, but it remains available and possible within 'folded' time.

Emily keeps turning up and back, like all those metamorphoses. Take the story of Apollo and Daphne as Chaucer's Knight tells it in Diana's temple:

> Ther saugh I Dane, yturned til a tree,
> I mene nat the goddesse Diane,
> But Penneus doughter, which that highte Dane.
>
> (1204–6)

The assonance of Dane, Diane and Dane, chimes the metamorphoses with which *A Midsummer Night's Dream* teems. The Knight does not mean to mention the goddess Diana but he can't help himself. The doubling of names is doubled back in Helena's description of her chase for Demetrius:

> . . . The story shall be changed:
> Apollo flies, and Daphne holds the chase.
>
> (2.1.230–1)

Helena rewinds the transformation rather as Theseus gets Diana's moon back to front: 'Wexynge it was, and sholde wanye soone' (*Knight's Tale*, 2078); '[h]ow slow / This old moon wanes' (*Dream*, 1.1.3–4). The moon, symbol of Diana, to whom Emily is votaress, crosses the Knight's – and Theseus's – desires, and neither man can subject the changes of the moon to his control. The shrinking moon with which Theseus is so impatient in *Dream* endangers the production of healthy progeny that is so vital to his marital plans.[25] Theseus's anxiety about Diana and her followers dogs his preoccupation with the moon. Joining forces with Egeus to exert his will over Hermia's desires, to dispose of her virginity, like Emily's, to the 'right' man, he threatens Hermia that she will be forced, 'to abjure / For ever the society of men' (1.1 65–6). But the continuation of his threat speaks his own anxieties:

> To live a barren sister all your life,
> Chanting faint hymns to the cold fruitless moon.
>
> (1.1.72–3)

Configurations: Voices/Bodies/Spaces, 1580–1690, ed. Gordon McMullan (Palgrave, 2001), p. 143.

[22] Andreas, 'Remythologising *The Knight's Tale*', argues that Chaucer's Emilye is 'doubled' in *Dream* and *Two Noble Kinsmen* as Hermia and Helena and the Jailer's Daughter, p. 53.

[23] Laurie Shannon, *Sovereign Amity: Figures of Friendship in Shakespearean Contexts* (Chicago, 2002), pp. 103–22.

[24] Valerie Traub, 'The Insignificance of Lesbian Desire in Early Modern England', in *Erotic Politics: Desire on the Renaissance Stage*, ed. Susan Zimmerman (London, 1992), pp. 158–9, and Richard Mallette, 'Same-sex Erotic Friendship in *Two Noble Kinsmen*', *Renaissance Drama*, 26 (1995), 34.

[25] For the waning moon as a threat to healthy progeny, see Hackett, *A Midsummer Night's Dream*, pp. 17–31 and Wilson, 'The Kindly Ones', p. 209.

While Chaucer's Knight and Theseus speak Emelye's desire to force it to their patriarchal will, their narrative determination towards a marital conclusion whose progeny will reproduce healthy versions of themselves must contain Emily and the childless moon to which she is avowed: sign of chastity, untimely menstruation and sisterly devotion. Once spoken, Emily's desire is let loose. The expressed will to its coercion or banishment unleashes its expression. Neither Emily, nor her cold fruitless moon, will be so easily packed up.[26]

The moon appears more often in *Dream* than in any other Shakespeare play. Even when the lovers are safely out of the wood and married at Theseus's palace, just at the point when Theseus might have felt in control the craftsmen stage his worst nightmare: not perhaps the play of Pyramus and Thisbe, whose tragedy of lovers divided by parental will dramatizes the plot that *Dream* must not fulfil, but their arduous attempts to bring the moon back into Theseus's court. The efforts of the craftsmen prompt much ribaldry amongst the 'gentle' characters, but Theseus's contribution has a particular edge. Ostensibly commenting on staging, he quips that 'the man should be put into the lantern. How is it else the man i'th' moon?' (5.1.241–3). This is not just a jape about a male-punctured moon: there is play on the proverbial expression: to 'be in the lantern', which means to be 'hanged from the post'.[27] Theseus's 'joke' threatens death by execution for the actor who has had such temerity to bring into his court, on the craftsmen's own terms, Theseus's dreaded moon, symbol of chastity and female bonding. Moonshine, as the craftsmen call the moon, contains even further horror. The word has the sense not only of 'the light of the moon' but also 'an appearance without substance; something insubstantial or unreal'.[28] The very thing, or name, of 'moonshine' that the craftsmen strain to produce for Theseus encapsulates *Dream*'s preoccupation with presences/absences, substances/shadows and actors/roles which Theseus attempts to explain away through 'cool reason' (5.1.6). 'I am invisible' says Oberon (2.1.186), standing on stage for all to see. The craftsmen, like the moonshine,

both are and are not here: present/absent; substances/shadows and actors/roles. In dramatic figure they body forth the shape, if not the name, of Emily, the intra-temporal threat to the play that insists on turning up.

Theseus's mockery of the moon prevents the grotesque merriment in *Two Noble Kinsmen*. The Second Queen, appealing to Hippolyta, 'most dreaded Amazonian' (1.1.78), to show Theseus her war-like strength to persuade him to wage war against Thebes, urges her to imagine her not-yet husband swollen 'i'th' blood-sized field... / Showing the sun his teeth, grinning at the moon' (1.1.99–100). *Two Noble Kinsmen* dramatizes, horrifically, what *Dream* and *The Knight's Tale* contain: Amazonian brutality, monstrosity, infanticide. The First Queen beseeches Theseus 'by warranting moonlight' to imagine 'rotten kings or blubbered queens' (1.1.176–9) when he kisses the sweetness of the 'twinning cherries' of Hippolyta's lips that will have been the kissing cherries that Demetrius sees in Helena's visage (*Dream*, 3.2.141), and Helena's and Hermia's 'double cherry' (3.2.210). The dove that according to Helena will chase the griffin (2.1.232) or the term of endearment which Flute (as Thisbe) addresses to the dead Bottom/Pyramus (5.1.323) will have been the brief kneeling gesture of an Amazonian woman which lasts no longer than 'a dove's motion, when the head's plucked off' (*Two Noble Kinsmen*, 1.1.98). The promise of healthy progeny at the close of *Dream*, unharmed by the vagaries of the moon, are the babies which Hippolyta and her Amazonian

---

26 Mark Taylor argues that Helena's preservation of her chastity in the wood is a product of the play's need for virginal and hence marriageable heroines at the end of the play. To have surrendered to desire before marriage would subvert the 'kind of play *A Midsummer Night's Dream* is trying to be, in which marriage is the fitting reward for chastity, faithfully preserved. It is only when the play's middle seems to forget about its end, so to speak, that this subversion seems capable of being actualised': 'Female Desire in *A Midsummer Night's Dream*', *Shakespeare Yearbook*, 2 (1991), 129.

27 Wilson, 'The Kindly Ones', p. 210.

28 *OED* 'moonshine', n.2a. It is used in this sense in *Love's Labour's Lost*: 'Thou now requests but moonshine in the water' (5.2.207).

soldiers 'broach . . . on the lance', broil in the brine of their tears, and devour (*Two Noble Kinsmen*, 1.3.20–2). *The Knight's Tale* and *Dream* contain the story of Amazonian Emily to which *Two Noble Kinsmen* gives full rein.

In *Two Noble Kinsmen*, while Emilia is handed in marriage first to Arcite and then to Palamon, her primary allegiance remains to Diana: to the company of women rather than the company of men.[29] *Two Noble Kinsmen* gives full dramatic expression to the Emilian desire that is prevented in *The Knight's Tale* and *Dream*, and not only in Emilia's speech about Flavina. When Palamon and Arcite spy Emilia in the garden she is engaged in sexy banter with her female attendant. 'Thou art wanton', Emilia tells her woman. 'I could lie down, I am sure', she replies. 'And take one with you?' asks Emilia (2.2.146–52). Whether the 'bargain' on which the two women 'agree' (2.2.153) is the punchline to a verbal sparring or, as it has been read, a mutual invitation to bed, the scene gives to Emilia a gynocentric scenario that makes a mockery of the two knights' rivalry as they gaze on her from their prison.[30]

Theseus forces Emilia to look at these two men to choose between them but, when asked for her opinion of Arcite, she replies:

> His mother was a wondrous handsome woman –
> His face methinks goes that way.
> (Two Noble Kinsmen, 2.5.20–1)

In Act 4, when Emilia reluctantly compares the kinsmen's pictures, she again looks beyond the men to women:

>   Two such young handsome men
> Shall never fall for me; their weeping mothers
> Following the dead cold ashes of their sons,
> Shall never curse my cruelty.   (4.2.3–6)
>
>   Palamon . . .
> He's swart and meagre, of an eye as heavy
> As if he had lost his mother . . .   (4.2.25–8)
>
> Two greater and two better never yet
> Made mothers joy –   (4.2.62–3)

Emilia may be forced to choose between men, but she sees through them to women. She remains unassimilated to the dynastic resolution, the 'concord from discord', which *Dream* must produce.

Emily's insouciant desire, prevented and unmoored in *Dream* and *The Knight's Tale*, is refracted in *Two Noble Kinsmen* through the role of the Jailer's Daughter. Unnamed, she is the woman who in performance steals the play. In her pursuit of Palamon through the wood and her wish to have him 'do / What he will with me . . . / [f]or use me, so he shall' (*Two Noble Kinsmen*, 2.6.28–30), the Daughter is Helena's contemporary, racing after Demetrius, begging him that as she is his spaniel, to use her as he would his dog (*Dream*, 2.1.203–10). The Daughter's desire for Palamon and her rejection of her Father's sanctioned wooer will have been Hermia's love for Lysander despite Egeus's preferment of Demetrius. Hermia's chastity must be preserved for a legitimate marriage bed, not taken on the dank and dirty ground, but the Daughter's chastity has no such protection. It is flaunted in the wood when – literally in the RSC 1986 production – she was caught up in the phallic exuberance of the countrymen's Morris.[31] And in her later mad scene, when she imagines she hoists a sail up on a ship, the 'nautical' commentary of the Jailer, Wooer and his brother disguises but very thinly what they see up the Daughter's skirts and what they desire to do there:

> *Brother.* Let's get her in.
> *Jailer.* Up to the top, boy! . . .
> *Daughter.* What kenn'st thou?
> *Second Friend.* A fair wood.

---

[29] Barry Weller, '*Two Noble Kinsmen*, the Friendship Tradition and the Flight from Eros', in Frey, *Shakespeare, Fletcher*, p. 95.

[30] Mallette, 'Same-sex erotic friendship', discusses the erotic potential of flirtation in what he calls this 'crucially and usually overlooked exchange', pp. 33–4. Shannon, *Sovereign Amity*, also argues that this scene has been completely neglected, pp. 118–19.

[31] The equation between Morris dancing and sexual prowess is spelled out in the Daughter's fantasy of Palamon's stamina, 'He'll dance the morris twenty mile an hour / And that will founder the best hobby-horse' (5.4.51–2).

Daughter. Bear for it, master.
Tack about!
[*Sings*] 'When Cynthia with her borrowed light...'
(4.1.147–151)

Once more, Diana/Cynthia is unable to protect a woman. The men imagine gang sex as the Daughter exposes her pubic hair ('[a] fair wood'), and instructs them to 'tack'.[32] Emilia's desire, thwarted and refracted, stages an unlicensed display of sexuality which would have Theseus howling at the moon in despair. The Daughter is not Emilia nor Emelye. She is their unruly, prevented part, dispersed in wrinkled time amongst her contemporaries: Hermia/Helena/Diana/the fair vestal/Emilia/Votaress/The Maid/Titania/Flavina/Emelye. All these parted women. What's in a name? Moonshine?

ARCITE

Moonshine: a name without a substance. Theseus may attempt to police the powers of the imagination which give to 'airy nothing /A local habitation and a name' (5.1.16–17), but the proliferation of names and persons to whom they attach are out of his reach.[33] *Dream* is full of 'airy nothings': Nedar, the changeling boy, Thisbe's mother, Titania's votaress and Lysander's widowed aunt.[34] And one whose role has been less discussed: Philostrate, Theseus's Master of the Revels. Shakespeare, we are told, takes the 'name' of Philostrate, from Chaucer's *Knight's Tale*.[35] In a play where there is so much sport with names and roles, what does it mean for Shakespeare to take the 'name' of Philostrate from Chaucer? Philostrate is the name which Arcite assumes when he defies his banishment by Theseus and returns to Athens. According to the wrinkle in time of the performed play of Orpheus, Philostrate ought to be somewhere at court, either in prison or acting as Emelye's squire. Philostrate is not just a name but a role and its player is Arcite. Philostrate's intratemporality marks the erasure of Arcite's history. The sounding of the name of Philostrate makes his 'other' self (Arcite as Palamon) available to the temporal imagination of a

knowing audience. And Arcite, like Emily, threatens the felicity of dynastic marriage. In *The Knight's Tale* and *Two Noble Kinsmen*, Arcite is the odd lover out – and he dies. Which is why he must be prevented in *Dream*.

In a play already filled with changelings, disfigurings and role-playing,[36] the craftsmen's amateur dramatics foreground the process of producing and transacting roles from names. Quince's pairing of 'disfigure' and 'present' (3.1.56) exposes the queasy relationship between name and person. In Act 5, the craftsmen's blatant exposure of the insubstantial relationship between name and thing confronts Theseus rather like their efforts with the moon, with a prevented truth that is staring him in the face. They repeat their concern not to frighten the court with their assumed roles: 'I, Pyramus, am not Pyramus, but Bottom the weaver. This will put them out of fear' (3.1.19–20), and:

---

[32] 'Tack' is not glossed in this play in a sexual sense, but cf. the reference to sexual activity in *Measure for Measure*, 'lost at a game of tick-tack' (1.2.178–9). The verb 'tack' describes driving pegs into holes: E. Partridge, *Shakespeare's Bawdy* (London, 1968), p. 262. The Prologue to *Two Noble Kinsmen* has the two dramatists 'tack about' (Prol. 26) their business which, given that new plays are likened to new maidenheads (Prol. 1), has clear sexual resonance.

[33] Maguire, *Shakespeare's Names*, p. 88.

[34] As discussed by Terence Hawkes, 'Or', in *Meaning by Shakespeare* (London, 1993), pp. 11–43, especially with reference to Nedar, Lysander's widowed aunt; Ania Loomba, 'The Great Indian Vanishing Trick: Colonialism, Property and the Family in *A Midsummer Night's Dream*', in *The Feminist Companion to Shakespeare*, ed. Dympna Callaghan (Oxford, 2000); Blackwell Reference Online accessed 27 July 2010. Michael Hoffman's film introduces a wife for Bottom; the 1909 Vitagraph silent film transforms Oberon into a woman and calls her Penelope; Kalyan Ray's *Eastwords* (London, 2004) reimagines the play across ages and continents with a host of metamorphoses, and additional and reinvented characters (from a range of Shakespeare's plays and other stories) and includes Sheikh Piru/Bardshah (Shakespeare).

[35] See Thompson, *Shakespeare's Chaucer*, p. 88; note the subsection entitled 'mere names' pp. 63–75. Holland, in glossing *Dream*, 1.1.11 (*A Midsummer Night's Dream*, ed. Peter Holland (Oxford, 1994)), notes that Philostrate is Arcite's 'assumed name when disguised', p. 132.

[36] Patricia Parker, *Shakespeare from the Margins* (Chicago, 1996), pp. 100–6.

You, ladies, whose gentle hearts do fear
The smallest monstrous mouse that creeps on floor,
May now perchance both quake and tremble here
When lion rough in wildest rage doth roar.
Then know that I as Snug the joiner am
A lion fell, nor else no lion's dam.
For if I should as Lion come in strife
Into this place, 'twere pity on my life.   (5.1.217–24)

Snug is both Lion and Snug, not one or the other, and he is both 'Lion' and 'a lion'.[37] L[l]ion worries he might terrify the court, but he also fears for his own life should he come in strife as Lion Proper. Wrinkled into Snug's speech are the terms of the threat of Philostrate's assumed role exposed: Philostrate presented in Theseus's palace as an 'Arcite' or Arcite *in propria persona*.

In *The Knight's Tale* Arcite is banished from Athens. He returns illicitly and, when he turns up at Theseus's court, he introduces himself presciently like one of the craftsmen in *Dream*, 'Philostrate seide that he highte' (1428),[38] but when the Duke catches him 'at strife' with Palamon in the grove, 'real' names are emphatically pronounced:

This is thy mortal foo; this is Arcite (1724)

For this is he that cam unto thy gate
And seyde that he highte Philostrate
Thus hath he japed thee ful many a yer.
(1727–9)

And this is he that loveth Emelye.   (1731)

I am thilke woful Palamoun . . .
I am thy mortal foo, and it am I
That loveth so hoote Emelye the brighte.
(1734–7)

The revelation of true identity is compulsively pathological. Palamon's use of the familiar 'thy' pronoun taunts Theseus with the identities of the men standing before him. Philostrate may have japed Theseus, but Palamon's brutal unmasking is tantamount both to suicide and fratricide. Revealed as 'themselves', both men are under Theseus's sentence of death.

Theseus's attempt to civilize this savagery by restaging the unlicensed brawl in the woods as a bloodless tournament in his exquisitely constructed amphitheatre is powerless to prevent Arcite's death (1851–62; 1881–1913). In curbing the autonomy of the kinsmen to stage their own fight, he merely postpones the inevitable tragedy. The unmasking of Philostrate as Arcite can lead only to death in *A Midsummer Night's Dream*. The craftsmen's fear for their own lives, which they project onto their audience, contains the fear of the consequences of exposing Arcite before Theseus. Philostrate must not be unmasked for, if Arcite is revealed as himself, the mathematical couplings do not work, and mortal confusion will have followed. Like Emelye, he must be prevented for he will have wrecked the procreative couplings on which Theseus's dynastic plans depend. But wrinkles of time unfolded, Philostrate has been 'here' all along; stalking the boards, the wings and the audience with the threat of his disclosure.[39]

Philostrate/Arcite's presence on, or off, stage is textually complex. In Act 1, the stage directions have Philostrate enter along with Theseus and Hippolyta and, at line 11, Theseus commands him by name, 'Go Philostrate', to stir up 'the Athenian youth to merriments' (1.1.11–12). That neither the Quarto nor the Folio marks his exit[40] perhaps matters less (though intriguing all the same) than the fact that the point at which he re-enters the play remains unclear. He could come back in Act 4, scene 1. According to the Folio's stage direction Theseus enters the wood with Egeus, Hippolyta and all his train. The Duke's Master of Revels could reasonably be expected to be included in Theseus's retinue but it would be difficult to stage;

37 Maguire, *Shakespeare's Names*, discusses the craftsmen's uncertainties as regards the difference between a proper noun and a name, p. 89. The confusion between actor, name and role is wonderfully preserved in the stage direction to the Folio version of 5.1.125 'Enter Tawyer with a trumpeter before them'; William Tawyer was an actor with the King's Men. This SD is absent from the Quarto.

38 Overt references to being 'highte' Philostrate occur also at lines 1558 and 1778.

39 Cf. Philostrate's 'double' Puck, who, overwatching the craftsmen's play in the wood, states that he will be an actor and an auditor too, i.e. visible to the audience, on and off stage at the same time (3.1.74–5).

40 The Stage Direction [Exit] is Theobald's.

the speeches which are assigned to Philostrate in Q.1 of *Dream* are, in the Folio, given to Egeus: 'Call Philostrate' (Q); 'Call Egeus' (F).[41] Tantalizingly, the role of the revels master is parted in this play between the two 'names' which Shakespeare took from Chaucer but not, ostensibly, their persons: Egeus is not Hermia's father in *The Knight's Tale* but the father of Theseus (2838). The implications for patriarchal and social order depending on whether Egeus is present or absent in Act 5 of *Dream* have been brilliantly analysed.[42] Philostrate has not received the same attention. If the speech prefixes of the Folio text are faithfully observed, then he is excised from the text; he becomes 'simply a name invoked in Act 1'.[43] Nothing, though, becomes simply a name in *Dream*. Even as the Folio systematically purges his name, a 'part' of him remains; one 'ghost' prefix: 'Phi' at the head of a page (sig. O2v). As Holland rightly observes, 'we can reasonably assume that the Folio version was intended to turn Philostrate into a mute in this scene, if indeed he is on stage at all'.[44] But perversely, if we court 'unreasonableness' instead, and give full play to the imagination that Theseus equates with irrational fear, then Philostrate/Arcite becomes one of Holland's 'men on the stair who refuses to go away'.[45] His presence lingers on even after the Folio tries to cut him out.

The textual redistribution of the parts of Philostrate wrinkles names from *The Knight's Tale* into a scene in which names and roles are most fearfully in question. This is, after all, the scene in which Theseus lets slip his conquest of Thebes. Q1 has Theseus overbearing the will of Philostrate/Arcite in the choice of entertainments; the Folio attempts to banish Philostrate as Arcite; but not only does half his name hang at the top of a verso, the conversation he has with Theseus gets split: not in two, but three. Theseus and Egeus share the warm-up act for the craftsmen's play with a new speaker: Lysander. Philostrate's role is shared out between two wandering Chaucer names, and one of the lovers. Unless Lysander is Philostrate/Arcite? The suggestion is fanciful but not without substance. The Folio's collaboration between Lysander, Theseus and Egeus

doubles a three-hander in the first scene of the play when Theseus calls Egeus and Demetrius to some off-stage business in preparation for his nuptials (1.1.123–6). But in Act 5, one lover's part is replaced by another on stage: Lysander replaces Demetrius. The plot of *Dream* requires the exchange of one male for another to secure the proper pairings of lovers; an exchange secured not by reason but because Demetrius's eyes are still coated with the magic love juice of the milk-white flower. In Act 5, Lysander takes Demetrius's place alongside Theseus and Egeus in a mirror image of Demetrius's replacing Lysander as the husband of Hermia.

The splitting of the lovers, stalked by Philostrate's on/off presence, contains Arcite's replacement by Palamon in *The Knight's Tale* and *Two Noble Kinsmen*. It prevents the triangular love entanglement of Arcite, Palamon and Emily which *Two Noble Kinsmen* and *The Knight's Tale* brutally contract into Jack-marries-Jill because Arcite is killed by his horse.[46] To regularize the asymmetrical surplus of lovers Theseus determines that Palamon take Arcite's place and marry Emily. No one dies in *Dream* (apart from Titania's votaress) and the play closes with three pairs of lawful, heteronormative couplings. But the name games, the textual uncertainty and the role reversals around Philostrate wrinkle Arcite, who like Emily, will have impeded

---

[41] Holland, ed., *Dream*, pp. 31 and 38 (5.1.37; 5.1.123–6).

[42] Philip C. McGuire, 'Egeus and the Implications of Silence', in *Shakespeare and the Sense of Performance*, ed Marvin and Ruth Thompson (London and Toronto, 1989), pp. 103–15 and Barbara Hodgdon, 'Gaining a Father: The Role of Egeus in the Quarto and the Folio', *Review of English Studies*, 37 (1986), 534–42.

[43] Holland, ed., *Dream*, p. 266.

[44] Holland, ed., *Dream*, p. 266.

[45] Holland 'Theseus's Shadows', p. 150.

[46] Boccaccio's *Teseida* at least grants Arcite the dignity of an apotheosis. In his textual afterlife, he ascends to the eighth sphere and looks down on the futility of human experience. Chaucer – or his Knight – cuts this. In Chaucer's *Troilus and Criseyde* Arcite's role is given to Troilus and he is granted an afterlife perspective that has no counterpart in Boccaccio's *Filostrato*, the major source for *Troilus*.

dynastic resolution, into the play. Puck's sweeping behind the door (5.1.380–1) to secure *Dream*'s happy ending is a figure for the play's mechanisms of prophylaxis. 'Now are frolic' he declares (378). Nothing is allowed to 'disturb this hallowed house': not hunger, weariness, woe, wild animals, death, nor gaping graves (361–72). Puck (whose stage double is Philostrate) speaks a catalogue of dangers in the compulsory 'now-frolic' which his broom may tidy, but cannot remove. Puck speaks and sweeps what *Dream* prevents: the death of one of the lovers in *The Knight's Tale* and the intensification of divisions, splittings and refractions in *Two Noble Kinsmen*.

In *Two Noble Kinsmen*, there are either not enough parts for Jack and Jill pairings, or too many.[47] The subplot multiplies arithmetic confusions. The Daughter, Emilia's parted self, is co-opted into the Morris dance in Act 3 because the male players find they are a woman short: '[h]ere's a woman wanting' (3.5.39), causing the players to fear that their business has become a 'nullity / Yea, and a woeful and piteous nullity' (3.5.55–6). Unmatched numbers of men and women bring all to naught. The play cannot go on. Mercifully, for the men, the Daughter wanders on stage, singing in madness, and is inveigled into the dance: 'we are made, boys!' (3.5.77), and the entertainment is saved. The Countryman's delight at resolution belies the textual confusion around normative pairings in this scene. The Quarto stage direction calls for 'Gerrold and 4 countrymen', which as Waith notes, is insufficient both for the names of the men whose names are called out and for them to partner the number of women expected.[48] Five countrywomen are named in the scene but the Quarto stage direction calls for only '2 or 3 wenches'. The textual asymmetry of men and women parallels the numerical complications of the Arcite/Palamon/Emilia plot. But Theseus-like, editors must sort out the pairings. So Waith supplies six countrymen and five women in his stage direction. Lois Potter gives us five of each which means that the figure of the Daughter, seized upon with glee, is then surplus to requirements. There are either too many – or two few – men

and women. For all the efforts to sort them out, someone is still left without a partner.

Two Noble Kinsmen proliferates the ill-matched and superfluous couplings that *Dream* contains. To whom is Hippolyta married? Theseus is split into Pirithous and, if there is any marital rite in the temple in Act 1, Pirithous must stand in for his friend.[49] For the rest of the play, the two men are inseparable: there are three people in Hippolyta's marriage. The textual crux at the close of Emilia's lament for Flavina encapsulates the obstacles to normative pairings. Emilia exalts 'the true love 'tween maid and maid . . . More than in sex dividual' (1.3.80–1). 'Dividual' is an emendation for the Quarto reading 'individuall' partly on metrical grounds (a line with not enough stresses), but also to improve the sense. But is it bettered or diminished? The sense of the word has been claimed as 'divided', 'singular', 'not able to be severed'.[50] Confusion over whether this term is a marker of individuality, division or inseparability, is writ large in the dramatization of the roles of Palamon and Arcite.

When Arcite is banished and subsequently discovered in the grove, there is no mention of his assumed name Philostrate. In keeping with many other roles in the play, Arcite-as-Philostrate has no Proper Name. The 'common' name of Arcite, however, predicates many different roles, including that of his rival Palamon. Here is Arcite, having just spied Emilia:

I am as worthy and as free a lover,
And have as just a title to her beauty,
As any Palamon   (2.2.183–5)

                              Am not I
Part of your blood, part of your soul? You have told me
That I was Palamon and you were Arcite.

                                            (2.2.188–200)

---

47 Masten, '*Textual Intercourse*', draws attention to the fact that both plots lack an available woman to shore up the cultural imperative on monogamous marriage, p. 49.

48 *The Two Noble Kinsmen*, ed. Eugene Waith (Oxford, 1989), p. 143.

49 As noted by Shannon, *Sovereign Amity*, p. 103.

50 Peter Stallybrass, 'Shakespeare, the Individual and the Text', in *Cultural Studies*, ed. Lawrence Grossberg, Cary Nelson and Paula A. Treichler (New York, 1992), pp. 593–610.

The exchanges between 'Arcite' and 'Palamon', between a Proper and a common name, and between 'parts', produce changelings whose roles are recursively transacted. Earlier in the scene when Arcite argues that their 'imaginations' can make their prison a space of freedom, he realizes Bottom's desire in *Dream* to play as many parts as possible (1.2.45, 62, 75):

We are an endless mine to one another:
We are one another's wife, ever begetting
New births of love; we are father, friends, acquaintance,
We are in one another, families –
I am your heir, and you are mine . . .   (2.2.79–83)

The extratemporal slippage between roles that are erotic, familial and social, and between singular and plural personal pronouns, makes the names of these two lovers endlessly available to play almost any part, and to exchange them at will. As an endless 'mine' to one another (79), they are both possessed of each other outside normative chronology and they are also a limitless supply of each other's parts.[51] Arcite, the lover who cannot be married to Emily, imagines the intratemporal danger he poses to the story which contains him in *A Midsummer Night's Dream*. In its disturbing obsession with 'parts', *Two Noble Kinsmen* is prescient of the role of 'dividual' Philostrate it dramatizes.

The triangle of Arcite, Emilia and Palamon is mirrored by Theseus, Hippolyta and Pirithous and doubled by the threesome of the subplot. While the Jailer's Daughter is courted by her nameless Wooer, she is madly in love with Palamon. Her unlicensed passion impedes Father's plans to marry her to Wooer. So the two men, assisted by a Doctor, undertake to 'cure' her. Their strategy to unstraighten the triangle has horrifying implications for the roles of Arcite, Palamon and Emilia, and all their contemporaries in *Dream*. The Doctor as Arcite convinces the others that the Daughter will be restored to sense if she has sex with the Wooer, and that she could be persuaded to do this if the Wooer plays the part of Palamon. The men succeed both in their fore-role-play,

and in the act which follows. 'Are you not Palamon?' asks the Daughter of the Wooer (5.4.83) to which he replies, 'Do you not know me?' 'Is this not your cousin Arcite?' she asks, pointing to the Doctor:

              Yes, sweetheart,
     And I am glad my cousin Palamon
     Has made so fair a choice.   (5.4.91–3)

The generic characters of Doctor and Wooer assume the name – and parts – of 'Arcite' and 'Palamon' to purge the Daughter of erotic desire that doesn't fit into their plans. The sight trick of *Dream*, achieved through the juice of the milk-white flower, turns bloody here. Parted I/eye gives way to parted thighs. Three men, working in collaboration, untangle the problem of one woman with two male lovers through a play, dreamt up and co-acted by 'Arcite', in which 'Palamon' coerces the Daughter to his sexual will. Arcite's part in *Dream* and *The Knight's Tale* will have been an accessory to rape of a woman he is unable to possess himself. It is a sick remedy that still doesn't solve the Jack and Jill problem.[52] Names, *Dream* teaches us, must be taken seriously. 'Palamon', in this play, gets the girl twice: first the Daughter, and then Emilia.[53] For all his interchangeability with Palamon and timeless supply of parts, Arcite fetches up with nothing: death; the failure of the Countryman short of a wench for his play. The Daughter, Emily's parted self, ends up with two men: Palamon and the Wooer. There are no happy nuptials in the story that *Dream* prevents.

TIME

In this article, I have tried to imagine the parts of Emily and Arcite in *A Midsummer Night's Dream* without fixing three texts in the sequence of

---

[51] *OED* 'mine', n.1c.

[52] Weller, '*Two Noble Kinsmen*', argues that the Daughter is 'worked into a marriage with a surrogate Palamon just as Palamon himself becomes, in effect, a surrogate Arcite for Emilia', p. 104.

[53] Cooper, 'Jacobean Chaucer', p. 199.

their historical composition; that is, without setting them in hierarchically bounded time. If no text 'can be temporally self-consistent, for the very reason that it does not own its own words and cannot specify their prehistories'[54] (or post, for that matter), then no text can be temporally self-sufficient. 'Source' study, so often a kind of reading which stabilizes an earlier text as a fixed point and leads to the inevitable conclusion of its latest avatar, is far more wrinkled. It may crinkle backwards or sideways; in starts or inconclusions. Of the three works under consideration here, arguably *Two Noble Kinsmen* is the 'earliest' in one sense. Its scene of Palamon and Arcite in Thebes (1.2) is 'before' *The Knight's Tale* except that the temporal sequence of *The Knight's Tale* confounds 'before' and 'after'. Set in 'adventure time',[55] its all-purpose temporal joiners of 'whanne/thanne' string out its many episodes. Told and glossed over, they lie like assortedly shaped beads on a necklace wanting spacers. With the absence of sustainedly specific co-ordinates of time and space, 'events' sort of follow on, or maybe have already happened sometime. Before which, quite how long since when is not spelled out. Which makes *Dream*'s variable 'now' presciently historical.

Narrative's closure lies at its end. Nor, of course, is it possible to set bounds on that end. *The Knight's Tale* 'ends' much later than *Two Noble Kinsmen* or *A Midsummer Night's Dream*. Emelye and Palamon are happily – and endlessly – married:

> Hath Palamon ywedded Emelye (3098)

> For now is Palamon in alle wele,
> Lyvynge in blisse, in richesse, and in heele,
> And Emelye hym loveth so tendrely
> And he hire serveth so gentilly
> That nevere was ther no word hem bitwene
> Of jalousie or any oother teene.
> Thus endeth Palamon and Emelye;[56]
> And God save al this faire compaignye! Amen.
>
> (3101–8)

The conclusion to *The Knight's Tale* contains its own temporal inconsistency. '[N]ow' in line 3101

sets the ending in the historic present, a tense conjoined snugly between now and then. '[N]evere was' in line 3105 reaches back into the endless past and points towards an unfulfilled future. And in whose time? The Knight's who speaks the words; Chaucer's who wrote them, or the 'compaignye''s who hears them; the Canterbury pilgrims, or a later audience? The temporal gap between lines 3107–8 yawns between the sometime of ancient Athens and the now of the Canterbury pilgrims.[57] Crucially, however, the last verb in the tale ('save', 3108) is in the subjunctive. Hovering somewhere between the jussive and optative, this final verb, following on from the interrupted sequence of historic presence, is a sign of incompleteness, a marker of vulnerability. The relationship of 'when' and 'now' floats somewhere in eternal time out of human reach. The Knight's attempt to use God to staple his story closed is a failure.

---

54 Strohm, 'Chaucer's *Troilus*', p. 81.

55 The term is Bakhtin's: 'all the days, hours, minutes that are ticked off within the separate adventures are not untied into a real time series, they do not become the days and hours of a human life. These hours and days leave no trace and therefore one may have as many of them as one likes': 'Forms of Time and of the Chronotope in the Novel', in *The Dialogic Imagination*, ed. and trans. M. Holquist (Austin, 1981), p. 94.

56 What 'ends' here? The story of Palamon and Emeyle, or the characters' lives?

57 A situation akin to the presence of 'English' craftsmen and Greek nobility in *Dream*. Paul Menzer notes how 'the play's ostentatious heterogeneity reaches an absurd peak in Act 5 where a group of early English craftsmen present the classical tale of Pyramus and Thisbe for a duke and duchess at their Athenian palace, after which a rural English fairy named "Robin Goodfellow" sweeps up': 'The Weavers' Dream: Mnemonic Scripts and Memorial Texts', in *A Midsummer Night's Dream: A Critical Guide*, ed. Regina Buccola (London, 2010), p. 95. Adrian Noble dramatizes temporal and locational discontinuity by dressing the craftsmen in costumes which recall the British TV comedy about the British Home Guard, *Dad's Army* (1968–77) while the Athenians wear exotic Indian-influenced costume, *A Midsummer Night's Dream* (Channel Four Films, 1996).

When the Royal Shakespeare Company opened the Swan Theatre in 1986, they chose *The Two Noble Kinsmen* as the premiere. *A Midsummer Night's Dream* was also part of that season's repertoire. What might a member of the audience on the Swan's first night have made of a later performance of *A Midsummer Night's Dream*? Some of the cast played roles in both performances, some were missing.[58] There were no parts assigned to Emily and Arcite. Not yet.

---

[58] Jailer (*Two Noble Kinsmen*)/Egeus (*Dream*); Emilia/Hermia; Wooer/Snout; Palamon/Oberon. Roberta Taylor played Hippolyta but did not perform in *Dream*; likewise Hugh Quarshie as Arcite and Imogen Stubbs as the Jailer's Daughter: *The Two Noble Kinsmen by William Shakespeare and John Fletcher* (RSC, 1987), p. iii.

'ENTER CÆLIA, THE FAIRY QUEEN, IN HER NIGHT ATTIRE': SHAKESPEARE AND THE FAIRIES

MICHAEL HATTAWAY

1. 'BELIEVING IN' THEATRICAL PERFORMANCES

Where to begin? From history? History of events and institutions? History of ideas? The history of what Max Weber called the 'external conditions' of the age? Alternatively, we might start from language, a category that comprises both verbal and visual language *systems* as well as *particular* words and images. I choose the latter option.

'*Enter Cælia, the Fairy Queen, in her night attire*' is a stage direction in the manuscript text of *Tom a Lincoln*, an anonymous theatrical romance that dates from around 1611.[1] The play's hero is the Red Rose Knight. Thomas Heywood may have written it, possibly for staging at Gray's Inn, but it was never published, and perhaps not even performed.

What does the stage direction signify? A search of the corpus of early modern drama reveals that a player in night attire was in fact a stock theatrical image, one that signified that his character was vexed or confused.[2] In the 'closet' scene of the first quarto of *Hamlet*, we find '*Enter the Ghost in his night gown*'. Heywood's Fairy Queen, accompanied by a court of night-tripping fairy Amazons, had been abandoned by her lover – like Dido. So, fairies or ghosts in night attire serve as *signs* requiring to be *read*, not as visible *representations* of substantial creatures, real or imagined that might be *seen*. Shakespeare frequently referred to players as 'shadows' – the word could also designate 'figures' or 'types'.[3] More particularly, the Swiss artist Henry Fuseli (a friend of William Blake), whose pictures of fairy topics are impressively both suggestive and informed, described dreams as 'personification[s] of sentiment': the implication is that, to be understood, they need to be translated.[4]

I propose that this sort of decoding may be more profitable than imputing beliefs to either authors or audiences. Indeed, summoning *Shakespeare*'s attitudes to the fairy faith is not only unnecessary but also impossible.

Why unnecessary? First, because 'the problem of belief' never disturbs sane adult spectators watching a performance of, say, *A Midsummer Night's Dream*. How should that be? Partly because *all* of the comedies bear some resemblance to fairy-tales,[5] and also because the play's title proclaims

---

This article is based upon my British Academy Shakespeare Lecture, delivered at the Royal Society in London on 22 April 2010. Pictures associated with certain productions mentioned in the text, namely those of *A Midsummer Night's Dream* by Peter Hall (1962), Ron Daniels (1981), Robert Lepage (1992) and John Doyle (1995), are to be found on the Arts and Humanities Research Board's 'Designing Shakespeare' website (www.ahds.rhul.ac.uk/ahdscollections). Some of these as well as further illustrative material can be found on the link to 'Presentation Slides' to be found on the British Academy's web-page for the lecture: www.britac.ac.uk/events/2010/shakespeare/index.cfm.

[1] *Tom a Lincoln*, ed. G. R. Proudfoot *et al.* (Oxford, 1992), line 1564.
[2] Another example at the entrance of Prester John and his queen: *Tom a Lincoln*, line 2494.
[3] *OED*, 'shadow', 6c.
[4] Henry Fuseli, *The Life and Writings of Henry Fuseli*, ed. John Knowles (London, 1831), p. 145.
[5] Catherine Belsey, *Why Shakespeare?* (London, 2007), pp. 19–20.

the informing metaphor of the play as a *dream*,[6] and dreams create a double time in which both the natural and supernatural are perceived.[7] In a dream, according to the Watford preacher Philip Goodwin, who was writing about 1657, men deceive themselves if they take 'the signs of things for the natures of things, mere shadows for substance. In a dream are thoughts of things, not the things thought.'[8] Fairies in a dream are obviously fictitious.

Second, we do not know what *particular signs* the Lord Chamberlain's men came up with when performing, either in a theatre or the hall of a palace or private house. Nor do we know whether or how they differentiated kinds of fairies: pucks, flower-fairies, bringers of fertility... (A 'puck', of course, is a hobgoblin: the character in the play perhaps ought to be given his ironic name, 'Robin Goodfellow' – although, as we shall see, that too is generic.[9]) There is a hint for fairy costumes in *The Merry Wives of Windsor*, where Mistress Page announces that child actors will take these parts:

> And three or four... we'll dress
> Like urchins, oafs, and fairies, *green and white*,
> With rounds of waxen *tapers* on their heads,
> And rattles in their hands.
>
> (4.4.48–51, emphasis added)

(An 'oaf' was an elf's child or changeling.) In *Tom a Lincoln* too the fairy ladies are green-coated,[10] and I guess that those tapers suggest that the text of *Merry Wives* was prepared for a private indoor performance.

What may a puck have looked like? In *Wily Beguiled*, an anonymous Paul's play of about 1602, the 'Robin Goodfellow' character appears primarily as a clown. The text reveals that he has a 'flashing [gleaming] red nose' and that he wears a jester's calf-skin coat, buttoned down the back – perhaps to display his buttocks: the motif of 'back to front' was common in carnival mockery, although it might also have been a means of keeping witches at bay.[11] Nine years later, in Jonson's 1611 court masque *Oberon*, the fairies are described as 'antics', a splendid word that has connotations of the antique, of revelry, and of the monstrous. One of Jones's

fairies has a large cod-piece, another *may* be wearing a coat buttoned at the back.[12] In Jonson's *Love Restored*, a masque presented at court the next year, Robin Goodfellow, speaking in prose, presents the action. Two ballads of *c.*1625, 'The mad-merry pranks of Robin Goodfellow', may have been written by Jonson, and are accompanied by woodcuts showing one puck naked except for a loin-cloth, the other with a tunic that makes him look rough and hairy.[13]

A late-Caroline night-wanderer with candle and broom, merry, demonized and ithyphallic appears on the title-page of Thomas Cotes's *Robin Goodfellow, his Mad Pranks and Merry Jests* (London, 1639).[14] Although Shakespeare's Puck seems to have brought a broom on stage as an index of his role (see 5.1.380), we just do not know exactly how fairies and pucks may have been presented in the amphitheatre or public playhouses.

Moreover, since 1595 there have been as many representations as there have been productions. They can be, and have been, ballet dancers or, as in Tim Supple's Indian production of 2006, gymnasts,[15] and sometimes they have appeared brazenly cross-dressed. Of course, children have

---

[6] For an excellent essay on dreams, see William Shakespeare, *A Midsummer Night's Dream*, ed. Peter Holland (Oxford, 2008), pp. 1–21.

[7] Katharine Mary Briggs, *The Vanishing People: A Study of Traditional Fairy Beliefs* (London, 1978), pp. 19–21.

[8] Philip Goodwin, *The Mystery of Dreams, Historically Discoursed* (London, 1657), p. 12, in Stuart Clark, *Vanities of the Eye* (Oxford, 2007), p. 302. Goodwin was quoting Philo, the Alexandrian philosopher.

[9] Holland (ed.), *MND*, pp. 35–49.

[10] Diane Purkiss, *Troublesome Things: A History of Fairies and Fairy Stories* (London, 2001), p. 63.

[11] Iona Archibald Opie and Moira Tatem, 'Clothes Inside Out', in *A Dictionary of Superstitions* (Oxford, 2005).

[12] The drawing is at Chatsworth: see http://art.chatsworth.org/image/673299/three-fays-c-1611.

[13] The images, from Pepys 1, 80–1, can be found on the 'English Broadside Ballad Archive': http://ebba.english.ucsb.edu/ballad/20274/image#.

[14] It has been frequently reproduced, for example in Holland, ed., *MND*, p. 37.

[15] There is illustrative material on www.britishcouncil.org/india-connecting-north-march-2006-tim-supple1.htm.

taken the parts,[16] particularly in amateur productions – and also in Peter Hall's 1969 film – and women have frequently played the puck's role.[17]

Third, belief in what? The signs or realities? Supernatural beings such as fairies are both signifiers and signifieds. They seem to have invisible inverted commas around them, and in *A Midsummer Night's Dream* they distinctively use trochaic rather than iambic metre (trochees are backward iambs). Ron Daniels, for a 1981 RSC production, created what was a memorable convention in which players, clad in black, operated large stick-puppet fairies. This made them obviously not only signs but what medieval theologians called 'types' – Elijah who ascended to heaven was a 'type' of Christ. In this context, certain of these puppets were visual quotations of the characters in the main play: signifiers and signified both lay within the text. In 'Pyramus and Thisbe' Shakespeare has a merry time mocking the mechanicals whose folly is that they consider that spectators crave or need artless theatrical realism, visual presentations of moonlight and substantial garden walls.

As Shakespeare obviously realized, theatrical images – and we can revert now to Heywood's Caelia and the Robin Goodfellow in *Wily Beguiled* – are elements in the *theatrical language system* of the early modern period. Many of the remnants of that system survive – and are not difficult to read – but 'Pyramus and Thisbe' reminds us that signs need not resemble what they signify. It follows, I would claim, that Shakespeare and his contemporaries were not '*thinking about*' fairies – whether they existed or not – but '*thinking with*' fairies, recording how people might use or react to what Philip Goodwin called the 'thoughts of things'. After all, young children think *with* their toys as they explore the world.

These Renaissance writers 'invented' fairies: in their time the word 'invent' did not mean 'to make up' or 'to devise for the first time', but 'to retrieve' or 'come upon'. Ben Jonson described the *mise en scène* and action of his *Entertainment at Althorp* as an 'invention' ('*The* invention *was to have a satyr lodged*

in a little spinet . . . who . . . advanced his head above the top of the wood').

Jonson again. In his tribute poem to Shakespeare, printed in the First Folio, Jonson reminds us that there is a 'thinginess' or substance in language – or 'inventions' – that, he claimed, using a blacksmith's metaphor, might 'turn' a poet:

> he
> Who casts to write a living line must sweat,
> . . . and strike the second heat
> Upon the muses' anvil; turn the same
> (*And himself with it*) that he thinks to frame
> (lines 58–62, emphasis added)[18]

As a poet transforms words into text on that metaphorical anvil, he may end by 'turning [or refashioning] himself', hammering out a sentence that he had not intended, even one in which he did not 'believe'. One can see why it is better for my investigation to begin with languages, poetic and theatrical, rather than with social or historical evidence.

Another way of orientating ourselves is to distinguish between '*believing in*' and '*believing that*': Theseus, in 'The lunatic, the lover and the poet', seems to distrust anything *in* which he cannot believe:

> *Theseus.*   I never may *believe*
> These antique fables, nor these fairy toys.
> Lovers and madmen have such seething brains,
> Such shaping fantasies, that *apprehend*
> More than cool reason ever *comprehends*.
> The lunatic, the lover, and the poet
> Are of imagination all compact.   (5.1.2–8)

His wife Hippolyta knows and *believes that* stories, 'turned' or fabricated out of fancy's images, can grow to something of great constancy (consistency and permanence).

---

16 Holland, ed., *MND*, pp. 25–34.
17 Ethna Roddy played the part in Kenneth Branagh's 1990 production for the Renaissance Theatre Company; Toyah Willcox in John Doyle's 1995 production for the same company; Angela Laurier for Robert Lepage at the National Theatre in 1992.
18 Ben Jonson, *Poems*, ed. Ian Donaldson (Oxford, 1975), p. 310.

Hippolyta. But all the story of the night told over,
And all their minds transfigured so together,
More witnesseth than fancy's images,
And grows to something of great *constancy*;
But howsoever, strange and admirable.

(*MND*, 5.1.23–27, emphases added)

This notion of 'believing in' is complex. There is no space for philosophical exposition, merely a chance to snap up fragments from two well-known texts, which, I submit, have made life difficult for those who teach Shakespeare. First, the Apostles' Creed: 'I *believe in* God, the Father Almighty . . . '. This text asserts '*belief in*' the three entities that constitute the Trinity. What does the verb mean? I think the recitation of these phrases betokens an assertion of faith or a *confidence in* or *commitment to* the Father, Son and Holy Spirit. By contrast, after Bertrand Russell, it has been common to argue that the use of phrases such as 'believing that' is a sign of a 'propositional attitude' used to indicate descriptive knowledge or assent to a verifiable statement: 'I *believe that*, when it is heated, an iron bar will expand.'[19] The words of the Creed do not constitute a proposition, an invitation to debate about whether the entities that comprise the Trinity have a real existence.[20] However, my hypothesis is that the two meanings, the one having to do with acquaintance and authority, and the second with knowledge and evidence, are frequently fused. In this new world of Richard Dawkins it would seem that many who now recite the familiar words of the Creed consider that they are staking a claim for the *real existence* of God. Their assumption is that propositions about God can be open to verification.

However, even if we are disinclined to *believe in* any deity, it may be good to *believe that* religious texts have a deal to offer us – the sort of belief of which Hippolyta was speaking. Indeed, today's uncivil society of nations might be a much happier gathering if the religious among its populations could clarify this distinction, and not brand unbelievers as infidels.[21]

A second phrase, Coleridge's 'willing suspension of disbelief',[22] has proved singularly unhelpful.

First, we must remember Coleridge was writing about *poetry*, not about *theatre*, and that, for the purpose of his argument, he associated that 'suspension' as much with *writers* as with *readers*. He was 'thinking with' his antique tale of an ancient mariner, and did not always postulate a categorical distinction between the wondrous visions of poetry and those of science – nor, more surprisingly, did his great friend Sir Humphry Davy, President of the Royal Society, who, around 1830, was to speculate that super-intelligent beings lived on the planet Saturn. They had wings made of 'extremely thin membranes . . . varied and beautiful . . . azure and rose-colour'.[23] These latter-day fairies told Davy that beings like themselves inhabited all of the solar system.

Coleridge's mantra, however, has been appropriated by generations of students of Shakespeare who have been programmed to 'believe in' his *characters*, whether in texts or on the stage, and consider them as though they were not *signifying clusters to be comprehended*, but substantial beings to be *apprehended*, resembling people like us. To tweak Philip Goodwin, playhouse characters are 'thoughts of people, not the people thought'. So let's try to staunch our addiction to realism – a drug that has been so successfully peddled by film-makers and admen.

2. FAIRIES AND REFORMATIONS

Now a glance at history, Weber's 'external conditions' in the particular context of English reformations, and for that we shall use an example. At

[19] Jerry A. Fodor, 'Propositional Attitudes', in *Perspectives in the Philosophy of Language*, ed. Robert Stainton (Peterborough, Ont., 2000), pp. 137–60.

[20] Compare Nicholas Lash, *Holiness, Speech and Silence: Reflections on the Question of God* (Aldershot, 2004), pp. 1–21.

[21] For a useful expansion of this position, see Stuart Clark, *Thinking with Demons: The Idea of Witchcraft in Early Modern Europe* (Oxford, 1997), pp. 3–5.

[22] Samuel Taylor Coleridge, *Samuel Taylor Coleridge*, ed. H. J. Jackson (Oxford, 1985), p. 314.

[23] Sir Humphry Davy, *The Collected Works*, ed. John Davy, 9 vols. (London, 1840), IX, p. 241.

the end of *A Midsummer Night's Dream*, Oberon, king of the fairies, blesses the chambers of the house, presumably Theseus's palace (5.1.382–413). How might we read this? How, in Shakespeare's time, might it have been performed? Oberon here seems to be a kind of fertility fairy,[24] but his speech expressly focuses on what, in pre-Reformation England, was termed a 'sacramental'.[25] Such a blessing would customarily have used holy water to drive away demons, and this, sprinkled on a marriage-bed, was supposed to promote fertility. However, the Protestant Archbishop Thomas Cranmer had scorned the blessing of objects, and this form of blessing, along with all other sacramentals, did not appear in *The Book of Common Prayer* of 1549. (Hardly surprising: a clergyman in Faversham had prescribed holy water as a specific against piles.)[26]

Players were prohibited from fostering such superstitions: there were repeated complaints from the Privy Council about the way 'players do take upon themselves certain matters of divinity and of state unfit to be suffered', and in 1589 the Archbishop of Canterbury was requested to nominate 'some fit person well learned in divinity' to join the Master of the Revels and a nominee of the Lord Mayor in order to 'view and consider' all texts that were to be publicly played.[27] In 1574, however, an Act of Common Council had exempted from this sort of injunction any 'plays . . . played or showed in the house of any nobleman, citizen, or gentleman'.[28] (Is this a shred of evidence to support the claims that *A Midsummer Night's Dream* originated as an occasional play for a private audience?) Would godly sixteenth-century Protestants in public audiences discern either sinister shades of papistry (Oberon's consecrated 'field-dew' as sham holy water), or an example of popular magic, open to opportunistic demonic interference? After all, only a couple of years later, in 1597, the future James I was to argue that fairies such as 'Diana and her wandering court' were demons, and the redoubtable Thomas Beard, schoolmaster to Oliver Cromwell, unequivocally branded the figure of Robin Goodfellow as the devil.[29] Is Oberon's blessing at the end of the play just 'charming' in the colloquial sense, or might the *ceremony* of charming have generated a frisson in performance?

In an analogous sequence in *The Merry Wives of Windsor*, contemporary with King James's *Demonology*, Mistress Quickly commands her elves and 'meadow-fairies' (5.5.64) to *scour* the 'chairs of order' (thrones) at Windsor Castle with 'juice of balm and every blessed flower', so preparing these for the ritual of the Garter. The text refers to cleaning and refreshing rather than blessing: Shakespeare seems to have shunned that shred of the precise Catholic sacramental of holy water, a relic of which remains in *A Midsummer Night's Dream*, and replaced it by a less contentious ceremony.

Overall, however, it is impossible to postulate a definitive interpretation of that consecration sequence in the *Dream*. The problem is paradigmatic: it is generally impossible to recover key details of practically any early *mise en scène*, any *locating tone* – any full meaning for parts of the play like this.

It follows that it is difficult to relate a theatrical experience involving the supernatural, when signs like this may be realized for performance in a myriad of ways, to our sense of the ideological contexts for magic and religion.

Does this therefore mean that we cannot use playtexts to test, say, a central thesis of Max Weber concerning modernity? Weber, like so many of his generation, argued that we should start from external conditions. He argued, in 'Science as a Vocation' (1918–19), that 'The fate of our times is

---

[24] Briggs, *Vanishing People*, pp. 154–6.

[25] Eamon Duffy, *The Stripping of the Altars: Traditional Religion in England 1400–1580* (New Haven, 2005), pp. 281–2, 439, 465–6; Charles Taylor, *A Secular Age* (Cambridge, MA, 2007), pp. 44–5.

[26] Duffy, *Altars*, p. 439.

[27] Glynne Wickham, Herbert Berry, William Ingram, eds., *English Professional Theatre, 1530–1660* (Cambridge, 2000), p. 94.

[28] Wickham *et al.*, *Theatre*, p. 76.

[29] King James, *Daemonologie* (Edinburgh, 1597) III.5, p. 74; Thomas Beard and Thomas Taylor, *The Theatre of God's Judgements* (London, 1642), p. 433.

characterised by rationalisation and intellectualisation and, above all, by the "disenchantment of the world".[30] Is there an unbridgeable divide between, on the one side, cultural history and cultural theory and, on the other, antiquarianism? More generally, can we ourselves push away regressiveness, along with the dominant attitudes of today, marinated as they are in nineteenth-century scientific rationalism and models of evolutionary development, and recover the ways in which popular magic and the fairy-faith were regarded in the age of Shakespeare?

3. *ROMEO AND JULIET* AND FORMS OF QUEEN MAB

It will be difficult. The first significant fairy in the Shakespearean canon is conjured by Mercutio in 1.4 of *Romeo and Juliet*, but of course his Queen Mab does not appear in person. It is surprisingly hard to work out the function of Mercutio's speech about her.

We might start from her name: the word 'mab' could mean a harlot or slattern.[31] This means either that 'Queen Mab' was an oxymoron, or perhaps that editors ought to print 'Quean Mab' – 'quean' meaning 'hussy'. Mercutio calls her 'the fairies' midwife': Warburton in the eighteenth century conjectured 'Fancy's midwife'. However, the emendation is unnecessary as the word 'midwife' was used figuratively for someone who 'helps to bring something into being' (*OED*).[32] Moreover, fairy midwives abound in folklore,[33] and bawdy or drunken midwives appear in satires of the period as stock examples of social degeneracy. Fuseli, as so often, seems to have got it pretty right with this gluttonous eater of junkets (that detail is from Milton's 'L'Allegro').[34]

Yet the Queen of the Fairies has a totally different role in *Merry Wives* (where she is not called 'Mab'). Rather, as a tormentor of the 'unclean knight', Sir John Falstaff, she leads a rout of fairies who pinch him. (In *Britannia's Pastorals*, William Browne gives us a Fairy Queen who 'did command her elves / To pinch those maids who had not swept their shelves' (Book 1, Song 2).)

However, in this tragedy of the calamitous loves of Romeo and Juliet, Shakespeare, unlike the choruses in Greek tragedy, is always careful not to impute *agency* to a supernatural being: all Mab can do is create signs that 'bode' misfortune (see 1.4.91). In this respect she resembles the witches in *Macbeth* – *inclinant, non necessitant* – they sway but they do not compel. Mercutio here is a kind of witch-finder, offering instances of mild maleficence, plaiting the manes of horses and tangling the hair of sluts. The first is widely recorded in

[30] Max Weber, *From Max Weber: Essays in Sociology*, trans. and ed. by H. H. Gerth and C. Wright Mills (New York, 1946), p. 155.

[31] As in Nicholas Udall (?), *Jacob and Esau* (London, 1568) V.vi, sig. Gj, 'Come out, thou mother Mab, out, old rotten witch' (cit. *OED*).

[32] *OED*, 3, although the dictionary only lists its first example of this meaning two years later in *Richard II*: 'So, Greene, thou art the midwife to my woe' (2.2.62). (There too the word is used between men who seem homoerotically bonded.) The detail may have come into Shakespeare's mind when he was reading Brooke's *Romeus and Juliet* (1562): 'His nurce he cursed, and the hand that gaue him pappe, / The *midwife* eke with tender grype that held him in her lappe: / And then did he complaine, on Uenus cruel sonne / Who led him first vnto the rockes. which he should warely shonne. / By meane wherof he lost, both lyfe and libertie, / And dyed a hundred times a day, and yet could neuer dye. / Loues troubles lasten long': (Geoffrey Bullough (ed.), *Narrative and Dramatic Sources of Shakespeare*, 7 vols. (London, 1957–73), IV, p. 340.

The state of midwives was an index of the moral condition of a commonwealth: Nicholas Breton evokes a golden age: 'When Gammore Widginne would not lose a Lamb / And Goodwife Goose would see her Chickens fed, / And Mother Midwife kindly where she came, / With merry chat would bring the wise a-bed, / And take the child and softly close the head: / Then take the babe and bring it to the mother, / God make you strong, to work for such another' ('Mad-cap's "Oh the Merry Time"', from *Old Mad-cap's New Gallymaufry* (London, 1602), lines 456–62). However, a few years later, in Robert Anton's 'The Philosopher's Fifth Satire, of Venus' we hear of 'the bawdy midwife, and the pifering nurse' (*The Philosopher's Satires* (London, 1616), p. 53).

[33] Briggs, *Vanishing People*, pp. 93–103.

[34] The painting is in the Folger Shakespeare Library: www.folger.edu/imgdtl.cfm?imageid=264.

folk literature[35] and the second was associated with elves. These would, if the 'trivial' acts had been enacted by the puck, have been called knavish tricks, but here they either portend trouble or, as we shall see, have to do with female sexuality.

Nineteenth-century Romantics, of course, wanted none of that: in Gustave Doré's picture Queen Mab is a guardian angel.[36] There is more edge in Turner's painting which I take to be a slightly misogynistic joke, a portrait of a busy-body who perhaps resembled Jane Austen's *Emma*, plonked into the centre of that fashionable back-ground, a 'landscape'.[37]

Mab had brought about Romeo's dream, pre-sumably a dream that prefigures his relation with Juliet. Dreams, of course, were much discussed in the early modern period. True dreams, according to classical authorities Homer, Virgil and Macro-bius, came through the Gates of Horn. Protes-tant thinkers accepted this explanation and then rehearsed the ancient categories of natural, divine and demonic dreams.[38] The debates are too com-plex to set out here, but Romeo had been con-vinced his dream was 'true' (1.4. 52), emanating from a supernatural source. Mercutio's reaction is to claim that Romeo has, in a demonic dream, been afflicted by his love for Rosalind and, more-over, that female desire is dangerous:

> This is the hag, when maids lie on their backs,
> That presses them and learns them first to bear,
> Making them women of good carriage.
>
> (1.4.92–4)

His Queen Mab is a night-hag, a form of Hecate, appearing in the form of an incubus (a sexual devil who lies on top), as in Fuseli's painting.[39]

How unlike Doré's version of the figure – and there's another Fuseli incubus to come.

We now move on to two Jacobean Fairy Queens, much less known, but more sensational, presum-ably because, as wielders of magic, they could be coupled with papistry.

The first, with whom we are already familiar, is from *Tom a Lincoln*. Here, the author's queen is not Mab but Cælia, but this is obviously ironic.

Heywood's 'heavenly one' seems to have internal-ized King James's opinion of fairies – Cælia aims to seduce the Red Rose Knight:

> *Enter Cælia, the Fairy Queen in her night attire*
> *Cælia.* Murder's black mother, Rapine's *midwife*,
>   Lust's infernal temptress, Guide to foulest sin;
>   Fountain of all enormous actions, night-
>   Horrid, infernal, dern [evil] and ominous Night,
>   Run not, oh run not with thy swarfy steeds
>   Too fast a course; but drive Light far from hence.
>   What is't that hates the light, but black Offence?
>   And I abhor it, going now to tempt
>   Chastest Hippolytus to hell-bred lust,
>   To thoughts most impious, actions most unjust.[40]
>
> (emphasis added)

She sees Red Rose as a Hippolytus figure and, like Phaedra in certain versions of the myth, is set to rape him. She succeeds . . . and Rose Cross departs to the court of Prester John.[41]

In the second example, the Queen Mab who appears in Drayton's *Nimphidia* of 1627, is wife to Oberon – but also an incubus. What she might do to young men is very explicit:

> And Mab, his merry queen, by night
> Bestrids young folks that lie upright [on their backs,
>   supine].
> (In elder times the 'mare' [nightmare] that hight)
> Which plagues them out of measure.   (sig. Q1v)

35 Stith Thompson, *Motif-Index of Folk-Literature*, 6 vols. (Copenhagen, 1955–8), F366.2.1.

36 The painting, in a private collection, may be viewed at www.leicestergalleries.com/19th-20th-century-paintings/d/gustave-dore/12877.

37 Provenance: Sale, Christie's, London, 8 June 1928, lot 127 (to Lefevre); Frick Art Reference Library negative number W4756. It was shown at the Royal Academy in 1846.

38 Clark, *Demons*, pp. 304–6.

39 The painting is in the Freies Deutsches Hochstift, Goethe museum. For an account of a related painting, see Lawrence Feingold, 'Fuseli, Another Nightmare: *The Night-Hag Visiting Lapland Witches*', *Metropolitan Museum Journal*, 17 (1984), 49–61; Fuseli took his inspiration from *Paradise Lost*, II, 662–6.

40 *Tom a Lincoln*, lines 1564–74 (emphasis added).

41 In Jonson's *Entertainment at Althorp* (1616) Mab appears as the Queen of the Fairies, and makes mischief in the manner of Shakespeare's Robin Goodfellow.

Drayton's lines are built around a *monde renversé* image: Mab is not just a tormentor but, on top, as *incubus*, must be for men an agent of effeminization.

Queen Mab, therefore, has four aspects, as nuisance, as a moral agent, as bringer of dreams and fancies and, most ominously, as incubus. In the late version of Fuseli's *The Nightmare*, one of his most notorious – and imitated – paintings, we see a furry demon with the face of a long-eared owl and looking rather feminine, eyeing minute fairies on the maiden's dressing table.[42] It may be impossible to banish or exorcise such demons or hags: at the end of Act 3 of the *Dream*, Puck says grimly, in prose, that, after the play is resolved, 'the man shall have his mare again, and all shall be well' (3.3.47–8). A 'mare' is actually a malign spirit[43] – but Fuseli, concurring with those who espoused the false etymology, obviously thought that the word referred to a horse for the ghostly head of a horse peers between the bed-curtains at the recumbent young woman.

Shakespeare, however, chose not to dwell long upon topics of malefic and sexual practice. Moreover, Mercutio's *tone* is quite different, although, ultimately, equally misogynistic. Much of the speech comprises the description of Mab's person, a listing of the dreams she brings to others, and concludes with a brief reflection upon the malefic she performs. What does it add up to?

First, the longish catalogue of dreams. Sir Keith Thomas has written on the way that self-fulfilment was difficult in the early modern period.[44] The dreams Mab brings are of fantasies, not only idle but also strait-jackets that prevent self-refashioning. All that men might do is labour in their vocation: their vocation is their destiny. This little woman is a dead weight for young men clambering up the slippery slopes of advancement. Indeed I would contend that political and religious ideology legitimized *occupations* by hallowing them as 'vocations' – Mab is an instrument in this process.

Alternatively we might want to say that Mercutio is indulging himself with an excessive feast of invention, at least in his description of the Queen's person, which feels pretty innocent. He goes 'off on one': it's as though someone had invoked

Murphy's law – 'if anything can go wrong, it will' – then amused his mates with a fantastical description in the manner of a bar-room comic. Anything demonic *seems* to have been purged away. Mercutio also stresses that Mab is very small, as in a 2009 Royal Mail stamp. It used to be said that the diminutive fairy was a Shakespearian innovation:[45] however, there are, in earlier texts, many references to small creatures, particularly elves, along with reports of the sighting of very small fairies.[46] I wonder whether this attribute was driven by Mercutio's mockery of Romeo at this moment in the play, and whether it carried over into some references in the text of *A Midsummer Night's Dream*. Perhaps we could compare the way that Milton, in *Paradise Lost*, reduced the size of the fallen angels to that of 'fairy elves' (Book 1, 781) as a way of marking their moral stature.[47]

Performances of *A Midsummer Night's Dream* however, demand humans to play the fairy parts: after all, Titania virtually propositions Bottom – she wants to be the ivy to his elm. Shakespeare seems to have playfully given the fairies names that suggest smallness,[48] while requiring the parts to be played by non-dwarfish players – whether boys or

---

42 Christopher Frayling, 'Fuseli's *The Nightmare*', in *Gothic Nightmares: Fuseli, Blake and the Romantic Imagination*, ed. Martin Myrone, Christopher Frayling and Marina Warner (London, 2006), pp. 9–21.

43 In Hieronymus Braunschweig, *A Most Excellent and Perfect Homish Apothecary*, trans. John Hollybush (Cologne, 1561), fo. 10, we read of 'the disease called incubus, that is, the mare, which is a sickness or fantasy oppressing a man in his sleep'.

44 Keith Thomas, *The Ends of Life: Roads to Fulfilment in Early Modern England* (Oxford, 2009).

45 William Shakespeare, *A Midsummer Night's Dream*, ed. R. A. Foakes (Cambridge, 1984), p. 8; William Shakespeare, *A Midsummer Night's Dream*, ed. Harold F. Brooks (London, Methuen, 1979), pp. lxxi–lxxv.

46 Purkiss, *Troublesome Things*, p. 6.

47 Julia Staykova reminded me of this.

48 Matthew 13:31–2 tells the parable of the mustard seed: 'The kingdom of heaven is like unto a grain of mustard, which a man taketh and planteth in his field. Which indeed is like the least of all seeds, but when it is grown, it is the greatest among of herbs and it is a tree, so that the birds of heaven come and build in the branches thereof' (Geneva Version).

adults we do not know. Perhaps the pigmy statures of Goodfellow, Peaseblossom and the rest of the trooping flower-fairies connoted their lowly positions in the hierarchies of faerie-land. In Greene's romance-play, *James IV* of 1590, five years earlier than the *Dream*, the bluff Bohan, in mocking King Oberon, dismisses the fairy king's attendants as 'antics' or 'puppets' (perhaps 'poppets') – the latter word suggests the parts were here taken by children. However, there is evidence from a seventeenth-century droll that the fairy roles in *Dream* were doubled with those of the mechanicals, parts that obviously demanded adult actors.[49]

Fuseli's Titania, as we have already seen, is the same size as Bottom, but some of her attendants are adult, and others, in the margins of Fuseli's picture, diminutive.[50] Most artists, however, overlooked *stage practice*, and it was Mercutio's fantastical speech that was the source of the plethora of images of tiny creatures in later illustrations of Shakespeare, in books of fairy tales and in Hollywood animations.

One more image from the romantic period: Richard Dadd's painting of nude fairies is intriguingly eroticized. Was this caught from sexualized representations of Queen Mab?[51]

I suspect, however, the speech is best explored in the context of laddish relationships and the ideology of gender.

To do this I leap back to 1450 and 1451, when bands of Kentish protestors, out to poach the deer of the Duke of Buckingham at Penshurst, 'painted on their faces with black charcoal, calling themselves "servants of the queen of the fairies"', intending that their names should not be known'.[52] Diane Purkiss intelligently asks how we should read this detail: to her suggestions we might add another, that these breakers of the king's peace were offering insult to injury, impugning the masculinity of any duke who could not stand up to puny creatures like fairies. In the same vein, Mercutio's speech is an insult to Romeo, implying that he has been unmanned by his infatuation with Rosaline, and become superstitious, 'believing in' his dream in the way that the dreams of women might make something of nothing. In 1601 at South Kyme in Lincolnshire during a derisive play against the Earl of Lincoln, a mock sermon was preached 'out of the Book of Mab'.[53]

Mercutio cunningly ends his catalogue of malefic acts, as practised by witches, when he describes the way Mab inducted maids into sexual practice, engendering that disturbing phenomenon of female desire, which might effeminize any man who reciprocates. By exposing Romeo's credulity, Mercutio must have scored a palpable hit, for in Act 3, just after Tybalt has killed his friend, Romeo laments:

> O sweet Juliet,
> Thy beauty hath made me *effeminate*,
> And in my temper softened valour's steel.
> (3.1.113–15, emphasis added)

Reginald Scot had gone further than Michael Drayton had in *Nimphidia*: he reported that young men could have 'their genitals taken from them by witches'.[54] Like so many womanizers, Romeo and his friends turn out to be misogynistic.[55]

In the description of Mab, was Shakespeare simply invoking an old-fashioned residual popular belief, in order for Mercutio, witty and agnostic (?), to mock it with attitude? Was he even implicitly accusing Romeo of false or heretical devotion?[56] Maybe, but one more comparison may complicate things even further. About sixty years later,

---

49 Holland, ed., *MND*, p. 24.
50 This convention of double-sized fairies was picked up in a painting, 'Mab, the Bringer of Dreams', by a contemporary American neo-realist, Howard David Johnson.
51 The painting is in the Harris Museum and Art Gallery in Preston: see http://museumpublicity.com/2011/04/21/harris-museum-acquires-19th-puck-painting. See also Charlotte Gere, Jeremy Maas and Pamela White Trimpe, *Victorian Fairy Painting* (London, 1997).
52 Purkiss, *Troublesome Things*, p. 67.
53 Martin Ingram, 'Ridings, Rough Music and the "Reform of Popular Culture"', *Past and Present*, 105 (1984), 79–113.
54 Reginald Scot, *The Discovery of Witchcraft* (London, 1584), p. 77.
55 In the same way Troilus feels his heroic self has been destroyed by his love for Cressida.
56 See the discussion of Gosson on 'Venus' nuns' in Julia D. Staykova, 'Adultery, Idolatry, and the Theatricality of False Piety', *Shakespeare*, 7 (2011), 170–91.

in 1653, Margaret Lucas Cavendish (1623–1673), Duchess of Newcastle, published *Poems and Fancies*, dedicated to her brother-in-law, Sir Charles Cavendish. It contains a long sequence of poems about fairies.[57] This is the penultimate poem in the book.

> Sir Charles into my chamber coming in,
> When I was writing of my Fairy Queen –
> 'I pray', said he, 'when Queen Mab you do see,
> Present my service to Her Majesty
> And tell her I have heard Fame's loud report
> Both of her beauty and her stately court.'
> When I Queen Mab within my fancy viewed,
> My thoughts bowed low, fearing I should be rude.
> Kissing her garment thin, which fancy made,
> Kneeling upon a thought, like one that prayed,
> In whispers soft I did present
> His humble service, which in mirth was sent.
> Thus by imagination I have been
> In Fairy Court, and seen the Fairy Queen.
> For why? Imagination runs about
> In every place, yet none can trace it out.[58]

Again there is no locating tone. Was Sir Charles gently mocking a degree of credulity in his talented sister-in-law, or making witty but courteous conversation? We can't tell, but I would submit that Cavendish is protective of her imaginary figure, conjured from the past, gently suggesting that her Mab may be, for women, a protective or tutelary spirit. Cavendish too is *thinking with* fairies – or, as she put it herself in the title of another poem, 'The fairies in the brain may be the causes of many thoughts.'[59] She may even have been remembering Hippolyta's 'something of great constancy' as well.

So can we define or fix Queen Mab? She was obviously a creature for all seasons – or we might quote Lewis Carroll: '"When *I* use a word," Humpty Dumpty said, in rather a scornful tone, "it means just what I choose it to mean – neither more nor less".'

4. *A MIDSUMMER NIGHT'S DREAM* AND ITS FAIRY PROGENY

Now for *A Midsummer Night's Dream* – but first another historical problem: *when* might fairy-lore

have become 'residual'? Well before the sixteenth-century Reformations, fairies had been associated with the olden days. In her 'Tale' Chaucer's Wife of Bath begins thus:

> In th'olde dayes of the Kyng Arthour . . .
> Al was this land fulfild of fayere.
> The elf-queene, with hir joly compaignye,
> Daunced ful ofte in many a grene mede.[60]

The Wife goes on to tell how fairies, practisers of heathen magical rituals, had been searched out and destroyed by the 'limiters', friars of an unreformed Catholic church. Later, we are told, Protestants also had separated magic from religion[61] so that, after the Reformation, fairies became, generally, malevolent beings whose 'magic' was branded as a species of the false religion said to be practised by that same Catholic church from which, two hundred and fifty years before, their inquisitional persecutors had been recruited. Reformations theoretically created a firmer time-line: Reginald Scot in 1584 wrote, 'In time to come, a witch will be as much derided and contemned, and as plainly perceived, as the illusion and knavery of Robin Goodfellow.'[62] Yet in 1610, when he wrote *Cymbeline*, Shakespeare, perhaps in deference to King James, invoked fairies as malevolent demons, threats to Imogen when she would sleep (2.2.9 and 4.2.218).

This is all registered in the first part of a ditty by Bishop Richard Corbet (1582–1635), written during the reign of James I,[63] who brilliantly evokes a world purged of magic, only to dismiss both fairies

---

[57] See Anna Battigelli, *Margaret Cavendish and the Exiles of the Mind* (Lexington, 1998), pp. 48–9.

[58] Margaret Cavendish, Duchess of Newcastle, *Poems, and Fancies* (London, 1653), pp. 213–14.

[59] Cavendish, *Poems*, p. 164.

[60] Geoffrey Chaucer, 'The Wife of Bath's Tale', in *Works*, ed. F. N. Robinson (London, 1957), lines 858–61.

[61] Keith Thomas, *Religion and the Decline of Magic* (Harmondsworth, 1973), pp. 27–57; Holland, ed., *Dream*, pp. 22–3.

[62] Scot, *Witchcraft*, p. 131.

[63] Claude M. Simpson, *The British Broadside Ballad and its Music* (New Brunswick, 1966), p. 740.

and their exorcism by his witty and disbelieving tone:

A Proper New Ballad, Entitled 'The Fairies' Farewell' . . .
To be Sung or Whistled to the Tune of 'The Meadow
Brow' by the Learned, by the Unlearned to the Tune of
'Fortune [My Foe]' 'Farewell, rewards and fairies',
   Good housewives now may say,
For now foul sluts in dairies
   Do fare as well as they;
And though they sweep their hearths no less
   Than maids were wont to do,
Yet who of late, for cleanliness,
   Finds sixpence in her shoe? . . .

Witness those rings and roundelays
   Of theirs which yet remain,
Were footed in Queen Mary's days
   On many a grassy plane;
But since, of late, Elizabeth
   And later James came in,
They never danced on any heath
   As when the time had been.

By which we note the fairies
   Were of the old profession,
Their songs were Ave Maries,
   Their dances were procession [Romish litanies
     sung in procession];
But now alas they all are dead
   Or gone beyond the seas,
Or further from religion fled –
   Or else they take their ease.[64]

By suggesting two tunes Corbet creates two perspectives on his text, one for the elite and one for rustics or the unlearned. Nevertheless, there *are* locating tones here: perhaps Shakespeare in the *Dream* and Corbet were quietly mocking the Calvinist position that men, having fallen, were peculiarly vulnerable to the snares of papistry. Edmund Spenser, after all, had desperately claimed that the words 'elves' and 'goblins' were derived from Guelphs and Ghibellines, the warring factions of Papist Florence.[65]

Another aspect of Reformation ideology is revealed in a country house masque, presented at Coleorton in Leicestershire in 1618.[66] As part of a lament for the cultural destruction wrought

by Puritanism, we learn fairies have been converted from holiday and helping with the harvest[67] in order to be conscripted into the Leicestershire coal-mines, rather like Bevan-boys. We have seen a puck as a mischief-maker and as a clown – here he is a gang-master:

Puck. O ho, ho, boy, hold thee there, and I'll bring thee acquainted with my new company.

Bob. Who are they, Puck?

Puck. Why, the black fairies, boy, the dancing spirits of the pits: such as look to Tom's Egyptians here, and help them hole and drive sharp their picks and mandrels [picks], keep away the damp, and keep in their candles, drain the sough [empty the drain] and hold them out of the hollows.[68]

Religion and the rise of capitalism indeed!

So, even if late medieval and early modern writers were aware that times were changing, it is almost impossible to specify dates for the changes. Moreover, Titania enters Shakespeare's play from classical antiquity; Robin Goodfellow, the puck, like the brownie or will o'the wisp, is a British type of neighbourhood spirit who can also fly.[69] We

---

[64] Richard Corbet, *Certain Elegant Poems* (London, 1647), pp. 47–8.

[65] E. K.'s Gloss to *The Shepheardes Calendar*, June, line 25, in Edmund Spenser, *The Shorter Poems*, ed. William A. Oram *et al.* (New Haven, 1989), p. 115.

[66] Philip J. Finkelpearl, 'The Fairies' Farewell: The Masque at Coleorton (1618)', *Review of English Studies*, 46 (1995), 333–51.

[67] Briggs, *Vanishing People*, p. 130.

[68] David Lindley (ed.), *Court Masques: Jacobean and Caroline Entertainments, 1605–1640* (Oxford, 1995), lines 72–9.

[69] Katharine Mary Briggs, *The Anatomy of Puck* (London, 1959), pp. 24, 186, 191. An oral tradition, which, it is claimed, derives from the time of Merlin, surfaces in the last stanza of a poem called simply 'Robin Goodfellow', once attributed to Jonson: 'From hag-bred Merlin's time have I / Thus nightly revell'd to and fro: / And for my pranks men call me by / The name of Robin Goodfellòw. / Fiends, ghosts, and sprites, / Who haunt the nights, / The hags and goblins do me know; / And beldams old / My feats have told; / So *Vale, Vale*; ho, ho, ho!' 'Robin Good-Fellow' (Thomas Percy, ed., *Percy's Reliques of Ancient English Poetry*, 2 vols. (London, Everyman, n.d.), vol. 2, pp. 316–17); see Simpson, *Broadside Ballad*, p. 204.

have to conclude that we are dealing with literary *topoi* with a long shelf-life, another reason for concluding that any particular or certain engagement with ideology is almost impossible. Or we might reasonably conjecture that it is the very *appearances* of fairies or evocations of fairyland in texts, signs of nostalgia and associated with nature as they are, that are indices of a general sense of cultural change.

Perhaps, however, these excavations in the soil of text and folklore do reveal some traces of slightly more specific ideological fault-lines. I have tentatively suggested that Shakespeare bowed to the pressures of Protestant thinking and rejected anything supernatural, anything akin to a miracle. However, I have no conclusions about whether or not he was happy with residual beliefs or, alternatively, generally 'disenchanted' and, living in the dawning of an age of scepticism, out to expose them. Did he write from the position of intellectual elitism? Or did he assume that, if his audiences were content with the quaint practices of popular magic, so was he? We just don't know.

By contrast, sixty odd years later, the goddess Reason had obviously snatched Samuel Pepys into her grip:

To the King's Theatre, where we saw *Midsummer's Night's Dream*, which I had never seen before, nor shall ever again, for it is the most insipid ridiculous play that ever I saw in my life. I saw, I confess, some good dancing and some handsome women, which was all my pleasure.[70]

We may presume that Pepys was thinking primarily about the fairies. Some fifty years after that, well into the Enlightenment, Weber's age of disenchantment, Alexander Pope was prepared to deploy fairy-like creatures, the sylphs that figure in *The Rape of the Lock*. He spelt out his intentions in the dedicatory letter to Arabella Fermor:

The 'machinery', Madam, is a term invented by the critics, to signify that part which deities, angels, or dæmons are made to act in a poem. For the ancient poets are in one respect like many modern ladies: let an action be never so trivial in itself, they always make it appear of the utmost importance. These machines I determined to

raise on a very new and odd foundation, the Rosicrucian doctrine of spirits.[71]

Pope therefore saw his use of spirits as a quaint rhetorical device, serving to make claims for human significance. More interestingly, he also – impishly – links belief to gender.

But might not ideological maps drawn by those who read as women indeed be different from those drawn by men? Witness Margaret Cavendish. Were the fairies in Shakespeare perceived by metropolitan or courtly elites in the way that Pepys perceived them, associated with rusticity and old wives' tales? Indeed how were they gendered? Were they more often harmless by virtue of being incorporated in amusing insets, as singers and dancers – as in Greene's *James IV* – or court masques such as Jonson's *Oberon*, presentational rather than representational?[72]

5. LANGUAGE AND GENDER: 'NYMPHS'

The actions of Oberon and the mistakes of the puck, a pastiche Cupid, are invoked to reveal to us the fragility of constancy:

Love looks not with the eyes, but with the mind,
And therefore is winged Cupid painted blind.
(1.1.234–5)

Casting spells upon the eyes of the lovers reveals that Helena's couplet may explain the iconology of the love-god, but it also implies that love *does* in fact originate in sight.

---

[70] Samuel Pepys, *Diary*, 29 September 1662; five years later Thomas Sprat was to announce the end of fairies: Thomas Sprat, *A History of the Royal Society of London* (London, 1667), pp. 29–30.

[71] Alexander Pope, *The Poems of Alexander Pope*, ed. John Butt (London, 1968), p. 217.

[72] Ben Jonson, *Selected Masques*, ed. Stephen Orgel (New Haven, 1970), p. 109; for plays in which fairies appear, see Alan C. Dessen and Leslie Thomson, *A Dictionary of Stage Directions in English Drama, 1580–1642* (Cambridge, 1999), pp. 87–8.

Not only do Titania's spell-bound eyes make her into a kind of incubus for Bottom,[73] but it is also notable that, after the men have been enchanted, Oberon calls after Helena 'Fare thee well, *nymph*' (2.1.245). If, as R. A. Foakes wrote, 'Shakespeare is playfully [absorbing] the lovers into a quasi-mythological world',[74] the gaze and word of the men transfigure the virgin Helena. In fact the word sexualizes her – because 'nymph' was a word that was applied both to those who were alive but doomed to die and also to man-snatchers like Calypso.[75] It was also applied to prostitutes – when Hamlet addresses Ophelia as 'nymph' just after 'To be or not to be' (3.1.91) many actors make the word sarcastic. When Demetrius awakens, he addresses Helena with the same word (3.2.138), and Helena echoes it when recalling the moment to Hermia (3.2.227) – these are the only instances of the word in the play. In his masque *Oberon the Fairy Prince*, Jonson has a pair of satyrs hoping to come upon sexually available nymphs (lines 33–4).

In his description of a performance of Macbeth at the Globe of 1611, Simon Forman begins:

there was to be observed, first, how Macbeth and Banquo, two noblemen of Scotland, riding through a wood, there stood before them three women, *fairies*, or *nymphs*, and saluted Macbeth, saying, three times unto him, 'Hail, Macbeth, King of Codon [*sic*]: for thou shalt be a king, but shalt beget no kings' . . . Then said Banquo, 'What? All to Macbeth, and nothing to me?' 'Yes', said the nymphs, 'hail to thee, Banquo: thou shalt beget kings yet be no king'. And so they departed and came to the court of Scotland, to Duncan, King of Scots, and it was in the days of Edward the Confessor.[76]

(emphases added)

Holinshed also refers to 'fairies or nymphs', so it is obvious that enchantment was a possibility for these chroniclers of both 'history' and performance. The fairies of Oberon and Titania have served to make everything seem double (4.1.188–9) – perhaps this double vision derives from the polarities of gender.

6. FAIRIES AND ROMANCE PLOTS

Having sketched the problems of relating texts to the forms and pressures of Shakespeare's time, I want to move further into *A Midsummer Night's Dream*. My suggestion is that Shakespeare had been treading very carefully: that use of a 'sacramental' indicates traces of explosive and Catholic beliefs, which Shakespeare carefully defused in *Merry Wives*. By contrast with his treatment of Mab, in his next play, *A Midsummer Night's Dream*, where the fairies are central to the action, was Shakespeare somehow *affirming* traditional fairylore, offering some 'retractation' (Spenser's word[77]) of Mercutio's implied mockery?

In the *Dream*, counter-intuitively – the fairies after all, drive the whole plot – Shakespeare's intention is completely invisible, nothing comes of nothing, and any interpretation we place upon the play belongs in our age not in Shakespeare's. The forest near Athens does not constitute a 'fairy-land' in the sense that Spenser created his: there *are* attendant fairies, but their controllers, Oberon and Titania, interest us because they are, almost disconcertingly, like humans, and we read the flower named 'love-in-idleness' as a metonym for the daily rigmaroles of being bewitched by others.

What might I mean by all this? Let's jump o'er times and think of Alfred Hitchcock. According to François Truffaut, who, in interview, questioned Hitchcock about *North by Northwest* (1959), the director had eschewed notions of cause and effect: 'the MacGuffin' he said, 'has been boiled down to its purest expression: nothing at all . . . The espionage that drives the plot does just that: it drives the plot.'[78] 'MacGuffin': a wonderful nonsensical nonce word for 'plot-driver' – or Pope's 'machines'.

---

[73] 'The divell plaieth *Succubus* to the man and carrieth from him the seed of generation, which he delivereth as *Incubus* to the woman' (Reginald Scot, *The Discovery of Witchcraft* [1586], ed. Montague Summers (London, 1930), III. xix, p. 41).

[74] Foakes, ed., *MND*, note to 2.1.245.

[75] Purkiss, *Troublesome Things*, pp. 38–46.

[76] Quoted in William Shakespeare, *Macbeth*, ed. A. R. Braunmuller (Cambridge, 1997), p. 57.

[77] Epistle to 'Fowre Hymnes', Spenser, *Shorter Poems*, p. 690.

[78] See François Truffaut, *Le cinéma selon Hitchcock* (Paris, 1966), *passim*.

The world of Hitchcock's cinematic romance resembles the world of Spenser's *Faerie Queene*, and its hero, Thornhill, played by Cary Grant, is, like Hamlet, 'but mad north-north-west', so protecting himself against an inscrutable and uncontrollable world. The film's screenwriter Ernest Lehman declined to attribute motivation to his characters, simply setting them in a Manichean world riven by the Cold War. We need to know little about the film's blonde double-agent heroine, who could be called Duessa, but is instead an Eve – her name proclaims her motivation. (Eve was played, of course, by the oxymoronically named Eva Marie Saint.) Lehman's characters are programmed according to the conventions of the genre, not motivated by a precipitating event in the past or particularized political or moral imperatives. By analogy, a warning over the power or moral stature of fairies might have been expected in the sixteenth century but Shakespeare did not offer one. Putting this another way: the fairies are the play's MacGuffin because there is a disconnnect between their dramatic function and their theatrical presence.

Hitchcock's fearsome narrative is defiantly episodic. In both his Illinois and Mount Rushmore identities are uncertain, locales fantastic, and perceptions are changed – by bourbon rather than love-in-idleness. There the film's Rosencrantz and Guildenstern, the sidekicks of the evil Phillip Vandamm, show up as inexplicably but conveniently as do pucks and fairies. This is not surprising, given that their names are marvellously Shakespearian: one sports the moniker of Valerian (a herbal sedative) and the other is called Licht ('Light'). The film's action is like what happens in the wood a league outside Athens. Indeed very many fantasies of this kind and science fiction films derive ultimately from medieval romances and, of course, for a Disney animator, the double size of fairies would be an opportunity rather than a challenge.

My point is that the fairies in Shakespeare's *Dream* serve as the play's 'MacGuffin'. They belong among the play's theatrical forms and their agency enacts its linguistic forms, metaphors of being 'enchanted', 'charmed' or 'spell-bound' (see 2.2.17).

In February 2010 Peter Hall inserted a MacGuffin into a production of Shakespeare's text when Judi Dench played Titania at the Rose Theatre in Kingston, near London. Shakespeare's Fairy Queen became Queen Elizabeth I – as always, in love. In a silent induction, Dame Judi, clad as Gloriana, seized a part from a member of a band of aristocratic but amateur players assembled to divert her, and stalked off to con the lines of Titania herself. She obviously knew the story and fancied a spot of doting with the handsome if bumptious young lord who was to play Bottom (Oliver Chris). It was all a bit absurd really – but it did demonstrate that Oberon's controlling but inscrutable will makes him a fit mate for this production's MacGuffin.

However, we should remember that in 1962 the young pointy-eared Dame Judi, again playing Titania, looked as though she had magical powers as strong as those of Oberon her husband. Putting all this yet another way, in *A Midsummer Night's Dream* the emphasis is on events and situations, not on *explanations* for them. And, even more generally, meaning depends as much upon directors as upon authors.

I am quite happy with Peter Hall's collaboration with Shakespeare: indeed it supports my hypothesis that the fairies in the *Dream* and *The Merry Wives of Windsor* carry a much lighter ideological burden than does Queen Mab, the 'less important' fairy in *Romeo and Juliet*. *Pace* Hall and Dench, I would argue that they are a kind of dramatic or theatrical shorthand, a way of portraying inwardness, dreams, and as Fuseli claimed, sentiments. It is legitimate to assume that Oberon and Titania are figures or types of the Duke of Athens and his bride, a way of portraying the tensions between Theseus and Hippolyta – a perception that informed that Ron Daniels production. The whole of the action during this summer night is a dream of the joys, fears and doubts of the lovers before they commit themselves to betrothal and marriage. All of this was allegorically inscribed in Peter Brook's great production of 1970 when he did what may well have been done in Shakespeare's time, doubled Theseus and Hippolyta with Oberon and Titania, as well as the fairies and the mechanicals. This was a MacGuffin-less production as both the powerful and the powerless were the same.

Given that fairies could have been branded as demons by the godly of the period, it is significant that Shakespeare's text does not seem to have drawn the attention of the censorious. Despite the precedent set by Spenser's *Faerie Queene*, Shakespeare obviously thought it might have done:

> *Robin.* My fairy lord, this must be done with haste,
>   For night's swift dragons cut the clouds full fast,
>   And yonder shines Aurora's harbinger,
>   At whose approach ghosts, wand'ring here and
>   there,
>   Troop home to churchyards; damnèd spirits all
>   That in cross-ways and floods have burial
>   Already to their wormy beds are gone,
>   For fear lest day should look their shames upon.
>   They wilfully themselves exile from light,
>   And must for aye consort with black-browed night.
> *Oberon.* But we are spirits of another sort.
>   I with the morning's love have oft made sport,
>   And like a forester the groves may tread
>   Even till the eastern gate, all fiery red,
>   Opening on Neptune with fair blessèd beams,
>   Turns into yellow gold his salt green streams.
>
> (3.2.379–94)

These fairy spirits can be more than harmless, in fact benign: the mother of the Indian boy, a 'vot'ress of [Titania's'] order' (2.1.123), was happy to confide her new-born son to Titania, the goddess of childbirth, a reversal of the topic of the changeling, a deformed baby substituted for one the fairies had snatched away. (As Diana, the same goddess had a habit of exiling or killing any votary who got herself pregnant.[79]) On the other hand they or at least their actions can be frightening: the translation of Bottom, which sends the mechanicals running from the stage, may be an index of the fear engendered by unpeopled spaces, in particular the wild wood. After punning on the word 'shadows' (actors and spirits), Robin as Epilogue disowns and hands to the *audience* the responsibility for conjuring fairies, banishing them from the land of fairy in the woods into a land of dreams – was this a safety precaution?

> If we *shadows* have offended,
> Think but this, and all is mended:
> That you have but slumbered here,
> While these visions did appear;
> And this weak and idle theme,
> No more yielding but a dream
>
> (Epi.1–6, emphasis added)

Rather than being agents, Shakespeare's fairy monarchs and their crew are markers, deftly evoking various kinds of transgression. They would be dangerous if they *were* abrogating laws of nature – raising tempests or blighting crops. They are not folkloric versions of the classical fates, although some scholars think the word 'fairy' derives ultimately from the Latin *fatum*. Perhaps we should not engage morally with the fairies: they are there to demonstrate something about human behaviour.[80]

Again Shakespeare treads delicately: when we hear of climate change, triggered by the actions of Oberon and Titania, we realize that the speech is rhetorical, setting out the limits of fairy power: 'on old Hiems' thin and icy crown / An odorous chaplet of sweet summer buds / Is, as in mock'ry, set' (2.1.109–11). It is important to note that the fairies had not *caused* the change but *provoked* it. Shakespeare's lines deploy the trope of what R. W. Scribner called a 'moralized universe'. 'Pre-Reformation religion . . . believed that certain human actions could provoke supernatural intervention in the natural world, either as a sign or a punishment', and Scribner argued that this nexus came more forcefully to the fore after the Reformation.[81] It obviously did: in July 2007 it was reported that the Bishop of Carlisle had claimed that gay marriages were responsible for floods that were widespread in England that year. In 2010 there were claims from Iran that earthquakes had been caused by promiscuous women.

---

[79] Purkiss, *Troublesome Things*, p. 178.
[80] Purkiss, *Troublesome Things*, p. 8.
[81] Robert W. Scribner, 'The Reformation, Popular Magic, and the "Disenchantment of the World"', *Journal of Interdisciplinary History*, 23 (1993), 475–94, at 485–6.

Shakespeare, however, is not obsessed by sexual transgression: he suggests that it was *dissension in the fairy court that* was responsible for that disconcertingly mild winter.

7. CONCLUSION

We have looked at *Romeo and Juliet* and *Cymbeline* (briefly), and at *The Merry Wives of Windsor* and *A Midsummer Night's Dream*. In the first two fairies are malignant, in the second, for the most part benevolent or at worst harmless. I do not think we can map cultural or ideological currents: all we can do is, as I have indicated, to watch Shakespeare thinking with his fairies. It may seem far-fetched, but I would like to propose a comparison with Archbishop Rowan Williams on Dostoyevsky:

I have assumed that Dostoyevsky is not presenting to us a set of inconclusive arguments about 'the existence of God', for and against, but a fictional picture of what faith and the lack of it would *look* like in the political and social world of his day.[82]

Let's ponder an aphorism by Philip Goodwin:

. . . man, as an animal creature, in dreaming sleeps;
And man, as a rational creature, in sleeping dreams.[83]

To end where I began: the devil may well have been exorcised from the imagined worlds of the playhouse, so naught shall go ill, although critics and directors will hunt their MacGuffins again, but all shall be well.

---

[82] Rowan Williams, *Dostoevsky: Language, Faith and Fiction* (London, 2008), p. 4.
[83] Goodwin, *Dreams*, p. 6.

THINKING WITH FAIRIES:
A MIDSUMMER NIGHT'S DREAM AND THE PROBLEM OF BELIEF

JESSE M. LANDER

There was an impenetrability about fairy-beliefs which protected them from easy exposure.

Keith Thomas

One of the recurring problems with fairies is that hard bony thought constantly melts into a jelly of aesthetics.

Diane Purkiss

The fairy vogue ... rested upon a kind of pleasurable half-belief.

Katharine Briggs

In 1662, the diarist, Samuel Pepys attended a performance of *A Midsummer's Night Dream* and came away famously unimpressed. Declaring it 'the most insipid ridiculous play that ever I saw in my life', Pepys allowed that there was 'some good dancing and some handsome women, which was all my pleasure'.[1] It is hardly surprising that Pepys, whose sexual energy is well documented in his diary, should have found pleasure in handsome women and dance. His dismissal of the play as insipid and ridiculous has usually been cited as evidence of a lack of discernment, a critical judgement so obviously wrong as to be valuable only as a provocation. Nonetheless, the terms of this rejection are significant. Pepys, after all, rehearses a position that is provided within the play by Duke Theseus, who dismisses the adventures of the lovers in the wood as so much childish nonsense. Moreover, it would be simple enough to align Pepys with an increasingly urban and urbane world in which a decisive separation between elite and common culture has occurred. According to such an account, a play like *A Midsummer Night's Dream* can only appear to the post-Restoration world as spectacle. The moment in which fairy-lore was widely accepted has passed; within the high culture of the metropolis it has become a merely poetic and aesthetic inheritance available to animate theatrical and literary productions. Consequently, Pepys signals some appreciation for the spectacle of dance and female bodies, but dismisses as foolish and dull the fairy matter that is central to the play.

Evidently, Pepys does not take the question of fairies seriously, but this raises another problem. As the position of Theseus indicates, even in Shakespeare's day there were plenty of people who dismissed fairy belief as childish superstition. Katharine Briggs has observed that fairy belief seems to be in perpetual decline and is invariably located elsewhere: in children, in old women, in an earlier age or an alien culture.[2] This disavowal, the imputation of false belief, has important implications for any attempt at historical understanding. Discussing the problem of religious unbelief, Stephen Greenblatt, following a line established by Lucien Febvre, declares 'not that atheism was literally unthinkable but rather that it was almost always thinkable only as the thought of another'.[3]

---

[1] Samuel Pepys, *The Diary of Samuel Pepys*, ed. R. Latham and W. Matthews, 11 vols. (Berkeley, 1970–83), III, p. 208.

[2] Katharine Mary Briggs, *The Anatomy of Puck: An Examination of Fairy Beliefs among Shakespeare's Contemporaries and Successors* (London, 1959), p. 22.

[3] Stephen Greenblatt, *Shakespearean Negotiations: The Circulation of Social Energy in Renaissance England* (Berkeley, 1988), p. 22; Lucien Febvre, *The Problem of Unbelief in the Sixteenth Century: The Religion of Rabelais*, trans. B. Gottlieb (Cambridge, MA, 1982). For an illuminating account, see

Of course, imputed unbelief is not the same thing as imputed belief, but the dynamic of disavowal is the same in both cases: misbelief is attributed to someone else. One major consequence of this dynamic is that talk about fairies invariably reflects upon the qualities and conditions of belief, and it frequently involves a historicizing of belief that posits a shift from a credulous past to a sceptical present. Given the always already dismissed status of fairy beliefs – in the words of Keith Thomas 'it seems that commentators have always attributed them to the past' – it is not surprising that scholars have sought to explain them in functional terms.[4]

The functionalism that Thomas offers regarding fairy belief is rudimentary: fairy-beliefs 'enforce a certain code of conduct'.[5] For example, the threat of fairy abductions increased the vigilance of care providers in the critical early days of an infant's life. Fairy hostility towards slovenly housekeeping provided a supernatural sanction for hygienic practices that reduced the spread of disease and the likelihood of food contamination. Somewhat more complexly, the changeling serves to absolve parents of the shame and guilt associated with a difficult or defective child. More recently Mary Ellen Lamb has criticized Thomas's functionalism for its effacement of agency.[6] As an alternative, she draws on the work of James C. Scott in order to position fairy-lore as a 'weapon of the weak', a means by which dominated groups resist social control.[7] A victim of rape, for instance, could describe herself as having been 'taken by the fairies', a euphemism that might preserve her honour and avoid accusing a member of the community of perpetrating an act of sexual violence. In addition to sexual acts, found money was referred to using 'fairy euphemisms'.[8] This interpretation posits a double consciousness: fairy explanations are alibis – white lies – that allow for smooth social functioning. Agency is part of the picture, but the agent's deployment of the alibi depends on unbelief – and not just on the part of the speaker but also on the part of the audience. The euphemism functions as an open secret: nobody actually believes that the child is a changeling, that the money is fairy gold.

Parsing the historical record in these terms involves a depth hermeneutic. Confronted by a documented claim about fairy practice, the cultural historian operates on the assumption that the proposition is not in fact about fairies, but is instead a code for something else. Lamb takes a surprisingly positive position on the use of fairy-lore as a subversive strategy, though her description of 'fairy euphemism' suggests that such speech acts preserved social harmony by denying the fact of violence. In particular, she associates Robin Goodfellow with an insurgent plebeian culture that transforms him into 'a hero who rights the wrongs suffered by the powerless and the poor'.[9] Moreover, Robin is not only a representation, an imagined solution for real social inequities; Robin can also be deployed as a weapon of the weak when men disguise themselves as 'fairies' to poach deer. Indeed, Lamb understands accounts of fairy gold to be about theft – such tales are a ruse to explain the sudden, and potentially awkward, acquisition of money. Lamb helpfully insists that fairy-lore was not simply identified with women (nurses and old wives); in her account, the disenfranchised of both genders resorted to the language of fairies as a way 'to forward their own interests'.[10] This argument seems attentive to agency: members of subordinated groups pursue clear-eyed and sophisticated representational strategies.

The model does not, however, consistently allow for a recovery of agency. At one point, Lamb observes that John and Alice West, a pair of swindlers who exploited fairy beliefs found

David Wooton, 'Lucien Febvre and the Problem of Unbelief in the Early Modern Period', *Journal of Modern History*, 60 (1988), 695–730.

[4] Keith Thomas, *Religion and the Decline of Magic* (New York, 1971), pp. 607–8.

[5] Thomas, *Religion and the Decline of Magic*, p. 611.

[6] Mary Ellen Lamb, 'Taken by the Fairies: Fairy Practices and the Production of Popular Culture in *A Midsummer Night's Dream*', *Shakespeare Quarterly*, 51 (2000), 277–312.

[7] James C. Scott, *Weapons of the Weak: Everyday Forms of Peasant Resistance* (New Haven, 1985).

[8] Lamb, 'Taken by Fairies', p. 285.

[9] Lamb, 'Taken by Fairies', p. 300.

[10] Lamb, 'Taken by Fairies', p. 284.

'their most gullible victims among the educated bourgeois or middle-class townspeople rather than among the illiterate farmers of the agrarian community, most of whom may have known better'.[11] But according to her model, they *must* have known better.[12] Townspeople are presumably vulnerable because they have lost contact with the practices associated with fairy-lore and consequently mistake an assemblage of alibis for an actual description of the world. It might be pertinent to point out that illiterate farmers tend to view strangers with suspicion and often lack the ready cash that would make them attractive targets for scam artists like the Wests. But the bigger problem is that the success of the Wests points to the existence of fairy belief, something that Lamb's account is only able to recognize as gullibility.[13]

Taking Peter Burke's claim about the withdrawal of 'great' culture from common culture as given, Lamb sees *Dream* effecting a 'conceptual separation that prepares for the eventual withdrawal of the dominant culture from popular roots'.[14] 'By engaging in the conceptualisation of a popular culture, defined within a mutually constitutive relationship with a more elite culture, *A Midsummer Night's Dream* represents', according to Lamb, 'a precondition for the denigration and eventual rejection of popular culture as vulgar by the eighteenth century.'[15] A crucial part of this argument concerns the way in which the play miniaturizes and aestheticizes its fairies – the weapons of the weak are neutered, denatured and domesticated – in order to construct 'a popular culture in the image desired by a dominant group'. However, the conservative aspects of the play are mitigated by its inability to enforce the cleavage that it initiates, and, in a familiar move, Lamb argues that the play also 'opens a space for rethinking the privileging of the "great" culture over the common culture'.[16]

A similar argument has recently been made by Wendy Wall, who is particularly interested in the connections between fairy-lore, domestic labour and Englishness.[17] According to Wall, 'Fairylore becomes a channel through which Shakespearian drama grapples with the class-specific practices that subtend debates about English community in the late-sixteenth and early-seventeenth centuries.' Wall's larger project explores the 'role that the household played in the project of conceptualising England's social order',[18] and as a consequence, she is especially attentive to the play's domestication of its fairies. Observing that many of the named fairies are associated with household remedies, Wall concludes, 'From this perspective the supernatural creatures of the exotic fairy queen devolve into mere Mustardseed, Peasblossom, Cobweb, and Moth – the stuff of kitchen gardens, condiments, and homey physic.'[19] The play affords a vision of the

social world predicated on a newly expanded domesticity that integrates rural tradition with courtly rule and middling-class concerns for work with aristocratic concerns for lineage. But this integration is not seamlessly accomplished. By revealing the palace's faulty housework and the dust it secret[e]s, Robin uncovers the fact that the tidy domestic closure rests on a reproduction as magical and contingent as fairylore (unacknowledged by the rational Theseus). Locating holy practices beneath the notice of aristocrats, Shakespeare makes daily labor the unacknowledged metaphorical basis for social order.[20]

The subtle suggestion here is that the play undermines its own conclusion by revealing the social reproduction that it seems to celebrate to be

---

[11] Lamb, 'Taken by Fairies', p. 291. Thomas, *Religion and the Decline of Magic*, pp. 613–14, provides details on the Wests. Their exploits are described in *The Severall Notorious and lewd Cousnages of Iohn West, and Alice West, falsely called the King and Queene of Fayries* (London, 1613).

[12] In fairness, Lamb does say, in another context, 'I would theorize a range of levels of belief among his informants, from simple "faith" to outrageous yarn-spinning' (Lamb, 'Taken by Fairies', p. 283, n. 20).

[13] For an extraordinary example of credulity of a later date, see J. Kent Clark, *Goodwin Wharton* (Oxford, 1984).

[14] Lamb, 'Taken by Fairies', p. 280.

[15] Lamb, 'Taken by Fairies', p. 303.

[16] Lamb, 'Taken by Fairies', p. 311.

[17] Wendy Wall, 'Why Does Puck Sweep?: Fairylore, Merry Wives, and Social Struggle', *Shakespeare Quarterly*, 52 (2001), 67–106.

[18] Wall, 'Why Does Puck Sweep?', p. 70.

[19] Wall, 'Why Does Puck Sweep?', p. 86.

[20] Wall, 'Why Does Puck Sweep?', pp. 87–8.

another version of magical thinking; moreover, Shakespeare appears as a staunch, if discreet, materialist who recognizes that labour is the basis for social order.

Given the role of folk-lore studies in the recovery of fairy material, the prominence of the popular in recent critical accounts of *A Midsummer Night's Dream* is not a surprise, but it is puzzling to find so little attention paid to the question of the supernatural.[21] Our sense of the deep connection between fairy-lore and the popular is fundamentally shaped by the polemical denigration of fairies in post-Reformation England; this association of fairy belief with the people was, of course, perpetuated by nineteenth-century folklorists who discovered authenticity where the reformers had found ignorance. Despite this long-running association, it is important to recognize that early modern fairies were not solely the property of the unlearned. Fairies were, indeed, one element in an elaborate constellation of superstitious beliefs that were attacked by reformers both Catholic and Protestant.[22] But this assault on superstition was part of a general contest over the place of the sacred and the proper line of division between the natural and the supernatural. A crucial element in the definitional ferment over the supernatural was the emergence of early modern demonology, the cultural centrality of which has been established by the recent work of Stuart Clark. However, despite the massive scope of his inquiry, Clark does not consider fairies.[23] Since demonologists were primarily concerned with the problem of witchcraft, fairies were not, indeed, a central preoccupation. Nonetheless, demonological tracts regularly mention them, and the standard position adopted is that fairies are demons. Following Clark, I will consider the ways in which early modern people habitually thought about fairies and the degree to which such thinking was neither deficient nor compromised but normal. Such an approach avoids the sort of functionalism that would explain beliefs in terms inexplicable to the historical actors involved. When Elizabethans spoke about fairies they were doing a great many different things, but it is possible to generalize. Fairy talk is concerned with

ontological questions about the extent and quality of the spirit world and epistemological questions about the possibility of knowledge of that world.

While such generalizations are valuable, the important point is to avoid positing a singular, collective 'fairy-lore' that is then understood to express popular belief or fulfil some specific social function.[24] Like witches, ghosts and demons, fairies were a source of controversy. The most pressing issue was not, in fact, their existence or non-existence, but rather their true identity. The consensus among the learned was that fairies were, in fact, demons. This is a limited form of scepticism – fairies are not what many have thought them to be. Edmund Topsell for example, argues that fairies 'arise from the praestigious apparitions of Deuils, whose delight is to deceiue and beguile the minds of men with errour, contrary to the truth of holye Scripture, which doeth nowhere make mention of such inchaunting creatures; and therefore if any such be, we will holde them the workes of the Deuill, and not of God'.[25] According to Topsell, fairy-like entities may exist, but it is an error to call them 'fairies'. This often strenuous demonisation of fairies is a response to an alternative position, associated with popular belief, holding that

---

[21] Regina Buccola, *Fairies, Fractious Women, and the Old Faith: Fairy Lore in Early Modern British Drama and Culture* (Selinsgrove, 2006) places fairies in a post-Reformation context and gives some consideration to questions of religion. However, Buccola's equation of fairies, women and Catholicism reproduces (in inverted form) an early modern English polemical taxonomy without sufficient attention to its limitations.

[22] Helen Parrish and W. G. Naphy, *Religion and Superstition in Reformation Europe* (Manchester, 2003).

[23] Stuart Clark, *Thinking with Demons: The Idea of Witchcraft in Early Modern Europe* (Oxford, 1997). Robert Hunter West, *The Invisible World: A Study of Pneumatology in Elizabethan Drama* (Athens, Georgia, 1939), acknowledges that fairies were a concern for demonologists, but declines to treat them because there is already an extensive literature on fairy belief in the period.

[24] For a critique of past approaches to fairy material that argues for a greater sensitivity to context, see Matthew Woodcock, *Fairy in the* Faerie Queene: *Renaissance Elf-Fashioning and Elizabethan Mythmaking* (Aldershot, 2004), pp. 9–16.

[25] *The historie of foure-footed beastes* (1607), p. 454.

fairies were neither divine nor diabolical. Precisely because they lacked a scriptural warrant and the imprimatur of orthodox theology, fairies offered an alternative to the cosmology of traditional Christianity and a challenge to the sort of binary categorization that was increasingly ubiquitous in the early modern period.[26] The tension between the notion that fairies are a third kind of spirit, neither angelic nor demonic, and the demands of Christian orthodoxy explain its relative rarity, especially in printed sources, but there are some interesting examples. Richard Greenham, a noted Protestant preacher and pastor with puritan inclinations, asked 'what he thought of fairies', answered 'he thought they were spirits: but he distinguished betweene them and other spirits, as commonly men distinguish between good witches and bad witches'.[27] Thinking of fairies as spiritual creatures of another sort encouraged the view that there were spirits in the world that were neither angels nor demons. At the very end of the seventeenth century, Richard Baxter, another Protestant divine, raises this possibility: 'Yea, we are not fully certain whether these Aerial Regions have not a third sort of Wights, that are neither Angels, (Good or Fallen,) nor Souls of Men, but such as have been there placed as Fishes in the Sea, and Men on Earth: And whether those called *Fairies* and *Goblins* are not such.'[28] Such alternative views are an important reminder that the far more common claim, that fairies are demons, has a decidedly polemical edge.

Just as the demonization of fairies has a long history, the positioning of fairy belief as past belief does not begin with the Reformation. Indeed, one of the most famous literary passages concerning fairies is found in Chaucer's 'Wife of Bath's Tale'. 'In th'olde dayes of Kyng Arthour', according to the Wife, 'was this land fulfild of fayerye . . . But now kan no man se no elves mo.' Their disappearance is blamed on the now ubiquitous friars whose incessant blessings 'maketh that ther ben no fayeryes'.[29] The Wife concludes with the sly suggestion that the friars are themselves sexual predators akin to the incubus, a standard piece of anti-fraternal satire that yokes ecclesiastical controversy to the language of disenchantment. While its

cultural politics are complex, the passage indicates that the idea that the fairies had disappeared was already current in the later fourteenth century. Despite such early evidence that fairy belief was in retreat and the historical hostility of the Church towards fairy belief, Protestant polemicists claimed that fairies were the invention of the Catholic Middle Ages. However, the historical claim for invention is less frequent than the sort of associative elision which identifies both fairy belief and Catholicism as twinned forms of superstition. A puritan wife in George Chapman's *An Humerous Dayes Myrth* (1599) puts it succinctly: 'Fairies were but in times of ignorance, not since the true pure light hath been reuealed.'[30] King James also held fairies to be 'one of the sortes of illusions that was rifest in the time of Papistrie'.[31] A more complicated example is provided by Edmond Bicknoll's *A Sword against Swearyng* (1579), a moral tract that inveighs against the laxity of the present time, which is

the unhappiest hindrance that now remayneth against the fulnesse and plentifulnesse of Gods kingdome: Whose kingdome, yf we buylde not vnto the ende, whose spirit yf we resist, and refuse, as heretofore (a fruite of infidelitie) we were geuen ouer to beleeue Hobgoblin, Robin goodfelow, Fayries, and suche other fancies, so hereafter we may be sure, hauenyng cast of[f] the spirite of grace, the Deuyll shal euery where in the terror of our conscience, appeare and shewe hym selfe vnto vs.[32]

---

[26] On this point, see Clark, *Thinking with Demons*, esp. pp. 31–79, and Peter Lake, 'Anti-popery; The Structure of a Prejudice', in *Conflict in Early Stuart England: Studies in Religion and Politics 1603–1642*, ed. Richard Cust and Ann Hughes (London, 1989), pp. 72–83.

[27] *The Workes of Richard Greenham* (London, 1599), sig. F5v. In the subsequent edition of 1612, Greenham's editor adds a saving gloss in the margin: 'Not for that they are good or lawfull, but of the blind people so called and reputed' (sig. E3v).

[28] *The Certainty of the Worlds of Spirits* (1691), sig. B2v.

[29] *The Riverside Chaucer*, ed. Larry D. Benson (Boston, 1987), pp. 116–17.

[30] George Chapman, *An Humerous Dayes Myrth* (London, 1599), sig. B1r.

[31] King James, *Daemonologie* (Edinburgh, 1597), p. 73.

[32] Edmond Bicknoll, *A Sword against Swearyng* (London, 1579), sig. A8r.

In a common dynamic, fairy belief is described as 'a fruite of infidelitie' – a failure of properly Christian belief makes a person susceptible to strange 'fancies'. The language of supersession identifies fairy belief, like Catholicism, as a thing of the past, but the consequences of refusing further reform are horrifyingly clear: the devil will 'appeare and shew hym selfe vnto vs'. Lest the phrase 'in the terror of our conscience' create the impression that this diabolical visitation will be entirely psychological, Bicknoll elaborates: 'So as hereafter it shalbe (I feare) as great a wonder to see many houses free from one or moe visibly possessed of the Deuyl, as heretofore it hath been strange to see one in a parish.' Bicknoll expresses a standard Protestant position that simultaneously restricts manifestations of the supernatural while amplifying the diabolical: hobgoblins, Robin Goodfellow, fairies, 'and such other fancies' are no longer credible, but an outbreak of demonic possession is a distinct possibility. Also typical is his vision of a world torn between 'the spirite of grace' and the devil.[33]

In addition to the common claim that fairy belief and Catholicism are varieties of superstition, occasionally Catholicism is identified as the cause of fairy belief, an argument offered in two different forms. In one version Catholicism is responsible for an increase in credulity which inevitably leads to the emergence of robust fairy belief; in another version, fairy belief is the direct creation of clerical imposture, part of the panoply of techniques that will come under the heading of priestcraft in the late seventeenth century. Thomas Cooper, for example, separates sexual intercourse between Satan and the witch (which is real) from fairies (which are not): 'This conversing of Satan with the Witch, hath been the ground of all these Conceits of Fairies &c. whereby the Papists kept the ignorant in awe.'[34] Another possibility is the facetious claim that the fairies are themselves practising Catholics. In Hesperides, Robert Herrick, for instance, suggests that the fairies are of 'a mixt Religion': 'Part pagan, part Papisticall'.[35] His elaborately detailed description of fairy ceremony is clearly satirical, but Richard Corbett's 'The Fairy's Farewell', which also identifies the fairies as having been of 'the old

profession', directs its animus against the puritans and voices nostalgia for an earlier, simpler time.[36]

Several of these elements appear in Reginald Scot's The Discovery of Witchcraft (1584), a deeply sceptical account of witchcraft that provoked a number of responses, including Daemonologie by King James VI. Though Scot was, in the words of one scholar, England's first demonologist, he was not an obvious candidate for the role. A member of Kent's minor gentry, Scot was initially known for his manual on hop farming, A Perfite Platforme of a Hoppe Garden, first published in 1574, a second and third edition appeared in 1576 and 1578. In addition to such practical agricultural pursuits, Scot was interested in engineering and was involved in the construction of a dam in Dover Harbour in 1583, a major project the details of which were deemed worthy of inclusion in the 1587 edition of Holinshed's Chronicles.[37] Scot is remarkable for the extent of his scepticism about spirit action in the physical world and for his use of sociological explanations for witchcraft belief. Indeed, Scot appears to have been the first to describe what has been termed the denial narrative, a scenario in which an impoverished woman, having been refused charity, cursed her neighbours, who then blamed subsequent misfortune on the diabolical interference of the 'witch'.[38] An updated version of this sociological explanation features largely in the work of Keith Thomas and Alan Macfarlane.[39] Scot is important,

---

[33] Nathan Johnstone, The Devil and Demonism in Early Modern England (Cambridge, 2006), pp. 27–59.

[34] Thomas Cooper, The Mystery of Witchcraft (London, 1617), p. 123.

[35] Robert Herrick, Hesperides (London, 1648), p. 102.

[36] Richard Corbet, 'The Fairies' Farewell' (1648): 'By which we note the Fairies / Were of the old Profession, / Theyre Songs were Ave Maryes, / Theyre daunces were Procession', Poetica Stromata or a Collection of Sundry Peices in Poetry ([Holland], 1648), p. 93.

[37] Philip C. Almond, England's First Demonologist (London, 2011).

[38] See Scott McGinnis, '"Subtiltie" Exposed: Pastoral Perspectives on Witch Belief in the Thought of George Gifford', Sixteenth Century Journal, 33 (2002), 670, n. 16.

[39] Alan Macfarlane, Witchcraft in Tudor and Stuart England: A Regional and Comparative Study (London, 1970).

for my purposes, not merely because he has a great deal to say about fairies but also because there is reason to think that Shakespeare was familiar with *The Discovery of Witchcraft*.[40]

In a famous passage, Scot identifies fairies as one among an extensive catalog of 'bugs' or 'vaine apparitions' that are used to frighten children:

But in our childhood our mothers maids have so terrified us with an ouglie diuell hauing hornes on his head, fier in his mouth, and a taile in his breech, eies like a bason, fanges like a dog, clawes like a beare, a skin like a Niger, and a voice roring like a lion, whereby we start and are afraid when we heare one crie Bough: and they haue so fraied us with bull beggers, spirits, witches, vrchens, elues, hags, fairies, satrys, pans, faunes, sylens, kit with the cansticke, tritons, centaurs, dwarfes, giants, imps, calcars, coniurors, nymphes, changlings, *Incubus*, Robin good-fellow, the spoorne, the mare, the man in the oke, the hell waine, the firedrake, the puckle, Tom thumbe, hob goblin, Tom tumbler, boneless, and such other bugs, that we are afraid of our owne shadowes. (M4v–5r)

Scot here uses the figure of congeries (or *accumulatio*) – a device common in anti-Catholic polemic – to insist on the irrational proliferation of such imagined creatures; his catalogue promiscuously mixes classical and native figures in order to suggest that all are illusory and insubstantial. Scot's emphasis on fearfulness is typical of early modern treatments of superstition, but he also implies that female domestics have promoted such anxiety in order to instil obedience.[41] John Deacon uses remarkably similar language in an attack on the exorcist John Darrel whose claims of exorcism will 'very shortly vanish away like snow in the Sunne, & be deemed no better in effect, then Hobgoblins, Bugboies, Night-sprites, or Fairies, to make the young children afraid with their supposed shadowes'.[42] Like Scot, Deacon assumes that fairy belief has been instrumentalized, used to make children afraid, though his phrase 'supposed shadows' points to the imagined creatures, whereas Scot's 'afraid of our own shadowes' offers a proverbial image of timorousness. Scot also uses the standard Protestant argument that associates such mistaken beliefs with the Catholic past: 'Well, thanks be to God, this wretched and cowardlie infidelitie,

since the preaching of the gospell, is in part forgotten: and doubtless, the rest of those illusions will in short time (by Gods grace) be detected and vanish awaie.'[43]

Fairy belief also features prominently in Scot's Epistle to the Reader. Partial readers are dismissed as beyond reclamation, they will never be convinced to read with 'indifferent eies': 'For I should no more preuaile herein, than if a hundred years since I should have intreated your predecessors to beleeue, that Robin goodfellowe, that great and ancient bulbegger, had been but a cousening merchant, and no diuell indeed.'[44] Having written off a portion of his audience as incorrigible, Scot shifts his attention to those he considers persuadable: 'Robin goodfellowe ceaseth now to be much feared, and poperie is sufficientlie discouered. Neuertheless, witches charms, and coniurors cousenages are yet thought efectuall.'[45] The orthodox Protestant reader is asked to entertain the possibility that, like other now discarded belief systems, witchcraft will also prove to be mere superstition.

Scot's identification of history as a progressive process of enlightenment combined with his dismissal of spirit action in the material world has led some recent scholars to argue that he does not believe in spirits at all. Sydney Anglo, for instance, claims that Scot did not believe in the reality of spirits, that he understood them as metaphors for good and evil.[46] James Sharpe adopts a similar position:

---

[40] Geoffrey Bullough, *Narrative and Dramatic Sources of Shakespeare* (London, 1957), vol. I, p. 394, includes Scot as a 'probable source'.

[41] On the affective aspect of early modern understandings of superstition, see Susan James, 'Shakespeare and the Politics of Superstition', in *Shakespeare and Early Modern Political Thought*, ed. David Armitage, Conal Condren and Andrew Fitzmaurice (Cambridge, 2009), pp. 80–98.

[42] John Deacon and John Walker, *A summarie ansvvere to al the material points in any of Master Darel his books* (London, 1601), p. 222.

[43] Scot, *Discovery*, sig. M5r.

[44] Scot, *Discovery*, sig. B2r.

[45] Scot, *Discovery*, sig. B2v.

[46] Sydney Anglo, 'Reginald Scot's *Discoverie of Witchcraft*: Scepticism and Sadduceeism', in *The Damned Art: Essays in the Literature of Witchcraft* (London, 1977).

'In effect (and despite his disavowals), the logic of Scot's arguments led to a denial of the reality of the spirit world as surely as it led to a denial of the reality of witchcraft.'[47] Such arguments confirm King James's claim that Scot was a Sadducee, but they exaggerate Scot's secularism and fail to recognize the seriousness of his commitment to non-corporeal spirit.[48]

Nonetheless, it is no surprise that contemporaries interpreted Scot's unorthodox theology as a denial of the spirit realm. The difficulties are apparent in a third passage where Scot comments on fairy belief during a discussion of the incubus. Scot here expresses general incredulity at the notion that a spirit entity, the incubus, could be capable of generation: 'But to use few words herein, I hope you understand that they affirme and saie, that *Incubus* is a spirit; and I trust you know that a spirit hath no flesh nor bones, &c: and that he neither dooth eate nor drinke.' This carnal image of the demonic spirit, a recurring preoccupation among demonologists recently examined by Walter Stephens, leads Scot to a remark on fairy belief: 'In deed your grandams maides were wont to set a boll of milke before him and his cousine Robin good-fellow, for grinding of malt or mustard, and sweeping the house at midnight: and you haue also heard that he would chafe exceedingly, if the maid or good-wife of the house, hauing compassion of his nakednes, laid anie clothes for him, besides his messe of white bread and milke, which was his standing fee. For in that case he saith, what haue we here? Hemton hamten, here will I neuer more tread nor stampen.'[49] Like the lusty incubus who desires the pleasures of human flesh, Robin Goodfellow is credited with carnal appetites despite his being a spirit. He enjoys a good bowl of milk, and yet the suggestion that he might clothe his body is deeply insulting. For Scot, the incoherence of a tradition that features a hungry body that is impervious to the cold is an aggravation, but the basic problem is that spirits are not corporeal. If it is 'granted that Robin could both eate and drinke', then the only conclusion is that he was 'a cousening idle frier, or some such roge'.[50]

Scot clearly wants to effect a strict segregation between the physical world and the spirit world: if an entity operates in the physical world seeking sexual intercourse or food and drink, then the only possible conclusion is that it is a fully material 'rogue'.[51] Not only does the analogy serve to connect the incubus to the now discredited Robin Goodfellow, but the contradiction that Scot sees in the practices of housemaids of his grandmother's generation is firmly lodged in the learned philosophical discourse of demonology. In pursuit of a strict segregation of the natural and the supernatural, Scot seeks to discredit accounts of spirit intercourse whether scholastic or popular.

A contrary view is provided by a manuscript copy of four spells to bind fairies produced around 1600 and now in the Folger Shakespeare Library. Written on a large piece of vellum, approximately 19 by 28 inches (48 × 71 cm), that has been folded, the spells provide access to a line of thinking about fairies that has received scant attention. Dirty and difficult to read in places, the document is a utilitarian object – there is nothing ornamental about it. The spell focuses on binding the fairies in order to have 'carnall copulacion' with them. After describing the necessary formula, the text continues:

This sayd goo to thy naked beed with her . . . & do with her what soo euer you please or canste doo for with owt dowt shee is a woman + & you needeste not to feare her for she shall haue no power to hurte the, beinge so bownde as is afore to the prescribed, nor the nether in the lyf hadiste soo pleasante a creature or lyvelye a /woman/

---

[47] James Sharpe, *Instruments of Darkness: Witchcraft in England, 1550–1750* (London, 1996), p. 55.

[48] Philip C. Almond, *England's First Demonologist: Reginald Scot & 'The Discoverie of Witchcraft'* (London, 2011), pp. 182–92.

[49] Walter Stephens, *Demon Lovers: Witchcraft, Sex, and the Crisis of Belief* (Chicago, 2002). Stephens argues that the fascination with demonic sex was a symptom of scepticism. Demon–human intercourse was not merely salacious or misogynistic, it promised to vindicate the existence of an otherwise intangible spirit world.

[50] Scot, *Discovery*, pp. 85–6.

[51] According to Clark, *Thinking With Demons*, 'Scot's most telling argument was his reduction . . . of all demonic agents to a non-corporeal condition, thus removing them from physical nature altogether' (p. 212).

in beed with the for bewtye & bountye nether / quene / nor / empres / in all the worlde is able to countervaile her.[52]

Written in a neat secretary hand, the spell refers to the practitioner's book (or grimoire), indicating that this particular document emerges from a cultural zone somewhere between what Keith Thomas identifies as the separate and distinct activities of popular and intellectual magic.[53]

The spells reveal a serious concern with the threat posed by the fairies; the binding charms, as usual, are extensive and legalistic. However, there is no indication that the fairy sisters are considered demonic. Indeed, the writer confirms that 'with owt dowt shee is a woman', a reassurance that uses gender to defuse the frightening possibility that the apparently companionable visitor is, in truth, a demon. Moreover, the fairy's female gender indicates that she is an embodied creature capable of sexual intercourse. Though the goal is 'carnall copulacion', one of the additional benefits of binding a fairy is that once 'thou haste accomplishe it & fulfilled thie will & desier with her then maiste Reason with her of any manner of thinges that thou desyreste to & in all Kynd of question you lyste to demmande of her'. However, the practitioner is warned not to ask her 'what shee is'. Both these elements are traditional: the notion that fairies provide secret knowledge is common as is the figure of the fairy lover who must not be questioned about her identity.[54] In the context of this document, however, the prohibited question of identity means that the fairy's status and the precise qualities of her body remain mysterious.

While the document may be an imposture confected to defraud an ardent fan of the fairies, it is evidence of a transaction between men at least one of whom was prepared to entertain the notion that sex with fairies was possible. Though the manuscript appears unprepossessing, the text is marked by a subtle persuasive rhetoric. Divided between invocations addressing the fairies that are to be repeated verbatim and commentary directed to the practitioner, the manuscript presents itself as a set of instructions offered by an accomplished master to a neophyte. These instructions include details concerning the furnishing of the room as well as provisions for failure (a common feature in early modern spells): 'This worde don & ended, yf she come note Reapete the counioracion agayne and bynde her by this bande as followeth.' Such provisos insist on the exacting nature of the conjuration; at the same time, they reassuringly suggest that failure is not final, that a careful repetition or an alternative formulation may finally do the trick. At the same time as it presents magical technique as arduous, the manuscript advertises the joys that await the studious artisan. Immediately after the passage extolling the sexual 'bewtye & bountye' of the fairy, the writer adds a personal testimonial: 'For I haue dyveres tymes provede her & haue had her with me.' This direct avowal of fairy experience echoes the often repeated scriptural injunctions to 'Try the spirits' (1 John 4:1) and 'Prove all things' (1 Thessalonians 5:21), but to an extraordinarily heterodox end.[55] Though the spell's anonymous writer is beyond recovery, his testimony remains significant. Unlike accounts of fairy sex produced through the legal machinery of prosecution, such as that of Andro Man who claimed to have had an ongoing sexual relationship with the fairy queen for some thirty years, Folger MS x.d.234 remains anonymous. It is also not the result of inquisitorial interrogatories, the responses to which have been recorded by a hostile scribe.[56] This is not to say that the Folger manuscript provides access to 'real' fairy belief; but it is evidence that fairy belief, and in particular an interest in fairy bodies and their sexual possibilities, existed amongst

---

52 Folger MS x.d.234. I would like to express my gratitude to Heather Wolfe, Curator of Manuscripts at the Folger Library, for her generous assistance with this document.

53 Thomas, *Religion*, p. 228.

54 Katharine Briggs, 'Human-Fairy Marriages', *Folklore*, 67 (1956), 53–4.

55 For the use of these texts in religious polemic, see Jesse M. Lander, *Inventing Polemic: Religion, Print, and Literary Culture in Early Modern England* (Cambridge, 2006), pp. 39–40.

56 For Andro Man, see Lizanne Henderson and Edward J. Cowan, *Scottish Fairy Belief: A History* (Toronto, 2001), p. 133 and Purkiss, *At The Bottom of the Garden*, pp. 134–9.

Elizabethans whose social status and education put them at some distance from the often illiterate and impoverished cunning men and women who claim in their confessions to have had physical contact with the fairies.

Shakespeare's *Dream* is further evidence of a late sixteenth-century interest in fairy bodies. The romance tradition that had been so recently renovated by Spenser presents fairies that are of human stature, and though there were precedents for tiny fairies, Shakespeare seems to have initiated the fashion for miniaturization – a tendency visible in the Queen Mab speech from *Romeo and Juliet* that gets a full articulation in *A Midsummer Night's Dream*. Usually this development is understood as a form of aestheticization – akin to the Elizabethan vogue for portrait miniatures. The classic account of Shakespeare's fairies, Minor White Latham's *The Elizabethan Fairies: The Fairies of Folklore and the Fairies of Shakespeare* argues that Shakespeare achieved a major innovation when he miniaturized the fairies of folk tradition.[57] However, Latham does not celebrate this aesthetic development; instead, he laments the way in which the vogue for precious, miniature fairies extinguished traditional beliefs. Katharine Briggs absolves Shakespeare by pointing to antecedents for his tiny fairies, but her interest is in 'fundamental beliefs' – and Shakespeare is capable of rehabilitation only to the degree that his fairies genuinely participate in a robust common culture: 'The whole conception of the fairies is true of its kind. They are creatures of another order, but definite, clear-cut and natural, with none of the flimsy quality that strikes one in later fairy stories.' The purveyors of flimsiness are presumably Herrick and Drayton, whose 'fairies became miracles of littleness and often very little else'.[58] An alternative account of this 'preoccupation with tiny things' has recently been offered by Marjorie Swann who argues that the fairy vogue was in part an attempt 'to indigenize a new form of material display rooted in the unsettled socioeconomic conditions of nascent capitalism'.[59] According to Swann, Shakespeare's depiction of the fairy queen as a 'tiny aristocrat engaged in conspicuous consumption' exposed both folklore and courtly myth

as mired in the pre-capitalist past. At the same time, Shakespeare's tiny fairies are not simply a new ideology for a nascent market society: 'Shakespeare underlines his own artifice and implicitly represents fairy lore as a cultural object available for manipulation.'[60] But what initially appears to be the commodification of fairy lore – Shakespeare was after all a huge success in what we now call the entertainment industry – is from a slightly different angle understood 'to satirize elite material display as grotesquely parasitic activity'.[61] The subsequent work of the Jacobean poets reveals a similar ambivalence; for Browne, Drayton and Herrick, fairy poetry expresses a deep alienation from Stuart culture: depictions of fairy courts reveal that the 'social rituals of the Caroline court have become ludicrously attenuated',[62] while tiny 'ceremonialist fairies' are a parodic version of the Laudian pursuit of beauty in holiness.

Miniaturization also develops an already established discourse on the precise quality of fairy bodies; their ability to change size and go invisible is directly related to their status as spirits, and the play deliberately presents fairies that resist precise measurement and strict classification. This indistinction is not the accidental, if predictable, consequence of a syncretic imagination combining popular lore and literary tradition with the philosophical and theological preoccupations of the moment; instead, it is a deliberate strategy, a response to the polemical positioning of fairies that was typical in the literate culture of late sixteenth-century England. Put crudely, the play can be read as a rejoinder both to Scot's *Discoverie of Witchcraft* and to the orthodox demonization of fairies. This does not mean that Shakespeare believed in fairies or that the play is an attempt to persuade its audience to believe

---

[57] Minor White Latham's *The Elizabethan Fairies: The Fairies of Folklore and the Fairies of Shakespeare* (New York, 1930).

[58] Briggs, *Anatomy of Puck*, p. 47.

[59] Marjorie Swann, 'The Politics of Fairylore in Early Modern English Literature', *Renaissance Quarterly*, 53 (2000), 449–73, 450.

[60] Swann, 'The Politics of Fairylore', p. 459.

[61] Swann, 'The Politics of Fairylore', p. 459.

[62] Swann, 'The Politics of Fairylore', p. 464.

in fairies; it is enough to say that the play presents belief in benign fairies as a plausible position within the world of the play. If fairy belief in the period is frequently imputed belief, the belief of some other person or people, the play can be seen to reproduce this dynamic in its representation of the young lovers, Bottom and Hippolyta. At the same time as the play makes an issue of belief, staging the controversy over fairies, it also provides tangible evidence for their existence, ensuring that the believers appear sympathetic.

The most sympathetic, if also the most inarticulate, of these believers is Bottom. In a play insistently concerned with change, Bottom's transformation into human-ass hybrid becomes an emblem for what Kristen Poole has recently described as the period's 'Ovidian physics', an understanding of the material world as 'eminently plastic'.[63] At the same time, there is an alternative tradition that denies the possibility of regular metamorphosis. Scholastic theologians had identified transmutation as the theoretical core of the miracle, an idea that undergirds the doctrine of transubstantiation, and were consequently committed to the position that non-miraculous changes were not true, substantial transformations.[64] Scot inherits the scholastic antipathy towards transmutation and combines it with a Protestant rejection of transubstantiation. In pursuing his case, Scot takes issue with a number of claims about diabolical transformation that appear in the demonological literature. In particular, Scot recounts, only in order to reject, a story told by Bodin of a young man transformed into an ass by a witch. The story appears in Book 5, which attacks the claim that humans can be bodily transformed into other creatures. Having reviewed Bodin's tale, Scot affirms: 'Whosoeuer beleeueth, that anie creature can be made or changed into better of worse, or transformed into anie other shape, or into anie other similitude, by anie other than by God himself the creator of all things, without all doubt is an infidel, and worse than a pagan.'[65] The position is affirmed by the Calvinist theologian William Perkins: 'The transmutation of the substance of one creature into an other, as of a man into a beast of what kind soeuer, is a worke simply aboue the power of nature, & therefore cannot be done by the deuill, or any creature. For it is the proper worke of God alone, as I haue said, to create, to change, or abolish nature.'[66] Scot explicitly connects such tales of transformation to the discredited doctrine of the Eucharist: 'I wonder at the miracle of transubstantiation.'[67] According to Scot, such narratives are bad physics and worse theology.

While Scot denies the possibility of a real, substantial transformation, he acknowledges that appearances can be manipulated in order to create the illusion of metamorphosis. In Book 13, treating the wonders of natural magic, Scot remarks: 'If I affirme, that with certeine charmes and popish praiers I can set an horse or an asses head upon a man's shoulders, I shall not be believed; or, if I doo it, I shall be thought a witch. And yet if I. Bap. Neap. Experiments be true, it is no difficult matter to make it seeme so.' The following detailed instructions, taken from Giambattista della Porta's *Magia naturalis*, describe the preparation of an ointment that will make men 'seeme to haue horrses or asses heads'.[68] Scot's apparently credulous reading of della Porta is produced by his theoretical commitment to the strict separation of the natural and the supernatural. The category of natural magic enables a strictly natural explanation for bizarre and

---

[63] Kristen Poole, *Supernatural Environments in Shakespeare's England: Spaces of Demonism, Divinity, and Drama* (Cambridge, 2011), p. 48.

[64] Caroline Walker Bynum, *Metamorphosis and Identity* (New York, 2001), pp. 77–111.

[65] Scot, *Discovery*, sig. I1r.

[66] William Perkins, *A Discourse of the Damned Art of Witchcraft* (London, 1608), sig. C1r.

[67] In an argument against the use of literary evidence, Scot writes, 'I doubt not but the most part of the readers hereof will admit them to be fabulous; although the most learned of my aduersaries (for lacke of scripture) are faine to produce these poetries for proofes, and for lacke of iudgement I am sure doo thinke, that *Actæons* transformation was true. And why not? As well as the metamorphosis or transubstantiation of *Vlysses* his companions into swine: which *S. Augustine*, and so manie great clarkes credit and report' (sig. K3r).

[68] Scot, *Discovery*, sig. Bb6r.

astonishing phenomena and precludes 'The inconvenience of holding opinion, that whatsoeuer passeth our capacitie, is diuine, supernaturall, &c.'[69]

Bottom's transformation is not illusory, yet it remains incomplete: he retains the powers of speech and reason, despite having the head of an ass. Bottom is a monster in the technical sense: a creature that combines animal and human parts. However, unlike the monsters of classical mythology, he is unfailingly gentle and, unlike the protagonist in *The Golden Ass*, he remains unaware of his transformation. When Quince responds to Bottom's new form – 'O monstrous! O strange! We are haunted. Pray, masters; fly, masters: help!' (3.1.99–100) – Bottom is merely convinced that his fellows are trying to trick him. Indeed, during his time with the fairies, Bottom never, despite developing an appetite for hay and dried peas, appears aware of his transformation. Despite this, the play embraces the possibilities afforded by Ovidian physics, most conspicuously in the characters of Bottom and Puck, who is capable of appearing as a roast crab apple, a joint stool, 'a hound, / a hog, a headless bear, sometime a fire' (3.1.103–4). Puck may be the play's most adept shape-shifter, but all the fairies exemplify a peculiar plasticity. Oberon's description of the sloughed off skin of a snake as 'Weed wide enough to wrap a fairy in' (2.1.256) serves, as do all the other indications of minuteness, to remind the audience that the fairies can vary their size.

Bottom's transformation, however, does not appear to be a liberation but rather a confinement that emphasizes the grossness of his bodily nature. Indeed, Bottom's demotion and his subsequent tryst with Titania has led one recent commentator to conclude that the play is 'patently about bestiality'.[70] There are many reasons to be sceptical about a hyper-sexualized Bottom; as Peter Holland has pointed out, such a characterization is difficult to square with the play's presentation of Bottom. Moreover, the emphasis on bestiality obscures the fact that the union in question is not between an ass and a human but between a human and a fairy.[71] The scenario plays out as a classic fairy abduction, but instead of terror, Bottom experiences lyrical

eroticism. The note of compulsion – 'Thou shalt remain here, whether thou wilt or no' (3.1.145) – is offset by the list of benefits Titania will confer: fairy attendants, jewels, a bed made of pressed flowers. But perhaps most important is her promise of another transformation: 'And I will purge thy mortal grossness so / That thou shalt like an airy spirit go' (3.1.152–3). Like Folger MS x.d.234, this episode concerns the prospect and the possibility of fairy sex but, unlike the ardent practitioners made visible by the manuscript, Bottom seems entirely innocent of sexual desire or understanding. Indeed, the episode is handled with a degree of decorousness that makes it impossible for the audience to know what exactly has happened.

Bottom's celebrated speech extolling the wonder of his recent experience refuses all specificity. Indeed, this speech has been celebrated as an expression of specifically religious awe, 'a rare vision', that conveys intimations of grace.[72] Such interpretations focus on Bottom's garbled quotation of St Paul – 'The eye of man hath not heard, the ear of many hath not seen, man's hand is not able to taste, his tongue to conceive, nor his heart to report what my dream was' (4.1.208–211) – and present him as a visionary, 'a mystic of sorts'.[73] The text in question, 1 Corinthians 2:9, reads, in the Geneva version: 'But as it is written, The things which eye hathe not sene, nether eare hath heard, nether came into mans heart, *are*, which God hathe prepared for them that loue him.' It is an affirmation of 'a secret and hidden wisdom of God' – a wisdom that includes the promise

---

[69] Scot, *Discovery*, sig. Bb4r.

[70] Bruce Thomas Boehrer, 'Bestial Buggery in *A Midsummer Night's Dream*', in *The Production of English Renaissance Culture*, ed. David Lee Miller, Sharon O'Dair and Harold Weber (Ithaca, 1994), pp. 123–50. For an earlier interest in the play's bestiality, see Jan Kott, *Shakespeare Our Contemporary* (New York, 1967), p. 182.

[71] Peter Holland, ed., *A Midsummer Night's Dream* (Oxford, 1994), pp. 72–3.

[72] For a representative example, see Ronald F. Miller, '*A Midsummer Night's Dream*: The Fairies, Bottom, and the Mystery of Things', *Shakespeare Quarterly*, 26 (1975), 254–68.

[73] Miller, '*A Midsummer Night's Dream*', p. 264.

of redemption, a spiritual truth only available to the faithful. As Richard Davies, a preacher, puts it, the faithful 'shall possesse ioyes that cannot be explicated with mortall tongues'.[74] In the words of Thomas Adams, 'The cheare is beyond all sense, all science.'[75] Approaches that emphasize this scriptural allusion too often devolve into allegories more attentive to the niceties of Pauline theology than to the exigencies of dramatic performance. Bottom's response to his experience is first of all extremely funny. Whereas the scripture passage is an affirmation of 'The things which . . . are which God hathe prepared for them that loue him', Bottom's version focuses on a fine derangement of the senses. Anthony Dawson insists that the religious material here is being appropriated and deployed in pursuit of particularly theatrical effects and that such moments contribute to a general secularization of society.[76] According to Dawson, Bottom's garbled reference is a 'clear example of the theatre cannibalising and carnivalising religious discourse and the authority that goes with it'. Dawson's argument is subtle and persuasive – he readily acknowledges the many ways in which the biblical text resonates in the scene – and his claim for the theatre as 'a secular, and secularising, institution' merits careful consideration.[77] However, a reading of *A Midsummer Night's Dream* benefits from a distinction between secularization and disenchantment. These two processes, though often identified, are conceptually distinct and, while the play conspicuously takes its distance from institutional religion, it presents a world that is decidedly enchanted, populated by the sort of spirit agents that are inadmissible in a disenchanted world.

Bottom's enchantment presents an affirmation not of Christian doctrine but of something far stranger. After all, he is recalling time spent in the bower of the fairy queen; his is an experience that escapes the categories of established religion and resists expression. Yet the notion that he is a mystic who has been given access to the transcendent and ineffable takes the episode far too seriously. To make Bottom into a mystic is to make Titania a god, and this would be to miss the play's serious consideration of fairies as spiritual creatures of

another sort. The fundamental point made by the second chapter of 1 Corinthians is that the mystery of God is not accessible through the senses, yet Bottom's experience is insistently sensual. Fairy sex provides access to the spirit world but it remains 'carnall copulacion'.

Like Bottom, the lovers attest to the existence of peculiar agencies in the woods outside of Athens. Unlike Bottom, who decides to remain silent, the lovers have described their experience, provoking the scorn of Theseus, who famously declares:

More strange than true. I never may believe
These antique fables, nor these fairy toys.
Lovers and madmen have such seething brains,
Such shaping fantasies, that apprehend
More than cool reason ever comprehends.
The lunatic, the lover, and the poet
Are of imagination all compact.
One sees more devils than vast hell can hold:
That is the madman. The lover, all as frantic,
Sees Helen's beauty in a brow of Egypt.
The poet's eye, in a fine frenzy rolling,
Doth glance from heaven to earth, from earth to heaven,
And as imagination bodies forth
The forms of things unknown, the poet's pen
Turns them to shapes, and gives to airy nothing
A local habitation and a name.
Such tricks hath strong imagination
That if it would but apprehend some joy
It comprehends some bringer of that joy;
Or in the night, imagining some fear,
How easy is a bush supposed a bear!   (5.1.2–22)

This indictment of the excesses of the imagination has an analogue, perhaps even a direct source, in the passage from Scot's *Discovery* discussed above. Especially susceptible to such 'bugs', according to

---

[74] Richard Davies, *A Funerall Sermon* (London, 1577), sig. C4v.

[75] Thomas Adams, *The Devill's Banket described in foure sermons* (London, 1614), sig. 2C2v.

[76] Anthony B. Dawson, 'Shakespeare and Secular Performance', in *Shakespeare and the Culture of Performance*, ed. Paul Yachnin and Patricia Badir (Farnham, Surrey, 2008), pp. 83–97.

[77] Dawson, 'Shakespeare and Secular Performance', p. 84.

Scot, are the sick, children, women and cowards, a catalogue that is replaced by Theseus's triad of the lunatic, lover, and poet. The position that Theseus articulates is startlingly similar to arguments offered by Scot: a strenuous rationalism and hostility towards the spirit world produce a strong form of disenchantment. Theseus historicizes fairy belief as 'antique' – a word that carries not only the sense of ancient but also that of 'antic' meaning grotesque, bizarre and fantastic. The sneering reference to 'more devils than vast hell can hold' brings a concrete literalism to the question of spirits and their extension, a question that had also exercised Scot.[78] Theseus's high-flying and dismissive account of poetic composition concurs with Scot's suggestion that the poets are at least in part responsible for a variety of false beliefs – their inventions having given 'airy nothing / A local habitation and name'. Indeed, the degree to which Theseus identifies metamorphosis as a strictly poetic operation echoes Scot's extensive engagement with Ovid.[79] Theseus goes on to offer a developed description of the psychological propensity to attribute agency to inanimate matter before concluding his critique with an appeal to proverbial wisdom. 'How easy is a bush supposed a bear' is a variation on 'Think every bush a bugbear' and 'afraid of every bush', two proverbs about the way fear produces misprision.[80] Indeed, Scot's dismissal of 'vaine apparitions', discussed above, includes a similar remark: 'in so much as some neuer feare the diuell, but in a darke night; and then a polled sheepe is a perilous beast, and manie times is taken for our fathers soule, especially in a churchyard, where a right hardie man heretofore scant durst passe by night, but his haire would stand vpright'.[81]

Proverbial wisdom is here deployed by Theseus precisely in order to dismiss received tradition. The critique that he offers is similar to that made by Mistress Page in *Merry Wives*. In order to humiliate Falstaff, she plans to exploit an old tale – regarding a dreadful spirit known as Herne the hunter – that is the product of 'superstitious idle-headed eld' (4.4.35). The disenchantment of suburban Windsor does not, however, carry over to the world of ancient Athens. As plausible as Theseus sounds to

modern ears, his scepticism needs to be understood within the context of the play in which he appears and in which his bill of indictment earns a quietly devastating response from Hippolyta:

> But all the story of the night told over,
> And all their minds transfigured so together,
> More witnesseth than fancy's images,
> And grows to something of great constancy;
> But howsoever, strange and admirable.
>
> (5.1.23–7)

In response to Theseus's individualizing psychology with its emphasis on the idiosyncratic and the aberrant, Hippolyta invokes the solidity of collective experience. Though her language hints at an Aristotelian respect for received belief as well as the explicitly Christian concept of a *consensus fidelium*, Hippolyta is referring specifically to a concurrence of witnesses, and her insistence on an event, a transfiguration that 'grows to something of great constancy', introduces an element of dynamism not usually found in the concept of tradition. This argument between Theseus and Hippolyta is broken off, not concluded, by the arrival of the lovers. Though the controversy over fairies is not resolved, it is they, not Theseus, who are given the final word.

First Puck appears and lists the night terrors that threaten: 'Now the hungry lion roars, / And the wolf behowls the moon . . . Now it is the time of night / That graves, all gaping wide, / Every one lets forth his sprite / In the church-way paths to glide' (5.2.1–12). But Puck declares nothing 'shall disturb this hallowed house'; he has been 'sent with broom before / To sweep the dust behind the door'

---

[78] Almond, *England's First Demonologist*, pp. 183–4.

[79] Abraham Fleming provided the English translations of Ovid that appear in *The Discovery*; Scot quotes Ovid approvingly at places (e.g. sig. I3r), but is contemptuous of those who misread him.

[80] Harold F. Brooks, ed., *A Midsummer Night's Dream* (London, 1979), p. 105; Holland, ed., *Dream*, p. 232. *The Oxford English Dictionary of Proverbs*, 3rd edn (Oxford, 1970), p. 813, lists 'He thinks every bush a boggard.'

[81] Scot, *Discovery*, sig. M5r.

(18–20). Here he plays the role of Robin Goodfellow, the household spirit who rewards good housewives and maids by sweeping at midnight, but he also assumes the role of guardian, a protector of the 'hallowed house'. He is immediately joined by Oberon, Titania and all their train. First the fairies sing and dance, then Oberon directs them to bless the beds and the chambers throughout the house 'with field-dew consecrate' (45). Oberon and Titania will themselves bless the 'best bride-bed': 'And the issue there create / Ever shall be fortunate' (33, 35–6). All three couples will, according to Oberon, 'Ever true in loving be' and their offspring will not be marred by 'the blots of nature's hand' (39). This fairy ritual clearly echoes the ancient practice of blessing the bridal bed found in the Sarum Missal, a practice that was dropped from the Book of Common Prayer.[82] But before concluding that we are dealing with Catholic fairies like those whose ritualism is lovingly described and gently mocked by Herrick, it is worth considering the episode from a slightly different angle.

Fairies, as we have seen, are frequently associated with the very night-terrors that Puck will ward off. Spenser's 'Epithalamion' has a similar passage in which the speaker expresses the wish that he and his bride be protected from a series of evils: 'Ne let the Pouke, nor other evill sprights, / Ne let mischivous witches with theyr charmes, / Ne let hob Goblins, names whose sence we see not, / Fray us with things that be not.'[83] Spenser, however, cannot resist a dig at folk belief even as he uses 'names whose sence we see not'. A more straightforward version is provided by Richard Brathwait, who, commenting on Chaucer's Miller's Tale, offers the following example of an 'old sylvan charm':

> Fawns and Fairies keep away,
> While we in these Coverts stay;
> Goblins, Elves, of *Oberon's* Train,
> Never in these Plains remain,
> Till I and my Nymph awake,
> And do hence our Journey take,
> May the Night-mare never ride us,
> Nor a fright by night betide us:
> So shall Heav'ns praise sound as clear,
> As the shrill voyc'd Chantecleer.[84]

Like the Chaucerian example, in which the Carpenter says a 'nyght-spell' in an attempt to recover the seemingly bewitched Nicholas, Brathwait's charm is directed against the fairies. More important than ritualism, then, is the fact that Shakespeare's fairies appear as guardians of the household and the natural order. The association between the fairies and the natural world, so conspicuous in Titania's description of the ill-effects of her struggle with Oberon (2.1.88–117), here returns in Oberon's claim that 'the blots of nature's hand / Shall not in their issue stand' (39–40). The resort to apotropaic ritual emphatically confirms Oberon's earlier response to Puck's description of 'damnèd spirits': 'But we are spirits of another sort' (3.2.383, 389).

Indeed, Shakespeare is usually credited with transforming the dark and robust fairies of folk tradition into the diminutive and benign creatures familiar to us now: from Puck to Ariel to Tinkerbell, a long term development that can be understood as a process of disenchantment, commodification, domestication or aestheticization. While acknowledging the interest and the importance of such long term changes, I have been arguing for a closer look at Shakespeare's fairies not as allegories, symptoms or social functions but as an important resource for thinking about the boundaries between the natural and the supernatural and the dimensions of the spirit world in early modern England. Despite the tactical retreat offered in Puck's epilogue, Shakespeare's fairies present a vital possibility: spirits of 'another sort'. This does not mean that Shakespeare believed in fairies; if pressed, I suspect he would have answered with Horatio, 'So have I heard, and do in part believe it' (*Hamlet*, 1.1.146). What *A Midsummer Night's Dream* does is entertain a belief in fairies in order to protest against

---

[82] Francis Douce, *Illustrations of Shakspeare and of Ancient Manners* (London, 1807), vol. I, pp. 199–200.

[83] *The Yale Edition of the Shorter Poems of Edmund Spenser*, ed. William A. Oram *et al.* (New Haven, 1989), lines 341–4.

[84] Richard Brathwait, *A Comment upon the Two Tales of our Ancient, Renowned, and Ever-Living Poet Sir Jefray Chaucer, Knight* (1665), p. 31. For Chaucer, see *The Canterbury Tales*, lines 3479–85.

the relentless dichotomizing and strenuous disen-chantment that accompanied the Calvinism that dominated England's universities and pulpits in the late sixteenth century. At the same time, there is no reason to read hostility towards strict Calvinism as an embrace of Catholicism. After all, the Church, even in the Middle Ages, was also hostile to fairy belief. Furthermore, even if traditional religion was able in practice to accommodate fairy belief, the Counter-reformation was militant in pursuit of popular error. Indeed, to see Shakespeare's fairies as an expression of recognisably Catholic dissent is to accept the polemical identification so commonly made by Protestants between Catholicism and fairy

belief. Instead, the fairies of *A Midsummer Night's Dream* afford a glimpse of a spiritual world beyond the confines of institutional religion and the rigidi-ties of polemic, an intimation that received theolo-gies, despite their claims to comprehensiveness, are something less than adequate.[85]

---

[85] A suggestive analogue is found in the work of Paracelsus whose *Book on Nymphs, Sylphs, Pygmies, Salamanders and other Spirits* describes elemental spirit-creatures who are neither angelic nor human. These creatures have bodies of flesh and blood, but are capable of preternatural feats; they bear children and our able to mate with humans; see, Paracelsus, *Four Treatises*, ed. Henry E. Sigerist, trans. C. Lilian Temkin, *et al.* (Baltimore, 1941), pp. 213–53.

'INDIA' AND THE GOLDEN
AGE IN *A MIDSUMMER
NIGHT'S DREAM*

HENRY BUCHANAN

An eastern 'India' for *A Midsummer Night's Dream* comes from an unscrutinized tradition, yet dominates interpretation. Recent studies by Margo Hendricks, Patricia Parker, Louis Montrose, R. W. Desai, Ania Loomba, Shankar Raman, Kevin Pask and Hugh Grady all posit an eastern India (region or country), but there is no evidence Elizabethans thought the Indian theme eastern.[1] An eastern interpretation appears to have originated in Purcell's opera *The Fairy Queen* in the late seventeenth century (which extensively orientalized Shakespeare's play and made Chinese additions) at a time when India (and China) had become the focus of imperial desire, but in the late sixteenth century the East Indies hardly figured in English affairs.

When the play was first performed in 1595–96, 'India', since the error of Columbus, often meant America. Of the fifty-odd references to 'India' and 'the Indies' in the *Calendar of State Papers, 1595–1597* there are only two minor ones to the east (none are to the country of India); the rest are American ('America' is seldom used at this time), and proportions are similar for the years before and after.[2] In *Love's Labour's Lost* (1595), love is compared to the 'savage' men of 'Ind' worshipping the sun, 'vassal' American Indians (4.3.220–3); in *1 Henry IV* (1596–97), the 'bountiful . . . mines of India' (3.1.164–5) appear located in the New World along with the 'mines' of the 'kings of India' in Marlowe's *1 Tamburlaine* (3.3.263–4);[3] in *Troilus and Cressida* (1601–02), Cressida's bed is an 'India' for Troilus until her infidelity becomes the 'hurricano' of his rage (1.1.100; 5.2.175), a new word in the language

describing a West Indian phenomenon;[4] when a *Play of Robin goode-fellow* (almost certainly *A Midsummer Night's Dream*) is performed for the new

---

[1] Margo Hendricks, 'Obscured by Dreams: Race, Empire and Shakespeare's *A Midsummer Night's Dream*', *The Shakespeare Quarterly*, 47 (1996), 37–60; Patricia Parker, *Shakespeare from the Margins: Language, Culture, Context* (Chicago, 1996), pp. 105, 311 n. 49; Louis Montrose, *The Purpose of Playing: Shakespeare and the Cultural Politics of the Elizabethan Theatre* (London, 1997), p. 170; R. W. Desai, 'England, the Indian Boy, and the Spice Trade in *A Midsummer Night's Dream*', *The Shakespeare Newsletter*, 48 (1998–9), 1: 3, 4, 26, 48; 2: 39, 40, 42; Ania Loomba, 'The Great Indian Vanishing Trick – Colonialism, Property and the Family in *A Midsummer Night's Dream*', in *A Feminist Companion to Shakespeare*, ed. Dympna Callaghan (Oxford, 2001), pp. 163–87; Shankar Raman, *Framing India: The Colonial Imaginary in Early Modern Culture* (Stanford, 2002); Kevin Pask, 'Engrossing Imagination: *A Midsummer Night's Dream*', in *The Shakespearean International Yearbook* (2003), 3: *Where are we now in Shakespeare Studies?*, ed. Graham Bradshaw, John M. Mucciolo, Angus Fletcher and Tom Bishop (Aldershot, 2003), pp. 172–92, p. 182; and Hugh Grady, *Shakespeare and Impure Aesthetics* (Cambridge, 2009), p. 53. Of the Shakespeare criticism surveyed, Alden T. Vaughan and Virginia Mason Vaughan, *Shakespeare's Caliban: A Cultural History* (Cambridge, 1991), p. 45, find it only 'remotely possible' that the 'Indian king' (2.1.22) 'is an east Indian potentate', and Kim F. Hall, *Things of Darkness: Economies of Race and Gender in Early Modern England* (Ithaca, 1995), p. 85, resists an eastern location of 'India' in favour of the 'new world'.

[2] *Calendar of State Papers (Domestic), 1595–1597*, ed. Mary Anne Everett Green (London, 1869) – hereafter *CSPD*.

[3] Christopher Marlowe, *The Complete Plays*, ed. Frank Romany and Robert Lindsey (London, 2003).

[4] Joan Pong Linton, *Romance in the New World: Gender and the Literary Formations of English Colonialism* (Cambridge, 1998), pp. 134–5.

court on 1 January 1604 the 'Indian' knights in the masque which accompanied it are American,[5] and for Globe theatre-goer Simon Forman 'India' is America too.[6]

A western 'India' resonates with events at the time of the play's first performance, for in August 1595, Sir Walter Ralegh, the Captain of the Queen's Guard who had fallen from royal favour, returned from his sensational Guiana voyage with an Indian prince. In September 1594 Ralegh said his voyage would be to 'India' (i.e. America),[7] while after his return in September 1595 court gossip Rowland Whyte reports that the queen had been informed that Ralegh had discovered the 'way to bring home the wealth of India',[8] for Guiana, the remote and unofficial Spanish province of 'Trinidad y Guayana', 'Manoa' or 'Dorado', had yet to be named. Ralegh 'coined' the name in English after the voyage;[9] it did not appear in print until his *Discoverie of the Large, Rich and Bewtiful Empyre of Guiana* was published in March 1596 and it is 1599 before it is located on a published English map, Edward Wright's *Hydrographiae Descriptio*, given equal prominence with Peru and Mexico. For audiences of the play in 1595–96, the 'farthest step of India' (2.1.69)[10] could have just as well suggested the destination of Ralegh's voyage as the east.

In *The Discoverie of Guiana*, Ralegh is promising a vast empire to rival Spanish conquests in the New World: gold, silver, pearls, precious stones, silk, spices, medicinal plants, timber and many other valuable commodities. With the good grace of the Indians, who would throw off the Spanish yoke and swear fealty to the queen, who still lived in the Golden Age and knew not Mine and Thine, the abundant land would become England's 'generall store' in the words of Chapman's *De Guiana, carmen Epicum* (1595).[11] Ralegh's voyage to the Orinoco delta was *the* imperial event of the era, and initiates what Charles Nicholl calls the 'Guiana craze' sweeping England;[12] on the reference to this time in *The Merry Wives of Windsor* (1597–98) – Falstaff's 'a region in Guiana, all gold and bounty' (1.3.61–2) – there is no dispute.

Crucially, it is likely that the Indian prince in *A Midsummer Night's Dream* alludes to Ralegh's Indian prince, and Puck's intimation that the 'changeling' was 'stol'n from an Indian king' (2.1.22–3) may be a topical humour. In *The Discoverie* Ralegh says his Indian prince was 'freely' given by Topiawari as a pledge for two of his men; yet contemporaries might have found too convenient his explanation that, as the Indian king was over a hundred years old and 'had but a short tyme to liue', he had assigned to himself the task of establishing his son Cayworaco as king of the 'Aromaia' region 'after his death'.[13] Rowland White and another eye-witness

---

[5] E. K. Chambers, *The Elizabethan Stage*, 4 vols. (Oxford, 1923), vol. 3, pp. 279–80.

[6] A. L. Rowse, *Simon Foreman: Sex and Society in Shakespeare's Age* (London, 1974), pp. 165, 255.

[7] Agnes Latham and Joyce Youings, *The Letters of Sir Walter Ralegh* (Exeter, 1999), p. 119.

[8] William A. Shaw, *Report on the Manuscripts of Lord D'Lisle & Dudley* (London, 1934), p. 165.

[9] John W. Shirley, *Thomas Harriot: A Biography* (Oxford, 1983), pp. 218–22.

[10] The first Arden edition, Henry Cuningham, ed., *A Midsummer Night's Dream*, 2nd edn (London, 1922), p. 39, preferred the Q2 reading 'steep of India' and promoted 'the idea of a lofty and precipitous range of mountains forming the extreme eastern boundary of India' (the Himalayas). This farthest 'steep' of India is rejected by the second Arden edition as a compositor's error (for the 'steppe' of Q1), pointing out that 'steep' is not used 'elsewhere' in the plays as 'a noun'. Harold F. Brooks, ed., *A Midsummer Night's Dream* (London, 1979), pp. 30–1.

[11] Walter Ralegh, *The Discoverie of the Large, Rich and Bewtiful Empyre of Guiana*, transcribed, annotated and introduced by Neil L. Whitehead (Manchester, 1997), passim. *De Guiana*, in *The Poems of George Chapman*, ed. Phyllis Brooks Bartlett (New York and London, 1941), pp. 353–7, p. 355. *De Guiana* was first published in 1596 in Lawrence Keymis's *A relation of the second voyage to Guiana* (London, 1596) immediately before Keymis's 'De *Guiana*, carmen Epicum', a Latin epistle to Thomas Harriot dated '1595'; as Chapman's poem is pleading for a 'seconding' voyage (p. 354), it would seem to date from the autumn of that year, i.e. after Ralegh's return from the Orinoco, but before the decision was made in late November or December not to sponsor a voyage, no later than Captain Keymis's (private) voyage in January.

[12] Charles Nicholl, *The Creature in the Map: A Journey to El Dorado* (London, 1995), p. 86.

[13] Ralegh, *Discoverie*, p. 197.

speak of 'hostages';[14] but stolen or freely given, Ralegh sought men and finance for another voyage to establish a colony in Guiana, what Chapman's *De Guiana* calls an '*Eliza*-consecrated sworde', and plans were made to present him to the queen in a 'Device' with a song by John Dowland, 'Behold, a wonder here'.[15]

Allusion to the real Indian prince and American voyaging would give a whole different *tenor* to the play, especially in relation to the Golden Age. That Titania's 'seasons' speech (2.1.81–117) describes a (fallen) Golden Age in 'Athens' is well established;[16] and if 'India' is America in her second speech (121–37) then this describes a Golden Age too, for that the Indians inhabited a primordial paradise was standard renaissance belief: in De Bry's series of engravings of Virginian Indians for Harriot's *A briefe and true report of the new found land of Virginia* (1590) a biblical Garden of Eden scene is placed first,[17] while for Montaigne's essay 'Of the Cannibals' (1603), a source for Gonzalo's 'Golden Age' speech in *The Tempest*, the Indians lived in a Golden Age surpassing that in Ovid. The notion of a Golden Age relates the two speeches, provides the substance to which Oberon's speech responds (148–74), and explains why he involves Queen Elizabeth (the 'imperial vot'ress' (163)) in the plot, ancient Greece notwithstanding.

GOLDEN AGE AMERICAN INDIANS

Titania describes how the Indian queen would

> sail upon the land
> To fetch me trifles, and return again,
> As from a voyage, rich with merchandise.
>
> (2.1.132–4)

This does not suggest commerce with the East Indies (which in any case is many years into the future). In Ania Loomba's interpretation of the play, although emphatically eastern, Titania's relationship with the Indians is actually more suggestive of the 'riches plundered from the Americas' than trade with the eastern India, observing that discourses about the New World 'routinely portray the natives as unable to comprehend the value of the riches that surround them, so they gift these valuables to Europeans, or trade them for worthless baubles'. East Indian potentates, she adds, can hardly be considered munificent, for in 'narratives pertaining to the East... the situation was to be reversed: European ambassadors to India... were frustrated by the fact that *they* had to become gift-givers in order to exact trading privileges'.[18] When England does start to trade with India in the early seventeenth century there was an eastward movement of some of London's gold reserves; there will be no gifts of 'trifles' as there are to Titania.

The 'trifles' fetched by the Indian queen are actually 'rich... merchandise' and better suit New World voyaging; this perplexes Margo Hendricks's eastern interpretation, since 'trifles', she concedes, is a term drawn from the 'early modern lexicon... [which] was generally used to describe the type of exchanges between Native Americans and English sailors'.[19] In writing on the New World 'trifles' was used since Columbus to describe the exchange of beads and bells for Indian gold and pearls. In a possible *Tempest* source, Richard Eden's seminal *Historie of Trauayle in the West and East Indies* (1577), the Indians encountered on Columbus's first voyage 'cast themselues by heapes into the sea, and came swimming to the shyppes, bringing gold with them, which they changed with our men for earthen pottes, drinking glasses, pointes, pinnes, hawks bels, looking glasses, & such other trifles'.[20] And for English voyaging to the New

[14] Shaw, *Report*, p. 165; Nicholl, *Creature in the Map*, p. 347.

[15] Chapman, *De Guiana*, p. 353; *CPSD*, pp. 130–3; Diana Poulton, *John Dowland* (London, 1972), p. 277.

[16] Marjorie Garber, *Dream in Shakespeare: From Metaphor to Metamorphosis* (New Haven and London, 1974), p. 71; Jonathan Bate, *Shakespeare and Ovid* (Oxford, 1993), p. 141 n. 25; Susan Baker, 'Chronotope and Repression in *A Midsummer Night's Dream*', in Dorothea Kehler, ed., *A Midsummer Night's Dream: Critical Essays* (New York and London, 2001), pp. 345–68, p. 356.

[17] Andrew Hadfield, *Literature, Travel, and Colonial Writing in the English Renaissance* (Oxford, 1998), p. 118.

[18] Loomba, 'The Great Indian Vanishing Trick', p. 169.

[19] Hendricks, 'Obscured by Dreams', p. 53 n. 47.

[20] Richard Eden, *The Historie of Trauayle in the West and East Indies* (London: 1577), fo. 9v.

World the word 'trifles' is used extensively to denote exchange with the Indians, from John Cabot in 1498 to Thomas Harriot's *A briefe and true report of Virginia* and the draft of Ralegh's *Discoverie*.[21]

The 'trifles' brought to Titania by the Indian queen are gifts, not an exchange, and these come from the Indians, not from the voyagers; but this looks like the typical Golden Age scene of American Indians *giving* to Europeans, a munificence which would disqualify Indians from the east. In Eden's *Historie of Trauayle*, the work which would have established the English myth of the New World, there are many passages where the Indians bring the Spanish food, gold or spices, usually in return for 'trifles', but often with no exchange of goods; this is because America is a 'golden worlde' of which 'olde wryters' speak where the uncultivated land produces in abundance, and the Indians, having no concept of 'Myne and Thyne', freely disburse their 'golde' or 'spyces' to the Spaniards.[22] Like the Indian queen (who knows not 'mine and thine'), native munificence is a standard feature of English writing on the New World: in the first account of Virginia in 1584, Arthur Barlowe describes the land as a 'golden age' paradise and tells how the 'loving' Indians bestowed on the colonists 'as much bountie . . . as they could possibly devise';[23] and on the stage, in Jonson, Chapman and Marston's *Eastward Hoe* (1605), the 'Indians are so in love' with the Roanoke colonists 'that all the treasure they have, they lay at their feet' (3.3.14–5; 22–4).[24]

A Golden Age 'India' in *A Midsummer Night's Dream* would play on the myth of America, of which the rhetoric surrounding the Guiana voyage was the latest manifestation. In *The Discoverie* Ralegh implores England to take advantage of this untouched paradise, this new American virgin, since 'Guiana is a countrey that has yet her Maydenhead';[25] and in De Bry's engraving of Ralegh's meeting with Topiawari (1599), where the Indians eagerly proffer flora and fauna, Charles Nicholl observes that the Indian king's outstretched arm symbolically offers the 'bounty' of the abundant land: the typical scene of 'Golden Age'

American Indians 'giving' to Europeans,[26] and not unlike the Indian queen in the play.

And in *De Guiana* Chapman proclaims that 'there doth plentie crowne their wealthie fields', imagines that for English colonists 'A world of Sauadges fall tame before them, / Storing their theft-free treasuries with golde', insists that Guiana's fruitfulness can compensate for the 'barrennesse' of the · irgin queen (like 'Virginia'), and pleads passionately with her to 'be the prosperous forewind to a fleet' and 'create / A golden worlde in this our yron age', not to be 'like a rough and violent wind, / That in the morning rends the Forrestes down, / Shoues vp the seas to heauen, makes earth to tremble'[27] – not to be like the 'winds' (2.1.88) which cause the devastations which befall 'Athens' in the play and threaten its Golden Age.

A FALLEN GOLDEN AGE

There is a Golden Age in 'Athens' – before the 'dissension' of Oberon and Titania over the Indian boy angers the winds (so Titania believes), floods the land and disrupts the seasons. For Susan Baker this is similar to the 'falling away of the golden age' in Ovid, for Jonathan Bate 'disruptions of nature' like the fall from the Golden Age after Pluto abducts Proserpina in the *Metamorphoses*:[28]

21 Richard Hakluyt, *The Principal Navigations, Voiages, Traffiqves and Discoueries of the English Nation*, 3 vols. (London, 1598–1600), vol. 3, p. 9; Thomas Harriot, *A briefe and true report of the new found land of Virginia* (London, 1590), p. 25; *Sir Walter Ralegh's 'Discoverie of Guiana'*, ed. Joyce Lorimer (London, 2006), pp. 178, 190.

22 Eden, *Historie*, fos. 15r and 24r.

23 Arthur Barlowe, 'The first voyage made to the coastes of America', in Richard Hakluyt, *The Principal Nauigations, Voiages, and Discoueries of the English Nation* (London, 1589), pp. 728–32, p. 731.

24 Ben Jonson, George Chapman, and John Marston, *Eastward Ho*, ed. R. W. van Fossen (Manchester, 1999).

25 Ralegh, *Discoverie*, p. 197.

26 Nicholl, *Creature in the Map*, p. 302.

27 Chapman, *De Guiana*, pp. 354, 357.

28 Baker, 'Chronotope and Repression', p. 356; Bate, *Shakespeare and Ovid*, p. 141 n. 25.

The ox hath therefore stretched his yoke in vain,
The ploughman lost his sweat, and the green corn
Hath rotted ere his youth has attained a beard.
The fold stands empty in his drownèd field,
And crows are fatted with the murrain flock.
The nine men's morris is filled up with mud,
　　. . . The spring, the summer,
The childing autumn, angry winter change
Their wonted liveries, and the mazèd world
By their increase now knows not which is which;
And this same progeny of evils comes
From our debate, from our dissension.

(2.1.93–8; 111–16)

Titania's speech to Oberon does not describe the classical Golden Age, which for Ovid was a time of everlasting spring and the abundant land was 'untouched of hoe or plough' (*Metamorphoses*, 1: 115),[29] where they would 'fleet the time carelessly as they did in the golden world', in the words of *As You Like It* (1.1.114–5), while the 'nine men's morris' (98) in her speech, the presence in the play of folk fairy 'Robin Goodfellow' (2.1.34) and an anglicized 'Duke' Theseus (4.1.214), above all Oberon's reference to 'the imperial vot'ress' (2.1.163) make the disruption of the seasons as much English as Athenian, and suggest a fall from the Elizabethan Golden Age. That the queen ruled over a *new* Golden Age was a common conceit of the time – Cranmer's speech in Shakespeare's *Henry VIII* describes the Elizabethan reign as one of 'peace' and 'plenty' (5.4.17–55; 47), parts of which are 'borrowed from the vision of the golden age that recurs throughout the Old Testament'.[30]

On account of their dissension over the Indian boy, the Golden Age has fallen, which Titania attributes to the 'winds':

　　　the winds, piping to us in vain,
As in revenge have sucked up from the sea
Contagious fogs which, falling in the land,
Hath every pelting river made so proud
That they have overborne their continents.

(2.1.88–92)

Oberon smugly assures Titania that once she gives him the Indian boy the seasons will be put back in order (2.1.118) – the Golden Age *restored* – which

it is by the end of the play when 'the heavy ploughman snores / All with weary task fordone' (5.2.3–4); but to his request for the Indian boy Titania delivers another speech on another Golden Age, that of the American Indians.

GOLDEN AGE AMERICA

Audiences in 1595–6 have heard that the 'changeling' is 'stol'n from an Indian king' and, since purloining New World natives was routine practice since the start of the sixteenth century, they are no doubt already going with the western 'India' when they hear Titania's account of her Indian queen fetching 'trifles' like Golden Age American Indians:

The fairyland buys not the child of me.
His mother was a vot'ress of my order,
And in the spicèd Indian air by night
Full often hath she gossiped by my side,
And sat with me on Neptune's yellow sands,
Marking th'embarkèd traders on the flood,
When we have laughed to see the sails conceive
And grow big-bellied with the wanton wind,
Which she with pretty and with swimming gait
Following, her womb then rich with my young
　　squire,
Would imitate, and sail upon the land
To fetch me trifles, and return again
As from a voyage, rich with merchandise.

(2.1.122–34)

Though modern critics are aware of the ambiguity of 'India' in the early modern period, ambiguity appears to be resolved by its conjunction with the word 'spiced' in Titania's lines and they favour an eastern location of 'India'. The linchpin of eastern interpretations, this 'spiced' Indian air is best understood as 'fragrant' or 'aromatic', complementing the many scented and 'fragrant flowers' in the play (2.1.249–52; 4.1.51): Titania is not saying that the 'embarked traders' seek to traffic for spice,

---

[29] *Ovid's Metamorphoses, Translated by Arthur Golding*, edited, with an Introduction and Notes, by Madeleine Forey (London, 2002).

[30] R. A. Foakes, ed., *King Henry VIII* (London, 1957), p. 175.

as is assumed in one analysis,[31] only describing the 'spiced' smell of the 'air'. For Columbus and subsequent voyagers, 'spiced' is how the west Indian air is described as well. In Eden's *Historie of Trauayle*, the main English authority on the New World: '[T]he soyle of these ilandes bringeth forth Mastir, Aloes, and sundry other sweete gummes and spyces, as doth *India*', the book states, describing how the Spanish could sense the 'fragrant sauors of spyces and sweet Gummes', talking of the many trees which have 'aromatical fruites and spyces', and finding the land 'ful of certayne spyces, but not such as we commonly use'.[32] And in *The Indian Nimph* by Robert Tofte, a contemporary poet who watched a performance of *Love's Labour's Lost* in the 1590s, 'Neptune' sends to America a 'breath' which 'she / Respires in soft perfumes of spicery'.[33]

Titania and the Indian queen sit on 'Neptune's yellow sands' and see ships that have embarked. The 'embarked traders on the flood' are 'images suggestive of an abundance of commercial traffic and the wealth of the Indian subcontinent' for R. W. Desai;[34] yet what looks like a voyage consisting of a few ships and a simple scene on the beach becomes magnified into some bustling city port on the Malabar coast. Fairy queen and pregnant Indian queen 'mark' the 'embarked traders on the flood' (not in the port), then laugh at the 'big-bellied' sails of the ships as they depart, which cannot be the departure of a whole port full of ships. Wealth and abundance are on the *land*, so much so that in one trip from the beach the Indian queen makes Titania 'rich with merchandise . . . as from a voyage'. Such abundance is made possible by the 'wanton wind' (resonating with the 'wanton green' (2.1.99), i.e. lush, overgrown) – surely the 'west wind' (mentioned in *The Two Noble Kinsmen*, 2.2.138), the gentle, fertile and luxuriant wind of the Golden Age before the 'penalty of Adam', the 'season's difference', the 'winter's wind' which epitomizes the fall from the Golden Age in *As You Like It* (2.1.5–7).

'Neptune's yellow sands' need only be a beach location fitting the maritime domain of the fairies: a 'beachèd margent of the sea' is a venue for the 'brawls' of Titania and Oberon (2.1.83–5; 87);

Oberon likes to look on 'Neptune' as dawn turns green sea to 'yellow gold' (3.2.392–4), a pure seascape; and in Prospero's speech in *The Tempest* where he abjures black magic, the 'elves' that 'on the sands . . . / Do chase the ebbing Neptune' (5.1.33–5) is an invented beach location adding to the magical domains ('hills, brooks, standing lakes and groves') of its source passage, Ovid's *Metamorphoses* (VII, 263–89). So can this really be the Queen of India (wife to the Great Akbar, mother to Prince Jahangir) come from the palace in Agra, here on the sea-shore dispensing 'trifles' to Titania like Golden Age American Indians? Such benevolence better suits an Indian queen of the New World in a delta of the Amazon or Orinoco ('a region in Guiana, all gold and bounty') for which the setting (beach or lagoon, no infrastructure) and the small number of ships would better apply (ships which no doubt seek to trade 'trifles' for rich merchandise).

The Golden Age myth of benevolent Indians is tested to the full in Caliban in *The Tempest*, who, though not actually an Indian, makes 'dams . . . for fish' (2.2.179) like the Virginian Indians,[35] can 'snare the nimble marmoset' (2.2.169), a monkey from the west Indies, and swears by 'Setebos' (1.2.375; 5.1.264), a Patagonian god

---

[31] Raman, *Framing India*, p. 244.

[32] Eden, *Historie*, fos. 11r, 12r and 19r.

[33] Robert Tofte, *The Indian Nimph*, in *The Poetry of Robert Tofte, 1597–1620: A Critical Old-spelling Edition*, ed. Jeffrey N. Nelson (New York and London, 1994), pp. 241–6, p. 241. Although voyagers failed to find eastern spices, West Indian spice was (and still is) a valued trading commodity. *Pimiento* or Indian pepper, for example, was traded all round Europe; it is catalogued as *Capsicum Indicum* in Gerarde's *Herball* (London, 1597) and it is *Capsicum frutescens* in later botany. When John Donne in 'The Sunne Rising' speaks of 'Both th'Indias of Spice and Myne' he is characterizing fantastic wealth, and does not try to convey the aromaticity of New World flora experienced by voyagers or imagined by creative writers. For Donne, in fact, 'Guyanaes harvest' would have been 'an India' for England: *The Complete English Poems*, ed. C. A. Patrides (London, 1991), pp. 54, 290–1.

[34] Desai, 'England, the Indian Boy, and the Spice Trade', p. 4.

[35] Hakluyt, *The Principal Nauigations*, p. 743.

mentioned in Eden's *Historie of Trauayle*.[36] Though at first Prospero 'made much' of him and Caliban was happy to show him 'all the qualities o'th' isle' (1.2.335; 339–40) and how to get food and water, rather like how a loving Indian queen brings Titania 'trifles', after time 'For every trifle' Prospero's 'spirits' are 'set upon' him (2.2.8) and he is whipped into compliance and falls from 'grace' (5.1.299). The illusion that benevolent natives can be depended upon for survival is exactly what in the dumbshow Prospero conjures for the hungry Europeans, where the 'banquet' presented by the 'strange shapes' (whose 'gentle-kind' 'manners' Gonzalo seems to take for American Indians) '*vanishes*' before it can be consumed (3.3.19; 30–3; 52).

And what of the *facility* with which the Indian queen fetches the 'trifles' from the 'land', the *leisurely* fashion, as if a *graceful dance*, in which 'with pretty and with swimming gait' she gets Titania's 'merchandise', the *carefree* way in which she fleets the time 'gossip[ing]' with the Fairy Queen? Such *ease* seems meant to suggest the abundant, Golden Age land of the American Indians – as in Barlowe's Virginia where the 'earth bringeth foorth all things in abundance, as in the first creation, without toile or labour';[37] or, since Golden Age America was European antiquity, a bountiful yet uncultivated nature like Ovid's classical Golden Age in the *Metamorphoses* in which 'The ground, untilled, all kind of fruits did plenteously afford' (1, 25). In relation to colonial discourse there seems an element of mockery in the antics of the Indian queen, for in *The Tempest*, as Jonathan Bate observes, though Caliban speaks of the 'island yielding up its own fruits in the ready abundance of the Golden Age' (2.2.164–8; 171–6), this is put into proper perspective by Prospero's betrothal masque in which the land is 'husbanded, not in a state of nature'.[38]

In *The Tempest*, counsel against an uncultivated nature is clearest in the contrast of Gonzalo's 'Golden Age' speech with Prospero's masque (4.1.60–138). Gonzalo's speech, 'Had I the plantation of the isle' he would 'excel the Golden Age' (2.1.149–74) – no 'tilth' or planting of 'corn', 'nature should bring forth / Of its own kind all

foison, all abundance' (158, 159, 168–9) – plays to the myth of New World *otium* which Prospero's masque corrects. As John Gillies shows, Gonzalo represents naïve perceptions of American colonization, 'just as Arthur Barlowe had imagined Virginia' producing 'golden age' abundance without toil, whereas Prospero's masque, stressing husbandry, reflects the more critical Virginia pamphlets like *A True Declaration of the Estate of the Colonie in Virginia* (1610) which censures the colonists for their idleness in tillage of the land and declares that '*Adam* himself might not live in paradice without dressing the garden'; Gonzalo's 'plantation' in which 'nature should produce / Without sweat or endeavour' (165–6) is therefore opposed by Prospero's masque which 'boasts those varieties of industrial foison that Gonzalo forswears' and 'affirm[s] agriculture'.[39] If *The Tempest* forbade that colonists should think that Virginia would yield Golden Age plenty without *negotium*, in 1595–6 it was the Guiana craze which required clear-headed perspective and what better than a fairyland scene in Golden Age America.[40]

---

36 Eden, *Historie*, fo. 434v.

37 Hakluyt, *The Principal Nauigations*, p. 731.

38 Bate, *Shakespeare and Ovid*, p. 257.

39 John Gillies, 'Shakespeare's American Masque', *English Literary History*, 4 (1986), 673–707, pp. 678, 689; *A True Declaration* quoted at p. 681.

40 In *The Historie of Trauayle* the New World is many times imagined as a fairyland (never the east, whose sections include many prosaic chapters on weights and measures, currency exchange, irrigation, etc.), for fairyland (along with spices, Amazons (fo. 13r–v) and orient pearls (46v)) moved to America with the new geography and is an Ovidian fairyland for translator Eden ('Fables much lyke Ouide his transformations', a side-note reads (51r)). America is likened to 'antiquitie' which 'beleued such fayries or spirites as they called *Dryades, Hamadryades, Satyros, Panes,* and *Nereides* to haue the cure and prouidence of the sea, woods, sprynges, and fountaynes'; where female '*Zemes*', idols with powers reminiscent of Ovid's Medea, are used in the invocations of the Indian shaman to 'raise wyndes, cloudes, and rayne . . . [and] geather togeather the waters which fall from the hygh hylles to the valleies, that being loosed, they may with force b[ur]ste out into great floodes, and overflowe the countrey' (52v and 53v).

ENGLAND'S GOLDEN AGE RESTORED

In response to Titania's story of her Indian 'vot'ress' and exit from the stage, Oberon brings the 'imperial vot'ress' (2.1.163) into the plot, an allusion to Queen Elizabeth which gives the story topical relevance. To compromise Titania in order to gain the Indian boy, he instructs Puck to gather the 'love-in-idleness' flower (168) made aphrodisiac when, at a royal entertainment, Cupid's arrow is deflected by the 'chaste beams' of the virgin queen:

> My gentle puck, come hither. Thou rememb'rest
> Since once I sat upon a promontory
> And heard a mermaid on a dolphin's back
> Uttering such dulcet and harmonious breath
> That the rude sea grew civil at her song
> And certain stars shot madly from their spheres
> To hear the sea-maid's music?   (148–54)

The word 'vot'ress' in Oberon's speech is the sole verbal link with Titania's speech on the Indian 'vot'ress', a juxtaposition of the 'imperial vot'ress' and the Indian 'vot'ress' which suggests contrast. And this contrast of the two votaresses, England's virgin queen and the pregnant Indian queen, is the same as colonial rhetoric for Virginia and Guiana that fertile America is recompense for the queen's virginity: in his 1587 Latin epistle to *De Orbe Novo*, Hakluyt writes that she can only 'bring forth new and most abundant offspring' (colonies) when he contrasts her with 'that fairest of nymphs', Virginia, while in *De Guiana* Chapman asserts that her 'barrennesse / Is the true fruite of vertue, that may get, / Beare and bring foorth anew' for Guiana, personified as an Indian queen.[41] The queen's barrenness is not mentioned in Oberon's speech; but 'fruitless' and 'barren' have already been used to describe Hermia's 'maiden' and monastic fate if she disobeys her 'father's will' (1.1.69–73, 75, 87), and prepare for a fuller profile of the 'maiden' (2.1.164) votaress and for a sharper contrast with the 'big-bellied' Indian votaress. In this reading, sensitivity to the queen's barrenness (and succession) would assume that she was not 'present' at

any of the performances,[42] for, as a contrast with the fruitful Indian queen, Oberon's praise of the queen's virginity is more mock panegyric than royal encomium.[43]

Oberon concludes his speech with his command to Puck to gather the magic herb and return 'Ere the leviathan can swim a league' (2.1.174), and Puck's reply that he will 'put a girdle round the earth in forty minutes' is usually taken as an allusion to Drake's circumnavigation of the globe (1577–80) which in Whitney's *Emblems* (1586) is represented by *The Golden Hind* attached to a girdle encircling the globe.[44] It certainly has, as Philip Armstrong notes, a 'cartographic tenor'.[45] So too does Oberon's 'We the globe can compass soon / Swifter than the wand'ring moon' (4.1.96–7), which, as Peter Donaldson observes, is a 'conjunction' of 'compass' and 'globe' which evokes both 'cartographic measurement' and 'actual travel'.[46] Actual travel and cartography in 1595–96 was Ralegh's Guiana voyage and Harriot's map for the queen,[47] so it is perhaps significant that Oberon's words come after Titania gives him the Indian boy (4.1.58–60) and immediately after his first dance in the play: for on the word 'compass' in *Eastward Hoe* the characters, taking supper aboard *The Golden Hind* docked permanently on London's river Thames, '*compass in Winifrid, and dance the*

---

[41] Richard Hakluyt, *The Original Writings and Correspondence of the Two Richard Hakluyts*, ed. E. G. R. Taylor, 2 vols. (London, 1935), vol. 2, pp. 367–8; Chapman, *De Guiana*, p. 354.

[42] See Stanley Wells, ed., *A Midsummer Night's Dream* (Harmondsworth, 1967), p. 13.

[43] For the view that the play was performed before the queen, see Harold F. Brooks, ed., *A Midsummer Night's Dream* (London, 1979), p. lv.

[44] Howard Horace Furness, ed., *A Midsommer Nights Dreame* (Philadelphia, 1895), p. 92.

[45] Philip Armstrong, 'Spheres of Influence: Cartography and the Gaze in Shakespearean Tragedy and History', *Shakespeare Studies*, 23 (1995), 39–70, p. 56.

[46] Peter Donaldson, 'All Which It Inherit: Shakespeare, Globes and Global Media', *Shakespeare Survey 56* (Cambridge, 1999), pp. 183–200, p. 186.

[47] Latham and Youings, *Letters*, p. 127.

drunken round' in celebration of Drake's circum-navigation and their own impending voyage to Virginia (3.3.169ff).

Oberon is 'Captain of our fairy band' (*Dream*, 3.2.110) and an imperial design would be consistent with other 'Oberons'. The assistance of 'Oberon' in the pre-Columbus romance *Huon of Bordeaux* helps Huon conquer the Saracens, amass much pagan treasure and rival the power of Charlemagne;[48] on the stage, the appearance of 'Oberon' in Thomas Dekker's *Lust's Dominion* (*c.*1600–05) dramatizes Eleazar's dastardly plot to compromise his wife Maria with the besotted King Fernando ('by her falling I must rise' (1.2.239)) so he can achieve 'Empery' (3.2.256), and brings to mind Oberon's plotting of Titania's fall from grace;[49] at the *Elvetham Entertainment* (1591), an event for the queen much resembling Oberon's description of his sighting of the 'imperial vot'ress', 'Auberon' is associated with an imperial suit – an American suit, since 'gould-breasted India' is a personage from the 'New World', not from the 'Indian sub-continent';[50] and in poetry, in Book Two of Spenser's *Faerie Queene* (1590), the founder of the royal line of 'Oberon' 'Was Elfin: him all *India* obayd, / And all that *America* men now call' (II.x.72).[51]

An imperial Oberon extending the Golden Age would play on the royal fairy entertainment. At the *Elvetham Entertainment*, long adduced as an influence[52] on Oberon's speech (Auberon, water spectacle, piscatorial imagery), the queen is complimented on her Golden Age of 'peace and plentie'; and, when the speech by the 'Fayery Quene' ('your Imperiall Grace') predicts that her reign will 'enlarge thy goulden dayes', enlargement of her empire is envisaged in the New World, for the 'jewel' bestowed on her is from 'gould-breasted India' (an American personage, an Indian queen), who, carried by a 'pinnace' sent by 'Neptune' across the Earl of Hertford's specially-built lake, 'leapt to the shore' and 'sprinkl[ed] endlesse treasure on this Isle'.[53] It is always the western 'India' which seeks royal assent in the queen's entertainments. In the fairyland of *The Triumphs of Oriana* (1601), for example, where Elizabeth is imagined in John Wilbye's madrigal as the 'Fair Queen of peace and plenty / . . . dight all in the treasures of Guiana', this combines compliment to her Golden Age with desire to extend her dominion to Golden Age America.[54] There is a similar possibility for the play: the restored seasons and a fruitful 'India' add up to an extended Golden Age, for once Oberon takes possession of the Indian boy his 'imperial vot'ress' (for whose fallen Golden Age Titania has shown unconcern by keeping him to herself) will reign over the bountiful land of the Indian 'vot'ress' as well her own Golden Age.

That Oberon *knows* the seasons will revert to normal once Titania gives him the Indian boy suggests it was he who raised the winds in the first place, a power of 'Oberon' in *Huon of Bordeaux* whose magic 'horne' can cause 'wynde . . . and tempest so horryble . . . that [it] semyd that heuen and the earth hade fought together and that ye worlde shoulde haue ended'.[55] Oberon's speech displays awe and admiration for how the supernatural effects of the 'dulcet . . . song' of the 'mermaid' becalmed the sea and 'shot' the 'stars' from their 'spheres' (Ariel's '*song*' makes possible Prospero's magical hold over Ferdinand in *The Tempest* (1.2.377ff)), and he is certainly shown to have

---

[48] *The Boke of Duke Huon of Burdeux; done into English by Sir John Bourchier, Lord Berners*, ed. Sidney Lee, 2 vols. (London, 1882–7).

[49] Thomas Dekker, *The Dramatic Works*, ed. Fredson Bowers, 4 vols. (Cambridge: 1953–61), vol. 4, pp. 115–231.

[50] Jean Wilson, ed., *Entertainments for Elizabeth I* (Woodridge, 1980), pp. 109, 115 and 163 n. 67.

[51] Edmund Spenser, *The Works of Edmund Spenser: A Variorum Edition*, 11 vols. (Baltimore: 1932–1957). Brooks, ed., *A Midsummer Night's Dream*, lxxxiv, cuts Spenser's line on 'America' then digresses to the eastern 'Oberon' in *Huon of Bordeaux*, giving the impression that Spenser's fairyland is eastern only and appearing to substantiate an exclusively eastern dominion for Oberon.

[52] Edith Rickert, 'Political Propaganda and Satire in *A Midsummer Night's Dream*', *Modern Philology*, 21 and 22 (1923), 53–87; 133–54.

[53] Wilson, *Entertainments*, pp. 102, 105 and 109.

[54] Edmund Horace Fellowes, *English Madrigal Verse, 1588–1632*, 3rd edn, rev. Frederick. W. Sternfield and David Grier (Oxford, 1967), p. 163.

[55] *Huon of Burdeux*, ed. Lee, p. 67.

the power to effect supernatural change when he orders Puck to 'overcast' the sky with 'drooping fog' when Lysander and Demetrius are about to fight (3.2.355–8). The disruption of the seasons in *A Midsummer Night's Dream* does not seem the harmless illusion Prospero gets Ariel to create with the 'dew' fetched 'From the still-vexed Bermudas' (1.2.230) in the opening 'shipwreck' scene: more like Prospero's confession of his younger and darker Medean magic (drawn from Ovid,[56] probably like Titania's 'seasons' speech):

> I have bedimmed
> The noontide sun, called forth the mutinous winds,
> And 'twixt the green sea and the azured vault
> Set roaring war. (5.1.41–4)

Oberon meddling with the seasons (as well as with love) provides the humour of the play: he has caused the fall from the Golden Age to get the Indian boy and restores it again once he takes possession of him, thereby enabling England's virgin queen to bear and rear up colonies in 'India' and extend her Golden Age. Titania had intended only to 'rear up' (2.1.136) the Indian boy in her garden of delights where she pampers Bottom, but Oberon will make him 'Knight of his train' (2.1.25) and seems set to return to the 'farthest step of India' (2.1.69) from where he has 'come' at the start of the play.

PARADISE REGAINED

For Marjorie Garber, Oberon contrives Titania's 'fall' from her 'Eden-like garden', and 'suggestions of the fall from paradise are unmistakable' in Titania's 'seasons' speech and in Hermia's romantic plight as well:[57]

> Before the time I did Lysander see
> Seemed Athens as a paradise to me.
> O then, what graces in my love do dwell,
> That he hath turned a heaven unto a hell? (1.1.204–7)

Hermia's fall from 'paradise' is suggested by her dream of the 'crawling serpent' eating her 'heart away' after Lysander makes an attempt on her

virginity in the wood (2.2.47–8; 152–5); indeed, after the 'love-in-idleness' enamours Lysander to Helena, he sees Hermia's romantic move on him as like a 'serpent' (3.2.262) which threatens to cause his own fall from grace (cf. Queen Isabel's reaction to the Gardener's speech, in 'Adam's likeness', in *Richard II*: 'What Eve, what serpent hath suggested thee / To make a second fall of cursèd man?' (3.4.74; 76–7)). For Renaissance thinking the end of the classical Golden Age merges with the fall from the biblical Garden of Eden (e.g. Golding's Epistle to Ovid's *Metamorphoses*, lines 469–70), and Hermia's fall from 'paradise' reiterates the Golden Age theme of Act 2; while details of her plight in Act 1 suggest affinities with the American Indians and New World conquest.

That against her 'father's will' she loves Lysander, scorns Demetrius's 'unwishèd yoke' and refuses to yield up her 'sovereignty' and 'virgin patent' to his 'certain right' (1.1.80–2) is not far away from colonial rhetoric that the American Indians under the Spanish yoke (and Papal decree) sought English love and vassalship instead; that she gives her love in exchange for Lysander's 'trifles' (1.1.34) echoes with the language of New World voyagers, draws parallels with the natives and locates 'India' as Golden Age America; and that her ordeal is tinged with allusion to Virgil's *Aeneid* – the 'Carthage queen' to Lysander's 'false Trojan' (1.1.173–4) – is more evocative of imperial conquest than of eastern trade (consider the influence of the *Aeneid* in *The Tempest*[58]). Shades of America in Hermia's plight would have been nothing new for readers of the violent taking of Lucrece's 'sov'reignty' (36) in Shakespeare's *Rape of Lucrece* (1594), for which Jonathan Bate remarks that 'Tarquin is like an ambitious Elizabethan adventurer setting out to conquer the virgin land of the New World'.[59]

'The course of true love never did run smooth' (1.1.134), but when Hermia emerges from the

---

56 Bate, *Shakespeare and Ovid*, pp. 249–51.
57 Garber, *Dream in Shakespeare*, p. 71.
58 See Stephen Orgel, ed., *The Tempest* (Oxford, 1987), pp. 39–40.
59 Bate, *Shakespeare and Ovid*, p. 72.

wood she is loved by Lysander, and, just as Titania is reunited with Oberon and order is restored to the seasons ('peace' (3.2.378) and plenty (5.2.3–4) in fairyland), 'paradise' is regained (thanks to Oberon's meddling). Bottom, as consort to the Fairy Queen in her uncultivated garden of fruits and flowers, experiences a sort of paradise too (his garbling of 1 Corinthians 2: 9 (4.1.203–12) expressing the indescribability of his 'rare vision', possibly a 'distant echo' of the 'paradise' in 2 Corinthians 12: 1–6; 4):[60] he is served like a king by Mustardseed and company in the same way Titania is served by the Golden Age Indian queen, the repetition of 'fetch' used for the 'trifles' brought by the Indian queen in her offer of the fairies to 'fetch'

him 'jewels from the deep' (3.1.150) and 'new nuts' (4.1.35) linking the passages, reinforcing symmetry and bringing unity to the play's themes.

Hermia's 'paradise' is linked to the Golden Age and this anticipates the Golden Age tenor of *The Tempest*, for Ferdinand praises Prospero's masque as 'a most majestic vision' which, now that he has fallen in love with Miranda, 'Makes this place paradise' (4.1.118; 124). For John Gillies, New World themes make *The Tempest* 'Shakespeare's American Masque' – and much the same may be said of *A Midsummer Night's Dream*.

---

[60] Peter Holland, ed., *A Midsummer Night's Dream* (Oxford, 1994), p. 227.

THE LIMITS OF TRANSLATION IN
A MIDSUMMER NIGHT'S DREAM

MICHAEL SAENGER

Translation theory (following on the work of Friedrich Schleiermacher) posits a distinction between two strategies of translation: foreignizing and nativizing.[1] 'Foreignizing', as used by translation theorists, describes a textual mode wherein the translator deliberately uses foreign-sounding words in a translation to create a feeling of textual strangeness. In the contrary, nativizing mode, the translated text is presented, to the greatest degree possible, as if it were always naturally at home in the new language. The foreignizing strategy encourages us to see translation; the nativizing (or 'domesticating') strategy encourages us not to. This binary was clearly relevant in the textual history of the English Bible, and it extends to content as well as vocabulary; Peter Burke has pointed out that the trade in translations in the Renaissance frequently involved adding or subtracting content, as well as 'transposition', wherein nativizing translators of Rabelais and Castiglione moved the *location* of events in their renditions closer to home.[2] Translation is motivated by the desire for foreign things, and the disparate lexical strategies point to that desire as a site for projection and introjection, an effort to appropriate potency, successful or failed. The tension between these alternate modes reflects a deep concern in the Renaissance with identity, desire and agency across borders, and unlike the mythic transformations of desire in Ovid's *Metamorphoses*, that tension plays itself out in lexical alternatives and grammatical strategies. *A Midsummer Night's Dream* is filled with erotic transformations that are primarily Ovidian, but those transformations also demonstrate a preoccupation

with the tensions inherent in textual appropriation. This essay examines this pattern, with a specific focus on Helena's erotic exploration of linguistic envy and Bottom's malapropistic exploration of socially tethered creativity. I suggest here that this tension between foreignizing and nativizing modes of translation can help to understand linguistic tensions that, at first glance, do not seem to involve foreign languages: Helena's desire to speak like Hermia, and Bottom's desire to speak English grandly. Both Helena and Bottom seek to learn a kind of new language without losing themselves, and in the process of desiring those new words, experience a transformation. However that ambition may work out for those characters, moments of translation in the play hint at the increasing richness of the English language.

Translation is both crucial and problematic in *A Midsummer Night's Dream*. Shakespeare was clearly fascinated with the ways in which our social sensation and construction of identity depends upon the quintessentially abstract framework of language, and efforts at translation point to this as an issue. Juliet famously pleads with Romeo to rename himself – a plea whose quixotic optimism and

---

I am grateful for the commentary of Peter Holland, Patricia Parker, Robert Watson, Sarah Gammill, Joe Wilson and Scott Newstok in the development of this article.

[1] See Mona Baker, *Routledge Encyclopedia of Translation Studies* (London and New York, 1998), pp. 240–4.

[2] Peter Burke, 'The Renaissance Translator as Go-Between', in *Renaissance Go-Betweens: Cultural Exchange in Early Modern Europe*, ed. Andreas Höfele and Werner von Koppenfels (Berlin, 2005), pp. 28–9.

essentialist assumption about what constitutes his identity make poignant the degree to which language irrevocably determines our sense of self and renders phantasmatic any dream of recovering a body without a name, without a history, without a discourse. Indeed a rose by any other name would not smell *as* sweet – our culturally overdetermined investment in that particular blossom makes it inevitable that we perceive – and even *feel* – a greater sweetness there than in many other fragrant flowers.[3] To Juliet's distress, language is not an interchangeable label for things.

If translation is foreclosed in *Romeo and Juliet*, it is pervasive in *A Midsummer Night's Dream*. The latter play is focused on acts of translation on many axes: rule-bound London and its wilder fringes are imaginatively translated into a similarly paired Athens and its magical purlieus, Demetrius is translated into the lover Helena wants him to be, and the efforts of the mechanicals are translated, by Theseus's gentle reception, into good art. But the play is equally littered with failed or incomplete acts of translation and vocal theft: Puck's mistaken translation of Lysander into a Helena-lover is central to the plot, and so is Bottom's transformation. When Quince exclaims that Bottom has been 'translated' (3.1.113), that word itself sounds estranged from the sentence; it has the feel of a poetically accurate malapropism. Bottom's translation is visible precisely because of its incompletion; he is (physically, vocally and mentally) only partly an ass. At stake in all of these events is agency across borders: Oberon successfully controls Demetrius, more falteringly controls Lysander. Translation (derived from the Latin 'to move across') often raises such issues of agency at boundaries, either implicitly or explicitly; domesticating translations compliment the target language's sense of agency by offering the feeling of completely successful re-situation, whereas foreignizing translations trouble that same sense of agency by signalling the protrusion of the untranslated in an otherwise translated text. Like Bottom's partially human shape, they remind us that translations often fail in one way or another. Indeed, they can fail in multiple ways; Oberon seems to think that he has succeeded in his intent to 'torment'

Titania (2.1.147), but there is no evidence that she suffers in any way. His partially failed translation has only partially accomplished its task, gaining him the changeling boy but only delighting his scornful compeer. One of the inevitable consequences of such visible translations is that all bushes and bears can be read as each other, potentially. The potential failure, and pervasive visibility, of translation means that things *per se* are almost impossible to find in the play; the mechanicals' efforts to put on a play force us to see the moon as a symbol of itself.

The thematic pattern of translation is closely related to the theme of control; *A Midsummer Night's Dream* is populated with people who seek to own and to contest ownership over other people. The play anchors itself around the lovers' quarrel wherein Lysander and Demetrius seek a judgement on who has the right to claim Hermia; the issue of Hermia's capacity to own herself is itself contested by her father. Theseus has conquered Hippolyta but seeks more fully to own her, Oberon and Titania contest custody of the changeling boy, Helena seeks to pry Demetrius away from Hermia, and Bottom wants to take almost every part in the mechanicals' play. Many of these efforts at ownership are urgently linked to language. When Bottom explains why he would be a good Thisbe and Lion, he focuses on the fact that he can make his voice high and lionish; he makes no reference to looking like a woman or a lion, which would seem to be important. Similarly, when Demetrius is confronting Lysander as they seek to defend Helena from Hermia, Demetrius says 'Speak not of Helena. / Take not her part' (3.2.333–4). To speak of, and to take a part, are both ways of referring to chivalric defence that oddly resonate with Bottom's thirst to take on more roles than he can adequately

---

[3] Recent research has shown that merely by raising the price associated with a glass of wine, the pleasure that test subjects physically experienced in drinking it was raised (see Claire Baldwin, 'Higher Wine Prices Boost Drinking Pleasure', *Reuters*, 15 January 2008). Subjects not only *reported* greater pleasure when tasting the same wine presented with a higher price – this might be chalked up to politeness in a discursive frame – they actually experienced greater pleasure due to the changed price, as revealed in brain scans.

maintain. Indeed, it is often noted that Thisbe (or her author, presumably Quince) seems to be comically unclear on classical mythology when she says that she will be trusty, 'like Helen, till the fates me kill' (5.1.196). Thisbe wants to claim allusive ownership of Helen, but her incomplete textual apparatus (i.e. the inadequate learning of her author) causes her only ineffectually to claim ownership both over Helen and over the tragic mode. In different ways, Quince mistranslates both Helen of Troy and the idea of tragedy.

Like Thisbe's citational Helen, Helena of Athens also can be seen as a mistranslation of her Homeric namesake; at one moment in the play, Helena is farcically pursued by two men, just as Helen was pursued epically. Further, Helena (and Bottom, examined below) is both translated and translating, both an object of textual transformation and, at least in desire, an agent of such transformation. In fact, Helena explains her envy of Hermia in terms that join translation to control:

Helena. Call you me fair? That 'fair' again unsay.
　Demetrius loves your fair – O happy fair!
　Your eyes are lodestars, and your tongue's sweet air
　More tunable than lark to shepherd's ear
　When wheat is green, when hawthorn buds appear.
　Sickness is catching. O, were favour so!
　Your words I catch, fair Hermia; ere I go,
　My ear should catch your voice, my eye your eye,
　My tongue should catch your tongue's sweet melody.
　Were the world mine, Demetrius being bated,
　The rest I'd give to be to you translated.

　　　　　　　　　　　　　　(1.1.181–91)

Helena wants to commit (in modern terms) identity theft, and she conceives of such a theft as a translation. The term 'identity theft' gestures to the fact that our identity can in some ways more accurately be located in an abstract social framework than it can be located within our bodies. This severability between (and consequently, interchangeability of) physical and social identity is a core characteristic of (early) modern urban life and of the burgeoning credit economy of early modern London; it is also both a basic condition of the acting profession and a continual fascination of Shakespeare's drama.

If Helena cannot have Demetrius as herself, she imagines adopting Hermia's identity so as to enjoy him. Of course, she does not want to *be* Hermia; that would come close to a situation where Helena is simply erased and Hermia is re-adored by Demetrius.[4] Self-translation without the retention of personal agency would only mean losing a core element of identity. Helena wants to *learn* everything that makes Hermia recognizable, while retaining Helena's own desire for Demetrius – a desire that, at this moment, Helena sees as the only aspect of herself that she wishes to retain. Either this would be transformation (translation's more common modern sense) or an Ovidian transfer of a spirit via erotic metempsychosis. Sensing the impossibility of both these options, she asks Hermia to instruct her: 'O, teach me how you look, and with what art / You sway the motion of Demetrius' heart' (1.1.192–3). This is a different idea: the notion of the affected assumption of a new identity (not a duplicate Hermia, but as it were a Hermia-ized Helena) to achieve a pre-existing goal.[5] Helena's repeated use of the word 'tongue'

4　In *Shakespeare's Imitations*, Mark Taylor examines a similar moment, in Titania's recollection of her interaction with the pregnant votaress (*Dream*, 2.1.122–37). For Taylor, the most interesting tension in this recollected scene is not between Titania and the votaress, but rather between the votaress – who is pregnant and playfully imitating the sailing ship – and the sailing ships, which are 'translated' by Titania's metaphor: 'In imitating the ships, the votaress, always conscious of her own act of imitation, retains her own identity, remains herself; conceived and grown big-bellied with the wanton wind, the sails lose their identity as sails and become pregnant women' (*Shakespeare's Imitations* (Newark, 2002), p. 39).

5　In Helena's transition from an imagined theft of Hermia's identity to an effort to acquire the craft to affect that identity we see something like Lacan's imaginary realm transitioning into the symbolic. At first, Helena projects herself onto the masterful image of Hermia, and then introjects that ideal image, in an attempt, to borrow from Philip Armstrong's treatment of *Hamlet*, to 'incorporate the mirrored image, by assimilating it "within" the archive of identifications that compose the "self"' (Philip Armstrong, 'Watching Hamlet Watching: Lacan, Shakespeare and the Mirror/Stage', in *Alternative Shakespeares 2*, ed. Terence Hawkes (London and New York, 1996), vol. 2, p. 221). This vocabulary of desire is not limited to erotic desire; Castiglione writes that 'He therefore that will bee a good scholler, beside the in that speech – she says it three times – puts an otherwise peculiar emphasis on the role of Hermia's voice in attracting Demetrius. One would not expect Demetrius to be primarily attracted to Hermia's voice over against other parts of her body, but that is Helena's focus, largely because it is the thing about oneself that one can most readily transform. However, that word also signals the elusiveness of Helena's ability to achieve her goal. The word 'tongue' itself is repeated enough to signal the profound challenge of this translation, if only because Helena's tongue is still the one saying every iteration of the word.[6]

Translation may come up in this context in part because, unlike most Shakespearian characters who want to take another character's identity,[7] Helena longs intentionally to adopt the identity of someone we and she know very well – Hermia – and it is especially complicated because, thanks to Puck's interference, Helena effectively *succeeds* in replacing Hermia's identity, at least in the demi-monde of the forest. Indeed it is interesting that when Helena is adored, Lysander praises her as being '[t]ransparent' (2.2.110); that word aptly characterizes the lure and danger of profound adaptability. He means that, like a gem, she transmits light and so he can 'see [her] heart' (2.2.111) through her bosom. The metaphor serves to mock his own erotic idolatry – it almost equates that mode of worship with a kind of autopsy – and it also resonates with Helena's fear and desire of being lost in translation. Initially, Helena's lack corresponds with Hermia's plenitude when it comes to men, self-esteem and identitarian solidity, but once Puck has destabilized the geometry of pursuit that impelled the lovers to enter the forest, Helena finally exhibits ego-formation, and Hermia experiences a corresponding crisis, culminating in abject loss when Hermia asks 'Am not I Hermia?' (3.2.274). When Puck causes Demetrius and Lysander to change their orientation, Helena is greeted with the realization of her dream. She finds herself in a situation where she has replaced Hermia almost completely, getting the attention of both men and the envy of her friend, and her response is – comically – one of outrage: 'I see you all are bent / To set

against me for your merriment' (3.2.146–7). Having nativized Hermia's identity almost completely, she finally distances herself from the words around her, hearing them as foreign.

Helena's desire for Hermia's vocal power is part of a larger thematic structure of voice-theft in the play, from Egeus stealing (and weirdly feeling) his daughter's desire to Oberon instructing Puck to mimic the voices of Lysander and Demetrius alternately, and thus incite them to rage (3.2.361–6); it is a theme that manifests most comically in Bottom's asinine desire for hay (4.1.32–3). At least one thread that links these vocal thefts is the play's exploration of human agency at the various borders – borders of patriarchal power, erotic fulfilment and ludic fantasy. Bottom in general, and in his waking in

---

practising of good thinges, must evermore set all his diligence to be like his maister, and (if it were possible) chaung him selfe into him' (Baldassare Castiglione, trans. Thomas Hoby, in *The Book of the Courtier*, ed. W. H. D. Rouse (New York, 1956), p. 45).

6 Shakespeare's engagement with these issues, and his particular linkage to an exploration of identity and desire in connection with Helena's name, is evidenced in the fact that a passage written by David McCandless on Helen in *All's Well That Ends Well* applies perfectly to this moment, if one allows for a substitution of the figure of Bertram with Demetrius: Helen's 'goal shifts from the fulfillment of desire to the achievement of desirability. Her desire is no longer simply the desire to wed but the desire to be desired. She thus identifies with, and acts through, the woman whom Bertram covets. In a Lacanian context, Helena says not "I wish to become a woman" but rather "I wish to be like her whom I recognize as a woman".' (McCandless, 'Helen's Bed-trick: Gender and Performance in *All's Well That Ends Well*', *Shakespeare Quarterly*, 45 (1994), 456). On the resonance of the name Helena, particularly in *All's Well That Ends Well*, see Laurie Maguire, *Shakespeare's Names* (New York and Oxford, 2007), pp. 104–9.

7 There is plenty of identity-switching in Shakespeare, but most of it occurs in instances where the danger of identity transfer is muted. This can happen because a character adopts an identity that has been newly created, and thus is stealing it from no one (Rosalind becoming Ganymede, Celia becoming Aliena, Viola becoming Cesario) or from an effectively uninhabited one (Portia and Nerissa becoming the Lawyer and Clerk). These swaps can also be muted when they are performed unintentionally, such as Antipholus of Syracuse playing his twin in *Comedy of Errors* or Sebastian playing his in *Twelfth Night*.

particular, presents a different vision of what translation does to identity. As part of Shakespeare's broader trope of poetic malapropism, Bottom plays with a desire for social status that is heard in English etymologically. But unlike many of Shakespeare's malapropists, Bottom ends up synthesizing his malapropistic habits into viable poetry with a biblical translation. Whereas Helena finds her ego as she loses her voice, Bottom finds a structure to his imagination when he refuses (intentionally) the structures of English grammar and hierarchical lexicology.

Shakespeare's malapropists tend to have trouble with Latinate roots. For example, in *Measure for Measure*, Elbow often begins sentences that make perfect sense while he uses Anglo-Saxon lexicon, but as he shifts into a more elevated Latin diction, he makes a mistake. It is such a direct mistake that it is audible as a substitution; we can almost hear the word he intends. He tells Angelo, 'I do lean upon justice, sir; and do bring in here before your good honour two notorious *benefactors*' (2.1.46–8, my emphasis), a mistake that Angelo corrects. Elbow follows this with, 'If it please your honour, I know not well what they are; but *precise* villains they are, that I am sure of, and void of all *profanation* in the world that good Christians ought to have' (2.1.51–4). His errors are partly comic (they flatter us for understanding his foolishness) and partly aesthetic; unbeknownst to him, Angelo is a malefactor who sounds like a benefactor, and the play could be seen as considering quite deeply Angelo's nature as a precise villain, and also asking how much profanation a Christian (like Isabella) ought to have. But because of the stratified nature of English as a hybrid tongue, the errors also distinctly resonate with social class. Elbow reveals his intrinsic affiliation with the lower class by his comfort with Anglo-Saxon English and broken striving for its more elevated Franco-Latin layers. Malapropism thus detaches intention from language: what the characters say is not what they mean and, unlike irony, the character is not in control of that palimpsest. The aesthetic and social patterning with which Shakespeare habitually invests his linguistic over-reachers testifies that,

though the speaker's intention may be detached from his or her words, another intention is audible, whether it be that of the artist (who uses the malapropist to hint at broader thematic patterns) or the invisible hand of social conservatism (that uses the malapropist as an example of failed ascension). Thus a malapropism is defined, grammatically, by its detached and reattached relationship to syntactic agents within its sentence (put bluntly, it does not fit), and it also performs a similar function on a more symbolic and societal level. Just as the erroneous word detaches from the other words in its sentence, and yet remains differently connected to them, so the figure of speech also detaches from the psychology of its speaker and yet regains attachment to something else; in Shakespeare those reattachments to more abstract agents are relatively transparent.

Bottom is another example. When he greets his fellows, he says a sentence whose Anglo-Saxon elements are perfectly sensible, but one of whose Latinate words obtrudes as visibly as an ass's head: 'You were best to call them *generally*, man by man, according to the scrip' (1.2.2–3, my emphasis). Bottom appears to mean, like Elbow, something like the opposite of what his Latin word makes him say, here and soon afterward: 'I will move stones. I will *condole*, in some measure' (1.2.22–3, my emphasis). He does seem to know that 'dole' means sorrow, but to condole is to sympathize with a person in sorrow, not to cause pain in a bystander. The antonymic vector of his errors makes his intention as clear as his mistake. Afterward, he boasts 'I will *aggravate* my voice so that I will roar you as gently as any sucking dove. I will roar you an 'twere any nightingale' (1.2.76–8, my emphasis), again intending the opposite of what his elevated diction says. Lexical ambition clearly parallels its social analogue. Dogberry, Elbow and Bottom all perform their roles ostentatiously for their betters (Leonato, Escalus and Angelo, and the Athenian court) as if hoping for advancement, and indeed, when Snug is fretting over Bottom arriving late for the final performance, he points to that performance as a transformative social event: 'If our sport had gone forward we had all been made men'

(4.2.16–17). We laugh at these characters because their words make audible their awkward efforts to translate their own social status: they *are* walking malapropisms. At the other end of the spectrum, Corin in *As You Like It* has no such ambition, makes no such mistakes, is the butt of no jokes, and speaks in emphatically Anglo-Saxon diction:

Sir, I am a true labourer. I earn that I eat, get that I wear; owe no man hate, envy no man's happiness; glad of other men's good, content with my harm; and the greatest of my pride is to see my ewes graze and my lambs suck.

(3.2.71–5)

Corin is as docile as the sheep he supervises, so he's not punished, but his grammar is as comically direct as his self-made wardrobe, and his lexicon is almost monolingual and monosyllabic. He may not be punished, but he implicitly resonates with a humble Englishness that will never rise beyond its sheep-shearing Anglo-Saxon roots on a rocky island. Some admixture of language systems, and some imported fabrics, are necessary for wider cultural advancement.

Famously, a key section of Bottom's post-dream monologue has a close relationship with a particularly soaring section of Paul's first epistle to the Corinthians, 2:9–10. The Protestant Geneva and Catholic Rheims-Douai versions of those verses appear below:

But as it is written, The things which eye hathe not sene, nether eare hathe heard, nether came into ma[n]'s heart, *are*, which God hathe prepared for them that loue him. But God hathe reueiled *them* vnto vs by his Spirit: for the Spirit searcheth all things, yea, the deepe things of God.[8]

But, as it is written, *That which eie hath not seen, nor eare hath heard, neither hath it ascended into the hart of ma[n], what things God hath prepared for them that love him.* but to us God hath revealed by his Spirit. For the Spirit searcheth al things, yea the profoundities of God.[9]

To which Bottom responds:

The eye of man hath not heard, the ear of man hath not seen, man's hand is not able to taste, his tongue to conceive, nor his heart to report what my dream was.

(4.1.208–11)

One of the interesting variations between the Geneva Bible and its Rheims counterpart is that in the former, divine inspiration is imagined (not) *coming* into the heart of man, whereas in the latter it is imagined (not) *ascending* there. Either way, only the spirit can access it, and then only via revelation. The Rheims version is foreignizing; the Latinate 'ascended' is cognate with the Vulgate, which has 'ascendit' here,[10] whereas 'come' is distinctly Anglo-Saxon. Indeed, the Geneva Bible is called the Breeches Bible because of the fact that in that translation, Adam and Eve wear (very English-sounding) *breeches* made of fig leaves. A similar contrast is seen in the second verse between the 'deepe things' and the 'profoundities' of God. The Geneva version thus nativizes the text, opting for a more familiar English root when possible, whereas the Rheims version retains a feel of Latinity in its syntax and lexicon. After all, the Catholic Church was reluctant to allow an English Bible at all, so it is understandable that that translation would register its tentative relation to the vernacular through the foreign-feeling choice of a Latin root.

In his revelatory state, Bottom quite surprisingly detaches Anglo-Saxon words from each other. It is difficult to say with any certainty whether he performs this metathesis (the transposition of words within a sentence) intentionally; he may be poetically approximating dream-like synaesthesia by misplacing his verbs, or he may be still in a dream-like state, speaking his own tongue wildly. Either way, a formerly stable satire of working-class pretensions of grandeur is released from any clear social location, just as Helena is released from erotic self-negation in the forest. One can take this to be a parody of Paul, as Harold Bloom does,[11] but the malapropistic patterning here is elaborate, and this

[8] *The Geneva Bible: A Facsimile of the 1560 Edition* (Madison, Milwaukee and London, 1969).

[9] *The New Testament of Jesus Christ: 1582* (London, 1975).

[10] *Biblia Sacra: Iuxta Vulgatam Versionem* (Stuttgart, 1994).

[11] Harold Bloom, *Shakespeare and the Invention of the Human* (New York, 1998), p. 167.

coherence hints at a function other than parody. He performs not just a simple metathesis but quite a complex pattern of substitution. Below are the nouns and verbs of this phrase, with Latin roots in boldface:

Past participle		Infinitive		
eye	ear	hand	tongue	heart
heard	seen	**taste**	**conceive**	**report**

On the left is a clear chiastic metathetic pattern, one which was probably audible as such even in its first hearing. But on the right, the substitution is more complex; at first glance, the tongue can *taste* and *report* (but not *conceive*) and the hand and heart are essentially irrelevant to all the verbs on the lower line. Many of the other malapropists, like Elbow, are quite clearly deflationary of the lower class. Snout stumbles in and on his prologue either because of its mispunctuation or his lack of ability to read that punctuation, thus emphasizing his difficulty with literacy. Orality and Anglo-Saxon diction seem like the proper place of the mechanicals, and they generally stumble when they attempt Latinate diction, written speech (such as scripts with cues) and classical mythology. Here, Bottom's words are metaphysically coherent and grammatically wild, finally harmonizing the Latinate and Anglo-Saxon streams of the English lexicon into a poesis that succeeds — perhaps the only such successful poetry Bottom speaks. The transformation he enacts is comically in a negative frame (hath not, not able . . .), but he nevertheless moves from (negated) present participles to (negated) infinitives, thus hinting at a progressive move from the present to the future, a movement that belies his ostensibly negative grammatical frame.

'Tongue' anchors the climactic second set of pairs; and 'tongue' can be a body part or a language. Like Paul's text, Bottom's is one of negation; his tongue *cannot* conceive his dream, just as Paul envisions an eye that cannot see the deep things of God. English, like Bottom's speech, was a lower-class hybrid tongue, never perceived as having the grace and elevation inherent in its social betters, such as French, Italian and Latin. Advancement for Bottom, and for English, is daunting if viewed by the standard rules of Athens, the same standard arithmetic that also frustrates Helena at the beginning of the play. But just as Helena can be transformed in the forest, so Bottom can be translated by his waking revelation, performing a kind of grammatical alchemy that turns the very clumsiness of the syntax-dependent English tongue into a poetic tool to translate Paul into dream poetry. Bottom wants Quince to write his dream, a desire that hints at a thirst for literary clarity — and even immortality. Quince would probably disappoint him if he tried, but Bottom himself is able, however fleetingly, to knit together the tendentious roots of English into something that creates as much beauty as he imagines he is unable to report.

Bottom breaks free from the strictures of rational thought (not to mention syntax), and he is particularly suited to doing so because he has never been very able to express himself. In this sequence of five paired verbs, he begins with an unorthodox German / German etymological pair that lacks sense, and then follows it with three German / Latin pairs. This defiance of reason in the native side of his native tongue thus opens the possibility for the second set of malapropisms to be something other than failed social climbing. If reason can be defied within the German root system, then Latinate roots can be mangled without the fear of exposing the language itself, and its dreamers, as being rude and mechanical; if Anglo-Saxon roots can be made to sound foreign, then the Latinate strata of English can (whether through poetry or malapropism) be nativized. Workmen, like Bottom, labour with their *hands* (as Philostrate puts it, he and his fellows 'never laboured in their minds till now' (5.1.73)). Physical *tongues* can taste and report, but linguistic tongues can, in a sense, both report and conceive. The thrust of Paul's text, and that of Isaiah which he cites (64:4), is to distinguish between earthly wisdom (which cannot properly know God) and inspiration (which can). Bottom's target of comprehension is not God, but only his dream, which is a relatively earthly thing. Helena's desire, and Bottom's dream, are in themselves hardly grand or serious, but through a poesis of personal translation and malapropism, the play implies that such ordinary things – and similar ordinary things, like (the English) language – can be transformed, if only fleetingly, into powerful and numinous visions.

VOICE, FACE AND FASCINATION: THE ART OF PHYSIOGNOMY IN *A MIDSUMMER NIGHT'S DREAM*

SIBYLLE BAUMBACH

Bottom: I see a voice. Now will I to the chink
To spy an I can hear my Thisbe's face.
Thisbe?

(*A Midsummer Night's Dream*, 5.1.191–3)

The revels have begun. After long rehearsals, the artisans finally perform their play in honour of Theseus and Hippolyta's wedding: 'A tedious brief scene of young Pyramus / And his love Thisbe: very tragical mirth' (5.1.56–7). The play within the play provides a comic reflection of the communication situation in the theatre insofar as it creates another space-within-a-space wherein observers observe other observers observing.[1] But, as Theseus notices ('"Merry" *and* "tragical"? "Tedious" *and* "brief"?' (5.1.58)), it also reconciles the irreconcilable: it makes the tragic comic; it makes visible what can only be heard; and it disembodies what can usually only be seen.

In the following, I will take up Bottom's cue and provide new perspectives on voices and faces as well as their interaction and translation in *A Midsummer Night's Dream*. As I will argue, much of the fascination with this specific play derives from the complex physiognomic discourse it reveals and with which it engages its audience(s).

I. THE ART OF PHYSIOGNOMY: ATTUNING THE EYE

The apparent confusion of eye and ear, which Bottom presents while playing Pyramus, is most prominent in his earlier reflections on his dream, which exceeds representation, partly because the senses are awkwardly mismatched: 'The eye of man hath not heard, the ear of man hath not seen, man's hand is not able to taste, his tongue to conceive, nor his heart to report what my dream was' (4.1.208–11). Bottom's parodic garbling of the biblical text from I Corinthians (2:9–10) has been read as a refusal of 'St Paul's easy supernaturalism, with dualistic split between flesh and spirit'.[2] First and foremost, however, it complements the characteristic acting style of the artisans, who are prone to confusions of all kinds, as indicated by Quince's mispunctuated prologue:

If we offend, it is with our good will.
That you should think: we come not to offend
But with good will. (5.1.108–10)

Perhaps dreading another imperfect speech of the same category as this 'tangled chain' (5.1.124), Theseus finally curbs the amateur performance. When Bottom asks whether he would like 'to see the epilogue or to hear a bergamask dance' (5.1.346–7), he cuts the play short: 'No epilogue, I pray you' (5.1.349). Robin will eventually [a]mend what needs [a]mending by declaring all the action on-stage to be an idle vision, '[n]o more yielding but a dream' (Epilogue 6) and its actors as 'shadows' (Epilogue 1), as immaterial beings that cannot be seen – but only heard?

---

[1] See Dietrich Schwanitz, 'Shakespeare stereoskopisch: Die Schule des Sehens und die Optik der Praxis', *Shakespeare Jahrbuch*, 129 (1993), 136–7.

[2] Harold Bloom, ed., *William Shakespeare: A Midsummer Night's Dream* (New York, 2010), p. 3.

'I see a voice'. Bottom's synaesthesia exceeds the kind of mere confusion of the senses that might occur in the aftermath of a mythic experience or a vivid dream. Voices can indeed be seen, as the voice in general conveys a strong sense of presentness. As Jacques Derrida claimed,

When I speak, it belongs to the phenomenological essence of this operation that *I hear myself* [je m'entende] *at the same time* that I speak. The signifier, animated by my breath and by my meaning-intention... is in absolute proximity to me. The living act, the life-giving act, the *Lebendigkeit*, which animates the body of the signifier and transforms it into a meaningful expression, the soul of language, seems not separate from itself, from its own self-presence.[3]

While we can imagine a number of situations and constellations where Derrida's assertion fails (one of the most significant for the theatre being the ability to alter one's voice deliberately, to 'make it strange'[4]), the voice accompanies visual presence. This is especially compelling in an age unfamiliar with techniques for recording or transporting a disembodied voice.

But it is also the case in *A Midsummer Night's Dream* that voices are always embodied and thus visible for the audience: we have witnessed Bottom's dream; Thisbe is on-stage when Bottom-as-Pyramus announces he will 'hear my Thisbe's face' (5.1.192); and even though Theseus refuses to 'see the epilogue' (5.1.346), he ends up watching the dance performed by Bottom and Flute. In their last appearance on-stage, the working-class weaver, who is transformed into one of the most memorable and hilarious visual images in Shakespeare's plays, and Flute, the bellows-maker, whose name is the most acoustic of all characters in the play, join forces in the panopticon or panacousticon of *A Midsummer Night's Dream* in a non-verbal, musical act of communication: they dance before they exit the play not to appear again.

While some critics have argued for the preference of the ear over the eye as mode of perception in early modern theatres, given the lack of decoration on 'the empty stage' (Peter Brook), Shakespeare's audiences came not only to hear, but also

to see a play.[5] In particular the architecture of the Globe allowed spectators a full view of actors' faces which offered a complex paratext in support of Shakespeare's word scenery. The gripping effect of this non-verbal communication was described by a spectator who watched a performance of *Othello* in September 1610. As he recalls, 'that famous Desdemona killed before us by her husband, although she always acted her whole part supremely well, yet when she was killed, she was even more moving, for when she fell back upon the bed she implored the pity of the spectators by her very face'.[6] The face is the key medium of communication both in the theatre and in everyday life. In Shakespeare's time, its legibility was proverbial: due to the immediacy with which emotions are translated onto the facial surface, it was deemed to be the index of the mind,[7] superior to verbal communication and more eloquent because it continues to 'speak' long after words have faded.

It is debatable, however, whether actors could produce various facial expressions with equal facility. A frown, a smile, an angry look – these are indeed 'actions that a man might play' (*Hamlet*, 1.2.84). When it comes to blushing, weeping, or growing pale on cue, it becomes more complicated. Tears could be produced with comparative ease, as suggested in *The Taming of the Shrew* when the boy-actor is advised to have an onion up his sleeve, whose acid will do the trick (Induction 1.122–6). Blushing, in contrast, is counted among the involuntary, somatic actions that can neither be produced nor repressed at will. The same applies to the loss of cheek colour, which results from shock,

---

3 Jacques Derrida, *Speech and Phenomena* (Evanston, 1973), pp. 78–9.
4 See Bruce Smith, *The Acoustic World of Early Modern England: Attending to the O-Factor* (Chicago, 1999), pp. 11–12.
5 Andrew Gurr, 'Hearers and Beholders in Shakespeare's Drama', *Essays in Theatre*, 3 (1984), 30–45.
6 Gāmini Sālgado, *Eyewitnesses of Shakespeare: First Hand Accounts of Performances 1590–1890* (London, 1975), p. 30.
7 See Martin Porter, *Windows of the Soul: The Art of Physiognomy in European Culture 1470–1780* (Oxford, New York, 2005), pp. 198 and 218; R. W. Dent, *Shakespeare's Proverbial Language* (Berkeley, 1981), p. 105.

surprise or fear, and is regarded as inimitable. Skin colour, such as the alabaster face or constant red cheeks, could be rendered by resorting to face-painting, a highly criticized, yet extremely popular practice at the time. It had Queen Elizabeth I as its most prominent exemplar: she is said to have taken great pains to keep her face *semper eadem* as an emblem of eternal youth.[8] In contrast, the sudden change of skin colour, such as in 'this silent war of lilies and of roses' (*Lucrece, 71*), exceeded both artificial representation and wilful enactment.

In keeping with Shakespeare's theatre of language, these essentially non-verbal expressions are verbalized on stage. Hence, Lysander purports to see a change in Hermia's face after Theseus's decree that forbids them to marry: 'Why is your cheek so pale? / How chance the roses there do fade so fast?' (1.1.128–9). Disregarding these physical limitations, actors were well-trained and must have been able successfully to 'frame [their] face[s] to [almost] all occasions' (*3 Henry VI*, 3.2.185). When this was not the case, all was not lost, as the audience was also trained to 'piece out [actors'] imperfections with [their] thoughts', as suggested in the prologue to *Henry V* (Prol. 23). Further, there might have been instances in which the physical and verbal texts were deliberately mismatched. Especially in the comedies, the effect of an intentionally repressed representation of a facial expression that could be conjured effortlessly but fails to show on the actor's face – or, conversely, the effect of any additional expressions that lie 'out of [his] text' (*Twelfth Night*, 1.5.222) – would have not only triggered laughter, but also heightened the metatheatrical awareness of the audience, who, in all of Shakespeare's plays, are constantly reminded that they are witnessing a performance.

Shakespeare's Globe provided the perfect arena for actors to do things with faces: just as the audience could scrutinize actors' features, actors could infer reactions to their performance from the faces of spectators. Hence Shakespeare's theatre enabled immediate feedback through facial expressions while providing the breeding ground for what theatre critics attacked as emotional contagion and infection through the eyes. The latter is anticipated by Bottom when he imagines his histrionic powers in the role of Pyramus: 'That will ask some tears in the true performing of it. If I do it, let the audience look to their eyes. I will move stones' (*Dream*, 1.2.21–3).

As a playwright who was not only concerned with the art of character portrayal, but who was an actor himself, Shakespeare must have taken a natural interest in psychophysiological and physiognomic theories of the time. While none of his characters is explicitly linked to the pseudo-science as, for instance, the Cardinal in John Webster's *The Duchess of Malfi* (1612–13) of whom Bosola wonders, '[d]oth he study physiognomy?' (1.2.152), Shakespeare obliquely acknowledges physiognomic theories in *The Rape of Lucrece* when Lucrece admires the portraits of Ajax and Ulysses: 'O what art / Of physiognomy might one behold! / The face of either ciphered either's heart' (1394–6). In portraiture, poetry and prose, and especially in the theatre, physiognomy is an indispensable tool for character construction. But theatre uniquely combines distinct modes of communication (verbal, visual and acoustic) and provides an arena in which playwrights and actors can experiment with the promise and the limits of facial rhetoric.

As I have argued elsewhere,[9] Shakespeare's drama is suffused with physiognomic knowledge. Fleeting emotions, such as blushing, trembling, smiling or blanching are frequently described together with the processes of transformation from the inside to the outside, and the challenges of rendering them. Shakespeare's descriptions of facial expressions reached such a level of perfection that

---

8 For face-painting, see Annette Drew-Bear, *Painted Faces on the Renaissance Stage: The Moral Significance of Face-Painting Conventions* (Lewisburg, 1994); for the face of Elizabeth I see Anna Riehl, *The Face of Power: Early Modern Representations of Elizabeth I* (Chicago, 2007).

9 Sibylle Baumbach, *Shakespeare and the Art of Physiognomy* (Tirril and Leicester, 2008) and *'Let me behold thy face': Physiognomik und Gesichtslektüren in Shakespeares Tragödien* (Heidelberg, 2007). For a discussion of facial evidence in *Othello*, see also Michael Neill, 'The Look of Othello', *Shakespeare Survey 62* (Cambridge, 2009), 104–22.

Charles Darwin quoted from his plays to support his own discoveries. Thus in his ground-breaking study *The Expression of Emotions in Man and Animals* (1872), he praised the dramatist as 'an excellent judge' with 'wonderful knowledge of the human mind'.[10] While references to facial expressions in Shakespeare primarily served as implied stage directions (thus faces could indeed be 'heard'), they also contributed to the physiognomic discourse of the time. They reflected the accepted physiognomic knowledge in early modern culture while serving to support, challenge or subvert popular physiognomic beliefs.

Physiognomic inference rests on the assumption that the exterior of the human body signifies specific traits, which by nature or habit leave their traces on the corporeal surface. While the face was the key object of physiognomic scrutiny, due to the complexity and versatility of its expressions, physiognomists examined the whole body, including static and dynamic (or, as they were referred to in the late eighteenth century, 'pathognomic') features. As defined in the pseudo-Aristotelian *Physiognomonica* (fourth century BC), the first physiognomic treatise, physiognomy explores 'movements, gestures of the body, colour, characteristic facial expression, the growth of the hair, the smoothness of skin, the voice, conditions of the flesh, the parts of the body, and the build of the body as a whole'.[11]

The sixteenth century experienced a renaissance of physiognomic thought and theory, stimulated by the increased interest in portraiture and strategies of self-fashioning, as encouraged in conduct books and manuals of rhetoric.[12] Numerous treatises were published that provided practical tools for the deciphering of man, including Thomas Hill's *The Contemplation of Mankind* (1571) and Giambattista della Porta's *De humana physiognomonia* (1586). However, possession of 'expert' knowledge about the signification of facial and bodily expression was a double-edged sword, as physiognomy aided not only the decoding of the face and body, but also their encoding. Thomas Wright, for instance, draws attention to the great potential of facial rhetoric, which, as he laments, has not yet been adequately recognized by his countrymen, who show a 'naturall inclination to Vertue and honestie'. In his *The Passions of the Minde* (1603), therefore, he aims at teaching them 'a certaine politique craftinesse', which allows them to control and alter their countenances 'by wit and will'.[13]

This is also the craft for facial composition in Shakespeare's plays. His most astute characters show a firm command of the 'art / Of physiognomy' (*Lucrece*, 1394–5), exploiting it to manipulate, as Richard Gloucester does, when he prides himself on his talent to 'smile, and murder whiles I smile' (*3 Henry VI*, 3.2.182).[14] Even if the art of physiognomy is initially dismissed as unreliable and deceptive, it emerges as a highly valuable tool for deciphering characters. Contrary to Duncan's claim – 'There's no art / To find the mind's construction in the face' (*Macbeth*, 1.4.11–12) – which is almost immediately countered by the cunning facial rhetoric of the Macbeths, there *is* an 'art / Of physiognomy'. The stress, however, is on the word 'art', the 'artifice' or 'artistry', which is indispensable for successful face-reading. As Levinus Lemnius confirms, 'in such as are marked with some visible note, Art finds out the truth'.[15]

In Shakespeare's plays, it is not the mere description of physiognomic features that is significant, but the manner in which these features are delivered,

---

[10] See Charles Darwin, *The Expression of Emotions in Man and Animals*, ed. Francis Darwin (London, 1989), p. 285.

[11] Ps.-Aristotle, *Physiognomonica*, 806a25 (Aristotle, *Minor Works*, trans. W. S. Hett (London and Cambridge, MA, 1936)).

[12] For a survey of the physiognomic discourse towards the end of the sixteenth century see Sibylle Baumbach, 'Physiognomy', in *A New Companion to English Renaissance Literature and Culture*, ed. Michael Hattaway, vol. 1 (Oxford, 2010), 582–97.

[13] Thomas Wright, *The Passions of the Minde in Generall* (London, 1620), p. 149.

[14] Cf. Michael Torrey, '"The plain devil and dissembling looks": Ambivalent Physiognomy and Shakespeare's *Richard III*', *English Literary Renaissance*, 30 (2000), 123–53. For further examples, see Baumbach, *Art of Physiognomy*, esp. pp. 125–78.

[15] Levinus Lemnius, *The secret miracles of nature in four books* (London, 1658), p. 130.

disclosed, and discussed on-stage. Face-readings are enacted in and as performance. Their validity ultimately depends on the physiognomic competence of the reader as well as on the legibility of the face that is being read. Consequently, relational contexts – who reads whom, who translates faces into words, and whose face is subjected to physiognomic scrutiny – shed new light on characterization strategies, power relations, and the (de)construction of gender in the plays. They illuminate concepts of performance, self-fashioning and the conditions of the theatre, which are reflected in Shakespeare's meta-discourse on physiognomy.

2. WHAT'S IN A FACE?

In a play where visions are blurred, giving way to imaginary forces – 'How easy is a bush supposed a bear!' (5.1.22) – and fairies dominate the stage, there seems little room for any facial or bodily descriptions. As Henry Morley argued, '[e]very reader of Shakespeare is disposed to regard the *Midsummer Night's Dream* as the most essentially unactable of all his plays . . . its characters are creatures of the poet's fancy that no flesh and blood can properly present'.[16] This notion of unrepresentability accords with William Hazlitt's severe criticism of the nineteenth-century illusionist stage and his indignation over the 'full-grown, well-fed, substantial, real fairies'[17] he encountered at the Theatre Royal, in a production by Frederic Reynolds in 1816. They are, after all, meant to be nothing but 'shadows' (Epilogue 1) that evaporate as soon as the final words of Robin's epilogue have faded. It is due to their gossamer, 'invisible' (2.1.186) being that we receive little information on their outer appearance, but have to content ourselves with their names – Peaseblossom, Cobweb, Mote, Mustardseed, which suggest non-human, abstract forms – and their voices, which we 'see' and follow (*Robin*. 'Follow my voice' (3.2.413)). Instead, we become more finely attuned to the properties of other characters, such as the artisans and the lovers, who exhibit corporeal presence on-stage. The lovers seem especially palpable:

they chase and embrace each other, and they fight, 'facing' each other.

When Hermia and Helena meet in the woods, they engage in a physiognomic combat. In a play where almost everyone addresses everyone else as 'fair',[18] fairness seems to have come to an end. Hermia attacks Helena's weak spot:

Hermia. Fie, fie, you counterfeit, you puppet, you!
Helena. Puppet? Why, so! Ay, that way goes the
    game . . .
  And are you grown so high in his esteem
  Because I am so dwarfish and so low?
  How low am I, thou painted maypole? (3.2.289–97)

The two women are rivals in love as well as in physiognomy. Difference in size is a feature that we find repeatedly in Shakespeare's female characters: in Rosalind and Celia, one being 'more than common tall' (*As You Like It*, 1.3.114), the other rather 'low' (4.3.88); in Hero, whom Benedick describes as 'too low for a high praise, too brown for a fair praise, and too little for a great praise' (*Much Ado*, 1.1.163–5), and in Beatrice, a role which, like Helena's, calls for an actor who is fair and tall.[19] Rather than type-casting, Shakespeare tailored these roles to two boys of his company, who embodied these opposites perfectly. One is said to have been tall and cheeky, and the other rather diminutive and reserved.[20]

While Shakespeare's plays are mainly concerned with the discursivation (in the Foucauldian sense of the term) of physiognomy, which involves engaging the audience in physiognomic (counter-) readings, we find some instances of physiognomic

---

[16] Henry Morley, *The Journal of a London Playgoer from 1851 to 1866* (London, 1866), p. 66.

[17] William Hazlitt, *A View of the English Stage* (London, 1818), p. 81.

[18] Thus 'fair Hippolyta' (1.1.1), 'fair Hermia' (1.1.117), fair Helena' (3.2.247), '[f]air lovers' (4.1.176), 'fair ladies' (3.1.36), 'fair Pyramus' (5.1.188).

[19] See John C. Meagher, *Pursuing Shakespeare's Dramaturgy: Some Contexts, Resources, and Strategies in His Playmaking* (London, 2003), p. 183.

[20] See Helmut Castrop, 'Das elisabethanische Theater', in *Shakespeare Handbuch: Die Zeit – Der Mensch – Das Werk – Die Nachwelt*, ed. Ina Schabert (Stuttgart, 2000), p. 111.

stereotyping, as, for instance, in Rosalind's portrayal of a man in love (*As You Like It*, 3.2.361–4). Distinct, static physiognomic features, are referred to for three main purposes: (1) to create antagonisms, such as between Helena and Hermia; (2) to prepare an anagnorisis, which is often accompanied by a face-reading[21] or its comic inversion, as in *Twelfth Night* where brother and sister identify each other by their shared knowledge of their father's mole (5.1.240–1); and (3) to establish genealogical relations that are revealed by the father's signature or 'imprint' on a face. Thus, in *All's Well That Ends Well*, the King links Bertram to his father, by both face and character: 'thou bear'st thy father's face . . . / Thy father's moral parts / Mayst thou inherit, too' (1.2.19–22).

Most *personae*, however, seem to play against the 'character' that has been designed for them. Within the dynamics of code-making and code-breaking, which is fuelled by cross-dressing, masking and self-fashioning, physiognomic clues emerge as a valuable tool for tracing processes of (self-)authorization. While the power of inscription and thus of creating 'characters' (the 'imprinted') has been traditionally attributed to man, who leaves his imprint on the (female) body, whereas women serve as interfaces in the process of creation, as passive receptors that follow and reproduce male scripts, Shakespeare's women run against their 'texts', gaining authority over their own bodies and faces. This process of authorization is at the heart of the conflict that sets off the action in *Dream*. Theseus reminds Hermia that it is not within her power to refuse her father's will:

> To you your father should be as a god,
> One that composed your beauties, yea, and one
> To whom you are but as a form in wax,
> By him imprinted, and within his power
> To leave the figure or disfigure it.   (1.1.47–51)

Hermia disobeys. Rebelling against paternal authority, she refuses to marry Demetrius and elopes with her beloved Lysander. After this upheaval against the determination of character, characters are set in motion: they are disguised, enacted, adopted and adapted, changed and exchanged, and also, as we will see in the case of Bottom, eventually overcome.

The 'translation' of Bottom into an ass-headed man, which symbolizes the 'continuous flow of human-animal, animal-human "translations"'[22] in Shakespeare's plays and marks a pivotal point in *Dream*, is the comic epitome of physiognomy. It stands in the tradition of the zoomorphic method of character-reading, which was first presented in detail in the pseudo-Aristotelian *Physiognomonica* and expanded by Hill, della Porta, and later also Charles Le Brun. Zoomorphism seeks to determine the human character by exploring analogies between the physical appearances of man and animal. The inference is straightforward: as the lion is associated with power, liberality and magnanimity, leonine features, such as a deep voice and full hair indicate a strong, just mind. The ass, on the other hand, was deemed idle, dull and arrogant. Consequently, a long face, extremely big ears, thick lips, protruding eyes and an unpleasant, deformed voice, point to a dull and languid mind,[23] as suggested in della Porta's woodcut that shows an ass's head and its human counterpart side by side (see Illustration 1).

In Shakespeare's *Dream*, we find these parallel physiognomies incorporated in Bottom, who seems smooth-faced – in contrast to Flute who claims to have 'a beard coming' (1.2.43–4) and has to play in a mask, Bottom has to beard himself for his role[24] – but finds himself to be 'marvellous hairy about the face' (4.1.24–5) after his translation. Moreover, Bottom claims that he can aggravate his 'monstrous' (1.2.48) voice into a frightening roar, and a great voice was seen 'as a sign of stupidity . . . irascibility, [and] often equated with an ass'.[25] Finally, Bottom's tendency to overestimate his acting capabilities combined with his

---

[21] See *Measure*, 5.1.201.
[22] Andreas Höfele, *Stage, Stake & Scaffold: Humans & Animals in Shakespeare's Theatre* (Oxford, 2011), p. 35.
[23] See *Scriptores Physiognomici Graeci et Latini*, ed. Richard Foerster (Stuttgart and Leipzig, 1994), pp. 137–8.
[24] Will Fisher, 'The Renaissance Beard: Masculinity in Early Modern England', *Renaissance Quarterly*, 54 (2001), 183–4.
[25] Porter, *Windows*, p. 178.

1. Giambattista della Porta, *De humana physiognomonia libri IIII* (1586).

ill-command of language, which is suggested by the numerous malapropisms, carefully prepare his transmutation into an emblem of folly, which in early modern iconology featured an ass.[26]

Regarding Bottom's characterization in the play, his 'translation' is almost the logical consequence. In fact, considering Michael Porter's remarks about 'the innate, iconic nature of the language of physiognomy',[27] it is quite likely that the audience has not only heard but also, to a certain extent, seen Bottom's ass-face, even before the transformation takes place. In his example, Porter refers to the widespread physiognomic association of an aquiline nose with magnanimity: 'given the frequency with which the aquiline nose was described as a sign of magnanimity in the early modern period', he writes, 'magnanimity itself would often have been automatically visually represented before the early modern mind's eye in the form of an image of an aquiline nose'.[28] The same might be claimed for the association of folly and stupidity with features of an ass – an image as latently present in early modern culture as the connection between magnanimity and the aquiline nose.

Having heard and seen his ass's face, the audience is urged by Bottom – awakening from his 'dream' – to qualify their perception: 'The eye of man hath not heard, the ear of man hath not seen . . . what my dream was . . . It shall be called "Bottom's Dream", because it hath no bottom' (4.1.208–13). We are reminded of another lover here, of Romeo who, when Juliet disappears from the balcony, ponders the nature of his vision: 'I am afeard, / Being in night, all this is but a dream, / Too flattering-sweet to be substantial' (*Romeo*, 2.1.181–3). Romeo's dream comes true. And Bottom's? Does it have no bottom because it was too 'flattering-sweet'? The (prognostic?) meaning of the dream cannot be determined: 'Man is but an ass if he go about t'expound this dream' (4.1.204). Nonetheless, Bottom determines to have it captured in writing. The realization and re-mediatization of his dream, however, does not end here: 'I will get Peter Quince to write a ballad of this dream' (4.1.211–12) – a ballad that Bottom intends to give a voice to immediately after its composition: 'I will sing it in the latter end

---

[26] See Joseph Rosenblum, 'Why an Ass? Cesare Ripa's *Iconologia* as a Source for Bottom's Translation', *Shakespeare Quarterly*, 32 (1981), 357–9. Deborah Baker Wyrick, 'The Ass Motif in *The Comedy of Errors* and *A Midsummer Night's Dream*', *Shakespeare Quarterly*, 33 (1982), 432–48.

[27] Porter, *Windows*, p. 228.

[28] Porter, *Windows*, pp. 228–9.

of a play' (4.1.213–14). Hence, while the weaver refuses to tell his friends about his experience ('Not a word of me' (4.2.30)), 'Bottom's Dream' has a 'Bottom', a voice that can be seen on-stage.

While it is suggested that Bottom's character remains unvarying throughout his (re-)translation – 'when thou wak'st with thine own fool's eyes peep' (4.1.83) – the asinity of this 'foolelosopher'[29] needs to be qualified. As Peter Holland remarks, Bottom cannot be reduced to a 'foolish, vain, and arrogant' character: 'he is also gentle, lovable, and admirable. The comedy lies in the disjunction between himself and the circumstances in which he finds himself, his existence beyond the bounds of his own competence.'[30] As ambitious actor, Bottom, the weaver, is out of his text: he fools about in a métier that is not his – just like the audience who have put down their tools and suspended their work to participate in the theatrical event.

The danger of reducing a character to a set of features which seem dominant in a particular situation is a problem inherent in the art of physiognomy. Physiognomic treatises, therefore, stress the necessity to consider not only individual features, but also the way which they interact with each other. Even then, the possibility of misreading persists, as indicated by Socrates, a prominent example of physiognomic misreading. As the story goes, the Syrian physiognomist Zopyrus, unaware of Socrates's identity, diagnosed him as dull and imbecile from his bulbous nose, protuberant eyes, bulky lips and overall Silenic appearance. Socrates defended this reading, but claimed to have overcome his natural disposition by reason.[31] Henceforth he was deemed an exception to the rule or, as Michel de Montaigne writes in his essay 'On Physiognomy': 'nature did him wrong'.[32] Bottom is not a second Socrates but the idea behind his transformation is the same: physiognomy is a tool that needs to be cautiously applied and scrutinized. It is an art of translation, in the process of which one or two misprints might creep in.

As David Marshall argued, the entire play is devoted to the question of representation: 'The question of the play is whether presenting and representing must mean misrepresenting; whether

figure must be synonymous with *disfigure*.'[33] The linchpin here is, of course, Bottom. Referred to as 'paramour' and 'paragon' 'for a sweet voice' (4.2.12–13), which amounts to 'a neat conflation of sexiness and exemplariness';[34] self-fashioned as multi-faced and -voiced actor; cast as 'sweet-faced' Pyramus, 'a most lovely, gentlemanlike man' (1.2.80–1) (information that causes Bottom to contemplate his choice of beard, as the beard had an important semiotic function, both as 'natural Ensigne of Manhood'[35] and 'ensigne of majesty'[36]); used as a medium for Oberon's playful revenge on Titania, and translated into the ass-headed lover of the fairy queen, Bottom emerges as both the agent and the subject of figuration and disfiguration. His physiognomic disfigurement does not end with the release from the ass's head. It continues in the play-within-the-play, which is deeply engaged in the process of figuration and disfiguration. The tragic story of 'Pyramus and Thisbe', which is dramatized in *Romeo and Juliet* (a play which in turn anticipates the world of *A Midsummer Night's Dream* in Mercutio's image of Queen Mab) and translated into the genre of comedy in *Dream*, awaits further transformation in the amateur performance: it stages the translation of Bottom into the role of Pyramus, and also includes another disfiguration of the 'sweet-faced' lover, sparked by a

---

[29] See Desiderius Erasmus, *The Praise of Folly*, trans. Sir Thomas Chaloner (London, 1965), p. 10.

[30] Peter Holland, ed., *A Midsummer Night's Dream* (Oxford, 2008), p. 81.

[31] Cf. Cicero, *De Fato* 10; Plato, *Symposium* 215b and *Apology* 21a.

[32] *Montaigne's Essays*, trans. John Florio, vol. 3 (London and New York, 1910), p. 314. See also Thomas Hill, *The Contemplation of Mankinde* (London, 1571), fo. x–xi; Richard Saunders, *Physiognomie and Chiromancie, Metoposcopie* (London, 1653), p. 144.

[33] David Marshall, 'Exchanging Visions: Reading *A Midsummer Night's Dream*', *ELH*, 49 (1982), 546.

[34] Ronda Arab, *Manly Mechanicals on Shakespeare's Stage* (Selinsgrove, 2011), p. 112.

[35] John Bulwer, *Anthropometamorphosis* (London, 1654), p. 193.

[36] Helkiah Crooke, *A Description of the Body of Man: The second Edition Corrected and Enlarged* (London, 1631), p. 70. See also Fisher, 'Renaissance Beard', p. 172.

face-reading: 'Asleep, my love? / What, dead, my dove? / . . . These lily lips, / This cherry nose, / These yellow cowslip cheeks / Are gone, are gone' (5.1.319–28). This comic inversion of the lethal misreading that leads to the tragic ending of *Romeo and Juliet*, when Romeo fatally misinterprets signs of life on Juliet's face (5.3.94–102), offers a description that fits a heroine, not a hero. Flute-as-Thisbe picks the wrong colours only to misapply them to the wrong features: 'Lily', often as 'lily-pale', is usually connected to skin colour, 'cherry' to lips, 'yellow' to hair, and the cowslip is completely out of place. Figuring or, rather, disfiguring the hero of the play in this *contre-blason*, tragedy transforms into comedy and the desire for physiognomic *evidentia* is again parodied. Considering the broader picture in *A Midsummer Night's Dream*, however, physiognomy is not lost in translation. Rather the opposite is the case as both the meta-theatrical dimension and Bottom's metamorphosis direct our attention to faces which we might have missed.

It is especially the notion of in-betweenness, created by an action which moves between different levels of stage reality and illusion, between Athens, governed by the tight reign of rational Theseus, the theatrical world of amateur performance and the 'green world' where imagination rules, that provides the perfect setting for comparing and contrasting opposing perspectives on this pseudo-science. Bottom's translatability carries to extremes what is a governing principle of nature. In this play particularly, physiognomy is intertwined with the notion of *magia naturalis*, which is conveyed through images of an anthropomorphic nature, whose character is rendered in physiognomic terms ('O grim-looked night' (5.1.168)). Titania's portrayal of nature is a case in point:

> the green corn
> Hath rotted ere his youth attained a beard . . .
> Therefore the moon, the governess of floods,
> Pale in her anger washes all the air . . .
> And thorough this distemperature we see
> The seasons alter: hoary-headed frosts
> Fall in the fresh lap of the crimson rose,
> And on old Hiems' thin and icy crown

> An odorous chaplet of sweet summer buds
> Is, as in mock'ry, set. (2.1.94–111)

Titania's quarrel with Oberon over the 'little changeling boy' (2.1.120) has left visible marks: 'These are the forgeries of jealousy' (2.1.81). Nature is about to lose its countenance as well as its temper. The corn has withered before maturity, the scattered frosty hairs of old Winter are mocked by the harbingers of spring, and the moon is outraged by what she sees on earth.

Advocates of physiognomic inference frequently stressed its connection to natural magic. Beyond Aristotle, one of the most influential proponents of this association was Giambattista della Porta. Following his *Magia naturalis sive de miraculis rerum naturalium* (1558), he wrote the highly successful *De humana physiognomonia* (1586), before turning to the physiognomy of plants in *Phytognomonica* (1588). Della Porta's observations are based on the doctrine of signatures and thus on the assumption that all elements of nature offer external signs that hold clues about their properties. Presenting physiognomy as the art to disclose these natural signatures and unlock the secret of Nature, he aims at distinguishing this art from any kind of charlatanism. Following Ps.-Aristotle, he embeds it within a scientific context to rehabilitate the pseudo-science, defy its bad press and pre-empt censorship.[37]

Moving between the rational world of Athens, the world of the theatre and the magical world of the fairies, physiognomy in *A Midsummer Night's Dream* can be seen as reflecting opposing views of this practice, which was degraded as mantic, divinatory art by some, and even prohibited at times,[38] while praised as 'lawdable science' by others.[39]

---

37 See William Eamon, *Science and the Secrets of Nature: Books of Secrets in Medieval and Early Modern Culture* (Princeton, 1994), pp. 210–14.

38 James I and IV, *The first Daemonologie*, ed. George B. Harrison (Edinburgh, 1966), pp. 21–2. In 1597, Elizabeth I decreed that whoever claimed 'to have knowledge in Phisiognomye Palmestry or other like crafty Scyence' shall be punished in public (39 Eliz. I c. 3 [1597]).

39 Hill, *Contemplation*, fo. 2.

Thus is born the notion of *magia naturalis*, which suffuses the play and serves to bridge and reconcile these divergent perspectives.

In particular the moon, 'th'inconstant moon' (*Romeo*, 2.1.151), remains a prominent image throughout the play, which takes on many names and many forms: it is not only embodied in the performance of the mechanicals (and thus cannot only be seen but also heard) but emerges as an instrumental player. It decelerates the 'nuptial hour' (*Dream*, 1.1.1) of Theseus and Hippolyta by allowing sufficient time for the four young lovers' journey into the green world ('Four happy days bring in / Another moon – but O, methinks, how slow / This old moon wanes! She lingers my desires' (1.1.2–4)); serves as guide to Hermia and Lysander who plan to elope 'when Phoebe doth behold / Her silver visage in the wat'ry glass' (1.1.209–10); and comments on the strange doings on earth: 'The moon, methinks, looks with a wat'ry eye, / And when she weeps, weeps every little flower, / Lamenting some enforcèd chastity' (3.1.190–2). It is debatable whether the moon's tears, which Titania refers to in this scene, mourn chastity violated by force, as a lunar Diana should, or whether the moon is lamenting a compelled preservation of chastity, as would become a 'more amorous Luna or Selene',[40] or Phoebe, as she is referred to in the play. While in either case, tears clearly signify distress, the uncertainty as to whether they imply a chaste or amorous moon complements the ambivalence inherent in many physiognomic features, including tears, which – depending on their context – can convey quite different meanings. In performance, these gaps in the visual or verbal text are filled by non-verbal actions on-stage, which make one reading more plausible than another. Titania's instruction to her fairies certainly allows for a reading of this scene in 'the most erotic of Shakespeare's plays',[41] as preparing the overcoming of 'enforcèd chastity': 'Tie up my love's tongue; bring him silently' (3.1.193).

Even if tongue-tied, the ass-headed Bottom will continue to 'speak'. Having heard, or rather read, a lot about faces, let us now revisit Bottom's remark, which was quoted at the beginning, and start 'seeing' voices.

3. WHAT'S IN A VOICE?

In physiognomic manuals, voice is ranked among the key components of analysis.[42] It not only delivers the body of language but is deemed as the most perceptible and most obvious trace of the body in language. Its particular texture, rhythms, tone, volume, tunes and dynamics carry information about the gender, age and character of its bearer. Hence, a shrill, high-pitched voice indicates an 'yreful'[43] person who is 'unstable, and vaine'.[44] A voice 'small and lowe', on the other hand, marks 'a creature to be fearefull and envious'.[45] A hasty one indicates wickedness; loud voices reveal 'talkative, bolde, and contencious'[46] characters; '[t]he creature with a verie bigge voice, is noted to be a servant, unto his owne belly';[47] and those blessed with a 'slowe, and bigge sounde of the voyce', are considered 'to be quiet, tractable, gentle, merie [and] verye iust'.[48]

Shakespeare was aware of this signifying quality, as suggested in Jacques's portrayal of the seven ages of man, in which the voice plays a prominent part: from the infant's '[m]ewling', the 'whining school-boy', 'the lover, [s]ighing like furnace' to the soldier that is '[f]ull of strange oaths, and bearded like the pard', 'justice, / In fair round belly . . . / With eyes severe and beard of formal cut', and the 'big, manly voice, / Turning again toward childish treble, pipes / And whistles in his sound'. Both the body of

---

[40] James L. Calderwood, '*A Midsummer Night's Dream*: Anamorphism and Theseus' Dream', *Shakespeare Quarterly*, 42 (1991), 421.

[41] Jan Kott, *Shakespeare Our Contemporary*, trans. Boleslaw Taborski (Garden City, 1964), p. 212.

[42] Hill, *Contemplation*, fo. 131–7.

[43] Hill, *Contemplation*, fo. 135.

[44] Hill, *Contemplation*, fo. 135.

[45] Hill, *Contemplation*, fo. 134.

[46] Hill, *Contemplation*, fo. 135.

[47] Hill, *Contemplation*, fo. 136.

[48] Hill, *Contemplation*, fo. 134.

the voice and the voice's body change substantially until the wheel comes full circle in 'second childishness and mere oblivion, / [s]ans teeth, sans eyes, sans taste, sans everything' (*As You Like It*, 2.7.144–66).

On the theatrical stage as in the *theatrum mundi*, one of the most immediate functions of the voice is identification. 'Who's there?' (*Hamlet* 1.1.1): the opening question of *Hamlet* requires no name, only a voice. 'Long live the King!' – 'Barnado?' (1.1.3). It is especially in scenes set at night that Shakespeare relies on the voice's kinetic qualities, which explains the prominence of the voice in *A Midsummer Night's Dream*, where '[d]ark night, that from the eye his function takes, / The ear more quick of apprehension makes' (3.2.178–9). The setting of many scenes at night and the magical events in the Athenian woods are impediments to vision, and the counter-illusionistic play within the play sets the stage for a voice to be 'seen'.

Bottom-*cum*-Pyramus is separated from his beloved by a wall when he purports to 'see a voice' (5.1.191). Indeed, he must have heard Flute-as-Thisbe lamenting her separation from her lover to the same wall, 'My cherry lips have often kissed thy stones, / Thy stones with lime and hair knit up in thee' (5.1.189–90). The references to facial features not only prepare for Pyramus's impression of 'seeing' a face, but also point to the visual paratext which accompanies these words. With Snout representing the Wall, not only the audience but also Pyramus must have had a good view of Thisbe. Imagine the scene in performance: it would have had a comic effect if Bottom-as-Pyramus asserted to have 'heard' instead of 'seen' Thisbe's voice, as he is almost facing Flute-as-Thisbe, because the imperfectly disguised Snout, who embodies the Wall, could hardly screen him from view. The fact that he goes on claiming to 'hear a face' can also be easily explained. During the casting, Flute complained about being assigned the role of Thisbe because he lacks the smooth skin required to play a female role: 'Nay, faith, let not me play a woman. I have a beard coming' (1.2.43–4). Quince promptly offers a solution: 'You shall play it in a mask, and

you may speak as small as you will' (1.2.45–6). These visors, however, are farcical as their potential for concealment is eroded by the players who are anxious to spotlight the fictitiousness of their masks. For their subversion, Bottom provides the text:

Nay, you must name his name, and half his face must be seen through the lion's neck, and he himself must speak through, saying thus or to the same defect: 'ladies', or 'fair ladies... If you think I come hither as a lion, it were pity of my life. No, I am no such thing. I am a man, as other men are.' (3.1.33–40)

We do not know what Flute's mask looked like; it might only have been a half-mask. In this case, it would not solve the problem. If it was a full mask, however, Thisbe's 'face' would have lacked mobility and therefore required verbal communication. Simultaneously, the repeated confusion of hearing and seeing underscores the counter-illusionistic mode of the artisans' performance while serving as an instruction to the audience to sharpen their eyes and attune their ears not only to what can be 'heard' or 'seen' on Shakespeare's stage, but also to what happens in translation from one to the other.

On an (almost) empty theatrical stage, the actor's voice together with his body is the key medium of communication. It translates the script penned by the playwright and sets its 'characters', in the literal sense of the word, in motion, by materializing or dematerializing them through performance. Flute's 'small' (1.2.46), probably high-pitched voice seems perfect for his role. What Shakespeare's Cleopatra is dreading – to be impersonated by '[s]ome squeaking Cleopatra' (*Antony*, 5.2.216) – Thisbe's character has to endure. Again, the question of whether Flute does a good job in presenting his lines in an adequately small voice or, as in Michael Hoffman's movie production of 1999, fails and becomes a laughing-stock, is another issue and depends on directors' choices. Even though Flute's aptness for a female role suggests a treble voice, his name implies a variety of tones and tunes, provided that its bearer knows the technique and is able to play.[49] Quite unlike Bottom's. And yet, Bottom's enthusiasm about acting is bottomless. Lover or tyrant, human or animal, man or woman – he wants to play them all and justifies the broad spectrum of adequate roles by referring to the great variability of his voice: 'let me play Thisbe too. I'll speak in a monstrous little voice: "Thisne, Thisne!"' (1.2.47–8); 'Let me play the lion too. I will roar that I will do any man's heart good to hear me' (1.2.66–7). On Quince's objection that his roar might frighten the ladies in the audience, Bottom immediately tries to qualify his 'monstrous' voice, but achieves the opposite when he promises, 'I will aggravate my voice so that I will roar you as gently as any sucking dove. I will roar you an 'twere any nightingale' (1.2.76–8).

Bottom's frequent malapropisms subvert his proclaimed ability to manipulate his voice according to his role. Even though the boastful weaver attests himself 'a reasonable good ear in music' (4.1.28), the image of the roaring nightingale parodies rather than supports the actor's talent to do things with voices. Hence, when Quince describes Bottom as 'a very paramour for a sweet voice' (4.2.11–12), Flute seems wrong in correcting him, '[y]ou must say "paragon". A paramour is, God bless us, a thing of naught' (4.2.13–14). Bottom is neither and both – he is the 'paragon' of the amateur actors and a paramour, i.e. 'a lover, . . . esp. in an affair or romance' (OED, 2a) of a sweet voice, of Titania the 'sweet queen' (4.1.74). The brief conversation between Quince and Flute therefore marks the transition of Bottom from Titania's paramour to the actor's paragon. Hence, Flute's demurring cannot be dismissed outright. After all, it is remarkable that Titania falls in love with Bottom's voice, not his face: 'What angel wakes me from my flow'ry bed? / . . . I pray thee, gentle mortal, sing again. / Mine ear is much enamoured of thy note; / So is mine eye enthrallèd to thy shape' (3.1.122–32). Titania sees a face through a voice; what is more, she demonstrates the concept of man as being situated somewhere between angel and animal, closer to the one or the other according to his conduct, as it was famously expressed in Pico della Mirandola's Oration on the Dignity of Man.[50] Enthralled by

Bottom's 'sweet' song, the eye follows the ear in its attraction to the ass-headed weaver: 'On the first view to say, to swear, I love thee' (3.1.134) – the ear informs the eye, the eye the voice, and reason is abandoned.

With their 'sound combat' in the casting scene, Bottom and Flute open a discourse on the quality of voices, which urges the audience to look behind the action on-stage, unveil the physiognomy of the theatre, and 'see' the mechanisms not only behind practices of cross-dressing but also of cross-voicing.

Flute-as-Thisbe's 'small' voice draws attention to the different physiological properties of the male and female vocal organs and 'the impact of sound on the performance of gender'[51] while alluding to the social (in)significance of the female voice, as it is unfolded in the opening scene. According to humoral theory, women's voices are inferior to men's because their bodies lack sufficient heat to produce full and variable voices. As Lemnius writes in The Touchstone of Complexions,

They . . . that have hoate bodyes are of nature variable, and chau[n]geable, ready, pro[m]pt, lively, lusty, and aplyable: of tongue, trowlyng, perfect, and perswasive, delivering theyr words distinctly, plainly, and pleasauntly, with a voice therto not squeaking and slender, but streinable, comly and audible.[52]

Audible and powerful – such is the voice of authority in Athens, which opens the play: eager to marry the defeated Amazon queen Hippolyta, Theseus sets the date and makes arrangements for their wedding, before passing judgement on Hermia's

---

49 Francis Bacon already describes the flute as a musical instrument with a broad soundscape: 'In flutes, the air, issuing by a hole nearer the breath, yields a more treble sound; by one more distant, a baser' (The Works of Francis Bacon, Lord Chancellor of England, ed. Basil Montagu, 3 vols. (Philadelphia, 1841), vol. 3, p. 540).

50 Giovanni Pico della Mirandola, On the Dignity of Man, trans. Charles Glenn Wallis et al. (Indianapolis, 1965), p. 5.

51 Gina Bloom, '"Thy Voice Squeaks": Listening for Masculinity on the Early Modern Stage', Renaissance Drama, 29 (1998), 39.

52 Levinus Lemnius, The Touchstone of Complexions, trans. Thomas Newton (London, 1581), fo. 46.

refusal to accept her father's arrangements for her marriage, while his future wife – except for a short interlude – remains silent: 'Come, my Hippolyta; what cheer, my love?' (1.1.122). The Duke of Athens has subdued the Amazon queen to his power, his will and also his voice. As Marshall has pointed out, 'her silence is an important key to the conflicts of *A Midsummer Night's Dream* ... As readers who must imagine Hippolyta represented on a stage, we must first hear her silence; we must recognise that she does not speak.'[53]

It is in these moments of silence when the rhetoric of face and body steps in, providing a 'voice' when none can be heard. To see Hippolyta's voice is to acknowledge her presence on-stage, a silent presence that can be far more powerful than one enforced by an audible voice. In the opening scene, Hippolyta and Hermia share the same fate: they both lack voices – one is meek, the other mute. While Hippolyta does not speak, Hermia should not speak. '[W]anting [her] father's voice' (1.1.54), she is not authorized to plead for the right to marry Lysander, as her voice lacks both male value and her father's consent. It is only after both Theseus and Egeus have left that Hermia regains her voice – a voice which Helena desires to imitate.

4. THE ART OF FASCINATION

Your eyes are lodestars, and your tongue's sweet air
More tuneable than lark to shepherd's ear ...
Sickness is catching. O, were favour so! ...
My ear should catch your voice, my eye your eye,
My tongue should catch your tongue's sweet melody.
Were the world mine, Demetrius being bated,
The rest I'd give to be to you translated.

(1.1.183–91)

Full of envy for Hermia's effect on both Demetrius and Lysander, Helena wants to exchange both her voice and eyes for Hermia's in order to charm Demetrius. She can 'see' the captivating quality of Hermia's voice that Egeus overlooks, because he silences his daughter. Instead, Egeus accused Lysander of having 'bewitched' her: 'Thou hast by moonlight at her window sung / With feigning voice verses of feigning love, ... With cunning

hast thou filched my daughter's heart' (1.1.30–6). Like Othello, whom Brabantio attacks similarly, Lysander is suspected to have seduced Hermia by the power of words, more precisely by his 'feigning voice'. As it turns out, however, it is Hermia who is responsible for this infatuation,[54] which is caused both by her voice and her visage. Even before the herb juice enters the play as a device for enchantment, there seems to be something magical in the air:

For ere Demetrius looked on Hermia's eyne
He hailed down oaths that he was only mine,
And when this hail some heat from Hermia felt,
So he dissolved, and showers of oaths did melt.

(1.1.242–5)

What Helena accuses Hermia of is the art of fascination, of exerting an 'irresistibly attractive influence'[55] that has charmed Demetrius. According to early modern psychophysiology, 'heat' in the naturally cold body of women indicates 'an inclination to love others'[56] and thus supports the emanation of spirits and passions onto other bodies.[57] As suggested by Francis Bacon, fascination is caused by two powerful affections, 'which draw the spirits into the eyes ... love, and envy'.[58] Whereas in love the eye sends out beams that enter the body of the beloved through the eyes, kindling in his heart the desire to return this affection to the body which emitted the glance, in envy the fire thus kindled is baneful, caused by the emanation of 'some malign or poisonous spirit'.[59] The power of fascination (from *fascinare* – to bewitch), therefore, was often intertwined with the notion of the

---

[53] Marshall, 'Visions', pp. 549–50.
[54] See Jay L. Halio, '"Nightingales That Roar": The Language of *A Midsummer Night's Dream*', in *William Shakespeare's A Midsummer Night's Dream*, ed. Harold Bloom (New York, 2010), p. 45.
[55] *OED*, 'fascination', 3.
[56] Gail Kern Paster, *Humoring the Body: Emotions and the Shakespearean Stage* (Chicago, 2004), p. 161, also pp. 77–134.
[57] See Paster, *Humoring the Body*, pp. 89–90.
[58] *Works of Francis Bacon*, vol. 2, p. 129.
[59] *Works of Francis Bacon*, vol. 2, p. 129.

evil eye and ranked among 'unlawfull Magicke'.[60] This magic, however, becomes natural when love is involved. As Robert Burton writes 'love is a fascination',[61] and as love is kindled by beauty and 'the face is beauty's tower', it is 'of itself able to captivate'.[62] Explaining 'the manner of fascination', Burton quotes Ficino, 'Mortall men are then especially bewitched, when as by often gazing one on the other, they direct sight to sight, and ioyne eye to eye, and so drinke and sucke in loue betweene them, for the beginning of this disease is the Eye.'[63]

Both love and envy abound in *Dream* and so does ocular contagion, which paves the way for a rich discourse of fascination that can be traced at verbal, visual and acoustic levels. While the voice has a certain captivating quality, 'fascination', as Bacon contends, 'is ever by the eye. But yet if there be any such infection from spirit to spirit, there is no doubt but that it worketh by presence, not by the eye alone: yet most forcibly by the eye.'[64]

While Helena insists that '[l]ove looks not with the eyes, but with the mind, / And therefore is winged Cupid painted blind' (1.1.234–5), there is not more to love than meets the eye, especially in Shakespeare. Phoebe's question, '[w]ho ever loved that loved not at first sight?' (*As You Like It*, 3.5.83) gets to the heart of '[y]oung men's love', which, as Friar Laurence laments, 'lies / Not truly in their hearts, but in their eyes' (*Romeo*, 2.2.67–8). The eyes serve as windows through which love and fascination enter the mind. Hence, Lysander purports to see in Helena's eyes '[l]ove's stories written in love's richest book' (*Dream*, 2.2.128) and Prospero observes with content that Miranda and Ferdinand 'have changed eyes' (*Tempest*, 1.2.445) at first sight.

In fact, in the classical tradition, Cupid was never painted blind.[65] Further, Helena herself, whose name brings to mind one of the most beautiful and fatally seductive women in cultural history, 'the face that launched a thousand ships',[66] does not believe in what she says. Instead she turns to Hermia, urging her to teach her this 'art': 'O, teach me how you look, and with what art / You sway the motion of Demetrius' heart' (1.1.192–3). Helena's demand will eventually be met, but not by

Hermia's instructions, nor by means of a bodily transformation, but by a change in Demetrius's eye. For this change to come to pass, the spell must be broken by removing the source of his infatuation (as Hermia promises, '[h]e no more shall see my face', 1.1.202) and fascinating Demetrius anew by 'love-in-idleness' (2.1.168).

As Oberon tells Robin, the juice of this flower 'on sleeping eyelids laid / Will make or man or woman madly dote / Upon the next live creature that it sees' (2.1.170–2). Once Robin circulates with the magic potion, Hermia's enchanting power has vanished. What is more, those formerly infatuated by her 'sphery' (2.2.105), 'bright' (98), 'blessèd and attractive eyes' (97) finally see her 'true' face: 'Away, you Ethiope' (3.2.258); 'Out, tawny Tartar, out; / Out, loathèd med'cine; O hated potion, hence' (3.2.264–5). Seen through eyes washed by the magic potion, Hermia's exotic fascination fades behind her dark complexion, which was thought to indicate a corrupted mind and to be entirely unalluring. Whereas Helena's 'tawny' skin seems to bar love from entering her heart, Lysander, whose true 'marshal to [his] will' (2.2.126) is now love-in-idleness, claims to look straight into Helena: 'Transparent Helena, nature shows art / That through thy bosom makes me see thy heart' (2.2.110–11). Against the sinister background provided by her former friend, Helena's beauty shines even more brightly, which explains Lysander's change of affection: 'Who will not change a raven for a dove?' (2.2.120).

It seems as if 'the pretty flow'rets' eyes' (4.1.54) have absorbed Hermia's power of fascination. This assumption is supported by the association of Hermia with Tartar and Tartar with Cupid. The

---

[60] Walter Ralegh, *The History of the World* (London, 1614), p. 209.

[61] Robert Burton, *The Anatomy of Melancholy*, ed. Democritus Junior (Philadelphia, 1857), p. 465.

[62] Burton, *Anatomy*, p. 465.

[63] Burton, *Anatomy*, p. 468.

[64] *Works of Francis Bacon*, vol. 2, p. 129.

[65] See Holland, ed., *Dream*, p. 14 n. 235.

[66] Christopher Marlowe, *Doctor Faustus*, 5.1.90 (ed. David Scott Kastan (New York and London, 2005), A-Text).

latter is exhibited in Oberon's reference to 'Cupid's archery' (3.2.103), which comes on the heels of Robin's '[s]wifter than arrow from the Tartar's bow' (3.2.101). Encapsulated between these two images stands the '[f]lower of this purple dye' (3.2.102). Once its juice, which gained its magic power from Cupid's misguided arrow, has entered Lysander's eye, there is no room for Hermia: 'Out, tawny Tartar, out.' These changes in agents and subjects of fascination are mediated by periods of sleep and dream, in which the mind can process impressions gathered during waking hours. In this time of transition, Hermia suffers from a nightmare that translates her loss into the image of a snake: 'Help me, Lysander, help me! Do thy best / To pluck this crawling serpent from my breast! / . . . Methought a serpent ate my heart away' (2.2.151–5). Serpents were associated with both apotropaic and lethal powers; they were attributed the greatest power of fascination, as epitomized by the basilisk that kills by a glance. Serpents were believed to petrify their prey, paralyzing it by their lethal gaze, holding it mute and unmoving before its death.[67] Hermia's association with a serpentine character is further supported by Lysander, who, 'freed' from her spell, threatens her, 'let loose, / Or I will shake thee from me like a serpent' (3.2.261–2). Despite forfeiting her fascination, which seems to have been sucked out by a new 'serpent', love-in-idleness, Hermia retains some serpentine qualities, which the audience are reminded of shortly before Robin reapplies the magic potion to set things and eyes right: she is reduced to 'crawling': 'I can no further crawl' (3.3.32). Weary from rejection and exhausted by the long wanderings through the woods, she finally falls asleep – only to awake with her charming powers over Lysander regained.

Apart from its 'force and blessèd power' (4.1.73), we know hardly anything about the physiognomy of the 'little western flower' (2.1.166), which holds the enchanting juice and 'changes' the eyes of Titania, Lysander and Demetrius. Love-in-idleness is a fancy name for a pansy. Etymologically, the name is derived from the French *pensée*: As speculations go, 'some unknown poet in ancient times believed that the flower had a thoughtful, pensive face'.[68] Hence, in addition to providing an image of metamorphosis, more precisely of Ovid's story of Pyramus and Thisbe, and serving as agent initiating the process of fascination, love-in-idleness emerges as an image of the fascination of and with faces in *A Midsummer Night's Dream*.

In the end, therefore, we shall heed Bottom's note of caution, which resonates throughout the play: 'let the audience look to their eyes' (1.2.22). To look to your eyes means to guard them against the perils of fascination, against being fixated on an eye, a face or a dream, because fascination is not only caused by sight but is also 'the power and act of imagination'.[69] It also means to look at yourself and 'see' yourself in the sense of *nosce te ipsum*. For the guarding of the eyes, Robin provides remedy when he releases the audience into the world (perhaps another dream?), before it is too late: 'Now to 'scape the serpent's tongue, / We will make amends ere long' (Epilogue 11–12). For the knowledge of the self and others, physiognomy provides the key. It offers a tool for translation and (re-)mediation and supports us in seeing and understanding interfaces between human and animal, body and mind, but also between dream and reality, comedy and tragedy: the theatre and *theatrum mundi*. The complexity, challenge and, not least the criticism of physiognomy contributed to its fascinating power, because what fascinates us most is the forbidden, the mysterious, the lure of the unknown and unattainable, which we find translated in Shakespeare's experimental physiognomic theatre in a playful nonchalance – like a dance for which all we need is a bass or 'bottom' and a flute.

---

[67] See Thomas B. Johnson, *Physiological Observations on Mental Susceptibility* (London, 1837), pp. 200–1.

[68] Robert Hendrickson, *QPB Encyclopedia of Word and Phrase Origins* (New York, 1998), p. 508.

[69] *Works of Francis Bacon*, vol. 1, p. 129.

A MIDSUMMER NIGHT'S DREAM
IN ILLUSTRATED EDITIONS,
1838–1918

STUART SILLARS

Throughout the eighteenth century, *A Midsummer Night's Dream* was a major source of visual treatments that illuminate both aspects of the play and elements of contemporary aesthetic and intellectual life – an intersection that was peculiarly rich, and remarkably diverse, in the work of Henry Fuseli, Joshua Reynolds, George Romney. Their work and those of others has been discussed in detail,[1] and resembles many of the best known paintings of the succeeding years in concerning itself almost exclusively with the world of the fairies, both in isolation and in the encounter between Titania and Bottom. Others, of which Sir Joseph Noel Paton's diptych[2] is perhaps the best known, and certainly the most expansive, focus more directly on the fairy world itself, and range from fantasies of the erotic imagination – John Simmons[3] – to those of the sombre unconscious – Richard Dadd.[4] All have their function in the Victorian assimilation of the play, and Shakespeare in general, into the larger contemporary consciousness, aided by a similar fascination with the world of faery that was presented by Perrault, Grimm and Andrew Lang and visualized in any number of non-Shakespearian paintings.

I

The Victorian period produced another visual practice that has been largely overlooked: the tradition of illustrated editions that, beginning with those of Charles Knight and Barry Cornwall in the 1830s, continued with the work of Henry Courtney Selous and John Gilbert, the latter being perhaps the most pervasive Shakespeare illustrator,

his work appearing in numerous editions aimed at different kinds of readers. After a lull in the century's final years, in which very few original illustrated editions appeared, tastes and techniques changed. In the years before the First World War, a shift towards lavish coloured illustration, ostensibly aimed at child readers, presented a final burst of activity, in which the play is offered new visual form in the work of Arthur Rackham and several less known, but equally important, figures. All these offer independent ways of seeing the play, using contemporary styles and production techniques to combine something of the immediacy of production with the full complexity of the printed text, often with the aid of critical apparatus borrowed from scholarly editions. The resulting compound reading experience was arguably the first involvement with the play for many more than those who initially encountered it in the theatre. The volumes, then, constitute a major force in the configuration and reception of the play, alongside the lavish productions of Charles Kean and Beerbohm Tree, the discussions of leading characters by Anna Brownell Jameson and Mary Cowden

---

[1] See, among others, W. Moelwyn Merchant, *Shakespeare and the Artist* (London, 1959); Stuart Sillars, *Painting Shakespeare: The Artist as Critic, 1720–1820* (Cambridge, 2006).

[2] *The Quarrel of Oberon and Titania*, 1849; oil on canvas, 99.1 × 152.4 cm (39 × 60 in) and *The Reconciliation of Oberon and Titania*, 1847; oil on canvas 76.2 × 123.2 cm (30 × 48$^1/_2$ in), both National Gallery of Scotland, Edinburgh.

[3] *Titania*, 1866; watercolour and gouache, 34.3 × 26.7 cm (13$^1/_2$ × 10$^1/_2$ in), Bristol City Art Gallery.

[4] *Contradiction: Oberon and Titania*, 1854–8; oil on canvas, 61 × 74.9 cm (24 × 29$^1/_2$ in), private collection.

Clarke, and the nascent critical explorations of the nature of comedy and the place of the *Dream* within its forms and traditions.

Like their contemporaries who worked in the more extensive and rhetorically distanced medium of oil on canvas, Victorian illustrators built on the tradition of intricately designed engravings that had developed since François Boitard's frontispieces to Rowe's edition of 1709 – a tradition that has also been much explored.[5] But the later illustrators of the plays had both more freedom and more challenges than those who came before. With very rare exceptions, eighteenth-century artists had only to present a single design, for use as a frontispiece, whereas later ones had to produce a series of images for presentation throughout the play's sequence. The former raised questions of selection, in that the moment chosen for the frontispiece would immediately lodge itself in the reader's mind as some kind of apex to the play's progression; but the latter brought with it problems not just of selection but of the rhythm of placement of images, the balance of settings and characters, and the larger concerns with variation of viewpoint and scale.

Some of these are unwittingly touched upon by Charles Knight in his 'Introductory Remarks' to the play. After discussing the sheer variety of character, mood and setting in the play, Knight talks of the futility of attempting to bring them all together, concluding that such an approach 'would be worse even than unreverential criticism'. Aside from the characteristic contemporary concern for reverence, the passage reveals a difficulty peculiar to the illustration of this play. In a play with as much diversity of setting as the *Dream*, the intertwined trinity of plot and character, and the complex variations of mood and tone, to say nothing of the comic yet intellectually teasing nature of the final interlude, the task of illustrator and designer, the unnamed figure responsible for bringing together word and image, was much increased. In production, especially in the Victorian theatre, lengthy intervals facilitate not simply changes of set but alterations of mood; in the more concentrated setting of the printed book, the illustrator must confront the multiple dimensions of diversity yet in

some way offer continuity of style to present an integrated experience of the play for the reader. In all the editions of the time these problems were addressed differently, to produce versions of the play that balance verbal and visual differently to offer new conceptual and aesthetic constructions that constitute a single, integrated experience for the reader that both parallels the blend of scenography, action and declamation in the theatre and offers something wholly dependent on the aesthetic identity of the printed book. The results offer a range of treatments of the play that if anything far outstripped the nature of contemporary performance in diversity and originality.

Charles Knight's *Pictorial Shakspere*, first issued serially between 1838 and 1843, reveals almost to an extreme the early Victorian concern for system and accuracy.[6] Knight's claim that the illustrations depicted 'the realities upon which the imagination of the poet must have rested',[7] which he enumerated as persons, places, scenes and costumes, is one dimension of this. For him, the plays are as much records of a specific space and time as dramatic entities, an approach which exemplifies the contemporary concern with antiquarian precision but somehow overlooks their origins within a much later imagination. Research in the Bodleian and the use, in carefully copied and reduced form, of images from the times of the plays' settings are matched by some efforts at serious scholarship in editing. System, too, is revealed in the rigorous structure applied to every play. Each scene begins

---

5 Most relevantly for this play, W. Moelwyn Merchant, '*A Midsummer Night's Dream*: A Visual Re-creation', in *Early Shakespeare*, ed. J. R. Brown and B. Harris (London, 1967), pp. 164–85; Kenneth Garlick, 'Illustrations to *A Midsummer Night's Dream* before 1920', *Shakespeare Survey 37* (Cambridge, 1984), pp 41–53; and, more generally, Stuart Sillars, *The Illustrated Shakespeare 1709–1875* (Cambridge, 2008).

6 *The Pictorial Edition of the Works of Shakspere. Edited by Charles Knight* (London, 56 monthly parts, 1838–43). Issued as 7 volumes, with an additional supplementary volume containing the life of Shakespeare. Subsequent versions included 'The National Edition', 3 vols. (London, 1858).

7 Charles Knight, *Passages of a Working Life during Half a Century: With a Prelude of Early Reminiscences*, 2 vols. (London, 1864), vol. 2, p. 284.

with a headpiece illustration, generally of a setting, and ends where space allows with a tailpiece, often of the same kind. After each act comes a series of 'Illustrations', mostly verbal annotations explanatory of textual allusions, but at times including visual material with the same purpose. The seriousness of the endeavour is relieved slightly by what Knight referred to as 'imaginative embellishment', but this was 'partially employed' and strictly 'where it is demanded by the character of the particular drama'.[8] All this sounds fairly forbidding in both plan and implementation: there is a hint that one may use illustrations as long as one doesn't enjoy them, which bodes ill for the *Dream*.

In operation, however, the approach is quietly effective. As in all illustrated editions, the initial image is fundamental in setting the tone and approach, and Knight's title-page, designed by J. Jackson (Illustration 2), is particularly successful. Rejecting the technique used elsewhere in the edition, in which events or characters are presented separately along the lines of much earlier synoptic frontispieces,[9] the design brings together moments from the fairy episodes in a loosely structured sequence that moves from close detail at the top to a distant scene at the foot, bracketing the play's title drawn in capitals constructed from rustic boughs, some of which trail tendrils to suggest a living forest. Titania decorates Bottom's ear with garlands; diminutive fairies war with insects larger then themselves among fronds and bluebells; at the foot, the whole is drawn together with a fairy ring on a twilit shore, above which hover Oberon and Titania. The whole suggests immediacy of the moment, the mingled vulnerability and power of the fairies in their natural setting, and the larger resolution in which the fairy king and queen are reconciled in a 'glimmering light' not of the palace but of the shore. It should be remarked that this is one of the earliest images to show Shakespeare's fairies on this scale, and it does so with a delicacy that avoids the saccharine or the erotic of later treatments. It also makes a direct statement about the play's main driving force. The presence of the fairies at the very outset suggests subliminally to the reader that they are the major power

2. Title-page by J. Jackson to the play in Charles Knight's *Pictorial Shakspere*.

of the play, moving the focus away from the mortal confusions with which they interact. This presents the play as very different from the idea of romance trajectory seen in other comedies. The framing threat hanging over the lovers from the first scene is itself enfolded within the fairy world, and exists in a mutually metaphoric relationship with it, as well as intersecting with it in narrative.

In the pages of the play itself, considerable efforts are made to integrate the play's levels of action. The lovers and fairies are shown in a wood that is

8 Knight, *Pictorial Edition*, 'Advertisement', Comedies vol. 1, unpaginated.
9 In *The Merchant of Venice*, for example. See Stuart Sillars, *Shakespeare, Time and the Victorians: A Pictorial Exploration* (Cambridge, 2011), pp. 47–9.

[*Bringing in the Maypole.*]

3. Unsigned engraving in Knight's edition, acting as a visual annotation to Act 1.

similar in scale and composition, and when Bottom awakes it is within the same setting. That this wood is nearer to Stratford than to Athens continues the Englishness of setting established in the title-page, and this is supported by some of the visual annotations, notably the engraving of 'Bringing in the Maypole' that is part of an extensive gloss to Lysander's line 'To do observance to a morn of May' (1.1.167; Illustration 3). The easy conversation between the play's worlds and Knight's commentary is continued in images of the Athenian world. The first image, accompanying a set of 'Introductory Remarks' which discuss the play's early printing and critical history, is a fragment of classical frieze above the quotation 'Hippolyta, I woo'd thee with my sword'; and this is balanced

against two similar fragments that accompany the discussion of costume, most likely by James Robinson Planché, adding a further level of notional authenticity. The plot strands are woven together again in the final image, the headpiece to Act 5 (Illustration 4). Hippolyta removes her wedding veil, assisted by Hermia and Helena; at the right, a shield and helmet stand unattended, recalling her courtship by the sword; above them the fairies soar in an arch, while at centre-rear, as in the position of the king on stage, Oberon wields his sceptre as if directing the performance.

The unity of all the elements of the mortal and fairy worlds thus presented is completed by the engraving's location, appearing above Puck's final words of command: 'Now, until the break of

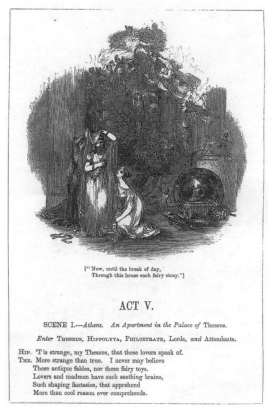

["Now, until the break of day,
Through this house each fairy stray."]

ACT V.

SCENE I.—*Athens. An Apartment in the Palace of Theseus.*

Enter THESEUS, HIPPOLYTA, PHILOSTRATE, *Lords, and Attendants.*

HIP. 'T is strange, my Theseus, that these lovers speak of.
THE. More strange than true. I never may believe
  These antique fables, nor these fairy toys.
  Lovers and madmen have such seething brains,
  Such shaping fantasies, that apprehend
  More than cool reason ever comprehends.

4. Unsigned engraving as headpiece to Act 5 of Knight's edition.

day, / Through this house each fairy stray.' That the human figures in the foreground are ignorant of the fairies suggests the ethereal, metaphoric nature of the equation between them; that the dark house, shown in a series of receding classical columns, resembles the forest, and the composition of the whole recalls the earlier headpieces showing fairies and mortals in the wood, suggests a concluding unity. From this, it might almost seem that Knight has succeeded in bringing together the play's action, the illustrations functioning cumulatively to climax in the final image that returns to the fairy world initiated on the title-page.

Almost, but not quite. There is no visual treatment of the wedding interlude, and the last we see of Bottom is his awakening in the wood. This is, perhaps, a final statement of Victorian order;

or perhaps its effect is to leave us with Bottom's dream, and his translation in the wood. More recent, more critically aware readers might see in these absences the inconclusiveness with which the so-called 'happy comedies' often address the closing issue of marriage, the lonely Bottom a prefiguration of the Shakespearian outsider often left solitary at the close. However we choose to read the images, they are striking in their approach to the play. Yet, with the partial exception of the first, they cannot be said to display an aesthetic fullness or visual imagination anywhere near the play's own richness, staying resolutely on the level of reductive mimicry of momentary event. In this, of course, they follow Knight's own instructions to the letter, even when trying to present 'imaginative embellishment', remaining earthbound in the presence of ethereal flight.

A different approach is taken by Kenny Meadows in the almost exactly contemporary edition by Barry Cornwall,[10] in the effort to present something of the harmonious confusion of the play's levels and moods. Immediately striking is its presentation of a far clearer single reading of the play, which makes the fairies far more dominant in action and mood. From the outset, too, the images impose and reflect on their identity as parts of an illustrated volume, to the level of metacritical reflection on the workings of a continuous visual-verbal sequence. The reader is at once greeted with a page opening that matches a frontispiece, turned at right angles from the printed text, with a combined title-page and cast list. The initial effect is one of incongruity, the two pages differing in scale and style, the result of their being by different designers and in different orientation. The frontispiece (Illustration 5) shows Bottom and Titania in the fairy bower, Bottom with an ass-head but a human body; unlike many twentieth-century productions, most illustrated editions of the earlier period remain true to

[10] *The Works of Shakspere revised from the best authorities with a memoir, and essay on his genius, by Barry Cornwall: and, annotations and introductory remarks on the plays, by distinguished writers: illustrated with engravings on wood, from designs by Kenny Meadows* (London, 1838–43).

5. Anonymous frontispiece to the edition of 'Barry Cornwall' (Bryan Proctor).

the text in stressing the duality, rather than making the character appear as completely animal. Titania's fairy identity is suggested by a pair of wings but, these apart, she is clearly human and seemingly adolescent: it is as if the wings have been placed on her as the head was placed on Bottom, suggesting their shared subjection to the spell. The youth of Titania places the image in the shadow of many Victorian images, from G. F. Watt's portrait of his child-bride Ellen Terry[11] to Julia Margaret Cameron's photographs of child nudes.[12] For contemporary onlookers, these were perhaps signs of innocence: for later readers, they are surely never less than troubling.

The facing 'Persons Represented'[13] page (Illustration 6) is embellished with marginal *grotteschi*, almost in the fashion of a medieval illumination – the Luttrell Psalter, say — in which what appear as playfully irrelevant figures become, on deeper acquaintance, elements that teasingly contradict and deepen the main concerns of the central text.[14] Meadows's fairies, ostensibly comic, are unsettling through the use of a technique recurrent throughout his Shakespeare work: they show

figures partially concealed, and so imply beneath their sensual shapes and supple movement the kind of unseen misdirections that take narrative form in the wood. They are largely comic in their elegance, but there is enough doubt to suggest a darker power of irritancy. The direct suggestion that they drive the action of the play in performance is matched by an element that binds them directly to the play as a printed form. With only two exceptions, all the figures are shown as if bursting through the printed

[11] *Choosing*, c.1864; oil on strawboard, 47.2 × 35.4 cm (18⅝ × 14 in).

[12] For example, *Cupid's Pencil of Light*, albumen print, c.1867. Cameron's *Ellen Terry at Age Sixteen*, carbon print, 1864, offers an interesting parallel to Watts's painting.

[13] The edition uses this form throughout, presumably to avoid the classical 'Dramatis Personae' as something intimidating to many of the target readers.

[14] Produced for Sir Geoffrey Luttrell at some time between 1325 and 1335, British Library Add MS.42130. Some pages are reproduced at www.bl.uk/collections/treasures/luttrell/luttrell_broadband.htm. See also Janet Backhouse (ed.), *The Luttrell Psalter*, Manuscripts in Colour series (London, 1989) and Michael Camille, *Mirror in Parchment: The Luttrell Psalter and the Making of Medieval England* (London, 1998).

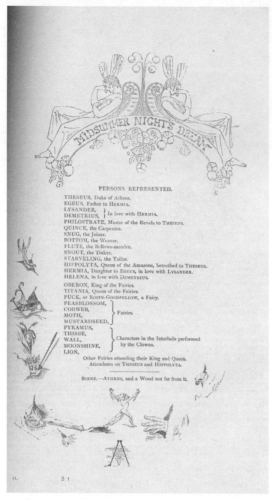

6. 'Persons Represented,' facing the frontispiece in Cornwall's edition.

7. Kenny Meadows: headpiece to Act 1, Cornwall's edition.

page, their bodies concealed behind the torn edges of paper drawn around their faces and, in one case, a hooked nose suggestive of a witch's face.

A greater sense of the reading that will dominate is given in the headpiece to Act 1 (Illustration 7). Instead of the Athenian couple shown by Knight, Meadows presents Titania enthroned, with the Indian boy and a surrounding cast of grotesques in a composition suggesting variations of scale and proportion through its absence of perspective. That the image appears above the first twenty-two lines

of the text places the altercation between Titania and Oberon physically and conceptually above that between Hermia and Egeus, a reordering confirmed by the later illustrations. The only visual treatment of the Athenians is a small image of Helena weeping against a tree; the mechanicals appear twice, once in a vignette at the foot of their first appearance in Act 1 and, more strikingly, in an engraving cut into the rehearsal scene in Act 3 where Puck's initial sight of them is shown from ground level, so that only their feet and legs are visible within the undergrowth of the forest (Illustration 8). The Pyramus and Thisbe interlude appears without illustration. Both the ironies of the Ovidian theme and the reflections on dramatic illusion are thus lost; but the loss of the first is balanced by the absence of the Athenians from the play's visual progress, and the latter are transmediated extensively through the self-reflective treatment of the play in print, announced on the title-page by the *trompe l'œil* torn-paper images.

Puck and the Players.

8. 'Puck and the Players', a wood engraving by Kenny Meadows cut into the text of Act 3 in the Cornwall edition.

As the play develops, the sense of the fairies' control is continued through a series of vignettes. Interspersed within the two columns in which the text is typeset, these also emphasize by implication the play's identity as a print object, and this is reinforced in other ways, for example in the opening image of the third act, where the figure of Puck at the foot thrusts upwards with an elongated spear at the ass-head above the inscription 'Act III'. On the facing page there is another treatment of Bottom and Titania (Illustration 9). Like the frontispiece, this is by a hand other than Meadows, and in yet another style. Upright, within an elaborate geometric floral frame, it shows the two figures seated apart, eyeing each other with something between fascination and suspicion. The more intricate engraving technique intensifies the mood of the exchange, the contrast from the frontispiece suggesting something very different and thus enhancing the shifting nature of the fairy world. The change of style and approach gives an uncertainty to the reading process, alternating between devotion and entrapment in the manner of the scene's dialogue, sharpened by the presentation of Titania as a mature woman, naked to the waist before Bottom's gaze. The relation between the two pages, and the text they enclose – the mechanicals' rehearsals, which further questions the idea of play and performance – imposes distance from the play's setting, mood and events, as well as constructively muddling its aesthetic identity as something on stage and in print.

Two further versions of Titania, both by Meadows, add to this complexity. The first again shows her with Bottom, this time from the undergrowth perspective used earlier, and surrounded by tiny fairies; the second is a full-face portrait, the dense stipple engraving giving an effect of misty softness, the foreground flowers adding to the imprecision of scale. These variations within the printed form, and the emphasis they throw on the play as printed object, climax in the final image (Illustration 10). Here, above his final words, Puck bursts through the page doffing his hat in mock courtesy to the reader: and the edition ends as it began, firmly under the control of the fairies. The apparent lightness of many of its illustrations is misleading; it would be a mistake to see the edition as merely another piece of Victorian whimsy. There is ambivalence and threat here, and the reading

Midsummer Night's Dream.
Act 3. Sc 1.

9. The second treatment of Titania and Bottom, again unsigned, from the Cornwall edition.

experience is unsettling as much because of this seeming lightness as despite it, aided by the constant dialogue between play and print. Meadows's reading offers a conception of the play quite different from Knight's, yet the presentation of the fairies as drivers of the plot in both suggests the force and the extent with which they occupied the contemporary visual imagination.

The two editions that appeared in the 1860s, again with curious synchronicity, again offer divergent approaches, but in a markedly different way. Henry Courtney Selous addresses the play in terms that are perhaps best described as high Victorian romanticism; John Gilbert takes a more serious, more reflective stance towards its layers of action. This perhaps suggests a shift of mood in

10. Kenny Meadows: the concluding image in
Cornwall's edition.

the decades that separate them from the earlier pair, a move towards what we would now regard as something more typically high-Victorian. Whatever the cause, they demonstrate the variety of visual treatments available in the period's central half-century, their availability suggesting that they were all-important in influencing readers in their approach to, and final concept of, the play.

Selous produced the images for what became known as *Cassell's Illustrated Shakespeare*, an edition in large-format volumes that presented the text in two columns above the Cowden Clarkes' footnote annotations.[15] The images are either half-page engravings spreading across both columns or designs occupying whole pages, both kinds being strict rectangles and all separated from the text by single or double rules. The result is to hold apart word and image, in strict rejection of the fluid overlappings of Meadows, and the separation is enhanced by the presence of two- or three-line quotations from the play as captions beneath each image. The result is to offer the reader something approaching a separate visual progression of event and character. The rigidity of layout is matched, or perhaps countered, by the use of a style of design

and manner of execution within each image that is representative of popular, but serious-minded, illustrated books of the period: Selous carefully lays aside the high-art intensity of the 'sixties style', settling instead on a style that would not be out of place in earnest publications such as *The Leisure Hour* or *The Girl's Own Paper*, the latter a periodical to which Mary Cowden Clarke herself made occasional contributions.[16]

The results are striking. Selous unbendingly separates the play's three orders of being; yet again the Athenians are given far less attention, having only one full-page and one smaller engraving. But what is apparent is that, apart from slight differences in costume and hair colour, the figures of Oberon and Titania and those of the mortal lovers are barely distinguishable. This offers quite a new reading of the play, taking things much further than the familiar on-stage doublings of Theseus and Hippolyta with Oberon and Titania. The interchange redefines all three pairs of lovers, suggesting something much younger and lighter in the fairy quarrel, perhaps in accord with the then current comedic reading of the play as a whole, as a sequence whose outcome is neither in doubt nor seriously threatened. The likeness is strengthened by the body language of the three pairs. All interact through what elsewhere I have termed the 'emotional choreography' associated with illustrations of popular romance.[17] There is sensuality in Titania's resting against Bottom's head, and more in her lying asleep with her head against his thigh; when she returns to Oberon after the removal of the spell, she leans against his chest in true Victorian affrighted maiden fashion (Illustration 11). It is not hard to place this sequence within Hermia's hand-to-head pose with

---

15 *Cassell's Illustrated Shakespeare. The Plays of Shakespeare. Edited and Annotated by Charles and Mary Cowden Clarke, authors of 'Shakespeare Characters', 'Complete Concordance to Shakespeare', 'Girlhood of Shakespeare's Heroines,' &c.* 3 vols. (London, 1864).

16 Most notably in 'Shakespeare as the Girl's Friend', *The Girl's Own Paper*, vol. VIII, no. 388 (4 June 1887), pp. 562–4.

17 Sillars, *Illustrated Shakespeare*, pp. 290–303.

11. Henry Courtney Selous: the reconciliation of Oberon and Titania, *Cassell's Illustrated Shakespeare.*

Lysander in 1.1 (Illustration 12), an image that might easily accompany an attack of the vapours at sudden plot reversal from Charlotte Mary Yonge or Mary Elizabeth Braddon. Even the classical setting is contemporary, recalling a design by Leighton or

Alma-Tadema, a Greek interior familiar in scale and ornament from reproductions in fashionable magazines.

If this equation is unfamiliar, and in a sense rather refreshing, the treatment of the mechanicals

102

12. Henry Courtney Selous: Lysander and Hermia, from Act 1 scene 1.

13. Frederick Barnard, engraved by J. Swain: the Pyramus and Thisbe interlude, from *Cassell's Illustrated Shakespeare*.

moves towards a kind of humour that begins subtly and then, in the last act, climaxes in grotesque. And none the worse for that: the final image (Illustration 13), by Frederick Barnard, shows Bottom in full histrionic flood as the dying Pyramus, while Thisbe waits placidly in the wings and Quince raises his hand in nicely observed directorial horror. All this comes together with the domesticated interiors and the shared emotional poses to suggest a directly contemporary re-enactment of the play, a world in which sensuality is under control, sexuality banished and humour robust. This is not the supreme visual richness of Charles Kean, nor the patterned restraint of Granville-Barker, but instead something that suggests a confident, untroubled, if perhaps rather too suburban, security. Selous's visual vocabulary reflects and validates the world of its readers, offering a

comforting sympathetic circularity through its visual vocabulary.

The fourth major Victorian edition, with illustrations by Sir John Gilbert,[18] adopts yet another approach. Integration of text and image is far harder to establish here, since the same images, from the same wood-block plates or stereos taken from them, were used in widely different editions. Their variation in page size meant that the rhythm of image and text was never constant; in some cases, too, it appears random. If Selous is the most typical

---

18 *The Plays of Shakespeare. Edited by Howard Staunton; the illustrations by John Gilbert; engraved by the Brothers Dalziel* (London, 1856–60). *A Midsummer Night's Dream* appeared as pages 337–88 in volume 1 of the three-volume edition published immediately after the issue of the separate parts, presenting them in the same order and the identical text.

14. John Gilbert: Bottom with the ass's head, from Act 3 of Howard Staunton's edition.

of Victorian style and attitude, then Gilbert is probably the most serious, the one that approaches most nearly the intense, finely worked engravings of the artist-designers who produced images complete in themselves or as presences in much smaller works than a complete Shakespeare. The first edition, in serial paper-bound parts, perhaps suffers from this at times; it is the later, larger Library Shakespeare that often achieves a better balance between word and image.[19] Yet the changes are not always deleterious, demonstrating instead a different, rather than less effective, treatment, especially in the images of the fairies. The most direct instance of this occurs at the beginning of the second act, where Puck's account of his actions to the Fairy is presented in three images which, after the headpiece that shows the two characters together, occur in the space of two page openings of the earliest, serial, edition. This gives Puck's rapid changes of form direct visual statement, creating a breathlessness that reflects the immediacy of the speech, converting it into direct rather than recorded action in a manner not only unique to the printed book but specific to this page-format. The later, larger edition allows greater physical space between each image, giving the reader more time for assimilation; the scene is

more reflective, but not necessarily more powerful. The two stand as alternative readings, and at a larger distance reveal the central importance of design and layout in the combined verbal-visual experience offered to the reader.

This episode forms part of a larger continuity of composition in the images that is remarkable for its balance of repetition and variation. The design showing a group of figures in flight before a single pursuer is employed in designs showing the mechanicals running from Bottom with the ass-head, Puck misleading night wanderers, and Puck leading Lysander 'up and down' in 3.2. Between these three there are images of stasis, the mermaid on a dolphin's back followed by a troop of fairies on a flower-stalk and the mechanicals before their rehearsal. Bottom with the ass-head is presented first in direct frontal composition, flanked by two mechanicals, the reader being given a direct experience of the new shape that is grotesque, a little alarming, certainly not just comic (Illustration 14).

---

[19] *The Library Shakespeare Illustrated by Sir John Gilbert, George Cruikshank and R. Dudley*, 3 vols. (London, 1873–75). For a discussion of the various editions using Gilbert's illustrations, see Sillars, *Illustrated Shakespeare*, pp. 305–6.

15. John Gilbert: headpiece to Act 1 of the Staunton edition.

The same is true of the title-page, which skilfully balances the two responses; and, while Titania is shown sleeping with her head on Bottom's massive temple, the scene is watched by Oberon, Puck and surrounding fairies, suggesting a kind of comic tenderness rather than sexual manipulation or the human sensuality of the Selous treatments.

What is most remarkable in Gilbert's treatment, though, comes in the relation between the first and last images, the headpieces to the first and last acts (Illustrations 15 and 16). The former shows Hippolyta seated on what can only be described as a throne, while Theseus stands beside her holding a staff which, along with his gaze, suggests that he is ordering Philostrate to 'Stir up the Athenian youth to merriment' and presaging the wedding celebration 'With pomp, with triumph, and

with revelling'. We should not be surprised that the darker resonances of 'Hippolyta, I woo'd thee with my sword' are unheard: only in more recent readings have these come to dominate. There is a hinted foretaste of celebration that places the wedding within the frame of governance and order, to which Philostrate is essential. This order is restated in the final image, through a subtle reference that balances the gentle suggestion of the first one: the headpiece to Act 5 gives direct statement to the ceremony of the wedding night, uniting the play's levels of action in quite a new way. Two diminutive forms, recognizable as child-fairies, hold processional torchères while between them the figure of Philostrate, in the same posture as his earlier depiction, holds a staff. This is the procession of fairies described by Puck that will 'through the house

105

16. John Gilbert: headpiece to Act 5 of the Staunton edition.

give glimmering light': the inclusion of Philostrate, the elderly retainer, is a fine interpretive stroke by Gilbert, bonding the fairy world with that of traditional rites of blessing.

Behind these figures is what first seems to be a wolf, echoing Puck's penultimate speech – 'And the wolf behowls the moon'. But a second glance shows it as held on a leash by a figure with a domed hat and lantern; we realize that it is Moonshine's dog, and the momentary threat is dispelled. Other figures behind the ceremonial group similarly reveal themselves, their dual identities maintained through likeness to earlier portrayals or by simple logic, maintaining the play-within-a-play concept and its implicit discussions of actuality. Thus Bottom is recognizably, and

importantly, revealed as himself rather than Pyramus – confirming a justifiable reading that the character is constantly performing his own identity rather than any assumed role. Flute as Thisbe, mask in hand, Snug as Lion and Snout as Wall, with Quince at the extreme right, complete the cast. The presence of these figures, with Philostrate before them, emphasizes the latter's function as master of the revels in the final act, but also as one whose presence enfolds the whole play as stage manager. The contrast to Meadows's presentation of Puck in this role is forceful, in both identity and manner. Philostrate represents the order that has been disrupted by the Athenian lovers, and by Oberon's theft of the Indian boy, at the outset, and is now restored in his participation in the ancient English wedding custom. It is a fine piece of directorial draughtsmanship, bringing together all the strands of action, not merely by overlapping the roles of fairies, mechanicals and aged courtier but by implication linking us, the readers, with the Athenian lovers, since we are placed in a position analogous to that of the three pairs of mortals as they watch the interlude. We may look with superiority on this piece of Victorian antiquarianism, for its sentimentality and its imposition of feudal hierarchy; but as a direct contemporary reading of the play it is a considered combination of levels that maintains the carefully controlled mix of sentiment and comedy apparent throughout the volume in Gilbert's engravings.

Comparing the four editions in terms of both their illustrations and the reading experiences they offer is revealing about the period's view, literal and conceptual, of the play. Most immediately, it confirms that there is no single characteristically – and by implication almost parodically – Victorian treatment of the play, since the four fall naturally into two pairs that are themselves opposed, the Knight and Meadows representing something rather different from the Selous and Gilbert. Knight's treatment suggests the extreme historical realism later to climax in the work of Charles Kean, unsurprising since Planché contributed notes on costumes, and the influence on Kean's productions of the 1850s is often clear. Meadows's imagination is quite without parallel in Shakespeare imaging, but if it can be pigeon-holed at all it would belong to an age before the onset of Victorian conformity, perhaps a last explosion of Regency exuberance. But his readings of textual ambivalences show no little insight, and the edition is also one of the earliest of printed books to exploit the technology of the wood-engraved block in integrating word and image, to produce a single unified experience for the reader. Gilbert's treatment is subtlest of them all, in its unobtrusive yet satisfying rhythm of compositional variation and contrast. His bracketing of the whole action within the Athenian court, and transformation of the closing ceremony to include all levels of action, remains a remarkable stroke of visual interpretation that makes simple, but

brilliant, use of the medium of the illustrated book. We are left with Selous, whose images come closest to the received ideas not just of Victorian illustration, popular but effective in form, but of the larger concepts of order and gender that the period most often seems to present.

The circulation of these editions is hard to estimate, but must have been very considerable when all the various forms in which they appeared are taken into consideration. To these should be added the versions of Knight's edition produced in Philadelphia from stereo plates shipped across the Atlantic to avoid import duty, and the use of some of Gilbert's images in the bewilderingly prolific versions of William J. Rolfe.[20] Given the number of readers – of image and word combined – that encountered one or more of the editions, they clearly have much to suggest about the way in which the play was presented and received during the central years of the century, an important extension to the better known paintings and stage productions of the time.

II

As hinted earlier, subsequent illustrated editions approach *A Midsummer Night's Dream* in different ways. Charles Knight's Imperial Edition,[21] another serial publication, included reproduction of paintings of the plays in steel engravings that had already appeared in the *Art Journal* or *Magazine of Art*. For *A Midsummer Night's Dream* the result was to bring the play far closer to the perception of the play as dominated by the fairy world as presented by the painters of the 1840s, through the presence of Huskisson's *There Sleeps Titania*[22] and Richard Dadd's *Puck*

---

20 *Shakespeare's Comedy of A Midsummer Night's Dream* (New York, Cincinnati and Chicago, 1877) uses some of Gilbert's smaller engravings. It was reprinted in 1898, 1903, 1905 and 1918, ensuring even further distribution of the images.

21 *The Works of Shakespeare with Notes by Charles Knight* (London, 1873–76).

22 Also known as *The Midsummer Night's Fairies*. 29.2 × 34.3 cm ($11^1/_2 \times 13^1/_2$ in), Tate Britain, London.

17. Lorna Burgoyne: 'Cupid is a knavish lad', from Act 3 scene 2 of her illustrations for a 1919 edition with the text of the Cambridge Shakespeare of 1863–66.

18. Lorna Burgoyne: Hippolyta as huntress, a colour plate from the edition of 1919.

and the Fairies.[23] A little later, 'The Henry Irving Shakespeare'[24] included images reflecting contemporary styles, from classical interior, through moral narrative to the emerging freer outdoor naturalism of the Newlyn School. Arthur Rackham's edition of 1910, using to the full the new four-colour Hentschel process, along with some fine, economical line-drawings, is a far more reflective and intelligent presentation than its popular following would suggest.

One further edition stands out for discussion here, because of the originality with which it treats the play, and the ways in which it moves towards a more detached, more mature reading that perhaps foreshadows the criticism and performance of the later twentieth century. This is the edition illustrated by Lorna Burgoyne that appeared just after the First World War, with forty full-page drawings and several full colour plates.[25] The levels

of action are kept separate in style, but brought together where the action demands. All the Athenian characters are shown in profile, extending the expedient of the classical medallion in simple but logical manner, but they are placed within luxurious woodland settings to suggest the play's richness. The fairies appear in similar, but more exaggeratedly exotic, settings, and are themselves just this side of grotesque. The coming together of the two is shown in Illustration 17, which also demonstrates Burgoyne's design style that adopts elements from Aubrey Beardsley, particularly in solid blocks of black and white and supple variation of line,

---

[23] 1841; 59.1 × 59.1 cm (23¼ × 23¼ in), Harris Museum & Art Gallery, Preston.

[24] *The Works of William Shakespeare edited by Henry Irving and Frank A. Marshall*, 8 vols. (London, 1888–90).

[25] *Midsummer Night's Dream: The Play of Shakespeare*. Illustrated by Lorna Burgoyne (London, 1919).

combining the classical features of the Athenians with the mechanicals' physicality and increased coarseness of body and expression. Most remarkable, perhaps, are the colour plates. The frontispiece, captioned 'His mother was a votaress of my order', shows Titania with an Indian woman within a classical Indian temple. At the beginning of the final act, to accompany Hippolyta's speech about her hunting expedition 'with Hercules and Cadmus once', there is a full-page colour plate of Hippolyta as huntress (Illustration 18). Coming near the close of the play, and the volume, it gives a wholly new thrust to the play's ending, turning the reader back to the opening allusions to Hippolyta's Amazon heritage and her violent courtship by Theseus. The resolution is still there at the close; but it is tempered and made astringent by this image: the power of the woman is clear; so, too, is a hint of the darker, more troubling readings of the play in the new century's later years.

BALANCHINE AND TITANIA:
LOVE AND THE ELISION OF HISTORY
IN *A MIDSUMMER NIGHT'S DREAM*

LAURA LEVINE

At the heart of Shakespeare's *A Midsummer Night's Dream* is the Indian child Oberon wants Titania to surrender to adorn his train and 'trace the forests wild'. Until Titania surrenders the child, she'll remain in love with Bottom; Bottom will remain an ass; Lysander will love Helena and no 'Jack shall have his Jill'. To get the child, Oberon must penetrate Titania's bower and afflict her eye with the love-in-idleness which makes her adore Bottom in the first place. In Shakespeare's text, the Indian child – described, but never seen – is the invisible pin that holds the play together. And Titania's bower is that world which will need to be penetrated in order for Oberon to get him. The Indian child's history, like his existence, is narrated and imagined, rather than witnessed as a physical set of facts upon a stage. We know him not through his physical presence – he is conspicuous, in fact, for the fact that he never appears in the play – but through the narrated histories he comes to stand for. 'She, being mortal, of that boy did die', Titania says of the votaress who was the boy's mother, 'And for her sake I will not part with him' (2.1.135–7).[1]

In Balanchine's *A Midsummer Night's Dream* – the one currently performed by New York City Ballet and, for practical purposes, the historical reconstruction we have that is closest to what Balanchine intended – both the Indian child and the bower Oberon must penetrate are physically realized.[2] Literalized and seen rather than described, they are presented to us as realities upon a stage. The histories behind both the child and the bower, however, are elided, passed over. What are the

[1] For important exceptions to this absence, see Margo Hendricks, '"Obscured by Dreams": Race, Empire, and Shakespeare's *A Midsummer Night's Dream*', *Shakespeare Quarterly*, 47 (1996), 37–60, and the production history it traces. My claim is not that productions do not choose to make use of the Indian child but that, in doing so, they ignore, as Balanchine does, his invisibility in the text, what Hendricks calls his imposed 'silence' (60). My thanks to Peter Herman, Lorraine Hirsch, Peter Holland, Julia Lupton, Pat Parker, Annie Saenger, Peter Saenger and Daniel Spector for wise input at earlier stages in drafts of this essay.

[2] Balanchine's *A Midsummer Night's Dream* opened at City Center in 1962 with Melissa Hayden as Titania and Edward Villella as Oberon. Five years later Balanchine supervised a film version of the original with much of the original cast but substituting Suzanne Farrell as Titania. See Anita Finkel, '*A Midsummer Night's Dream*', in *Reading Dance*, ed. Robert Gottlieb (New York, 2008), p. 168. In an interview Balanchine said, 'I wanted to leave my own ballet, as I have done it myself, for the future.' The film appeared to great critical acclaim briefly but disappeared 'when its producer Richard Davis, lost the rights to it in a poker game' (account from programme, Walter Reade Theater, 2004, archived at http://filmcomment.net/archive/wrt/programs/10-2004/midsummer04.htm). As such the question of what constitutes the best record of the 'original intention' is a particularly troubled one. Although a 're-mastered' and 'colour-corrected' version made by the British Film Institute and released by the Film Society of Lincoln Center with the cooperation of the George Balanchine Trust and the Cinémathèque de la Danse in Paris exists, its claim to capture the 'original' seems to me no more secure than any of the competing 'inferior' versions at the Cinémathèque de la Danse, all of which, with the camera's inevitable selective focus, are, in any case, partial. I have therefore based my reading on the current NYC ballet production(s) comparing key moments with the Cinémathèque de la Danse's version where necessary.

interpretive consequences of such trade-offs in Balanchine's production? What does the replacement of history with a set of visual images do to the argument of Shakespeare's play?

To answer this question we need to place these changes in the context of other alterations and elisions that Balanchine makes and to compare them to the moments of text from which they derive. First, let us look at the text Balanchine drew from and then, in roughly chronological order, at some of the changes he made. I want to argue first that it is not the case that any translation of a text into ballet, a virtually wordless medium, necessarily erases history but rather that Balanchine systematically erases a specific history: by removing Theseus's abduction of Hippolyta – his 'woo[ing]' of his bride with his sword – as well as other moments in the play which resonate with Oberon's theft of the child, Balanchine presents Oberon's penetration of Titania's bower as an isolated event, outside that history of coercion which (in the play) it epitomizes. In so doing, he dismantles a complicated and important argument Shakespeare makes. Second, I want to look at the question such a claim logically raises: does this mean that all Balanchine does is erase history? In fact, such a thing turns out to be impossible. What the ballet suggests is that visual images themselves carry histories: in stripping the histories that permeate *A Midsummer Night's Dream* from the objects and humans they belong to, Balanchine has necessarily created an alternative history, one he conveys iconographically.

Shakespeare's play begins with the memory of something like a rape, an act of sexual coercion, which Theseus plans to transform into a legitimate marriage.[3] 'Hippolyta, I wooed thee with my sword', he says, 'And won thy love doing thee injuries. / But I will wed thee in another key – / With pomp, with triumph, and with revelling' (1.1.16–19). No sooner has Theseus made this resolution though, than he undermines it by ordering another woman, Hermia, to yield what she calls her 'virgin patent' up to the man she explicitly does not want to marry. 'Stir up the Athenian youth to merriments', he tells Philostrate (1.1.12), but a moment later, when the Athenian youth show up in person,

he squelches them. 'Take time to pause', he tells Hermia, who wants to marry Lysander, 'and by the next new moon – / The sealing day betwixt my love and me / ... that day either prepare to die / For disobedience to your father's will, / Or else to wed Demetrius' (1.1.83–8). The play begins with the memory of something like a rape, which it has its ruler threaten to repeat as soon as he's said he will correct and transform it.

What begins by seeming like Theseus's personal past turns out to be built into Athenian law itself. 'I beg the ancient privilege of Athens', Egeus says, 'As [Hermia] is mine, I may dispose of her, / Which shall be either to this gentleman / Or to her death, according to our law' (1.1.41–4). Theseus himself suggests the disposal of a daughter's 'virgin patent' as property is a prerogative of Athenian law, not his personal wish, when he tells Hermia to 'fit [her] fancies' to her father's will, 'Or else the law of Athens yields you up – / Which by no means we may extenuate' (1.1.118–20). Thus, though the play starts out by imagining sexual coercion as a feature of Theseus's own personal past, by the end of Act 1 it is a principle built into Athenian law itself.

Nor does such coercion remain peculiar to Athens. As the play progresses, it seems increasingly as if sexual coercion is built into the nature of existence itself. Lysander, trying to persuade Hermia to elope, says he has a rich aunt whose house is seven leagues from Athens and that they can marry there, where 'the sharp Athenian law / Cannot pursue' [them] (1.1.162–3). But when the

---

[3] For extended discussion of this, see Laura Levine, 'Rape, Repetition and the Politics of Closure in *A Midsummer Night's Dream*', in *Feminist Readings of Early Modern Culture: Emerging Subjects*, ed. Valerie Traub, M. Lindsay Kaplan and Dympna Callaghan (Cambridge, 1996), pp. 210–28. For a brilliant discussion of rape as a founding principle of states and marriages, see Susanne L. Wofford's 'The Social Aesthetics of Rape: Closural Violence in Boccaccio and Botticelli', in *Creative Imitation: New Essays on Renaissance Literature in Honor of Thomas M. Greene*, ed. David Quint, Margaret W. Ferguson, G. W. Pigman III and Wayne A. Rebhorn (Binghamton, 1992), pp. 189–238.

lovers leave Athens for the forest, the forest turns out to be a mirror image of Athens. For there, Oberon plans to seize and redirect Titania's sexuality in order to get the child he covets. 'I'll watch Titania when she is asleep', he says, 'And drop the liquor of it in her eyes. / Be it on lion, bear, or wolf, or bull, / On meddling monkey, or on busy ape – / She shall pursue it with the soul of love' (2.1.177–82).

In Shakespeare's play, the world of the woods comments on the world of Athens by suggesting that rape is not simply a feature of Theseus's individual make-up, nor even simply embodied in the state, but built into existence, built into nature itself. (Later, Titania, preventing Bottom from leaving the wood, will say that even the flowers weep, lamenting some enforced chastity.) If inside the state fathers have the power of patriarchy, the power to dispose of daughters as property, fleeing the state doesn't solve but exacerbates this problem. Outside, in 'nature', rulers drug and violate their spouses for control over children.

In contrast, Balanchine's *A Midsummer Night's Dream* virtually erases any memory of rape. Balanchine begins in the forest, which seems to exist independently and without any reference to Athens. What we see first are the children of the company listed as butterflies, but appearing in various ladybug, moth-like and butterfly costumes. Oberon enters from 'his' side of the stage. Titania enters from 'hers' with her cavalier, the ballet's most conspicuous addition to the dramatis personae, carrying a huge leaf by way of canopy over her and her fairies and the Indian child. Oberon gestures to the Indian child. Titania mimes 'no'. Oberon picks up the Indian child and places his train in the child's hand. Titania gestures vehemently no. Oberon exits from the direction he came from. Titania and her train do the same. The scene yields to a spot of light in the middle where three drunken mechanicals circle each other with an ale can. The mechanicals yield to Oberon and Titania who repeat (almost) identically what they've done before, and as they exit they're replaced by Theseus and his Athenian advisors.

Before we see any scenes at Theseus's court, then, any scenes between Athenians at all, we see the dispute between Oberon and Titania. The ballet reduces the scenes in Athens to a kind of parenthesis, stripping what happens to Titania of its context and history. When Theseus does appear, his court is distinctly male, Hippolyta conspicuously absent, so that when she finally appears in scene 5 it is without any history of victimization.

Balanchine, then, presents as primary and central the world of the woods and as marginal and parenthetical the world of Athens. What are the consequences of this shift, which shaves off Theseus's and Hippolyta's history and most of what is said about Athenian law? Gone is any analysis about whether the criminality in the play lies in its ruler, its state or is simply a given of existence. Gone is the criminality itself. Gone (for the most part) is the question of how a state should conduct itself, whether, for instance, it should run on the principle of patriarchy, that daughters are property, or whether it should entertain ideas of personhood when dealing with women, acknowledge that daughters, like others, are persons. In Shakespeare's play this analysis is central. 'Demetrius is a worthy gentleman', Theseus says to Hermia, and when she tells him 'so is Lysander', his answer is:

> In himself he is,
> But in this kind, wanting your father's voice,
> The other must be held the worthier. (1.1.53–5)

Like so much else of Shakespeare's work, the play is involved in an ongoing analysis of whether people derive their worth, even their properties, from values others confer on them, or whether there is such a thing as an internal self, a state of personhood and hence an internal worth to a given person. The theory of patriarchy Theseus adopts assumes that value is conferred by the father. The theory of 'true love' Hermia adopts depends on the premise that each human is unique and not interchangeable. Thus one cannot be substituted for another. In Balanchine's opening scenes, this analysis has been removed. What we have instead – in the words of Wendy Whelan, New York City Ballet principal – is a custody suit, presented as the dilemma of the performance.[4] If Shakespeare's play begins by asking questions like 'What responses are possible when the state has a crime at its origin?' or 'Is it possible to transform a rape?' or 'To what agency should we attribute sexual violence: a single person with power, an institution, or an inevitable part of the make-up of the world?', Balanchine's production opens with questions like 'Who should get the child?'

The other characteristic of Balanchine's opening is its isolation and romanticization of Helena. Even before Oberon and Titania appear in response to the insects and fairies who summon them, Balanchine has Helena cross the stage, alone and sad. The insect world slows down to watch her, and Puck holds a leaf over her head, which she picks and puts to her eye. Puck makes a gesture of sympathy and the little insects flutter around her as she exits. By centralizing Helena and her sadness, the ballet presents much of what happens subsequently from her 'point of view', elevating her above the rest of the lovers, ennobling her. This point of view presupposes an answer to the question of whether there are persons, for in endowing any one point of view with superiority over another, and in that way differentiating it, the ballet implicitly imagines a state of personhood. In Shakespeare, when Egeus presents his problem to Theseus, he says, 'Stand forth, Demetrius – My noble lord, / This man hath my consent to marry [Hermia].' Identifying Lysander, he says, 'Stand forth Lysander. – And, my gracious Duke, / This hath bewitched the bosom of my child' (1.1.24–7), as if Theseus wouldn't otherwise be able to tell the difference between the two.[5] Although the distinction clearly serves the needs of exposition, it also playfully suggests the lovers are, but for what love confers on them, interchangeable. In some ways, Balanchine preserves this tweedledee/tweedledum aspect of things. Helena wears magenta, Hermia pale blue; their respective partners wear tunics to match. But by giving Helena this moment of isolated sadness, Puck's attention, the insects' attention and her own impassioned solo later in the ballet, Balanchine begins to differentiate Helena. In so doing, he further erodes the question

the play poses of whether humans are essentially interchangeable.

In Shakespeare, the world of the forest is 'real' in a metaphysical sense: it governs the world of the mortals below. But it is not the point of view the play opens from. In Balanchine, the world of the forest is primary in both ways. And if the ballet opens by presenting the forest as central, it also presents as 'real' (in the sense of being consummately visual and physical) what is only verbally described in Shakespeare's play. In Shakespeare, before we see anyone invade the bower, we already know of it as a place of beauty, an amalgam of smells and touch. We know it through words before Oberon enters it. He himself describes it in 2.1:

> I know a bank where the wild thyme blows
> Where oxlips and the nodding violet grows,
> Quite overcanopied with luscious woodbine,
> With sweet musk-roses, and with eglantine.
> (2.1.249–52)[6]

'Luscious', redolent with sexuality, spice and flower, violet and thyme, the bower is a container enclosing Titania: 'There sleeps Titania sometime of the night, / Lulled in these flowers with dances and delight' (2.1.253–4). Not only is it shaped like an enclosure or container, being 'overcanopied', but the bower contains within it other enclosures, other replications of the female body: 'And there the snake throws her enamelled skin, / Weed

---

[4] Wendy Whelan in conversation in 'Dances With Shakespeare: A Midsummer Night's Dream', Danny Kaye Playhouse, Hunter College, 8 June 2009.

[5] For a discussion of this indistinguishability or willed failure to differentiate, see René Girard's seminal discussion in 'Myth and Ritual in Shakespeare: *A Midsummer Night's Dream*', in *Textual Strategies: Perspectives in Post-Structuralist Criticism*, ed. Josué V. Harari (Ithaca, 1979), pp. 189–212, as well as my discussion in Levine, 'Rape, Repetition and the Politics of Closure', pp. 221, 225.

[6] Nancy Dalva claims that Balanchine was particularly enamoured with Oberon's description of the bower: 'Many of its [*A Midsummer Night's Dream's*] lines stayed with him, and as an adult he could recite (in Russian) many of the speeches, seeming particularly to like "I know a bank where the wild thyme blows, Where oxlips and the nodding violet grows".' See Nancy Dalva, 'We Can Dream, Can't We?', *danceviewtimes* (1 May 2006), 4:17.

wide enough to wrap a fairy in' (2.1.255–6). Even those objects with typically phallic associations like the snake have come to replicate the shape of containers.

The bower's intoxicating beauty is itself a kind of continuation of the history Titania provides of the child's meaning to her.[7] For in the 'spicèd Indian air' at night she used to engage in a kind of intimate play possible only between women: 'His mother was a vot'ress of my order, / And in the spicèd Indian air by night / Full often hath she gossiped by my side', Titania tells Oberon (2.1.123–5). She describes the way she and the votaress sat on Neptune's yellow sands:

Marking th'embarkèd traders on the flood,
When we have laughed to see the sails conceive
And grow big-bellied with the wanton wind,
Which she with pretty and with swimming gait
Following, her womb then rich with my young squire,
Would imitate, and sail upon the land
To fetch me trifles, and return again
As from a voyage, rich with merchandise.

(2.1.127–34)

As the bower physically replicates the female body, the story behind the child celebrates that capacity unique to women, the capacity to bear children. It is a nostalgia for this capacity, and the bond it creates between women, which lies at the centre of the play. It is precisely this bond, however, which has to be destroyed for the plot to advance. That the bower, the physicalization of femininity, is violated is only the externalization of what is happening elsewhere in the play – in the destruction of the promise Titania made to the votaress, in the violation of Titania's control over her own sexuality, in the replacement of Demetrius and Lysander in Hermia's and Helena's affections for each other. Because all this context – the various costs of the happily ever after – has been stripped from Balanchine's ballet, Titania's bower, like the forest itself, seems to exist outside of history.

Before the first dancer has even moved, there's what it's like to see the bower: the fairies, like Titania, are costumed in a shade of pink as close to the colour of flesh as possible. Although a screen of green leaves falls behind it, what the eye is drawn to is Titania's throne. Scallop-shaped and, like the fairies who surround it, covered in pale peach-pink coloured velvet and feathers, it is vulva-like. The eye keeps being drawn, somewhat uncomfortably, back to it. In its enclosure, Titania sits clad in the same pink flesh-coloured material. We see her silhouette before we see her, before the lights go up and in front of pairs of fairies and the Indian child, she and her cavalier begin to dance. In Balanchine, it is as if the spectator were complicit with Oberon in the act of penetrating the bower, as if what were on display were the openness of the female body itself. At this moment, rather than historicizing the female body as Shakespeare does, rather than presenting it in the context of the story of troubling transactions which have come to define it, the ballet appears to naturalize it, to render it up to us for the explicit pleasure of viewing as if this pleasure could be separated from its history. Here, the viewing of the female body and the elision of history go hand in hand. To look is to enjoy the specific illusion that bodies – female bodies in particular – can exist outside of history.

This illusion is deepened and textured by the actual *pas de deux* Titania has with her cavalier, one of Balanchine's most startling additions to the story line, for though Oberon jealously rages over the Indian child, neither he nor anyone else in the ballet seems particularly disturbed by the existence of the cavalier. The scene is built around the theme of interruption; the greater the pleasure, the more energetic the interruption. Titania and the cavalier dance. The music builds in a crescendo, and Puck interrupts just as Titania's body, in various combinations, opens. His interruption is always preceded by the music announcing him, and as it sounds Titania withdraws, hiding

---

7 For the two histories of the child, see Louis Montrose's seminal discussion in 'Shaping Fantasies of Elizabethan Culture: Gender, Power, Form', in *Rewriting the Renaissance*, ed. Margaret Ferguson, Maureen Quilligan and Nancy J. Vickers (Chicago, 1986) as well as the earlier and longer version of the essay '"Shaping Fantasies": Figurations of Gender and Power in Elizabethan Culture', *Representations*, 1 (1982), 61–94.

behind the throne, the cavalier either with her or exiting the stage. Puck approaches the Indian child, runs his hands through the air around the child's body or even picks him up, but the fairies always return to drive him off-stage. Before each interruption, though, Titania and the cavalier's *pas de deux* culminates in a series of lifts, in the most dramatic of which the cavalier raises her up as she does a *développé en avant*, her back arched and her legs open to us in what is almost a crotch shot. Here, too, we, like Oberon, gaze.

It is as if the ballet were intent on licensing, if only for a moment, the intimacy and the pleasure between Titania and her cavalier.[8] What Puck keeps trying to interrupt finally happens: the music is allowed to reach its climax and the cavalier carries Titania aloft and triumphant. The Indian child runs to the throne and watches and, a moment later, the tableau has transformed itself in to a kind of holy family, child enthroned, cavalier and fairies in attendance, the pleasure domesticated and contained within the tableau, the moments arguing in effect for a kind of alternate family.

Where the repetition of sexual coercion in Shakespeare's play argues, in effect, 'if you think you can escape institutionalized rape by leaving this city, see what happens when you turn to nature', the effect of the repetition of Puck's failed attempt to invade the bower is to heighten what he is not able to spoil, an idyllic alternative to Oberon himself. Framing the attempt with Titania, her cavalier, child enthroned and fairies in attendance, mutes the danger and dangles the possibility of an alternative family arrangement in front of us, even if only briefly.

This particular moment is symptomatic of the ballet's general impulse towards idealization and thus compatible with the kind of ennobled Oberon whose magnificent solo dominates the next scene.[9] In contrast to the upper body movements of the butterflies grouped in circles around him – they mostly do arm-waving movements to give the impression of flying – Oberon's solo isolates his kicks, his legs and the lower half of his body for viewing.[10] And indeed he does seem to defy gravity. Like the attention given to Helena at the

[8] For Finkel, '*A Midsummer Night's Dream*', p. 172, this *pas de deux* is one of a series of failed or incomplete *pas de deux*, incapable of reciprocity and therefore sterile. For her, because Act 1 is essentially preparatory, a series of 'blunted' dances between men and women, which will eventually yield to the ideal love of the *pas de deux* in Act 2, this *pas de deux* is interesting chiefly for what it lacks: 'Act 1 cannot have a real pas de deux in it, or Balanchine defeats his thematic purpose.' In its important focus on the *pas de deux* as part of a larger pattern, this brilliant essay nonetheless seems to me to ignore the specifically sexual details of the scene and particularly of its final moments.

[9] Finkel, '*A Midsummer Night's Dream*', p. 170, calls both Titania's *pas de deux* with the cavalier and Oberon's scene 3 dance 'partnered solos': 'Oberon and Titania may not dance with each other, but each *does* dance, and each has a partner – a partner in both cases so perfunctory as to be "not there". In Act 1 Titania and Oberon dance what are, in fact, partnered solos . . . Titania, "at home" . . . While observers have been puzzled by the dance of Titania and the cavalier, they have at least noticed the man in green; virtually no one has noted that Oberon's dazzling bravura scherzo is not solo but a dance with a female dancer who also executes difficult steps.' Where Finkel sees a symmetry between Titania and Oberon in the ballet – both, though dancing with partners, are in effect alone – Skiles Howard sees an asymmetry between the dances Oberon and Titania are imagined to do in the play: Titania's as communal, Oberon's as solitary. For the argument that Oberon not only rejects Titania's invitation to dance, but actually impedes it ('But with thy brawls thou hast disturbed our sport') and for the discussion of 'brawls' as French dances, see Skiles Howard, 'Hands, Feet and Bottoms: Decentering the Cosmic Dance in Shakespeare's Comedies', in *The Politics of Courtly Dancing in Early Modern England* (Amherst, 1998).

[10] See Edward Villella's account in '*A Midsummer Night's Dream*' of the way he had to keep his back straight, moving legs only: 'In the second sequence of the variation, he [Oberon] does a series of brisées ouvertes, behind. What I tried to do is not move any part of my upper body, just let my legs do all the work, as if I were floating, buzzing over the tops of the trees or above the ground fog . . . I had to be careful not to tense my muscles, not to hunch my neck and shoulders. Nothing in this role can be done abruptly. No shortcuts can be taken. The steps must be elongated; in preparation for the jump, the plié must be articulated in its entirety. I was beginning to understand the concept of slower being faster: in order to dance quickly, I had to take the time to articulate everything to acquire the speed': '*A Midsummer Night's Dream*', in *Reading Dance*, ed. Robert Gottlie (New York, 2008), pp. 1027–8. For an extended description of the way he learned the part (and shaped it), see pp. 1024–9.

beginning of the ballet, the solo has an ennobling function.

After gesturing his various butterflies off the stage, Oberon holds his conch shell up to his lips, a chord sounds and Oberon holds up his conch again. Puck enters landing on one knee. Oberon draws a semi-circle, pointing to what the lights coming up in the back reveal as a white flower. It is at this point that Balanchine presents us with the love-in-idleness, framing it in such a way that its history too is diminished: an arrow is discharged from off-stage. It goes into the flower, which turns red. The audience laughs.

In the arrow which turns the flower red Balanchine telescopes the whole history of the love-in-idleness. For in the story as Oberon tells it in the play, a mermaid on a dolphin's back uttered 'such dulcet and harmonious breath / That the rude sea grew civil at her song' (2.1.151–2). Although the song civilized the sea, certain stars were so excited that they 'shot madly from their spheres / To hear the sea-maid's music' (2.1.153–4). Cupid, flying between the 'cold moon' and the Earth, shot at a virgin (commonly assumed to be Elizabeth) but missed and his love bolt fell on a flower, then white but now 'purple, with love's wound', the love-in-idleness. All of this, the song which simultaneously civilizes and drives stars wild, the virgin queen, also a fairy queen, who escapes being shot and the 'wound' of the flower are here telescoped into the flower which lights up red on-stage at which the audience laughs (or claps depending on its mood). Balanchine leaves out the history of the flower as he does that of the bower, the Indian child and Titania's body. Here though, rather than naturalizing the thing he dehistoricizes, he does the opposite: the performance calls attention to the artificiality of the flower's elaborate history and provenance. Shakespeare has become the 'history' to which the production comically alludes. Like Brecht's titles which simultaneously narrate and diminish the events playing out on-stage beneath them, the electrical flower diminishes by comically framing the story of the love-in-idleness. It elides history by reducing it to a comic allusion.[11]

If scene 3 strips the love-in-idleness of its history by calling attention to the artificiality of the story, the next moments of the ballet cut, foreshorten and exaggerate details in Shakespeare, blunting many of the play's arguments about sexual violence. Thus, Oberon watches the pairs of lovers enter (Lysander and Hermia happily, Demetrius spurning Helena who weeps). While he goes off to find Puck, Hermia and Lysander re-enter coyly, look to make sure no one sees them kiss, and separate, blowing kisses to each other. Lysander exits to pick Hermia flowers. While he's picking them, Demetrius sneaks up on Hermia, who flees with him in tow. Oberon points Puck in Demetrius's direction, but Puck mistakes Lysander for Demetrius and switches the love-in-idleness with Lysander's bouquet. What Balanchine erodes from these whimsical moments are the threats of sexual violence which Shakespeare sounds throughout the play. There Lysander exits not to pick flowers but because Hermia fears for her virginity and sends him to sleep elsewhere. In Shakespeare Hermia dreams about danger and on awakening describes her dream ('Methought a serpent ate my heart away' (2.2.155)). Removing both the threat to Hermia's virginity and the sexually charged image of the serpent, Balanchine sends Lysander off to pick flowers. Gone too is Demetrius's implied threat to rape Helena. Vacillating between the threat that he'll leave her to the 'wild beasts' ('I'll run from thee . . . / And leave thee to the mercy of wild beasts' (2.1.227–8)) and the threat that he'll leave her to his own impulses ('You do impeach your modesty too much, / To leave the city and commit yourself / Into the hands

---

[11] In Brecht's work, one might argue, the titles work in the opposite way. Thus when Brecht begins the third scene of *Mother Courage* with a title that says '[Mother Courage's] honest son dies', we are supposed to be prevented from feeling too much about the loss of the son by knowing in advance it was going to happen. In theory, at least, the effect Brecht seeks when he 'sets forth the text' is historicization. See 'The Modern Theatre Is the Epic Theatre' for discussion of 'setting forth the text' (pp. 33–42) and 'Alienation Effects in Chinese Acting' (pp. 91–9) for his concept of historicization in John Willett, ed., *Brecht on Theatre* (New York, 1982).

of one that loves you not', he tells Helena, 'To trust the opportunity of night, / ... / With the rich worth of your virginity' (2.1.214–9)). Demetrius both embodies and warns of the sexual violence that always seems imminent in this world. Balanchine has cut such warnings.

Similarly, by foreshortening what takes two acts to unfold in the play into one extended scene, and exaggerating Puck's mistakes, Balanchine strips the material between the lovers of most of its sexual content, and heightens its comic potential. Thus Balanchine has Helena cross the stage three times as Puck grows increasingly frustrated before allowing her to virtually trip over the drugged Lysander, who wakes to love her. In the ultimate 'fore-shortening' he has Hermia, Helena and Lysander do a *pas de trois*, both women entwined around the same man. Puck has to actually peer under Hermia's hair before he recognises he's doctored the wrong Athenian man, and Oberon kicks him in the butt when he sends him off-stage to find Demetrius. In a repetition of the same pair of exaggerated gestures (the lover pleads; the beloved throws back the plea) Balanchine has Helena reject Lysander, Lysander Hermia, Hermia Demetrius and Demetrius Helena again, all in a matter of minutes. Here too, the audience's laugh, like the laugh at the electrical love-in-idleness lighting up red, signals the reduction of a complicated history to an absurdity.

In Shakespeare, Helena, like Titania, has a long speech about the bonds between women. 'O is all forgot?' she asks Hermia, cataloguing the moments of oneness they shared as girls. Sewing one sampler, sitting on one cushion, warbling one song, they grew together, 'Like to a double cherry: seeming parted, / But yet an union in partition' (3.2.210–11). 'And will you rend our ancient love asunder', Helena asks (3.2.216). Gone too is the echo of this kind of nostalgia. Helena's dance of grief, though it sets her apart, is not 'about' the bonds between women.

But if the lovers' scenes have been stripped of their arguments about sexuality, Titania's have not. Set in Titania's bower, dramatically the goal of scene 4 is to get Titania to sleep. To effect this,

the bower descends. The fairies emerge in a line, holding hands, weaving between each other, in and out of the chain they themselves form. Titania enters with long, loose hair and dances. The fairies' lullaby song begins. Titania moves into her throne. The fairies dance. There is more song. The song ends and Titania sleeps. The fairies turn her throne around.

To say this, though, is hardly to get at the heart of the scene. First, there is the song itself, which is sung aloud in the ballet:

> You spotted snakes with double tongue,
> Thorny hedgehogs, be not seen;
> Newts and blindworms, do no wrong;
> Come not near our Fairy Queen.

> (2.2.9–12)

The song itself constitutes a break with all that has come before in that it is the first moment in which words from the play are articulated, albeit as song. But the first fairy soprano who sings the verse has such an extraordinarily high operatic voice that most of what is audible is the repeated line 'Come not near our fairy queen'. From the chorus 'Philomel with melody, / Sing in our sweet lullaby; / Lulla, lulla, lullaby; lulla lulla lullaby', most of what is audible is 'lullaby'. In having the first articulated words of the ballet be 'come not near our Fairy Queen' (in making an exception to the wordlessness that is ballet for these words) the scene both titillates our desire to 'come near' and calls attention to the prohibition against us doing so. We are made to want to gaze even as we are frustrated in this endeavour, for we are voyeurs only until the throne is turned around from us as well. If the principle is that the more energetic the interruption, the greater the pleasure, then here we might speculate the greater the prohibition, the greater the desire to see. There is a drama going on between the spectacle and the audience: the drama of what and when we are allowed to see.

The desire to look is ultimately going to be satisfied in the scene, but it is fulfilled in a way that reinvents what it is we are looking at. If the scene began by singing about Titania's vulnerability, it very soon presents us with an image of her strength and power. Before this can happen though, a number of other events must take place: first, the fairies must exit and Hermia dance her dance of grief. The mechanicals must arrive, Quince holding up the scroll that is Wall, which Puck must knock over. Bottom must get the ass's head put on him and Quince mime shrieking gestures, while Puck laughs hysterically. When all this has happened, and the mechanicals have exited, Puck will need to point in front of Bottom (now wearing the ass's head) and Bottom will need to point back in reply (apparently meaning 'I should follow?') as he indeed follows Puck off-stage.

A moment later, Oberon will enter, turn the throne around and pull it further front downstage, the better for us to see. We will watch as he (not Puck) waves the love-in-idleness under Titania's nose, and Puck leads Bottom out and places him seated with ass-head in front of Titania and Titania wakes, stretches, yawns and rises. It is here that what we are looking at seems to have changed. It is here that iconographically Titania, with long, loose hair on her scallop shell throne, begins to draw on another set of associations. If one turned the shell on its side and captured, as a still, single frame, the moment of Titania rising out of it, she would be Botticelli's Venus, rising from the half shell. The leaves that covered her bower in scene 2 would be the leaves in *La Primavera*, Botticelli's other depiction of Venus, which Diaghilev showed Balanchine and which Balanchine said 'stayed with [him] for [his] whole life'. The flowers that cover Titania's train would be those that adorn Flora. Charles Dempsey writing about the Graces in that painting comments on the idea of *beneficium* – one grace gives, another receives and the third gives and receives, forming an unbroken chain, because the nature of benefits is to keep replenishing, flowing from giver to receiver.[12] The fairies who weave in and out of their own chain, hands clasped, are those graces, in their transparent, flowing gowns. Rising, erect and loose-haired in front of her scallop shell, Titania assumes the properties of Botticelli's Venus. If scene 2 made us complicit with Oberon's gaze, and this scene began by frustrating our desire to see, in the moment Titania rises we are again allowed

to look, but what we are looking at is not an image stripped of history, but a picture with a long and complex history. What we are looking at is a Botticelli Venus.[13]

---

[12] For Balanchine's description of seeing *La Primavera* in the Uffizi see Solomon Volkov, *Balanchine's Tchaikovsky: Interviews with George Balanchine* (New York, 1985). After trashing Prokofiev, who he says was bothered by the success of Stravinsky's music, Balanchine says: 'Diaghilev not only helped me to understand the subtleties of Stravinsky's music, he explained painting to me, too. He opened my eyes to Botticelli. We were in Florence together. Diaghilev led me to the Uffizi Gallery, sat me in front of Botticelli's *La Primavera*, and said, "Look at it". Then he went off with Lifar and Kochno to have lunch . . . When Diaghilev returned to the Uffizi, full, I was sitting in front of the Botticelli, hungry and angry. Diaghilev asked me, "Well, do you understand anything?" Of course I had seen that *La Primavera* was a wonderful painting, but I was angry with Diaghilev. Lifar and Kochno were his favorites, he dressed them well and fed them well. And, of course, they played at being great connoisseurs of art. To spite Diaghilev, I said I didn't understand a thing: well, a painting like any other, so what? Nothing special. Diaghilev lost his temper then. But actually I had liked Botticelli very much. And his *Primavera* has stayed with me for my whole life. Natasha Makarova recently sent me a Christmas card, and on it is Botticelli's *Primavera* . . . I know that Natasha wants that card to suggest a ballet idea to me. She somehow realized that I liked Botticelli' (pp. 211–12).

Despite Balanchine's denials about the influence of painting in general ('Still, even though I have worked with many now-famous artists, I don't get my ideas from looking at paintings') it is clear that both the *Primavera* and *The Birth of Venus* stayed with him in meaningful ways during *A Midsummer Night's Dream*. Interestingly, the *Primavera* and *The Birth of Venus* are perennially confused by those who write about Titania's throne in ways that suggest the generative conflation of the two. Thus Peter Harvey repeatedly calls Titania's throne her 'Primavera throne' though, of course, the throne draws on the shell in *The Birth of Venus*. See Peter Harvey, 'Designing for George Balanchine: Diaries of Ballet Productions, Part Two', *Dance Chronicle*, 20 (1997), 295–326. For Charles Dempsey's discussion of the differences between the two Venuses – the *Primavera* one clothed, the other naked – as well as a discussion of their mythical ancestors, see Dempsey, *Portrayal of Love* (Princeton, 1997) quoted at length below, especially pp. 44–9.

[13] See Charles Dempsey's definitive and masterful *The Portrayal of Love* as well as his earlier 'Botticelli's Three Graces', *Journal of the Warburg and Courtauld Institutes*, 34 (1971), 326–30, for the description of the graces, the transparent, loose-fitting dresses they wear and the concept of *beneficium* and

If Balanchine erases various problematic aspects of his characters' pasts, it is a touchstone of his method, his tendency towards citation, to do just the opposite with forms. Thus the *pas de deux* that follows interrogates its own form. It does so, characteristically, through inversion, for when Titania and Bottom begin to dance they offer a complete inversion of what it means to dance a *pas de deux*.[14] After placing Bottom in her throne (the second character to enjoy that place) and crowning him with garlands, Titania dances with Bottom until he falls to the ground, where he crawls around on all fours. Tempting him with ferns, she lifts him (in a kind of parody of the lifts she herself has performed in the cavalier's arms) and eventually partners him from behind. The scene offers an inversion of what it means to dance a classical ballet, both because of Bottom's clumsiness and his exaggerated fumbles and because the scene reverses the positions between women and men. But even as it inverts the grace and polarity a *pas de deux* strives for, this *pas de deux* breaks down into highly exaggerated and ill-executed actions those things assumed to be necessary to partner another person. In so doing it not only indicates what these actions are but what they historically have been: As Bottom 'dips' Titania, at the climax of the scene, he breaks any semblance of the fourth wall, and looks out slowly and directly at the audience, as if to say, 'What am I getting myself into?' By isolating and freezing 'the dip' in a method analogous to the way the choreography isolated Oberon's kicks, or froze the lovers in positions during the funny *pas de trois*, Balanchine offers a series of juxtapositions: this *pas de deux* to the tradition of romantic ones that have preceded it, this moment in a bower to its antecedents both within the ballet and outside in Italian paintings. Even as he rewrites the histories of bodies within his ballets, he calls attention to the way the ballets themselves are rewritings: this is one of the tensions of Balanchine, that while the ballets' 'stories' may eclipse various elements in their sources, the forms themselves are virtually citational, acknowledging the various traditions they quote.

Everything lyrical and languorous about Titania's bower scene is replaced by the turbulence of scene 5, the last scene in Act I. At the scene's centre, and in contrast to Puck's frantic, exhausted activity – his impersonations of Demetrius and Lysander to each other, his shadow-boxing with himself, his desperate attempts to catch Helena's tears, interrupted by the need to carry off Hermia pummelling the air – is Hippolyta with her bow, hunting with her spectral white hounds. She is both spatially at the centre of the stage and her motion – the *fouetté* after *fouetté* at the heart of her solo – is 'centred', balanced, circular, poised, while Puck pantomimes the breathlessness of

---

its sources. Here is Dempsey in *The Portrayal of Love*, quoting Seneca's essay *De benificiis*: 'Why do the sisters hand in hand dance in a ring which returns upon itself? For the reason that a benefit passing its course from hand to hand returns nevertheless to the giver; the beauty of the whole is destroyed if the course is anywhere broken, and it has most beauty if it is continuous and maintains an uninterrupted succession' (pp. 33–4). Dempsey's gloss a moment later ends: 'Described purely in terms of gesture, the cycle of the giving, receiving, and returning of benefits could hardly be more poetically and accurately limned, and it is especially fitting that the cycle of liberality should be indicated by gesture alone – in fact purely as dance – since benefits are abstract and intangible in nature' (pp. 34–5). For his discussion of the graces as both unclothed and clothed in loose transparent gowns, see his discussion on p. 34: 'Seneca characterises the Graces as clothed in loosened and transparent gowns (*soluta et perlucida veste*), dancing with their hands intertwined, and accompanied by Mercury. These are exactly the features that distinguish Botticelli's Graces.' For the complicated chain of evidence about the meanings of the clothed versus unclothed Graces, see Dempsey, *Portrayal of Love*, p. 44.

14 For Finkel, '*A Midsummer Night's Dream*', p. 169, this is only one of the ballet's 'very apparent and entertaining variations on the pas de deux'. She says, 'To face the awesome task of abstracting Shakespeare from its verbal context, the choreographer chose one very simple, strong, basic dance image . . . one feature of classical dancing which is the cornerstone of ballet, its eternal subject matter: the pas de deux . . . At the very end of *A Midsummer Night's Dream* is one of Balanchine's most lyrical and romantic pas de deux. But to reach this vision of perfect beauty and harmony, Balanchine takes us, delightfully, through a series of other pas de deux that illustrate stages at various distances from that ideal.' For Finkel, Titania's and Bottom's inversion is one in this series.

dragging bodies across the stage and nearly (again) mismatches lovers, by putting Demetrius next to the sleeping Hermia.

Before the end of the scene, Theseus will propose to Hippolyta on bended knee and they will hug – any suggestion of the play's original violence being cut. Hippolyta appears for the first time in this scene. Puck will get the lovers sorted, and they will appeal to Theseus, who will bless them, Hippolyta reminding him to include Helena and Demetrius. Titania will lead Bottom out with garlands and Oberon will 'cure' her of her folly. She will voluntarily, even cheerily it seems, hand the Indian child over to Oberon. Before the end of the ballet we will see what Shakespeare would never show us, not the botched 'Pyramus and Thisbe' the mechanicals present as an alternative to 'The battle with the centaurs, to be sung / By an Athenian eunuch to the harp' (5.1.44–5) but a full-fledged wedding masque, in which ideal love is danced for (and by) the three wedding couples. Before any of this can happen, though, what we see is Hippolyta with her dogs and her bow, the fogs spilling out into the orchestra pit. This is Hippolyta triumphant, not Hippolyta abducted with a sword.

In Act 4 of Shakespeare, Theseus offers his bride-to-be the chance to hear the 'music of [his] hounds' (4.1.105), and Hippolyta remembers having heard a similar sound when Spartan hounds bayed a bear in Crete. She claims she never heard so 'musical a discord' (4.1.117). In Balanchine both future promise and past memory are simply interpolated into the present tense as if they were happening. Dogs bound through the scene in a kind of eternal present. Balanchine doesn't just de-historicize Hippolyta's past here (or Theseus's promise). He presents 'history' as if it had become the present. If Titania is Venus rising from the half shell, Hippolyta, doing flawless *fouetté* after *fouetté*, bow in hand, is Artemis chaste and transformed, Diana with her dogs, capable of dismembering Actaeon for looking.[15] In juxtaposing the two for us, Balanchine simultaneously invites us to look and warns of the danger of doing so.

We might imagine that if Balanchine erases the history that Shakespeare patiently (and patently) exposes, he is in effect erasing history itself. But this would be a fallacy. For in rewriting the iconography of the play, he has instead offered us a different history. If Titania's body offers us the fantasy that we may gaze on the female body with impunity, Hippolyta reminds us of that body whose sight destroyed the male who gazed upon it. Balanchine does not present us with a set of images divorced from history. For in divorcing these images from the histories that they belonged to, he inevitably and necessarily attaches to them alternative histories. Instead of the body wooed with the sword he brings us Venus and Diana as emblems of female power, with all the long histories those images have worn.

---

[15] For Titania *as* Diana, see Leonard Barkan, 'Diana and Actaeon: The Myth as Synthesis', *English Literary Renaissance*, 10 (1980), 317–59.

A MIDSUMMER NIGHT'S DREAM
ON RADIO: THE OREGON SHAKESPEARE
FESTIVAL'S RADIO SERIES

MICHAEL P. JENSEN

Shakespeare plays produced for the mass media tend to be studied as texts, in the larger context of television or filmed Shakespeare, and sometimes as part of the work of an auteur such as Kenneth Branagh or Laurence Olivier. It is rare to study mass media productions for what they tell us about the organization that created them. Such an approach can be of interest, as it is with the three radio series produced by the Oregon Shakespeare Festival (OSF).[1]

OSF is unusual in a number of ways. It is the longest-lived Shakespeare Festival in North America, producing its first two plays in 1935.[2] OSF boasts of its outdoor stage designed to the dimensions of the Fortune Theatre contract in its backstage tours and publicity materials.[3] In 1983, OSF became the first Shakespeare festival to win a Regional Tony Award.[4] It is the only US Shakespeare festival to have a contract with an audiobook publisher: Blackstone Audiobooks' *Hamlet* used most of the cast of OSF's 2010 production. It was released in May 2011 and nominated for a Grammy Award, a unique honour. The Festival's 2011 production of *Measure for Measure* is being recorded the week I write this and should be available by the time you read it.[5] The Old Vic and OSF are the only Shakespeare companies to have had radio series.[6]

OSF thrived in the small town of Ashland located in sparsely populated Southern Oregon, then more than six hours from a major city,[7] in part because of exposure on its national radio programme. My premise is that these broadcasts helped the Festival build an audience large enough

to sustain its growth until OSF became a modern, self-sustaining, and fully professional regional

My thanks to the archivists at the Oregon Shakespeare Festival for their help researching this article: Lead Archivist Maria DeWeerdt, Archivist Debra Griffith, Fellowships Assistantships Internships and Residencies Archives Assistant Gwyn Hervochon, and especially now retired Archivist Kathleen F. Leary who knew where everything was buried. Thanks also to my wonderful friend and mentor Bernice W. Kliman, who died as I was completing this article.

1 The company was known as the Oregon Shakespearean Festival until 1988. The shorter name was often used by others prior to the official change. See note 58 for an example.
2 The Old Globe Theatre in San Diego opened the same year as an exhibit in the California Pacific International Exposition and was retired with the Exposition. The current Old Globe administration began in 1954. See Franklin J. Hildy, 'Why Elizabethan Spaces?', in *Elizabethan Performances in North American Spaces*, vol. 12, Theatre Symposium Series, (Tuscaloosa, 2004), pp. 98–120.
3 The 1599 contract supplied the dimensions for the stage, which was first used when OSF reopened in 1947. The choice of the word 'boasts' was deliberate. OSF is proud of its 'authentic' stage, mentioning its imitation of the Fortune stage often but seldom noting that the Fortune lacked the steps leading to the stage from the voms and that the tiring house at the back is an original design. The Fortune stage was elevated above the level of OSF's stage.
4 The Arena Stage in Washington DC won the first Regional Tony in 1976. OSF is one of just three self-identifying Shakespeare organizations to win the award, with the Utah Shakespearean Festival following in 2000 and the Chicago Shakespeare Theatre in 2008. The Old Globe Theatre in San Diego won in 1984. It has a summer Shakespeare programme, but does not identify itself as a Shakespeare festival.
5 My thanks to actor Anthony Heald, who plays the Duke, for telling me about the latter release in a conversation on 1 August 2011.

theatre. Obviously, any successful enterprise as large as OSF has many factors contributing to its success. We should bear in mind Ashland's charm as a town, the many outdoor recreational activities that made not just OSF but the greater Rogue Valley a tourist destination, plus the Festival's other marketing efforts: direct mailings, newspaper and magazine advertising, television and radio commercials, newspaper interviews, community outreach, newsletters, education programmes and recommendations from satisfied audience members. Each contributed to the Festival's growth and success. This article looks at OSF's broadcast of *King Lear*, their first annual programme from the National Broadcasting Company (NBC) in 1951, then three broadcasts of *A Midsummer Night's Dream* in 1966, 1971 and 1979.[8] Each will be accompanied by a look at the corresponding growth of OSF in reputation and attendance, summarized in a statistical table at the end. The *A Midsummer Night's Dream* broadcasts will be studied in some detail to understand the challenges of turning this text into a radio play, looking at the cultural features that both informed and challenged the content of the broadcasts. This concentration on a single play has the additional benefit of showing the different ways that OSF approached this script, and the Festival's growth can also be seen in these comparisons. To set the context, I begin with a look at OSF's radio programmes prior to 1951 and comment on the nature of radio drama in the US at that time.

The Festival's first broadcast was a thirty-minute *The Taming of the Shrew* on NBC that went out live from the Golden Gate International Exposition on Treasure Island in the San Francisco Bay, where the Festival had travelled and sold out two performances in the summer of 1939. Though the network would later become OSF's radio home for more than twenty years, there is no direct connection between this broadcast and the series that began in 1951.

The Festival received more radio exposure in 1950, though not in the United States. The government-sponsored Voice of America, which mostly broadcast behind the Iron Curtain, produced a thirty-minute programme about the

Festival, possibly airing as early as 20 August 1950. It included a history of the Festival by founder Angus Bowmer, a lecture on why Shakespeare should be performed and not just read by Stanford professor and OSF education director Margery Bailey, and excerpts from that season's four plays, *Henry IV, Part 1*, *The Comedy of Errors*, *Antony and Cleopatra* and *As You Like It*.[9] This one-off

---

[6] The Old Vic presented an eight-part serial adapting both *Henry IV* plays in forty-five minute instalments on Thursday evenings from 31 May to 19 July 1945 on the BBC. The BBC also used Old Vic casts to broadcast abridgements of *Richard II* and *The Merchant of Venice* for schools in 1929, and the company supplied two thirty-minute episodes for the series *From the Theatre in Wartime* in 1942, *The Merchant of Venice* and *Othello*. Other Old Vic and Shakespeare Memorial Theatre plays were heard many times on the BBC, but these were occasional broadcasts using the casts of a stage production. The Stratford Festival of Canada appeared on the Canadian Broadcasting Corporation infrequently for several years from 1998 but, again, not as a regularly scheduled programme. There have been several series in which networks aired their own Shakespeare companies or hired actors for special Shakespeare broadcasts. Most notable are BBC Wales (1923–24), BBC London (1923–present), the CBC (1937–38, 1944–45, 1947–57), the Australian Broadcasting Corporation (1936–38) and NBC Radio in the US on the programmes *Radio Guild* (1929–36), *Streamlined Shakespeare* (1937), *Great Plays* (1938–41) and the *Columbia Shakespeare Cycle* on the Columbia Broadcasting System (CBS, 1937). All broadcast occasional Shakespeare programmes as well as these series.

[7] With the completion of Interstate Highway 5, Ashland is now about five hours from both Portland, Oregon and San Francisco, California.

[8] This play was chosen because it is one of only five that were presented in all three of OSF's radio formats, the broadcast dates are uniquely placed to map the ways that OSF evolved as a company and, unlike some of the broadcasts of other plays, each is available to study in script or audio form, though the third of the four disks of the 1979 broadcast is missing.

[9] Anonymous, 'Ashland Festival Gains Approval of Voice of America', *Medford Mail Tribune*, 20 August 1950, no page number. The date of the broadcast is not given, but the article does say that a tape of the programme was flown to New York, perhaps indicating some haste to get it on the air. This clipping, like most in this article, was found in the OSF Archive. In these early days, newspaper and magazine articles and reviews of Festival shows were cut out and pasted in a scrapbook. Page numbers, and occasionally the article title and name of publication were clipped off before the article or review was glued to the scrapbook page. Reporters are

broadcast did not directly influence NBC's decision to put OSF on the air, though the programme was engineered by KMED in Medford, Oregon which was instrumental in getting OSF on NBC.

Radio drama was in decline by 1951 when OSF began its annual broadcast. Comedy, variety, soap opera and dramatic programmes had already begun to migrate to television, increasingly leaving radio to recorded music. With even the most popular radio programmes losing audience and sponsors, the Festival's show could only exist as a sustaining programme.

Sustaining programmes kept US networks on the air. The first networks in most English-speaking nations were government run, broadcasting Shakespeare as part of their educational and cultural programming. The British, Canadian and Australian Broadcasting Corporations are still organized this way.[10] The United States Government decided against running radio, instead licensing commercial companies to broadcast.[11] Without government financing, these companies were run for profit by selling air-time to sponsors. Martin Esslin exaggerated when he wrote that US radio was 'little more than a minor branch of the advertising business',[12] but exaggerations sometimes make a valid point.

Because radio frequencies are legally owned by the public, broadcasters were required to prove themselves worthy of this public trust by broadcasting some non-commercial, educational and public service programming. If they did not, their profitable licences would not be renewed. While all but ignored today, this requirement was taken very seriously from the twenties into the seventies. Broadcasters took pride in meeting their obligation with programmes intended to be of high quality even if they drew a very small listenership. These non-commercial shows were called sustaining programmes, because they were not sponsored but sustained by the network.[13] Nearly all Shakespeare broadcasts in the United States were sustaining programmes. Though NBC regarded the OSF broadcast as sustaining fare, the Festival created a long commercial to increase attendance at its theatre.

Jennings Pierce worked at NBC's Los Angeles headquarters as the West Coast Stations Relations Manager before coming north in 1950 to manage NBC affiliate KMED, twelve miles north of Ashland. Pierce gave the station a high profile, creating several national programmes.[14] As part of this initiative, Pierce enticed an old friend from his NBC years, Andrew C. Love, commonly called Andy, to visit the Rogue Valley for the hunting and fishing and to see if Love thought the Festival was worth putting on the air. Love and his wife Hazel came during their 1950 vacation and were charmed by Ashland and the Festival. Love persuaded the network to air a show the next year. As with the Voice of America programme, the engineering would be handled by KMED.

Other people could probably have produced OSF for radio, but no one was more ideal than Andy Love. Love began his career in music, working for RCA Victor and Columbia records before going to NBC in 1931. At the network he

---

not always indentified on even the intact articles. Citations include all identifying information in the OSF Archive. I hope that all these articles may be consulted in the future, though as I write OSF Archivists are purging selected clippings.

10 New Zealand broadcasting is more difficult to summarize with the government authority emerging years later to organize and standardize independent stations. I leave them out of consideration because I have been unable to document any Shakespeare broadcasts on New Zealand radio until much later. I have not studied English language broadcasting in Africa.

11 The US government finally got into publicly financed radio when the Corporation for Public Broadcasting was established in 1967, and it in turn created National Public Radio, which began broadcasting in 1970. See Ron Lackman, *The Encyclopedia of American Radio: An A–Z Guide to Radio from Jack Benny to Howard Stern* (New York, 2000), p. 205.

12 Martin Esslin, 'Contemporary English Drama and the Mass Media', *English*, 18:5 (1969), 6.

13 A second type of sustaining programme was a promising commercial-type show that had not found a sponsor. It was broadcast in the hope of finding one.

14 Art Chipman, *KMED The First Half Century: 'The Biography of a Great Radio Station'* (Medford, OR, 1972), pp. 29–30, 33.

produced and directed[15] *The Kraft Programme*, a variety show (1933), *The Eternal Light*, soap opera style dramatizations of religious dilemmas (1948), the quiz show *Noah Webster Says* (1950), the sitcom *The Truitts* (1950–51) and, though they came later, Frank Sinatra's adventure show *Rocky Fortune* and live broadcasts of the Academy Awards (both 1953–54). Love was a well-rounded producer who broadcast everything except news and documentary programmes. He won a Christopher Award and three Peabody Awards for excellence in broadcasting.[16] Most to the point, Love was then producing literary adaptations for sustaining broadcasts. *NBC University Theater* adapted novels for the air, running weekly from 30 July 1948 to 14 February 1951. The short story adaptation programme *NBC Presents: Short Story* began the next week, airing from 21 February 1951 to 30 May 1952. Love was NBC's current producer of adapted literature.

Andy Love came to Ashland every year for three decades to put the Festival on the air. He added a syndicated programme upon his retirement from NBC, about which there is more below. The first NBC broadcast, *King Lear*, was presented on 11 August 1951. An excerpt from the play split airtime with a shameless plug for the Festival. It was a thirty-minute commercial.

The first fourteen minutes are the most commercial-like. Starting with a bold fanfare, OSF is introduced with these words from the announcer:

In Ashland, Southern Oregon, sixteen years ago, in the lush valley of the River Rogue, on a stage like the one Shakespeare used to use, a play was produced as he saw it produced in his own day. The results were a little amazing. Suddenly, Shakespeare had returned to the people.

The entire introduction is overwritten. The grander sounding 'River Rogue' replaces Rogue River, the correct name. Embellishing words such as *lush* and *amazing* add to the effect. The introduction positions OSF as Shakespeare's ambassador to the world in several ways. The point making 'a stage like the one Shakespeare used to use' replaces what OSF usually calls its 'Elizabethan stage'. Listeners are later told that the plays are produced in repertory, 'in the manner that Shakespeare himself did them'. The announcer sounds impressed throughout, especially when he says 'Ashland is the Shakespeare center of America'.[17] He later says that 'Shakespeare is fun', and notes the Festival's 'important stature', without explaining what that means. Noted are the souvenir booths, Elizabethan flower gardens, strolling madrigal singers and Elizabethan country dancers, each contributing to the illusion that visiting Ashland is like visiting Shakespeare's England. Pierce then comes to the microphone to interview Bowmer, Texas-born actress Barbara Huggins, English actor John Brebner, New York-based actor Richard Graham and Professor Bailey.

Bowmer claims that Shakespeare is 'the greatest showman of them all', and that people of every age love to see Shakespeare performed. He adds that 'gifted, experienced and successful actors' perform at OSF. This cues the interviews with three of the gifted, experienced and successful actors. Huggins says that she would rather act in Ashland than with Maurice Evans, which she did a short time before. Brebner prefers Ashland too, though he recently worked with Katherine Cornell. Graham claims OSF gives audiences a more authentic experience than productions in England, and that OSF does Shakespeare better than English companies. Bailey adds that it is better to see Shakespeare's plays performed than to read them, that OSF offers 'living theater, presenting living Shakespeare', and makes it clear that the company does not traffic in the

---

15 Working differently from the standard practice in film and television where producers and directors seldom have the same job, radio producers usually directed their broadcasts. Dates are for the years Love produced these series and do not indicate all of the years a series was on the air.

16 Faith McCullough, 'Andrew Love Again Visits, Does Festival Recording Work', *Medford Daily Mail*, 29 March 1970, no page number.

17 This phrase may have been taken from a headline in the *New Haven Register* newspaper. The 17 June 1951 article about the Festival was titled 'City in Oregon Becomes US Shakespeare Center', no page number. This was pasted on the same scrapbook page as articles about the *King Lear* broadcast.

'experimental nonsense' that mars some productions. She ironically concludes that 'there is no commercialism in Ashland'.[18]

Each interview contributes to the Festival's underlying message that listeners should come to Ashland for the best, most authentic Shakespeare in the world delivered in a way that everyone will like. This seems hyperbolic today, and perhaps did at the time, but the speakers sound sincere. Not mentioned is the fact that the shows were directed by and cast with volunteers, mostly acting students and teachers. People from the community sewed costumes, made props, erected sets, brewed coffee and worked the souvenir booths. There was seldom more than one equity actor in the cast at this time, though OSF put on a pretty good amateur show. In addition to this fourteen-minute preamble, the broadcast included an introduction to the play and closing credits. This left a scant thirteen minutes for the excerpt from *King Lear*, so only the first scene was given. This excerpt should also be seen as an advertisement for OSF, since it was the Festival's chance to demonstrate the high quality of their performances. This required some trickery.

King Lear played to near capacity crowds for three weeks, actors filling the 1200-seat Elizabethan Theatre with performances large enough to reach the back row. Large playing comes across as bombastic on radio, and that was Love's challenge. Taking the material staged by director William Oyler, Love taught the actors to give smaller performances directed to the microphone. Bits of bombast linger in the performances of Huggins's Goneril and Thornton Shively's Kent, while Jean Leonard (Cordelia) and Ross Hogue (France) sound like the amateurs they were, but overall the *King Lear* portion of the broadcast comes off well.[19] Listeners hear the stage characterizations, but with the intimate approach of a professional radio drama.

There are few cuts, so the scene feels fairly whole and satisfying, and ends with an invitation for listeners to enjoy the complete play in Ashland. The programme was heard on about a hundred NBC affiliates all over America.

Results were immediate and lingering. Louis Wright of the Folger Shakespeare Library praised the programme in the Washington, DC papers.[20] An 'unusually large number of actors' auditioned for the 1952 season,[21] which was lengthened from three weeks to a full month to accommodate the extra demand for tickets.[22] The second broadcast in the series went out that year, with the result that in 1953 OSF was visited by people from all forty-eight states, two future states and ten other countries, boosting total attendance by fifty per cent. OSF announced plans to build balcony seating to accommodate its growing audience.[23] The programme went onto Armed Forces Radio in 1954, giving OSF a limited international audience. *Shakespeare Quarterly* began reviewing OSF on a regular basis starting with a look at the 1954 season,[24] and national publications such as the *Christian Science Monitor* and the *National Review* sent reviewers from the mid-fifties.

The time given to overt self-promotion shrank quickly. OSF realized that the best advertisement was to give listeners a taste of their quality by making the play the thing that dominated the show. This change was made by 1953 when pre-play

---

[18] The statement is ironic for two reasons. The first is that the programme had already mentioned the Festival's souvenir booths and the broadcast was designed to get tourists to visit OSF. Second, though the commercialism in Ashland was modest compared to today, OSF soon made tourism Ashland's major industry. When I quoted Bailey in a lecture at the Festival on 17 July 2010, the audience laughed heartily because Ashland in now so obviously commercial. Most of the shops in the downtown area cater to tourists, and the number of hotels and nearly 100 restaurants are far out of proportion to the town's size.

[19] Acting styles have changed since 1951; these are generally competent in the style of the era. All comments about performances in this article compare the actors to contemporary audio performances.

[20] Angus L. Bowmer, *As I Remember, Adam: An Autobiography of a Festival* (Ashland, OR, 1975), p. 215.

[21] Anonymous, *Ashland Daily Tidings*, 17 April 1952, no page number.

[22] Anonymous, *The Oregon Journal*, 23 March 1952, no page number.

[23] Anonymous, *The Shakespeare Newsletter*, 3:5 (1953), 1.

[24] Horace W. Robinson, 'Shakespeare, Ashland Oregon', *Shakespeare Quarterly*, 4 (1955), 447–51.

comments were kept to just a page of the script.[25] The broadcast now more closely resembled other sustained broadcasts of plays, with a short introduction followed by the abridgement. A standardized opening was devised in 1955 that continued mention of the beauty of the region, the Elizabethan stage's natural setting and the Festival's authentic way of producing Shakespeare. Bowmer made an almost annual announcement that the current season was OSF's most successful ever. The Festival's first broadcast of *A Midsummer Night's Dream* was in 1966.

There are fewer challenges in adapting *A Midsummer Night's Dream* for radio than there are with many of Shakespeare's plays, especially those that have more physical action and/or several scenes with many speakers, but each of Shakespeare's plays presents unique problems for adapters. Because radio audiences cannot see the performers or any of the properties that might be used on stage, careful listeners with long attention spans have an advantage over those whose minds wander. Familiarity with a play will neutralize some difficulties, though not all. Radio producers are aware of those problems, and have strategies to make stories clear.

Identifying speakers is the most pervasive problem. When Theseus, Hippolyta and Egeus enter in 4.1, listeners have not heard them speak since 1.1, but nobody says, 'Here come Theseus, Hippolyta and Egeus' and so it may not be clear that it is they who are conversing. Similarly, Puck has not been on stage since 2.1 when he enters in 3.1.71 and says, 'What hampen homespuns have we swagg'ring here / So near the cradle of the Fairy Queen?' Only casting the part with an actor possessing a distinctive voice will help listeners know that Puck is the speaker. In the same scene, theatre audiences can tell that Puck is invisible because the mechanicals do not look at him and are confused by his antics. Listeners, however, cannot see the mechanicals overlook Puck and may wonder why they do not answer his question.

This is the scene in which Puck gives Bottom the head of an ass, usually done by the off-stage placing of an elaborate mask on the actor playing Bottom. Bottom's new look is not described when he returns to the stage, only acknowledged. Peter Quince says 'O monstrous! O strange! We are haunted. Pray, masters; fly, masters: help!' (99). This tells listeners that something is wrong, but not that Bottom has something on his head. Neither Snout's, 'O Bottom, thou art changed. What do I see on thee?' (109), nor Quince's, 'Thou art translated' (113) explain what Bottom is changed or translated into. Audiences listening to the play instead of seeing it thus spend more than a hundred lines without specifically knowing what is going on until 3.2.17, Puck's line, 'An ass's nole I fixèd on his head'. Only then do listeners understand that Bottom has a new head, and only if the radio adapter changes the word *nole* to one that is more familiar.

The more speakers in a scene, the more challenging it is to keep track of who is speaking, though the nature of a scene can increase the difficulty. There are six speakers in 1.1, but Hippolyta has only one speech and does not present much of a problem. The other five speakers can usually be told apart because each character has a different goal in the scene, and what each says is distinctly in pursuit of those goals. The scene is harder to follow than a two-person scene, but not hopeless. It is more difficult to differentiate the same number of speakers in 3.2, when the four lovers plus Oberon and Puck are together. Many of the lines are short and delivery is often fast to give the scene a comic punch. It quickly becomes difficult to follow the rapidly changing speakers. Adding to the confusion, Demetrius and Lysander now have the same goal: to achieve Helena's love. Their lines are less distinctive now that they are on the same emotional trajectory. An added complication comes when Puck imitates Lysander to Demetrius and Demetrius to Lysander.

---

[25] The script for the 1952 broadcast of *Much Ado About Nothing* is missing and the tape is too fragile to review, so just how much of the broadcast was overtly commercial in the second year is unknown.

Listeners can mistake Puck for either or both of them.

Act 5 can be followed well enough until the interlude begins. The heckling then comes thick and fast. It is difficult to know which noble is heckling the performers. There is nothing distinguishing about Theseus's, 'I wonder if the lion be to speak' (5.1.151), Demetrius's 'He should have worn the horns on his head' (236), and Lysander's 'This lion is a very fox for his valour' (228). It is true that Demetrius and Lysander add the words 'my Lord', when addressing Theseus.[26] Not all listeners will pick up on this subtlety, and even those who do will need to remember the voices of Demetrius and Lysander to know which is speaking.

Does it matter if listeners identify each heckler as they speak? For many it may not, as long as listeners realize the speakers are the nobles and not the performers. However, it is frustrating for anyone who lost track of the speakers earlier in the broadcast to lose track of them again. Seeing characters is always helpful.[27]

As with the adding of Bottom's nole, there are times when listeners need to see the action. The text is usually clear about who has the juice of a flower put into their eyes, who puts it there, when it is done, and if it is the love juice or the antidote. Still, without being able to see the action and the actors, a listener must have remarkable attentiveness to follow all the variations. Listeners cannot see the other fairies exit the stage and Puck come to the apron to address his final lines to the audience, so the epilogic character of these lines is not clear at first.

Shakespeare does something in this play that he does in no other: have characters fall asleep in one scene, 2.2, and keep then on stage until they awake two scenes later in 3.2. One is frequently conscious of these characters while watching this play, and surely Shakespeare wanted his audience to be conscious of them. The sleepers are out of a listener's sight on the radio, and so are likely to be out of a listener's mind for most of these scenes. We can argue about what Shakespeare wanted to achieve by keeping these characters on stage but it is hard to argue that forgetting about them, as listeners likely will, was part of the plan.

Can radio listeners compensate for being unable to see the characters and the action by reading along with the broadcast? They can try. This can be rewarding, but it goes against the point in creating the production, at least in theory. Radio plays are designed to make sense without listeners reading along. To that end, broadcasters employ different strategies to compensate for the problems created by audio-only storytelling. The BBC usually casts actors with contrasting voices to help listeners identify speakers, and makes changes to the text for audio clarity. Scenes are often transposed or shortened, with the result that listeners may lose their place if they read along.[28] The BBC's most recent radio broadcast of *A Midsummer Night's Dream* cut a few dozen lines, replaced several antiquated words with more familiar terms, and moved one of Bottom's speeches up several lines.[29] Even these slight alterations challenge those reading along. Productions that make more radical changes, such as the 2001 BBC *Othello*, make reading along quite impossible.[30]

---

[26] Examples are Demetrius's lines 152–3 and Lysander's 119–20, but there is nothing to distinguish their lines from Theseus's lines when they do not speak to him.

[27] I confess these comments are informed by personal experience with an audio recording of the play heard before I knew the story well enough to quickly regroup from any inattentiveness. I believe these comments address the frustrations that many non-specialist listeners have with audio and radio productions. A scene with a similar problem, though simpler, is 3.2.155, when Peaseblossom, Cobweb, Mote and Mustardseed are introduced to Bottom. The *Oxford Complete Works* does not indicate which fairy speaks, giving the first words to 'A Fairy', and the other words in the shared line to the other fairies in three speech prefixes, each labelled, 'Another'. The same is true when the same characters 'Hail' Bottom in 166–9, though those lines are not shared.

[28] Strategies used by the BBC to adapt plays for the ear are explained in Michael P. Jensen, 'Lend Me Your Ears: Sampling BBC Radio Shakespeare', *Shakespeare Survey 61* (Cambridge, 2008), p. 176.

[29] Broadcast on Radio 3 on 11 September 2011, directed by Celia de Wolff.

[30] Broadcast on Radio 3 on 30 September 2001, directed by Jeremy Mortimer. For a description of selected changes,

Any adaptation of this play needs to deal with these textual challenges, but there are additional demands from the cultural baggage the play has picked-up since it was first performed. Two have special impact on radio productions. The first of these is music.

Over the centuries, the play has gained a soundtrack. Shakespeare's script has songs, most of his plays do, but other music was soon added. As Richard Noble writes, 'A greater part of this comedy has been set to music than is the case with any of the others.'[31] This began as early as 1692 when spectacular interludes of dances and songs, the music by Henry Purcell, were included in a version called *The Fairy Queen*. The show only used about half the text. David Garrick's 1755 version, *The Fairies*, had twenty-seven songs, included songs from other Shakespeare plays and more that incorporated music set to verses by John Dryden, George Granville, John Milton and Edmund Waller. The text was even more severely cut so as to exclude all the mechanicals' scenes, though the off-stage Bottom is mentioned.[32] The best-known music for the play is Felix Mendelssohn's, created for the Ludwig Tieck production at Potsdam's court theatre in 1843, amounting to roughly forty-five minutes of music.[33] The score continued to be used until well into the twentieth century. The play thus gained a musical tradition, usually the Mendelssohn musical tradition, which became intrinsic to the play's cultural identity.

Williams makes the point that Tieck's staging also shared in the tradition of nineteenth-century pictorial productions, calling designer J. C. Gerst's set a 'compromise between the Elizabethan and [the] pictorial stage'.[34] Highly pictorial productions include Sir Herbert Beerbohm Tree's now notorious staging in 1900. Like many producers before him, Tree emphasized what the eye sees more than what the ear hears. It seems significant that it took two designers, Joseph Harker and Hawes Craven, to create all the splendour. They put the columned buildings of ancient Athens on stage to stand for Theseus's palace and included live rabbits for the scenes in the woods. To accommodate the elaborate set changes, the text was severely trimmed and rearranged to reduce the number of breaks. This approach seems ridiculous today, but contemporary critics were dazzled.[35] For some of his indoor productions, Max Reinhardt put Titania and some of her attendants on wires so they could fly or hover above the stage,[36] and Peter Holland notes the tradition of flying Puck.[37] Listeners familiar with the play on stage could hardly help but have expectations for music and spectacle as they tuned to the BBC at 20:00 GMT on 25 July 1923 and waited for their radios to warm up so they could hear the first 'full-length'[38] production of *A Midsummer Night's Dream*.

The broadcast would only satisfy one of these expectations. Mendelssohn's music was used on the programme, both the overture and at least some

additions, and restructurings in this programme, see Michael P. Jensen, 'Radio: Play by Play', in Richard Burt, ed. *Shakespeares After Shakespeare: An Encyclopedia on the Bard in Mass Media and Popular Culture*, vol. 2 (Westport, CT and London, 2007), p. 553.

[31] Richard Noble, *Shakespeare's Use of Song With the Text of the Principal Songs* (Oxford, 1923), p. 54.

[32] George C. D. Odell, *Shakespeare from Betterton to Irving*, vol. 1 (1920; reprint, New York, 1966), pp. 358–9. Bottom is not named in *The Fairies*, but Titania is said to keep company with a 'patched fool'.

[33] It comes to 49 minutes on the Sony Classical compact disk with Claudio Abbado conducting the Berlin Philharmonic, released in 1996. There are a few spoken parts on the disk read by Kenneth Branagh. Some of these are spoken with no music, reducing the time of Mendelssohn's score slightly. See Simon Williams, *Shakespeare on the German Stage, 1586–1914* (Cambridge, 1970), vol. 1, pp. 103–9, for a description of Tieck's production.

[34] Williams, *Shakespeare on the German Stage*, pp. 104–5.

[35] Williams, *Shakespeare on the German Stage*, pp. 131–9. Williams reproduces stills that show the exterior and interior palace, and the wood sets. Information about the rabbits comes from Bernard Grebanier, *Then Came Each Actor: Shakespearean Actors, Great and Otherwise, Including Players and Princes, Rogues, Vagabonds and Actors Motley, from Will Kempe to Olivier and Gielgud and After* (New York: 1975), p. 375.

[36] Williams, *Shakespeare on the German Stage*, p. 168.

[37] Peter Holland, ed., *A Midsummer Night's Dream* (Oxford, 1994, reissued 2008). p. 45.

[38] 'Full-length' was BBC-speak for a slightly abridged play that kept the story-line essentially intact.

of the incidental music,[39] with the songs sung by Winifred Fisher.

Mendelssohn's score was probably soothingly familiar, but in the long passages of speech in-between the actors delivered the words straight to the ears of the radio audience without visual filters such as sets, costumes and flying fairies. Though abridged, the broadcast emphasized the words of the play, and had to because radio cannot do visuals. This concentration on language is radio's strength.

OSF adjusted to this limitation in different ways for their broadcasts of *A Midsummer Night's Dream*. Each was strongly musical, but the Festival had to discard their own visuals in order to put the play on the air.

'Our audiences are demanding more performances than we can manage without a major change', Bowmer said in 1966.[40] It was felt that no nights could be added until a second theatre was built, so the Festival announced a half-million dollar drive to build an indoor theatre to supplement the Elizabethan stage. Fundraisers for the new building were held around the state two months before the season opened, kicked off by a poorly attended performance of the Duke Ellington Orchestra in Ashland. Ellington included excerpts from *Such Sweet Thunder*, a set of musical impressions from Shakespeare. That fundraising continued on the air.

Bowmer would pitch the new building in his opening remarks, but which of the 1966 plays would draw listeners to hear those remarks? *A Midsummer Night's Dream* was the one sure crowd-pleaser in production, and Peter D. Smith writes that it was OSF's best offering that year.[41] Certainly, it was the show most likely to attract an audience.

Which part of the play to excerpt was decided late in the process. The *Gazelle Times* reported on 29 August 1966 that the 'presentation will incorporate scenes from all parts of the play'.[42] An unidentified clipping in the Festival archive, hand dated with the 30 August 1966 date of the broadcast, reports that OSF would present 'excerpts from the woodland fantasy scenes'. OSF actually presented neither of these, opting for the Pyramus and Thisbe

interlude and the blessings that end Act 5. Festival publicist and radio adapter Carl Ritchie realized broadcasting Act 5 solved most of the adaptation problems by simply excerpting the Pyramus and Thisbe playlet. It stands more or less on its own as one of the show's stronger set pieces. Smith felt that the cast of mechanicals, led by Angus Bowmer's Peter Quince, was the best part of the production. 'He set a splendid example of verse speaking.' Smith also liked Jim Baker's Bottom for 'his crude but winning exuberance'.[43]

Stage director Hugh Evans introduces the play with generalities:

Call it a woodland fantasy; call it a play of bewitching charm and haunting beauty; call it the happiest of Shakespearean comedies; rich in memories of youth – the search for marvel – the yearning for melody and mystery and the candle-lit night when all things are well. But, whatever you call it, William Shakespeare's 'A Midsummer Night's Dream' walks with moons and warm evenings and the thrill of that mystic adventure which may be *commanded*, *compounded*, or *come-across*. Shakespeare sets his idea that way with the initial conversation of Theseus, Duke of Athens, and his bethrothed [sic] Hippolyta.[44]

---

39 The programme, produced by Cathleen Nesbit and directed by Cecil A. Lewis, was broadcast live and was not recorded. No scripts are known to have survived, so how much of Mendelssohn's music was used is unknown. The music was probably excerpted since the programme was followed by an audio history of the motorcycle industry, and that was followed by a programme of extracts from Mendelssohn's score, perhaps the portions of the score not used in the dramatization. Details come from the *Times* broadcast listings on 25 March 1923.

40 Anonymous, 'Ashland Notes Record Season', *The Oregonian*, 13 September 1966, no page number.

41 Peter D. Smith, 'The 1966 Festivals at Ashland, Oregon, and San Diego, California', *Shakespeare Quarterly*, 17 (1966), 412–17.

42 Anonymous, headline missing, *Gazelle Times*, 29 August 1966, no page number.

43 Smith, 'The 1966 Festivals', p. 416. Quince actually speaks prose except for the prologue in Act 5. Smith was reviewing all of Bowmer's scenes from the stage production and not just the brief bit of verse in Act 5, so he probably meant that Bowmer spoke Shakespeare's language well.

44 Emphasis as given in the radio script. The tape of the broadcast is not available for review.

The next half-page of script is the opening of the play through Theseus's instruction to Philostrate to 'Stir up the Athenian youth to merriments', just twelve lines, 1.1.1–12. Evans then returns to summarize the story up to the merriments, after which the actors return to the microphone to present most of Act 5. These excerpts hardly do the play justice, but they served the needs of the now twenty-four minute broadcast very well.[45] There are no traditional sound effects but the nineteen-page script has twenty-one music cues composed by W. Bernard Windt.[46] The cues include the standard opening fanfare and a bridge between the first scene and Act 5 but are mostly used to punctuate the Pyramus and Thisbe scene. Peter Quince gets a drum fanfare as he enters, and something, 'PERHAPS A CYMBAL', musically introduces Snout.[47] Each new player receives a fanfare as he enters the scene, a clue to audiences that the next person speaking has not been heard before. These are short bursts of music, to be sure, not the prolonged pieces introduced by Mendelssohn and Tieck, but this play, so associated with music, averages a music cue for nearly every minute it was on the air.

Carl Ritchie made notes on all the Festival recordings in 1997. His comment about this show is, 'Fairly tight script with the accent on the cast', and this is how the script reads. Ritchie commends the 'fine cast',[48] who also impressed newspaper reviewers.

Reviewers further noted the visual aspects of the stage production. Ruth Acklen commented on 'the breathtakingly beautiful scenes', and found the fairy costumes 'gorgeous', though she wanted them to be a bit more 'sylvan in character'.[49] Another reviewer identified only as B. G. notes that 'Perhaps the most memorable [scene] is [when Bottom] twitches his last . . . Wearing a helmet too large and awkward armor . . . he clumsily draws his broadsword and stabs himself, then drags on his death for several minutes, to the complete amusement of the audience.'[50] Nothing in the radio script indicates that Bottom's death was comically prolonged. Also not on the air was an 'ingenious prop', Bottom's donkey head. Linda Dahl

describes its 'movable pink ears, flutterable eyelashes (with sparkles on them) and a red tongue which moves as the weaver speaks'. She also mentions the 'brilliantly colored costumes. The blending of the shades of purples and lavenders and yellows and browns were extremely effective and pleasing to the eye. The appropriateness of costume to character . . . projected its own feeling for the individuals.'[51] A dog named Shag was cast as Moon's dog but, lacking a speaking part, Shag was not on the air. Love redesigned the show for the ear.

If the script gives an accurate indication of the programme and if Ritchie's opinion can be trusted, the broadcast was a very good advertisement for OSF: a show lean of everything but the play's funniest scene, some of Shakespeare's most memorable closing lines and the pitch for the building fund. Those who accepted the invitation to Ashland found a company that was perhaps less polished than they sounded on the air but nonetheless saw a visually rich and imaginative production that was inventive in ways that radio simply cannot represent.

I have set up three threads that come together in 1971: OSF's syndicated programme, the opening of the new theatre and the second radio broadcast

---

[45] NBC took back six minutes of air time for commercials and news in 1957.

[46] The script is numbered at eighteen pages, plus an additional page of credits is inserted between pages 17 and 18.

[47] Carl Ritchie, adapter, *The Oregon Shakespeare Festival: A Midsummer Night's Dream* script. The cue for Peter Quince is on p. 4 and the cue for Snout is on p. 5. Sound cues are typed in capital letters. In 4.1.29, Bottom calls for 'the tongs and the bones', which are percussive rustic instruments. I cannot tell if the choice of percussive music for Act 5 on the broadcast was influenced by this but it is an appropriate choice.

[48] Carl Ritchie, Audio Notes Volume 4, The Plays IV, p. 12.

[49] Ruth Acklen, 'Shakespeare Opener Delights Playgoers', *Daily Courier*, 25 July 1966, no page number.

[50] B. G., 'Opening Night's Play Within a Play Called "Best Done"', *Medford Mail-Tribune*, 25 July 1966, p. A11.

[51] Linda Dahl, 'Off the Best', *Gazelle Times*, 30 August 1966, no page number.

of *A Midsummer Night's Dream*. I shall look at these chronologically.

OSF started a second radio series in 1960. The fifty-nine-minute programme[52] was structured like the shorter show. Love still produced, listeners were still invited to see the plays in Ashland, and OSF still made its dubious claim of giving audiences an 'authentic Shakespeare experience'. The first syndicated show was *Antony and Cleopatra*, which was sent free to any station willing to air it. The programme was immediately picked-up by Radio Free Europe and the Armed Forces Radio Service, so US soldiers and international listeners in their vicinity heard the invitation to visit Ashland.

The Angus L. Bowmer Theatre opened in 1970.[53] Fundraising and building took four years, partly due to a final cost of $1.4 million, nearly three times the original estimate. With the opening of the Bowmer, host Philip Davidson could boast on the air that for the first time OSF would produce 'over 200 performances over six months', which included an increase in the non-Shakespearian drama produced by OSF.[54] The 1971 production of *A Midsummer Night's Dream* was the first time that play was produced in the Bowmer and the only time it was produced for the Festival's syndicated programme.

Raye Birk's introduction takes an abstract line, mentioning the multiple plots without describing them, and contrasting ideas and images. He includes, 'people/sprits, love/hate, rational/passionate, wet/dry, summer/winter, sensual/cerebral', without giving concrete examples. The feeling is of something grand, magically 'Shakespearian', not grounded in the sod of the Athenian wood. He makes even the most base and bawdy parts of the play seem ethereal and fine.[55] This heady narrative evokes a dream state, or at least a dreamy state, in which traditional narrative gives way to Birk as the dream-casting storyteller, a strategy that allows adapter Andy Love to skip over the adaptation problems in this play.

Birk mostly describes the pastoral aspects of the story, and Love's script supports this by minimizing other scenes. The heaviest cuts in 1.1 are between Theseus and Hippolyta, putting the emphasis on

the wooing of Hermia which will continue in the wood. Most of the trimming overall is done to the mechanicals, then to lines that do not move the story forward. The entire scene of Bottom's transformation into an ass is off-mike, which actually makes radio sense since, as we have seen, Bottom is not described as wearing the ass-head when he comes on stage. Birk eventually refers to it as an established fact when he says, 'Titania approaches with Bottom, his ass's head garland [*sic*] with flowers'. This is not only the first mention of Bottom's new head, but the first mention that Bottom and Titania have met. The power of Birk's dreamy narration makes these cuts seem almost natural. Bottom and Titania do share 4.1, a lovely scene that is only slightly abridged.

The mechanicals are cut from Act 5, so the show moves from the reconciliation of the fairy kingdom to the fairies giving their blessings. There is a logical progression between these events, so those who do not know the play will not miss the interlude. It is not true to say that Act 5 was presented in 1966 and the rest of the play in 1971, but story-wise each broadcast has much of what the other lacks.

Most of the actors speak clearly, using good radio technique even though many of the younger players were new to broadcasting. The cast is strong,

---

52 The sixtieth minute was broken in two, starting with a thirty second break after thirty minutes for a legally required air check. All stations were required to announce their call letters, city and the time every thirty minutes of their broadcast day. 'This is KMED, Medford. It's 7:30', was a typical air check. The other twenty-five seconds were typically used for station announcements. The thirty seconds at the end of the programme would be used for another air check and, usually, more announcements.

53 The name came as a surprise to Bowmer. Naming rights were given to the Carpenter family who contributed the most to the building fund.

54 Bowmer was on sabbatical that year, so company actor Davidson hosted the show. The figure is rounded down. There were 223 performances. See Table 1 for details. The first non-Shakespearian play produced by OSF was George S. Kaufman and Moss Hart's *You Can't Take it With You* in 1939.

55 His opening comment is nearly word-for-word his 'Director's comments' from the Souvenir Programme (Ashland 1971), p. 4.

with good to very good performances from most. Standouts include Garry Moore (Theseus), Julian Lopez-Morillas (Egeus), Fredi Olster (a weepy Helena), and Dan Johnson (Peter Quince). American actor Michael Winters uses a lower-class English accent as Bottom, but the accent is mostly convincing, adds to the character's eccentricity, and serves to distinguish Bottom's voice from the American-sounding voices of the other actors when the audience cannot see who is speaking.[56]

There is music in abundance, though it is very odd music. The soundtrack for the fairy scenes was created by a Moog synthesizer, composed and played by Daniel LeBlanc. The synthesizer's electronic squeals make a moody and other-worldly soundtrack for these other-worldly characters, and emphasize stage actions as when it makes the 'twinkling sound of dropping fairy dust'.[57] Just as Mendelssohn presented a soundtrack for a nineteenth-century fairy world, the Moog created a soundtrack for the fairies of the seventies, a sound informed by science fiction films. Margery Bailey may well have called much of this 'experimental nonsense'.

Though hardly avant-garde, this was a modern production by the standards of 1971. The Bowmer Theatre allowed new staging opportunities, for this show a circular playing area that would have been difficult on a stage built to the dimensions of the Fortune Theatre. In this circle were dances choreographed by Judith Kennedy. The design elements consisted of projected photographs of the sky, a scrim, a four-foot boulder, a seven-foot boulder, a panel, steps that could be adjusted in seven configurations, elaborate costumes and some hand-held props.

Robin Carey identified 'two stage moments' that 'crystallized' the magic effects on stage. In one, 'Titania metamorphosed her Indian boy into a troll to prevent his capture' and, in the other, 'an invisible wall of sound . . . protected the sleeping Titania [from] the powers of Oberon'.[58]

It is not possible to show the translation of the Indian boy into a troll on the radio. A moment that for Carey was a hallmark of this production is simply lost, and so was the wall of sound. The Moog synthesizer could not have been used in the Elizabethan Theatre which simply was not wired for it,[59] and visually can only become a wall of sound if characters are seen attempting to breach that wall. Radio does not accommodate either of these staging choices without adding new dialogue to explain these actions. Birk's production experimented with the new Bowmer space, technology, dance and special effects, but these experiments are meaningless in a medium where imaginative space is created by sound alone.

Another change is mentioned by Carl Ritchie, who writes that Birk used the play to celebrate love, but notes that the darker themes come through on the air. Unfortunately, Ritchie does not explain what caused this change in tone.[60]

I described business performed on stage in the 1966 and 1971 shows that are not audible in the broadcasts in order to give a sense of what it may have been like for those who heard the broadcast and then visited OSF. Love presented polished radio plays that lacked everything visual on stage. A lot was missing. Obviously the scripts used for the stage are longer, delivering more story and characters, and obviously the longer running times presented more of the music than could be used in the broadcast, but there is also Moon's

---

56 Michael Winters confirmed that he is US born in an e-mail dated 11 May 2011. He played Bottom again in 1975 at the Pacific Conservatory of the Performing Arts TheaterFest in Santa Maria, California, under the direction of Laird Williamson. This time he used a dialect 'meant to have the sound & flavor of Old Middle English, like the sound of Chaucer'. My thanks to Mr Winters for supplying most of this information, and to Craig Shafer of PCPA TheaterFest for an e-mail dated 13 May 2011 that supplied the year of this production.

57 Michele LaBounty, *Ashland Daily Tidings*, 20 March 1971, no page number.

58 Robin Carey, 'Oregon Shakespeare Festival – 1971', *Shakespeare Quarterly*, 12 (1971), 377.

59 Hasso Hering, headline missing, *Ashland Daily Tidings*, 17 March 1971, no page number.

60 Carl Ritchie, Audio Notes Volume 4, The Plays IVB, p. 11. Comparing the records in the OSF Archive with the broadcast did not reveal the reason to me. Possibly it is no more that the result of the way that Love reduced the script and redirected the actors for the broadcast.

dog, the costumes, fairies with silver skin, insurmountable walls of sound, projections of clouds, the moon, and trees, sets that allow characters to sit or stand at vital moments, lighting, visual magic such as disguising the Indian boy as a troll, and even showing this character on stage, the ass head, and Bottom getting his ass's head presented dramatically. If hearing the broadcast was good, seeing the play was better, because OSF delivered a lot more on stage. All those comments about the beauty of the Rogue Valley, the charm of Ashland, the quality of the actors, the authenticity of the Shakespeare experience, and mounting the plays paid off. Over the years, thousands of people learned about the Festival on the radio, visited Ashland, liked it and came back for more. Yet, in the late seventies and early eighties the broadcasts more closely reflected the productions as OSF actually staged them, and the programme sank in quality.

The last NBC show was broadcast in 1974. The number of affiliated stations that aired the programme dwindled over the years until there were about thirty, too few for NBC to continue. The annual broadcast appears to be the last dramatic programme on network radio in the US.[61] The syndicated programme continued until 1979, when it was retired for similar reasons. Andy Love produced both shows until the end. Ronald Kramer, however, arrived two years earlier to give OSF a third broadcast home in a new format.

Kramer managed Ashland's National Public Radio (NPR) affiliate KSOR. As Jennings Pierce had with KMED, Kramer wanted to raise KSOR's national profile, and saw broadcasting the Festival's plays as a way to do this. He put the opening night production from the Festival's Elizabethan stage on the air locally, and through transmitters the signal was heard throughout Southern Oregon and the northernmost cities of California.[62]

Kramer copied the format of New York's Metropolitan Opera broadcasts.[63] The introductions and summary of the plot at the beginning are similar, though the Festival's introductions lasted a full half-hour, and occasionally longer. Instead of

an intermission 'Opera Quiz', a staple of the Met broadcasts, KSOR presented a 'Shakespeare Quiz'.

The obvious difference between the KSOR broadcasts and the abridgments is length. Less obvious, but more revealing, are the different approaches taken by Love and Kramer.

Like all mediums, radio has strengths and limitations. Good programmes play to radio's strengths. Bad programmes ignore its limitations and the quality of the programme suffers as a result. Andy Love's broadcasts were generally good radio because he took work that originated on stage and turned it into fully realized broadcasts. The KSOR shows are bad radio because Ronald Kramer simply miked stage productions. The difference is immense. As OSF took the final steps in becoming a fully professional company, their radio broadcasts became more amateur because the acting was not delivered by the voice alone, but with the entire body, plus everything else on stage that listeners could not see.

This is not really the fault of either OSF or KSOR but a problem with the concept. OSF made the best theatre it could, unconcerned about what makes good radio. Kramer broadcast an event: three, sometimes four-hour events, including the front and back matter with the intermission. These are very long events, especially when heard at home with all the distractions there and no actors, sets or costumes to draw the eye and help listeners concentrate.

The 1979 *A Midsummer Night's Dream* was hosted by actor and Festival publicist Peggy Rubin and Ed Brubaker of Franklin and Marshall College,

---

61 CBS attempted to revive radio drama that year with the *CBS Radio Mystery Theatre*, which lasted until 1982. The programme was produced by CBS but it was actually syndicated.

62 Susan DeRosia, 'Jefferson Public Radio Boosting the Signal', *Daily Tidings*, 2 January 2004, pp. 1–2. KSOR is still the station's legal name, though it is now popularly known as Jefferson Public Radio (JPR).

63 That this was a conscious imitation was confirmed in a phone conversation with Ronald Kramer. My thanks to Mr Kramer for his several helpful conversations, voice mail messages, and e-mails in November 2004.

actor, educator and a director with the Festival. The broadcast began at 8:00 pm Pacific Standard Time but the play did not begin until 8:50. The time was given to filler. The hosts comment about the specialness of opening nights, discuss why Bowmer thought Shakespeare was popular, lament Bowmer's death earlier in the year, and plug Ashland, OSF, and especially this play.

After eight minutes of this chatter, longtime CBS announcer Dick Joy, who retired to Ashland, interviews *Dream* director Dennis Bigelow and actors Dan Kremer (Bottom) and Gary Sloan (doubling Puck and Philostrate) about the production. This is followed by bagpipe music, after which Joy interviews composer Todd Barton about the music he created for this play. The show then returns to Rubin, who says with typical Rubinesque hyperbole that Barton's compositions for this production are 'the most beautiful music in the world'.[64]

This summary covers just the first twenty-five minutes of the programme, but gives a sense of what the entire introduction is like. The problem is not that the material is uninteresting but that there is so much of it. Listeners tuned in to hear the play, not fifty minutes of chat about the play. Though the introduction is badly conceived, the performance is incompetent radio because neither the script nor the performance was adapted for the ear.

The voices are big, broad and loud enough to be heard in a 1200-seat outdoor theatre. Sound levels change as actors move around the stage, and are farther from or nearer a microphone. People can be heard walking across the stage during the song in 2.2.

There are unexplained gaps starting with a fourteen-second pause between Lysander's, 'I will, my Hermia', and the rest of the line, 'Helena, adieu' (1.1.224), with no explanation why. There is an additional eleven seconds of dead air between the exit of Oberon and the entrance of Lysander and Hermia, and another fifteen seconds between the sleep of Lysander and Hermia and the first words of Puck, both in 2.2. The line, 'This man,

with lantern, dog, and bush of thorn' (5.1.134) gets a big laugh, though the line is not particularly funny. This is probably due to stage business, but the prompt book does not indicate what the actors did at this point. Between 'Let him approach' (5.1.106–7) and the start of the Prologue are thirty-six seconds during which there are some shuffling sounds, tittering from the audience, something that may be a horn, and a thud or two. This catalogue of silence and unexplained sounds is far from complete. There are dozens of similar incidences in the broadcast. First nighters could see the action on stage but radio listeners had no idea what was going on. In this way, the visual aspects of the performance, though unseen, were a constant part of the broadcast.

The 1979 production was visually elaborate. One photo shows a beautiful shot of Titania and Bottom in front of a tree with clouds and the moon projected above them. At the start of Act 5, Theseus, Hippolyta and their train come on and meet the lovers. The costumes are very elaborate and Theseus and Hippolyta ride modified hobby-horses. To create the chink in the wall, Snout held up two stones with space between them, so Bottom did indeed kiss the stones and not Thisbe. The visual aspects of the production are lovely, expertly crafted, and enriched a visit to the Elizabethan Theatre. Taken together, however, these lovely visuals helped derail the rhythm of this broadcast.

All visual elements contribute to the rhythm of a show on stage, but stage rhythm is not the same as radio rhythm. Stage rhythm is partly

---

[64] This example of Rubin's constant hype should not reflect badly on Barton, who is one of the most prolific but under-known Shakespeare composers of our time. As of this writing, Barton has composed music for the thirty-seven plays in the standard canon twice, with the exception of *King John*, for which he has composed only once. He has also scored *Two Noble Kinsmen* just one time. He has composed music for many of Shakespeare's plays four or five times, including *A Midsummer Night's Dream*, *Romeo and Juliet* and *As You Like It*. While most of this work has been for OSF, Barton has worked at other theatres as well.

devised during rehearsal, and depends on the characterizations the actors work out with their director, blocking, props, physical interactions between characters, the distance between characters, the set, any visual effects, and even how an actor must move in costume. Once the show is in front of an audience, the rhythm changes if the actual stage tweaks the blocking, and shifts with audience reaction to the actors: which lines get laughs, how long the laugh lasts, if an actor senses the audiences is bored and needs a boost of energy, and similar things. Stage rhythm can change from performance to performance and moment to moment. Since this portion of stage rhythm is reactive and depends not just on what an audience hears but on what they see, stage rhythm can be a bad fit for radio listeners. This broadcast has dozens of rhythm changes to accommodate the theatre audience that come over as oddities on the air.

Jeffrey King, who recently recorded the role of Claudius for the Festival's audio-book *Hamlet*, described the difference between stage rhythm and audio rhythm this way.[65] 'You have to take all the things that made your performance corporeal... meaning everything your body does: the turns, the looks, the movement through space, even the breath, and focus them in your voice... you have to, in some way, change everything that was seen into something that can be heard. And all these things affect rhythm. Dead air is bad, so you have to play things faster.'[66] The 1979 broadcast did not, could not, allow the actors to refocus their performances for the ear, and the broadcast suffered for it.

Despite the lateness of the play due to nearly an hour of introduction, the inconsistent sound levels, performances too big for broadcasting, visual aspects of the staging that created dead air, unexplained laughs and its odd rhythm, the broadcast succeeded in its goal of presenting an opening night event, but it is bad dramatic radio. In 1951, Andy Love took a company with good but amateur productions and polished them to a professional level of broadcasting. Ronald Kramer took a nearly professional company and inadvertently made them sound like amateur broadcasters because he

did not adapt this play for the ear, but included the visual and physical aspects of the production that listeners could not see.

To contrast the 1979 company with the company in 1951, the year of the *King Lear* broadcast, OSF had just three professional actors in 1951. The company grew gradually until there were thirty-seven performing on the Festival's two stages in 1979, some with credits in major houses such as the Kennedy Center. OSF was on the verge of being a fully professional company during that 1979 broadcast. Those watching this production of *A Midsummer Night's Dream* saw that professionalism on stage. One critic wrote that the play, 'gets the good treatment it deserves in the festival's hands', and another that it 'is an unmitigated delight.' Alan Dessen called it, 'funny, visually attractive... and full of surprises', though he did not like all of the surprises.[67] The event-style broadcast failed to deliver that experience.

In 1981, the KSOR show moved up to selected stations on the NPR network and up to three broadcasts on consecutive weeks. OSF opens the three plays in their Elizabethan Theatre on successive nights, Friday through Sunday. Stations were not willing to devote three nights in a week to OSF, so KSOR broadcast the first Friday show live, then recorded the Saturday and Sunday openings for broadcast on the two following Fridays. The programme was never popular, starting with about the same number of affiliates as the last NBC broadcast, and then lost stations the next year. The last plays were broadcast in 1983, though there was a preview of the OSF season on NPR in 1984. The lack of public support is hardly surprising given that America had generally lost interest in radio drama

---

[65] For our purposes, I take radio rhythm and audio rhythm to be virtually synonyms.

[66] E-mail dated 27 June 2011. My thanks to Mr King for commenting, and also to actors Marti J. Cooney, Kyle Haden, and Geoffrey Ridden for comments I did not use.

[67] Don Bishoff, '"Dream" a well-balanced presentation', *Register Guardian*, 17 June 1979, no page number; Ted Mahar, '"Midsummer" Fast, Delightful', *The Oregonian*, 17 June 1979, no page number; and Alan Dessen, 'Oregon Shakespeare Festival', *Shakespeare Quarterly*, 31 (1980), 279.

Table 1 Oregon Shakespeare Festival 1951–2010

	1951[a]	1953	1966	1971	1979[b]	2010
Attendance	11,700	16,733	63,093	155,143	265,054	414,783
Performances	25	29	59	233	574	770
Box Office ($)	17,000	28,032	171,655	566,923	1,744,643	18,473,563

In addition to data for the years of the broadcasts studied in this article, I include the figures for 1953, the year of the first real explosion of national and, to a lesser extent, international attention.

[a] Box office records through 1952 were destroyed in a fire. These numbers are the Festival's estimates. The number of performances is correct, not an estimate.

[b] A third space, the Black Swan Theatre, opened in 1977, adding to the number of performances, tickets sold, box office revenue and the number of non-Shakespeare plays performed by OSF each year. The Black Swan was replaced by the slightly larger New Theatre in 2001.

by the sixties. It is to the Festival's credit that they broadcast for so long.

Despite my reservations about the quality of the KSOR and NPR shows, and despite the limited exposure OSF received throughout the country, the three broadcasts in 1982 won second place in the spoken arts category at the National Public Radio conference.[68] OSF also won the Regional Tony Award the next year, the year their last plays were broadcast. I have not found a statement from anyone on the Regional Tony committee who has said that the broadcasts made a difference in picking OSF for the honour, but it seems likely that the broadcasts kept the Tony organization aware of the small-town festival and its work.

OSF has not had a radio home since 1984, nor does the Festival need one.[69] It is difficult to pin down a date because different years achieved different milestones, but during the seventies OSF gradually lost most of the benefit brought to it by broadcasting. The broadcasts continued partly out of habit and partly because there is always some kind of benefit to having national exposure, however small that exposure is, but the rewards were also small. OSF simply outgrew the need to broadcast a few years after broadcasting outgrew its need for radio drama. Ashland's growing population,[70] more traditional forms of publicity, and the 125,000 tourists who now visit

the Festival each year[71] demonstrate that OSF has an audience large enough to sustain it without broadcasting. Radio helped bring that audience to Ashland in the first place, and many of these people returned because they liked the OSF brand.

---

[68] These were *The Comedy of Errors*, *Romeo and Juliet*, and *Henry V*.

[69] JPR and local television stations still do stories about OSF, and company members occasionally appear on JPR interview shows.

[70] The US Census is conducted every ten years, so figures are for the closest census year. The population of Ashland in 1950, the year before the first NBC broadcast, was just 7,739. It nearly doubled to 14,943 during the thirty years between 1950 and 1980, the year after the last *A Midsummer Night's Dream* broadcast. The town population grew at a very slightly slower rate during the next thirty years, to 20,095 in 2010. I have looked for a study that breaks down emigration to Ashland by reason(s) for moving, but cannot find one and suspect this has never been studied. Anecdotally, after discussing this with several dozen people, all but six of them moved to Ashland after visiting OSF several times. I have the impression that many have relocated for this reason, though, the result may be skewed since the people I am most likely to meet are those most likely to be OSF supporters. The combination of being drawn to the Festival and liking the town during visits appears to be at least a major reason that many relocate, and certainly a consistent reason. The increasing population adds to the Festival's local audience base, again making OSF less dependent on broadcasting to bring audiences to the Festival.

[71] E-mail from Katherine Flanagan of the Ashland Chamber of Commerce, dated 27 July 2011.

Clearly, the broadcasts made a tremendous difference to the Festival and made OSF an internationally recognized institution. Angus Bowmer said, 'Andy's impact here is almost immeasurable; because, literally, he has carried the story of the Festival around the world.'[72]

SELECTED RADIOGRAPHY[73]

King Lear, NBC, 11 August 1951, 30 minutes

William Dawkins (adapter), William Oyler (stage director, narrator), Andrew C. Love (radio director), Angus L. Bowmer (host)

A Midsummer Night's Dream, NBC, 30 August 1966, 24 minutes

Carl Ritchie (adapter), Hugh Evans (stage director/narrator), Andrew C. Love (radio director), Angus L. Bowmer (host)

A Midsummer Night's Dream, Syndicated, recorded 23 May 1971,[74] 59 minutes

Andrew C. Love (adapter/radio director), Raye Birk (stage director/narrator), Philip Davidson (host)

A Midsummer Night's Dream, KSOR, 15 June 1979, approximately 225 minutes[75]

Dennis Bigelow (stage director), Ronald Kramer (radio director), Peggy Rubin and Ed Brubaker (hosts).

---

[72] Carl Ritchie, 'Festival Magic Broadcast to the World: the Love connection', in *Ashland Oregon Shakespeare Festival 50th Anniversary Season* programme, Summer/Fall 1985, p. 55.

[73] All other OSF programmes are listed in the radio section of Burt, ed., *Shakespeares After Shakespeare*, pp. 508–84.

[74] Stations played the syndicated show at the time, day, and even month of their convenience, so there is no traditional broadcast date for the syndicated show. I have supplied the recording date instead.

[75] The length is based on notes about the show in the OSF archive and is an educated guess. The missing disk makes it impossible to determine the exact running time with certainty. The play was not adapted for radio, but was slightly trimmed for the stage in the latter acts.

BENJAMIN BRITTEN'S DREAMS

RUSS McDONALD

A minor but telling moment in the history of operatic performance occurred in São Paolo in November 2003. Gerald Thomas, director of what we might call an imaginative production of *Tristan und Isolde*, was greeted at the curtain call with a hostile chorus of boos, whereupon he dropped his trousers and mooned the audience. Charged with an act of public indecency – for the exposure, not the *Tristan* – he thus supplies a convenient introduction to the topic of directorial creativity and, since the focus of my analysis is Benjamin Britten's adaptation of *A Midsummer Night's Dream*, it is a happy accident that the composer should have treated the noun 'moon' with great playfulness in the last act of his opera. The following discussion considers three important productions of Britten's *Dream*, attending particularly to the aims and achievements of the different creative teams. They are Peter Hall's 1981 staging for Glyndebourne, frequently revived and available on video; Robert Carsen's much travelled production, which originated at the festival in Aix-en-Provence in 1991 and was filmed in Barcelona in 2005; and Christopher Alden's recent version for the English National Opera, premièred in London in May 2011. These three major realizations serve as epitomes of three different directorial styles, offering a range of interpretations of Britten's take on the Shakespearian original and collectively providing a useful survey of the changing modes of opera production at the end of the twentieth and the beginning of the twenty-first century.

My larger aim in studying these three stagings is to address the question of directorial licence. The escalation of directorial authority and innovation over the past two decades has reached so extraordinary a pitch as to require a rigorous debate over the production team's proper role. Most of the responses in the opera houses and in the popular press constitute no more than emotional evacuation: journalists delight in trumpeting the latest excesses of the most recent bad boy or girl and his or her directorial outrages. Such discourse adds little substance to the conversation. In America this radical or avant-garde style of production, seen with less frequency than in Europe, was until recently known as Eurotrash; the more neutral term is *Regietheater*; I prefer to call it Director's Opera. What exactly is the status of the director in the modern opera house or theatre? Is the director on a creative par with the composer and librettist or playwright? When the production 'plays against the text', or the director 'reads against the grain', what should we call the result? Is it representation? Interpretation? Adaptation? Desecration? Creativity? Art?

What is needed now is measured discussion of the status of the text or score to be staged and the contribution of the director in relation to that text: some relevant topics would include an analysis of what constitutes interpretation, the limits of representation, the difference between production and adaptation. To study the stage history of Britten's *Dream* is to raise questions and problems that are also becoming increasingly pertinent to the production of Shakespeare's plays. One caveat, however. It is essential to remember that the comparisons and contrasts I shall develop cannot be exact, owing to the difference in media: the Hall and Carsen productions I have seen only on DVD, videotaped versions of productions done originally for the stage, directed for video by David Heather and François Roussillon, respectively. Each of these might be termed a production of a production, and I have watched and studied them repeatedly. The Alden staging, although it may eventually make its way onto DVD, I saw live, and only once, on 23 May 2011. These differences necessarily affect interpretation.[1]

Britten's *A Midsummer Night's Dream* was originally performed at Aldeburgh, and indeed was conceived and written for the reopening of the tiny Jubilee Hall at the 1960 Festival. Britten began composing in the autumn of 1959, he and his partner, the tenor Peter Pears, having devised the libretto together beginning in the summer of that year. In an article published in *The Observer* just before the première, entitled 'A New Britten Opera', the composer declares that he and Pears worked mainly from facsimiles of the 1600 Quarto and the 1623 Folio,[2] but scholarship has determined, on the basis of archival material, that this claim may have been a bit pretentious. The facsimiles in the Suffolk archives are virtually clean and, based on the scribbles and deletions mostly in Pears's hand, the real work seems to have been done with the old English Penguin edition, edited by G. B. Harrison.[3] The choreographer John Cranko directed the first performances, with sets and costumes by John Piper, the composer conducting. From the conception of the project, Britten had settled on casting the countertenor Alfred Deller as Oberon. Deller was then exclusively a concert singer with no stage experience, but Britten wanted the distinctive strangeness of the countertenor sound – especially strange in 1960, a period without the gaggle of countertenors available in our day – to denote the otherworldliness of Oberon. The singer Robert Tear reports an anecdote about a German woman who, on meeting the countertenor, inquired, 'You are eunuch, Herr Deller?', to which he replied, 'Surely, madam, you mean *unique*'.[4] Britten had wanted the Swiss tenor Hugues Cuénod for Flute/Thisby,[5] but since he was unavailable, and since Pears's performing

schedule kept him from taking a larger part such as Lysander, Pears sang Flute. Puck, the speaking, non-singing part, was performed by the fifteen-year old son of Leonid Massine, the great French dancer and choreographer.[6]

After the initial brief run, the company, Britten's own English Opera Group, took the show to the Holland Festival. In February of 1961 a follow-on production was mounted at Covent Garden. Cranko's directorial efforts had neither pleased many nor pleased long, and so John Gielgud was engaged to direct the new version (although Britten's first choice for the replacement was Peter Hall, who was unavailable). And there were other substitutions. Since Deller was entirely innocent of the theatre and Cranko had given him no help with movement and gesture, his performance had seemed wooden: he was replaced by the American countertenor Russell Oberlin. Britten, ill that winter, yielded the podium to the Royal Opera's music director, the composer confessing himself pleased to find in Georg Solti an international conductor sympathetic to the score and willing to apply his considerable talents to it. Major productions followed throughout Europe, at Milan, Hamburg,

---

[1] I am grateful to Professor Peter Kazaras of the University of California at Los Angeles for making this point in response to an oral version of this paper. The occasion was *Shakespeare and Opera: Found in Translation?*, a conference held at UCLA on 6 and 7 November 2011.

[2] *The Observer*, 5 June 1960.

[3] See Andrew Plant, 'Night's Caressing Grip: The Evolution of the *Dream*', in *A Midsummer Night's Dream: Benjamin Britten*, Overture Opera Guides (London, 2011), pp. 10–11.

[4] Humphrey Carpenter, *Benjamin Britten: A Biography* (London, 1992), p. 394.

[5] 'Thisby' and 'Tytania' are the altered spellings preferred by Britten and Pears.

[6] Shakespearians will be interested to know that in Christopher Renshaw's production for the Royal Opera, Covent Garden, in 1986, Mark Rylance was cast as Puck. For more detailed information about the process of preparing the opera and the reception of the first performances, see Carpenter, *Benjamin Britten*, pp. 390–6; *Letters from a Life: The Selected Letters of Benjamin Britten, Volume Five, 1958–1965*, ed. Philip Reed and Mervyn Cooke (Woodbridge, 1958), pp. 168–306; and Plant, 'Night's Caressing Grip', pp. 9–21.

Berlin (directed by Walter Felsenstein, who had over six months of rehearsal), and in Moscow as well. Happily we have the audio recording that Britten made for Decca in 1966, with Deller back in as Oberon. Analysis of these early performances is mostly confined to press reviews, although Howard Taubman wrote two extended pieces in the *New York Times* about the Aldeburgh production. The world-wide approval found a dissenter in Britten's erstwhile friend W. H. Auden, who wrote to Stephen Spender about seeing the London production and finding it 'Dreadful! Pure Kensington'.[7]

One of the delights of Britten's *Dream* is that the *Pyramus and Thisby* interlude in Act 3, designed originally by Shakespeare as a parody of old-fashioned drama, presents a succession of operatic parodies, with the composer in mischievous mood: indeed, although the musical directions throughout the rest of the score are written in English, all these pages contain markings strictly in Italian. Thisby's final lament over Pyramus, 'Asleep, my love? / What, dead, my dove?' lampoons the conventions of a Donizetti mad scene, complete with flute obbligato, and thus one of the highlights of that first run was Peter Pears's devastating mimicry of Joan Sutherland, who had only the year before created a sensation in *Lucia di Lammermoor* at Covent Garden. Britten was not altogether delighted with the expanded Royal Opera production of *A Midsummer Night's Dream*; this is hardly surprising from a composer who detested Jon Vickers's performance as Peter Grimes. As one writer puts it, the composer tended to be 'proprietorial' about his productions.[8]

REPRESENTATION: PETER HALL, GLYNDEBOURNE 1981

At Glyndebourne in 1981 Peter Hall created a *Dream* that quickly achieved iconic status. Hall was Director of Production at Glyndebourne at the time, as well as Director of the National Theatre and formerly Founding Director of the Royal Shakespeare Company – in other words, a natural

for this assignment. Received with almost universal rapture, his staging was considered by many to be the benchmark (and by some still is so considered) for what a staging of the opera ought to be. Peter Pears told John Christie that 'he wished Ben had lived to see it, that he would have loved it'.[9] Bernard Haitink, Music Director of Glyndebourne at the time, conducted to great acclaim, emphasizing the passion in the score and achieving, according to one reviewer, 'a Mahlerian intensity in the Prelude to Act 2'.[10] On the videotape (as in the first performances) James Bowman sings the King of the Fairies, having become the Oberon of choice beginning in the late 1960s (and continuing to perform it until the 1990s); Ileana Cotrubas is Tytania; among the lovers, the notable performance is Felicity Lott's tall, gangly Helena. The mechanicals (or 'rustics', the noun Britten uses) underplay their scenes, relatively speaking. Bottom's asinine head looks exactly right, like an illustration in a children's book, both ridiculous and slightly sweet.

Hall's staging is straightforward but by no means unimaginative. Like most of his work both in the theatre and the opera house, it is perspicuous in narrative detail and always attentive to the text. The designs, by John Bury, look as if they are realistic, but that 'realism' is deceptive. The forest, for example, is both naturalistic and not, dimly lit and shrouded in fog, representing the liminal world of night and nature. For it, Bury created trees that embody this medial state: their crowns and leaves are realistic, but the trunks are actors, cloaked in dark attire and moving slightly to magical and perhaps sinister effect. The decision by composer and librettist to cut Shakespeare's first Athenian scene, beginning the show with the quarrel between Oberon and Tytania, places the emphasis

---

[7] Reported in Humphrey Carpenter, *W. H. Auden: A Biography* (Oxford, 1992), p. 428.

[8] David Nice, 'Reinventing the *Dream*: *A Midsummer Night's Dream* on Stage', in Overture Opera Guides, p. 43.

[9] Michael Kennedy, ''Tis almost fairy time', Glyndebourne Festival Programme Book (2001), p. 83.

[10] Richard Fairman, *Opera*, Festival Issue (1989), p. 26.

squarely on the supernatural plot, and its theatrical centrality emerges immediately from the elaborate costumes and hair for the fairy king and queen, from their demeanour and posture, and from their high-lying musical declamation. The chorus of fairy boys are dressed in a witty combination of the fantastic and the historical, gossamer wings and Elizabethan ruffs. Nothing is entirely straightforward or uncomplicated, and yet this mixture of periods and realms of being is always subtle, never heavy-handed.

The wedding celebrations of Act 3 are held in the great hall of a Tudor house, from which the camera pulls back slightly to acknowledge the presence of an audience in the opera house, breaking for the first time the diegesis that has so far been scrupulously observed. This manoeuvre may be the producers' attempt to capture the Shakespearian strategy of worlds arranged within worlds: the mechanicals in the centre; the Athenians in the next circle; the fairies outside; beyond them the theatre audience; we, the video viewers, watching all; and then perhaps a celestial audience observing us as we both watch and play our parts. This breaking of the fourth wall, possible for the videotaped performance in a way that it would not have been in the opera house, is consistent with the fluid quality characteristic of Hall's vision. The musicologist Roger Parker, writing about the last of several revivals of the show at Glyndebourne, acknowledges and applauds the 'simple matching of visual and musical means':

aspects of the staging mirror the famed ambiguity (or, perhaps better, ambivalence) of Britten's musical language. That shifting forest, for example, gradually reveals itself to be operated by shadowy human figures, 'scene shifters' who seem to be poised delicately in some liminal space, between the fictional and the practical world – are these bush carriers and tree shakers part of the opera or part of the production? And this uncertainty, this blurring of theatrical edges, is something also explored in the music: think of the way in which, in the last act, the most intense moments of musical parody (those passionate, Italian violin melodies) threaten to break out of the comic and flood the orchestra with 'real' emotional charge.[11]

This perception about the work's musical liminality is especially pertinent because it is consistent with contemporary productions of Shakespeare's play: in the past few years it has become almost *de rigueur* for directors and actors to try to make Thisbe's final lament truly moving as well as absurd.

RE-PRESENTATION: ROBERT CARSEN, BARCELONA

Robert Carsen gets a lot of mileage out of his productions. Much sought after as an opera director, especially in Europe and the UK, he came to prominence partly on the strength of his widely seen staging of Boito's *Mefistofele*. His *Dream* began life in the early 1990s in Aix-en-Provence, played in numerous European festivals and cities, and was filmed in connection with performances in Barcelona in 2005. Eros is the overriding theme this time, and the highly stylized designs (Michael Levine) are calculated to emphasize the erotic throughout the several spheres. The stage is dominated by an enormous green bed with two extremely large pillows: this is the forest. It is backed by a blue cyclorama with a crescent moon above. Smaller beds make their appearance later, for Tytania and Bottom and for the lovers. The sexual current – undercurrent would be understatement – the sexual torrent is embodied in a variety of details: as one reviewer of the La Scala performances put it, 'we'd be remiss to not mention [Bottom's] 20-inch strap-on that would make Dirk Diggler blush'.[12] The Indian boy is an infant swaddled in an earth-coloured blanket. Puck is played not by a child or adolescent but by an ageing actor, the exceedingly athletic Emil Wolk: this clown's vexed relationship with Oberon makes for considerable comedy during the confusion over the love lotion. The fairy chorus is extremely stylized, a disciplined line of miniature bellboys or butlers, with painted moustaches instead of wings.

---

[11] Review in *Opera* (2006), p. 987.
[12] www.operachic.com (June 8, 2009). Dirk Diggler is a porn star in the film *Boogie Nights*.

Carsen succeeds in creating meaning with the use of colour. The greensward of a bed is recapitulated not only in the same vibrant green of Oberon's majestic robes but also in the tint of his hair: clearly this realm is dominated by the king of the fairies. His queen is clothed in the equally assertive blue of the sky, not only her gown but also the matching blue wig. The fairy-servants wear green trousers (aligning them with Oberon) and blue swallowtail coats (signifying their allegiance to Tytania). The lovers enter dressed in white and cream, very posh, Hermia in a gown of flouncing ruffles and carrying hatboxes and valises also in cream; Helena, by contrast, resembles a stylish intellectual or executive secretary, stiffly costumed in a tight white Chanel-style suit with eye-glasses on a chain and chopsticks in her French twist. The young men appear à la *Brideshead*, white sporting jackets and trousers. As the shifted alliances and ensuing quarrel proceed, these pristine outfits become increasingly soiled with grass-stains, taking on the green of the forest bed, and by the end of their struggles the mortals have stripped to their hopelessly green-streaked underwear. One critic felt that 'to show the young lovers in white costumes which became progressively more tattered and filthy – a symbol of their loss of purity? – is surely a somewhat shopworn idea'.[13] Apparently this sour reviewer has seen too many recent productions of the play, for which the increasingly tattered clothing has become a standard turn. But in the last act of Carsen's *Dream*, when the lovers awaken for their magical quartet, their knickers are miraculously cleansed.

Although superstar directors are not usually known for their *Personenregie*, the careful direction of their actors, Carsen has drawn detailed, meaningful performances from his singers. As George Hall writes, reviewing the DVD release, 'The four lovers in particular, who in a sloppy staging can be a wan and indeterminate lot, emerge here with their identities and shifting emotional allegiances strikingly intact.'[14] And, as is characteristic of most of Carsen's productions, the staging abounds with invention and humour. Here some of that wit explores class conflicts arising from the interaction of the three different realms. For example, the fairies, standing on the dignity of their position as royal servants, are having none of Bottom. Thus when Peaseblossom is obliged to scratch the ass's head, the diminutive fairy pulls a face indicating extreme distaste and then takes from his pocket a surgical glove for his hand (already gloved) before commencing with the scratch. When the fairy king and queen are reunited and Oberon gives the swaddled Indian boy into the keeping of Puck, the actor looks as if he has been handed something rotten.

Reporting on one of the live performances of Carsen's *Dream*, Joel Kasow notes the popular and critical success of the production but suggests that it 'would probably not have gone down well with the composer or librettist'.[15] That judgement is probably accurate, although it says more about Britten's conservatism with the staging of his work than it does about Carsen's achievement. Although abstract and non-specific in its *mise-en-scène*, the Barcelona *Dream* is brilliant to look at but hardly radical. It recreates the action as Shakespeare and Britten imagined it, cleverly and colourfully, always seeking new means to realize, not to alter or subvert, the magic spirit of the piece. And the *Pyramus and Thisby* interlude is genuinely funny, the giant bed now converted to a platform stage and the aristocratic audience looking on from behind. In its way this staging of the opera is as emotionally powerful as Hall's – decidedly hip in appearance but *re*-presenting rather than departing from the fundamental aims of playwright and composer.

INTERVENTION, OR SUB-TEXT ON STILTS: CHRISTOPHER ALDEN, ENGLISH NATIONAL OPERA 2011

If Carsen's work is likely to have displeased Britten, one shudders to imagine the composer's reaction to the most recent version staged at the English National Opera in May 2011. Since one predictable

---

[13] Joel Kasow, 'Major and Minor Modes', *Opera*, Festival Issue (1991), p. 68.

[14] George Hall, *Opera* (May 2006), p. 618.

[15] Kasow, 'Major and Minor Modes', p. 67.

feature of modern opera production is directorial resiting of the action, in Christopher Alden's concept (read CONCEPT) we remove from 'A Wood Near Athens' to an English urban state school, all grey brick and high windows, the noun BOYS carved into the lintel above the door. But the student body now includes girls, at least two of them, Hermia and Helena, and the opera's three character groups are distributed according to their function in the school. The fairies who begin the opera are pupils, as is Puck, and among this lot there is a good deal of smoking, loitering in shades and trying to look grown up. The King and Queen of Fairies have been translated into Head Teachers, male and female, Oberon as the Latin Master, Tytania the music mistress. The mechanicals are the custodial staff of janitors and maintenance men. One reviewer pointed out that the soprano Anna Christy as Tytania was made to resemble Imogen Holst, daughter of the composer Gustav, she who lived with Britten and Pears in Suffolk and acted as a kind of amanuensis, PA, musical assistant, and sounding board.[16]

Alden, however, has added a character, whom I introduce by citing the first line of the Synopsis in the ENO programme: 'On the eve of his wedding, a man returns to his old school. Long-forgotten memories of his schooldays come back to him in the form of a dream.' As the orchestra sounds out Britten's famous musical snore, the man (played by Paul Whelan) is joined by a younger version of himself, a schoolboy dressed identically, down to the rep tie. The teenager is Puck, as we recognize from his 'How now, spirits!' The dreaming figure, we will discover in Act 3, is Theseus, undergoing a kind of dream therapy before being wedded to an Amazon. According to Michael White in *The Daily Telegraph*, Alden's 'big idea – which is both fascinating and clever – is that Puck's traumatic dream happens on the eve of marriage. He has grown up to be Theseus, and he needs to confront these childhood memories before he can make a good relationship with Hippolyta.'[17] The first act introduces the mortal lovers, in this case schoolboys and schoolgirls, with Hermia and Lysander snogging behind the rubbish bins but, appropriately,

the action is given over mainly to the dispute over the changeling boy – a new pupil. Oberon seems to have thrown over Puck for the new favourite of Tytania. She leads him away from the Latin master past a blackboard on which is written the conjugation of *amare*; when Oberon punishes Puck with a beating, the blackboard reads 'Out of this wood do not desire to go.'

The second act is nightmarish. Shakespeare's and Britten's nocturnal fantasy – Tytania's erotic obsession with Bottom and the mortal lovers' quarrel – becomes a frightening inversion of all things pedagogical. The sullen fairies lounging on the steps or in the schoolyard smoking cigarettes (or something stronger) help to spark the saturnalia. Tytania's attraction to Bottom is induced by Oberon's having drugged her apparently with marijuana, whereupon, stripping to her brassière, the music mistress has her way with the building's custodian. He is the distinguished baritone Sir Willard White, here not ass-like in the least: no visual transformation occurs, merely the removal of his shirt as he is doted upon and twinèd in her arms. The lovers in their school uniforms join the schoolyard confusion. The end of the act brings a genuine *coup de théâtre*, a violent conflagration in which the fairies set the school afire and flames lick from the windows. All is finally calmed with the entrance of a white veiled figure – she will turn out to be Hippolyta – and a very orderly line of singing boys.

The third act presents restored harmony between Oberon and Tytania (or such harmony as there can be in this institution), the awakening quartet for the lovers, the entrance of Theseus (post-dream) with Hippolyta, the presentation of the custodians' interlude, and finally the blessing of the – er – house. The mechanicals seemed as sullen and joyless as the rest of the cast. The *Pyramus and Thisby* episode, unfailingly funny, was not funny. Very colourful – all red and gold costumes and bunting – their show seemed desperate and

---

[16] Michael White, 'ENO's shocking new paedophile *Midsummer Night's Dream* is brilliant, and I hated it', *Daily Telegraph*, 20 May 2011.

[17] White, 'ENO's shocking *Midsummer Night's Dream*'.

gratuitous, so unashamedly sexual that during Thisby's final number, one of the other mechanicals masturbates wildly at the side of the stage. (As Anna Russell says, 'I'm not making this up, you know.'[18]) The conclusion returns us to the beginning. According to the critic Mark Berry:

we were in for another turn of the screw. [Theseus] is a tormented man, turned tormentor, who, following the rustics' departure, manages to free himself from his respectable, echt-1950s wife, [and] returns to the school to revisit Puck... Puck, whom one might expect now to be triumphant, appears broken, perhaps literally. The abuse, and abuse it undoubtedly is, has taken its toll. Rather than force himself upon the boy again, the Duke, perhaps chastened, as a Puck himself in later life, slinks away. Puck's final words are defiant, but we know that this boy will remain troubled.[19]

Almost to a person, reviewers referred to the production as the 'Paedophile Dream'.

The immediate question raised by Alden's interpretation concerns the director's exploitation of Benjamin Britten's well-known attraction to adolescent males. What kind of attraction? It is worth attempting to analyse the nature of that impulse and the extent of its reach: there is a great deal of evidence, much of it conflicting or at best inconclusive. The ENO programme is of little help, and in one case downright dishonest. It reprints an extract from 'A Suitable Boy', a magazine article by Don Boyd originally published ten years previously, in which the middle-aged writer, now married with two children, describes his earliest sexual experiences with his male French teacher, encounters that surely warrant the name of sexual abuse. 'I now realize that, for all my protestations that "it has done me no harm" and that what occurred was "one of life's rich experiences", what [he] did to me was appallingly cynical and inexcusable... I am still living with the consequences of [his] behaviour, and have only just begun to analyse its impact on my life and relationships.'[20] Boyd's is a compelling story, well told and furnishing recognizable detail about early foreign-language training with a charismatic instructor, but its relevance to the biographical and artistic history of Benjamin

Britten is precisely zero. Indeed its prominence in the programme invites the spectator to make connections and draw inferences for which there is no justification whatever. Another programme piece is more responsible, a judicious essay by John Bridcut that locates Britten's lifelong devotion to children, particularly boys, in the composer's own schooldays. Author of a serious monograph on the subject, Bridcut illuminates Britten's ambiguous attitude towards boarding school, complaining to his parents about the privations and miseries of Gresham's but apparently liking the place and retaining throughout adulthood a fondness for its associations and memories, fixed in the crucial age between twelve and fifteen.[21] (For example, for the rest of his life he preferred cold baths.) Britten's homosexuality was indisputably a dominant feature of his life from early on, and his partnership with Peter Pears, beginning in the 1930s, was apparently the focus of his sexual life. We know that Britten made and sustained for a time close relationships with several adolescent boys between the 1940s and the 1960s: these included Ronald Duncan, David Hemmings and other less well-known names. Given Britten's sexual drives, these relationships almost certainly evoked erotic feelings. But there is no evidence that the composer acted upon such sexual impulses.[22] Alden,

---

18 Anna Russell is the English-Canadian singer and comedienne (1911–2006), whose most popular piece is her comic narration of Wagner's *Ring of the Nibelungs*, available on audio disc. The quotation occurs when she notes that Gutrune is the first woman Siegfried has seen who wasn't his aunt.

19 http://boulezian.blogspot.com/2011/05/midsummer-nights-dream-english-national.html

20 'A Suitable Boy', English National Opera Programme for *A Midsummer Night's Dream*, May 2011, p. 17. The extract is from an article first published in the *Observer Magazine*, 19 August 2001.

21 'A Precocious Schoolboy,' English National Opera Programme Book (London, 2011), pp. 10–13. Bridcut's book is *Britten's Children* (London, 2006).

22 Philip Brett, one of the pioneers of gay musicology, states that the composer 'seems never to have forced himself on his young friends': 'Britten's *Dream*', in *Music and Sexuality in Britten*, ed. George E. Haggerty (Berkeley, 2006), p. 114.

however, grafts his salacious reading of the composer's emotional biography onto the narrative of *A Midsummer Night's Dream* and teases the audience with an imaginary scenario almost entirely alien to the spirit of the work.

There is no denying the cleverness of Alden's idea or the brilliance of its execution, and in some respects his production is faithful to Britten's text. It offers, for example, a pointed critique of authority and power, two concerns that thread themselves constantly through the letters of the pacifist composer. But these are not the only topics subjected to doubt. Love, imagination, theatre, self-discovery, joy – all are treated sceptically, at times even scornfully. Alden inflects Britten's operatic text with sinister implications and colourings, trading disingenuously on the cheapest, ugliest construction of the composer's emotional life. It has been suggested that the negativity of such a production resembles the case of a pianist's or conductor's giving prominence to a usually subordinated musical phrase.[23] Or we might say that the dark reading complicates the affirmations of the score by adding a kind of chromatic dissonance, a complementary shadow to balance the brightness. But what if this added layer contradicts or cancels the significations of the score? When does representation tip over into misrepresentation? Is every representation a misrepresentation? What rights does the composer have? Or the playwright? Might not Alden defend his staging on the grounds that every representation is a commentary and that the composer has already distorted the original Shakespearian object in adapting the dramatic text? In the case of the ENO *Dream*, what matters is whether this dubious narrative represents a legitimate basis for staging Britten's adaptation of Shakespeare.

The negativity of the production is almost total, its promotion of subtext at the expense of text and score a distortion. Early analysts of Britten's opera, musicologists such as Wilfrid Mellers and Michael Kennedy, felt compelled to remind readers that neither play nor opera is exactly a trip to the moon on gossamer wings, that dreams could be not only delicious but also terrifying. As Kennedy put it in 1981, 'Enchantment can be for good or

evil and part of the flavour of this score is the menace which lurks behind the exchanges between Oberon and Tytania, not entirely exorcised by their rapt slow saraband when Tytania is reunited with him in Act III after her nightmare experience with Bottom.'[24] Now, however, the proportions have been almost entirely reversed and the 'menace' so exaggerated that, conversely, reviewers of Alden's production have felt it appropriate to remind readers that dreams can be pleasurable and that neither Britten's nor Shakespeare's *Dream* is a product of the theatre of cruelty. Also germane to the problem of interpretation is the delicate complementarity built into Britten's score. For all the potential terrors of the dark, the harmonic, rhythmic and melodic textures are exceedingly ambiguous and thus hard to evaluate. As Kennedy notices, with reference to Tytania's liaison with Bottom, 'it is for this "nightmare" . . . that Britten composed the most seductive, passionate and lyrical music of the opera – of any of his operas'.[25]

This question of interpretation has become central to the discussion of operatic performance in the twenty-first century. The growing prominence of certain avant-garde directors, particularly in Europe, has divided audiences, delighting some and enraging others. Moreover, readers of *Shakespeare Survey* will be aware that the questions raised here are hardly less pertinent to the direction of Shakespeare's plays. As I write, Stratford audiences are enduring Rupert Goold's production of what has been referred to as *The Merchant of Vegas*.[26] Whatever one's response, it seems clear first that these provocative directors and their teams are here to stay, both in the opera house and the theatre, and second that their arrival has created a need for theorizing or at least responsible debate about the differences between presentation, re-presentation and

---

[23] Professor Daniel Albright of Harvard University made this point during the discussion period at the conference on *Shakespeare and Opera: Found in Translation*, UCLA, 7 November 2011.

[24] *Britten*, Master Musicians Series, ed. Stanley Sadie (London, 1981), p. 221.

[25] Kennedy, "Tis almost fairy time', p. 221.

[26] See the review by Carol Rutter on pp. 480–3 below.

misrepresentation. So far little of value has been published. Linda Hutcheon, whose critical study called *Theory of Adaptation* we might expect to be suggestive, argues the thesis that adaptation is second but not secondary, but she is virtually silent on the question of performance as adaptation.[27] The rest of the library doesn't take us very far either: the critical maps of this terrain are very crude. Perhaps surprisingly, the internet, although it necessarily attracts and disseminates its share of nonsense, offers much cogent analysis and debate about these interpretive and artistic questions.[28]

Having posed a series of questions and implied some answers, I conclude by being more direct. It is risky to draw sweeping conclusions about questions of taste, interpretation and performance, so my practice, when it comes to Directors' Opera, has been to proceed on a case by case basis. On successive nights at Bayreuth I attended two performances that I loathed and loved: Katherina Wagner's unspeakable *Meistersinger*, the worst production of an opera I have ever seen, and Stefan Herheim's thrilling *Parsifal*, with a concept much more radical than Ms Wagner's but one in which the young Norwegian director employed his imaginative flights in a sympathetic engagement with the musical and verbal text. Creative adaptation is not necessarily good adaptation, and it is not necessarily bad adaptation. Certainly every production need not follow to the letter the stated preferences of the artist who created it: the end of that approach yields a performance that might be described as late D'Oyly Carte. Objection to directorial adventurism does not necessarily imply reactionary politics or artistic conservatism. Nor is innovation always new: sometimes, in the words of the poet Donald Hall, 'it's novelty, old novelty again'.

Are there guidelines for discriminating between intervention and interpretation? Pre-production publicity can be useful; reviewers may post warnings; certain names are to be avoided. To be fair to the ENO, their advertising campaign indicated that Alden's would be a non-traditional *Dream*. At times the desire to hear an infrequently performed opera will lead me to ignore what I know about a production team or to suppress my misgivings. The experience of the potential audience has some pertinence here: I can risk an off-the-wall reading of a familiar piece for myself, but I would not want the lab-rat *Lohengrin* to be anybody's first performance of the opera.[29] To be blunt, I would say that the criterion for success or failure is the degree to which the director's style is consonant with the work's imaginative structure; legitimate production entails observing the limits established by composer and librettist. I applaud productions that attempt to interpret the piece; I deplore those that seek mainly to comment on or subvert it. What is wanted is invention, not intervention. For me, the ENO *Dream* was an act of vandalism, a violation of the work's spirit that substituted the director's vision for the composer's. Britten's opera is not inhospitable to darkness or irony but in this case those tones tyrannized all other responses. While admiring the verve and creativity with which the director translated the original into its new context, I believe that Christopher Alden is probably less talented than William Shakespeare and Benjamin Britten, and that his production occludes their achievement, which I had paid to see and hear. Perhaps Linda Hutcheon needs to rethink her axiom, acknowledging that adaptation is always second but sometimes also secondary. And I look forward to someone else's version of Britten's version of Shakespeare's version of love and imagination.

---

[27] Linda Hutcheon, *Theory of Adaptation* (London, 2009).

[28] See particularly the series of articles under the title 'Rough and Regie' by James Jorden, posted on the *Musical America* website. Jorden is the originator of the 'queer opera zine' *Parterre Box* and music critic for the *New York Post*.

[29] I refer to Hans Neuenfels's Bayreuth production (2010), in which the chorus were costumed as rats.

STAGING *A MIDSUMMER NIGHT'S DREAM*: PETER HALL'S PRODUCTIONS, 1959–2010

ROGER WARREN

During the last fifty years, Peter Hall has been closely associated with *A Midsummer Night's Dream*: six productions and a film. He began at Stratford-upon-Avon in 1959; the production was revived there, much modified, in 1962, and still further revised at the Aldwych Theatre, London, in 1963. These stagings formed the basis of the film that he made in 1967, released in 1969. He returned to the play in a somewhat different form, Benjamin Britten's operatic version, at Glyndebourne in 1981, revived many times since then. *A Midsummer Night's Dream* was one of the two productions he staged at the Ahmanson Theatre, Los Angeles, in 1999; and he returned to it yet again at the Rose Theatre, Kingston-upon-Thames, in 2010. Each production, he said, was 'a development of previous knowledge'.[1]

Although the productions certainly did develop, some basic assumptions about the play remained constant; so it is useful to begin with Peter Hall's brief statement about these, taken from the programme of his most recent production, at the Kingston Rose:

Shakespeare's play is set in Athens, but this classical device is to distance and romanticise what is, in fact, a very Elizabethan and very English play. Bottom and his mates are the workers of Warwickshire. Theseus is no pagan warrior, but a country duke who practises an essentially English brand of pragmatism when things get difficult, especially with the young. The Renaissance conceits of the four young lovers belong to the Elizabethan love-lyrics. And the fairies in their wilfulness and sexiness are not classical, but sprites of Hallowe'en.

The play is earthy and passionate, about Beauty and the Beast and the anguish of young love. Its world is Northern rather than the Mediterranean. Athens, for Shakespeare, is an English country community suffering, as usual, a very bad summer. The quarrel between Oberon and Titania has upset the seasons, giving torrential rain, frost in June, and ice on the rose. Shakespeare knew that fairy tales must be concrete if they are to be human and not whimsical.

Oberon's 'I know a bank where the wild thyme blows' is one of the supreme pieces of lyric writing in English, yet he is talking about a flower which is going to wreck Titania's life. English lyricism is always harsh, or rather, realistic. It is rarely sentimental. It's about the actuality of passion, the pain of sex, the difficulty of it, and the essential desire on everybody's part to achieve love.

However much they varied in other respects, two features have been common to all Peter Hall's productions: the creation of an Elizabethan world, and specifically of an Elizabethan court world, together with a very detailed presentation of a rural world – thus reflecting that combination of the courtly and the rural which distinguishes the play and gives it its special flavour.[2]

---

[1] Quotations from Peter Hall are from conversations, from the rehearsals for the Rose production, or from his statements made at the time of his earlier versions. I saw all of them except the Los Angeles one, upon which I cannot therefore comment, although I prepared the performing text for it, which was also used at the Rose. Quotations are from that text, based on the 1600 quarto.

[2] A shortened version of the 1959 production, made for American television, can be viewed at the Shakespeare Centre library, Stratford-upon-Avon; the 1967/9 film has been issued

19. Theseus's country house, transformed into the wood, Stratford-upon-Avon, 1959.

STRATFORD 1959, 1962; LONDON 1963; FILM 1967/9

In his first production of the play in 1959, Peter Hall drew on a theory, current at the time, that the play might have been written for, or at least performed at, an aristocratic Elizabethan wedding. So his set, designed by the distinguished Italian artist Lila de Nobili, was the rush-strewn great hall of an Elizabethan manor house – as it might be Charlecote, near Stratford – which, thanks to the cunning use of painted gauzes, was effortlessly transformed into a wood. (Illustration 19 shows this transformation taking place.) The Elizabethan costumes for the mortal court were subtly modified for the fairy one: they were Elizabethan in shape but made of a fabric which suggested the cobwebs, dew and gossamer of the fairies' natural environment.

Within this setting, Theseus was very much the pragmatic country duke of Hall's description, particularly when Tony Steedman played the part in

1962 and 1963. T. C. Worsley caught his tone neatly: 'Things are always, his manner implies, arrangeable' (*Financial Times*, 14 June 1963). This treatment brought out the way in which, when Theseus sees the lovers correctly – 'fortunately' – paired, he does what in the opening scene he says he couldn't do, and bends the strict letter of the law when it is in the interests of his subjects to do so. It was here in particular that what Hall calls Theseus's 'humanity and wisdom' emerged most clearly. The character seemed much more interesting than in most modern productions.

It was perhaps in his treatment of the four lovers that Peter Hall's handling of the play developed most significantly over the years. In 1959 they were played for broad humour; this drew some adverse

---

on DVD by an American company (WBF 8043); and the Glyndebourne production was recorded by Southern Television and is available on DVD (Warner PC49348).

20. Charles Laughton as Bottom, Stratford, 1959.

criticism, and Hall modified this approach subsequently, and beneficially, especially at Glyndebourne and at the Rose, although the humorous potential of these scenes was never entirely forgotten; and in any case it chimes well with the way in which these lovers fall into the clichés and chinking rhymes of conventional Elizabethan lyric, even to the point of parody:

O Helen, goddess, nymph, perfect, divine!
To what, my love, shall I compare thine eyne?

Hall subsequently stressed the 'dangers' of being in love, and the way in which the lovers' experiences in the wood helped them to 'define the demands of love and loyalty'.

Hall emphasized the warm humanity of the mechanicals' scenes. These were often taken at a strikingly slow pace, not simply because the characters were slow on the uptake, but because they were thinking things out. They took their play very seriously indeed, and were the funnier for it. This

is, of course, a basic principle of playing comedy: the more seriously you take your character, the more laughs you will release. The chief innovation here was that, when he was transformed, Bottom did not have a complete ass's head, but only 'fair large ears' and ass's hooves on his hands and feet (Illustration 20). This had the advantage of allowing Charles Laughton's and later Paul Hardwick's facial expressions full play, and also of emphasizing how, even when he is 'translated', Bottom remains very much himself. His scenes with Titania were at the heart of the production, especially when Judi Dench joined the company in 1962.

Judi Dench is another of the constant elements in Peter Hall's (Illustration 21; Illustration 22) productions, since she also played Titania in his film and at the Rose in 2010. She has the full range of qualities that the part requires: natural authority, a spontaneous impish sense of humour, and the ability to speak formal verse with both clarity and sensuous beauty. In her scenes with Bottom, for example, she showed a delicious combination of sensuality and delicacy as she stroked his 'fair large ears'; she used her irresistible sense of humour in her chuckling appreciation of Bottom's wit and wisdom, yet she could move from that to instant authority at 'I am a spirit of no common rate.' And in her long speech about the bad weather that has resulted from her quarrel with Oberon, she used that characteristic little catch in the voice to express her sympathy with the 'human mortals' who 'want their winter cheer'. The whole speech, magnificently delivered and sustained, drew much critical acclaim; but Judi Dench herself attributes her success to Peter Hall's guidance: 'he knew *exactly* what he wanted. He knew precisely. I remember the *Dream* rehearsals being exceptionally *easy*.'[3] And when he came to film the speech, he supported her with constantly varying images of the seasonal chaos she describes, changing the shot, as he put it, 'at the end of the line, or at the caesura'; even when making a film, Peter Hall observes Shakespeare's verse structure.

---

[3] Cited by David Addenbrooke, *The Royal Shakespeare Company: The Peter Hall Years* (London, 1974), p. 99.

21. Judi Dench as Titania, Stratford, 1962.

22. Judi Dench as Titania, Rose Theatre, Kingston, 2010.

Opposite Judi Dench in 1962, Ian Richardson's Oberon was 'a fop in his bearing and a poet in his speaking, like a dandy such as Lytton Strachey in his book on Elizabeth and Essex [which was, incidentally, an influence on Hall's 2010 production],

represented as being typical of the period' (*The Times*, 18 April 1962). So the fairy court mirrored the mortal one.

Such mirroring was the element missing from the film that Peter Hall made in 1967, with many of the casts from his Stratford versions, in the house and wood at Compton Verney, near Stratford, thus sustaining the Warwickshire connection. The main difference was that Hall came to feel that even Lila de Nobili's imaginative costumes for the fairies were too substantial and mortal in a real wood, so they were pared away until the fairies were nearly naked. This certainly accorded with Hall's view that he had always sought to make the fairies 'more sensual than the mortals'; and if they no longer suggested an alternative court to that of Theseus and Hippolyta, they were certainly 'spirits of another sort' – inhabitants of Warwickshire woods.

GLYNDEBOURNE, 1981

To say that Peter Hall's interpretation of *A Midsummer Night's Dream* reached a climax at Glyndebourne in 1981 may seem paradoxical but Britten recreates the essence of the play so successfully that Peter Hall's work on the opera marked a significant stage in his interpretation of the play. Britten, who had admired Hall's 1959 staging, had asked him to direct the original production of his opera at Aldeburgh in 1960 but, since 1960 was the first season of Peter Hall's creation of the Royal Shakespeare Company at Stratford, that was impossible. Even so, Hall says, 'the piece haunted me. Britten was a genius at setting English. I can't read Oberon's "I know a bank", or see it, without thinking of Britten's setting. What fascinated Britten was the nature of the wood, the nature of night, and the nature of dreams, and those extraordinary motifs for the orchestra, strange haunting glissandos.' Those glissandos were the key to the Glyndebourne production.

Responding to Shakespeare's vivid poetic evocation of it, Britten makes the wood a living presence, expressed in orchestral sighs marked 'slowly animating'. Hall and his designer John Bury in their turn responded to this by creating a moving wood:

23. A moving wood at Glyndebourne, 1981.

branches, bushes and logs were animated by black-clad actors, so that from the very first bars the wood moved mysteriously in the moonlight, precisely matching the musical phrases (Illustration 23). This was the most striking development from the Stratford versions; but Oberon and Titania were, more than ever, Elizabethan grandees, and their connection with the rural world was even more marked: Oberon's wig, for example, was brushed back and streaked with black, like a badger's. But perhaps the most memorable moment came in the fairies' blessing of the palace (one of Britten's most inspired passages): they could be seen gathering outside the casement windows of Theseus's palace before coming through them – a potent image of a country house surrounded by a wood and its inhabitants.

When I reviewed the first night of this production in these pages,[4] I thought that the four lovers gave the best performances of these characters that I had seen, in any version, up to that point: they were subtle, eloquent and impassioned. They were greatly helped by the composer, especially in their quartet of amazement just before they leave the wood. Britten seizes his opportunity for an ensemble, building upon Helena's 'Mine own and not mine own', which is one of the jewels of the score and was a major climax of this production. This certainly represented a notable development from Hall's first version in 1959, where the lovers' quartet was cut completely, perhaps in line with his broadly humorous approach to the lovers at that time; it was restored in 1962 and thereafter.

I suggested in my review that these lovers were so powerful and eloquent as to draw attention away from Oberon and Titania, whose music suggests that they are the composer's centre of interest. But watching the DVD of that production,

---

4 *Shakespeare Survey 35* (Cambridge, 1982), pp. 144–6.

I now think that was unfair to James Bowman's Oberon, in particular, which is a remarkable performance. He has unusual power for a countertenor – and unusual stage authority, too. I said in 1981 that he lacked clarity of diction; on the first night maybe, but not by the time the production was filmed for television, where he relishes both Shakespeare's text and Britten's setting of it. He also maintains an Olympian distance: he is a 'king of shadows' whom it will be dangerous to cross. This emerges notably when he plans to anoint Titania's eyes with the magic juice. 'I'll make her render up her page to me' is delivered smilingly, with just a hint of sadism; he turns away, but then half turns back to us, implying coolly, 'Don't tangle with me.'

The weakness of the opera lies in Britten's handling of Theseus, who doesn't appear until the play scene, and even then you can hear, from his vocal line, that Britten isn't interested in him. This is the main departure from the play, as Peter Hall observes: 'The play is about marriage, the necessity of it, and how we can learn to *be* married. Shakespeare pegs the whole thing round the marriage of Theseus and Hippolyta. Theseus and Hippolyta don't enter the opera until the end, and they're ciphers, they're hardly anything. But the centre of the humanity and wisdom of the play is Theseus. There isn't any wisdom in the opera; it's an evocation of the dark forces of lust – very beautiful and very seductive, but rather alarming.'

THE ROSE, KINGSTON

Any account of a production at the Kingston Rose requires a brief statement about its stage, which is a scrupulous reconstruction of the Elizabethan Rose theatre, whose foundations were revealed during an archaeological dig in 1989. There, amazingly, preserved in the London mud of four centuries, were some of the timbers of the original Rose stage – or rather, *two* stages, the first one of *c.*1587 and the modification of 1592. The shape of each stage was clearly visible, and they called into question received opinion of what an Elizabethan stage might have looked like. For it did

not 'thrust' deeply into the audience, as the pencil sketch of the Swan theatre or the contract for the Fortune theatre imply; instead, the Rose stage was 'lozenge' shaped: wide and narrow, tapering towards the front. The entire audience was in front of the stage, not clustered around its sides. Advocates of the 'thrust' stage argue that it enables the actor to get well forward, amongst the audience, and so increases communication. But when actors advance to the front of the thrust, they leave a significant proportion of the audience *behind* them; those spectators are certainly not being communicated with. At the Rose, by contrast, the actor could communicate with the whole house, as they were all in front of him.

Peter Hall has been an impassioned advocate of the Kingston Rose and is now its Director Emeritus. What, then, were the advantages of this stage, to him, for presenting *A Midsummer Night's Dream*? First, he said, 'it frees the actor to talk to the audience, to encourage their laughter or tears', a freedom of which Charles Edwards, playing Oberon, took full advantage, inviting the laughter of collusion at 'I am invisible' or 'I wonder if Titania be awaked', or sharing with them both the lyrical beauty and the malicious intent of 'I know a bank', to which Hall refers and always emphasizes. The width of the stage allowed plenty of room for scenes that can seem cramped on other stages: when the lovers were put to sleep, for example, each pair lay down on either side of the 'lozenge' at the front. Bottom was asleep on Titania's bower at the back; so there was plenty of space in the centre for the dance of reconciliation between Oberon and Titania, and later for Theseus's hunting party. It was also an ideal space for the lovers' quarrel, where Hall stressed the darkness and dangers more fully than in his previous versions. And whereas those versions had used elaborate settings, here there was virtually no scenery at all: Hall relished the opportunity to exploit the potential of the Rose stage as it stood. The Elizabethan world was created instead by Elizabeth Bury's magnificent costumes; many of them were in fact those she had designed for the Glyndebourne production, generously loaned by the opera house.

Whereas at Stratford the Elizabethan court had been 'local', provincial, it was very grand indeed at the Rose, for there the production was set in Elizabeth's own court – as it might be Hampton Court, down the road from the Rose, rather than Charlecote in the Stratford versions. At its centre was the Queen, intervening in a court performance to play Titania herself. When he was preparing the production, Peter Hall wondered if the Queen ever saw the play. The court records tell us that Shakespeare's company regularly performed before her from 1594, but not, maddeningly, what they played; still, as a popular part of their repertoire – the 1600 Quarto says that it 'hath been sundry times publicly acted' – *A Midsummer Night's Dream* is a likely candidate for court performance too. But in any case, Hall's approach arose not from external factors of this kind but – as always with this director – from scrupulous attention to Shakespeare's text, for the Queen is part of the fabric of the play, most strikingly in Oberon's vision of the 'fair vestal thronèd by the west', obviously an elaborate compliment to the Queen. But she is evoked elsewhere in the play as well: the hierarchy of the fairy court reflects her own; even the cowslips are Titania's equivalent of Elizabeth's 'pensioners' or personal bodyguard of handsome aristocratic youths, and in this production Titania's attendant fairies were played by young male actors. Elizabeth's court was simply, economically established.

Looking back on the Rose production, Peter Hall felt that one advantage of setting the play in Elizabeth's court was that it 'increased the distance' between the characters, from mechanicals to courtiers to Queen. And from 'different species' too: in the scenes between Titania and Bottom, they find 'they have things in common: Bottom's love-making is the most natural thing a country boy could do – not a terrible perversion' (as in many, perhaps most, modern productions). While at Stratford Bottom's ass's head had been a matter of 'fair large ears', at Glyndebourne and at the Rose it was a complete head, 'a work of art', said Hall. It had a moveable mouth, and eyes that could close when Bottom falls asleep. There was

a rather wonderful sense that the head, instead of masking Bottom's reactions, could reflect them. It was a curious but very effective fact that Oliver Chris's Bottom, far from going into eclipse under his ass's head, was more, rather than less, expressive. Hall likens this to the use of masks in Greek drama, and cites one of Oscar Wilde's aphorisms: 'Give a man a mask, and he will tell you the truth.' Oliver Chris was a youthful Bottom ('a country boy' in Hall's formulation), and this, too, relates to the context of the production and to Elizabeth's addiction to youthful favourites. This version made it clear that *A Midsummer Night's Dream* is an Elizabethan play in a more precise sense than simply a play written in the last decade of Elizabeth's reign.

And in the double role of Elizabeth/Titania, returning to the part that she had last played for Peter Hall over forty years before, was Judi Dench, the production's centre and its *raison d'être*. Astonishingly, she didn't even have to relearn it. As she says in her recent book, 'It was extraordinary. I did remember every single word of the whole play.'[5] Her delivery of the text, especially the speech about the seasonal chaos, was as riveting as it had been in 1962 and 1967 – but no great performer simply repeats the past. In the scenes with Bottom, for instance, there was a mixture of old and new. In all of Peter Hall's versions, Bottom punctuated his lines with an ass's bray but now Titania joined in. Judi Dench says, 'This time I played some scenes quite differently. When Bottom was wearing the ass's head, he laughed with a hee-haw, so I hee-hawed back. That just happened one day in rehearsal. I thought, if she loves him so much, she wants to try and speak like him too.' Hall agreed: 'It's the new court language.' Director and actress were at one: Peter Hall's developing interpretation of *A Midsummer Night's Dream* was Judi Dench's too (Illustration 24).

Together, they took that development of previous knowledge of which Peter Hall speaks to new heights. The production was enthusiastically

---

[5] *And Furthermore* (London, 2010), pp. 235–6.

24. Judi Dench as Titania, Oliver Chris as Bottom, and Richard Keightley as a fairy, Rose Theatre, 2010.

received, for example by Charles Spencer: 'one of the most lucid and beautifully spoken productions of the *Dream* that I have ever seen' (*Daily Telegraph*, 17 February 2010). This was the fullest and richest of Hall's many versions of the play. His note in the programme concluded: 'The *Dream* is a masterpiece which, while looking honestly at the absurdity of human behaviour, ends up celebrating it.' A celebratory play, then, and at the Rose a celebratory production.

A MIDSUMMER NIGHT'S DREAM AT THE MILLENNIUM: PERFORMANCE AND ADAPTATION

CAROL THOMAS NEELY

This article tests and extends Margaret Kidnie's definition of the Shakespeare 'work' in *Shakespeare and the Problem of Adaptation* as 'not an object at all, but rather a dynamic *process* that evolves over time in response to the needs and sensibilities of its users', one that 'continually takes shape as a *consequence* of production'.[1] These 'users' include its critics, producers, adapters and audiences. She claims: 'The criteria that are sufficient to mark out "the work" – and so to separate it from adaptation, or what is not "the work" – constantly shift over time, sometimes subtly, sometimes suddenly and drastically, in response to textual and theatrical production... What might count as "genuine" production can therefore be only provisionally known by recognizing adaptation' (7–8). Because 'work recognition in practice depends in large part on the contextual influence of historical, national, and even institutional circumstances' (41), different bodies of users may understand the work differently.[2] The same context influences adaptation and production alike and, because both shift, the first may be absorbed into the second. Hence, 'it is as hard to sustain a category of adaptation that is entirely independent of a fluid work as it is to make the boundaries of that work impervious to production' (69).[3] Here I analyse how criticism, production and adaptation together define what counts as the 'work' *A Midsummer Nights Dream* in our historical moment.[4] Instead of seeking boundaries, I examine the process of convergence. I also explore how, as users reinvent this 'work' over time, the less yielding shape of the comic genre with its drive towards resolution and celebration

Thanks to Michael Shapiro and Andrea Stevens for their invaluable comments on drafts of this article.

[1] Margaret Kidnie, *Shakespeare and the Problem of Adaptation* (New York and Milton Park, 2009). Kidnie's italics, pp. 2, 7.

[2] Kidnie's assessment of the boundary between productions and adaptations shifts, appropriately, throughout the book. This line is discernible in the title of the second chapter: 'Defining the work through production – or what adaptation is not' and in formulations that divide the two: 'the limits of the work are continually redefined by distinguishing what can be recognized as legitimate productions from adaptations or illegitimate productions' (Kidnie, *Problem of Adaptation*, p. 65). Elsewhere, because 'writing back to Shakespeare [the aim of many adaptations] is always writing *with* Shakespeare' (p. 87), over time, adaptation and production become entwined and the line between them vanishes. In Chapter 3, 'Entangled in the Present', Kidnie shows how 'Shakespeare's works can, logically, never be made free of their adaptations' (p. 65). I analyse how adaptations and criticism are incubated by the same cultural conditions that shape productions so that all three feed into the work's journey.

[3] One example of this process is visible in watching the theme of incest become a part of the work, *King Lear*. In a provocative essay, 'The Avoidance of Love in *King Lear*', Stanley Cavell subtly analysed a 'particular kind of love' between Lear and Cordelia: *Must We Mean What We Say* (New York, 1969), repr. in his *Disowning Knowledge in Six Plays of Shakespeare* (Cambridge, 1987), pp. 58–144; p. 71. Attention to incest was further fuelled by increasing feminist attention to this core abuse of patriarchal power in the 1970s and widely publicized sensational revelations of recovered memories of incest and child abuse in the 1980s, and criticism began to suggest this interpretation. An adaptation dramatized the theme when the Woman's Theatre Group and Elaine Feinstein's prequel, *Lear's Daughters* (performed first in 1987 and 1988) represented the effects of the (absent) King's incestuous relationships with his three daughters and the fool. Its run was limited, but its influence spread when it was published – first in *Herstory: Volume 1* in 1991 and again in Daniel Fischlin

may exert a counter-pressure that partially contains available meanings. I analyse this convergence in three widely disparate millennial re-productions of *A Midsummer Night's Dream* that similarly foreground its erotic circulations, negotiate its gender battles, test its class divisions and adjust all these to retain its comic form. Taken together they provide a snapshot of where this 'work' is now.

The three iterations are produced – and re-produced – at different moments on different continents and for different audiences. J. (Jean) Betts and W. Shakespeare's *Revenge of the Amazons* is a feminist hybrid, first performed at the Circa Theatre in Wellington, New Zealand in 1983, published in 1998, 2006 and 2008, and remounted at Bats Theatre in Wellington in 2007. Set in the seventies, it parodies, satirizes and revises both the patriarchy in Shakespeare's play and seventies' radical feminist critiques of it. While the four lovers remain in Shakespeare's plot and speak his (slightly revised) lines, the power dynamics of the older couples (in a pastiche of Shakespeare and Betts) are reversed, and the mechanicals become a newly scripted feminist theatre troupe, the Fallopian Thespians, whose consciousness-raising play, 'Labia's Lament', is mounted to stop the marriages. BBC's TV adaptation of the play in its 2005 series, *ShakespeaRetold* carries the same title as the original; its advertising and website claim it is an 'updating' or 'interpretation' (Kidnie, 134). But it is completely re-scripted with just a few lines of Shakespeare's text remaining. The principals arrive in the Dream Park resort in contemporary England to celebrate Hermia's engagement to James Demetrius – only to have the party interrupted by her flight with Zander. Here too the young couples' plot is intact but the other three are revised especially when the roles of Theseus and Egeus are amalgamated in Theo Moon, the longtime husband of Polly and father of Hermia, and the Dream Park workers put on a revue. The University of Illinois Theater Department's March 2011 production, *A Midsummer Night's Dream – It's a Bacchanal!*, set at Carnival in the Caribbean uses Shakespeare's text (only minimally cut) but its altered title and advertising warning

'For mature audiences' hint that it might be an adaptation.[5]

All three, taken together, make visible what counts as *A Midsummer Night's Dream* in the decades surrounding the millennium, blurring distinctions between adaptation and production. Situated within the same global milieu, the three versions intersect as they represent issues of sexuality, gender and class that preoccupy this period. At the centre of each is the fairy love juice, the play's central marker, catalysing character, plot and theme. Drawn from flower or vial, administered to eyes with similarly elaborate flourishes and

---

and Mark Fortier's collection, *Adaptations of Shakespeare* (London and New York, 2000), widely used in classrooms. Jane Smiley's best-selling novel, *A Thousand Acres* (New York, 1991) retold the plot in a contemporary setting and circulated the motif of Lear's incest, with Ginny (Goneril) and Rose (Regan), to an American culture prepared to accept it. The 1997 film of the novel made this interpretive extension of Lear's power commonplace, and it was more often suggested in productions.

[4] For Kidnie, 'Shakespeare's play is whatever a dominant consensus of voices agrees to recognize as Shakespeare's play': 'Where is *Hamlet*: Text, Performance, and Adaptation', in *A Companion to Shakespeare and Performance*, ed. Barbara Hodgdon and W. B. Worthen (Blackwell, 2005), 101–19; p. 116. One problem with this identification of the 'work' through the negotiations of reception is that most of the voices in the consensus – playgoers, teachers at all levels, students of the plays of all ages who see them, read them or encounter them in books, performances, adaptations, ads or online parodies like 'Sassy Gay Shakespeare' – remain unregistered. Hence assessing consensus, whether across national boundaries or in local communities, remains approximate and difficult. This article offers my own analysis as a long-time reader and viewer, but I have tried to be alert to other responses, for example those of my University of Illinois, spring 2011 honours seminar who discussed these three versions with me. But there are not enough responses to these productions to pinpoint widespread consensus.

[5] J. Betts and W. Shakespeare, *Revenge of the Amazons* (The Play Press, 1998, repr. 2006, 2008). *ShakespeaRetold: A Midsummer Night's Dream.* Written by Peter Bowker. Director: Ed Fraiman. Producer: Pier Wilkie. Performers: Imelda Staunton, Bill Paterson, Lennie James, Sharon Small, Johnny Vegas. BBC1, 28 November 2005. BBC Video, 2007. *A Midsummer Night's Dream – It's A Bacchanal!* By William Shakespeare. Director: Lisa Gaye Dixon. Dramaturg: Andrea Stevens. Performers: Jess Pritchard and Jessica Dean Turner. Colwell Playhouse, Urbana, Illinois. March, 2011.

musical accompaniments, it signifies slightly differently. It stands for male lust in *Revenge of the Amazons*, false and true vision and romantic love in the BBC's updated tale, and for the pleasures of untrammelled desire in the Illinois production. All three versions highlight a second motif – gender wars – staging the attempted patriarchal control of women and its confrontation by Hippolyta's extended resistance, Titania's power and pleasure in her liaison with Bottom, and the (promised) reform of Theseus and Oberon. Third, although the adaptations reinvent the workers more than does the production, all three versions redesign class divisions and exploit the inner play to produce a comic finale that elicits audience pleasure and acquiescence. All three conclusions register unresolved tensions but only one partly dislodges comic resolution.

The long historical process whereby these motifs – transforming (or reforming) magic, erotic play, gender trouble and class exploitation – became the work began just after the middle of the twentieth century when *A Midsummer Night's Dream*, defined as a green world comedy, was notable for its harmony in multiplicity achieved through its two settings, five couples, four plots and ten major characters. Such comedy achieved, according to Northrop Frye in 1949, 'an individual release which is also a social reconciliation' and moved, in the well-known formulation of C. L. Barber in 1959, 'through release to clarification', producing *Something of Great Constancy* as David Young titled his 1966 book. But even as that consensus emerged, it was being challenged. Jan Kott's landmark 1964 essay interpreted the play as a nightmare of bestial erotic couplings where 'exchangeable' lovers are seen 'passing through animality' to shame, as is Titania, whose affair with a brutal phallic monster is engineered by a 'menacing devil' Puck.[6] The essay is informed by Kott's fantasies of the homo- and hetero-erotic behaviour of original spectators at a drunken wedding celebration (217, 222). Related interpretations are staged in Peter Hall's 1969 film with its apparently nude Titania and its increasingly muddy, dishevelled and disoriented lovers and in Peter Brook's 1970–73

stage production with its highly physical, sensual and acrobatic lovers, its powerful Titania, and its granting to Bottom of a giant phallus and a wedding celebration complete with confetti and Mendelssohn's march.[7]

In the decades after these interventions, critics of all sorts, including feminists, queer theorists, cultural materialists and historicists, denying that state-sponsored and enforced heterosexual

---

[6] C. L. Barber, *Shakespeare's Festive Comedy* (Princeton, 1959), p. 4. Northrop Frye, 'The Argument of Comedy', in *Modern Shakespearean Criticism*, ed. Alvin Kernan (New York, 1970), p. 167. David Young, *Something of Great Constancy: The Art of* A Midsummer Night's Dream (New Haven, 1966). Jan Kott, *Shakespeare Our Contemporary*, trans. Boleslaw Taborski (New York, 1964, repr. New York, 1974), pp. 213–36; pp. 219, 225, 215.

[7] Peter Hall's film was developed out of his 1959 RSC production, remounted in 1962–63. Both Brook's production, as I vividly remember it, and Hall's, revisited, seem somewhat tame now. Other productions representing the play's dissonant aspects include: John Hancock's in 1966 at San Francisco Actor's Workshop where Hippolyta in animal skins was pulled on stage in a cage; Liviu Ciulei's 1985 interpretation of the play at the Guthrie as 'a power struggle that threatens the world with chaos' and Robert Lepage's 1992 famously wet and muddy show at England's National Theatre. On the Guthrie production, see Thomas Clayton who above quotes reviewer Robert Collins on KSJN Radio in 'Shakespeare at the Guthrie: *A Midsummer Night's Dream* (1985)', in Dorothea Kehler, ed., *A Midsummer Night's Dream: Critical Essays* (New York and London, 1998), p. 404. On the stage productions, see also Gary Williams, *Our Moonlight Revels:* A Midsummer Night's Dream *in the Theatre* (Iowa City, 1997) and Jay L. Halio, *Shakespeare in Performance: A Midsummer Night's Dream* (Manchester and New York, 2003, 2nd edn). On the films see Jack J. Jorgens, *Shakespeare On Film* (Bloomington and London, 1977) and Halio. Other histories of performance are Trevor R. Griffiths, ed., *A Midsummer Night's Dream* (Cambridge, 1996) and Jeremy Lopez whose history, 'written backwards' shows how productions of the play, no matter how apparently new, recycle elements of past productions also remembered by informed spectators. See '*Dream*: The Performance History', in *A Midsummer Night's Dream: A Critical Guide*, ed. Regina Buccola (London and New York, 2010), pp. 44–73; p. 52. For example, in the production still from *Revenge of the Amazons* (Illustration 25 p. 160 below), the twiggy, lit up headdress Oberon wears seems a distressed version of that worn by the Fairy King (Victor Jory) in Max Reinhardt and William Dieterle's still powerful 1935 film. For a photograph of Jory's head-dress, see Williams, *Our Moonlight Revels*, Fig. 40, p. 180.

marriages are anything to celebrate, brought new attention to the multiple erotic circulations and gender and class conflicts of the play. Wendy Wall, examining Puck in the contexts of popular folk and fairy tales, finds the figure Kott fantasized: a devil known for phallic prowess, erotic pranks and subversive mischief. Valerie Traub analyses the text's circulation and containment of non-normative desires in the relegation to the past of women's deep eroticized bonds – those of Hippolyta and her Amazonian sorority, of Titania and her Indian votaress, of Hermia and Helena's girlhood friendship. Douglas Green explores the play's sodomitical potentials centring on the character and name of Bottom. Shirley Garner, with other feminists, laments Titania's humiliation and the silencing and subordination of all four women characters in marriage to secure male bonds and male desires. Louis Montrose and later others examine the infantilizing and exploitation of the working man by both rulers, by Titania with Bottom and by Theseus who patronizes his subjects for his own gratification.[8] The three productions I discuss have absorbed and reimagined such critical concerns – whether or not their directors and designers have read such criticism.

These current emphases of the work, especially its gender battles, are most exaggerated, as its title signals, in Betts and Shakespeare's *Revenge of the Amazons* where conventional gender roles are reversed in the plots of the older (but not younger) lovers. Hippolyta becomes the protagonist (played in leather with one breast bare) who struggles to reconcile her own women-dominated Amazon life with Theseus's society which, she has trouble believing, 'accepts *men* as *equals*' (2). In a parody of patriarchal *and* feminist assumptions, she embodies male traits and Theseus displays those of a stereotypical woman: 'Men are such an absurd mixture of logic and sentiment. So frightened of the truth, of love, of men prettier than they are. Such vain little things! And so emotional!' (2). She and Hermia voice outrage, as feminist critics have, at Theseus's edict that Hermia must marry Lysander: 'What kind of a sick joke is this?' (6), Hippolyta asks, and ever-pliant Theseus promises to change the law –

tomorrow. At the finale, Hippolyta mollifies the feminist theatre troupe with her promise to fight against women's oppression and at the same time she reaffirms her commitment to Theseus because he is 'kind', 'patient' and 'has never treated me as anything less than his equal' (67).

The BBC tale in a realistic contemporary setting where Hippolyta's subordination would be unacceptable, also completely revises this plot; instead of representing Polly's strength, this version focuses on Theo's flaws and reforms them through Oberon's counselling sessions. Theo's 26-year marriage to Polly is in trouble due to his blustering, controlling anger. Hermia ignores him and elopes; Polly first endures his flare-ups then tells him off, complaining that his anger requires her to maintain self-control. This made-for-TV Shakespeare has a patly therapeutic resolution, one perhaps designed to be especially satisfying to the BBC's likely audience demographic of older women.[9] Oberon, also having marital difficulties himself, avuncularly advises Theo that he can solve his problems with Polly by reciting three phrases: 'Forgive me. I'm sorry. I love you.' When he dutifully follows the advice, Theo and Polly go happily to bed and he graciously accepts Hermia's choice of husband. Going further, Theo, to replace the aborted engagement party, arranges a reaffirmation of their marriage

---

8 Wendy Wall, 'Why Does Puck Sweep?: Fairylore, Merry Wives, and Social Struggle', *Shakespeare Quarterly*, 52 (2001), 67–106. Valerie Traub, 'The (In)significance of "Lesbian" Desire in Early Modern England', in *Queering the Renaissance*, ed. Jonathan Goldberg (Durham and London, 1994), pp. 70–3. Douglas E. Green, 'Preposterous Pleasures: Queer Theories and *A Midsummer Night's Dream*', in Kehler, ed., *Midsummer*, pp. 369–97. Shirley Garner, '*A Midsummer Night's Dream*: "Jack Shall Have Jill; / Nought Shall Go Ill,"' in Kehler, ed., *Midsummer*, pp. 127–43. Louis Adrian Montrose, '*A Midsummer Night's Dream* and the Shaping Fantasies of Elizabethan Culture: Gender, Power, Form', in *Rewriting the Renaissance*, ed. Margaret Ferguson, Maureen Quilligan and Nancy Vickers (Chicago and London, 1986), pp. 65–87.

9 Ruth Morse, 'Twice-telly-ed Tales', *Shakespearean International Yearbook*, 10 (2010), 281–97, notes that 'All three plays emphasized the adults, rather than the young lovers, at their core' (288) in her discussion of *Dream*, *The Taming of the Shrew* and *Much Ado about Nothing*, the three comedies of the four BBC *Retold* tales. *Macbeth* is the fourth.

vows where he recites his poem in praise of Polly. By its quick fix for marital inequity, this version acknowledges and easily resolves the play's gender troubles. And because the younger couples, although sorted out, do not marry in the course of the play, their future is left open.

A Midsummer Night's Dream – It's a Bacchanal! likewise fully represents Hippolyta's hostility towards and resistance to Theseus – in part by doubling the pair with Titania and Oberon. But the Illinois production also motivates and enacts her gradual, tentative acceptance of the marriage as Theseus subtly changes as well. Her love is, ultimately, bestowed, not 'won' (1.1.17). This Hippolyta is a tall, regal, black woman, wearing at the start, a red top and long beige skirt covered with an awkwardly constricting beige corset and yellow flounced overskirt representing her confinement and self-division in Athens. Until the last act, the couple are far apart on stage: Hippolyta often has her back turned to Theseus (as when he implores 'I will wed thee in another key', 1.1.18) or stalks off angrily (when he commands that Hermia marry Demetrius).[10] Their disagreements are expressed in speeches of equal length (with Theseus's lines often cut down) and her attitude and aloof posture begin to change only when day returns and Theseus changes. As he encounters the four lovers at daybreak (4.1), his long, wild, full black wig (worn by Theseus in the opening scene and by Oberon throughout) is gone. He dismisses Egeus's demand and accepts the love matches. Hippolyta, now wearing a colourful patterned skirt instead of the beige one, moves closer to him in response to his acceptance of the couples. Later, when they agree to disagree about what the night meant, Theseus's declamation becomes an exchange when his 'Lunatics, lovers and poets' speech is cut from 21 lines to just 7; its disdain for imagination is muted, and it is counter-balanced by Hippolyta's certainty that 'something of great constancy' has transpired (5.1.1–27). Finally Theseus's expressed concern for low status players, 'Love, therefore, and tongue-tied simplicity / In least speak most, to my capacity' (5.1.104–5), elicits Hippolyta's sympathy for them

and also for him, so for the first time she sits next to him.

The dangerous power of male rulers is likewise acknowledged and re-formed in representations of the Oberon/Titania/Bottom triangle that exaggerate class distinctions. All three iterations represent the Fairy Queen's power, her satisfaction (without shame) at the juice-induced coupling with Bottom, and Oberon's ultimate capitulation to *her* demands.[11] *Revenge of the Amazons* wittily reverses the Titania/Oberon plot by giving to Titania Oberon's (slightly adjusted) lines and vice versa. She punishes his outrageous promiscuity (he attempts to rape the female Puck, Titania's sidekick and his own fairy, Peaseblossom) by using 'Rata juice' (squeezed from the bright red flower of the rare Rata tree which blooms only once every three or four years in Northern New Zealand) to induce besotted love with Barbara, the radical socialist of the theatre troupe, who is transformed by Puck into a parodic playboy bunny with long red ears and a tail and a bra with 'flashing lights' (SD, 33). Not one to be led around, Barbara, a socialist feminist, humiliates Oberon (Illustration 25).[12] She repeatedly knocks him to the ground

---

[10] These have been commonplace performance choices for decades. Clayton, 'Shakespeare', p. 405 quotes J. C. Trewin, *Going to Shakespeare* (London and Boston, 1978), p. 103, on standard production choices for Hippolyta: '(1) tall and coffee-colored; (2) aloofly disdainful; (3) urgently in love; (4) scuffling with Theseus on the ground; or, just as implausibly . . . (5) ironic and in manacles'.

[11] The absence of the Indian boy in *Revenge* and the BBC's production requires new motives for the quarrel. Theseus's demand for the boy and Titania's refusal to give him up for love of his mother remain in the production, but the boy does not appear on stage.

[12] Stage directions indicate that 'She should not, of course, look titillating but hilarious' (Betts, *Revenge*, p. 33), and Illustration 25 shows her bonding with Peaseblossom (left) and Puck (right) while Oberon begs a kiss. Alas I have not seen this play produced. My analysis is based on the text and its stage directions and introduction by the author, on exchanges with Jean Betts and some production stills she sent, all these based on the 1983 production as well as on three reviews of the 2007 production (with a slightly updated script). Laurie Atkinson, 'Explodes with Energy, Laughs, and Disco', Review of *Revenge*

25. Aileen Davidson as Peaseblossom, Chrissie Chronis as Barbara, Lindy Hatherley as Puck, Peter Sakey as Oberon in the 1983 *Revenge of the Amazons.*

for his seduction moves and allows him a kiss only after negotiating a tough prenuptial agreement that stipulates his fidelity and housework duties as well as her right to work, to have children only if she chooses and be sure of unlimited gym time. The desperate Oberon begs Titania on his knees to 'free me from this love disease' which she does only after he promises 'henceforth absolute fidelity' (48–9).

BBC's retelling also represents Oberon as the cause of the king and queen's quarrels, attributing them to his egotism ('you don't need me' Titania says) and his desire to control his wife (paralleling Theo's flaw). He too is reformed. Titania usually sarcastically disregards him. Her lover, Bottom, played by comedian Johnny Vegas, is a Dream Park security guard and a British working-class stereotype, short-haired, stubble-chinned, with a huge beer belly and a Northern accent and ears more like pig's than ass's.[13] He is not sweet and

of the Amazons, Bats Theatre, Wellington, 3 December 2007, *New Zealand Performing Arts Review and Directory*, www.theatreview.org.nz/reviews/review.php?id=1964. Gemma Freeman, Review of *Revenge of the Amazons*, Bats Theatre, Wellington, December 2007, www.lumiere.net.nz/reader/item/1472. John Smythe, 'Ebullient Satire: Treat Yourselves', Review of *Revenge of the Amazons*, Bats Theatre, Wellington, 1 December 2007, *New Zealand Performing Arts Review and Directory*, www.theatreview.org.nz/reviews/review.php?id=1062.

[13] The actors in the BBC production are known for their film, TV and stage roles, especially in Britain, and their acquired personas inflect their characters here. Imelda Staunton (Polly) is especially well-known for her performances in other Shakespeare films. She played Margaret in Kenneth Branagh's *Much Ado about Nothing*, the nurse in *Shakespeare in Love* and Maria in Trevor Nunn's *Twelfth Night*, three strong women characters who challenge the system but also make their peace with it. Sharon Small (Titana) is best known to BBC viewers for her role as Detective Sergeant Barbara Havers, rebellious lower-class

26. Sharon Small as Titania and Johnny Vegas as Bottom in the 2005 BBC *A Midsummer Night's Dream* in *ShakespeaRetold* series.

touching like some Bottoms or funny like others but unattractive, especially sexually, but happily compliant. (My students found the class stereotyping troubling but many British viewers responding on the website loved him.) Titania is charmed. She coos, 'I love a rough man', and takes him off to her elaborate bower where we see her clearly post-coital bliss (Illustration 26). After the encounter, his grin as he pulls thong panties out of his sweater pocket confirms their one-night stand. Titania's reacceptance of Oberon is dependent, like Polly's with Theo, on his blaming himself for what goes wrong: 'It was my fault not hers', he tells Puck before she wakes. When he dutifully deploys those three surefire (superficial) phrases, she gives in only reluctantly and sassily. She asks, 'Why should I believe you' and retorts: 'I dreamt I was enamoured

of an ass – and I still am' and extracts his promise to eschew jealousy and promiscuity. As they punt on the lake, he redeclares his love with a poem, as Theo did, in this case with a pastiche of lines from Shakespeare's sonnets.[14]

---

side-kick to aristocratic Inspector Lynley in his series on *Mystery* based on Elizabeth George's books. Johnny Vegas (Bottom) is a stand-up comedian with successes and failures who fronted his own show, *18 Stone of Idiot*, on Channel 4 when the Shakespeare series appeared. See the BBC *ShakespeaRetold* website for additional information, updated August 2006. Accessed 15 October 2011, www.bbc.co.uk/drama/shakespeare/midsummernightsdream/index.shtml.

[14] Hermia likewise blames her break-up with James Demetrius on his failure to say the words, 'I love you', and Helena continues to refuse him, even after he wakes up with changed affections and woos her, until the last scene when he shouts

27. Jessica Dean Taylor as Titania and Jess Pritchard as Oberon in University of Illinois's 2011 *A Midsummer Night's Dream – It's a Bacchanal!*

The Illinois production represented Titania's erotic and political power as fully as the adaptations, but not by diminishing Oberon's charisma. Costumed in a racy red bra, trimmed, like her hair, with multi-coloured flowers and in a flowing red transparent skirt, she stunningly enters the forest with her fairies in a vigorous sensual dance to the beat of Soca music, a branch of Afro-Caribbean music indigenous to Trinidad and Tobago, often highly sexual and performed by competing bands at Carnival celebrations. The king and queen each have their competing fairy bands and their own signature entrance songs; their first fiery encounter kept them on opposite sides of the stage; each used magic (musical and sound effects), force and verbal swordplay to best each other (Illustration 27). Later, Titania, delighted, leads off 'silently' the younger, slighter, modest Bottom whose 'translation' was represented by an open-work donkey

mask that left his charmed and vulnerable face visible (Illustration 28). The liaison unfolds in a kaleidoscopically lit Caribbean landscape at the foot of a banyan tree draped with Spanish moss and led, following 4.1.48, to what director Lisa Dixon described to me as 'an orgasm that rocks the forest'. On top of a mostly invisible Bottom, upright from the waist, Titania enacted – visibly and audibly – a prolonged sexual coupling ending in orgasm. The enactment was magnified by lighting effects and by a chorus of similarly rhythmic gasps and

'I love you' to her before all the guests at the remarriage reception. He is also dripping wet from the pond, like Zander in the first scene. Getting wet, often the price of love in productions of this play, here provides proof of its authenticity. The empty swimming pool that helped define a sterile stark Athens in the Illinois production was perhaps an ironic nod to many earlier sodden productions.

28. Jessica Dean Taylor as Titania and Robert Montgomery as
Bottom in the University of Illinois's 2011
A Midsummer Night's Dream – It's a Bacchanal!

moans from fairies all over the stage and was doubled by the simultaneous anal coupling (including full frontal male nudity) of a male–male fairy couple next to Titania and Bottom in the bower. This Titania then returned to Oberon out of desire for him, not disgust with Bottom, and made the first advances, flirtatiously offering him oral sex, then leading their dance. Whereas the adaptations tamped down or warned against even heterosexual eroticism, this production joyously represented multiple, polymorphously perverse and queer erotic possibilities, not only through the main characters but through the stage business of the ten beautifully choreographed fairies who were on stage throughout and engaged in pleasurable erotic play of every sort. The production did achieve, as the programme noted, 'the

rejection of normative definitions of sexuality', and the 'transgression' and breaking of 'social ties and social hierarchies' permitted by Carnival.[15]

But if this stage production represented multiple desires without salaciousness and rendered gender conflicts highly visible and only contingently resolved, like the others it exploited the play within the play to interpolate laughing audiences into a happy ending. In the text, the workers and their performance are the most complex element of *A Midsummer Night's Dream*'s ensemble. First, the Pyramus and Thisbe play parodies the inadequate and outmoded theatre practices of a company not unlike Shakespeare's to assert his own play's superior art; second, it counterpoints, tragicomically, the play's main theme, romantic love (or desire); third, it generates laughter from on-stage and off-stage audiences that displaces conflict with shared delight. *Revenge of the Amazons* innovatively revises all three functions of the play within the play. The inept outmoded theatrical content and practices of the Fallopian Thespian troupe parody the feminisms of Hippolyta, of the author and of the collective devisers of the play itself. Feminist collaboration fails hilariously when troupe members, each with different back stories, motives and brands of feminism, fight about the story, the script, the parts. Their play counterpoints the power of Hippolyta and Titania in their plots with a didactic tale of women's suffering under patriarchy. Its history of Labia, Everywoman, exposes her systematic subordination from the trauma of first menstruation, through her sexist education and rape to her economic imprisonment in patriarchal marriage. During the performance, characters miss cues and costume changes, forget their lines and actions, and ad lib in despair. Just as the Pyramus and Thisbe performance botches love, this one botches thoroughly – in rehearsal and performance – the rape that is its centrepiece exemplar of male aggression.

---

[15] Quotations are from the Krannert Center programme for the University of Illinois production, *A Midsummer Night's Dream – It's a Bacchanal!*. The first is from Andrea Stevens, 'Dramaturg's Note', p. 10. The second is from a 'Lexicon', and is part of the definition of Carnival, p. 8.

Georgiana, playing the rapist, only feebly recites her lines, 'Like all men I throb with vile desires', and merely paws at her victim. Barbara playing the rape victim, just as feebly resists the 'Raw red tape', forgetting to scream and fall down (32, 63–4). But the troupe carries on to conclude with a rousing separatist anti-marriage chorus: 'We will not take their beatings and become their wretched slaves, / we will not join their system for it's totally depraved, / in everything to do with them we're goddesses or whores, / So turn on your new husbands and knee them in the balls!!! . . . we take the name New Amazons and forge a path for all / so throw away your wedding rings and hear our call!!' (67). Although Hippolyta toasts them in support, she reaffirms her marriage choice and a shouting match between the newly-weds and players derails any resolution of conflicts over sex, gender roles and marriage, leaving unanswered Hippolyta's plaintive question, 'What is a feminist??' (69).

Sulamith. All men are bullies!
Lysander & Demetrius. All women are wimps!
Angela. Fascist!
Lysander. Communist!
Sulamith. Rapist!
Demetrius. Housewife! Feminist!
Lysander. Manhater!
Angela. (to Hermia *and* Helena) Cabbages! Traitors!
Helena: (to Angela/Shulamith) Ugly Bitch!   (68–9)

The happy ending that comic form demands is parodied when Puck freezes the characters with magic glitter and delivers a revised epilogue that neither asks pardon (not even of Shakespeare: 'perhaps he's laughing and approves?') nor promises amends but merely suspends conflict (69).

The BBC version likewise uses 'magic' at the ending, not to freeze conflict but to extract laughter from discomfort. At Theo and Polly's party celebrating their remarriage, the performance by the patently lower-class resort security guards is a series of nightclub acts: illusions, juggling, card tricks, a song, a stand-up routine. It parodies bad TV variety shows perhaps but provides no counterpoint to the tale's therapeutic reforms and does not, on its own,

produce laughter. The players' failed card tricks and bad jokes are not funny in the way that bad tragic acting is. When the party guests pay little attention to the show, the (supposedly) invisible audience of Titania, Oberon and Puck intervene. Snout's illusions and tricks succeed when Puck blows his magic dust on them. Bottom's stand-up routine, that repeatedly falls flat in rehearsal, is still less funny on stage. He is subjected to nasty heckling (not by principals but by nameless party guests) and comes close to drying up. Titania, watching with a dreamy smile that remembers their liaison, saves him. She does not improve his bad performance, but blows laughter-inducing magic on the audience via that familiar TV convention, the laugh-track. The track goes on and on as the camera pans the cast couples, all laughing uproariously, then returns to a surprised and delighted Bottom – whose routine we scarcely see. But the device failed to cue any laughter from the student audience I watched with. Instead it had the effect of exposing how both Theseus and the production exploit the embarrassed players. In this adaptation they are literally turned into passive 'mechanicals' whose lack of talent is irredeemable and whose audience response must be artificially, magically generated, widening class divisions and those between the on-stage and off-stage audiences.

In contrast, the Illinois production's Pyramus and Thisbe play exposed acting so bad it was brilliant, recapitulated the play's erotic plots and promoted shared laughter. The players, all but one undergraduate theatre majors, brought more than usual earnestness to their acting challenges and were assured a wildly enthusiastic reception from their peers. Most of the heckling remarks by the on-stage audience were cut, as is regularly the case today. Wall's chink was an indiscriminately erotic zone, now a commonplace in performance. Quince, stage left, script in hand, hysterically cued the ensemble, mouthing all the words, mimicking all the gestures and reminding Flute to keep his voice high-pitched. But most hilariously the death of Thisbe parodied and recalled the athletic and erotic encounters in the woods. Pyramus died sprawled on his back on the upper level with his head hanging down to his right. Thisbe, dying, fell forward on top of Pyramus and down to her left, her thighs gripping his head to stop her fall, twisting it down and nearly off – or so it seemed – and they froze. The visual effect was of Pyramus and cross-dressed Thisbe locked precariously in a grotesque, post-mortem act of queer oral sex. This 'love death' not only recalled erotic positions and couplings in the forest but counterpointed them by emphasizing the link between eros and death that is articulated in the playtext by Puck's monologue (5.2.1–20).

The production's conclusion followed rapidly, capitalizing on audience delight in the Pyramus and Thisbe play. After Theseus urged: 'Lovers, to bed; 'tis almost fairy time' (5.1.357), Hippolyta turned towards him, opening her arms and he moved in for their first kiss. As they embraced, the rectilinear Athens set disappeared, absorbed into the Caribbean landscape. She led him off to bed through a corner of the woods where she stopped to caress a female fairy. Following Puck's epilogue, the lights went down, then up, and the play ended not with fairies entering the court, but with the whole cast joining the fairies' dance in the woods, the space of carnival transgression. They were led by an exuberant Hippolyta and Theseus with Puck, then joined by the lovers, Egeus and Philostrate, the workers and the prop-movers in another athletic and sensual dance to a powerful Soca beat. The audience (mostly students) began clapping early and continued as the dancing went on through the curtain calls. Most stood to applaud and many danced along at their seats or in the aisles. This production certainly solicited audience pleasure and participation in the play's ending. Yet that conclusion celebrated not the joys of marriage but those of dirty dancing.

The text of *A Midsummer Night's Dream* acknowledges 'darkness' and death at its ending moments when Puck mentions a 'hungry lion', 'graves, all gaping wide' and 'a shroud' (5.2.16, 1, 10, 8), and Oberon acknowledges the possibility of infidelity for the newly-wed couples or birth defects in their children (5.2.37–44). Although none of the three re-productions include either

speech, all three iterations of the work negotiate its darkness and joy, its conflicts and resolutions in collaboration with the demands of those millennial audiences who don't all find male domination, normative heterosexual eroticism, patriarchal marriage or exploitation of those lower in status a cause for happy celebration.

These three productions provide a snapshot of the irreducible components of the 'work' *A Midsummer Night's Dream* in their current articulation and interpretation. Work recognition, however, can also emerge from only a handful of key elements as we can see by examining what counts as the recognizable core of two other Shakespeare plays, visible in unlikely places. First, the work, *Hamlet*, Kidnie shows, can be recognized in a nine-second playlet, performed by three male Reduced Shakespeare actors in 'renaissance' costumes to serve as a clue on a *Jeopardy!* programme. A ghost in a white sheet with a crown scares a doublet-and-hose-attired character ('Boo-oo!') and exits; the character blithers 'Bl-bl-bl-bl! Mad!', then is nicked on the arm by a sword held by an unseen assailant ('Ow'). A male actor in drag enters, drinks from a cup, screams 'Poison!' and dies; the protagonist cries 'Mother!' and stabs another man with a crown while crying, 'Treachery!' The stabbed man dies ('Agh-hh-hh-hh!') as does the stabber ('Ugh!'). A contestant answers immediately and correctly 'What is *Hamlet*?'[16] These few actions and elements – a ghost, madness, mother, poison, treachery, and deaths in rapid succession – are sufficient to cue widespread recognition of the 'work', *Hamlet*. Missing from this playlet, but central to the Reduced Shakespeare Company's thirty-second *Hamlet* forwards, then backwards, is Ophelia, whose drowning (throwing water in her face) and un-drowning (spewing water out of her mouth) was the hilarious high point of the two productions I saw long ago and of their online

---

[16] Margaret Kidnie uses this example of work recognition, quoting its script (*Shakespeare*, p. 140). The filmed performance can be found on the 26 April 2005 show on *J! Archive* at www.j-archive.com.

performance now.[17] In another rich example of the convergence of production and adaptation, when those interviewed by the Nature Theater of Oklahoma company's devisers recount what they remember of the work, *Romeo and Juliet*, there is agreement on core elements as well as amalgamation of the playtext, the films and the adaptation, *West Side Story*.[18] Respondents remember that Romeo and Juliet are very young lovers whose families forbid the match and who die. Key scenes/settings are vivid: a party/ball/dance, a balcony, a sword fight and a 'morgue' (90). Fragments of iambic pentameter surface, often telling ones marking key encounters: the lover's first meeting's shared sonnet ('Pilgrim Hands!! / What does she say?, Pilgrim hands touching... Let me taste the sin again') and their balcony declarations: ('But light – ! What DAWN through / yonder window breaks! / It is the EAST! / And Juliet is the Sun!', 'Romeo, Romeo where art thou Romeo!' (77, 76). Plot, actions, scenes, lines are remembered but there is confusion too. Interviewees remember a mid-play sword-fight in which someone is killed but who or why is muddled. Juliet's two 'deaths' by potion and by sword create ubiquitous confusion about how the lovers die or in what order. Some suggest that Romeo dies in the fight and Juliet takes poison afterwards, although some remember a fake death too. The Nature Theater of Oklahoma's *Romeo and Juliet* production is created out of these communal remembrances of the work, strung together and scripted into free verse, becoming fuller and fuller, and acted in renaissance costumes with theatrical panache. This performance becomes, in its turn, a re-creation of the 'work' *Romeo and Juliet* which, reconstituted by memories of the play, unfolds gradually within it.

The complete re-productions of the 'work' that I analyse contain many more elements, represented complexly and coherently. *A Midsummer Night's Dream* today consists of characters, plot, scenes, its central prop and its key lines and much else. The dominant characters today are the older pairs and the cross-class or cross-species Titania/Bottom match. The fairy love juice remains powerfully at the centre in each version and signifies male lust, true love and vision or polymorphous desire. It is given rich representation even in the BBC's updated script where it becomes a vial of shimmering richly hued liquid. Oberon's mythic explanation of the magic juice's origin is quoted in all three retellings. While the reference to the chaste maiden (Elizabeth) that Cupid aims at is omitted in each, even the BBC rescripting has Oberon say 'Remember the night I heard the mermaids singing. Oh in maiden meditation fancy free. Yet marked I where the bolt of Cupid fell. It fell upon a little western flower, before milk-white, now purple with love's wound, and maidens called it love-in-idleness' (cf. Betts, 20–1 and Shakespeare 2.1.148–72).[19] In all three productions the flower (or vial in the BBC version) is vividly represented and the anointing of eyes is elaborately staged. In *Revenge of the Amazons*, we learn (accurately) that

---

[17] The Reduced Shakespeare Company's reduced Hamlets can be seen in a 29 March 2009 performance at: video.google.com/videoplay?docid=17033555007759599, accessed 11 October 2011.

[18] The script, conceived and directed by Pavol Liška and Kelly Copper, is available in *Theater*, 40 (2010), 74–113, where it is introduced by Karinne Keithley, 'Uncreative Writing: Nature Theater of Oklahoma's Romeo and Juliet', *Theater*, 40 (2010), 67–73. One re-teller castigates herself: 'And really what I'm remembering is the movie! Which one? The Leonardo DiCaprio... Claire Danes movie! 1999 or something?' (85). Another confuses the play with *West Side Story* (80). I learned about Nature Theater of Oklahoma's *Romeo and Juliet* and saw clips from it in W. B. Worthen's talk, '"What light through yonder window speaks?" De-dramatizing Shakespeare', on a panel, 'Experimental Shakespeare in Theory and Practice', at the Annual Meeting of the Shakespeare Association of America in Bellevue, Washington, 9 April 2011.

[19] Morse, 'Twice', pp. 293–4, notes that in the BBC tale, Oberon often quotes or paraphrases Shakespeare's text; so does Puck, likewise licensed by his fairy status, and he delivers an epilogue to conclude all three versions. In the Illinois production, it is intact; Betts cuts and adds, and the BBC's Puck paraphrases. In each, Puck addresses the audience intimately and urges them to consider the play a dream. In the BBC version he cements his connection with the audience by drawing on the resources of film. He concludes by dropping the liquid into the viewers' eyes (onto the camera lens in closeup) and we then experience a flashback montage of key moments and desires from this filmed dream.

the Northern rata tree that is the source of the flower drops its seed in the top of another tree, sends roots down and grows up, choking off its host, an apt symbol of the lust the flower juice catalyzes. In the BBC version we see the juice's effects each time it is administered in a montage of images representing the characters' shifts of vision and affection. Unlike many adaptations and productions that omit key plot elements (for example, the Fortinbras plot from *Hamlet* or the Induction from *The Taming of the Shrew*), these three reiterations retain all of the multiple and intricately intertwined aspects of *A Midsummer Night's Dream*. But the dramatic emphasis is placed, as I have shown, on expressions of sexual desire, on the older couples, their gender wars and their negotiation of equality. The other key feature, the artisans – whether feminists, resort staff or ordinary workmen – parody in their performance each work's techniques, counterpoint its plots, and crucially catalyse the comedy's happy ending.

Each production, of course, remains more fixed in its own historical and cultural moment than is the mobile work. The New Zealand *Revenge of the Amazons* farcically enacts the battles of feminism vs. patriarchy in the 1970s and 80s; since these remain unresolved in the play as in the culture, the adaptation can still succeed in revival in 2007. The BBC's *ReTold Dream* continues the channel's legacy as the guardian of British traditional and accessible Shakespeare by keeping the play heterosexual and remarkably modest and by giving women power to demand reform from their husbands, the twenty-first century's post-feminist default position. The University of Illinois's American production, *A Midsummer Night's Dream – It's a Bacchanal!*, by concluding the play in the world of Carnival, postpones any return to normative erotic desires, gender relations and marriage in tune with its audience of open-minded college students with open-ended lives. But the work, in process, will continue to move on.

SHAKESQUEER, THE MOVIE: *WERE THE WORLD MINE* AND *A MIDSUMMER NIGHT'S DREAM*

MATT KOZUSKO

There is a conceptual glitch in the climactic moment of *Shakespeare in Love*. It has nothing to do with historical inaccuracies or the film's fanciful depiction of public performance, which though not factual is oddly plausible. Rather, it's a bait-and-switch, or a sort of sleight of hand in which the forceful beauty of Shakespeare's plays – the magic that makes them so moving to read or perform or behold – is argued with the tropes and *topoi* of Hollywood melodrama. Shakespeare's power, that is, is made visible not in the staged performance that the film depicts at its dramatic climax but in the techniques and technologies that structure the film itself. The power of Shakespeare's plays turns out to be incommunicable in any objective sense, a quality that is impossible to demonstrate as self-evident. It is an assumed power, something that needs to be in place for the film's central gesture to work, but it is fundamentally something that cannot be established objectively or straightforwardly. At once the premise and the argument of the story, Will Shakespeare's dramatic genius turns out to be something we take on faith.

Having framed the public performance of Will's new drama *Romeo and Juliet* as a test of whether a play, in the Queen's words, can 'show us the very truth and nature of love', the film offers its audience an originary Shakespeare playing Romeo in the original public performance.[1] At stake in this performance is the very foundation of the myth of Shakespeare as the poet laureate of humanity: failure to capture life – here, love – in a stage play means that Will the character will lose a £50 bet, but it also implies the failure of Shakespeare's dramatic artistry, which in turn undermines the myth constructed in the centuries since. While the movie toys playfully throughout with a continuum between playwright and screen writer, between early modern drama and contemporary Hollywood, the authenticity of the performance *as a stage play* is central to the test: this is Will Shakespeare himself on stage, at the Rose theatre, in a recreation of Elizabethan staging. That staging is central to contemporary notions of Shakespeare and authenticity, as is evident in the widespread insistence on Shakespeare in his native medium and in the growing popularity of 'original practices' approaches to performance itself. This Rose performance will do what it does – win the hearts and minds of the audience by representing on stage something never before quite captured in dramatic narrative – because Shakespeare, as we know, has a way with words. On the original London stage, the magic of the words, spoken by and speaking through the cast, will function at the height of their power.

The premise of 'actual performance', however, is supplemented throughout, and ultimately supplanted, by the medium of film. The death scene, figured here as the final, perfecting argument for true love, makes the usual cuts to the play text in order to keep the clutter of Paris and the Friar from disrupting the focus on Romeo/Will and Juliet/Viola. But as the climactic moment

---

[1] *Shakespeare in Love* (Director: John Madden. Performers: Gwyneth Paltrow, Joseph Fiennes, Geoffrey Rush. Miramax, 1998; DVD edition 1999), ch. 17.

approaches, the pretence of a stage performance of *Romeo and Juliet* before thousands of people collapses altogether. Will and Viola's final moments together, and the validation of Shakespeare the playwright, is a series of whispered exchanges of lines possible only in film. Though the sweeping camera movements and the alternating angles effectively suggest audience lines of sight, the viewer's perspective is actually an aggregate of all perspectives; it is comprehensive and all-seeing, and it depends heavily on close-up, particularly for the lovers' final lines, which are – which would be – inaudible to the Rose theatre audience.

Perhaps most important, the power of the play's language is established not via its recitation, but in external cues: the swelling score and the gasps, sobs and exclamations of the rapt audience. We know the performance is a success because the music, the tears and the reactions of the in-film audience tell us so. *Shakespeare in Love* thus ends up situating Shakespeare's power as a function of the movies, not of the poetry. After invoking an originary Shakespeare, the film substitutes the technologies and conventions of Hollywood for the technologies and conventions of Shakespeare's theatre.

The substitution is subtle. It might even be read as incidental, ultimately immaterial, just a minor media tweak to a fundamentally sound story in which Shakespeare's words host a transformative moment for the troubled protagonists working through their interpersonal dramas. It is an old story, after all, one we in the west have been telling for decades. But I think the story, and its sleight of hand, is emblematic of a dynamic that defines the way we produce and consume Shakespeare today: it is a dynamic of substitution and circularity, a dynamic in which what is to be demonstrated turns out to be what is assumed and in which the climactic, transformative moment – Shakespeare's genius at work – turns out always to be a function of something else. Shakespeare, I would argue, no longer has a native medium; Shakespeare is itself a medium. It is a space, sanctioned by the cultural status of the plays and adorned with their language, in which a certain kind of story can take place.

To explore this thought, I want to look at two recent films that make extensive use of *A Midsummer Night's Dream* in telling stories of the power of Shakespeare to bring about transformations in audiences who watch the plays and in the actors who perform them. My focus is on Tom Gustafson's 2008 romantic musical, *Were the World Mine*, but I want to discuss it in the context of Peter Weir's 1989 drama, *Dead Poets Society*. In some senses, the films are quite different. They are separated by genre and nearly two decades, and *Dead Poets Society* is only peripherally concerned with Shakespeare. Yet both are set in US prep schools, and both match their central male characters to the role of Puck, an empowering experience that gives each young man an opportunity to confront hostility and ignorance in hopes of reforming it. Both operate in the mode of melodrama, which means that despite the significant difference in tone, both are concerned to elicit sympathy for a beset protagonist in whom the film's audience recognizes a truth, an innocence, a virtue that is undervalued or altogether unseen by the world around him. And together, the films demonstrate the flexibility of Shakespeare to accommodate the needs and desires of whoever is speaking the language. They show us, that is, the sense in which Shakespeare is a text that always speaks on behalf of the person who wields it, even when all that text means is 'Shakespeare'. Perhaps especially then.

This form of 'meaning by Shakespeare', as Terence Hawkes has called it, cares less and less to attend to the language as it advances a cause under the Shakespeare banner. The 'latent semantic potentiality' – Michael Bristol's phrase – that drives most instances of meaning-by-Shakespeare remains, in the tradition to which these films belong, latent.[2] What matters isn't the lines' ability to speak to the current situation, even if getting the lines to speak means putting some interpretive torque on them, but simply their status as Shakespeare. To put it another way, what's important

---

[2] See Terence Hawkes, *Meaning By Shakespeare* (New York, 1992); and Michael Bristol, *Big-time Shakespeare* (New York, 1996), pp. 3–29.

in films of this genre, and particularly in *Were the World Mine*, is not the rich, famously flexible content that allows Shakespeare to be mobilized on behalf of potentially contradictory positions, but the archaic syntax and diction that give the lines a 'Shakespeareness'. *Were the World Mine* proposes to put to work the intricate, complexly wrought poetry; what it actually uses is the dense, eccentric sound of early modern verse, coupled with the conventions of melodrama. Like *Shakespeare in Love*, these movies bet on Shakespeare but win with a trick play.

In *Dead Poets Society*, Neil Perry (Robert Sean Leonard) has struggled to accept and to meet his father's expectations. Neil is supposed to go to Harvard and become a doctor: 'you don't understand, Neil. You have opportunities that I never even dreamt of, and I'm not going to let you waste them.'[3] But it is of course Neil's father who does not understand. Parents in *Dead Poets Society*, like textbooks and headmasters and the school's administrative machinery, are figures of the status quo. They're not evil – they mean well – but as the J. Evans Pritchards of the human experience, they plot success in life as a product of numerical scores on a graph.[4] Fine arts in general are tolerated, not celebrated, presumably as a means of eking out character. Tom Anderson, Neil's fellow student at Welton Academy, gets the same desk set every year for his birthday from his parents. It is an expression of their cluelessness and a perfect metonymy for the kind of education experience that English teacher John Keating (Robin Williams) wants to move his students to see beyond. 'Medicine, law, business, engineering: these are noble pursuits, and necessary to sustain life', he tells them, 'but poetry, beauty, romance, love; these are what we stay alive for' (ch. 5).

Shakespeare is the film's key metonymy for poetry, beauty, romance and love; it is the stand-in for all noble pursuits, the opposite of desksets. Parents don't hear it, and J. Evans Pritchard doesn't quite get it. Even Keating's students need to be convinced. And while poetry, beauty, romance and love each play an important part as the various students meet their various challenges, the

Shakespeare story gets top billing, because among the characters' transformative encounters with art, Neil's performance of Puck has the biggest consequences. It marks both the power of the transformative experience hosted in this film by Shakespeare and the gravity of its implications. When Neil wins the part of Puck in *A Midsummer Night's Dream*, he pursues it against the proscription of his father. He forges consent forms and lies even to Keating about permission. When Mr Perry unexpectedly turns up at the performance, Neil, glimpsing him from behind the curtain, is unsettled for a brief moment, but he takes the stage anyway. The story is familiar, and we know already how it will end: Neil will find in Shakespeare the power he needs to confront his father.

The performance scene itself is noteworthy for several reasons. First, its conventions follow a pattern common to filmic representations of Shakespeare on stage. While the stage play is the ostensible focus of the sequence, we rely largely on external cues, such as music and shot sequence, to guide our reading of the performance. As in *Shakespeare in Love*, it is difficult for the performance to be moving on film, so shots of audience reaction are especially important in establishing the power of the play. Here, we know that Neil is good as Puck not simply because he appears to be competent on stage, but because Neil's audience in the film tells us so – they are rapt, they clap, they laugh, they remark aloud ('he's really good!').[5] Most striking, though, is the performance's climactic moment, Puck's epilogue. If 'successful play' is the argument

---

[3] Quotations from *Dead Poets Society* (Director, Peter Weir. Performers, Robin Williams, Robert Sean Leonard. Touchstone, 1989) are keyed to the DVD edition (Touchstone Home Video, undated). This line is from ch. 19.

[4] In one of *Dead Poets Society*'s iconic scenes, the John Keating character instructs his students to tear our of their poetry textbooks a page that explains how a poem's greatness can be determined as a matter of 'area', by plotting its perfection and importance on a graph. Pritchards is the fictional analogue of Laurence Perrine, whose 1956 book, *Sound and Sense: An Introduction to Poetry*, is presumably the source for the model of evaluation derided in the film.

[5] Quotations here are taken from ch. 18.

of the performance sequence, its larger narrative function for *Dead Poets Society* surfaces in the final stretch of verse, in which the drama external to the stage play is brought simultaneously into focus with the drama internal to the stage play. Shakespeare's words provide a resolution to the play and to the story's enclosing conflict as Neil uses Puck's epilogue to confront his father and to plead his case. The arrangement of shots – first Neil, then his father, three times – shows us that the lines are spoken as part of the play, to the audience, but also as part of the Perry family drama, from father to son: 'if we shadows have offended / Think but this, and all is mended'. The words resonate with an overdetermined significance – the actors' transgressions, but also Neil's transgression in acting, are merely 'a dream'; the vision of the Harvard-bound son profaning his time with weak and idle themes is not something worthy of reprehension; the father's expected rebuke is a serpent's tongue; and finally, 'give me your hands, if we be friends', is not merely a solicitation for applause, but also a plea for understanding. With Neil empowered by Puck, by Shakespeare, the exchange between father and son, Nick loquacious and Mr Perry compelled to listen, reverses the dynamic we see elsewhere in the film, in which father issues commands as son falls silent. Shakespeare's language is sanctioned and sacred. It can't be interrupted or answered. Its argument is irrefutable.

Typically, the inspiring performance story leads to a happy ending. Friendships are mended, love is rekindled, personal shortcomings are addressed and resolved. The lesson that cast and audience take away is always that the performance was thrilling, that the ensemble was exhilarating, and that the experience was enfranchising. There are always *senex* characters who don't get it and whose failure to get it complements the lesson that all the right-thinking characters learn – Lord Wessex in *Shakespeare in Love*; Holly Day in the first season of *Slings & Arrows*. In *Dead Poets Society*, the lesson is ultimately devastating, partly because the *senex* character is neither converted by the play's power – Shakespeare's irrefutable argument is simply ignored – nor compelled to a cave or some

other obscurity in the story's margins. Neil's father remains very much in power, and his renewed proscription forbidding any more acting drives Neil to despair. Brought by Shakespeare to a final and full awareness of his calling, his talents and the intolerability of his father's plans, Neil kills himself with his father's gun in his father's study.

Were the World Mine fits comfortably in the tradition of Shakespeare appropriations and adaptations in which Shakespeare hosts a transformative experience. The film loosely reproduces language and plot points from *A Midsummer Night's Dream*, and it draws its tropes and *topoi* partly from Shakespearean comedy and partly from the filmic tradition in which it participates. The beset protagonist, Timothy, struggles to be accepted by his peer group. He is a surrogate for the viewer's subject position, and his triumph at the film's conclusion marks the comedy's happy ending, with all the right-thinking people brought over to his side. Timothy's guide is a sage theatre-director figure, Miss Tebbit, who knows Shakespeare cold and who silently identifies Timothy's problems and works to resolve them. She is a surrogate for Shakespeare himself, the ultimate source of wisdom, personal empowerment, and right-thinking, well-adjusted people – people, that is, who get Shakespeare and who are part of the happy conclusion. Timothy's misfit friends, Frankie and Max, navigate their own romantic difficulties, while his mother, Donna, struggles with personal empowerment issues, also under the guidance of a (parody) tutor figure. Both sub-plots provide a comic complement to Timothy's problems. The various iterations of institutional power – a private school's headmaster and its thick-skulled coach; the homophobic, scripture-quoting locals of Kingston, Illinois – serve as blocking figures before they are made, along with everybody else, to see the world from Timothy's perspective.

The film manages the conventions of the genre in interesting ways, following the general contours of a saved-by-Shakespeare story but opening up new spaces within that story and putting creative stress on some of its standard devices. It is alternately subtle and overstated, queer and oddly heteronormative. In its tame but open affection for male–male sexual embraces, the film offers a kind of 'gay gaze' and frankly celebrates same-sex coupling. But it falls short of doing anything radical to the genre – of queering it – just as it falls short, ultimately, of being a queer film. In this sense, it is governed more by the requirements of Shakespearian comedy than by anything else, with *A Midsummer Night's Dream* providing the function of Green World. Because the Green World itself requires a world outside, a containing narrative that is necessarily *not* green and a world that is normative in every functional sense, there is no opportunity for any of the film's queering gestures to take root and spread. And in a final move, a move at the end out of the magic and the world of Shakespeare's *Dream* and into Timothy's dream world, the film returns to the genre conventions sketched here in my brief accounts of *Shakespeare in Love* and *Dead Poet's Society*. Despite its various departures from the formula, it is finally a traditional, which is to say 'straight', saved-by-Shakespeare story.

'IT DOESN'T MAKE SENSE!'

The first scene frames Timothy, openly gay, as the tormented outcast at a prep school populated with homophobic rugby players. Even the rugby coach, Driskill, mocks Timothy, calling him 'fancy feet' and grinning derisively when he is smacked in the face during a game of dodgeball. In the ensuing exchange among players in the locker room, the film establishes 'Shakespeare' as a reference point opposite the masculine norm:

Cole (to Cooper, who is dressing). Hey, you're gonna be
    late to that Shakesqueer crap.
Cooper. Who cares? The guy's like 400 years old; it
    doesn't make sense!
Henry. It does to anyone with a brain.
Player Two. A brain – but no dick!
Henry (mocking Cooper). 'Duh . . . hey, all I know is
    rugby'
Cooper. Rugby rocks; give it up![6]

The lines are crude and ostensibly insignificant – almost background noise, with an improvised quality that would seem to minimize their

importance. I will come back to them frequently, however, partly to help structure this discussion and partly because they serve as well as anything else to sketch the film's central concerns. Rugby and masculinity are set up in opposition to Shakespeare, which is 'queer' in the sense that it's archaic and difficult to understand, and perhaps in that it's associated with theatre, but principally because it isn't rugby. The point here, apparently, is not that these students hate Shakespeare; rather, they're not especially interested in anything outside of sports and the heteronormative, masculine identity that governs participation in sports. They are the high-school athlete equivalent of a stock character – the *discipulus gloriosus*, perhaps, with the suggestion that the drama will discipline them and bring them around to better integration in a renewed social order at the conclusion. As the students work through the play, there is no aggression towards Shakespeare beyond the usual struggling with the awkward language. Even the reflexive aversion to cross-dressing quickly subsides.

Where *Dead Poets Society* figures Shakespeare as the metonymic representative of fraught humanity, articulated in poetry, *Were the World Mine* offers a less anxious version. 'Shakespeare' is a stand-in for thoughtfulness and abstraction, and the fact that the plays are 400 years old lends them a kind of virtue. Shakespeare makes no sense, perhaps because the material is old, but mostly because an absence of understanding is the precondition for enlightenment. And of course, the complaint here functions as a guarantee that in the end, Shakespeare *will* make sense; the film itself is the story of how that comes to be. The stakes are lower, however, and the investment in the poetry is less. *Were the World Mine* features far more language drawn from the plays than does *Dead Poets Society*, but it treats that language more casually. This treatment is attributable in part to the extent to which the film is a version of *Dream*, as opposed to a film about a

---

[6] Quotations from *Were the World Mine* (Director: Tom Gustafson. Performers: Tanner Cohen, Wendy Robie, Judy Mclane and Zelda Williams. SPEAKproductions, 2008) are taken from a video file (Wolfe Video, 2009) without chapters.

production of *Dream*. Many saved-by-Shakespeare appropriations in which a Shakespeare play is staged tend to create plot parallels between the play's action and the action of the containing narrative. *Shakespeare in Love*, for example, works through proscriptions against class exogamy that echo the intra-class social boundaries of *Romeo and Juliet* but do not reproduce them precisely. The first season of *Slings & Arrows* turns on mentor-student relationships that suggest Hamlet's struggles with the will of his dead father, but the festival company is not living through *Hamlet*. By contrast, *Were the World Mine* is closer to being *A Midsummer Night's Dream* than to echoing it and, as a result, the need to make the language a precise focal point, to make it do specific work, is rarely urgent.

Instead, it works by association and suggestion. The film is littered with Shakespeare quotations, but with a few exceptions, none of them seems strictly necessary at any given point. Shakespeare in *Were the World Mine* is more a disposition than a presence with agency; it is a marker of enlightenment and understanding, and that enlightenment is reached not by way of precise signification but when characters are able to 'unite rhythm with words', as the film's English teacher and sage figure, Miss Tebbit, puts it. In the second scene, she starts her class by saying to her students, 'today I challenge you to write in verse. / Remembering William Shakespeare, scribe away / your thoughts and feelings, boldly on a page.' She is aligned with Shakespeare – functions as his surrogate, even – via her affection for verse. Presumably by design, she herself speaks throughout the scene entirely in iambs, and typically in pentameter. She follows her verse challenge by reciting lines from *Dream* aloud, with an emphasis on the metrics:

What angel wakes me from my flow'ry bed? (3.1.122)
I pray thee, gentle mortal, sing again (3.1.130)
Love looks not with the eyes, but with the mind,
And therefore is winged Cupid painted blind.
                                                    (1.1.234–5)

Shakespeare is associated with love poetry, with thoughts and feelings, with archaic diction like 'scribe away'. The lines Miss Tebbit quotes are not contiguous in the play, and they have no qualities immediately relevant to the moment. They are chosen because they sound like Shakespeare and because they fit the subject matter: love. Indeed, the 'Shakespeareness' of the lines is arguably overdone. In straight iambic pentameter, 'wingèd' would be monosyllabic, and 'flowery' would be disyllabic, but the film goes out of its way to emphasize the extra syllables in order to suggest 'verse'.

Elsewhere, the film deals flippantly, almost irresponsibly, with Shakespeare's language. That is, while the sanctity of the poetry is the film's entry point into an understanding of Shakespeare's power, it seems to have a pronounced need to crowd the language with other vaguely metaphysical agents of power and inspiration, from song and dance to poetry written in the style of early modern verse but not taken from Shakespeare. 'Awaken and empower what's within' is Miss Tebbit's invitation (pentameter, but not Shakespeare) to Timothy to take the part of Puck in the production. She issues the invitation twice, in fact, the second time to Timothy and his love interest, Jonathon, but Timothy is slow to catch on. He initially shows no interest in it ('I'm not an actor'), and he has no native affinity for the verse. Reading from 3.2 at auditions, he acknowledges, 'I don't even know what I'm saying', and stumbles on one of Puck's signature lines, 'Lord what fools these mortals be!' Miss Tebbit responds preemptively, 'agreed, indeed'. She then oddly invokes an alternative to the poetry of Shakespeare, inviting Timothy to set aside one script and take up another – the lyrics to one of the film's musical numbers. 'Let's sing', she suggests, before putting Timothy through an audition we have just watched another student fail.

We fairies that do run
From the presence of the sun
We follow darkness like a dream
Chorus
Be as thou wast wont to be
See as thou wast wont to see

Timothy sings beautifully, displaying an affinity that was lacking in the line reading, and here the film introduces yet another incremental remove from the straight, which is to say typical, take on Shakespeare's language. While its songs borrow extensively from *Dream*, the film here thinks of 'fairies' not in the *Dream* sense but in the Timothy sense, and the chorus, as yet without any plot anchor in charmed sight – that will come later – seems to invite Timothy to be himself. It reads not the word 'wont', but rather 'want' – be as you want to be, see the world that you want to see. In other words, the film slips not into Shakespeare, but into a musical fantasy sequence, and one in which the rugby team smothers Timothy with attention. Shakespeare presides over the moment but the film asks the language to do something new, something that signifies with the authority of Shakespeare but without straight semantics.

Later, as Timothy continues to struggle with Puck's language, Miss Tebbit offers an instruction:

Unite rhythm with words, and they will unlock to empower you, like a midsummer night's dream come true. Take pains, be perfect, adieu.

The central episode in *Were the World Mine* involves this instruction, the notion of empowerment, and Timothy's discovery of a recipe for a real-life, fully functional version of the love potion. Working through another of Puck's iconic lines, 'I'll put a girdle round about the earth', he discovers its animating rhythm. As he begins emphasizing the iambs aloud to himself – 'I'll *put* a *gird*le *round* a*bout* the *earth*' – the page in his text becomes luminous, and words begin to fade. The word 'REMEDIES' appears, then a recipe:

#3
Cupid's Love Juice

Secure upon-sat stones of promontory,
Spark'd essence of the madly shooting stars,
One drop or two of anything wat'ry
Some semblance of a milk-white western flower
Fulfill a pot of purely mineral with
Ingredients which you've gathered carefully.
Upon said bowl, bestow harmonious breath
Til thou remember'st pure whose love you seek.
Allow this precious time to meditate;

Their quenched thirst your just deserved prize!
United they conspire to charm your mate
With purple liquor destined for Love's eyes.
 Now with a deft and musical note, rejoice
 To give your deepest love-desire strong voice.

The sonnet appears only briefly, and it would be a stretch to imagine its importance goes any further than another instance of the ' Shakespeareness' first introduced via Miss Tebbit. The vaguely archaic gestures in the verse, mostly anastrophe and various figures of omission, and the diction ('promontory', 'liquor') have an appropriate quality, but there is nothing imperative in their content. Like Miss Tebbit's dialogue, the lines recall Shakespeare without suggesting that they are Shakespeare.

Nonetheless, with its investment in Shakespeare's verse, *Were the World Mine* follows a convention of the saved-by-Shakespeare genre in privileging the language of the plays and assigning to the poetry the abstract power to bring about the change that will drive the narrative towards conclusion. The mode of that change is essentially melodramatic, in the sense established by Peter Brooks in *The Melodramatic Imagination* and since developed by film theorists such as Linda Williams and Christine Gledhill.[7] Because the effect is valid across genre lines (in *Dead Poets Society*, recall, the conclusion is dark), the point is not a happy ending so much as a recognition of virtue or innocence or some other instance of ethical or moral integrity. Keating's understanding of the importance of seizing the beauty in life and Neil's realization that he is not suited to a conventional career are celebrated, even though they cause great pain, because they are discovered in the course of the narrative to be sound. In other films, such as Hank Rogerson's 2005 prison Shakespeare documentary, *Shakespeare Behind Bars*, the effect of Shakespeare's language is

---

7 See Peter Brooks, *The Melodramatic Imagination* (New Haven, 1976; repr. with new preface, 1995); Christine Gledhill, 'Signs of Melodrama', in *Stardom: Industry of Desire*, ed. Christine Gledhill (London, 1991), pp. 207–29; and Linda Williams, *Playing the Race Card* (Princeton, 2001), especially ch. 1.

more dispersed, but it is not fundamentally different. It is consistently understood to provide both the challenge and the solution to the character, or person, who must work his way through it as the story unfolds. As I have argued elsewhere, this is true in genres even as distant as the radio documentary and actor training literature, where the importance of Shakespeare's language to the transformative process is even more pronounced.[8] But whether the transformation is effected by a performance of Shakespeare or a reading of such a performance, the result is enlightenment, revelation, vindication; and whether the result is comic or tragic, it is brought about in a space provided by Shakespeare.

'THAT SHAKESQUEER CRAP'

Much of the film's mild comedy comes from watching young male students stumble through line readings and struggle with the unfamiliar demands of playing Shakespeare. The more pointed of these jokes depend on the tension between heteronormative, rugby-ready masculinity and Shakespeare, whose encroaching on rugby territory becomes more aggressive as the film proceeds. 'I'm not shaving', says a student cast as woman, to which another replies 'at least you're not the jackass'.[9] 'At least the jackass doesn't have to wear a dress', says the first. The student implicitly cast as Bottom – 'the jackass' – teases the student implicitly cast as Flute: 'What is Thisbe? Is that a chick?', he asks, and we recall 'Flute' begging Miss Tebbit not to cast him as a woman, because he is growing a goatee. The name 'Thisbe', of course, isn't on the cast list – only Flute – and the joke here depends on Flute's line, 'Nay, faith, let not me play a woman. I have a beard coming' (1.2.43–4). It is a reward for viewers who know the play, but it also registers a growing concern with the power of Shakespeare to affect students who have to play it.

Coach Driskill's fears are less specific, but more serious. His initial objection is to rehearsals, which will compete for time in students' schedules with rugby practice. Miss Tebbit reads the objection

differently. In this exchange, Tebbit is confronted by Driskill and the school's headmaster:

Dr. Bellinger. Miss Tebbit, this year's varsity rugby time is one of the best in the history of our institution.
Ms. Tebbit. So this has nothing to do with time requirements.
Dr. Bellinger. We're concerned about the tradition. Members of the rugby team portraying females . . .
Ms. Tebbit. Truth be told –
Coach Driskill. It's bad for morale; you're embarrassing them!
Ms. Tebbit. Only because you've trained them to cast judgment upon each other.
Dr. Bellinger. Miss Tebbit, the academy is concerned that we're sending the wrong message.
Ms. Tebbit. The academy has been staging Shakespeare in this fashion for fifty-six years.
Coach Driskill. We live in a different time.
Ms. Tebbit. Your ignorance of the history of this academy, and the history of the theatre, is offensive.
Dr. Bellinger. Miss Tebbit –
Ms. Tebbit. Women were prohibited by law to act on the Elizabethan stage; men filled the void. If this confabulation is about your insecurities with sexuality, or the sexuality of your Warriors –
Coach Driskill. I don't have any issues with my sexuality!
Ms. Tebbitt. A Midsummer Night's Dream is the senior play; the cast is chosen.

Tebbit emerges here as a figure of some power. Her knowledge, of theatre and of the academy's history, evidently trumps community concerns and the fears of a coach, even though those fears have the headmaster's backing. We later learn (perhaps we sense already) that Tebbit has some of Oberon's magic; she can help Timothy to the love potion, but she can also work on the larger community when it is necessary – as when she later defuses a call to cancel the performance by raising her

---

[8] See Matt Kozusko, 'Actors, Audiences, Inmates and the Politics of Reading Shakespeare', *Shakespeare Bulletin*, 28 (2010), 235–51.
[9] The camera lingers briefly on the cast list, though the students' names as listed there do not correspond perfectly with the names in the film's credits.

hands and intoning, 'the play must go on'; nobody questions her, and everybody turns up for the performance. Here, her function is to draw to the surface some of the film's submerged logic. Tebbit imagines the play as a means of bringing about her own confrontation: she isolates the cause of the community's homophobia as a matter of training – 'you've trained them to cast judgment upon each other' – and her Shakespeare production, not merely a device to help Timothy, will be a means to rehabilitate the rugby team's relationship with a queered, which is to say Shakespearian, masculinity.

I use the word 'queer' throughout this article rather loosely, both as adjective and as transitive verb, in order to suggest the film's project of disrupting the ostensibly natural bond of masculinity with heterosexuality, and by extension, with heteronormativity and homophobia.[10] The male body and the male disposition as established in the opening scene of the film carry all these traits, and the film pursues various strategies for stripping them away. Insofar as simply to denaturalize heterosexuality is to queer it, *A Midsummer Night's Dream* itself does some of the work by proxy. Cupid's love juice may be the material embodiment of a 'natural' attraction, but that naturalness is consistently trumped, in my reading, by the love juice's power to affect and manipulate human behaviour – behaviour which thereby comes to seem always determined, never natural or inevitable. But *Were the World Mine* has more precise designs. It wants everyone to see the world from Timothy's perspective, and so it queers rugby, and rugby's containing narrative, masculinity, first in the musical fantasy scenes that turn the homophobic jocks into gay dancers, and later by virtue of Puck's love potion, which turns them into romantic partners. Along with Coach Driskill, in love with Dr Bellinger (the school's headmaster), and Nora Bellinger (his wife), in love with Donna, the cast and most of the town are also paired up in same-sex couples as Timothy wanders the night, wearing his Puck wings and spreading the love potion, at a firehouse, at a church and at a bar. The town wakes up the next morning to a kind of gay mania. The streets are filled with assorted same-sex couples, embracing and beaming at each other. The mayor has declared gay marriage legal, drawing swarms of same-sex lovers from neighbouring areas. Bellinger's wife won't acknowledge him, and Coach Driskill won't leave him alone. Parents of suddenly-gay children demand action during an emergency meeting at the academy. 'It's that alternative teacher and her Shakespeare!', someone shouts. 'Shakespeare was queer too!', adds another. The odd thing is that the hysterical fears, for once, are accurate. Shakespeare in the film *is* queer, and the play has most certainly turned the entire cast queer. In a sense, it is Puck's love potion that is figurative, and it is the play itself that is literally responsible: participation in *A Midsummer Night's Dream* has realized the worst fears not merely of the rugby coach but of the scripture-citing community.

Much of the film's comedy happens in this Green World space opened by the play. We are invited to enjoy the squirming of the characters who have to this point aligned themselves against Timothy's camp. The midsummer night's dream here is Timothy's, whose midday fantasies, presented as a sequence of musical dance numbers, begin in the first scene and punctuate the film intermittently. Components of the fantasies make their way into the waking world – a large tree from the first number, for example, suggestive of release, freedom and respite from the abuse of the rugby squad, forms the central set piece in the play. But under the effect of the love potion, the centrepiece of those fantasies, the male body in erotic motion, is moved to the waking stage. The camera falls short of caressing the bodies it captures outside the fantasy sequences, and whether the camera's gaze is still Timothy's is debatable. Its disposition and point of view are sympathetic to him, but they do not transfer from the fantasies to the containing narrative as the queered rugby players make the same move. The bodies are no longer aggressively

---

[10] The term seems to have lost some of its urgency and some of its danger, at least in academic usage. For a recent overview, see Nikki Sullivan, *A Critical Introduction to Queer Theory* (New York, 2003), especially chs. 7 and 11.

sexualized; we see them now from the traditional perspective of observers in a love story. But it is also difficult to isolate Timothy's point of view in a stable sense once the move is made; indeed, it is difficult in the final fantasy sequence, in which Timothy is exhorted to undo the confusion he has created as Puck, to distinguish midday fantasy from an ordinary night's dream. Once the love potion takes effect, the world of the film is suddenly and irreversibly Timothy's.

This move from fantasy to reality begins with Coach Driskill, one of the potion's first victims. While his campy parody of homosexuality is entertaining, it also provides an organizing function for the now-gay rugby team: as an authority figure, he helps focus the gay madness that engulfs unaffected characters, giving that madness a purpose and an institutional validity. The dance routines are already governing the players' movements, as Driskill's entrance into the gym is framed by two students forming an archway over the door with rugby balls. 'Gentlemen! This afternoon, we focus on balance and coordination', he announces, and then he slips into verse: 'essential *skills* to *hone* for *rug*by *one*', he intones, accompanied by claps to emphasize the iambs. When his players respond with assent by way of a short dance exchange, he exclaims 'Excellent! Onward to the field, gentles!' People under the spell, which is to say people in love, which is to say people in homosexual love, speak Shakespeare, and when they aren't speaking Shakespeare, they tend towards the archaic syntax and diction ('gentles!') that suggest Shakespeare. To work at the point from the other direction, Shakespeare has all along been associated with love, and love – true love, the course of which never did run smooth, as any number of the film's characters now insists – is queer; thus, *Shakesqueer*.

Watching formerly homophobic characters under the spell of Shakesqueer makes us laugh, but laughter is merely a secondary effect of the comedy. Its primary function is the reforming of ignorance, which it effects by queering masculinity to allow for a renewed social order. The film does not explicitly decide whether the love potion's victims remember their behaviour once they have

been released from its effects. In one of the subtleties that lends the project an intelligent nuance, they simply smile and go about their business with a new attitude. The polarizing issue that made normalized behaviour homophobic behaviour has been resolved, and while a heteronormative masculinity is restored, that standard no longer requires, or even seems to recognize, homophobia. That is, while nobody remains under the effects of Puck's potions, nobody is returned to the precise position he or she formerly occupied. Homosexuality is not the new standard, but it is accommodated in the new understanding of masculinity.

What looks like a renewed social order at the film's conclusion may most easily be explained as a function of Shakespearian comedy, though my suggestion is that the film silently drops, in its final moments, the Shakespeare conventions it has been employing and replaces them with modern analogues and with key *topoi* of the saved-by-Shakespeare genre. Just as it moves out of its performance of *A Midsummer Night's Dream* as the play comes to an end, so the film begins to shore up the power of Shakespeare to effect change by resorting to the usual external cues – soundtrack, audience approval, cast celebration and so forth. This move, I will argue, ultimately un-queers the movie, Shakespeare, and maybe Timothy himself.

As with the Neil story-line in *Dead Poets Society*, the focal point of the final scenes is Puck's epilogue and the audience response. The familiar sequence of shots draws all the film's characters into easy harmony. All of Timothy's doubters and detractors, together with his supporters, watch in approving wonder. Donna smiles from the audience and fields compliments about her son. The cast engages in mutual congratulations, realizing that they have delivered a first-rate performance, and the audience's enthusiastic approval grows to a standing ovation when Timothy, like Neil, appears for a final bow. The magic of the performance, and of Timothy's performance in particular, registers primarily in these effects, not in Shakespeare's language, because that language does no real work here. Puck's epilogue provides a sanctioned space in which Timothy can emote, but he doesn't use the lines to make amends. His delivery is suffused with a sadness, because he has just released Jonathon from the potion's spell and – he thinks – sent him back to the heterosexual, heteronormative world of rugby that exists outside of Shakespeare, outside of the play. Where the words have some careful significance for Neil, they are for Timothy simply an opportunity to lament the dream he must give up as the play closes.

In a corresponding move, the film chips away at the integrity of *Dream*'s language by breaking off some of its defining components and reassigning them to other genres and other media. The Pyramus and Thisbe play becomes a rock song, the film's structural analogue to the play's lowbrow but earnest entertainment. Shakespeare's language is lost entirely in the lyrics. It has to be there, reminding us that we are watching Shakespeare at work – and it is important work, even here, because it allows Max publicly to proclaim his love for Frankie but, in the thrashing of drums and guitars, words are not united with rhythm, in Miss Tebbit's phrasing, so much as overridden and overwritten with rhythm. *Were the World Mine* begins with words, then proposes that their power can be activated when they are intoned aloud, with rhythm, only to crowd out the words in the end, subjecting them to props that were supposed to empower them. Shakespeare, supplemented throughout with scenery, costumes and dance routines, ultimately disappears, taking most of the film's queerness with him.

'RUGBY ROCKS: GIVE IT UP!'

Timothy can use Puck's lines without any obligation to their *Dream* function because Timothy isn't entirely an honest Puck. Shakespeare's Puck delights in leading Athenians up and down and contributing to the confusion that baffles the rude mechanicals and the other mortals. He is a knavish sprite with little interest in renewing or restoring order. Without the benevolent impositions of Oberon, there is no reason at all for Puck to set things right. But Oberon, with problems of his own – and motivations clearly more complex than

simple benevolence – is compelled to restore order. He is in fact an embodiment of order, together with Titania, and we understand that in the play, the quarrels that occupy the Athenians in the opening scene are merely an effect of a larger cosmic imbalance that needs to be addressed and resolved. At the level of comic formula, however, Puck is a device, as is 'love' itself, used to bring about a realignment. Puck can do the work he does because he has no investment in the human passions that drive the lovers and animate the mechanicals. In this respect, he fills the role allotted elsewhere in Shakespeare to the clown or fool, a character who looks on at the play's core actors with a bemused indifference. While Puck's commentary – 'Lord what fools these mortals be' – doesn't fully develop into the wit and wisdom of Feste or of Lear's Fool, his perspective on the events of the play is similarly privileged.

Were the World Mine makes an important adjustment here. It gives Puck, as Timothy, a significant investment not only in the renewed social order but also in the resolution of the lovers' confusion. He leads Kingstonians up and down, with the help of Miss Tebbit, but he shares with her the function of Oberon in recognizing the need, the imperative, to return to the townspeople their wonted sight. Both are happy to incite the madness that occupies the film's middle third, because both recognize that the world is out of order already, but both also understand the obligation to resolve the confusion – Miss Tebbit because she is Oberon, an agent of a benevolent status quo that will be homo-tolerant but that is ultimately heteronormative; and Timothy, because he has internalized those heteronormative obligations and understands their imperatives.

One way to put this is to say that Timothy is gay but, like the film, not quite queer. It is a troublesome word for the film generally. When he first identifies himself as 'queer', Donna objects to the word. 'Why are you gay? What did I do?', she asks, in an early confrontation. Timothy responds by beginning to explain, 'you didn't make me queer', but she cuts him off: 'don't use that word to me'. Timothy finishes, 'nobody did; I'm just queer, okay? So deal with it', but Donna does not budge, insisting that she shares the problem and complaining that his homosexuality is as much a burden to her as it is to him. She slowly sheds this attitude. Her growing understanding is signalled when she volunteers the word 'queer' in a conversation with a client at a makeover:

Mrs. Boyd. I would love to have you stay for Bible study.
Donna. I have wings to make.
Mrs. Boyd. It's a potluck.
Donna. No, for my son; he's a fairy.
Mrs. Boyd. A fairy . . .
Donna. In a play!
Mrs. Boyd. Oh!
Donna. Well, in real life, too. He's gay. My son is gay. Or queer. But the wings are for the play.
Mrs. Boyd. 'A man shall not lie with a man' –
Donna. Do you want the damn eye cream or not?

Mrs Boyd embodies the intolerance Donna initially understands but is coming to reject. Faced with a decision either to support her son or to thrive in a much-needed position as a cosmetics salesperson, she ultimately sides with Timothy. But this is perhaps less a matter of Donna reconciling herself to the word 'queer' than of the film allowing the word 'queer' to be absorbed by the word 'gay'; the movement is not towards radical acceptance, but towards a normalization of queer sexualities so that queerness is merely gay. For every move the film makes to queer masculinity, it makes a corresponding move to take the edge off 'queer', creating a stable but sterile medial space in which homophobia is expelled from heteronormativity, but in which queer is co-opted by something more acceptable, more demotic, more ordinary.

The film works deliberately at points to maintain this space. There is for example a somewhat jarring attempt to clear Shakespeare's name from homosexuality, when Miss Tebbit responds to the comment 'Shakespeare was queer, too!' by noting, 'firstly, Mr. William Shakespeare has never been proved to be a homosexual'. The phrasing not only calls into question Miss Tebbit's all-important knowledge of the 'the Elizabethan stage', but its

attitude is weirdly incongruous with the film's larger project.[11] Instead of critiquing the value of the judgement – 'homosexuality is bad' – she challenges its provability, leaving the notion of a homosexual Shakespeare firmly in the negative. Her next rejoinder, 'bi-sexual, perhaps', doesn't quite undo the ideological oddity of the moment, which lingers as a kind of concession to some unnamed but powerful force.

Let's call that force *rugby*. In successfully rehabilitating masculinity's relationship with homosexuality, *Were the World Mine* manages a happy ending that is a challenge to read. On the one hand, Timothy wins acceptance from the rugby team, and a romantic partner in its captain and star player, Jonathon. As we now recognize, Jonathon has been gay the whole time, or has been waiting to discover that he is gay. 'Don't you feel . . . different?', Timothy asks, supposing that Jonathon's love for him has been a function only of the love potion and thus surprised by a dressing-room kiss. 'I feel like myself', Jonathon says. At this moment, Cooper, who has been Timothy's primary tormenter throughout the film, appears and enjoins the couple to attend the cast party: 'you two love birds better be at my party tonight; it's gonna be beyond, alright?' All would seem to be well.

On the other hand, rugby still rocks. In the sense that this new world is Timothy's, there is no incongruity here, since rugby, ground zero of the eroticized male body, is now gay-friendly. But in the sense that 'Shakesqueer' gives way to the force framed in the opening scene as Shakespeare's ignorant opposite, the *discipulus gloriosus*, there is a sense of loss and of missed opportunity. The final fantasy-dream sequence in which Timothy is persuaded to return the charmed mortals to their wonted sight darkens the marks of concession sketched elsewhere. All the film's songs are

---

[11] Miss Tebbit elsewhere advertises her understanding of Elizabethan theatre – 'women were prohibited by law to act on the Elizabethan stage; men filled the void' – but it does not occur to her here that the question 'was Shakespeare a homosexual?' is not historically valid.

reprised in an ensemble musical number. Tebbit, the rugby team, and several others plead with Timothy as the lines 'see as thou wast wont to see / Be as thou wast wont to be' reacquire their straight, which is to say Shakespearian, meaning. Timothy gives in, agreeing to the world as it was wont to be, rather than the world he wants to see. In moving us from Shakesqueer to a Shakespeare that has itself been emptied of danger, and emptied of poetic significance, *Were the World Mine* threatens at the end to take away the very magic that can make things queer. Having teased us with the allure of a world elsewhere, it returns us to a standard romantic comedy, swapping in the conventions of a very conventional story. 'Who's next?', Miss Tebbit taunts, as she aims one of Timothy's squirting prop buds at the camera, threatening to turn us all queer. But at this moment, under the cumulative weight of the film's concessions and substitutions, you can't help feeling she's holding the wrong flower.

LETTER FROM THE CHALK FACE: DIRECTING *A MIDSUMMER NIGHT'S DREAM* AT THE STAUNTON BLACKFRIARS

JACQUELYN BESSELL

The writings of theatre practitioners are letters from the chalk face rather than 'theories'. Practitioners practise first, and make their discoveries on the studio or rehearsal-room floor in much the same way as the scientist conducts experiments in a laboratory. However, these are not as readily codifiable as a scientific experiment, where a mathematical equation may offer a solution to the problem. In theatre, experiments constitute a constant search which will never reach a quantifiable conclusion. Experiments may, however, reach a qualitative conclusion: 'it works or it doesn't' is the maxim, where the measuring stick is an informed artistic sensibility.[1]

I find Dymphna Callery's confidence in the 'informed artistic sensibility' encouraging, because I am a theatre practitioner. I direct plays. In my parallel career as an academic working in the UK higher education sector, I have found that 'letters from the chalk face' such as Callery describes are included in a wider range of outputs and publications known collectively as 'practice-as-research'. My own practice-as-research methodology typically takes three forms: firstly, I search for practical solutions to perceived challenges presented by textual, material and logistical elements of plays in production; secondly, I follow my own curiosity and desire to create something genuinely new, in productions that speak directly to their audiences; thirdly, I attempt to record and contextualize some of the discoveries made in the rehearsal room, in print publications. This particular 'letter from the chalk face' shares my experience and reflections on practice, rather than labouring with theory, but this is not to suggest that the substance of what follows is purely anecdotal and reflective. Rather, this article considers a range of playable solutions to a set of perceived challenges posed by a Shakespearian text, in this case, *A Midsummer Night's Dream*. Further, the article suggests ways in which theatre practice can refresh (rather than reject) certain established literary-critical readings of the text, giving them renewed dramatic agency.

My work in the theatre supports Callery's view that '[t]he rejection of theory does not mean the rejection of training. Quite the reverse, in fact ... training is fundamental'[2] because my work as a director is methodologically linked to my ongoing activities as an acting coach. So what follows is an examination of the role played by specific strands of modern actor training techniques in an 'original practices' production of *A Midsummer Night's Dream* which played at the American Shakespeare Center's reconstructed Blackfriars Playhouse in Staunton, Virginia,[3] as part of a year-long national tour of the USA.

The role of modern actor training has been largely overlooked in the critical discussion of the 'original practices' approach to Shakespearian

---

[1] Dymphna Callery, *Through the Body: A Practical Guide to Physical Theatre* (London, 2007), p. 13.

[2] Callery, *Through the Body*, p. 14.

[3] I directed the production in 2006 for the American Shakespeare Center on Tour. The production opened and closed at the reconstructed Blackfriars Playhouse in Staunton, VA, and in between enjoyed a nine-month run, playing in venues across the USA. A recording of the production's première performance is held in the American Shakespeare Center's archives.

performance in today's reconstructed early modern theatres. On one level, this should hardly be surprising; the 'modern' aspect alone offends a historical sense of authenticity, and a modern understanding of actor training differs radically from the experience of the early modern acting apprentice as articulated by the best scholarship we have. John H. Astington identifies the historical gap between modern theatre practice and the experience of the early modern players. Astington locates 'original work on text and character simultaneously with attention to an ensemble style, overseen by one guiding intelligence, the kind of approach practised at the Royal Shakespeare Company, for example, from about 1960 onwards' as a practice invented in the nineteenth century by the Duke of Saxe-Meiningen.[4] Scholarship enjoys a close (if occasionally vexed) relationship with what might be called 'original practices-as-research' at the reconstructed Globe and Blackfriars, and when the subject of actor training surfaces in relation to the first ten years of performance at the Bankside Globe, Christie Carson emphasizes the primacy of theatre architecture in the complex of meaning-making at the Globe, suggesting that '[s]tandard acting training becomes inadequate, even detrimental, in this space'.[5] While such a statement reflects a popular and attractive appraisal of the Globe as a unique performance space, it does not necessarily reflect the experience of many of the actors involved.

Later in the same volume, the actor Paul Chahidi offers a different perspective. For him, the specific technical challenges of the Globe space offer opportunities to hone established techniques:

you have to flex all your acting muscles in a way you definitely would not have to in a conventional theatre. Because you do not have lighting to help you and tell the audience where to look, you just have some other actors, the costume and the music . . . It really forces you to work out your techniques, your voice production, the way you would use an audience.[6]

I would agree with Chahidi's assessment and go further, to suggest that this period of Globe

production was in fact underpinned by a range of widely disseminated actor training principles. In the capacity of Head of Research at the Globe from 1990–2002, it was my job to document the development of the productions and the performers, in the *Globe Research Bulletin* series.[7] Leaving aside a consideration of the collective training experiences of the acting companies themselves, it should be noted that the theatre's first artistic directorate instituted ongoing, season-long, on the job training for the actors, in the form of verse classes with Giles Block, movement classes with Glynn Macdonald, jig choreography with Sian Williams and voice classes with Stewart Pearce.[8] At the risk of over-simplifying the contributions of these individuals (who, like their actor-clients, draw on a very wide range of training and professional experience) it is fair to say that, at the very least, the actors' work at the Globe has been informed by the approach to verse speaking pioneered by Peter Hall, the movement training system of F. M. Alexander, the dance training and notation system developed by Rudolf Laban, and the voice work of Cicely Berry, since at least 1999.

But this does not alter the fact that modern actor training methodologies still fail to register in most serious discussions of the 'original practices' performances at the reconstructed theatres. This could be due to the connection between modern training regimes and modern rehearsal approaches; with respect to the latter, Don Weingust suggests that to adopt any systematic approach to group rehearsal

[4] John H. Astington, *Actors and Acting in Shakespeare's Time: The Art of Stage Playing* (Cambridge, 2010), p. 140.

[5] Christie Carson and Farah Karim-Cooper, eds., *Shakespeare's Globe: A Theatrical Experiment* (Cambridge, 2008), p. 8.

[6] Mark Rylance, Yolanda Vazquez and Paul Chahidi, 'Discoveries from the Globe Stage', in Carson and Karim-Cooper, eds., *Shakespeare's Globe*, pp. 204–5.

[7] The Globe Research Bulletin series can be found at www.globelink.org/research/researchbulletins/(accessed 12.10.11).

[8] Many other freelance voice and movement specialists (too numerous to name here) have contributed to the work of individual productions at the Globe, but the practitioners named here have provided a kind of methodological continuum over the past decade or so.

is to take an anachronistic step which compromises any engagement with early modern theatre practice. In Weingust's view, Patrick Tucker's Original Shakespeare Company (OSC) has developed a historically informed model of rehearsal which emphasizes private study over group rehearsal, and as such, this model has a distinct advantage over the Globe's more recognizably modern rehearsal methods.[9] In an argument that engages with W. B. Worthen's understanding of performativity[10] Weingust argues that the OSC's approach,

> while involving a most detailed attention to their written texts, eliminates many of the other elements of production input that stabilize the performance texts of most contemporary western theatres. Without a codifying rehearsal regimen, OSC work is more greatly variable in performance, the audience a much larger factor in the schema, having more immediate bearing on the production of the OSC performance text.[11]

Weingust seems to be suggesting that an actor working within conventional rehearsal structures is less able to bring variety to subsequent iterations of his/her performance, because structured group rehearsals necessarily undermine the role of the live audience in the process of making meaning. Director Mike Alfreds recognizes that audiences 'have a will of their own . . . and the energy of their collective concentration has a huge influence on the nature of a performance',[12] but he argues that the best way for the actor to engage with the audience is through extensive preparation in group rehearsals:

> I believe, in fact I *know* from my own practice, that a production can be developed through rehearsals in such rich depth that the WORLD OF THE PLAY becomes profoundly absorbed into the actors' psyches. They feel so familiar with this world, its space, its conventions and the relationships within it, that it gives them the security to play openly and freely every night. The external structure of fixed patterns and deliveries is replaced by strong inner structures. Each performance should be a *disciplined* improvisation in which the '*what*' (text and, to a certain degree, ACTIONS and OBJECTIVES) remains unchanged, but the '*how*' (the execution of these) can vary . . . The performance is open to the possibility of

increased fluidity, sudden revelation, greater intensity, *creative joy*.[13]

The emphatic strength of Alfreds's convictions may be inferred from his typographical choices in the quote above. His vocabulary reflects the influence of Stanislavski (amongst others) in his own work, and his practice – developed in the 1970s through his company Shared Experience and later disseminated through his activities as a freelance director at the RSC, the National and the Globe – has influenced the work of many directors, including my own. Budgetary constraints as well as the 'original practices' brief adopted by the American Shakespeare Center (ASC) at the Blackfriars effectively vetoed the ten weeks of rehearsal implied in Alfreds's preferred model, but I was able to adapt my own model to a three-week period of structured group rehearsals, to give the actors the best chance to explore a range of playable choices. This seemed to me to be the best way to equip the actors with the necessary confidence to choose the most appropriate action, spontaneously and appropriately, in the moment of performance itself. It has been my experience – and, I would venture, that of many actors – that the more thorough the preparation, the better able the performer is to act with real 'immediacy' and the kind of spontaneity that Weingust attributes to the OSC's productions. The key function shared by most modern rehearsal structures and most actor training methodologies is to equip the actor with that essential confidence, the confidence to play.

The ASC's reconstructed Blackfriars Playhouse is in many respects an entirely different animal

---

[9] For a comprehensive account of the Original Shakespeare Company's approach to performance, see Patrick Tucker, *Secrets of Acting Shakespeare* (London, 2002).

[10] See W. B. Worthen, *Shakespeare and the Authority of Performance* (Cambridge, 1997).

[11] Don Weingust, *Acting from Shakespeare's First Folio: Theory, Text and Performance* (London, 2006), p. 121.

[12] Mike Alfreds, *Different Every Night: Freeing the Actor* (London, 2007), p. 23.

[13] Alfreds, *Different Every Night*, p. 25.

to the reconstructed Globe, and the ASC's own experiments with 'original stage practices' occupy a central position within the company's mission; this is arguably no longer the case at the Bankside Globe. The ASC is prescriptive about its 'house style' of performance, and engages directly with current scholarship on early modern theatre practice, going so far as to write elements of this into its contractual agreements with actors. As I have discussed elsewhere,[14] the ASC's 'Actors' Renaissance Season' represents the company's most rigorous experiment to date with the kind of rehearsal practices set out by Tiffany Stern,[15] and for these productions the very brief period of group rehearsal allows little time for ensemble work to address more than basic staging.

As a guest director for both the touring and resident troupes at the ASC, I have directed at the Blackfriars on several occasions in recent years.[16] My work there and elsewhere is decidedly low-tech, prioritizing actors' contributions to narrative and characterization over designers' contributions to metaphor and concept. So, in most important respects my approach is highly compatible with the ASC house style, which, in espousing its own definition of 'original practices', eschews sets, lighting and other mod cons. But important differences between the 'house' approach and my own remain, with regard to the role of actor training methodologies. Though the ASC's house style certainly embraces current scholarship on early modern performance practice, it contains no formal recognition of current actor training techniques.

Outside of professional directing work, I have spent much of the last fifteen years coaching actors in training. This has obviously shaped my directing style, determined how I speak to actors, and influenced the way I look at performance more generally. I don't so much direct as facilitate, and I do a lot of coaching in rehearsals. It has been my experience that prioritizing the actors' performances, their ownership of their words, and their relationships with their audiences is an engrossing and satisfying way to work, regardless of the venue or performance context. It is an ergonomic way

to work, as it makes use of the training structures common to so many different institutions, and as I will explain, it sometimes obviates the need for elaborate directorial 'concepts'.

METHODOLOGIES, NOT CONCEPTS

One of the truisms modern directors of *A Midsummer Night's Dream* face sooner rather than later is that the play demands three carefully delineated 'worlds'. More often than not, this demand is met with recourse to modern theatre technology, and big concepts. The 2011 RSC production[17] employed kaleidoscopic lighting gobos to signal when magical forces are at work, with a leather sofa transforming into a kind of vertical shuttle between the mortal and fairy worlds. The RST's fly system was put to further use as chairs painted in primary colours were flown in to various heights, to suggest a forest of the imagination.

But another truism directors of plays by Shakespeare may encounter is that conceptualizing any production can be an exercise in diminishing returns. According to this view, sooner or later, a line, a character or even great swathes of text will emerge which need to be cut because it/they will not fit the chosen conceptual framework. 'Our gods must not be concepts but the words that are in the text',[18] warns Barton and, while I am never shy

---

14 See 'The Actors' Renaissance Season at the Blackfriars Playhouse', in *Performing Early Modern Drama Today*, ed. Pascale Aebischer and Kathryn Prince (Cambridge, forthcoming).

15 The ASC contract includes quotations from Tiffany Stern, *Making Shakespeare: From Stage to Page* (London, 2004).

16 I directed the touring productions of *Much Ado About Nothing* (2005–06) and *A Midsummer Night's Dream* (2006–07), as well as *Love's Labour's Lost* (2007) for the resident company. As a member of the teaching faculty in ASC's partnership MLitt/MFA programme with Mary Baldwin College, I also directed three MFA showcase productions, *Twelfth Night* (2006), *Hamlet* (2007) and *King Lear* (2008).

17 The production was directed by Nancy Meckler, designed by Katrina Lindsay, with lighting by Wolfgang Göbbel.

18 John Barton, *Playing Shakespeare* (London, 1984), p. 23.

about cutting Shakespeare's scripts,[19] the notion of a 'concept' imposed by a director remains a vexed one for me. However, I have found that training methodologies import a structure into the work in rehearsal very much as concepts can, without imposing the kind of creative restrictions which concepts often bring with them.

To put it another way, staging concepts most typically manifest themselves in concrete visual or aesthetic *forms*, whereas methodologies are typically manifested as playable *activities*. If a company of actors are all engaged in the same activity, each can find his/her own expression of that activity, rather than having to repeat a form, with varying degrees of success. I have found that methodological structures, manifested as activities, provide a happy and fruitful 'freedom within structure' for the actor. Back in 1984 Barton reminded his actors that 'although it's up to us to analyse the verse as well as we can, in the end we must treat it intuitively. We must trust it and let it be organic rather than conscious',[20] and it is this kind of thinking which still informs the frequent comparisons between accomplished jazz musicians and good Shakespearian actors. In fact, I would argue that 'freedom within structure' is now as distinctly a Shakespearian 'concept' as any current working definition of 'original stage practices'. So, actor training methodologies have a lot to offer Shakespeare's plays in rehearsal, especially for those productions which embrace aspects of 'original practices' research, precisely because they provide structures designed to support, amplify and make legible a range of individual actors' creative impulses.

Using the experience of directing this play for the ASC's touring company, I will demonstrate how actor training techniques help actors to delineate and reveal character, create a sense of place and establish helpfully different modes of storytelling. In performance conditions which do not include or embrace 'high production values', actor training techniques can help a director side-step some of the potential pitfalls associated with that conceptual hurdle, the 'three worlds' of *A Midsummer Night's Dream*.

DIRECTING *A MIDSUMMER NIGHT'S DREAM* FOR THE ASC TOURING TROUPE

The vocabulary of my rehearsal room was drawn from widely disseminated actor training techniques common to a large number of American conservatories, but specifically that developed by Rudolf Laban (1879–1958). Laban's approach to theatremaking is not exactly avant-garde these days, but in its somatic foundation it differs considerably from the psychologically motivated, post-Stanislavski school of occidental realism. Laban's theories on movement are extensive, and have found many different applications in dance, theatre and physical education pedagogy, but my own use of Laban technique is limited to what he calls the eight effort actions.[21]

As I have argued elsewhere,[22] the application of Laban's eight effort actions to Shakespearian text not only emphasizes the inherent rhythmic possibilities contained in the text, it also emphasizes the extent to which the way words sound and feel determines their meaning in the theatre. As such, I found it a useful comprehensive approach to use for *Dream*. Laban's effort actions became the *lingua franca* of our rehearsal room.

To choose the appropriate Laban effort action for a particular segment of text, one must first consider whether the effort may be described as direct or indirect. To illustrate the difference between the two, it might be useful to imagine the efforts of a tennis player as direct, and the efforts of the ball s/he hits as indirect. Next, the performer must

---

[19] My recent work includes a 90-minute version of *Antony and Cleopatra* for two actors and a musician, which opened at the 2010 International Shakespeare Conference.

[20] Barton, *Playing Shakespeare*, p. 46.

[21] For more information on Laban's methodology, see Rudolf Laban, *The Mastery of Movement*, 4th edition revised and enlarged by Lisa Ullmann (Plymouth, MA, 1998). For more on the eight effort actions, see Rudolf Laban and F. C. Lawrence, *Effort* (Plymouth, MA, 1974).

[22] See 'The Early Modern Physical Theatre', in *Speaking Pictures: the Visual/Verbal Nexus of Dramatic Performance*, ed. V. M. Vaughan, F. Cioni and J. Bessell (Cranbury, 2010), pp. 181–201.

decide whether the effort is strong (as if moving against resistance) or weak (moving against no resistance). This might be described as the difference between walking through treacle and walking through air. Finally, the performer must choose between a sudden effort and a sustained effort, for example the difference between knocking on a door (sudden) and trying to push a door open (sustained). When these three pairs of components are combined, eight archetypal effort actions emerge:

Direct + Strong + Sudden = Punching	Indirect + Strong + Sudden = Slashing
Direct + Weak + Sudden = Dabbing	Indirect + Weak + Sudden = Flicking
Direct + Strong + Sustained = Pressing	Indirect + Strong + Sustained = Wringing
Direct + Weak + Sustained = Gliding	Indirect + Weak + Sustained = Floating

Laban's effort actions are effective tools for performers wishing to expand their vocal and somatic palette. Laban's labels come from observation of course, and readers might usefully reflect for a moment on their own habitual patterns (some of us are by nature punchers; others, left to our own devices, are floaters, and so on) before considering the extent to which the Laban efforts can assist performers seeking to break with their own habitual patterns of vocal or physical behaviour. By limiting the variables to three pairs of components and therefore eight archetypal patterns, Laban provides performers with that most valuable commodity: freedom within structure. The effort actions are not repeatable forms but repeatable qualities of movement, with endless possibilities for individual variation and adjustment. The efforts might in fact be best described as activities in which all performers can engage, without fear of replicating or contradicting anyone else's engagement with the same activity.

Another advantage in using this technique is that it allows for the same notation system to be used for vocal work. So, the somatic and vocal aspects of Laban's approach offered us transformative possibilities in physical and vocal aspects of characterization that would prove invaluable in creating the 'other worldliness' of Titania, Oberon and the fairies.

In other words, the efforts defined how the fairies moved, but also how they spoke. Choral movement for Titania's 'train' of fairies could be generated by the actors in less time than it would take to learn formal choreography by rote, simply by asking all of the fairies to adopt the same effort action for a given period of time. This movement provided a physical underscore for the entrance and exit of Titania and her train in 2.1. The movement was itself enhanced by the sound of the fairy train breathing together, again using the effort actions. Usually, performers adopted the same effort for breath as for movement, but occasionally it seemed theatrically interesting, for instance, to have Titania's train advance as one on Oberon, using a sustained pressing effort, while breathing audibly with a lighter, sudden, dabbing effort.

Laban efforts also help performers find something playable in passages of well-beloved poetry (which can all too often feel more like poisoned chalices than gifts to the actor). I have included the effort action annotation for the speech below, illustrating choices played by Henry Bazemore as Oberon. At this point, readers may wish to withdraw to a place where they may not be overheard, and try this orchestration out for themselves:

[FLOAT] I know a bank where the wild thyme blows,
Where oxlips and the nodding violet grows,
Quite overcanopied with luscious woodbine,
With sweet musk-roses, and with eglantine.
[GLIDE] There sleeps [DAB] Titania sometime of
   the night,
[GLIDE] Lulled in these flowers with dances
   and delight;
[DAB] And there the snake throws her enamelled skin,
[FLOAT] Weed wide enough to wrap a fairy in;
[WRING] And with the juice of this I'll streak
   her eyes,

And make her full of hateful fantasies.
[DAB] Take thou some of it, and seek through this
  grove.
[GLIDE] A sweet Athenian lady is in love
[PUNCH] With a disdainful youth. [DAB] Anoint his
  eyes;
But do it when the next thing he espies
May be the lady.   (2.1.249–63)

To help establish the language of Laban from day one of rehearsals, I replaced the typical first read-through of the play with a 45-minute workshop, guiding the actors through each of the key methodological strands that would underpin the rehearsal period – specifically, approaches to verbal and somatic storytelling. Taken as a whole, the range of exercises worked through in this 45-minute primer provided an extremely time-efficient means of establishing a common technical vocabulary within the group. The company moved forward into all subsequent rehearsals with a shared set of technical references, which in turn expedited the process of giving directorial notes towards the end of the rehearsal period. Small or radical adjustments to what the audience will ultimately read as the playing style could be prompted using the same specific technical vocabulary in notes to the actor.

As Laban effort actions are rooted in somatic impulses, using them as a foundation can make other kinds of somatic approaches to characterization easier to develop in subsequent rehearsals. The most physically expansive element of the actors' work for *Dream* was in the area of animal work.

ANIMAL WORK

This describes an approach to physical characterization which is hard to document, but exceedingly easy to pastiche. Nigel Planer's monstrous creation and *nom-de-plume* Nicholas Craig does this better than most, in the thinly-veiled parody of Simon Callow's autobiography, *Being An Actor*. In a section ostensibly addressed 'To the Young Actor',

Craig gives advice on 'Choosing a Drama School' which bears repeating:

Do not be seduced by glossy prospectuses. You only need to know two basic facts: how many prizes and medals are handed out at the end of the final year . . . and how often are the study trips to the zoo (imitating animal behaviour is of course the most important skill for a young actor to acquire) . . . While the alumni of the Birmingham School of Speech Training and Dramatic Arts loyally defend the virtues of the aviary in the botanical gardens at Edgbaston, a better all-round bet is the Bristol Old Vic Theatre School – a goodly clutch of awards, and practically next door to Johnny Morris's old stamping ground [Bristol Zoo].[23]

If the reader is moved to hollow laughter at this point, perhaps they, or someone they know, attended one of the posher *conservatoires* in the 1980s. Animal work is a recognized (if freely adapted) approach to physical characterization, and it is true that many generations of budding thespians have been sent down to Regent's Park Zoo to observe the minutiae of a specific animal's movement and physical habits. Since the nearest zoo in Virginia was over two hours' drive away, actors in the *Dream* company had to use their imagination (and, I should add, numerous clips on YouTube) when choosing an animal as the basis for somatic characterization.

One advantage of incorporating animal work into rehearsal is that it generates large amounts of physical material very quickly. Refining this work to create more 'authentic' movement takes time, however, and the *Dream* company's rather ad hoc research methodology – observing animals in a virtual or notional way – presents its own distinct challenges to any notion of authenticity, making this work hard to evaluate in a systematic way. Laban effort actions share a somatic emphasis with animal work, and this suggested to me that Laban's notation system could potentially be

---

23 Nicholas Craig (with Christopher Douglas and Nigel Planer), *I, An Actor*, 2nd edn (London, 2001), pp. 132–4.

adapted to annotate the animal work brought in by the actors. To effect this, the actors were asked at an early stage of animal work to translate the essence of what they had discovered into one or more Laban effort actions. This meant that an actor who had chosen a smallish bird chose 'flicking' as the somatic default for this character, while another found 'pressing' best encapsulated the movements of a panther. Choosing a default mode of movement is very useful precisely because this allows for variation, and using the established Laban vocabulary allowed me to communicate effectively and actively with the actors, to find a range of minor and major variations on their default mode. Put simply, the Laban spectrum opposite of 'flicking' is 'pressing', and this is somehow a more credible proposition than suggesting the bird-character finds variety by adopting panther-esque movement every now and then.

SHAPE-SHIFTING ANIMAL WORK: OBERON

At the risk of contradicting the last sentence, I should add that Oberon's superior magical powers can be suggested through an imaginative actor's audacious facility with animal work, too. Henry Bazemore and I decided that to assign a different animal physicality and movement to each of Oberon's entrances in the plot against Titania might be a good way to ensure that the audience didn't get ahead of the physical storytelling, as well as making his line 'But who comes here? I am invisible' (2.1.186) a little easier to swallow. With a long black tunic that could suggest wings very easily, Oberon 'flew' in as a hawk, carrying the 'love in idleness' flower in his 'beak'. Anointing the sleeping Titania's eyes with the same affected a physical transformation into a larger predator, in this instance, a puma. Later on, as an altogether more jovial Oberon, Henry elected to listen to Puck's news of Titania's tryst with Bottom (3.2.6–34) with the screeching glee of an overexcited orang-utan, bouncing up and down as he did so.

In common with such 'big' choices in the area of animal work, Laban's effort actions are arguably most legible and/or audible to the audience when externalized and amplified by the actor, using their voices and bodies to explore the effort to its fullest extent. This tends to result in a physically expansive gestural language and playing style, but, like most genuinely useful systems, Laban's effort actions are flexible and fully adjustable to taste and style. An effort action can be fully physically realized, or cloaked, or internalized, to a point where the effort is only discernible by the audience in a subtle way. Internalizing an effort action, giving it a less expansive gestural scope, creates the impressions of an altogether different performance style. The cliché of the swan that masks its strenuous underwater paddling by appearing to glide on the water's surface is perhaps a useful model when considering the relationship between internal efforts and those which are externalized. The cloaking of physically expansive gestural language corresponds nicely to the process of making physical characteristics more 'natural' or, in the broadest sense, more 'human'. This cloaking process also suggests to the performer that naturalism is not an absence of style but a carefully orchestrated appearance of the natural.

In a nutshell, for this production, characters from Athens internalized their effort actions, while the fairies externalized their effort actions and chose to give physical actions their fullest scope. So, the approach to characterization for the mortal characters retained the same Laban vocabulary underpinning work on the fairy characters, while a distinctly more naturalistic, 'human' form was achieved by first decreasing the scope of the efforts or impulses being explored by the actors.

CHARACTERIZING THE MECHANICALS: SEND IN THE CLOWNS

To delineate the creative endeavours of the community theatre enthusiasts in Peter Quince's company from the behaviour of their social betters in the court of Theseus, the next step was to add in some of the gestural language of clown work, another readily legible, somatic approach to storytelling.[24] Taken as a whole, the mechanicals' narrative lends itself to self-consciously theatrical playing styles, even pastiche (there's a long and glorious tradition of laughing at the am-dram characters in this play) but, without a reasonably robust methodological framework, I feared that too much pressure might be felt by individual actors to invent gags, some of which might not support the overall narrative the company had agreed upon. So, I asked the company to consider these few 'ground rules' that have their roots in basic clowning principles.

Clown Rule 1: Everything is a Proposition

First, in devising the performance style for the *Pyramus and Thisbe* show, all of the company involved in these scenes recognized the importance of accepting propositions and investigating them fully, rather than jettisoning new ideas without trying them out. This very basic rule – what Keith Johnstone calls accepting (not blocking) an offer[25] – is the foundation of all forms of improvisation. The explicitly democratic nature of this way of working was compromised, of course, by the pressure of time. Our expedited rehearsal period could not reasonably accommodate unlimited exploration of every proposition from each performer, and so a pragmatic 'if it ain't broke . . .' attitude among the cast played a key role in deciding which propositions were ultimately adopted as performance choices and which jettisoned. I would add that one huge benefit of 'Clown Rule 1' is that it avoids the potentially limiting imposition of a single performance style or concept, by effectively sidestepping the notion of a single authoritative presence in the rehearsal room.

Clown Rule 2: When you're on, you're on . . .

It has been my experience that actors performing at the Bankside Globe and the Staunton Blackfriars very quickly become aware that 'when you're on, you're *on*'. The bare stage and universal lighting conditions combine to create a particularly exposed performance environment for the actor. This can be no bad thing, as long as the performer exploits it successfully, and it starts with their entrance. The entrance is always part of the performance at the Globe and Blackfriars, never a mere transition into it.

Given that the flanking doors provide the location for most of the entrances and exits in any production, good clowns will give serious attention to these features of the Blackfriars' architecture. Obeying the conventions of popular farce also helped to delineate the mechanicals' own playing style. Actors were encouraged from the start to ensure that none of their entrances or exits were 'neutral'; in practice, this meant experimenting with extremes in tempo and duration of entrances and exits, as well as the comic potential contained in revelation or concealment of space or action, effected by doors which swing open or shut unexpectedly. Doors, we found, are a clown's best friend. Leaving both doors open allowed for a high-speed, figure-of-eight chase sequence between Puck, the mechanicals and the donkey-headed Bottom that borrowed equally from the comic stylings of Benny Hill and *Scooby Doo*.

Clown Rule 3: Everything is Potentially Animate

Investing significance in certain props by animating them can pay theatrical dividends in the immediate and longer term. Put more simply, carefully setting up Bottom's choice of headgear for the rehearsal scenes in the forest – a helmet in Roman gladiator style in our case – will add a kind of comic poignancy to a later moment when Flute pays

---

[24] Clowning is a very general term, and can refer to a wide range of performance traditions. Readers with an interest in the methodological roots of companies such as Theatre de Complicite and Théâtre de la Jeune Lune will enjoy Jacques Lecoq, *Theatre of Movement and Gesture*, ed. David Bradbury (London, 2006). A good general overview of clowns at work today can be found in Louise Peacock, *Serious Play: Modern Clown Performance* (Bristol, 2009).

[25] Keith Johnstone, *Impro: Improvisation and the Theatre* (London, 1981), p. 97.

tribute to his missing colleague, holding the same prop very much as though it were Yorick's skull. The difference between the helmet as prop and any old hat as a piece of costume is that the helmet is treated as potentially animate, and invested with significance accordingly.

There are many textual precedences for such investment in objects in Shakespeare's plays. The most obvious instance from *A Midsummer Night's Dream* surrounds the flower, love-in-idleness. The allusions in the speech in which Oberon tells the tale of Cupid's botched archery (2.1.155–74) may require glossing for some, but its chief *function* – to invest enormous significance in a small prop which is shortly to appear – is transparent to all.

Clown Rule 4: Everything is exaggerated

Dymphna Callery identifies traits common to all physical theatre styles as the 'paradigm of progressing from impulse to movement to action to gesture to sound to word'[26] which nicely traces the development of the mechanicals' devised approach to the *Pyramus and Thisbe* play within the play very succinctly. Laban effort actions can be exaggerated, as well as internalized. In creating the performance style for the *Pyramus and Thisbe* show, the mechanicals' amateur company used Laban efforts *in extremis*, to appropriately comic effect. Aaron Hochhalter's performance as Wall was characterized by 'pressing' throughout, in both somatic and vocal choices. This relentlessly strong, direct and sustained effort most literally encapsulated his role. For Wall's main speech (5.1.154–63) Hochhalter developed a technique of breathing which allowed him to give the impression of speaking all of his lines in one breath, at a regular pace, with no spaces between words. Hochhalter used pitch modulation to provide increasing levels of suspense (comically inappropriate for the purely expositional quality of the lines Wall actually speaks) by using a single monotone pitch for each weighty, sustained line, before raising the next verse line by a perfect half tone. The overall effect was almost too much to bear, for audience and performer alike.

PHYSICAL COMEDY AND STAGE COMBAT (LOVERS IN THE FOREST)

Of course, all somatic approaches to performance require actors who are physically fit, flexible and on occasion quite brave. As well as the transformations achieved by changes in Laban efforts, the lovers in particular had to undertake a lot of unreconstructed slapstick and knockabout comedy. We spent most of these actors' physical comedy capital in 3.2, the scene in which all four appear and a four-way squabble ensues. There is very little in the script which absolutely demands a full-on brawl between the four lovers, but the lengthy speeches contained therein present directors and actors with questions. Chief among these questions is, what, exactly, *are* the men doing during Helena's lengthy speech to Hermia on the theme of female friendship and double cherries (3.2.193–220)? While the Globe stage is sufficiently large for proxemics to do some of the work (and, despite their many detractors, those pillars arguably earn their keep as 'trees') the Blackfriars stage is tiny in comparison, and so this scene, unlike all the others, required at least some 'blocking', a term and a practice I dislike and usually avoid. Realistic fight choreography was very effectively employed for this scene, which provided a useful contrast to the 'magical' strength and prowess of fairy monarchs who could move entire gangs of mortals with the concentrated wave of a hand. We agreed as a company that the physical transactions between the mortal lovers could be very brutal, very literal, profoundly unimaginative. The anti-heroic altercations between Lysander and Demetrius owed a stylistic debt to Peter Brayham's hugely popular fight choreography for *Bridget Jones' Diary* (2001), and the set pieces needed to be orchestrated carefully, to time out perfectly and to avoid drawing all focus away from what was being said about double cherries and female friendship in another part of the forest, a few feet away.

---

[26] Callery, *Through the Body*, p. 8.

SUBTEXT AND INTERNALIZED EFFORTS IN THESEUS'S COURT

Audiences do not typically come away from performances of *A Midsummer Night's Dream* raving about the scenes which take place in Theseus's court. Traditionally there is little joy in the Athens of 1.1, owing to the famous tradition of doubling Theseus/Oberon and Hippolyta/Titania. Once this casting decision has been taken, the opening scene necessarily settles itself in the gloomier end of its possible subtexts, often at the expense of the text itself.

My production contributed to this tradition, by characterizing Hippolyta as a less-than-thrilled wife-to-be, even though the text of her initial response to Theseus does not indicate any explicit unhappiness on her part. To communicate this unease is thus to engage with subtext and action, rather than rhetoric and narrative. Initially, I suspected these difficult scenes might be best played with a strong emphasis on clearly delineated objectives, clear choices of tactics, and an overriding concern to clarify relationships between the characters. Had we been allocated a further two weeks of rehearsal I would have encouraged the actors to tackle the Athens scenes using Stanislavski's system, thus rooting the scenes in an altogether different theatre tradition to the scenes in which the fairies take control. But as we had insufficient time to integrate Stanislavski's system formally into the rehearsal process,[27] Laban's effort actions once again proved an effective and highly adaptable methodology. Further adjustments to the scope of physical and vocal gestures meant that the same eight efforts could be deployed on a scale that audiences would read as psychological realism. The 'score' for Hippolyta's speech is provided below:

[PUNCH, internalised] Four days will quickly steep
  themselves in night,
[PRESS, internalised] Four nights will quickly dream
  away the time;
[GLIDE, internalised] And then the moon, like to a
  silver bow

New bent in heaven, shall behold the night
Of our solemnities.   (1.1.7–11)

Internalizing the efforts does not require any less physical engagement on the part of the performer, but the effect produced remains very much in the realm of realism. In this case, Lillian Wright's 'punchy' opening gambit almost interrupted Henry Bazemore's impatient observations about the passing of time. Having secured his attention, the sustained (but subtextual) weight of the 'pressed' second line ensured that Theseus could not mistake Hippolyta for a pushover. By choosing to lead the rest of this short speech with an internalized 'gliding' effort, Lillian created an effect that suggested a dignified but disengaged Hippolyta, one who suddenly and tragically realized that her fate was inevitable.

SO, WHAT DID WE DISCOVER?

We discovered that the 'three worlds' of the play could be delineated by the somatic characterization of the actors. The fairies enjoyed a full range of vocal and physical scope, and their externalized efforts, coupled with animal work, produced a style of performance which richly suggested alien supernatural forces were at work. The mechanicals' style of clowning was achieved by cloaking the effort actions a little, and blending this with some tried and tested principles of clowning. Titania and Oberon's mortal counterparts sublimated their effort actions to produce the appearance of almost cinematic naturalism, without the complications of a Stanislavskian back story. The common Laban methodology provided the performers with many opportunities to suggest links between their variously doubled roles, and made transitions between different characters and scenes simple and

---

[27] Another good reason not to switch the methodological focus of the rehearsal process (towards a formal consideration of Stanislavski's system) is that the overwhelming majority of actors trained in conservatoires on both sides of the Atlantic are exposed to some elements of Stanislavski's system as part of their basic training.

technical, and 'mood proof'. We discovered that using three variations on a single methodological theme can refresh and make playable the literary-critical notion of the 'three worlds' of *A Midsummer Night's Dream*, without recourse to elaborate or costly theatre technology, in keeping with the spirit of 'original practices as research'. The play's narrative depends as much upon difference as it does upon connections between roles, and adjustments to the same basic Laban frameworks effectively resulted in qualitatively different, but methodologically linked, playing styles. In purely practical terms, a shared technical vocabulary helped to produce an identifiable and *consistent* performance style for each 'world', without the need for lengthier rehearsal periods.

Ultimately, this production suggested the extent to which 'character' and 'performance style' are phenomena located in the eyes and ears of the audience, as well as the extent to which apparently radical shifts in performance style can be effected using relatively small adjustments to a single methodological approach. It is often the director's job to judge the effects of the actors' work on the likely perceptions of the audience, and it has been my experience that this job is made easier using an adaptable methodology, one rooted in actions that are easily executed, which uses simple language as the prompt for a range of beautifully complex variations which can be orchestrated 'in the moment'. The common Laban vocabulary promotes an ensemble sense of ownership of the work, as well as a common structure based in activities, not repeatable forms. Activities are flexible, and may, as we found, be amplified, scaled down, internalized, externalized, endlessly modified and engaged with in a purely personal way, thus creating the impression of distinct playing styles for each 'world'.

Placing value in the notion of an ensemble 'ownership' of the methodological means of production locates my approach firmly in the camp of moderns, of course, and marks a radical departure from most published strands of 'original practices' methodology, which historically and necessarily de-emphasizes the role of group work.

Weingust again engages with Worthen in this context, and identifies recognized theatre practices as inadequate:

While in traditionally prepared Shakespearean theatre today each company's *production* of a play may be said to destabilise the text, in actuality the individual *performances* of that production tend to vary – and hence further destabilise the text – only little. Productions tend to replace the stability of a printed text with the stability of an aural and physically embodied text... Particularly in long commercial runs, or by touring companies such as the RSC, once a production has been up and running, further destabilising of the written text, or any significant destabilising of the performance text, is generally quite minimal indeed.[28]

But I would argue that our shared performance vocabulary was not an attempt to impose a kind of false stability and authority in the performance text, but rather to provide a formal space in the rehearsal for a contract to emerge between all members of the company, that defined the parameters of the narrative they would undertake to tell, over the course of the tour. Using a common but adaptable methodology provided the freedom to play, as well as the structure to play well, together.

The myriad ways in which this touring production developed whilst on the road – too numerous, and perhaps too indulgent, to mention here – challenges any general assumption that a rehearsed production equates to a 'sealed' production. A more mature production returned to the Blackfriars in the spring, after almost eight months on the road, having apparently seized every opportunity to mature and refine itself in the area of audience engagement. This, perhaps, is the area most discussed in current scholarship on reconstructed early modern theatres and the companies who work in them, and it is also an area where a whole company's experience will trump any individual director's theory. For both of these reasons, I did not use rehearsal time to impose any hard and fast policy on 'audience engagement' methods and

---

[28] Weingust, *Acting from Shakespeare's First Folio*, p. 122.

strategies, electing to let the company develop and refine these on the road.

Finally, and most importantly, the common technical vocabulary provided the performers – some of them young and inexperienced – with no small degree of confidence. Weingust's argument for a production that honestly responds to its audience is in many respects a strong one,[29] but I would suggest that the production discussed here provides one model to achieve this, using, not jettisoning, modern actor training methodologies. I remain convinced that for all but the most

self-confident actor (itself a mostly oxymoronic concept, in my view) it is better to face an audience of strangers – and easier to play spontaneously and honestly with that audience – feeling that one is well prepared to do so.

---

[29] The ASC's 'Actors' Renaissance Season' provides perhaps the best case study of this branch of original practices scholarship – that is, the theories of Stern and Tucker – in practice. As well as the chapter mentioned above, readers may wish to learn more about the Actors' Renaissance Season, from the ASC website: www.americanshakespearecenter.com.

A *DREAM* OF CAMPUS

ANDREW JAMES HARTLEY

One of Shakespeare criticism's singular blind spots concerns theatrical productions staged on university campuses. Apart from the occasional review in *Shakespeare Bulletin*, for instance, most campus shows go unnoticed by the larger scholarly community, unanalysed, unarchived, unobserved, consigned to obscurity with all their imperfections on their heads. Those imperfections are, of course, part of the reason for the omission. Those of us who attend college productions do not go expecting to be dazzled by the standard of acting or awoken to new ideas and resonances in the play, as we might be in the professional theatre. Yet while it is a practical necessity that most theatrical overviews of a play's production history stray but rarely from the RSCs, the Nationals and their ilk, it is worth remembering that in these days where we look to performance criticism for more than insight into the play as text, a wealth of theatrical endeavour which could provide insight into questions of Shakespearian meaning in larger cultural terms is being ignored. More particularly, the campus shows we consign to oblivion are – regardless of their merits – often instrumental in defining the very nature of theatrical Shakespeare (and thus of Shakespeare more generally) in the popular consciousness.

The case I want to make has few claims to large-scale argument. Quite the contrary, in fact. As Michael Dobson's work attests, the impact of amateur performance (of which, I will argue, university production is a very specific subset) is not assessed in global, national or even regional terms, and tracking its shifts and developments is rarely the mapping of coherent or extensive trends. Amateur performance tends to remain a strictly local phenomenon with productions in different places affecting each other in only the most indirect of ways. Assessment of such productions must thus take the worm's eye view, and that is what I would like to do here, remaining deliberately at the level of specifics and the immediate shaping pressures of the local as seen from inside the production.

I begin by exploring the curious and telling ways in which campus production tends to straddle the categories of professional and amateur theatre. I will argue that the particular model of college or university production which I am describing – one driven by faculty as part of a theatre department's season but performed almost exclusively by students – is unique in form, methodology and the way it shapes its audience.

With these generalities established I will engage with the specifics of a single production of *A Midsummer Night's Dream* which I directed in the spring of 2011 on the University of North Carolina's Charlotte campus. I aim to offer neither a pure review of the show nor an equally pure scholarly analysis of the play, though my method must partake of both in some measure. What I want to offer is an account of how a particular production came to be, the things which shaped it, its goals and strategies, and something of its effect, all told by someone implicated in the whole not simply as the director but as a member of a particular community defined by the production's campus context. I will focus, therefore, on the way this show generated meaning as, through and for

UNC Charlotte. What I am sketching here, then – and perhaps abler pens than mine will map college productions elsewhere – is a particular cultural moment focused by the production as the nexus of various impulses rooted in the institutions of education and the Shakespeare industry, but also in popular youth culture and the specifics of college experience. Such productions may not rank with the best the world has to offer in matters of insight or execution, but they cannot be consigned simply to amateur diversion or pedagogical exploration, forming as they do a crucial and potent element in the popular definition of what Shakespeare in the twenty-first century is, how it is made, and what it is worth.

I. THE CAMPUS PRODUCTION

Michael Dobson's excellent recent study of amateur performance uses that loaded adjective's emphasis on doing something for the love of it, as opposed to the professional theatre which tends to be tied to both commerce and a monolithic, state-sponsored notion of Shakespeare. School productions and those staged in prisons are, Dobson says, 'of their very nature much less voluntary than other forms of non-commercial performance and as such they can readily be assimilated to the established history of Shakespeare's co-option by the State'.[1] I suspect that the schools he is thinking of here tend to be of the middle and high variety, and I want to offer what amounts to a friendly amendment in thinking expressly about university production, as a subset of the amateur which he does not discuss.

Plenty of work has been done on the use of performance as a teaching tool, but there has been to my knowledge no serious study of the plays in performance on the college and university stage simply as theatre.[2] What is remarkable about this omission is that it is in such productions that many students get their first taste of theatrical Shakespeare, as either audiences or company members, and for some (more, perhaps, than we would care to admit) such experiences become, in the absence of anything later in life, the only touchstone they

have for what Shakespeare on stage is. Though Charlotte is a thriving city the opportunities to see Shakespeare on stage in the surrounding area are almost nil, so for those students who stay close to their alma mater after graduation, their college theatrical experience looms especially large.

I want to begin by teasing at that remark about school productions being 'less voluntary' than the amateur dramatics of local community theatre. In one sense it is obviously and unequivocally true, and not just of middle and high school productions where students may be pressured in various ways to participate. My school, the University of North Carolina at Charlotte, requires its theatre majors to audition once a year, and students in the department must earn performance practicum credits to graduate. That said, we mount approximately five major shows a year so students need not feel obligated to participate in a Shakespeare play, which will only ever fill one of those slots. Even the audition requirement is a little misleading, because it does not obligate actors to take a role in the show for which they auditioned. Moreover, the department permits the casting of non-theatre majors in departmental shows, something I was obligated to do for the *Dream* production I'm going to discuss, and those students participate in a purely voluntary fashion. Non-majors can get production/performance practicum credit for their involvement, but that is only useful on their transcript if they subsequently declare a theatre major or minor. It goes without saying that while students who are theatre majors may feel more pressure to be involved in a Shakespeare production, they are in no way constrained to be theatre majors at all. Indeed, most are involved in theatre to the unease, and sometimes outright displeasure, of their families.

---

[1] Michael Dobson, *Shakespeare and Amateur Performance: A Cultural History* (Cambridge, 2011), p. 20.

[2] See for instance *Shakespeare in Education*, ed. Martin Blocksidge (London and New York, 2003) or *Shakespeare and Higher Education, a Global Perspective*, ed. Sharon Beehler and Holger Klein (Lewiston, 2001).

It might be argued that however voluntary the decision to be a theatre major may be, the course of study is effectively pre-professional training for a career on the stage, so the amateur status of the shows in which students perform is tainted, the work actually being apprenticeship for professional employment. This is certainly true of conservatory programmes producing professional theatre practitioners. UNC Charlotte, however, is no such school. We are the urban research campus of a state university and the theatre department offers a BA degree, not the BFA usually preferred by those intending to make a life on stage, nor do we have the Masters programmes considered necessary for that life. A few of our students go on to graduate school or otherwise find a way to work professionally in the theatre, but the vast majority – 90 per cent based on recent numbers – go into entirely different professions. For them the theatre degree has limited practical application beyond the usual critical thinking skills which are the hallmark of most BA degrees, coupled with discipline-specific insight and some tools for self-presentation. Most of our students choose theatre over, say, English, because they enjoy it but do not seriously indulge the idea of becoming professionals. They are, I would argue, amateurs in Dobson's sense.

One of the advantages of performing outdoors in daylight as we did is that you can take a pretty accurate survey of who is in the audience and who isn't. To begin with the latter category, there were no reviewers working for off-campus publications of any kind, nor were there professional directors or actors in attendance.[3] A small percentage of the audience came from the city, but UNC Charlotte continues to struggle to draw members of the area community to campus events. At each performance there was a scattering of faculty, mainly from our department, but the vast majority of the audience were students, and the friends and families of people connected to the show, a surprisingly large number of whom came back to watch two or more times.

As an outdoor production which rehearsed and performed in a central campus location, we got a great deal of attention from the university community (and the show was the salvation of an otherwise dismal year at the box office) but virtually none at all from outside. This production will not become part of a larger conversation about the play on stage as, for instance, an RSC show does automatically. It isn't going to be archived for study. It didn't even get covered in the local papers whose arts coverage has been systematically gutted over the last few years. It won't be discussed at Shakespeare conferences by scholars who experienced its two-week run in person. In short, our *Dream*'s effects were both local and transitory and, while this is always true of live theatre, the extent to which its effects stayed within the immediate community (an essay such as this notwithstanding) is on a par with any other strictly amateur production. The nature of the community is, however, significantly different from those attending most amateur performance because student populations are in constant flux as they (hopefully) matriculate, so the audience built for one show will not exist for the next. Instead of the community theatre's geographically and socially rooted audience, or that of the professional theatre which may draw from further afield in proportion to its scale and reputation, the student production constructs an audience which is both spatially and temporally a campus phenomenon. I write this only four months after the show closed, but many of those involved have since graduated. They – and the friends and family they drew to see the show – will not return, and their memories of the production will be forever intertwined with the people and events of their collegiate past.

Few productions are more bound in terms of their final meanings to the nature of their process than those staged on campus. Company members talk to their peers (their audience) about everything they've done along the way and what they

---

[3] The exception was Peter Holland, who was visiting campus to present a paper as part of the events surrounding the production and who subsequently reviewed the production for *Shakespeare Bulletin*.

finally think the show is about. The rehearsal process itself is unusual in college, borrowed from an idealized professional model few companies can actually afford, a model rarely observed in amateur dramatics, or in all but the best endowed (usually European) companies. We cast our show in mid-January (delayed a week by a rare snow fall) and were working by the first week of February, focusing on general issues of voice, metrical awareness and, for those who would be in the forest/fairy world, physical work on animals. From there we moved into two weeks of table work, before we started physically exploring scenes, then to preliminary blocking, partial run-throughs, complete run-throughs, then technical rehearsals including dress rehearsals. We opened in mid-April, so the rehearsal process lasted about eleven weeks, four nights a week, four hours a night. It's a huge time commitment for all involved, and though our rehearsal day is much shorter than those at large professional houses we still wind up with considerably more time to work than most mid-level and lower (in terms of budget) professional outfits. Amateur companies also tend to rehearse in the evenings and on weekends because of their members' day-job commitments but my (admittedly anecdotal) sense of such groups is that, though there are exceptions, their rehearsal period tends to be considerably shorter than ours.[4]

Once more it is worth saying that amateur dramatic/community theatre companies and the smaller professional and semi-professional outfits which often resemble them are essentially idiosyncratic organizations, so it is impossible to generalize meaningfully on their rehearsal practices, but I can offer specifics which pertain to our immediate community. In visiting the rehearsals of local semi-professional Charlotte theatres I was struck by how much closer their rehearsal system is to that of the amateur dramatics society for which my father worked for decades in England than to the university model. Since the demise of Charlotte Repertory Theatre in 2005, the area's only LORT theatre, the city has lost the majority of its Equity actors to Atlanta, to Charleston and Columbia in South Carolina, and to Wilmington, a seaside town

with a growing film industry. With the exception of the Children's Theatre, which is one of the nation's leading companies geared to young audiences, Charlotte theatre is spotty at best and only nominally professional, offering few or no Equity contracts and requiring the kind of auxiliary work (actors who also make costumes, directors who are also performers and so on) which few full-time professionals would consider acceptable. Payment is nominal, production runs brief, so that making a living wage as an actor doing nothing but theatre in Charlotte is not feasible. What money there is in acting in the region tends to come from commercials and industrial training films. The theatre which audiences actually go to is almost exclusively Broadway touring shows staged in the large and impressive roadhouses down town, spaces the local companies cannot come close to either affording or filling.

There are two ad hoc local companies performing Shakespeare annually free of charge. One of them recently invited me in to their rehearsals of *King Lear* which was being mounted in a mind-boggling three weeks, rehearsing only at night. Blocking was done in the first week and the rest of the rehearsal period was a series of runs conducted as the cast learned their lines. There was no table work and minimal abstract discussion of larger issues or character. It was a workmanlike process designed to get the script on its feet as quickly as possible but it seriously limited what the production might achieve. In Charlotte, alas, where Shakespeare off-campus is concerned (whether we call it professional or amateur, the distinction being hazy at best) this is the rule rather than the exception.

---

4 Brownsea Open Air Theatre, for instance, in Dorset, begin work in February for shows that open in August. Such lengthy rehearsal periods are, however, misleading since (as Michael Dobson pointed out to me in private correspondence) the companies may only work one or two nights per week, so that lines learned early in the process have to be relearned before the end. Such a process often leads not to constant exploration and innovation but the endless repetition of early choices which then calcify.

It might be argued that our lengthy rehearsal period stems from the fact that students need more time to rehearse because their skills are less advanced than their 'adult' counterparts, but this is not the case. Student actors, paradoxically, tend to approach their craft seriously, through youthful earnestness and because they have caught a rhetoric of professionalism from the institution. I was able, for instance, to mandate that all actors be off book by the time we blocked each scene and, though we had people calling for occasional lines right into March, I generally got my wish. This was a far cry from the 'professional' rehearsal I had sat in on two days before their dress rehearsal, where virtually no one was close to knowing their lines and where the process was geared to getting them through the scene, rather than exploring or polishing it. Again, this problem arose from the brevity of their rehearsal period, a fact driven less by company apathy than by the costs involved in securing rehearsal space and access to the theatre, a familiar problem in amateur dramatic circles. It is hardly surprising that so many struggling professional directors are delighted when they come to academia and find that there are considerably more resources – of time, materials, budget and access to facilities – than they are used to in all but the largest and best financed professional companies. Simply put, the model of theatrical Shakespeare we aspire to in our campus shows is one not seen in the Charlotte area *except* on university campuses. More arguably, perhaps, but in ways that sidestep the troublesome amateur/professional binary which I have already alluded to, I would make the case that ours is the only *serious* theatrical Shakespeare in the area. I make no claim for the quality of our execution, though I think it on a par with comparable institutions, perhaps a little better: the seriousness I mean is one of intent, reach and methodology.

College productions are necessarily inflected by the academic world, particularly the scholarly network which trickles down through the teachers who inevitable work as directors and dramaturgs, privileging an intellectual investment in the production. This is perhaps to draw a distinction between productions generated entirely by students from those operating under official departmental aegises, though I'd be prepared to bet that even productions with nary a faculty member in sight are touched by what the students have gleaned from their Shakespeare classes. Dramaturgs, for instance – real dramaturgs who do more than preshow chats and programme synopses – are still treated as luxury items in most professional theatres, and (though I admit to a bias on this) I think that such an assumption often reveals a less than determined wrestling with the play's intellectual dimension. Dramaturgs in university productions are commonplace; dedicated faculty, often from outside the theatre department, who are excited about the material and invested in its theatrical realization. In my case I had a faculty dramaturg from English, Kirk Melnikoff, and a graduate student serving as his assistant, who were involved in rehearsals from casting onwards. Again, this represents a hybrid status; what we have in the college dramaturg is an idealized version of the professional theatre motivated by the passion and esprit de corps of the equally idealized amateur dramatic society. No one, after all, gets tenure based on dramaturging campus shows.

And it isn't just the presence of dramaturgs which beef up a college production's intellectual and professional dimension. Faculty Directors are encouraged to model what might be called 'best practices' for their casts, and though the form of this will depend on their bent and training, such an impulse tends to produce a greater aspiration towards intellectual and creative rigour. In the hands of a director with a scholarly background, it is inevitable that the production will at least be informed by current academic debate, even if it does not further that debate especially. Faculty are, after all, educators and, while a conservatory programme might focus exclusively on craft and aesthetics, a programme such as ours with its liberal arts slant and BA degree, will always be anchored in the realm of intellectual discussion and analysis.

Perhaps the results tend towards RSC-Lite, and it is certainly true that college productions of Shakespeare are more suited to a 'concept' approach where the work of the director and designers (who are usually faculty) drive the actors (usually students) in ways more obviously manifesting a 'take' on the play than is possible with a semi-professional company mounting *King Lear* in three frantic weeks. The rise of the concept production comes, as is often pointed out, with the rise of the director, but the full impact of this on a notion of normalcy for college productions, where directors are faculty modelling a version of what professional theatre *should be*, goes less commented on. For college Shakespeare productions driven by faculty, the archaism of the language combined with an apparent lack of spatial and temporal rootedness invites directorial mediation, interpretation and construction. Conceptual frames – be they aesthetic, intellectual or defined by the specifics of a single choice such as period setting – are the rule, not the exception. Campus productions, I would argue, mirror their larger academic surroundings in being effectively thesis-driven, even if their argument is made at the level of aesthetic choice.

2. THE TREE OF HEAVEN

From the outset the plan was to stage our production neither inside our new and nicely appointed 300-seat modified proscenium theatre nor in our flexible black box lab space. It was to be outside.

The logic of this was only partly driven by the play's woodland setting. The theatre department, like many others across the country, had been feeling the economic pinch in its publicity and marketing budgets: audiences and departmental visibility more generally had been shrinking, and some of our best work was going unnoticed. An outdoor production, it was felt, would draw attention to our programme by creating a sense of 'event', something much hallowed in those marketing circles which value interaction over presentation.

The initial plan was to make the production fully in promenade, moving from the black box space (Athens) out through the set shop (the first mechanicals scene) and then out into UNC Charlotte's pleasant, wooded campus. We would process from location to location among the trees and around the lake beside the theatre building, finally going back into the lab theatre for the final scene. The logic of this was initially to be represented literally in the production itself which, I thought, might work as a metaphor for the college experience. The first scene would be a high school graduation party strung with banners adorned with the lovers' names. We would then move onto the campus, led by mechanicals in UNCC groundskeeper attire, and the fairy scenes would have a distinctly college feel, the outside venues augmented with stacks of oversized books, pizza boxes and beer can sculptures. The woods would trace the kind of exploration and self-discovery/fashioning that happens on college campuses everywhere. The final scene would be a return home, transformed.

In the months after I proposed the production, however, the logistics of this came under question and it was eventually determined that we did not have the resources to execute this approach effectively, and some argued that our audience would not play along. I was doubtful of the latter point, but had to concede the former, and my faith in the rather literal forest-as-college and vice versa concept stalled. The core theme remained, I think, as a psychological through-line which, given the nature of our cast and cultural environment, was inescapable, but it was completely stripped from the show's obvious and measurable semiotics.

As to the physical space issue, compromise was reached as compromises always are in practical theatre. The show would take place entirely outdoors and two locations would be established, one for Athens, one for the fairy world, each with its own seating and distinctive ambience (insofar as that could be achieved with a 'found space' aesthetic and budget). The audience would move twice, from Athens into the forest and back, with an intermission inserted after Bottom was taken to Titania's bower. We chose a broad quadrangle in front of the theatre building (partly so we would have access to dressing rooms and bathrooms inside) which was dotted with large trees. There was also a central angular metal sculpture on permanent loan from the Mint Museum officially titled 'Celtic knot' though referred to throughout the design process as the Rubik's cube, which could not be moved, modified, climbed on or even touched. There was also a scaffolding 'pavilion' recently erected by the architecture department which was intended to be used as a kind of performance space but which, being too small, oddly placed and obscured by the metal of its own structure, we could use only as the mechanicals' final act tiring house.

I have directed outdoors before but only once (a production of *Twelfth Night* in Georgia) and on a simple platform stage with a preset auditorium space. This time there were no set parameters and no institutional memory on which to draw, since no one had performed in the venue we had selected. The dynamics of blocking, of audience interaction, the acoustics, even the ground plan of the performance space itself would have to be discovered through rehearsal.

In addition to demanding that we spent a lot of time outside, our playing space meant that we would have none of the usual theatrical bells and whistles to help carry the show. Neither Athens nor the fairy woods had a clear perimeter, there were no natural screens to keep sightlines focused on the action, and our 'found space' aesthetic prohibited us from building any. Even if we could have afforded to, it made little sense to commit to an outdoor production and then recreate the dynamics of an interior space. There would thus be no set changes, the only shift in look created when the audience moved from Athens to the fairy world on the other side of a large southern magnolia where their orientation would be reversed. There would be no lighting effects (though we later discovered that some simple work lights were necessary for the play within the play because we could not get the entire show completed before sundown), and though the actors would have to wear microphones in order to be heard in a space so prone to sudden winds, there would be no canned music of any kind. There would be, in short, nothing to hide behind: anything which was to sway the audience fell to the cast. It was, frankly, terrifying.

As the lack of a traditional offstage made it impossible to change sets so it also meant that costume changes, the introduction of props, even

simple actor exits and entrances became vexed. We began work in a rehearsal room (North Carolina is cold and dark in winter) which reinforced the false sense that we were doing a conventional production in which actors could enter and exit their scenes as usual. The moment we started walking through those scenes outside (bundled up in the dark, and using flashlights to pick our way over tree roots) it became clear that much of what we had planned was logistically untenable. We opted for a Grotowski-esque 'poor theatre' approach in which the cast remained seated on benches arranged around the playing space with their backs to the action whenever they were not on stage. When entering, each actor would stand, pause for a second as themselves, then get into character and move directly into the scene. Costume changes were kept to a minimum and effected either in full view of the audience or, in the cases of the wedding party at the end, in the Athens section before the audience had moved from the forest world.

It was a measure of our anxiety about the space, and a nagging awareness of how crucial that space would be to the production's generation of meaning as well as aesthetics, that I became neurotically obsessed with a particular tree. There were two which figured in our playing space. One, the southern magnolia which I have already referenced, was large and central and evergreen. Like all southern magnolias it is a solid, shaggily conical tree with huge glossy green leaves which drop and lie on the ground like the soles of ancient shoes. Its foliage is so dense that it provided us with the closest thing to a wall we had to work with, but also made real interaction with the plant itself virtually impossible. Titania's bower, which had originally been conceived in a cavalier fashion as being somehow under or inside the tree, had to be moved to a spot more generally at its foot, so that there was a reasonable chance of the actors (a) being visible, and (b) getting out again without a chain saw. This, however, was not the problem tree.

The problem tree was on the other side of our fairy world. It was a spreading plant whose main trunk separated into four almost immediately above the ground, each stem arcing out and branching in ways both elegant and eminently climbable. How perfect a place it would be, I had thought, strolling the grounds the previous fall, for the male fairies to literally hang out! The image of Oberon and Puck shinning up to lounge like leopards in the dappled foliage of the canopy seemed a particularly beautiful way to embrace our verdant setting, one that would speak to who these characters were and what the fairy world meant.

But as we got enough evening light to work in and rehearsals drifted outside, an unpleasant truth began to insert itself into the proceedings. February turned to March and March chuffed purposefully into April but our tree remained not so much verdant with dappled foliage as bare and brown. The tree, it seemed, had died over the winter.

I sought counsel, amateur and professional, on the chances of the tree reviving and coming into leaf in time for opening. Cast members regularly plucked at the outermost twigs and studied them for signs of green. A groundskeeper, watched anxiously by the cast for whom this had become a matter of some weight, pronounced it a Tree of Heaven, and still alive. A great rush of relief went through the assembled company.

'So it will be covered in leaves by mid April', I persisted, as if he might personally see to it.

'Yeah', he mused, perversely as it turned out. 'Yeah, that's not going to happen.'

In fact, however, it did. Just. The buds had turned to the frailest leaflets by dress rehearsal, and by opening it might be said that the tree was in leaf, though for the first few shows the green was not so much a verdant dappled canopy as a baby's breath haze. It didn't screen out the buildings behind as much as I had hoped, but it gave the actors a sense of being surrounded by something alive, and that was what counted. By the second week of the run they were having to adjust their positioning so they could still be seen amongst all that verdant dappling.

The slow-leafing tree wasn't the only space-related inconvenience which had to be negotiated in ways shaping the final production. The

29. Oberon (James Shafer) watches from the tree of heaven.

sun turned out to set a little earlier than expected, emitting side-light which blinded half of the audience for much of the forest scenes. Blocking was adjusted and seats were moved but we never completely solved the problem. The work lights brought in to combat the darkness which draped itself over the final act, though a source of great concern, turned out to be simple to use, and gave the final scenes a magical quality I could not have anticipated. Other insistent realities were more minor but no less formative. Rehearsal and performance were marked by the rhythms of campus: the chiming of the carillon tower, the sudden floods of students going to and from classes, the gathering of architecture majors talking and smoking on a nearby balcony. Skateboarders rumbled passed only yards from the playing space. Fire engines on the main road once competed with

Bottom's antics as Pyramus for five full minutes. Squirrels invaded Titania's bower and Canada geese came roaring overhead like great honking Stukas. In the forest, the seats at the back were too low and the audience took to standing up and shifting, sometimes moving into what were effectively voms which actors used as entrances and exits, thereby generating much ad-libbing and adjustment. Passers-by (including campus police) would congregate behind the action to see what was going on, sometimes for an hour or more at a time. In the second week of the run, work began upstage of our fairy world playing space to erect three massive pickaxes, part of the university's 'branding' programme (Go, forty-niners) which seemed to wryly magnify the pick brandished by our butch Flute.

These are the material conditions of performance. They aren't in the script, but they become part of how the company rehearses, how audiences perceive the show and therefore how its meanings are made. All of these extra-textual additions/distractions/flourishes have analogues in other outdoor spaces, but their specifics were ours alone, defined not simply by the material geography of the space, but by its conceptual limits as a university campus.

3. CONCEPTUAL THROUGH-LINE AND WORKING WITH ACTORS

The play, as I saw it, was a journey from constriction to liberation, something figured particularly in the lives of the lovers and registered through gender. I wanted the production to begin in tension and under the shadow of two forced marriages, Hermia's and Hippolyta's. The former would be overturned by the events of the play because it was against Hermia's wishes. The latter would be ratified in a more complex negotiation of power and desire played out through the central characters' alter egos in the forest. This meant doubling Theseus/Oberon, Hippolyta/Titania and, to provide continuity, Philostrate/Puck. The Indian boy was a constant throughout, a real child for Hippolyta and as much a source of tension in Athens as he

was the centre of the fairy squabble. I knew this going in, and approached casting accordingly with my dramaturg, Kirk Melnikoff, keeping a close eye on the incidentals which might be introduced into this larger agenda by different actors, particularly in terms of cross-gendered and racial casting.

Student productions rarely have the breadth of talent they would like on which to draw and (again) compromises have to be made. Even so I was dismayed to find that in the initial round of auditions I had barely enough to cast the show, and not enough men, even with some creative cross-gendered casting. Calls were made and deals successfully struck, but though we remained stretched very thin we were from the outset determined not to use so-called colour or gender 'blind' casting, committed as we were to the idea that such things signify on stage. With the minor exception of Hermia, who was Hispanic, though her father was not (we rationalized this in terms of an absent Hispanic wife for Egeus), all the cross-casting choices made sense according to the logic of the production. None were intended to be invisible. Lysander was African-American, something which both helped to distinguish him from Demetrius and gave an edge to Egeus's opposition to his marriage to Hermia. The opening scene (particularly with Egeus's accusations of witchcraft, however figurative) evoked *Othello*, hinting at a prejudice which could not be overcome by Theseus's 4.1 ruling. Egeus stormed out of the final forest scene with a dismissive gesture to Hermia and did not reappear until the curtain call. The students seemed a little baffled by our decision to play a racial tension because they think of themselves (or profess to think of themselves) as post-racial in their attitudes, but in our last performance a cast member alerted us to the possibility that a family member who would be in the audience and who opposed interracial relationships should be expected to disrupt the show. It was an alarming situation and the police were notified. In the event, the family member did attend the production, but kept quiet, and the performance passed without incident. Even so, the warning was a curious reminder of the region's all too recent past, and left us wondering what went unarticulated by some of our audience. Again, the specific dynamic of the campus audience signifies here, since family ties to company members draw people to material they would otherwise avoid and not only because they consider the material hard or archaic. My (again anecdotal, local and arguable) sense of amateur Shakespeare at the community theatre level suggests that productions off campus are less likely to make the kinds of edgy socio-political choices which may alienate their audience.

Hippolyta, who doubled as Titania, was played by a black actress, and her difference from the faintly Prussian uniforms of the Athenian court figured in the strong colours of her costume and in the beads and shells which made up her corsetry as Titania. As Hippolyta she opened the production performing a vigorous exercise with a curved two-handed sword quite different from the dress swords worn by Theseus and the Athenian attendants who interrupted her. The changeling, who mimicked her, and who was, to Theseus, an inconvenient link to a former life, was played by a dark-skinned Asian boy. Whether he was supposed to be a blood relative to Hippolyta rather than being an adoptee (like Titania's), the production did not attempt to clarify.

Predictably, it was the fairies and mechanicals who were subjected to the most cross-casting. Oberon was assigned a single male fairy in addition to Puck, while Titania got all female fairies, one of whom (Mustardseed) was also black. Quince was a woman as were Snout (who was also African American) and Flute. This last required some finessing of both the script and the performance, since the original cross-gendering was lost. Our Flute was tall and big boned, a miner with a pick-axe, who chewed seed, spat and generally comported herself in pointed contrast to her lady-like superiors in the court. Her resistance to playing a woman as Thisbe (she *brought* a beard to the first rehearsal) was about despising frailty and refinement. It was a working-class sensibility (something most UNCC students get intuitively) and one constantly in comic tension with the part she had to play. That she was able, as Thisbe, to express real feelings for Bottom in her own voice was part

of her character arc, and her sincere kiss of the dead Pyramus was a moment of pathos as well as comedy. Frankly, if we had had more men to pick from at audition (a recurring problem when casting student Shakespeare) we wouldn't have made this choice, but, as in other choices, we were fortunate that the problem generated a logic from outside the text, one that worked within the frame of the production and breathed a little freshness into the character dynamics.

The above sense that necessity is the mother of theatrical invention is perhaps a mantra for student production where one never seems to have quite what one envisages in resources and talent. As I have said, our production stood or fell on the shoulders of the cast who had to play out in full sunlight, making eye contact with an audience sitting only feet (sometimes inches) away from them, and who could never completely escape the stage except at the intermission and the end of the show. Yet many of our actors were performing Shakespeare for the first time. Many – as is not uncommon in American theatre programmes where naturalism generated from inside is still the default approach – had little formal training in voice work, verse speaking, or in a physical approach to acting. I set up some voice and movement sessions with a colleague, Kelly Mizell, but much of their learning was going to have to be on the job.[5]

Given their comparative lack of experience, this was troubling, though some of the solutions we found proved some of the most successful moments of the production. Our lovers, for instance, were

---

[5] A second, and more surprising, difficulty was that talk of love was alien to many of the cast. Their first response to the play's subject matter even in its most simple articulation was sceptical, even cynical. Moreover, on several occasions when I was giving notes which prompted the actors to recall what it was like to be in love, I was told by several that they had never been in love. At first I put this down to a lack of life experience, but I soon realized that it was more than that. At their age, after all, I had been in love several times, usually unhappily, as had almost everyone I knew! What I was seeing in my cast was, in ways I couldn't quite pinpoint, a generational difference. They thought of relationships, of privacy, of sexuality, differently from the way I did, and very differently from the play.

badly mismatched in terms of experience, the ladies having done a lot of theatre including Shakespeare, while the men had not. Both had distinctive looks, Lysander black, athletic and graceful of movement, Demetrius pale with fashion model good looks and a winsome smile. Both were nervous around the language, something that manifested itself also in a physical tentativeness.

We ran into our first real problems in the Demetrius and Helena scenes in the woods beginning with the latter part of 2.1. The gist of the moment is simple enough: Helena is bewailing the way Demetrius treats her, while Demetrius demands that she stop following him. The problem is that in the course of their 56-line exchange, nothing of consequence happens. No one changes, no new information is presented, no obvious discoveries are made. Two people talk, and one of them (Demetrius) talks primarily about why he wants to be elsewhere, thereby raising the question of why he doesn't just leave. Student actors are often so focused on the text (something that the sudden concentration on scansion, breathing and imagery exacerbates) that they find it intensely difficult to be as inventive as they might if they were playing a modern script or – better still – if they were improvising a scene in their own words. We ran the scene over and over, but it felt wooden, static, and the more we pressed and prodded at it the more I got close to my Helena's modern (or post-modern) frustration with her own character's self-deprecation. She was irritated particularly by the 'spaniel moment', in which she requested that Demetrius use her as he used his dog, a sentiment no notion of love would allow her to embrace. Demetrius, meanwhile, didn't know why he was still talking to her at all. Both of them wanted the scene heavily cut.

Helena, being the more experienced actor, was able to swallow down her feelings about the lines she had to say, but Demetrius's lack of purpose continued to be a problem. We tried playing the scene in contemporary English, but this illuminated the difficulty rather than solving it, since it died after about ten lines. Once someone has rejected someone else's advances, they felt, what else was to be

said? They thought of love and sex in direct terms while the characters' words were all fatuous sparring and indirection. Demetrius had to be told that 'nymph', a word he used several times of Helena elsewhere, meant something closer to goddess than it did, as he had taken it, nymphomaniac, and wildly wrong though that second meaning was, it made more sense to him, gave him something with which his twenty-first century (lady-killer) self had more experience. I insisted that we did not take Helena down that particular cul-de-sac (not that the actress would have gone there anyway), but this left my Demetrius even less sure of himself.

We returned to the text and picked our way through Demetrius's strategies to get her to leave him alone of her own accord, trying to find a different approach for each (cajoling, entreating, threatening, etc.). This gave us something of a psychological frame, but left dead spots during Helena's lengthy responses where Demetrius didn't know what to do. Since he was not coming up with ideas of his own, I tried walking through each moment with him, resorting to all kinds of tricks to keep him in the space. He was looking for Hermia, he said, so we gave him a compass and a map. We had him running his hands over the ground like a tracker or a scout looking for footprints. We had him trying to get a phone signal so he could text her (the show was eclectic in terms of period, and went for specificity of character and theme rather than historical verisimilitude). It was all very busy, and none of it worked.

Eventually I threw up my hands, took Demetrius aside and told him that if he felt like leaving at any point in the course of the scene, he should do so. Then I told Helena that whatever happened, she could not let him go. It was an absurdly simple note but, from that point on, the scene directed itself. It became fast and physical, earnest and funny, and was never precisely the same each time. As the dynamic became more honestly about what the actors themselves were doing as actors, they began to escape the strictures of the text. Suddenly Demetrius was punctuating his exasperation with shouts and gestures that were completely spontaneous and believable where his former speechifying had been obviously conned with cruel pain. At one point he closed on her menacingly as he spoke:

> You do impeach your modesty too much,
> To leave the city and commit yourself
> Into the hands of one that loves you not;
> To trust the opportunity of night,
> And the ill counsel of a desert place,
> With the rich worth of your virginity.
>
> (2.1.214–19)

The rape threat was a feint, of course, another strategy to get her to leave him alone, but he found the absurdity of her response ('Your virtue is my privilege. For that / It is not night when I do see your face') so confounding that he dropped the threatening posture and retreated shrieking (as only students can do) a wholly extra-textual 'Oh my God!' We kept it. It was a moment so real, so utterly plausible, and one so clearly growing out of the clash of modern student sensibility and Shakespearian heroine at her most ridiculously high-minded, that it brought the house down.

Navigating the effects of the magic flower was similarly tricky. The students' wariness of Shakespearian love,[6] coupled with their sense of the verse as larger than normal speech meant that they saw (perhaps rightly) little difference between the speech of lovers who had been treated or infected by Oberon's love juice and those who hadn't. It is not unusual, of course, to have the lovers played this way, with no clear difference between the two versions of love the play offers. I was committed, however, to a genuinely happy ending, and read backwards from there. This meant that Demetrius's supposed love for Hermia at the beginning had to be more about his rivalry with Lysander than it was about true feelings for his proposed bride, and Lysander's love for Helena in the forest was magically induced and therefore empty. Indeed, we decided that the love juice could not force love per se, only a kind of obsessive doting, and that Demetrius's final love for Helena was only real because he had been in love with her before the action of the play began, his fascination with Hermia a kind of illness from which he finally recovers:

> The object and the pleasure of my eye
> Is only Helena. To her, my lord,
> Was I betrothed ere I see Hermia.
> But like a sickness did I loathe this food;
> But, as in health come to my natural taste,
> Now do I wish it, love it, long for it,
> And will forever more be true to it.
>
> (4.1.169–75)

The love juice then came to represent something quite different from the relationships which concluded the production. On a deep psychological level it allowed experimentation, taking the lovers out of their former roles and inverting them (so the beloved became despised and vice versa) in ways ultimately teaching empathy and self-knowledge. In romantic terms, the love juice exploits the familiar Shakespearian notion of love – or rather 'love' in its doting, obsessive and unselfconscious manifestation – as transformative. Which is all well and good, but pretty heady for student actors to grasp, many of whom (as they said) had had precious little experience of romantic love in any form, even while they were quite comfortable with sex.

Solutions emerged as we talked about how popular culture represented love, particularly that notion, so useful for the love juice scenes, that the lover is crucially not himself. This tapped into their own scepticism about the love which was shown on television, and after a while the actors playing Demetrius and Lysander each came up with an angle based on their own interests. Lysander homed in on popular music, specifically the slick seductions of boy bands, complete with mini dance routines, soppy facial expressions and choreographed gestures which illustrated his words. From the moment he awoke with the taint of the love juice, Lysander pulsed with a gentle rhythmic throb whenever he looked at or thought of Helena. The actor playing Demetrius, who paid his way through college as a Calvin Klein-esque model, generated a sultry and provocative persona such as one might find in cologne ads or on the covers of romantic novels. He strutted, posed and

---

[6] See note 5 above.

30. Helena (Amy Scheide) confronts the 'love juiced' Lysander (Harmony Andre).

exposed as much of his chiselled body as we could get away with. The key to both performances was a lack of self-consciousness that nicely demonstrated how empty their obsessions had made them. It was a little like watching people who were drunk or high, people who were free to indulge their narcissism, unaware of their absurdity. I kept saying they had been stripped of superego. The students said they had lost their filter. Most importantly, of course, both approaches were funny and this was finally the key to their success. Initially both men were hesitant and understated, and didn't really come into their own until they found themselves in front of an audience who laughed uproariously. From that point on, they were unstoppable. Lysander worked in some Michael Jackson crotch grabs. Demetrius supplemented his striptease jacket removal by dunking a cup of water over his chest a la *Flashdance* . . . It was all gloriously over

the top and nicely underscored the hollowness of this particular brand of love in which performance negated any kind of actual connection between the lover and the object of his affection. Here was only performativity and the shallowest of appetites given unselfconscious shape by the trappings of a culture for which there is rarely a serious alternative.

Such a position requires, of course, a leap of faith that the love found in the final marriages is any better. We chose to make that leap, based partly on resonant snippets in the way the awoken lovers spoke of and to each other (particularly Helena's 'mine own and not mine own' (4.2.191) a far cry from her earlier doting 'in idolatry' (1.1.109)) and partly because that was simply what we wanted to present. It is one of the benefits of being a teacher among students that the director's reading runs into less resistance than it might with professionals. Such moments finally hinge on the idea that the production is a constructor of meaning, not merely an interpreter or transmitter of what resides in the text. In this case, the body language of the awoken lovers as they tentatively reconnected with each other, and their brand of intimacy thereafter, made the difference clear and incontrovertible within the show. They had passed through a period of play, of role reversal, and of acting on impulse without thought for consequence to self or others, and they had emerged wiser, humbler and with a clearer sense of who they were and what they valued. That several relationships blossomed among the cast in the course of the rehearsal process (four couples that I knew of) surely fuelled the heady atmosphere.

The fairy world was wilder than the constrained world of Athens, and married two contrasting aesthetic impulses. The first was animal. Since costume changes would be minimal I had determined early on that the shift from Theseus to Oberon, Hippolyta to Titania, and Philostrate to Puck would be made largely through the bodies of the actors. We studied animal posture and behaviour through nature documentaries and hit on two broad categories. The female fairies of Titania's court would be roughly feline, while the male fairies, including Oberon and Puck would be equally roughly canine, and not only because the two groups fight like cats and dogs. The female fairies were more solitary, though they groomed each other. They were more elegant and sensual, particularly in repose. The men had a different sense of the pack, a stronger sense of group play and suddenly asserted status: Oberon was wolfish, Puck more the hyena, playful but with an edge of menace. These roles were chosen before we got into scene work, and their specifics took a long time to evolve as the actors got comfortable with their different ways of moving, of watching, of interacting, but the result, I think, went a long way to eradicate confusion over who they were at any given time and gave a powerful sense of the world in which they lived. That world influenced the lovers the longer they stayed there, so that as their faintly Victorian Athenian garments

were stripped away, they became more like the bestial fairies and by the time squabbling turned towards the possibility of real combat at the end of 3.2 both men and women had grown (literally and figuratively) a good deal closer to the ground. Demetrius and Lysander squared up to each other like coyotes and Hermia's threats to Helena (nails bared like claws) were punctuated by a dangerous hiss which echoed Titania's to Oberon at the end of 2.1.

But the fairy world wasn't simply animal. I had been discussing the differences between Athens and the forest with the set and costume designers (Anita Easterling and Paula Garofalo) before rehearsals began, working through the final blending of the two as the fairies cross over into the Athenian court and something of the forest is brought back with the three married couples. The designers latched onto the idea that the fairies (as is suggested by Oberon and Titania's sparring over their respective dalliances with humans (2.1.64–80)) crossed over to the human world from time to time. So our fairies became collectors of human knick-knacks, refashioning them to suit their world. The result was largely what fantasy writers and artists have come to call 'Steampunk' or 'retro futurism': a mode of alternate history in which the materials of the late nineteenth century take on a sci-fi twist à la Jules Verne or H. G. Wells.[7] Our fairies wore clothes with Victorian silhouettes, but trimmed with animal fur and accessorized with brass goggles and combat boots. Oberon had a mechanical arm and his henchman had a backpack spouting tubes and copper pipes. Moth sported collapsible copper-etched wings, Cobweb brandished a recycled parasol, and Pease Blossom wore a hat with a delicate metal bird attached: happy whimsies all. They browsed and flirted and groomed

---

[7] For some of steampunk's dazzling and whimsical delights, see Art Donovan's *The Art of Steampunk: Extraordinary Devices and Ingenious Contraptions from the Leading Artists of the Steampunk Movement* (East Petersburg, 2011), Jay Strongman's *Steampunk: The Art of Victorian Futurism* (London, 2011), or Jema Hewitt's *Steampunk Emporium: Creating Fantastical Jewelry, Devices and Oddments from Assorted Cogs, Gears and Curios* (Cincinatti, 2011).

31. Moth (Ashton Smith) as steam punk aviator.

each other around a makeshift fountain fashioned from an old mattress. The idea was to prevent the fairy forest from becoming a bucolic idyll utterly separate from the human, suggesting instead a playful and inventive space which was both rooted in the ground, in life which sends the sap shooting, and in an alternate version of humanity unshackled by the authoritarian patriarchy which was our Athens. Rendered in quasi-realist character terms, our fairies were filchers, borrowers with a long history of covert incursion into Athens, and their appropriated human trappings balanced their bestial natures and complicated the familiar romanticization of pop-culture fairies and Victorian prettiness.

Steampunk is of a similar order to what we were doing with Shakespeare, a whimsical remaking of the past in ways anticipating present or future concerns and interests. Both steampunk and our version of Shakespeare on stage announce themselves as un-historical history, a version of the world whose fantasy makes the past prologue to something outside the original's temporal, spatial and cultural dimension, generating an airy nothing to which it grants a particularly local name and habitation. Steampunk is, moreover, a performance mode, even a lifestyle which does not need an actual stage, tapping as it does into one of the more inventive subcultures associated with the fantasy and sci-fi communities. I defy anyone not to be impressed by some of the steam punk costumes and associated gadgetry that you see at conventions like Dragon Con, built – to return to Michael Dobson's sense of amateur – for the love of it. I knew some students would be aware of – even invested in – the movement already but it never occurred to me that as the run progressed we would develop a contingent of steampunk audience members. Yet night after night I would glance around to see the house sprinkled

32. Helena (Amy Scheide) plays and sings for the final dance as Demetrius (Sammy Harley)
looks on.

with top hats, corsets and goggles, some of them worn by people coming back to the show for the second or third time. It was a nice illustration of the way that the barriers between performer and audience had grown steadily more permeable without disrupting the basic semiotics of the production itself: again, I think, this grew out of our campus location.

The students often remarked on their own similarity to the rude mechanicals, not in the denigrating sense of being unprofessional, but because they felt a comparable sense of enthusiasm and group identity. Our mechanicals had a journey from mutual suspicion and a sense of clearly defined hierarchy to community and close (in some cases romantic) personal relationships. Their rustically exuberant bergomask (lyrics borrowed from the play, music written and played by the cast) always felt completely sincere to me, because it so clearly capped the entire production process, making the distinction between actors and roles impossible to draw. It helped that the audience seemed to find it infectious too, but that was at least partly

because they were themselves participants by virtue of both the day-lit space, and because those on stage were their peers, their siblings, their friends, their alter egos in this curiously local and momentary population.

Whatever the production achieved as a staging of Shakespeare, as an educational tool, even as a form of three-dimensional literary criticism, its greatest success, it seems to me now, was simply as an event which embraced the half-discovery I began with: that staging campus theatre is the construction of a particular geographically, culturally and temporally rooted community. For weeks afterwards that community's facebook pages buzzed with new pictures and anecdotes, new outpourings of mutual love and delight at having been part of something. Versions of this exist in all theatre, of course, amateur and professional, but the college production's particular blend of inexperience, daunting material mastered, youthful fervour, the tackling of Big Ideas, all pursued out of love and the impulse to support one's fellow company members makes it, I think, unique. Such things cannot be separated from what a production finally meant. They are an infectious part of the live experience, into which they are sealed, capable of casting only the faintest shadows for those not present. It is always true of live theatre that you had to be there to fully grasp the show, but on campus, where the larger event – including as it does issues of the educational and social community, of landmarks in the emotional and intellectual development of young people for whom the world seems full of possibilities – it seems doubly so. It's time we paid this ubiquitous phenomenon more attention.

THE PLURALITY OF SHAKESPEARE'S SONNETS

PAUL EDMONDSON AND STANLEY WELLS

For at least two and a half centuries Shakespeare's Sonnets have suffered from the attentions of readers who have falsely assumed imaginary biographical contexts and have lazily accepted mistaken assumptions about the poems. Their originality has still not been adequately acknowledged. They have too often been read as if their aims were identical to those of sonnet sequences of the 1590s. Critics and biographers have persisted in writing about 'the Dark Lady' and 'the Young Man', figments of (initially) an eighteenth-century biographical sensibility, and one which continues to hold too much sway in sonnet criticism. Unquestionably Shakespeare's Sonnets invite biographical readings. But biographical readings of any kind – like political and multi-cultural interpretations – are only at best a by-product of a poem's literary impact.

This article falls into five sections. In the first we revisit and assert the originality of Shakespeare's Sonnets, particularly by questioning the notion that they follow any model set by writers of sonnet sequences in the 1590s. For this reason, we consciously refer to Shakespeare's Sonnets as a collection rather than a sequence. Second, we attempt to identify critical cobwebs that need sweeping away. In our view too many biographical accounts of Shakespeare's life, as well as critical discussions of the Sonnets, lazily assuming that the Sonnets tell some kind of discernible story about real or imagined protagonists, attempt to identify real people behind the poems. Third, while not wanting to deny the possible relevance of the Sonnets to Shakespeare's life, we argue that this should be thought of in relation to limited and precise biographical readings of individual poems. Fourth, we wish to interrogate the common terms 'the Dark Lady', 'the young man' and 'the rival poet'. Finally, we make the plea for all approaches to the Sonnets to focus on the poems themselves, rather than on assumptions about their interrelationships.

I

Many of the ideas we question derive from the notion that this collection of poems falls into the generic category of amatory sonnet sequences such as were popular from the posthumous publication of Sir Philip Sidney's *Astrophil and Stella* in 1591 through to 1597. These years saw the publication of at least nineteen single-authored collections of sonnets as well as the composition of others that were not published. There are so many ways in which Shakespeare's collection differs from any of these that it seems quite wrong to regard it as merely a late specimen of a well-established genre. For one thing, with 154 poems it exceeds the longest of the others, Sidney's, by almost 50 per cent. Unlike other collections, Shakespeare's does not tell a story, nor does it hang together as a complete, uninterrupted cycle or sequence. Almost all the earlier collections have titles, most of them including, or consisting simply of, the name of a woman who is the object of the poet's love – titles such as *Delia* (1592) by Samuel Daniel, *Diana* (1594) by

An earlier version of this essay was jointly delivered to a plenary session of the British Shakespeare Association's annual conference at King's College, London in September 2009.

Henry Constable or *Fidessa, More Chaste than Kind* (1596) by Bartholomew Griffin. *Shakespeare's Sonnets* on their first publication were called simply that: a third-person label which, in conjunction with the title-page phrase 'never before imprinted', appears anxious to suggest that their publication is eagerly awaited by a reading public. And omission of Shakespeare's given name is surely a measure of his fame. The third-person form of the title-page inscription might also suggest that the poems are not appearing under their author's own auspices.

Shakespeare's Sonnets are not easy to read; at least, it is challenging fully to experience more than three or four at one sitting. This in itself should give us pause before we consider them as a sequence. When compared to John Donne's *La Corona*, for instance, which self-consciously links all of the sonnets by causing the last line of one to form the first line of the next, Shakespeare's Sonnets clearly resist sequentiality. They tell no story (though they occasionally hint at one). The fact that there are linked pairs of sonnets, and even small, thematic sequences of three or four poems within Shakespeare's collection, is itself revealing of an ordering mind at work, trying to bring intermittent unity and sequentiality to an otherwise disparate collection of poems. It is possible that their composition extended over a quarter of a century. The 1609 quarto is a miscellany (in some ways resembling *The Passionate Pilgrim* of 1599), a collection, even an anthology. It is not a unified sequence.

Shakespeare's Sonnets differ in other ways, too, from their ostensible prototypes. One is that some of his poems, on the evidence of forms of address and of personal pronouns, are clearly addressed to a male, not to a female person. Among previous sonneteers, only one, Richard Barnfield, in his playfully homoerotic poems, had done this. By our reckoning only twenty of Shakespeare's poems unambiguously concern a male (far fewer than is usually assumed.)[1] All of these occur among the first 126 poems as originally printed. Only about seven poems, all among the last twenty-eight, are unambiguously addressed to a female; for the remainder of the poems considered individually – that is without our being influenced

by their position relative to other poems in the collection – it is impossible to determine the sex of objects of the poet's sometimes conflicted real or imagined affections. Furthermore the title does not name an addressee, nor do any of the sonnets in the volume, unless we regard the unromantically and firmly masculine name 'Will' of Sonnets 134, 135, 136 and 143 as the name of the beloved as well as of the poet or his persona.

Shakespeare's collection is exceptional too in that whereas other sonneteers typically idealize the loved one, some of the persons in Shakespeare's collection (both male and female, and we should keep our minds open to there being more than one of each – Sonnet 31 refers pluralistically to 'the trophies of my lovers gone') are presented as seriously flawed in their appearance and behaviour (for example in Sonnets 127 and 130).[2]

Shakespeare's originality extends too to the content of the poems: some of them are far more explicit in their sexual references than other sonneteers', or indeed than most other poets' of the period writing in any other poetic form. We think for example of Sonnets 135 (with its obsessive repetition of the sexually loaded word 'will') and 151, of which the final words – 'for whose dear love I rise and fall' – might be spoken by the poet's penis. Sonnet 94, 'They that have power to hurt and will do none', stands apart from the rest of the collection as a philosophical enquiry in its own right. So does Sonnet 116, with its famous beginning 'Let me not to the marriage of true minds / Admit impediments.' Furthermore, although this poem is printed among those that are usually supposed to be addressed to a male, it is frequently read at heterosexual marriages and partnership ceremonies. And the great but damaged Sonnet 146, 'Poor soul, the centre of my sinful earth', would be more at home in a religious than in an amatory collection. There

---

[1] By our reckoning only the following sonnets, on the evidence of unambiguous pronouns, can confidently be identified as relating to male subjects (real or imagined): 1, 3, 6, 7, 9, 13, 16, 19, 20, 26, 33, 39, 41, 42, 63, 67, 68, 101, 108 and 126.

[2] As noted by Michael G. Spiller, *The Development of the Sonnet* (London, 1992), p. 156.

are formal irregularities, too: Sonnet 99 has fifteen instead of the usual fourteen lines, Sonnet 126 is a twelve-line poem written in rhyming couplets, and Sonnet 145 is written in iambic tetrameter.

Another important aspect of the originality of Shakespeare's collection is that, with only two exceptions, its poems are far less literary in origin than those of other Elizabethan sonneteers. Many of its supposed predecessors make extensive use of continental sources, especially poems by Petrarch and Ronsard. Shakespeare occasionally draws on his reading in, for instance, Erasmus and Ovid, but his poems contain few direct classical or other literary allusions, and only two of them depend heavily on a single literary source. These are the last two, both of which are straightforward though different reworkings of a single Greek epigram by Marianus Scholasticus, known probably through Latin translations. In English it reads:

Beneath these plane trees, detained by gentle slumber, Love slept, having put his torch in the care of the Nymphs; but the Nymphs said to one another 'Why wait? Would that together with this we could quench the fire in the hearts of men.' But the torch set fire even to the water, and with hot water thenceforth the Love-Nymphs fill the bath.[3]

Here, though nowhere else, Shakespeare is clearly conducting a literary exercise, as if he were a student required to translate the same poem in two different ways. Could it be that these two poems were written while Shakespeare was still at school, even before Sonnet 145 with its puns on 'hath' and 'away'? The references in the original poem to the bath in which maidens quench Cupid's ardent flame ought to dispose of the common notion that Shakespeare's Sonnets refer to the city of Bath. Even the idea that the cure effected for the 'strange maladies' of Sonnet 153 is of a venereal disease rather than simply of the pains that love brings is an inference (more plausible through Sonnet 153 than in Sonnet 154). The fact that the last two sonnets in the collection are translations, or imitations, ought to give us pause before interpreting them biographically. On the other hand, the collection's overall independence from literary models may support the belief that the poet is writing frequently from personal experience.

There are two other common beliefs that we should like to challenge. One is that the first seventeen of the Sonnets were written to commission by a mother who was anxious that her son should beget an heir. It is true that these sonnets are unusually closely related in subject matter, though there is no evidence of a commission. We challenge, too, the common assumption that the 'Mr W H' to whom Thomas Thorpe dedicated the volume is to be identified in any way with the poems' addressees. The notion that the 'begetter' of the Sonnets is the – and the only – male person to whom the poet addresses himself is not in our view substantiated by the poems themselves. In the first place 'begetter' could mean simply the procurer of the manuscript; and in the second place we shall argue for the plurality of addressees.

2

A selective survey of major biographical interpretations of these poems during the last decade will show how deeply ingrained are some of the preconceptions that we wish to challenge.

Park Honan takes an even-handed approach to the Sonnets in his 1998 biography.[4] He posits an either/or scenario by asking 'did he [Shakespeare] write lyrics to please a nobleman other than Henry Wriothesley?' (p. 181). This takes for granted the common belief that some of the poems are addressed to a young aristocrat, a dubious proposition. Honan goes on to consider, and obliquely to dismiss, the claims of William Herbert as the alternative to Wriothesley. He accepts the critical commonplaces that 'most of the first 126 sonnets focus on a lovely youth', that the poems paint 'their speaker's – or Poet's – portrait' (p. 185), and, whilst appreciative of the sonnets in the context of Shakespeare's wider creative output, still

---

[3] Quoted from *The Complete Sonnets and Poems*, ed. Colin Burrow (Oxford, 2002), p. 686.

[4] Park Honan, *Shakespeare: A Life* (Oxford, 1998).

perceives a narrative, albeit a 'slender' one: a 'triangular love-story of a Poet who loves a youth and a Dark Woman' (p. 186).

A year later, Anthony Holden's biography[5] separates the dedicatee of the Sonnets – whom he sees as the procurer of the manuscript – from their addressee, 'the fair youth'. Holden's survey of candidates for the Dark Lady especially notes the 1973 argument by A. L. Rowse in favour of Emilia Lanier. But Holden prefers 'to think of the Dark Lady in Shakespeare's own fictional terms' (p. 121), rooted in the character of Rosaline in *Love's Labour's Lost*, a play which Holden then goes on to read biographically, casting the Earl of Southampton as the King of Navarre and Shakespeare himself as Biron.

In Katherine Duncan-Jones's 1997 Arden edition (revised, 2010[6]) she assumes that only one 'young man' is involved, and during the course of seventeen of her introductory pages she assumes 'that "Mr. W. H." is the same individual as the original of the young man addressed and celebrated within the sonnets', and sets out 'the case for his being based on William Herbert' (pp. 56–7). She exaggerates what she calls the 'outrageous misogyny' (p. 49) of the 'dark lady' poems, describing Sonnets 127–152 as a consistent and misogynistic attack on a woman who 'has a muddy complexion, bad breath and a clumsy walk' (p. 47). Comparing this woman to Audrey in *As You Like It*, she says that 'Shakespeare's speaker seems, like Touchstone, to brag to other men in his audience that he can make satisfactory sexual use of a woman too stupid to realize that she is also being set up as the butt of his wit' (p. 47). But notice her evasion of the praise lavished on the mistress – whom she regards as 'no more than a sexual convenience' (p. 50) – in some of the sonnets she takes to task: 'And yet, by heaven, I think my love as rare / As any she belied with false compare', says the poet in Sonnet 130, and in Sonnet 132 he declares of the loved one

And truly, not the morning sun of heaven
Better becomes the gray cheeks of the east,
Nor that full star that ushers in the even
Doth half that glory to the sober west,
As those two mourning [black] eyes become thy face.

Sonnets 127, 128, 139 and 141 also include praise for their addressee. To suggest that these poems are uniformly misogynistic is simply wrong.

Duncan-Jones's dim view of the morality of the relationship between Shakespeare and 'the' mistress informs her further biographical claims that Shakespeare frequented a brothel kept by George Wilkins in Turnmill (also known as Turnbull) Street and that there he contracted syphilis, which she writes about in her 2001 book *Ungentle Shakespeare: Scenes from his Life*.[7] She combines what she calls 'graphic images of sweating tubs and venereal infection' with close references to the endings of *Troilus and Cressida* and *Shakespeare's Sonnets* in an attempt to support a supposition that Shakespeare's visits to Turnmill Street – all of them figments of her imagination – 'had left him with an unwanted legacy of infection, or at the very least, that he may have believed that they had done so' (p. 258).[8] Poetry does not always have to be informed by personal experience. And Duncan-Jones's speculations harden into filmic reality in the portrayal of a brothel called 'Cupid's Arrow' presided over by a distinctly seedy George Wilkins in William Boyd's 2005 BBC television screenplay *A Waste of Shame* on which she served as academic advisor for The Open University. Overt fictionalizations of Shakespeare's life are fine, but not when they claim academic authority.

Peter Ackroyd's 2005 critical handling of the Sonnets in relation to Shakespeare's life in his biography[9] gives as much as it takes away. He glimpses the Sonnets' plurality: 'the poems are perhaps best seen as a performance' (p. 287), and 'it is not even clear that the sonnets are addressed to

---

[5] Anthony Holden, *William Shakespeare* (London, 1999).

[6] References are to the revised edition.

[7] Katherine Duncan-Jones, *Ungentle Shakespeare: Scenes from his Life* (London, 2001); references are to the edition 'with additional material' (2010).

[8] Bizarrely she remarks that 'it makes very little difference whether, from about 1608, he was indeed venereally infected, or whether he merely thought he was' (p. 224). One might have thought that it would have made a great deal of difference to him.

[9] Peter Ackroyd, *Shakespeare: The Biography* (London, 2005).

the same persons throughout' (p. 286), and quotes John Donne's 'I did best when I had least truth for my subjects' (p. 287). At the same time, though, Ackroyd cannot resist listing different candidates for Mr W. H. (pp. 452–3), the rival poet and the Dark Lady (p. 288), and seems happy to wheel out Emilia Lanier and William Herbert as the most appropriate (pp. 284 and 289).

In 2007, Dympna Callaghan, in a study of the poems,[10] assumed three main protagonists: the mediated or unmediated voice of the poet (a real or imaginary 'Shakespeare'), the young man and the Dark Lady. Callaghan says 'it is typically assumed that the sonnets refer to a single male addressee rather than to different young men. Similarly the remainder of the poems, Sonnets 127–154, are understood to be about a single "woman color'd ill"' (p. 2). Although she admits these as assumptions, she continues as though they were facts, with the result that her readings are locked into a pre-determined biographical approach.

In the same year Tom MacFaul's *Male Friendship in Shakespeare and His Contemporaries* was published.[11] Like Callaghan, MacFaul acknowledges that 'some have questioned the prevailing view that the *Sonnets* have only one male addressee' (p. 30), whilst himself preferring to perceive only one. MacFaul consistently refers to 'the young man' and suggests that 'the sense of discontinuity may come from the fact that Shakespeare finds himself forced to reconstruct his addressee from poem to poem' (p. 30).

René Weis's vibrantly engaging *Shakespeare Revealed* (also published in 2007) seeks to find 'the dark lady', countenancing Emilia Lanier as 'the most plausible candidate'.[12] Weis imagines Shakespeare dispatching sonnets to the Earl of Southampton from Stratford to London in the plague years of 1593–94. Sonnet 104 becomes a 'birthday gift to the Earl, who was now officially of age' (p. 145). Christopher Marlowe is identified as the Rival Poet (p. 125) and Weis refers to 'the possibility that Marlowe and Southampton may have enjoyed ganymedic relations, neither of them for the first time and in Southampton's case probably not for the last' (p. 138). Weis's approach resembles

those of other critics who read the Sonnets as imperfectly concealed and intermittently coherent biography.

2007 also saw Germaine Greer turning to the Sonnets as a crucial resource for her to imagine the relationship between Shakespeare and his wife.[13] She suggests that Sonnet 27 might be a poem written by a strolling player who was missing his wife:

Weary with toil I haste me to my bed,
The dear repose for limbs with travel tired;
But then begins a journey in my head
To work my mind when body's work's expired:
For then my thoughts, from far where I abide,
Intend a zealous pilgrimage to thee,
And keep my drooping eyelids open wide,
Looking on darkness which the blind do see:
Save that my soul's imaginary sight
Presents thy shadow to my sightless view,
Which like a jewel hung in ghastly night
Makes black night beauteous, and her old face new.
    Lo, thus by day my limbs, by night my mind,
    For thee, and for myself, no quiet find.

This is valuable as an alternative interpretation. But by imposing her own biographical reading (albeit a fresh one), Greer does not quite succeed in defamiliarizing the poems from the long-ingrained contours of critical commonplaces. Take for instance the following summation:

All of which is not to say that Shakespeare's sonnets are addressed to his wife, but that perhaps once, before they were prepared for publication, some of them had been meant for her. Praise of the beloved for constancy, as in Sonnet 53, seems ill directed towards the young man. If Shakespeare assumed different masks for different sequences and different imagined readers, it is no more than we should expect. It seems not unreasonable that one of his masks was the aspect that he showed to his wife. (p. 262)

Greer admits plurality but does not fully detail which of the Sonnets she sees as being especially related to Mrs Shakespeare. Also, why should praise

---

[10] Dympna Callaghan, *Shakespeare's Sonnets* (Malden, 2007).

[11] Tom MacFaul, *Male Friendship in Shakespeare and His Contemporaries* (Cambridge, 2007).

[12] René Weis, *Shakespeare Revealed* (London, 2007).

[13] Germaine Greer, *Shakespeare's Wife* (London, 2007).

for constancy in Sonnet 53 be 'ill directed towards the [*sic*] young man'? Here Greer's characteristically deconstructive eye uncritically accepts a critical commonplace which could prompt at best an anti-male and at worst a homophobic critique.

Jonathan Bate's 2008 book *Soul of the Age*[14] appreciates that the Sonnets 'are more than anything else a drama of love's perplexity' (p. 219), and that 'Shakespeare's original intention was to circulate them among his private friends, so perhaps we should be content to let them remain private' (p. 220), but he himself cannot resist invading their privacy. William Herbert again becomes the candidate for Mr W. H. and John Davies bursts onto the scene as the rival poet, the scribe for the copy of the Sonnets that went to Thomas Thorpe the printer, and the author of *A Lover's Complaint*. Literary and historical biography become once again irresistibly conflated.

In surveying a sample of writings since 1997 which attempt to identify real life characters behind the personae of the Sonnets we look back with something almost like regret to 1996 and to Heather Dubrow's *Shakespeare Quarterly* article, '"Incertainties now crown themselves assur'd": The Politics of Plotting Shakespeare's Sonnets'.[15] There Dubrow pointed to the 'curiously positivistic claims' that the Sonnets have long attracted. 'In particular, critics who differ on many interpretive problems are nevertheless likely to agree that the direction of address of these poems can be established with certainty: the first 126 sonnets refer to and are generally addressed to the Friend, while the succeeding ones concern the Dark Lady' (p. 291). Dubrow is interested in how this 'generates assumptions about the presence of a linear plot', 'the basic assumptions' of which 'are still widely and firmly accepted' (pp. 291–2). Our survey shows how these same assumptions which Dubrow powerfully questioned in 1996 continue nevertheless to inform Shakespeare criticism and biography.

3

We do not deny that some of Shakespeare's Sonnets may refer outwards to events or facts that are likely to have been meaningful to the person or persons who first read them but whose significance is lost to us, and which indeed might not have been clear even to those who first bought the book. We accept Andrew Gurr's 1971 suggestion that the irregular Sonnet 145, with its puns on 'hate away', is likely to be a poem of Shakespeare's courtship.[16] This biographical reading seems plausible because it arises from a carefully focused close reading of an individual poem. We think it entirely reasonable to attempt to identify significant phrases such as 'the mortal moon hath her eclipse endured' (107), or 'Thou art thy mother's glass' (3), or 'In act thy bed-vow broke' (152), or 'every alien pen' (78), or 'that affable familiar ghost / Which nightly gulls him with intelligence' (86), but we think that each such referent should be considered on its own, not as part of an implied narrative affecting other sonnets in the collection. And we have to allow for the possibility that Shakespeare was imagining himself into fictitious situations that no one but himself would have known about, as if, for example, he were writing imaginary speeches from an unrealized play.

4

Dubrow's 1996 article might be regarded as a failed assassination attempt on the Young Man and the Dark Lady. We should now like to try out a renewed attack in the hope that it might kill them off once and for all.

Neither phrase is used among the 154 poems in the collection. 'Dark Lady' was first used in the eighteenth century and is laden with cultural assumptions; why not call her 'dark *woman*', for example? Any notion of 'the Dark Lady' can be

---

[14] Jonathan Bate, *Soul of the Age: The Life, Mind and World of William Shakespeare* (London, 2008).

[15] '"Incertainties now crown themselves assur'd": The Politics of Shakespeare's Sonnets', *Shakespeare Quarterly*, 47 (1996), 291–305; reprinted in James Schiffer, ed., *Shakespeare's Sonnets: Critical Essays* (New York and London, 1999).

[16] Andrew Gurr, 'Shakespeare's First Poem: Sonnet 145', *Essays in Criticism*, 21 (1971), 221–6.

based on only five sonnets, all of which suggest differently 'black' attributes. The mistress described in the third person in Sonnet 127 has a 'raven-black' brow and eyes; in Sonnet 130, she has (conditionally) 'black wires' for hair and 'dun'-coloured breasts. Sonnets 131, 132 and 147 directly address an intimate 'thee' (whose sex in these poems is not revealed), who does 'black' deeds (Sonnet 131), whose eyes, as though in mourning, 'have put on black', whose 'complexion' itself seems black and in mourning (Sonnet 132), and who is 'as black as hell, as dark as night' (Sonnet 147). The phrase 'woman coloured ill', who is the 'worser spirit' of Sonnet 144, might refer to any number of colours in costume, or make-up, or even to a sickly countenance. So, five sonnets refer to a subject who is 'black' and of those, three might be addressed to a male or female. In re-examining these sonnets it is important to notice the distinction between sonnets which are addressed *to* an imagined or real addressee and sonnets which are literally *about* a male or female object. Anyone interested in female identity will find among the collection just four which unequivocally discuss a female subject (127, 130, 138, 145), and only a further three which are directly and unambiguously addressed to a woman (139, 141 and 151).

What about 'the Young Man'? Four relevant categories of sonnets can be identified. First, six sonnets relate to a male subject in the third person (19, 33, 63, 67, 68 and 101). Only two of these suggest intimacy: 'my love' (Sonnet 19) and 'my sweet love' (Sonnet 63). Age is only intimated by Sonnet 63's 'his youthful morn'. Second, eight sonnets directly address an intimate male 'thee' (1, 3, 6, 7, 9, 20, 26 and 42). Sonnet 26 is the most explicit and refers to the 'lord of my love'. None of these sonnets refers to age. Third, two sonnets directly use the more formal pronoun 'you' (13 and 16), and one of these, Sonnet 13, refers to him as 'love' and 'dear my love'. Again, the age of this addressee is unknown. Fourth, three sonnets address a young and intimate male 'thee': Sonnet 41's 'straying youth', Sonnet 108's 'sweet boy' and Sonnet 126's 'lovely boy'. That makes six sonnets which are about male subjects (only one of whom

is described as young), and fourteen sonnets which are addressed directly to a male (only one of which refers to youthfulness and two of which refer to boyhood).

All of this adds up to the quite startling revelation that 'the Dark Lady' and 'the Young Man' who continue to enjoy the attention of critics, and who amble through Shakespearian biographies, can only be made tentatively (and inconsistently) present through a total of nine sonnets (41, 63, 108, 126, 127, 130, 131, 132 and 147). These nine poems are the only ones among all 154 which might excuse the conventional attempt to identify characteristics relating to a particular male or female addressee. Even then, it does not follow that these sonnets are about, or addressed to, only two subjects. Black hair is not the same as black deeds; a young man is not the same as a boy; looked at even more rigorously, three of these nine poems – Sonnets 131, 132 and 147 – could be addressed to either a male or a female. Margreta de Grazia drew attention to the sonnets' pronouns in her 1994 essay 'The Scandal of Shakespeare's Sonnets' when, in the course of defending John Benson against the charge of having tried 'to convert a male beloved to a female' in his 1640 volume, she pointed out that 'because none of the sonnets in question specifies the gender of the beloved, Benson had no reason to believe that a male beloved was intended'.[17] But, as with both Shakespeare's own Beatrice and Dubrow, no one has marked her.

With these critical lenses in place, we are now going to offer a reading of Sonnet 5 which, along with the rest of Sonnets 1 to 17, is usually assumed to be addressed to a man whom the poet is persuading to beget a child. If read as individual poems not all even of these sonnets can be confidently assigned to a male addressee. Consider Sonnet 5:

---

[17] Margreta de Grazia, 'The Scandal of Shakespeare's Sonnets', *Shakespeare Survey 46* (Cambridge, 1994), pp. 35–49; reprinted in James Schiffer, ed., *Shakespeare's Sonnets: Critical Essays* (New York and London, 1999) and in *Shakespeare and Sexuality*, ed. Catherine M. S. Alexander and Stanley Wells (Cambridge, 2001), pp. 146–69.

Those hours that with gentle work did frame
The lovely gaze where every eye doth dwell
Will play the tyrants to the very same,
And that unfair which fairly doth excel;
For never-resting time leads summer on
To hideous winter, and confounds him there,
Sap checked with frost, and lusty leaves quite gone,
Beauty o'er-snowed, and bareness everywhere.
Then were not summer's distillation left
A liquid prisoner pent in walls of glass,
Beauty's effect with beauty were bereft,
Nor it nor no remembrance what it was.
    But flowers distilled, though they with winter
      meet,
    Lose but their show; their substance still lives
      sweet.

There are no telling personal pronouns to signify a male addressee. Summer being led on to 'hideous winter' is gendered as masculine in line six, but that doesn't necessarily reveal anything about the addressee. Rather, the imagery of flowers being distilled by meeting with the by-now-masculinized winter is more suggestive of a female subject. Further ambiguity occurs in line eight with the reference to 'Beauty o'er-snowed, and bareness everywhere', where, as Colin Burrow points out in his exemplary Oxford edition, 'bareness' could imply 'barrenness'. This is surely a word more associated with the female than with the male body. At the epicentre of Sonnet 5, Shakespeare hints at a womb which is unable to bear children, as much as at a womb which should be desirous for them. And the final couplet could refer to a woman's inherent beauty which lives on in spite of age.

What about the so-called 'rival poet'? Traditional criticism of the Sonnets has regarded Sonnets 78–84 as a mini-sequence about a poet who is competing with Shakespeare for the attentions and affections of the masculine beloved. In our view only one of these sonnets is properly specific in alluding to another writer, that is Sonnet 83 in its statement that

There lives more life in one of your fair eyes
Than both your poets can in praise devise. (13–14)

How might this traditional grouping be differently considered? Why do these sonnets have to be about a 'rival poet'? Sonnet 78 refers to 'every alien pen' and 'others' works', which suggest rivalry in general. Sonnet 79 refers to 'whilst I alone', 'my verse alone', and says that 'my sick Muse doth give another place'. This sonnet seems to be more about the poet feeling unworthy to write well about the beloved than about another rival who is already so doing. Sonnet 80's 'a better spirit doth use your name' might refer to any rival in love – in the way that in *The Two Gentlemen of Verona* Sir Thurio might regard Proteus, for example, and contains no certain reference to a rival writer. Nothing at all suggests a rival writer; the phrase is 'better spirit'. In Sonnet 81 no rival of any kind is mentioned. Instead this sonnet itself becomes a transcendent work which, each time it is read, makes the lover present 'even in the mouths of men'. Sonnet 82's reference to 'the dedicated words which writers use' is again about rivalry in general, rather than an allusion to another, single poet. Sonnet 84 seems again to be about rivalry in general as well as an appreciation of how the addressee is a subject for writing.

So, let us reconsider Sonnet 83 with its reference to 'both your poets' in the light of biographical assumptions. First, even if we were to accept the notion of a mini-sequence from Sonnets 78 to 84, the most accurate observation we might make is that the poems are about rivalry in love. None of them unambiguously reveals the sex of the addressee. Sonnet criticism which accepts the generic division that all of the first 126 sonnets are addressed to a man presumably imagines a biographical love-triangle between two poets competing for the attentions of their male subject in this so-called 'rival poet' sequence.

Having critically relieved Sonnets 78 to 84 from the burden of this identification, we would now add that a reader confronted with Sonnet 83 on its own might be more likely to take it to be addressed to a female than to a male. It begins 'I never saw that you did painting need' (if nature, or, as Viola says, 'God did all'[18]); even in Shakespeare's time women were more likely to use cosmetics than men. Its beginning relates it closely to the end of Sonnet 82 in which the poet compares language to make-up and collapses the distinction between the two:

> Thou, truly fair, wert truly sympathized
> In true plain words by thy true-telling friend;
>   And their gross painting might be better used
>   Where cheeks need blood: in thee it is abused.
>   (11–14)

Earlier in the collection, the first line of Sonnet 20, 'A woman's face with nature's own hand painted', alludes to feminine use of cosmetics. Editors, as if wishing to deflect readers from supposing that the first line of Sonnet 83 is spoken to a woman, are liable to evade the cosmetic sense and to gloss 'painting' as a metaphor for 'decoration' or 'ornamental rhetoric' – so for example Stephen Booth (in his note on the same word in Sonnet 82) says 'description, depiction . . . decoration; adornment (i.e. extravagant praise').[19] Duncan-Jones suggests 'falsely profuse rhetoric' or 'delineation' and Helen Vendler takes 'painting' to mean 'praise'.[20] So Sonnet 83 is the only poem which might suggest a rival poet, and it remains ambiguous about the sex of its imagined addressee. We hope that we have here almost erased the rival poet's role in possible biographical readings and that at best he, – or indeed she – is now left gasping for life, and then only in so far as Sonnet 83 will allow.

5

So far we have been deconstructive. How could we adopt a more positive approach? Let us sketch some of the advantages of freeing ourselves from the traditional framework of discussion. One is that it enables a closer concentration on the poetical and rhetorical techniques that have gone into the creation of individual poems, on their form and style. Another is that it encourages us to see the poems within a broader perspective – for example, in relation to Shakespeare's plays, with which there are many links.[21] Furthermore it helps us to appreciate the originality of these poems. It should enable us to question the belief that in them Shakespeare speaks on his own behalf, even to countenance the possibility that he may at times be adopting an imagined female perspective.

★★★

So, to sum up, let us not speak of Shakespeare's Sonnets as 'a sonnet sequence'. Better to describe them as a 'collection'. Let us not assume they were written in the order in which they were first printed. Let us not assume the sex of the addressee of individual sonnets, unless this is revealed through personal pronouns or other forms of address. Let us use no proper names – and especially not Shakespeare's own – as if they have indisputable referents in the poems. Better to use 'poetic voice', or 'imagined "I"'. Let us not speak of 'the first seventeen sonnets' as if they formed an identifiable unit and as if they were necessarily the first to be composed. And above all, let us not speak of 'the young man', 'the dark lady' and 'the rival poet'. It is time for these three Shakespearian ghosts to be laid well and truly to rest. Virginia Woolf famously killed 'the angel in the house' (the idealized, domesticated woman) by flinging the bottle of ink at her whenever she started to appear. We propose that some of that same ink should be flung at the young man, the

---

18 *Twelfth Night*, 1.5.226.

19 Stephen Booth, ed., *Shakespeare's Sonnets* (New Haven and London, 1997).

20 Helen Vendler, *The Art of Shakespeare's Sonnets* (Cambridge, MA, 1997). A further thought. Why might not the word 'painting' in Sonnet 83 refer to visual painting, as in an oil painting or a miniature? The reference to 'both your poets' in close relationship to the 'life' of the 'fair eyes' might then mean the poet who writes about you and the poet who paints you. But, even granting this line as referring to a rival who writes poetry rather than paints does not make it form part of a mini-sequence of the six sonnets on either side of it.

21 See Chapter 7, 'The Sonnets as Theatre', in Paul Edmondson and Stanley Wells, *Shakespeare's Sonnets* (Oxford, 2004), pp. 82–104.

rival poet and the dark lady. To follow these pre-
cepts is to demand a far greater than usual degree
of accuracy in our criticism and readings of these
remarkable poems. Killing 'the young man', 'the
rival poet' and the 'dark lady' is a way of acknowledging the Sonnets' plurality and complexity, an
act of literary critical murder which by our indulgence will set the Sonnets free.

THE PROPERTIES OF WHITENESS: RENAISSANCE CLEOPATRAS FROM JODELLE TO SHAKESPEARE

PASCALE AEBISCHER

In 1974, an appendix in Janet Adelman's *The Common Liar* for the first time considered, with an unprecedented seriousness and application, the skin colour of Shakespeare's Cleopatra. Surveying the textual evidence, from Philo's condemnation of Cleopatra's 'tawny front' with which the play opens (1.1.6), through Cleopatra's reminder to Antony to 'Think on me, / That am with Phoebus' amorous pinches black' (1.5.27–8) to her assertion of white racial purity in her reference to her 'bluest veins' (2.5.29) and Antony's description of Cleopatra's 'white hand' (3.13.140),[1] Adelman was unable to pin Cleopatra down to a specific racial category. 'Perhaps all we can conclude', she wrote, 'is that Cleopatra's tawniness contributes to the sense of her ancient and mysterious sexuality, whether or not she is thought of as African.'[2]

Spurred on by the development of a strong school of postcolonial criticism and early modern race studies and by an increasingly strong popular reappropriation of the figure of Cleopatra as a black 'sister', more recent critics have been more readily inclined to ignore the evidence of Cleopatra's whiteness and insist, as does Mary Floyd-Wilson, on the 'conspicuous blackness' of Shakespeare's Cleopatra.[3] Ania Loomba was one of the critics who led the way with her description of Shakespeare's queen as 'the non-European, the outsider, the white man's ultimate "other"' who

embodies all the overlapping stereotypes of femininity and non-Europeans common in the language of colonialism . . . The images that cluster around Cleopatra are

specifically Orientalist in nature: her waywardness, emotionality, unreliability and exotic appeal are derived from the stereotypes that Said identifies as recurrent in that discourse.[4]

For Arthur Little, Shakespeare's is 'the only black Cleopatra to grace the pages of early modern drama'.[5] Imtiaz Habib equally sees her as a 'black

---

This article has evolved over several years and has benefited from the feedback and help of many colleagues and friends. Thanks are particularly due to Gordon Campbell, Jennifer Feather, Sarah Hatchuel, Farah Karim-Cooper, Rick Rylance and Catherine Thomas, whose feedback has left visible traces in my argument. Thanks are also due to Kate McLuskie, Tony Mortimer, Francesca Royster, Andrew van der Vlies and Rick Waswo for inviting me to present my work in seminars and lectures in Stratford, Fribourg, Geneva, Sheffield and, funded by the British Academy (to whom many thanks), Chicago.

[1] On Cleopatra's 'bluest veins' as an explicit assertion of her white racial purity, see Ania Loomba and Jonathan Burton, who trace the expression back to Inquisition terminology: 'The phrase "blue blood" is a translation of the Spanish *sangre azul*, a concept that evolved from the claims of Spanish families who declared they had never been contaminated by Moorish or Jewish blood' (*Race in Early Modern England: A Documentary Companion* (Houndmills, 2007), p. 16).

[2] Janet Adelman, *The Common Liar: An Essay on* Antony and Cleopatra (New Haven, 1973), pp. 187, 188.

[3] Mary Floyd-Wilson, 'Transmigrations: Crossing Regional and Gender Boundaries in *Antony and Cleopatra*', in *Enacting Gender on the English Renaissance Stage*, ed. Viviana Comensoli and Anne Russell (Urbana, 1999), pp. 75, 73, 77.

[4] Ania Loomba, *Gender, Race, Renaissance Drama* (Manchester, 1989), pp. 74, 78–9.

[5] Arthur L. Little, Jr., *Shakespeare Jungle Fever: National-Imperial Re-Visions of Race, Rape and Sacrifice* (Stanford, 2000), p. 167.

female subject',[6] and even though Geraldo U. de Sousa speaks of 'the Egyptians' dual racial nature', he, too, emphasizes Cleopatra's blackness and points out her connection to a fourteenth-century manuscript that 'depicts Cleopatra as black African'.[7] Cleopatra's physical indeterminacy in Shakespeare's play – what Lynda Boose in 1994 still called 'the unrepresentability of Cleopatra's racial status' – has thus become increasingly fixed.[8] By 2001, and in reaction against Mark Rylance's cross-dressed performance at the Globe in 1999, which she described as a 'cultural hijack' of the role of Cleopatra, Carol Rutter could vigorously argue for a critical and performative recovery of Cleopatra's blackness: 'I want to argue that Shakespeare wrote a black narrative at the centre of *Antony and Cleopatra*, a narrative marked by racial self-reference as explicit as Othello's.'[9]

Carol Rutter's determination to 'think black' about Shakespeare's Cleopatra and Francesca Royster's question, in *Becoming Cleopatra: The Shifting Image of an Icon*, 'Is Cleopatra Black?' are the critical context into which I want to insert my consideration of Cleopatra in the plays of Shakespeare's predecessors:[10] Etienne Jodelle's *Cléopâtre captive* (1553), Robert Garnier's *Marc Antoine* (1578), its translation into English as *Antonius* by Mary Sidney Herbert, the Countess of Pembroke (1590/1592)[11] and Samuel Daniel's *The Tragedy of Cleopatra* (1594). All four plays are concerned with the death of Cleopatra and follow Plutarch in either Jacques Amyot's translation or Thomas North's translation of Amyot. All four present distinct visions of Cleopatra, whose racial make-up, I will argue, is a crucial ingredient in the characterization of the queen as a body natural and body politic. As the dramatic representation of Cleopatra moves from sixteenth-century France to late Elizabethan England, some of the resplendence of Cleopatra's whiteness is lost in translation. From being a theatrical and cosmetic property that can index the wearer's exoticism or nobility, whiteness becomes a Petrarchan metaphor before disappearing altogether in Daniel's disembodied, exotic double of England's queen. Understanding the history of Cleopatra's whiteness in early modern French

and English drama has important implications for our understanding Shakespeare's portrayal of the queen, as I will suggest in my brief closing comments. When racial markers of whiteness reappear in Shakespeare's play, they regain the performative character they had possessed in the French text, but are set aside signifiers of blackness in such a way as to undermine any essentialist understanding of race.

As Francesca Royster reminds us in her important discussion of *Titus Andronicus*, in the early modern period white was not necessarily 'accepted ... as a kind of default setting for human skin color, regarding other races as deviations from this norm'.[12] 'Thinking black' about the sixteenth-century Cleopatra plays, therefore, requires us to stop taking the implied and ostensible whiteness of their queens for granted and to start questioning both *why* and *how* they are white. Bearing in mind Richard Dyer's contention that 'there is implicit racial resonance to the idea ... of sexual desire as itself dark',[13] 'thinking black' also requires us to consider Cleopatra's racial representation in relation to the sexuality she so conspicuously uses as a political tool in all the plays I want to consider.

---

6 Imtiaz Habib, *Shakespeare and Race: Postcolonial Praxis in the Early Modern Period* (Lanham, 2000), p. 158.

7 Geraldo U. de Sousa, *Shakespeare's Cross-Cultural Encounters* (Houndmills, 2002), p. 141.

8 Lynda E. Boose. '"The Getting of a Lawful Race": Racial Discourse in Early Modern England and the Unrepresentable Black Woman', in *Women, 'Race', & Writing in the Early Modern Period*, ed. Margo Hendricks and Patricia Parker (London, 1994), p. 47.

9 Carol Chillington Rutter, *Enter the Body: Women and Representation on Shakespeare's Stage* (London, 2001), pp. 88, 62.

10 Francesca T. Royster, *Becoming Cleopatra: The Shifting Image of an Icon* (New York and Houndmills, 2003), pp. 17–18.

11 Following the title-page of the 1595 edition of the tragedy, the play is often also referred to as *The Tragedie of Antonie*. I use the abbreviated title of the 1592 edition, which calls the play *Antonius: A Tragedie*.

12 Francesca T. Royster, 'White-limed Walls: Whiteness and Gothic Extremism in Shakespeare's *Titus Andronicus*', *Shakespeare Quarterly*, 51 (2000), 433–55.

13 Richard Dyer, *White* (London, 1997), p. 36.

PROPERTIES OF WHITENESS: JODELLE'S *CLÉOPÂTRE CAPTIVE* (1553)

Etienne Jodelle's *Cléopâtre captive* is the first of Shakespeare's dramatic pre-texts.[14] Staged in front of King Henri II and his court, in celebration of a military victory and a royal wedding in 1553,[15] the play is, in fact, the first neoclassical tragedy to be written and performed in French. Strikingly, in Jodelle's play, Cléopâtre's beauty is never described, nor is her skin colour referred to. Nevertheless, as I will argue, the conflict between Cléopâtre's political standing and her private femininity is articulated through the 'properties' – in both senses: the theatrical props and characteristics – of whiteness, which, as a signifier, evolves from denoting magnificence and exoticism to standing for innate royalty.

The first two acts of the play emphasize a contrast between the former pomp, pride and seductiveness of the Egyptian queen and her current state. Antoine's resentful ghost paints the picture of a serpentine and seductive Cléopâtre. In a striking iconographic reversal of the image of Cleopatra with the asp, it is Antoine who describes himself, at the beginning of the play, as 'nourishing at [his] breast [his] deadly female serpent' ('Nourissant en mon sein ma serpente meurtrière', 1.46). While Antoine thus associates Cléopâtre with a serpent, the Chorus links the queen's former seductive glory with Cléopâtre's garments which, when dressed as the goddess Isis, were of 'sumptuous white' (2.711):

> *Strophe* Elle qui orgueilleuse
> Le nom d'Isis portait,
> Qui de blancheur pompeuse
> Richement se vêtait,
> Comme Isis l'ancienne,
> Déesse Egyptienne,
> *Antistrophe* Ores presque en chemise,
> Qu'elle va déchirant   (2.709–16)

[*Strophe* She who in her pride took the name of Isis, who dressed richly in sumptuous white, like ancient Isis, the Egyptian Goddess, *Antistrophe* Now almost in her shift, which she is tearing]

Whiteness is a theatrical costume and is associated with the moment of Cléopâtre's greatest pride and arrogance, when she identified herself performatively with Egyptian exoticism and deity. Not for nothing were white garments, in sixteenth-century France, considered metonymic signifiers of their wearers' social superiority, considered 'representative of their person, as if inherent to their being, like veritable ontological attributes'.[16] Now, however, the *Antistrophe* of the Chorus says, the queen has exchanged her proud assumption of Egyptian whiteness for something far more secular and close to home: something that resembles a torn shift, which, by implication, is not of the same resplendent white. The transformation of the goddess ('la Déesse', 2.703) into an enslaved mistress ('l'esclave Maîtresse', 2.705) is articulated through a change of costume. The ripped-up undergarment Cléopâtre now appears in is a stage property that allows her to perform her new-found properties of humility, vulnerability and ordinariness. 'Sumptuous white', in Jodelle's play, is not a neutral signifier: it is magnificent, erotic and exotic and belongs to Cléopâtre's body politic. Cléopâtre's renunciation of it makes her more human, European (the 'chemise' is homely and French), and pitiable: in her shift, what we see is the body natural. The queen's vulnerability is underlined when she appears in person, with her hair cut and her chest torn and beaten, physical signifiers of grieving private femininity.

In the middle of the play, when Cléopâtre meets her antagonist, Octavian, the breasts she describes

---

[14] Etienne Jodelle, *Cléopâtre captive*, ed. Françoise Charpentier, Jean-Dominique Beaudin and José Sanchez (Mugron, 1990). All quotations from the play will refer to this edition, and all the translations are mine.

[15] For a discussion of the doubly festive circumstance of the premiere of *Cléopâtre captive* in spring 1553, see Enea Balmas, *Etienne Jodelle: Un Poeta del Rinascimento francese: la sua vita – il suo tempo* (Firenze, 1962), pp. 295–7. French dates in this essay follow the Julian calendar, whereas English dates follow the Gregorian calendar.

[16] Catherine Lanoë, *La Poudre et le fard: une histoire des cosmétiques de la renaissance aux lumières* (Seyssel, 2008), p. 246. All translations from Lanoë's work are mine.

as skinny and scratched ('ces deux mamelles, / Qu'ores tu vois maigres et déchirées', 3.882–3) signal her loss of political agency with which she tries to convince Octavian that she has indeed been reduced to the body natural of a feeble woman ('la pauvre faiblette', 3.863). The scene of the antagonists' encounter is remarkable for the thoroughly indecorous action it suggests between the lines. Having failed to sway Octavian and having been betrayed by her treasurer, Cléopâtre flings herself on the traitor and gives him the thorough hiding that left an indelible mark on Shakespeare's characterization of the temperamental queen.[17] Exhausted with the exertion of pulling the traitor Séleuque's hair, punching and kicking him, she then launches into a magnificent assertion of her power: 'moi, Reine d'ici, / De mon vassal accusée ainsi' – 'I, the Queen of this land / Thus accused by my vassal' (3.1033–4) – is unambiguous in its claim of authority. The episode serves as a turning-point in the play in which Cléopâtre's physical violence serves to wipe out Séleuque, upstage Octavian, and establish her body as flamboyantly strong, royal and female not so much in spite of as *because of* the marks of violence it bears. All the connotations of femininity as weak and concerned with motherhood and love rather than politics and honour are kicked out of existence by Cléopâtre's regal wrath. Her beautiful complexion, as the Chorus regretfully notes, might well be tarnished by deadly worries, complaints and a dry fever ('Quelles plaintes mortelles, / Quel souci meurtrissant ont terni son beau teint? / Ne l'avait pas assez la sèche fièvre atteint?', 4.1242–4), but this only emphasizes the way she has come to embody both vulnerability and a form of royalty that no longer connotes decadence and pride.

When Cléopâtre reassumes her royal robes and crown for her suicide in the last act, which takes place in her closet and is narrated by a messenger, this may therefore be read as an acknowledgement that the pomp of her robes and the whiteness of her deathly pallor are now no longer an effect of arrogance, but a right, paid for by her death. This reading of Cléopâtre's regal self-display is endorsed by Charmium's dying assertion that the suicide is an 'act of nobility that bears witness to Cléopâtre's descent from . . . a long line of Egyptian kings' (5.1490–2). No longer the abject body of a woman of tarnished complexion who has cut her hair, torn and beaten her chest, in death Cléopâtre's body is intact (5.1543) and pale ('blême', 5.1485); it is shrouded in a mystery which will baffle Octavian and force him to yield to Cléopâtre's constancy (5.1548). The disappearance of Cléopâtre's former pompous whiteness, the tearing of her body and her resumption of a smooth body surface and whiteness at the end of the play hence show her evolution from pride to humility and, through that humility, to a more intrinsic sense of royalty. It is her acknowledgement of female vulnerability that allows Cléopâtre to die in a whiteness that speaks, once more, of her nobility, mystery, transcendence of sexuality and ultimate invincibility to which even Octavian must give way. Whiteness, in Cléopâtre's final self-display, is the outward signifier of a moral and political victory: Jodelle's Cléopâtre succeeds in upstaging all the male players in this political theatre.

THE SAINTLY QUEEN: ROBERT GARNIER'S *MARC ANTOINE* (1578)

In the twenty-five years that separate Jodelle's play from the *Marc Antoine* of Robert Garnier,[18] France saw six wars of religion and, in 1572, the St Bartholomew's Day Massacre of several thousand Huguenots in Paris and across the country under the influence of Catherine de Médicis, who is also credited with introducing Italian courtly manners and whitening cosmetics into the Valois court.[19]

---

[17] See, in particular, Kenneth Muir, 'Elizabeth I, Jodelle and Cleopatra', *Renaissance Drama*, 2 (1969), 197–206.

[18] Robert Garnier, 'Marc Antoine', in *Robert Garnier: Two Tragedies*: Hippolyte *and* Marc Antoine, ed. Christine M. Hill and Mary G. Morrison (London, 1975), pp. 105–66. All references to the play cite this edition and the translations are mine, unless explicitly acknowledged as Pembroke's.

[19] Janine Garrison, *A History of Sixteenth-Century France, 1483–1598: Renaissance, Reformation and Rebellion*, trans. Richard Rex (Houndmills, 1995), p. 358; Lanoë, *La Poudre*, pp. 50, 242.

Marc Antoine is probably the play that was performed on 11 May 1578 at Saint-Maixent,[20] in one of the few years of peace in the period. The plays of Robert Garnier, a Catholic playwright who briefly became militant, are deeply marked by the internal divisions of his country. In his depiction of Cleopatre, the political responsibilities of the ruler towards her war-torn country are articulated through tropes of whiteness derived, on the one hand, from Petrarchan love poetry, popularized in France by the work of the 'Pléiade' poets, and on the other hand from ubiquitous Catholic iconography. The play portrays a shift from a secular sainthood associated with political and sexual power to a religiously inflected understanding of sainthood as a transcendence of human sexuality and vanity for the sake of a greater love. Once more, signifiers of whiteness play a key role in the dramatist's conception of the relationship between the queen's body and political power.

The play opens with Marc Antoine's lament, which portrays Cleopatre as a clichéd goddess of love poetry, whom he idolatrously adores (1.77, 104, 106), and as the exotic ruler of an alien fertile land, whom he desires. By Act 2, a cluster of references to racial markers make her skin colour a central issue at the same time as they deny the exoticism of Marc Antoine's desire-fuelled fantasies of Cleopatre and Egypt. Diomede, an Egyptian, laments Cleopatre's loss of beauty, which he links to the loss of power evident from the fact that her voice is no longer heard in Asia and 'black Africa' (2.100). Asia and the 'blackness' of Africa are in this way clearly dissociated from Cleopatre at the same time as their evocation as regions formerly under Cleopatre's influence establishes an oblique link between the white queen and the 'black' continents, between her white-skinned seductiveness and the black passions of Africa and Asia. Such a link is also suggested by Cleopatre's reference to the 'people burned with the rays of the Sun' ('les peuples brulez / Des rayons du Soleil', 2.461–62), which aligns Africans with the burning of the lovers' passion and of Cleopatre's own 'ardent jealousy' ('ardente jalousie', 2.464). That her complexion is nevertheless white is clear from

Eras's reference to the 'beautiful alabaster' (2.421) of her face, which she evokes in the context of Cleopatre's royal descent ('Race de tant de Rois', 2.423).

Most strikingly, her whiteness is in this scene identified with the beauty of a political *femme fatale* who causes the downfall of the powerful men she entraps. Diomede launches into a Petrarchan blazon of Cleopatre in which he itemizes the components of the Queen's 'saintly', golden-haired whiteness and concludes by redefining her features as military weapons to be used to 'fight against Octavius'. Her white beauty and seductiveness are thus represented as a means of political power:

> L'albastre qui blanchist sur son visage saint
> Et le vermeil coral qui ses deux lévres peint,
> La clairté de ses yeux, deux soleils de ce monde,
> Le fin or rayonnant dessur sa tresse blonde,
> Sa belle taille droitte, et ses frians attraits,
> Ne sont que feux ardans, que cordes, et que traits.
>
> (2.713–8)

[The alabaster that whitens on her saintly face and the red coral that paints her two lips, the lightness/brightness of her eyes, two suns of this world, the fine gold that shines on her blonde tresses, her beautiful straight waist, and her appetising attractions, are nothing but fires, ropes and arrows.]

As in Jodelle's play, Cleopatre's fair beauty is significantly located in the past. Diomede's blazon of Cleopatre's beauty serves as a way of lamenting Cleopatre's loss of this powerful weapon and the consequent misfortune of her people, since her willingness to use her 'amorous charms / To render Caesar a vassal to her will', would 'secure the sceptre for her and her descendants' ('si . . . elle avoit recours à ses amoureux charmes / Pour se rendre Cesar serf de ses volontez / . . . le sceptre [serait] asseuré pour elle et pour sa race', 2.735–40). As Marie-Madeleine Mouflard bluntly puts it, Diomede clearly sees Cleopatre's political

---

[20] See the entry of the *Journal* of Michel Le Riche as quoted by Marie-Madeleine Mouflard, *Robert Garnier, 1545–1590: L'Oeuvre* (La Roche-sur-Yon, 1963), p. 259.

responsibilities as extending to 'her prostitution to Caesar'.[21]

What is noteworthy in Diomede's blazon is the way it invites a reading of the whiteness that is key to Cleopatre's 'amorous charms' as *cosmetic*:[22] it appears that Marc Antoine is not entirely off the mark when complaining that the beautiful face that seduced him was 'feigned' and nothing but a 'mocking semblance' ('son visage feint', 1.16; 'le semblant moqueur', 1.111). The reference to whiteness in the blazon is not adjectival but a verb, whose grammatical subject is alabaster. Alabaster, in turn, does not seem to be used as a metaphor: what Diomede is describing corresponds to alabaster face powder, a whitening cosmetic.[23] Equally, the coral-coloured vermilion referred to is a cosmetic ingredient with which Cleopatre's lips used to be 'painted'.[24] The redness of her rouged lips is another signifier of whiteness, since rouge was used as a counterpoint to heighten the whiteness of the complexion.[25] Even the blonde hair, upon closer consideration, seems to have been enhanced: the fine gold on her hair is likely not to denote the hair itself, but fine gold jewellery or netting of the type worn by ladies at court in the 1570s.[26] The Cleopatre described here is accessorized and made up to look like the perfect embodiment of Renaissance ideals of female beauty, with the literal cosmetics used − alabaster, coral, gold − taken from the metaphorical repertoire of Petrarchan love poetry, so as to invite, as a political reality, the subjection of the lover that is a convention of that most fashionable of poetic styles in mid to late sixteenth-century France.[27]

The precious ingredients listed in the blazon have an additional meaning in the period: as Catherine Lanoë points out, such valuable and rare ingredients were seen as the outward signifiers of political power for the Renaissance prince, whose ability to purchase and use expensive cosmetics make his power visible on his face. Regardless of gender, cosmetics, in sixteenth-century France, were an external signifier of nobility and courtly values, the artificial whiteness of the skin testifying to and reaffirming its bearer's social rank.[28] Conversely, renouncing cosmetics gradually became a codified, even theatrical, way of enacting the transition from a courtly life to a life of retirement and contemplation.[29]

Cleopatre's alabaster face in Garnier's play, then, demands to be read as a combination of Petrarchan and political signifiers of femininity and power, both of which can be renounced in a theatrical ritual. For Garnier's Cleopatre, the Petrarchan lady's white-and-red beauty is a mask that can be put on for political and sexual purposes and that can just as easily be scraped and washed off. Cleopatre's tears, dishevelled hair and her beating and tearing-up of her stomach and breasts constitute a deliberate, ritualistic destruction of this constructed ideal of white princely beauty and

---

[21] Mouflard, *Robert Garnier*, p. 171, my translation.

[22] Significantly, the word 'cosmétique' enters the French language in 1555, as cosmetics become more important in French court culture. See Lanoë, *La Poudre*, p. 21.

[23] Fenja Gunn, *The Artificial Face: A History of Cosmetics* (Newton Abbot, 1973), p. 76, who notes that white powder was made not only from ceruse (white lead), but also 'from ground alabaster or starch with perfume added as an ingredient'. See also Christopher Hibbert, *The English: A Social History, 1066–1945* (London, 1987), p. 224.

[24] Farah Karim-Cooper, *Cosmetics in Shakespearean and Renaissance Drama* (Edinburgh, 2006), p. 23; Lanoë, *La Poudre*, p. 54.

[25] Lanoë, *La Poudre*, p. 49.

[26] See, for instance, the contemporary portrait of Diane de France, Duchesse d'Angoulême in the Musée Carnavalet, Paris, in which her hair is covered with delicate gold and pearl jewellery. For an account of similar fashions for caps or cauls 'made in net mesh of gold' at the Elizabethan court, see Georgine de Courtais, *Women's Headdress and Hairstyles in England from AD 600 to the Present Day* (London, 1973), p. 50. Maggie Angeloglou even suggests that 'gold dust' may have been used as a hair powder to lighten dark hair (*A History of Make-up* (London, 1970), p. 50).

[27] See Karim-Cooper's observation of how the authors of printed recipe manuals 'draw heavily upon this archetype of beauty repeatedly imaged in literature and art as they include in their cosmetic recipes ingredients such as flowers, stones, minerals and jewels that correspond to the common conceits found in many sixteenth and seventeenth-century love lyrics' (*Cosmetics*, p. 6).

[28] Lanoë, *La Poudre*, pp. 241, 246, 248.

[29] Lanoë, *La Poudre*, pp. 251–2.

frustrate Diomede's expectation of political prostitution. The Petrarchan cliché of 'saintliness' associated with Cleopatre's painted face here begins its transformation into the sanctity of the beautiful woman who, for the sake of a holy love ('nos saintes amours', 2.658), abnegates the worldly power and princely identity signified by the cosmetically whitened body, subjecting it to self-mortification. Whiteness, in this scene, begins its shift from signifying secular and erotic power towards a more metaphorical conception of inner purity.

Once Cleopatre's beauty has been destroyed, her body seems to disappear from the play. It is only with the messenger's account of Marc Antoine's suicide and his hoisting up to Cleopatre's monument at the end of Act 4 that Cleopatre's body is once more given tragic, if not queenly, standing. Tellingly, she is now no longer defined through her seductive whiteness but rather through her body's martyrdom for love. Even before Marc Antoine's suicide, the messenger says, Cleopatre in her grief has torn her stomach to the bone (4.1575). From Act 4 onwards, her grief is depicted as a form of martyrdom that sanctifies her love for Marc Antoine through its alignment with the Virgin Mary's selfless devotion to Christ. Certainly, her assertion that she is 'the unhappiest of all women' – 'malheureuse entre toutes les femmes' (4.1576) – cannot help but convey to Garnier's Catholic audience the Annunciation, as ritually repeated in the rosary prayer 'Hail Mary', in which the Virgin is greeted as 'bénie entre toutes les femmes' – 'blessed [art thou] amongst women'. Cleopatre's loss of her lover is, through this phrasing, figured as the opposite of Mary's gain of a son. By implication, then, she acquires the sexless nobility and whiteness of mind and body of the Virgin, whom Richard Dyer describes as 'a pure vessel for reproduction who is unsullied by the dark drives that reproduction entails'.[30]

Cleopatre's unvarnished, asexual, physicality is particularly striking in the messenger's description of the 'hideous' lovers' reunion in her monument, in which 'All the attention . . . is on her body in pain':[31]

Jamais rien si piteux au monde ne fut veu:
L'on montoit d'une corde Antoine peu à peu,
Que l'ame alloit laissant, sa barbe mal peignee,
Sa face et sa poitrine estoit de sang baignee;
Toutesfois tout hideux et mourant qu'il estoit
Ses yeux demy-couverts sur la Roine jettoit,
Luy tendoit les deux mains, se souleboit luy mesme,
Mais son corps retomboit d'une foiblesse extréme.
La miserable Dame, ayant les yeux mouïllez,
Les cheveux sur le front sans art esparpillez,
La poitrine de coups sanglantement plombee,
Se penchoit contre bas, à teste recourbee,
S'enlaçoit à la corde, et de tout son effort
Courageuse attiroit cet homme demy mort.
Le sang luy devaloit au visage de peine,
Les nerfs luy roidissoyent, elle estoit hors d'haleine.

(4.1634–49)

[Never was anything this pitiful seen on earth: they were pulling Antony up little by little with a rope, while he was letting go of his soul, his beard unkempt, his face and chest bathed in blood. Yet all hideous and dying as he was, he cast his half-closed eyes on the Queen, stretched his two hands towards her and raised himself up, but his body fell back because of his extreme weakness. The unhappy Lady, her eyes wet, her hair artlessly spread over her forehead, her chest beaten bloody with her strokes, was leaning down, her head bent, clasped the rope and with all her strength bravely pulled this half-dead man towards her. The effort made the blood rise to her face, her nerves stiffened, she was out of breath.]

The pathos-filled description stresses the lovers' physical suffering, down to the detail of Marc Antoine's unkempt beard and Cleopatre's bloodied chest, breathless flush and stiffened nerves, only to negate their sexuality and represent their love as transcending physicality. The early treacherousness of Cleopatre's artfully white 'feigned face' is now replaced with the simplicity of a flushed face distorted in effort and of hair that is 'artlessly' spread over the forehead. While courtly etiquette in sixteenth-century France required perfect

---

[30] Dyer, *White*, p. 29.

[31] Eve Rachele Sanders, *Gender and Literacy on Stage in Early Modern England* (Cambridge, 1998), p. 103.

control over one's facial expressions and emotions, Cleopatre in this scene lets go of courtly decorum and gives way to the expression of passion forbidden by aristocratic rules of behaviour.[32] The image of a limp, wounded male body hoisted with pulleys and surrounded by feeble, grieving women is that familiar from the thirteenth station of the cross: Jesus taken down from the cross in the presence of the grieving Virgin, now the unhappiest of all women, a devotional motif that was the object of meditation on Good Friday in every Catholic church.

Cleopatre's association with the grieving Virgin is carried over into the last act, where she sheds her role as a ruler and definitively identifies herself as the wife of Marc Antoine, whom she must join in death as a demonstration of their 'faithful love' (5.1950, 5.1944). She sends away her children to be looked after by the othered 'black Ethiops with curly hair' ('Ethiopes noirs aux cheveux refrisez', 5.1839). Like 'tearful Niobe' ('Larmoyante Niobe', 5.1886), she bewails her losses, marvelling that the 'stern heavens' refrain from transforming her into 'weeping marble' ('le ciel rigoureux / Ne me transforme point en un marbre pleureux', 5.1894–5). This reference to statuary, and specifically to the representation of a mother's grief over the loss of her children, compounds Cleopatre's visual connection with the Virgin Mary and her move from a Petrarchan and aristocratic to a Christian mode of white sainthood: in the final scene of the tragedy she adopts the physical and spiritual pose of the *pietà*, the familiar image, made famous by Michelangelo, of the distraught mother weeping over the corpse of her adult son. The kisses she gives him with her dried-out mouth are devoid of eroticism. Cleopatre now transforms Diomede's blazon of her beauty into an almost literal disassembly of her once so seductive body parts, which she consecrates to the embalming and incineration of Antony's corpse:

Je veux mille sanglots tirer de mes entrailles,
Et de mille regrets orner tes funerailles;
Tu auras mes cheveux pour tes oblations,
Et mes boüillantes pleurs pour tes effusions;

Mes yeux seront tes feux, car d'eux sortit la flamme
Qui t'embrasa le coeur amoureux de ta Dame.

(5.1976–81)

[I want to pull a thousand sobs out of my entrails, decorate your funeral with a thousand regrets, you shall have my hair for your oblations, and my boiling tears for your effusions, my eyes will be your fires, for from them emerged the flame which burnt the heart in love with your Lady.]

Lest we miss the point that this is a deliberate renunciation of sexuality, Cleopatre orders her women to similarly mortify their bodies because their beauties must not now be preserved for anyone (5.1986–9).

Having thus defaced herself, torn open her body and shed the golden tresses that had signified her white Petrarchan beauty and political power, Cleopatre has attained the moral, saintly whiteness of the Virgin Mary. Her self-mortification allows her to redirect attention to the prostate body of her lover in her blazon of Antony's body:

Que je vous baise donc, ô beaux yeux, ma lumiere!
O front, siege d'honneur! belle face guerriere!
O col, ô bras, ô mains, ô poitrine où la mort
Vient de faire (hà! mechef!) son parricide effort!

(5.1992–5)

[That I may then kiss you, oh beautiful eyes, my light! Oh forehead, seat of honour! Fair war-like face! Oh throat, oh arms, oh hands, oh chest where death has just (oh! misery!) made its parricidal attempt!]

The play articulates not only the Queen's abandonment of political and erotic power for the sake of a holier type of love, but also the redirection of the spectator's gaze from the painted female to the wounded male body as an object of contemplation and devotion. Garnier's tragedy transforms Cleopatra from the artificial whiteness of the Petrarchan lady to the artless spiritual whiteness of self-abnegation and the transcendence of 'dark' sexual desire as informed by a deeply Catholic, Mariological, aesthetic.

---

[32] Lanoë, *La Poudre*, p. 245.

LOST IN TRANSLATION:
PEMBROKE'S *ANTONIUS* (1590)

In view of Garnier's deployment of Catholic imagery in his play and his documented temporary allegiance to extremist Catholicism in France, it is surprising that Mary Sidney Herbert, the Countess of Pembroke, a 'spokesperson for the Protestant alliance' in England, should have chosen to translate this text in 1590.[33] The Countess of Pembroke's play was first published in 1592 alongside her translation of Philippe de Mornay's *Discourse of Life and Death*.[34] Because of the two texts' joint publication, and in view of Pembroke's additional (though unpublished) translation of Petrarch's *Triumph of Death*, Mary Ellen Lamb has concluded that the play reveals Pembroke's 'interest in the art of dying'. In Lamb's reading, which has proved so influential as to be adopted by most critics of Pembroke's translation up to and including Karen Raber in 2006,[35] the Countess's concern with women's heroic deaths was designed to counter the cultural perception of female authorship and speech as linked to sexual looseness: 'through translating works about women who died well, she cleansed her writing from the contamination of the illicit sexuality inherent in female authorship'.[36]

In order to establish Pembroke's status as 'a turning point in the development of the woman writer',[37] the tragedy has had to be salvaged from its condemnation, by earlier critics, as 'almost grotesque' and 'agonizingly bad poetry'.[38] The text's contorted, elliptical syntax – a result of Pembroke's condensation of Garnier's twelve-syllable alexandrines into an equivalent number of pentameter lines – is turned into a virtue in S. P. Cerasano and Marion Wynne-Davies's contention that this 'allowed for more naturalistic dialogue and, consequently, permitted [Pembroke] to strengthen the characterization with powerful and moving speeches. Cleopatra, in particular, becomes a believable and sympathetic protagonist, rather than a stereotypical villainess.'[39] Instead of stressing the 'faithfulness' of the line-by-line translation to the French original, critics now stress the 'independent artistry' of Pembroke's 'remarkably free'

translation:[40] for Eve Sanders, the Countess is 'an inventive and rigorous translator' whose 'style is pithy, direct and clear' and whose text 'marks an act of authorship'.[41] Following on from Sanders's analysis, Joyce Macdonald goes as far as to suggest that Pembroke 'radically . . . revises her French original . . . creating a virtually new work which emphasizes and vindicates the power of Cleopatra's sexuality'.[42] Most recent readings of Pembroke's tragedy thus see its primary context in the common gender of the protagonist and the translator and are keen to identify, in *Antonius*, features that allow for an interpretation of the play as 'a bold feminist statement'.[43]

A cornerstone of this interpretative strategy is the now almost commonplace suggestion that 'Cleopatra is set up in this translation as a wife

---

33 Margaret P. Hannay, *Philip's Phoenix: Mary Sidney, Countess of Pembroke* (Oxford, 1990), p. x. Pembroke's translation is based on the 1585 edition of Garnier's play. See Alexander Maclaren Witherspoon, *The Influence of Robert Garnier on Elizabethan Drama* (New Haven, 1924), p. 85. I follow Diane Purkiss, 'Introduction', *Three Tragedies by Renaissance Women*, ed. Diane Purkiss (Harmondsworth, 1998) in identifying the Countess by her title rather than her maiden name (p. xiv).

34 Victor Skretkowicz, 'Mary Sidney Herbert's *Antonius*, English Philhellenism and the Protestant Cause', *Women's Writing*, 6 (1999), 8.

35 Karen Raber, *Dramatic Difference: Gender, Class, and Genre in the Early Modern Closet Drama* (Newark, 2001), pp. 62–3.

36 Mary Ellen Lamb, *Gender and Authorship in the Sidney Circle* (Madison, 1990), p. 120.

37 Elaine V. Beilin, *Redeeming Eve: Women Writers of the English Renaissance* (Princeton, 1987), p. 121.

38 Marilyn L. Williamson, *Infinite Variety: Antony and Cleopatra in Renaissance Drama and Earlier Tradition* (Mystic, 1974), p. 133 and Russell E. Leavenworth, *Daniel's* Cleopatra: *A Critical Study* (Salzburg, 1974), p. 11.

39 S. P. Cerasano and Marion Wynne-Davies, '*The Tragedy of Antonie*: Mary Sidney, Countess of Pembroke', in *Renaissance Drama by Women: Texts and Documents*, ed. S. P. Cerasano and Marion Wynne-Davies (London, 1996), p. 16. All references to Pembroke's play will be to this edition, which uses the 1595 text as its copy-text.

40 Cerasano and Wynne-Davies, 'Mary Sidney', pp. 16, 15.

41 Sanders, *Gender and Literacy*, pp. 103, 110, 103.

42 Joyce Green Macdonald, *Women and Race in Early Modern Texts* (Cambridge, 2002), p. 37.

43 Skretkowicz, 'English Philhellenism', p. 7.

and mother' in order to purge her of her illicit sexuality.[44] Possibly one of the most difficult facts to face for anyone investigating Pembroke's translation with the hope of finding in it the 'bold feminist statement' resulting from her 'radical revision' of her source text, is that *Antonius* is astoundingly close to Garnier's *Marc Antoine* in line-by-line content. Stylistically, on the other hand, the condensation into blank verse leads to broken-up, contorted and compressed syntax that bears no relationship to the easy elegance and expansiveness of Garnier's alexandrines. Such modifications of the original content as there are in Pembroke's rendering happen within single lines rather than across a sentence, speech or scene. These subtle shifts of emphasis mostly hinge on Pembroke's selections from a range of synonyms, on deletions or additions of single words, or on changes in the subject of a sentence when an active construction is translated in a passive voice or *vice versa*. Often, these modifications are clearly the result of the formal constraints Pembroke has imposed on herself with her verse translation and are thus not meaningful. At other times, a change, for instance of 'Cleopatre' in Garnier (4.1593) to 'queen' in Pembroke (4.249), which would suggest a shift towards a political view of Cleopatra in the translation, is cancelled out by another change a few lines down, in which Garnier's 'Roine' (4.1628) is depoliticized by Pembroke's rendering of the term as 'she' (4.284). It is the more telling, therefore, that the most significant cluster of genuine revisions accrues precisely around Cleopatra's status as a wife, the holiness of her love and her illicit sexuality.

Contrary to expectation, Pembroke's interventions amount to a pretty much systematic denial of Cleopatra's wifeliness and a toning down of allusions to her sexuality and the sanctity of her love: looking for the vindication of Cleopatra's sexuality vaunted by Sanders and Macdonald, what I found in my word-by-word comparison of the two texts was a combination of extraordinary 'fidelity' to the original combined with sexual coyness. The subtle attenuation of Cleopatra's sexuality begins in Antoine's opening soliloquy, in which his complaints about Cleopatra's sexual duplicity are partly erased. Pembroke bizarrely translates Cleopatra's treacherous face – the 'visage feint' (1.16) or 'feigned face' – as 'feeble face', removing not only the allegation of Cleopatra's duplicity but also the first indication of her beauty's cosmetic constructedness. Cleopatra's 'blandices' (1.101), her 'flatteries,' are rendered simply as 'words' (1.101) and, most importantly, the implication of sexual betrayal inherent in Antoine's 'Cesar qu'elle va cherissant' (1.136) is removed in Pembroke's 'Caesar to please, whose grace she seeks to gain' (1.136).

It is in Act 2, in which Garnier's Cleopatra defends herself against accusations of sexual betrayal and counters these with an insistence on her marital bond with Antonie, that Pembroke's interventions are most obvious. Consistently, she finds ways of translating 'amie', which in early modern French carries a sexual meaning, in ways that remove this implication. 'D'avoir esté d'Antoine en son bonheur amie' (2.620) thus for instance becomes 'With Antonie in his good haps to share' (2.384), while 'moy . . . qui fut sa chere amie' (2.580) becomes 'I . . . who was his hope' (2.344). Yet more blatantly, wherever possible, Cleopatra's claim to marital status is denied in the translation. Pembroke shows great ingenuity in finding unambiguously non-marital alternatives to words and phrases such as 'alliance' (2.527), 'un amy si conjoint' (2.550), 'mon espous' (2.586 and 2.588), and 'Veuve de son amour' (2.673; also 5.1907), which all denote or connote marriage. The sober rendering of the last phrase as 'Without his love' (2.438; also 5.116) is the more remarkable since Pembroke elsewhere,

---

44 Irene Burgess, '"The Wreck of Order" in Early Modern Women's Drama', *Early Modern Literary Studies*, 6 (2001), 10.4. See also Cerasano and Wynne-Davies, 'Mary Sidney', p. 17; Danielle Clarke, 'The Politics of Translation and Gender in the Countess of Pembroke's *Antonie*', *Translation and Literature*, 6 (1997), 159; Lamb, *Gender and Authorship*, pp. 131–2; Skretkovicz, 'English Philhellenism', p. 7; Tina Krontiris, *Oppositional Voices: Women as Writers and Translators of Literature in the English Renaissance* (London, 1992), pp. 70–1. Krontiris is the only critic in this group to qualify her statement by noting that in the end the play shows Cleopatra's instincts as a lover to be stronger than her instincts as a mother (p. 72).

in a context unrelated to Cleopatra, has no trouble translating the expression 'L'univers captivant veuf de sa liberté' (4.1355) literally as 'Making the world *widow* of liberty' (4.12; my emphasis in both quotations). When Pembroke does translate words with a marital meaning accurately, this is either because the text requires a specific contrast, as in the opposition between Charmion's accusation 'Hardhearted mother!' and Cleopatra's riposte 'Wife, kindhearted, I' (1.320), or because Garnier's text undermines Cleopatra's marital pretensions, as in Charmion's 'And you, for some respect of wifely love / (Albee scarce wifely), lose your native land' (2.354–55). In the only instance in the entire play in which Pembroke adds a marital meaning, it is applied to Antonie's tomb, and not to Cleopatra, and furthermore refers to an action – 'To shed some tears upon a widow tomb' (2.386) – which Cleopatra refuses to do. Pembroke seems intent on undermining Cleopatra's insistence on her marriage to Antonie and on rendering the lovers' union as sexually neutral as possible.[45]

Hand-in-hand with this neutralization of Antonie and Cleopatra's relationship goes Pembroke's extermination of the few references to the 'saintliness' of either Cleopatra or her love. Her 'saintes amours' (2.658) hence become 'true loves' (2.422), her 'visage saint' (2.713) is 'her face' (2.477). This is not entirely the result of her general Protestant coyness about the use of the words 'saint' or 'holy', for Pembroke is quite happy for Octavius to speak of his 'holy' war against Antonie (4.100) and even to allow the affection of fellow-soldiers Antonie and Lucilius to be described as 'holy love' (3.112). It is *only* when applied to Cleopatra and to her all-too-pagan goddess/double Isis, who is turned from 'la sainte Isis' (5.1847) into 'good Isis' (5.57), that Pembroke shies away from saintliness.

Bearing in mind the importance Cleopatra's wifely status and her elevation of her love to 'holiness' have in Garnier's text, and the way Catholic Garnier makes use of both verbal and visual Mariological imagery in his final act, Pembroke's sabotage of this cluster of features strikes at the heart of Garnier's portrayal of Cleopatra. Even though, in

Pembroke's final act, Cleopatra retains most of her claims to wifely status and is even allowed a reference to her 'holy marriage' (5.155), Pembroke has done enough to render it difficult, if not impossible, to see in Cleopatra a figure of the Virgin of the thirteenth station of the cross and the *pietà*. This is not only so because of the revisions to Act 2 and the translation of the Marian allusion of 'malheureuse entre toutes les femmes' (4.1575) as the not remotely biblical 'Of women, her, the most unhappy called' (4.232), but also because of Pembroke's other major change to the tragedy: her shutting of Cleopatra into the genre of closet drama. All the available evidence about Pembroke's play suggests that its 'performance' was restricted to readings within a small circle.[46] Pembroke's tragedy was hence 'situated within a playreading *tradition* rooted in the humanist pedagogical program and thus predicated upon a model of readership as labor rather than leisure',[47] that is, a mode of reading that sought moral edification through the debates presented in dramatic dialogue rather than through the visual contemplation of bodies in conflict, grief or death. Hence Garnier's visual evocation of the *pietà*, with its consequent shift of Cleopatre from

---

45 In this context, it is revealing that, as Cerasano and Wynne-Davies note, 'Mary Sidney presented herself to the court as a woman of culture, and *not* as a wife and mother' (p. 13). For an interpretation that seeks to argue for heightened references to eroticism in Pembroke's translation, see Sanders, *Gender and Literacy*, pp. 115–16.

46 See Coburn Freer's well-substantiated hypothesis that 'a play like *Antony* would have been read in the manner of a production in a reader's theater, with different voices taking different parts . . . It is most unlikely that in such a performance there would have been either costumes or action' ('Countess of Pembroke: Mary Sidney', in *Women Writers of the Renaissance and Reformation*, ed. Katharina M. Wilson (Athens, GA, 1987), p. 486. See also Hannay, *Philip's Phoenix*, p. 120. Gweno Williams's attempt to argue for a performance history of Pembroke's play does not manage to produce any conclusive evidence ('Translating the Text, Performing the Self', in *Women and Dramatic Production, 1550–1700*, ed. Alison Findlay and Stephanie Hodgson-Wright (Harlow, 2000), pp. 15–41).

47 Marta Straznicky, 'Closet Drama', in *A Companion to Renaissance Drama*, ed. Arthur F. Kinney (Oxford, 2002), p. 422; emphasis in the original.

lover to mother and her iconographic transcendence as a martyr for love, is lost in translation. In comparison with the saintly martyr of Garnier's play, Pembroke's Cleopatra is secular and down-to-earth.

This is also borne out by a close look at how Pembroke deals with Cleopatra's whiteness. In the translation, Cleopatra's whiteness, along with her saintliness, remains a Petrarchan metaphor rather than a literal truth, a signifier of aristocratic status or an expression of spiritual purity. In Diomede's speech, the 'black Africa' ('l'Afrique noire' 2.700) of Garnier's text is turned into 'sunburnt Africke' (2.464), not only giving a climatic explanation for racial difference,[48] but also making it easier to see a continuity between the sunburn of Africans and the complexion of Egypt's Queen that may be subject to tanning. In his blazon, a very few, very focused alterations mean that Cleopatra's skin colour is less unambiguously white than in Garnier, reminding us that, as evident in the alabaster tomb of Bess of Hardwick in Derby Cathedral, the yellowish-brown variety of the stone was known and used in England to memorialize powerful noblewomen:

describing the physical process that enables Cleopatra to turn herself into a political/sexual weapon, what Pembroke provides is a conventional Petrarchan metaphor. The same is true of her Cleopatra's 'fine and flaming gold' hair: with the omission of 'dessur' ('on top of'), no trace is left of the gold accessories that made this metaphor literal in the French text. By translating 'peint' as 'engrains', Pembroke has removed the explicit reference to face-painting. The actual cosmetic ingredient of vermilion is furthermore replaced by the 'coral colour' that can denote naturally red lips. Still an idealized Petrarchan beauty, Pembroke's Cleopatra is no longer the regally white painted queen of the French text, whose face-paint suggests a political performance of the role of the Petrarchan mistress.

The reason for Pembroke's endeavour to turn literal face-paint into metaphorical whiteness and to neutralize Cleopatra's sexuality may be that in England any representation of this female monarch invited a comparison between Cleopatra and Elizabeth I. The English queen's 'red and white painted beauty . . . was a symbol of virtuous beauty' and 'a signifier of political authority and the stability of that authority',[49] to the extent that white

Antonius, 2.474–82	*Marc Antoine*, 2.711–18
She is all heavenly; never any man	Elle est toute celeste, et ne se voit personne
But seeing her **was ravished with her sight**	La pouvant contempler, **qu'elle ne passionne**
The **alabaster covering** of her face	**L'albastre qui blanchist** sur son visage **saint**
The **coral colour** her two lips **engrains**	Et le **vermeil coral** qui ses deux lévres **peint**
Her beamy eyes two suns of this our world	**La clairté de ses yeux**, deux soleils de ce monde
Of her fair hair the fine and flaming gold	Le fin or **rayonnant dessur** sa tresse blonde
Her brave straight stature, and her winning parts	Sa belle taille droitte, et ses frians attraits
Are nothing else but fires, fetters, darts	Ne sont que feux ardans, que cordes et que traits

The active force of Cleopatre's seductiveness is lost in the passive construction of 'was ravished with her sight'. Gone are the saintliness of Cleopatre's face and the light colouring of her eyes. More significantly, the single explicit reference to the whiteness of alabaster has disappeared. The 'alabaster covering' of Cleopatra's face in Pembroke's rendering appears more metaphorical than literal and could refer as much to smoothness as to colour: instead of

[48] On the commonplace climatic explanation of Africans' pigmentation in sixteenth-century Europe, see Alden T. Vaughan and Virginia Mason Vaughan, 'Before *Othello*: Elizabethan Representations of Sub-Saharan Africans', *The William and Mary Quarterly*, 54 (1997), 23.

[49] Karim-Cooper, *Cosmetics*, p. 18.

became a dominant colour at court in the 1590s.[50] In the 1590s in particular, ambassadors at Elizabeth's court had 'noted [the ageing queen's] extravagant attire and low-cut dresses' and reported that she was still using 'the "game" of courtship' as 'her most effective tool of policy'.[51] Hence the portrayal of a cosmetically whitened Cleopatra's active sexuality, especially when, as in Garnier, it is imbued with the conventions of courtly love and mixed in with politics, becomes a potentially dangerous comment on Elizabeth. It is this perception of Cleopatra as a potential focus for political anxieties which impelled Sir Fulke Greville to burn his own tragedy on the subject of Antony and Cleopatra for fear that it be 'construed, or strained to a personating of vices in the present Governors and Government'.[52] The portrayal of Cleopatra's decision to deface herself rather than enhance her physical attractions for political ends, as Garnier's Diomede suggests and Elizabeth practised, could be interpreted as an implied criticism of Elizabeth's increasingly indecorous mixture of flirtation and policy-making.

Pembroke's translation attenuates such criticism and, when the opportunity arises, enhances a passage which could be construed as flattering the queen. In her translation, Garnier's praise of Cleopatra's linguistic skills can be read as a more pointed allusion to Elizabeth's own facility with languages, as Garnier's

Mais encor ce n'est rien aupres des **artifices**
De son esprit divin, **ses mignardes blandices**, ...

(2.719–20)

is rendered as:

Yet this is nothing to th' **enchanting skills**
Of her celestial spirit, **her training speech**,
Her grace, her majesty, and forcing voice,
Whether she it with fingers' speech consort,
Or hearing sceptred kings' ambassadors
Answer to each in his own language make.

(2. 483–88)

Instead of the 'artifices' and 'mignardes blandices' or 'precious flatteries' of the French original, which both imply falsehood, Pembroke's text

gives us a more positive view of the Queen's speech and ability to persuade, for 'training', which Diane Purkiss glosses as 'alluring',[53] can also mean 'instructing' or 'drawn-out' (OED). With the additional translation of the assertion of Octavius's linguistic force in 'tout fremist a sa voix' ('everything shakes at the sound of his voice', 4.1370) as bland 'All Caesar do, both awe and honour bear' (4.27), it seems clear that Pembroke is reserving powerful speech for her Queen. Even though all these modifications in the translation can in no way be legitimately described as a 'radical revision', the context of the translation itself thus makes certain parts of the text resonate differently and gives the very act of translation and dissemination political significance. In that sense, Garnier's *Marc Antoine*, born out of the French wars of religion, and Pembroke's *Antonius*, a product of late Elizabethan court culture, are indeed different plays, with Pembroke's Cleopatra somewhat less saintly, less wifely, less artificially white than Garnier's, to suit her Protestant Elizabethan readership.

BEYOND REPRESENTATION: SAMUEL DANIEL'S *TRAGEDY OF CLEOPATRA* (1594)

Samuel Daniel's *Tragedy of Cleopatra* of 1594, which he links to Pembroke's play in his dedication, picks up where Pembroke left off and transforms the Egyptian queen into an intangible Elizabethan icon

---

[50] Little, *Shakespeare Jungle Fever*, p. 161.

[51] John Guy, 'Introduction. The 1590s: the Second Reign of Elizabeth I?', in *The Reign of Elizabeth I: Court and Culture in the Last Decade*, ed. John Guy (Cambridge, 1995), p. 3.

[52] Quoted in Clarke, 'The Politics of Translation', p. 155. See also Clarke's discussion of Greville's comments, 155–6. For readings of the play that see it as a topical intervention in contemporary political debates, see also Skretkowicz, 'English Philhellenism'; Anne Lake Prescott, 'Mary Sidney's French Sophocles: The Countess of Pembroke Reads Robert Garnier', in *Representing France and the French in Early Modern English Drama*, ed. Jean-Christophe Mayer (Cranbury, 2008), pp. 68–89; Anne Russell, 'The Politics of Print and *The Tragedie of Antonie*', *Research Opportunities in Medieval and Renaissance Drama*, 42 (2003), 92–100.

[53] Purkiss, 'Introduction', p. 192.

of female royalty.[54] As Daniel acknowledges in his dedication, the very act of literary production is political insofar as it demonstrates the ascendancy of 'great *Eliza*'s reign', which has 'bred' music that 'Might now be heard to *Tiber, Arne, and* Po: / That they might know how far the Thames doth out-go / The Music of declined *Italy*' (93, 94, 86–8). Daniel here suggests an English succession to impe-rial Rome, whose own succession to Egypt is, later in the play, couched in terms of the Tiber's domi-nation over the Nile (5.1702–29). Through Daniel's river imagery, Elizabeth, the fruitful mother of the arts, is flatteringly portrayed as the inheritor of both Octavius and Cleopatra, of the imperial West and the exotic, fertile East.

In recent criticism, Daniel's play has been described as an antagonistic gesture by the poet towards his patron and as a staging of 'the uni-versal condemnation of Cleopatra as an example of lust, vanity, and inconstancy', reinforced by the fact that 'the speeches of Daniel's Cleopatra resem-ble the dicta of conduct manuals'.[55] Mimi Dixon goes as far as to suggest that 'Daniel's play gives us an entirely different Cleopatra', 'a stereotypical femme fatale, who serves as a warning for men who love too much'.[56] While it is certainly true that much of the play is dedicated to a condemna-tion of the lust that has led to Cleopatra's downfall, these readings ignore the discrepancy between the former decadence that is thus condemned in the play and Daniel's portrayal of Cleopatra on her last day. As she is preparing for her death, Daniel's queen is an intrinsically royal and majestic figure whose intense anxiety for her children is second only to her deep – if admittedly belated – concern for the welfare of her country and her fierce sense of honour (1.94–8). If Daniel does indeed respond to his patron's translation in a critical manner, it is in order to counter her, and Garnier's, portrayal of Cleopatra's denial of responsibility towards chil-dren and country for the sake of love with a stress on Cleopatra's determination to put her duties as Egypt's queen above all else, in much the same way that Elizabeth liked to represent herself as renounc-ing private emotions for public duty. Reflecting the deepening anxieties provoked by the English

succession crisis, Daniel also goes one step fur-ther than Pembroke by emphasizing, through Cho-ruses and action, how Cleopatra's death entails the destruction of an entire native dynasty and how one of the queen's enduring concerns is the provision of an heir.

Throughout the play, Cleopatra consistently rep-resents her body natural as inextricably connected to her body politic. Her plea that Octavius should leave her, at the very least, 'The Kingdom of this poor distressed corse' (2.349) explicitly makes of her physical body the last surviving remnant of her country – Egypt, she said earlier, is already in the 'grave' (1.22). Cleopatra's politicization of her body is matched by Octavius's perception of her: he lays great stress on her status as a queen and suspects that she aims to deceive him *because* she is a queen: 'private men', he says, 'sound not the hearts of Princes / Whose actions oft bear con-trary pretences' (2.383–4). The duplicity of Daniel's Cleopatra is not sexual, but political, and therefore considered, even by her most entrenched enemy, as a sign of princely bearing.

Cleopatra's skilful use of her charms is portrayed by Daniel as one of her chief political strengths in a manner specifically designed to flatter Eliz-abeth. Daniel's Cleopatra is not only adept at manoeuvring her wooers, but her royal beauty is such that it transcends a boundary which Elizabeth had increasing trouble ignoring: her age. Though Daniel does, to an extent, follow Plutarch and his dramatic predecessors in speaking of Cleopatra's defacement through grief, and although he does, in passing, refer to her 'martyred breast' (2.303),

---

54 Samuel Daniel, 'The Tragedie of Cleopatra', in *The Com-plete Works In Verse and Prose of Samuel Daniel*, vol. 3, ed. Rev. Alexander B. Grosart (New York, 1963), pp. 21–94. All quotations from this play will refer to this edition. I am modernizing the spellings to establish an equivalence of practice between quotations from Pembroke and Daniel's plays.

55 Sanders, *Gender and Literacy*, pp. 119, 121.

56 Mimi Still Dixon, '"Not Know Me Yet?": Looking at Cleopatra in Three Renaissance Tragedies', in *The Female Tragic Hero in English Renaissance Drama*, ed. Naomi Liebler (New York, 2002), p. 81.

the chief obstacle to seduction for Cleopatra is not her self-mortification, but her age:

> And yet thou cam'st but in my beauties wane,
> When new appearing wrinkles of declining
> Wrought with the hand of years, seem'd to detain
> My graces light, as now but dimly shining,
> Even in the confines of mine age   (1.171–5).

Yet this supposed 'Autumn of [Cleopatra's] beauty' (1.181) does not get in the way of Antony loving her, nor does it stop her from unwittingly seducing Dolabella. If Pembroke did indeed tone down her Cleopatra's sexuality because of a concern about how Garnier's Queen would be received by her late Elizabethan readership, Daniel goes in the opposite direction by repeatedly stressing the continued attractiveness of Cleopatra, whom he ages beyond her historical thirty-six years at the time of her death. Daniel seems intent on showing how an ageing queen's persistent use of her charms can be a sign of political wisdom notwithstanding her advancing years.

In praising Cleopatra's beauty and drawing attention to the political uses to which it may be put, Daniel's Dolabella is the successor of Garnier's and Pembroke's Diomede. But where Diomede's blazon served the purpose of itemizing Cleopatra's beauty and codifying each of her features according to a strict Petrarchan model of feminine beauty, Dolabella's description conspicuously avoids pinning down any of Cleopatra's features. In fact, though this is the play in which most space is devoted to a praise of Cleopatra's attractiveness, this is also the play which, sexy wrinkles apart, manages not to give a single physical detail about her away. The queen's racial identity thus becomes the ultimate mystery of 'Mysterious Egypt' (4.1201). Though Cleopatra repeatedly speaks of her 'race' as denoting either her offspring or her ancestry, at no point does she use it in the modern sense, as denoting '[a] group of several tribes or peoples, forming a distinct ethnical stock' or '[o]ne of the great divisions of mankind, having certain physical peculiarities in common' – the earliest occurrences of the usage of the word 'race' with these meanings being dated by the OED to 1842 and

1774 respectively.[57] Daniel's Act 5 offers us a vague image of Cleopatra's utterly enchanting, but ultimately unrepresentable, racially elusive, exoticism and eroticism.

In that last act Cleopatra not only displays herself with all the accessories of pompous royalty, but she does so in a way that deliberately exoticizes her by making her Venus-like appearance the wonder of 'Asia' (5.1479). It is in her address to the asp that Cleopatra's exoticism and her affection for, if not connection with, Africa and the Nile becomes most obvious:

> O rarest beast (saith she) that Afric' breeds,
> How dearly welcome art thou unto me?
> The fairest creature that fair Nylus feeds
> Me thinks I see, in now beholding thee.
>   (5.1509–12)

Cleopatra's exoticism is what allows her to be both desirable and undefinable, always one step ahead and just out of the reach of the men who want to seize her. Appropriately, it is her exotic connection with Africa and the Nile which withdraws her from their grasp altogether. Having applied the asp to her arm, Cleopatra gently dies. Only once she is dead, Daniel tantalizingly gives us a glimpse of her skin while still, and forever, denying us any specific knowledge of her body:

Yet lo that face the wonder of her life,
Retains in death, a grace that graceth death,
Colour so lively, cheer so lovely rife,
That none would think such beauty could want breath.
And in that cheer th'impression of a smile,
Did seem to show she scorn'd death and Caesar,
As glorying that she could them both beguile,
And telling Death how much her death did please her.
                                  (5.1639–46)

The woman who in life had called herself a 'corse' is, in death, more lovely and 'lively-coloured' than ever: there is no trace, here, of the deathly pallor that had been such an important feature in Jodelle. In this disturbingly necrophilic description

---

57 On the early modern meanings of the word 'race', see Loomba and Burton, Race in Early Modern England, pp. 13–14.

in which everything is ultimately left to the reader's erotic imagination, Daniel's Cleopatra transcends age, race and death itself. Her smile speaks of her triumph over Octavius, but it also speaks of her triumph over representation: even in death, Daniel's Cleopatra is beyond the reach of anyone trying to pin down her body. 'The Kingdom of [her] . . . corse' (2.349) resolutely remains her own. 'Dying like a Queen' means eluding the 'control' of physical representation (4.1197–9).

Possibly the most extraordinary aspect of Cleopatra's death scene in Daniel's play is its insistent use of theatrical metaphor at the same time as theatricality is denied by the double remove at which the scene takes place, narrated, as it is, within the confines of a closet drama. Daniel's combination of theatricality and invisibility renders Cleopatra's race impossible to ascertain even though the whole play seems obsessed with the idea of Cleopatra's identity, of who her 'real' self is, of whether it is located in the body or the mind, in life or in death. This crisis of identity comes to a climax when we are told that her 'union of her self' in death is equivalent to 'perform[ing] that part / That hath so great a part of glory won' (5.1610) and that her dying words invoke the 'earth, the Theatre where I / Have acted this' (5.1623–4). Both death and life are thus presented as Cleopatra's 'act', her 'performance'.

What Daniel's theatrical metaphors, and his linking of theatricality to royalty, thus emphasize is the unknowability of Cleopatra's performative body. Ultimately, for Daniel's Cleopatra, royalty thus appears to entail freedom from the body and its physical representation altogether. His Cleopatra is known to us merely through her words and the effect she has on people around her – her 'self' is disembodied from the outset, always already dead, always already beyond gender, beyond age, beyond race; a sign whose referent is insistently out of reach. In that sense, closet drama is the only genre in which the body of the queen can be portrayed accurately, since a move into visibility would pin down her 'infinite variety' (Shakespeare, 2.2.242).[58] 'Thinking black' about Daniel's Cleopatra means acknowledging the void

of her racial representation: claiming, as does Mimi Dixon, that Daniel's Cleopatra is 'dangerously "other" . . . dark, seductive, exotic',[59] involves ignoring the fact that the queen's potent exoticism is, in this tragedy, carefully dissociated from skin colour. It is in Daniel's closet, at the farthest remove from intrusive gazes, that the Eurocentrism of the sixteenth-century dramatic and pictorial representations of Cleopatra is genuinely challenged for the first time by Daniel's implicit admission that the exotic, desirable 'other' is by definition beyond reach, beyond representation – that it is a fantasy. Revealingly, the features of this fantasized 'other' also almost perfectly fit the mould of the ultimate incarnation of the 'self' in the uncanny resemblance Daniel's Cleopatra bears to Elizabeth.

PROPERTIES OF RACE: SHAKESPEARE'S *ANTONY AND CLEOPATRA* (C.1606–07)

I deliberately invoke Shakespeare's 'infinite variety' at this point because his *Antony and Cleopatra*, and the controversies about racial casting it has given rise to, was the starting-point of this exploration of Cleopatra's body in sixteenth-century drama. As Jodelle's violent queen anticipates Cleopatra's rage against the hapless bearer of bad news in Shakespeare, and as Garnier's evocation of the 'Hail Mary' prepares for Shakespeare's use of a similar allusion to the Annunciation in her demand that the messenger 'Ram [his] fruitful tidings in [her] ears, / That long time have been barren' (2.5.24–5),[60] Daniel's tragedy with its unrepresentable, disembodied queen paves the way for Shakespeare's Cleopatra in yet another way. The body of Shakespeare's Cleopatra, like Daniel's, is beyond

---

58 Daniel was to revise his play under the influence of Shakespeare's *Antony and Cleopatra* as a stage play. This revision is beyond the scope of this article, which focuses on the background to Shakespeare's Cleopatra rather than on Shakespeare's influence on later representations.

59 Dixon, '"Not Know Me Yet?"', p. 83.

60 For a reading of this allusion, see Little, *Shakespeare Jungle Fever*, pp. 158–60.

representation, situated, as it were, in the gaps between the words the play consists of.[61] Understanding the history of Cleopatra's racial representation in the plays of Shakespeare's predecessors allows us to add a racial twist to the insights of the many critics who have commented on the elusiveness and theatricality of Shakespeare's Egyptian queen: not for nothing does Theodora Jankowski write of '[t]he dramatist Cleopatra',[62] for Shakespeare's queen is the culmination of a long line of Cleopatras who carefully stage-manage their appearance(s) and racial attributes. Crucial to this ability to stage herself is the lack of importance of Cleopatra's real, as opposed to her theatrical, body. As Linda Charnes cannily observes, 'descriptions of Cleopatra in [Shakespeare's] play are never more than descriptions of the effect she has on the onlooker'.[63] Meanwhile the woman herself stays beyond reach, hovering somewhere between the blackness of her 'tawny front' and the whiteness of her ladylike 'white hand' (1.1.6, 3.13.140), between being draped 'In th'habiliments of the goddess Isis' and needing to ask Charmian to 'cut [her] lace' (3.6.17, 1.3.71).

As these references to culturally specific sartorial markers demonstrate, racial identity, in Shakespeare's tragedy, is as dependent on properties as it is for Jodelle's queen in her royal Egyptian robes and her homely French shift. Cleopatra's beauty and exoticism, as Enobarbus's account of the queen's seduction of Antony on her barge famously shows, is expressed through extras, accessories, theatrical properties. The queen herself remains elusive. For Shakespeare's Cleopatra, racial characteristics, black *and* white, can be performed according to situation and need, regardless of the actual skin colour of the queen or the actor performing her: racial difference is not located in bodies, but in objects. Whiteness is thus denaturalized as the 'default setting for human skin colour';[64] it is as racially marked as is blackness and is harnessed whenever Cleopatra wishes to present herself as a Petrarchan mistress who demands the submission of her Roman lover, or when, as with the cutting of her lace, she appeals to the audience to identify with her actions and distress.

The implications for the debates with which I opened this article are twofold. Firstly, the play's performative approach to racial markers challenges casting decisions based on an essentialist understanding of race. As scripted, the part demands of a white-skinned actor that s/he be able to perform both white skin and tawny gypsyhood just as it demands of a dark-skinned actor that s/he be able to perform sunburn and blue veins: neither actor can assume a continuity between her/his racial identity and that of Cleopatra. If it is nevertheless important that black women be cast in the role – and I do think it is – then that has everything to do with present-day politics and cannot be justified as 'authentic' either by reference to Shakespeare's sources or to his characterization of the queen. We must accept that Shakespeare's Cleopatra is neither black nor white, but that should not stop us from appreciating the political significance of casting choices, nor should it fool us into thinking that, for a character like Cleopatra, any casting choice will ever be 'colourblind'.[65] Secondly, it becomes obvious that Cleopatra's politically and sexually motivated performances of race dismantle the binaries

---

[61] For Shakespeare's use of Daniel's play as a source, see Geoffrey Bullough, *Narrative and Dramatic Sources of Shakespeare*, vol. 5 (London, 1964), pp. 231–6; Arthur M. Z. Norman, 'Daniel's *The Tragedie of Cleopatra* and *Antony and Cleopatra*', *Shakespeare Quarterly*, 9 (1958), 11–18; Ernest Schanzer, 'Daniel's Revision of His *Cleopatra*', *Review of English Studies*, 8 (1957), 375–81; Muir, 'Elizabeth I, Jodelle and Cleopatra'; Michael Steppat, 'Shakespeare's Response to Dramatic Tradition in *Antony and Cleopatra*', in *Shakespeare: Text, Language, Criticism*, ed. Bernhard Fabian and Kurt Tetzeli von Rosador (Hildesheim, Zürich, New York, 1987), pp. 254–79; Brents Stirling, 'Cleopatra's Scene with Seleucus: Plutarch, Daniel, and Shakespeare', *Shakespeare Quarterly*, 15 (1964), 299–311.

[62] Theodora A. Jankowksi, *Women in Power in the Early Modern Drama* (Urbana and Chicago, 1992), p. 161.

[63] Linda Charnes, *Notorious Identity: Materializing the Subject in Shakespeare* (London, 1993), p. 127.

[64] Royster, 'White-Limed Walls', p. 433.

[65] See Harry J. Lennix's recent denunciation of supposedly colourblind casting as 'the very definition of irresponsibility' in 'A Black Actor's Guide to the Scottish Play, or, Why *Macbeth* Matters', in *Weyward Macbeth: Intersections of Race and Performance*, ed. Scott L. Newstok and Ayanna Thompson (New York, 2010), p. 114.

of Rome vs. Egypt, self vs. other which Romans and critical tradition alike have used as a means of fixing her identity. For Shakespeare's theatrical queen, a 'wonderful piece of work' that carefully constructs itself anew in every scene (1.2.145–6), racial attributes are not properties that are embodied, but theatrical properties to be deployed and discarded at will.

'THIS IS THE STRANGERS' CASE': THE UTOPIC DISSONANCE OF SHAKESPEARE'S CONTRIBUTION TO *SIR THOMAS MORE*

MARGARET TUDEAU-CLAYTON

'Your "if" is the only peacemaker; much virtue in "if".'
As You Like It, 5.4.100–1

I. PARLIAMENTARY DEBATE AND PLAYTEXT: IRRECONCILABLE 'ARGUMENTS ON BOTH SIDES'

In March 1593 a bill was introduced for debate in the House of Commons 'against Aliens selling by way of retail any Foreign Commodities'.[1] The debate broadened to address the place of 'aliens' in the city – whether to 'entertain' or expel them – as well as their impact on the economy – whether, for instance, they were to blame for the 'beggaring' of 'home' retailers and the draining of English coin from England. Adapting the classical *topoi* of *honestas* and *utilitas* – moral honour and expediency – '[a]rguments on both sides' were made, for the bill on behalf of the shopkeepers and freemen of the 'City of *London*' who had introduced it, and against the bill on behalf of 'the Strangers'. As Walter Ralegh, himself fiercely hostile to the strangers, would summarize two days later, those who argued against the bill did so on the grounds of charity, honour and profit. Honour and profit had been urged principally by Sir John Wolley who argued that 'the Riches and renown of the City cometh by entertaining of Strangers, and giving liberty unto them', citing the examples of Antwerp and Venice that thereby 'gained all the intercourse of the World' – an argument echoed, as James Shapiro has noted, by Antonio of Venice in *The Merchant of Venice*.[2] Charity had subsequently been urged by

the member for Canterbury, Henry Finch, whose closing appeal 'so let us do as we would be done

I am grateful to the *Shakespeare Survey*'s reader for raising important questions and to Paul Seaward and Andrew Thrush for helping me answer them.

[1] All quotations from *The Journals of all the Parliaments during the reign of Queen Elizabeth collected by Sir Simonds D'Ewes* (London, 1682), pp. 505–11. Compiled sometime before 1630, the journals, though incomplete, are judged generally reliable. With reference to this debate D'Ewes comments that the speeches, 'being omitted in the original Journal-Book of the House of Commons, are *in respect of the great weight of this matter touching Aliens*... supplied out of the... Anonymous Journal' (my emphasis). This unique anonymous journal of the 1593 parliamentary session, which, like the 'original Journal-Book', is now lost, is itself indicative of interest in, and circulation of the contents of the debates; this is underscored by the several extant copies made from it. The most substantial is reproduced in *Proceedings of the Parliaments of Elizabeth I*, ed. T. E. Hartley, 3 vols. (London and New York, 1981–95), vol. 3, pp. 134–48. Scholars' accounts of the debate are necessarily selective; the most detailed are: Irene Scouloudi, *Returns of Strangers in the Metropolis: 1593, 1627, 1635, 1639: A Study of an Active Minority* (London, 1985), pp. 64–71; David Dean, *Law-making and Society in Late Elizabethan England* (Cambridge, 1996), pp. 155–7. Traces of earlier attempts to pass similar bills are recorded in Hartley, *Proceedings*, vol. 2, p. 95 (1585), p. 399 (1587); pp. 480–3 (1589; see note 39).

[2] Antonio: 'the commodity that strangers have / With us in Venice... the trade and profit of the city / Consisteth of all nations'. *Merchant*, 3.3.27–31. See James Shapiro, *Shakespeare and the Jews* (New York, 1996), p. 183. The case for the implication of *Merchant* in the 'alien' question has been argued, though without reference to the parliamentary debate, in Andrew Tretiak, 'The Merchant of Venice and the "Alien" Question', *Review of English Studies*, 5 (1929), 402–9; and John Michael Archer, *Citizen Shakespeare. Freemen and Aliens in the Language of the Plays* (New York and Basingstoke, 2005), pp. 39–46.

unto' finds echo, as others have noted, in the contribution to the playtext of *Sir Thomas More* by 'Hand D', widely, if not unanimously, agreed today to be Shakespeare's.[3]

What has not been observed is, first, that 'Hand D' – let us suppose Shakespeare – re-presents Finch's appeal as a response of conviction – 'Faith, a says true. Let us do as we may be done by' (6.156) – uttered by a stage audience of xenophobic artisan-citizens moved to a change of heart by the eponymous protagonist's representation of 'the strangers' case' (154); second, that, in making this case, Shakespeare's More echoes the hypothetical mode used by Finch to urge his appeal. 'They are strangers now, we may be strangers hereafter' Finch had urged, grounding his hypothetical case, as we shall see, on collective memory of persecution and exile as well as biblical precedent, while the figure of More, summoning likewise a hypothetical future experience of exile and persecution for his audience of citizens, calls upon them rhetorically: '[w]hat would you think / To be thus used? This is the strangers' case' (153–4). If Finch's 'we' has become More's 'you', both speakers project a hypothetical change of case, from subject/citizen/insider to object/stranger/outsider, which they invite their respective xenophobic citizen audiences to imagine as theirs in order to produce a change of heart from a will to violent exclusion to a will to the mutual charity of the biblical exhortation. This is itself a call to an ethical praxis grounded on the exercise of self-splitting in a subjunctive as well as hypothetical mode – imagining oneself as the object of one's (consequently charitable) actions as subject: 'Whatsoever ye would that men should do unto you, even so do unto them; for this is the Law and the Prophets'.[4]

If, however, Shakespeare's More succeeds in his efforts at persuasion Henry Finch did not. No change of heart took place in the House of Commons where the appeal on behalf of the strangers was met with counter-appeals to 'our Countreymens grief'.[5] Shakespeare's re-presentation of Finch's appeal as a response of conviction is thus itself an exercise in the hypothetical mode,

imagining Finch's as the 'decisive argument' that it is taken to have been by the playtext's Revels editors, no doubt misled by Hand D.[6] For, if the bill was eventually rejected by the House of

---

[3] First noted without comment in P. Maas, 'Henry Finch and Shakespeare', *Review of English Studies*, 4 (1953), 142, the echo has been almost entirely ignored by subsequent scholarship. The Revels editors take it as indicative of the 1593 date of composition but without considering its extent and implications. See *Sir Thomas More*, ed. Vittorio Gabrieli and Giorgio Melchiori (Manchester and New York, 1990), pp. 26–7. The specificity of the echo is questioned by B. J. Sokol who cites a speech, perhaps from an earlier debate (discussed below), and a sermon preached not in 1572 as he assumes, but in 1594 (discussed below), which separately express ideas combined by Finch and echoed by Shakespeare. B. J. Sokol, *Shakespeare and Tolerance* (Cambridge, 2008), pp. 60–3. Scott McMillin does not mention the parliamentary debate, though he takes the general parallels with the context of anti-alien agitation as evidence of the 1592–93 date of the composition of the original play, if not of the revisions; Scott McMillin, *The Elizabethan Theatre and 'The Book of Sir Thomas More'* (Ithaca and London, 1987). McMillin is followed by Lloyd Edward Kermode who, again, does not mention the debate, though it is germane to his subject. Lloyd Edward Kermode, *Aliens and Englishness in Elizabethan Drama* (Cambridge, 2009), pp. 76–8. The 1592–93 date is questioned, though not the authorship, most recently in MacDonald P. Jackson, 'The Date and Authorship of Hand D's contribution to *Sir Thomas More*: Evidence from "Literature Online"', *Shakespeare Survey 59* (Cambridge, 2006), pp. 69–78. Jackson adds to the linguistic and textual evidence for the later date of 1603 (which is also preferred by the Oxford editors), admirably summarized in Brian Vickers, *Shakespeare, Co-Author* (Oxford, 2002), pp. 36–43, 87–90, 128–9, 131–2. It is presumably in part because he assumes this date for the revisions as well as 1600 for the original version that John Jowett makes no mention of the parliamentary debate in his recent Arden edition of the playtext, *Sir Thomas More*, ed. John Jowett (London, 2011). The linguistic evidence is impressive and if what follows raises again the question of date, it is important to bear in mind that extant copies of the anonymous journal date from the early seventeenth century: Hartley, *Proceedings* vol. 3, pp. xi–xii.

[4] Matthew 7.12 (from the Sermon on the Mount) as given in the 1552 edition of *The Book of Common Prayer* where it features as one of the 'sentences' to be spoken before the taking of communion. Subsequent biblical quotations are taken from the Authorized King James Bible (1611).

[5] D'Ewes, *The Journals*, p. 507.

[6] *Sir Thomas More*, ed. Gabrieli and Melchiori, note to line 152.

Lords,[7] it was passed by a substantial majority in the House of Commons.[8] Its subsequent suppression triggered considerable social unrest, if not the 'Citizens . . . in uproar' that one of the supporters of the bill had envisaged[9] and that Shakespeare stages as contained by a reprise of Finch's argument in the speeches of his More.

In taking a stand on behalf of strangers Henry Finch and Shakespeare align themselves, like the House of Lords, with court policy.[10] In the case of Shakespeare's More this is underscored by the line of his argument foregrounded by critics, namely the imperative of obedience to royal authority (6.101–28).[11] Though not voiced in the parliamentary debate, this imperative was implicit as 'royal power and prerogative' were one of the stakes in the recurring conflict between court and parliament/city over strangers or 'aliens'.[12] In the play-text this line of argument is shadowed, as others have commented, by the irony of More's own subsequent refusal to submit to royal authority.[13] The irony is pointed up by other authorial hands who capitalize on its implications by drawing a parallel between the death of More and the death of the rebel citizen leader Lincoln (see below). At the same time, More's own later case serves to strengthen his second, relatively neglected line of argument which directly concerns the strangers. For More himself becomes a stranger when exiled from court, 'estranged', as he puts it, 'from great men's looks' (14.131).[14] His own case, that is, illustrates the contingency of 'the strangers' case', which is crucial to his, as it is to Henry Finch's argument on behalf of strangers.

This will be recalled in the last of the history plays in which Shakespeare had a 'hand', *Henry VIII* (*All is True*). Indeed, the contribution to the earlier play is precisely recalled by an echo of the resonant image of 'men, like ravenous fishes' (6.96), which Shakespeare's More uses to represent the generalized state of predatory mutual destruction that would follow were the citizens to achieve their will to the violent exclusion of strangers. In a similar hypothetical mode – '[i]f I am / Traduced' (1.2.72–3) – Cardinal Wolsey, in the later play, describes as 'rav'nous fishes' (80)

'malicious censurers' (79) who would thus seek to do him harm through misinterpretation of his

---

[7] 'House of Lords Journal Volume 2: 31 March 1593', *Journal of the House of Lords: volume 2: 1578–1614* (1767–1830), p. 184, www.british-history.ac.uk/report.aspx?compid=28189 (date accessed, 18 May 2011). See W. Chitty, 'Aliens in England in the Sixteenth Century', *Race*, 8 (1966–67), 141; Laura Hunt Yungblut, *Strangers Settled Here Amongst Us: Policies, Perceptions and the Presence of Aliens in Elizabethan England* (London and New York, 1996), p. 41; Andrew Pettegree, *Foreign Protestant Communities in Sixteenth Century London* (Oxford, 1986), pp. 291–2; Dean, *Law-making*, p. 157. Dean cites economic motives for the suppression and points out that no further such bills were introduced under Elizabeth.

[8] According to D'Ewes a majority of 80 (D'Ewes, *The Journals*, p. 511), according to the version reproduced by Hartley a majority of 40 (Hartley, *Proceedings*, vol. 3, p. 148).

[9] 'The Exclamations of the City are exceeding pitiful and great against these Strangers', and, if many hadn't already returned home, 'the Citizens would have been in uproar against them: The which if the Government of the City repress not, they will be apt enough to it' (D'Ewes, *The Journals*, p. 506). For the unrest that followed the suppression of the bill, see Chitty, 'Aliens', pp. 141–2; Yungblut, *Strangers Settled*, pp. 41–2, and below.

[10] As Yungblut shows, court policy was divided between security fears and economic interests which finally tipped the balance in favour of the alien communities: Yungblut, *Strangers Settled*, pp. 61–94; see too Pettegree, *Foreign Protestant Communities*, especially pp. 262–309.

[11] This critical focus goes with the ongoing assumption that the central theme of Shakespeare's contribution with parallels elsewhere in the corpus is the threat of revolt against a ruler and the attendant disorder. This has not been questioned since it was first proposed by R. W. Chambers in 'Shakespeare and the Play of *More*', in *Man's Unconquerable Mind* (London, 1939), pp. 204–49.

[12] Yungblut, *Strangers Settled*, p. 63. This may well have been one of the reasons for the interest in the debate. The parliamentary historian Andrew Thrush has suggested (in private communication) that 'the level of interest in acquiring copies of speeches may have been directly related to the level of conflict between the Monarch and the House of Commons'. For the interest indicated by the extant copies, see note 1.

[13] Among others, Vittorio Gabrieli, '*Sir Thomas More*: Sources, Characters, Ideas', *Moreana*, 23 (1986), 32.

[14] Robert Miola points out the parallel, though it tends to contradict the view he expresses earlier that Shakespeare appears not to have read the rest of the playtext. Robert B. Miola, 'Shakespeare and *The Book of Sir Thomas More*', *Moreana*, 48 (2011), 28.

actions.[15] The mutual destructive violence that More figures in this image represents, as we shall see, the negative counterpart or double of the mutual benevolence to which he calls xenophobic citizens, urging, like Finch, the contingency of the strangers' case. In the later play this contingency is urged through the re-presentation of the case of More as one in a series of change of case, or fall, from insider at court to outsider/stranger and/or heretic, exemplified by Buckingham and Katherine as well as by More's predecessor Wolsey whose expressed hope that More may 'do justice / For truth's sake and his conscience' (3.2.397–8) resonates with the irony of the future history dramatized in the earlier play. Highlighting through repetition the shared case of those who have viewed each other as antagonists (notably Katherine and Wolsey), the later play again calls for the recognition of kinship beyond differences and a consequent practice of mutual charity. If, in the earlier play, the appeal is to a common humanity beyond the differences between citizen and stranger, as we shall see, the appeal in the later play is rather to a common Christian identity beyond the differences that find their origin in the historical moment to which the play returns. Like the earlier play's appeal on behalf of strangers, the later play's appeal for reconciliation across the religious divide was again in line with royal policy – here James's aspiration to a reconciled Christendom – and again at odds with the sympathies of city and parliament.[16]

As well as this likeness, the hypothetical, 'put case' mode of argument used by Shakespeare's More finds telling parallels and echoes both within the Shakespearian corpus and within the playtext. For if change of case – from insider/subject to outsider/stranger/object – is recurrently dramatized by Shakespeare as a function of contingencies of time (history) and place (geography), the argument 'make the case yours' (5.2.90) is explicitly urged by the Lord Chief Justice to a newly crowned Prince Hal in 2 Henry IV in a speech that carries at least one other echo of More.[17] Specifically, the newly crowned king is invited to imagine the case of the Chief Justice faced with an unruly

prince as his own, in the same way that the unruly xenophobic citizens are invited by More, likewise a figure of judicial and political authority, to imagine as theirs the strangers' case.

While such parallels tend to strengthen further the case for Shakespeare's authorship of the contribution by 'Hand D', continuities within the playtext suggest the complexity of its intratextual purpose. In a prior scene worked up by other hands mainly from biographical sources,[18] the figure of More stages the 'put case' mode as lived theatre, setting up a judge in order to correct him '[f]or blaming others in a desperate case, / Wherein

---

[15] The echo is noted in Caroline Spurgeon, 'Imagery in the Sir Thomas More fragment', *Review of English Studies*, 23 (1930), 265, where it is compared to similar images in the corpus (notably from *Coriolanus*), and again in Jackson, 'The Date and Authorship', p. 73, but neither in the Arden 3 edition of *Henry VIII* nor in editions of *Sir Thomas More*. As Gary Taylor, following John Jowett, points out, the phrase is also used by Henry Chettle (though not in association with the hypothetical mode) in *The Tragedy of Hoffman* (?1603–04, published 1631), which, in Taylor's view, exhibits still more telling parallels that, like Jowett, he takes as indicative of the 1603–04 date of composition of Shakespeare's contribution. Gary Taylor, 'The date and auspices of the additions to *Sir Thomas More*', in *Shakespeare and Sir Thomas More: Essays on the Play and Its Shakespearian Interest*, ed. T. H. Howard-Hill (Cambridge, 1989), pp. 118–19. Certainly the parallels suggest Chettle had Shakespeare's contribution in mind, though this does not necessarily imply it had only just been written.

[16] See William B. Patterson, *King James VI and I and the Reunion of Christendom* (Cambridge, 1997). James's preference for the terms 'Christian' and 'Christendom' (pointed out by Patterson) is followed in the play.

[17] Shakespeare's More uses 'the majesty of law' (6.136), the Lord Chief Justice '[t]he majesty and power of law' (5.2.77); see Jackson, *The Date and Authorship*, p. 74; *Sir Thomas More*, ed. Jowett, p. 194; for similar images elsewhere in the corpus, Spurgeon, 'Imagery', pp. 264–5. Within Chambers's thematic frame, Karl Wentersdorf notes the phrases in a convincing demonstration of the parallels between More's speeches and the speeches of Henry to his son Hal about his 'revolt' in *2 Henry IV* (Karl Wentersdorf, 'Linkages of Thought and Imagery in Shakespeare and *More*', *Modern Language Quarterly*, 34 (1973), 393–5).

[18] Thomas Stapleton's *Life of More* (1588) supplemented from other sources; see *Sir Thomas More*, ed. Gabrieli and Melchiori, pp. 245–6; Gabrieli, '*Sir Thomas More*: Sources, Characters, Ideas', pp. 17, 28–9.

himself may fall as soon as any' (2.92–3).[19] The staged drama here obliges a figure of authority to live the case of a social inferior who is the object of his judgement in order to bring about a change of heart/perception/judgement. Whether or not this was perceived by the authorial hands responsible for it, the scene serves to illustrate not only the proverbial witty wisdom and humanity of the historical More, but also his appreciation of the ethical potential of theatre to bring about change in human relations as well as (and through) summoning awareness of the precarious contingency of one's position as subject.[20] Implicit to Shakespeare's recurrent dramatizations of 'change of case', this ethical potential is extended to the hypothetical mode of imaginary representations in his contribution to the playtext. For the 'change of case' is here not staged but summoned verbally by More who, like Finch, invites his hearers to imagine the strangers' case as their own lived experience in order to bring about a change of perception/heart. This intratextual continuity, which has not been discussed by critics, skilfully contributes to the coherence of the playtext even as it strengthens the case made on behalf of strangers. This is opposed to the case made against strangers on behalf of citizen-artisans through the actions and speeches of the first scenes by other hands (discussed below). True then to the dramatist's ethical vocation, Shakespeare's contribution, I want to suggest, addresses itself to fellow hands, calling upon them to see strangers differently, that is, to a change of perception/heart and, perhaps, of 'hand' (i.e. further revision). Specifically, by re-presenting Finch's appeal to Christ's exhortation as a response of conviction from xenophobic citizens Shakespeare calls upon fellow hands to imagine the 'virtue in "if"' as Touchstone puts it – to imagine, that is, the efficacy of the hypothetical mode in bringing about a change of heart to which they are themselves called.

Arguing the contingency of the strangers' case – into which one 'may fall as soon as any' – Finch and Shakespeare sought then respectively to persuade other speakers/hands who argue rather on the side of the citizens and the city, whether in a House of Commons heavily weighted, as the outcome of the vote indicates, on this side, or in a playtext similarly weighted by authorial hands, notably Anthony Munday and Henry Chettle who were both Londoners.[21] For if, as the Revels editors suggest, the playtext is structured around the poles of the city and the court[22] the bias is towards the city, the court being for the most part an off-stage – off-centre – place. Not only is the city of London 'the protagonist' in the first part, as they suggest, but it is above all as a citizen of London that More is portrayed in the second part and he dies a citizen-martyr to royal power like the rebel citizen leader Lincoln to whom he is pointedly compared.[23] The playtext's city-oriented hands thus add more (and More) to their case against strangers on behalf of citizens. In the opening scenes this case is made through actions and speeches that imply arguments like those made in parliament, notably the privileges enjoyed and abused by strangers and perceived injustices of treatment.[24] Indeed, if it combines history play and domestic tragedy, the play might best be described as a city tragedy, a

---

19 At the back of this scene is another of Christ's exhortations in the Sermon of the Mount: 'Judge not that ye be not judged': Matthew 7.1.

20 Recognition of this precarious contingency is of course one of the ethical purposes claimed for tragedy by Philip Sidney in *The Defence of Poesy* (1595). The historical More's appreciation of theatre is well documented; see Gabrieli, 'Sir *Thomas More*: Sources, Characters, Ideas', p. 37.

21 Gabrieli and Melchiori, 'Introduction', p. 16; Jowett, 'Introduction', pp. 9, 16.

22 Gabrieli and Melchiori, 'Introduction', p. 29.

23 Giorgio Melchiori, '*The Book of Sir Thomas More*: dramatic unity', in *Shakespeare and Sir Thomas More*, p. 93; cf. Jowett, 'Introduction', pp. 37–41.

24 For example: 'Shall these enjoy more privilege than we / In our own country?' (4.28–9; there is no parallel in the historical sources given in the Revels edition). Compare: 'Their priviledge of Denization is not to be allowed above the priviledge of Birth, and our Natives are not allowed to retail and Merchandize as they do': D'Ewes, *The Journals*, p. 505. Perceived injustice was a recurring complaint; for the mutual recriminations leading up to the bill which included complaints about how the 'strangers' were 'extraordinarily favoured', see Scouloudi, *Returns of Strangers*, p. 57. On 'denization' as a privilege bestowed by Royal Patent, see below.

counterpart to the emergent genre of city/citizen comedy which places city and citizen ideology centre-stage.[25] As an outsider to the city, an internal immigrant, or 'Englishman foreign', connected rather to the court and the 'stranger' communities,[26] Shakespeare was perhaps called in to lend a 'hand' to mediate between such a heavily weighted playtext and the court censor.[27] Yet, if the contribution in his hand 'would have pleased the royal censor',[28] its skilful appropriation of the character of More to argue the strangers' case may not have pleased city-oriented fellow hands disinclined to respond to the change of heart/hand it calls for. Unlike his More, that is, but like Henry Finch, Shakespeare did not bring about a change of heart. For, despite the continuities I have discussed, critics are right finally to judge as discontinuous Shakespeare's contribution, which is described by the Revels editors as a 'discordant note' that breaks an achieved unity in the rest of the playtext.[29] Rather, I would suggest, in playtext as in

parliament, there was a failure to find a compromise or synthesis between 'arguments on both sides' put by speakers/hands trained in a habit of mind as formative of the drama as of political debate.[30] In a context of acute 'economic and social distress' with 'feelings running high', negotiation of arguments,

---

25 *Sir Thomas More* is included by Janette Dillon in her list of playtexts that illustrate the shift to London as a focus of the drama, though she does not distinguish between genres. Janette Dillon, *Theatre, Court and City, 1595–1610: Drama and Social Space in London* (Cambridge, 2000), pp. 4–6. More generally, she argues that these playtexts 'play' between court and city interests, although she does acknowledge occasional tensions. Her argument illustrates how disabling the theoretical concept of indeterminate 'play' can be when, as here, it fails to register the lived experience of struggle in a context of severe economic stress, which was the reality of London in the 1590s, as historians remind us (see below).

26 E. A. J. Honigmann, 'Shakespeare, *Sir Thomas More* and Asylum Seekers', *Shakespeare Survey 57* (Cambridge, 2004), pp. 225–35; Archer, *Citizen Shakespeare*, pp. 9–12; Sokol, *Shakespeare and Tolerance*, pp. 63–4.

27 This applies whether the contribution was part of the original composition, as McMillin argues, or, as most others have argued, a revision added after the intervention of the censor. This raises of course the question of the character of the original version of this scene: was it discontinuous, like the Shakespearian version, or more consistent with the rest of the playtext? (My thanks to *Shakespeare Survey*'s reader for raising this question.)

28 McMillin, *The Elizabethan Theatre and 'The Book of Sir Thomas More'*, p. 143; following Chambers, McMillin argues this is due to its staging of 'a riot being brought to order by a persuasive official' not for its adherence to court policy on strangers, which he does not mention.

29 Gabrieli and Melchiori, 'Introduction', pp. 27, 30; compare A. J. Hoenselaars's comment that More's speech 'serves to divert attention' from the 'real issues' (sic), namely the carefully worked out 'causes of the revolt' in the opening scenes. A. J. Hoenselaars, *Images of Englishmen and Foreigners in the Drama of Shakespeare and his Contemporaries: A Study of Stage Characters and National Identity in English Renaissance Drama, 1558–1642* (Rutherford and London, 1992), pp. 51–2. It is principally this, and the related discontinuity in the representation of the citizen-artisans (turned from dignified individuals to ignorant mob), that critics have emphasized. Less attention has been bestowed on the differences in representations of the strangers (though see note 38). Jowett suggests that the 'fracture' should not be 'over-emphasised': 'Introduction', p. 47.

30 First pointed out by Joel B. Altmann, this has been taken up by subsequent critics, including Stephen Greenblatt whose discussion of it in relation to Thomas More I comment on below (note 58). Joel B. Altmann, *The Tudor Play of Mind: Rhetorical Inquiry and the Development of Elizabethan Drama* (Berkeley, 1978). For a recent discussion that highlights 'how the form of early modern political thought also shaped its content', which this parliamentary debate illustrates, see David Armitage, Conal Condren and Andrew Fitzmaurice, 'Introduction' in *Shakespeare and Early Modern Political Thought* (Cambridge, 2009), pp. 5–6; for detailed analyses of the modes of argument used in parliamentary debate, which show their derivation from school and university education, see Peter Mack, *Elizabethan Rhetoric: Theory and Practice* (Cambridge, 2002), pp. 215–52. In 1622 Henry Peacham would explicitly advise gentlemen who wanted to acquire practical eloquence: 'Procure then, if you may, the Speeches made in Parliament:'; Henry Peacham, *The Compleat Gentleman* (London, 1622), p. 53. This was relatively easy from the early seventeenth century when copies of speeches even began to be sold; see Harold Love, *Scribal Publication in Seventeenth Century England* (Oxford, 1993), pp. 9–22. It was, however, more 'unusual' in the Elizabethan era for which there is less evidence (Paul Seaward in private correspondence). As I have indicated, the 1593 session was precisely unusual in having been fully recorded in an anonymous journal from which copies were subsequently made. The interest thus shown was, however, not for the form so much as the content of the speeches, which covered the sensitive topics of the royal subsidy and recusants as well as strangers, all issues that highlighted the tension between court and parliament (see note 12).

however dexterous, in parliament as in playtext, reached an impasse.[31] In parliament the irreconcilable positions voiced in the debate, the subsequent suppression of the bill by the House of Lords and the social unrest that followed all fed into the developing stand-off between court and parliament/city. The 'alien' question was indeed an exacerbating instance as well as symptom of a widening fissure to which this playtext bears testimony.[32] It also bears testimony to the playtext as a potential site of conflict between city and court ideologies where accommodation of the arguments on both sides – whether in a suspended 'play' or unifying containment – could not always be achieved.[33]

2. THE STRANGERS' CASE: MEMORIES OF EXILE AND VISIONS OF COMMUNITY

The tension between court and parliament/city was not, however, all that was at stake. For

neither Shakespeare nor Finch simply toed a court line in their respective interventions. In parliament it was, as I have indicated, John Wolley, a Privy Councillor, 'ever the queen's good servant', who assiduously toed this line when he made the argument from honour and economic profit.[34] This was an argument Henry Finch might well have made, given the prosperity that his constituency of Canterbury enjoyed thanks to a large Walloon community of skilled workers.[35] He directs attention, however, rather to 'profit' of another kind in order to make the argument from charity, urging that the strangers are 'profitable among us' for their exemplary piety, thrift, hard work and honesty.[36] This is entirely at odds with the views expressed by hostile speakers such as Walter Ralegh, who describes the strangers, especially the Dutch, as cunning self-interested profiteers who 'eat out our profits' and operate 'by policy'.[37] The playtext proposes similar – and similarly irreconcilable –

---

[31] Scouloudi, *Returns of the Strangers*, pp. 58, 61. For the high level of tension, see too Peter Clark, 'A Crisis Contained? The Condition of English Towns in the 1590s', in *The European Crisis of the 1590s*, ed. Peter Clark (London, Boston, Sydney, 1985), pp. 44–66.

[32] For the expression of resentment towards the court through hostility towards strangers, see Yungblut, *Strangers Settled*, p. 54; for the assimilation of 'strangers' and 'the crown' in the construction of city solidarity through the use of 'Ill May Day' as watchword, see Nina Levine, 'Citizens' Games: Differentiating Collaboration and *Sir Thomas More*', *Shakespeare Quarterly*, 58 (2007), 41.

[33] Critical discussion has focused on questions of authorship, date and occasion, perhaps in part to avoid still sensitive political and ideological issues. Recently, Tiffany Stern's important work on the fragmentary production of playtexts has led Robert Miola to suggest, in explanation of the discontinuities, that Shakespeare wrote the part he was assigned 'as if he had not 'read any other part of the play at all'. Miola, 'Shakespeare and *The Book of Sir Thomas More*', p. 16; cf. John Jones, *Shakespeare at Work* (Oxford, 1995), p. 9. Vickers suggests the discontinuities, which he attributes to 'inadequate co-ordination', would not have disturbed an audience. Vickers, *Shakespeare, Co-Author*, p. 439. Though invaluable as an interpretative constraint, the current emphasis on the material conditions of production, whether of playtext or performance, tends to evacuate content of explanatory significance. If Shakespeare may be supposed to have held

religious views, may he not be supposed to have held ethical views on pressing topical issues? And is it not possible that collaborators, like members of parliament, fell out over such issues?

[34] Glyn Parry, 'Wolley, Sir John', *Oxford Dictionary of National Biography* (Oxford, 2004–10).

[35] Anne M. Oakley, 'The Canterbury Walloon Congregation from Elizabeth I to Laud', in *Huguenots in Britain and their French Background, 1550–1800*, ed. Irene Scouloudi (Basingstoke, 1987), pp. 56–71. Clark notes 'unrest at Canterbury over the strangers' in 1587, but it was not on the scale of the unrest in London. Clark, 'A Crisis Contained?', p. 52. In his intervention Finch actually makes a point of the difference of London from the rest of the nation in this respect. The crucial importance of European immigrants to the development of skills and industries in England is pointed out in L. A. Clarkson, *The Pre-Industrial Economy in England 1500–1750* (London, 1971), pp. 110–13, and still more fully in Lien Bich Luu, *Immigrants and the Industries of London, 1500–1700* (Aldershot, 2005).

[36] The version of the anonymous journal reproduced by Hartley is explicit here: 'He used the argument of charitie'. Hartley, *Proceedings*, vol. 3, p. 138.

[37] D'Ewes, *The Journals*, p. 509. This is accompanied by a pragmatic, sceptical call not to grant privileges to strangers that Englishmen did not enjoy abroad. The distinction between doing as you *are* done by (Ralegh) and doing as you *would be done by* (Finch) is a distinction pertinent to *Merchant* as well as to Christopher Marlowe's *The Jew of Malta* performed, as McMillin notes, in this period (1592); McMillin, *The*

views of the strangers: represented in the opening scenes as predatory and profiteering abusers of privilege, they are represented by 'Hand D' rather as scapegoats and victims of exclusionary violence.[38] It is as victims of exclusionary violence that Finch proceeds to represent the strangers, first more implicitly by citing one of three places in the Old Testament where the Israelites' lived experience of persecution and exile in Egypt is given as the grounds for the command to practise charity towards strangers.[39] He follows this up by inviting his audience to remember the collective trauma of 'the days of Queen Mary when our Cause was as theirs is now', when, that is, English protestants were constrained to flee as exiles, or face death, like the forty-five 'Kentish martyrs' burned at the stake at Canterbury and memorialized by John Foxe in 1563.[40] '[T]hose Countries' he urges, 'did allow us that liberty, which now we seek to deny them.' Mobilizing collective memory as well as biblical example Finch thus illustrates the contingency of the strangers' case which he thrusts home by evoking a hypothetical future recurrence: 'They are strangers now, we may be strangers hereafter.'[41]

Finch's appeal to biblical example, if not to collective memory, is taken up in a response two days later by Thomas Palmer who argues for limits to be set to charity, citing another biblical verse from 'the apostle' Paul – '[t]hat he that provideth not

for his Family is worse than an Infidel'[42] – to urge that priority be given to 'our Country and our poor Country-men'. What is at stake then in the 'arguments on both sides' is a vision of community and its attendant ethics. Citing the exhortation which is declared by Christ himself to be a fulfilment of the Mosaic law[43] Finch brings together

---

38 The contrast is noted in Gabrieli, 'Sir Thomas More: Sources, Characters, Ideas,' pp. 34–5, and Miola, 'Shakespeare and *The Book of Sir Thomas More*', pp. 18–19.

39 Exodus 22.21. Cf. Leviticus 19.33, Deuteronomy 24.17–22; 'of charity' is the summary given at the head of this chapter in the King James version, which gives a marginal cross reference to another earlier verse: 'Love ye therefore the stranger: for ye were strangers in the land of Egypt': Deuteronomy 10.19. This verse is cited together with the verse from Leviticus in an argument from the 'law of God' made in a speech on behalf of strangers attributed to the MP Henry Jackman which may have been given in a prior debate in 1589, though Dean argues that it belongs to the 1593 debate, while Hartley suggests it may not have been delivered at all. Dean, *Law-making*, p. 157 n. 95; Hartley, *Proceedings*, vol. 2, pp. 409, 480–3. As Sokol points out, the speech evokes the 'golden rule of justice' – to give others what we would receive from them. Sokol, *Shakespeare and Tolerance*, pp. 62–4. This is, however, treated as a natural law not as the law of Christ cited by Finch and Shakespeare's More. It may be that Finch reworked Jackman's arguments, though he did not sit in the parliament of 1589. Jackman sat in both sessions, though, unless Dean is correct, he did not intervene in the 1593 debate on strangers.

40 A memorial to the martyrs, first raised in 1899, still stands in Canterbury. Allusions to Mary's reign as well as biblical citations were typical features of Elizabethan parliamentary oratory: see Mack, *Elizabethan Rhetoric*, pp. 232–3.

41 The contingency of the strangers' case ('their case may be our case'), illustrated by biblical example (Leviticus 19.33) as well as the memory of the 'refuge' given the English 'in the bloodie persecution' under Mary all feature in a representation of the 'disposition' of the 'wise and godly' towards strangers in a sermon preached in Oxford by George Abbot towards the end of 1594 and not, as Sokol assumes, in 1572 (when Abbot was 10); Sokol, *Shakespeare and Tolerance*, p. 63. Rather then casting doubt on the specificity of the Shakespearian echo (as Sokol suggests), this suggests how, once leaked, Finch's intervention circulated amongst those committed to international protestantism, as I discuss in Margaret Tudeau-Clayton, 'Shakespeare and Immigration', forthcoming in *SPELL*, 27.

42 I Timothy 5.8; D'Ewes, *The Journals*, p. 508.

43 See above, p. 240. In his first publication Henry Finch, a lawyer, had sought to bring English common law 'into

---

Elizabethan Theatre and 'The Book of Sir Thomas More', pp. 68–9. As he comments, Marlowe was implicated, if obscurely, in the social unrest surrounding the stranger communities, as Shapiro also notes, quoting the so-called Dutch church libel signed 'Tamburlaine', posted in May 1593, i.e. shortly after the suppression of the bill (Shapiro, *Shakespeare and the Jews*, pp. 184–5). Matthew Dimmock has recently attributed this libel to Thomas Deloney, who, like Marlowe, was an associate of Ralegh's, though he does not point out that it echoes Ralegh's intervention in parliament even as it lumps European strangers and Jews together: 'Like the Jews you eat us up as bread.' Matthew Dimmock, 'Tamburlaine's Curse', *TLS*, 19 November 2010, pp. 16–17. In this libel as well as in another posted in April the strangers are also described, as they are by Ralegh, as hypocrites and cowards who use religion as 'a counterfeit'. See John Strype, *Annals of the Reformation* (Oxford, 1824), vol. 4, pp. 234–5. These echoes again suggest a leaking of the content of the debate, whether through the anonymous journal or through Ralegh.

Old Testament and New to urge an ethical practice of mutual charity grounded on recognition of a shared condition of precarious contingency to which relatively recent lived experience as well as biblical example of persecution and exile bear testimony. As a transnational, universalist vision this is at odds with the priority given by the bill's advocates to the more locally defined communities of nation, city and (merchant) class and the 'doctrine of self interest' (see below).[44]

The vision of community advanced by Shakespeare's More is still more explicitly universalist when, like Finch, he closes his intervention by calling on his audience of xenophobic citizens to imagine themselves 'in the strangers' case' (6.141–55). Where Finch evokes a hypothetical future experience grounded on local collective memory and biblical example of persecution and exile, More paints a vivid picture of the 'hideous violence' (6.147) the citizens would suffer in exile should they be treated with the hostility with which they treat strangers in England. He illustrates this with an imagined scene of hostile locals who would '[w]het their detested knives against your throats, / Spurn you like dogs' (6.149–50). A conflation of representations of Shylock's treatment of Antonio and Antonio's treatment of Shylock in *Merchant*, as others have noted,[45] the scene underscores how differences yield to likeness in the bond of reciprocal hatred dramatized in the later/earlier play. Anticipated in the image of men that 'like ravenous fishes, / Would feed on one another' (6.96–7, discussed above), this is the negative counterpart, or double, of the bond of reciprocal 'neighbourly charity', in which differences again yield to likeness, that Shakespeare's More here summons through representation of its opposite – an opposite that is also implicit in the shared memory of persecution evoked by Finch.[46] More, however, goes on, as Finch does not, to denounce such hatred as a denial of a common human condition that he defines, first, in relation to God: 'like as if that God / Owed not nor made not you' (6.150–1); then, still more tellingly, in relation to a nature that belongs to all: 'nor that the elements / Were not all appropriate to your

comforts, / But chartered unto them' (6.151–3), 'chartered', that is, to those whose violent exclusion of other humans implies an appropriation of nature as private property.[47] 'What would you think / To be thus used?' (or 'propertied', as Shakespeare elsewhere puts it[48]), More concludes,

---

closer conformity with the law of Moses'; Wilfred Prest, 'Finch, Sir Henry', *Oxford Dictionary of National Biography* (Oxford, 2004–10).

44 Finch's transnational aspirations culminate in a work (1621) announcing 'the establishment of a universal Judaeo-Christian empire as a glorious end in itself': Prest, 'Finch, Sir Henry'. See too Shapiro, *Shakespeare and the Jews*, p. 178. As Jeffrey Knapp has argued English Protestants were divided as to where their allegiances lay: Jeffrey Knapp, *Shakespeare's Tribe: Church, Nation, and Theatre in Renaissance England* (London and Chicago, 2002), especially chapters 2 and 3. Knapp's argument touches on mine, although his view of Shakespeare as a member of a theatrical community that shared an 'Erasmian', supranational, inclusive form of Christianity precludes the possibility of disagreement within this 'tribe' such as I am suggesting this playtext illustrates.

45 See note to 145–6 in the Revels edition, and William H. Matchett, 'Shylock, Iago, and *Sir Thomas More*: with some Further Discussion of Shakespeare's Imagination', *PMLA*, 92 (1977), 217–30. While there is no further comment by the Revels editors, Matchett takes this as further confirmation of Shakespeare's authorship and of the (later) date of composition.

46 '[N]eighbourly charity' is itself taken from *Merchant* (1.2.76) where it is used ironically of relations between the English and their old, local enemies the Scots and the French in a comic vignette that, as I have suggested elsewhere, anticipates the deadly drama which follows: Margaret Tudeau-Clayton, 'The "trueborn Englishman": *Richard II*, *The Merchant of Venice* and the Future History of (the) English', in *This England, That Shakespeare*, ed. Willy Maley and Margaret Tudeau-Clayton (Farnham, 2010), pp. 74–5.

47 Though there are eight instances in the Shakespearian corpus of 'charter', which all imply privilege and/or possession, the striking word 'charter'd' is used again only once in the corpus and in connection with one of the elements, the air, 'a chartered libertine' in *Henry V* (1.1.49) as Jackson, following John Jowett, notes: 'The Date and Authorship', p. 76. See too J. M. Nosworthy, 'Shakespeare and *Sir Thomas More*', *Review of English Studies*, 6 (1955), p. 16. Unnoticed by the Revels editors of *Thomas More* and editors of *Henry V*, the echo again reinforces the connections between Shakespeare's contribution to *Sir Thomas More* and the second tetralogy.

48 *Twelfth Night*, 4.2.93; *King John*, 5.2.79.

'[t]his is the strangers' case, / And this your mountainish inhumanity' (6.153–5).[49] With this arresting phrase More closes his picture of the 'hideous violence' the citizens would suffer were they to meet with what he earlier describe as 'a nation of such barbarous temper' (6.146). 'Barbarous' and 'inhuman' are thus aligned as interchangeable, mutually defining terms in the spirit of the inclusive Christian humanism of More's *Utopia* as well as of sceptical interrogations of the word 'barbarous' by such as Puttenham[50] and Montaigne whose condemnation of 'the barbarisme in eating men alive' witnessed in Europe's wars of religion echoes More's anticipation of this scene in the image of men feeding on each other like ravenous fishes.[51] Indeed, insofar as the mutually defining terms, 'barbarous' and 'inhumanity', frame a scene of exclusionary violence they are turned against the habitual use of 'barbarous' precisely to exclude as, in the playtext, the near synonym 'outlandish' (4.27) is used of the strangers by the rebel citizen leader.[52] Habitually used as synonymous with, and in early dictionaries glossed by 'uncivil', 'cruel' and 'rude', but not by 'inhuman', 'barbarous' continued, that is, to be used, as its etymon was by the Greeks, of those others through whose exclusion a community defined its linguistic and cultural identity as well as its territorial boundaries. It continued, in short, to be used to produce such exclusions as Shakespeare's More condemns as

an 'inhuman' denial of a shared human condition. As the discussion above indicates, this anticipates (or recalls) *Merchant* where the denial of a common humanity in mutual assertions of exclusionary difference by Venetian Christians and their other, the Jew, exposes their ironic resemblance in a reciprocal hatred that illustrates the 'barbarous' 'inhumanity' condemned by More. It bears too on the later Venetian play, *Othello*, where a similar oppositional difference likewise collapses, having

---

[49] 'Mountainish' has proved a stumbling block, though the Revels editors' citation of the line in *Twelfth Night* where 'mountains' are associated with 'barbarous caves' (4.1.47) seems to me sufficient to confirm this reading; the proposed alternative would, of course, exclude muslim 'infidels' from the category of the human. See K. P. Wentersdorf, 'On "Momtanish Inhumanyty" in "Sir Thomas More"', *Studies in Philology*, 103 (2006), 178–85. For the association of mountains with the limit of the civilized/barbarous, see George Puttenham's sceptical comment: 'The Italian at this day by like arrogance calleth the Frenchman, Spaniard, Dutch, English, and all other bred behither their mountains Apennines, *Tramontani*, as who would say "barbarous"' (George Puttenham, *The Art of English Poesy*, ed. Frank Whigham and Wyne A. Rebhorn (Ithaca and London, 2007), p. 337).

[50] See note 49.

[51] Montaigne's sceptical interrogation comes in his essay 'Of the Caniballes' which Shakespeare will recall in *The Tempest*. Observing first how the word is used simply to label those who are different – 'Now . . . I finde . . . there is nothing in that nation, that is either barbarous or savage, unless men call that barbarisme which is not common to them' – Montaigne later collapses the Christian civilized/pagan barbarian opposition by asserting, with reference to the wars of religion, that 'there is more barbarisme in eating men alive, then to feede upon them being dead' concluding: 'We may then well call them barbarous, in regarde of reasons rules, but not in respect of us that exceede them in all kinde of barbarisme.' *The essayes or morall, politike and millitarie discourses of Lo: Michaell de Montaigne . . . now done into English by . . . John Florio* (London, 1603), pp. 101, 104. The historical More too interrogates the word when, in his discussion of translation of the Bible, he dismisses as 'fantasye' the claim that English is a barbarous tongue: 'For so is . . . every straunge langage to other': *A Dialogue Concerning Heresies* (1531), in *The Complete Works of St. Thomas More*, vol. 6, Part I, ed. Thomas M. C. Lawler, Germain Marc'hadour and Richard C. Marius (New Haven and London, 1981), p. 337. It is of course with reference to language that 'barbarous' is most frequently used in this exclusionary sense.

[52] Cf. John Cheke in 1550: the 'grecian called everi contree . . . beside theer own *barbarous* . . . We now call them *strangers* and outborns, and *outlandisch*': *The Gospel according to Saint Matthew and Part of the First Chapter according to Saint Mark*, ed. James Goodwin (London, 1843), p. 48 (emphasis mine). In the Shakespearian canon 'barbarous' is used of behaviour, qualities, language or peoples from which a character is, or wants to be differentiated. It is used most often in one of the Roman plays *Titus Andronicus* where its use illustrates Shakespeare's knowledge of its original sense to define those outside the community of the privileged nation (barbarian = not Roman). As in *Merchant* and *Othello*, however (see below), the barbarous/civilized opposition is also collapsed as John Drakakis points out in an unpublished paper 'English Renaissance Drama and the Aesthetics of Violence' given at a workshop on 'Violence and Aesthetics' at the University of Zürich, June 2011.

been asserted by the eponymous protagonist in a condemnation of a 'barbarous brawl' – 'For Christian shame, put by this barbarous brawl' (2.3.165) – that, ironically, marks the outset of a descent into the 'hideous violence' of 'barbarous' 'inhumanity', brought about by a European Christian of Venice whose hatred of the other that is the Moor is expressed through an exclusionary representation of him as an 'erring barbarian' (1.3.355).[53]

3. VISIONS OF COMMUNITY: SHAKESPEARE'S MORE AND THOMAS MORE'S UTOPIA

As I have indicated, this turning of 'barbarous' and 'inhuman' as mutually defining terms against the exclusionary use of 'barbarous' is in the spirit of the inclusive Christian humanist vision of the historical More's *Utopia*. This intertextual filiation is advertised by a textual echo in the first description through which Shakespeare's More seeks to change the xenophobic citizens' view of the strangers. Evoking a vivid scene, as he will again in his closing speech, he invites the citizens to '[i]magine that [they] see the wretched strangers, / Their babies at their backs, with their poor luggage, / Plodding to th' ports and coasts for transportation' (6.84–6). As others have noted, though without exploring the implications, this echoes a description of victims of enclosure by the figure of Raphael Hythloday in the first book of the *Utopia*, as rendered in Ralph Robinson's 1551 translation.[54] In a fierce denunciation of the practice Hythloday describes how those who are thus deprived of their means to live are forced to depart, 'wretched souls, men, women, . . . woeful mothers with their young babes . . . [a]way they trudge . . . finding no place to rest in'.[55] Advertising a filiation between his More and the radically dissonant voice of Raphael Hythloday in the historical More's *Utopia*, Shakespeare invites those who hear it, including fellow authorial hands, to recognize the strangers as in the same case as the victims of enclosure. A practice that continued throughout the sixteenth century, enclosure drove many, including many from Shakespeare's home region, the West Midlands, to London where they were classed alongside the immigrants from continental Europe as 'Englishmen foreign' in surveys conducted by the city authorities to address the social unrest attendant on the consequent strain on resources (housing and food).[56] As others have pointed out, there were far more internal immigrants than European strangers but it was the strangers who were the objects of citizen violence.[57] With an insider's knowledge of internal exile Shakespeare echoes the historical More's description of the victims of enclosure to insist rather on the likeness between 'the strangers' case' and the case of English men

---

[53] The link to *Othello* has recently been strengthened by the establishment in it of the highest overlap of what are called 'Hand D's rare words' in Timothy Irish Watt, 'The Authorship of the Hand-D Addition to *The Book of Sir Thomas More*', in Hugh K. Craig and Arthur F. Kinney, eds., *Shakespeare, Computers and the Mystery of Authorship* (Cambridge, 2009), p. 155. The notion of 'barbarism' in More's speech is added to Chambers's series of linked images by Wentersdorf who misreads it as signalling the anti-Christian character of *revolt*. Wentersdorf, 'Linkages of Thought and Imagery in Shakespeare and *More*', pp. 401–4. In Stephen Greenblatt's sceptical reading Iago shows not only hatred, but fellow feeling – precisely the empathy that Shakespeare's More calls for – which Greenblatt describes in language redolent of the image of 'ravenous fishes' as 'a ruthless . . . absorption of the other'. Stephen Greenblatt, *Renaissance Self-Fashioning: From More to Shakespeare* (Chicago and London, 1980), p. 236.

[54] See note to 80–2 in the Revels edition and to 85–7 in the Arden edition; Gabrieli, 'Sir Thomas More: Sources, Characters, Ideas,' p. 42, note 24; Miola, 'Shakespeare and *The Book of Sir Thomas More*', p. 19. Miola usefully notes that the passage from the *Utopia* is cited at length in Francis Trigge, *The Humble Petition of Two Sisters* (London, 1604), a contemporary tract against enclosure

[55] *The Utopia of Sir Thomas More, Translated by Ralph Robinson*, introduced by H. B. Cotterill (London, 1958), p. 29.

[56] Clark, 'A Crisis Contained?', p. 52; one of these surveys was conducted in April–May 1593 in an attempt to stem the unrest attendant on the suppression of the bill.

[57] It is difficult to establish definite figures (Sokol, *Shakespeare and Tolerance*, p. 186), but Scouloudi puts the percentage of the 'stranger' population in the survey of 1593 at 3.69%, a 'negligible figure' as she comments. *Returns of the Strangers*, p. 76; Clark notes how, if complaints were made about the English 'foreigners', aggression was directed to the alien immigrants: Clark, 'A Crisis Contained?', pp. 52–3.

and women driven into internal exile by the practice of enclosure. The likeness is then underscored when, in his closing speech, More represents the violent exclusion of strangers as an inhuman denial of nature as a common good, 'chartered' 'as if' private property.

For the rejection of private property – with the contrary doctrine of all things in common – constitutes of course the ground of the community imagined in the sustained exercise in the hypothetical mode that is the second book of the *Utopia*.[58] Like Shakespeare's More this advocates mutual charity between peoples on the grounds of a natural bond between humans.[59] Nature too 'equally favoureth all that be comprehended under the communion of one shape' as humans and this equality before nature implies the ethical imperative: 'do not so seek for thine own commodities that thou procure others incommodities'.[60] The objection to the practice of enclosure was precisely that it served the profit of a few to the harm of many, but the objection was countered and defeated by the argument from profit.[61] 'Self love', in short, 'hath exiled charitie', as Henry Chettle succinctly puts it in a denunciation of unscrupulous landlords in *Kind-Hartes Dreame* (1592), a tract which one critic at least has suggested is significantly connected to the playtext of *Sir Thomas More* in which Chettle himself had a 'hand'.[62] The 'strangers' and the evicted English were, indeed, historically speaking, in the 'same case' inasmuch as they were victims of what might be described as a deep change in structures of feeling – the triumph of the 'doctrine of self interest' over charity as a legitimate 'guide to ... behaviour' which, together with the 'institution of private property' that the practice of enclosure served, marked England's ineluctable transition to a market economy in the sixteenth century.[63] Like Finch's evocation of the memory of persecution and exile under Mary, the evocation of enclosure – not only a historical memory but an ongoing brutal reality – served then to underscore the lived experience of precarious contingency and exclusionary violence shared by 'our countrey-men' and 'strangers' alike.

But Shakespeare's combination of the radical voice of the historical More's *Utopia* with the voice of Henry Finch serves to draw attention away from religious to ethical differences evoking as it does an alliance across the religious divide of those who speak on behalf of the dispossessed and excluded of all nations. At the same time the allusion to the historical More's *Utopia* adds the force of an ironic reminder to Protestant/puritan fellow hands who betray their protagonist's inclusive pre-reformation social vision even as they misrepresent his 'case'. For this is treated as a legitimizing instance of the authority of individual conscience over state

---

[58] Thomas More's skill in the hypothetical mode is brilliantly discussed by Stephen Greenblatt who, however, does not consider how this is taken up in *Sir Thomas More*: Greenblatt, *Renaissance Self-Fashioning*, pp. 231–2. Though the specific echo has been noted, there has been no further exploration of the relation to the *Utopia* as far as I know; the assumption appears to be that there is 'not even an allusion to *Utopia*' in the whole playtext. G. Harold Metz, '"Voice and credyt": The Scholars and *Sir Thomas More*', in *Shakespeare and Sir Thomas More*, p. 11.

[59] Robinson: 'For what purpose serve leagues? say they; as though nature had not set sufficient love between man and man. And who so regardeth not nature, think you that he will pass for words?' *The Utopia*, p. 115.

[60] Robinson, *The Utopia*, p. 97.

[61] Clarkson, *The Pre-Industrial Economy in England*, pp. 20–1; cf. Trigge: 'these enclosers respect only their own commodities, and therefore it is against charity ... they think that they may doe it lawfully; that is, they may make their own commoditie, howsoever that their brethren fare': Trigge, *The Humble Petition* (no pag.).

[62] The critic is Peter Blayney whose argument that the playtext is a source for *Kind-Hartes Dream* has been convincingly challenged in Gary Taylor, 'The Date and Auspices of the Additions to *Sir Thomas More*', in *Shakespeare and Sir Thomas More*, pp. 101–29. That Chettle was involved in the production of the playtext is indisputably demonstrated by John Jowett's essay in the same volume as well by his recent edition: John Jowett, 'Henry Chettle and the Original Text of *Sir Thomas More*', in *Shakespeare and Sir Thomas More*, pp. 131–49; Jowett, 'Introduction', pp. 15–18. For a later recollection by Chettle of Shakespeare's contribution to the playtext see note 15.

[63] Clarkson, *The Pre-Industrial Economy in England*, p. 21; cf. Trigge: 'these covetous men, that for their own private lucre and gaine, doe take Commons from men' (Trigge, *The Humble Petition* (no pag.)).

authority,[64] which is to (mis)take More as an advocate for a 'private ownership of the self', as Greenblatt puts it, a private, *enclosed* self that has no more place in the radical social vision of the *Utopia* than land enclosed as private property.[65]

In the speeches of his More Shakespeare then weaves together two intertexts: Henry Finch's appeal in parliament to Christ's exhortation as the logical, ethical response to a hypothetical projection grounded on local and biblical testimony to the contingency of the strangers' case; and the historical More's *Utopia* – at once the foundational principles of the ideal community imagined in the second book's extended exercise in the hypothetical mode and the historical realities with which this ideal is engaged in dialectical opposition, notably the practice of enclosure and the institution of private property it serves, which are directly denounced in the first book.

It is, however, important to underscore that it is the radical voice of Raphael Hythloday that is evoked in the speeches of Shakespeare's More and not the prudent, pragmatic and accommodating voice that is actually named 'More' in the *Utopia*. Indeed, this figure of 'More' takes a distance both from Hythloday's imagined community and his fierce critique of contemporary English society. Hythloday is even taken to task by 'More' for his uncompromising stand. This is done in terms which, as it happens, bear not only on the dissonance of Shakespeare's contribution to *Sir Thomas More*, but also on what I call the ideology of Shakespearian linguistic practices which, I want to suggest in conclusion, is consistent with this contribution. As critics, justly, take Shakespeare to task for a contribution that breaks the aesthetic integrity of the playtext, the figure of 'More' likens Hythloday's uncompromising refusal to accommodate his speech to time and place to a breach of generic decorum that disrupts the formal integrity of a drama, 'rehearsing that which served neither for the time nor place to have made such a tragical comedy'.[66] To this the translator adds a gloss, 'or gallymalfrey', perhaps to emphasize the critical thrust of the comparison. According to the

OED this is the first recorded instance of this figure (from French) which came to be used in the last decades of the sixteenth century to represent (usually negatively) social as well as generic mixes that breach 'proper' boundaries. Above all it was used of the linguistic mix of the national language produced through the practice of latinate and romance neologisms which make 'our English tongue a gallimaufray or hodgepodge of al other speches', as 'E.K.' puts it in the introduction to *The Shepheards Calender* (1579).[67] As I have argued elsewhere, Shakespearian linguistic practices, including the practice of latinate and romance neologism, tend to the gallimaufry. This figure is, moreover, explicitly set in opposition to the figure of 'the King's English' in Shakespeare's one essay in the genre of city comedy (to which I have suggested *Sir Thomas More* is a tragic counterpart) and the only play in which he evokes this figure of an emergent norm, *The Merry Wives of Windsor*, itself a generic as well as linguistic hodge podge.[68] Evoking 'the King's English' (*Merry Wives*, 1.4.5) Shakespeare ironically exposes the arbitrary, necessarily exclusionary boundaries of this – any – norm and its implied ownership of the vernacular. He

---

[64] The Revels editors comment that 'freedom of conscience' was 'a question that interested the Puritan and nonconformist London middle class' ('Introduction', p. 16). It is a question that critics still see as central to the meaning of the playtext in which, as they note, More's 'Catholicism' is repressed. See, for example, Gabrieli, 'Sir Thomas More: Sources, Characters, Ideas', pp. 23–6, 38.

[65] Greenblatt, *Renaissance Self-fashioning*, p. 38; as Chambers points out it was rather for an absolute belief in a united Christendom that More died. R. W. Chambers, *Thomas More* (Brighton, 1982), p. 365.

[66] Robinson, *The Utopia*, p. 50.

[67] *Elizabethan Critical Essays*, ed. G. Gregory Smith, 2 vols. (Oxford, 1904; repr. London, 1964), vol. 1, p. 130. Other examples are given in Margaret Tudeau-Clayton, 'Richard Carew, William Shakespeare, and the Politics of Translating Virgil in Early Modern England and Scotland', *International Journal of the Classical Tradition*, 5 (1999), 524–6.

[68] Margaret Tudeau-Clayton, 'Shakespeare's "welsch men" and the "King's English"', in *Shakespeare and Wales: from the Marches to the Assembly*, ed. Willy Maley and Philip Schwyzer (Farnham, 2010), pp. 121–49.

thus invites the question *whose* English is 'the King's English' even as, in his practice, he celebrates rather English as a gallimaufry – a changing, mobile and inclusive vernacular without 'proper' defining boundaries, a common good, we might put it here, like nature, not to be 'chartered', enclosed as private property. This is indeed how we might describe 'the King's English': introduced from the mid-sixteenth century by self-appointed, Protestant bourgeois linguistic legislators 'the King's English' was consistently mobilized in negative performatives to constitute the centre it represents through exclusion of linguistic 'strangers', notably the romance and latinate neologisms practised by nomadic gentlemen, like Falstaff in *Merry Wives*, who is said to 'love' the 'gallimaufry' (2.1.110). The opposed figures of 'the King's English' and 'the gallimaufry' imply then ideas of community which rhyme exactly with the oppositions I have looked at in the playtext of *Sir Thomas More* and the parliamentary debate that the playtext echoes: on the one hand, a mobile, inclusive mix of linguistic/human 'strangers' ('the gallimaufry'), on the other, a fixed, homogeneous community of a 'proper' bounded nation/language to be constituted through exclusion of 'strangers' ('the King's English').

The rhyme is underscored, more generally and more precisely, by two discrete texts that, as it happens, belong respectively to the two preferred alternative dates for Shakespeare's composition of his contribution to the playtext: 1592–94 and 1603–04. In the prologue to his *Midas* (first performed 1592) John Lyly represents the contemporary '[g]allimaufrey' of cultural and linguistic forms as at once a reflection of, and response to, the 'Hodge-podge' of the world as of its epitome, London, with its mix of professional and social classes – soldiers, courtiers and countrymen – and European nationals – Italian, Spanish, German and English – each with their own cultural preferences.[69] Still more relevantly a passage at the close of Samuel Daniel's *A Defence of Rhyme* (?1603) evokes the stand-off between parliament and court around the question of human 'strangers' even as it criticizes the introduction of linguistic 'strangers' as 'unnatural to our own native language':

I cannot but wonder at the strange presumption of some men, that dare . . . to introduce any whatsoever forraine wordes, be they never so strange, and of themselves, as it were, without a Parliament, without any consent or allowance, establish them as Free-denizens in our language.[70]

The application of the language of citizenship to the status of words was a commonplace practice inherited from the Romans.[71] It is turned here, however, in terms of administrative procedures specific to Elizabethan and Jacobean England. For while naturalization of 'aliens' required an act of parliament, they could be made denizens by 'Kings letters Patents'.[72] The court had, moreover, been successfully lobbied by the 'stranger churches' (the centres of the alien communities) for a major enrolment of strangers as denizens in 1561, while in 1574 the city authorities had sought restraint from the Privy Council in the granting of denizenship.[73] If these events point

[69] *The Complete Works of John Lyly*, ed. R. Warwick Bond, 3 vols. (repr.) (Oxford, 1967), vol. 3, p. 115.

[70] Samuel Daniel, *A Defence of Rhyme*, in *Elizabethan Critical Essays*, ed. G. Gregory Smith, vol. 2, p. 384.

[71] Frederick M. Rener, *Interpretatio: Language and Translation from Cicero to Tytler* (Amsterdam, 1989), pp. 56–8; as I point out in a discussion of further examples: 'the practice illustrates . . . how the imagined totalities of the English nation and the English vernacular are homologous, constructed according to a common logic of inclusion/ exclusion through the drawing of more or less arbitrarily determined categorial boundaries of the "pure" and "proper"': Margaret Tudeau-Clayton, 'Shakespeare's Extravagancy', *Shakespeare*, 1 (2005), 146.

[72] This is from the gloss to 'denizen' in Henry Cockeram's 1623 'hard word' English–English dictionary. On this point see Chitty, 'Aliens in England', p. 132; Shapiro, *Shakespeare and the Jews*, p. 181; Yungblut, *Strangers Settled*, p. 78. Scouloudi observes that there were a far greater number of patents of denizations than acts of naturalization (Scouloudi, *Returns of the Strangers*, p. 4).

[73] Pettegree, *Foreign Protestant Communities*, pp. 145–9, 288. Pettegree's excellent account underscores court support and protection of the stranger communities and (from the 1570s) opposition from the commons and the city.

up the tension between court and parliament/city around strangers in the Elizabethan era that came to a head, as we have seen, in the parliamentary debate of 1593, the 'matter touching Aliens' (D'Ewes) clearly continued to carry 'great weight' in the Stuart era.[74] Aligning himself with parliament Daniel criticizes the court for its entertaining of linguistic as well as human strangers, setting peremptory acts of particular sovereign wills – *a* rather than *the* king's English[75] – in contrast and opposition to the authority of parliament, the established institutional apparatus for political negotiation (for which, regarding the language, there was, as yet, no equivalent[76]). In the 'entertaining' of linguistic 'strangers' there was implied the entertaining of human 'strangers', and at stake in both was the stand-off between court and parliament/city.[77]

In his linguistic practices as well as in his contribution to *Sir Thomas More* Shakespeare appears then to have aligned himself with the court. But, as I have argued more fully elsewhere in relation to his linguistic practices and here in relation to his contribution to the playtext, there is more at stake, since both imply an inclusive vision of a 'mixed' transnational community of human 'strangers'.[78] In the playtext this vision is communicated through the speeches of Shakespeare's More that recall two dissonant voices: the radical voice of Raphael Hythloday in the historical More's *Utopia* and the voice of the Protestant lawyer Henry Finch who, urging the contingency of the strangers' case, appeals for the practice of what Hythloday calls the 'norma Christi' – the law of Christ. This is in his reply to the criticism of 'More' (quoted above) when he comments that, in a time and place where private property prevails, the Utopian principle of all things in common must indeed 'seem . . . out of place', but no more so than Christ's teachings which 'are more dissident from the manners of the world nowadays than my communication was', although this is occluded precisely through such accommodations as 'More' urges.[79] In his appeal to the 'norma Christi' Henry Finch was likewise 'dissident' from a time and place where the self-interest of local, national and class

communities prevailed. So too was Shakespeare when he re-presented Finch's appeal as a response of conviction to urge, as I have suggested, fellow authorial hands as well as xenophobic citizens to imagine the 'virtue in "if"', the force of utopic

---

74 Tension may even have increased since James regarded foreigners as a resource: in his *Basilicon Doron* (1598) he advises his son and heir to 'permit and allure forraine Merchants to trade here' citing the example of England, 'how it hath flourished both in wealth and policie, since the strangers Craftes-men came in among them': King James VI and I, *Political Writings*, ed. J. P. Sommerville (Cambridge 1994), p. 30.

75 As others have pointed out, 'the King's English' has never been practised by royalty, or even by the highest class of speakers. The sign of 'the King' is thus used at once to legitimize and to conceal the arbitrary boundaries of inclusion/exclusion that the first, self-appointed Protestant, bourgeois linguistic legislators seek to draw. I develop this point in an unpublished paper given at the ESSE conference in Turin (August 2010), 'Shakespeare and "the King's English"'.

76 Not yet, but, in the following year, Robert Cawdrey will invoke 'the King's English' in his preface to the first English–English hard word dictionary (London, 1604), which echoes nearly verbatim the first recorded instance, in Thomas Wilson's *Art Of Rhetoric* (1553). See Tudeau-Clayton, 'Shakespeare's "welsch men"', pp. 92–3, 96.

77 For discussion of the implication of these politics in cultural forms see too Richard Helgerson, 'Barbarous Tongues: The Ideology of Poetic Form in Renaissance England', in *The Historical Renaissance*, ed. Heather Dubrow and Richard Strier (Chicago University Press, 1988), pp. 273–92; *Forms of Nationhood: The Elizabethan Writing of England* (Chicago and London, 1992), ch. 1.

78 Tudeau-Clayton, 'Shakespeare's Extravagancy', pp. 142–7.

79 *The Utopia of Sir Thomas More*, pp. 51–2. As Logan and Adams point out, 'communism', approved as it was by classical authorities (notably Plato) and practised as it was by the first Christians (as recorded in the New Testament), 'had long been respectable'; they quote a wry comment by More's close friend Erasmus that it is 'extraordinary how Christians dislike this common ownership of Plato's . . . although nothing was ever said by a pagan philosopher which comes closer to the mind of Christ': Thomas More, *Utopia*, eds. George M. Logan and Robert M. Adams, rev. edn repr. (Cambridge, 2003), pp. 37–8 n. 87. Trigge gives 'the practice' of 'all things Common' in 'the Primitive church' as an illustration of the 'Christian charitie' which is betrayed by enclosure (Trigge, *The Humble Petition*, fol. E2v).

dissonance to bring about a change of perception/ heart even as they are themselves called upon to see strangers differently. History was not on their side as it was not on the side of Shakespearian linguistic practice.[80] History was rather on the side of local self-interest and private property as it was on the side of 'the King's English', in short, on the side of the modern bourgeois order of things. If, however, at odds with time and place then, Shakespeare's utopic dissonance speaks to us now, in this post-modern moment, as the modern bourgeois

order dissolves and the King's English disappears into the Englishes of a world culture. Indeed, the imperative to imagine ourselves as members of a single, global community and nature as a common good is today not so much a matter of Christian charity as of self-interested survival.

---

[80] A similar point about Shakespearian linguistic practice is made, though from a very different angle, in Stephen Mullaney, *The Place of the Stage* (Chicago and London, 1988), pp. 76–87.

A COLLABORATION: SHAKESPEARE AND HAND C IN *SIR THOMAS MORE*

JOHN JOWETT

Studies of Shakespeare's involvement in the manuscript play *Sir Thomas More* usually have sought to confirm, question or deny that the writer nominated by W. W. Greg as Hand D can be identified as Shakespeare.[1] That debate is no longer so pressing. A review of wide-ranging evidence and collocation study by MacD. P. Jackson and the vocabulary analysis of Timothy Irish Watt leave the matter in little doubt, and there is no longer any need to treat the question as controversial.[2] The present article, taking the identity of Hand D as Shakespeare as its premise, will move forward to re-evaluate Shakespeare's contribution to the revision in two specific ways. First, it will offer a new explanation for a textual crux at the beginning of the Hand D section; this will challenge the usual view that Shakespeare was working in isolation from the other revisers. Second, it will reassess Shakespeare's overall contribution to the revision by considering his involvement in two short further additions that were copied out and pasted into the main manuscript. One of them is generally accepted as by Shakespeare already. The other has been hitherto unattributed, but it will be argued here that it may well combine lines by Shakespeare and by Heywood.

Shakespeare's role in the revision is distinctly complex. Nevertheless, one aspect of Shakespeare's contribution is his willingness to collaborate by way of deferring some matters to Hand C. As a result, Hand C, the theatre scribe and annotator who is the key figure in the making of the revision, was prompted to make a sustained and variegated series of interventions in the revision, introducing detailed adjustments to the Shakespeare passage that are almost anxious in their complexity.

The following discussion is developed on grounds that will not be argued in detail but summarized here.[3] The Original Text is a fair copy in the hand of Anthony Munday. The complete script, including leaves subsequently removed, was submitted for licensing to the Master of the Revels, Edmund Tilney. Tilney returned it with instructions to leave out the entire insurrection episode that dominates the first half of the play, and he made further deletions affecting the portrayal of More's arrest in the second. He did not mark any of the revisions, and probably saw none of them. The statistics relating to the revision itself suggest a wholly remarkable enterprise. Probably in 1603–04, a

---

[1] In his Malone Society Reprints edition (Oxford, 1911), pp. viii–ix. The manuscript is British Library MS Harley 7368.

[2] Jackson, 'Is "Hand D" of *Sir Thomas More* Shakespeare's? Thomas Bayes and the Elliott–Valenza authorship tests', *Early Modern Literary Studies*, 12 (2007), 1, online at http://extra.shu.ac.uk/emls/12-3/jackbaye.htm; Watt, 'The Authorship of the Hand-D Addition to *The Book of Sir Thomas More*', in *Shakespeare, Computers, and the Mystery of Authorship*, ed. Hugh Craig and Arthur F. Kinney (Cambridge, 2009), pp. 134–61. Both contributions present a convincing case for Shakespeare's authorship. Both also critique the most significant study to question Shakespeare's authorship, Ward E. Y. Elliott and Robert J. Valenza, 'Two Tough Nuts to Crack: Did Shakespeare Write the "Shakespeare" portions of *Sir Thomas More* and *Edward III* ?', online at www.claremontmckenna.edu/govt/welliott/UTConference/2ToughNuts.pdf.

[3] For this, and for references to the relevant scholarship, see my edition in the Arden Shakespeare series (London, 2011), pp. 344–94 and 415–60. Line references follow this edition.

team of four revisers contributed the five Additions. These amount to no less than eight separately scripted passages occupying seven leaves and two paper slips.[4] The revisions replace all or almost all of five scenes in the Original Text, and add new material in a further two scenes. In the redeveloped play, the insurrection is not abandoned but largely reworked. The scene depicting the long-haired ruffian Falconer is split in two; the sections are positioned before and after the scene showing the visit of Erasmus in a single scenic sequence.

Of the revisers, Henry Chettle and Thomas Dekker can be identified with confidence purely on the basis of their handwriting.[5] Shakespeare's part-authorship of this play is far more rigorously demonstrated than it is, for instance, of *Pericles*, or, for instance, George Peele's part-authorship of *Titus Andronicus*, or Thomas Middleton's of *Timon of Athens*. Heywood is another matter: the attribution is very plausible but not wholly secure, and when I refer to 'Heywood' it should be understood with an appended query: 'Heywood(?)'; nevertheless, the correlations that will be noted later between part of Addition V and Heywood's works strengthen the ascription, and there is little reason to doubt it.

ADDITION II

The theatrical provenance of the revisions would no doubt illuminate the matters considered here if it was known, but must remain tantalizingly beyond the scope of the present investigation. Shakespeare's collaboration with Chettle, Dekker and Heywood poses a problem that has given a particular inflexion to textual study of the manuscript, and in particular the insurrection sequence in Addition II, which contains the work of Shakespeare, Heywood, Dekker, and at least one other dramatist. Peter W. M. Blayney offers a precise and elaborated account of how Shakespeare worked separately from the other playwrights.[6] Rejecting the simpler interpretation that Tilney saw only the Original Text, Blayney envisages a sequence in which Tilney first required alterations to the insurrection episode; Shakespeare acted as

the first reviser, scripting the Hand D passage; Tilney then reviewed the manuscript again and disallowed the whole insurrection; then the other revisers, with what Blayney himself calls 'surprising optimism', attempted to preserve the insurrection in modified form.[7] Blayney's case rests on two foundations: the stage direction 'Manett Clowne' at the end of the revised scene 4, along with the absence of an entry direction for More in scene 6 as revised by Shakespeare. These are clues, Blayney argues, that point to a lost original, which has been replaced by the existing scene 5.[8] In it, the insurrection would have continued unabated. The missing sequence would have begun with the Clown on stage and would have developed towards More's entrance, before resuming at the top of the first page of the surviving Shakespeare addition.

Blayney's work influences much subsequent thinking about Shakespeare's role. For instance the Revels editor Giorgio Melchiori argues that the Hand D passage was the first section of Addition II to be written.[9] When Hand C later reviewed Heywood's revised scene 4, he envisaged that the

---

4 The date was first proposed by Scott McMillin, in *The Elizabethan Theatre and The Book of Sir Thomas More* (Ithaca and London, 1987), p. 94, and more fully elaborated by Gary Taylor, in 'The Date and Auspices of the Additions to *Sir Thomas More*', in *Shakespeare and 'Sir Thomas More': Essays on the Play and its Shakespearian Interest*, ed. Trevor Howard-Hill (Cambridge, 1989), pp. 101–29.

5 For a summary of evidence and scholarship for these two dramatists and Heywood, see Harold Jenkins's supplement to W. W. Greg's Malone Society Reprint, revised edition (Oxford, 1961), pp. xxxiv–xxxvi.

6 Peter W. M. Blayney, 'The Booke of Sir Thomas More Re-Examined', *Studies in Philology*, 69 (1972), 167–91.

7 Blayney, 'The Booke of Sir Thomas More', p. 175.

8 Scene numbers are based on those in Greg's Malone Society Reprint, except that Greg identifies Sc. 5 in the revised version as Sc. vᵃ. For issues affected by page layout such as the 'Manett Clowne' stage direction, see John S. Farmer, ed., *The Book of Sir Thomas Moore (Harleian MSS. 7368, c. 1590–96)*, Tudor Facsimile Texts, Folio Series (London, 1910; repr. New York, 1970), or the digital facsimiles on CD-ROM in the British Library.

9 Giorgio Melchiori, 'The Booke of Sir Thomas Moore: A Chronology of Revision', *Shakespeare Quarterly*, 37 (1986), 291–308, p. 302. Melchiori's position is summarized in the Revels edition: Anthony Munday and others, *Sir Thomas*

Clown would remain on stage as if to address the audience, but that this business would be pre-empted by the return of the other rebels as at the beginning of scene 6; subsequently the revisers changed their mind and decided to revive the Guildhall scene, scene 5 (p. 307). All this, according to Melchiori, happened after an initial concern about the possibility of censorship but before Tilney actually saw the manuscript. Melchiori avoids Blayney's posited double submission to Tilney and speculated lost passage of first-stage revision. But the revision in two or more stages with Shakespeare as the first reviser is still fully in place, with the 'Manett Clowne' direction offering vital evidence.

Since Melchiori wrote it has been established that the supposed problem of the Clown remaining on stage at the end of scene 4 is imaginary. The manuscript page containing the scene (fo. 7a) is in Heywood's hand. In it, Heywood wrote a two-line speech for the Clown up the right margin of the page; Hand C added the stage direction 'Manett Clowne' below it (that is to say, alongside the right edge of the page). Hand C's additional ink-marks are crucial. He inscribed a half-box around the stage direction, and further lines leading from it via the bottom right-hand corner to the end of the speech at the bottom of the page, which is spoken by Lincoln. Eric Rasmussen has convincingly pointed out that these establish that the stage direction takes effect at the end of Lincoln's speech. 'Manett Clowne' therefore stipulates that the Clown remains on stage to make his final speech.[10] Consequently there is no reason to suppose that he remained on stage after that speech.

Equally, the first lines of scene 6 as it survives at the top of a new leaf (fo. 8), this being the beginning of the passage in Shakespeare's hand, lend no support to the idea that the leaf continues action that would have begun on a censored and now lost preceding leaf. The passage shows all the characteristics of a new scene:

Lincoln. Peace, hear me! He that will not see a red
    herring at a Harry groat, butter at eleven pence a
    pound, meal at nine shillings a bushel, and beef at
    four nobles a stone, list to me.   (6.1–4)

The dramatic effect of the main speaker claiming his platform amidst a general hubbub is similar, for example, to the opening of *Titus Andronicus* 3.1, 'Hear me, grave fathers; noble Tribunes, stay!', *Julius Caesar* 1.2, 'Peace ho! Caesar speaks' (after Caesar calls 'Calpurnia'), and especially *Coriolanus* 1.1, 'Before we proceed any further, hear me speak.' It would, moreover, be an odd and very unexpected coincidence if this Shakespearian scene-opener were actually a mid-scene passage that just happened to fall precisely at the top of a new leaf of paper.

The one and only substantial difficulty in the surviving script lies in the omission of an entrance for Thomas More. At the foot of fo. 7b, after the end of scene 5, Hand C wrote a detailed stage direction to initiate scene 6:

Enter Lincoln. Doll. Clown. George betts williamson others / And A Sergaunt at armes

This accurately and in detail identifies the requirements for the first passage in the scene. Arguably this is not the place where More's entrance would occur. Some lines into the scene, after 6.31, Shakespeare himself supplied a stage direction for the entry of the law-and-order party who are going to confront the rebels:

Enter the L. maier Surrey
Shrewsbury

This is probably the more logical point for More to enter, but again he is not named. Sixteen lines later, More has his first speech. It is well recognized that the stage directions in early modern play scripts are often incomplete or inconsistent. But, in a situation where the stage directions are specific and detailed, the omission of an entrance for the play's titular role and the scene's leading speaker is of a different order

---

More, ed. Vittorio Gabrieli and Giorgio Melchiori (Manchester, 1990).

[10] Eric Rasmussen, 'Setting Down what the Clown Spoke: Improvisation, Hand B, and *The Book of Sir Thomas More*', *The Library*, 13 (1991), 126–36, p. 136. Fo. 7b is reproduced on p. 133. Rasmussen understands the direction to anticipate further improvisation by the Clown, but as he is given lines to speak this inference is superfluous.

from the relatively minor matters of detail that are usually left unnoted. It requires explanation.

My suggestion is that, here as elsewhere, part of Hand C's technology for co-ordinating this exceptionally complex revision lay in the manipulation of paper.[11] He copied the new scene 5 and the stage direction for scene 6, not after the revisions of scene 4 and scene 6 as Blayney proposes, but before either of them. When fo. 7 was given to Heywood, it would already have contained on the verso scene 5 and Hand C's opening direction for scene 6, leaving the blank recto into which he was to write his revision of scene 4. As for the purpose of the stage direction itself, far from indicating that Hand C was clearing matters up after Shakespeare had submitted his work, it indicates that he was anticipating the revised passage before it was written. It either gives Shakespeare an initial steer when revising the scene as it appeared in the Original Text, or provides a basis for Hand C himself to review the script when marrying the sections together – perhaps Hand C had both objectives in view. The stage direction contrasts with Hand C's annotation of the Hand D passage, as its position on the previous leaf indicates in itself. Hand C wrote the opening direction on fo. 7 rather than fo. 8, the first Hand D leaf, because he was not at that stage dealing with the Hand D leaves – for the simple reason that Shakespeare had not yet written onto them.

But there was an unintended consequence. Shakespeare took no benefit from Hand C's stage direction. Nor could he have done so if, as I propose, fo. 7, where it was written, was in Heywood's hands when Shakespeare was writing. As already indicated, Shakespeare supplied no opening entry for the scene. He might have been aware that Hand C had dealt with the matter already. Or perhaps he understood, as did Heywood in revising both scene 4 and scene 9, that the provision of opening stage directions was a task that was to be left to Hand C at the reviewing stage, when his audit of stage directions at the beginning of each addition would play an important role in his co-ordination of the various sections into a continuous script.

In contrast, when Shakespeare reached the mid-scene arrival of the earls and the Mayor he supplied the needed stage direction. But there may have been a question about More's entrance in his mind. The words he wrote would comfortably have fitted on a single line; the division into two lines allows very ample space both to the left and right, as it were inviting Hand C to annotate. Shakespeare may have recognized that a key staging issue was unresolved. The layout suggests that even as he took responsibility for the ongoing action, he was inviting and indeed legitimizing the work of the annotator, anticipating that he would make alterations. His approach is just the same as when, earlier in the same passage, he left speech-prefixes for 'other' (6.5, 9), or, more briefly 'oth' (6.14) or merely 'o' (6.21): the decision as to which citizens should speak was thereby handed over to Hand C.

But the cogency of assuming that fo. 7b had already been completed before Heywood got to work on it has not as yet been fully demonstrated. Two points will emerge. First, despite Hand C's role as co-ordinator, when he annotated the Shakespeare section he faced exactly the same predicament as had Shakespeare before him, with even more idiosyncratic results. Second, his annotation of the Shakespeare pages was discontinuous with his writing of the opening stage direction in fo. 7b. When these two conclusions are put together, it becomes clear that in terms of the sequence of events the opening stage direction is separated from Hand C's annotation of the Shakespeare pages quite simply by Shakespeare's own writing. The clarity of the staging requirements in

[11] The paste-in slips are a conspicuous example. Otherwise, the main revision was conceptualized as a series of leaves as follows: scenes 4–5 (Heywood and ?Chettle), one leaf; scene 6 (Shakespeare), two leaves; scene 8 (Dekker), two leaves; Heywood, end of scene 9, one leaf. Some of the extant pages are not those prepared by the dramatists but contain Hand C's transcriptions. If Chettle drafted the revised Sc. 5 as copied by Hand C, each of the four dramatists would have been initially given two leaves (though Heywood's included a page filled by Hand C, and none of the dramatists completely used his allocation).

both Shakespeare's script and Hand C's annotation of it suffer as a result.

In revising Shakespeare's contribution, Hand C made a series of very particular and detailed alterations. The speeches Shakespeare had vaguely given to 'other' were distributed cogently between the citizens. Clown Betts, a new role introduced into the revision mainly by Heywood, was given two of these speeches. Hand C, aware of the possible confusion between the Clown and his brother George, wrote 'Ge' against Shakespeare's prefix 'bettes' at 6.36. Shakespeare had supplied two ambiguous and apparently contradictory speech prefixes for 'Sher' at 6.32 and 35 against speeches that cannot be uttered by the same speaker; Hand C gave one of them to the Lord Mayor and the other to the rioting citizen Williamson. Hand C also sought to strengthen the role of the rebel leader Lincoln, assigning to him a speech that Shakespeare had given to Betts (6.99) and another that he had given to 'all' (6.158). Further, Hand C deleted three lines that Shakespeare had written, and wrote the words 'tell me but this' (6.129) to bridge over his cut; he was evidently reading the passage for intelligibility and introduced the cut because he could not follow the sense. These changes are all practical, looking forward to the play as it could be staged rather than backward to Shakespeare's intentions. They assert in strong terms the theatrical ownership of the script. They are compatible with alterations he made elsewhere in the play that will be described below in demonstrating a degree of fine-tuning that brings the script very close to the requirements of the stage. The scrutiny is remarkably detailed and thorough. Yet the generous space around Shakespeare's stage direction remained vacant. In the script as Hand C left it, More still remained without an entry. Hand C, like Shakespeare, failed to make any connection between the stage direction he himself had supplied and the script as Shakespeare had written it.

One further alteration that Hand C made to Shakespeare's script relates directly to the problem of More's missing entrance. Against the first speech-prefix for the Sergeant-at-arms, which

appears at 6.21 (a few lines before Shakespeare's entry for the Mayor, Surrey and Shrewsbury), Hand C wrote the word 'Enter'. Compared with the missing entry for More, this is fine-tuning. But here, uniquely, the annotation causes a new difficulty. In the stage direction initiating the scene, as quoted above, Hand C had already provided an entrance for '*A Sergaunt at armes*'. This is forgotten at the point where he annotated the conflicting direction 'Enter' opposite the Sergeant's speech. The resulting duplication falls in the same passage, beginning with Hand C's stage direction at the foot of fo. 7b, as the manuscript's silence over that most crucial matter, getting More on stage. Nowhere else in the entire play is Hand C incompetent in this fashion even once, let alone twice. A simple conclusion follows. It is not hard to understand why Hand C should follow Shakespeare in proceeding without reference to fo. 7 if this, the leaf onto which Hand C had previously written the opening stage direction for the scene, inconveniently remained with Heywood throughout.

The absence of the main character, rather than testifying to Shakespeare's isolation, therefore reflects the nature of the script as an exceptionally intricate collaboration between him and others. It is inevitable that one part of a manuscript in preparation is detached from another part when writers work in physical isolation one from another. The assumption that Shakespeare was scripting in parallel with Heywood explains the key difficulties in the complex sequence of revisions identified collectively as Addition II. We see the advantage and the disadvantage of using multiple revisers. The advantage is that progress can be speeded up by having them work simultaneously; the disadvantage is that while they are doing so they are blind to each other's endeavours. In other words, the unusual failure of both an experienced dramatist and an assiduous annotator to deal with a key matter of staging is an immediate consequence of the fragmented process of the revision. The complexities lie, not as Blayney supposed, in the intricacies of lost stages of revision, but in the simultaneity of different parts of the revision as it survives.

ADDITION V

But this is not the only time that Shakespeare and
Heywood were composing the revisions in parallel. They are the two dramatists who come into
view once again in Additions III and V. These revisions were written after Hand C had copied out
the long Addition IV, which contains the scene
that conflates the Falconer and Erasmus episodes
(scene 8). Hand C then copied Additions III and
V into slips that had been cut from the same leaf of
paper. After Hand C's transcription, the slips were
pasted onto cancelled pages of the Original Text
in positions that establish the place of each passage
within the sequence of the revision: Addition III
between the Original Text and Addition IV; Addition V between Addition IV and the reversion to
the Original Text.

Addition III is a short soliloquy of twenty-one
lines spoken by More. It introduces scene 8. More
in his new capacity as Lord Chancellor meditates
on his mistrust of high office. His words act as a
prologue to his game of dressing his manservant
as himself to test whether Erasmus can spot the
deception. The speech is a key passage for articu-
lating More's awareness of his humble origin, and
his bemused wariness towards the dangerous accessory of political power. Addition V also consists of
a soliloquy by More, and, like Addition III, it had
no other content when Hand C first copied it.
Its obvious function is to connect the revised and
now composite scene 8 with scene 9, in which
the interlude, *The Marriage of Wit and Wisdom*, is
performed before city dignitaries at More's house.
In Addition V More notes how 'Friends go and
come' (9.6): Erasmus has sailed away for Rotterdam, but now the Lord Mayor is about to arrive.
The implication, as in Addition III, is: such it is
to be famous. The powerful lead lives of episodic
encounter with other great men, and if you are
Thomas More you value their friendship. Seen in
conjunction, the two soliloquies show the revisers'
desire to give stronger coherence to the play's fragmented middle scenes. They both use More as the
adhesive, placing him in a semi-choric role. They
both also develop the audience's awareness that he

is the play's central figure, and they both elaborate
on his state of mind. They are, indeed, More's only
soliloquies in the entire play. In all these respects
the design is palpable.

Addition III has been convincingly attributed
to Shakespeare on stylistic grounds.[12] The parallels
that have been identified with Shakespeare would
provide a fair basis for attributing the speech to
him even if he were not elsewhere identified in the
play. Shakespeare is by a very considerable measure likelier to have written the speech than any of
the other dramatists involved in the play, and the
case for his authorship is indeed strong relative to
any other dramatist of the period.

The overall authorship of Addition V has not
previously been considered in any detail. The first
five and a half lines, spoken by a Messenger, are a
late addition to the original soliloquy, copied into
the margin by Hand C. They can safely be ascribed
to Heywood, because Hand C copied them from a
draft Heywood had written at the end of Addition
VI. The main soliloquy is as follows:

> Why, this is cheerful news. Friends go and come.
> Reverend Erasmus, whose delicious words
> Express the very soul and life of wit,
> Newly took sad leave of me, with tears
> Troubled the silver channel of the Thames,
> Which, glad of such a burden, proudly swelled
> And on her bosom bore him toward the sea.
> He's gone to Rotterdam. Peace go with him!
> He left me heavy when he went from hence,
> But this recomforts me: the kind Lord Mayor,
> His brethren aldermen, with their fair wives
> Will feast this night with us. Why, so't should be.
> More's merry heart lives by good company.
> Good gentlemen, be careful; give great charge
> Our diet be made dainty for the taste.
> For, of all people that the earth affords,
> The Londoners fare richest at their boards.
>
> (9.6–22)

---

[12] R. C. Bald, 'Addition III of *Sir Thomas More*', *Review of
English Studies*, 7 (1931), 67–9; J. M. Nos-
worthy, 'Shakespeare and *Sir Thomas More*', *Review of English Studies*, ns 6
(1955), 12–25.

No investigation of authorial traits can hope to amass quantitative evidence from such a short sample. Even if one attempts instead to identify individual items that correlate the text with the work of other dramatists of the period, it cannot be expected that a short passage will yield many items of evidence that would not individually be paralleled in the work of more than one dramatist. But if the pool of dramatists is reduced to those who can be identified on prima facie grounds as credible candidates, there are good chances of discovering affinities and disaffinities between the passage and the particular writers in question. Indeed, in attribution study it is common to assess the competing claims of as few as two collaborators. In the case of *Sir Thomas More*, two is too small a number, as there were four known dramatists involved in the revision, with Munday potentially present also as author or co-author of the Original Text.

I conducted a study for locutions unique to one dramatist among these five, by searching the online databases *Literature Online* (*Lion*) and *Early English Books Online* (*EEBO*). It is necessary to deploy both databases as *Lion* has fuller records of plays, particularly in that it includes the major manuscripts, whereas *EEBO* contains a much wider range of prose, which is a significant part of the output of Munday, Dekker and Heywood. Single words provided no clear evidence; the most distinctive word 'recomforts' has no exact parallel but does have parallels based on variant forms in Munday, Shakespeare and a work attributed to Chettle. The evidence depends, then, on phrases and sequences of words. Searches can be limited to the exact phrase or, if that provides no parallels, extended to variations on the phrase or its constituents identified by conducting proximity searches (identifying two or more elements in proximity but not necessarily adjacent) or searches of variant forms (identifying parts of a verb, singulars and plurals, adverbials, etc.).

This investigation reveals no significant evidence in favour of Chettle or Dekker. In contrast, Shakespeare, the putative author of the equivalent soliloquy in Addition III, and Heywood, the author

of the first lines of Addition V, are firmly in the frame. There are two parallels with Munday, which are different in kind. These may be considered first. Where Addition V has 'give great charge' (9.19) Munday writes 'gave great charge'. Heywood comparably has 'gives him great charge', so Munday is not uniquely singled out. More noteworthy, the passage '*the Thames, / Which, glad of such a burden, proudly swelled / And on her bosom bore him* toward the sea' (9.10–12) has an unusually strong parallel in 'as *the very Thames* appeared *proude of this gallant burden, swelling her breast to beare them* with pompe and Majestie' (*London's Love*, 1610, sig. C3).[13] Unlike 'gave great charge', this goes beyond a coincidence of ordinary locutions and indeed it exceeds in significance any other individual parallel between More's speech and any other dramatist. It suggests conscious and specific reuse of a known pre-existing text. The specificity can be measured by noting that *EEBO* identifies no more than three of the five components in any early modern text. This single parallel might testify either to the presence of Munday in the writing of Addition V or the influence of the revised play on his later writing. The paucity of distinct parallels with Munday elsewhere in the speech, and the absence of any other indication that he was involved in the Additional Passages at all, point to the latter explanation, and suggest that Munday is consciously drawing on the speech in his later pageant. The provisional conclusion that Munday was familiar with the play in its revised version is interesting in its own right, but takes us no further in analysing the authorship of the speech.

Phrases paralleled in Shakespeare's work include: 'this is [adj.] news' (9.6; *Coriolanus*, 5.4.52; *Anthony and Cleopatra*, 1.2.93), '[plural noun] go and come' (9.6; *Henry V*, 3.2.8), 'burden... swelled... bosom' (9.11–12; 'Swell, bosom, with thy freight', *Othello*, 3.3.452), 'proudly swelled' (9.11; 'proud swelling', *King John*, 4.3.148, the only instance of an immediate collocation of 'proud swell' and variants), 'He's

---

[13] Quotations from printed texts by Heywood are from the original editions as reproduced in *EEBO*.

gone . . . Peace go with him' (9.13; 'Art thou gone too? All comfort go with thee', *2 Henry VI*, 2.4.88), 'left me heavy' (9.14; cf. 'heavy leave', two instances, the only ones of 'heavy' qualifying 'leave' and its variants, both with 'take': cf. 'take sad leave', 9.9), 'merry heart lives' (9.18; *2 Henry IV*, 5.3.49, but from an existing song: 'light heart lives', *Love's Labour's Lost*, 5.2.18, with 'merry' at 5.2.16), 'our diet' (9.20; *Twelfth Night*, 3.3.40, here also referring to a diet that is to be arranged: 'I will bespeak our diet'), 'dainty for the taste' (9.20; i.e. 'dainty for . . . [noun]', 'dainty for such tread', *Love's Labour's Lost*, 4.3.277; i.e. 'dainty' qualified by phrase with 'taste', 'Dainties to taste', *Venus and Adonis*, 164, 'the daintiest that they taste', *2 Henry VI*, 3.2.326).[14] Of these, the qualification of 'leave' or 'to be left' with 'heavy' is found in no other play of the period; '[plural noun] go and come' is found only twice in any other plays offering parallels (by John Lyly and William Alexander), 'dainty for' and 'proud swell' are properly paralleled in only one play each (by Christopher Marlowe and John Fletcher respectively), and the few instances of 'our diet' in the drama lack the shared idea of an arrangement that is to be made.

Two lines deserve special consideration, as they contain conflicting evidence not so far presented. 'Express the very soul and life of wit' (9.8) has Shakespeare parallels for 'words express the [. . .] of' ('words express / The manner of', Sonnet 140.3–4) and 'the very soul and life of wit' (8; 'the soul of wit', *Hamlet*, 2.2.91). But it has Heywood parallels in 'express the . . . life' (cf. various instances of 'expressed to the life', etc., though this is a set expression of different meaning) and 'the very soul and life of' (cf 'the very life and spirit of'). These phrases all break down into commonplace ideas except in one respect: 'the soul of wit' is probably a Shakespeare coinage, as the earliest instance identified in *EEBO* is dated 1603, a few years after the probable earliest text *Hamlet* was written. The line 'Troubled the silver channel of the Thames' (9.10) has affinities with both Shakespeare and Heywood. But there is a particularly striking Shakespeare parallel for the image in *Julius*

Caesar, where 'tears' are wept into a 'channel' until it swells: 'weep your tears / Into the channel, till the lowest stream / Do kiss the most exalted shores of all' (1.1.58–60). Where Addition V has 'troubled the silver channel', Shakespeare writes 'Troubles the silver spring', *2 Henry VI*, 4.1.72. *Lion* offers no other instance of 'troubl* the silver' in drama of the period, making it a strong parallel. Heywood, for his part, has the more mundane 'channel of the' (but compare Shakespeare's 'the sweet channel of her'); he writes 'Faire Thamesis, upon whose silver breast' (but the image is Spenserian, and Shakespeare describes another English river, the Trent, as *silver* in *1 Henry IV*, 3.1.99), and the collocation 'channel . . . swell' (but Shakespeare has 'channel . . . o'erswell'). The reference to the Thames is firmly locked into Shakespearian imagery.[15] The balance of probability for this line too lies firmly with Shakespeare.

Elsewhere in the passage, the specifically Heywood-favoured expressions are: 'which, glad of such a burden' (9.11; 'who glad of such a purchase', *Gynaikeion*, 300), 'with their faire wiues' (9.16; *Hierarchy of the Blessed Angels* (1635), 501), 'will feast this night' (9.17; *Silver Age* (1613), sig. C4), 'so't should be' (9.17; 'so't must be', *Life of Merlin* (1641), 250; 'so it must be', *Pleasant Dialogues* (1637), sig. L2), 'of all people' (9.21; one straightforward instance, one in collaboration and one in translation), 'all . . . that the earth affords' (9.21; 'all that the earth brings', *Hierarchy*, 441; 'the earth affords', *Hierarchy*, 421), 'the earth affords . . . richest' (9.21–2; cf. 'Scarce can the world affoord a richer prize', *Four Prentices* (1615), sig. G4v) and the rhyme 'affords . . . boards' (9.21–2; *Troia Britanica* (1609), 224). Several of these features are combined in Heywood's:

---

[14] The collocation of *dainty* and *taste* is also in Heywood, but not *dainty for*.

[15] It might be observed that the Shakespeare parallels under immediate consideration belong to the years immediately before the revision of *Sir Thomas More*, where Heywood's works are later; Heywood could therefore have been influenced not only by Addition V itself but by Shakespeare's writing elsewhere. But no such special explanation is necessary.

Numa Pompilius, who did oft inuite
The best of Rome to feast with him by night,
Neuer made vse of market to afford
Rich choice of dainties to his sumptuous bord
(*Hierarchy*, 507)

In Addition V the feasters are Londoners; 'Londoners' is Heywood favoured, and in one passage he notes 'How great and magnificent the Londoners feasts be even amongst themselves . . . as also the ordinary Tables of the Lord Maior and the Sheriffes' (*Whittington*, sig. C3v). Heywood is evidently the only one of the five dramatists to use the contraction 'so't'. The passage with the rhyme in Heywood's *Troia Britanica* happens to be close in content to ideas in the soliloquy:

I passe the Citty gates, my Barke I boord,
The fauourable winds calme gales affoord,
And fill my sailes, vnto your Land I steare,

Turning beyond the revisers to the larger picture, *Lion* and *EEBO* identify two instances of 'with their fair wives' in all literature in the period, of which one is by Heywood. He also wrote 'with faire wiues', describing London citizens 'in the *richest* sort being garnish't out' and 'good Citizens / And their faire wiues' (*2 If You Know Not Me*, sigs. E1v, E2v). Heywood's is the only other instance of 'will feast this night'; the absence of any other parallel to the internal collocations 'will feast this' and 'feast this night' testifies that the full four-word collocation is a particularly strong one. He is the only professional dramatist to use the phrase 'so't [modal] be' before Richard Brome.

Considering the shortness of Addition V, the evidence for both dramatists is moderately strong and, in contrast with Munday, recurrent. With the doubtful exception of 1.8 and 1.11, where Shakespeare is nonetheless quite distinctly favoured, the indications of two different dramatists are far from mutually cancelling. The mix of parallels coherently suggests a history of initial drafting by Shakespeare and revision by Heywood. Outside the two lines with mixed affinities, the Heywood parallels occur in two short clusters:

The kind Lord Mayor,
His brethren aldermen, with their fair wives
Will feast this night with us. Why, so't should be.

For, of all people that the earth affords,
The Londoners fare richest at their boards.

The city consciousness is clear. Moreover, five of these six lines are consistent to the point of duplication with the information in the Messenger's speech that Heywood had initially drafted at the end of Addition VI:

My honourable lord, the Mayor of London
Accompanied with his lady and her train
Are coming hither, and are hard at hand
To feast with you. A sergeant's come before
To tell your lordship of their near approach.

It is Heywood who would have been most immediately aware of the speech's content.[16] If the Heywoodian lines are omitted, the residual passage reads:

Why, this is cheerful news. Friends go and come.
Reverend Erasmus, whose delicious words
Express the very soul and life of wit,
Newly took sad leave of me, with tears
Troubled the silver channel of the Thames,
Which, glad of such a burden, proudly swelled
And on her bosom bore him toward the sea.
He's gone to Rotterdam. Peace go with him!
He left me heavy when he went from hence,
But this recomforts [and delights my soul].
More's merry heart lives by good company.
Good gentlemen, be careful; give great charge
Our diet be made dainty for the taste.

The bracketed words conjecturally restore a pentameter, on the assumption that Heywood altered these or similar words to make way for 'the kind lord Mayor'. It is of course possible that he cancelled or altered more, or that the conjectured words are off the mark. Nevertheless, the passage as presented above can otherwise be offered as a tentative addition to the canon of Shakespeare's writing.

---

[16] It is at least possible that Heywood intended to replace the Messenger's speech with his additions to More's speech, but that Hand C misunderstood or took a different view.

It is proposed, then, that Heywood undertook in the soliloquy to provide extra information to set the scene and to underscore the social importance of the Mayor's visit. The celebration of Londoners' 'richest' diet, suggests London's ascendance as a trading city – as does 'the silver channel of the Thames' once it is set in relation to these lines. This is entirely compatible with the London-oriented patriotism of Heywood's work elsewhere.

Shakespeare, unlike Heywood, did not engage in celebration of London's civic dignity. Moreover, if Shakespeare wrote on the Shakespearian theme of citizens rioting partly over food shortages in Scene 6, he is unlikely to have written 'The Londoners fare richest at their boards' without a trace of irony. The highly metaphoric language in the first half of the speech, however, is distinctly Shakespearian. The description of the Thames that 'proudly swelled' (9.11) when bearing Erasmus away has a suggestive parallel in the Hand D passage of *Sir Thomas More* itself: 'Whiles they are o'er the bank of their obedience / Thus will they bear down all things' (6.46–7). The proudly swelling river recalls various similar personifying images in Shakespeare more specifically: 'I have seen / Th'ambitious ocean swell' (*Julius Caesar*, 1.3.6–7), 'The ocean, overpeering of his list' (*Hamlet*, 4.5.97), or 'Proud Cleopatra when she met her Roman, / And Cydnus swelled above the banks' (*Cymbeline*, 2.4.70–1). Enobarbus's description of Cleopatra's barge also involves the personified elements taking on themselves the emotional resonance of the occasion, in much the same manner as More's description of Erasmus's ship: 'The winds were love-sick', and the water was 'amorous' of the oar-strokes (*Antony and Cleopatra*, 2.2.201–4). The two descriptions of Cleopatra both come from plays written later than the revisions of *Sir Thomas More*, demonstrating that the influence does not flow from Shakespeare to another reviser. The part-erotic, part-maternal tenor of More's lines – tears, channel, burden, proudly swelled, bosom, bore – are entirely in Shakespeare's manner. So too is the fluidity of syntax and metre, as indicated by the high incidence of enjambment.

The provisional conclusion is that Shakespeare undertook to write both of the soliloquies for More that appear in Additions III and V. Addition III remained unaltered (and indeed is rather awkwardly bedded into the scene that follows), whereas Addition V was expanded by Heywood. The provisionality in this statement has to be acknowledged. The searchable databases available at the present, though huge, are not complete. The conflicting indications in 9.8 and 9.11 point to a vulnerability in the method – though one that leaves the evidence locally ambiguous rather than invalidating the method itself. Findings presented here are based on soft evidence; the parameters for inclusion and exclusion are malleable, and the value attributable to the findings varies. Although every effort has been made to pursue the investigation in a rigorous and even-handed way, the possibility remains that there may be undetected counter-evidence – or, for that matter, undetected evidence in support. The case presented here is a far cry from, for example, Ian Watt's investigation of Hand D, and his claims for near certainty are not echoed here. Nevertheless, it is very hard to imagine, in the light of the present findings, that a more persuasive account of the writing of Addition V will emerge. A fair summation of the case would be that it is significantly more probable than improbable that Shakespeare and Heywood both played a part in the writing of Addition V.

Shakespeare's involvement in *Sir Thomas More* is often explained in terms of his established skill in treating scenes of popular tumult in such a way that they would not be disallowed by the Master of the Revels. More's speeches in the Hand D section have been admired for their arrestingly expressive quality and their articulation of a humane and passionately reasoned opposition to xenophobia. But if we take into account Shakespeare's probable involvement in Additions III and V, different perspectives emerge. Shakespeare now is the dramatist who makes More deeply articulate. Of course More has plenty to say in the play's later scenes showing his arrest and its aftermath. But they are all of a similar tone, one that contrasts with the earlier scenes. In the later part of the play More's whimsy becomes a mask that conceals introspection, no doubt with the intention of forestalling the attention of the Master of the Revels, though the note of reserved pious stoicism has its own dramatic logic. In contrast, Shakespeare's More speaks openly and generously. His words are not constrained by the need to avoid religious controversy. He is indeed an entirely secular figure, who is concerned with the *polis*, with the individual's role within the *polis*, and with the vulnerable theatricality of power. In the paste-in soliloquies he talks about his father; he describes his guests as his friends; in both instances he places his sense of self within the wider pattern of emotive relationships.

In short, to attribute Addition III and the first draft of Addition V to Shakespeare is to posit his responsibility for dimensions of character not seen elsewhere in the play except in the Hand D section. But the highlighting of More's role has a structural as well as characterological aspect. If scene 6 places More at the heart of things, Additions III and V place him in threshold positions. The episodes that neighbour these passages are connected and put in context; and the audience is assured that More's interiority is the space to watch. Such an account places Shakespeare in a specific and crucial role in the process of revision: no longer ignorant and isolated, but knowingly and responsibly shaping the action.

HAND C

Even on this view, it remains far from the case that Shakespeare was the key player in the overall inception of the revisions. That role can belong only to Hand C. We have seen how his transcription of scene 5 and his manipulation of the leaf into which it was written were a purposeful steering device, and it is likely that throughout his work he used the distribution of leaves of paper as a method of controlling the work of his contributors.[17] From the point when he transcribed scene 5 in Addition II and scene 8 in Addition IV, his measures to orchestrate the revision were persistent and multifaceted. His inscription, and presumably cutting and pasting, of Additions III and V provide an obvious case

in point. But Addition V is fascinating because it reveals the full complexity of the revision process alongside the diversity of Hand C's interventions as he sought to rein in the textual dispersal and co-ordinate the components.

The full history of Addition V runs something like this.[18] As I have posited, Shakespeare wrote a short soliloquy, and Heywood expanded it. In this state it was copied by Hand C and pasted into the main manuscript. Heywood supplemented the soliloquy, using spare paper in another leaf. Hand C incorporated these lines into Addition V, writing them up the left margin of both the underlying leaf of the Original Text into which the slip was pasted and the slip itself. As his original transcript lacked an opening stage direction, he now added the direction 'Enter a Messenger to moore.' The last line of the marginal insert, '*Moore* why this is cheerful &c', serves both to supply the otherwise missing speech-prefix and to connect the Messenger's speech to More's soliloquy at 9.6 by means of a short duplication.

But Hand C had not finished. Subsequently he wrote in the corner below the insert at the beginning of Addition V (or to the left of it if the leaf is turned to read it) a boxed stage direction, reading '*Mess / T Goodal*'. This establishes that the messenger who speaks to More is to be played by the actor Thomas Goodale. Demonstrably, Hand C considered the script as requiring fine and, one might expect, late-stage adjustment for performance. The annotations are informed by a clear eye to casting requirements that extended to minor roles. But Hand C had another object in view, which was to reinforce the point of textual connection between Addition IV and Addition V. To this end, he wrote a second and equivalent stage direction in the margin of Addition IV itself to the left of 8.247–8:

---

17 The paper of the revisions is of a single but mixed stock. On the import of paper in stocks combining the product of different manufacturers in a single locality, see Allan H. Stevenson, 'Watermarks are Twins', *Studies in Bibliography*, 4 (1955), 60.

18 Apart from the present proposal about the authorship of the Addition, the sequence was first fully described in Melchiori, '*The Booke of Sir Thomas Moore*'.

'Enter a messenger heere'.[19] As with Hand C's interventions elsewhere in the manuscript, he used duplication as a technique for highlighting the link between separated sections of text.

Dekker subsequently broke this link when he wrote a new ending to scene 8 (258–91), taking advantage of a blank half page below Hand C's transcription. Hand C was alert to the situation. It was presumably he who scribbled out his own direction halfway down the page for the messenger to enter. He wrote two reference marks consisting of a cross in a circle, one at the foot of Dekker's new end to scene 8, the other inside the box he had drawn around the opening entry of scene 9. Elsewhere, the same reference mark was used to link the Original Text and Addition VI. By this device, in both cases, the continuity of the text across the two sections is clearly indicated. The reference marks are therefore a shorthand equivalent to the duplication of stage directions.

Hand C's interventions around Addition V resemble those in the Hand D passage in scene 6 only insofar as they are detailed and complex. In other respects they differ completely. Rather than reflecting a single review, they are individual acts in a cumulative sequence. Rather than responding to the internal difficulties and uncertainties presented by a rough draft, they respond to a sequential growth in the text through three stages of revision. Where for the circumstantial reasons explained above Hand C was unable to make an effective transition between authorial stints in Addition II, here he takes repeated and effective measures to ensure that very continuity. The contrast in procedure again highlights the peculiarity of his failure to establish a good join between fos. 7 and 8. He co-ordinated the writing of at least three dramatists in Additions IV and V, work completed in five separate stages; he did so successfully.

The word 'co-ordinate' is here possibly a misleading understatement: dramatic writing was usually commissioned rather than being spontaneously offered, and Hand C may have had a role here too. The persistence of Shakespeare, Heywood, and Dekker in all putting forward new material after the initial job of reworking scenes 4–6 and

scenes 8–9 had been completed is one of the more remarkable aspects of what was already a remarkable project: why did they not consider the job done? It should be noted further that the revisions cannot be broken down into a simple two-stage pattern whereby the add-ons were agreed at a specific moment: as we have seen, at the point where Hand C added stage directions to Additions IV and V he had not anticipated that Dekker would supplement Addition IV. The peculiar sequence of add-ons may well testify not to the dramatists' individual urges to generate more and more passages of new dialogue, but to Hand C's evolving awareness of dramatic requirements. The fragmented nature of the writing and the complexity of Hand C's work are closely related.

The soliloquies of Additions III and V have been explained already in terms of character and play structure. No more might be said about them if it were not that Addition V is found in an area of the text where Hand C was demonstrably preoccupied with issues of casting. Apart from its dramatic effectiveness, a short soliloquy is a convenient device for creating a wider gap in time between adjacent scenes. In *2 Henry IV*, for example, Shakespeare provided a soliloquy for Falstaff at the end of 3.2, the scene in which Falstaff recruits soldiers from the peasantry of Gloucestershire; it certainly made excessive demands on the theatre company. In *Sir Thomas More*, as we have seen, Addition V contains the play's only annotation in which an actor is named. The space between the previous scene, scene 8, and the main action of the scene begun in Addition V, scene 9, was widened further by Dekker's last-minute new ending for scene 8. The adding of both the Addition V soliloquy beginning scene 9 and the extra Falconer–Morris dialogue at 258–91, and the expansion of the Addition V soliloquy with the extra Messenger speech, suggest a common tactic of filling out the dialogue in order to manage the action more effectively. The

---

[19] The stage direction was written a few lines before the end of Addition IV as Hand C had copied it; either the final exchange between Falconer and Morris was added after the stage direction, or its position is anticipatory.

annotation naming Goodale gives further testimony to the difficulty in doing so.

The reason is clear if we present all the stage directions for the early part of scene 9 as Munday had written them:

Enter Sʳ. *Thomas Moore*, M. *Roper*, and Seruing men setting stooles.

Enter his Lady.

Ent. Player.

En. Lady.

The waytes playes, Enters Lord Maior, so many Aldermen as may, / the Lady Maioresse in Scarlet, with other Ladyes and Sir Thomas / Moores daughters, Seruaunts carying lighted Torches by them.

After this, the players enter in role to perform the interlude. Irrespective of how many or few aldermen enter, this passage makes heavier demands on the cast than any other moment in the play. Like the recruiting scene in *2 Henry IV*, it presents exceptional demands of costuming – the aldermen's and ladies' robes, and the players' costumes and properties for their parts (the Vice carries a bridle). It also requires special lighting effects, which need both the preparation of torches and the nomination of actors to carry them. There are also musical demands, which are already flagged up in the Original Text itself where a duplicating marginal note reads 'waites play / hautbois'.[20] If the role-changes and the spectacular requirements of the scene presented an exceptional difficulty, the extra playing time beforehand would be welcome if not necessary.

Seen thus, it becomes clearer that it was Hand C, the theatrical annotator demonstrably thinking about acting personnel, who most likely called for the added passages. As for the dramatists, Dekker's extension of Addition IV (like Heywood's extension of scene 9) is primarily a comedic filler whose effect on the play is purely local. Heywood and Shakespeare take a more extended view. Heywood concentrates on the comic roles of the clown in the insurrection sequence and the player in scene 9. Even here the thinking is theatrically oriented in

that Heywood symptomatically writes the speech-prefix 'clo' against one of the speeches for the vice Inclination, suggesting that he was developing both episodes to bolster the parts for the same comic actor. Shakespeare too was supplying lines mainly for a single actor, the player of More himself. If there still remains some truth in the observation that Shakespeare writes as if without full awareness of the work of his fellow revisers, much the same is true of the other three. The personal consciousness that overarches the revisions is Hand C's, and Hand C's only.

Plays have different dimensions of creative organization, and this article presents an account of two contrasting types of play-making. Shakespeare writes as a theatre poet, Hand C as a theatre co-ordinator. If it is no revelation that they conformed to their functions, the diversity and range of both contributions is remarkable. Hand C does far more than would be expected of a theatre functionary, or than can be found in the work of other annotators in play manuscripts of the period. Indeed, he plays an astonishingly full and diverse role in the artistic co-ordination of the revision. I would argue that he is one of the co-authors of the revisions: the only identifiable figure to understand them and organize them as a whole, the only figure working directly and more or less in alignment with the intentions of all the dramatists, the only figure who can be described as having overall intentionality for the revision, and so in a real sense its maker.

The work of each segment of the revision seems isolated, dependent on a process of co-ordination that he alone supplied. But in the case of Shakespeare the contribution is essential to securing the theatrical effectiveness and dramatic coherence of the first two-thirds of the play. Even in the disadvantaged and hemmed-in position from which he

---

[20] This annotation is transcribed by Greg as 'waites play / here', and ascribed to Hand C. If so, it would be his only intervention in the Original Text, and in fact the script looks more like Munday himself. The present reading and attribution are Blayney's, as recorded and adopted in the Revels edition.

writes as one collaborator on a revision, he nudges the play towards greater eloquence and intensity. The constraints under which he wrote were those of his colleagues as well, but he made a greater virtue of this necessity. John Jones has described the Hand D passage, in contrast with his work on plays of sole authorship, as lacking in imaginative involvement with the play as a whole; it is not quite 'wonderful through belonging to a particular masterpiece, this and no other'.[21] Yet Shakespeare indeed thought beyond the needs of the local moment, and partly shared with Hand C in sensing the dramatic work.[22] In Addition II, the purely circumstantial and local difficulty arising from the distribution of sheets of paper was not overcome. Shakespeare deliberately held back from the kind of theatrical fine-tuning that would be best done when his contribution to Addition II was placed in the context of the other revisions. But from the present account it emerges that there is no slackness in Shakespeare's imaginatively mature involvement in the play's dialogue and structure.

---

[21] John Jones, *Shakespeare at Work* (Oxford, 1995), p. 28.

[22] Heywood's contribution is also diverse in terms of the range of interventions he makes (including, for instance, annotation of the Original Manuscript), though for circumstantial reasons such as paper-saving that fail to indicate an overall co-ordination of the project.

THREE'S COMPANY:
ALTERNATIVE HISTORIES OF LONDON'S THEATRES IN THE 1590s

HOLGER SCHOTT SYME

When theatre historians talk about the Chamberlain's Men, their stories almost inevitably turn into narratives about Shakespeare and the plays he wrote in the 1590s. In one sense, this move is simply dictated by the available evidence: not only are most of the surviving texts that can be securely linked to the company by Shakespeare, he was also among the first members of the troupe to be named in official records: 'To Will[ia]m Kempe Will[ia]m Shakespeare & Richarde Burbage seruantes to the Lord Chamb[er]leyne vpon the councelles warr[an]t dated at Whitehall xv^{to} Martii 1594 for twoe seuerall comedies or Enterludes shewed by them before her Matie in [Christ]mas tyme last paste.'[1] By March 1595, the Chamber Accounts inform us, Shakespeare had joined the company in which he would remain a sharer until his retirement almost twenty years later. It has generally been assumed that he was a founding member of the troupe when it was first set up sometime in the spring of 1594, but there is no documentary basis for this belief. All the same, his works dominate our impression of the company's repertory: with the single exception of the anonymous *Warning for Fair Women* (1599), all plays attributed to them on sixteenth-century title-pages are Shakespeare's. Of *all* the plays that can unequivocally be linked to the Chamberlain's Men, seventeen are his, as opposed to a mere eight by other playwrights. Of these, Ben Jonson's *Every Man In His Humour* (1601), Thomas Dekker's *Satiromastix* (1602), *Thomas Lord Cromwell* by 'W. S.' (1602), and the anonymous *A Larum for London* (1602) list the company on their title pages. We may add Jonson's *Every Man Out of His Humour*,

first printed in 1600 without company attribution but linked to the Chamberlain's Men in his 1616 *Workes*; *The Merry Devil of Edmonton*, assigned to the King's Men on the title-page of its first quarto in 1608, but on stage by 1602/3, since it is mentioned in Middleton's *Black Book*;[2] and possibly the anonymous *Mucedorus* (advertised as performed by the King's Men in 1610, but first printed in 1598 without attribution).

These strong connections between author and company have served to obfuscate the fact that neither was in any sense coterminous with the other – the Chamberlain's Men never were the 'Shakespeare Company', even if they may appear that way in retrospect, nor was Shakespeare always a Chamberlain's Man. A significant part of his oeuvre was written before the troupe came into being and, although scholars have long presumed that all his plays – all the plays printed in the 1623

I am grateful to Douglas Bruster, Peter Holland and Sally-Beth MacLean for their generous comments on this article, and to the members of a 2011 SAA seminar on 'Lacunae in Theater History', particularly Peter Greenfield, David Kathman, Ros Knutson and Leslie Thomson, for their responses to the section on Sir John Harington's Christmas festivities; John Jowett deserves special thanks for pointing out an extraordinarily foolish mistake.

[1] E. K. Chambers, *The Elizabethan Stage*, 4 vols. (Oxford, 1923), vol. 4, p. 164. The year in the entry reflects old style dating, with the year starting on 25 March.

[2] Thomas Middleton, *The Black Book*, ed. G. B. Shand, *Thomas Middleton: The Collected Works*, ed. Gary Taylor and John Lavagnino (Oxford, 2007), pp. 204–18, esp. p. 216. *The Black Book* was likely written in late 1603 and was published in 1604.

Folio, that is – entered the new company's repertory together with the playwright, there is next to no evidence to support such an assumption, however near-universally it may have been adopted.[3] In fact, the Folio never so much as mentions the Chamberlain's Men – or any other company – by name. In this article, I will argue that we know almost nothing of the Chamberlain's Men's activities before 1597 and even less of the fate of Shakespeare's early plays. Decoupling author from sharer and playwright from play will enable us to question common convictions about the development of the theatrical scene in mid-1590s London, and allow us to construct new and more complex narratives of Shakespeare's place in that development than have hitherto been proposed.

I

Let me begin with the plays Shakespeare probably wrote before the summer of 1594 and therefore for a company other than the Chamberlain's Men. Three of them can be shown to have become part of the new troupe's repertory at a later date: *Titus Andronicus* belonged to them by 1600, when they were listed on the title-page of the second quarto, but its status before that year is uncertain, as I will demonstrate below. *Richard III*, which most scholars date earlier than 1594, was printed in 1597 'As it hath beene lately Acted by the Right honourable the Lord Chamberlaine his seruants', the first instance of its attribution to any company. *Love's Labour's Lost* similarly is often seen as an early work but the Chamberlain's Men seem to have performed it at court in 1596/7 or 1597/8,[4] and the play may well not predate the new group's establishment.

This leaves a number of Shakespearian plays that cannot be linked to the Chamberlain's Men at all: *The Two Gentlemen of Verona*, *The Taming of the* – or *a* – *Shrew*, *The Comedy of Errors* and all three parts of the first Henriad. *The Comedy of Errors* belonged to the King's Men by December 1604, when they staged it at Whitehall, and they also performed *Shrew* at court in November 1633,[5] so those two texts presumably made their way to the company

at some point between their composition and the later stagings. Yet no evidence exists to show that either was ever staged by the King's Men's predecessors. *Two Gentlemen* may be the earliest of Shakespeare's surviving plays, but we know neither who first performed it nor whether it was revived at any point. That Francis Meres mentioned it in 1598 suggests that it remained in *someone's* repertory.[6] The *Henry VI* trilogy offers perhaps the most intriguing challenge. Its final part was published in octavo in 1595 as *The True Tragedy of Richard Duke of York* and attributed to Pembroke's Men; the same stationer, Thomas Millington, issued part two, *The First Part of the Contention of the Two Famous Houses of York and Lancaster*, in quarto in 1594 and scholars generally assume that this, too, was staged by Pembroke's company despite the title-page's silence on the matter. *1 Henry VI* first saw the light of day in printed form in the 1623 Folio. Its date of composition and authorship have occasioned much scholarly debate over the past century,[7] and while it is often alleged to be the 'harey the vj' Strange's

---

[3] To the best of my knowledge, the assumption has never been seriously questioned, and is introduced as indubitable fact in almost every discussion of the theatrical history of Shakespeare's works. For representative instances, see, e.g., Leeds Barroll, 'Shakespeare, Noble Patrons, and the Pleasures of "Common" Playing', in *Shakespeare and Theatrical Patronage in Early Modern England*, ed. Paul Whitfield White and Suzanne R. Westfall (Cambridge, 2002), pp. 90–121, esp. p. 118; Randall Martin, 'Introduction', *Henry VI, Part Three* (Oxford, 2001), p. 127 ('the ultimate transfer of the entire early body of Shakespeare's early plays to the Chamberlain's Men'); Andrew Gurr, *The Shakespearian Playing Companies* (Oxford, 1996), pp. 72–3; E. K. Chambers, *William Shakespeare: A Study of Facts and Problems* (Oxford, 1930), vol. 1, p. 289.

[4] Gary Taylor, Stanley Wells et al., *William Shakespeare: A Textual Companion* (Oxford, 1987), p. 117.

[5] John H. Astington, *English Court Theatre, 1558–1642* (Cambridge, 1999), pp. 239, 260.

[6] See Francis Meres, *Palladis tamia Wits treasury being the second part of Wits common wealth* (STC 17834) (London, 1598), sig. Oo2r. *Two Gentlemen's* early date has recently been disputed by John Peachman in 'Why a Dog? A Late Date for *The Two Gentlemen of Verona*', *Notes and Queries*, 54 (2007), 265–72, though his remains a minority position.

[7] See, for instance, Gary Taylor, 'Shakespeare and Others: The Authorship of *Henry the Sixth, Part One*', *Medieval and Renaissance Drama in England*, 7 (1995), 145–205; Hanspeter Born,

Men staged sixteen times at the Rose from March 1592 to January 1593,[8] there is nothing beyond a desire for certainty to suggest that Henslowe's diary entries refer to Shakespeare's play.[9] It is possible that *1 Henry VI* was Strange's, but Henslowe's reference is as opaque as his later listings of a 'harey the v' (staged fifteen times between November 1595 and July 1596) and of a 'long shancke' (performed fourteen times between August 1595 and July 1596),[10] neither of which clearly corresponds to the other plays about those monarchs that survive from the 1590s, Shakespeare's, Peele's, or the anonymous *Famous Victories of Henry the Fifth*.[11]

That it appears so difficult to determine exactly who owned the plays Shakespeare wrote before 1594 should indicate just how daunting a proposition writing about these early years ought to be, even if recent scholarship has tended to suggest otherwise.[12] In fact, the sum of what little we actually know of the Lord Chamberlain's Men, 1594–97, is easily accounted for. In June 1594, Henslowe noted in his 'Diary' that 'my Lord Admeralle men & my Lord chamberlen men' had begun playing 'at newing/ton'. Henslowe's entries, recording ten performances (from 3 to 13 June) with extraordinarily low receipts ranging from 4 to 17 shillings, are a puzzle critics prefer to gloss over, but it is worth noting that we have no idea why Henslowe had any involvement with income generated at a theatre that did not belong to him, raised by companies that had next to no prior connection with him (the Admiral's Men played at the Rose for three days in May 1594); nor do we know why the plays made so little money; nor do we know who these 'Lord chamberlen men' were or where they had come from. We have some idea where they went – and it may not have been James Burbage's Theatre, as most narratives have it. They received 2s 8d at Marlborough sometime before Michaelmas 1594,[13] and their next recorded appearance was not in Shoreditch but at court, on 26 and 27 December of the same year and again on 26 January 1595. For the next years, all we have are a few dates and a handful of names. Mostly, these come from court performances, 13 of them by the end of the 1597/8 Christmas revels.[14] A couple of provincial records

show that the Chamberlain's Men toured on occasion – in 1594/5 they were in Cambridge, in 1595

'The Date of *2, 3 Henry VI*', *Shakespeare Quarterly*, 25 (1974), 323–34; Chambers, *William Shakespeare*, vol. 1, pp. 277–93.

[8] R. A. Foakes, ed., *Henslowe's Diary*, 2nd edn (Cambridge, 2002), pp. 16–20.

[9] Henslowe's entries more or less coincide with the mention of a popular play about the same subject matter in Thomas Nashe's *Piers Penniless*, but whether either instance refers to Shakespeare's play is anything but certain (although the conjecture can be justified). The usual scholarly manoeuvre, however, has been to dismiss such doubts and focus instead on the even murkier question of *which* Henry VI play(s) lie(s) behind Henslowe's entries; see, for instance, Michael Taylor, 'Introduction', *Henry VI Part One* (Oxford, 2003), p. 3. Following that path, some recent scholars can confidently (if baselessly) envisage *3 Henry VI* on 'the Rose's thrust stage': John D. Cox and Eric Rasmussen, 'Introduction', *King Henry VI, Part 3* (London, 2001), p. 7.

[10] Foakes, ed., *Diary*, pp. 30–48. Both plays are marked 'ne' by Henslowe, his usual annotation for a first performance of some kind. See also Roslyn L. Knutson, 'Play Identifications: *The Wise Man of West Chester* and *John a Kent and John a Cumber; Longshanks* and *Edward I'*, *Huntington Library Quarterly*, 47 (1984), 1–11; and on the issue of duplicate or multiple plays about the same events or figures, see Knutson, *The Repertory of Shakespeare's Company, 1594–1613* (Fayetteville, 1991), pp. 48–50.

[11] *Edward III* (newly granted admission to the canon, first in the second edition of the Riverside Shakespeare in 1997, and subsequently by the New Cambridge Shakespeare, the second edition of the Oxford Shakespeare, and the forthcoming third edition of the Norton Shakespeare) probably predates the establishment of the Chamberlain's Men, but its 1596 quarto only advertises it as having been 'sundrie times plaied about the Citie of London'. This reticence may suggest that it was not performed by one of the troupes that survived the shake-up of the catastrophic plague of 1593, and thus might never have entered the Chamberlain's company's repertory either.

[12] Andrew Gurr's recent books on the Chamberlain's and Admiral's Men in particular project a surprising degree of confidence in their narratives; see *The Shakespeare Company, 1594–1642* (Cambridge, 2004) and *Shakespeare's Opposites: The Admiral's Company, 1594–1625* (Cambridge, 2009). The opening sentence of the latter book provides a representative example: 'For six years from May 1594 the English government gave two acting companies the exclusive right to entertain Londoners' (p. 1). None of the factual assertions in that sentence are supported by documentary evidence – nor could they be, since no such evidence exists.

[13] Gurr, *Companies*, p. 303.

[14] Astington, *Court Theatre*, pp. 234–6.

in Ipswich, around 1 August 1596 in Faversham, in 1596/7 in Dover, Marlborough, Faversham and Bath, and in 1597 in Rye (in August) and in Bristol (in September).[15]

However, it is unclear precisely when the company took up residence at the Theatre. They were probably there by September 1595, when the Lord Mayor and Aldermen complained to the Privy Council about the goings on at 'the Theator & Bankside', even if this specificity is somewhat tempered by 'as in all other places about the Cytie' – presumably referring to the Curtain and possibly already the Swan.[16] By late 1598, Burbage's playhouse could be described as 'unfrequented',[17] having been abandoned by its occupants, who had probably moved to the Curtain sometime after they returned from the summer tour that took them down the Great West Road in 1597.[18] But in essence all connections between the Chamberlain's Men and a specific playhouse rely on the assumption that they would have performed at a venue controlled by James Burbage – there is scant independent evidence that they ever played at the Theatre (although they almost certainly did), and their theatrical home can be established with certainty only after the opening of the Globe in 1599.

Finally, to cap off my list of factual fragments, we know the names of some of the company's members but only spread out over a number of years; there is no record of who formed the initial core of the troupe. Between 1594 and 1597, as we saw, Burbage, Kempe and Shakespeare are among them; from 1595/6, we can add John Heminges and George Bryan; and as of 1596/7, we can be sure that Thomas Pope was one of their number as well.[19] By 1598, if Jonson's cast-list in *Every Man in His Humour* is to be trusted, Augustine Phillips, Henry Condell, William Sly, Christopher Beeston and John Duke had joined their ranks (though they *may* also have been there from the start);[20] and if David Kathman is right in his dating of the *2 Seven Deadly Sins* plot, we can name most members of the Chamberlain's Men, sharers and hired men alike, by 1597/8.[21] However, before then we only know six of them and we cannot say with certainty who the company sharers were.

II

The relative opacity of these collected fragments – we do not know who the Chamberlain's Men were, where they performed (and from when to when), or what plays they staged – has largely been downplayed in most recent accounts of the company's early history, which project a sense of confidence in assigning them a membership, a venue, a repertory and commercial dominance. Such accounts also bypass, ignore or dismiss evidence that would affirm other, competing narratives. For while the archive may be relatively devoid of data about the Chamberlain's Men in the mid-1590s, it contains a rather larger set of references to other companies. The Admiral's Men are the obvious example, since their performances at the Rose were documented

[15] Gurr, *Companies*, p. 303.

[16] Chambers, *Elizabethan Stage*, vol. 4, p. 318; on the specificity of the phrase 'about the City', see Paul Menzer, 'The Tragedians of the City? Q1 *Hamlet* and the Settlements of the 1590s', *Shakespeare Quarterly*, 57 (2006), 162–82.

[17] Everard Guilpin, *Skialetheia*, quoted in Chambers, *Elizabethan Stage*, vol. 2, p. 398n.

[18] On the 1597 tour, see Peter Davidson, 'Introduction', *The First Quarto of King Richard III* (Cambridge, 1996), pp. 38–42. When the Burbages abandoned the Theatre is unclear; all that is certain is that the building was empty by September 1598. When the Burbages' lease ran out in March 1597, their landlord granted them an extension, either 'for the space of a year or two' or 'for divers years', an extension for which they paid rent: Glynne Wickham, Herbert Berry, and William Ingram, eds., *English Professional Theatre, 1530–1660* (Cambridge, 2000), pp. 367–8. It is thus unlikely that they moved before they had to – or before they decided to dismantle the entire playhouse in late 1598.

[19] Based on their appearance in court payment records; see Chambers, *Elizabethan Stage*, vol. 4, pp. 164–5. By 1597, then, four of five members of Strange's Men listed in a 1593 travelling licence can be confirmed as Chamberlain's Men; a year later, the fifth name on that list, Augustine Phillips, is documented as a member of the new company as well (see Chambers, *Elizabethan Stage*, vol. 2, p. 123).

[20] Excerpted in Gurr, *Shakespeare Company*, p. 250.

[21] Kathman, 'Reconsidering *The Seven Deadly Sins*', *Early Theatre*, 7 (2004), 13–44. Kathman's conclusions have been challenged by Andrew Gurr, in 'The Work of Elizabethan Plotters, and *2 The Seven Deadly Sins*', *Early Theatre*, 10 (2007), 67–80, whose rebuttal has in turn been refuted by Kathman in '*The Seven Deadly Sins* and Theatrical Apprenticeship', *Early Theatre*, 14 (2011), 121–39.

in Henslowe's 'Diary', a document that has little to say about market dominance and rather speaks, at least obliquely, to the presence of other troupes and venues in London. In April 1594, there are the Queen's Men and Sussex's Men, playing at the Rose; in May of the same year, Henslowe's nephew Francis receives a loan to buy a share in the Queen's Men; in June 1595 he takes out another loan to purchase 'his hallfe share w[i]th the company w[hi]ch he dothe play w[i]th' (which may or may not have been the Queen's Men); in October 1597, a number of Admiral's Men who had previously left to join Pembroke's Men returned to the company, an event Henslowe records as the two *companies* coming together to 'playe at my howse'.[22]

Beyond the 'Diary', the title-pages of printed plays advertise a host of acting groups, even as they remain silent about the Chamberlain's Men until 1597. These books mention the Queen's Men, the Admiral's Men, Pembroke's Men, less frequently Sussex's Men, and by the end of the century the relaunched Derby's Men and Oxford's Men. Overwhelmingly, the attributions convey an impression of theatrical currency; the only playbooks informed by any sense of nostalgia are those staged by the Children of Paul's – a company that certainly had ceased to exist by the time their plays were printed. In her 1591 quarto of Lyly's *Endymion*, the widow Broome took special care to highlight the retrospective quality of her publications, announcing that 'certaine Commedies' had 'come into my handes by chaunce' 'since the Plaies in Paules were dissolued'.[23] No such notion of print as a medium of access to a bygone theatrical era can be found in any of the playbooks that had their origins in the adult companies.

Given how commonly they are dismissed as negligible, it is worth dwelling on the reliability of title-pages as theatre-historical evidence. They are certainly not unproblematic witnesses, since what wound up being advertised varied from book to book and from stationer to stationer: some listed authors' names, some merely noted that a play had been performed (but not by whom), some gave no information beyond the title.[24] The majority of 1590s title-pages, however, mentioned the

company who had staged, or was still staging, the play – and this information turns out to be remarkably accurate. In all cases where we can independently confirm stationers' claims, they are correct. Almost no title-pages appear to refer to companies no longer in existence and, in many instances, attributions clearly strive for precision.[25] Thus the first quarto of *Romeo and Juliet* was issued as performed by 'the right Honourable the L. of *Hunsdon* his Seruants' in 1597, when George Carey had succeeded his father as the company's patron but not yet in the office of Lord Chamberlain.[26] In January 1594, when Richard Jones entered *A Knack to Know a Knave* in the Stationers' Register, he listed it as 'plaid by Ned Allen and his companie', a description later repeated on the title-page.[27] The play had previously been performed by Strange's Men, but that company had lost its patron and no longer operated under its old name by early 1594. Jones's phrase precisely reflects the unstable nature of company compositions and affiliations after the theatres reopened in late 1593: whatever troupe Jones could have mentioned might well have been defunct by the time the play reached booksellers'

---

22 Foakes, ed., *Henslowe's Diary*, pp. 7, 9, 21, 60.

23 John Lyly, *Endymion* (London, 1591), sig. A2r.

24 For detailed statistics about title-pages, see Alan B. Farmer and Zachary Lesser, 'Vile Arts: The Marketing of English Printed Drama, 1512–1660', *Research Opportunities in Renaissance Drama*, 34 (2000), 77–166.

25 The single exception to this rule is the 1599 quarto of *George a Greene*, which was advertised '*as it was sundry times acted by the seruants of the right Honourable the Earle of Sussex*', a company that as far as we know no longer existed by the late 1590s, although they do reappear in the records in the early seventeenth century: *A Pleasant Conceyted Comedie of George a Greene, the Pinner of Wakefield* (STC 12212) (London, 1599). It is, of course, entirely possible that in this instance the title-page is accurate and our historical assumptions are at fault.

26 *An Excellent conceited Tragedie of Romeo and Iuliet* (STC 22322) (London, 1597).

27 *A most pleasant and merie new Comedie, Intituled, A Knacke to knowe a Knaue* (STC 15027) (London, 1594). For the Stationers' Register entry, see W. W. Greg, *A Bibliography of the English Printed Drama to the Restoration* (London, 1939–59), vol. 1, p. 194.

stalls, but Alleyn's popularity likely remained a constant, no matter whom he served.

This impression of stationers striving for exactitude quickly fades when we look beyond first editions. Reprints routinely reiterated the information on the original title-pages, no matter whether it remained accurate and regardless of its potential absurdity. Hence *The Troublesome Reign of King John* was reissued in 1611 as performed by the Queen's Men, a company that had vanished eight years before; *The Taming of a Shrew* was still advertised as Pembroke's in 1607, as was *Edward II* in 1612 and 1622; *Shoemaker's Holiday* remained the Admiral's Men's in print until 1657, the sixth, last and most amusing time its claim to having been performed for the queen (of unspecified name) 'on New-years-day at night' was repeated.[28] Very occasionally, stationers updated their title-page attributions, as when *Romeo and Juliet* became the Chamberlain's Men's in 1599 and then correctly switched to the King's Men in the 1609 third quarto; Ben Jonson showed a fine if rare sense of historical specificity in the 1616 *Workes*, noting that *Every Man in His Humour* was performed by the '*then* L. Chamberlayne his Servants' rather than updating the company's name.[29] But these examples are exceptions and reprint title-pages in general make for poor theatre-historical evidence.

The distinction can be explained from a marketing perspective. When a play was first printed, its commercial potential was directly linked to its success in the theatre, and a clear connection to a current, abidingly popular company of players could provide a reminder of such stage success.[30] Some scholars have recently argued that printed plays could serve as advertisements for performances, particularly for revivals, which, if true, would additionally strengthen the likelihood that newly issued playtexts tended to be accurately attributed.[31] But stationers in any event had an inherent interest in harnessing their publications' connections to popular success in another medium irrespective of what the players wanted them to do. Unlike the overtly nostalgic boy-play quartos, most new playbooks did not thrive on remedying an otherwise irretrievable loss; on the contrary, they were marketed

with a view to riding the wave of relatively recent theatrical success. By the time a play was being reprinted, however, its status had shifted: its ability to attract a readership as well as an audience had been established, and the performance occasion recorded on the title-page had lost much of its importance. Stationers accordingly seem to have cared more about getting the initial claim to theatrical currency right than about keeping that original reference up to date. Given all this, I would argue that we ought to feel more confident – and more obliged – to take first-edition title-pages at their word.[32]

If we do that, however, the picture of London's theatre scene in the 1590s changes radically. Suddenly, the Queen's Men are back as a major, if perhaps old-fashioned, force – not just on the touring circuit but in the capital as well. Troupes such as Derby's Men or Sussex's Men are no longer marginal companies barely worth noticing, but well-known enough that stationers thought their names could sell books. And Pembroke's Men emerge as a dominant force of late Elizabethan theatre, staging some of the most recognizable and still canonical plays of the era: *Titus Andronicus, The*

---

[28] *The First and second Part of the troublesome Raigne of John King of England* (STC 14646) (London, 1611); *A Pleasaunt Conceited Historie, called The Taming of a Shrew* (STC 23669) (London, 1607); *The troublesome raigne and lamentable death of Edward the second, King of England* (STC 17439) (London, 1612); *The troublesome raigne and lamentable death of Edward the second, King of England* (STC 17440) (London, 1622); *The Shoomakers Holiday, or the Gentle-Craft* (Wing D683) (London, 1657).

[29] Excerpted in Gurr, *Shakespeare Company*, p. 250.

[30] I develop this argument at greater length in 'Thomas Creede, William Barley, and the Venture of Printing Plays', in *Shakespeare's Stationers*, ed. Marta Straznicky (Philadelphia, forthcoming).

[31] See Peter W. M. Blayney, 'The Publication of Playbooks', in *A New History of Early English Drama*, ed. John D. Cox and David Scott Kastan (New York, 1997), pp. 383–422, esp. p. 386, and Roslyn Lander Knutson, *Playing Companies and Commerce in Shakespeare's Time* (Cambridge, 2001), pp. 68–9.

[32] On title-pages and especially their relationship to playbills, see further Tiffany Stern, *Documents of Performance in Early Modern England* (Cambridge, 2009), pp. 53–62.

Taming of a Shrew, Edward II and at least the final two parts of *Henry VI*. What is more, the mention of the company on the title-pages of those playbooks would have to be seen as prima facie evidence that the company was well and active in 1594, and the attribution of *The True Tragedy of Richard Duke of York* to them in the 1595 octavo would have to be treated as an indicator that their fortunes had not changed markedly since the previous year.

Distressingly (perhaps), we would also have to acknowledge that the surviving evidence indicates that at least four of Shakespeare's plays did not make it to the Chamberlain's Men in 1594, and at least one of Marlowe's plays did not become the Admiral's Men's property either. What is more, these plays were performed by other companies *after* the formation of the two court-favoured troupes; neither of them appears to have had an exclusive right to associate itself with the works of the recently deceased rebel or the rising star. At least one of these plays, *Titus Andronicus*, allows us to connect various types of data: it is mentioned by Henslowe, has two distinct sets of title-page attributions (the second quarto featuring a rare update on its performance history), and we know that it was staged by a London company during New Year's celebrations in Rutland in 1596. Typically, all these pieces of evidence have been arranged to confirm that the play belonged to the Chamberlain's Men from their beginning. In what follows, I will demonstrate in some detail that they cannot easily be made to cohere in a way that would support such a narrative.

III

In one way or another, *Titus* can be associated with five different companies: Henslowe lists three performances by Sussex's Men in January and February 1594 and two further stagings by the Lord Admiral's and/or Chamberlain's Men at Newington Butts in June; the title-page of the first quarto, published that same year, lists Derby's and Pembroke's Men in addition to Sussex's; and the second quarto of 1600 adds the Chamberlain's company to its three predecessors. How exactly these constellations are to be parsed has been subject to much debate, focusing in particular on the challenge of the 'ne' annotation Henslowe placed against *Titus*'s first performance (which probably suggests that the play was new in January 1594) and on the question of whether the first quarto title-page ought to be read as documenting a sequence or an amalgamation of companies staging the tragedy.[33] What most scholars agree on, though, is that the two shows at Newington Butts were put on by the Chamberlain's Men, who consequently must have become the play's owners from then on. This view seems to be confirmed by the already-mentioned title-page of the second edition of 1600 and by the record of a private performance of *Titus* at Sir John Harington's home in Burley-on-the-Hill in Rutland on 1 January 1596. It is further supported by the fact that the play does not appear in Henslowe's diary after the Newington Butts entries, implying that it never became the Admiral's Men's property.

The attractiveness of this narrative of *Titus*'s (re)union with its only begetter partly rests on what looks, for once, like positive evidence: Henslowe *tells us* that the Chamberlain's Men staged the tragedy; the Rutland record confirms that it remained in the repertory; and the 1600 printing of the text reveals the seamless transition from the old, defunct companies to the new duopoly troupe. Unfortunately, however, none of these fragments of information can speak for itself quite so unambiguously – they are all subject to and in immediate need of interpretation. This is especially true of the Rutland performance, even though uncertainty has hardened into apparent fact since the reference to this staging was first discovered by Gustav Ungerer in 1961. In his analysis of the letter in which the French secretary Jacques Petit describes the

---

[33] See, for instance, David George, 'Shakespeare and Pembroke's Men', *Shakespeare Quarterly*, 32 (1981), 305–23; Jonathan Bate, 'Introduction', *Titus Andronicus* (London, 1995), pp. 69–79.

arrival of 'les commediens de Londres' at Haring-ton's house and their apparently spectacle-oriented staging of 'la tragedie de Titus Andronicus', Ungerer took a relatively circumspect stance on the players' identity: 'there is no conclusive evidence', he argued, 'which justifies the assigning of the Bur-ley performance to any one of the [known] com-panies', although the Chamberlain's Men appeared to be his favourite.[34] By 2008, this tentative atti-tude was gone, allowing him to refer to 'Shake-speare's *Titus Andronicus* as performed at Burley-on-the-Hill by the Chamberlain's Men on Jan-uary 1, 1596'.[35] We can find a similar spectrum of certainties and scepticism among more recent scholars. Thus Leeds Barroll cautions that 'one cannot uncompromisingly identify [the group] as Shakespeare's company . . . Yet, under certain cir-cumstances . . . the company could have made the trip'.[36] Jonathan Bate is rather less hesitant, declar-ing that 'on 1 January 1596 *Titus* was performed by one of the London companies, presumably Shake-speare's Chamberlain's Men';[37] and Andrew Gurr simply states as a matter of fact that 'a winter jour-ney happened' when Harington 'summoned' the Chamberlain's Men to Rutland.[38]

Let us pretend for a moment – heuristically – that Henslowe's 'Diary' did not survive, thus removing the only pre-1600 connection between *Titus* and the Chamberlain's Men, and examine the plausibility of these accounts of the Burley perfor-mance independently of what we think we know about 1594. The Chamberlain's company played at court on 28 December 1595 and 6 January 1596. Between these two dates, both pre-arranged engagements more lucrative than any other per-formances the players would put on in any given year (at a guaranteed £10 per show), they are supposed to have taken to the road, travelling a long way north and back, in order to appear at the house of an ambitious knight – and in the depth of winter, precisely the time of year when even playing at the Theatre seemed such a sea-sonal inconvenience that they had attempted to gain permission to use the Cross Keys' yard in October 1594.[39] Perhaps this seems implausible enough on its face – but there is more. Gurr

asserts that the 'seventy miles up the Great North Road from London to Rutland . . . was a three- or four-day trek in each direction that they must have felt obliged to do', a questionable state-ment on multiple counts. For one thing, the jour-ney was considerably longer. Gurr uses Harri-son's *Description of England* (1587) to determine distances and routes, but even Shakespeare's near-contemporaries recognised this as a highly inac-curate source for such information. By 1679, John Ogilby's *Pocket Book of Roads* offered a more reliable and consistent guide, and by Ogilby's computation, the most likely and well-maintained route, through the market towns of Waltham, Ware, Royston, Huntington, Stilton and Stamford, would have been almost 83 miles long – and beyond that, the players would still have faced at least another ten miles on much less well-travelled roads west across Rutland to Burley-on-the-Hill.[40]

How long such a journey might have taken is extremely difficult to determine, but three or four days has to be an unreasonably optimistic estimate.

---

[34] 'An Unrecorded Elizabethan Performance of *Titus Andron-icus*', *Shakespeare Survey 14* (Cambridge, 1961), pp. 102–9, esp. pp. 102 and 107.

[35] 'The Presence of Africans in Elizabethan England and the Performance of *Titus Andronicus* at Burley-on-the-Hill, 1595/96', *Medieval and Renaissance Drama in England*, 21 (2008), 19–55, esp. pp. 19 and 38.

[36] Barroll, 'Pleasures of 'Common' Playing', p. 118.

[37] Bate, 'Introduction', p. 43.

[38] Gurr, *Shakespeare Company*, p. 56.

[39] See Chambers, *Elizabethan Stage*, vol. 4, p. 316.

[40] John Ogilby, *Mr. Ogilby's pocket book of roads . . . the Third Impression* (Wing O177a) (London, 1679), sig. A2r. Ogilby dismissed the old calculations of distances as 'vulgar com-putations' (sig. B2v). Gurr also seems to think that the per-formance took place at Exton, Harington's other residence, a few miles closer to Stamford, but there is no evidence to support such an assumption. Burley House was evidently a suitable venue for theatrical productions. It later came into the possession of George Villiers, Marquis of Buckingham, who had Ben Jonson's masque *The Gypsies Metamorphosed* staged there for James I in 1621: see *The Complete Masques*, ed. Stephen Orgel (New Haven, 1969), p. 316. For a his-torical description of the house and its situation, see James Wright, *The History and Antiquities of the County of Rutland* (Wing W3696) (London 1684), sigs. E2v–E4r.

The conventional rule of thumb in discussions of touring holds that '25 miles a day'[41] was the usual average speed, but recent studies of the royal post make this assumption look overly generous. On the one hand, Elizabethan regulations demanded that messengers riding in post, carrying important government letters, had to maintain speeds of seven miles per hour in the summer and five in the winter;[42] the distance between London and Stamford could thus have been covered in 17 hours. But in reality, these speeds were almost never reached. A more realistic estimate, reflecting post-room ledger figures, would be a travelling time of 30 hours – and even that may be too optimistic, since average delivery speeds rarely seem to have exceeded 3 miles an hour. If a letter's destination lay off the main post road those low averages declined even more rapidly.[43] None of these times, however, refers to the journey of one person on the same horse. They merely show how long it took one particular *parcel or letter* to reach its destination, carried along its way by a sequence of riders switching horses at great frequency as they proceeded from post to post along the major routes. No individual messenger normally rode in post for 30 hours on end. A company of players, even if they travelled on horseback, would likely not have switched horses at every station, nor could they have moved at speeds as high as a single rider;[44] unlike the composite messenger in post, they would have to stop for meals and sleep, and likely did not continue their journey after nightfall.[45] Finally, we must assume that the troupe that performed *Titus* did not travel lightly since our epistolary witness valued the spectacle of their show ('la monstre') so much more than the subject matter ('le suiect').[46] The play also requires a fairly large cast: even by the most limited estimates, it would still have been a group of at least twenty men and boys riding north that December.[47]

Taking all these factors into account, then, completing the journey from London to Burley in four days would have been an impressive feat. A month earlier, Jacques Petit himself had covered the same distance in the company of the Earl and Countess of Bedford in four days, but they spent each

night being accommodated as became their social rank and continued on with fresh, well-rested and

---

[41] See, for instance, Arthur F. Kinney, *Shakespeare by Stages: An Historical Introduction* (Oxford, 2003), p. 53. In support of his estimate Kinney cites Shakespeare's description of the distance between Tamworth and Bosworth Field as 'one day's march' in *Richard III* (5.2.13), but those two places are about 15 miles apart, not 25.

[42] See 'Orders agreed vpon, and set downe by the right honourable Sir VVilliam Brooke Knight', The National Archives: PRO SP 12/176/1 fo. 32r (29 January 1585).

[43] See Mark Brayshay, Philip Harrison and Brian Chalkley, 'Knowledge, Nationhood and Governance: The Speed of the Royal Post in Early-Modern England', *Journal of Historical Geography*, 24 (1998), 265–88, esp. pp. 277–8 and 281, and Brayshay, 'Royal Post-Horse Routes in England and Wales: The Evolution of the Network in the Later-Sixteenth and Early-Seventeenth Century', *Journal of Historical Geography*, 17 (1991), 373–89.

[44] See also William Ingram, 'The Cost of Touring', *Medieval and Renaissance Drama in England*, 6 (1993), 57–62, esp. p. 58.

[45] For an example of impressively fast travelling times, take Lady Anne Clifford's two-day journey from 'Tittenhanger, my Lady Blount's house' (near St Albans) to Rockingham Castle in Leicestershire, a distance of about 65 miles. Her company spent the night at Wrest House in Bedford, having covered about 22 miles between noon and night the first day, and rode another 40 miles between early morning and night the next day. However, that journey took place on sunny summer days – and the company maintained such a murderous pace that they killed three horses in the process: see J. H. Wiffen, *Historical Memoirs of the House of Russell from the Time of the Norman Conquests* (London, 1833), pp. 69–70.

[46] Ungerer, 'Unrecorded', p. 102.

[47] T. J. King assumes a principal cast of ten men and four boys, but also calls for up to an extra thirteen men for minor and mute parts: *Casting Shakespeare's Plays: London Actors and Their Roles, 1590–1642* (Cambridge, 1992), p. 81. David Bradley argues for a similarly large cast of at least sixteen men and four boys: *From Text to Performance in the Elizabethan Theatre: Preparing the Play for the Stage* (Cambridge, 1992). Among editors, Alan Hughes stands alone in maintaining that the entire play could be staged by fourteen men and boys, but admits that 'as a spectacle' such a production 'would not have been impressive'; he also allows the boys playing Tamora and Lavinia to double as senators and Goth soldiers, which seems a rather far-fetched proposition: 'Appendix 2: Performance by a Small Company', *Titus Andronicus*, New Cambridge Shakespeare, rev. edn (Cambridge, 2006), pp. 174–5, esp. p. 174. Bate suggests that 'an absolute minimum company size of between twenty-five

well-fed horses.[48] A troupe of twenty actors travelling with a wagon or some other carriage for their props and costumes, on the road for maybe ten hours of a short winter day could hardly have gone more than twenty miles a day under the best of circumstances – and even at that speed, they would nearly have matched the Bedfords' pace. But unlike them, the players did not have four days. The Chamberlain's Men performed at court in Richmond on 28 December, and since court entertainments took place late at night, they could not have set off before the early afternoon of the 29th, having returned from Surrey to Shoreditch to collect whatever they needed to stage *Titus*. Petit writes that they 'son[t] venus icy' on New Year's Day, and they were clearly ready to put on their play by the late evening.[49] And yet even in the best-case scenario I have sketched above, a company leaving London on 29 December could not seriously have expected to make it to Burley within three days (without killing their horses). It would have meant significantly outpacing the Earl and Countess of Bedford, despite the shorter days of late December, almost certainly travelling with a larger and less well-equipped company, and carrying heavier luggage.

But that is still not all. The Chamberlain's Men were due back in London on 6 January, to play at court – surely an unmissable date if ever there was one. They could not have departed from Rutland before midday on 2 January, leaving only four days of travel time to return to London, prepare their evening performance, and make their way to Richmond – at least another eight miles, what John Astington has called 'a considerable journey'.[50] My point is not that no one could have pulled off such a feat. But it seems highly improbable that the players would have taken the chance of beating the odds both going to Rutland and coming back while deliberately taking the risk of standing up the queen – an entirely likely outcome given the distances and potentially bad weather conditions involved.

Add to all these factors the complication that the Chamberlain's Men are never recorded anywhere north of Cambridge on any of their brief touring excursions, and appear to have favoured the western and southern circuits, and take into consideration that the Christmas season commonly was among the most profitable periods of the year for London companies, as theatres were full – and it may begin to seem somewhat unlikely that Shakespeare and his fellows would have thought it a good idea to race back to Shoreditch right after their court performance in the early hours of 29 December, travel at breakneck pace north (where they had never been before and where they would never return) in order to stage a play that required a large cast and impressive costumes, only to then immediately turn around, hurtle back to London and the court, always in the knowledge that they might easily fail to keep their appointments with either their Rutland sponsor or the queen herself, if not both, and all while missing out on the income from at least six additional high-grossing shows at the Theatre. But since the actors that arrived at Burley on 1 January were 'les commediens de Londres' and since they staged *Titus Andronicus*, they necessarily must have been the Chamberlain's Men – because there were only two companies 'de Londres' in 1595/6 and the 1600 quarto of *Titus* tells us that it was a Chamberlain's play. Or so the logic goes.

And that is still not all. It might help to say a little more about the lord of the manor of Burley-on-the-Hill. Sir John Harington was born in 1539/40 as the son of Sir James Harington and his wife Lucy, daughter of Sir William Sidney. Lucy Sidney was Sir Henry Sidney's sister – Philip and Mary Sidney's aunt – and John Harington's cousin Mary was the wife of Henry Herbert, second Earl

---

and twenty-seven . . . is necessary for the first scene' ('Introduction', p. 94). Gurr counts *Titus* as one of the 'large' plays of the early 1590s (see *Playing Companies*, pp. 59–60).

[48] See Petit's letter to Anthony Bacon (20 December 1595), Lambeth Palace Library MS 654, fos. 70r–71r; and Gustav Ungerer, 'Shakespeare in Rutland', *Rutland Record*, 7 (1987), 242–8, esp. p. 242.

[49] Ungerer, 'Unrecorded', p. 102.

[50] 'Court Theatre', in *The Oxford Handbook of Early Modern Theatre History*, ed. Richard Dutton (Oxford, 2009), pp. 307–22, p. 310.

of Pembroke. His uncle, Henry Sidney, was not only Pembroke's father-in-law but also his predecessor as Lord President of the Council in the Marches of Wales.[51] The ties between the branches of the family were close: in 1602, when Harington hosted what John Chamberlain described as a 'royal Christmas', the festivities were attended by both Sir Robert Sidney (Mary and Philip's brother) and William Herbert, who had succeeded his father as the third Earl of Pembroke.[52] Harington's daughter Lucy married Edward Russell, the third Earl of Bedford, and the couple were in attendance in 1596 as well as in 1602 – and Lucy Countess of Bedford is, of course, a familiar figure to literary scholars as one of her age's leading patrons of the arts.[53] None of these genealogical connections amount to evidence, exactly, but if they point to any of the late Elizabethan playing companies, it is not the Lord Chamberlain's. If anything, they point the other way: in the autumn of 1595, a match had been proposed between William Herbert and Elizabeth Carey, George Carey's daughter and the Lord Chamberlain's grand-daughter. However, Pembroke's son objected and the proposal fell through, leading to a lasting division between the Herberts and the Careys. In early December 1595 Rowland Whyte wrote to Robert Sidney that 'Sir George Carey takes it unkindly that Lord Pembroke broke off the match between Lord Harbert and his daughter.'[54] Given this climate, it would have been a less than canny decision by the Chamberlain's Men to risk missing a court performance to play for the close relative of a man who had just entered himself into their patron's bad books in egregious fashion – nor does it seem likely that Harington would have chosen to offend his most prominent and powerful kinsman by making Carey's troupe a centrepiece of his own lavish Christmas celebrations.

From a multitude of perspectives, then, it appears extremely unlikely that the Burley performance was staged by the Chamberlain's Men, and highly probable that it was put on by a different company of London actors. I can see only two arguments against this conclusion: one has a documentary basis of sorts, the other does not. The

former, drawing on Henslowe's diary and its references to the Newington Butts shows, will need to be addressed in some detail. The latter, the theory that there were only two companies of note in London in the years after 1594, can be dealt with more directly.

The two-company hypothesis dictates that Harington could not have had another company at his disposal, since the Admiral's Men were unquestionably tied up at court, where they performed that very New Year's Day in 1596. Therefore, no matter how improbable the proposition may be, the Chamberlain's Men must have been the troupe that travelled to Rutland; and once that claim has been accepted, the Harington performance becomes further evidence that *Titus* belonged to that company as of 1594. Aside from its circularity, the major problem with this theory is that it assumes much more about London and the new companies than can be confirmed. In fact, the only honest answer to the question of who staged *Titus* at Burley is that we do not know and likely never will – just as we also do not know who staged most plays in London that year and in the years surrounding it. As I have argued above, the fragmentary evidence we have about the Chamberlain's Men in the mid-1590s shows only that they were a dominant company at court and did

---

[51] See Jan Broadway, 'Harington, John, first Baron Harington of Exton (1539/40–1613)', *Oxford Dictionary of National Biography* (Oxford, 2004); online edn, Oct. 2005; Wallace T. MacCaffrey, 'Sidney, Sir Henry (1529–1586)', *Oxford Dictionary of National Biography* (Oxford, 2004); online edn, Jan. 2008; and Penry Williams, 'Herbert, Henry, second earl of Pembroke (b. in or after 1538, d. 1601)', *Oxford Dictionary of National Biography* (Oxford, 2004); online edn, Jan. 2008.

[52] 'Sir John Harrington meanes to kepe a royalle Christmas in Rutlandshire, having the Erles of Rutland and Bedford, Sir John Gray and Sir Harry Carie, with theire ladies, the Erle of Pembroke, Sir Robert Sydney, and many more gallants': *Letters written by John Chamberlain during the Reign of Queen Elizabeth*, ed. Sarah Williams (London, 1861), p. 171.

[53] See Helen Payne, 'Russell, Lucy, countess of Bedford (*bap.* 1581, *d.* 1627)', *Oxford Dictionary of National Biography* (Oxford, 2004); online edn, Jan. 2008.

[54] Quoted in Margaret P. Hannay, *Philip's Phoenix: Mary Sidney, Countess of Pembroke* (Oxford, 1990), p. 159.

indeed share a duopoly with the Admiral's Men when it came to courtly performances. But we have next to no knowledge of their *commercial* fortunes. They probably did well, but who their competition was in London and whether the situation at court mirrored the situation of the public stages is completely unclear. If anything, the references on title-pages I discussed earlier point to a striking disparity between courtly order and public diversity, as does the fact that there were three viable playhouses on the outskirts of the city throughout much of the 1590s (the Theatre, the Curtain, and the Rose), to which a fourth, particularly lavish one (the Swan) was added in 1595. Given the available data, I would argue that the only justification for concluding that the Chamberlain's Men dominated the theatrical scene unrecorded in the Accounts of the Chamber in the same way that they dominated the Christmas Revels is our desire to think of Shakespeare's company as a hegemonic and near-uncontested cultural force.[55] It may be time to take our eyes off the court records, and off the Folio, and rethink what the day-to-day life of a theatrical company in London may have been like.

IV

In this spirit of unconventional hypothesizing, let me now try to identify a more suitable candidate for the Burley show. I already listed some of the troupes that probably played in London besides the court-duopoly companies. The information gleaned from title-pages and Henslowe's 'Diary' can be supplemented by touring records, however incomplete and inconclusive. Of the companies active before the 1593 plague, Sussex's Men disappear from the archive until the seventeenth century. Most known members of Strange's Men wound up as colleagues of Shakespeare, with Alleyn joining the reformed Admiral's Men; whoever remained presumably formed the company that continued to tour in subsequent years under the patronage of Ferdinando Stanley's brother, the sixth Earl of Derby. This troupe may well have performed in London and certainly did by the end of the century, when they were using the Boar's Head.[56] The

Queen's Men continued to be the touring powerhouse they had always been,[57] and presumably still staged plays in the capital as they had done in the past – as prolonged pit stops, not as a more or less residential company. Lastly, Pembroke's servants were in Ipswich in April 1595, and at some point in 1595/6 in Oxford, where they were paid at the same rate as the Admiral's Men (both received 10 shillings that year).[58] And here we also find a connection with Harington's family: as we saw, the company's patron was married to Sir John's cousin, Mary Sidney, and the idea that she was the driving force behind Henry Herbert's decision to support a company of actors has intrigued many recent scholars, even if no tangible evidence exists to confirm or disprove the notion.[59] Pembroke's Men are also named on the title-page of the 1594 quarto of *Titus* as one of the three groups that performed the play. And finally, of all the companies I have mentioned, they were the ones least likely to be asked to act at court, given the fraught relationship between the Lord Chamberlain and their patron – and thus, they would seem to fit the profile for a troupe that may have been active in London but invisible in court records.

---

55 For a longer version of this argument, see my 'The Meaning of Success: Stories of 1594 and Its Aftermath', *Shakespeare Quarterly*, 61 (2010), 490–525.

56 See Gurr, *Companies*, pp. 273–5; and Herbert Berry, *The Boar's Head Playhouse* (Washington, DC, 1986).

57 See Scott McMillin and Sally-Beth MacLean, *The Queen's Men and their Plays* (Cambridge, 1998).

58 John R. Elliott, Jr., *et al.*, eds., *Record of Early English Drama: Oxford* (Toronto, 2004), p. 240.

59 See, for instance, Hannay, *Philip's Phoenix*, pp. 124–5; Gary Waller, *The Sidney Family Romance: Mary Wroth, William Herbert, and the Early Modern Construction of Gender* (Detroit, 1993), p. 225. The actor Simon Jewell made provisions for his 'share of such money as shalbe given by my ladie Pembrooke or by her meanes' in his will, a reference some scholars have treated as evidence that Jewell was a member of Pembroke's Men, and that the countess took an active interest in the company: Mary Edmond, 'Pembroke's Men', *Review of English Studies*, 25 (1974), 129–36, esp. p. 10. See also J. A. B. Somerset, 'The Lords President, their Activities and Companies: Evidence from Shropshire', in *The Elizabethan Theatre X*, ed. C. E. McGee (Port Credit, 1988), pp. 93–111, esp. pp. 109–10.

Pembroke's Men, however, as any diligent student of the period is aware, went bankrupt in 1593. Gurr writes of their 'rapid death', and other scholars also generally subscribe to the belief that the troupe's existence came to an end that year, even if a distinct new version of the group emerged later on.[60] The single basis for this idea is a letter Henslowe wrote to Alleyn, then on tour, in late September 1593. Henslowe reports that 'my lorde a penbrockes . . . are all at home and hauffe ben t<his> v or sixe weackes for they cane not saue ther carges <w>th trauell as I heare & weare fayne to pane the<r> parell for ther carge.'[61] Four often-ignored points are worth noting about this letter. For one, it says nothing about a break-up – in fact, Henslowe still refers to the players assembled in London as 'my lorde a penbrockes'. They may be inactive and in financial trouble, but they still constitute a recognizable entity. The letter also says nothing about Pembroke's Men *selling* anything, neither their costumes nor their books. Rather, what the actors have been forced to do (or perhaps merely to consider) is *pawn* their wardrobe: not necessarily a final transaction, but a means of raising cash that was ultimately reversible.[62] Furthermore, Henslowe refers to London as the company's *home* – to his mind, these are players resident in the city and away from home when on tour. London is where they belong. And finally, the date of the letter is important. On 28 September neither Henslowe nor Alleyn could know that the theatres would reopen at the end of the year, nor could the idle members of Pembroke's company – but as things turned out, they only needed to bridge a few more months before business picked up again, and without the need to travel.[63] The letter, if taken seriously and as literally as possible, does not tell quite as clear-cut a tale of commercial death as theatre historians have commonly suggested.

But even if I am right in asserting that Pembroke's Men survived their troubled 1593 and continued to perform in London along with a sizeable number of other troupes, assigning *Titus Andronicus* to them remains a problem – precisely because of Henslowe's references to the play, none of which mention a company under Pembroke's patronage.

On 23 January 1594, Sussex's Men are entered as performing *Titus* for the first time, an entry Henslowe marked 'ne'. This is usually taken to mean that the play was new at that point, or at least new to that particular company at the Rose. Such a reading of the entry would mean that Shakespeare's tragedy was staged by the three companies mentioned on the first quarto's title-page – Derby's, Pembroke's and Sussex's – between January and June, when either the Admiral's or the Chamberlain's Men, or both, are listed as performing it at Newington Butts. Sussex's Men left the Rose in early February and did not perform the play when they came back for a brief stint with the Queen's Men in early April, so there is a span of about four months during which *Titus* may have switched ownership and been put on by the two other troupes elsewhere. This would fit with Scott McMillin's hypothesis that one or more players in possession of the script moved from one group to the next.[64] On the other hand, it is equally possible that, as some critics have argued, the three troupes listed in the quarto acted as an amalgamated company, possibly the one Henslowe refers to as 'the earle of susex his men'.[65] Alternatively, we might follow William Ingram's lead in

---

[60] Gurr, *Companies*, p. 272.

[61] Foakes, ed., *Henslowe's Diary*, p. 280.

[62] I am grateful to Christopher Matusiak for information on the early modern trade in clothing; he discusses Christopher Beeston's involvement in that trade in his PhD dissertation, 'The Beestons and the Art of Theatrical Management in Seventeenth-Century London' (University of Toronto, 2009).

[63] This realization may lead us to ask just how long the stranded Pembroke's Men expected to be out of work, and if they would have pawned all their stock in August 1593. If Simon Jewell was a member of the company, they owned £117 worth of apparel and equipment in August 1592 (see Edmond, 'Pembroke's Men', p. 9). Even if they only realized half that value when pawning their possessions, they would have raised significantly more money than they would have *needed* to live on, especially given how brief a period they eventually had to bridge. This increases the likelihood that the company could have bought back at least some of their apparel when the theatres reopened.

[64] McMillin, 'Sussex's Men', pp. 220–1.

[65] See George, 'Pembroke's Men'.

querying the very notion of company identities,[66] and propose that the play was performed by the same set of players acting as three different companies in succession, though likely not in the order stipulated on the title-page (which is, coincidentally or not, alphabetical). While scholars thus disagree about who staged *Titus* when, they commonly share the assumption that the printed text must have been published before June, since otherwise it would list the Chamberlain's Men as well[67] – in other words, that none of the companies on the title-page corresponds to the new troupe created in 1594. This supposition may indeed be correct: the play was entered in the Stationers' Register in February, long enough in advance of the Newington Butts shows that it may have been printed before its return to Henslowe's records. It also seems plausible, however (though I do not think the notion has been proposed before), that the company Henslowe called the Chamberlain's in June would not have been readily recognizable by that name to a book-buying audience at that point: they were brand new after all. It may thus have made better economic sense to reference the household names of the companies from which the actors came that made up the new troupe, particularly if these companies had not folded (yet). The title-page may thus reflect both past and current ownership of *Titus Andronicus*; it certainly reflects, like the *Knack to Know a Knave* attribution, the fluid state of London's theatrical world in 1594.

But there is yet another possibility. The quarto's attribution may chart, in alphabetical rather than chronological order, the staging of the play from its first appearance in the 'Diary' in January (Sussex's Men) through its second appearance in June (at the hands of two companies that between them shared the major figures associated with Strange's, or, by 1594, Derby's Men) to what was by the time the book was published later in the year its final owners, the servants of the earl of Pembroke. This reading retains my earlier suggestion that in 1594, a company called the 'Chamberlain's Men' was not a widely known quantity, even if that was the name they gave Henslowe; it is entirely conceivable that a stationer may still have thought of them as Derby's

(or Strange's) Men. If this seems like an unnecessarily contorted explanation, consider the similar case of *The Taming of a Shrew*. That play, also listed by Henslowe among the works staged by the Admiral's Men and the Chamberlain's Men together, was likewise published in 1594 as staged not by either of them but by Pembroke's Men. Its Stationers' Register entry on 2 May only predates Henslowe's listing on 11 June by a little over a month. It is possible, though somewhat unlikely, that the book was printed within little more than a month of being entered; in that case, one could surmise that the title-page attribution no longer reflected theatrical reality when it appeared. Pembroke's Men had finally collapsed in May (for no clear reason), while players that moved on to the Chamberlain's Men took the play with them and staged it in June. Alternatively, Peter Short and Cuthbert Burby, the stationers responsible for the quarto, chose to list on their title-page a troupe that had been defunct for almost a year (since August 1593) and because of plague closures had likely not appeared on London stages for over a year and a half, while ignoring the fact that the play was alive and well in theatres in the hands of the exciting new Chamberlain's Men.

Unless, of course, it wasn't. Unless, that is, both the *Titus* and the *Shrew* quartos offer perfectly accurate, up-to-date and marketable attributions to a company that had come back from the doldrums of 1593, just like the troupes that would become the Admiral's and Chamberlain's Men; like, perhaps, the Queen's Men; like, possibly, others. How could giving the quartos such credit (and allowing *Shrew* to have been published anytime in 1594, not rushed out in weeks) be reconciled with Henslowe's entries? I think we should entertain the notion that the two companies that performed at Newington Butts in June 1594 were not yet fully formed, and that out of the instability and

---

[66] Ingram, 'What Kind of Future for the Theatrical Past: Or, What Will Count as Theater History in the Next Millennium?' *Shakespeare Quarterly*, 48 (1997), 215–25, esp. p. 222.

[67] Cf. Gurr, *Companies*, p. 279, arguing that *Titus* 'had been put into print as a Pembroke's play' by the time it was staged at Newington Butts.

flux of those days emerged not two, but at least three leading troupes, one of which had no favour at court. The Admiral's and Chamberlain's Men were to dominate the Christmas Revels, but they did not have a duopoly in the commercial world of the public theatres. There, Pembroke's Men served as a healthy competition, staging a repertory that included plays both by the Chamberlain's increasingly well-known playwright, Shakespeare, and by a dramatist whose works were relatively dominant during the Admiral's Men's first year at the Rose, Marlowe.[68] They presumably would have made the Curtain their home at first, competing with the Chamberlain's Men next door but also earning some of their members good money if they already held shares in that playhouse then (Thomas Pope was a sharer, as his will shows, and the theatre 'is to be found only in the hands of players' from the 1590s on).[69] Pembroke's Men might not have stayed for long, though: William Ingram has speculated that Francis Langley may have hosted a company related to the Queen's Men at the Swan in 1595/6, but I would propose that Pembroke's Men are a more likely candidate.[70] The agreement they signed with Langley in February 1597 would thus appear as the formalization of an already established relationship. From this point of view, the decision of three of the Admiral's players to jump ship and join the company at the Swan in 1597 begins to appear like a rational choice, since the troupe they went to may have had a history of giving the Rose a run for its money. Otherwise the desertion of Richard Jones and Thomas Downton, both established members of Alleyn's group, seems difficult to comprehend.[71] Whether Pembroke's Men were the Rose's next-door competitors for a few years or merely a rival from the other side of London, it remains a puzzle why they would have needed new players in 1596/7 anyway – death or retirement of leading men lost to history may be the most convincing explanation. If the company continued to perform Shakespeare's early histories, *Titus* and *Shrew*, as those title-pages indicate, they must have been fairly large (as all those plays have unusually large cast requirements) and, given that they must have been subject to the same fluctuations as the

other groups, they likely had to recruit new actors fairly frequently.

Without the reliable source of income at Christmas that the two privileged companies had, Pembroke's Men may well have been open to invitations like Sir John Harington's but, unlike the Chamberlain's Men, they could have taken their time, stopping in the numerous market towns along the Great North Road to render the journey both more leisurely and more lucrative. Their scattered touring records suggest that they travelled west, east and north, without the clear preference for the southern parts of the country that the Chamberlain's servants displayed.[72] I would assume that, wherever they went, they would rarely have taken plays like *Titus* or the *Henry VI* series on the road, given their cast requirements; a bespoke performance like that in Rutland would have been a different matter, but it is hard to imagine that they would have willingly chosen the financial and

---

68 I do not mean to replace the conventional duopoly narrative with a model in which three resident companies split the market between them. Given that there were at least four theatres in operation in London in 1595 and 1596 (not counting the inns), it is reasonable to assume that either there was a fourth troupe more or less permanently in place at the Curtain after the Swan opened or that companies such as the Queen's Men continued to play there frequently and regularly.

69 See William Ingram, *The Business of Playing: The Beginnings of Adult Professional Theater in Elizabethan London* (Ithaca, 1992), p. 235.

70 William Ingram, *A London Life in the Brazen Age. Francis Langley, 1548–1602* (Cambridge, MA, 1978), pp. 116–20, 142–50. Ingram also admits for the possibility that 'the Earl of Pembroke may have been the patron' of the company performing at the Swan in 1595/6 (p. 154).

71 See Ingram, *Brazen Age*, pp. 151–96, and David Mateer, 'Edward Alleyn, Richard Perkins and the Rivalry between the Swan and the Rose Playhouses', *Review of English Studies*, 60 (2009), 61–77.

72 See Gurr, *Companies*, pp. 276–7, 303; Gurr, *Shakespeare Company*, pp. 54–9; Terence G. Schoone-Jongen, *Shakespeare's Companies: William Shakespeare's Early Career and the Acting Companies, 1577–1594* (Aldershot, 2008), pp. 217–18. On touring routes in general, see Sally-Beth MacLean, 'Tour Routes: "Provincial Wanderings" or Traditional Circuits?', *Medieval and Renaissance Drama in England*, 6 (1993), 1–14.

logistical burden of moving that many men and props. In any case, they were certainly the company most closely associated with Harington's family, and as such as ideal a fit as could be imagined for the 1596 staging of *Titus Andronicus*.

V

This revisionist account of Pembroke's Men not only unsettles the conventional narrative of how London's theatrical scene developed after 1594; it also has a profound effect on our understanding of the Chamberlain's Men's early repertory. Put in stark terms, if someone wanted to see a Shakespeare play in January 1595, say, he or she may have been as well advised to go to see Pembroke's company at the Curtain as Carey's servants next door at the Theatre. What is more, if a new reader of plays had just discovered the gory spectacle of *Titus Andronicus* or the sexist hilarity of *Taming of a Shrew*, that theatrical novice would have had to turn not to the playwright's own troupe but to a rival company to hear the lines spoken and see the characters come to life. In this version of history, Pembroke's Men no longer serve the useful function they served in the past, as a temporary stopover for both Shakespeare and his plays.[73] That, after all, is why most accounts of the period are interested in them at all: since they seem to have owned more than a few of Shakespeare's early plays, he also must have been one of them, and as Shakespeare's old company, they gained cultural capital in the twentieth century.[74] But how reliable is this conventional belief that playwrights and plays went hand in hand – that as his plays went, so went Shakespeare and vice versa?

There is clear evidence that long-lasting relationships existed between particular companies and playwrights, some of whom were actors in those companies. What we do not know is whether actors who also wrote scripts sold them only to their own troupe, especially if they were not sharers but hired men. What little data exists yet again suggests the opposite is true: Thomas Heywood sold the Admiral's Men a 'bocke' in 1596 but cannot otherwise be linked to the company before

March 1598, when he bound himself to Henslowe as a player for two years.[75] Either he was with another company when he sold his play to the Admiral's in 1596 or he was not acting at all at that time. Intriguingly, the 1598 bond specifies only that Heywood may not '*playe* any wher publicke a bowt london',[76] but has nothing to say about his activities as a dramatist; and in fact those seem to have been considered distinct and separate from what he contributed as an actor, since he continued to be paid at the usual rate for scripts after he signed the bond.[77] He was prominent enough as a writer by then that Francis Meres listed him among 'the best for Comedy' in 1598, but little trace of Heywood's output survives in the Admiral's Men's repertory – though some of his works may of course lie hidden behind the dozens of titles of lost plays in the 'Diary'. By 1602, after he became a sharer in Worcester's company, however, we can link his dramatic works to his own company much more securely. It is impossible to say whether this pattern was representative or not. But at the very least it casts doubt on the direct connection between Shakespeare's company membership

---

73 That the company has functioned in this way is surely also why so much of the scholarship on Pembroke's Men is concerned with where they came from and who their early members were, but not with where they went and what happened to them once Shakespeare became a Chamberlain's Man. See, e.g. Chambers, *William Shakespeare*, vol. 1, pp. 49–50; G. M. Pinciss, 'Shakespeare, Her Majesty's Players and Pembroke's Men', *Shakespeare Survey 27* (Cambridge, 1974), pp. 129–36; George, 'Pembroke's Men', pp. 313–15; Scott McMillin, 'Casting for Pembroke's Men: The *Henry VI* Quartos and *The Taming of A Shrew*', *Shakespeare Quarterly*, 23 (1972), 141–59.

74 This theory goes back to Chambers, *Elizabethan Stage*, vol. 2, pp. 129–31, informs (and in a sense justifies) most accounts of the company since then, and has recently been tentatively reaffirmed by Gurr, who is 'almost convinced that Shakespeare was with his plays in Pembroke's Company at the Theatre in 1592 and 1593' (*Companies*, p. 271). However, no new evidence has been discovered since Chambers first stated the hypothesis; the idea has no more of a factual basis now than it did in the 1920s.

75 Foakes, ed., *Henslowe's Diary*, p. 50.

76 Foakes, ed., *Henslowe's Diary*, p. 241, my italics.

77 See Foakes, ed., *Henslowe's Diary*, pp. 102, 207.

and his plays. And as that connection disappears, so does the argument that he may have been a member of Pembroke's Men. For all we know, he may have been a hired hand in Strange's Men while selling his plays to Sussex's and Pembroke's companies at the same time.

Writing for multiple troupes 'on spec' undoubtedly was the standard practice for playwrights in the period and, beyond Shakespeare's example, it is difficult to find any deviations from this pattern until well into the seventeenth century, when long-term exclusivity contracts between authors and companies begin to appear.[78] Figuring Shakespeare himself as writing only for the group with whom he performed is not a choice determined by the available information but an a priori assumption that distorts not just our understanding of the early Chamberlain's Men but of the entire world of London theatre in the 1590s. Ultimately, these distortions may seem less than momentous: I am, after all, concerned with a mere four or five years in the mid-1590s. What is more, wherever Shakespeare's early plays were in those years, most of them certainly wound up with the Chamberlain's or King's Men at some point. But, as I shall try to show in my final section, narratives about Shakespeare's development as a playwright are so deeply anchored in long-held convictions about the 1590s that a recalibration of our views of what may have happened in those years directly affects how we conceive of the dramatist's career, the relationship of his works to each other, and the role of the Folio in turning him into an author figure.

VI

My hypothetical story of Pembroke's Men as a major London company ends in 1597, when some of their sharers were imprisoned as a consequence of the 'Isle of Dogs' affair, the Swan was at least temporarily shut down, and a number of their actors joined the Admiral's Men, bringing a set of plays with them.[79] A troupe under Herbert's patronage continued to travel and may have performed in London after this date, but the evidence is even thinner on the ground than before. I would suggest that just as the Newington Butts players (and probably others) wound up forming three troupes, the suppressed Pembroke's Men split into three: some (William Bird, Thomas Downton, Richard Jones, Robert Shaa and Gabriel Spencer) began acting at the Rose, some remained with their old group, taking the show on the road, and some became members of the Chamberlain's Men, bringing *Titus*, possibly *Shrew* and maybe even *Edward II* with them. They may very well have had other Shakespearian wares to offer, including in particular *Richard III*. There is some basis for believing that this play might have belonged to Pembroke's Men at one point: as John Jowett has recently pointed out, it contains passages seemingly inserted simply to praise the earl's family.[80] The play also, of course, joins up quite naturally with *3 Henry VI* (or *The True Tragedy* for that matter). And finally, it appeared in print at just the right moment.

The Swan was not the only theatre shut down in 1597: probably as a consequence of the 'Isle of Dogs' scandal, all playhouses in London were closed for a while, and all the companies can be found on the road that summer. When they returned home in the autumn, the Chamberlain's Men almost immediately sold *Richard III* to Andrew Wise, who entered the play in the Stationers' Register and printed it later the same year, as the first or second volume ever to mention the

---

[78] See G. E. Bentley, *The Profession of Dramatist in Shakespeare's Time, 1590–1642* (Princeton, 1984), esp. pp. 111–44; Bentley distinguishes between 'ordinary poets' (p. 112) contractually bound to specific companies and drawing steady salaries, and 'unattached professionals' like Jonson, Marston or Ford (p. 264). Cf. also Richard Dutton, 'Shakespeare: The Birth of the Author', in *Licensing, Censorship, and Authorship in Early Modern England: Buggeswords* (Basingstoke, 2000), pp. 90–113.

[79] See Ingram, *Brazen Age*, pp. 167–96; Foakes, ed., *Henslowe's Diary*, pp. 60, 239–40.

[80] Jowett, 'Introduction', *Richard III* (Oxford, 2000), pp. 5–7. Karl Wentersdorf made a similar case years ago, on very different grounds, in 'The Repertory and Size of Pembroke's Company', *Theatre Annual*, 33 (1977), 71–85.

company on its title page.[81] While this may not mean anything, it makes for a rather intriguing sequence: Pembroke's Men lose their theatre and, once playing resumes in London, the Chamberlain's Men aggressively advertise their ownership of what was destined to be one of Shakespeare's most successful plays in print. Perhaps the gesture was designed to remind the public of an old favourite, long familiar as a play in the company's repertory; but alternatively, it may have been meant to let the theatre-going and play-reading audience know that they could now see this play in a new context, staged by new players including the rising star of the theatrical world, Richard Burbage. Certainly the phrasing of the company attribution highlights the play's particular (and given its likely age, peculiar) currency: 'As it hath beene *lately* Acted by the Right honourable the Lord Chamberlaine his seruants'.[82]

Identifying Burbage as the key attraction, however, means falling into the predetermined thought patterns I am arguing against here. Burbage came to be associated with the role of Richard a few years later, as is evident from John Manningham's well-known anecdote about Shakespeare as a sexually victorious William the Conqueror.[83] But no such association can be documented in the 1590s. Burbage, it turns out, cannot be linked to any Shakespearian characters before the turn of the century, nor to any other major roles at all before the *2 Seven Deadly Sins* plot, around 1597/98. Despite this evidentiary void, scholars have routinely assumed that the largest part in every one of Shakespeare's early plays was written for his company's leading man, and that that leading man was Richard Burbage. Hence also the frequently stated belief that they *both* must have been members of Pembroke's Men (especially since a complicated connection can be constructed between Pembroke and the Burbage family via the latter's links to the Earl of Leicester).[84] Roslyn Knutson has proposed that 'seeing Burbage in the part of Edward II' with Pembroke's Men might have given Shakespeare the confidence to write Richard III for him, which makes for an intuitively credible narrative[85] – but largely, I would suggest, because it is difficult for

us to imagine the great actor in smaller parts, and because the direct connection between the player's skills and the playwright's ever more challenging and complex dramaturgical experiments has been such a staple of Shakespeare criticism for so long.

As far as I can see, however, there is no reason to assume that Burbage was a member – let alone a leading member – of Pembroke's Men at all. Nor do I see much basis for surmising that he was the undisputed lead actor of the early Chamberlain's Men. The thought may be strange and unfamiliar, but other actors, including John Heminges and George Bryan, had more experience and seniority, and could well have eclipsed him in the troupe's early days – Shakespeare may initially have been writing with them in mind. Titus, Petruccio, Gloucester, Richard III – whoever these parts were first composed for, whoever first played them, it is entirely possible that it was someone other than the future star. Nor do we know for whom mid-1590s parts such as Richard II or even Romeo were conceived.

Rethinking Burbage's importance to Shakespeare's development as a writer means contemplating a rupture in the traditional narrative. It also means indulging, self-consciously, in the same kind of speculative storytelling that tacitly underpins that traditional account. But to my mind, figuring Burbage as on the verge of greatness rather than

---

81 The Chamberlain's Men were also listed on the title-page of *Richard II*, printed in 1597 and registered in August, two months before *Richard III*.

82 *The Tragedy of King Richard the third* (STC 22314) (London, 1597), my italics.

83 Chambers, *William Shakespeare*, vol. 2, p. 212.

84 The idea that Burbage was a member of Pembroke's Men was still considered 'without foundation' by W. W. Greg (*Dramatic Documents from the Elizabethan Playhouses* (Oxford, 1931), vol. 1, p. 44), but has since gained popularity. See Karl P. Wentersdorf, 'The Origin and Personnel of the Pembroke Company', *Theatre Research International*, 5 (1979–80), 45–67, esp. pp. 53–4; Gurr, *Shakespeare Company*, p. 222. For the Burbage–Leicester connection, see Gurr, *Companies*, pp. 267–8.

85 'Marlowe, Company Ownership, and the Role of Edward II', *Medieval and Renaissance Drama in England*, 18 (2005), 37–46, esp. p. 37.

always already famous opens up alternative scenarios at least as intriguing as the familiar story. Can we perhaps read the conflict between characters such as Richard II and Bollingbrook, or the contrast between the old-fashioned Petrarchan Romeo and the cynically modern Mercutio, as representative of the relationship between the rising star and his somewhat older colleagues? Would it make sense to understand the Hal of *1 Henry IV* as the character that marks Burbage's arrival as the new leading man, the moment of Harry's self-coronation mirrored in the ascendancy of the player? That a developmental narrative offers more interesting perspectives than one in which nothing happens (Burbage is and remains great from beginning to end) does not make it any more true or likely – but if we can choose between two equally probable interpretations of the available evidence, why not opt for the richer version?

If I am right in supposing that the early Shakespearian works I listed above were with Pembroke's company until 1597, the reunion of playwright and plays would doubtless have increased the tensions among established and emergent stars in the Chamberlain's Men. The major characters of those plays, after all, were certainly performed by other leading actors, actors who would have expected to continue in the roles they already knew. If one wanted to speculate about their identity, it might be worth considering one prominent member of the Chamberlain's Men who cannot be documented as an actor in the company before 1597, although he rose to prominence shortly thereafter and became one of the original sharers in the Globe in 1599: Augustine Phillips. We can name only five of the leading members of Pembroke's Men (the ones that sued Langley over their financial dealings in connection with the Swan in 1597) but the other sharers remain tantalizingly anonymous, and Phillips could well have been one of them.[86] This proposition is nothing more than guesswork, but so is the idea that he was a member of the Chamberlain's Men from 1594. However, it provides another glimpse of an alternative narrative, one in which the Chamberlain's Men slowly take on the shape they would retain for years over the course of the late 1590s

and do not emerge from their shell full-fledged in 1594. A Phillips that had been used to playing Gloucester in *3 Henry VI* and the same character in *Richard III* would have had to defend his roles against the demands of his new company's established leading men, but he may also have found a fascinatingly overdetermined Richmond in Burbage.

The infusion of new (old) plays and new actors into the Chamberlain's Men in 1597 may have caused productive frictions in the casting process, which would presumably have had a significant impact on Shakespeare's development as a playwright – and on how his dramatic output was regarded by contemporary audiences. As of the autumn of that year, the company's repertory (in my account) suddenly featured two versions of its chief writer: on the one hand, the new Shakespeare, exploring the lyrical flights of fancy of *Midsummer Night's Dream* and *Romeo and Juliet*, maybe returning to figures of otherness in a newly contemporary, urbane setting in *Merchant of Venice* (with Burbage as Bassanio?), and revisiting the history play from a new point of view in *Richard II*; on the other hand, the Shakespeare of the early 1590s, with the more episodic, more heavily rhetorical *Richard III* and a much wilder, both more and less radical take on otherness in *Titus*. *Taming of a Shrew* might suddenly have run before or after *Much Ado* – a play that may just possibly have been inspired by the re-encounter with the older (and more simple-minded) portrait of a shrewish figure. If *Edward II* came with

---

86 For the lawsuit, see C. W. Wallace, 'The Swan Theatre and the Earl of Pembroke's Players', *Englische Studien*, 43 (1911), 340–95; Ingram, *Brazen Age*, pp. 152–6. The five actors who sued Langley had all signed bonds for £100; Phillips may well already have been of solid enough financial standing to be good for such a sum, given that when he died in 1605, he was a wealthy gentleman and landowner in Mortlake, Surrey, who could leave well over £100 in gifts and donations in his will: see E. A. J. Honigmann and Susan Brock, eds., *Playhouse Wills, 1558–1642* (Manchester, 1993), pp. 72–5. In 1604, he was solvent enough to lend out £100 at interest: see Wickham, Berry and Ingram, eds., *English Professional Theatre*, p. 197.

the remnants of Pembroke's Men, the Chamberlain's company could have staged Marlowe's drama of a conflicted king in conjunction with the play it likely inspired, *Richard II*. And so on. Figuring the Chamberlain's Men's repertory as non-linear in its development, as open to the introduction of older works, thus brings into view another possible rupture in the received narrative of Shakespeare's career. It allows for an account that sees the playwright as involved in a productive dialectical relationship with his own earlier efforts, efforts that the re-emergence of plays from the past both fuelled and forced. In this account, the repertory of the Chamberlain's Men loses some of its orderly shape and linear logic, in which they begin with what was written before 1594, adding to that stock, cycling older offerings out of the rotation and occasionally reviving possibly revised and updated versions of popular favourites. Instead, external events, such as the collapse of another successful troupe, now have an impact on the repertory, as previously inaccessible works become newly available and create both new opportunities and new challenges – in Shakespeare's case, the challenge of coming face to face with an earlier version of himself.

At the same time, and this is the third potential rupture I would highlight in the conventional narrative, the *Henry VI* trilogy may very well not have been among the plays that made it into the Chamberlain's Men's stock and became a staple of their repertory. For one thing, all three works make fairly extraordinary demands on a company's cast, requiring easily over twenty actors in speaking parts, and in the case of *1 Henry VI*, over twenty-five.[87] Such large-cast plays were *en vogue* in the early 1590s, and Pembroke's Men may have continued to stage them until their demise. But Shakespeare's later plays – almost all of the ones written after 1594 – are far less demanding, and the same is true of other surviving texts. We cannot say with any certainty how many Chamberlain's Men there were, but given the disparity between the post-1594 plays and the earliest histories, we can plausibly posit that they may not routinely have had enough actors on hand to stage the first tetralogy without making major strategic cuts or taking on extra players.[88]

Notably, this does not apply to *Richard III*, which could be 'performed by a small to average-sized theatre company' – possibly an indication that it would have been one of the texts Pembroke's Men might have taken on tour with them.[89] *Taming of a Shrew* and *Edward II* likewise can be performed by eleven to fourteen players, about average for a Chamberlain's Men play.[90] *Titus*, as we already saw, is the odd one out in calling for a large company, though its casting requirements still fall short of those of the first Henriad.

These figures call for two modifications to the received theatre-historical account. For one thing, they suggest that while Pembroke's Men certainly must have been a large troupe, at least in the early 1590s, they probably did not specialize exclusively in large-scale productions, and their penchant for such plays was probably not why they were in financial trouble in 1593.[91] The assumption that the company went bankrupt because they tried to take their big shows on the road and discovered too late that large-cast productions did not travel well treats them as shockingly ignorant of the economic basics of their trade. I do not think the surviving evidence warrants such a degree of condescension.

---

[87] See Gurr, *Companies*, pp. 59–50; King, *Casting*, p. 254; also Scott McMillin, *The Elizabethan Theatre and the Book of Sir Thomas More* (Ithaca, 1987), pp. 55–8. For McMillin's revised casting estimates for some of those plays, see McMillin and MacLean, *Queen's Men*, pp. 100–1.

[88] Theatre historians often point out the shift from large to medium-sized cast requirements in the mid-1590s, but almost never ask what this change meant for plays originally written for big companies: could they still be used at all? How? I am not aware of any text that survives in an original large-cast state as well as in a significantly altered version possibly intended for a later, much smaller company. The likelihood is that these earlier and more demanding plays were often simply dropped from the repertories of the newer, more streamlined companies.

[89] Jowett, 'Introduction', p. 75.

[90] See McMillin and MacLean, *Queen's Men*, p. 101.

[91] For the argument that the company's economic woes were connected to their dramaturgical preferences, see Gurr, *Companies*, pp. 59–61. For a very useful summary of theatre historical debates about origins, personnel and repertory of the company, see Schoone-Jongen, *Shakespeare's Companies*, pp. 119–46.

The more significant revision concerns the fate of Shakespeare's plays in the repertory of his own company. It seems to me not just possible but highly likely – simply as a logistical matter – that the first Henriad died with Pembroke's Men as a work of live theatre and was never staged by the Chamberlain's or King's Men. The one argument against this theory rests on the inclusion of the trilogy in the 1623 Folio and the concomitant belief that that volume records Shakespeare's plays *as his company's*. In fact, no such connection exists between the Folio and any playing company. Its title-page advertises only the author's name and works and announces the authoritative status of the texts it reproduces. The centrality of authorship to the Folio's project has often been discussed,[92] but the foregrounding of the playwright and the simultaneous erasure of the troupes that staged his plays have not been taken seriously as a theatre-historical challenge. And yet, the sole reminder of the theatrical origins of the plays is the well-known list of 'principal players' – a list that is not organized into distinct groups or any kind of chronological order and leaves the actors' diverse company affiliations almost deliberately obscure. Jonson's lists of actors in his 1616 *Workes* form a stark contrast to this approach. There, as we have seen, the reader is given a historically specific run-down of who took part in productions by, for instance, the 'then Lord Chamberlain's Men'. The Shakespeare Folio lacks such indications of chronological accuracy, all the more surprisingly given that both men responsible for its compilation were members of the Chamberlain's as well as the King's Men. From this point of view, we may question whether the Folio really offers versions of Shakespeare's plays 'presenting themselves as the Chamberlain's' – a claim recently made by James Marino in an otherwise highly astute essay on the textual history of *Taming of the Shrew*.[93] The Folio, remarkably, makes no claims at all for a persistent continuity between Shakespeare and the Chamberlain's/King's company; on the contrary, it remains totally silent on the issue. What it emphatically offers instead is a composite picture of its myriad-minded author, of the continuity of his oeuvre as a coherent whole suitable for readerly consumption. But such a vision has little to do with the theatre and its rhythms of repertorial innovation, repetition, and revival – and in particular, it smooths over the ruptures and shifts in the history of Shakespeare's 1590s plays as I have sketched it here.

We could call this the Folio effect: Shakespeare's works are always with him, part of him just as he is part of them; the oeuvre grows organically with its author, without separation or alienation. The duopoly narrative buys into this vision of a playwright wholly at one with himself, his works and his company. My account here, by contrast, has attempted – in as speculative, but no more speculative a fashion – to open the way for an alternative view of Shakespeare and his theatrical world that takes seriously the messy, the non-linear and non-teleological, the commercial and market-driven, the fluid and sometimes out-of-control elements of that world; that recognizes the reality that plays lived and died with companies, not with playwrights, and that Shakespeare was no more born a sharer than Burbage was born a leading man. Three may well have been company in mid-1590s London, but four or five would still not have been a crowd.

92 See, for instance, David Scott Kastan, *Shakespeare and the Book* (Cambridge, 2001), pp. 63–78.
93 Marino, 'The Anachronistic *Shrews*', *Shakespeare Quarterly*, 60 (2009), 25–46.

THOMAS GREENE:
STRATFORD-UPON-AVON'S TOWN CLERK AND SHAKESPEARE'S LODGER

ROBERT BEARMAN

A feature of recent Shakespeare biography has been a shift away from the recycling of the surviving material facts which document Shakespeare's life towards a study of the broader issues of the age in which he lived or the lives of those who knew him well.[1] This may not reward us with direct knowledge of Shakespeare's attitude towards those many issues which preoccupied his contemporaries but it does at least remind us that, as a man of his time, he too must have been beset with daily problems concerning his and his family's welfare and that he would have discussed such things with friends and acquaintances. Had more archive material survived, we would have to take account of a whole range of interests and activities in our assessment of Shakespeare's outlook and behaviour in response to such considerations; the reverse of the temptation, in the absence of such evidence, to imagine he lived isolated from the issues of immediate concern to those around him.

One man well acquainted with Shakespeare was Thomas Greene, on one level an unremarkable representative of a minor town gentry family, who for fifteen years was town clerk, or steward, of Stratford-upon-Avon. But Greene also lived and worked in the town at the same time as William Shakespeare, for some years as his tenant. He also went to law with him over their shared interest in the Stratford tithes and the two men later worked together closely during the controversy arising out of the proposed enclosure of the open fields at Welcombe, Greene writing to Shakespeare more than once, and personally recording a conversation they had, the only person to have done so.[2] He

also described Shakespeare as his cousin, a statement which has led to attempts to unravel his precise meaning, notably by Rupert Taylor in 1945 and Christopher Whitfield in 1964.[3] Both studies are helpful in the rehearsal of much of the surviving data concerning Greene's life but they do their subject an injustice by seeking primarily to establish this supposed family relationship. A broader study, taking account of claims to kinship as part of the process of seeking out patrons and influential contacts, might have uncovered more subtle elements in the relationship, revealing not only similarities between the two men in terms of social origin and literary ambition but also a dramatic contrast when it came to worldly success.

Many people have kindly read drafts of this article and I would particularly thank Katherine Duncan-Jones, David Ellis, Wilfrid Prest, Kate Pogue and John Taplin for their helpful comments.

[1] James Shapiro, *1599: A Year in the Life of William Shakespeare* (London, 2005); Charles Nicholl, *The Lodger: Shakespeare on Silver Street* (London, 2007); Germaine Greer, *Shakespeare's Wife* (London, 2007).

[2] Below, p. 299. But conversations with Shakespeare were retrospectively reported in legal evidence submitted in the Bellott/Mountjoy case: E. K. Chambers, *William Shakespeare: a Study of Facts and Problems*, vol. 2 (Oxford, 1930), pp. 90–1, 93.

[3] Rupert Taylor, 'Shakespeare's Cousin, Thomas Greene, and his Kin: Possible Light on the Shakespeare Family Background', *PMLA*, 60 (1945), 81–94; Christopher Whitfield, 'Thomas Greene: Shakespeare's Cousin. A Biographical Sketch', *Notes and Queries*, 11 (1964), 442–55.

Thomas Greene set out his ancestry in an ambitious pedigree submitted to the heralds in 1623.[4] It begins with a John Greene, five generations back, said to be the third brother of Thomas Greene of the distinguished Greene family of Greens Norton in Northamptonshire. The reliability of this claim is open to question: suffice to say that in no way did such ancestry confer on him or his father, also Thomas, the status of men of independent means. When, in 1581, Thomas the elder emerges into the light, it is as a man of business, that of mercer, in the borough of Warwick, he having moved there from the nearby village of Tanworth some years previously; and although Thomas the younger, in the 1623 pedigree, did his best to emphasize his ancestors' gentry origins, the reality was that his paternal grandfather, Oliver Green, was barely of yeoman status.

Thomas the elder became a man of some standing in Warwick. In 1586, as an Assistant Burgess and Master of the Company of Mercers, Grocers and Haberdashers (and as an indication of his religious leanings), he is found supporting the controversial nomination as Member of Parliament for Warwick of the radical Puritan, Job Throckmorton, a likely candidate for the authorship of the notorious Marprelate Tracts.[5] He made his will on 22 July 1590, clearly on his deathbed.[6] The bequests it contained, and the accompanying inventory (valuing his assets at over £113), indicate a man of considerable means. His executor, Thomas junior, also charged with responsibility for his two under-age brothers, was not, however, liberally provided for, suggesting a lack of warmth between father and son.[7] In addition to a 'gray mare', some items of silver and other household effects, his principal legacy was of an uncertain and complicated nature – a forfeited bond in the sum of £80 in his father's hands entered into by two fellow Warwick townsmen, which may or may not have been discharged.

By then Thomas the younger, presumably educated at the town's grammar school (though no records to substantiate this have survived), had apparently already decided to pursue a career in the law. To this purpose, he had sought admission to Staple Inn, one of the lesser inns

originally set up to train young men for service as clerks in the Chancery, but which by the later sixteenth century had become a more general training ground for attorneys and those wishing to achieve entry to one of the more prestigious inns of court. Records of these lesser inns are virtually non-existent and Thomas's years there are thus largely undocumented, though he is probably to be identified with the 'Mʳ Grene' with whom members of the Stratford-upon-Avon Corporation sat down for dinner during a trip to London on legal business in May 1590.[8] Be that as it may, in November 1595, he was admitted from Staple Inn to the Middle Temple as the son of Thomas Greene of Warwick, gentleman, deceased.[9]

Greene's sponsors for his admission to the Middle Temple were two existing members, the lawyer, John Marston, and his son of the same name, who later achieved fame as a poet and dramatist. John the elder had entered the Middle Temple in 1570.[10] Originally from Hayton, near Ludlow, in Shropshire he had, by the mid 1580s, established himself in Warwickshire, being appointed counsel for the city of Coventry in 1585 and its steward in 1588.

---

4 *The Visitation of the County of Gloucester, Taken in the Year 1623*, ed. John Maclean and W. C. Heane, Harleian Society, vol. 21 (1885), p. 69.

5 *The Black Book of Warwick*, ed. Thomas Kemp (Warwick, 1898), pp. 385–7. Thomas is first recorded in Warwick in July 1581, when he was assessed for the poor rate, as a resident in High Pavement (Warwickshire County Record Office, CR 1618/W18/1, unpaginated); and see *Book of John Fisher*, ed. Thomas Kemp (Warwick, 1900), p. 81.

6 Worcestershire Record Office, wills, 1591, no. 61. His inventory was dated seven days later.

7 Thomas junior must therefore have been born by 1569 but probably not long before. His younger brother, John, was born in 1575: Edgar Fripp, *Shakespeare Man and Artist*, vol. 2 (Oxford, 1938), p. 890.

8 *Minutes and Accounts of the Corporation of Stratford-upon-Avon, 1586–1592*, ed. Richard Savage and Edgar Fripp, Dugdale Society, vol. 10 (London, 1929), p. 87.

9 *Middle Temple Records*, ed. C. H. Hopwood, vol. 1 (London, 1904–05), p. 357.

10 For John Marston, father and son, see James Knowles, 'Marston, John, 1576–1634', *Oxford Dictionary of National Biography* (*ODNB*) online; Whitfield, 'Thomas Greene', p. 250.

In 1590, he had been consulted by the Stratford Corporation concerning an appeal to the Privy Council.[11] John Marston junior had entered the Middle Temple in 1592, just three years earlier than Greene. The Marstons' involvement in sponsoring Greene's admission clearly implies a connection of sorts between them, most probably derived from these local ties.

Greene spent seven years at the Middle Temple before his call to the bar in October 1602.[12] Many of his fellow Middle Templars were sons of gentry who had moved on from university to attend the Inns of Court for a few years as part of their education. But Greene was from no such background. As far as is known, he had only the uncertain bequest from his father as a means of support and was therefore constrained to regard his years at the Middle Temple as ones of preparation for a career in the law. However, as was the case with other contemporaries of slender means, he might have hoped that a successful bid for patronage would provide him with an opportunity to pursue his interests freed from those financial pressures which had probably dogged him since his father's death. This would be sufficient to explain an early attachment to the young Henry Rainsford, who had been admitted to the Middle Temple in October 1594 at the age of nineteen.[13] He was the wealthy son of the late Hercules Rainsford of Clifford Chambers, a mile or so from Stratford, completing his country gentleman's education before his marriage in 1596 to Anne daughter of Sir Henry Goodere of Polesworth. We have to wait a few years for documentary confirmation of this friendship (until September 1604, by which time Greene was acting as his steward at Clifford Chambers[14]) but later evidence establishes a strong and lasting link between the two men, surely first forged at the Middle Temple.

This friendship may have taken on an added dimension on Rainsford's marriage to Anne Goodere in 1596. Anne, born in 1571, was the daughter of Henry Goodere, in whose household, and that of his younger brother, Thomas Goodere, had lived the young Michael Drayton, in the capacity of page or servant.[15] Following Henry Goodere's

death in 1595, Drayton initially sought patronage elsewhere but he did not forget the Gooderes: in 1597 he dedicated one of his *Englands Heriocall Epistles* to Goodere's elder daughter, Frances, and another to her husband (and cousin), Henry Goodere the younger. He also maintained contact with Goodere's other daughter, Anne, who had married Rainsford a year after her father's death. The popular notion that Anne was the subject of Drayton's sequence of fifty-one sonnets published in 1594 and that she remained his lifelong platonic mistress has been questioned in recent years.[16] However, in Drayton's *Barrons Wars*, published in 1603,[17] there is a veiled reference to Anne Rainsford and the River Stour, on which Clifford Chambers stands, repeated more strongly in an eclogue included in a collection of Drayton's poems published three years later.[18] Drayton also composed an elegy to commemorate the death of Anne's husband, Henry Rainsford, in 1622 in which Rainsford features as his 'Incomparable Friend' who 'would have sworn that to no other end / He had been borne: but only for my friend'.[19] Even allowing for poetic exaggeration, this, together with Drayton's poetic allusions to Clifford Chambers, would surely confirm a relationship between the two men following Anne's marriage to Rainsford. It would therefore have been another consequence that Thomas Greene, as one of Rainsford's fellow students at the Middle Temple, became acquainted with Drayton; for the two men were clearly known to each other by

[11] *Minutes and Accounts of the Corporation of Stratford-upon-Avon, 1586–1592*, p. 117.

[12] *Middle Temple Records*, I, p. 426.

[13] *Middle Temple Records*, I, p. 346.

[14] Below, p. 295.

[15] Bernard H. Newdigate, *Michael Drayton and his Circle* (Oxford, 1941); Jean R. Brink, *Michael Drayton Revisited* (Boston, 1990); Anne Lake Prescott, 'Drayton, Michael (1563–1631)', *ODNB* online.

[16] By Jean Brink, *Michael Drayton Revisited*.

[17] See below.

[18] 'Driving her Flocks up the fruitfull *Meene* [Meon hill] /Which daily lookes upon the lovely *Stowre*': *Poemes Lyrick and Pastorall* [1606] (STC: 7225.5).

[19] Michael Drayton, *The Works of Michael Drayton*, 5 vols. (Oxford, 1931–41), III, p. 232; V, p. 217.

1603 when Greene penned a sonnet in Drayton's honour, prefacing the latter's quasi-epic poem, *The Barrons Wars in the Raigne of Edward the Second*, published that year,[20] to be reprinted in a collection of Drayton's poems published in 1605.[21] In the same year appeared a more ambitious work, by 'Thomas Greene, Gentleman', *A Poets Vision and a Princes Glorie dedicated to the high and mightie Prince, James King of England and Ireland*, one of many similar offerings to the new king presented by those looking for some advancement.[22] These were not the only works with which Greene can be credited. In 1602 there had also appeared a new edition of *The Hystorie of the Seven Wise Maisters of Rome*, prefaced by an epistle from 'Thomas Greene Gentleman', in which he explains why he had agreed to undertake the work of correction.[23] We might also note, whilst considering Greene's literary pretensions, some Latin verses on death, apparently his, composed by 1614 though not published in his lifetime.[24]

This aspect of Greene's activities during his Middle Temple years raises significant issues. That he was called to the bar in 1602 establishes that he had applied himself to his legal studies. But he would also have been aware of the wider literary interests for which the Inns of Court were well known. We have already noted not only the admission of John Marston, the future playwright, to the Middle Temple in 1592 but also his sponsorship of Greene when he was admitted three years later. Another future playwright, John Ford, entered the Middle Temple in November 1602,[25] the same year that fellow student, John Manningham, noted a performance of Shakespeare's *Twelfth Night* there.[26] Manningham himself was a personal friend of Greene's, judging by a note made in his diary earlier that year of one of Greene's witticisms.[27] Greene's friendship with Drayton, though facilitated by Rainsford's marriage, might also have grown closer during the years immediately following 1597 when Drayton was in London collaborating in the writing of a succession of plays for the Admiral's Men.[28] At the same time, Greene's contact with Marston might also have led to his meeting with William Shakespeare, given the possibility of Shakespeare

and Marston co-operating at that time in providing contributions to Robert Chester's *Love's Martyr* published in 1601.[29] And binding all three men together – and a fourth was Henry Rainsford – were their local Warwickshire ties.

There is, however, a more worldly reason why Greene might first have come to Shakespeare's notice. Whilst at the Middle Temple, Greene had looked to supplement his income by undertaking legal work. One of his clients (not surprisingly, given his Warwickshire origins) was the Stratford Corporation, for whom he may have initially been employed as early as 1590.[30] Leading aldermen, and notably Richard Quiney, regularly travelled to London, both on town business and in connection with their own affairs. At some point the decision was made to re-engage Greene's services and in January and February 1601, when Quiney was in London preparing the Corporation's case against Edward Greville, Stratford's lord of the manor, with whom the Corporation had been at war since the previous summer, we find listed in his expenses a

---

[20] STC 7189. This was a re-publication, with many alterations, of his *Mortimeriados*, published in 1596.

[21] STC 7216. 'Poems. By Michaell Draiton Esquire'.

[22] STC 12311. It has been suggested that this, and the tribute to Drayton, might have been the work of the actor, Thomas Greene, though there is no material, nor even circumstantial, evidence to support this (Herbert Berry, 'Greene, Thomas . . . actor', *ODNB* online). See also Mark Eccles, *Shakespeare in Warwickshire* (Madison, 1961), p. 128.

[23] STC 21299.5.

[24] Shakespeare Centre Library and Archive (SCLA), BRU 15/13/26a (v): now published in C. M. Ingleby, ed., *Shakespeare and the Enclosure of the Common Fields of Welcombe* (Birmingham, 1885), p. 4; Edgar I. Fripp, *Shakespeare's Stratford* (Oxford, 1928), p. 60.

[25] *Middle Temple Records*, I, p. 427.

[26] *The Diary of John Manningham of the Middle Temple*, ed. Robert Parker Sorlein (Hanover, 1976), pp. 48, 265. For a list of dramatic performances at the Middle Temple during these years, and at the other inns of court, see *Records of Early English Drama: Inns of Court*, ed. Alan H. Nelson and John R. Elliott, 3 vols. (Cambridge, 2011), II, pp. 759–61.

[27] *Diary of John Manningham*, pp. 172, 374.

[28] Newdigate, *Michael Drayton and his Circle*, pp. 101–4.

[29] STC 5119. For this, see Katherine Duncan-Jones, *Ungentle Shakespeare* (London, 2001), pp. 137–45.

[30] Above, p. 292.

payment of 10 shillings to 'Mr Greene our Sol-
liciter for hys paines' and a further 3s 4d which
Greene had 'layed out in the searche of Recordes
for us', presumably at some point before Quiney's
arrival.[31] We are also told that Greene accompanied Quiney on three unsuccessful attempts to see
the Lord Chief Justice, Edward Coke, 'butt colde
nott have hym att Leasure'. This can hardly have
been the first occasion that the two men had met.
Quiney had been making regular visits to London
since October 1593. On two of these trips, over
the winters of 1597/98 and 1598/99, we know
with some certainty that he met up with William
Shakespeare,[32] and no doubt would have done so
at least by the time of the later visits, in the autumn
of 1600 and then again in February 1601, when we
first read of Greene's renewed activities on behalf of
the Corporation. Given Greene's literary interests,
it would therefore surely not have been surprising
if, towards the end of this period, he had sought an
acquaintance with Shakespeare through Quiney's
intermediation, if he had not already done so as a
result of a shared friendship with Marston.

In June 1601, Quiney was back in London, his
expenses again revealing the extent of Greene's
assistance.[33] On 22 July, following Quiney's return
to Stratford, Greene wrote to him, with an update
on the progress of the case which Edward Greville was to bring against the Corporation at the
forthcoming Warwick assizes,[34] following this up
with another letter, written in September, letting
Quiney know that he had succeeded in engaging
Edward Coke as the Corporation's counsel in the
Greville dispute.[35] The two men met up again in
London in November 1601. This time Quiney paid
him over £5 for 'hys paines with us in the terme',
not forgetting to claim 15 pence for the breakfast
they enjoyed together on 9 November.[36]

The year 1603 was for Greene an important one.
Having been called to the bar in October 1602,
he now saw his way clear to marry, taking as his
wife Lettice, the daughter of Henry Tutt of West
Meon in Hampshire. The Tutts were respectable
local gentry though it has not yet been established
how Greene came to know them, nor the precise
date of the marriage or where it took place.[37] His

bride was under twenty-one and unmarried when
her father made his will in 1589, leaving her 100
marks (£66).[38] She was still unmarried in May
1598, when her uncle Richard left her a further
£20.[39] On the other hand, the Greenes' first child
was baptized on 18 March 1604, implying the early
summer of 1603 as their date of marriage.[40]

It was also in 1603 that Greene decided to
return to Warwickshire. His closest Stratford contact, Richard Quiney, had died in May 1602 but
Greene may still have been aware of the increasing
likelihood of securing appointment as Stratford's
town clerk or steward. The existing steward, John
Jeffreys, who had succeeded to the post back in

---

[31] *Minutes and Accounts of the Stratford-upon-Avon Corporation, 1599–1609*, ed. Robert Bearman, Dugdale Society, vol. 44 (2011) (*Minutes*), p. 124; Edgar I. Fripp, *Master Richard Quyny* (Oxford, 1924), pp. 174–6. See also above, n. 8, for evidence that, as early as 1590, the young Thomas Greene, in London, may have been acting in a legal capacity on behalf of the Stratford Corporation.

[32] Robert Bearman, *Shakespeare in the Stratford Records* (Stroud, 1994), pp. 24–6, 32–6.

[33] 'Geeven to Mr Greene for hys paines, 20s.', and 'Paied hym for thatt he layed out for us in searcheinge in the Rowles in the tower [of London] and othe where, 13s. 4d' (*Minutes*, p. 137). In forwarding to Greene a letter he had just received from Stratford, Quiney adds: 'My wante of good health lettethe my cominge to yo^w att thys tyme. I praye yo^w be att home after supper' (*Minutes*, p. 131).

[34] *Minutes*, pp. 139–40.

[35] *Minutes*, p. 146.

[36] *Minutes*, p. 186.

[37] For the family's pedigree, see *Pedigrees from the Visitation of Hampshire . . . continued with the Visitation made by John Phillipott in A^o 1622 . . . as Collected by Richard Mundy*, ed. W. Harry Rylands, Harleian Society, vol. 64 (1913), pp. 212–15. This includes Lettice's marriage to Thomas Greene, though perhaps as a later addition.

[38] The National Archives (TNA), PROB 11/89, fos. 169–170v.

[39] TNA, PROB 11/94, fos. 129v–130v.

[40] *The Registers of Stratford-on-Avon . . . Baptisms, 1558–1652*, ed. Richard Savage, Parish Register Society, VI (1897), p. 69. Fripp's complicated argument that on her marriage to Greene she was already the widow of one Chandler of Leicester, whose stepson by her husband's first marriage, also widowed with a child, came with her to Stratford (Edgar I. Fripp, *Shakespeare Man and Artist*, vol. 2 (Oxford, 1938), p. 785) is seriously flawed for reasons that John Taplin has kindly pointed out to me.

1587, was by 1601 beginning to attract criticism. In that year he missed eight out of fifteen meetings, and in 1602 five out of ten.[41] By then he had moved to Wolverton and on 22 December 1602 the Corporation agreed that, unless Jeffreys gave an undertaking to return to the town, he would be relieved of his post.[42] His record, however, failed to improve and on 31 August Greene was therefore appointed to succeed him.[43]

Another major incentive for his move to Stratford would have been his wish to remain close to Henry Rainsford, who had never completed his studies at the Middle Temple, returning to Clifford Chambers on his marriage in 1596. He was to play an important part in Greene's later life and Greene's wish to exploit the friendship formed during those years at the Middle Temple is easily understood. A second relationship possibly forged in London, this time with William Shakespeare and as the result of his literary ambitions, may also have been a factor. Greene apparently still had no means of financial support beyond what he could earn in legal work (of which there is very little evidence): on the other hand, both Henry Rainsford and, by 1603, William Shakespeare might have been willing to help him. In Rainsford's case, this becomes evident in his appointment as Rainsford's steward on his manor of Clifford Chambers by at least September 1604.[44] For Shakespeare, the evidence is less conclusive, namely Greene's famous, and oft-quoted, remark in September 1609 that he would be able to remain at New Place (the house which Shakespeare had purchased in 1597) for another year, presumably as Shakespeare's tenant.[45] Whether or not this landlord/tenant arrangement had existed from the time of Greene's arrival, with his new wife, in Stratford in 1603, is uncertain. Until the note of 1609, there is only the fact that he is not known to have resided elsewhere in the town which would allow us to assume that New Place had been his home since 1603.[46] Nevertheless his family had remained a small one for some years. His second child had died in infancy in August 1606 so that his household had only increased to four by the time of the birth of a son, William, in January 1608;[47] and New Place was a property large enough to have

accommodated the Greenes. The size of Shakespeare's family, even if it included his mother and his two unmarried siblings, was also static if not decreasing, following his mother's death the following year.[48] All this, of course, is circumstantial but it surely remains a strong possibility that Greene came to Stratford as Shakespeare's tenant and remained so until, as we shall see, he decided to purchase a home of his own; and further that such an arrangement would be a natural corollary to his having nurtured an acquaintance with Shakespeare through shared literary interests.

This also raises the much discussed question of a possible family relationship, as Greene three times refers to Shakespeare as his cousin, between November 1614 and January 1615, though only in his personal diary concerning the attempted enclosure of land at Welcombe.[49] By 1603, Shakespeare was a man of some standing and it would clearly have been of advantage if he could be claimed as kin.[50] Negotiating a lease of a portion of New Place, for instance, would have been made smoother by such an appeal to family ties. However, no such family link has yet been established. There was a family of Greenes in Little Alne and another in neighbouring Wilmcote and, though neither is known with certainty to be related to the Greenes of Tanworth (whence Thomas's father

[41] *Minutes*, pp. 147–8, 150–2, 164–5, 167–8, 196–8, 201–2, 209–10.

[42] *Minutes*, p. 207.

[43] *Minutes*, p. 266.

[44] SCLA, DR 33/59.

[45] SCLA, BRU 15/12/103; Chambers, *William Shakespeare*, II, p. 96.

[46] But he was leased a barn in Bull Lane, now Bull Street (SCLA, BRU 15/3/27).

[47] *Registers of Stratford-on-Avon . . . Burials 1558–1652/3*, ed. Richard Savage, Parish Register Society, vol. 55 (1905), p. 73; *Registers of Stratford-on-Avon . . . Baptisms*, p. 75.

[48] Shakespeare himself may not initially have been much in residence, though theatre closures due to plague for much of 1608 and all of 1609 may have led to his spending more time in Stratford at this time.

[49] Ingleby, *Shakespeare and the Enclosure of the Common Fields of Welcombe*, pp. 1, 4, 7.

[50] See also below, p. 298.

hailed) or to the Ardens of Wilmcote, a claim to kinship through this coincidence of names and places could well have been invoked by a man eager to seek patronage.[51]

The stewardship of the borough of Stratford only carried with it a modest fee of £5, though Greene astutely managed to persuade the Corporation to pay him an additional £2 for additional duties.[52] He was therefore obliged to look further afield to supplement his income. We have already noted that by 1604 Henry Rainsford had appointed him steward for the manor of Clifford Chambers: by way of reciprocation, perhaps, he stood surety for Rainsford's son, when in November 1616 he too was admitted to the Middle Temple.[53] In 1608 we find Rainsford and Greene witnessing the will of the wealthy Stratford townsman Thomas Combe[54] and from 1607 to 1617 Greene was acting as steward for the Throckmorton family of Coughton on their manors of Coughton, Sambourne and Oversley in Warwickshire and Throckmorton in Worcestershire.[55] In November 1610 Sir Edward Conway of Ragley also awarded him an annuity of 40 shillings a year in return for his advice.[56] A link with another local gentry family is suggested by his standing surety for William the son of Sir William Somerville of Edstone, near Wootton Wawen, on his admission to the Middle Temple in 1608, and in 1614 he was engaged as one of the arbitrators to settle a dispute between Henry Ferrers of Baddesley Clinton and fellow Middle Temple lawyer, Anthony Ludford, concerning the manor of Kingswood.[57]

Despite these other calls on his time, there is no evidence to suggest, especially in the early years, that he did not perform his duties to the Stratford Corporation other than to its general satisfaction. There were inevitably occasions when he was unable to attend Council meetings, especially during the four legal terms when he was often in London. But the Corporation's own business would have taken him to the capital anyway and it must also have been understood that the town's barrister-steward on only £7 a year would need to look beyond the town to supplement his income. In any case, his absences from Corporation

meetings were few and far between. During his years as steward, he was present at the great majority: some 144 meetings out of 196, some 73 per cent. Evidence of the Corporation's general confidence is therefore to be found in his nomination as steward in the town's second charter granted in July 1610.[58]

We must now consider the important issue of Greene's purchases of property in Stratford, the consequences of which may well have had a bearing on his decision to leave the town some years later. In September 1609, he was living at New Place where he anticipated he 'mighte stay another yere', a remark made in the context of his having purchased the freehold of a substantial house adjoining the Stratford churchyard, known as St Mary's.[59] There was a delay in the completion of the purchase, or at least of the Greenes moving in, as the result of difficulties with a sitting tenant, George Browne, whose unwillingness to

---

[51] For further discussion of this, see Taylor, 'Shakespeare's cousin, Thomas Greene'; Whitfield, 'Thomas Greene'; Irvine Gray, 'Shakespeare's cousin, Thomas Greene', *Transactions of the Bristol and Gloucestershire Archaeological Society*, 92, (1973), 213–15.

[52] This payment first occurs in the chamberlain's accounts rendered in January 1605 'for assisting Mr Balife & Mr Alderman with his counsell in affaires pertainienge to their offices' (*Minutes*, p. 322) but became annual thereafter.

[53] *Middle Temple Records*, I, p. 611.

[54] TNA, PROB 11/113, fos. 99v–100.

[55] SCLA, DR 5/2200, 2203, 2287, 2291, 2293–6, 2391, 2393–5, 2397, 2400, 3291–2, 3294; BRU 12/7/152; BRU 15/5/92.

[56] SCLA, BRU 12/7/144.

[57] *Middle Temple Records*, II, p. 488; SCLA, DR 3/468–9, 616.

[58] SCLA, BRU 1/2. In 1611–12, as further evidence of favour, Greene's brother John was elected a capital burgess and considered for appointment as deputy town clerk and the Corporation's solicitor (SCLA, BRU 2/2, pp. 206, 230, 236, 243; below, n. 104).

[59] This had previously belonged to the Stratford College but at the Reformation had been confiscated by the crown when in the occupation of Thomas Whitley. In November 1607, it had been sold, with other College property, to two speculators, Richard Lidell and Edmund Bostock (TNA, C 66/1740, part 20) following which Greene had subsequently entered into negotiations for a sale to him (SCLA, BRU 15/11/1).

leave had prompted Greene's note, embedded in a statement of the case which he put to his friend, Henry Rainsford, asking that 'I desire I may have the possession at our Lady Day next [25 March 1610] that then I may begyne to make yt reddy agaynst Michaelmas next'.[60] Whatever the result of this plea, Greene had certainly moved his family there by 21 June 1611 when an order was made by the Corporation 'to repare the churchyard wall at Mr. Green's dwelling-house, and to keepe yt sufficiently repar'd for the lenth of too hundred nintye and seaven foote of wallinge'.[61] Greene later claimed to have paid out more than £400 for St Mary's. This cannot be verified from surviving documentation but was probably an exaggeration: a few years later, as we shall see, he agreed to sell it for £240.

His other major purchase was of a share in Stratford's tithes. Until the Reformation, Stratford's tithes had belonged to the Stratford College but on its suppression these were confiscated by the crown. In 1553, a portion of these tithes, valued at £34 a year, had been granted to the Corporation, mainly in return for paying salaries to the vicar and curate. But there was a complication. In 1543, shortly before the College's suppression, the last warden, Anthony Baker, had granted a 92-year lease of these tithes to a member of his own family.[62] This lease was allowed to stand despite the transfer of the ownership of the tithes first to the crown and then, of part of them, to the Corporation, who thus had to be satisfied with receiving only £34 a year for the duration of this lease rather than the much larger sum the tithes were worth. Over the years this lease was assigned from one party to another, divided into parts, and these parts even sub-let. In 1580, for instance, John Barker, the descendant of the original lessee, had assigned the original lease to Sir John Hubaud, who in his will, proved in 1583, left one half of the Corporation's share to his brother, Ralph.[63] This was the half that William Shakespeare acquired in 1605.[64] The other half went to George Digby, whose widow, Abigail, sublet it to the Combe family in 1595 for twenty-one years.[65] Subsequently, the principal lease of this half passed though several hands,

ending up with Humphrey Colles, of the Middle Temple, who in 1609 agreed to assign it to his fellow Middle Templar, Thomas Greene. The asking price was £360, £60 of which was to be paid immediately, and £300 in 1613 when the sub-lease to the Combes was nearer expiry.[66] In 1609, then, Greene had made a substantial commitment, first, and immediately, to find the money to purchase St Mary's (allegedly £400 but probably less), together with £60 as an initial payment for the lease of the tithes, and secondly to raise a further £300 in four years' time to complete the purchase.[67]

His purchase of the tithes inevitably had an effect on his relationship with the Corporation. Ever since the charter of 1553, the Corporation, as explained above, had had to be satisfied with the annual rent of £34 reserved to them under the 92-year lease despite the fact that the tithes would have yielded much more if under its immediate control. The acquisition of an interest in a share of tithes by its own steward was thus a sensitive issue, laying Greene open to accusations of a conflict of interest. As the Corporation's steward, he was expected to support the Corporation's efforts to recover its control over the tithes; on the other

---

60 SCLA, BRU 15/12/103. Browne, the sitting tenant, had married Frances Barnes in 1594, possibly a relative of William Barnes, Rainsford's stepfather, hence Greene's appeal to him: *The Registers of Stratford-on-Avon . . . Marriages 1558–1812*, ed. Richard Savage, Parish Register Society, vol. 16 (1898), p. 16.

61 J. O. Halliwell, *An Historical Account of the New Place, Stratford-upon-Avon, the Last Residence of Shakespeare* (London, 1864), p. 25.

62 Robert Bearman, 'The Early Reformation Experience in a Warwickshire Market Town: Stratford-upon-Avon 1530–1580', *Midland History*, 32 (2007), 74.

63 TNA, PROB 11/66, fos. 232–5v.

64 Bearman, *Shakespeare in the Stratford Records*, pp. 41–2.

65 SCLA, BRU 8/17/3.

66 SCLA, BRU 8/17/9. Colles was presumably a little older than Greene, admitted to the Middle Temple in August 1592 (*Middle Temple Records*, I, p. 330) but was clearly a man he would have studied with.

67 Another indication of his intention to acquire property at this time is reflected in his application in July 1610 to have first refusal on the lease of a Corporation barn in Ely Street (SCLA, BRU 2/2, p. 196).

hand, he could be seen as one of the tithe holders benefiting from the fact that the Corporation's hands were tied by the 92-year lease. When news of the deal with Colles leaked out, there was clearly unease, if not outright criticism, to the extent that in April 1610, it was reported at a Corporation meeting that 'Thomas Greene . . . standeth secretlie scandalised and unjustli sklaundred bie unknownen authors That he hath hearetofore deceaved and dealt evillie with us in the byinge of one Humfrie Coles, esquier, an intereste in tithes, the inheritance wheareof is in us.' At this stage, however, opposition was muted and the majority view was to dismiss the accusation 'for his fidelitie and endevors in our behalfes allwaies used us verie well'.[68]

It was this purchase of an interest in the tithes that brought Greene closest to Shakespeare in his business dealings. Almost immediately, either in 1610 or 1611, he was persuaded by two fellow tithe-holders, Shakespeare himself and Richard Lane, to go to law against other holders of the local tithes over a somewhat obscure but important point. When, back in 1580, the Barkers had in effect assigned the lease of all the tithes to John Hubaud, they had reserved to themselves an annuity of £27 13s 4d, payable by the assignees. The payment of this annuity became a complicated matter once the lease fragmented, and the tithes divided between growing numbers of assignees. In 1605, when Shakespeare was assigned half the Corporation's share in the tithes, a proportion of this charge − £5 − was carefully specified. But such care had not been taken in other cases with the result, it was claimed, that Shakespeare and Richard Lane, 'and some fewe others', were being forced to make up the payment to the Barkers, on threat of dispossession, due to the failure of fellow tithe-holders to contribute a fair share.[69] It is not clear why Greene allowed himself to become involved in the dispute at this point. Although he had just agreed to purchase a half-interest in the lease of the Corporation's tithes, the other half of which was already held by Shakespeare, he was not due to enter into his lease or to complete the purchase until 1613. Perhaps he was persuaded to be a party as the result of his legal background

and because, at that point still Shakespeare's tenant, he could not easily refuse to help. Certainly, intriguing evidence still survives which points to a working relationship between the two families. In July 1613, Thomas Greene and Shakespeare's son-in-law, John Hall, were appointed trustees of an arrangement whereby Richard Lane settled land on his children.[70] But a more intimate connection is indicated in December 1611 when Lettice Greene, Thomas's wife, alongside her husband Thomas and Shakespeare's daughter Judith, witnessed a conveyance by Elizabeth Quiney and her son of a house in Wood Street − Lettice signing with some competence but Judith restricting herself to a mark.[71] Thomas Greene, and another witness, Edmund Rawlins, were there as legal advisors to the parties involved, Greene probably acting for the Quineys.[72] But the presence of two women who would have come to know each other well during the Greenes' tenancy of New Place indicates a considerable degree of social familiarity, both with each other and with the Quineys.

Greene's interest in the tithes, and his position as town clerk, also drew him into the much more serious dispute which broke out in the autumn of 1614 when news surfaced of a plan to enclose lands at Welcombe, the progress of which Greene carefully recorded in diary form. Enclosure could have affected both Shakespeare's and Greene's interests if the scheme were to lead to a reduction in tithe

---

[68] SCLA, BRU 2/2, pp. 188–9.

[69] The undated bill of complaint (SCLA, BRU 15/2/11) is printed in full in J. O. Halliwell-Phillipps, *Outlines of the Life of Shakespeare*, 9th edn, 2 vols. (London 1890), II, pp. 25–31. An abstract of the answer of William Combe, one of the defendants, sworn in Chancery on 13 February 1611, is also extant (SCLA, BRU 15/10/9). See also Chambers, *William Shakespeare*, II, pp. 122–7.

[70] Thomas Greene's brother John had married Margaret Lane, Richard Lane's niece, providing another link.

[71] SCLA, ER 27/11. For a facsimile of these signatures, see Frederick Wellstood, *Catalogue of the Books, Manuscripts . . . exhibited in Shakespeare's Birthplace* (Stratford-upon-Avon, 1944), p. 52.

[72] Rawlins was appointed to take seisin on behalf of William Mountford, the purchaser.

income as the result, for example, of converting arable land to sheep pasture. During October, November and December, Greene's diary is therefore peppered with references to his attempts to make sure he would not suffer; and at an early stage he managed to get his name inserted into an agreement between Shakespeare and William Replingham, agent for the enclosure party, that both he and Shakespeare would be recompensed should their tithe income be affected by 'by reason of anie inclosure or decaye of tyllage'[73] – or, as Greene put it, 'Mr Replyngham 28 Oct[o]bris articled w[i]th Mr Shakspeare & then I was putt in'.[74]

The Corporation, as over-arching owner of the tithes, was also fearful of a drop in their value at a time when increasing demands were being made on its resources. It therefore took up a position of absolute resistance on the assumption that Greene, as its steward, would do his best to help thwart the scheme. This inevitably led to difficulties. As early as 15 November, when Greene met Replingham in London, he was assured, as far as his own interests were concerned, that 'I should be satisfyed'; but as for the town he was told 'he [Replingham] car[ed] not for their consents'.[75] Two days later Greene button-holed Shakespeare when he came up to London with his son-in-law, John Hall, to discuss the forthcoming enclosure plans.[76] On 22 November he heard via a third party that 'I was much excepted unto' by the enclosure party 'for makeing such mighty opposicion agaynst the Inclosure', albeit on the Corporation's behalf. He attempted to defend himself on the grounds that 'I did it accordyng to the trust in me reposed by the Baylyff etc. & howe I was tyed to them etc'.[77] By this time, the Corporation too was having doubts about Greene's loyalty, which surfaced at a council meeting held on 12 December. As Greene again noted, after some dispute over his agreeing to toe the Corporation line, 'I at their instance did write [in the order book] that I declare my provins to be by all lawefull & reasonable meanes to assist them as their Steward and Counseller to w[i]thstand the inclosure & howe I hadd given my word for it.'[78] On 23 December he records two letters he

sent to Shakespeare. One was in his capacity as town clerk, signed by members of the Corporation, doubtless urging Shakespeare to support the town's opposition campaign. The other was to 'my Cosen Shakspeare' couched no doubt in less formal terms in which he discussed 'the Inconvenyences wold g[row] by the Inclosure'.[79] By then both men would have felt fairly safe due to their agreement reached with Replingham back in October, though no doubt kept secret from the Corporation. Indeed, an indication of Shakespeare's willingness to go along with the enclosure is probably reflected in Greene's note of 10 December that he had called at New Place in the hope of meeting Replingham, a fair indication that, if Replingham were not actually lodging there, he was at least received as a guest.[80] On 9 January, Greene was visited by William Combe, the principal champion of the enclosure, and his contemporary at the Middle Temple, who subjected him to more pressure, willing 'me to propound a peace, promised me x[li] to buy a geldyng to doe yt'.[81] Greene protested that 'yt was knowen that he [Combe] was here & that I thought I did nothing but both sydes heard of yt & therefore I caryed myself as free from all offence as I could'. Greene did agree, however, to urge a treaty on 'some of the principall of them' but pleading that Combe would not take it as 'unfashionable dealyng' on his part if the Corporation continued to press its case in the London courts. Then Combe, 'aftir some speches that he should think himself beholdyng unto me yf I could bring an end to passe, he, aftir many promises &

---

73 SCLA, ER 27/3; Bearman, *Shakespeare in the Stratford Records*, pp. 53–5.
74 Ingleby, *Shakespeare and the Enclosure of the Common Fields of Welcombe*, p. 6 (Ingleby, Enclosure).
75 Ingleby, *Enclosure*, p. 1.
76 Ingleby, *Enclosure*, p. 1.
77 Ingleby, *Enclosure*, p. 2.
78 Ingleby, *Enclosure*, p. 3; SCLA, BRU 2/2, pp. 276–7.
79 Ingleby, *Enclosure*, p. 4.
80 Ingleby, *Enclosure*, p. 3.
81 Ingleby, *Enclosure*, p. 6. For Combe's years at the Middle Temple, from 1602 to at least 1612, see *Middle Temple Records*, I, pp. 425, 427; ii, pp. 496, 503, 555–6.

protestacions that I should be well dealt w[i]thall, he departed'. Two days later, Greene dined with Replingham, who 'assured me . . . that I should be well dealt w[i]thall confessyng former promisses by himself . . . & his agreement for me w[i]th my Cosen Shakspeare'.[82] In September, Greene not only recorded an enigmatic conversation in London between his brother John Greene and Shakespeare about the proposed enclosure but also gave an account of a visit to his patron, Henry Rainsford at Clifford Chambers.[83] He was told there that Combe had been to visit Rainsford, emphasizing that 'he would gyve me satisfaccion so as I would procure the townes consent' to enclosure. Greene was interested enough 'to see what composicion in reddy money he would offer me for otherwise I would not deale with him'. However, when Rainsford put this to Combe he replied that 'he would not agree with me unles he agreed with all the rest'.[84]

Certainly, then, Greene's tenancy of the tithes had placed him in a difficult position. Initially, though the Corporation's steward, he was seeking to derive an income from a source which the Corporation could regard as at its expense; and, when enclosure was proposed at Welcombe, he had both to defend his personal position by entering into an agreement, probably secret, with the enclosure party whilst assuring the Corporation that he was doing all he could to thwart the scheme. Forced to reassure the Corporation by subscribing to an order that he would 'assist them agaynst the seyd inclosure',[85] but pestered by Combe with sweeteners tempered by threats, he may well have come to regret his investment. In fact, there is no evidence that it ever brought him any real benefit. The balance of £300, due to Humphrey Colles on 25 March 1613 to complete the purchase, had been duly paid[86] but, until the expiry in 1616 of the sub-lease to the Combes, his income from this source would have been very limited. Moreover, on 18 March, a few days before the payment to Colles had been made, comes evidence of indebtedness, Greene acknowledging that he owed £10 to Thomas Rawlins of Long Marston.[87] We cannot be certain that this debt had been contracted

as the direct result of his having within a few days to find £300; but, when Greene, some four years later, eventually decided to sell up and leave Stratford, it is clear that this was only one of several obligations he had contracted during his later years in Stratford. In the winter of 1616/17 he informed the Corporation of his intention to resign his post and last made entries in the Corporation's order book following the meeting of 19 March 1617.[88] Greene may, of course, have been finding his position as steward increasingly difficult as the result of the conflict of interest as tenant of part of the Corporation's tithes, a situation exacerbated by the controversy over the Welcombe enclosures. But, though this issue dragged on after Greene left the town, it is clear from his increasingly brief diary entries before his departure that, having ridden out the crisis of 1614 and 1615, he would have been able to deal with the aftermath had he not been under pressure from a different quarter.

As explained, in 1609 Greene had committed himself to laying out £500 or £600, £300 of which was due for payment in 1613. It is unlikely that he would have been able to accumulate such a capital sum beforehand and that he would therefore have needed to borrow, on the security of future income, especially from his share in the tithes. Shakespeare's investment in his share, for instance, had been yielding him some £60 annually since 1605. But Greene's share had been sublet to the Combes until 1616, and his income from this source would thus have been very limited and his ability to repay any loans to increasingly impatient creditors compromised. And the arrangements made for the sale of his Stratford property, when considered alongside later evidence of Greene's slender resources, certainly indicate strongly that his decision to leave Stratford arose

---

82 Ingleby, *Enclosure*, p. 7.
83 Ingleby, *Enclosure*, p. 11.
84 Ingleby, *Enclosure*, pp. 11–12.
85 SCLA, BRU 2/2, p. 276; Ingleby, *Enclosure*, p. 3.
86 SCLA, BRU 8/17/11; BRU 15/12/120.
87 SCLA, BRU 15/12/115.
88 SCLA, BRU 2/2, p. 325.

mainly out of a need to satisfy creditors rather than as a response to Corporation pressure.

Negotiations now followed whereby Greene sold his Stratford property – St Mary's house and his share in the tithes – to the Corporation. He set out his stall early in May, asking £870 in all, made up of £280 for the house though he claimed it had cost him much more ('A pretty, neate, gentleman like howse, with a pretty garden & a lyttle yonge Orchard standinge very Sweete and quiett; the place and buildinge within this 6 yeres Cost above 400ˡⁱ'); a further £550 for his share of the corn tithes, again a bargain in his view as he estimated he would have enjoyed an annual income of 100 marks (£66) over the remaining twenty years of the lease ('soe here ys 20 Cropps to Come – worth 100 markes per Annum'); and finally £40 for his leasehold interest in the privy tithes.[89]

The Corporation had no such financial reserves to meet this offer and it in turn had to borrow. On 9 May seventeen of the aldermen and capital burgesses agreed to make personal loans, ranging from £80 down to £10, totalling £650.[90] A contract was drawn up, dated 13 May, to which Henry Rainsford put his name, offering Greene a total of £640, Rainsford standing surety for Greene's completion of the deal by 14 June.[91] Greene, now at the Middle Temple, received this on 15 May, and replied on 22 May, somewhat aggrieved, having compared the figures. 'I . . . do see . . . that I must lose a hundred marks in the true value of my things I sell to the place which have more reason (yf I may speak yt without offence) to gyve me recompense to a greater value for my golden dayes and spirits spent in Stratfordes Service.'[92] He also made it clear that he wished to receive most of the cash in hand except (and this can surely only have been to meet his debts) 'some little which I accounted I might thereof persuade you . . . to become bound to pay yt to others'. He closes: 'I shall I hope see Sir Henry Raynsford this day and upon some explanacions by him wryte further unto you.' But if he hoped for any support from that quarter he was to be disappointed: Rainsford, no doubt influenced by the fact, as we shall see, that he was one of

Greene's creditors, urged settlement. On 27 May Greene wrote again from the Middle Temple: 'I have . . . hadd conference with Sir Henry Raynsford and in regard he hath gone soe farre with you I shall be much ruled by him.'[93] Final copies of the deeds for the sale of St Mary's and the surrender of the tithes have yet to come to light but both were executed in June 1617, with £340 of the purchase money paid over to Greene on 23 June, together with an undertaking to pay the balance of £300 on 3 February following.[94] But it is the arrangements for the payment of this second instalment which indicate Greene's indebtedness, for most, if not all of it, was to be paid to those who could only have been his creditors. Two lists of these recipients survive, one of which, in Greene's fair italic hand, breaks the £300 down into seven parcels: £100 to be paid to Rainsford himself at Clifford Chambers, £50 to George Thorpe, esquire (a near contemporary of Greene's at both Staple Inn and the Middle Temple),[95] also at Clifford, £42 to John Hall, Shakespeare's son-in-law, £34 to Timothy Wagstaffe, another of Greene's Middle Temple contemporaries,[96] £34 to Francis Collins, £25 to Robert Lee, lord of Billesley, and £15 to Edmund Pyke, one of his wife's relatives, at

---

89 SCLA, BRU 15/7/125.

90 SCLA, BRU 2/2, p. 329.

91 SCLA, BRU 15/7/128.

92 SCLA, BRU 15/1/1.

93 SCLA, BRU 15/1/2.

94 For drafts of the sale of St Mary's and of the assignment of the lease of the tithes, see SCLA, BRU 15/10/23; BRU 15/11/1.

95 George Thorpe of Wanswell, in Gloucestershire, was admitted in February 1598 (*Middle Temple Records*, I, p. 382). His sponsors were Greene himself and Oliver Style with whom Greene had shared chambers since November 1595 (*Middle Temple Records*, I, p. 360). In 1611 Greene appears to have acted as his attorney (London Metropolitan Archives, ACC/0819/001).

96 Timothy Wagstaffe, son of Thomas Wagstaffe of Harbury, admitted in May 1598, three years after Greene (*Middle Temple Records*, I, p. 375) and called to the bar in 1605. His wife, whom he married in 1605, was twice treated by John Hall, once as his wife and once as his widow: Joan Lane, *John Hall and his Patients* (Stroud, 1996), pp. 85–7.

Clifford Chambers.[97] The other list, in Greene's cursive hand, differs in several respects.[98] Rainsford's portion, still to be paid at Clifford, now appears as £80, and John Hall's, to be paid at New Place, as £40. Wagstaffe's portion, now standing at £30, was to be paid at the College, where he was presumably a guest of William Combe. Francis Collins was to receive only £25, instead of £34, also to be paid at New Place, whilst Robert Lee's £25 was to be taken to Billesley. Neither George Thorpe nor Edmund Pyke feature in this list. Instead, Greene asks for £100 to be paid to him directly at New Place.

Neither list is dated so various interpretations may be offered. For instance, the list, in his fair hand, might be the later one, including debts (principally to Pyke and Thorpe) which had come to light since he had compiled the other. But this second list was drawn up to serve a different purpose. It is in two columns, the first listing the names of those Corporation members who had agreed to raise the necessary £300, with the sums offered, ranging from £40 to £10, entered against each name. The right hand column specifies to whom the money should be paid. Thus the bailiff's £30 was to be paid to Wagstaffe, and the £40 apiece from the chief alderman and Henry Wilson were to go to Rainsford. Greene's £100 was to be made up of seven small contributions, including all those at the modest rate of £10. Out of this, he may have been intending to pay off Thorpe and Pyke and bring the other sums up to the level specified in the first list. But whatever the explanation, it is at least clear that these direct payments are a far cry from the 'some little' which he had earlier requested should be paid to 'others'. And of particular significance is surely the £40 to be handed over to John Hall at New Place, where Francis Collins and Greene himself were also to receive their payments. This may represent money lent to him by Hall but may equally represent a debt owing to William Shakespeare, who had only died the previous year. Surprise has sometimes been expressed, given the known connection between Greene and Shakespeare, that Greene does not feature as a beneficiary in Shakespeare's will. But a substantial debt

owing to the family may, of course, have been the reason.

Another important aspect of Greene's sale of his property concerns his wife Lettice, at the same time throwing further light on Rainsford's involvement in Greene's affairs. When, on 14 May, the Corporation agreed to go ahead with the purchase, the condition was made that 'the Companie are Contented to give M^{irs} Greene five poundes for her Love in the name of a gratuetie, At Sir the Right woor^{pll} Sir Henry Rainsford his Request'.[99] Whilst this might imply a high personal regard, there were also practical reasons for the parties involved to show such appreciation; for it had been proved necessary to include her as a party to the deed whereby St Mary's was conveyed to the Corporation.[100] Moreover, this same deed included a proviso that the purchasers would be warranted against any claims subsequently made against them by Lettice's cousin, Sir Alexander Tutt, or her brother Chiddock Tutt. Such clauses, though standard, served a real purpose were there any likelihood that third parties might later challenge title to the property conveyed. In this instance, the possibility that members of Lettice's family might take such steps would most likely have arisen out of their role as trustees appointed on her marriage. No formal settlement survives for Thomas's and Lettice's marriage but, if it had conformed to the usual pattern, it would have provided her with some security, in the event of widowhood, proportionate to assets represented by her marriage portion. We know, for instance, that in his will her father had left her 100 marks to which her uncle had added £20 a few years later.[101] If this, or any other money which she had brought with her, had been used by Greene

[97] SCLA, BRU 15/7/129. For Pyke's relationship to Alexander Tutt, Lettice's cousin, see Wiltshire and Swindon Archives, 1300/112; 9/8/16; 9/24/42 & 44. But Pyke's will had been proved in January 1616 so this could be a reference to his son, also Edmund (TNA, PROB 11/127, fos. 49–50).

[98] SCLA, BRU 15/7/127.

[99] SCLA, BRU 15/7/126.

[100] SCLA, BRU 15/11/1.

[101] Above, p. 294.

to purchase land or other investments, then the subsequent purchasers of these assets, in this case the Corporation, would need assurance that the sale was with her consent and secure against any objections her family might subsequently make.[102]

The Corporation may not have been displeased to see Greene out of the way. Not only had it been able to resume direct control of his share of the tithes, at the same time ridding itself of a tenant who, though its servant, might have been suspected of profiting at its expense; it also made a saving, when a successor was appointed the following October, by discontinuing the payment of the £7 fee which Greene had enjoyed, at the same time ignoring a request that Greene's brother, John, should succeed him.[103] An earlier Corporation order, of 20 November 1611, entitling Greene, and his deputy to a half-share in the profits of the local court of record, may also have been a charge the Corporation was glad to see put on hold.[104]

What befell Greene thereafter is far from clear, though his continuing association with the Middle Temple is well documented. As we have seen, he had been careful in his attendance there at least during the law terms and only once, in Michaelmas term 1605, was he fined for not attending the formal reading.[105] In 1619 he was appointed 'to stand at the cupboard', as junior reader during the following year, followed by his election as Reader (and thus a Bencher) for the years 1621 and 1622.[106] In 1627, as a Master of the Bench, he was admitted to new chambers and in 1629 was nominated as Treasurer for the following year.[107] One would have expected this steady promotion to be accompanied by evidence of a thriving legal practice and a comfortable income. Evidence for this, however, is largely lacking. On the contrary, whilst Reader he took advantage of one of the privileges of that office to have his son William, aged only thirteen, admitted without the payment of a fee;[108] and during his term as Treasurer he arranged to have his chambers in Elm Court rebuilt 'and convenienced' at the Temple's charge.[109] Greene had had to wait twenty-six years before his call to the bench, considerably longer than average, and he only reached

that position on the basis of seniority as opposed to acquisition of valuable office or through the assistance of influential patrons.[110] In comparison with the careers of close on 400 Benchers called in the first half of the seventeenth century, it is also clear that Greene was one of a very small minority who failed to secure further advancement in the law, promotion to government office, appointment as Justice of the Peace or Recorder, or election as a

---

102 Rainsford's intervention on her behalf may have been prompted by other considerations, currently obscure but perhaps reflected in further favour from the same quarter: when Henry Rainsford's widowed mother had remarried, she brought her second husband, William Barnes, to live at Clifford Chambers. In his will, of 1621, Barnes left 30 shillings to Lettice and £5 to her son, William, recently admitted to the Middle Temple, to buy books: TNA, PROB 11/138, ff. 231–231v.

103 John Greene had been acting for the Corporation in a legal capacity since c.1610, and in 1613 was briefly considered for the post of deputy town clerk (SCLA, BRU 2/2, pp. 206, 212, 243, 250). He had been proposed as his brother's successor as steward by George Lord Carew but had been passed over in favour of Francis Collins who had died, however, in September (SCLA, BRU 15/17/1; BRU 2/2, p. 326). When Anthony Langston was appointed town clerk in October, he was merely 'to have and receive such fees as to the place doth appertayne' (SCLA, BRU 2/2, p. 339). In the interval, however, another lawyer, Thomas Lucas, under Clement Throckmorton's patronage (despite allegations against him concerning 'the genarall Carridg of his Lyfe') and with whom both Collins and Greene had quarrelled, became the Corporation's additional legal adviser in return for an annual fee of only £2 which he received until his death in 1625 (SCLA, BRU 2/2, p. 328; BRU 15/13/7, 38; ER 1/1/79–81; BRU 4/1, pp. 305, 310; BRU 4/2, pp. 2, 6, 15).

104 SCLA, BRU 2/2, p. 215. Greene had doubtless negotiated this additional income through implementation of clauses in the Corporation's new charter of 1610 which authorized the appointment of a deputy town clerk and required weekly, instead of fortnightly, sittings of the court of record (SCLA, BRU 1/2).

105 Middle Temple Records, II, p. 458.

106 Middle Temple Records, II, pp. 646, 653, 655, 660, 664, 673.

107 Middle Temple Records, II, pp. 753, 757.

108 Middle Temple Records, II, p. 665. See also Middle Temple Records, II, pp. 684, 770.

109 Middle Temple Records, II, pp. 765, 771, 790.

110 Wilfrid R. Prest, The Rise of the Barristers: A Social History of the English Bar 1590–1640 (Oxford, 1986), pp. 137, 139.

Member of Parliament.[111] Though many lawyers, especially those buttressed by inherited wealth and with the support of powerful friends, ended their days in very comfortable circumstances, it was not unknown for some Benchers to die in poverty.[112] This, or something like it, proved to be Thomas Greene's fate.

On his departure from Stratford in 1617, Greene had decamped with his family to Bristol where the following year he presented himself, though unsuccessfully, as candidate for the post of steward of the mayor and sheriff's court there.[113] In February 1619 he made an equally unsuccessful approach to the influential lawyer, Henry Sherfield, asking him to bear his name in mind as a candidate for the post of under-steward of the court of the Honor of Gloucester, he having heard that the present incumbent, Edmund Estcourt, was 'exceeding ill'.[114] In 1621, as Master Greene of Bristol, he is found advising the borough of Thornbury, near Bristol, on a matter concerning its management of what was known as the Poors Land.[115] Of other notices of him in Bristol, there are very few, although much later, in February 1638, by then in his sixties, he once again offered his services as steward to the 'Courtes houlden before the Sherriffes & Bailiffes of this Cittie of Bristoll'. On this occasion he was duly chosen 'to enjoye all the Fees & proffitts incident to the said office'.[116] What this brought him by way of income is not known but his will, made on 5 November 1640, indicates a man with very little money at his disposal.[117] He did make a bequest of 3s 4d to the cathedral church of Bristol and 12 pence to 'every Almesbody of the Hospitall of St Johns Churchyard in Bristoll'. But beyond that he left only 40 shillings to his son William to make him a ring; to his daughter Elizabeth, now the husband of John Gifford, 25 shillings, and to her husband, 30 shillings, again to make rings; to his other married daughter, Ann Holloway, £5 and to her children, Humphrey and Thomas, £3 6s 8d each; and to his daughter Margaret, baptized in December 1618 and still unmarried, £10. The unspecified residue went to the long-suffering Lettice, 'my most deare & loveing wife, being sorry I have noe more (than I have)

to leave to soe good a woman; And her I make my whole & sole Executrix of this my last will, Given under my hand & seale which I use at London...not appointinge any Overseers because I know her very justly minded'. Of any freehold, or even leasehold property, there is no mention. Greene was buried on 8 May 1641 as 'Master Thomas Greene, counsellor at law and steward of this city' in the churchyard of St John the Baptist[118] and Lettice proved the will some eight months later, on 1 July 1641.

This study of Greene's career may have thrown little new direct light on the life of William Shakespeare but the contention here that previous accounts have overlooked a crisis in Greene's affairs, coinciding with his sudden departure from Stratford in 1617, may modify our opinion of the relationship between the two men. They clearly knew each other well: indeed, more evidence exists to document Shakespeare's dealings with Greene than with any other of his contemporaries. He was a tenant of Shakespeare's in New Place, perhaps for as long as six years; he was persuaded to go to law with Shakespeare in 1609/10; he worked closely with Shakespeare during the controversy over the proposed enclosures at Welcombe; and he may even have borrowed money from him. Yet their careers were very different. Shakespeare, like many of his grammar school contemporaries who sought to earn a living with his pen, may, like Greene, initially have sought patronage; but he escaped the fate that befell many jobbing playwrights by gaining access to the comparative security offered by membership of a theatrical company. Greene, on

---

[111] These careers are tabulated in Prest, *Rise of the Barristers*, pp. 340–406.

[112] Prest, *Rise of the Barristers*, pp. 155–6.

[113] Bristol Record Office (BRO), M/BCC/CCP/1/2, fo. 70.

[114] Hampshire Record Office, 44M69/L50/9. Sherfield had been appointed steward by the earl of Salisbury and Greene had initially discussed becoming under-steward when he had met Sherfield 'in the Courte of Wardes'.

[115] Gloucester Archives, D282/C1A.

[116] BRO, M/BCC/CCP/1/3, fo. 82.

[117] TNA, PROB 11/186, fos. 295–295v.

[118] BRO, P.St JB/R/1/a, unpaginated.

the other hand, though he too may have had literary ambitions, failed to attract patronage sufficient to develop them; or, indeed, even to carve out for himself a profitable career in the law. Early connections with Henry Rainsford, and perhaps with Shakespeare, may have led to his decision to move to Stratford; but, whereas he would thereafter have been witness to Shakespeare's investment of significant capital in the purchase of property in and around Stratford, his own attempt to pursue such a course ended in dismal failure from which he never recovered. The diary he kept during the enclosure controversy also provides insight into personal life of a kind rarely found at this time. In December 1614, for instance, after a formal meeting with William Combe and others at the College, he notes a subsequent anxious conversation in the street 'at my pale door' during which Combe reassured him that, as far as his personal interests were concerned, 'noe Advantage' would be taken of anything he had said.[119] We read of a meeting in 'my best Chamber' at St Mary's in December 1614 and on 1 January 1615 he records evening prayer 'in my study at home' as a prelude to further discussion of enclosure business with other interested parties.[120] In April 1615, he and Thomas Combe met in Greene's garden to discuss business and on several other occasions he records information passed on to him from his wife Lettice, sometimes acquired by her in conversation with their near neighbour in Old Town, Mistress Frances Reynolds.[121] This was a man, then, beset by conflicting interests as the town's steward and a prospective tenant of its tithes but unable, even with the aid of money from his wife's jointure, to provide his family with a secure home. In many of his business dealings he was also close to Shakespeare who himself was not immune from such worries. In or soon after 1613, for reasons that are not entirely clear, Shakespeare appears to have surrendered his shares in both the Globe and Blackfriars theatres, thus forgoing what until then had been his principal source of income. Though he had made investments, the yield from these would not have compensated him for this loss, a likely explanation of the fact that it is precisely at that time that he is found working closely with Greene in a joint attempt to protect the value of their investments. Shakespeare was clearly the more successful – or at least he died some six years later as a man still possessed of considerable means. But Greene was less fortunate, forced to sell up and leave Stratford in order to discharge debts, notably to his erstwhile patron, Henry Rainsford, but also, in all probability to Shakespeare's family as well. There is, of course, another difference and a very striking one. Lettice clearly played an active and well-testified role in Greene's life and one of which, judging from his tribute to her in his will, he was clearly well aware. Ann Shakespeare could hardly stand in starker contrast. Barely mentioned by name between her marriage and burial – not even in her husband's will – her low profile suggests that Shakespeare might have been troubled with other worldly concerns during this period.

Most sources reassure us that, following his departure from Stratford, Greene went on to enjoy a career as a successful barrister. Some writers appear to have taken this almost as a matter of course for a man who claimed to have been Shakespeare's cousin. But, whilst it was certainly the case that by a process of seniority he eventually reached high office at the Middle Temple, this did not make him a wealthy man. On the contrary, his will indicates the very opposite: a man of only very modest means which in turn may well have been the result of his earlier over-ambitious attempts whilst living in Stratford to set himself up as a man of property, in emulation perhaps of his more successful landlord. Such a reappraisal of his career may serve to remind us that very few people, especially in the early years of the seventeenth century, would be free from the day-to-day worries of seeking to provide for themselves and their families; and, moreover, that Shakespeare was well acquainted with such people and may, particularly in his later years, have even shared some of their concerns.

---

[119] Ingleby, *Enclosure*, p. 4.

[120] Ingleby, *Enclosure*, pp. 4–5.

[121] Ingleby, *Enclosure*, pp. 8–9.

SHAKESPEARE AND THE INQUISITION

BRIAN CUMMINGS

One of the oddest single surviving copies of the works of William Shakespeare is a Second Folio of 1632, which once belonged to the library of the Real Colegio Seminario de los Ingleses (or English Seminary College) at Valladolid. The copy was first described by Sir Sidney Lee in an article in *The Times* in April 1922.[1] The questions to which Lee sought an answer were glaring enough. First, why were young Jesuits, training for the mission in Spain, reading an English dramatist in the mid-seventeenth century? A second issue was why the book bears inside its front end-papers the certificate of Guillermo Sánchez, a censor for the Holy Office, or in other words, the Spanish Inquisition:

Opus auctoritate Sancti officii permissum et expurgatum eadem auctoritate per Guilielmum Sanchaeum e Soc^te Jesu.[2]

A third question, obviously related closely to the second, was why the entirety of just one play, *Measure for Measure*, had been neatly cut out using a sharp instrument.

Like so many objects in the Shakespearian archive, the Valladolid Shakespeare has become both a fetish and a shibboleth. It can hardly be said to be unknown. Its discoverer was the author of the article on Shakespeare in the first *Dictionary of National Biography*. Lee himself supposed the copy would return for ever to the English College, but it was shortly afterwards acquired by the Folger Library.[3] It could not be in a more prominent place; yet despite discussion by Roland Frye in *Shakespeare and Christian Doctrine* in 1963, and more recent dissemination at the Folger Institute,

many Shakespearians and Catholic historians have never heard of it.[4] What can explain the widespread indifference to such a sensational object, placing Shakespeare face to face with the Inquisition?

As always with repression, the reasons for unconscious knowledge are deep-seated and complex. They form in this case an index of Shakespearian study and its motivations from one

This article is a revised version of the Inaugural Lecture for the Centre for Early Modern Exchanges at UCL, London, given in April 2010. I thank the Directors, Helen Hackett and Alex Samson, for inviting me. I also thank Andreas Höfele for the opportunity to present the argument in December 2010 at the Sonderforschungsbereich 573, *Pluralisierung und Autorität in der frühen Neuzeit* at Ludwig-Maximilians-Universität, Munich. The discussion of censorship originated at the colloquium *Politics, the Press and Public Debate in the Seventeenth Century* at the European University Institute in Florence in December 2007; I would like to thank the organizers, Henk Looijesteijn and Freya Sierhuis, for an inspiring occasion.

[1] Sir Sidney Lee, 'Shakespeare and the Inquisition. A Spanish Second Folio. How the Plays Were Expurgated. Politics and Drama', *The Times*, Monday, 10 April 1922, p. 15. Lee was first asked to describe the volume when a valuation was sought in 1914. A second article completed the description, *The Times*, Tuesday, 11 April 1922, p. 12. The two articles were reprinted as a unit in Sidney Lee, *Elizabethan and Other Essays* (Oxford, 1929), pp. 184–95.

[2] Folger Library, Washington, DC, shelf mark: STC 22274 Fo.2 no.07, title page (A2r). On the following leaf (A3r) the ownership mark is given in a different hand: 'Collegii Sancti Albani Anglorum Vallisoleti'.

[3] The copy was bought by Henry Folger via Maggs Bros in June 1928.

[4] Roland Frye, *Shakespeare and Christian Doctrine* (Princeton, 1963), pp. 275–93.

LONDON,
Printed by *Tho. Cotes,* for *Iohn Smethwick,* and are to be fold at his fhop
in Saint *Dunftans* Church-yard. 1632.

*Opus auctoritate Sancti officij permissum et expurgatum eadem
auctoritate per Guilielmum Sancœum e Soc: Jesu.*

33. Folger Shakespeare Library, shelf mark: STC 22274 Fo.2 no.07, title page (A2r), showing the signature of the censor William Sankey.

generation to another. In the twentieth century, in the wake of Lee's article, explanation can be found in the profound assumption of Shakespeare's secularity. Henry Folger himself considered the Folio to be 'only a curiosity, with but little literary value'.[5] Frye used the copy to support his general thesis that Shakespeare had no particular investment in Christian belief: this peculiar Second Folio should 'put us on our guard... against the overly eager identification of Shakespeare's plays with Christian teachings in general and with the Catholic tradition in particular'.[6] The censoring of a play was a Jesuit problem; it told us nothing about Shakespeare. Shakespearians were not very interested in Jesuits, and probably thought that shredding playtexts was what they did all the time. Lee, without feeling the need to supply any evidence, averred that the cutting out of the offending play was standard practice for the Inquisition.[7] As for why, this only served to confirm Shakespeare's secular identity: his plays naturally offended the religious.

In the twenty-first century, this situation has reversed. Shakespeare scholars talk of little else but Jesuits: the current vogue could be called *cherchez la messe.* The repression of the Valladolid copy now performs a different kind of displacement. Since Shakespeare is now readily assimilated with recusant and more specifically with Jesuit sympathies, the idea of his works being censored and even mutilated by Jesuit readers seems counter-intuitive or even perverse. Recent response to the Valladolid Shakespeare, and especially to the destruction of *Measure for Measure,* has shown a collective sign of confusion. David Daniell finds in it a formal disproof of the whole Catholic Shakespeare

thesis.[8] Richard Wilson, contrarily, feels it shows how Jesuit attitudes *after* Shakespeare's death hardened, and the action of the censor confirmed his view that Shakespeare increasingly distanced himself from the Jesuits, while retaining his underlying Catholic identity.[9] Richard McCoy, more circumspectly, calls it 'one of the most striking traces of the Counter-reformation', and a unique Shakespearian survival.[10] Sir Frank Kermode, meanwhile, in one of his last books, gave voice to the older, secular, view of Shakespeare in finding the whole affair 'baffling'.[11] By far the most arresting comment is made by Stephen Greenblatt, in an interview on the enduring mystery of Shakespeare in the *Washington Post.* As Greenblatt speaks to the journalist, the Head of Reference at the Folger Library, Georgianna Ziegler, dramatically (or ritually, in the journalist's sensational account) holds up the Valladolid Shakespeare as a testament to the power of books.

---

[5] Henry Folger to Maggs Bros, 10 March 1928, Folger Library, STC 22274 Fo.2 no.07, provenance file, MS letter.

[6] Frye, *Shakespeare and Christian Doctrine,* p. 293.

[7] It is 'torn out bodily in accordance with a common usage among expurgators of the Holy Office', *The Times,* 10 April 1922, p. 15.

[8] 'Shakespeare and the Protestant Mind', *Shakespeare Survey* 54 (Cambridge, 2001), pp. 1–12, this ref. p. 2.

[9] Richard Wilson, *Secret Shakespeare: Studies in Theatre, Religion and Resistance* (Manchester, 2004), p. 288.

[10] Richard C. McCoy, Introduction to 'Redefining the Sacred in Early Modern England', NEH Summer Institute at the Folger Library, June 1998. www.folger.edu/html/folger_institute/sacred/essay.html, accessed 19 September 2011.

[11] Frank Kermode, *The Age of Shakespeare* (London, 2004), p. 33.

By way of formal explanation, it is suggested that the missing text of *Measure for Measure* could be due to the play making light of certain Catholic doctrines. But there is something still unexplained, the interview continues: '"People do things to sacred texts", Greenblatt says.'[12]

Greenblatt's sly conflation of Shakespearian Folio and holy writ is not meant to be bibliographically accurate. He knows perfectly well that religious censorship is more subtle and venal in its motivations than this. In respect of the Valladolid Folio's curious relationship to Shakespeare studies in general, however, he takes us straight to the heart of the matter. What the Catholic Shakespeare argument has become, perhaps without quite knowing it, is a proxy debate about the authenticity of Shakespeare's personal identity. Shakespeare's religion is controversial because religion itself is controversial, of course. But it is also controversial because it appears to set the seal on who Shakespeare was, and how he felt himself to be. Ever since Coleridge, the very lack of evidence about Shakespeare's personality has been used as an ideological plinth that sets him apart. Shakespeare the artist and the man is beyond explanation. He did not have personality, but he gave personality to others who read him or watched his plays: 'while SHAKSPEARE becomes all things, yet for ever remaining himself'.[13] This view prevailed right through to the time of Samuel Schoenbaum, who argued that Shakespearian biography was always constructed in the image of the biographer. Shakespeare's religion amounted to projection on the part of his readers: 'Thus does each man convert Shakespeare to his own belief.'[14] Harold Bloom also found consolation in this idea in asserting Shakespeare as secular: he is our 'secular scripture', because he writes for us, and thus supplants the need for theocratic scripture.[15] Catholic Shakespeare has challenged this orthodoxy. At the same time it has given renewed authorization to biography. That Shakespearian biography regained its fashion at precisely the same time as the 'religious turn' is not an accident. Wilson, with acute insight, put the two together in using the clandestine habits of recusant writing to give historical explanation for the emergence of the myth of Shakespeare's impersonality.[16]

Greenblatt's comment attests to the aura of the uncanny surrounding this textual artefact, something that censorship (ordinarily understood) does not quite explain. Yet in return, the material oddity of the Valladolid Folio has the capacity to speak across the debate about Shakespeare's religion and to ask questions of it. For in all of this, the significance of this unique copy of the complete works has been all but lost from view. In its own right, the Valladolid Folio is a highly important copy. Firstly, by remaining so long in the library of the English College in Valladolid, it represents a Shakespeare Folio locatable in the hands of a single owner for three hundred years. Its provenance can be traced back almost to its original purchase, and then forwards right through to its resting place in a modern international library. Secondly, the Valladolid Folio is unique in the extent of its annotation. The dearth of early readers marking copies of Shakespeare is a constant source of grief to Shakespearian bibliographers. Here, as well as a missing play, we have a mass of markings of expurgation, of words, or sometimes lines, or sometimes virtually whole speeches, crossed out and removed. There are even a few, if cryptic, words of comment.

As often with Shakespeare and religion, the first problem has been that we have posed the wrong question. Frye wanted to find in the expurgated text some sign of what Shakespeare's own religious opinions might have been, which the censor was reacting to, revealed, as it were, in ideological negative relief, like in the impress of a seal.[17] But this

---

[12] Linton Weeks, 'Stephen Greenblatt, Rockford-Upon-Avon: A Shakespearian Detective Sifts for Goodly Clews', *The Washington Post*, 18 October 2004 www.washingtonpost.com/wp-dyn/articles/A40960–2004Oct17-3.html, accessed 19 September 2011.

[13] Coleridge, *Biographia Literaria*, ed. James Engel and W. J. Bate, 2 vols. (Princeton, 1983), vol. 2, p. 28.

[14] S. Schoenbaum, *Shakespeare's Lives*, new edn (Oxford, 1991), p. 331.

[15] *Hamlet: Poem Unlimited* (Edinburgh, 2003), p. 3.

[16] Wilson, *Secret Shakespeare*, pp. 22–3.

[17] Frye, *Shakespeare and Christian Doctrine*, p. 275.

is a text printed in 1632, and examined sometime after that, in relation to plays written mostly at least a generation before. The window opened by the Valladolid Folio is not so much directly onto Shakespeare's soul, as onto how Catholics read and viewed Shakespeare. There are some comparisons to be made with other such readings. Right at the end of the seventeenth century, six plays were transcribed in manuscript from the Second Folio by an English Catholic at Douai.[18] This may have been for performance. Martin Wiggins has also uncovered evidence of another, sympathetic, Jesuit reader, Father Clarke of St Omer, writing before 1660.[19] Amid all the controversy over 'Catholic Shakespeare' it has somehow been assumed that a Catholic author easily makes himself known to a Catholic reader; perhaps even that all Catholic readers implicitly read the same way. But the three known seventeenth-century cases are all different. In the case of the Valladolid Folio, the immediacy of the page brings stark evidence of the specificity of one form of Catholic reading. It is nothing like what we have been led to expect.

However, just because one Jesuit reader reacted to Shakespeare's text with censorial violence, we need not assume its general relevance. A symmetry between the mind of the author and of an audience has been one of the most corrupting temptations of the 'religious turn' in Shakespearian criticism. If we cast our eyes beyond Shakespeare, this is not something we find in other aspects of Elizabethan and Jacobean literary confessionalization. Robert Southwell, often discussed in alliance with Shakespeare, circulated his poems in manuscript among the coterie of the faithful. But the same poems, transferred to print, were disseminated without demur by the Archbishop of Canterbury's own censors. Some of Southwell's readers knew who they were reading, but many did not. Protestant devotion as well as Catholic was aroused by his poetry, and presumably many hybrid forms of sensibility in between. There is no such thing as intrinsically 'Catholic' writing.

There is also no such thing as intrinsically Catholic reading. The Valladolid Folio reminds us of the singularity of the reading process, even as it tenders itself (in the most explicit way possible) as a template for the reading of others, by showing subsequent readers what not to read and what not to think. While it narrows its eyes towards the text it represents, it broadens our conceptual framework for interpreting early modern Shakespearian reading practices. The copy thus makes us think about some key methodological and philosophical issues. One concerns the use of markings in an individual copy to make judgements about 'the history of reading'. This method has had strong currency as that field has developed in the last twenty years. But it is a fragile method. Every surviving copy of an edition is a *unicum*, a singular object. We have to learn to decode it in its own context.

The Valladolid Folio is thus at once an odd and idiosyncratic object, one which forces us to contextualize and particularize historical argument at the most intimate level; but it also leads us to speculate about more general kinds of cultural exchange: what happens to a book between its appearance in the press and its arrival in front of an individual reader; what happens to a book in its longer history, as Shakespeare continued to be read, long after his death, in very different places and times; and how those historical readings relate to readings we make of Shakespeare now. Furthermore, because we are dealing with a symbolic instance within the history of censorship, we are made to consider the public value of books; how they are authorized and come to have public meanings; and how they test ideas of public control and orthodoxy and acceptability.

I

But first there are more local concerns. One of the oddities of this copy is that it represents a reading taking place outside of England. Early readers and owners of Shakespeare in continental Europe are

---

[18] G. Blakemore Evans, 'The Douai Manuscript: Six Shakespearian Transcripts (1694–95)', *Philological Quarterly*, 41 (1962), 158–72.

[19] Martin Wiggins, 'Shakespeare Jesuited: The Plagiarisms of Pater Clarcus', *The Seventeenth Century*, 20 (2005), 1–21.

rare. This was Lee's interest, and he compared the (possibly apocryphal) tale of another copy owned, in Valladolid itself, by the Count of Gondomar. The Valladolid Shakespeare, while it has been used primarily to say things about Shakespeare himself, needs to be considered from the point of view of the relationship between English and Spanish culture and the presence of English literary texts in Spain and how they were read. Apart from the Gondomar story, there is no other known copy of Shakespeare in Spain before the late eighteenth century.[20] This copy can therefore help us think about the formation of a library within Spain containing English books. What is this copy of Shakespeare doing there, and how did it come to be there? Beyond this, the Valladolid Folio can only be understood when we consider the procedure for censorship in Catholic Europe and in Spain in particular.

To answer these questions we begin with who it was that made the examination. Lee in *The Times*, perhaps romantically, thought he was encountering Guillen Sánchez, if so one of a very select group of Spanish clerics reading in English in the seventeenth century. However, was Sánchez Spanish at all? Patrick Ryan, SJ, wrote a letter to *The Times* the day after Lee's article, making the brilliant suggestion that Guillermo or Guillen Sánchez is the Spanish *nom de plume* of Father William Sankey.[21] Sankey's dates gleaned from the *Records of the English Province* certainly fit. He was born in Lancashire in 1609; he entered the novitiate at Watten (near St Omer) in the Spanish Netherlands in 1628. In 1639 he was in Ghent.[22] From the records of the College in Valladolid, we find that he first arrived in Spain from Flanders in January 1641.[23] He was professed of the four vows in 1643. He is described at different points as a procurator, confessor and consultor.[24] For a couple of months in 1649 he was in temporary charge of the College in an interval between two official Rectors (who were usually Spanish).[25] In 1651 he moved to Madrid, where he became Rector of St George's English College until 1662.[26] The nineteenth-century Jesuit *Records of the English Province* suggest that he then went to England in 1666, labouring for the mission for a while in London; but this seems doubtful: he was still keeping the books in Madrid in March 1667, and he was in Bilbao in September that year.[27] He did visit England briefly, but it can be shown that he was travelling back and forth: there is a letter by Sankey from San Sebastian in 1670, and another from London in 1673.[28] Both letters are in Spanish and deal with his continuing concerns with his time in Madrid. He died in Flanders in 1682, aged 73.

The first reader of this Spanish Shakespeare was therefore English, not Spanish. There is also one other personal trace of readership in the volume – the signature 'Joannes Lucas' which appears alongside Ben Jonson's poem in praise of Shakespeare in the front matter.[29] This is of another English student and priest at Valladolid, who entered St Alban's in 1691. While the book may have had Spanish readers at some point, there is no evidence for it.

---

[20] See the survey by Henry Thomas, 'Shakespeare in Spain', *Proceedings of the British Academy*, 35 (1949), 4–24.

[21] 'Letters to the Editor', *The Times*, Wednesday, 12 April 1922, p. 13.

[22] Henry Foley, *Records of the English Province of the Society of Jesus*, 7 vols. in 8 parts (London, 1877–83), vol. VII, part 2, 'Collectanea' [biographical dictionary], pp. 685–6.

[23] Edwin Henson, *Registers of the English College at Valladolid*, Catholic Record Society (London, 1930), p. xxviii. The records are taken from the *Liber Alumnorum*, an MS volume with entries commencing in 1589 and continuing until 1677.

[24] Sankey is referred to as Procurator in a visitation of 22 March 1666; later in 1666 he was appointed confessor and consultor: Henson, *Registers of the English College at Valladolid*, p. xxxi.

[25] Michael E. Williams, *St Alban's College Valladolid: Four Centuries of English Catholic Presence in Spain* (London, 1986), p. 262.

[26] Edwin Henson, *Registers of the English College at Madrid 1611–1767*, Publications of the Catholic Record Society, 29 (London, 1929), p. ix. Sankey is referred to as Rector and secular priest.

[27] Henson, *Registers of the English College at Valladolid*, p. xxxi.

[28] Henson, *Registers of the English College at Madrid*, p. 312 and p. 320.

[29] Folger Library, STC 22274 Fo.2 no.07, 2r. Lucas's handwriting resembles that of one or two other doodles in the text.

Yet Sankey is a very distinctive kind of English reader. The Sankeys were a Lancastrian family. Like much of the neighbouring gentry, they adhered to the Roman Church in the Elizabethan changes. In the small hours in February 1584, a raid was made on Sankey House, in Great Sankey.[30] Edward Sankey in 1590 was classed among those who came to church but were not communicants.[31] Francis and Lawrence, as well as William Sankey, became Jesuits in the early part of the seventeenth century. Lawrence served in his native Lancashire from 1638 to 1649. William's nephew Thomas also served as a missionary in Lancashire from 1663 to 1676.[32] However, William himself lived almost all of his adult life, from his teens to his seventies, in exile communities in continental Europe. He was never a missionary. This singular fact has, I think, completely escaped Shakespearians, who, to the extent they have noticed him at all, have treated him as a kind of honorary recusant. But Sankey was a career priest and bureaucrat, and a long-term expatriate domicile. All his surviving words, spoken or written, apart from a handful of English words in the copy of Shakespeare, are in Spanish. To all intents and purposes he is a naturalized reader.

Sankey was part of a very specialized English community. The English College was founded in 1589, as Spain was proposed as an alternative and perhaps more stable home to the English Jesuit mission as it moved between Douai and Reims.[33] St Alban's, Valladolid (romantic English names were chosen for all these seminaries) was the project of the superior of the English Jesuit mission, Father Robert Persons.[34] King Philip II granted his official patronage (he visited in person in 1592), and a house was purchased in Calle de Don Sancho with monies from a Spanish aristocratic benefactress; it is still there.[35] Of the first six students, three had already been at Reims, and three at the English College in Rome. Among early graduates was Henry More, the great grandson of Thomas and future historian of the Jesuits, who entered in 1603. Numbers at first were high: in the first two decades between 30 and 60 students were enrolled at the College in any one year.[36] The purpose of St Alban's Valladolid was to train missionaries to go

back to England, and between 1600 and 1643 it is not surprising to find seventeen alumni who were either executed or died in prison in England.

After 1603 numbers of students declined. The purpose of the mission lost some of its urgent clarity; the position of the English students began to be interpreted differently. While Spain waited patiently for the conversion of England, expatriate English students became sometimes a little embarrassing. The College had Spanish members, too; in some years there were no new English students at all. When a parallel foundation was opened in Madrid, there were fears in the Spanish court that it would become an obvious target for English spies sent from the Stuart court in London. The records also show that there was often conflict between the English community and its Spanish neighbours. According to the contemporary opinion of Father Christopher Mendoza, the Spanish and English Jesuits 'not only did not work together but were violently opposed'.[37] In Valladolid, control of the College was deliberately placed in the hands of a rector who was Spanish; in Madrid, he was at first English, although Sankey turned out to be the last of this line.[38] The records in Madrid are full of simmering antagonisms between the English contingent and local administrators who dealt with taxes and fees, and for that matter the ordinary Spanish people who served the Church and provided its furnishings and candles and supplies of sacramental wine and oil.[39]

---

[30] Foley, *Records of the English Province*, II, pp. 116–18.

[31] State Papers (Domestic), Eliz. (1590), ccxxxv, no. 4.

[32] Henson, *Registers of the English College at Valladolid*, p. 167n.

[33] Williams, *St Alban's College Valladolid*, p. 4.

[34] Williams, *St Alban's College Valladolid*, pp. 6–9.

[35] Victor Houliston, 'Persons [Parsons], Robert (1546–1610)', *Oxford Dictionary of National Biography* (2004), www.oxforddnb.com/view/article/21474, accessed 22 September 2011.

[36] Williams, *St Alban's College Valladolid*, pp. 21–2.

[37] Henson, *Registers of the English College at Madrid*, p. 115.

[38] Williams, *St Alban's College Valladolid*, Appendix D, pp. 261–3, gives a list of the Rectors at Valladolid. On the different practice in Madrid, see ibid. p. 36.

[39] Henson, *Registers of the English College at Madrid*, pp. 109 and 112.

The English Jesuits in Spain therefore had a distinctive identity. Once we reconnect the Second Folio with this context, rather than think of it in isolation as a book which refers only inwards, we can see that the Valladolid Shakespeare fits in with this sense of Anglo-Spanish identity. The Library of the English College in Valladolid substantively survives, and the seventeenth-century library can to some extent be reconstructed from surviving early books in its modern counterpart. The bulk is of course mainly scholastic and theological. But there are some other books concerning especially English history which place Shakespeare in an intriguing and coherent context – a copy of Matthew Paris's *Historia major* in Archbishop Parker's edition (London: R. Wolfe, 1571); a Froissart's *Chroniques* from Lyon of 1588; and Henry Savile's collection of chronicles including William of Malmesbury (1596) in a Frankfurt edition of 1601.[40] There are also Thomas More's Latin works in a Louvain edition of 1566, Ralegh's *History of the World* and Francis Bacon's *History of the Reign of King Henry VII*. While no early catalogue survives to explain the rationale of the collection, Shakespeare has a logical place. If Richard Wilson's description of the Second Folio as a Jesuit 'set text' is wilfully enthusiastic, the English seminarians were provided with a variety of lenses through which to view the history and culture of their native and perhaps future land.[41] Libraries acquire books by accident but, once there, the copy of Shakespeare could do useful work. Jesuit syllabuses made full use of rhetorical and poetic materials in the education of a secular priest. Poetry taught the seminarian an emotional language of profound pastoral importance. In this instance, Shakespeare's plays also taught acquaintance with a language that might seem distant to a student who had left England at an early age, like Sankey himself at eighteen. Although we have no idea how or how much the Valladolid Folio was used, it is not impossible that plays might have been copied out for performance; although in the case of the bowdlerized versions, as we will see, it must have created special performance difficulties.

When was the Second Folio acquired by the library? Many books were acquired in seminary libraries as gifts of entering novitiates, who in any case at this point gave up their worldly possessions. It is not possible to tell whether this book came with Sankey, but it is unlikely, since he left England in 1628. In any case, the act of censorship is quite different from the occasion of donation. The censor acted with authority within a determined system. But there is one piece of evidence to help date this. One other book bears the signature Sánchez as expurgator – intriguingly also in English; it is the third edition of John Speed's *History of Great Britain*, published in the same year of 1632. Here the authority of the Holy Office is invoked, and the date is given of 1645:

Historia haec expurgata est et permissa auctoritate Sancti Officii huius Tribunalis Vallisoletani anno 1645 Gulielmum Sanchaeum.[42]

It seems reasonable to think that the Shakespeare was examined around the same time. In any event, it cannot have been earlier than 1641 when Sankey arrived in Spain, and probably not as late as 1649, when his duties increased.

I turn, now, to Sankey's reading of Shakespeare. The first thing to realize here is that almost all of the interventions by Sankey as a reader are of course expurgations, the blacking out, with pen and ink, of words, lines and passages. There is more to say about this, about the very special form of textuality constituted by *deletion*, a subject of special interest to Jacques Derrida, who constructed what we might call a grammatology of erasure, but which has not received the same sympathetic attention from historians.[43] Apart from deletion, there are few marks in the Valladolid

---

40 *Rerum Anglicarum scriptores post Bedam praecipui.*
41 Wilson, *Secret Shakespeare*, p. 288.
42 Lee examined this book also: *The Times*, 10 April 1922, p. 15.
43 Following Heidegger's use of the term *das Sein* ('Being'), Derrida deliberately employs the crossing out of a word within a text, but allowing it to remain legible and in place.

Folio. The English word 'Good' appears above four plays; but despite the hopeful description of this by Frye as 'positive comment', the handwriting does not belong to the censor, appearing to be eighteenth-century.[44] A still more enigmatic word, 'rare', appears above *Cymbeline*, another play which is left unexpurgated.[45] We are left longing for some further indication of literary appreciation. Nevertheless, we can at least note that all the words added to the text are English.

A rather different kind of mark does deserve comment. Lennox's words in *Macbeth*, Act 3 scene 6 inspire in a reader black lines in the margin alongside:

> *Lennox.*   Some holy Angell
> Flye to the Court of England, and unfold
> His Message ere he come, that a swift blessing
> May soone returne to this our suffering Country
> Under a hand accurs'd.[46]   (*Macbeth*, 3.6.45–9)

The same marking occurs in the Valladolid Folio (VF) in Act 4 when Malcolm declares 'I thinke our Country sinkes beneath the yoake, / It weepes, it bleeds' (VF 205v). This is the nearest we have to a personal response in the book. It cannot be the hand of Sankey; it is in pencil not ink. It has nothing to do with the performance of censorship. Indeed it may counteract the motion of censorship entirely, showing a sympathetic reading of the play in opposition to the moments of deletion alongside. It is certainly the nearest thing we have in the annotation of this book to a Catholic reading in accord with Shakespeare's text. The marked lines have everything to say to English Catholics in Spain, contemplating the heretical yoke of the native country and interpreting Lennox's and Malcolm's words as a kind of prophetic yearning for national redemption.

As for expurgation, Sankey's methods are both tireless and yet not exhaustive. The first point to make is that many plays are untouched – slightly more than half of the 36 plays in the Folio. He makes marks in exactly 7 out of 14 comedies and 5 out of 10 histories, while in the case of the tragedies, he only deletes in 3 out of 12. It is possible that he did not inspect all the plays. Lee felt, indeed, that the touch of the censor was comparatively light, and even speculated that this was the one aspect of the book which lent credence to the idea of Shakespeare as Catholic. Perhaps it is more accurate to say that Sankey gives mixed messages. His expurgations follow noticeable patterns but he is not consistent in their application; not only do features he deletes occur frequently in plays he completely ignores, but even within a single playtext he lets slip in one place something he is rigorous about elsewhere.

However, Sankey cannot be accused of lacking either industry or purpose. Many deletions are of individual words or of short phrases. The major categories are (first) the use of oaths:

> *Falstaff.* By the ~~Masse~~ Lad, thou say'st true
>   (*1 Henry IV*, 2.4.355; VF e4v)

A second category is sexual propriety. On the first page of *The Tempest*, the words 'as an unstanched wench' (VF A1r) are struck through.[47] Another sexual reference to women is excised in *Hamlet*:

> *Oph.* I thinke nothing, my Lord.
> *Ham.* Thats a faire thought ~~to lye between Maids legs~~.
> *Oph.* What is my Lord?
> *Ham.* Nothing.   (*Hamlet*, 3.2.117–20; VF 2q4r)

In the bowdlerized text, for a moment maybe we are tempted to see in Sankey a penchant for the Pinteresque ('nothing, my lord / That's a fair thought / What is, my lord? / Nothing'). A cooler

---

[44] The word appears at the head of *The Merry Wives of Windsor* and *The Comedy of Errors*, which are free from deletions; also *Much Ado About Nothing* and *The Merchant of Venice*, which have minor deletions.

[45] Folger STC 22274 Fo.2 no.07, 3b1r.

[46] All subsequent references taken from the Valladolid Folio (VF), are given in the text using an abbreviation and the signature number, e.g. here VF 204r. Act and scene numbers are supplied from the Arden Shakespeare.

[47] In general, the censor uses heavy curled penstrokes to delete words, sometimes doubled so as to make the words illegible. Occasionally a word can still be read underneath.

glance shows what may be complete inattention paid to the incomprehensible text that remains. The censor is not so much interested in what the reader reads, as what the reader does not read. In just one case, in *1 Henry IV*, the censor appears to correct the text, where a stage direction is emended from '*Enter Hostpurre*' to '*Enter Hostesse*' (f1v). In some cases, he removes words but leaves a full grammatical sense; but where deletion creates an awkward sense or even nonsense, he does not worry.

The key therefore is not what is there but what is not there. In general, Sankey does not like references to sex, especially to the act of sexual penetration. If in Shakespeare this might sometimes leave little left, Sankey most often does not notice. The text is clearer of interference than a school edition of the nineteenth century; just three out of eight codpieces in Shakespeare are removed.[48] Only one 'prick' offends (L6r). More interestingly, in some places it is possible to witness Sankey hesitating to see what goes just far enough. He is especially prone, hardly surprisingly, to eliminate references to sexual activity involving brothers and sisters in religious orders. Thus here the Clown in *All's Well That Ends Well*:

Clown. As fit as ten groates is for the hand of an Atturney, as your French Crowne for your taffety punke, as *Tibs* rush for *Toms* forefinger, as a pancake for Shrovetuesday, a Morris for May-day, as the naile to his hole, the Cuckold to his horne, as a scolding queane to a wrangling knave, ~~as the Nuns lip to the Friers mouth~~, nay as the pudding to his skin. (*All's Well That Ends Well*, 2.2.28; VF V4v)

None of this is anything less than filthy, indeed the friar kissing the nun is one of the more innocent activities going on, but it is easy to identify Sankey's inhibition. It is his only mark in the whole play.

Of course, it is not only a question of sensitivity to his own kind, or natural prurience. The reputation of religious orders, of the priesthood, especially of the secular clergy or members of the Society of Jesus, were prime areas of controversial dispute in anti-Catholic literature circulating in England. Sankey is visibly keen to intervene

in these areas. In *King John*, he takes the trouble to remove (twice over) the libel that the king has been poisoned 'by a Monke' (b5r). A third category of expurgation, which obviously often crosses over with those of blasphemy and innuendo, is therefore obviously doctrinal and theological. A good example is from *As You Like It*, in an exchange between Rosalind and Celia:

Ros. I' faith his haire is of a good colour.
Celia. An excellent colour:
Your chestnut was ever the onely colour.
Ros. ~~And his kissing is as full of sanctitie,~~
~~As the touch of holy bread.~~
Celia. Hee hath bought a paire of chast lips of *Diana*.
(*As You Like It*, 3.4.14–5; VF R3v)

Here the worry is the doctrinal status of the bread in the mass, as well as a blasphemous sexualisation of 'holy bread'. In *1 Henry VI*, the word 'Indulgences' along with a reference to 'the Pope, or dignities of Church' are the only excisions from this play (1.3.35 and 50; VF l6r). Elsewhere, Sankey is frequently concerned with the cult of saints, both in references such as 'Saint *Cupid*' in *Love's Labour's Lost* (VF M2r) and 'Saint *Denis* and Saint *Cupid*' (VF M4r), and also in the elimination of the word 'holyday' in 'holyday-foole' in *The Tempest* (VF A5r), Sankey worrying here about the derogatory lightness expressed over saints' days in Protestant England.

II

Yet to understand the meaning of deletion, we cannot treat Sankey the reader or the censor in isolation. E. M. Wilson the Hispanist criticized Frye's account of Sankey for exactly this reason, that he did not consider the context of censorship in Spain in the seventeenth century.[49] Since Wilson's time,

---

[48] The offensive codpieces are on L5r and 2s6v; the codpiece in *Much Ado About Nothing* (K2v) remains, despite some heavy sexual censorship on the facing leaf.

[49] Edward M. Wilson, 'Shakespeare and Christian Doctrine: Some Qualifications', *Shakespeare Survey 23* (Cambridge, 1970), pp. 79–89.

especially in the last decade with the opening up of the archives by the Vatican in the 1990s, there has been enormous ground made in the understanding of the local practices of the Holy Office. Sankey acted under the aegis of the Valladolid *tribunal*, and the purpose of the tribunal in Valladolid was to follow rules laid out in Rome to examine a book before it was available to read. Usually this process would happen before a book came to be printed, so it could be given its imprimatur of orthodoxy. The special status of the Valladolid Folio as a foreign book therefore again makes it an unusual object: a book left in a library with the deletions there for all to see.

This gives us the prospect of what we might call a comparative approach to censorship. Of all subjects censorship lends itself to overwhelming generalization. Often this historiography is divided between glib extremes of sensationalism and revisionism. Lee is heavily influenced in his account by the *leyenda negra* of the Inquisition that then prevailed in England. Here we have to compare how an English book might be dealt with in continental Europe as opposed to England. One difference in England is that as a practical process it was left in the hands of the Stationers' Company, thus inveigling the printing industry in a kind of veiled self-censorship. Cyndia Clegg has argued that this process was neither efficient nor ideologically consistent.[50] Catholic Europe did things in a way that was both more systematic and more complex. The Roman expurgators were fabulously meticulous. The late sixteenth and early seventeenth centuries are the highpoint in the idea of the 'universal index'. In 1596 the Congregation of the Index expanded the concept of the Index from the early editions of 1559 and 1564 to cover the censorship of individual editions of individual books rather than the outright condemnation of whole authors. From single editions they passed on to the examination of single passages or sentences or even words within single editions. This is the origin of the Sankey method, part of a distinctive literary culture of supervision. There is a ratchet process at work: an ever more intricate procedure of reading applied to an ever more selective set of texts conforming to an ever more precise and rigid standard of orthodoxy.

In Europe, unlike England, there exists the physical evidence of books which show the mark left by the censor's hand. Nonetheless, we should be mindful of the doctrine of the doyenne of modern censorship scholars, Gigliola Fragnito: 'the censorial apparatus was not the well-oiled machinery that has often been depicted; rather, it frequently jammed, and changes of mind, reversals and dithering gave it a markedly erratic course'.[51] Indeed, Fragnito argues, the very ambition of the Index, the increasingly Herculean scale of its operation, was largely a response to its own sense of failure, perhaps we might say its sense of the inevitability of its own failure.

In the twenty-five years following the third Index of 1596, a kind of bureaucratic mania ensued – with all the inadvertent farce and incompetence that energetic bureaucracy brings with it. After a while specialization was introduced to assist the process. Works on medicine and philosophy were sent to Padua; those on astrology to Venice; historical texts to Milan; books on duelling to Parma, Piacenza and Cremona; texts on canon law to Bologna; those on civil law to Perugia; and literary works to Florence.[52] There was a complaint in Padua that after they had finished with an author from their point of view, it had to go on to other cities for further expurgation, perhaps even undoing their own work (p. 42). Yet the Congregation of the Index itself worried about arbitrarily local decisions. It aspired instead to a comprehensive collation of variant expurgations. Naturally, these processes are full of irony and contradiction. One cardinal worries that when more than half of a sentence is removed, the rest may become hard

---

[50] In her trilogy finishing with *Press Censorship in Caroline England* (Cambridge, 2008), covering the period leading up to Sankey's time.

[51] Introduction to Gigliola Fragnito, ed., *Church, Censorship and Culture in Early Modern Italy*, trans. Adrian Belton (Cambridge, 2001), p. 4.

[52] Fragnito, *Church, Censorship and Culture*, p. 40.

to understand.[53] Are the censors permitted to add to the text to restore the sense of what they have removed?

In Fragnito's words, 'The central apparatus had been crushed by the weight of a project for the dis-infestation of an unmanageable quantity of books' (p. 46). A number of factors brought it down: the slowness of the expurgators; the habitual meanness in paying them fees; the inefficiencies of transfer-ring material from person to person. Beyond the impossible magnitude of the task in hand there were further questions: what if, in the effort of voluminous, inexhaustible expurgation, the cen-sors had omitted, or still worse misinterpreted or transgressed, matters of orthodoxy or doctrine themselves? This is the ultimate paradox of expur-gation: that it is itself an act of interpretation, and by revealing itself lays itself open to further censorship.

If Italian censorship by 1620 was running out of steam, in Spain it now entered its high triumphant phase. In Valladolid, it was administered by a local *tribunal*. It is possible to see, then, in the signa-ture of William Sankey inside Shakespeare's book, a kind of after-burn of the Roman Inquisition after the first quarter of the seventeenth century. It is a specialized form of censorship in relation to the Roman Inquisition in that it concerns a foreign book. Sankey does not treat it either as an orthodox or as a heretical text. Instead he attempts to clear it of any material which is contrary to the truth of the Church. Of this material he finds much to object to, more than in any other English book in the Valladolid library. As Susannah Brietz Monta argues, his motivation seems to have been theo-logical rather than political.[54] Yet he also leaves the marks of his mind by showing what he has blot-ted out. Here we encounter a deep epistemological problem within the process of censorship. In some sense we are always dealing with an argument from silence, from what is *not there*. We encounter simul-taneously, that is, both the act of censorship and the thing censored.

This is especially true of the most glaring cases of interference by Sankey in Shakespeare's text. These are congregated in two places. One is the heavy deleting in *King John*, for instance of the speeches defying the Papal Legate, and all references to the 'usurped authority' of the Pope:

> *K. John.* Though you, and all the Kings of
>   Christendome
> Are led ~~so grossely by this medling Priest,~~
> ~~Dreading the curse that money may buy out,~~
> And by the merit of vilde gold, drosse, dust,
> ~~Purchase corrupted pardon of a man,~~
> ~~Who in that sale sels pardon from himselfe:~~
> Though you, and all the rest ~~so grossely led,~~
> ~~This jugling witch-craft with revenue cherish,~~
> Yet I alone, alone doe me oppose
> Against the Pope, ~~and count his friends my foes.~~
>
> *Pand.* Then by the lawfull power that I have,
> Thou shalt stand curst, and excommunicate,
> And blessed shall he be that doth revolt
> From his Allegeance ~~to an heretique;~~
> ~~And meritorious shall that hand be call'd,~~
> ~~Canonized and worshipp'd as a Saint,~~
> ~~That takes away by any secret course~~
> ~~Thy hatefull life.~~   (*King John*, 3.1.168–79; VF a5r)

How do we interpret this as a textual act? Con-ventionally, we interpret by reverse: we look for the missing text to explain what is going on here, showing for instance how in the mid-seventeenth century English Catholics reinterpreted arguments about the sovereignty of the Protestant monarchy. Sankey can thus be seen as showing a later Jesuit line over the one familiar from recusant politics in the period of Cardinal Allen. He allows the reference to justified rebellion but removes the Protestant slur of disloyalty.

Yet this is to allow the missing text to be leg-ible in a way that the violence of the erasure makes impossible. Perhaps instead, we should fol-low the example of Derrida and consider the tex-tuality of deletion itself. The Valladolid Folio is

[53] Cardinal Valier to the inquisitor of Ferrara, 10 October 1600, cited in Fragnito, p. 44.

[54] '"Thou fall'st a blessed martyr": Shakespeare's Henry VIII and the Polemics of Conscience', *English Literary Renais-sance*, 30 (2000), 262–83, at p. 282.

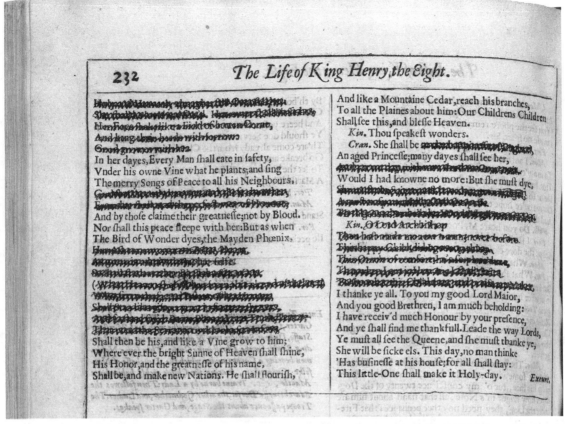

34. Folger Shakespeare Library, shelf mark: STC 22274 Fo.2 no.07, y6v (*Henry VIII*, 5.4.29–75), showing the deletions of the censor.

palpably written *sous rature*, 'under erasure'.[55] Sankey's text is not so much an emended version of Shakespeare, as a visible form of defacement. It shows a loyal Catholic reader the material sign of heresy: indeed the defacement is like a declaration of doctrinal hygiene. Yet if so, we have to acknowledge that it is written in the opposite spirit to that suggested by Derrida. It is Shakespeare's writing which represents the sense of deconstruction, 'the end of the book and the beginning of writing'.[56] Sankey wishes to undo the duplicity of writing and restore the totality of the signifier by reconstituting the 'idea of the book'. He gives the text back 'la protection encyclopédique de la théologie' (p. 31). By a savage Derridean irony, he does so precisely through the act of violence.

Perhaps this is most obvious in another case within the Valladolid Folio of a blank wall of black ink, that of *Henry VIII*, where the visible presence of the English Reformation makes its interpretation in English Spain almost a textual fetish. Every favourable reference to Archbishop Cranmer (the adjectives 'virtuous', 'good', 'honest') is scored through. This is visually comical when King Henry is made to say:

Was it discretion Lords, to let this man,
This ~~good~~ man (few of you deserve that Title)

---

55 *De la grammatologie* (Paris 1967), p. 80. Translation by Gayatri Chakravorty Spivak, *Of Grammatology*, corrected edn (Baltimore, 1997), p. 60.
56 'La fin du livre et le commencement de l'écriture' is the title of the first chapter of *De la grammatologie*.

This ~~honest~~ man, wait like a lowsie Foot-boy
At Chamberdore? and one, as great as you are?
                                    (*Henry VIII*, 5.2.171–4, VF y5v)

There is a kind of typographical flyting going on; not only is Cranmer not 'honest', he is '~~honest~~'. Sankey's text acquires its own improvisatory energy in the finale to the play, where the prophetic eulogies at the baptism of Princess Elizabeth are savagely reduced. The virtues ascribed via the Queen of Sheba to the future heretic queen and her 'Princely Graces' and 'Holy and Heavenly thoughts' are eliminated (VF y6r). More specifically, the prophecy that 'God shall be truly knowne' in her time, a Protestant boast of savage travesty to a Catholic of the next generation, is anathema, as is the reference to the peaceful reign of King James that follows. In a bravura performance of censorship, twenty-five out of fifty lines on the last page of the final scene of the play are removed. All mention of the future 'happiness of England' is excised, leaving only the barest outline of narrative sense: it is foretold only that Elizabeth will one day be 'an aged Princess' and that she 'must die'. In this condemnation of the Protestant Reformation to non-existence, King Henry's speech is rendered as a theatrical mockery, in which he has a complete memory lapse about the future and then thanks the Archbishop, as if for nothing:

Cranmer. She shall be ~~to the happinesse of England~~,
    An aged Princesse; many dayes shall see her,
    ~~And yet no day without a deed to Crowne it~~.
    Would I had knowne no more: But she must dye,
    ~~She must, the Saints must have her; yet a Virgin~~,
    ~~A most unspotted Lilly, shall she passe~~
    ~~To th' ground, and all the World shall mourne her~~.
King.   ~~O Lord Archbishop~~,
    ~~Thou hast made me now a man, never before~~
    ~~This happy Child, did I get anything~~.
    ~~This Oracle of comfort, ha's so pleas'd me~~,
    ~~That when I am in Heaven, I shall desire~~
    ~~To see what this Child does, and praise my Maker~~.
    I thanke ye all.   (*Henry VIII*, 5.4.56–68, VF y6v)

This is a text showing every visible sign of its own doctrinal and historiographical torments. The marks of deletion grow more urgent: single curled lines of the pen are doubled up once he reaches the most reprehensible lines, the reinforcement giving physical sign of the censor's anxiety. It is also by virtue of this a new form of text: the Valladolid Folio demands to be read in its own unique way as a book showing its readers what not to think as well as what to think.

III

In conclusion, I return to the most extreme act of censorship of all. What happens when *Measure for Measure* is removed altogether, the final act of violence?[57] This is not writing under erasure but writing in oblivion. What brings this into being? I can hardly have a proper answer to this question. Indeed, the whole problem here is that strictly I can have *no* answer to this question, since anything I say must be a form of argument *ab silentio*. Censorship always contains a tension between what is there and what is not there, between the text seen and unseen. Here, however, I am suggesting that censorship opens up different ways of reading, which have been obscured by our looking too quickly for answers. Instead, we need to be more imaginative, and see what happens when we look between the lines.

Indeed, with the missing text of *Measure for Measure*, I am being self-consciously speculative. How can we even know Sankey cut it out? The answer, of course, is that we do not. Yet this space of uncertainty precisely enables us to think further about the volatility of religious experience which surrounds the watching and reading of this play. As it happens, I believe Sankey in all probability was responsible. Here the parallel history of Spanish censorship of plays, described by E. M. Wilson, provides a fascinating commentary on Sankey's Shakespeare. Bartolomé de Torres Naharro, of Jewish *converso* descent and who himself took holy

---

[57] The missing text is VF F1r–G6v. The excision appears to have been made using an instrument like a razor; the cuts are sharp, although with occasional reverse movements as the instrument catches the paper.

orders, wrote plays which were published in 1517 in a volume entitled *Propalladia*. It was only after his death and after the Reformation that they ran into trouble. A ban was placed by the Inquisition in 1559, and in 1573 a full expurgation was undertaken. Just as in Shakespeare's text, expressions similar to 'by the Mass' were removed; in the case of *Propalladia*, they were replaced with euphemistic phrases such as 'si plaze a Dios'. Obscene expressions, like *desvirgar* ('to ravish') and *mear* ('to piss'), were cut, and also references to the Virgin, Church and Saints.[58] The corrected text was then released. But in one copy of Torres Naharro in the Biblioteca Nacional at Madrid, the examiner (a friar in the monastery of St Jerome at Seville) went further. He dated his act 2 June 1585: 'The comedy called *Jacinta* was taken out and torn up because it was prohibited in the catalogue printed in 1583' (p. 82). Yet the excision was incorrect; the play had not been officially banned. The excess zeal of the friar was in turn mitigated by a later reader who added the play back, copied out by hand.

Wilson thought this meant we should be wary of making any judgement about *Measure for Measure* as an expression of the Inquisition in Valladolid. But perhaps instead it provides another kind of insight into the process of examination. Is the excision of *Measure for Measure* an example of an excess of zeal or paranoia? Probably both things are present. However, this may lead us to an as yet unnoticed kink in the historiography of censorship. The model of censorship usually offered is inherently functional and instrumental. Censorship aims to remove something offensive from a text. By definition it therefore knows what it is looking for. In this model, then, a settled version of orthodoxy always pre-exists for censorship to act on. Yet the expurgators were often using censorship to work out what orthodoxy was. This suggests that there is something more mysterious and less practical about the operation of censorship. It does not always know what it is looking for, and it does not always know what it has found when it has finished looking. What appears like the most transparent possible statement of meaning – crossing out a line of text – gives us rather an opaquely physical action. What the act of crossing means, what the word that is crossed out means *when it is crossed out*, what the difference is between the word scored and unscored, what the words to one side or the other of the purged word mean, all of this is open to interpretation. In this context, the act of interpretation is anything but free: the mind making sense of the text on the page is now backed into a corner, recognizing the palpable fact of error, perhaps reeling from it, and trying to work out how to manoeuvre around it.

The case of the missing play in the Valladolid Folio, however, gives us something else, perhaps the truest form of censorship, properly defined. It is the case of the totally obliterated, the absolutely expurgated, the absent text. What can be said between the lines of a text where all the lines have been removed? Where there is not even a proclamation outlawing this text, or giving a reason for its removal?

In the past the mutilation of the Valladolid Folio has been used to place a window on Shakespeare, but perhaps instead we should look to *Measure for Measure* in order to understand the examiner. For Sankey has himself become the victim of a kind of simplification. Shakespearians, whether horrified like Lee by the black legend of the Spanish Inquisition, or sympathetic in their exposition of Shakespeare in the context of Catholic recusancy, have reduced Sankey to a cipher, a straw man, transparently pious and simple-minded.[59] It is said, in this context, that we know hardly anything about the examiner in Valladolid. But we know more about William Sankey than about the considerably more mysterious William Shakespeare. Not only in Valladolid, but in the records in Madrid, where he arrived in 1651 (shortly after the censorship of Shakespeare), a good deal of information on Sankey emerges. Henson, the historian of Madrid, is not an admirer: 'The papers were very badly cared for during the time of

---

58 Wilson, 'Shakespeare and Christian Doctrine', p. 80.
59 Foley, *Records of the English Province*, vol. VII, part 2, p. 686 describes him as 'humble' and 'sweetly pious'.

Fr. William Sankey, as can easily be imagined when the account of his financial administration of St George's is read.'[60] Depositions were presented by Don Aquiles Napolitano against Sankey over many years involving his time of office as rector.[61] Sankey was accused of swindling the Spanish sacristan of the church of the payments for wine and oil used in the sacraments. Sankey at first refused to answer the charges, or to hand over the accounts; he was answerable only to the Nuncio and the Papal see, he claimed. When the accounts were examined, there were discrepancies with the records of the Procurator Fiscal; Sankey's goods were sequestrated and he was removed from office in 1663.[62] It would be wrong to believe every calumny about Sankey, based on only one side of the litigation; but the records show the friction between English and Spanish over decades, a cultural antagonism of a different colour from missionary idealism. One report in particular vividly describes the high emotions: Sankey came up to the sacristan (we are told) at thanksgiving after mass at the high altar, saying unto him impudently 'Salga aqui fuera al patio', 'Get out of here into the courtyard.'[63] A group of English seminarians then threw the sacristan onto the street and trashed his room, pitching out his bed and furniture and knocking him over again. On another occasion, Sankey is accused of tearing up a demand to pay a *Censo* to the Discalced Carmelites, and was put in prison for forty days, 'which is sufficient to give an idea of what he is like, and what he is capable of'.[64]

The relationship between exiled English Jesuits and their Spanish hosts was not always mutual and reciprocal. It involved unexplained, perhaps unacknowledged, tensions and anxieties. This could also help to explain the state of the copy of Shakespeare in the library at the Colegio. The Valladolid Folio shows a book which is not fully assimilated, either into the culture surrounding it, or even into the Anglophone culture which sits uneasily in its estranged context. What happens if we try for a moment to impersonate the enigmatic William Sankey in front of this English book? What was he looking for, and what did he find when he had finished, when he had blotted out whole scenes

to the point of incomprehensibility, or cut out an entire play with a razor?

Of course there are instrumental reasons for expurgation. The play can be seen (at least if you are looking for it, if you want to see it, if you think that everybody in England thinks this way) as anti-Catholic. The play is explicitly insinuating about religious houses and openly and often gruesomely sexual. But the censor also does not know in advance exactly what is problematic here. It is not because the censor knows what he is doing that he cuts out an entire play. If he could so readily understand the play, then as with *Henry VIII*, he would just take out words and speeches. It is because he cannot make complete sense of the play that he finds it troubling enough to remove it altogether.

What is different about *Measure for Measure*? In this respect, it is interesting to consider how the play itself mirrors the action of religious censorship, and in the process ambiguates the boundaries of religious orthodoxy. It is a play in part about the discovery of orthodoxy, the enforcement of it, and the triumphant display of it. Yet it is also a play about the dismantling of orthodoxy, not by outward rebellion but by a kind of decay from within. The play gets into the heart and mind of the censor himself, and it appears that the censor does not enjoy this. The play is concerned throughout with systems of religious control, with the desire to enforce religious and moral conformity by violent means. It articulates the rigour of social control down to the interior thoughts of the citizens. In the process, it also investigates the physical means orthodoxy uses to carry out this scrutiny, including torture. This peculiar mix between political authority and confessional zeal is very post-Reformation.

However, the worst thing for Father Sankey is the investment of authority in the person of the

---

[60] Henson, *Registers of the English College at Madrid*, p. viii.
[61] Henson, *Registers of the English College at Madrid*, p. 109.
[62] Williams, *St Alban's College Valladolid*, p. 37.
[63] Henson, *Registers of the English College at Madrid*, p. 114.
[64] Henson, *Registers of the English College at Madrid*, p. 114.

Duke. The Duke disguises himself in the habit of a friar and impersonates a priest. Here, one or two other instances of censorship in the Valladolid Folio may be relevant to the extreme case of *Measure for Measure*. We have already seen how in *King John*, the slandering of a monk as a poisoner arouses the anxiety of the censor. In *2 Henry VI*, in the exorcism scene in Act 1, scene 4, there is a more curious case of excision. The stage direction mentions the entrance of the witch Margery Jourdain with '*two Priests*', but in the Valladolid Folio the words '*two Priests*' are cut out (o1r). More strangely, the identity of one of the priests, 'Iohn Southwell' is twice crossed out. Southwell is mentioned in Edward Hall as a priest and canon of St Stephen's Westminster, but it is presumably another Southwell Sankey is worried about. Robert Southwell was the Jesuit martyr second only to Edmund Campion in the order's English pantheon. The depiction of a priest carrying out a satanic conjuration and raising of spirits is too close to anti-Catholic satire. On the following leaf, there is further considerable excision, this time of a scene of torture and false miracles (2.1.136–55; VF o2r).

What Sankey agonizes about most in Shakespeare, apart from the legal rights of the Pope in *King John* and the glorification of the English Reformation in *Henry VIII*, is the Protestant calumny, well known to the Jesuit order, that Catholic priests were conjurors and charlatans, forever prone to acting in disguise or fabricating extravagantly theatrical miracles. He also winces at the portrayal of priests as moral enforcers, agents of the Inquisition in extracting secret information under the ecclesiastical power of pardon, indulgence or confession. In *Measure for Measure*, the caricature of a fake priest is displayed in excruciating detail, supervising the conscience of Isabella, and then in turn almost everybody in the play. No intervention by the Duke as friar is more extreme than when he takes on the role of her brother Claudio's confessor, the night before his execution. This is an extraordinary scene, one of the most remarkable in all Shakespeare. It is a scene of *quietus*, of deathly silence and extreme unction. The figure of the father-confessor here could not be more

ambiguous. One fact which must trouble Father Sankey the confessor in reading this is that the friar abuses his position to play games with the minds of the penitent. Another – enough perhaps to ban the play – is that the friar breaks the seal of confession in order to achieve his grand manipulation of events. The Duke plays God, and pretends to hear the last confession of Claudio before his death in order to encourage him into following the Duke's plans. But perhaps Sankey is most troubled, as many viewers of the play are, by the agony of confrontation between brother and sister which the friar forces them into conducting. He leaves them alone in a scene of pitiless intimacy. 'Now sister, what's the comfort?' asks Claudio.[65] Isabella at first tries to cheer him up with thoughts of eternity: 'Why / As all comforts are: most good, most good indeed.' Angelo intends him as an ambassador to speak in heaven; Claudio must make ready his appointment with the almighty.

Despite the tenderness of their banter, this scene quickly gets worse. Claudio is offered the temptation of his own release from prison. Isabella is there to tell his brother he must die. But she will also tell him that he has a chance to escape death, only it is a choice he must not take, since it is a choice that will imperil both his soul and hers. It is another of those scholastic bargains with theology that the play is so full of:

> Isabella.   dost thou thinke *Claudio*,
> If I would yeeld him my virginity
> Thou might'st be freed?
>
> (*Measure for Measure*, 3.1.96–8; F2, F6r)

Claudio is steadfast: 'Thou shalt not do't.' Isabella retorts, with the ease that imagination gives, that if it were only her life she would willingly give it up. 'Thankes deere *Isabell*', Claudio replies, perhaps a little curtly. Is there a more intimate scene in Shakespeare? It is all the more charged with emotion in that it is shared between brother and sister and not between lovers, and that it faces up to death and

---

[65] The missing text in the Valladolid Folio is filled out here from the facsimile of the Second Folio (London, 1909); this citation sig. F6r.

not to love. It is also a moment caught on the knife-edge of Reformation theological politics. Indeed, it is a scene straight out of the Inquisition. The inquisitor was always instructed to make this particular bargain with the condemned. The afterlife, the dying man is reminded, is worth more than this present life. He must, then, willingly choose death. Claudio hesitates on the edge of death and chooses life. He makes one final theological bargain with his conscience:

> *Claudio.*   Sweet Sister, let me live.
> What sinne you doe, to save a brothers life,
> Nature dispenses with the deede so farre,
> That it becomes a vertue.
>
> (*Measure for Measure*, 3.1.132–5; F2, F6r)

And yet, just at the point where we have learned to empathize with Claudio in his desperation, the play makes him turn again. He hates himself for having put his sister in this position. Death is his ultimate reconciliation with God. Like the condemned heretic, he has no choice but to recant his life of sin and embrace his own execution as the ultimate kindness of the church and of God. Is there a more disturbing scene in Shakespeare, in its moral ambiguity, its astonishing privacy and exposure, its closeness to the promise of mortality? If it was this that drove the censor to his ultimate act of amputation, and reach for his razor, for a moment we can perhaps feel some sympathy.

THE COWELL MANUSCRIPT OR THE FIRST BACONIAN: MS294 AT THE UNIVERSITY OF LONDON

K. E. ATTAR

The Library also possesses a number of manuscripts, including a Latin Bible on vellum written and rubricated in Italy in the early part of the fifteenth century; the unpublished manuscript of Sir Charles Cornwallis's Discourse of the State of Spain, 1607, written while Ambassador in Spain; and an unpublished poem by George Herbert inserted in a copy of the original edition of Bacon's Translation of certain [i.e. seven] Psalmes into English verse, 1625. Another interesting manuscript contains Some Reflections on the Life of William Shakespeare, in a paper read before the Ipswich Philosophic Society in 1805, by James Corton Cowell, a Quaker, who is thereby established as the first critic known to have raised doubts publicly as to Shakespeare's authorship of the literature which passes under his name and to have attributed it to Bacon. In a second paper the author revealed, under a unanimous promise of secrecy from members of the society, his indebtedness to the Rev. James Wilmot, D.D., Rector of Barton-on-the-Heath near Stratford-upon-Avon, an alleged author of the 'Letters of Junius', who desired to remain anonymous lest he should incur the resentment of the inhabitants of Stratford-upon-Avon. The earliest dissenter from the Shakespeare tradition mentioned by Sir Sidney Lee is Joseph C. Hart in his *Romance of Yachting*, 1848.[1]

This passage is from the 1931 annual report of the University of London's Library Committee. The paragraph is the third from the end of an anonymous three-page description of the Durning-Lawrence Library, bequeathed to the University by Edith Jane, Lady Durning-Lawrence in 1929 and received into the University Library in August 1931. Its author is uncertain: conceivably Reginald Arthur Rye as the Goldsmiths' Librarian of the University of London at the time; possibly the

Shakespearian scholar Allardyce Nicoll, then Professor of Queen Mary College at the University of London, and a member of the Library Committee. What is certain is that the discovery of the so-called Cowell manuscript, had it remained confined to the library report, would have languished, at least for a while.[2] But on 25 February 1932, Nicoll published an article entitled 'The First Baconian' in the *Times Literary Supplement*, summarizing the manuscript's content (including Wilmot's reasons for preferring Bacon to Shakespeare as the author of the Shakespearian canon) and providing biographical background about Wilmot.[3]

---

[1] London, Senate House Library, University of London, University Archive, UL 1/1/4.

[2] The next published description of the Durning-Lawrence Library, excerpted from the Library Committee report, mentions the fifteenth-century Latin Bible and the Cornwallis manuscripts, but not Cowell. See 'Notes and News: The Durning-Lawrence Library', *Library Association Record*, 3rd ser. 2 (1932), 178–9.

[3] Allardyce Nicoll, 'The First Baconian', *Times Literary Supplement*, 25 February 1932, 128. The Library Committee report precedes the newspaper article. Minute 322 of the Library committee meeting for 23 May 1932 begins: 'Arising out of the Minutes of the last meeting of the Committee and the Report on the University Library for 1931, the Chairman drew the attention of members of the Committee to an interesting article on "The First Baconian"' (London, Senate House Library, University of London, University Archive, UL 1/1/4). The previous meeting referred to, at which Nicoll was present, took place on 18 January 1932. It had considered the draft report of the University Library for 1931 and resolved to approve it (ibid., minutes 309–10). The most detailed account of Wilmot is Olivia Wilmot Serres, *The Life of the Author of the 'Letters of Junius', the Revd. James Wilmot,*

An editorial in that day's *Times*, rehearsing disparagingly the history of the Baconian theory, highlighted the import of Nicoll's piece,[4] for, in publishing it, Nicoll transformed literary scholarship on the Baconian controversy. Henceforth, public expression of doubt in the authorship of Shakespeare's plays was accepted as having originated not with Joseph C. Hart in 1848, but with James Wilmot, via James Corton Cowell's lectures of 7 February and an unspecified day in April, 1805.[5]

Nicoll and others outlined the argument of the lectures and cited sentences from them. Yet the lectures themselves have never been published. In 2010 James Shapiro cast doubt on their authenticity, noting vocabulary not widely used and facts about Shakespeare not known until later in the nineteenth century.[6] While Shapiro was not quite the first to query the genuineness of the manuscript, he was the first to do so in a monograph and on factual and linguistic grounds.[7] Like Nicoll's

discovery nearly seventy years earlier, Shapiro's findings were promulgated widely through publication in the *Times Literary Supplement*.[8] It therefore seems timely to publish the manuscript and to explore its background.[9]

This background is suspect. The Ipswich Philosophic Society to which Cowell allegedly delivered his lectures in 1805 is presumably a careless mistake for the Ipswich Philosophical Society, a body which did not come into being until 1 January 1842, with the object of providing 'such a course of reading on science as was not attainable by reference to established libraries or book clubs of town',[10] and the few records in the local press of its fortnightly lectures are of scientific subjects.[11] The identity of James Corton Cowell is questionable. In common with the Arthur Cobbold who presided at his lectures, the Mr Neame with whom Cowell states that he lodged in Stratford the evening before visiting Wilmot, and Dr Bayford, he is not recorded as having attended an English university.[12] This agrees with Cowell's description of himself as not being a man of letters, and lacking acquaintance with Latin and Greek authors, and could have led to Nicoll's belief that he was a

---

D.D. (London, 1813); this work refers to Wilmot's respect for Bacon (pp. 89, 195–6) and avers that Wilmot considered Milton 'the greatest poet any age had produced, for sublimity and elegance of stile' (p. 192). It does not mention Shakespeare. For a briefer, more recent account of Wilmot, see Philip Carter, 'Wilmot, James (1726–1807)', *Oxford Dictionary of National Biography* (Oxford, 2004); online edn, September 2010, www.oxforddnb.com/view/article/29622, accessed 4 Jan. 2011.

4 'The First Baconian', *The Times*, 25 February 1932, 15.

5 See H. N. Gibson, *The Shakespeare Claimants: A Critical Survey of the Four Principal Theories concerning the Authorship of the Shakespearean Plays* (London, 1962), pp. 17–18; S. Schoenbaum, *Shakespeare's Lives*, new edn (Oxford, 1991), pp. 397–9; John Michell, *Who Wrote Shakespeare?* (London, 1996), pp. 102–3, and, most recently, Warren Hope and Kim Holston, *The Shakespeare Controversy: An Analysis of the Authorship Theories*, 2nd edn (Jefferson, NC, and London, 2009), p. 4.

6 James Shapiro, *Contested Will: Who Wrote Shakespeare?* (London, 2010), pp. 12–13. Shapiro points out that Shakespeare's activity as a money-lender first became known in 1806, that his dealings in malt were first published in 1844, and that the word 'unromantic' was not yet commonly used.

7 Earlier suspicion of the Cowell manuscript appears in Nathan Baca, 'Wilmot Did Not: The "First" Authorship Story Called Possible Baconian Hoax', *Shakespeare Matters*, 2 (2003), [1], [7] and [33]; noted by Shapiro, *Contested Will*, pp. 319–20, and available at: www.shakespearefellowship.

org/Newsletter_Archive/SM2.4z3a.pdf, accessed 4 January 2011.

8 James Shapiro, 'Forgery on Forgery: Not the First Baconian: The Strange Case of James Corton Cowell', *Times Literary Supplement*, 26 March 2010, 14–15. They have also been taken up in Carter, 'Wilmot, James (1726–1807)'.

9 I should like to thank Senate House Library, University of London, for permission to reproduce the transcription of the manuscript. Thanks are also due to Warwick Gould and James Shapiro for their encouragement and comments.

10 John J. Glyde, *The Moral, Social and Religious Condition of Ipswich* (Ipswich, 1850), p. 183.

11 E.g. the state of health in Ipswich (*Bury and Norwich Post, and East Anglian*, 22 November 1843, *et al.*); the potato disease and its remedy (*Hampshire Telegraph and Sussex Chronicle*, 28 November 1846, *et al.*); artificial light and the usual mode of obtaining it (*Ipswich Journal*, 11 April 1857); organic chemistry and its probable results (*Ipswich Journal*, 25 April 1857).

12 Cowell MS, p. 1 (Cobbold); p. 59 (Neame); p. 73 (Bayford). See Joseph Foster, *Alumni Oxonienses: The Members of the University of Oxford, 1715–1886*, 4 vols. (Oxford, 1888); J. A. Venn, *Alumni Cantabrigienses: A Biographical List of all*

Quaker.[13] However, Cowell is recorded in none of the major Quaker biographical sources, neither in *Quaker Records*, nor in the *Quaker Digest of Suffolk*, nor in the manuscript Dictionary of Quaker Biography held at the Society of Friends Library in London.[14]

The manuscript, numbered MS294, is from the Durning-Lawrence Library at Senate House Library, University of London. It has no markings or accompanying documentation to shed any light on previous provenance. The Durning-Lawrence Library, of about 5,750 items, was primarily collected by the prominent Baconian Sir Edwin Durning-Lawrence (1837–1914) who, in the words of his wife, purchased every book 'with one aim, and that aim was to prove that Francis Bacon was at the head of a great literary and scientific society, from whence emanated all the Elizabethan and Jacobean literature'.[15] For content, it sits well in the Durning-Lawrence Library, which contains several shelves of books about Bacon and the Baconian controversy. It has an evident place, too, among Durning-Lawrence's manuscripts with their Baconian connection. Most of these are from the seventeenth century or earlier, but others include a copy of a manuscript of Bacon's essays in John Payne Collier's hand (MS291; dated 1867–1883) and a notebook with information from various sources about early editions of Shakespeare, partly written in Collier's hand, originally owned by the lawyer and evangelical activist John Poynder (1779–1849) (MS306).[16]

Like earlier provenance, the immediate source of acquisition of the Cowell manuscript is unrecorded. Durning-Lawrence himself is unlikely to have seen it. The manuscript is listed neither in his register of accessions nor in his manuscript catalogue, and Durning-Lawrence's voluminous scrapbooks of receipts, 1890–1914, contains no receipt for it.[17] The only reference to it is, as noted by Shapiro, a half-sheet of blank paper, measuring 124 × 203 mm, in a folder of looseleaf invoices and receipts, stating: 'Cowell MSS | £8=8=0 | Lady Durning-Lawrence holds the Receipts.'[18] Moreover, the manuscript lacks the letters 'D S' stamped in mauve ink, with numbers indicating

the bookcase and shelf after each letter, which regularly mark Durning-Lawrence's acquisitions.[19] It is also worth noting that Durning-Lawrence had already attempted in the final chapter of his *Bacon is Shakespeare* to bolster his argument that Bacon was Shakespeare by citing 'a few of the utterances of men of the greatest distinction who, without being furnished with the information which

Known Students, Graduates and Holders of Office at the University of Cambridge from the Earliest Times to 1900 Pt. 2, From 1752 to 1900, 6 vols. (Cambridge, 1940–54). The Cobbolds were an old brewing family of Ipswich, with the earliest Arthur Cobbold recorded on the family tree being Arthur Thomas Cobbold (1815–1898; see The Cobbold Family History Trust, www.cobboldfht.com/index.php, accessed 22 November 2011).

13 For Cowell's lack of letters and classical learning, see Cowell MS, p. 60 and p. 72 respectively.

14 *Quaker Records: Being an Index to 'The Annual Monitor' 1813–1892, Containing Over Twenty Thousand Obituary Notices of Members of the Society of Friends, Alphabetically and Chronologically Arranged, with Reference to 'The Annual Montor'*, ed. by Joseph J. Green (London, 1894); *Quaker Digest of Suffolk: Index of Births 1641–1837, Marriages 1662–1837, Burials 1655–1837* (22 August 1998); London, Library of the Religious Society of Friends in Britain, Dictionary of Quaker Biography (no ref. number).

15 Alexander Gordon, *Family History of the Lawrences of Cornwall* (West Norwood, 1915). For a detailed overview of the Durning-Lawrence library and the position of Durning-Lawrence in Baconian debate, see K. E. Attar, 'Sir Edwin Durning-Lawrence: A Baconian and his Books', *The Library*, 7th ser., 5 (2004), 294–315.

16 For a list of manuscripts owned by Durning-Lawrence, see the printed handlists of manuscripts in the Durning-Lawrence Library and of manuscripts in the University of London Library in the Special Collections reading room of Senate House Library, University of London MSS 285–320), and the archives and manuscripts catalogue of the University of London Research Library Services, at http://archives.ulrls.lon.ac.uk.

17 London, Senate House Library, University of London, Durning-Lawrence Archive, DLL/1/2: Library catalogue vol. II, L–Z (heading: manuscripts); DLL/1/3: Accessions list, 1–2500: Baconiana and Manuscripts; DLL/1/7–9: Invoices and receipts, 1890–1914.

18 London, Senate House Library, University of London, Durning-Lawrence Archive, DLL/1/10: Receipts and invoices for book purchases, 1910–1925. see also Shapiro, *Contested Will*, p. 320.

19 See Attar, 'Sir Edwin Durning-Lawrence', p. 306.

we have been able to afford to our readers, were possessed of sufficient intelligence and common sense to perceive the truth respecting the real authorship of the Plays' and thereby 'prove to the reader that he will be in excellent company when he himself realises the truth that BACON IS SHAKESPEARE'.[20] Durning-Lawrence followed up *Bacon is Shake-Speare* with pamphlets and with letters to the press about Baconian authorship.[21] Had a manuscript which, by pushing the Baconian theory back by over fifty years, appeared to give it extra credence been at his disposal, Durning-Lawrence would surely have wished to publicize it to support his case. Either Sir Edwin Durning-Lawrence ordered the manuscript before his sudden death on 21 April 1914 but it arrived afterwards, or Lady Durning-Lawrence acquired it. The latter is feasible: Alexander Gordon, a family friend, recorded that she continued to add to her husband's library,[22] and although she did not purchase on a large scale, receipts or invoices are extant for items such as seven shillings for two copies of Sir George Greenwood's pamphlet *Ben Jonson and Shakespeare* from David E. Reeves, 21 December 1921; £60 for a two-volume edition of *Don Quixote* from Davis & Orioli (21 December 1923), and twelve guineas for unspecified manuscripts (21 April 1925).[23]

The manuscript is a quarto volume, bound in twentieth-century half-morocco and marbled boards, measuring 25.5 × 21 cm. The pages are attached to stubs. The paper is handmade off-white wove drawing cartridge of a kind first made in the mid-1790s. It is typical of paper produced by Robert Edmeads and John Pine at the Great Ivy Mill and Little Ivy Mill in the Loose Valley near Maidstone, Kent, and continued to be made by the firm under changing partnerships until about 1820.[24] The page size is 23.9–24.3 × 18.3–18.8 cm. The first lecture ends mid-sentence at the foot of page 36. Seven blank leaves follow. The second lecture occupies pages 55–87. Three blank pages follow before the back flyleaf and endpaper. Pages 23–4 have been torn, affecting three lines on p. 23 and five on p. 24. Page numbers have later

been pencilled continuously on the recto pages, including on the blank leaves. The first lecture contains between fifteen and seventeen lines per page, the second between fourteen and seventeen, with twelve lines on the final page.

The manuscript has been rather carelessly written, as shown not only by 'Philosophic Society' for 'Philosophical Society', already noted, but by some thoughtless spelling errors, corrected by the writer (e.g. 'rights' for 'rites' on p. 13), and by grammatical errors or the omission of words: 'no evidence exists that this man of learning who must have read many hundreds of books never left a single volume' (p. 21); 'We have in the writer of [the] Plays' (p. 32); 'I found that the account of Dr Wilmot's erudition given me by Mr Neame to have b[ee]n in no degree exaggerated' (p. 64). Cowell was furthermore an inaccurate copyist. Citing Alexander Pope's edition of Shakespeare on pages 12–13, he omitted 'from' in 'whether he has it from one language or from another' and 'a' in 'still a nicer distinction'. He adapted Pope, changing 'But as to his want of learning' to 'With regard to his learning' and 'natural philosophy' to 'English history'; omitting 'at least, if they will not call it learning' after ''tis plain he had much reading at least', and a sentence 'His reading in the ancient historians is no less conspicuous . . . and the speeches copy'd from Plutarch in Coriolanus may, I think, as well be made an instance of his learning, as those

[20] Edwin Durning-Lawrence, *Bacon is Shake-Speare* (London, 1910), pp. 178–182.

[21] Durning-Lawrence's Baconian pamphlets are Sir Edwin Durning-Lawrencc, *The Shakespeare Myth* (London, 1912) and *Macbeth Proves Bacon is Shakespeare* (London, [1913]). For a list, which does not claim to be exhaustive, of Durning-Lawrence's letters to the press, see Gordon, *Family History*, pp. 78–9. Some of these letters are included in scrapbooks of correspondence on the Bacon-Shakespeare authorship question in the Durning-Lawrence Archive: see London, Senate House Library, University of London, Durning-Lawrence Archive, DLL/2/2, DLL/2/4–6 and DLL/2/8.

[22] Alexander Gordon, *Memoir of Lady Durning-Lawrence* ([no place], 1930), p. 33.

[23] London, Senate House Library, University of London, Durning-Lawrence Archive, DLL/1/10.

[24] Shapiro, 'Forgery on Forgery', p. 15.

copy'd from Cicero in Catiline, of Ben Johnson's between 'of the latter' and 'The manners of other nations', and 'in general, the' after 'other nations'; and adding 'ancient' before 'Egyptians'.[25]

The handwriting shows several inconsistencies. Sometimes the writer indents new paragraphs; often he does not. He capitalizes adjectives and common nouns at whim, with the greatest inconsistency being 'new light' as the catchword on p. 14, 'New Light' as the first words on p. 15. He employs two forms of some capital letters, an upper case letter, and a larger version of the lower case letter. Occasionally in double s combination he uses a long 's' (amassed, p. 32; assurance, p. 58; association, p. 70); but 'assured' appears on p. 58 as two short letters, four lines above 'assurance', and 'dissenter' appears with two short letters 's' in the same line as 'assurance'. The first lecture contains catchwords; the second does not. Sometimes the catchword comprises two words ('of Enquiry' (p. 7); 'the greatest' (p. 8); 'to lay' (p. 9); 'of the' (p. 12), 'new light' (p. 14), 'My Friend' (p. 19), 'But the' (p. 21), 'My Friend' (p. 22, with 'My' omitted on p. 23), 'to let' (p. 26; 'to' is the last word on p. 26, 'let' the first word on p. 27)); sometimes the writer neglects to repeat the catchword as the first word of the subsequent page (e.g. 'then' as the catchword on p. 17; 'his' as the catchword on p. 31; 'allurement' on p. 33 is a supralinear addition on p. 34), suggesting that he was writing the catchwords before beginning the next page (perhaps copying a source). Some words are abbreviated, but not consistently, notably 'would', 'which', 'could', 'should' (appearing in full in the first lecture and, except for its first occurrence, in abbreviated form in the second) and 'the'. The latter sometimes appears as a symbol resembling the 'h' of Pitman shorthand or an upside-down lower-case Greek gamma; on three occasions it appears as a Greek gamma.[26] Crossings out are sometimes of oblique strokes (\) through individual letters, sometimes of whole words.

The transcription follows the paragraph indentation, punctuation and the capitalization of the original, except that I have added missing full stops silently. Where a letter (typically 'm', 'n' or 'c')

follows a lower case form but is slightly above the line, and it is unclear whether it is meant to be upper or lower case, I have used lower case. I have followed the writer's abbreviations where feasible, but expanded the symbol for 'the', not reproducible on a computer, with square brackets. Vertical bars followed by a number in square brackets indicate page breaks. Angular brackets indicate that the writer has crossed out a word. Square brackets indicate editorial insertions and occur only where the manuscript has been torn or a word is illegible or uncertain. The position of words added above the text is indicated by an upwards arrow at each end of the supralinear insertion; words existing only below the text (chiefly catchwords which have not been repeated on the following page) are indicated by a downwards arrow at each end.

[1] Some Reflections on the Life of
William Shakespeare
A Paper Read before the
Ipswich Philosophic Society
by
James Corton Cowell
February 7 1805
~
Arthur Cobbold Esq[re] President

|[3] M[r] President & Members

It will be within your memories that during the Session of 1803 I read a paper on the Genius of the Poets Shakespeare and Milton compared and that in consequence of the kind appreciation expressed by the several members who took part in the Discussion and in Response to the expressed wish of our late lamented President I undertook the Task of enlarging yet farther on the Life of Shakespeare. – As you are all aware a serious Visitation of |[4]

---

[25] William Shakespeare, *The Works of Shakespear in Six Volumes*, ed. Alexander Pope (London, 1725), vol. 1, pp. ix–x and later editions.

[26] 'unless the members of [the] Society' and '[the] promise I have made', p. 58; 'his strange knowledge of [the] ways of Courts', p. 74.

sickness prevented my carrying out my Promise at the time; but I cannot but see in that a Divine Interposition since the long and otherwise tedious interim of my slow recovery was provided with an employment at once entertaining and useful. It was the opportunity for careful study thus Providentially afforded that has brought me to the strange pass wherein you now find me, — a Pervert, nay a Renegade to the Faith I have proclaimed and avowed before you all. I am prepared to hear from you as I unfold my strange and surprising story cries of disapproval and even of execration; but I pray of you to bear in mind that while I |[5] may be suspected of assailing a cherished and deeprooted Belief I am but expressing the just claim of all who would know the Truth; nay more, I do but point out sundry discoveries and seek for aid in carrying them to that stage when they shall no longer be doubts but <u>Certainties</u> proved by others more fit than I to adjudge on evidence.

I only ask that my material may be used by others regardless whence it came for it matters little who made the axe so that it cut. Also I am but the discoverer of doubts not the maker of them, and it is the province of an |[6] Association such as this to Investigate doubts even as a Judge and a Jury at Assize hear and examine into a cause be it never so unsavoury and the witnesses never so infamous. I am moved to making this petition since I know how even in this age of advancement and Intellect he who gives cause for doubting an old and established Belief may look for much and strong Opposition, even from those who adjudge themselves of Philosophic minds.

|[7] When I set out on my quest of knowledge wherewith to carry out my enquiry into the things that had made for the Genius of the Wonderful Poet who is the Ornament of English Literature I was stopped on the threshold by want of guidance. "Where (thought I) shall I find that which will give me light on the life of the man Shakespeare? I sought it in the many volumes that have of late fallen from the Press. During many weeks I sought diligently, reading and studying all that came my way as the result |[8] of enquiry of Booksellers and friends who by their taste for and

acquaintance with polite Literature were likely to have the knowledge I sought. I even at great inconvenience and expense proceeded on a journey to the town of Stratford on the Avon thinking not unreasoningly that I might in the birthplace of the Poet encounter those better fitted than others to inform me on matters appertaining to the personality of the Poet who has shedd [sic] lustre on their town; but everywhere was I met by a strange and perplexing silence, and I was driven to the conclusions that have prompted this Paper, namely that of |[9] the greatest Poet of England less is known touching him apart from his works than of many lesser Geniuses who lived and died hundreds of years before he arose.

It was the contemplation of this surprising discovery that set me on the path wherein I now stumble — though perhaps there are among you those who will think that I have wilfully strayed and that my search for light is but the natural consequence of my inability to and unwillingness to see it where it exists. I am not sufficiently puffed up in my own conceit to believe that that does not exist which I cannot discern, and that is why I have come to you |[10] to lay before you my difficulties and to ask your aid in resolving them.

The first aspect of the matter that occurred to me when I became awake to the immense ignorance of those whom I sought guidance from was the marvel that one who was filled with the vast store of world knowledge that Shakespeare had should have been unknown and that at a time when men of Parts stood like Saul Head and shoulders above their fellows. I first applied myself to discovering at what School or College Shakespeare got his learning and I was filled with |[11] amazement to discover that there is no sign left that he was ever at any School. At Stratford on Avon it is believed that he was taught at the School there, but no one has ever seen any record of this. All is but conjective. Certes: if he had been to a University his name and achievements if any would exist in the Books of his College as is the Case with all men who have won fame. Indeed it would be hard to find a man of note during the past Hundred or more years whose first steps on the road to knowledge could |[12] not be traced with ease. This point I apprehend to be of great importance inasmuch as the testimony of his works show Shakespeare to have been a man of more than usual learning, that is, more than was usual in a man brought up as he was in a place remote from sources of polite learning and certainly remote from such learning and knowledge of men and Cities as is revealed in the writings of the Poet who described Italy so well. On this point I may quote Pope as I did on the first occasion. Says he

"With regard to his learning, there is certainly a vast difference between learning and languages. How far he was ignorant |[13] of the latter I cannot determine, but it is plain he had much reading nor is it any great matter if a man has <learning> knowledge whether he has it from one language or another. Nothing is more evident than that he had a taste of English History, Mechanics, Ancient and modern History, Poetical learning & Mythology. We find him very knowing in the Customs, <rights> rites and manners of Antiquity. In Coriolanus and Julius Caesar not only the spirit but the manners of the Romans are exactly drawn, and still nicer distinction is shown between the Manners of the Romans in the time of the former and of the latter. The manners of other Nations, Ancient Egyptians, Venetians, French &c are drawn with equal propriety. Whatever |[14] object of Nature or branch of Science he either speaks of or describes it is always with competent if not extensive knowledge."

Now I must confess that although I as an admirer and Student of Shakespeare have ever been impressed by the vast variety of his knowledge it never struck me as strange that a man reared in a rural surrounding and away from sources of information should know so keenly the affairs not only of his own country but of Foreign countries both ancient and modern. Since I have devoted more time to the contemplation of the subject I have seen new light, and let me further confess that the |[15] author of this new Light was not myself but an ingenious gentleman of the neighbourhood of Stratford on Avon with whom I discussed the subject at great length on the occasion of my visit.

I have not his permission to make public his name since as he rightly pointed out the Townsfolk of Stratford on Avon have of late years taken such a vast pride in the connexion of the Poet with their town that they would bitterly resent any attempt to belittle the Poet. Therefore he has been for reasons of loyalty careful not to offend by making public his views which |[16] he expounded freely to me. I was much taken with his answer to my objection that Shakespeare being a genius would account for his vast knowledge. Nay, said he, Genius enables a man to apprehend quickly, but no genius would enable a man who had never seen a foreign country to describe it and its people as accurately as Shakespeare has described places and peoples he could never have seen. And least of all would it permit a man who had never seen ought but plain and simple folk to describe with accuracy the speech and manners of Courtiers, for it is a fact that Shakespeare describes the |[17] life at Courts even more completely than he does that of the Common people whence he sprung. I replied that Shakespeare might have learned much of these matters during his life in London, but my friend retorted very justly that being an Actor, one of a Profession held in great disrepute at that period he was scarcely likely to mix with the people habituated to the life of Courts. Even admitting that a few such might be among his acquaintances it was improbable that even the most observing of men could learn in the course of brief talks so much of the manners and spirit of others as Shakespeare revealed. ↓Then↓ |[18] he pointed out how notorious is the fact that the ill bred never acquire the habits thought and manners of those of a higher station, for however well they may simulate them they never fail to reveal their lowly origin. Even said he were it true that Genius does so much to teach and make a man adaptable to new surroundings the process of learning must be long, and if as seems probable Shakespeare was busily engaged in the arduous duties not only of managing his Theatre but in writing the numerous plays and poems ascribed to him he would not have the leisure to consort with |[19] people and at places where alone he could learn to know them as Shakespeare does. The habit of speech and writing is an art that takes long to acquire, and to one who did not take to it until comparatively late when ones early habits have been formed it w^d come so hard that the artificiality would reveal itself. Yet there is nothing in the writings of Shakespeare that does not argue the long and early training of the School-man, the Traveller and the associate of the Great and learned. Yet there is nothing in the known life of Shakespeare that shows he had any one of these qualities.

|[20] My Friend laid great stress upon a fact which I am persuaded must produce upon the minds of impartial men such as you much the same weight and surprise as it has on me. He pointed out that it is a strange and perplexing circumstance that of all the many thousand sheets of writing that must have gone to make up the plays and Poems of this marvellously industrious writer not a scrap is in existence, or at any rate has never been produced. Were it that Shakespeare lived even a Century earlier this w^d not be such matter for sur-prise but seeing that he flourished only 200 years agone it is indeed a cause for astonishment. Surely somewhere a page or two of his |[21] handwrit-ing would have escaped the general holocaust that w^d appear to have destroyed every vestige of his unparalleled industry as a producer of manuscript. My friend has calculated that even supposing he made few transcriptions he must have filled over a quarter of a million sheets of paper with his writ-ings. Then there is the strange fact that no evi-dence exists that this man of learning who must have read many hundreds of books never left a sin-gle volume, not even a note book or record of his business. True the fact that no literary writings remain might also account for the non-existence of other manuscript records. |[22] But the circum-stance, whatever the explanation is significant. My Friend has an explanation that is so startling that it is easy to understand his timidity in putting it forth boldly and I share his reticence. He goes so far as to suggest that the reason for the non-existence of the manuscripts is that they were the work of some other person who had good reason for concealing his connection with them and that they were either

destroyed purposely to conceal that Connection or were returned to the owner.

And now comes the very natural question, If these Plays and Poems were not the work of Shake-speare whose were they? ↓My↓

|[23] friend has a theory which he supports with much ingenuity that the real author of the Plays attributed to Shakespeare was Sir Francis Bacon, Lord Verulam of St Albans, and that the manuscripts were destroyed to conceal the fact that one so exalted in dignity should have descended to association with What was at that period the lowest form of literary art. He points out very many striking circumstances in support of this view, and notably the fact that very many of the scenes described in the Plays are of persons and places with which Bacon [had an] intimate connection [. . . like? . . .] |[24] with life at the English Court at the period when Bacon was at his zenith. Then it is a surprising circumstance that the Foreign countries and people described are all those of which we know Bacon had personal acquaintance while on the other hand there is no reason for believing that Shakespeare was ever out of his own country.

This briefly is the proposition that I have had the boldness to suggest [for] the discussion of this Association [. . . Havi]ng opened my case I shall [. . .]with the rules proceed [. . .]the details in a [. . .].

|[25] As I have frankly avowed I make no claim to being the Author of this very original and sur-prising Theory but am only the mouthpiece of another, I shall not further overload my disserta-tion by referring to him, feeling that he himself w^d prefer to be left in the modest position whi^h he has been content to occupy for some 20 years, as he told me is the time that has elapsed since he first began to think on his new view of the Author-ship of the Plays and Poems Commonly ascribed to Shakespeare. Let it suffice for me to say of him that he is a man of deep learning, College learned and blest by Providence with a Competency and condition that permit him to devote much |[26] time to the study and Contemplation of the high-est forms of literary excellence. It is also just that

I sho^d record my firm trust and Confidence in his good judgement and having devoted some time to the study of the Law he may be Considered to have that equipment for the impartial consideration of a matter such as this.

And now having made it clear that I am but a Recorder of Anothers words I would fulfil that office as justly as I can.

It is within the power of all of you to verify such arguments and illustrations as are drawn from the works of the Poet we are Considering, so I w^d ask you to |[27] let your memories wander over such of the Plays of Shakespear as reveal the close familiarity of the author with the life of the Courts of Queen Elizabeth and Henry VIII. It is reasonable to presume that one who like Bacon lived for years in [the] atmosphere<s> of Courts and was old enough to know men who were in the same or a corresponding position to his own in the days of Henry, would be well acquainted with the stories gossip and traditions that are reflected and revived in the "Merry Wives of Windsor." It is on the other hand hard to believe that a man in [the] position of Shakespeare – a member of a dishonorable calling – could have got that atmosphere so thoroughly. We know that |[28] it is easy to detect the difference between the narrative of one who records or repeats the experience of Ano.^r and one who narrates his own. The one lacks that filling in of little incidents that the other insists on often with tiresome disregard of [the] time and patience of his hearers. It is a thing difficult to describe, but plainly apparent when listened to. The careful reader of Shakespeare cannot fail to experience this feeling – a sense of reality, of assurance that the man who describes had seen and known that which he wrote. His is [the] correct and natural speech of the man of parts and of genteel education, and not the imitation of the clever actor.

|[29] The very circumstance of Bacon occupying so exalted a position wo^d be a just and reasonable cause for his concealment of his associatioⁿ with what the age contem^d. I confess that in the absence of another explanation it wo^d be hard to understand why any man capable of producing such triumphs of literary Genius sho^d be content to let the glory go to another, for it may be justly presumed that any author is proud of his work and there must be good reason for his neglecting to accept such credit as it may bring him. It is a point of much consideration that Bacon has proved himself the Master of every species of literary production save that of Poetry and [the] Dramatic, nor is it a strain upon our imagination to suppose that he would neglect a branch of Literature that has ever been most attractive to the cultured writer – the Poetic.

My Friend assures me of what is a most telling fact, though my own unfamiliarity with the life of Bacon does not permit me to support it – that the plays of Shakespeare were produced only at such times as Bacon's abstention from his public duties gave him leisure. He gave me a list of the order in which the Plays were produced and a corresponding list showing that Bacon was absent from Public life at those periods, but I have unfortunately mislaid that important record, so I do not ask you to |[31] attach great importance to it at least for the present. I hope later to present in a more substantial <form> and seriatim form the arguments and facts bearing on this very considerable evidence in support of this theory. At present I do not purpose more than a bare indication of the main points that will supply material for you to check and follow up the proposition for debate.

Perhaps [the] greatest might attaches to that part of [the] case wh my Friend has devoted most of his time to studying on the spot, and which shows how ill that part of the character wh: we know of Shakespeare fits in with what we might justly expect from what is shown of the Man by ↓his↓ |[32] writings. We have in the writer of [the] Plays – whoever he may have been, one who had not only been habituated to the Society of the learned and Polite, but himself one of the most learned men of his age, yet having by the pursuit of his calling in London amassed what was for that period Wealth, retiring to end his days not among people of culture and intelligence like himself, but among the simple and coarse folk of a small rural town. Nor is this strange taste this perversion of all that had been his true character – if his writings are an Index – explained <by> when we bear in |[33] Mind <great> how great was the animosity Shakespeare showed in his Writings toward that very class among whom he chose to end his days. His Plays abound with contemptuous remarks and allusions to the Common people. His sympathy and interest was ever <dear> with [the] great and Exalted. True it may be argued that it is a common thing for people who have made their fortunes away from their place of birth to return to their old friends; but it is strange that Shakespeare whose best years had been spent in a profitable and Literary vocation sho^d return to an obscure village offering no intellectual |[34] ↑allurement↑ and take up the very unromantic business of a Money lender and dealer in Malt. We can only liken it to Alexander the Great returning after his crowning triumphs to dig in the fields of his native district. I must confess that this circumstance weighs much with me, for I know as the result of years of experience and observation that it is the rarest thing for a man to abandon in his later years all interest and connection with the vocation where out he has made his fortune. For often such an one becomes tedious and wearisome in reviving stories of his |[35] past achievement in the field of Commerce. It is inconceivable to me that a mind such as the Author of "Hamlet" must have had could find solace in the company of small tradesmen and farmers. And what are we to offer in explanation of the fact that the greatest Literary character England has produced sh^d be unknown to his literary contemporaries; never be referred to by name in the letters and writings of those who must have known him. It is passing strange that Bacon who was so vastly appreciative of Literary genius and was contemporaneous has no allusion to the Works of a Master mind which could not but have excited in him an admiration that he was in the best ↓position↓ |[36] to mark his appreciation of by the exercise of his vast influence, and that at a period when Literary men sought the patronage of the great. It could not be jealousy if we are to accept the suggestion that Bacon did not indulge in Dramatic and Poetic composition. And again is it not a strange circumstance that this simple country bred Poet should have pursued exactly the same line of thought, the same studies of Foreign

tongues, the same Law, made the same journeyings and exhibited the same Patrician prejudices as the man whose life was spent ↓among↓ [*ends here*]

[55] April 1805

When at the opening Meeting of the Session I introduced on Alien Authority some very unusual − not to say startling views as to the Authorship of the Plays & Poems that have during 200 years been ↑regarded as↑ the unquestioned work of William Shakespeare of Stratford on the Avon I was neither surprised nor disappointed to find the proposal met with such scanty approval. Indeed I should have been more surprised had the reverse happened for I confess that the grounds on which you as members of a Learned Society were approached with a view to asking you to abandon the fixed opinions of a life, |[56] were not so greatly strong that I could justly feel agrieved [*sic*] by their rejection. It is a fair presentation against any change that the thing ↑it is↑ proposed so to alter has served well for two centuries or more and further that noone hath seen or given good reason for a change. But strongest justification of all I confess is the unbiden [or imbeden?] way wherein the new & strange theory is advanced, that is to say, on the authority not of the Author of the paper, but of a person who prefers to remain behind a veil. It was because of my knowledge of this weakness that I was so careful to avoid in my essay anything that might sound like the arrogance of assurance. I feel certain that all of you |[57] who heard me will agree that I erred much farther in undervaluing than in overvaluing such arguments as I used.

Regarding as I must the extreme weight of the objections raised on the Score of the Anonymous Authority I made it my affair as soon as Convenience permitted to <bring> take steps to produce − if not my Witness, at least some stronger support than I was able to offer on my first introduction of this subject. I am pleased to be able to Announce that I have received in response to my request the full permission of my Authority to give his name. But he put one Condition, i.e. that no printed announcement be made of his name |[58] without his Consent; and to that Condition I have subscribed on my own Authority. I have assured him that I would not disclose his name unless the members of [the] Society before whom I had made the first Announcement would without a single dissenter agree to be bound by my assurance. I therefore now, before proceeding with the declaration and amplification of the subject ask you to declare by vote and through our President that you assume <the> upon yourselves [the] responsibility of [the] Promise I have made.

|[59] On my arrival at the town of Stratford on the Avon in pursuit of the knowledge I needed for the better fulfilment of my undertaking I lost no time in making such enquiries as wo^d bring me into association with such as might prove of assistance in my quest. I laboured under the g^t disadvantage of having no Acquaint^{ce} there, but was fortunate in being directed to such a lodging at the House of Mr Jas Neame, a gentleman of somewhat broken Estate, but whose Cultivated mind has stood him in good stead in his adversity, since it has qualified him to serve as Instructor to the sons of such of the local gentry as have not yet |[60] thought fit to send them to a University. I need not press the fact that I found Mr Neame both well-nourished and informed as an Appreciative reader of Shakespeares writings, & even moved to a grateful enthusiasm by the fact that the Poet was of his own Town — for although not born in Stratford on the Avon Mr Neame has been a townsman of Shakespeares birthplace since early manhood and regards it as his Native Town.

I confided to him that I had Come in quest of material for a paper on the Life of the great Poet whereat he expressed his pleasure that one like myself, not a man of Letters, sho^d deem the subject |[61] of such moment as to persuade myself to undertake a Pilgrimage. We discoursed very fully on Shakespeare for some hours, but it was not till the next day that my Host remembered that there was in the neighbourhood a learned man who was known to have meditated writing a Life of Shakespeare. It may be, said he, that he wo^d be glad to oblige a fellow student, for he must have much material, for to my own knowlege he has been engaged on his Task many years.

Then he gave me his name as the Revd Jas Wilmot DD, the Rector of Barton on the Heath, a small village about six or seven miles north of |[62] Stratford on the Avon. He was then a very old man but vigorous beyond his years and a man held in g^t esteem by the gentry of the neighbourbood wherein he had dwelt he & his kinsfolk for many generations.

I sent forward by messenger a letter begging the favour of an audience and avowing my motive to profit by his vast knowledge on a subject wherein I was so solicitous for wisdom yet so ignorant. The Doctor sent an oral reply that he w^d be glad to receive me on the morrow to dine and converse, so hiring a horse because the badness of the road wo^d have made travel by wheel painful to me, I arrived at his Rectory House about noon, and was welcomed by my newfound |[63] host as chearfully as if an old friend, this amiability to strangers being a quality of his character which with others equally agreeable makes him much beloved & esteemed.

I found there certain gentry of the neighbourhood who though pleasant enough were plainly not of the kind who take pleasure in such matters as I had come to discuss, and the Doctor playfully rallied them on the subject saying they wo^d much rather feel the pants of a fat beast than the point of a literary jest, which from their later converse I can readily believe.

It was not until these bucolic guests had departed near 4 o'clock that the Doctor and I were able to approach the subject of our |[64] colloquy, and then we set to. I found that the account of Dr Wilmot's erudition given me by Mr Neame to have b[ee]n in no degree exaggerated. He had been a Fellow of Trinity College Cambridge and was distinguished as a Scholar in all matters pertaining to the Literature and Learning Sacred & Prophane of the period of the men of the Stuart days. It was this which had turned his thoughts towards the writings of Shakespeare and caused him to yield readily to an offer by a London Bookseller of Repute to write a life & Commentary upon Shakespeare to meet the great demand that has arisen during the late two decades for more knowledge on the matter of the greatest of all English writers. He showed me many books filled with |[65] his writings, and his Library though small contained, said he, all that was to be had to assist him in the work he had started with a light heart to compose. But, said he, although the material may seem great in bulk it is but so much chaff. This, said he, pointing to a few pages of manuscript, contains all that I have been able to glean, dig & gather of the life of the most prolific of Authors for some years, with the aid of the Bookseller, himself a student of the Poet he had sought for more, but the tale was but a few paltry lines that w^d compare but feebly with that |[66] which was known of the life of the least notable of Shakespeares fellows. Finding it necessary to abandon his project of a full & fitting life of the Poet he resolved to make amends by producing a new & full critical exposition of the plays & Poems. Twice or thrice when I had given expression to high praise of some evidence of the wide knowledge of men & things exhibited by Shakespeare he had observed "Marvelous indeed. Where did he obtain it?" On the last questioning I hesitated, for it had begun to arrest me that my own mind was not clear on this point. The Doctor perceiving my hesitation said Has it had never come to you that it was perplexing to resolve how a young |[67] man, country bred, with no advantage of <a> Scholarship or the Society of the learned & cultured could in the brief space of ten years or less acquire such worldly wisdom as co^d only come of Scholarship and the Society of the learned?

Then he proceeded to narrate how he had devoted years to <for> searching for some light on this great mystery, but had found only that the young man Shakespeare was at best a Country clown at the time he went to seek his fortune in London, that he c^d never have had any School learning, and that that fact would render it impossible that |[68] he could be received as a friend and equal by those of culture and breeding who alone could by their intercourse make up for the deficiencies of his youth. It was he observed, a strange fact that the writings of Shakespeare dealt most largely with persons & things which he by his humble origin and want of learning co^d never

have had Association. It wo^d have been reasonable to suppose that if Shakespeare had suddenly manifested capacity and taste for play writing that he wo^d have dealt with persons & things with which he was familiar. Yet it is strange that he shows less knowledge of matters appertaining to his own sphere in life than he does of |[69] Courts, Courtiers & Scholars and particularly Lawyers of whom he co^d have known nothing. Nor co^d the quickest intellect acquire in so brief a time the vast and intimate acquaintance with them that his writings reveal. It is easy said he for a man of quick perception to copy and emulate the ways of strangers, but howsoever good that Copy it must ever, as in the efforts of the Pupil to emulate the Copy set by the Schoolmaster, show signs of immaturity. There are no such signs in those comments of Shakespeare when dealing with Worldly knowledge or the speech and Conduct of the Great. The knowledge he shows of Law, Divinity, of |[70] Statesmanship was that of a Man of deep learning and familiarity with those subjects and not to be easily acquired by the mear [sic] association with those who had that knowledge. X I think every impartial mind must agree that it wo^d be a wonder approaching the miraculous if an ignorant country bred youth at a period when learning was so rare sho^d with no previous training acquire not only a familiarity with Greek, Latin, French Italian, but with the manners, speech and even the Secrets of the Statesmen of his own and past epochs.

It is I admit, one thing to doubt that Shakespeare wrote the Plays and Poems that bear his name, but quite |[71] another to fill the void by saying who did. Dr Wilmot does not venture so far as to say definitely that Sir Francis Bacon was the Author, but through his great knowledge of the works of that writer he is able to prepare a Cap that fits him amazingly.

I deeply regret that my own acquaintanceship with the Latin & Greek writers is not sufficient to permit me to follow much less check the numerous examples he gave me in proof of the extraordinary likeness in style that he has discovered between Shakespeare and Bacon, but there are Members of this Society so qualified, and I propose to them that they would find |[72] an agreeable source of play in following up all pursuit on these lines.

I am myself most interested with that aspect of [the] case which calls for an explanation of the immense difficulty of what the Doctor rightly calls the sudden advance in Culture and worldly knowledge displayed in [the] writings of a man who had had no opportunity of acquiring a tithe of the wisdom he displayed within a few years. Dr Wilmot rightly as I think points to one great and convincing piece of evidence that Shakespeare c^d not have written one part of the Play of Coriolanus Since it displays a knowledge of a medical fact not known during his life. In Act II Scene I will be found a reference to the |[73] Circulation of the Blood so accurate and opposed to the accepted belief current in the time of Shakespeare that it co^d not have been known to him, and it is significant that it sho^d occur in a Play that was published after his death. As our friend Dr Bayford will agree the discovery of Harvey was not made known until 1619 when Shakespeare had been dead Three years, and the Play of Coriolanus was not published till 1623, Four years after the Discovery of Harvey and Seven years after the death of Shakespeare.

This I say is a fact and Circumstance of vast import and by itself alone demands that any claim on behalf of the Authorship of Shakespeare sho^d |[74] be regarded as a subject for careful consideration and least of all sho^d we dismiss as [commonly?] such objections as are put forward by a man of such Intellectual preeminence as Dr Wilmott.

There is another very surprising piece of evidence which if it does not prove the hand of Bacon certainly calls for explanation. I have Commented on Shakespeares familiarity with people in a condition of Life very much above his own and his strange knowledge of [the] ways of Courts. We have a remarkable case in the Play "Loves Labour Lost." The scene of this Play is in Navarre and three Lords are |[75] Named as attending the King named Biron, Dumain and Longaville. It is certainly remarkable that these sho^d be the names of the ministers who were at that Court at the time when Anthony Bacon a Brother of Sir Francis Bacon was residing at that Court & writing

and Corresponding with Sir Francis. Dr Wilmot points out that Navarre at that period was so obscure and unknown to the general [public] that it is extremely improbable that a person in the position of Shakespeare – a man of no degree or standing in the Polite world – sho^d be aware of |[76] the constitution of a Foreign Court of such obscurity.

There are many similar instances to be met with by students who are familiar with the life of Bacon and Dr Wilmot is particularly informed on this important aspect of the business. He has also during many years and with the opportunity of local knowledge gleaned much information as to the times of Shakespeare and his contemporaries at Stratford on the Avon and though this information is necessarily but based on Tradition it is as good as much if not most of the informat^n |[77] whereon we rely for historic facts. Among his curious collection are notes as to certain odd characters living at or near Stratford on the Avon with whom Shakespeare must have been familiar and whom it is reasonable to suppose he wo^d have introduced into some of his Plays particularly his Comedies. There was for example a certain man of extreme ugliness and tallness who Blackmailed the Farmers under threat of bewitching their cattle. He was it appears held in such fear that no one dare say him nay, not even the Justices. And it is even said that they |[78] connived at the misdeeds of the Wizard in order to secure safety for themselves. Dr Wilmot is strongly of opinion that Shakespeare when safe in London from the possible malevolence of this creature wo^d not have refused [the] opportunity to introduce him by way of exposure of the Justices whom he had no occasion to love. There is also a local legend of that period that makes the Devil remove a church building, a legend of showers of cakes at Shrovetide with stories of men who were rendered cripples by the falling of these cakes. |[79] The neighbourhood abounds in Curious legends <for> of people and events, but Dr Wilmot has been unable during his long study of the writings of Shakespeare to discover any evidence that Shakespeare made use of his local knowledge which must have been great seeing that the only literary accomplishment of the people at that period co^d have been the narration of such stories. Shakespeare having an imaginative mind could hardly fail to have noted these stories and have drawn upon them when writing his Plays. |[80] Dr Wilmot has further examined the Records of the Corporation, the Church books and many private local collections of letters and documents which his position as a Clergyman gave him easy access to but not a scrap of evidence has come to light that tends to show that the Gentry of the District had heard of Shakespeare. He is of opinion that had his fame been such as it is supposed to have been local pride wo^d have induced some one of authority to have drawn attention to the credit won for the town by one of its Sons. There are frequent allusions to one Taylor who won some distinction as an armourer attached to the Court of Elizabeth and a |[81] Sea Captain who made a successful voyage to America was made much of by the townsfolk who knew him as a youth. At that period fame was not a transient thing by the very reason that people having little to talk of made much of such as they had.

Dr Wilmot has made great efforts to trace any evidence of books that might have belonged to Shakespeare. He argues that if Shakespeare had left books at his death they wo^d have soon passed for money from his poor and illiterate next of kin into the hands of the local gentry who alone purchased Books. He said he had |[82] covered himself with the dust of every private bookcase for 50 miles round, often coming upon rare and Ancient volumes but never one that bore any Sign of having been through the hands of a man like Shakespeare who must have devoured many hundreds of volumes.

Dr Wilmot makes another point of the circumstance that none of Shakespeares family were able to write and thinks it unlikely that any exception wo^d be made in the case of himself when a youth who had no prospect in life of ever |[83] having need of <the> an art that was confined to those who intended to employ it in their calling. He is of opinion that at the period when Shakespeare was in Stratford on the Avon not one person in a

hundred of the inhabitants were able to write and it is extremely improbable that the son of a Butcher sho^d prove an exception. The strange absence of any writing by Shakespeare is in the opinion of Dr Wilmot one of the strongest pieces of negative evidence <supo> in support of his belief that the Plays were written by another.

|[84] Dr Wilmot has made a calculation of the Books he has been able to trace as having been drawn upon by the writer of the Plays and Poems of Shakespeare and makes the number to be

English	153
French	21
Italian	4
Greek & Latin	18

|[85] Of names used in the Plays he has been able to trace only about a dozen that were known in Stratford on the Avon at the time of Shakespeare, and none of these were exclusively local. There are many names peculiar to the county of which he has a complete list; but none of them appear in Shakespeares plays – a very significant fact.

Neither are any purely local words or phrases met with, yet they |[86] were very numerous. It is impossible says Dr Wilmot to trace throughout the whole of the writings any sign of the origin of the author so far as it shows his connection with Stratford on the Avon.

|[87] <u>Coriolanus Page 126</u>
"True is it, my incorporate Friends" quoth he, "that I receive the Food at first which you do live upon"

Stratford on the Avon Names

Percy	Westerley	Seeby}
Bates	Jurers	Zeebie}
Jargy	Sendall	Jooser
Timmy}	Carlon	Weerdly
Timmie}	Guyton}	Weirdy
Seconders	Gylon}	
Nathan	Galesworth	
Margoty	Jamberswell	
Jontess		
Seccombe		

~

THE SPECTRE OF FEMALE SUFFRAGE IN *SHAKESPEARE'S REVELATIONS BY SHAKESPEARE'S SPIRIT*

TODD BORLIK

If I am getting ready to speak at length about ghosts, inheritance, and generations, generations of ghosts, which is to say about certain *others* who are not present, nor presently living . . . it is in the name of *justice*. Of justice where it is not yet, not yet *there* . . . It is necessary to speak *of the* ghost, indeed *to the* ghost and *with* it, from the moment that no ethics, no politics, whether revolutionary or not seems possible and thinkable and *just* . . . One can never distinguish between the future-to-come and the coming-back of a specter.

– Jacques Derrida, *Specters of Marx*[1]

Few dead authors can claim to be as prolific as William Shakespeare. Every decade or so an apocryphal play, anonymous poem or previously unknown painting is unveiled, for which evidence is marshalled pointing to a Shakespearian pedigree. Invariably, and the recent publication of *Double Falsehood* under the impress of the respected Arden Shakespeare Series is no exception, a brouhaha erupts over the authenticity of the work. Since Thomas Betterton's first visit to Stratford in the early eighteenth century, antiquarians have raided every attic and archive in Warwickshire in hopes of recovering even the faintest blips Shakespeare left on the documentary record. Yet when over 450 new poems filled with Shakespeare's personal confessions and assorted musings surfaced in 1919, the reaction was one of utter and contemptuous silence.

Most readers probably never made it past the title page:

Shakespeare's Revelations
by
Shakespeare's Spirit

Through the medium of his pen
SARAH TAYLOR SHATFORD
Dictated exactly as herein found.
No illiteracies, no obliterations,
Chargable to the Medium. My
Hand and seal hereon.
W.S. In spirit

Contact was first established, according to Shatford, in her New York apartment on 19 December 1916, when the Immortal Bard employed an ouija board to compose three new lyric meditations on the need for peace, the reality of heaven and the evils of war. Soon afterwards Shakespeare's Spirit dispensed with the board altogether and began to whisper a torrent of words directly into the right ear of this self-styled 'clairaudient'.

To be blunt, *Shakespeare's Revelations by Shakespeare's Spirit* ranks among the most bizarre and inept attempts at literary ventriloquism ever perpetrated.

Somewhere mortals hope to find a heaven
Where is no pain, no loss, and no despair;
Such promises have been to mortals given,
That when they 'die' they'll find this place
'somewhere'.[2]

Even Donald Foster, who sent shockwaves through the world of Shakespearian scholarship by

I would like to thank Tom Postlewait and Peter Holland for their feedback on early drafts of this article.

[1] Jacques Derrida, *Specters of Marx*, trans. Peggy Kamuf (New York, 1994), pp. xix, 38.
[2] Sarah Taylor Shatford, *Shakespeare's Revelations by Shakespeare's Spirit* (New York, 1919), p. 145. Hereafter cited in text.

identifying the W.S. who wrote the *Funeral Elegy* as none other than the Swan-of-Avon, has demurred as to the authenticity of these verses.[3] In the three follow-up books dictated by the Bard's Ghost – *For Jesus' Sake*, *Jesus' Teaching* and *My Proof of Immortality* – Shakespeare turns his talents to composing rather cloying prayers and to railing against the evils of birth-control, Darwinian evolution, and Freudian psychology.[4]

With their kooky occultism and reactionary Christianity couched in insipid verse, Shatford's books would seem to deserve to moulder away in dusty oblivion and Shakespeare's perturbed spirit allowed to rest in silence. Even today, when Shakespeare and Appropriation has become a thriving sub-sector of Shakespeare studies, no critic has made a serious examination of this text. Shatford's forgeries are mentioned, when at all, only as an eccentric specimen of Shakespeariana. In his magisterial survey of Shakespearian biography, Samuel Schoenbaum disposes of Shatford's contribution, in two pages with his usual snide erudition, classifying them under the heading 'Studies Mad and Bad'.[5] Helen Sword grants Shatford a mere one-sentence cameo in her otherwise astute chapter on Shakespeare and spiritualism.[6] As biography, Shatford's book is an utter sham; as poetry, it is for the most part ghastly drivel; as a cultural document, however, the *Revelations* is a tremendously complex and fascinating text that merits further attention than a bemused footnote.[7]

Since disproving the attribution of these poems need not detain us, the real question they provoke is why Shatford chose to pass her writings off as Shakespeare's in the first place. Did she believe that Shakespeare was uniquely qualified to deliver communiqués from beyond the grave because his most famous play, *Hamlet*, sanctioned such messages? Perhaps. But more likely she recognized that Shakespeare possesses a cultural cachet far surpassing any other writer in history. His status as 'The Greatest Writer of All Time' was being re-inscribed with a vengeance in 1916, the tercentenary of his death.[8] When Shatford claimed that Shakespeare's Spirit appeared in her parlour in 1916, his ghost must have truly seemed *hic et*

ubique. With the quadricentennial fast approaching, Shatford's response offers a timely reminder of how the commemorations of anniversary-year births and deaths perform periodic transfusions to

---

[3] Donald Foster, 'Commentary: In the Name of the Author', *New Literary History*, 33 (2002), 391.

[4] One might think that Shatford's mission to convert Shakespeare into a spiritual authority and upright Christian would shipwreck upon the innumerable bawdy passages. But she hits upon a clever expedient, going a step beyond Bowdler's expurgations to provide a posthumous authorial retraction: 'much of my work (Shakespeare) should be burned and future generations purified thereby' (p. 13).

[5] Samuel Schoenbaum, *Shakespeare's Lives* (Oxford, 1991), pp. 492–3.

[6] Helen Sword, *Ghost Writing Modernism* (Ithaca, 2002), p. 51.

[7] Far from an aberration, attempts to channel the playwright's spirit constitute a prominent motif in Shakespearean criticism. The seventeenth-century Cavalier playwright, William Davenant, was known to boast in his cups 'it seemed to him that he writt with the very spirit that did Shakespeare' (*Aubrey's Brief Lives*, ed. Oliver Lawson Dick, 3rd edn (London, 1958), p. 85). In 1755, Shakespeare's Ghost penned a review in a London theatre journal critiquing Garrick's performances of his work. Forty years later, he again spoke out in defence of his legacy against William-Henry Ireland and his forgeries (Schoenbaum, *Shakespeare's Lives*, p. 65). Not long after Shatford's works appeared, Hester Travers Smith, the daughter of famed biographer Edward Dowden, published *Psychic Messages from Oscar Wilde* (1923) in which Shakespeare's Spirit, under the sobriquet 'Old Mole,' also contributes some verses. In the 1940s the Anti-Stratfordian Percy Allen called upon Dowden's talents to summon the spirits of Bacon, Oxford and Shakespeare and interrogate them on the authorship question. Though serious interest in spiritualism has waned, Shakespeare as figurative revenant continues to stalk modern criticism. In *Shakespeare's Ghost Writers* (New York, 1987), Marjorie Garber illustrated the extent to which critical theory was the offspring of intellectual titans like Freud, Marx, Nietzsche, Derrida and de Man grappling with the Bard's ghost. Spiritualism might even be taken as an unconscious conceit under-propping New Historicism, given the infamous opening line of Stephen Greenblatt's *Shakespearean Negotiations*: 'I began with a desire to speak with the dead.'

[8] An overview of some of the tercentennial performances and publications, including a new edition of Sidney Lee's *Life* (which Shatford likely read), is given in 'New Year Plans of Publishers and Authors', *New York Times*, 2 January 1916. For a look at the political overtones of the celebration focusing on Israel Gollancz's 1916 *A Book of Homage to Shakespeare*, see Coppélia Kahn, 'Remembering Shakespeare Imperially: The 1916 Tercentenary', *Shakespeare Quarterly*, 52 (2001), 456–78.

the author function. Perhaps it is not a coincidence that 1916 was also the year Shatford published her first book of poems, *Birds of Passage*, written in her own voice. Disappointed by the scant attention paid to her literary labours, Shatford may very well have found the accolades piled upon the Immortal Bard somewhat galling. Rather than the mere raving of a delusional theosophist, her subsequent claim to have become Shakespeare's medium could thus be seen as a desperate yet strategic attempt to appropriate *the* voice of literary immortality. As the Bard's chosen scribe, Shatford acquired for herself an unparalleled authority, an authority of which women – as both writers and citizens (as we shall see) – were all too often allotted only a meagre ration.

A product of its time, *Shakespeare's Revelations* attests to the vogue for spiritualism in the early decades of the twentieth century, one that seduced many brilliant modernists from W. B. Yeats to Arthur Conan Doyle. Theosophy exerted a particularly hypnotic charm in the years during which Shatford allegedly channelled the playwright's ghost, when the First World War was decimating an entire generation.[9] In the Foreword, Shakespeare's Spirit inveighs against small-minded scientists who would discredit his efforts to comfort a 'torn world bereaved at loss'. Warfare comprises one of the central subjects ruminated upon in the poems, especially those composed after America officially entered the war in 1917. At one point Shakespeare dictates a letter to Arthur J. Balfour, the British War Commissioner to America, to express his support for the war effort, and obligingly rewrites the 'To be or not to be' soliloquy as a spiel for military recruitment. Enlisting soldiers need not fear death since 'God knows no soul that dies' (215). In the war poems, the collaboration between a dead English poet and an American medium becomes an apt platform for expressing Anglo-American solidarity. But the impending alliance between Britain and America was not the only political development on the horizon motivating Shatford's imposture.

Perhaps a better approach to understanding *Shakespeare's Revelations* would be to situate it in

the context of modernism, and its acute sense of a radical rupture with the aesthetic and political ideals of the past. In her incisive study of 'Necro-Bardolatry' Helen Sword shows that Shakespeare haunts many modernist manifestos and compares Joyce's treatment of the Bard as a literary father figure in *Ulysses* with Hester Dowden's attempt to emerge from the shadow of her own father by communicating directly with the ghost of Shakespeare himself.[10] Like Joyce and Dowden, Shatford, too, seeks to assert her own authority and originality by negotiating with the writer who incarnates the idea of the Western literary tradition; the result is a book that is in some ways staunchly conservative and in others radically progressive. Though *Shakespeare's Revelations* reveals nothing about Shakespeare the man, it is crammed with revelations on the nature of literary authority. In particular, it testifies to the enormous obstacle Shakespeare's legacy posed to women writers struggling to find a 'voice' at a time when women were fervently campaigning for a voice in the democratic process. In 1916, while the popular and literary press blazed with encomia to Shakespeare's genius, the American media were also following another story: the emergence of the suffragette movement as a viable political force.

Situating *Shakespeare's Revelations* in the context of the suffragette movement demands that we, if not exonerate, at least reconsider Shatford's sham. As Penny Farfan has remarked, early twentieth-century women writers were sometimes compelled to wrest authority from male authors by commenting on canonical texts,[11] or even resorting to outright forgery:

Though it has commonly been suggested that the door-slam at the end of *A Doll's House* signalled the advent

---

[9] Jenny Hazelgrove has recently challenged the widespread notion that the sudden popularity of spiritualism can be explained simply as a response to 'mass bereavement' from the First World War in *Spiritualism and British Society between the Wars* (Manchester, 2000), p. 6.

[10] Sword, *Ghost Writing Modernism*, p. 74.

[11] Even commenting on Shakespeare in print was no easy feat. Of the 166 tributes compiled in Israel Gollancz's 1916 anthology, *A Book of Homage to Shakespeare*, only five are by women writers.

of both modern drama and the woman's movement, Nora's forgery of her father's signature is in fact the act of transgression that sets the drama in motion; and indeed, authorship and authority are linked throughout Ibsen's 'women's plays', so that acts of writing [and] reading . . . signify the female protagonists' respective degree of critical engagement with hegemonic cultural texts that deny women status as authoritative subjects. Correspondingly, feminist artists in the late-nineteenth and early-twentieth centuries engaged with the texts of the culture at large through their relationships to the texts of the theatre, so that their responses to dramatic literature and theatrical practice in effect constituted feminist critical discourse.[12]

Like Nora forging her father's signature, Shatford's audacious scheme to pass off her poems as Shakespeare's reflects the widespread efforts of female authors, actresses, and activists to claim the status of authoritative subjects in charge of their literary and political destiny. Fittingly, Shakespeare's Spirit even makes a passing tribute to the actress Sarah Bernhardt: 'God kissed her in her cradle (Bernhardt) and never left her after' (20). Considering that Bernhardt had notoriously performed the role of Hamlet as a crypto-woman, she seems a model heroine for Shatford's own scheme to impersonate the Bard. The *Revelations*, in its clumsy attempt to channel Shakespeare's voice, can thus be recuperated as a kind of feminist discourse *avant la lettre*. Specifically, it provides an uncanny commentary on the struggle for female suffrage in the United States.

A bill to enfranchise women had first been brought before the House in 1915, the year before Shakespeare's Spirit began to frequent Shatford's parlour. The proposal was introduced, defeated and re-introduced four times over the next five years until the 19th Amendment was officially ratified in 1920 – just one year after Shatford's book reached print. The three-year period during which she composed the poems was thus a time of vociferous public debate over whether women deserved a voice in the political process. The battle had been particularly heated in Shatford's home state of New York, which was the birthplace of the suffragette movement. Thanks to vigorous campaigning, New York managed to anticipate the federal action by approving an amendment to the State Constitution in 1917 granting women the vote in local elections.[13] In October of that year, suffragette activists had picketed a meeting of Congress's Emergency War Session and been thrown in jail. Their subsequent trials, hunger strikes and indignant demands to be treated as political prisoners made headlines in all of the national newspapers.[14] Though she passed much of her time on a higher spiritual plane, Shatford was by no means oblivious to these developments. In a poem entitled 'Universal Suffrage', Shakespeare's Spirit proudly endorses the movement.

> When womenkind take up the spade and plow
> And till and reap the fields, and take up arms,
> There's wisdom in old England's parliament
> In giving sufferance, stilling its alarms!   (p. 179)

Here Shakespeare applauds the British government for passing a landmark bill in 1918 that granted voting rights to women, albeit with certain limitations: to be eligible, she had to be over the age of thirty and belong to a family who owned property with an annual rent over £5. As the stanza suggests, the war had played a decisive role in shifting public opinion behind the measure. The poem continues by arguing that the earth would be a gentler and virtually crime-free place if women wielded power.

> If men were made of metal just as fine
> And carried in their hearts one image true
> And loyal, moral, sane, as womankind,
> The courts of Justice would have less to do!
>
>   (p. 179)

Though Shakespeare never issues a formal apology for *The Taming of the Shrew*, he comes fairly close in this poem by crowing, 'The world has come to know its women's worth!'

Poetry was, naturally, a major weapon in the suffragettes' campaign to win over hearts and minds.

---

[12] Penny Farfan, *Women, Modernism, and Performance* (Cambridge, 2004), pp. 1–2.
[13] Ida H. Harper, *History of Woman Suffrage*, vols. 5 and 6 (Rochester, NY, 1922), vol. 5, p. 518.
[14] Linda Ford, *Iron-Jawed Angels: The Suffrage Militancy of the National Woman's Party: 1912–1920* (Boston, 1991), p. 174.

In Britain, Eva Gore-Booth and Sylvia Pankhurst wrote dozens of verses bemoaning the subjugation of women, and in 1908 Cicely Hamilton and Bessie Hatton co-founded the Woman Writer's Suffragette League whose members deployed their literary talents to whip up support for the cause.[15] In 1907 the League's president, Elizabeth Robins, wrote an agitprop drama entitled *Votes for Women*, which was staged by Shakespearian enthusiast Harley Granville-Barker at the Court Theatre in London.[16] Across the Atlantic, American women activists also composed countless poems and protest songs. Among the more illustrious contributors to this genre was Charlotte Perkins Gilman (of *Yellow Wallpaper* fame) who published a collection entitled *Suffrage Songs and Verses* decrying gender inequality and prophesying the birth of a new breed of woman:

> A mind where Reason ruleth over Duty,
> And Justice reigns with Love;
> A self-poised, royal soul, brave, wise and tender,
> No longer blind and dumb;
> A Human Being, of an unknown splendor,
> Is she who is to come![17]

Rather than mystical dispatches from the spirit world, several of Shatford's poems bear a conspicuous similarity to these suffragette verses. Though only one poem of the 450 or so in the *Revelations* explicitly addresses female suffrage, a sizeable number of them are directly or indirectly engaged with the contemporary debate over the moral and political status of women.[18]

Curiously, Shatford's interest in the woman question predates her interest in spiritualism. Her 1916 poetry collection, *Birds of Passage*, contains a poem entitled 'Marriage à la Suffrage' in which Shatford revises the standard wedding vows so the promise of political equality between the sexes redefines and ennobles the institution of marriage:

> Our country's laws the same
> Shall each defend!
> Equality shall reign for you, for me.[19]

Although there is no mention of Shakespeare or spiritualism in the 510-page tome, clearly

Shatford was inspired by suffragette verse well before she adopted the persona of the clairaudient. *Shakespeare's Revelations* contains what amounts to a sequel to this poem, entitled 'Marital Miseries', in which the Bard pours out his heart for widows and bereaved mothers who have lost loved ones in the war:

> Oh woman of the silent grief who bears
> Her sorrows as a faithful woman can,
> What have ye not withstood and suffered,
> For the perfidy and deceit of man.   (p. 377)

A principal cause of Shatford's grief, however, turns out to be men's veneration of silence as a cardinal female virtue.

> Silence a woman and she is you [sic] enemy. Let her loquacious tongue wag both ways and reprove her not, and, thinking herself admired she will be your friend. (pp. 12–13)

And yet, even as her poems valorize her own outspokenness and criticize men for infringing on a woman's right to express herself, Shatford's act of literary ventriloquism ironically re-inscribes female deference to the male author. Likewise, her views on gender are, by the standards of second-wave feminism, crudely essentialized. Shakespeare's Spirit tends to describe women as a 'gift' or 'a balm' (p. 178).

---

15 Glenda Norquay, *Voices and Votes: A Literary Anthology of the Suffragette Campaign* (Manchester, 1995), pp. 172–8; Deborah Tyler-Bennet, 'Suffrage and Poetry: Radical Women's Voices', in *The Women's Suffrage Movement: New Feminist Perspectives*, ed. Maroula Joannou and June Purvis (Manchester, 1998), pp. 117–26.

16 For more on Robins, see Sheila Stowell, *A Stage of Their Own: Feminist Playwrights of the Suffrage Era* (Manchester, 1992), pp. 9–39, and Farfan, *Women, Modernism, and Performance*, pp. 11–33. Robins was, incidentally, fascinated by Bernhardt's performance of Hamlet: 'On Seeing Bernhardt's Hamlet', *North American Review*, 171 (1900), 908–919.

17 Charlotte Perkins Gilman, *Suffrage Songs and Verses* (New York, 1911), p. 24.

18 The very first poem by Shakespeare's Spirit is, generously, a dedication to Shatford's mother, which opens with the words 'God made all women fair.'

19 Shatford, *Birds of Passage* (New York, 1916), p. 314.

A woman's smile and charm...
Makes a vaster happiness for creatures
Than anything on earth since Adam's fall!

(p. 178)

As keepers of the sacred hearth whose feminine 'charm' turns the home into another Eden, their raison d'être is defined primarily in relation to men. Yet Shatford's claim that women were the more spiritually advanced of the sexes was shared by many suffragettes and their allies in the theosophic community.

In addition to a love for poetry, a fascination with spiritualism was fairly widespread among feminist activists. Historian Ann Braude has documented the overlap between these movements, observing that both originated in upstate New York in the mid-nineteenth century and 'intertwined continually as they spread throughout the country. Not all feminists were Spiritualists, but all Spiritualists advocated women's rights, and women were in fact equal to men within Spiritualist practice, polity, and ideology.'[20] The monumental four-volume *The History of Woman Suffrage* edited by Elizabeth Cady Stanton, Susan B. Anthony, and Matilda J. Gage, commended Spiritualists as 'the only religious sect in the world . . . that has recognised the equality of woman'.[21] Stanton herself personally dabbled in theosophy and attended several séances with the British medium Annie Besant, a disciple of the renowned Madame Blavatsky.[22] Benjamin Fish Austin, the former principal of a prestigious girls school in Canada and the author of *On Woman* (which advocated female suffrage), was also the editor of a spiritualist journal (with the somewhat incongruous title *Reason*). He met with Shatford in Los Angeles in 1920 and actually wrote her a letter of support (appended to one of her later works) touting her authenticity as a medium.

A predilection for occult philosophy among advocates for women's rights was so well known it eventually became a target of parody. In H. G. Wells's novel *Ann Veronica* one high-minded suffragette expresses the same sort aversion to the carnal iterated in Shatford's poems: 'Bodies! Bodies! Horrible Things! We are souls. Love lies on a higher plain!'[23] Spiritualism no doubt appealed

to many in the movement as a strategic retreat to a discursive matrix where they wielded an equal if not superior authority to men. In response to the positivist philosophy then in its heyday, some early twentieth-century feminist thinkers began to promote an essentialized notion of women as more spiritually evolved beings. The *Revelations* abounds with panegyrics to the new enlightened woman, epitomized by none better than the medium herself, Sarah Taylor Shatford. Several times Shatford even attempts to reconcile this idea with the biblical account of creation in Genesis, as evident in this stanza where Shakespeare posits the following definition of WOMAN:

The last, most perfect work of the Almighty:
The equal of Himself in many ways:
The one gift that perfected His creation:
The only solace of man's earthly days.   (p. 29)

Shatford here portrays woman (and female theosophists in particular) as the paragon of animals: in her apprehension of divine mysteries how like a God, in the 'solace' her companionship provides how like the late Victorian ideal of 'the angel in the house'.[24] If her views now seem outdated,

---

[20] Anne Braude, *Radical Spirits: Spiritualism and Women's Rights in Nineteenth-Century America* (Boston, 1989), p. 3. A corollary to my argument can be found in John Kucich's investigation of the role of spiritualism in movements for abolition and Native American rights: *Ghostly Communion: Cross-Cultural Spiritualism in Nineteenth-Century American Literature* (Hanover, NH, 2004).

[21] *The History of Woman Suffrage*, ed. Elizabeth Cady Stanton, Susan B. Anthony and Matilda J. Gage, 4 vols. (Rochester, NY, 1881–1902), vol. 3, p. 350.

[22] Kathi Kern, '"Free Woman Is a Divine Being, the Savior of Mankind": Stanton's Exploration of Religion and Gender', in *Elizabeth Cady Stanton: Feminist As Thinker*, ed. Ellen Carol DuBois and Richard Candida Smith (New York, 2007), p. 101.

[23] H. G. Wells, *Ann Veronica* (New York, 1909), p. 176.

[24] While some feminists had begun to question the institution of marriage altogether, others sought to re-invent it so that the wife's role would no longer be to merely keep house and satisfy her husband's physical needs; instead she would minister to his spiritual life. This same mentality later prompts the Shakespeare's Spirit, guilt-stricken by his lascivious sonnets to the Fair Youth, to confess he should have known 'no

Shatford was ahead of her time in her insistence on the spiritual, emotional and political intelligence of women, and her tacit indignation at men's de facto monopoly on literary authority, which the figure of Shakespeare appears to embody.

In the epigraph for this article, Derrida ponders the necessity of speaking *with* the ghost in the name of social justice. The ghost, for Derrida, is not only a reminder of the persistence of the past within the present, but also a rhetorical method for annexing the future. In so many political diatribes, the ideal future-to-come arrives, paradoxically, in the guise of a revenant, the coming-back of a spectre. Derrida's insight makes it easy to see why suffragette activists found theosophy attractive. Shatford's text is an uncanny specimen of Derrida's 'hauntology'.[25] Just as Hamlet's ghost haunts, according to Derrida, Marx's invocation of the spectre in *The Communist Manifesto*, Shakespeare's ghost would stalk the women's suffrage movement. Despite the fact he wrote for a stage in which women were not permitted to perform, his plays had become, at the start of the twentieth century, a rare public forum in which women could speak and act out in ways that challenged not only Elizabethan, but also Edwardian gender norms. Shatford was not the only woman writer to speak with Shakespeare on behalf of her sex. Thanks to his complex portraits of witty and outspoken women, Shakespeare would prove to be a robust catalyst for first-wave feminism.

As 'The Greatest Writer of All Time' and the pre-eminent authority on the art of public speaking, Shakespeare was a logical model for suffragettes to imitate in their poems and lectures. He was also, however, a somewhat problematic one given the occasional outbursts of misogyny scattered throughout the plays. In a speech delivered before the New York legislature in 1854, Elizabeth Cady Stanton professed herself to be appalled by the way Petruccio treats Katherine as chattel. Milton, too, would come in for his share of criticism as someone 'who talked of liberty for men – but who held man to stand in God's place toward woman'.[26] But Shakespeare, due to his unrivalled reputation and the sheer diversity of

his representations of women, ultimately proved the more alluring ally. As the movement gained momentum there would be a concerted attempt to conscript Shakespeare into the suffragettes' camp. In 1892 Stanton no longer denounces Petruccio but reads the play of 'Titus and Andronicus' [sic] as a feminist fable, identifying the tongueless Lavinia as an icon for the status of women of the nineteenth century silenced by men who denied them the vote.[27] Suffragettes found another powerful voice in the Shakespearian actress, Ellen Terry, who, along with Elizabeth Robins, Cicely Hamilton and Edith Craig, was a member of the Actresses' Franchise League. Between 1910 and 1921, Terry travelled the globe delivering a lecture on 'Shakespeare's Triumphant Women', in which she hailed Rosalind, Beatrice and Portia as prototypes of the modern emancipated woman.[28] Striking a similar note (albeit in a lighter key), an anonymous reader of the *New York Times* in 1914 penned a letter to the editor which half-jestingly depicts Shakespeare as a proto-suffragette, citing a line from *Merry Wives of Windsor*: 'I'll exhibit a bill in Parliament for the putting down of men' (2.1.26–7).

Despite the reactionary streak that colours much of Shatford's text, the *Revelations* is, nonetheless, a remarkable feminist document. A decade after it was written Virginia Woolf would paraphrase an Anglican bishop who had opined 'cats do not go to heaven. Women cannot write the

---

man / Could serve as woman too!' (p. 88). Yet Shatford's status as a spokeswoman for modern feminism should not be taken too far. In a poem entitled 'The Woman God Forgot' she enlists Shakespeare to condemn what was sometimes referred to as a 'Boston marriage': God will apparently not remember to save the 'she who dwells without an [sic] he, – / The woman who bans man' (p. 165).

[25] Derrida, *Specters of Marx*, p. 10.

[26] *The History of Woman Suffrage*, vol. 1, p. 779.

[27] *The History of Woman Suffrage*, vol. 4, p. 190.

[28] Ellen Terry, *Four Lectures on Shakespeare*, ed. Christopher St John (New York, 1969), pp. 79–122. Terry's lecture received an enthusiastic review in the Suffragette magazine, *The Vote*, 4.92 (29 July 1911), 180. See Stowell, *A Stage of Their Own*, p. 41, and Farfan, *Women, Modernism, and Peformance*, p. 46.

plays of Shakespeare.'[29] Woolf then conducts her famous thought experiment of the playwright's gifted sister to illustrate why perhaps a woman could not have written *Hamlet* in 1600, while insinuating that circumstances had altered to the point that a modern woman can produce works of artistic genius. In her own eccentric fashion, Shatford with a pen and a parlour of her own had essentially set out to prove Woolf's thesis. Though few will agree she succeeded as Woolf did, the *Revelations* advances bold claims for the spiritual and literary prowess of women. Shatford repeatedly vaunts the fact that Shakespeare, after vetting all the specimens of humanity born after 1616, deemed her alone worthy to be his medium.

> To hold the hand of an immortal poet,
> And be his own through time, and yet not know it,
> This is the rare relationship of Her,
> Who shall one day set mortal-hearts astir.   (p. 96)

The epithet 'immortal', so commonly applied to Shakespeare, here acts as a sliding signifier – again subliminally fostering belief in the theosophists' spirit world. More importantly, this monomaniacal outburst asserts a spiritual kinship with the undying poet. No mere humble scribe, Shatford envisions herself as his equal, describing herself as holding hands with Shakespeare in language that suggests a marriage of souls. Repeatedly she compares herself to an instrument or harp plucked by his Spirit. From the fact that many of the poems so belabour the conceit that it is really, truly Shakespeare's ghost speaking – as if insisting on it ardently in four hundred poems might somehow erode our incredulity – one can infer that Shatford is not simply leeching off the playwright's reputation to promote spiritualism. She is exploiting the current fascination with spiritualism to appropriate the cultural authority of the Author par excellence. Shatford was not alone in this quest.

Nor was Shakespeare the only writer to have his eternal slumber disrupted. It is, I believe, highly significant that all five of the 'Alleged Posthumous Writings' examined by Arthur Conan Doyle in his spiritualist manifesto, *Edge of the Unknown*, were composed by female mediums speaking in the voice of renowned male authors.[30]

Shakespeare, of course, remained the most attractive quarry. If some feminists were content to cite Shakespeare simply as proof of their intelligence and education, Shatford goes a step further by proclaiming herself his spiritual and literary equal. By assuming Shakespeare's voice she grants herself an instant cultural authority that reinforces the idea that women possess the creative intelligence and moral capacity to participate in the democratic process. Feminist critics of Shakespeare, perhaps understandably put off by the zany occultism and doggerel verses, or simply unaware of this scarce publication, have neglected to comment on Shatford's work. The oversight is regrettable as the *Revelations* is a literal demonstration of Shakespeare's positively spectral presence in Anglophone culture.

---

[29] Virginia Woolf, *A Room of One's Own* (London, 1929), p. 48.

[30] Arthur Conan Doyle, *Edge of the Unknown* (New York, 1930). The five authors are Wilde, London, Lord Northcliffe, Dickens and Conrad. As previously mentioned, Hester Dowden also received dictations from Wilde's spirit. Northcliffe's messages were delivered to 'a lady living in a small town in New Zealand' (p. 147). Dickens and Conrad contacted a Mrs von Reuter from London, the former to express his disapproval of recent efforts to complete *Edwin Drood*, the latter to ask someone to finish his book on the Napoleonic era. The musings of Jack London's spirit, recorded by an unnamed 'woman of considerable culture' (p. 141), bear a striking similarity to Shatford's Shakespeare. The medium has the author recant aspects of his writings that conflict with spiritualist doctrines: in London's case, this meant retracting his materialist philosophy and Marxist-tinged assaults on religion.

SHAKESPEARE, WORD-COINING
AND THE *OED*

CHARLOTTE BREWER

We do not need to be historical lexicographers or experts in Early Modern English language to guess that Shakespeare was an experimenter with language. The inherent relish in combinations of words such as 'butt-end of a mother's blessing' (*Richard III*, 2.2.98), 'summer-seeming lust' (*Macbeth*, 4.3.87), 'fleshment of this dread exploit' (*Lear*, 2.2.120), 'To lip a wanton in a secure couch' (*Othello*, 4.1.70), 'paddling palms and pinching fingers . . . virginalling / Upon his palm' (*Winter's Tale*, 1.2.117, 127–8), 'underpeep her lids' (*Cymbeline*, 2.2.20), 'Come, you spirits . . . / unsex me here' (*Macbeth*, 1.5.39–40) – to take a random handful of many possible examples – is self-evident, and readily appreciated by any modern reader or auditor of his plays. And if we turn to what is still the most comprehensive authority on English vocabulary for the late sixteenth and early seventeenth centuries, the *Oxford English Dictionary*, in order to see just how innovative Shakespeare was in using such characteristically vivid words and compounds, we often find good justification for the intuition that Shakespeare was lexically creative. On countless occasions he is identified there either as the sole user of the locution in question, or as the first user, with other writers coming after him whether in conscious imitation or coincident adoption of the same usage. So, in the examples above, Shakespeare is uniquely cited for *summer-seeming, fleshment* and the verb *virginal* ('to tap with the fingers as on a virginal'); and he is recorded as the first person to use *butt-end* in a non-literal sense, *lip* to mean 'kiss', *paddle* to mean 'finger idly or playfully', *under-peep* and *unsex*. The more of Shakespeare's words one

looks up, the more one discovers that, time after time, according to the *OED*, he turns out to have used language in wholly individual ways or (more often) to have originated usages that subsequently became established in the language.

Pursuing individual words in this way is interesting but scarcely adds up to a general picture. Can we come up with a systematic and reliable estimate of how many new words Shakespeare contributed to the language? And what assumptions are involved in investigating this subject? This article attempts to begin to answer this question, in the first place by considering the character and reliability of our main investigative tool, the *OED* itself, and secondly by reviewing its successive record of a number of first citations from Shakespeare – i.e. words and usages recorded by *OED* as first used by this writer. The *OED* was originally compiled over the late nineteenth and early twentieth centuries, and although it was supplemented in the 1970s and 1980s with more modern vocabulary, its treatment of the sixteenth and seventeenth centuries remained unrevised and uncorrected until 2000.[1] In this year, online publication began of

---

[1] There are a handful of exceptions to this generalization, where the four Supplement volumes edited by R. W. Burchfield (Oxford, 1972–86) newly identified senses, current in twentieth-century English but unrecorded in *OED1*, whose history could now be traced back to earlier centuries and for which pre-nineteenth-century quotations were therefore inserted or rearranged. Often these were sexual senses, for example, *die* meaning 'experience a sexual orgasm', added to the Supplement in 1972, with Shakespeare cited as first user ('*Much Ado* iii. ii. 70 *Claudio*. Nay, but I know who

the first stages of an entirely new version of *OED*, often referred to as *OED3* (the previous two editions being *OED1*, published between 1884 and 1928, and *OED2*, published in 1989, which amalgamated *OED1* with supplementary twentieth-century vocabulary). At the time of writing (July 2011), *OED3* has revised about a third of the alphabet in a consecutive series of entries over letters *M* to *R*, along with revisions of many other entries dotted across the alphabet (amounting to around 30 per cent of the original dictionary in all). This means the majority of entries have remained unrevised from their original form, as composed 80–125 years ago. This present unevenness in *OED*'s treatment of Shakespeare – a mixture of Victorian and Edwardian scholarship, now out-of-date, with utterly recent research – places a series of important qualifications on any conclusions we draw from *OED*'s testimony. Not least, we need constantly to bear in mind that *OED*'s testimony is at present a 'moving picture', which will not stabilize for another couple of decades, when *OED3*, or the third edition of the dictionary, is relatively complete.

OED1 AND OED2

To try to unravel the complexities involved in assessing *OED*'s evidence on Shakespeare, we should begin by considering the circumstances under which the bulk of today's *OED* was compiled – that is, those prevailing in the 1880s to 1920s. The plan for constructing this enormously ambitious dictionary is simple enough to state: read through as many printed works as possible from 1150 to the recent past, extract quotations showing how words had been used from their earliest use to their latest, and deduce from these the senses of words as manifested throughout their history. Texts of all kinds were drawn upon to determine when a word came into the language and what it meant – novels, plays, poems, printed letters and diaries, histories, newspapers, works relating to arts, sciences, commerce, crafts and so on – but overall there was a strong literary bias. This was due partly

to the availability of literary texts for all periods, and partly to the predominant view in the late nineteenth century (as both earlier and later) that literature had an especially formative role in creating and preserving the nation's language – so that *OED*'s chief editor, James Murray, named 'all the great English writers of all ages' as his principal quotation sources.[2] Shakespeare's unparalleled cultural and literary status in British culture meant that the original *OED* editors (and their hundreds of volunteer readers) were extremely keen on recording his language in as much detail as possible, and almost every word attributed to him got into the dictionary one way or another, sometimes several times over. This virtually comprehensive treatment was not meted out to anyone else, of any period: however generous *OED* has been to other great writers who used language in singular ways (Milton, Carlyle, James Joyce), it has drawn the line at recording *all* their vocabulary. It follows, inevitably, that the original *OED* – and therefore the second edition too, since it didn't revise any of the pre-1800 material in *OED1* – will have exaggerated the significance and extent of Shakespeare's contribution to the language. New words of the period, if used by Shakespeare, would have been more likely to be found in his writing than in that of other authors who were less closely trawled by the lexicographers, and hence Shakespeare rather than anyone else will have been recorded by *OED* as their first user. And Shakespeare's once-off usages – made-up words which didn't catch on in the language

---

loues him . . . and in despight of all, dies for him. *Prince*. Shee shall be buried with her face vpwards'); *possess* to mean 'have sexual intercourse with (a woman)', added in 1982, with Shakespeare cited as second user ('*A.Y.L.* iv. i. 144 Now tell me how long you would haue her, after you haue possest her?'). On *OED1*'s occasional reluctance to specify sexual senses of words see further below, also Charlotte Brewer, *Treasure-House of the Language: The Living* OED (New Haven and London, 2007), pp. 203–5, 289 n35 (on *possess* and William Empson) and Lynda Mugglestone, '"Decent Reticence": Coarseness, Contraception, and the First Edition of the *OED*', *Dictionaries*, 28 (2007), 1–22.

[2] See further Charlotte Brewer, 'The Use of Literary Quotations in the *Oxford English Dictionary*', *Review of English Studies*, 61 (2010), 93–125.

for whatever reason (the technical term is *hapax legomena*, Greek for 'once-spoken') – will also have been more likely to get into *OED* than those created by other writers of the time. *1 Henry IV*, 2.1.76, for example, mentions 'Bourgomasters, and great Oneyers', and *oneyers* is a baffling word which the first *OED* editors didn't attempt to define, but which they entered in the dictionary nevertheless, noting that its 'origin and meaning [was] uncertain' (the first edition of *OED* included around 300 examples of such apparently unique usages in Shakespeare's writings).[3]

The unusualness of Shakespeare's treatment in the *OED* emerges when we look at comparative figures: with his 33,000-odd quotations (often several in the same entry) he is easily the most cited writer in the dictionary, towering over the next most cited author Walter Scott (just over 15,000 quotations), who is in turn followed by Milton and Chaucer (11–12,000), Dryden (8,000), Dickens (7,000) and Tennyson (6,000).[4] Almost certainly these figures tell us about the relative cultural importance of these writers in the late nineteenth-century rather than about their contribution to the language. But that is not to say that Shakespeare – and probably some of the other writers too, particularly Milton and Chaucer – have not influenced the language significantly. Given Shakespeare's unmatched cultural standing, his vocabulary and especially his phrases have often been picked up and reused just because they were his: *OED3* has recently revised the entry for *oneyer*, which it suggests means 'sheriff', and has found three twentieth-century examples of the word which allude to Shakespeare's original use, and there are many other such instances – *out-Herod Herod*, meaning to outdo Herod in cruelty and evil, for example.[5]

OED's pre-eminence as a record of English vocabulary means that its treatment of Shakespeare has been extraordinarily influential on histories of the language and on studies and editions of Shakespeare's works. Even when scholars have been able to turn up occasional omissions or errors in the *OED* – dialect words used by Shakespeare which antedate or postdate *OED*'s record, for example –

such studies have inevitably relied on *OED*'s unparalleled scholarship for the bulk of their analysis, whose validity they are obliged to take on trust.[6] And after the second edition was digitized in the 1990s, and became available in searchable electronic forms (a succession of CDs, with online access to the database 2000–2011), it became much easier to access its data on Shakespeare systematically and to begin to quantify this writer's recorded contribution to the language (according to the *OED*). The fullest treatment of such electronically accessible evidence was Crystal's analysis of *OED2* in *The Stories of English*. Searching an edition of the CD-Rom, he found that Shakespeare was recorded as the first person to use over 2,000 lexemes (a useful linguistic term which can be applied to the item of vocabulary recorded in the head word of a dictionary's entry, and avoids counting different

---

[3] As counted by David Crystal, *The Stories of English* (London, 2004), p. 320. Under *oneyers* *OED1* quoted the Folio text (reproduced here) but assigned the First Quarto date (1598). The Oxford Shakespeare emends 'Oneyers' (spelled thus in the Folio but 'Oneyres' in the First Quarto) to '"oyez"-ers (or, in 'original' spelling, 'Oiezres'), a conjectural nonce-word: see Stanley Wells and Gary Taylor, *William Shakespeare: A Textual Companion* (Oxford, 1987), p. 334.

[4] Figures derived from the online version of *OED2* available up to March 2011 which has now been removed from public access (see further below). See further Charlotte Brewer, 'Examining the *OED*' (http://oed.hertford.ox.ac.uk/main/). All *OED3* data quoted in this article is taken from the website www.oed.com, at latest in its June 2011 form, and elsewhere at the date indicated.

[5] For a list of Shakespearian phrases which have become standard modern idioms – 'to the manner born', 'more in sorrow than in anger', etc. – see Crystal, *Stories of English*, pp. 330–1.

[6] See Hilda M. Hulme, *Explorations in Shakespeare's Language: Some Problems of Lexical Meaning in the Dramatic Text* (London, 1962); Vivian Salmon, 'Some Functions of Shakespearian Word-Formation', *Shakespeare Survey 23* (Cambridge, 1970), pp. 13–26; Bryan A. Garner, 'Shakespeare's Latinate Neologisms', *Shakespeare Studies*, 15 (1982), 149–70. Qualifications and doubts about *OED*'s reliability in treating Shakespeare have from time to time been expressed, from W. S. Mackie, 'Shakespeare's English: And How Far It Can Be Investigated with the Help of The "New English Dictionary"', *Modern Language Review*, 31 (1936), 1–10, through to Jürgen Schäfer, *Documentation in the O.E.D: Shakespeare and Nashe as Test Cases* (Oxford and New York, 1980) and beyond.

forms of the same word, such as plurals or varying verb forms, twice over) – 2,079, to be precise, which he narrowed down to 2,035 after excluding malapropisms and nonsense words. Given that Shakespeare's entire recorded word stock comes to something under 20,000 lexemes (a figure extracted from Spevack's concordance of Shakespeare, whose total of 30,000 words used by Shakespeare counts different forms of the same lexeme and therefore needs to be shrunk down), this finding is, on the face of it, quite breathtaking: *OED*'s evidence suggests that one in every ten of Shakespeare's lexemes was a new usage, a proportion matched by no other post-medieval writer whose usage is intensively recorded in the *OED*.[7] Similarly, no other post-medieval writer is recorded as having so many new usages in absolute terms either. The nearest contenders from his own period seem to be Philemon Holland, with around 1,000 first citations, i.e. half as many – though as a translator from classical sources he is a special case – and the prose writers Thomas Browne and Henry More (*c*.830 and 690 respectively), both of whom use a much more academic and difficult lexis than Shakespeare. Ben Jonson (*c*.560) and Sidney (*c*.400) trail way behind as his nearest contemporary poetic and/or play-writing rivals, and the most lexically productive writers (according to *OED*) from later periods – Milton (*c*.650), Carlyle (*c*.565), Coleridge (*c*.520) – cannot come close to Shakespeare's record either.[8]

But how far can we trust the *OED*'s witness here? As we might expect, many complicating considerations come into play (fully recognized by Crystal). First of all, as already indicated, *OED*'s preferences for citing Shakespeare, along with the reduced number of sixteenth- and seventeenth-century texts available over the time *OED1* was compiled, will have resulted in the dictionary favouring Shakespeare over his contemporaries. Fresh reading in other works of the time may reveal – in fact, *does* reveal – that Shakespeare was not the first person to use some of these 2,000-odd lexemes attributed to him in *OED2*. So *newsmonger*, for example, can be found a few years earlier in Thomas Nashe, as can *merited, protractive,*

reprieve, repure, roguery, sportive – all words revised since Crystal's analysis by *OED3*, which in many other cases too has managed to antedate *OED*'s record quite considerably – *ratcatcher*, first recorded by *OED* in *Romeo and Juliet* (3.1.74) in 1592, has now been found in an earlier text of 1565; *ransomless* (*Titus Andronicus*, 1.1.274) has now been antedated with an example in Lydgate's *Troyyes Book* of 1425; *melted* in the sense 'liquefied by heat' (*Henry V*, 3.5.50), has been pushed back not just to the fifteenth century but is also now illustrated with a quotation from an Old English text. (In fact, however widely you read, you can never be sure that you have found the first example of a word – it is always potentially antedatable, so that many of such new findings by *OED3* may themselves be superseded). Secondly, even when fresh reading does not unearth preceding examples, we have to be careful about what we deduce from Shakespeare (or anyone else) being recorded as originator of a word. The *OED* confines itself to printed sources, so it is quite possible that a 'new' word will have been in oral use for some time before being used by Shakespeare, and one can see that newly current vocabulary would have had a special value for his audience, just as the use of buzzwords or innovative coinages do in newspapers, journals, cinema, television, plays, novels, and poetry today. As Crystal pointed out, Shakespeare is unlikely to have invented the word *clack-dish* (for a bowl with a lid that beggars 'clacked' to encourage donations) – a word also recorded in Middleton only five years later – and surely cannot have been the first person to swear '*sBlood* ('by God's blood'), though his plays are cited as first, second and third use respectively (in 1598, 1599 and 1604), or to use the term *madame* to refer to French women (*Henry V*, 3.5.28: 'By Faith and Honor, Our Madames

---

7 *OED2* attributes around 2,040 first usages to Chaucer, but its record on Middle English will only have been able to draw on editions of Middle English texts available at the end of the nineteenth century, then dominated by Chaucer.

8 Quotation figures from *OED2 Online* (March 2011).

mock at vs').[9] More individualistic coinages would seem to be unusual words such as *conceptious, rejoindure, reprobance* (and many others). But here again we may pause. These words look unusual not least because they have not survived today. We can guess that Shakespeare may have made them up, but can we really say that he thereby contributed to the language, given that such words have never achieved general currency (and in the case of *conceptious* and other such *hapax legomena* may have got into the *OED* only because they were used by Shakespeare)?[10] The problem of identifying a really successful neologizer begins to make itself plain: the more successful the word coiner – i.e. the faster that coinages are seized on and enthusiastically adopted by the rest of us – the harder it is to be sure that one particular person has been sole originator of a specific usage (two or more people may have coined a word simultaneously).

To tackle some of these considerations, and in particular to take into account *OED*'s likely bias in citing Shakespeare over his contemporaries, Crystal devised an ingenious method of sorting and discriminating among Shakespeare's neologisms as recorded by the *OED*. Studying the dictionary record for each of the 2,035 items, he compared the rate at which the word (or sense) was subsequently recorded from another source – the reasoning being that if a word was recorded again within a few years of Shakespeare's usage (as in *clack-dish* and *'sBlood* above, also *'slid* 'God's eyelid', *ajax* 'privy', etc.), then Shakespeare was a lot less likely to have been its originator than if the word didn't turn up again for several decades or so. The results of this analysis are most interesting: 640-odd lexemes had a presence in the language within twenty-five years of Shakespeare first using them; a further 1,100 or so, first used by Shakespeare, are recorded again only after twenty-five years. It would seem fairly safe to say that those in the latter category were invented by Shakespeare, but that a reasonable proportion – say a half? – of the first category may have been in the process of entering the language independently. So Crystal suggests we add up as follows: 300 lexemes recorded in *OED* only in Shakespeare (so presumably invented by him),

plus 1,100-odd first recorded in Shakespeare but not used again for a significant time, plus 320-odd (i.e. half of 640) that Shakespeare may have made up and which were swiftly adopted by his contemporaries. That gives us a total of around 1,700 or so lexemes altogether – still a really enormous number for a single individual to have made up.

This is a most attractive analysis. The problem with it, unfortunately, is that it places too much weight on *OED*'s consistent recording of quotation evidence. Sometimes the lexicographers chose to print two or more quotations from the same decade to illustrate a particular usage, and sometimes they left a gap of several decades or more at a time – the official policy was to have only one quotation per century! It is hard to explain this inconsistency except as the result of different editors working over many years; but certainly it is unwise, even today, to treat *OED* as a corpus which registers frequency of use, and can therefore be used to measure how quickly a usage becomes adopted in the language. This means that some of the neologisms attributed to Shakespeare and not recorded in the dictionary again over the next twenty-five years – and therefore eligible, according to Crystal's analysis, to be regarded as bona fide inventions by Shakespeare – may well have existed in other late fifteenth- or early sixteenth-century sources known to the lexicographers, but that they chose (for cultural, i.e. non-linguistic reasons) to print the Shakespeare quotation in the *OED* rather than the 'non-Shakespeare' quotation.[11]

---

[9] Entries, dates and quotations for all these terms are cited from *OED2* (unchanged from *OED1*).

[10] *conceptious* (*Timon of Athens* 4.3.188) is recorded only in Shakespeare; *rejoindure* (*Troilus and Cressida* 4.4.35) is subsequently recorded in 1650 and 1749; *reprobance* (*Othello* 5.2.216) was used again in 1878 by Swinburne, in an echo of *Othello*.

[11] Three examples will variously illustrate the point. *OED1* cited *Measure for Measure*, dated 1603, as the first example for *merited* ('you may most vprighteously do a poor wronged Lady a merited benefit'; 3.1.202), followed by a quotation of 1797 (Frances Burney's diary). *OED3* has now antedated the Shakespeare quotation with one of 1593 from Nashe and one of 1602 from Marston's *Antonio and Mellida* (1602), the latter work quoted 775 times elsewhere in *OED1*. Did

So was Crystal too generous with his figure of 1,700 Shakespearian neologisms? In fact, as he himself observes, he may not have been generous enough. This is because the pre-2011 searchtools in the *OED* identified only one quotation in a dictionary entry as being the first recorded evidence of use, regardless of how many senses the entry had in total. But under the verb *ruin*, recorded from 1585, Shakespeare is listed as the first user (in 1613) of four of its sixteen distinct senses; under the adjective *unfledged*, he is the first to use three of its four distinct senses; he is the first to use the noun *water-fly* both literally (*Antony and Cleopatra*, 5.2.58) and metaphorically (*Hamlet*, 5.2.84, of Osric: 'Dost know this water-fly?', also *Troilus and Cressida*, 5.1.30, 'how the world is pestered with such waterflies'); and so on.[12] This looks like lexical creativity of quite a significant sort – but we can only discover it if we happen to look the word up and count the Shakespeare quotations manually, as *OED2* electronic searches did not identify the *ruin* examples at all, and found only the *Hamlet* instances (since they are the earliest ones) of *unfledged* and *water-fly*. These examples can be replicated many times over, and any casual browsing of the *OED* will reveal that Shakespeare pops up again and again as the first quoted example of individual senses identified in an entry, if not the oldest sense itself. Using existing words in new ways may well be just as significant a form of lexical innovation as inventing a word in its entirety – indeed this technique is arguably more significant, since it develops the resources of the language in directly communicative ways. Many of Shakespeare's most striking examples of inventive language use do just that: so *Antony and Cleopatra*, 2.2.234, 'She made great Cæsar lay his sword to bed. / He ploughed her, and she cropped', supplies the *OED* entries for *plough* and *crop* with their first examples of specific senses for each of these verbs, although the verbs themselves had both been long established in the language before Shakespeare chose to exploit them in this way.[13] But it was impossible to extract any quantitative information about such instances of Shakespeare's lexical innovation from the electronic tools with which *OED2* was supplied.

OED3

All this is changing as the new version of *OED* gathers steam. This long overdue revision of the first edition has so far covered around a third of the alphabet, and is transforming every element of the dictionary as it goes – identification of headword, etymology, pronunciation, recording of spelling variants, selection and dating of quotations, and finally the analysis of the history and development of a word's senses which the newly amassed and configured quotations enable.[14] A sustained and expanding reading programme is fuelling many of the changes taking place, and it is this which promises to contextualize, and (one might expect?) to correct, *OED*'s representation of Shakespeare. Since the first edition was completed, our knowledge of sixteenth- and seventeenth-century language and literature has greatly increased: there are many more editions in print, of a far wider range of sources (scientific, technical, historical, colloquial) than there were a hundred years ago, and consequently much more linguistic material, especially non-literary material, available against which to measure and assess Shakespeare's vocabulary use.

---

the *OED1* lexicographers simply miss the Marston usage, or did they choose to cite Shakespeare's example rather than Marston's, despite the fact Marston's was earlier, and that printing both quotations would have given a better idea of the word's currency? By contrast, *OED3* will always print the first example of usage found but they may then, just like *OED1*, skip many years before printing a second example, even if they know that such exists. Thus in revising *majestically*, *OED3* antedate Shakespeare's first quotation of 1596 (*1 Henry IV*, 2.4.359) with one from another author of 1595. The next quotation they print for this word is 1670 – so they drop the Shakespeare quotation altogether. Yet in revising *movingly*, *OED3* print the original Shakespeare quotation *and* put in two others of around the same date. If one were to try to infer relative rates of usage from these entries one would be misguided.

12 *OED* quotes no other metaphorical examples of *water-fly*.

13 This characteristic has often been observed; see e.g. N. F. Blake, *Shakespeare's Language: An Introduction* (London, 1983), pp. 51–5.

14 See John Simpson, Edmund Weiner and Philip Durkin, 'The *Oxford English Dictionary* Today', *Transactions of the Philological Society*, 102 (2004), 335–81; Brewer, *Treasure-House of the Language*, pp. 237–55.

In particular, searchable databases (Early English Books Online, Eighteenth Century Collections Online, and many collections of nineteenth- and twentieth-century texts) now give the lexicographers access to a much more sizeable proportion of the material that issued from printing presses from 1485 onwards. At the same time, substantial research has been carried out both on Shakespeare's language (in numerous scholarly editions of his plays, for example) and on Early Modern English more generally, and the lexicographers have been able to draw upon this scholarship as well as upon the raw lexical material available in all these newly visible texts. So is Shakespeare's reputation as linguistic innovator par excellence in the English language going to be sustained, increased or undermined?

The answer is that Shakespeare's key role in the language is certainly being sustained – and in some respects at least, it is being increased; though a number of qualifications and explanations apply to this verdict, not least in view of the fact the *OED3*'s revision is unfinished and that its character seems to be changing as it moves through the alphabet. What follows is an attempt to create as much clarity as possible at this stage.

A caveat is in order first of all, rendered necessary by substantial changes which have taken place on the *OED Online* website since research for this article was originally carried out. To discover what *OED3* is doing to *OED2* in its record of Shakespeare (or of any other author or text, or indeed any other respect one can think of), we need to compare like with like: to take the entries that *OED3* has revised and measure them systematically against the equivalent ones in *OED2* so as to contrast and compare. But on 1 April 2011 the dictionary's publisher Oxford University Press took down the separate electronic version of *OED2* from its website, making such searches impossible. This is most regrettable. The data presented here is therefore taken from comparisons of the two versions which were by good fortune made prior to that event, in November 2010. As *OED3*'s revisions continue to progress through the alphabet, it will be impossible to measure and assess its treatment of *OED2* in any

comparable way in future, unless OUP decides to re-introduce an electronically searchable version of *OED2* which can be set against *OED3*.[15]

The March 2011 removal of *OED2* from public access was part and parcel of a general make-over and relaunch of *OED Online*, most of which took place in December 2010. This included a striking new feature which allows one, for the first time ever, to count up all the times an author is cited as the first user of an individual *sense* of a word. The innovation addresses the point made at the end of the previous section of this article, that the limited electronic searches possible on *OED2* will have significantly under-rated the degree to which the first edition represents Shakespeare as lexically innovative. Shakespeare's total of first uses of a sense, at December 2010, was 8,207, an immense figure – especially bearing in mind, as noted before, that his total word- (or lexeme-) stock was around 20,000. The nearest post-medieval competitor was again the translator Philemon Holland, but this time, rather than having half Shakespeare's total – as was the case when we were counting first use of a *word* – he had less than a third: he was cited 2,456 times as first user of a *sense*. Holland was followed in ever-decreasing proportions by Walter Scott (2,267), Milton (2,149) and Carlyle (1,830).[16] While Shakespeare's markedly increased pre-eminence in lexical productivity in this respect looks very significant, we must remember that these figures told us about *OED2* plus *OED3*. That is, they are derived from a state of *OED* which merged the *unrevised* three-quarters of the dictionary with the *revised* one quarter as it stood at the end of 2010. Perhaps Shakespeare's count of new senses is going

---

15 OUP are most helpful in their responses to individual researchers and have kindly made a downloadable form of *OED2* available to individual users on request. However this has primitive search tools and cannot be used to conduct the systematic searches required (e.g. of first quotations) to make comparisons between the second and third editions. On the relaunched website one can also click through, entry by entry, to the previous (*OED2* version): but the *OED2* pages are not cumulatively searchable.

16 Jonson came in at 1,742, Spenser at 1,709, Browne at 1,640.

down in the revision, as the lexicographers discover new texts and realize Shakespeare was not as original as *OED1* thought he was? Very probably, since the same search conducted six months later (June 2011), after two further tranches of revised entries have been substituted for the original *OED2* ones, yielded a lower result: 8,181.[17] We cannot be sure, however, without comparing *OED3*'s rate of recording new senses in Shakespeare with *OED2*'s rate. But we cannot now make this comparison, since the electronically searchable *OED2* has disappeared from the website (and no figures are available from past searches since, as already explained, the previous *OED2* search tools could not identify the number of individual new senses for which an author was responsible).

So in trying to see what *OED3* has done and is doing with Shakespeare, the relaunched website does not help us. Instead, we must turn to data collected before the old website disappeared. In its previous incarnation as in its new, *OED3* was alphabetically merged with *OED2*, so the only practicable way to compare like for like in November 2010 was to take the alphabetically consecutive set of entries revised at that date, viz. *M–rotness*. This yielded a substantial sample, comprising the majority of entries then revised, and also covering the entire period over which *OED3* had then been engaged in working on its revision (i.e. the mid-1990s to the end of September 2010).

The result was unambiguously clear. In *OED2*, there were 406 entries over this stretch of the alphabet which recorded Shakespeare as first user of its head-word, compared with 263 entries over the same stretch in *OED3*. Of course this is a substantial decrease, telling us that as *OED3* revisited the work of its parent dictionary up to November 2010, in the light of all the new lexical evidence then available, it was finding earlier usages for around *one third* of the lexemes previously attributed to Shakespeare. Considerable as the reduction seems, however, it continues to leave Shakespeare preeminent among English language word-coiners. Assuming that the sample is a trustworthy predictor of the likely results of the revision as a whole, it suggests that by the time *OED3* is complete,

Shakespeare's outline total of 2,000-odd new lexemes will have dropped to 1,200 or so — a total which is still unmatched by any other postmedieval writer recorded in the dictionary.[18]

We can get a more nuanced picture of the changes *OED3* is making in the lexical record by looking at individual instances within the sample. I scrutinized the first quotations over *M–misprized* and *R–reportingly* respectively, which comprise 50 consecutive items each at either end of the sample, and I also dipped into other entries across the sample where it was clear that interesting revisions had been made. As we would expect, there are many instances where *OED3* has managed to find earlier examples of usage whose first use was previously attributed to Shakespeare. In my two sub-samples 17 out of the 50 items (or 34%) had been antedated in the *M–misprized* range (henceforth ss1), and 26 out of 50 (or 52%) in the *R–reportingly* range (henceforth ss2). That the latter alphabet stretch yielded more than the former may be explained by the fact that the revisers have been able to use a much greater range of databases in the recent stretches of their revision than when they started off their work, in the mid 1990s. It is likely that this higher rate of antedating will continue or increase as the revision progresses over the next few years.

Some of *OED3*'s antedatings seem more significant than others, however. Five items in ss1, and six in ss2, had disappeared from the list of Shakespeare

---

[17] The June 2011 totals of first citations for use of an individual sense by the other competitive authors are 2,470 for Holland, 2,248 for Scott, 2,142 for Milton, and 1,819 for Carlyle.

[18] One of the current *OED* lexicographers has recently reviewed *OED3*'s treatment of Shakespeare over a smaller sample of words attributed to Shakespeare as first user in *OED2* (117 words over *P–Ra*), to show that nearly half have been antedated in *OED3*; see Giles Goodland, 'Shakespeare's First Citations in the *OED*', in *Stylistics and Shakespeare's Language*, ed. Mireille Ravassat and Jonathan Culpeper (London and New York, 2011), pp. 8–33. In the same collection, Ward E. Y. Elliott and Robert J. Valenza are similarly sceptical about attributing spectacular lexical productivity to Shakespeare ('Shakespeare's Vocabulary: Did it Dwarf All Others?', pp. 34–57).

first usages not because of *OED3*'s new lexical discoveries but because of its new dating policy. Plays
cited from the first folio, published in 1623, are now
dated 'a1616' (i.e. 'before 1616', Shakespeare's date
of death), which means that a number of *OED2*'s
first citations have been demoted on arguably artificial grounds. *OED2* quoted *Julius Caesar*, which
it dated 1601, as the first example of *majestic* ('the
Maiesticke world'),[19] and in fact a Swiss doctor,
Thomas Platter, recorded seeing a production of
this play in 1599. But since the first copy of *Julius
Caesar* is the 1623 Folio, in *OED3* Shakespeare
has been pipped to the post for this word by a
1606 quotation from *Bien Venue* by John Davies of
Hereford. Similarly, first citations from *Two Gentlemen of Verona*, commonly reckoned Shakespeare's
first play and thought to have been written around
1590, have in a number of cases surrendered their
status to other texts, also cited in *OED2*, since the
play is now dated a1616 (*OED3* takes the Oxford
Shakespeare edition as its base text, though like its
predecessors it looks in detail at textual variants and
prints in original spelling).

One is not surprised to find *OED3* reducing Shakespeare's count of neologisms. It is more
startling to discover that the revision is simultaneously recording additional, newly identified neologisms. Somewhat disappointingly, many of these (3
out of 8 in ss1, and 4 out of 6 in ss2) turn out to be
due to methodological changes: *OED3*'s splitting a
first-edition entry into two or more new entries,
throwing into new prominence a quotation previously tucked away in a sub-entry. So the verb *re*
(used in *Romeo and Juliet* as a humorous threat to a
musician, 4.4.144–5: 'I will carry no crotchets. I'll
re you, I'll fa you'), recorded by the first edition
under the noun *re*, now has its own separate entry.
In both editions it is the only quotation for this
sense, but could not be electronically identified as
such in *OED2* owing to the limited search tools
available for this edition. The same is true, one
way or another, of *mappery*, previously recorded
under *map*, *made-up* ('consummate', as in *Timon of
Athens*, 5.1.97: 'he's a made-up villain', previously
recorded under the past participle *made*), *memento
mori* (*1 Henry IV*, 3.3.29–30), *repairing* ('opposites of

such repairing nature', *First Part of the Contention*,
5.5.27), *reprobance* (*Othello*, 5.2.216), and *reeling ripe*
(*Tempest*, 5.1.282). Much more potentially exciting
is the handful of freshly identified new usages that
have come to light under *OED3*'s newly directed
search beam.

In my samples, ss1 and ss2, three newly identified additions to Shakespeare's total of neologisms
(*masoned*, *meditance* and *misbecomingly*) come from
Two Noble Kinsmen and are therefore straightforwardly explained by a change of authorship attribution: *Two Noble Kinsmen* had been read and cited by
OED1 (which recorded twenty-seven first usages
from its pages in all, of which seven were from
the alphabet range *M–rotness*) but had not ascribed
its quotations to Shakespeare.[20] A tiny handful
of other additions resuscitate textual variants, e.g.
related in *Hamlet* 1.2.38, a first Quarto (1603) reading usually rejected by editors, which antedates
the record for this word by one year.[21] Others
are due to some form of re-analysis of Shakespeare's language. The *OED* records and defines
'words', but the decision as to what constitutes a
word is not a straightforward one. When Adonis,
in Shakespeare's early poem *Venus and Adonis* (413),
described love as a 'life in death', the first edition
lexicographers understood the phrase syntactically,
but their modern-day descendants have construed
it as a single word, anticipating Coleridge's Ancient
Mariner's 'The Night-mare LIFE-IN-DEATH was
she' and thus meriting its own entry, with Shakespeare recorded as first user and Coleridge as second. Whether they will do the same with other

---

[19] Followed by *The Tempest* (1610: 'a most maiestice vision')
then by a quotation of 1664 from John Evelyn.

[20] The other first usages identified by *OED1* in *Two Noble
Kinsmen* over *M–rotness* were *operance*, *out-breast*, *piglike* and
port (verb), to which *OED3* has now added *precipitance*, first
use of which had in *OED1* been attributed to Milton.

[21] The Q1 reading is not noticed by Wells and Taylor, *Textual
Companion*; cf. p. 402 on editorial policy in recording Q1
variants and also pp. 403, 411. A study of which Shakespeare
editions were used, with what results, by *OED1* editors,
and how *OED* documentation was influenced by Schmidt's
Shakespeare Lexicon and Quotation Dictionary (to which *OED1*
editorial notes often refer), would be most useful.

Shakespearian formulations remains to be seen (the hyphenation of Elizabethan compositors is too variable to be relied upon to solve such puzzles). Unsurprisingly, given the length of time over which the original dictionary was compiled, as well as the difficulties of texts and interpretation, the first edition was not always consistent in its decisions about how and whether to treat such terms: *crafty-sick* (*2 Henry IV* Induction, 37), *heady-rash* (*Comedy of Errors*, 5.1.217) and *honest-true* (*Merchant of Venice*, 3.4.46) were recognized as compound adjectives but not *heavy-sad* (*Richard II*, 2.2.30) or *secret-false* (*Comedy of Errors*, 3.2.15);[22] *Cymbeline*'s 'our hence-going' (3.2.63) and *Winter's Tale*'s 'my hence departure' (1.2.450) were recorded but not *Macbeth*'s 'my here-remain' (4.3.149). Whether Shakespeare's rate of lexical innovation in total rises or falls will be in part determined by *OED3*'s policies on such items (all untreated in the revision as yet).

Shakespeare's fondness for macaronic language – dovetailing one language with another, and foreign borrowings of various sorts – may also push up his neologism count in *OED3*, owing to its more generous interpretation of what counts as an English word: so *manus*, as in Holofernes's use ('when he was a babe, a child, a shrimp, / Thus did he [*sc.* Hercules] strangle serpents in his *manus*', *Love's Labour's Lost*, 5.2.584–5), is now regarded as a bona-fide English word and placed at the head of the new entry, and the same may also happen to *canus*, two lines above (though as yet *quoniam*, two lines below, is untreated: the criterion for inclusion may be whether or not the word has been found in other sources, as is the case with *manus* but not *quoniam*). In my minutely examined set of two sub-samples, only the lexeme *merry-meeting* emerged as a Shakespeare first usage genuinely missed out by the first edition.[23] Defined as 'a festive or convivial gathering', *OED1* had recorded this compound from the 1650s onwards, entirely overlooking *Richard III*'s 'Our stern alarums changed to merry meetings' (1.1.7). Other examples outside the sub-samples include *pleading*, newly spotted in *Venus and Adonis* (217): 'Impatience chokes her pleading tongue', whose record in *OED2* began with a quotation

from Shelley of 1818, and *plebs*, as in *Titus Andronicus*, 4.3.92, 'I am going with my pigeons to the tribunal plebs', which *OED* had previously dated 1835 onwards.

As the figure of 8,207 quoted above would suggest, there is a profusion of examples of *senses* for which Shakespeare is newly identified as first user. Random dipping suggests that a renewed scrutiny of compounds and phrases may contribute importantly to his enhanced role as language-originator. *OED1* had Shakespeare down as the first person to use three examples of *never*, yoked with a participle to make an adjective – 'What never-dying honour hath he got' (*1 Henry IV*, 3.2.106); 'That hand shall burn in never-quenching fire' (*Richard II*, 5.5.108); 'If you refuse your aid / In this so never-needed help' (*Coriolanus*, 5.1.33–4) – but had only dated *never-conquered* from 1631. *OED3* has now turned up 'Vnder that colour am I come to scale Thy neuer conquered Fort', from *Lucrece* (481–2), and though it has antedated *never-dying* (found in a pre-Shakespearian text of 1567) it should also add *never-resting* (as in 'never-resting time leads summer on', Sonnet 5, line 5) and *never-surfeited* ('the never surfeited sea', *Tempest*, 3.3.55) to the list of Shakespearian first usages for *never-* combinations.[24]

---

[22] *OED1* quoted the *Comedy of Errors* example of *secret* but did not identify the adjective as attached to 'false'. On compound forms see further Salmon, 'Shakespearian Word-Formation'.

[23] Of the 14 new *OED3* first citations found in ss1 and ss2, 9 were attributable to reorganizing existing entries in *OED1/2*, *related* and *merry-meeting* are discussed above, and *masoned*, *meditance*, *misbecomingly* were recorded from *Two Noble Kinsmen* but not ascribed to Shakespeare.

[24] *OED3* presently dates *never-resting* from a1637 and has no entry at all for *never-surfeited* (though the *Tempest* quotation turns up twice elsewhere in the dictionary, under *belch* and *surfeited*). Curiously, *never-resting* was listed in Schmidt's Shakespeare *Lexicon* of 1874, on which the *OED1* lexicographers were presumably heavily reliant. Shakespeare also uses *never-daunted* (*2 Henry IV*, 1.1.110), *never-ending* (*Lucrece* 935), *never-erring* (*Two Noble Kinsmen*, 1.2.114), *never-heard-of* (*Titus Andronicus*, 2.3.285) and *never-withering* (*Cymbeline*, 5.5.192). *OED1* had recorded *never-daunted* from 1590 but missed the other three, dating *never-ending* from 1667 (*Paradise Lost*), *never-erring* from 1679, and *never-heard-of* from 1600 (*Titus* was dated 1588 or 1594 by *OED1*, so its example

Substantial date-shifting has also taken place: the *OED* Supplement of 1976 had noticed a specific sense of 'new' as applied to snow and ice ('recently formed snow deposit'), which it found only from 1860, but now *OED3* is able to quote *Romeo and Juliet*, 3.2.19: 'thou wilt lie upon the wings of night / Whiter than new snow on a raven's back' (the next quotation is from Thomson's *Seasons*); *pretty fellow* ('fop, dandy'), first recorded in *The Tatler* of 1709, is now documented from 1600 with *Merchant of Venice*, 3.4.63: 'When we are both accoutered like young men, ile proue the prettier fellow of the two'; *night owl*, in the sense 'A person who is up or active late at night' – another definition newly identified in the Supplement of 1976, with quotations from 1847 onwards – is now quoted from *Lucrece*, 'The doue sleeps fast that this night Owle will catch.' All three of these examples may raise dissenting or at least questioning eyebrows: to interpret *night owl* as *OED3* suggests, for example, simply spells out (as a dictionary arguably need not do) the metaphor already present in *dove*.

Sometimes, as with the *never-* compounds, the revision suggests a pattern, indicating either a locution apparently favoured by Shakespeare or (as in the following example) a sensitivity to colloquial speech otherwise unrecorded for centuries. So *OED3* now credits Shakespeare with first use of the familiar form of address *old son* (*Richard II*, 5.3.144: 'Come my old son. I pray God make thee new') – the next example being Dickens[25] – thus matching his similarly first recorded use (in *OED1*) of both *old lad* and *old boy*. Shakespeare retains his first quotation in *OED3* for *old lad* (*Titus Andronicus*, 4.2.120: 'Looke how the blacke slave smiles vpon the father, As who should say, olde Lad, I am thine owne'), a term not used in print again – according to *OED3* – until 1977 (in James Herriot's *Vets might Fly*), but owing to dating conventions has lost *old boy* to Jonson: Tucca, in Jonson's *Poetaster*, of 1602 – 'Thou shalt impart the wine, Old boy' – now trumps Toby Belch's 'Did she see thee the while, old boy, tell me that' (3.2.7), since *Twelfth Night* in *OED3* is dated, in accordance with the new policy, to *a*1616.[26]

A different type of example, likely to proliferate, is due to changed social mores over the last hundred years. *OED3* has now spelled out the specifically sexual senses of *medlar* ('The female genitals', 'a prostitute'), for which *Romeo and Juliet* supplies the first example (2.1.36) 'Now will he sit under a medlar tree, And wish his mistress were that kind of fruite, As maids call medlars, when they laugh alone') and *Measure for Measure* the second (4.3.167, 'They would . . . haue married me to the rotten Medler'),[27] and it has identified a new sense of the noun *mark*, namely 'The female genitals, regarded as a sexual target', for which *Love's Labour's Lost* furnishes the first quotation: 'A mark saies my Lady. Let the mark haue a prick in't, to meate at, if it may be' (4.1.130). Studies such as Gordon Williams's *Glossary of Shakespeare's Sexual Language* (1997) and Jonathan Green's huge *Dictionary of Slang* (2010), the latter supplementing and often antedating *OED* in its collections of historical quotations, may guide the *OED* lexicographers to many more instances of sexual metaphor shied away from in previous editions.[28]

---

of *never-heard-of* should have antedated the 1600 one). *OED3* has now found an earlier instance of *never-ending* (?1592), and of *never-erring* (1589), while it quotes *never-heard-of* from *Edmund Ironside*, which it dates *a*1594 (as compared with *OED3*'s 1594 date for *Titus*). All in all, the evidence suggests that Shakespeare's use of these adjectival *never*-compounds – eleven in all – was innovative and distinctive. Disappointingly, *OED* has not attempted to tackle Ulysses's tricky 'Never's my day, and then a kiss of you' (*Troilus and Cressida*, 4.6.53).

25 Like *new snow* and *night owl*, *old son* only entered the *OED* in one of the Supplement volumes (1982), with quotations from 1916 onwards.

26 Cf. *my boy*, newly attested from the 1594 First Quarto text of *Titus Andronicus*, 4.1.109 '(Ay, that's my boy! Thy father hath full oft For his ungrateful country done the like') – significantly antedating *OED*'s previous record of this term, from 1902 onwards. (*OED3*'s entry begins with a quotation from Gascoigne of 1575, referring to a dog). *Old lad* also occurs in *1 Henry IV*, 1.2.41: 'As the honey of Hybla, my old lad of the castle'.

27 Three further seventeenth-century quotations are supplied.

28 Green identifies many sexual senses, unrecognized by *OED*, in Shakespeare's language, furnishing them with an historical lineage in subsequent or previous writers. The dictionary

How can we use all this information in ways that help us better understand Shakespeare's works? One technique, under-exploited in Shakespeare criticism so far, is to compare rates of neologisms in the different plays – though we must also keep an eye on how that neologism rate is changing between *OED2* and *OED3* as the revisers (re-)read texts by Shakespeare's contemporaries and predecessors. *Hamlet*, for example, is recorded as having 23 neologisms in *OED2* over *M–rotness*, compared with 18 in *OED3*; by contrast *Love's Labour's Lost* has 33 neologisms in this same stretch in *OED2*, now reduced to 14 in *OED3*. Whatever conclusions may be ultimately drawn from those figures and proportions (and comparison is immediately beset with complications the moment one looks at the detail, since as before *OED3* has found new neologisms in this alphabet range while antedating *OED2*'s examples), and however risky it is to use them to predict the direction of travel of *OED3*'s revision of the remaining three-quarters of the alphabet, it is easy to see that *OED3* is changing the lexical landscape so far as Shakespeare is concerned. Another technique would be to attempt to discriminate between the value and significance of different neologisms. This may look promising but is not straightforward. Are coinages like *miching malicho*, *mobled*, *imploratory*, *primy* (all from *Hamlet*, all recently revised in *OED3* and confirmed in their status as neologisms) more significant, because more unfamiliar to us today, than the new verb *pander* (also from *Hamlet*)? Or should it be the other way round?

Setting detail aside, is it still justifiable to claim Shakespeare as more influential on the English language than any other writer? All the evidence presented in this essay would confirm that this is so – and that his status is resoundingly affirmed by the most up-to-date lexical scholarship. A substantial doubt persists, however, largely because Shakespeare remains the writer most intensely quoted in the *OED*, and almost certainly the most intensely scrutinized one too. The new *OED* website tells us he has just over 1% of its total number of quotations, but anyone who looks up sets of non-scientific or non-technical words systematically in

the dictionary will be struck by his unmatched dominance of entry after entry. To take, as a random sample, the words in the sentence beginning this paragraph: he is quoted once in the *OED2* entry for *setting* (for first usage of a sense), 5 times in that for *aside* (once for first usage), 20 times for the pronoun *it* (4 times for first usage), 6 times in the entry for the adverb *still* (3 for first usage), twice for the verb *claim* (once for first usage), 11 times for *as* (once for first usage), 12 times for the adjective *more* (once for first usage), 3 times for *English* (once for first usage), 7 times for *language* (3 times for first usage). The suspicion must remain that a portion of Shakespeare's influence, as recorded by the *OED*, is the preference for Shakespeare as a quotation source independently of the lexical value (or contribution) of his language. Since *OED3* is rarely discarding Shakespeare quotations as it revises, this influence is hardly likely to fall off – indeed, so far *OED3* is increasing the number of Shakespeare quotations, not reducing them.[29]

It is not surprising that a writer whose usage is subjected to such meticulous and exhaustive scrutiny will be found to have originated many new senses. The witty coinage *uncolted*, for example, created by Prince Harry in retorting to Falstaff's rebuke when his horse has been taken away (Falstaff: 'What a plague mean ye to colt ['trick'] me thus?' Prince: 'Thou liest, thou art not colted, thou art uncolted'; *1 Henry IV*, 2.2.37), which puns on *colt* to mean 'horse' as well as 'trick', has not since been used in the language; it would almost

---

is not yet electronically searchable but a list kindly sent me by the editor includes *beef* ('vagina': *Measure for Measure*, 3.1.323: 'Troth, sir, she hath eaten up all her beef, and she is herself in the tub'), *lance* ('penis', *Troilus and Cressida*, 1.3.280: 'The Grecian dames are sunburnt and not worth / The splinter of a lance'), *lap* ('vagina', *1 Henry IV*, 3.1.224: 'Come, Kate, thou art perfect in lying down. / Come, quick, quick, that I may lay my head in thy lap'), and many more examples.

[29] A count kindly carried out for me by *OED* staff on 29 July 2010 recorded an increase of 597 Shakespeare quotations over the alphabet range *M–rococoesque*. Of these new quotations 20 were from *Two Noble Kinsmen* (so newly attributed to Shakespeare rather than, necessarily, new to the *OED*).

certainly have gone unrecorded by *OED* if found in another writer's work, not least because it is clearly motivated by the immediate verbal and physical context (Falstaff's use of the verb *colt* in connection with his losing his horse). The same is true of many of the words and phrases already mentioned, such as *night owl* or *new snow*, newly admitted to the dictionary owing to fresh semantic analysis. Shakespeare's language continues to be scoured for puns and metaphors which it is always ready to yield, but which other poetic texts too might easily offer were they similarly examined: all poetry works through connotative suggestion, and its language will therefore surrender to many possible interpretations.[30] If *OED3* were to decide, as it progresses through the alphabet, to scrutinize the language of other writers with the unremitting intensity and thoroughness it has applied to Shakespeare, it is certainly not beyond the bounds of possibility that his record might be challenged.

---

[30] See e.g. *OED3*'s fine distinctions of sense giving Shakespeare newly identified first quotations s.v *pent* (adjective, sense 2), *move* (verb, 25h), *obscure* (verb, 2b).

SHAKESPEARE'S NEW WORDS

ROBERT N. WATSON

I. A WORD-WAR WON

That Shakespeare invented – or, at least, successfully promoted – more new English words than anyone else in history is a truth universally acknowledged.[1] But how and why did he do that? An otherwise superb exploration of 'Some Functions of Shakespearean Word-Formation' identifies many technical purposes – 'To ensure coincidence of metrical and lexical stress',[2] for example – but does not attend to what were surely important functions for Shakespeare: to draw paying customers to his plays by appealing to their need for cutting-edge social tools, and to articulate the complexities of mood and consciousness that are a hallmark of his literary achievement. This double business – selling to a wide popular audience, while also serving a fathomless interior intellect – may seem contradictory, but the combination is surely essential to Shakespeare's greatness.

The shared life of the vernacular, granted new range and prestige by the printing press, was extended by the English stage; as poets, notably Spenser, reached backward for archaisms, perhaps to appeal to a fading aristocratic economy of patronage, playwrights pushed ahead. The Elizabethan theatre was a 'knowledge marketplace',[3] and a key commodity in that market was lexical. English was evolving rapidly, not only because print and trade were accelerating exchange with other languages (to which English has always been unusually receptive) and because social and technological revolutions were requiring new terminologies, but also because the disappearance of grammatical inflections in English allowed words to be easily converted from one part of speech to another, as Shakespeare liked to do, by what linguists call 'zero derivation'[4] and Renaissance rhetoricians called *anthimeria*. As I have argued

[1] Like the precept that opens *Pride and Prejudice*, this is more assumed than proven. Others such as Thomas Nashe and (as a translator) Philemon Holland were also aggressive minters of words. But (unlike associated claims about the supposedly extraordinary size of Shakespeare's overall vocabulary) it is probably true, even if – because the *OED* was overly reliant on Shakespeare from its inception – the numbers are inflated by over-reliance on the *OED*; see Jürgen Schäfer, *Documentation in the O.E.D.* (Oxford: Clarendon, 1980), and Jonathan Culpeper and Phoebe Clapham, 'The Borrowing of Classical and Romance Words into English: A Study Based on the Electronic OED', *International Journal of Corpus Linguistics*, 1 (1996), 199–218. I will therefore be using several databases – most often, *Literature Online* (http://lion.chadwyck.com) and *EEBO* – to determine how new or uncommon certain words or usages probably were among other writers in Shakespeare's lifetime.
[2] Vivian Salmon, 'Some Functions of Shakespearean Word-Formation', in *A Reader in the Language of Shakespearean Drama*, ed. Vivian Salmon and Edwina Burness (Amsterdam, 1987), pp. 193–206, esp. p. 198.
[3] Paul Yachnin, *Stage-Wrights: Shakespeare, Jonson, Middleton, and the Making of Theatrical Value* (Philadelphia, 1997), ch. 4.
[4] Geoffrey Hughes, *A History of English Words* (New Jersey, 2000), p. 149, notes that such conversion becomes 'possible only after the loss of grammatical inflections'. Much of that loss is already evident in Middle English, but the Elizabethans were well situated to exploit its near completion. See also Dick Leith, *A Social History of English*, 2nd edn (New York, 1997), p. 99: 'the loss of distinctive form for, say, nouns and verbs, could offer enormous syntactic possibilities for a poet and dramatist like Shakespeare'.

elsewhere, these new products were manufactured and sold by Shakespeare and his rival playwrights.[5]

Scholarship on Elizabethan and Jacobean drama has almost entirely overlooked a battle for market-share in this sideline business of compiling and vending a fresh verbal repertoire at a moment when social advancement and humiliation were extraordinarily dependent on mastering the latest tricks of speech. Thomas Dekker's satiric 1609 'How a Gallant should behave himselfe in a Play-house' observed that 'The *Theater* is your Poets Royal-Exchange, upon which, their Muses (ye are now turnd to Merchants) meeting, barter away that light commodity of words . . . your *Groundling*, and *Gallery Commoner* buyes his sport by the penny, and, like a *Hagler*, is glad to utter it againe by retailing.' That upwardly mobile commoner is advised to 'hoord up the finest play-scraps you can get' in order to banter with gentlewomen.[6] In *The Return from Parnassus* (1599), Gullio values poets, especially Shakespeare, because he can 'take some of there wordes and applie them to mine owne matters by a scholasticall imitation'. Public-theatre dramatists therefore sought, like Chapman's Monsieur D'Olive, to 'have my chamber the Rende-vous of all good wits, the shoppe of good wordes, the Mint of good jests, an Ordinary of fine discourse' (1606; sig, B2v). Even if these lexical innovations were only a small bonus added to the main value of the product, the competitive situation helps to explain several quirks in the so-called War of the Theatres (involving Jonson, Marston and others), as well as the 'inkhorn controversy', the publishing of the first English dictionaries and guides to the 'canting' languages of London's criminal underclass, and the economic language persistently associated with the literary 'coining' of new English words.

Costard's folly in mistaking 'remuneration' and 'guerdon' for units of money in *Love's Labour's Lost* (3.1.128–68) contains an element of insight.[7] In the alchemy of the Shakespearian stage, words could be turned to gold – could be coined.[8] Calling Don Armado's neologisms 'fire-new words' (1.1.176) suggests a minting of metal.[9] Mocking pretentious verbal mannerisms to the paying audience at such a verbally mannered play as *Love's*

Labour's Lost was an audacious act of brinkman-ship on Shakespeare's part, calculated to let him

---

5 Robert N. Watson, 'Coining Words on the Elizabethan and Jacobean Stage', *Philological Quarterly*, 88 (2009), 49–75, analyses the purveying of the rapidly evolving English language to a partly illiterate audience at theatres around 1600. The topic united a philological approach with what is commonly supposed its opposite, namely, an emphasis on drama's social functions and material conditions. The thesis was that dramatists competed in a theatrical economy that was partly a store of new words and a demonstration of new ways of assembling them. The basic rules of marketing applied: convince customers that your product can turn them into suave, sexy and successful people, whereas competing products would sicken or humiliate them. Groundlings must have wondered whether they too would seem heroic, or instead simply ridiculous, if they mimicked Tamburlaine's 'high astounding terms' (*Tamburlaine*, Part I, 1587–8, Prologue). The latest and most ear-catching modes of speech were especially precious – and precarious – in a city of sudden social mobility such as London *c*.1600.

6 Thomas Dekker, 'How a Gallant should behave himselfe in a Play-house' in *The Guls Horne-booke* (London, 1609), pp. 27–8; 32.

7 As if in ironic fulfilment of this point, the 2008 Scripps National Spelling Bee prize was won by spelling 'guerdon'. Shakespeare seems aware that Costard is doing what the audience would also be doing: recognizing the words as presumptively nouns by their endings (the obvious '-ation' and the less obvious '-on'; Donka Minkova, private communication, 2009, reports that all English words ending in '-on' are nouns, except 'common' and 'wanton'). Costard again speaks truer than he realizes with 'contempts' at 1.1.187.

8 With a noteworthy persistence, the coining of words was associated with the coining of money in this period. Jonson, in *Timber, or Discoveries*, calls custom 'the most certaine Mistresse of Language, as the publicke stampe makes the current money' (*Ben Jonson*, ed. C. H. Herford, Percy Simpson and Evelyn Simpson (Oxford, 1947), vol. VIII, p. 622). In *Christ's Tears Over Jerusalem*, vol. 4 of *The Complete Works of Thomas Nashe*, ed. Alexander Grosart (London and Aylesbury, 1883–4), p. 6, Nashe even argues that the characteristic English monosyllables are like small change, and that his more elaborate diction enables his countrymen to trade profitably in larger sums. For a more extensive discussion of this point, see David Crystal's entry in *The Cambridge Encyclopedia of the English Language* (Cambridge, 2003), pp. 60–1.

9 Terttu Nevalainen, 'Shakespeare's New Words', in *Reading Shakespeare's Dramatic Language: A Guide*, ed. Sylvia Adamson et al. (London, 2001), esp. p. 238. Debates about imported words regularly took on the shape and even the vocabulary of mercantilist economic controversies; cf. Watson, 'Coining Words', p. 53.

have his fancy Euphuistic layer-cake and – through Berowne's renunciation of Russian performances and French courtesies in favour of 'russet yeas, and honest kersey noes' (5.2.413 ff.) – forswear it too. In fact, many of the words that character-ize Armado's excess turn up elsewhere in Shake-speare's works in all earnestness.[10] *Love's Labour's Lost* provides the interest of both high Latinate neologism (through the schoolmaster Holofernes) and the more free-wheeling continental variety (through Armado), while at the same time taking a dismissive commonsensical position against the vanity of such literary innovations when balanced against domestic common sense and the biolog-ical facts of life. It does the accused Costard no good to change the wench to a damsel, virgin, or maid: the sentence is the same (1.1.276–88). The linguistic show-offs can't stop renaming naming: Nathaniel's 'intitulated, nominated, or called' is framed by 'Armado hight' in the opening scene and Holofernes's 'ycleped' in the final one, encompass-ing some twenty other uses of 'name' itself. When Holofernes and Armado use affected neologisms to attack each other's affected neologisms, they repli-cate a contradiction that pervaded the Elizabethan 'inkhorn controversy'. If many of the *OED*'s first-use citations from this play, but few from *Hamlet*, can be antedated by electronic database searches (as Charlotte Brewer has provisionally noted), it may reflect the difference between a comedy that was mocking some recent ways of talking, and a tragedy that struggled to articulate some nascent ways of thinking.

Like many new businesses, the buying and selling of verbal riches involved risks as well as opportunities. The final scene of *Love's Labour's Lost* attacks, as mere regurgitators, those who seek socio-economic advantage by pilfering witty speech. Berowne thus belittles, yet also envies, Boyet, and puns on 'utters' as both 'saying' and 'selling':[11]

This fellow pecks up wit as pigeons peas,
And utters it again when God doth please.
He is wit's pedlar, and retails his wares
At wakes and wassails, meetings, markets, fairs.

And we that sell by gross, the Lord doth know,
Have not the grace to grace it with such show.

(5.2.316–21)

For every such Boyet, there must have been many boys who lacked the suavity to succeed in this manoeuvre; amorous plagiarists abound but do not thrive in Renaissance drama. For every Henry V, who wins Katherine's favour by deflating the grand rhetoric of formulaic courtship and mocking his own efforts to reach from English into French, there must have been dozens of Navarres who earned only the mocking laughter, not the sub-missive hands and disputed lands, of the princesses they courted in a high literary style. Although he is not one of the fools in plays from this period who acknowledge learning their overblown verbiage at the theatre – such as Tomkis's Trinculo, who woos 'with compliments drawn from the plays I see at the Fortune and Red Bull, where I learn all the words I speak and understand not'[12] – Andrew Aguecheek offers a memorable cautionary exam-ple, vowing to master '"Odours," "pregnant," and "vouchsafed" – I'll get 'em all three already', but unable to handle 'accost' or (despite his vaunted linguistic skills) '*pourquoi*' (*Twelfth Night*, 3.1.89–90, 1.3.46–56, 88–9). Shakespeare and his colleagues were already making the basic joke of Cole Porter's song 'Brush up your Shakespeare': no classy dame is really going to fall for a street-tough just because he can quote (in an incongruous accent) a few exalted words from Elizabethan drama.

At the risk of complicity in a professorial ten-dency to underrate the sheer playfulness of plays and to overrate their pedagogical intent, this arti-cle will emphasize Shakespeare's diligence and ingenuity as a teacher of vocabulary in a one-large-room schoolhouse. Through Holofernes, he could make fun of the sixteenth-century humanist

---

[10] Paula Blank, *Broken English: Dialects and the Politics of Lan-guage in Renaissance Writings* (London, 1996), p. 51.

[11] *Oxford English Dictionary*, definitions verb 1.II.5.a and verb 1.I.1a (e.g. *Romeo*, 5.1.68); this pun recurs at 4.4.185 of *The Winter's Tale*; both link back to the sense of 'coin, issue currency,' verb 1.I.2a.

[12] Thomas Tomkis, *Albumazar* (1614), 2.1.

method that taught language by corny *copia*: 'The deer . . . hangeth like a jewel in the ear of *caelo*, the sky, the welkin, the heaven, and anon falleth like a crab on the face of *terra*, the soil, the land, the earth' (4.2.3–7). But Shakespeare recognized the sanity in this method, and put it to his own uses, regularly finding ways to make the innovations both memorable and – notably in the case of *Othello* – thematically important. In this as in other areas, he deftly combined *dolce* with *utile*, Ariel with Caliban, the delights of his art with the practical business of his theatre. As Edmund Gayton observed, 'men come not to study at a Play-house, but love such expressions and passages, which with ease insinuate themselves into their capacities'.[13] In Elizabethan London, the mastery of new language was pleasure and profit conjoined.

Clearly Shakespeare's original audiences enjoyed his language, not because (as modern readers tend to assume) they knew all those strange locutions, but partly because they didn't yet. Ralph Alan Cohen – a key figure in reviving the original experience of Jacobean drama – has written that 'Shakespeare's audience went to the playhouse not in possession of the language they would hear there but in search of it . . . The only advantage the Elizabethan audience had over today's audience was a delight in new words.'[14] Even if one doubts the 'only', the implications for teaching and editing are immense, and support the already compelling case against modernized-diction texts of Shakespeare. This is especially true for younger students, who are generally the ones most avidly protected from Elizabethan diction, but also the ones best equipped mentally, developmentally, to learn unfamiliar words and constructions, as they must do every day by seeing them in context and, ideally, surrounded by memorable explanatory actions, as they would be in the materialized memory-palace of the theatre.

2. SHAKESPEARE'S TECHNIQUE

However small his Latin and less his Greek,[15] Shakespeare proved a daunting competitor for the scholar-neologists of his time. His commercial success in his own time, like his influence on modern English, depended partly on a talent for finding the right degree of variation to make neologisms attractive – and offering contextual definitions that made them comprehensible. In an era of multicultural anxieties, remaking English from within (by exchanging parts of speech or adding prefixes and suffixes) proved at least as effective as high humanist importations, and Shakespeare was willing to attempt both, willing even to jumble them together.[16]

Though, to my unhappy surprise, I have not found any satisfactory list of the famous Shakespearian neologisms,[17] many instances can be located simply by noticing that seeming redundancies are often actually glossaries. The system was far from flawless, and about a third of Shakespeare's neologisms have not survived.[18] But he cares for his young conscientiously, surrounding them with their kin, and there are few *hapax legomena* – words strutted once on stage, and then heard no

---

[13] Edmund Gayton, *Pleasant notes upon Don Quixot* (1654), p. 271.

[14] Ralph Alan Cohen, *ShakesFear and How to Cure It!* (Clayton, 2007), p. 109.

[15] T. W. Baldwin, *William Shakespere's Small Latine and Less Greeke* (1944) and Stuart Gillespie's *Shakespeare's Books* (New Brunswick, 2001) have helped clarify that these diminutives are misleading by modern standards. Jonson was always ready to take a more-classicist-than-thou stance, but Shakespeare received and demonstrated a good classical education.

[16] On Shakespeare's high tolerance for such combinations, see Bryan A. Garner, 'Latin-Saxon Hybrids in Shakespeare and the Bible', in *A Reader*, pp. 229–34.

[17] Garner, 'Latin-Saxon Hybrids'; also Garner, 'Shakespeare's Latinate Neologisms', in *A Reader*, pp. 207–28; Jürgen Schäfer, *Shakespeares Stil: Germanisches und romanisches Vokabular* (Frankfurt, 1973); and the more recent and accessible David Crystal, *'Think on my Words': Exploring Shakespeare's Language* (Cambridge, 2008). A perfect list may be impossible, since we certainly cannot recover and date the full spoken lexicon of the period, and what to count as a new and distinct word is open to many different interpretations. Jeffrey McQuain and Stanley Malless, *Coined by Shakespeare* (Springfield, 1998) is written for a non-academic audience and deals with a limited set of words (many of which were not quite as new as it supposes), but still helpful.

[18] Garner, 'Shakespeare's Latinate Neologisms', p. 214.

more – among his many creations. Regan's neologistic claim that she is 'alone felicitate' in Lear's affection is prepared by her synonymous claim, two lines earlier, that she is 'an enemy to all other joys' (1.1.73–5). When Goneril urges Lear 'A little to disquantity your train' (1.4.227), Shakespeare accompanies the new verb with enough discussion about numerical reduction to make the meaning obvious: one hundred, fifty, twenty-five, ten, five, one, zero (this is a particularly bold example, because Latin would not permit 'dis-' to be added to verbs; but Goneril is not much for rules, and often puts a thin veneer of sophistication over her transgressions). The definition of 'decimation' – a word Shakespeare probably learned from North's translation of Plutarch, but otherwise unknown in this sense during the sixteenth century – becomes similarly mathematical: a Senator urges Alcibiades, 'By decimation and a tithèd death, / . . . take thou the destined tenth' (Timon, 5.5.31–3). Falstaff's 'dwindle' was another novelty for the idea of diminution (here spatial rather than numerical), but Shakespeare offers plenty of help: 'Bardolph, am I not fallen away vilely since this last action? Do I not bate? Do I not dwindle? Why, my skin hangs about me like an old lady's loose gown. I am withered like an old apple-john' (1 Henry IV, 3.3.1–4). The only other recorded use before 1610 was also by Shakespeare (if the scene is), and again he nestles it amid synonyms: 'dwindle, peak, and pine' (Macbeth, 1.3.22).

Consider the two uses of a more elaborate word, once in a new form and once in a still-rare one:

1. *Sir Toby.* Am not I consanguineous? Am I not of her blood?   (*Twelfth Night*, 2.3.74)

2. *Cressida.* I have forgot my father.
   I know no touch of consanguinity,
   No kin, no love, no blood, no soul, so near me
   As the sweet Troilus.   (*Troilus*, 4.3.22–5)

Earlier in *Troilus and Cressida* (1.3.106), Ulysses discusses 'The primogenity and due of birth' (the Folio has the equally unprecedented 'primogenitive' here); so we may sense Shakespeare repeatedly offering Latinate replacements for Teutonic

roots (such as 'blood' and 'birth') as the classical story stands in satirically for Renaissance England – though Jonson would surely observe that Shakespeare ought here to be using Greek rather than Latin forms. In fact, the first scene set in the Greek camp is replete with doublets (within a single speech at 1.3.4–29, Shakespeare gives us 'Tortive and errant', 'Bias and thwart', 'artist and unread', and a half-dozen others)[19] and with neologisms derived from both classical languages.[20] Presumably Shakespeare is signalling – along with a shortfall of language that matches the inefficacy of vows – the alien character of that world, in this weirdly alienating play. This is, and is not, English.

Antony offers an instant gloss when he complains that his former followers 'discandy, melt their sweets' (*Antony*, 4.13.22). 'Dwarfish' was extremely rare elsewhere in the literary record – Marlowe's *Hero and Leander* provides a lonely but prominent precedent – but not in Shakespeare, who seems to have enjoyed its sound (like Marston, he enjoyed playing with blunt, body-based Teutonics, as well as with grander classical constructions) and made its meaning obvious every time.[21] He makes special use of its Teutonic bluntness when Hermia complains that Helena

> hath urged her height,
> And with her personage, her tall personage,
> Her height, forsooth, she hath prevailed with him –
> And are you grown so high in his esteem
> Because I am so dwarfish and so low?
> How low am I, thou painted maypole? Speak,
> How low am I? I am not yet so low
> But that my nails can reach unto thine eyes.
>
>   (*Dream*, 3.2.292–9)

Hermia mockingly replaces 'height', based in Old English and German, with the Norman-French

---

19 Simon Palfrey, *Doing Shakespeare* (London, 2005), p. 51.

20 David Crystal, *The Cambridge Encyclopedia of the English Language* (Cambridge, 1995), pp. 166–7.

21 E.g. 'this dwarfish war, these pigmy arms' (*King John*, 5.2.133–5); 'a giant's robe / Upon a dwarfish thief' (*Macbeth*, 5.2.21–2). Even with the simpler form, Shakespeare offers guidance: Berowne calls Cupid 'This Signor Junior, giant dwarf' (*Love's Labour's Lost*, 3.1.175).

'personage', then corrects it back to 'height', to deride Helena's implied assumption that stretching implies superiority. Aided by the courtly etymology, the length of 'personage' implies *hauteur* based on height; and the assonant suggestion that Helena will cease to 'prevail' when Hermia wields her 'nails' performs the same kind of work, as the tough little monosyllables chase the lengthy speech to its close.

Lady Macbeth's rejection of 'compunctious visitings of nature' (1.5.44) is escorted by multiple definitions of natural conscience, and Banquo's 'exposure' arrives already defined as nakedness, in opposition to hiddenness: 'when we have our naked frailties hid, / That suffer in exposure' (2.3.125–6). For an antonym to 'exposure', *Macbeth* places a new adjectival form between two less novel versions: 'cabined, cribbed, confined' (3.4.23). Isabella's reference to Angelo's 'circummured' garden is attended by redundant, overdetermined imagery of surrounding walls (*Measure*, 4.1.27–32).

Prospero's obsessive anxieties allow Shakespeare to offer redundant contexts for a nearly-new word, 'sanctimonious', and a brand-new word, 'abstemious'. Prospero admonishes Ferdinand that, until

> All sanctimonious ceremonies may
> With full and holy rite be ministered, . . .
> Look thou be true. Do not give dalliance
> Too much the rein. The strongest oaths are straw
> To th' fire i'th' blood. Be more abstemious,
> Or else, good night your vow.
>
> (*Tempest*, 4.1.16–17, 51–4)

Unlike a seemingly simpler neologism for the same concept – 'unfix', which Shakespeare repeatedly accompanied with overlapping contextual definitions (*2 Henry IV*, 4.1.202–7; *Macbeth*, 4.1.110–13) – 'deracinate' has survived, perhaps because Shakespeare aired its roots: Burgundy laments the leas that weeds 'root upon, while that the coulter rusts / That should deracinate such savagery' (*Henry V*, 5.2.46–7). 'Savagery' too was apparently a Shakespearian formulation, and when

he first presented it, he did so with plenty of explanatory parallels:

> *Salisbury*. this is the bloodiest shame,
> The wildest savagery, the vilest stroke
> That ever wall-eyed wrath or staring rage
> Presented to the tears of soft remorse.
>
> (*King John*, 4.3.47–50)

'Invulnerable/vulnerable' turns up four times, with due explanatory diligence performed in each instance:

> 1. *King Philip*. Our cannons' malice vainly shall be spent
>   Against th'invulnerable clouds of heaven.
>
>   (*King John*, 2.1.251–2)
> 2. *Ariel*.   The elements
>   Of whom your swords are tempered may as well
>   Wound the loud winds, or with bemocked-at stabs
>   Kill the still-closing waters, as diminish
>   One dowl that's in my plume. My fellow ministers
>   Are like invulnerable. If you could hurt,
>   Your swords are now too massy for your strengths
>   And will not be uplifted.   (*Tempest*, 3.3.61–8)
> 3. *Macbeth*. Thou losest labour.
>   As easy mayst thou the intrenchant air
>   With thy keen sword impress as make me bleed.
>   Let fall thy blade on vulnerable crests;
>
>   (*Macbeth*, 5.10.8–11)
> 4. *Marcellus*. For it is as the air invulnerable,
>   And our vain blows malicious mockery.
>
>   (*Hamlet*, 1.1.126–7)

Hamlet – the dysfunctional home of 'words, words, words' – abounds with instances. The tautology in 'windy suspiration of forced breath' (1.2.79) is also a built-in glossary. When Claudius agrees with Laertes that 'No place indeed should murder sanctuarize', Shakespeare has already established the vivid and specific image of murder in a church in the previous line, and then rephrases the meaning in the next one: 'Revenge should have no bounds' (4.7.100–1). When the Ghost calls Claudius an 'adulterate beast' (1.5.42), Shakespeare again packs the gift in more extensive and familiar definitions of the crime. We know that 'malefactions' must be bad doings, even if we miss the etymology, by the example that follows (2.2.593–4). Nor would anyone have had much trouble understanding 'survivor' or 'condolement' – the latter also used and instantly glossed in *Pericles*, but with a different meaning[22] – thanks to the way Shakespeare has Claudius frame them:

'Tis sweet and commendable in your nature, Hamlet,
To give these mourning duties to your father;
But you must know your father lost a father;
That father lost, lost his; and the survivor bound
In filial obligation for some term
To do obsequious sorrow. But to persever
In obstinate condolement is a course
Of impious stubbornness, 'tis unmanly grief
(1.2.87–94)

To help 'survivor' survive (it was seldom used outside of legal discussions), Shakespeare will revisit it in *Coriolanus*, 5.6.17–8: 'the fall of either / Makes the survivor heir of all'. 'Impious', we will see, receives extensive aid through 'pious', which is itself repeatedly defined. An exception proves the rule: Shakespeare might have been able to save 'cerements' – a rare term for burial wrappings – had his parallelism not misleadingly implied that it was merely a synonym for 'sepulcher':

Hamlet. Why thy canonized bones, hearsèd in death,
Have burst their cerements, why the sepulchre
Wherein we saw thee quietly enurned
Hath oped his ponderous and marble jaws
To cast thee up again. (1.4.28–32)

Another technique emerges when Claudius (at 3.1.169) worries about 'the hatch and the disclose' of whatever Hamlet is brooding over. Claudius uses two words unfamiliar as nouns to help us recognize not only what they mean, but also how he is redeploying them: the former one of the first such uses in English (along with Shakespeare's similar 'the hatch and brood of time' in *2 Henry IV*, 3.1.81), the other only the second, according to the *OED* (indeed, even as I write this, Microsoft Word's grammar-checker is protesting the placement of 'disclose' as a noun). This double verb-to-noun move is reversed when Hamlet warns Gertrude not to let rationalization 'skin and film the ulcerous place' (3.4.138). When the Ghost worries about making Hamlet's 'knotty and combinèd locks to

part' (1.5.18), the familiar first term illuminates the second, which was apparently a neologism, though it has since become common. To support 'pious', which was then extremely unusual (especially outside theological tracts), Polonius warns Ophelia against 'unholy suits' proffered 'like sanctified and pious bawds' (1.3.129–30); Polonius later laments that 'with devotion's visage / And pious action we do sugar o'er / The devil himself' (3.1.49–51); and during the subsequent decade Shakespeare repeatedly offers 'pious' conjoined with synonyms such as 'holy' and 'saint-like'.[23]

So, in addition to the thematic function of this doubling of nouns (and sometimes verbs) as masterfully traced by William Empson, George T. Wright, Frank Kermode and Patrick Cheney,[24] and the pairing of Germanic and Romance roots masterfully tracked by Jürgen Schäfer,[25] the rhetorical structure called 'hendiadys' also allowed the definition of new words by edging towards *synonymia simplex*. Linguists who assume that synonyms exist to permit alliteration and prevent repetitiveness tend to neglect this pedagogical function.[26] Even

---

22 Scene 5, line 193; see Hilda M. Hulme, *Explorations in Shakespeare's Language: Some Problems of Lexical Meaning in the Dramatic Text* (London, 1962), pp. 279–80.

23 'Pious,' which the Literature Online database suggests was almost never used in the sixteenth century, became a decade-long project for Shakespeare. Duke Vincentio's speech to Friar Thomas goes from 'My holy sir' to 'Now, pious sir' (*Measure*, 1.3.7–16). Belarius in *Cymbeline* speaks of 'pious debts to heaven' (3.3.72). Norfolk's sarcasm about Cardinal Wolsey builds (with references to souls and angels and submissive blessings) towards the then-unusual word: 'How holily he works in all his business, / And with what zeal! . . . / . . . is not this course pious?' (*Henry VIII*, 2.2.23–36). Two scenes later Queen Katherine is praised as 'saint-like . . . and pious' (2.4.135–7). See similarly *Macbeth*, 3.6.27 and *Timon*, 4.3.136–41.

24 William Empson, *Seven Types of Ambiguity*, 3rd edn (London, 1956), pp. 88–101; George T. Wright, 'Hendiadys and *Hamlet*', *PMLA*, 96 (1981), 168–93; Frank Kermode, *Shakespeare's Language* (New York, 2000), pp. 100–2, 167–9; Patrick Cheney, *Shakespeare's Literary Authorship* (Cambridge, 2008), pp. 142–5, 204–6.

25 Schäfer, *Shakespeares Stil*.

26 Inna Koskenniemi, *Repetitive Word Pairs in Old and Early Middle English Prose* (Turku, 1968), p. 109, similarly assumes

Rosencrantz – half of a human hendiadys – joins in with 'mortised and adjoined, / . . . small annexment, petty consequence' (3.3.20–1).

Other plays employ the same tactic: for example, 'Th'inaudible and noiseless foot of time' (*All's Well*, 5.3.42), 'fertile and conceptious womb' (*Timon*, 4.3.188) or 'Countless and infinite' kisses (*Titus Andronicus*, 5.3.158). 'Critical' – though occasionally used in astrology and medicine – almost never carried the sense of 'censorious' until Theseus rejects 'some satire, keen and critical, / Not sorting with a nuptial ceremony' (*Dream*, 5.1.54–5). Sometimes, with a not-quite-new word, an escorting synonym is sufficient: 'most courtly and fashionable' (*Timon*, 5.1.26–7), or 'ceremonious and traditional' (*Richard III*, 3.1.45). 'Affined' was almost unknown, so it generally travels with an assistant: 'affined or leagued'[27] (*Othello*, 2.3.211), and 'affined and kin' (*Troilus*, 1.3.24).

The technique itself was hardly new. The juxtaposing of synonyms, arguably derived from William Caxton's fifteenth-century translations, emerged as a tool for teaching Latin in Erasmus's *De Copia* (1512), developed into a kind of thesaurus-function, and then into a stylistic quirk of sixteenth-century humanist rhetoric.[28] When he could not find an English synonym that would be familiar to ordinary readers of his 1550 translation of Peter Martyr Vermigli's Latin treatise, Nicholas Udall 'added suche circumstaunce of other words, as might declare it and make it plain'.[29] Sir Thomas Elyot's *Boke of the Governour* (1531) 'sensibly followed the practice established from Middle English of pairing neologisms with established words and phrases to make the newcomers comprehensible',[30] a practice continued in Puttenham's domestications of Latin rhetorical terms. Thomas Cooper's *Thesaurus Linguae Romanae et Britannicae* (1565) – a book which Shakespeare clearly knew, perhaps from the copy a schoolmaster bequeathed to the Stratford grammar school – could have suggested not only Shakespeare's thesaurus-like method of explaining new words, but also many of the specific instances cited here, including 'abstemious', 'condolence',

'consanguinity', 'adulterate' (Cooper offers the Hamlet-friendly example of 'adultry with his brothers wife'), 'affined', 'compunctious', 'audacious', 'suspiration' and perhaps 'relume', by glossing their Latin roots into English.

No one, however, seems to have taught by tautology as industriously as Shakespeare himself. Nor were others as ingenious in using hendiadys to establish the meaning of the plays as well as of the words: when, just before the first battle-scene in *Henry V*, the Chorus says that every Englishman of 'pith and puissance' has joined the invasion of France (3.0.21), the near-synonyms not only match the itinerary of the expedition they describe and help define each other, they also capture in miniature exactly the difference between blunt Anglo-Saxon earthiness and Gallic vainglory that the play repeatedly suggests will enable the 'bastard Normans, Norman bastards' (3.5.10) to conquer the French. This trick of sliding from the native term to its exotic near-synonym would become crucial to Shakespeare's characterization of Othello just a few years later.

The production and elucidation of neologisms seems to drop off significantly in Shakespeare's

---

that two symbols expressing a single meaning must be – if not 'pathologic' – intended 'to convey a message more accurately and more effectfully than one word would'. She does acknowledge cases pairing 'a loan-word and a native synonym', but supposes these are usually the result of 'the authors' wish to display a knowledge of two languages, or to various stylistic motives' such as 'a search for alliterative synonyms' (116), rather than anything pedagogical. M. Görlach, *Introduction to Early Modern English* (Cambridge, 1991), p. 195, assumes that the main use of synonymy is 'to avoid repetition'.

27 The First Folio and First Quarto read 'league', which Alexander Pope plausibly emended to 'leagued'. Iago's use of 'affin'd' at 1.1.39 is an exception.

28 Sylvia Adamson, 'Synonymia, or in Other Words', in *Renaissance Figures of Speech*, ed. S. Adamson, G. Alexander and K. Ettenhuber (Cambridge, 2007); this excellent study of *synonymia* recognizes it as an outgrowth of Erasmus's Latin pedagogy, but (even when citing Shakespeare) does not recognize it as a tool for teaching within English.

29 Preface; quoted by R. F. Jones, *The Triumph of the English Language* (Stanford, 1953), p. 83.

30 Hughes, *A History of English Words*, p. 156.

late plays. Perhaps the boom of verbal innovation was tapering off in England (the tic of *copia*
had certainly gone out of fashion); perhaps the
extended absence from London in 1607–10 posited
by Jonathan Bate[31] withdrew Shakespeare from
what was left of the neologistic ferment; perhaps
he was well enough established that he no longer
needed to offer vocabulary as a supplement to the
other pleasures of his plays; and perhaps his innovative energies went instead into the syntactical
rigours of his late verse, which Russ McDonald has
explored so masterfully.[32] Perhaps, in the building
of the new English language, Shakespeare eventually moved from brick-making towards early-post-
modern architecture.

3. SHAKESPEARE'S VERBAL PALETTE

Shakespeare's neologisms – and this category
inevitably includes words he did not absolutely
originate but helped to popularize – were certainly
not merely items for display and sale. Like several
of his younger contemporaries,[33] he waged pro-
tracted campaigns on behalf of some locutions that
filled gaps in his expressive palette. The previous
section briefly traced his development of several
words ('compunctious', 'abstemious', 'exposure',
'critical', and 'pious') that articulate a boundary
between the ethical, thoughtful, withheld or withholding inner self, and an external world consisting
of that self's objects and obstacles. His half-dozen
efforts to sustain the dying sense of 'revolve' and
'revolving' as pondering an idea at length – turning it over in the mind – suggest the same need.
Twice 'revolve' comes paired with 'ruminate' (*1
Henry VI*, 5.7.101, *Troilus*, 2.3.185–6), as it does
in Cooper's gloss on *ruminatio* – and 'ruminate',
while not new as a term for human meditation,
was evidently returning from obscurity, since it
appears in a series of fashionable new words that the
foolish Juniper mishandles in Jonson's *The Case is
Altered* (published in 1609, but probably written in
the late 1590s).[34] Shakespeare seems to have seized
on this revived verb for the process of thoughtful,

artful planning, and dutifully explained it: 'Then
she plots, then she ruminates, then she devises'
(*Merry Wives*, 2.2.294–5), 'ruminate strange plots'
(*Titus Andronicus*, 5.2.6), 'ruminated, plotted' (*1
Henry IV*, 1.3.268), 'Sit patiently and inly ruminate' (*Henry V*, 4.0.24), 'To ruminate on this so
far until / It forged him some design' (*Henry VIII*,
1.2.181–2), 'a studied, not a present thought, /
By duty ruminated' (*Antony*, 2.2.144–5), 'speak
to me as to thy thinkings, / As thou dost ruminate' (*Othello*, 3.3.136–7), and 'the sundry contemplation of my travels, in which my often
rumination wraps me in a most humorous sadness' (*As You Like It*, 4.1.17–19). These add up
to more uses than the *Literature Online* database
shows in all the plays of Shakespeare's competitors
combined.

The boundary these words explore corresponds
to a pervasive scholarly recognition of Shakespeare as a withdrawn figure (a Romantic biographical tradition developed by Dowden, and
more recently, with an emphasis on philosophical scepticism, by several other fine scholars),[35]
and as an inventor of human interiority and

---

[31] Jonathan Bate, *Soul of the Age: A Biography of the Mind of William Shakespeare* (New York, 2009), p. 46.

[32] One possible deduction from Russ McDonald's excellent study of *Shakespeare's Late Style* (New York, 2006) is that those final works show an author more determined to please his own rhetorical intelligence with difficult innovations than to offer socially viable forms of speech to his audience.

[33] Jones, *Triumph of the English Language*, p. 272 n. 1: 'The Elizabethans borrowed from necessity, vanity, or sheer exuberance. One senses a different spirit, something akin to the metaphysical, a seeking for the strange and out of the way, perhaps a striving for certain imaginative or sound effects, in the borrowing of men like Burton, Donne, Taylor, and Browne.'

[34] Ben Jonson, *The Case is Altered*, 1.4.16; in *Ben Jonson*, ed. C. H. Herford, Percy Simpson and Evelyn Simpson (Oxford, 1947), vol. III.

[35] Graham Bradshaw, *Misrepresentations: Shakespeare and the Materialists* (Ithaca, 1993); John D. Cox, *Seeming Knowledge: Shakespeare and Skeptical Faith* (Waco, 2007); Hugh Grady, *Shakespeare, Machiavelli, and Montaigne: Power and Subjectivity from Richard II to Hamlet* (New York, 2003); Anita Gilman Sherman, *Skepticism and Memory in Shakespeare and Donne* (New York, 2007); Ellen Spolsky, *Satisfying Skepticism* (Burlington, 2001).

subjectivity (a more recent and high-theoretical view).[36] In other words, several of Shakespeare's most assiduous developments of vocabulary would seem to confirm, at a microscopic level, some of the largest speculations about his character and characterizing practices.

Shakespeare makes three further attempts (four, if we count 'retirement') to invent and promote new words for the concept of pious retreat or isolation, of withdrawal from the world compelled by principle or psychology. 'Lonely' is now so common that it is hard to believe that it once needed such direct definition, but it did: hence, 'I go alone, / Like to a lonely dragon' (*Coriolanus*, 4.1.30–1), and later, 'I keep it / Lonely, apart' (*Winter's Tale*, 5.3.17–18).[37] Observers of Prince Hal 'never noted in him any study, / Any retirement, any sequestration / From open haunts and popularity' (*Henry V*, 1.1.58–60). Othello invents another noun form to prescribe, for the dangerously social and passionate Desdemona, 'A sequester from liberty; fasting, and prayer, / Much castigation, exercise devout' (3.4.40–1).[38] 'Reclusive' gets similar conceptual support:

> Friar Francis.   you may conceal her,
>   As best befits her wounded reputation,
>   In some reclusive and religious life,
>   Out of all eyes, tongues, minds, and injuries.
>
>   (*Much Ado*, 4.1.242–5)

Both the glossary function and the contemplative emphasis are stark when the Bishop of Winchester condemns Gloucester for coming 'with deep premeditated lines? / With written pamphlets studiously devised?' (*1 Henry VI*, 3.1.1–2). In a clearly Shakespearian section of *Two Noble Kinsmen* (1.1.134–7), the audience receives similar guidance with an otherwise unknown form of the same word, followed by a rare one grown from the same root: 'what you do quickly / Is not done rashly; your first thought is more / Than others' laboured meditance; your premeditating / More than their actions.'

Perhaps I am cherry-picking my instances – many of Shakespeare's new words lack this intellectual character – but he does seem to spend a remarkable amount of neologistic energy on expressing these mental states, or more tellingly, states of mental reservation: we may add 'deceptious' (*Troilus*, 5.2.125), 'denotement' (*Othello* 2.3.310), 'tranquil' (*Othello*, 3.3.353), 'dishearten' (*Henry V*, 4.1.112, and *Macbeth*, 2.3.32–3), 'the pauser, reason' (*Macbeth*, 2.3.111), and 'give preceptial medicine to rage' (*Much Ado*, 5.1.24). Those who believe that Shakespeare was a recusant may be especially inclined to add 'equivocator' (extensively defined in *Macbeth*, 2.3.8) and 'equivocal' to this list; they may also be intrigued to learn that the only evident precedent for Shakespeare's use of 'rumination' was in the works of the famous Jesuit Robert Parsons.[39]

Literature Online shows only two instances of the word 'dejected' in plays prior to 1599, but four others appeared by 1600 – a good indication that it was a word coming into fashion (perhaps because melancholy was also). Shakespeare made sure it was always well defined, either by context or by counter-point:

---

36 Catherine Belsey, *The Subject of Tragedy* (London, 1985); Joel Fineman, *Shakespeare's Perjured Eye: The Invention of Poetic Subjectivity in the Sonnets* (Berkeley, 1986); Harold Bloom, *Shakespeare and the Invention of the Human* (New York, 1998); John Lee, *Shakespeare's Hamlet and the Controversies of Self* (New York, 2000); Francis Barker, *The Tremulous Private Body: Essays on Subjection* (New York, 1984).

37 The First Folio reads 'Louely', probably an accidental inversion of the 'n' in reading or typesetting process; the fact that Hanmer could tell this emendation was needed shows how clearly Shakespeare has signalled the idea of 'lonely'. 'Lonely' appears fairly often in the *EEBO* database, but several instances are actually 'alonely', and others are typesetting errors for 'lovely'. Its only real advocate seems to have been Sir Philip Sidney, who uses 'lonely' at least seven times in *The Countess of Pembroke's Arcadia* (1593).

38 Notice that 'castigation', then quite rare, receives a gloss here as 'exercise devout', in a context emphasizing chastity. At 1.3.345, Iago uses 'sequestration', but seems to mean 'sequel'.

39 Parsons also surrounds the neologism with related ideas to a degree that not even Shakespeare normally attempts: 'to beare it in mynde, to ponder in harte, to studdie & meditate upon it both day and night . . . to make it our cogitation, our discourse, our talke, our exercise & our rumination': Robert Parsons, *A Christian directorie* (1585), p. 9.

1. *Hamlet.* No, nor the fruitful river in the eye,
   Nor the dejected haviour of the visage,
   Together with all forms, moods, shows of grief
   That can denote me truly.   (*Hamlet*, 1.2.80–3)

2. *Edgar.*   To be worst,
   The low'st and most dejected thing of fortune,
   Stands still in esperance . . .   (*Lear*, 4.1.2–4)

3. *Scarus.*   Antony
   Is valiant, and dejected, and by starts
   His fretted fortunes give him hope and fear . . .
                          (*Antony*, 4.13.6–8)

Shakespeare persistently teaches his audiences that 'speculation' has to do with seeing, but also with the limitations and partiality of seeing[40] – an important topic for an endlessly questioning playwright in an era whose revival of classical scepticism emphasized visual differences and distortions. For what is kept unreliably unseen, Shakespeare launches 'undivulged', and sends several paraphrases after it to make sure the meaning cannot be missed:

> *Lear.*   Tremble, thou wretch
> That hast within thee undivulgèd crimes
> Unwhipped of justice; hide thee, thou bloody
>   hand . . .
>   close pent-up guilts,
> Rive your concealing continents . . .
>   (*Lear*, 3.2.51–8)

Shakespeare also spends considerable effort, especially in the history plays, developing antonyms to mark the polar opposites on a spectrum running from rebellious boldness to humble yielding. 'Audacious' was fairly scarce[41] until Shakespeare made it a project early in his career, always signalling a combination of daring and insubordination.[42] Duke Theseus prefers 'the modesty of fearful duty' to 'saucy and audacious eloquence' (*Dream*, 5.1.101, 3). Somerset admonishes York, 'Obey, audacious traitor; kneel for grace' (*2 Henry VI*, 5.1.108). *Love's Labour's Lost* offers 'audacious without impudency' (5.1.4–5) and 'fear not thou, but speak audaciously' (5.2.104). 'Submissive' – essentially an antonym of 'audacious' – is another early but temporary favourite, nurtured through its infancy.[43]

This palette allowed Shakespeare to explore some boundaries repeatedly embattled in his plays: between inward and outward selves, between perception and knowledge, between passion and deliberation, and between self-assertion and assimilation into the social order. In *Othello*, Shakespeare discovers a new way to integrate this expansion of the lexicon with his exposition of a character in the grip of those dilemmas.

4. THE CASE OF OTHELLO

It is easy to understand 'fleers' when Iago speaks of the 'fleers, the gibes and notable scorns' that the arrogant Cassio will cast on a disdained mistress (4.1.81). Before Othello laments, 'I know not where is that Promethean heat / That can thy light relume', Shakespeare gives us eight lines on the problem of restoring extinguished lights (5.2.12–13). But here the glossary game turns tragic, with doublets providing a microcosmic index to the divided affiliations that tear the hero apart.

Character criticism has often been dismissed in recent years on the grounds that plays are really 'only words'; but words can be constitutive of character, both on stage and off. C. S. Lewis's complaint that Shakespeare's near-repetitions (and those of other Elizabethan dramatists) offer mere *'variation'* where Milton's involve *'construction'*[44] overlooks not only the pedagogical function of Shakespeare's synonyms but also the way those doublets construct Othello's character, by implicitly

---

[40] E.g. *Troilus*, 3.3.100–6; *Macbeth*, 3.4.94–5; *Lear*, 3.1.15; *Othello*, 1.3.270, 3.3.365.

[41] Although the *Literature Online* database finds only 27 entries for 'audacious' in sixteenth-century prose, poetry, and drama, the fact that 'audaciousness' was in use by 1599 suggests that the root word was well enough established for the compound to be viable.

[42] *1 Henry IV*, 4.3.43–7; *1 Henry VI*, 3.1.8–15, 25–6; 4.1.124–7.

[43] *1 Henry VI*, 3.8.3–12; *Love's Labour's Lost*, 4.1.89; *Shrew*, Induction, 1.51.

[44] C. S. Lewis, 'Variation in Shakespeare and Others', in *Selected Literary Essays*, ed. Hooper (Cambridge, 1969), p. 76. On similar flaws Lewis detects in the work of Shakespeare's contemporaries, see pp. 77–80.

reflecting the doubleness the hero must endure inwardly and project to the world outside.

Othello's efforts to introduce himself to the Senate in his new role as Venetian husband, as they overlap with Shakespeare's efforts to introduce him to us in his full hybridity, provide a particularly telling example – and one that shows the interpretive as well as historical potential of attention to neologisms. Both for Shakespeare's purposes and for Othello's own, Othello must seem both exotic and accessible – a double-bind often lamented by racial-ethnic minorities, who find themselves required to stand out and yet to assimilate, at once to exemplify and reject the stereotyped expectations of the majority. After a disarmingly simple first line – ''Tis better as it is' (1.2.6) – Othello's first speech contains three neologisms, each created by attaching an ordinary Anglo-Saxon prefix to change a common word into a new part of speech:

> My services which I have done the signory
> Shall **out-tongue his complaints**. 'Tis yet to know –
> Which, when I know that **boasting** is an honour,
> I shall **promulgate** – I fetch my life and being
> From men of royal siege, and my demerits
> May speak **unbonneted** to as proud a fortune
> As this that I have reached. For know, Iago,
> But that I love the gentle Desdemona
> I would not my **unhousèd free** condition
> Put into **circumscription and confine** . . .
>
> (1.2.18–27)

'Out-tongue' uses an outré tongue to override – might one hear a trace of Shakespeare the anti-Petrarchan here? – the mere 'complaints' of a Venetian insider. Othello then amplifies 'boast' into 'promulgate' (or the Quarto's 'provulgate'), and familiarizes 'unhousèd' with 'free', and 'circumscription'[45] with 'confine'. Thereafter, Othello – unlike Shakespeare's deliberately less appealing African characters such as Aaron or Morocco – often employs a compressed form of the socially driven practice that linguists call 'code-switching', juxtaposing a common word with a new or rare one of similar meaning, making him a kind of familiar stranger, appealing in both aspects of the oxymoron.

Hendiadys often implies a neologism residing in the unarticulated space between the paired words; in Othello's case, it implies an uninhabitable oceanic space between his two worlds. Sometimes this tactic involves pairing an Anglo-Saxon word with a Romance-language import; sometimes it involves pairing an idiomatic with a non-idiomatic usage of native words, with the charm of a foreign speaker offering us a fresh look at the contingency of our speech. Not all the highlighted phrases below include an outright neologism in the pairing (though some of Othello's other words here, such as 'hint' at 1.3.165, were surprisingly rare), but they suggest the many ways Othello gathers customary and unaccustomed language together in this scene in order to represent himself effectively. To these 'Most **potent, grave, and reverend signiors**, / My very **noble and approved good masters**', he will 'a **round unvarnished** tale deliver / Of my whole course of love, what drugs, what charms, / **What conjuration and what mighty magic**' he used on Desdemona (1.3.76–92). He told her

> Of **moving accidents** by **flood and field**,
> Of **hair-breadth scapes** i'th' **imminent deadly breach** . . .
> And of **the cannibals that each other eat**,
> **The Anthropophagi** . . .
>   of some **distressful** stroke
> That my youth **suffered**.
>
> (1.3.134–5, 142–3, 156–7)

These struggles, Othello adds, have made 'the **flinty and steel** couch of war / My thrice-driven bed of down. I do agnize / A **natural and prompt alacrity**' for such martial hardships (1.3.229–31). For Desdemona, however, he demands 'Due **reference of place and exhibition**, / With such **accommodation and besort** / As levels with

---

45 Richard Mulcaster, *The First Part of the Elementarie* (1582), p. 140, remarks on 'the enfranchising of such words, as circumscription', which means that the word was hardly new when *Othello* was written; but the same evidence suggests it had been recognized during Shakespeare's adult life as an imported novelty, and outside of a couple of theological uses it is very scarce before *Othello*. 'Confine' was common, though not as a noun without the terminal 's'.

her breeding' (1.3.236–8). He asks permission to bring her along to Cyprus, not

> to **comply with heat** – the young **affects**
> In me [or, my] **defunct**[46] – **and proper satisfaction**,
> But to be **free and bounteous** to her mind . . .
>   No, when **light-winged** toys
> Of **feathered** Cupid seel with wanton dullness
> My **speculative and officed** instruments,
> That my disports corrupt and taint my business,
> Let housewives make a skillet of my helm,
> And all **indign and base** adversities
> Make head against my estimation.   (1.3.263–74)

This remarkable flurry, in a span of fewer than two hundred lines, seems designed to present Othello, to both the on-stage and off-stage audiences, as cool enough to produce chills, and yet communicative enough to generate the warmth of connection.

Pierre Bourdieu has rightly argued against an excessively decontextualized understanding of language that once dominated the field of linguistics, but his model may benefit from an even more complex model of power and language here replicated by Shakespeare. According to Bourdieu, 'language is worth what those who speak it are worth, i.e. the power and authority in the economic and cultural power relations of the holders of the corresponding competence'.[47] My claim – which gives the *tu quoque* to Bourdieu's condemnation of ahistorical linguistics, and reflects in miniature the complaint that Bourdieu's theory underrates the potential of resistance – is that this speaker (like others in the humanistic Renaissance) will be deemed worth approximately what his language is worth. Othello's acceptance bears no simple correspondence to his subjugation of his native discourse to that of the dominant community. His position is certainly strengthened at this moment by Venice's pressing needs for his military abilities. But to reduce language to either a mystification of power or a quantity of capital[48] – even including the cultural capital (and the IOUs) Othello's introductory and valedictory speeches deploy – is to overlook the complex relationships of local buyers and alien sellers, and what rarities those sellers have to offer. 'Symbolic capital' may be 'inseparable from the speaker's position in the social structure',[49] but a shrewd speaker can negotiate favourable exchange-rates for that capital and thereby improve his accounts.

Othello's verbal mode fits Mikhail Bakhtin's category of 'hybridisation': 'a mixture of two social languages within the limits of a single utterance, between two different linguistic consciousnesses, separated from one another by an epoch, by social differentiation, or by some other factor'; and this mixing is important not so much for the linguistic forms themselves as for 'the collision between different points of view on the world that are embedded in these forms'.[50] Othello does not aim merely at what Bourdieu would predict: to 'be believed, recognised, obeyed'.[51] By making his verbal self partly astonishing and partly recognizable, he intends to be charming – to exercise (as he half-jokingly acknowledges at 1.3.168) an alternative kind of witchcraft through his diction. He replicates, at the level of vocabulary, the charm already cast on Desdemona at the level of story – something that demands admiration (for being

---

46 Hulme, *Explorations*, pp. 153–4, suggests that 'defunct' here might mean 'free – of danger, punishment'; so eliminating the emendation of 'my' to 'me' and the punctuation imposed by modern editions on this sentence would make 'defunct and proper' another pairing of the sort I am describing. Othello would then be saying that, with his marriage authorized despite Brabantio's complaints, his bodily proximity to Desdemona would be legal and suitable, even though that is not, he insists, his motive for welcoming her company.

47 Pierre Bourdieu, 'The Economics of Linguistic Exchanges', *Social Science Information*, 17 (1977), 645–88, esp. 652.

48 'The structure of the linguistic production relation depends on the symbolic power relation between the two speakers, i.e. on the size of their respective capitals of authority': Bourdieu, 'The Economics of Linguistic Exchanges', p. 648.

49 Bourdieu, 'The Economics of Linguistic Exchanges', p. 646.

50 Mikhail Bakhtin, *The Dialogic Imagination: Four Essays*, ed. Michael Holquist, trans. Caryl Emerson and Michael Holquist (Austin, 1981), pp. 358, 360.

51 Bourdieu, 'The Economics of Linguistic Exchanges', p. 648.

something she in her Venetian domesticity could never experience) but also somehow enables sympathetic identification. To recognize fully the tragedy of 'he that was Othello', audiences must say, with her, ''twas strange, 'twas passing strange, / 'Twas pitiful, 'twas wondrous pitiful' (5.2.290; 1.3.159–60).

Several otherwise excellent scholarly commentators feel obliged to resist this spell and judge it as Iago does (before we have heard Othello speak a word), dismissing Othello's unusual diction as 'bombast circumstance / Horribly stuffed with epithets of war' (1.1.13–14). Lynne Magnusson – elsewhere admirably alert to Shakespeare's recognition of the complex social matrices shaping characters' speech[52] – criticizes Othello for 'bombast . . . an impulse to linguistic overreaching'.[53] Kenneth Gross diagnoses 'self-conscious excesses of ornament, almost ludicrous neologisms'.[54] George T. Wright (despite having noticed some subtle functions of hendiadys in *Hamlet*) dismisses the Moor's pairings as the mere 'orotundity' of an 'incorrigibly extravagant' man 'excessively disposed to use the doublet theatrically'.[55] Simon Palfrey – although he recognizes acutely that 'Othello's bloated and half-borrowed discourse is a crucial marker of his incipient tragedy' – hears mostly 'a snip and paste job gleaned from some unholy mix of official documents and ancient romance', and perceives these doublets as 'over-stuffed padding' in which 'the second noun is pretty much redundant'.[56]

Much virtue in 'pretty much': Othello's doublets are obviously different from the mere repetitiveness of Anglo-Saxon monosyllables mustered by Justice Shallow (*2 Henry IV*, 3.2.95–9) or, more winningly, Cordelia. They also differ from the mode of hendiadys that pairs words to complicate or compromise the meanings of those words; Othello's doublets instead signal his own complications and compromises. Sylvia Adamson recognizes that Shakespeare's matching of high-style words with their low-style synonyms can produce the illusion of a rounded character; but she reads the effect of Othello's diglossia as 'a glimpse of a private man behind the public hero, of a sincere feeling behind

the rhetorical splendor'.[57] I see a murkier and more politically constrained division.

If 'hendiadys is a principle that asserts conjunction and *thwarts* it',[58] so is multiculturalism. If we recognize the double-bind of Othello's social situation, we can find those pairings fully apt to the play's tragic theme. Iago declares 'I am not what I am'; Othello is constantly declaring (as if to a Customs and Immigration officer) more than one self. Frank Kermode characterizes Othello's language as 'innocent pompousness', and notes that to 'use a strange word rather than a familiar one' is something Othello 'does on a good many other occasions'.[59] My claim is that Othello often uses a strange word *along with* a familiar one that glosses it – a device that Shakespeare had tested on the Ghost in *Hamlet*, another figure caught between worlds, who must seem unsettlingly alien and distant yet also eligible for sympathy.

What produces Othello's 'language habitus' (to use Bourdieu's term, but to go beyond his limitation of that concept to 'a dimension of class habitus'[60]) is his habitation of two worlds, in neither of which he feels fully at home. The locus of Othello's speech is always already Cyprus – indeed, in his speeches to the Senate he may be displaying his unique suitability for that posting, offering a

---

[52] Lynne Magnusson, *Shakespeare and Social Dialogue: Dramatic Language and Elizabethan Letters* (Cambridge, 1999).

[53] Lynne Magnusson, '"Voice Potential". Language and Symbolic Capital in *Othello*', in *Shakespeare and Language*, ed. Catherine M. S. Alexander (Cambridge, 2004), esp. p. 219; Magnusson does notice the insistence of doublets in Othello's introductory speeches, but sees them instead as ordinary embellishments signalling insecurity.

[54] Kenneth Gross, 'Slander and Skepticism in *Othello*,' *ELH*, 56 (1989), 819–52, esp. 826.

[55] Wright, 'Hendiadys and *Hamlet*', pp. 168–93, esp. pp. 175–6.

[56] Palfrey, *Doing Shakespeare*, pp. 52–3.

[57] Sylvia Adamson, 'With Double Tongue: Diglossia, Stylistics and the Teaching of English', in *Reading, Analysing and Teaching Literature*, ed. Mick Short (London, 1989), pp. 221–2.

[58] Cheney, *Shakespeare's Literary Authorship*, p. 144.

[59] Kermode, *Shakespeare's Language*, p. 180.

[60] Bourdieu, 'The Economics of Linguistic Exchanges', p. 660.

rhetorical resumé, at the moment he most needs to be needed there – and Cyprus, significantly, is the locale of the secondary bloom of neologisms in the play, as several characters attempt to speak to this liminal territory, claimed by two empires.[61] Throughout *Othello*, neologistic speech remains a significant index of alienation, and not just for the title character. This may explain why Michael Cassio, scorned by Iago as a vain, over-educated Florentine seducer among the salt-of-the-sea Venetians, has more than his share of minor neologisms, created by small prefix alterations: it marks him as a little bit foreign, and a little bit affected. More centrally, Shakespeare has Iago – the 'Turk' disguised as a loyal Venetian, the man who swears 'By Janus' in 1.2 – introduce himself through doublets such as 'duteous and knee-crooking knave' and 'timorous accent and dire yell' (1.1.45; 75, with other examples here and at the end of 1.3) that reveal his characteristic satiric and nativist mode, deflating the pretensions of others by dropping from exotic and exalted terms to their blunt Anglo-Saxon equivalents. He thus does in small what he will do to undo Othello in the plot at large, reducing romance to materiality, and the foreign-word-weaving aristocrat thereby to a mere beast. As with 'honest',[62] Iago often balances the old and new meanings of single words to conceal his real intentions, whereas Othello balances old words with new ones to display his complex self.

Othello's near-repetitions serve, not so much to provide Erasmian *copia*, as to imply Laingian schizophrenia; the Shakespearian doublet that William Empson identifies as a type of ambiguity[63] may function here instead as a symptom of dual citizenship. The tension persists even at the micro-level of Othello's name, decipherable as 'Ottoman' with an Italian suffix;[64] and at the overarching level of the play's title, *The Tragedie of Othello, the Moore of Venice*. Othello evinces small resurgences of this verbal tic as his split identity reasserts itself around the murder of Desdemona. The temptation scene adds 'contract and purse thy brow together', 'exsufflicate and blowed surmises', 'icy current and compulsive course', and 'destiny unshunnable' (3.3.117, 186, 457, 279). His soliloquy opening the final scene, as he prepares the murder, begins with forty-one monosyllables and one bi-syllable before exploding, like a chilly firework, into 'monumental alabaster' (5.2.1–5). He calls the handkerchief – at once the most lowly domestic and most exotically magical item – a 'recognizance and pledge of love' (5.2.221), and then tells Desdemona's corpse that 'When we shall meet at count [Quarto; 'compt', Folio] / This look of thine will hurl my soul from heaven, / And fiends will snatch at it' (5.2.280–2). The moment audiences spend wondering what 'count' or 'compt' is, before the next line explains it as Last Judgment, provides another opportunity to wonder at Othello's beautiful strangeness just when we have been repelled by his horrible deed – committed partly because he could not reconcile a Christian discourse of gratuitous love (from 'the divine Desdemona', 2.1.74) with a paganistic discourse (echoed and amplified by Iago) that says love must be earned and can be quantified.[65]

When Othello speaks, finally, of his 'subdued' eyes (5.2.357), the adjective is unusual (though not as novel as the *OED* suggests), but prepared by Desdemona's use of the common verb form at 1.3.250; and Othello's combination of the etymological senses ('deceived' and 'purged') with the homophonic hint of 'dewed' is fulfilled when the sentence goes on to describe his guilty teardrops. The domesticated Othello then silences the exotic one – not just in his allegorical construal of his suicide, but also in his terribly simple dying

---

61 Shakespeare may also be signalling the strangeness of the place, and the dramatic grandeur of both the storm and the emotional reunion with 'ruffianed', 'chidden', 'enchafèd', 'ensheltered', 'banged', 'designment', 'aerial', 'arrivance', 'blazoning', 'engineer', 'ensteeped', 'enclog' and 'Enwheel' (2.1.7–88).

62 William Empson, 'Honest in *Othello*', in *The Structure of Complex Words* (Cambridge, 1989), pp. 218–49.

63 Empson, *Seven Types*, pp. 88–101.

64 David Schalkwyk, *Speech and Performance in Shakespeare's Sonnets and Plays* (Cambridge, 2002), pp. 180–3, observes that this name was created 'supposedly by adding to the first syllable of "Oth-oman" the Italianate "-ello"', and goes on to discuss perceptively the dangers represented by such 'splitting of self across two names'.

65 Watson, 'The Reformation Othello', *passim*.

words – 'I kissed thee ere I killed thee. No way but this: / Killing myself, to die upon a kiss' (5.2.368–9) – just when he has made us love that verbal exoticism most, set against the blank foil of Lodovico's official Venetian rhetoric that closes the play. In short – I should say, 'in other words' – Othello is sold to the audience partly as Shakespearian drama as a whole is sold to the audience: as a purveyor of new words that offer a glimpse into wonderful and terrible new worlds.

Less than two years after Othello first spoke, Thomas Middleton similarly signalled the liminal social status of the usurer Harry Dampit by peppering his ordinary speech with neologisms (thus also linking the morally dubious coining of money to the coining of words).[66] Within that same brief aftermath, Shakespeare himself used the collapse of Lear's exalted diction into brutally blunt Anglo-Saxon monosyllables in the final scene to convey the plainness with which Lear has come to perceive the brutality of life and death; and used the leap from extreme verbal simplicity into neologistic elaboration to convey Macbeth's slippage from selfish determination to self-alienating rationalization:

> If it were done when 'tis done, then 'twere well
> It were done quickly. If th'assassination
> Could trammel up the consequence, and catch
> With his surcease success . . .   (1.7.1–4)

The double character of Macbeth, at war with himself, is similarly signalled by a division between high and low diction when he complains that 'this my hand will rather / The multitudinous seas incarnadine, / Making the green one red' (2.2.59–61). The aptly multi-syllabic 'multitudinous' – not attested before 1603 – is set against its aptly simple antonym 'one'; in the same pair of lines, Shakespeare alters the form, the former function, and the previous meaning of the rare and difficult 'incarnadine', and then defines it vividly in simple monosyllables. The device of delineating characters by their neologisms – as in *Love's Labour's Lost* and *Troilus and Cressida* – thus becomes a much subtler tool, a brush for tragic portraiture rather

than broad comic caricature or satiric disorientation.

5. THE POWER OF SPEECH

Rhetorical knowledge was real power, in the collective mind of Renaissance humanism. Words mattered not only for persuasion in courtship, courtiership, and the law-courts. They mattered greatly in geopolitics, as Shakespeare's second history tetralogy demonstrates through Richard II's rhetoric-riddled fall, Prince Hal's mastery of Eastcheap dialects, his inspirational unification of the British as Henry V, and Princess Katherine's word-by-word preparation for the subjugation of France (*1 Henry IV*, 2.5.4–32; *Henry V*, 3.4). The expansion of world trade and the emergence of vernacular literatures made the development of English into an essential work of patriotism, as many writers eagerly asserted. Words mattered no less in soteriology, where Catholics and Protestants had very different ideas of how words would save, and in which language, but no doubt that they were indispensible for salvation. And they were a matter of survival – for swinging a deal, finding a laugh or a friend, or demanding respect – on the mean streets of Elizabethan London.

The early modern period 'exhibits the fastest growth of the vocabulary in the history of the English language, in absolute figures as well as in proportion to the total', with 'an extremely rapid increase in new words especially between 1570

---

[66] In *A Trick to Catch the Old One*, Dampit's personality and social status are both 'registered in his inventive language: 'trampler', 'fooliaminy', 'infortunity', 'gernative', 'mullipood'. Dampit's speech is familiar, colloquial, and alien at once. His penchant for neologisms in conventional, if energetic, exchanges highlights the oddity of his role in the community: he is successful within the law but operates beyond its bounds; he is widely known but close to no one' (Eric Leonidas, 'The School of the World: Trading on Wit in Middleton's *Trick to Catch the Old One*', *Early Modern Literary Studies*, 12 (2007), 1–27, esp. 24–5; available at http://extra.shu.ac.uk/emls/12–3/leontri2.htm). The technique is different – fewer doublets or lexical affixations – but lexical innovations again signal liminality: a borderline personality in a man of the borderlands.

and 1630'.[67] This corresponds to the prime of the English drama, which drew on those new verbal energies and (after skimming off a little middleman profit) fed them back into the system. Nearly a third of the neologisms created in English during the entire Renaissance emerged between 1588 and 1612,[68] which is to say, within the quarter-century scope of Shakespeare's career as a playwright. A mass of newcomers to London, arriving from all over an England far more diverse in its dialects than we can now imagine, would have both faced and presented great linguistic challenges; and – in a society where, as Philip Sidney acidly remarked, Londoners were inclined 'to jest at straungers, because they speake not English so well as wee doe'[69] – people would have had special incentives to catch up on the latest parlances.

If writers lured clients by promising social ascent and seductive graces, they also depicted the humiliation of those who acquired their words from some inferior supplier. Shakespeare's unwitting masters of malapropism such as Dogberry, Bottom, Elbow, Mistress Quickly, and the Gobbos constitute a kind of negative advertising. In fact, Shakespeare and his colleagues provide more examples of people embarrassing themselves by trying to echo theatrical grandiosities than examples of people actually succeeding with such echoes. Auditors often recorded appealing locutions in commonplace books; the learning of single words may not have required such a record, but it was a miniature of the same process, prying loose a piece of artful language to take home – where it often ended up looking ridiculous rather than magnificent, as when Polonius savours 'mobbled queen' (*Hamlet*, 2.2.506). Perhaps the rhetorical commodity was then so saleable that drumming up demand was less important than diverting market-share from rival manufacturers.

Alternatively, the predominance of failed mimics may derive from the ambivalence of English Renaissance drama generally towards social volatility: plays implied they could teach the means of social advancement, but they also assured people that their inferiors would only demonstrate their insufficiencies for higher rank if they

tried to ascend through borrowed rhetoric.[70] The malaprops tend to be lower-class characters attempting dignified forms and seeking access to professional vocabularies – Bottoms aspiring to the top – and their mangling of a privileged lexicon made an essentialist case against social levelling. This contradictory function matches the way Shakespearian drama has been presented for centuries: on the one hand, as a resource whereby menial classes could improve themselves into sensibility and respectability, and non-white races could participate in a shared and therefore equalizing human essence, yet on the other hand, as an

---

67 Görlach, *Introduction to Early Modern English*, pp. 136–7. The surge was noted in 1668: 'this last Century may be conjectured to have made a greater change in our Tongue, then any of the former, as to the addition of new words': Wilkins, quoted by Görlach, p. 138.

68 Garner, 'Shakespeare's Latinate Neologisms', p. 209. Blank, *Broken English*, p. 40, claims that 'the period 1500–1659 saw the introduction of between 10,000 and 25,000 new words into the language, with the practice of neologism culminating in the Elizabethan period'; see also p. 44: 'The period from 1580 to 1619, the era of Nashe and Shakespeare, seems to have been the heyday of neologizing in England.' Culpeper and Clapham, 'The borrowing of Classical and Romance words', endorse a figure of 'somewhat above 12000' during the Renaissance, as well as the idea that this constituted a notable acceleration; they also endorse the belief that 'borrowing from Latin peaked in the period from about 1580–1660' (pp. 210–11). Nevalainen, 'Shakespeare's New Words', p. 246, observes that 'English was gaining new functions as a standard language in the public sphere, and was therefore in the process of acquiring a wealth of new vocabulary' in the Renaissance.

69 Sir Phillip Sidney, *An apologie for poetrie* (1595), sig. K3r. Cf. Blank, *Broken English*, p. 3: 'The Renaissance saw the rise of dialect comedy, and juxtaposing a peasant dialect with the King's English was, often enough, played for laughs. One of the first genres to incorporate dialect was the early sixteenth-century popular jest book; many jests hinge on provincials and foreigners being unable to speak the language properly.'

70 Adamson, 'Literary Language', in *The Cambridge History of the English Language*, ed. Roger Lass, vol. 3 (Cambridge, 1999), pp. 539–95, 575–6, perceives a bias in the modern tendency to call the verbal novelties of lower-class characters 'malapropisms' and those of higher-class characters 'neologisms'; but this accusation seems to me to overlook the ways that Shakespeare marks the malapropisms as comically erroneous (and usually antonymic) rather than innovative.

implicit (and sometimes explicit) validation of aristocratic culture and Eurocentrism.

The Elizabethan and Jacobean theatre offered verbal rungs for a social climb, even if there was always danger of a humiliating fall. As Cathy Shrank observes, Renaissance reformers of English such as Thomas Wilson worried that 'language overburdened with foreign neologisms threatens to drive apart, not bring together, the national community by hindering communication, particularly for the less educated, accentuating social difference'.[71] Wilson's solution is to 'banishe al suche affected Rhetorique', but a ban was unlikely to hold when the use of such rhetoric conferred status. Instead, we see a progression: 'Where, in the 1540s, Andrew Borde used "difficult" Latinate words to flatter an educated elite, and in the 1550s Wilson sought to remove them, the dictionary writers of the late sixteenth and early seventeenth centuries were concerned to explain and "democratize" them.'[72] We may trace a parallel evolution in the English drama of the same era, moving from the university wits to the public-theatre playwrights, and it may explain why the elaborate classicist neologisms of Marston – clearly designed to 'flatter an educated elite' – were mocked by Jonson (who makes a Marston-figure vomit up such indigestible terms in *Poetaster*) and eventually superseded by Shakespeare's determination to offer a public audience the power of a rapidly expanding language. If Renaissance drama 'retails elements of high culture to the middling sorts',[73] one such element was surely lexical.

The lyrics accompanying the famous 'Othello music'[74] exemplify transmission of vocabulary laterally, by reaching across into a foreign culture – a version of colonial commerce. The high-humanist innovations in English are versions of domestic social-climbing. Learning downward was also important, however: partly for the sheer pleasures of billingsgate (many teachers now arrange 'railing' or 'flyting' contests, using insults culled from the plays, to introduce schoolchildren to the energies of Shakespearian language), but also to avoid being gulled or cozened (two verbs the drama itself helped popularize) by the many predatory schemers who – aided by the anonymities of the new urban landscape – lurked as parasites, using a secret 'cant' or jargon.

The street-slang lesson Prince Hal offers to Poins, Shakespeare offers to us at the same time: 'They call drinking deep "dyeing scarlet"' (*1 Henry IV*, 2.5.14–15; see also *2 Henry IV*, 4.3.68–71). A popular early Elizabethan tract also offered translations of a new criminal language 'halfe myngled with Englishe when it is familiarly talked'[75] – a lowly version of Othello's mixed parlance. Tricksters lived on the boundaries of normal speech. A poem in dialogue form depicting a con-artist pretending not to know English – 'me non spek englys by my fayt / My servaunt spek you what me sayt'[76] – may anticipate Princess Katherine's coy tactics in the final act of *Henry V* distinctly enough to remind us that the niche of obscured language has always been a haven for disempowered people. Opening that niche to the ruling class through coney-catching guidebooks presumably limited the effectiveness of that sanctuary. Doubtless there was an element of salesmanship, even a kind of linguistic protection-racket in offering defences against criminal language at least partly invented by the author. We need not take these tracts at face value, as purely objective revelations of real dangers, to

---

[71] Cathy Shrank, *Writing the Nation in Reformation England, 1530–1580* (Oxford, 2004), p. 190.

[72] Shrank, *Writing the Nation*, p. 190. Adamson, 'With Double Tongue', p. 209, perceives a shift from early dictionaries which are fundamentally remedial and focused on written language, to those of the later eighteenth century, which provide 'the social aspirant [with] instruction in prestige forms of speech'. I believe that the theatrical instances I have been describing bridge the gaps between those two types.

[73] Charles Whitney, *Early Responses to Renaissance Drama* (Cambridge, 2009), p. 118.

[74] G. Wilson Knight, *The Wheel of Fire* (London, 1993), pp. 97–100; for my purposes, it seems noteworthy that Knight claims that Othello offers 'no fusing of word with word, rather a careful juxtaposition of one word or image with another'.

[75] Thomas Harman, *A Caveat or Warening for Commen Cursetors* [1567] (London, 1573), sig. G3v.

[76] Robert Copland, *The hye way to the spyttell hous* (London, 1535–36?), sig. C1r.

recognize that they sold access to an emerging lexicon, and thereby control over a perceived threat from below.

That the theatre was a marketplace – and vice versa – is not a new idea.[77] Materialist readings of Shakespeare's theatre have become prominent, even dominant, in recent years. Yet no commercial analysis of what Dekker called 'that light commodity of words' has emerged. Perhaps the fact that language is evanescent, almost *im*material, has discouraged analysis of how it was sold, and how that trade affected the class-system. Yet Bakhtin himself recognized that the rapidly evolving common language was essential to the marketplace of the Renaissance, and to its hierarchies.

Western cultures have long relied on popular writers to enliven their verbal style and update their lingo; and recent research suggests (and literature professors will like to believe) that an extensive vocabulary may be sexually alluring, just as complexity of song can be as important a display for a mate-seeking nightingale as plumage is for a peacock.[78] Disputes over which kinds of verbiage were healthy and which were merely garish – George Gascoigne aspired 'to make our native language commendable in it selfe, than gay with the feathers of straunge birdes'[79] – only confirm that there were incentives for the right kind of display. The phenomenon I have been describing is hardly unique to Elizabethan and Jacobean England.

That does not mean, however, that it is entirely trans-historical. Other types of rhetorical self-help books evidently became saleable around the year 1600 in England: along with the aforementioned exposés of 'canting' terms came collections of similes for all occasions, and handbooks promising new and improved ways of writing letters, poems, and sermons. In popular medical texts, 'An aid to comprehension was occasionally provided by word pairs, with the foreign terms followed by common equivalents or interpretations.'[80] English dictionaries are another genre that emerged during Shakespeare's years as a playwright. The first, Robert Cawdrey's *Table Alphabetical of Hard Usual English Words*, appeared in 1604, the same year that *Othello* was first performed; in 1623, the year

Shakespeare's First Folio was published, Cockeram's *English Dictionarie* included a Latinizing section where 'any desirous of . . . a more refined and elegant speech . . . shall there receive the exact and ample word to express the same'. Shakespeare's ascent to the rank of gentleman was a direct result of economic developments – the social fluidity produced by urbanization and emergent capitalism – but also an indirect result of that fluidity as it coincided with the diachronic evolution of language.

The question so central to ongoing controversies in the social sciences as well as the humanities – whether the chief work of cultures is performed by individual will and genius or instead by large impersonal collective historical forces – is replicated in miniature when we ask whether Shakespeare's astonishing productivity of lasting neologisms was an index of his greatness or, instead, of his moment. The safe answer may also be the correct one: both, irreducibly so. Clearly others tried to become large-scale merchants of new ways of speaking, but they did not succeed on Shakespeare's scale, because (I believe) they lacked his instinct for making neologisms accessible and memorable, and for linking them to the settings of the plays and the psychology of the speakers. No wonder, then, that the schoolman Robert Greene complained about this 'upstart crow, beautified with our feathers'.[81] Artful words – including 'ruminate', which Shakespeare may have learned from Greene – were the plumage of the new social elites, and those who could produce them in quantity and quality could find thousands of customers on the South Bank.

---

77 Mikhail Bakhtin, in *Rabelais and His World*, trans. Helene Iswolsky (Bloomington, 1984) sees the marketplace as a theatre; Jean-Christophe Agnew, in *Worlds Apart: The Market and the Theater in Anglo-American Thought, 1550–1750* (Cambridge, 1986), sees the anxieties of the early modern marketplace reinforced by theatrical practice.

78 Geoffrey Miller, *The Mating Mind: How Sexual Choice Shaped the Evolution of Human Nature* (New York, 2001), pp. 369–92.

79 Jones, p. 115, quoting from Gascoigne's *Complete Works*, ed. J. W. Cunliffe (1907), vol. I, p. 6.

80 Görlach, *Introduction to Early Modern English*, p. 148,

81 Robert Greene, *Greene's groats-worth of witte, bought with a million of repentance* (London: 1592), p. 40.

Clearly these diction-lessons are part of a broader trade in *habitus*-upgrades for an era of social fluidity: 'as merchaundise, so also new words', according to the influential 1561 translation of Castiglione's *Book of the Courtier*.[82] Although the emphasis in the sixteenth century was more on words than on syntax,[83] the teaching of rhetoric (professed explicitly by Peacham and Puttenham, and indirectly by Shakespeare and his rivals) often involved larger units. What Shakespeare accomplished by combining words far outweighs what he accomplished by inventing them. But the study of neologisms offers a narrow aperture that brings an overlooked aspect of early modern theatre and Shakespearian technique into focus. This aperture may also bring into view, if not yet into focus, the question of what teachers of language and literature – of vocabulary and sensibility – may have to offer in the marketplaces of the twenty-first century.

---

[82] *The courtyer of Count Baldessar Castilio*, trans. Thomas Hoby (1561) sig. C1r.

[83] Russ McDonald, *Shakespeare and the Arts of Language* (New York, 2001), p. 36, drawing on the scholarship of Jane Donawerth and Judith Anderson, observes that 'sixteenth-century educators and commentators wrote much more extensively about words than about grammar and syntax'.

HAMLET IN PLETTENBERG: CARL SCHMITT'S SHAKESPEARE

ANDREAS HÖFELE

I. ABOUT SCHMITT

There is a typewritten note among Carl Schmitt's papers in the North Rhine Westphalian state archives in Düsseldorf:

I make a bet that the Democratic candidate in the upcoming presidential election in the USA, Adlai Stevenson, will <u>not</u> be elected. I base my prognosis solely on the fact that Adlai Stevenson is called 'Hamlet', the 'Hamlet of Illinois'.

Plettenberg, 28 October 1956
Prof. Carl Schmitt[1]

There is also a list of correspondents (among them the writer Ernst Jünger) to whom Schmitt intended to – or actually did – communicate his thought, along with Schmitt's handwritten remark: 'Agree entirely: Americans don't deserve an intellectual president. Joseph H. Kaiser 29/10.'[2] The note, coming about six months after the publication of *Hamlet or Hecuba*,[3] is one of several records indicating Schmitt's abiding interest in Shakespeare's most famous play and character. Slight as his little witticism about the doomed Democrat from Illinois may seem, Schmitt liked it enough to use it in a public lecture on Hamlet in January 1957; and he returned to it again and again at what he saw as decisive historical junctures, adding further scribbled glosses: 'Bet overrun by the wheel of world history (Hungary – Egypt – Suez October 1956)'; 'But meanwhile (end of 1960) Kennedy elected (with minimal majority)'; 'Meanwhile August 1968 (occupation of Prague)'; 'Meanwhile Jimmy Carter November 1976'.

In Shakespeare's melancholy prince Schmitt saw not only 'a primal image of the human condition' (*HH* 7) but also a usable persona for newly emerging actors on the contemporary political stage. 'Hamlet-spotting' apparently became a kind of hobby with him. A slip of paper headed *Hamlet-Galerie* lists the Italian Socialist Giuseppe Saragat, 'Pope Montini (Paul VI)', Paul Sheffer[4] and once more Adlai Stevenson and Kennedy, the latter with a question mark and the explanatory term *Ko-Existenz*.[5] An article Schmitt – by then aged 91 – found in *Der Spiegel* (26 November 1979) and kept in his stack of Hamlet-related press-cuttings adds

---

1. Landesarchiv NRW, Abteilung Rheinland, Standort Düsseldorf (Nachlass Carl Schmitt) RW 265–21086. I would like to thank Jürgen Becker, trustee of the Schmitt estate, for kindly granting me permission to quote from the unpublished materials in the Düsseldorf archive. A shorter version of this article was presented in a seminar on political theology at the SAA conference in Seattle 2011 organized by Jennifer Rust and Nichole Miller. My thanks to the convenors and members of the seminar and especially Martin Moraw for his helpful response.

2. Joseph H. Kaiser (1921–1998), a constitutional law professor, was a student of Schmitt's in Berlin and later trustee of his estate.

3. Carl Schmitt, *Hamlet oder Hecuba. Der Einbruch der Zeit in das Spiel* (Düsseldorf, Cologne, 1956). Published in English as: Carl Schmitt, *Hamlet or Hecuba: The Intrusion of the Time into the Play*, trans. David Pan and Jennifer Rust (New York, 2009). References are identified as *HH* and given in brackets.

4. Paul Sheffer, originally Scheffer (1883–1963), was a journalist whom Schmitt had known since the 1920s. Why he is on this list remains obscure.

5. Landesarchiv NRW, Abteilung Rheinland, Standort Düsseldorf (Nachlass Carl Schmitt) RW 265–20313.

another candidate to the file: Enrico Berlinguer, the leader of Italy's Communist Party, whom the *Spiegel* article styles 'Red Hamlet'.[6] Trivial though this pursuit of latter-day Hamlets may seem, it is grounded in serious existential concerns. For Schmitt, Hamlet becomes a primal image of the condition of the post-war world and of his own place, or rather displacement, in it.

In what follows I want to look at Schmitt's engagement with *Hamlet* in a perspective that takes full account of its personal and political contexts. Following the 'discovery' of *Hamlet or Hecuba* in Anglo-American criticism, there has been a spate of publications that have sought to demonstrate it to be a major statement of Schmitt's politico-cultural thought and to link it with other major twentieth-century thinkers like Benjamin or Adorno.[7] My attempt here is to obtain a fuller view of what Schmitt is doing and why, by giving more attention than has hitherto been done to his situation in post-war Germany. One way to illuminate this context is to relate *Hamlet or Hecuba* to the theatre discourse of its time; another, to collate it with Schmitt's other Shakespearian writings. These consist of his 1952 preface to Lilian Winstanley's book on *Hamlet*, which is now available in an English translation,[8] the brief 'defence' of *Hamlet or Hecuba* that Schmitt delivered in June 1956, and the *Hamlet* lecture he gave in January 1957. The defence, entitled 'Was habe ich getan?' (What have I done?), has been published;[9] the unpublished lecture – part typescript, part notes – is among the Schmitt papers in the Düsseldorf archive.[10]

Regarding these writings as a coherent though by no means homogeneous ensemble will cast a somewhat different light on *Hamlet or Hecuba*, making it less easy to ignore what has been politely described as Schmitt's 'sometimes blunt allegorical reading of Hamlet'[11] and less politely as 'crass'.[12] It means that the more dubious features of the essay will not be quite so hastily cleared away as they usually are when critics draw a bead on what they regard as the genuinely valuable core of Schmitt's 'remarkable', 'crucial' or even 'key' text. Most recent articles on *Hamlet or Hecuba* are at pains to separate the wheat, as it were, from the

chaff; to pass over, in other words, the cranky literary detective, Lilian Winstanley, to whom Schmitt is massively indebted, in order to reach the loftier plane on which Schmitt 'corresponds' with Walter Benjamin.[13]

I want to linger on the chaff here, not least because this seems in keeping with Schmitt's own approach. A crucial argument in *Hamlet or Hecuba* is Schmitt's insistence that Shakespeare's art cannot be cordoned off from the public sphere of the Elizabethan popular theatre, from the 'filthy

---

6 RW 265–21086 vol. 1. Other press-cuttings in the Schmitt archive refer to J. Robert Oppenheimer as the 'Hamlet of modern physics' (obituary in *Die Zeit*, 3 March 1967, 9) and to Pope Paul VI, the 'Hamlet of Milan' (*Deutsches Allgemeines Sonntagsblatt*, 25 September 1977, 12) on the occasion of his eightieth birthday. A piece from *Rheinischer Merkur*, 29 November 1957, quotes Marcel Brion as calling Hamlet 'a prototypical European'. All in RW 265–20311.

7 For the latter, see David Pan, 'Afterword: Historical Event and Mythic Meaning in Carl Schmitt's *Hamlet or Hecuba*', in Schmitt, *Hamlet or Hecuba*, pp. 73–86.

8 Carl Schmitt, 'Foreword to the German Edition of Lilian Winstanley's *Hamlet and the Scottish Succession*', trans. Kurt R. Buhanan, *Telos*, 153 (2010), 164–77. References to this translation, cited as FW, are given in brackets.

9 Carl Schmitt, 'Was habe ich getan?' *Schmittiana*, V (1996), 13–19. This text is cited in brackets as WH. The translation is mine.

10 Carl Schmitt, 'Hamlet als mythische Figur der Gegenwart' (Hamlet as a mythical figure of the present), RW 265–20311. This text is cited in brackets as HM. The translation is mine.

11 Jennifer R. Rust and Julia Reinhard Lupton, 'Introduction: Schmitt and Shakespeare', in Schmitt, *Hamlet or Hecuba*, p. xix.

12 Michael Dobson, 'Short Cuts' (review of Schmitt, *Hamlet or Hecuba*), *London Review of Books*, 31:15 (6 August 2009), p. 22.

13 Rust and Lupton, 'Introduction', pp. xv–li at xv–xvi, speak of 'Schmitt's correspondence with Walter Benjamin'. We know that Benjamin wrote an adulatory letter to 'Esteemed Professor Schmitt' in December 1930. But we do not know what Schmitt wrote back or whether he wrote back at all, though it is perhaps unlikely that he did not acknowledge Benjamin's praise. To speak of a correspondence is misleading. For an English translation of Benjamin's letter and a discussion of his debt to Schmitt, see Samuel Weber, 'Taking Exception to Decision: Walter Benjamin and Carl Schmitt', *Diacritics*, 22 (1992), 5–18.

reality' he mockingly cites as the bugbear of ide-
alist aesthetics.[14] It is a misconception, he wrote
in a letter to Wolfgang Clemen, to conceive of
Shakespeare 'after the model of our great classics: Goethe, Schiller, Grillparzer, Hebbel' as 'a
writer working in his study, a literary homeworker
who submits his finished literary work to a literary
publisher'.[15] The *im*purity of Shakespearian drama,
its non-exclusiveness, provides a strong argument
for Schmitt's fundamental critique of the liberal-
bourgeois notion of a tidily separable autonomous
sphere of the aesthetic. Shakespeare's art, its very
greatness, Schmitt argues, is inseparable from its
'seat in life', from the rough, 'barbaric' time in
which Shakespeare and his audience lived, and
whose 'intrusion into the play' elevates *Hamlet* to
the status of authentic myth and effects its quantum
leap from *Trauerspiel* to tragedy.

It seems only appropriate then to approach
Schmitt's *Hamlet* with the same openness to the
intrusion of the time that Schmitt himself deemed
indispensable for a proper understanding of Shakespeare. Schmitt represents his *Hamlet* essay as an
attack on a 'purity taboo deeply rooted in the tradition of German *Bildung*, a taboo which does not
permit one to speak of intrusions of the time into
the play' (WH 17). It would hardly be consistent,
then, to swaddle Schmitt's attack in a similar purity
taboo and dissociate *Hamlet or Hecuba* from the
ghosts of its author's past and from the ghost he
himself raised from one of the weirder cold case
files in the annals of Shakespeare scholarship.

Carl Schmitt's career has been the subject
of endless debate.[16] A staunch Catholic anti-
parliamentarian of the right, he rose to eminence
during the Weimar Republic as one of Germany's
most brilliant constitutional lawyers, an eminence
that carried him seamlessly into the Third Reich.[17]
Though he eventually failed to secure the position of 'Hitler's crown jurist'[18] – a label that has
nonetheless stuck to his name – this was not for
want of trying. Deploying his legal expertise to justify the dismantling of constitutional and civil rights
by the Nazis between 1933 and 1936, Schmitt
applauded both the 'night of the long knives'[19] and
the Nuremberg race laws.[20] The pre-eminent jurist

of the Third Reich, he fell victim nevertheless to
an intrigue hatched by Nazi rivals within the legal
profession.[21] Their attack, ironically, was abetted

---

[14] *HH* 47. The English translation has 'miserable reality',
which does not quite capture the German '*dreckichte Wirk-
lichkeit*'.

[15] Copy of an excerpt from a letter to Professor Wolfgang
Clemen in Munich, 14 July 1954. RW 265–21087. The
thought, including the term 'literary homeworker', recurs
almost verbatim in *HH* 34.

[16] For a lucid exposition of the controversial issues see Peter C.
Caldwell, 'Controversies over Carl Schmitt: A Review of
Recent Literature', *The Journal of Modern History*, 77 (2005),
357–87. Reinhard Mehring, *Carl Schmitt: Aufstieg und Fall*
(Munich, 2009) has been hailed by one reviewer as the
definitive biography. Although Mehring deserves praise for
his painstaking fairness (if not for the quality of his writing) this seems premature. Large parts of Schmitt's personal
diaries still await transcription (the provisional transcription
in the Düsseldorf archive ends with the year 1934) and large
parts of his huge correspondence still await study.

[17] Schmitt did not actively support Hitler's takeover in 1933
but served as legal adviser to General von Schleicher who
sought to prevent that takeover. But his views needed no
major adjustments in order to be compatible with, indeed
emphatically supportive of, the new regime. See e. g. Dirk
Blasius, *Carl Schmitt: Preussischer Staatsrat in Hitlers Reich*
(Göttingen, 2001).

[18] The term '*Kronjurist*' was apparently first used with reference to Schmitt in an article by Hellmut von Gerlach,
'Schleicher und sein Stahlhelm', *Die Weltbühne*, 28 (1932),
343, which castigates the anti-republican militarism of General von Schleicher, minister for the *Reichswehr*, and Schmitt
as a legal apologist of anti-parliamentarian measures. Prus-
sia, von Gerlach said, had a history of jurists like Schmitt
who would legally justify any breach of international or
constitutional law committed by the Crown.

[19] Schmitt celebrated Hitler's liquidation of the SA leader
Röhm on trumped-up charges of high treason as the
epochal transition from the obsolete liberal *Rechtsstaat* to the
'*unmittelbar gerechte Staat*' (immediately just state) in which
the (merely formal) principle of legality is superseded by
the '*Lebensrecht des Volkes*' (a people's right to live): Carl
Schmitt, 'Der Führer schützt das Recht' (The Fuehrer pro-
tects the law) (1934), in his *Positionen und Begriffe im Kampf
mit Weimar – Genf – Versailles 1923–1939*, 3rd edn (Berlin,
1994), pp. 227–32.

[20] Carl Schmitt, 'Die Verfassung der Freiheit' (The Constitution of Liberty), *Deutsche Juristen-Zeitung*, 40 (1935),
cols. 1133–5.

[21] See Blasius, *Carl Schmitt*, pp. 153–80; Mehring, *Carl Schmitt*,
pp. 339–40 and 355–80.

by some articles published in a Swiss emigré journal in which Schmitt's former student Waldemar Gurian – one of those emigrants whose expulsion from Germany Schmitt had warmly welcomed[22] – exposed inconsistencies between Schmitt's Weimar opinions and his Nazi zealotry.[23] Gurian's points were avidly taken up by Schmitt's Nazi enemies. In an attempt to clear himself from charges of opportunism, Schmitt organized a conference on *Das Judentum in der Rechtswissenscʃhaft* in October 1936 which he addressed with a rabidly anti-Semitic keynote lecture on the perniciousness of the Jewish element in German jurisprudence.[24] Fighting the Jews, Schmitt declaimed, was an 'exorcism' accomplishing, now quoting Hitler, 'the work of the Lord'.[25] But the public campaign his enemies had launched against him in the SS-journal *The Black Corps* had already gone too far. Schmitt lost all his positions in the Nazi hierarchy. Only personal intervention by Hans Frank and Hermann Göring prevented further reprisals and saved Schmitt the title of Prussian state councillor as well as his chair at Berlin University.

Despite this reversal of fortune, Schmitt continued to publish and lecture in Germany and abroad throughout the war. But his glory years under the Nazis were not forgotten in 1945. While many an active supporter of National Socialism was quietly absorbed into the new system, with the legal profession in particular notoriously prone to turning a blind eye to its members' pasts, Schmitt was never readmitted into the fold. He had simply been too visible. Thwarted in his ambition to become the Third Reich's authoritative legal spokesman, he was now also thwarted in the hope to earn some credit for the hardships he had undergone at the hands of his SS adversaries. He thus felt doubly punished, the victim of both Hitler and Allied victors' justice. Never regaining a university professorship, he retreated to his provincial Westphalian hometown of Plettenberg, where he spent the remaining forty years of his long life, at first in the cramped family home of his childhood, then in a modest abode he christened 'San Casciano' after Machiavelli's refuge in exile. Unreconciled to post-war West German democracy, he

cultivated the role of the outcast, the victim of history, more sinned against than sinning, 'the King Lear of public law' as he styled himself in a

---

[22] Following the introduction of the law excluding non-Aryans from public service (7 April 1933), Schmitt wrote in a celebratory article in the Nazi paper *Westdeutscher Beobachter*: 'The new regulations...cleanse public life from non-Aryan, alien elements...We are learning again how to distinguish. But principally we are learning to distinguish correctly between friend and enemy.' ('Das gute Recht der deutschen Revolution', 2 May 1933). Among those who fled Germany because of the new law was Schmitt's famous colleague Hans Kelsen: 'Schmitt helped in ousting Kelsen, the Jewish liberal enemy, from the Law Faculty at Cologne (shortly after personally securing Kelsen's help to get himself appointed there)': David Dyzenhaus, *Legality and Legitimacy: Carl Schmitt, Hans Kelsen and Herman Heller in Weimar* (Oxford, 1997), p. 84. In another article for *Westdeutscher Beobachter* ('Die deutschen Intellektuellen' (The German intellectuals), 31 May 1933) Schmitt reviled emigrants as scum: 'may they be spit out for all times!'

[23] Between October 1934 and December 1936 Gurian published ten articles about Schmitt's role in the Third Reich in *Deutsche Briefe 1934–1938: Ein Blatt der katholischen Emigration*, 2 vols., ed. Heinz Hürten (Mainz, 1969).

[24] Gopal Balakrishnan, *The Enemy: An Intellectual Portrait of Carl Schmitt* (London, 2000), p. 207, calls this event 'a well-organized intellectual pogrom' but then goes on to speculate that 'perhaps Schmitt thought that if the role and presence of Jews in German legal culture could be precisely delimited, libelous, indirect insinuations of Jewish influence could be curtailed'. There is not a shred of evidence for such an apologetic assessment. What the publication of Schmitt's diaries reveals with ever more irrefutable clarity is, on the contrary, his deeply ingrained anti-Semitism. See Wolfgang Schuller, ed., *Carl Schmitt: Tagebücher 1930 bis 1934* (Berlin, 2010). Raphael Gross, *Carl Schmitt und die Juden: Eine deutsche Rechtslehre* (Frankfurt am Main, 2000) (Carl Schmitt and the Jews: A German legal doctrine) makes anti-Semitism the very core of Schmitt's thinking. Although this overstates the case, George Schwab much more seriously *under*states it when he claims that anti-Semitism was 'a trait Schmitt...acquired overnight' (as late as 1936) and that this 'lip service to the Nazi vogue' constituted the whole extent of Schmitt's post-1933 opportunism: George Schwab, 'Carl Schmitt: Political Opportunist?' *Intellect*, 103 (1975), 334–7 at 336–7.

[25] Carl Schmitt, 'Die deutsche Rechtswissenschaft im Kampf gegen den jüdischen Geist. Schlusswort auf der Tagung der Reichsgruppe Hochschullehrer des NSRB vom 3. und 4. Oktober 1936', *Deutsche Juristen-Zeitung* 41 (1936), col. 1193–9 at 1197.

letter to a former student in 1950.[26] Banished from the public arena, the dethroned king of jurists turned to literature. Ever '*unzeitgemäss*' (untimely, but not so much premature as belated), the 'last representative of the *ius publicum Europaeum*', he also became the last in a long line of German writers, poets and intellectuals to find in *Hamlet* 'the form and pressure' of their own life and times. Schmitt, it is true, sought to distance himself from this tradition, which he dismissed as romantic and subjectivist. But in this, as in much else, he doth protest too much. If Hamlet, as Schmitt says in his 1957 lecture, 'has become the mythical figure of the European intellectual' (HM 1), then the nineteenth-century Romantic legacy is the enabling condition of the myth's continuing discursive presence. And it is this legacy that enables Schmitt to use Hamlet as a mirror of his own present.

2. WHAT'S JAMES TO US?

In its 5 November 1952 issue, *Der Spiegel*, Germany's investigative weekly news magazine, ran an article titled 'Hamlet war Jakob' (Hamlet was James). 'Carl Schmitt', the article begins, 'the ostracised Nestor of German constitutional law, has written the preface to a book that his daughter, the stage designer Anima Schmitt, has translated for the first time into German.'[27] Schmitt's notoriety apparently made for a good opening. The rest of the article, which summarizes Winstanley's main propositions and the critical responses her book elicited from English reviewers in the 1920s, mentions neither Schmitt nor his preface again.[28]

How and when exactly Schmitt chanced upon Lilian Winstanley's *Hamlet and the Scottish Succession*[29] has to my knowledge not been ascertained. By 1952 the book had clearly outlived its moment of critical attention and was gathering dust as one of the more eccentric fruits of Shakespeare philology. For Schmitt's daughter Anima, who subsequently translated several of her father's works into Spanish, the rendering of Winstanley's book into German was the first step into a career as a translator. The preface by her famous father

certainly helped to promote the book, as did the more in-your-face title *Hamlet, Sohn der Maria Stuart* (Hamlet, Son of Mary Stuart),[30] which cleverly flags not just one but two icons of German literary culture.

Winstanley's study was first published in 1921 to mixed and in some cases unsparingly vitriolic reviews. Given its medley of speculative ingenuity and sheer Fluellenism, this is hardly surprising. At the heart of her argument is the hypothesis that Shakespeare's play owes more to contemporary history than to the 'Nordic saga' from which its protagonist derives his name, more to the turbulent life of Mary Queen of Scots as chronicled by George Buchanan[31] than to the Amleth of Saxo Grammaticus. Hamlet, she claims, is a covert portrait of James I, whose father, Lord Darnley, was murdered

---

[26] Letter to Karl Lohmann, 21 July 1950. RW 569–490. One of the issues Caldwell seeks to clarify in his review essay is 'whether Schmitt served in the Federal Republic as an enemy of democracy or as a mentor to some of the most important political thinkers of the postwar democratic order': Caldwell, 'Controversies over Carl Schmitt', p. 358. The answer must be that he did both. For the complexities of Schmitt's post-war affiliations and influence, see Jan-Werner Müller, *A Dangerous Mind: Carl Schmitt in Post-War European Thought* (New Haven and London, 2003).

[27] Unsigned review, 'Hamlet war Jakob', *Der Spiegel*, Wednesday, 5 November 1952, 26–7.

[28] Four years later, *Der Spiegel* also ran an article on *Hamlet or Hecuba* ('Die Mutter ist tabu', *Der Spiegel*, 35 (1956), 29 August 1956). Rudolf Augstein (1923–2002), founder and part-owner of *Der Spiegel*, was another influential public intellectual of the post-war period who maintained contact with Schmitt. Apropos of *Hamlet or Hecuba* he wrote to Schmitt: 'I almost like this even better than your former piece on the same subject' (quoted in Mehring, *Carl Schmitt*, p. 496 (my trans.)).

[29] Lilian Winstanley, *Hamlet and the Scottish Succession: Being an Examination of the Relations of the Play of 'Hamlet' to the Scottish Succession and the Essex Conspiracy* (Cambridge, 1921). Page references to this book are given in brackets in the text.

[30] Lilian Winstanley, *Hamlet, Sohn der Maria Stuart*, trans. Anima Schmitt (Pfullingen, 1952).

[31] George Buchanan, *Ane detectioun of the duinges of Marie Quene of Scottes, touchand the murder of hir husband, and hir conspiracie, adulterie, and pretensed mariage with the Erle Bothwell. And ane defence of the trew Lordis, mainteineris of the Kingis graces actioun and authoritie. Translatit out of the Latine quhilke was written by G.B.* (London, 1571).

in February 1567 and whose mother Mary Queen of Scots married the murderer, the Earl of Bothwell, in 'most wicked speed' just over three months later. In addition, Hamlet's character also contains features borrowed from the Earl of Essex. A veritable forest of resemblances proliferates round this central cluster of identifications. The circumstances and manners depicted in Shakespeare's Denmark, Winstanley writes, 'are, in the highest degree, distinctive and strange; but they can *every one* be paralleled in the case of sixteenth-century Scotland'(7). A mix of barbarism and erudition, of Protestantism and Catholicism, with notorious drinking habits, Shakespeare's fictitious Denmark is the spit and image of historical Scotland. In the play, 'a councillor is murdered in the presence of a queen' (9); the same fate befell Mary's secretary, Rizzio. At the Danish court we find a Guildenstern, a Rosencrantz and a Francisco; at the Scottish court, a (Danish!) Guildenstern and 'a Francesco, a friend of Rizzio's' (10), with an Eric Rosencrantz figuring marginally in the later life of Bothwell. No doubt, then, Horatio must be the faithful Earl of Mar, the only loyal friend of James's troubled youth; and Hamlet's self-accusations must echo the many letters in which Elizabeth I enjoined her hesitant successor-to-be not to bear the whips and scorns of his proud enemies, but to take arms against them. Exasperated by James's lack of resolution, Elizabeth writes: 'And since it so likes you to demand my counsel, I find so many ways your state so unjoynted, that it needs a skilfuller bone-setter than I to joyne each part in its right place' (81). 'One may compare this', Winstanley says, 'with Hamlet's bitter cry: The time is out of joint: O cursed spite / That ever I was born to set it right.' And she continues: 'In exactly the same way as Elizabeth piles up the indignities James has suffered, so Hamlet piles up those he endures himself' (81). 'So the thirty-year-old Shakespeare', a Swiss reviewer scoffed in 1924, 'had cognizance of Elizabeth's letter in 1592, or the words "unjoynted" and "joyned" were passing from mouth to mouth between London and Edinburgh ten years later! The whole book is built on such *salti mortali*.'[32]

Horatio says of Old Hamlet that 'A was a goodly king' (1.2.185), Darnley's dead body was eulogized by Buchanan as 'the goodliest corpse of any gentleman' (61). The Ghost wears full armour; Darnley was noted for often doing the same. Hamlet's father is killed in an orchard; so was Darnley. Hamlet's father has poison poured in his ear; so had – at least according to Mary's detractors – her first husband, François II. Darnley, too, was said to have been poisoned. He survived the attack, but the 'black Pimples breaking out all over his body' (53) parallel the 'vile and loathsome crust' that covers 'all [the] smooth body' (1.5.72–3) of Hamlet's dying father. Once this kind of paper-chase is set in motion, there is no stopping it. It generates evidence with the same snowball momentum that immunizes Anti-Stratfordians from doubt. 'Today the author is firmly convinced of the reality of her discoveries', the same Swiss reviewer concludes, 'but when, in years to come, she will calmly reread her book, she will recognize that she went flying to *Neverland* with Peter Pan.'[33]

Schmitt must have read a different book altogether. Winstanley's great achievement, he declares, the achievement that 'real critics' have recognized all along, is a turning away from the vagaries of subjectivism towards 'the objective' (FW 176). 'The mists of fanciful interpretation dissipate, the flickering (*Geflimmer*) of psychological possibilities ends. One sees the granite rock of a singular historical truth emerge, and the figure of a real king with a concrete fate appears' (FW 170, trans. modified). Thinly disguised as the 'old Scandinavian Hamlet saga' (FW 164), the true core of Shakespeare's *Hamlet* drama is to be found in its 'most immediate actualization of the directly lived event, the directly experienced fate' (FW 169). Shakespeare has not invented the dramatic plot but found it in contemporary historical reality.

---

[32] Bernhard Fehr, untitled review, *Beiblatt zur Anglia*, xxxv (1924), 1–16 at 6 (my translation). Fehr, featuring anonymously as 'a well-known Anglicist in Zurich' who sought to 'destroy' Winstanley's 'disruptive book', in turn receives a sound dressing down in Schmitt's foreword (FW 176).

[33] Fehr, *Beiblatt zur Anglia*, p. 6 (my trans.).

Schmitt's 1952 preface is even more emphatic about the immediacy and presence of the dramatized events than *Hamlet or Hecuba* would be four years later. Shakespeare's play is 'the most amazing instance of immediate proximity to its time that the history of great drama has ever seen' (FW 165, trans. mod.). The events it stages are as much 'topical present' for Shakespeare and his audience as 'the death in 1889 of Crown Prince Rudolf von Habsburg and the "tragedy of Mayerling" would have been for a Viennese audience or the Röhm affair for a Berlin audience in 1934' (FW 168, trans. mod.).

Such hammering home of real-life immediacy is yoked up with an equally forceful thrust towards a time-transcending essence or 'core'. As a key passage in the preface argues, it is 'the timely core of its presence' (FW 169) that 'holds the mysterious power to carry the drama from the present of its time and place of origin into posterity and to make possible the thousand interpretations and symbolizations of later centuries, without the drama losing its hero or its countenance (*Gesicht*)' (FW 169, trans. mod.).[34] The more closely Shakespeare's play is linked to its historical present, the more it can transcend that present. The logic of Schmitt's argument is encapsulated in an oxymoron: 'infinite singularity' (*unendliche Einmaligkeit*) (FW 169, trans. mod.).[35] It is in this coincidence of opposites – time-bound *versus* time-transcending, but also time-bound *ergo* time-transcending – that the mythical force of *Hamlet* has its origin.

Schmitt's argument is based on a linking of two oppositions: the opposition of historical truth and poetic invention, in which *Hamlet* is firmly located on the side of history; and the opposition of accidentals and essentials, surface and core. The latter proves somewhat harder to maintain. Shakespeare's *Hamlet*, Schmitt says, 'is a mirror, but not a mere copy (*Abbild*) of this historical reality. It is not a *pièce-à-clef*, nor an old-fashioned form of what we would now call a newsreel' (FW 165, trans. mod.). But a *pièce-à-clef* (*Schlüsselstück*), whose every detail can be traced to a current event or living person, is precisely what Winstanley's relentless hunting for

historical parallels makes of *Hamlet*. A *pièce-à-clef* is also what Schmitt suggests when he speaks of the 'transparent *incognito*' that 'heightens the tension and the participation of the knowing spectators' (*HH* 37) in *Hamlet*. And how if not as a *pièce-à-clef* are we to imagine Schmitt's hypothetical play about the killing of Röhm and his associates in the so-called night of the long knives? '[H]unting for resemblances', Drew Daniel cautions, 'is to miss Schmitt's point.'[36] But then, it seems, Schmitt sometimes missed his own point, too. His praise for Winstanley – boosted, no doubt, by a feeling of affinity with a fellow outsider – insists that her 'astounding findings' prove the factual basis of Shakespeare's dramatic plot 'down to the finest detail' (FW 164); 'her evidence', he maintains, 'is clear and simple' (FW 170). Topical allusions confirm 'the most intense historical presence and the most immediate contemporary reality' (FW 167). This makes *Hamlet* the essential modern drama. And yet, he says, 'my claim here is not that sheer topicality makes great art' (FW 168).[37]

In order to reconcile these somewhat contradictory assertions, Schmitt introduces a three-tiered distinction in *Hamlet or Hecuba*. History enters either in the form of 'simple allusions' which are of limited scope and hence little interest, or in the form of 'true mirrorings' – reflections of a major contemporary event such as the Essex rebellion. But only the third and most important type, the 'genuine intrusion' of a truly epochal event or figure, has the capacity to unsettle the stage play in a way that raises it to the level of tragedy and generates myth. The fate of James I constitutes such an intrusion. The taboo of his mother's alleged complicity in the murder of his father accounts for the major blind spot in *Hamlet*: the irresolvable

---

34 The translator, Kurt Buhanan, renders *Gesicht* as 'vision'. This makes sense, but is not what Schmitt wrote.

35 Buhanan drops the adjective *unendlich*.

36 Drew Daniel, '"Neither Simple Allusions Nor True Mirrorings": Seeing Double with Carl Schmitt', *Telos*, 153 (2010), 58–9.

37 See also FW 175 (trans. mod.): 'I have not said that every writer who puts the events of his own time on the stage is therefore a greater dramatist than Schiller.'

question of Gertrude's guilt. And what Schmitt calls the 'Hamletization of the avenger' is directly due to the figure of James himself, the overly thoughtful, hesitant prince entangled in 'the fate of the European religious schism' that killed his mother and his son Charles and would eventually shatter the whole royal line of 'the unhappy Stuarts' (*HH* 52).

The distinction goes some way towards separating the Schmittian wheat from the Winstanleyan chaff, towards untangling 'one of the leading political thinkers of the twentieth century' from the embrace of his dubious British muse.

Some way, but not all the way. The real stumbling block for Schmitt's reading is not that he swallows Winstanley's 'findings . . . down to the finest detail' (*FW* 164); the details, after all, are of little consequence compared to the myth-generating historical 'core'. The problem, rather, has to do with the core itself. It results from the inclusion of what Schmitt professes to categorically exclude: psychological interpretation. Psychology intrudes not so much as a 'flickering of . . . possibilities' but as a floodlit psychodrama of revelatory veracity. Schmitt prefaces his reading of Hamlet with T. S. Eliot's *bon mot* that, although 'it is probable that we can never be right' about Shakespeare, 'it is better that we should from time to time change our way of being wrong' (*HH* 6). But Schmitt leaves the reader in no doubt that his own effort is invested with a truth claim far beyond such relativist modesty. This claim is inseparable from what could best be described as an empathetic psychogram of the troubled Stuart monarch. In this, too, Schmitt takes his cue from Winstanley.

Viewing Shakespeare through the lens of nineteenth-century psychology, she argues, can only produce anachronistic distortion. What needs to be explored instead is '[t]he point of view of an Elizabethan audience'. This 'can only be understood by means of a careful study of the history of the time' (31). Careful study reveals not only that James and Hamlet are of the same age (thirty), build (fat) and dressing habits (sloppy) (94–6), but also, more importantly, that they are plagued with the same incapacity for resolute action. Time and

again, in her letters, Elizabeth chiding James for his lethargy sounds like Hamlet chiding himself for the same weakness. 'Does it not look', Winstanley asks, 'as if the mental malady in the two were identical?' (83). Of course it does, and the reason is not hard to find: 'Elizabeth and Shakespeare were both people of genius and they were analysing one and the same case' (83).

The operation that leads to this breathtaking conclusion is not, as Winstanley would have us believe – and no doubt believed herself – a replacement of fallacious psychology by reliable history. It is in fact quite the opposite: a takeover of history by psychology, the very kind of psychology – not sixteenth- but nineteenth-century – that has produced the myriad-faceted modern image of Hamlet, Eliot's 'Mona Lisa of literature'. This image, the cumulative result of a century of character criticism, is by no means discarded; rather, it is the lens through which Winstanley looks at James, the template from which she constructs her image of the Scottish successor. What she finds in Elizabeth's letters, what directs her choice of quotations from the letters, is determined by this image. And so is her neglect of all those of James's personality traits that were anything other than Hamlet-like. Dramatic fiction, in other words, precedes, and determines, historical 'fact'. In this way, Winstanley's James becomes the *doppelgänger* of Shakespeare's Hamlet, the historical king an offshoot of the fictional prince, not, as she claims, vice versa.

Schmitt, too, could not be more categorical in his rejection of psychological interpretation. Psychology has nothing to offer but sundry ways of being wrong about Shakespeare. Echoing Winstanley, Schmitt maintains that the only way to be right about Hamlet is to turn to history: 'it is clear that the distortion (*Abbiegung*) of the avenger figure *can only be explained* by the historical presence of King James' (*HH* 30, my italics). But in order to explain Hamlet, Schmitt, like Winstanley, must first Hamletize James. In his account, James becomes a tragic character, laden not only with his own troubles, past and present, but also with those that would befall his doomed progeny in the course of the seventeenth century (*HH* 52).

The two-and-a-half pages Schmitt spends on his portrayal of James draw a picture of unrelieved doom and gloom. The cataclysmic rifts of the age are ingrained unmediated in the existential angst of a 'philosophizing and theologizing' intellectual (*HH* 25) who 'conducted . . . great – although, of course, quite fruitless' learned debates (*HH* 29, transl. mod.), whose 'being was torn' (*HH* 29, transl. mod.) and whose 'ideological position was simply hopeless' (*HH* 29). This last attribute connects the Hamletized James to another of Schmitt's favourite figures: the fighter for a lost cause, defeated by history, as exemplified by the Spanish Catholic antiliberal Donoso Cortés and, of course, Schmitt himself.[38] The emphatic claim to objectivity and 'the granite rock' of historical truth thus loops back to the undeniably subjective.

Schmitt's highly dramatic version of history clenches the fate of a whole era not just in a single man but in a single moment. If James personifies the conflicts of the age, 1603 becomes the *catastrophe*, the turning point, not just for England but for the whole of European history. To 'Shakespeare and his friends', the new king 'was their hope and their dream in a desperate moment of crisis and catastrophe' (*HH* 30–1).[39] James disappointed these hopes. 'But hope and dream had by then found their way into the brilliant play. The figure of Hamlet had entered into the world and its history, and the myth began its journey' (*HH* 31).

But, one may well ask, what's James to us? To Shakespeare's contemporaries, Schmitt avers, the fate of this tragic hero was a matter of life and death. 'The spectators', he maintains in characteristic hyperbole, 'were not mere spectators; rather, their lives were . . . at stake in the drama as it played out before their eyes' (FW 167). They felt the brute force of history burst (*einbrechen*) into the play. But what is at stake for 'us'? How are 'we' supposed to respond? If we weep for Hamlet, Hamlet becomes a mere Hecuba to us, Shakespeare no more than a superior Schikaneder, supplier of second-rate librettos for enlightened *Kunstgenuss*, for pure, self-indulgent aesthetic pleasure.[40] Should we, instead, weep for James, the tragic victim of history? One answer the text suggests is that we definitely should

not – for how could we weep for anyone we aren't even supposed to think of? 'I do not expect anyone to think of James I when they see Hamlet on stage. I would also not want to measure Shakespeare's Hamlet against the historical James I or vice versa' (*HH* 38; transl. mod.). 'It would be foolish to play Hamlet in the mask of James. This would be either a historical panopticon . . . or . . . the attempt to pump blood into a spectre, a kind of vampirism' (*HH* 51).

In the conclusion of the essay, however, the spectre comes very much alive and another, rather different answer as to whether Shakespeare's Hamlet should make us weep for James seems to emerge. Schmitt retracts his rebuttal of historicism or, rather, extracts the historical figures of James and Mary Stuart from the historical past, transplanting them into what one might call a continuing historical present. What matters here is not, to quote Eliot, 'the pastness of the past, but . . . its presence'.[41] 'Mary Stuart is still *for us* something other and more than Hecuba. Even the fate of the Atreidae does not affect us as deeply as that of the unhappy Stuarts' (*HH* 52; my italics). To Schmitt, the historical moment that gave birth to the tragic myth of *Hamlet* is not over. It is clearly *his* moment. Flanked by the Catholic Spanish Don Quixote and the Protestant German Faustus, Hamlet occupies the centre panel of a symbolic triptych: he 'stands between them in the middle of the schism that

---

38 See, for example, Carl Schmitt, 'Historiographia in Nuce: Alexis de Tocqueville', in his *Ex Captivitate Salus: Erfahrungen der Zeit 1945/47*, 2nd edn (Berlin, 2002), pp. 25–33.

39 According to most historical accounts, there actually was no crisis. The Scottish succession, well prepared and shrewdly managed, went as smoothly as anyone could have hoped. James's 'peaceful accession was welcomed with practical unanimity, and, we are told, "the like joy, both in London and all parts of England, was never known"', Godfrey Davies, *The Early Stuarts 1603–1660* (Oxford, 1959), 1, quoting *Hist. MSS. Com., Salisbury MSS.* (1930), pp. xv, 26.

40 Cf. Schmitt's scathing critique of Mozart's *Magic Flute* (libretto by Emanuel Schikaneder). *HH* 30 n. 21, translator's comment.

41 T. S. Eliot, 'Tradition and the Individual Talent', in *Selected Prose of T. S. Eliot*, ed. Frank Kermode (London, 1975), p. 38.

has determined the fate of Europe' (*HH* 52), a schism that in Schmitt's view continued to determine it. This continuity explains the seamless transition from Shakespeare's Elizabethan audience to 'us' in the central section of the essay. Shakespeare would not intend 'us' 'to weep for Hamlet as the actor wept for the Trojan queen' (*HH* 43) because in doing so 'we would divorce our present existence from the play on the stage', '[w]e would no longer have any purpose or cause', indulging in merely 'aesthetic enjoyment' (*HH* 43) and that 'would be bad, because it would prove that we have different gods in the theatre than in the forum and the pulpit' (*HH* 43; transl. mod.).

But in the autonomous sphere of post-Enlightenment art, we do of course have 'different gods', or, more precisely, 'gods' of different valency, in the theatre than in the other social domains.[42] To Schmitt this division is precisely what is wrong with liberal modernity. His vision is a regressive utopia. What he seeks to recuperate is a pre-modern unity of art, religion and the political in a theatre that offers more than just play. In a sense that Schmitt would probably not be willing to accept, this unity is the myth, the sustaining historical fantasy,[43] to which *Hamlet or Hecuba* pays tribute.

3. EINBRUCH

In hankering after this mythical unity – and especially in singling out the theatre as the site of its consummation – Schmitt's Hamlet essay is more typical of its historical moment than hitherto recognized.

Schmitt's approach, so the standard view has it, is the great exception at a time when (West) German professors of literature sought to distance themselves as far as possible from the *völkisch* brand of *Geistesgeschichte* (history of ideas) and their own involvement in it by embracing a safely a-political formalism. By launching his intrusion of the political into this reserve of literary autonomy, Schmitt trespassed against the 'purity taboo' (WH 17) observed by the professional guardians of literary study. This view conforms with Schmitt's own assessment of his role, except that he also saw

himself as challenging 'the monopoly' of another critical orthodoxy – that which prevailed east of the Iron Curtain:

He who endangers the monopoly is a reactionary and a class enemy. Between *Diamat*[44] and *schöner Schein* (beautiful appearance),[45] a German is caught between the horns of a dilemma. My way of seeing Hamlet historically endangers the monopoly of the dialectical-materialist history of art. I have learnt to my own cost what that means in practical terms. (WH 18)

Engaged in a fight on two fronts, Schmitt fashions himself as the embattled outsider (though a stand against Communism hardly qualified as a dissident

---

42 An increasing differentiation of society into systems and subsystems is the hallmark of the modern world according to 'modernity's most meticulous theorist', Niklas Luhmann: William Rasch, *Niklas Luhmann's Modernity: The Paradoxes of Differentiation* (Stanford, 2000), p. 10.

43 More specifically than he ever does in *Hamlet or Hecuba*, Schmitt defines myth in his 1923 essay 'Die politische Theorie des Mythus' as a belief that empowers a people, a nation or a mass movement with a collective vision, a vital sense of historical mission. It is symptomatic of the degeneracy of parliamentary democracy, Schmitt argues, that it lacks a myth. It is equally symptomatic and a sign of genuine vitality that Fascism has one. Schmitt cites Mussolini's famous rallying speech before the 'march to Rome' approvingly: 'We have created a myth, this myth is a belief, a noble enthusiasm; it does not need to be a reality, it is a striving and a hope, belief and courage. Our myth is the nation, the great nation which we want to make into a concrete reality for ourselves': Carl Schmitt, *The Crisis of Parliamentary Democracy*, trans. Ellen Kennedy (Cambridge, MA, 1988), p. 76.

44 *Diamat* is an abbreviation of 'dialectical materialism'. The version of 'What have I done?' that was printed on the initiative of Piet Tommissen in the Flemish nationalist journal *Dietsland-Europa* (1957) has '*Diamant*' (diamond) instead of '*Diamat*'. In a handwritten note in the typescript of 'What have I done?' (RW 265 21087), Schmitt comments on the grotesque typo: 'Note for the Schiller year 1959: most educated Germans of 1959 are no longer able to read this last sentence; they will not know where the "dilemma" comes from and be inclined to read "Diamant" rather than "Diamat". The Schiller speeches and Schiller celebrations of 1959 will be held on the basis of such diluted education.' Oddly enough, the typo survives into Tommissen's 1996 re-edition of the text in *Schmittiana*, 18.

45 '*Schöner Schein*', a key concept of Schiller's aesthetics, is used here metonymically for the doctrine of artistic autonomy.

stance in Cold-War West Germany). Letting history 'intrude' into the rarefied confines of pure art, he himself becomes the intruder, 'the troublemaker, the taboo-violator, the anti-monopolist' (WH 18).

'Intrusion', the trope under which Schmitt stages his trespass, has, however, a familiar ring in cultural criticism of the post-war era. 'Irruption' would be closer in meaning to the German word Schmitt uses, *Einbruch*, which conveys a violent breaking or bursting into. In its most common use the word denotes the offence of breaking and entering. Compounds with the verb *brechen* (break, rupture) and its concomitant noun *Bruch* abound in writings of the late 1940s and 50s. This is, of course, because the *Zusammenbruch* (breakdown) of the Third Reich constituted a radical *Bruch* (rupture) in German history, the rupture from which the post-war situation derived, most obviously the rupture of the country itself. An article by Wilhelm Backhaus (a journalist, not the pianist) published in the 1946/47 *Theatre Almanach* speaks of '*Einbruchstellen*' (break-in points) at which 'political and social mass hysteria' had engendered 'devastations of the world':

But salvation from all of these spiritual and material troubles can only come from a new cultural wholeness . . . Only from a renovation or rather re-creation of the religious or . . . mythical cultural core can a living vital form (*lebendige Lebensform*) arise that will embrace all intellectual, spiritual and material aspects of humanity.[46]

Cloaking the events of the recent past in vague generalizations, Backhaus employs a strategy common in the writings of the time. Equally vague and no less typical is his vision of future remedy. The same sense of mission and the same pathos can be found in hosts of contemporary articles, essays and pamphlets. What is remarkable and perhaps uniquely German is the fact that so many of these publications identify the theatre as the prime site of a break with the past, the crucial source of cultural and spiritual renewal. 'The theatre', claims a writer from East German Gotha in 1949,

influences people more strongly than any other art form, it works more immediately, more deeply and more

unsettlingly. It has a special significance in times of social upheaval (*Umbruch*). This was so at the end of the eighteenth century as it is today.[47]

In 1945, just weeks after Germany's capitulation, theatrical activities resumed in the devastated country. Driven by a veritable 'theatre frenzy', people thronged to improvised stages amid the rubble of the bombed-out cities.[48] This theatre craze – hardly to be expected after the end of a total war – was accompanied by a rash of publications advocating a theatre that was emphatically not a place of mere entertainment but a site of spiritual regeneration. Typically, this was conceived as a return to cultic origins, to a religious Ur-theatre.[49] A favourite trope for this theatre was the catacomb, the beleaguered early Church becoming the model for a theatre congregation in search of spiritual guidance in the basements and air-raid shelters of the ruined cities.[50]

---

[46] Wilhelm Backhaus, 'Bretter, die die Welt nicht mehr bedeuten?' *Der Theater-Almanach 1946/47* (Munich, 1946), pp. 168–81 at pp. 175–6 (my trans.).

[47] Erich Nippold, *Theater und Drama* (Gotha: Engelhard-Reyher-Verlag, 1949), p. 5 (my trans.).

[48] 'German theatre after 1918 had been proudly revolutionary. After 1945 it tried to regain its spiritual bearings by going conservative.' Wilhelm Hortmann, *Shakespeare on the German Stage: The Twentieth Century* (Cambridge, 1998), pp. 174–181 at p. 179; cf. also Andreas Höfele, 'From Reeducation to Alternative Theater: German-American Theater Relations', in Detlef Junker, ed., *The United States and Germany in the Era of Cold War*, Vol. 1: 1945–1968 (Cambridge, 2004), pp. 464–71.

[49] The classic rejoinder to the adherents of theatre sacralization is Brecht's quip: 'Theatre may be said to be derived from ritual, but that is only to say that it becomes theatre once the two have separated.' Bertolt Brecht, 'A Short Organum for the Theatre', in *Brecht on Theatre: The Development of an Aesthetic*, trans. and ed. John Willett (London, 1964), pp. 179–205 at p. 181.

[50] Cf. Paul Th. Hoffmann, *Theater und Drama im deutschen Geistesschicksal* (Hamburg, 1948), p. 116: 'From all this it becomes clear what an upheaval (*Umbruch*) and what new developments the theatre in Germany . . . is facing. Nearly all the major German theatre cities are in ruins. A time of such affliction that causes a complete change in our way of life will deeply affect our theatre' (my trans.).

What makes these woefully dated, ephemeral writings interesting here is their affinity to Schmitt's vision of a pre-modern theatre as outlined in both *Hamlet or Hecuba* and his Winstanley foreword. Born, as Schmitt says of *Hamlet*, of 'a desperate moment of crisis and catastrophe' (*HH* 31), this emphatically non-playful, deeply serious post-war discourse demanded a theatre where the audience's 'lives were at stake in the drama as it played out before their eyes' (FW 167), where it would be impossible to 'divorce our present existence from the play on the stage' (*HH* 43). The stage would be a place where the divisions of modernity would be revoked and where we would *not* indulge in merely 'aesthetic enjoyment', but recognize the same 'gods [we recognize] in the forum and the pulpit' (*HH* 43, transl. mod.).

An explicit marker of Schmitt's affinity to this discourse is his mention of Egon Vietta (*HH* 24).[51] A year before Schmitt's book appeared in print, Vietta had published what was both the culmination and the swansong of the theatre discourse I have just described. With its melodramatic title, *Catastrophe or Turnabout of the German Theatre*, the book flags its claim to address an issue of national importance.[52] In 1955, the collocation of 'catastrophe' with 'German' would inevitably evoke associations with 'the German catastrophe', Germany's destruction through the Nazi regime and the lost war.[53] But with the 'economic miracle' in full swing, Vietta's catastrophe does not refer to the national disaster of 1945 but to a present in which this catastrophic rupture had already been smoothed over by the oblivious normality of a society bent on prospering and forgetting. Already, Vietta argued, theatre had become a formal routine, a vehicle of subsidized higher entertainment subsumed into the economy of the modern state. Against this normalization Vietta called for a catastrophe, a radical reversal or turning back to the theatre's archaic roots. For the theatre, and not just the theatre, the question was: 'To be or not to be'.[54] In order to regain its vital core, the theatre, Vietta demanded, must 'descend into the catacombs and found the cells where life becomes cult'.[55] Nothing less ground-shaking than 'another man' (*ein anderer*

Mensch) would arise from a theatre which, instead of mechanical mass entertainment, offered 'a sacral bonding place'.[56] 'The closer the stage moves to its true being', Vietta concluded, 'the sooner it will find its way home. – When will the stage enter into its true being?'[57]

Vietta's text, typical of the time both in its nebulous religiosity and its trendy Heideggerism, is also unmistakably Schmittian. There is the haughty contempt for 'neutralization',[58] the thrust from normality to the extraordinary – the longing for catastrophe as a state of exception. There is also the world-historical, more specifically salvation-historical, perspective of theatre as 'epiphany'. In an appendix Vietta gives a one-page outline of theatre history from its origins to the present. From epiphanic *Ur*-theatre to Athenian tragedy to the 'waning of the epiphany' in Aristophanic comedy, the survey credits the gospels and medieval mystery plays with the 'return of the epiphany'. Early modernity brings the 'irruption (*Einbruch*) of the technical-scientific age' and the twentieth century the 'beginnings of film' and 'epiphany-less theatre'.[59] At this point only a catastrophe can bring salvation, can guide us 'home'. 'Theatre', Vietta declares, 'is Janus-faced; it shows the

---

51. Egon Vietta (1903–1959), a travel writer, dramatist, critic and author of a book on Heidegger, was a student of Schmitt's and a lifelong correspondent. Schmitt mentions Vietta's death in a letter to Armin Mohler, adding that he was 'very devoted'. *Carl Schmitt – Briefwechsel mit einem seiner Schüler*, ed. Armin Mohler in cooperation with Irmgard Huhn and Piet Tommissen (Berlin: Akademie Verlag, 1995), p. 266.

52. Egon Vietta, *Katastrophe oder Wende des deutschen Theaters* (Düsseldorf, 1955).

53. The 'German catastrophe' was a catch-phrase launched by the historian Friedrich Meinecke's influential post-war book, *Die deutsche Katastrophe* (1946).

54. Vietta, *Katastrophe*, p. 115.

55. Vietta, *Katastrophe*, pp. 182–3 (my trans.).

56. Vietta, *Katastrophe*, p. 185.

57. Vietta, *Katastrophe*, p. 228.

58. Vietta, *Katastrophe*, p. 80 and esp. p. 115, where Vietta denounces 'the neutral formalism on which our Weimar Republic foundered'.

59. Vietta, *Katastrophe*, p. 229.

struggle over departing gods and the advent of new ones. If theatre is living poetry, it gives us world-historical intrusions (*Einbrüche*) which only much later are converted into political currency.'[60]

The quality of Vietta's writing may be several rungs below Schmitt's, but his conservative cultural critique and theology of history give a good idea of the intellectual environment in which Schmitt's Hamlet essay originated. The severance of aesthetics from politics – the 'purity taboo' which Schmitt infringes upon – was the norm in literary studies, a norm which was by no means maintained only by those who had a Nazi past to cover up.[61] Theatre, however, was seen as the one domain where 'play' failed in its responsibility if it 'led away from life',[62] if it did not contribute to the regeneration of society in 'the struggle for a new order of values'.[63] 'The tragic', said the Catholic writer Reinhold Schneider in 1955, 'is that which is inherited from the past and at the same time absolutely new'; it is 'the harrowing challenge of history to us . . . Again and again peoples have found themselves . . . on the tragic stage, rising – in utmost danger – . . . to the stature of history.'[64]

The overblown pathos of these post-war pronouncements – even those coming from individuals who, like Schneider, had resisted the Nazis[65] – is often virtually indistinguishable from the rhetorical tone of just a few years before. In the *Berlin Theatre Almanach* of 1942, the actor Mathias Wieman enthused about how he felt playing Faust, the epitome of the 'Faustian German fighting man' whom other nations would never fully comprehend, during the 'tremendous process of transformation'[66] in which 'the decision over our continent is being decided on the battlefield'[67] – at the very moment, in fact, when the *Wehrmacht* was invading Norway. Faust under these circumstances 'was no escape from reality, no lapsing into an oasis of peace or circled-off spiritual enclosure . . . The hot breath of our time also courses through our theatre.'[68] That Wieman (1902–1969) was a friend and 'welcome guest' of the Schmitt family,[69] that his was the sonorous voice reading the Nativity story from the

Bible on German radio on Christmas Eve during the 1950s and 60s is of merely incidental interest. More relevant here is the continuity of a discourse

[60] Vietta, *Katastrophe*, 113.
[61] This is the misleading impression given by David Pan in his 'Afterword' in *HH* 71–2. Pan is right in speaking of an 'institutionalized cover-up of *Germanistik*'s Nazi past' (*HH* 72). But his next assertion does not hold up: 'To insist on the separation of art from politics is to argue that the Nazi movement was simply a political movement with no cultural underpinnings.' It is precisely their awareness of how much Nazism had in fact permeated German culture, German universities and especially *Germanistik* that made post-war literary scholars (not just ex-Nazis and fellow-travellers) want to steer clear of politicizing literature. That this was in itself a highly political evasion was the standard reproach of the student generation of '68 against their professors. Pan's attempt to make Schmitt the only man honestly facing realities when everyone else (except Theodor W. Adorno) was not gives too much credit to Schmitt's own version of himself. On the role of *Germanistik* and *Anglistik* in the Third Reich, see Gerhard Kaiser, *Grenzverwirrungen: Literaturwissenschaft im Nationalsozialismus* (Berlin, 2008); Frank-Rutger Hausmann, *Anglistik und Amerikanistik im 'Dritten Reich'* (Frankfurt am Main, 2003).
[62] Oskar Wälterlin, *Die Verantwortung des Theaters* (The Responsibility of the Theatre) (Berlin, 1947), p. 78 (my trans.).
[63] Backhaus, 'Bretter', p. 176.
[64] Egon Vietta, ed., *Darmstädter Gespräch: Theater* (Darmstadt: Neue Darmstädter Verlagsanstalt, 1955), p. 216 (my trans.). Reinhold Schneider (1903–1958) was a prominent public intellectual in the 1950s. The 'Darmstadt Dialogues' (1950–1975) were a series of symposia on such 'big' themes as 'Man and his Future' (1960) or 'Fear and Hope in our Time' (1963). Among the 1951 panellists ('Man and Space') were the philosophers Heidegger and Ortega y Gasset; guests at the 1955 meeting on 'Theatre' (which was co-organized by Vietta) included Adorno and the dramatist Friedrich Dürrenmatt.
[65] Schneider's 1938 play *Las Casas vor Karl V* (Las Casas before Charles V), contained a critique of political oppression, racism and religious fanaticism. In 1941 he was prohibited from publishing, and in April 1945 was charged with high treason, narrowly escaping execution at the end of the war.
[66] Mathias Wieman, '"Faust" im Kriege', *Berliner Theater-Almanach 1942* (Berlin, 1942), pp. 253–6 at p. 253 (my trans.).
[67] Wieman, 'Faust', p. 255.
[68] Wieman, 'Faust', p. 256.
[69] See Armin Mohler's note in *Carl Schmitt – Briefwechsel mit einem seiner Schüler*, p. 100.

in which the 'play' of theatre is construed as serious, socially important and fatefully implicated in the process of history. In view of this, the question why *Hamlet or Hecuba* had so little impact at the time needs to be reconsidered.[70] Schmitt's own claim that this was because he had broken 'the taboo that does not permit [one] to speak of intrusions of the time into the play' (WH 17) can hardly be credited, given that German theatre discourse had been speaking of little else for the last ten years. And given also that Theodor W. Adorno, who broke the same 'taboo', could be heard on German radio so often that some listeners complained of an 'Adorno inflation'.[71] But Adorno, despite a leftism that jarred with the conservative climate of the Adenauer era, was politically correct; Schmitt wasn't.

But the problem was not just Schmitt's association with Nazism, it was also his association with Lilian Winstanley. That his book left not a trace in the review sections of scholarly journals[72] has at least as much to do with Winstanley as with politics. The one important professional reader who deemed *Hamlet or Hecuba* worthy of attention took issue not with Schmitt's politics but with his literary views. This was Hans-Georg Gadamer whose *opus magnum* of 1959, *Truth and Method*, devotes a two-page appendix to refuting Schmitt's critical method.[73] The appendix takes up Gadamer's discussion of 'occasionality', the integral function that the imprint of historical realities has in the work of art.[74] Gadamer agrees with Schmitt that

it is right, in principle, to exclude the prejudices of a pure aesthetics of experience (*Erlebnis*) and to situate the play of art within its historical and political context, [but] it seems to me wrong to expect one to read *Hamlet* like a roman à clef . . . Thus, in my opinion, Schmitt falls victim to a false historicism when, for example, he interprets politically the fact that Shakespeare leaves the question of the Queen's guilt open, and sees this as a taboo. In fact it is part of the reality of a play that it leaves an indefinite space around its real theme . . . The more that remains open, the more freely does the process of understanding succeed – i.e., the process of transposing what is shown in the play to one's own world and, of course, also to the world of one's own political experience.[75]

The last statement could not be better illustrated than by the way in which Schmitt's reading of *Hamlet* reflects, and is inflected by, his own view of the contemporary world.

4. THE HIEROGLYPH OF THE WESTERN WORLD

Hamlet is James: this is the proposition on which Schmitt's whole argument depends. Without it, no tragedy, and without tragedy, no myth. What this makes of *Macbeth*, *King Lear* or *Othello*, not to mention *Romeo and Juliet*, we can only guess. Are these plays just so-called tragedies, but in fact mere *Trauerspiele*? Or would at least *Macbeth* and *King Lear* qualify as genuine tragedies, though perhaps to a lesser degree than *Hamlet* and only on the condition that they be unlocked with a *clef* provided by Lilian Winstanley?[76] The question obviously never

---

70 Tommisen's claim that Schmitt's Hamlet book found greater resonance than Schmitt suggests in WH has little evidence to support it. WH 14 fn. 5.

71 Michael Schwarz, '"Er redet leicht, schreibt schwer": Theodor W. Adorno am Mikrophon', *Zeithistorische Forschungen/Studies in Contemporary History*, 8:2 (2011), 286–94 at 286, estimates that Adorno recorded no fewer than 300 radio broadcasts in the 1950s and 60s with some 300 public appearances in the same period. Thus, Schwarz concludes, 'one could hear Adorno speak somewhere almost every week'.

72 *Shakespeare-Jahrbuch*, for example, reviewed the 1952 Winstanley translation but ignored *Hamlet or Hecuba*.

73 Hans-Georg Gadamer, *Truth and Method*, 2nd rev. edn, trans. Joel Weinsheimer and Donald G. Marshall (London, New York, 2004), pp 498–500.

74 Gadamer, *Truth and Method*, p. 141.

75 Gadamer, *Truth and Method*, pp. 498–9.

76 Cf. her two later monographs: *'Macbeth', 'King Lear' and Contemporary History: Being a Study of the Relations of the Play of 'Macbeth' to the Personal History of James I, the Darnley Murder and the St Bartholomew Massacre and also of 'King Lear' as Symbolic Mythology* (Cambridge, 1922); *'Othello' as the Tragedy of Italy: Showing that Shakespeare's Italian Contemporaries Interpreted the Story of the Moor and the Lady of Venice as Symbolizing the Tragedy of Their Country in the Grip of Spain* (London, 1924).

occurred to Schmitt. In this, he is typical of the German Shakespeare tradition, which has tended to treat *Hamlet* as not just the pinnacle but virtually the sum total of Shakespeare's work.

Schmitt is, of course, very much aware of this tradition, especially of its political dimension. He quotes the catch-phrase, 'Germany is Hamlet', together with parts of Ferdinand Freiligrath's poem from which it comes[77] in the introductory section of *Hamlet or Hecuba*, where he cursorily surveys the history of Hamlet interpretation. From Goethe, who turned Hamlet into a Werther, to Freud, for whom 'every neurotic is either an Oedipus or a Hamlet', 'an excess of psychological interpretation' (*HH* 7) has clouded rather than clarified Hamlet. A particularly blatant instance of such distortion, Gerhart Hauptmann's 1935 play *Hamlet in Wittenberg*, 'remains trapped in psychologizing and contains painfully embarrassing digressions in which a subjectivist of the first half of the twentieth century seeks to foist his own erotic complexes onto Hamlet' (*HH* 8). Though spared such scathing censure, Freiligrath's 'Germany is Hamlet' is cited as another instance of such projection. Only in this case, the psychology of Shakespeare's melancholy procrastinator is not foisted on an individual, but a whole 'tattered and fractured' people (*HH* 9). 'In this way', Schmitt concludes, 'the labyrinth becomes ever more impenetrable' (*HH* 9). It comes as something of a surprise that Freiligrath's poem receives honourable mention in the climactic final paragraph of *Hamlet or Hecuba*. The poem's allusion to Wittenberg, Schmitt says, shows 'an inkling' of 'the final and greatest aspect of the Hamlet issue', the religious 'schism that has determined the fate of Europe' (*HH* 52). No longer exemplifying misguided psychologism, 'Germany is Hamlet' now bears witness to the procreative power of the Hamlet myth.

In *Hamlet or Hecuba*, Schmitt is clearly more interested in the 'birth' of this myth than in its later 'journey'[78] – more, in other words, in the proposition that Hamlet is James than in the proposition that Germany is Hamlet. But the fact that he uses the same adjective, *zerrissen* (torn, tattered), to characterize both 'the unhappy Stuart'

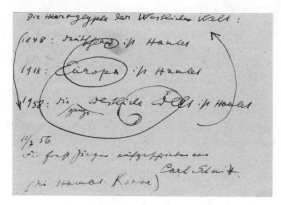

35. Carl Schmitt's Hamlet-Curve.

and the Germany of 1848 can be taken as a hint that Schmitt saw the predicament of the 'torn' king and that of the 'torn' nation as in some way connected; that he saw them both as being part of the same tragic history, a history that was far from over.

No sooner was *Hamlet or Hecuba* published in April 1956 than Schmitt redirected his priorities from James to Germany, from the historical origin of the Hamlet myth to its continuing historical momentum. On the back of a letter to Ernst Jünger, dated 1 August 1956, we find this 'hieroglyph of the Western world' (Illustration 35):

> 1848: Germany is Hamlet
> 1918: Europe is Hamlet
> 1958: the whole Western world is Hamlet
> II/7 56
> Written down for Ernst Jünger by
> Carl Schmitt
> (The Hamlet-Curve)[79]

---

[77] Ferdinand Freiligrath, 'Hamlet' (1844), *Freiligraths Werke in einem Band*, ed. Werner Ilberg (Weimar, 1962).

[78] Both terms are Schmitt's; see 'Preface', p. 170: 'The Birth of a Myth out of a Play of Contemporary Historical Presence'; and *Hamlet or Hecuba*, 31: 'The figure of Hamlet had entered into the world and its history, and the myth began its journey.'

[79] *Ernst Jünger / Carl Schmitt: Briefe 1930–1983*, ed. Helmuth Kiesel (Stuttgart, 1999), p. 310. The 'hieroglyph' also appears in a letter to Armin Mohler, 15 July 1956: Mohler, ed., *Carl Schmitt – Briefwechsel*, p. 220.

Jünger responded by drily observing that 'this would give us another two years' (1956–58), adding: 'Hamlet seems to have come much into fashion – whether this is a good sign is another question.'[80]

The present significance of *Hamlet* was also the main theme of 'What have I done?' (*Was habe ich getan?*), the statement Schmitt prepared as an introduction for a discussion of *Hamlet or Hecuba* at the home of the publisher Eugen Diederichs on 12 June 1956.[81] 'Hamlet is a very popular theme', Schmitt says, citing recent offshoots of Shakespeare's play, a novel by Alfred Döblin and a play by Stefan Andres with a 'Hamlet Europe' character:[82]

I have not seen the play, but I remember that Paul Valéry said in 1919, after the First World War: Europe is Hamlet. In the previous century, before 1848, the German liberal revolutionaries used to say: Germany is Hamlet. A curious progression from Germany to Europe that should give us pause as Germans and make us apprehensive as Europeans.   (WH 15)[83]

The term 'presentism', denoting a way of 'reading the literature of the past in terms of what most "ringingly chimes" with "the modern world"'[84] did not exist in 1956 but serves to capture the embattled urgency of Schmitt's engagement with Shakespeare, an urgency not lost on his early reviewers. They responded to this urgency, and he in turn seems to have responded to them by moving more determinedly in a 'presentist' direction. This would not be the first time that Schmitt, as it were, became the student of his students,[85] and it would help explain the shifting of his interest from the Jacobean Hamlet to his nineteenth-century and Cold War descendants.

'Was habe ich getan?' opens with Schmitt's declaration that it took the reviews by Walter Warnach and Rüdiger Altmann to make him realize what 'I have actually done' (WH 15). From the defensiveness of his statement – the tone of maligned innocence is vintage post-1945 Schmitt – one would assume the reviews to have been hostile. But in fact they were nothing of the kind. Given that they were both written by card-carrying Schmittians, this is hardly surprising. Warnach leaves the

reader in no doubt that he is on Schmitt's side in a very contemporary culture war. Applauding Schmitt for taking the same stand against the 'bad subjectivity' of Romantic occasionalism as in his *Political Romanticism* of 1919, he calls *Hamlet or Hecuba* a 'most impressive example of intellectual continuity'.[86] But Romantic subjectivism which regards the world in general – and Hamlet in

---

[80] Ernst Jünger to Carl Schmitt, 5 August 1956. *Ernst Jünger / Carl Schmitt: Briefe*, p. 310 (my transl.).

[81] Schmitt also circulated 'What have I done?' among his friends. On the initiative of one of them, Piet Tommissen, the text was first published in the Flemish nationalist journal *Dietsland-Europa* (1957) and then once more in Tommissen's own periodical, *Schmittiana*, 5 (1996), 13–19.

[82] *Hamlet oder Die lange Nacht nimmt ein Ende* (1956) is the last novel by Alfred Döblin (1878–1956), author of *Berlin Alexanderplatz* (1929), one of the major works of German modernism. A Social Democrat and a Jew, who converted to Catholicism, Döblin escaped the Nazis and returned to occupied Germany in 1945 as a member of the French cultural administration. Neglect of his work and the hostility he experienced – as did many other returned emigrés – induced him to move to Paris in 1951. *Hamlet Europa* is a character in Stefan Andres's (1906–1970) play *Tanz durchs Labyrinth. Dramatische Dichtung in fünf Bildern* (1948).

[83] One of the typescript copies of the text in the Düsseldorf archive (RW 265 21087) has a hand-written footnote appended to this paragraph, which gives the same 'Hamlet-curve of the West' (1848 – 1918 – 1958) as the two letters.

[84] Ewan Fernie, 'Shakespeare and the Prospect of Presentism', *Shakespeare Survey 58* (Cambridge, 2005), pp. 169–84 at 169, quoting Terence Hawkes, *Shakespeare in the Present* (London and New York, 2002), p. 22. Schmitt has also been claimed as a New Historicist *avant la lettre*, but this goes to show that the antithesis between 'Presentism' and New Historicism is more rhetorical than real. The 'history' explored by the New Historicism is shaped by very present, late twentieth-century, concerns and attitudes. Greenblatt's desire 'to speak with the dead' leads, after all, to his realization that 'the dead' are accessible only 'under the terms of our own interests and pleasures and in the light of historical developments that cannot simply be stripped away': Stephen Greenblatt, *Shakespearean Negotiations* (Oxford, 1988), p. 20.

[85] Willy Haas, 'Eine neue politische Lehre' (review of Carl Schmitt, *Der Begriff des Politischen*, 2nd rev. edn 1932), *Die literarische Welt* 21 (20 May 1932), notes sardonically that 'Carl Schmitt has become the disciple of his disciples' (*der Jünger seiner Jünger*).

[86] Walter Warnach (1910–2000), 'Hamlet-Mythos und Geschichte' (review of Schmitt, *Hamlet or Hecuba*), *Frankfurter Allgemeine Zeitung*, 2 June 1956, 'Literaturblatt'.

particular – as just a 'grandiose occasion for self-reflexion' is only, as it were, one side of a bad coin. The other, more pernicious, is Marxism. Schmitt's reading of *Hamlet*, Warnach writes, defies both the false autonomy of Romantic art and the Marxist subjection of art to the 'hollow sham' of 'economic realities'.

Altmann, too, is duly respectful of the master's 'magnificent' interpretation, and he castigates the usual Schmittian suspects, liberal and leftist, with George Lukács being held responsible for a 'Marxist descent into the hell of rationalism'.[87] At the same time Altmann insists that the consideration of what Hamlet meant to an Elizabethan audience should lead on to the more important question of what Hamlet means to us now. 'But if a myth can be begotten and attested to (*gezeugt und bezeugt*), not produced, then it does not only hit the core of a *historical* reality – it must in some way also concern the *present* fate of the European intellectual' (italics original). It is not entirely clear whether Altmann thinks that Schmitt has actually addressed this issue or not, or has addressed it but not rigorously enough. In one place, Altmann seems to be saying that Schmitt's whole point is 'to elevate [Hamlet] to the status of a modern myth, the myth of the intellectual'; in another, that Schmitt only hints in this direction while being more interested in delving into the foundations of modern thought. '[D]oes Don Capisco[88] intend to leave the antagonism of the present aside in order to . . . explore the bedrock of thought (*das Urgestein des Denkens*)?'[89] The word 'intellectual' appears in *Hamlet or Hecuba* only once, near the end, where Schmitt notes that 'all three great symbolic figures' of European literature, Don Quixote, Hamlet and Faust, 'are oddly enough readers of books and thus intellectuals, so to speak' (52). Still, the final climax of the essay is not devoted to the modern intellectual but to the tragic fate of the Stuarts.

The 'antagonism of the present' (Altmann) takes centre stage in 'What have I done?' and in the *Hamlet* lecture which Schmitt was invited to deliver at Aachen Technical University in January 1957 and for which he chose 'Hamlet as mythical figure of the present' as his topic.[90] He begins by asking

'what image comes to mind when we hear the name Hamlet':

We see a distinct figure, a prince dressed in black, who is given and takes on a great task and who for thinking and philosophizing cannot get down to action; who suffers from his own nature and the people around him; who behaves towards others with condescending irony and torments himself with self-reproach in his soliloquies until he is finally overrun by the course of events. In other words: we see what we could call a typical intellectual. What is typical here is the discrepancy between thinking and doing, the immobilization caused by reflection and self-observation, superior intelligence and irony but a failure to act in reality. Thus Shakespeare's Hamlet has become the mythical figure of the European intellectual.[91]

---

87 Rüdiger Altmann, 'Hamlet als mythische Situation', *Civis: Zeitschrift für christlich-demokratische Politik*, 18 (1956), 39.

88 Don Capisco was the sobriquet Schmitt was given by Ernst Jünger. It became a password among his devotees.

89 Another disciple of Schmitt's, the young historian Reinhard Koselleck, had drawn similar front lines as Warnach and Altmann in a brief unpublished review of *Hamlet, Sohn der Maria Stuart* (1952). Jean-Paul Sartre's call for a *littérature engagée*, Koselleck declared, had produced nothing but 'laboured artifice' (*künstlichen Krampf*); a 'four-year-plan for productive literature' would never engender 'the inner bond between historical presence and genuine poetry'. Winstanley, by contrast, showed that truly great literature was rooted in history. She – and, of course, Schmitt – were to be thanked, Koselleck wrote, for 'opening our eyes to the fundamental precondition of all poetry, the historical roots from which any work of art must spring if it is not to be a product of pure ideology'. Reinhard Koselleck, 'Hamlet, Sohn der Maria Stuart', unpublished typescript, 2 pp., RW 265–226, No. 9 (my trans.). Koselleck (1923–2006), a doctoral student whose 1954 dissertation *Kritik und Krise* was strongly influenced by Schmitt, became one of the most influential German historians of the post-war era and the leading theorist of 'conceptual history' (*Begriffsgeschichte*). Cf. his *Practice of Conceptual History: Timing, History, Spacing Concepts* (Palo Alto, 2002).

90 The role of the intellectual was a widely debated topic at the time, as is borne out by the international resonance of Raymond Aron, *L'opium des intellectuels* (Paris, 1955), *The Opium of the Intellectuals*, trans. Terence Kilmartin (New York, 1957). Schmitt knew the book, whose first part is titled 'Political Myths', and consulted it for his lecture.

91 Carl Schmitt, 'Hamlet as a mythical figure of the present' (my trans.). The lecture was held on 21 January 1957. The

From the typed introduction and the handwritten notes for the rest of the paper, it is clear that the lecture expanded Schmitt's three-stage 'hieroglyph' of the Western world into a history of the Hamlet myth from Voltaire, 'the greatest Church father of the European intelligentsia', to the present. From the philosophers of the French Enlightenment to the Romantics and the German liberals of the *Vormärz* to the turn of the twentieth century and the Dreyfus affair, Schmitt traces the transformations of the role of the intellectual and of Hamlet in a continuous parallel. After World War I the myth undergoes an identity crisis with Paul Valéry, and there is 'a sharp division between bourgeois and Marxist intellectuals'. Lenin becomes the archetype of the Marxist intellectual as 'the bearer of progress', whereas Hamlet becomes simply 'uninteresting', the slightly ridiculous figure of Brecht's Hamlet sonnet ('Here is the body, puffy and inert').[92] Schmitt draws a predictably gloomy picture of the present state of affairs: 'the intellectual has been made to fit in (*eingepaßt*) . . . the old myth is at an end. The Hamlet myth will no longer do for what is left of the intellectual. Should we then bury Prince Hamlet?'

The lecture notes, partly in longhand, partly in Schmitt's notoriously cryptic shorthand, are not easily decipherable. In conclusion, Schmitt protests that he did not intend to spoil his audience's enjoyment of 'one of the greatest plays of world history'. 'On the contrary', he says, 'I wanted to clear the way for a view unclouded by self-deception.' In the cultural cold war of the 1950s this is a political, not just an aesthetic imperative: 'Perceiving works of art without illusions must not remain the monopoly of dialectical materialism.'

5. RESTRAINING HISTORY: THE *KATÉCHON*

Schmitt's Aachen lecture helps us to put his Hamlet-spotting in perspective. Five latter-day Hamlets, including Adlai Stevenson and the British prime minister Anthony Eden, are mentioned to demonstrate the continuing presence of Shakespeare's melancholy prince in the collective imagination. These examples may be trivial, yet even the most blatant trivialization may have a non-trivial significance. The sobriquet 'Hamlet' applied to a politician, Schmitt says, 'need not be more than a journalistic tag' for indecisiveness:

But there are also deeper uses of the name, explicable by the fact that, in the age of mass democracy, simplified and reduced symbolic figures are unavoidable ersatz-myths for the millions of viewers, listeners and readers of cinema, radio and the press. The newspapers need them and convert genuine myths into slogans, just as they convert whole primeval forests into newsprint.   (HM 2)

The dividing line between genuine and ersatz is a thin one here. The ersatz, so the passage suggests, becomes indispensable for the sustenance and perpetuation of the real thing, just as being convertible to slogan is the best proof of the vitality of the myth thus converted.

Not only does this tally with Schmitt's contention that Shakespeare's art was only properly understood in its popular, even vulgar setting, it also reveals the connection between Schmitt's Hamlet-spotting and another far from trivial pursuit of his. Alongside his search for latter-day Hamlets, Schmitt scanned the modern world for embodiments of the *katéchon*, the holder-up, delayer or restrainer. This concealed, but all-important figure took on a pivotal role in Schmitt's theology of history starting around 1942.[93] According to a single biblical mention

---

untitled typescript (RW 265–20311) breaks off into handwritten notes after two pages. In a letter to Ernst Jünger (26 January 1957) Schmitt refers to it as 'Hamlet als mythische Figur der Gegenwart': *Ernst Jünger / Carl Schmitt: Briefe*, p. 320. A summary of the argument is given by Mehring, *Carl Schmitt*, pp. 503–4.

92 'On Shakespeare's Play Hamlet', Bertolt Brecht, *Poems 1913–1956*, trans. John Willett and Ralph Manheim (London, 1987), p. 311.

93 Schmitt himself dates his 'theory of the *katéchon*' back to 1932: Carl Schmitt, *Glossarium: Aufzeichnungen der Jahre 1947–1951*, ed. Eberhard Freiherr von Medem (Berlin, 1991), p. 80; but see Heinrich Meier, *The Lesson of Carl*

(2 Thessalonians 2: 6, 7), the *katéchon* is one who holds up or slows down the Antichrist's seizure of power before the Second Coming. 'The whole Christian aeon', Schmitt explains, 'is not a long march but a single long waiting, a long interim between . . . the appearance of the Lord in the time of the Roman Caesar Augustus and the Lord's return at the end of time.'[94] Within this all-embracing interim 'numerous larger or smaller earthly interims constantly emerge' (ibid.) and for each the question as to the Antichrist and the *katéchon* must be asked and answered anew.[95] 'For each epoch of the last 1948 years', Schmitt noted in December 1947, 'one must be able to name the *katéchon*. His place was never vacant, or we would not exist.'[96] However, as Heinrich Meier points out, from the obligation that we must be able to name the *katéchon* it does not automatically follow that we actually are able to do so. 'Schmitt "knows" that the restrainer exists but he does not know who the restrainer is . . . From the *Imperium Romanum* down to the Jesuit order, Schmitt can offer a number of quite different candidates.'[97] These include, in the twentieth century, Emperor Franz Joseph of Austro-Hungary, the Czech president Masaryk and Marshal Pilsudski of Poland.

The analogy to Schmitt's search for Hamlets is more than just an analogy. If the 'Hamlet-curve' can serve as a 'hieroglyph' for the downward trajectory of the entire Western world, then it is part and parcel of the larger eschatological scheme of Schmittian history. Both the historical figure 'behind' Shakespeare's dramatic character and that character's later doubles have a role to play in the great Manichean struggle between the forces of the Antichrist pushing the world headlong towards doom and the forces that oppose this push by 'standing in the way', 'withholding', 'restraining' it (2 Thess. 2: 6, 7).

Schmitt's portrayal of James I makes 'the unhappy Stuart' a *katéchon*, but a *katéchon manqué* whose insights into what a king should rightly be and do are woefully at odds with what he actually was and did. In holding up a tragic mirror to this royal procrastinator, Shakespeare assumes the part of what we might call a second-order *katéchon*. 'Shakespeare's *Hamlet*', Schmitt writes in his 1952 preface, 'is but an urgent entreaty addressed to James I not to expend the divine right of kings in reflections and discussions' (FW 171, trans. mod.). Seeking 'access to the power-holder',[98] the author of *Hamlet* is the double of the author of *Hamlet or Hecuba*, who had offered his advice to the ill-fated General von Schleicher, the last chancellor of the Weimar Republic, but to no avail.[99] It is here that the author's personal investment in the Hamlet myth emerges. Shakespeare's tragic hero serves as a 'transparent incognito' (*HH* 37) for Schmitt's own role in Germany's recent past, wishing to 'hold up' but failing. Schmitt's efforts towards saving the presidial system of Weimar in the last throes of the Papen and Schleicher administrations lend some credence to this version of himself. His career after Hitler's seizure of power clearly does not, though some of Schmitt's apologists would insist that even at the height of his pro-Nazi campaigning he was 'trying to prevent worse' – the standard excuse of many active supporters of the regime.

Schmitt's writings give no indication that he thought himself to be in any way culpable. Instead there is a towering sense of the injustice done to him. His feeling that, no matter what he did, he

---

Schmitt: *Four Chapters on the Distinction between Political Theology and Political Philosophy*, trans. Marcus Brainard (Chicago and London, 1998), p. 161 n. 106. I follow Meier's exposition of Schmitt's concept of the *katéchon* here.

[94] Carl Schmitt, *Political Theology II: The Myth of the Closure of Any Political Theology*, trans. and ed. Michael Hoelzl and Graham Ward (Cambridge and Malden, MA, 2008), p. 86.

[95] Meier, *The Lesson of Carl Schmitt*, p. 163.

[96] Schmitt, *Glossarium*, p. 63 (my transl.).

[97] Meier, *The Lesson of Carl Schmitt*, p. 161.

[98] Access to the power holder (*Zugang zum Machthaber*), a key notion in Schmitt. Cf. Carl Schmitt, *Gespräch über die Macht und den Zugang zum Machthaber* (Pfullingen, 1954).

[99] Gabriel Seiberth, *Anwalt des Reiches: Carl Schmitt und der Prozess 'Preußen contra Reich' vor dem Staatsgerichtshof* (Berlin, 2001).

was inevitably in the position of the accused[100] seeps from every sentence of the explanatory statement on *Hamlet or Hecuba* which he delivered in June 1956. Its very title, 'What have I done?', suggests – no doubt deliberately – the situation not of someone explaining what he has tried to do in a piece of literary interpretation but of someone standing trial on much graver charges, the charges faced before a de-Nazification tribunal. Flaunting his outcast image, Schmitt plays up this association by harping on the word unobjectionable (*einwandfrei*) – not unlike Mark Antony harping on 'honourable' in the forum speech (*Julius Caesar*, 3.2):

So what have I actually done? At first sight, something good or at least unobjectionable. I have written a book about Hamlet. Hamlet is a very popular subject. Tens of thousands of unobjectionable people have written about Hamlet. I thus find myself in unobjectionable company.   (WH 15)

The defence of a little book about *Hamlet* is staged as a defence of its author in the court of history – the self-styled martyr, the scapegoat, 'the white raven who is missing from no black list'.[101] In Schmitt's literary thinking, the political is inextricably bound up with the personal. Great works of literature, so his writings on *Hamlet* suggest, are great because they encapsulate the experience of historical crisis in the 'concrete universal' of myth. 'Myth' is Schmitt's term to describe a two-way traffic of symbolization: giving concrete, individual shape to collective meaning and, conversely, raising an individual figure to the level of collective significance.[102] Schmitt never doubted his entitlement to regard himself as such a figure, least of all when his public career was over. It was then that he took on the role of the exem-

plary victim of the century's cataclysms, proclaiming his 'identity with the fate of Germany'.[103] If the 'hapless Stuart' caught up 'in the middle of the schism that has determined the fate of Europe' (*HH* 52) became the entry point for Schmitt's self-inscription into the tragic myth of *Hamlet*, the apocalyptic 'hieroglyph of the Western world' offered an even stronger identificatory potential to this 'outlawed' law professor who, like the Oscar Wilde of *De Profundis*, thought of himself as 'a man who stood in symbolic relations to [his] age'.[104] Carl Schmitt's engagement with Shakespeare can hardly serve as a model of how to read *Hamlet*. But it makes fascinating reading as a critical appropriation haunted by the unlaid ghosts of one of the twentieth century's most controversial thinkers.

---

[100] 'Me, I am always treated unjustly; I am *hors la loi* and outlawed' (10/12/1947) Schmitt, *Glossarium*, 59.

[101] Schmitt in a letter to Armin Mohler, 6 January 1955 (quoted in Mehring, *Carl Schmitt*, p. 13).

[102] Herman Melville's novella *Benito Cereno* is a parallel case. From 1941 onwards Schmitt regarded the story of the Spanish captain, seemingly in command of, but in reality held hostage by the slaves who have taken over his ship, as the perfect encryption of his situation under the Nazis and, more generally, as 'a symbol of the intellectuals in a mass-system': Schmitt, *Ex Captivitate Salus*, pp. 21–2.

[103] In the brief biographical note submitted for a *festschrift* for Ernst Jünger in 1954, Schmitt states that he lost his readership at Strasbourg university 'as a result of the outcome of the first World War' and his Berlin chair 'as a result of the outcome of the second World War'. 'The identity with the fate of Germany', he wrote to Armin Mohler, the editor, 'becomes clear enough from these dates' (quoted in Mehring, *Carl Schmitt*, p. 13).

[104] *Complete Works of Oscar Wilde*, introd. Vyvyan Holland (London, Glasgow, 1969), p. 912.

BEHIND THE RED CURTAIN OF VERONA BEACH: BAZ LUHRMANN'S *WILLIAM SHAKESPEARE'S ROMEO + JULIET*

TOBY MALONE

It's inconceivable that Romeo is not caught [in Juliet's bed]: that's what Red Curtain Cinema means.[1]

Extraordinary suspension of disbelief is a hallmark of Baz Luhrmann's 1996 film, *William Shakespeare's Romeo + Juliet*.[2] Ruptures in logic like Romeo's bedroom near-miss are accepted by filmgoers conditioned to conventions of fantastical escapism alongside extreme verisimilitude. Luhrmann successfully collides the familiar (of verisimilitude) with the unfamiliar (of escapism), and meshes 1996 fashion, music and physicality with Elizabethan language, laws and social restraints. Luhrmann's combined aesthetic is established within a distinctive, created world, uniquely crafted and microscopically detailed, in which every piece of text and dialogue is an intertextual reference from almost the entire breadth of the Shakespearian canon.

The difficulty of naturalizing Elizabethan language, customs and themes on film has, over the past century, yielded adaptations set in specific time-frames or places to establish distance, aesthetics employed by filmmakers including Olivier and Branagh. The perils of neglecting distance are seen in Michael Almereyda's 2000 *Hamlet*, set in modern-day Manhattan. Almereyda's hindrance was too-strong familiarity and blurred division between the fictional and the actual, where modern New Yorkers speak verse in well-known settings. This choice permits the audience to linger on anachronisms or overt familiarity, which undermines the story and draws attention to artificiality. The world of the director's vision is essential to the success of the adaptation. This article examines the comprehensive world of Luhrmann's *William Shakespeare's Romeo + Juliet* and the extraordinary lengths taken – on a series of sliding levels – to ensure the film's internal verisimilitude.

'Red Curtain Cinema' is conceptually central to the development of Luhrmann's film world. Luhrmann coined the term as an overarching definition of his filmmaking process while promoting his 2001 movie musical *Moulin Rouge!*. Luhrmann noted the structural continuity, common crew and stylistic through-line that linked his three films – *Moulin Rouge!*, *Strictly Ballroom* (1992) and *William Shakespeare's Romeo + Juliet* – and dubbed it 'The Red Curtain Trilogy'. The Red Curtain offers 'a self-conscious nod to the audience in the storytelling that eschews realism',[3] and adheres to three conventions: (1) setting in a *heightened creative world*; (2) use of a *recognizable story shape*; and (3) audience awareness that *what they are watching is not meant to be real*.[4] Unlike the Sydney of *Strictly Ballroom* and the Paris of *Moulin Rouge!*, however, the

---

[1] Marius de Vries, *William Shakespeare's Romeo + Juliet: Music Edition*, DVD Commentary (Twentieth Century Fox/Bazmark Inq.), 2006.

[2] *William Shakespeare's Romeo + Juliet*, Dir. Baz Luhrmann (DVD, Twentieth Century Fox/Bazmark Inq., 2003/2006; Blu-Ray, Twentieth Century Fox/Bazmark Inq., 2010), 1996.

[3] Anton Monsted, personal e-mail correspondence, September 2010. Monsted is formerly Luhrmann's assistant, and is now General Manager of Luhrmann's company, Bazmark Inq.

[4] 'Strictly Ballroom'. *IFI Study Guides*. www.irishfilm.ie/downloads/ifi_strictly_sg.pdf, accessed 31 August 2011, p. 8. *Moulin Rouge!* is prefaced with a literal red curtain parting as if it were a theatrical première.

'Verona' of *William Shakespeare's Romeo + Juliet* is so heavily removed from the geographical location of Verona that it is rebranded entirely. For Luhrmann, this is not Verona. This is Verona Beach.

This is a version of Verona never before committed to film: a 'shimmering no-place',[5] a distinctive world of its own, one 'made up of collage... visual collage, written collage, sonic collage, and... musical collage'.[6] The 'pastiche visual nightmare known as Verona Beach'[7] is a dusty, urban coastal wasteland whose architecture, weather, and style variously evoke Mexico City, California, Miami and Rio. Familiar fashion, music and accents encourage audience identification, but Luhrmann avoids an identifiable American city to emphasize Verona Beach's other-worldly location. Production briefs called for 'a heightened created world... recognizable to a contemporary audience but... laden with and informed by the world indicated by the language of Shakespeare'.[8]

Verona Beach, then, in its heightened style, conscious verisimilitude and exacting detail, might be called a 'possible-world', a setting where the logically impossible is authorized through exhaustive authenticity. I will return to the possible-world theory in relation to Luhrmann's 'collage' in greater detail below. Luhrmann's heightened milieu emphasizes its fictionality, with fine detail which enfolds a generation's distaste for perceived Shakespearian archaism – a major studio concern – into the world's very construction material.[9] Luhrmann's intertextual basis for Verona Beach allows space to exist where real-world rules need not apply, be they legal, linguistic or geographical. Verona Beach is a place that does not exist in our world and, strikingly, it is built from the very text that Luhrmann's film is often criticized for disregarding.

Shakespearian citation informs every aspect of Verona Beach. The humorous intertextuality of the film's production design – pistols branded 'sword' and 'rapier', for example – is frequently glossed elsewhere, usually dismissed as gimmickry. Rather, the intertextual development of Verona Beach relies on audience collusion for interpretation of a complex network of visual and

aural references, foregrounded by the Red Curtain's very real artificiality. Verona Beach's comprehensiveness establishes a local dialect, constructed with visual, verbal and musical signifiers perceptible in concentric layers of detail. This discourse completes the world's construction, authorizes the use of Elizabethan language, and envelops the viewer so completely that every detail becomes part of a discursive vernacular.

PROJECT GENESIS

This investigation began after I rewatched the opening moments of *William Shakespeare's Romeo + Juliet* for perhaps the tenth time. As the 'Montague Boys' are introduced, a vaguely inaudible piece of text is spoken, external to Shakespeare's play. Being familiar with Luhrmann's production design, I came to suspect that there was more to this exclamation than had been previously acknowledged. The official DVD captioning of the film's first dialogic scene (Shakespeare's 1.1) confirmed this suspicion: Phrases shouted by Samson and Gregory (absent from the published screenplay) are captioned as follows:

> SAMPSON:
> Excrement – In a Urinal –
> SAMPSON AND GREGORY:
> Go rot![10]

---

[5] Alfredo Michel Modenessi. '(Un)Doing the Book "without Verona walls": A View from the Receiving End of *Baz Luhrmann's William Shakespeare's Romeo + Juliet*', in *Spectacular Shakespeare: Critical Theory and Popular Cinema* (Madison 2002), p. 70.

[6] Baz Luhrmann, *Romeo + Juliet: The Music. William Shakespeare's Romeo + Juliet: Music Edition DVD* (Twentieth Century Fox/Bazmark Inq.), 2006.

[7] Courtney Lehmann, *Screen Adaptations: Shakespeare's Romeo and Juliet* (London, 2010), p. 170.

[8] Monsted, e-mail correspondence.

[9] Baz Luhrmann, *William Shakespeare's Romeo + Juliet: Special Edition, DVD Commentary* (Twentieth Century Fox/Bazmark Inq.), 2003.

[10] *William Shakespeare's Romeo + Juliet*, Dir. Baz Luhrmann. *Closed Captioning* (DVD, Twentieth Century Fox/Bazmark Inq., 2003/2006), 1996.

A close examination of the actors' faces reveals that words are omitted from this gibberish. After some analysis, it became clear that the boys in fact say:

> SAMPSON:
> Pedlar's excrement! King Urinal!
> SAMPSON AND GREGORY
> Go rot!

With this adjusted text, the lines remain nonsensical but they become direct citations. Luhrmann recontextualizes Autolycus's 'Let me pocket up my pedlar's excrement' (*Winter's Tale*, 4.4.713–14), which signals interest in source, even for incidental lines. To the same end, both the Host's 'Thou art a Castilian-King-urinal!' (*Merry Wives of Windsor*, 2.3.31) and Leontes's 'Make that thy question, and go rot' (*Winter's Tale*, 1.2.326) are reincorporated as slang. Luhrmann appropriates and regroups these lines so that their primary meanings (if not original intentions) are irrelevant, and foregrounds the use of such vernacular in this society.[11]

Having puzzled out the provenance of these lines, I saw that there was more textual depth to this film than had previously been acknowledged. In fact, Verona Beach incorporates intertextuality in production design, music and verbal text on what I have categorized as large-scale medium-scale and microscopic levels.

VERONA BEACH AND THE BARD WITH THE FOREHEAD

As I analysed the extraordinary intertextual detail that comprises Verona Beach, it became quickly apparent that its focus is centralized on the written word. The film's textual grounding is immediately signalled with an onscreen prologue, detailed billboards and newspapers. The film's soundtrack producer, Marius de Vries, suggests 'these cultural sign-posts and cross-references are so blatant that they become . . . common ground by which those watching the film are seduced into collaborating with the world which the movie is postulating'.[12] This centralized immersion is developed on multiple levels.

The varying levels of identified detail were the result of an exhaustive, intricate process, which created what production designer Catherine Martin calls an 'intense society around Romeo and Juliet' which reinforced the text within a world of 'contemporary myth'.[13] Courtney Lehmann, wary of the connection between 'myth' and the supernatural, defers instead to the legendary;[14] regardless, these vernaculars highlight Verona Beach's Red Curtain-influenced heightened plane, in 'a time and place caught between here-after and no-where, unidentified and identifiable'.[15] Verona Beach is a collection of pop-culture images which invoke religion, consumerism and iconography, headed by the presence of Shakespeare, in a society which 'not only most stridently advertises itself as a product of global capitalism but also knowingly flaunts how that culture consumes "Shakespeare"'.[16]

Critically, to these 'Veronese', Shakespearian expression and citation are not ironic, they are unremarkable. Luhrmann winks at the knowing audience as the camera pans across storefronts for 'The Merchant of Verona Beach' and 'Globe Theatre Pool Hall', yet none of the characters wink at one another. Verona Beach is not a society preoccupied with citing Shakespeare; it is a society where Shakespeare's words are a common parlance, with no citation necessary. The film's Shakespearian images, quotations and references are more about the audience's interpretation of a constructed world than they are about living in a giant Shakespeare-themed amusement park where stores are named for an idolized absent figure. In fact, Hodgdon's observation of the truism that 'the Shakespeare

---

11 The captioning programme has been updated for the 2010 Blu-Ray edition and more accurately reflects many of the Shakespearian references included in this paper.

12 De Vries, *Music Edition DVD*.

13 Jo Litson, '*Romeo and Juliet*', *Theatre Crafts International*, 30 (1996), 47–9; pp. 47, 49.

14 Courtney Lehmann, 'Strictly Shakespeare? Dead Letters, Ghostly Fathers, and the Cultural Pathology of Authorship in Baz Luhrmann's *William Shakespeare's Romeo + Juliet*', *Shakespeare Quarterly*, 52 (2001), 189–221; p. 190.

15 Modenessi, '(Un)Doing', p. 72.

16 Barbara Hodgdon, '*William Shakespeare's Romeo + Juliet*: Everything's Nice in America?', *Shakespeare Survey* 52 (Cambridge, 1999), pp. 88–98; p. 89.

myth insists on the physical spectre of the Bard with the Forehead'[17] is ironized within Verona Beach, because the one Shakespearian icon that never appears is the Droeshout portrait.

Despite his ubiquity in Verona Beach, Hodgdon's 'Shakespeare myth' is uneasily absent here, as is Shakespeare himself, aside from one sly in-joke clear perhaps only to the filmmaker. Prior to the lovers 'meeting' through a decorative fish-tank, Romeo passes a man at a urinal dressed in a Renaissance-style costume. We see only the man's back for a brief second; according to Luhrmann, that man is Shakespeare.[18] The man wears an elaborate hat, so no 'Forehead' is apparent; it is a citation for insiders alone, yet its significance lies in Shakespeare's anonymous, background presence. Indeed, the surprising fact that the word 'Shakespeare' is not used as a brand name removes the author's identity and emphasizes citation as normalized speech. Critics who identify Verona Beach as a 'post-Shakespearian world'[19] disregard that world's construction; more accurately, Verona Beach is 'post-Shakespearian' only for the audience. Luhrmann does not ever suggest that the film's characters are quoting Shakespeare; rather, Verona Beach is a world beyond the realms of contemporary culture, where Shakespeare is a one-way cultural icon, ironically absent for anyone within the film but ubiquitous in the interpretation of canny moviegoers.

LARGE-SCALE INTERTEXTUALITY

While the bulk of this investigation will focus on Verona Beach's easy-to-miss intertextual details, large-scale citation plays its role in the construction of the broader universe. In creating Verona Beach, production crews went to great lengths to generate the extraordinary detail required to build the world literally from nothing.[20] Cars, branding and costumes were tailored to individual personalities. As the Red Curtain-heightened world of Verona Beach rose from sketchbooks and screenplay drafts, an ontological construction ensured all elements were considered. The social development of Verona Beach required consistency and rigorous

verisimilitude to effectively crowd out the outside world.

To this end, extant products, customs and locations were consciously excluded from all aspects of production design. Importantly, however, the constructed world bears just enough resemblance to reality that familiar imagery reinforces both Verona Beach's alienation and alliance to reality. For example, Luhrmann reuses a large, familiar 'Enjoy Coca-Cola' billboard (also featured in *Strictly Ballroom* and *Moulin Rouge!*), translated to 'Wherefore L'Amour'. The familiar design sweep appeals to the viewer's semiotic understanding of that sign, while the otherness of seeing different words in place of the iconic drink logo distances Verona Beach from the actual world. The sign sits alongside enough familiar elements to encourage us to be comfortable there.

The familiar and unfamiliar are also rendered musically, to provide a familiar, sonically extensive base amidst what might be alien text.[21] Luhrmann's inclusion of music from popular recording artists attracted teenaged audiences and ensured ongoing association between certain songs and the film. The musical score and pop soundtrack specifically incorporated the text, and intertwined music around Shakespeare's words and Catherine Martin's images to complete a comprehensive picture of Verona Beach.

[17] Hodgdon, 'Everything's Nice', p. 88.

[18] Baz Luhrmann, *William Shakespeare's Romeo + Juliet: Music Edition, DVD* Commentary (Twentieth Century Fox/Bazmark Inq.), 2006.

[19] Richard Vela, 'Post-Apocalyptic Spaces in Baz Luhrmann's *William Shakespeare's Romeo + Juliet*', in *Apocalyptic Shakespeare: Essays on Visions of Chaos and Revelation in Recent Film Adaptations* (Jefferson, 2009), p. 99.

[20] Luhrmann, *Special Edition DVD*. Large sets, such as the impressive wasteland of Sycamore Grove, were built from scratch, at such a high degree of craftsmanship that they withstood a hurricane.

[21] Luhrmann, *Music Edition DVD*. Luhrmann produced the film's soundtrack in conjunction with assistant Anton Monsted, orchestral composer Craig Armstrong, music producer Paul Andrew (Nellee) Hooper, and producer/composer Marius de Vries.

The combination of extant pop songs with custom-made pieces inspired by the film and Shakespeare's play is a point of disjuncture for flashes of the familiar in the unfamiliarity of Verona Beach. Choric re-orchestrations and remixes of popular songs contrast the familiar and unfamiliar, a shock that delays the viewer's recognition of the recontextualized lyrics. Music reinforces the world's un-alien distinctiveness, both familiar in tone but unfamiliar in content to its audience, undistinguishable in immersive, remixed layers.

Far beyond a reliance on familiar signifiers, however, is the actual construction of the world central to the authenticity of Verona Beach. Built on a devotion to physical verisimilitude, Verona Beach is much less a set than a world in which people live. The world's strength is the detail which renders features ubiquitous and unremarkable. The majority of Verona Beach's distinctively designed pieces – set dressings, product placements, text citations and social constructions – are *ignored* by characters. Of all created elements, far more props, signs, furniture and pieces of text exist than are actually foregrounded, a technique which serves to emphasize the completeness of this world. The sheer volume of design features ignored by actors and the camera – as opposed to self-conscious indication of a carefully placed prop – harmonizes elements. Crucially, the citizens of this world share the blasé acceptance of familiar features of a city street on which citizens live; eventually details are taken for granted. Luhrmann begins at this saturation point, where the worn-down city streets of Verona Beach are not worthy of a second glance from figures presumably born there. Excepting the lurid expository zoom-shots on selected items, Luhrmann rarely lingers on clever detail long enough for the audience to absorb its full meaning.[22] In fact, as I shall observe, much of Luhrmann's detail is minute and fleeting, with an especial reliance on intertextual citations not readily familiar to the casual filmgoer, all of which serves to validate Verona Beach's comprehensiveness.

To ensure the authenticity of the many slogans, products and hoardings of Verona Beach, an Australian commercial artist was engaged to design the world's details. Working with a team of designers, Tania Burkett's role was to ensure that Verona Beach resembled a world where appropriate, unique products were available for sale, all of which were created from references found throughout Shakespeare's canon. Burkett's responsibilities ranged from large-scale elements to minute details, with 'Shakespeare as [her] copywriter' to develop images and products as needed.[23] Burkett and her colleagues designed dozens of items that adorned the sets which featured both prominently and fleetingly in the film. Many ideas occurred out of necessity or inspiration, such as the *Othello*-inspired delivery service Post-Post-Haste-Dispatch.[24]

The first large elements emphasized are Catherine Martin's trademark advertising billboards, which '[communicate] clearly to an audience that this is where we are and this is what we're doing'.[25] Recontextualizing Shakespeare's words for commercial branding, citation is varied, creative and often humorous. Beyond the *L'Amour* sweep, billboards advertise 'Thunder bullets' which 'Shoot Forth Thunder' (*2 Henry VI*, 4.1.104); 'Sword 9mm

---

[22] Luhrmann's distinctive camera work has attracted enough critical attention to obscure the detail it encompasses. Courtney Lehmann suggests that 'Luhrmann invents a whole new language [with] whip pans, lightning cuts, super macro slam zooms, static super wide shots, tight on point-of-view shots, and other vertigo-inducing angles courtesy of crash crane camerawork' (Lehmann, *Screen Adaptations*, p. 145) but grounds the translation of that language solely in the film's broader mechanics, as opposed to its finer detail.

[23] Tania Burkett, personal telephone correspondence.

[24] Burkett, telephone correspondence. 'Post-Post-Haste-Dispatch' delivery service was originally 'Speed dispatch', from Friar Laurence's 'I'll send a friar with speed / To Mantua, with my letters to thy lord' (4.1.123–4). According to Burkett, studio lawyers called for an alternative so as not to be confused with the many authentic delivery businesses with 'speed' in their names. Burkett chose Brabantio's 'Write from us to him post-post-haste. Dispatch' (*Othello*, 1.3.46) with the correct tone. The subsequent emendation of Laurence's line, to 'I'll send my letters post haste / To Mantua,' was suggested by actor Pete Postlethwaite, and is a rare textual alteration. Close-up angles on the delivery envelope include the line 'A local habitation and a name' (*A Midsummer Night's Dream*, 5.1.17).

[25] Litson, '*Romeo*', p. 49.

Series S'[26] handguns are 'Thy pistol [*sic*] and thy friend' (*2 Henry IV*, 5.3.94); and 'Prospero Scotch Whiskey' promises 'Such stuff as dreams are made on' (*Tempest*, 4.1.156–7). Capulet Industries claims that 'Experience is by industry achieved' (*Two Gentlemen of Verona*, 1.3.22), while a skyscraper is 'Retail'd to Posterity' (*Richard III*, 3.1.77) by Montague Construction.[27] As suggested above, it is significant that not all intertextual citations are necessarily familiar to the casual filmgoer, although the majority of these large-scale references are presented in such a way that it is clear that 'something' is being quoted. Despite this pointed branding, of the above quotations, arguably only Prospero's is widely familiar. The employment of Shakespearian citation spreads to almost the entire canon at one stage or another; yet not every citation is iconic.

Luhrmann emphasizes the importance of familiar media framing to bridge a 'language gap': 'because we're constantly seeing a vocabulary which for some viewers will be deeply unfamiliar in familiar contexts, on advertising hoardings, in newspapers, on the covers of magazines, [so the] framing is not as alien as the language might be'.[28] On top of establishing a familiarity of style, Luhrmann incorporates packaging, services, media, advertisements and vernacular into a uniform familiarity which allows an entry point for viewers.

Crucially, these broad strokes work to achieve the first and third steps in the Red Curtain cinema mandate, of building a heightened creative world while simultaneously reminding the audience of the deliberate distance from the real world. Intertextuality serves as a constant visual reminder of the world's unreality but does so by ensuring exhaustive authenticity within it.

MEDIUM–SCALE INTERTEXTUALITY

A more delicate negotiation comes in the finer details around Verona Beach: these flourishes have often attracted the greatest criticism as gimmicks. Where large-scale intertextuality represents the wider *universe*, medium-scale details fill out *the everyday* in Verona Beach, fine enough to reflect and refract reality through the viewer's biases. From incidental signage to added dialogue and tongue-in-cheek citation, Luhrmann's medium-scale elements are conspicuous enough to be easily noted (and emphasize the otherness of Verona Beach in keeping with the Red Curtain conventions) but are unremarkable enough to be subtly used and discarded by characters through the course of the film.

Production design structures smaller products and establishments not necessarily in camera focus but glimpsed peripherally. Citations are plentiful and are often not pointed enough to be clearly Shakespearian, particularly to the casual viewer. Among the dozens of included citations are the set dressings in the opening scene's Phoenix Gas station, where customers are invited to 'Add more fuel to your fire' (*3 Henry VI*, 5.4.70), amidst packaging for 'Hotspur Filters' cigarettes, a 'Shylock Bank' storefront, and 'Argosy Cars' taxis ('Hath an argosy cast away coming from Tripolis', *Merchant of Venice*, 3.1.94). The 'Sycamore Grove' amusement park features bars/brothels called 'Pound of Flesh' (*Merchant of Venice*), 'Midnite Hags' (*Macbeth*, 4.1.64) and 'Shining Nights' (*Love's Labour's Lost*, 1.1.90) alongside signage for 'Rozencrantzky's' burgers, an over-sized prop bottle of 'Bolingbroke Champagne', and cabana bars called 'Mistress Quickly' and 'Cheapside'. 'Sack: Good Double Beer' features the almost unreadable slogan 'Let a Cup of Sack be your Poison' (*1 Henry IV*, 2.2.45–6).

---

[26] Martin Brown, personal telephone correspondence. All guns used were working firearms, and were specifically designed by an armourer to act as both status symbols and costume jewellery. Custom pieces included Romeo's 'Sword', Tybalt's 'Rapier', Benvolio's 'Sword 9mm Series S', and Mercutio's 'Dagger'.

[27] Other unused construction slogans include 'Montague: A Tower of Strength' (*Richard III*, 5.3.12) and 'Montague Constructions: The Houses He Makes Last Till Doomsday' (*Hamlet*, 5.1.59)

[28] Luhrmann, *Music Edition DVD*.

The walls of Sycamore Grove and the Globe Theatre Pool Hall are papered with posters advertising concerts for bands with names such as 'Jack Cade's Venom'd Vengeance' (2 Henry VI; Troilus and Cressida, 5.3.49) and 'Feigned Ecstasies' (Titus Andronicus, 4.4.21) who advertise a new album called 'Our ears vouchsafe it but your legs should do it' (Love's Labour's Lost, 5.2.217). The creation of two fictional bands demonstrates that in Verona Beach, there is a social world beyond Shakespeare's characters. Each of these cited references are large enough to be read but too small to be clear at a glance, an effect which places the work at risk of appearing gimmicky. Crucially, however, embellishments point towards the completeness of Verona Beach as a society which extends beyond the camera's gaze.

Luhrmann not only creates Verona Beach as a visual world, but additionally, true to the Red Curtain rule of audience distancing, he further anchors this society through linguistic vernacular. For Luhrmann and co-adapter Craig Pearce, 'the story dictated the world, and the world dictated the story at all times'.[29] In keeping with the development of Verona Beach as a society which normalizes Elizabethan language, incidental lines of dialogue were consciously lifted from Shakespeare, often recontextualized, and used to fill linguistic gaps along the same lines as the above typographical interpolations.

Fittingly, many of Luhrmann's interpolated spoken lines are insults between young men, which build the raw, aggressive, evolving street vernacular into the fabric of Verona Beach. Some interpolations are unremarkable, such as Abra[ham]'s lascivious 'Double, double, toil and trouble' prior to the opening brawl sequence (Macbeth, 4.1.10). Many are difficult to interpret and harder again to identify within the canon: for example, in the Queen Mab scene, Sampson shouts 'you taffeta punk! [All's Well That Ends Well, 2.2.21] Die a beggar! [Antony and Cleopatra, 1.5.64].' The original meaning of the second half of this line ('Who's born that day / When I forget to send to Antony / Shall die a beggar') is refigured as youth vernacular, where intent trumps meaning. In the fatal duel scene, Tybalt

attacks Romeo with 'Thou art my soul's hate' ('There is the man of my soul's hate', Coriolanus, 1.6.10), refigured as an enraged epithet. Each interpolation was initially unplanned and unstructured: no additions are published in screenplay form, a fact which emphasizes the process of ongoing textual development. When in need, Luhrmann would call for necessary lines during the shooting process. Co-producer and script supervisor Martin Brown's role was (in part) to furnish a list of Shakespearian insults that could be adopted at short notice, or, as Brown colourfully noted, 'Baz asked me for a list of words that might be used if an Elizabethan wanted to tell someone to fuck off.'[30]

Another intriguing adjustment of the youth slang comes as Romeo greets Benvolio and Mercutio at Sycamore Grove, with a familiar 'Ho ho, you taffeta punks!' (All's Well That Ends Well, 2.2.21). Benvolio returns his greeting with a slangy 'Ro-MAY-oh', altering his name with affectionate familiarity without straying from the text, while simultaneously evoking a play on words from the published screenplay, omitted from the film:

> BENVOLIO
> Here comes Romeo, here comes Romeo!
> MERCUTIO
> Without his roe . . .
> BENVOLIO
> Me, O.
> MERCUTIO
> . . . like dried herring.[31]

The pun is excised but the familiarity remains, firmly rooted within a local dialect based on citation.

Other inventive verbal citations come from the 'newsreader' Chorus, overheard on a television saying ' . . . this costly blood (Julius Caesar, 3.1.61), never anger made good guard for itself (Antony and Cleopatra, 4.1.9–10). The law hath not been

---

[29] Brown, telephone correspondence.
[30] Brown, telephone correspondence.
[31] Baz Luhrmann and Craig Pearce, William Shakespeare's Romeo + Juliet: The Contemporary Film, the Classic Play (New York, 1996), p. 82.

dead . . . (*Measure for Measure*, 2.2.92)' before focus shifts away. These inserted lines are, importantly, barely heard and are hardly iconic. Luhrmann might be forgiven for deciding to mute the newscaster or to substitute filler lines, yet he maintains his Red Curtain consistency by giving the Chorus a local casual, deliberate citation similar to that of the street youths.

This distinctive street vernacular extends prominently to the music that accompanies Verona Beach life. Half of the soundtrack's songs were specifically commissioned, often inspired by the film. One such track, *Pretty Piece of Flesh*, acts as more than a simple reference to Sampson's early boast. The song is a triumphant theme for the Montague boys, who repeatedly sing the song's chorus ('I am a pretty piece of flesh') in place of Sampson's lines, and again later as the Montague boys celebrate their successful conquest of the Capulet Ball. Luhrmann co-opts and recontextualizes this dialogue and incorporates local vernacular into the world's popular commercial culture.

Specific references similarly shape two custom-made soundtrack songs free-associated from preview footage: *Whatever (I Had a Dream)* and *Local God*. Both songs are heard in fragments in the body of the film, remixed, played at different speeds and sampled. Neither song's overt Shakespearian references are heard in the film proper: they are present only to a consumer listening to the songs separately. *Whatever* is a raucous, jumbled piece which blends Romeo's dream state, Verona Beach references and assorted familiar pop culture icons: references range from Romeo's 'I dreamt a dream tonight' (1.4.50) and Juliet's death to sordid imagery of illegal narcotics, John Wayne and Bette Davis. Similarly, *Local God* uses lyrics that incorporate the experience of being a Montague in Verona Beach. The song's first line, '*You do that Romeo / Be what you wanna be . . .*' appropriates 'Romeo' as a generic local action: 'do[ing] that Romeo' is a stylistic choice. In Verona Beach, to be a 'Romeo' is non-ironic and un-Shakespearian. It is the joyous act of gang life, where 'a Romeo' is one to be both emulated and lovingly mocked, and recalls Benvolio's 'Ro-MAY-oh'. The chorus catches the spirit

of the Montague boys: '*I feel just like a local god when I'm with the boys / We do what we want, we do what we want . . .*' In Verona Beach, the warring boy-gangs *are* local gods who *do* 'do what [they] want': this sense of invincibility colours their gang experience.

Medium-scale detail further embeds the Red Curtain mentality of creating a heightened creative world, and it is clear that the audience is expected not to interpret all developed details fully, but instead to treat citation as part of the world's structure. The achievement of surface verisimilitude provides an assured sense of consistency for the casual viewer, and the potential for greater detail to be noticed on further viewings.

MICROSCOPIC INTERTEXTUALITY

Doležel has suggested that in literature, all fictional worlds are incomplete, and that eventually a world's verisimilitude will be compromised.[32] Doležel's assertion is complicated when applied to film, as the demands of verisimilitude and continuity seek completion, even though in all cases that completion is illusive. The challenge for filmmakers is to insist on extreme detail to emphasize the world's completeness. No fictional world can hope for actual perfection: indeed, often errors are unnoticed until after release. While many filmmakers settle for completeness in areas framed by the camera, Luhrmann's Red Curtain called for a comprehensive world inside which his cameras could freely operate without fear of straying outside, which means that every detail had to be exacting.

To this point, designer Tania Burkett related that Luhrmann only loosely planned his daily filming process, so designers were obliged to presume that slight details would be incorporated in the finished product. Burkett and her collaborators were expected to be as 'authentic [to the world] as possible' in case Luhrmann focused his lens on a package or a piece of graffiti, for example. This sense of multilayered authenticity created

---

[32] Lubomir Doležel, *Heterocosmica: Fiction and Possible Worlds* (Baltimore, 2000), p. 22.

a world whose tiniest products shared a unified feel.[33] As such, miniscule details like a 'Butt-Shaft' Cigarette brand – which I spotted in the extreme background of the gas-station sequence and asked Burkett about – were placed on set in anticipation of their potential use. Ultimately, the reference to 'the blind bow-boy's butt-shaft' (*Romeo and Juliet*, 2.3.15–16) is almost undetectable; yet, as Burkett recounted, the shelves of the Phoenix Gas Mart and other places of Verona Beach commerce were fully, authentically stocked in case they were ever filmed.[34] Other references, including 'Maiden milk', 'Hark Communications' public telephones and 'Mercury Special Filter Cigarettes' are glimpsed peripherally, but these products' ubiquity is most effective in the fact that characters never linger over a product placement for the sake of the reference. These designs are effective precisely because the citizens of Verona Beach *pay them no attention* and, what's more, many are so subtle that it is impossible to absorb every layer of meaning and design in a single viewing, given the extraordinary volume of design.[35]

The microscopic detail that characterizes the production design extends to sonic construction: right from the film's opening moment, citation musically establishes the world with the memorable, grandiose homage to Orff's *O Fortuna*, knowingly renamed *O Verona*. The choric gesture opens with an accelerated sound effect, a pastiche achieved by sampling 'segments of every musical cue in the movie, [which were then] laid on to half-inch tape, speed-manipulated with tape stops and tape starts, re-sampled, reversed and layered up'.[36] Furthermore, the lyrics to *O Verona* are a Latin translation of Shakespeare's Prologue, a fact not immediately apparent: layered orchestration, vocals, sound effects, and recitation of the actual Prologue text render almost all of *O Verona's* de-emphasized Latin text virtually inaudible, and in any case almost certainly irrelevant to the film's teen demographic.[37] Both the soundtrack pastiche and Chorus translation speak to Luhrmann's tendency for precision, where the smallest points are carefully detailed despite the fact that they almost certainly go unnoticed by casual filmgoers.

Visually, details and citations flash across the screen too quickly to be read, such as numerous newspaper articles which fill the frame for fractions of seconds. A careless designer might fill these articles with dummy text or gibberish to infer detail: rather, every Verona Beach newspaper is intertextually comprehensive. The film's first textual signifier is a newspaper article which coincides with the Chorus's speech, featuring headlines with citations such as 'War Against God's Peace', (*1 Henry VI*, 1.5.73–4); 'Violent Ends', (*Romeo and Juliet*, 2.5.9); and 'A Rash Fierce Blaze of Riot' (*Richard II*, 2.1.33). The many fleetingly glimpsed newspapers and magazines are virtually unreadable, yet every piece contains appropriate (if disjointed) Shakespearian citation from at least twelve different plays.[38] For example, as Laurence fantasizes over the potential of the lovers' union, an oddly disjointed but thematically linked newspaper article briefly materializes:

Brother Capulet [*sic*], give me your hand. For this alliance may so happy prove, to turn our [*sic*] households' rancor to pure love [*Romeo and Juliet*, 5.3.295, 2.2.91–2]. Why ring not out the bells aloud throughout the town? Prince, [*sic*] command the citizens make bonfires and feast and banquet in the streets [*1 Henry VI*, 1.8.12–13]. Loyal, just and upright gentlemen never did captive with a freer heart! Cast off your chains of bondage and embrace [*Richard II*, 1.3.87–8]. A contract of true love to celebrate,

---

33 Burkett, telephone correspondence.
34 Burkett, telephone correspondence.
35 Bazmark generously granted me access to some of these products, many of which were not seen on film. These included 'Crystal Tresses' shampoo (*1 Henry VI*, 1.1.3), to 'rend off thy silver hair' (*Titus Andronicus*, 3.1.259) and to 'be an amber-colour'd raven' (*Love's Labour's Lost*, 4.3.85); SilverBright toothpaste (*King John*, 2.1.315, 'To clean between thy teeth'); 'Out Damn'd Spot Dry Clean' (*Macbeth*, 5.1.33), 'Fortune's Cap' restaurant (*Hamlet*, 2.2.231) and 'Goodly Gear' clothing (*Romeo and Juliet*, 2.3.93).
36 De Vries, *Music Edition DVD*.
37 An early draft of *O Verona* supplied by Fox Music utilized words from a modified thirteenth-century hymn, *Dies Irae*, contemporary with and similar in structure to the *Carmina Burana*.
38 With at least five fully-developed newspapers featuring in the film, the breadth of detail in each featured article is too broad to cite here in full.

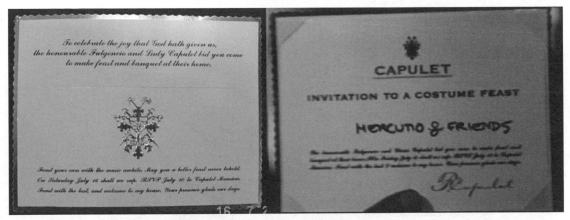

36. Detail from two distinct Capulet Ball invitations: an early prototype (left) and the final product (right), featuring unique textual references.

and some donation freely to estate on the blest lovers! [*Tempest*, 4.1.84–86] We'll celebrate their nuptials, and ourselves will in that kingdom spend our following days. Our son and daughter shall in Verona [*sic*] reign [*Pericles* 22.103–5]. To hear the rest untold, sir, lead's the way [*Pericles* 22.107]. To celebrate the joy that God hath given us [*1 Henry VI*, 1.8.14], come in, and let us banquet royally after this golden day of victory! [*1 Henry VI*, 1.8.30–1] The gods today stand friendly that we may, lovers in peace, lead on our days to age! [*Julius Caesar*, 5.1.93–4]

The breadth of cross-canon citation compiled for newspaper articles demonstrates interest in coherently communicating a layered world in part through the media: the inclusion of the essentially everyday newspaper dedicated to chronicling the minutiae of society suggests cultural depth consciously left to the audience's inference.

The written word continues as the site of local verisimilitude: custom-made publications include *Timely* magazine, a news glossy with the motto 'Matter for a Hot Brain' (*Winter's Tale*, 4.4.684). *Timely*'s cover feature on 'Dave Paris' as 'Bachelor of the Year' talks of his 'Excellent breeding (*Merry Wives of Windsor*, 2.2.218), sums of love and wealth (*Timon of Athens*, 5.2.37), absolute power (*King Lear*, 5.3.276), and a good name' (*Cymbeline*, 2.3.83). *Prophecy* runs a feature on 'Music Frightful as a Serpent's hiss' (*2 Henry VI*, 3.2.330); *BulletIN*

magazine notes that 'The Golden Bullet Beats it Down' (*Passionate Pilgrim*, 18.18). Public, pervasive written signifiers reinforce a local dialect consistent with the Red Curtain Cinema's construction and offer a fleeting glimpse into inferred areas of Verona Beach society.

Furthermore, the written word extends to the personal, which includes 'I love thee' engraved inside Juliet's wedding ring, Romeo's jotted poetic musings, and a meticulously detailed invitation to the Capulet Ball. The detail on this prop (Illustration 36) is onscreen for barely two seconds, and the only clearly legible words it bears are 'Mercutio and Friends', yet the citation is typically detailed:

To celebrate the joy that God hath given us [*1 Henry VI*, 1 1.8.14], The Honourable Fulgencio and Lady Capulet bid you come to make feast and banquet at their home [*Titus Andronicus*, 5.2.114]. Feast your ears with the music awhile [*Timon of Athens*, 3.7.33–4]. May you a better feast never behold [*Timon of Athens*, 3.7.87]. On Saturday July 16 shall we sup. RSVP July 10 to Capulet Mansion. Feast with the best, and welcome to my house [*Taming of the Shrew*, 5.2.8]. Your presence glads our days [*Pericles*, 7.19]. – F. Capulet.[39]

---

[39] This text is based on a prop (above, left) that Bazmark kindly supplied me; it differs slightly from that in the film.

37. Distressed Agincourt Cigarette package, featuring obliterated text (left) alongside the slightly different original studio design (right).

Usefully, much of the cited text is recontextualized, with original meaning removed and Shakespeare's language established as common vernacular. As such, the designers present their information entirely without irony: Timon's misanthropic invitation to feast is cited with sincerity.

At an even finer level, intertextual detail exists on the tiniest of props. One notable example is the detail on a package of 'Agincourt Cigarettes,' where a decorative embellishment is, on close examination, an obscured, obliterated excerpt from W. H. Auden's 'O Where Are You Going': one of several text citations from sources as disparate as Eliot and Marlowe (see Illustration 37). These items demonstrate commitment to poetic verisimilitude beyond Shakespeare's canon, even for unreadable text, and even fancifully hint at communities external to Verona Beach where Eliotian and Marlovian citation is standard, such is the itinerant nature of cigarette packages.

The textual branding of Verona Beach reaches its logical conclusion – as a worn-down urban centre home for restless youth – through the literal marking of the walls and blank spaces of the world. Vandalism is ubiquitous, with most walls and businesses bearing local names including 'Romeo', 'Benvolio' and 'Rosaline'. More detailed are two pieces of graffiti which enjoy no close-up, but appear in the background in stages. On a wall behind the Globe Theatre Pool Hall, a large, ornate piece of graffiti reads, in its first appearance, '... THOU WERT CL... / ... PI...'. The camera misses parts of the phrase, and others are distressed to the point where they are quite unreadable. Several more angles reveal more letters, but the entire phrase – 'Would thou wert clean enough to spit on' (*Timon of Athens*, 4.3.361) – is never revealed in its entirety (Illustration 38). Further down the wall, another blurred piece of graffiti is readable only in part: 'How N... Fat...', or 'How Now Ye Fat Kidneyed Rascal', an appropriation of 'Peace, ye fat-kidneyed rascal, what a brawling dost thou keep!' (*1 Henry IV*, 2.2.6–7) (Illustration 39). Aside from the use of Shakespeare as linguistic slang, vandalism is used as a territorial claim of ownership and street language consistent with the world's construction.

Even more than the large- and medium-scale citations that adorn Verona Beach, the microscopic shifts the focus of the design from a constructed 'set' to a constructed 'world', where the ignored detail furnishes the day-to-day lives of its citizens. The fact that such attention was paid to this element reinforces the idea of what the creators of the Red Curtain Cinema were attempting.

38. Large-scale graffiti shows the partially obscured reference to *Timon of Athens*.

39. A fleeting reference to *1 Henry IV* is almost completely undecipherable as a citation.

VERONA BEACH AS
POSSIBLE-WORLD

The many layers of Luhrmann's Red Curtain world emphasize its exhaustive construction and its ambition for verisimilitude. To reach beyond the company's artistic mission statement, however, Verona Beach is uneasily defined. Verona Beach is no 'alternate universe', a category ubiquitous in literature, film, comic books and drama. Constructions similar to our own world yet slightly different, alternate worlds 'indulge the "what if" syndrome',[40] which firmly grounds the adaptation in 'our' world with slight variation. Verona Beach is clearly not part of our world: the film features no national flags or suggestion that Verona Beach is American, aside from (many of) the actors' accents.[41] Alternative universes are often engaged by characters from one world (usually the actual world) interacting with the unfamiliar, to note contrast between what they see and what we know to be true.

Different but related concepts are variously defined: Hutcheon considers the 'heterocosm', 'literally an "other world" or cosmos, complete ... with the stuff of a story – settings, characters, events, and situations' in which the 'res extensa ... of that world, its material, physical dimension' is deployed for the totality of experience.[42] Ruth Ronen considers 'fictional worlds', which are 'based on a logic of parallelism that guarantees their autonomy in relation to the actual world'.[43] Both theories are compelling to a point, but the extensive interaction between Shakespeare's canon and the detail of Verona Beach requires more separation for the interpreting audience member beyond a simple dismissal of a world as simply fictional or parallel.

More useful is a train of thought common to the fields of logic, literature and philosophy: the possible-world. Distinct from an alternate universe, a possible-world revolves on a 'heterogeneous paradigm that allows various conceptions for possible modes of existence'.[44] Possible-worlds apply to any possible version of our world so long as it adheres to the laws of physics. The semantically compelling sense that possible-worlds represent a version of our actual world rather than a simple fiction is useful in allying the familiar and unfamiliar and fits the Red Curtain approach.

Rod Girle notes that possible-worlds 'usually have some sort of internal consistency, or some sort of internal logic, even when they are quite unrealistic',[45] a position consistent with the structure of Verona Beach. Furthermore, the actual world and possible-worlds are 'utterly and completely distinct from each other from a causal and spatiotemporal point of view across all spatiotemporal dimensions'[46] and, most critically, are designed to be interpreted by spectators who live within our actual world.

The possible-world perspective authorizes the use of Elizabethan language by constructing a place where all vernacular and advertising mirror the local language. To repeat a contrast, Almereyda's *Hamlet* draws attention to the disjunction between the setting and the words as spoken. Almereyda's presentation of the possible-world of Manhattan as Elizabethan is too familiar to be effective, because the world's logic is anachronistically compromised. In contrast, Luhrmann's immersive world creation authorizes Elizabethan language through imagery derived from the Shakespearian canon. The distinction between 'natural' and 'artificial' languages lies in the complexity and richness of the former and the limitations of the latter.[47]

---

[40] Robert Boswell. *The Half-Known World: On Writing Fiction* (New York, 2008), p. 110.

[41] The only national signifier in the film is on Paris's astronaut costume, with what appears to be an American flag with the Verona Beach crest in place of stars.

[42] Linda Hutcheon. *A Theory of Adaptation* (New York, 2006), p. 14.

[43] Ruth Ronen. *Possible Worlds in Literary Theory* (Cambridge, 1994), p. 8.

[44] Ronen, *Possible Worlds*, p. 21.

[45] Rod Girle, *Possible Worlds* (Montreal, 2003), p. 1.

[46] Girle, *Possible*, p. 2.

[47] Girle, *Possible*, p. 6.

Luhrmann's achievement was to turn Elizabethan English into *a natural language for his world* by appropriating Shakespeare's canon to create a Verona Beach vernacular. The result is an intertextually extended world with a natural dialect grounded in what Hutcheon calls 'truth-of-correspondence', or believability that such events could feasibly occur in that artificial setting.[48]

Most importantly, Verona Beach features recognizable elements alongside possibly unfamiliar Shakespearian language to create a place parallel to (yet significantly different from) late-nineties America. The material familiarity of the world draws the audience to the cinema, but it is the self-evident disconnect between Verona Beach and contemporary America that authorizes unfamiliar actions. The possible-world revolves on 'the simple idea that something is possible if it is so in at least one possible-world'.[49] Logically, behaviour sanctioned in Verona Beach but considered antisocial, illegal or immoral in our contemporary society is physically *possible*, meaning that logically it is possible in this *possible-world*. As noted at the beginning of this article, Romeo escapes Juliet's bedroom unnoticed; teens legally and openly tote pistols; Romeo is banished without trial for the crime of murder; Juliet is buried without question or autopsy; and every character, from the lowest to the highest status, speaks in poetic, heightened Elizabethan language. None of these concepts are physically impossible or illogical by the laws of physics. Each is unthinkable in our actual world, yet all are unflinchingly accepted in Verona Beach, which 'posits a reality of [its] own that casts doubt on basic notions in logic and semantics'.[50]

The independent reality of Verona Beach, complete with aspects that defied conventional belief, is seamlessly incorporated into the created world of the film and emphasizes its completeness. Extraordinary focus on the world's verisimilitude through detailed design emphasizes the reality of this new society for the figures that exist within it, which in turn endorses the linguistic and societal logic that would jar in a familiar setting.

AFTERWORD

Alfredo Michel Modenessi has noted that in watching Luhrmann's film, 'the viewer is assaulted with signs but is as helpless to decode them as Shakespeare's fated protagonists',[51] yet this response is certainly part of the point. Luhrmann's entire world is not designed to be immediately interpreted; it is designed to be experienced. Were it constructed as a world to be read, Verona Beach would be little more than a highly decorated set. The achievement of Luhrmann's production team was to create a detailed and vibrant location where characters feasibly live and grow. It is significant that the intertextual world of Verona Beach is entirely public: there are no Shakespearian slogans in private homes, only in places of commerce. In private homes decorations are chosen and strategically placed, while in the public world haphazard collections of signs exist at every turn, so frequently that they can never be kept straight, through the universal (large-scale) to the everyday (medium-scale) to the microscopic.

The intricacy and layering of Verona Beach, in Luhrmann's 'visual, . . . written, . . . sonic, . . . and musical collage',[52] belies Lucy Hamilton's suggestion that Luhrmann's film is made up of 'disrespectful elements to disturb the establishment [including] a number of visual Shakespearian jokes'.[53] Verona Beach has little to do with 'the establishment' and is comprised of more than just a 'number' of 'Shakespearian jokes': in all, Luhrmann

---

48 Hutcheon, *A Theory*, p. 14.
49 Girle, *Possible*, p. 3.
50 Ronen, *Possible Worlds*, p. 1. Hodgdon notes that '*Romeo + Juliet* makes no overtly tactical alignment with melting-pot ideologies [and echoes] an America where such blurrings and crossings of ethnic, racial, gender, and class boundaries occur daily' (p. 96).
51 Modenessi, '(Un)Doing', p. 77.
52 Baz Luhrmann, *Romeo + Juliet: The Music. William Shakespeare's Romeo + Juliet: Music Edition DVD* (Twentieth Century Fox/Bazmark Inq.), 2006.
53 Lucy Hamilton, 'Baz Vs. the Bardolaters, or Why *William Shakespeare's Romeo + Juliet* Deserves Another Look', *Literature/Film Quarterly*, 28 (2000), 118–25; p. 121.

cites from at least thirty-two of Shakespeare's plays, as well as the works of several contemporaries.[54] Luhrmann's filming process is summed up by Martin Brown: 'many directors start with the text, and then film what is given. Baz builds a world first and then films the visual, he builds a soundscape and visual-scape [*sic*] and lets them interact to create an interwoven cinema experience – text, music, and visuals intersect and heighten one another.'[55] The 'seamless' world of Verona Beach is effective precisely because a willing audience member can be swept up in the film's energy and can believe that these events could feasibly occur within such a society. If the film were set in modern Los Angeles, Rio or Mexico City, as several commentators have guessed, landmark-spotting and awareness of illogical moments would potentially mar the integrity of the piece.

Furthermore, as Anton Monsted recalls, textual or visual decisions were never made lightly: 'we were ambitious about infusing every element of the film – visually, in the graphics, the guns, the music, and the lyrics with Shakespearian verse,

Elizabethan stage convention, and the stage in general'.[56] The conventions of 'Red Curtain Cinema' are without doubt observed in the construction of Lurhmann's world. The great achievement of the Red Curtain possible-world is the creation of a place which oscillates between the familiar and the unfamiliar in a totality of citation and extreme attention to detail, and forces the admission that, as a possible-world, Verona Beach is as comprehensive as may be wished.[57]

---

[54] This count is doubtless incomplete: there is a great likelihood that plays not cited (including *As You Like It*, *The Comedy of Errors* and *Henry VIII*) are present yet unnoticed.

[55] Brown, telephone correspondence.

[56] Monsted, e-mail correspondence.

[57] I am indebted to Anton Monsted, Tania Burkett, Martin Brown, Marius de Vries, Nikki Di Falco, Fox Music and Bazmark Inq. for their invaluable assistance in providing me with production materials and their time to compile this paper. In addition, my colleagues Jill Levenson, Linda Hutcheon, Colette Gordon, Jacqueline Johnson and Carrie Cole were generous in their proofreading and structural ideas, for which I am particularly grateful.

THE ROYAL SHAKESPEARE COMPANY AT THE SWAN: THE FIRST TWENTY-FIVE YEARS

MARGARET SHEWRING

From its opening in 1986, the Royal Shakespeare Company's Swan auditorium in Stratford-upon-Avon has been hailed by directors, actors, audiences and critics as a warm, visually-appealing performance space with a strong 'feel-good factor'.[1] Theatre critic of *The Guardian*, Michael Billington, asked after the first three seasons, 'How on earth did the British theatre manage without the Swan?'[2] Now in its twenty-fifth season, the Swan remains widely popular. What makes it so distinctive? What has been its contribution to staging productions in the late twentieth and early twenty-first centuries, both in the context of the repertoire of the RSC and in the wider context of its contribution to theatre in Britain?

The generosity of American philanthropist Frederick Koch enabled the Swan to be built as 'an act of defiance' at a time when the Arts Council of Great Britain was facing declining funds and a period of retrenchment.[3] Its repertoire was to be drawn from the wealth of lesser-known plays written between 1570 and 1750, with the express intention of locating the familiar Shakespeare canon in its wider context. In 1989 Trevor Nunn (then Artistic Director) wrote that as the home of a unique and much-lacked repertoire 'the Swan is dedicated to exploring our past, assessing our influences, living through our heritage and preserving humility and sanity in a mercantile world'.[4]

From the outset, the Swan has offered an alternative theatrical experience sitting comfortably between the traditional Shakespearian repertoire of the RSC's main 1000-seater auditorium and the smaller (second) Other Place which has frequently featured new writing in its 150-seater, flexible, studio-style space. The Swan has served as a catalyst, forging its own identity while carrying its audiences with it as they became accustomed to the theatrical satisfactions offered by playwrights such as Jonson, Ford, Shirley and Marlowe, collaborative pieces by Shakespeare and Fletcher, and the satirical comedies of the Restoration, including plays by Wycherley and Etherege. The Swan has also housed a 'Gunpowder Season', a 'Jacobean Season' and hosted plays from the RSC's 'Complete Works Season'.

Comparatively little has been written about this innovative theatre space. Drawing on interviews with Michael Boyd, Gregory Doran, Michael Billington, Max Stafford-Clark and Roger Howells as well as on the resources of the RSC's archive at the Shakespeare Birthplace Trust, this article assesses the contribution of the Swan's construction and design to the English theatre of the last twenty-five years, drawing on a selection of the 167 productions staged there.[5]

---

[1] Michael Attenborough, 'Directing for the RSC: The Classic and the New', in *Making Space for Theatre*, ed. Ronnie Mulryne and Margaret Shewring (Stratford-upon-Avon, 1995), p. 89.

[2] Michael Billington, 'The Critic's View', in *This Golden Round: The Royal Shakespeare Company at the Swan*, ed. Ronnie Mulryne and Margaret Shewring (Stratford-upon-Avon, 1989), p. 53.

[3] Trevor Nunn, 'Preface', in *This Golden Round*.

[4] Nunn, 'Preface'.

[5] This total includes special shows and one-night performances. For a full list see the Appendix to this article.

In 1976, stage designers John Napier and Chris Dyer had been responsible 'for a variant [of the RSC's Main House]...stage which carried the balconies through the concealed proscenium arch and round behind the acting area' in a manner suggestive of the Elizabethan 'wooden O'.[6] This reflected the Company's need to get closer to the audience, breaking out from the proscenium arch and extending the stage to curve outwards across the first rows of the stalls. The result was a compromise – but it was to point the way forward. The inspiration for the auditorium of the Swan came from a sketch and model drawn up by the same stage designer, John Napier, in consultation with Trevor Nunn (1979). Further inspiration emerged from an RSC small-scale regional tour which included the theatre in Christ's Hospital School in Horsham.[7]

Architect Michael Reardon, with his associate Tim Furby, was responsible for the eventual design of the Swan, taking Napier's work as a starting point. Constructed on the site of the old Memorial Theatre, the Swan accommodates audiences to a middle-scale capacity of approximately 430 spectators wrapped around three sides of its thrust stage within what was described in *The Observer* at its opening as a 'pale golden galleried playhouse'.

Given the acoustic difficulties associated with many theatres, Reardon was sensitive to the need for 'tuning' the new space.[8] When the Swan opened, Guy Woolfenden (Head of Music for the RSC) commented that the 'natural acoustic in the Swan is wonderful'.[9] With its thrust stage 24 feet across and 35 feet deep, 'the interior of the Swan combines features of church and theatre but its major source is, of course, the accumulated evidence for the design of Renaissance stages'.[10] This pedigree has created a dynamic space appropriate for the plays of Shakespeare, his predecessors and his contemporaries by recapturing, in Christopher Baugh's words, 'some of the essential qualities of Elizabethan and Jacobean theatre architecture'[11] without offering a listless reconstruction of either an outdoor or an indoor Elizabethan or Jacobean playhouse.

Reardon recalls being asked why, 'in a theatre specifically designed for the performance of Renaissance drama, we did not design a classical building using elements derived from Renaissance architectural theory?' His response was that this would have placed 'a historicist emphasis on the theatre and on productions...the Swan's rather minimalist architecture, its rhythm of post and beam, avoids this constricting historicism'.[12]

Like its Elizabethan predecessor, as is clear from the famous De Witt sketch, the Swan's lay-out confirms Richard Eyre's assertion that 'the human figure is the central inalienable fact about theatre performance'.[13] What is captured so successfully in the Swan's 'very human space' is the relationship between performer, stage and audience.[14] As Peter Holland wrote in 1986: 'The combined effect of the woodwork, the stage lighting and the deliberate decision of the architect to make it impossible to take out the house-lights completely is to leave the audience in a visible half-light aware of their visibility to the actors and, to a marked degree, expecting the actors to take notice of them.'[15]

Reardon and Furby worked towards a flexible stage and auditorium from the outset, one which

---

[6] Iain Mackintosh, *Architecture, Actor and Audience* (London, 1993), pp. 96–7.

[7] For details of Christ's Hospital Theatre, see *Making Space for Theatre*, pp. 164–5.

[8] Nunn, 'Preface', p. ix. Michael Reardon also took inspiration from the Teatro Farnese in Parma and from the Renaissance Theatre in Sabionetta.

[9] Guy Woolfenden, 'The Music of the Swan', in *This Golden Round*, p. 143.

[10] Peter Holland, 'Style at the Swan', *Essays in Criticism*, 36 (1986), 194.

[11] Christopher Baugh, *Theatre, Performance and Technology: The Development of Scenography in the Twentieth Century* (Basingstoke and New York, 2005), p. 179.

[12] Michael Reardon, 'Designing the Swan Theatre', in *This Golden Round*, p. 14.

[13] Richard Eyre, 'Space and the Director', in *Making Space for Theatre*, p. 94.

[14] Author's interview with Max Stafford-Clark, theatre director and founder of Joint Stock and Out Of Joint, 21 February 2011.

[15] Holland, 'Style at the Swan', p. 195.

40. The interior of the refurbished Swan auditorium, 2011.

could be conveniently adapted to an almost unlimited number of plays and performance styles: 'the stage itself is made of demountable rostra and can be removed to leave a flat trapped floor . . . The front of the seating rakes can also be removed, leaving a space in which the audience can stand, promenade or sit on the floor. The stage rostra may also be used centrally with an audience on all four sides.'[16] Michael Reardon has commented that, looking back, one of the Swan's weaknesses 'is the lack of an axial entrance point for actors . . . When the Swan was being designed we discussed whether we should have a major axial entrance, opposite the stage, with a central gangway; I am sorry that in the end we decided not to on the grounds that it would have divided the audience into two.'[17] Yet the auditorium, with its 'vomitories' (gangways) from the front corners of the stage running diagonally through the auditorium (at stalls level), is energized by the potential for audience interaction with the performance experience.

Michael Attenborough, a former Principal Associate Director of the Royal Shakespeare Company, asserts that performance spaces 'have different personalities' and each has a 'distinctive atmosphere'.

He believes that 'the personality of a theatre space is also to do with where it is sited'.[18] In this respect, the Swan fulfilled a need within the RSC's repertoire, for the community in its local area, and for the theatregoing community as a whole – in terms of space, repertoire and integration into the long-standing traditions of the theatre in Stratford. It was designed to occupy part of a listed building that linked the RSC back to the Shakespeare Memorial Theatre of 1897 (burned down in 1926), by converting the surviving shell of the old building from a Conference Room used for rehearsals to the core of the new auditorium. The local community was engaged with the process every step of the way, as Michael Reardon's working papers, recently deposited in the Archive of the Shakespeare Birthplace Trust, demonstrate.

For RSC actors the Swan posed a host of challenges – both in terms of the physical space and

---

16 Reardon, 'Designing for the Swan', p. 14.
17 In Peter Holland, 'Stratford Stages: Two Interviews', *Shakespeare Survey 47* (Cambridge, 1994), p. 119.
18 Attenborough, 'Directing for the RSC', p. 89.

of the demanding language of the chosen repertoire. The thrust stage required actors to develop a performance style that could respond to audiences surrounding them on three sides and looking down from the galleries. It was all too easy to obstruct the sight lines of individual audience members and so exclude them. Yet from its earliest seasons actors enjoyed playing the Swan – once they had mastered the dynamics and vocal demands of the space. For Simon Russell Beale the Swan is, simply, 'the most beautiful space in England',[19] yet while it is 'one of the warmest theatres' it is 'quite a treacherous place to play . . . technically it's very demanding' because 'you can't hide on the Swan stage'.[20] Tony Church shares this sense of risk: 'it's the most demanding space I've worked in. But what it gives back to the actor, in terms of audience contact, is quite extraordinary.'[21] For Trevor Nunn the 'Swan style' was most evident in his own production of *The Fair Maid of the West* (which opened on 11 September 1986). Looking back at the opening season in 1989 he noted: 'This production expressed everything I believed about the Swan when I talked about it being a public space. The show quite literally stormed the audience, surrounded them, took place amongst them and demanded from them an imaginative response.'[22]

The plays of Shakespeare's contemporaries, or near contemporaries, have formed the backbone of the repertoire at the Swan. Each has extended knowledge of the performance climate in which Shakespeare was writing as well as encouraging the audience to view Shakespeare's plays in a rich and, sometimes, directly comparative context. So, for example, in 1997 Michael Boyd directed *The Spanish Tragedy* by Thomas Kyd, probable author of the 'ur-*Hamlet*'. In the same season Matthew Warchus directed *Hamlet* in the main house. Similarly, in 2003, Gregory Doran directed Shakespeare's *The Taming of the Shrew* in the main auditorium and Fletcher's *The Tamer Tamed* in the Swan, allowing the relationship between the plays to emerge whilst still permitting each play to speak in its own voice.

Doran has developed a long-standing familiarity with the Swan, performing in two productions and directing sixteen. He is passionate about the Company's 'real responsibility to do the repertoire of Shakespeare's contemporaries'. So many plays, he says, are 'waiting to be done'.[23] In an interview in 2010, Doran strongly endorsed the RSC's decisions to gather plays together, in seasons, so that they 'gained strength' by being 'in company with each other'.[24]

Arguably, one of the Swan's most successful seasons was the repertoire of lesser-known Jacobean plays in 2002. John Barton, talking about his scriptwork with the so-called 'Jacobean' company, highlighted the way in which 'what [the Swan] allows is a conversation with the audience'.[25] Sadly, the RSC does not have a space equivalent to the Swan in London. When the Jacobean season transferred to the Gielgud Theatre (London), a number of asides that had worked well in the Swan had to be cut – and with them went the 'sense that the play is an act of complicity with the audience'.[26] The season's five plays, *Eastward Ho!*, *Edward III*, *The Roman Actor*, *The Island Princess* and *The Malcontent*, ranged from Jonson's collaboration with Chapman and Marston on a 'bawdy immorality tale' (*Eastward Ho!*) to 'Stratford's psycho-drama' (*The Roman Actor*) in which Antony Sher led the company in a 'drama of sexual jealousy and carefully anatomised imperial power'.[27]

Each of the plays used relatively simple settings. For *Edward III*, for example, there were 'few stage props, apart from cleverly-used ladders, a rope and tent pegs. But [Anthony] Clark's use of finely choreographed battle and chivalry rituals, bolstered

---

[19] Simon Russell Beale, 'Space and the Actor', in *Making Space for Theatre*, p. 107.

[20] Tony Church, 'Acting in the Swan', in *This Golden Round*, p. 135 and p. 136.

[21] Church, 'Acting in the Swan', p. 104.

[22] Trevor Nunn, 'The Director in the Swan', in *This Golden Round*, p. 65.

[23] Gregory Doran, interview with Ronnie Mulryne and Margaret Shewring, Stratford-upon-Avon, 26 August 2010.

[24] Interview, 26 August 2010.

[25] Recalled by Doran, interview, 26 August 2010.

[26] Doran, interview, 26 August 2010.

[27] Rachel Halliburton, *Evening Standard*, 26 April and 3 May 2002.

by Conor Lineham's musical and choral accompaniments' created 'a strong sense of an anarchic society at war'.[28] Perhaps the most inventive use of stage space was for Fletcher's tragicomedy, *The Island Princess*. This draws on a colonial mentality and exploits religious insecurities in its Indonesian setting in the Spice Islands. Staged in London in the late 1680s in a version by Nahum Tate, it had not been seen in its original version for around three hundred and seventy years. Paul Taylor, in *The Independent*, describes the evocative setting: 'Bolts of silk hang in warm pearly-pink columns from the top of the balcony . . . an onstage gamelan orchestra adds a reverberant urgency to the proceedings or a dreamy, chiming sense of the sybaritic. Behind the instrumentalists, the totem of a huge female-breasted god sits with palms raised' (8 July 2002).

In 2005 Doran co-ordinated another very successful group of productions, known as the 'Gunpowder Season', bringing together Middleton and Rowley's *The Old Law; or, a New Way to Please You*, the anonymous *Thomas More*, Massinger's *Believe What You Will*, Ben Jonson's *Sejanus* and a new play by Frank McGuiness, *Speaking Like Magpies*. The season as a whole concentrated on violence and terrorism, and on the use and abuse of power.

Sejanus, directed by Doran himself, was the latest Jonson play to be staged in the Swan since 1986. The only other professional production of *Sejanus*, since that in the Globe in 1604, was William Poel's in 1928. Benedict Nightingale, in *The Times*, played up the modern relevance of Doran's production saying it combined 'dramatic momentum with clarity . . . The folly of hubris is the play's subject, but so is the fear, self-interest and corruption of politicians' (28 July 2005). Billington in *The Guardian* defended the production against the charge of obviousness: 'by preserving the Roman setting, Gregory Doran's magnificent production . . . allows us to deduce the modern parallels for ourselves' as we respond to the play's 'blend of psychology and politics'. Nevertheless, he writes, 'what truly . . . exhilarates is the rediscovery of a play that shows Jonson's understanding of both the practical mechanics and insane corruption of power' (28 July 2005).

Thomas More, a play often attributed to Anthony Munday but believed to have significant contributions from Dekker and Shakespeare, by contrast, brought an understanding and humanity to events in More's life, concentrating as it does on the time spent by More as a popular sheriff in London, on his domestic circumstances and on his entertainment of Erasmus, before concluding with More leaving his family to go to the Tower. The familial emphasis worked well in the intimate surroundings of the Swan.

Shakespeare's plays were not to be understood solely in the context of other plays by his English contemporaries, but by those of continental European writers, too. Another of Trevor Nunn's original hopes for the Swan was to be fulfilled with the Spanish Golden Age project, celebrated in *The Times* by Benedict Nightingale (10 April 2004) along with its 'begetter and co-ordinator', Laurence Boswell. In an article that included an interview with Boswell, Nightingale explained that this season was 'the fruit of two years in which he [Boswell] read 100 plays, commissioned translations of 30 and ended up selecting four' for performance in the Swan. Boswell had been fascinated by Spanish Golden Age plays during his years as artistic director at the Gate Theatre, London, in the early 1990s. He told Nightingale he had chosen plays for the Swan that 'ask profound questions about the relationship of love and honour', while explaining that Lope de Vega (1562–1635) had 'much in common with his contemporary, Shakespeare: above all, a determination to reach every class of audience, groundlings upwards, and a refusal to obey the neo-classical "rules" then in intellectual vogue in Europe'.

Boswell himself directed the first show of the season, Lope de Vega's *The Dog in the Manger*, in a script freshly translated by David Johnston. The review in the *Evening Standard* described Es Devlin's 'bare stage set, with . . . gleaming brass floors and rear-centre doors' which suggested 'a world of expensive, cold decorum' (22 April 2004). Richard

---

[28] Nicholas de Jongh, 26 April 2002.

Edmonds, writing in the *Birmingham Post*, confirmed the praise heaped on the production by a number of critics: 'this take on de Vega combined with sumptuous costumes and high-speed playing plus crashes of guitar music and castanets to underline the significant points of the evening' and made 'Boswell's attractive production deeply pleasurable' (23 April 2004). For the matinee and evening performances of the *Dog in the Manger* on 24 July, the Company even went so far as to experiment with replicating the segregated audience configuration of the Spanish theatres of the Golden Age, with men seated in the stalls and women in the galleries, an experiment referred to within the Company as 'Girls on Top'.

Each of the plays in Boswell's Golden Age season was directed by a different person: Nancy Meckler directed Sõr Juana de la Cruz's *House of Desires* while Mike Alfreds marked his debut at the RSC with a world première of Cervantes's last play, *Pedro, the Great Pretender* (translated by Philip Osment). The season's darkest play was Tirso de Molina's *Tamar's Revenge: A Tale of Rape and Retribution*, adapted for the RSC by James Fenton and directed by Simon Usher. Following the previews, the opening night was delayed by six weeks as the company tried to get the measure of this bleak, violent story of incest that marked the end of the biblical House of David. Overall, the Spanish Golden Age season, invited to play Madrid in October 2004, was a triumph, 'opening up new realms of dramaturgy and putting the English canon into arresting new perspectives', so that, as Paul Taylor wrote in *The Independent*, 'Boswell's season is exactly what the RSC should be doing and makes a supreme case for its public subsidy' (22 April 2004).

Jonson's plays have featured in each decade since the Swan opened, with productions of nine plays staged over nineteen years. These plays cross a wide range of genres including city comedies written for the Men's companies, satirical works for the Boys, and tragedies in the classical style for Men's companies on the public stage and at Court. Jonson, 'the cartoonist of contemporary abnormality' (Michael Billington, *The Guardian*, 7 July 1989), stocks his plays with uncompromising caricatures. Of *The Devil is an Ass*, Nicholas de Jongh wrote, 'if ever there was a play for today from a distant London yesterday it is this Jacobean comedy of loose morals and manners ... Warchus's spectacular knock about production, with Bunny Christie's fancy set of little model houses resting on stilts ... goes for winsome razzle-dazzle rather than any governing malevolence' (*Evening Standard*, 5 April 1995).

A number of Jonson's plays staged in the Swan were not familiar to late-twentieth and twenty-first-century audiences. John Caird's production of Jonson's *The New Inn* was 'a rarity'.[29] The play had not been seen on the professional stage since 1629 and Michael Coveney, in the *Financial Times*, described it as 'a real surprise and a real treat' (12 November 1987). Sometimes the realization that the modern audience would be new to a play led the Company to capitalize on audiences' ignorance, for example by asking reviewers from the national press not to reveal the full plot of *Epicene, or the Silent Woman*.

Billington's *Guardian* review described Danny Boyle's *Epicene* as 'a comedy rancid with misogyny', 'a hard, cruel comedy that lacks any real moral centre' (7 July 1989) yet it proved, perhaps unsurprisingly, thoroughly appealing to today's Swan audience. Kandis Cook's design, however, was a limited success. It included a 'colourful backcloth reminiscent of Wenceslas Hollar's Long View of London', although, as Billington notes, 'there is little to suggest the teeming, noisy, bustling nature of life in and around London's Strand: a pity since London itself is a principal character in the play'.

Jonson's plays use detailed props to assist the creation of a physical as well as imaginative space. For the Swan's first Jonson production, *Everyman in his Humour*, Sue Blane's initial design included 'an idea of surrounding the edges of the stage with all sorts of objects'. In *This Golden Round* she explained why she changed the design during the rehearsal period, recalling: 'I hadn't

---

[29] J. C. Trewin, *Birmingham Post*, 11 November 1987.

realised...how much this [cluster of objects] would disturb the actors...It wasn't very high, but it was enough to create a psychological barrier...the stage needs to be totally accessible. It's such a warm space.'[30] This accessibility was used to good effect in Sam Mendes's 1991 production of *The Alchemist* when, as Paul Taylor wrote, at the end of the show the actor playing Face tried 'to bribe the audience to acquit him', by hinting at the audience's complicity in his, and the other tricksters', schemes. The theme of deception was complete when Face threw what looked like 'a heavy handful of sovereigns into the stalls' but, instead of crashing down, they fluttered in the air as 'sparkling, weightless confetti' (*The Independent*, 29 August 1991).

Most of the Swan's productions of Jonson drew on period costume to evoke the atmosphere of early-seventeenth-century London or, as appropriate, Italy. Billington, writing in *The Guardian* about Lucy Pitman-Wallace's 2002 production of *Eastward Ho!* hailed the show as 'Jacobean comedy at its documentary best: a salty, vivid report on the eternal clash between the puritan ethic and spendthrift snobbery' (26 April 2002). Laurence Boswell's *Bartholomew Fair*, by comparison, was strikingly modern, a production that was 'sparky, up-to-date, slightly surreal, and at every point brightly characterised' (Alastair Macauley, *Financial Times*, 17 December 1997).

The inclusion of such an extended range of Jonson's plays may go some way to readjusting an audience's sense of his contribution to the Jacobean stage in relation to that of Shakespeare. Unsurprisingly, it was not to be many seasons before the repertoire of the Swan began to embrace Shakespeare's plays, too, initially concentrating on those that offered less-than-secure box-office returns if staged in the main auditorium.

Of Deborah Warner's pared down yet emotionally powerful production of *Titus Andronicus* Alan Dessen notes that 'the word repeated constantly among *Titus* personnel was *trust* in the script, in the audience, in the Swan (a major component in the success of the show), in each other'.[31] This trust was to result in what Robert Hewison described as the

'stripped simplicity of means' that was the key to the production's success.[32] This was the Swan at its best, emphasizing the 'immediacy' of the production, foregrounding powerful rhetoric along with dark comedy and poignant pain.[33]

A great strength of the Swan has been its ability to facilitate some of the most difficult of Shakespeare's plays, eliciting their meaning with clarity. Sam Mendes's debut production, *Troilus and Cressida*, is a case in point. The play is episodic, with an unusual emphasis on verbal devices (from political debates to satirical jibes). All its elements are moulded by the destructive force of a long-drawn-out war and the victimization of women. Anthony Ward's set was dominated by 'a massive stone Grecian female mask, one side perfect, the other decayed'.[34] The remainder of the thrust stage was left as a promontory – uncluttered, with the exception of a well, used for cleansing the swords of the returning Trojan fighters after a day in the field. This economy with stage sets carries a bonus. As Mendes has said: 'There is something about the Swan which I have never experienced in any other theatre. It allows you to achieve the fluid and simple technique of shifting from one world to another, to be both epic and domestic. So it's an ideal theatre in which one can move from the inside of a tent onto the battle plains of Troy, and then back into a man's mind.'[35] Occasionally a more widely popular Shakespeare play made its way into the repertoire: David Thacker's *The Tempest* (1995), and Gregory Doran's *Macbeth* (2000) and *Antony and Cleopatra* (2006), all played the Swan. Sam Mendes's production of *Richard III* opened in the Other Place and then went on tour

---

30 Sue Blane, 'Designing for the Swan', in *This Golden Round*, p. 89.

31 Alan C. Dessen, *Shakespeare in Performance: 'Titus Andronicus'* (Manchester, 1989), pp. 58 and 61.

32 Quoted by Dessen, *Shakespeare in Performance*, p. 58.

33 Peter Holland, 'Shakespeare in the Twentieth-century Theatre', in *The Cambridge Companion to Shakespeare*, ed. Margreta de Grazia and Stanley Wells (Cambridge, 2001), p. 201.

34 *English Shakespeares*, p. 71.

35 Holland, 'Stratford Stages: Two Interviews', p. 121.

before reaching the Swan where according to many observers it 'came into its own'.[36]

Shakespeare Survey has included the Swan's productions of Shakespeare among its regular reviews. It is, therefore, unnecessary to document the full range of the Swan's Shakespearian repertoire here. Suffice it to say that the number of Shakespeare productions has increased. What has become clear is that the dimensions of the Swan are not a bar to staging even the largest of the plays, both in scope and cast. Doran's *Antony and Cleopatra*, designed by Stephen Brimson-Lewis, succeeded in combining the intimacy of the Swan to remarkable effect with the play's wide range of locations and tragic theme. Michael Dobson vividly evokes the prelude to the performance: 'The theatre is crammed and expectation is high, and, as I take my seat and start admiring the understatedly Romano-Egyptian cracked terracotta finish of the stage's back wall, I notice that Doran has cannily placed into this opening of his show a reflection of our own impatience for the arrival of the star performers we have paid to see.'[37] Such complicity draws on the strengths of the Swan, with its intimate auditorium/stage relationship.

Shakespeare's English history plays have been mounted in the Swan with varying degrees of success. Michael Attenborough staged the two parts of *Henry IV* on a somewhat hazardous, steeply-raked stage, while Michael Boyd worked with a separately cast ensemble on his 'This England' project, staging the three parts of *Henry VI* and *Richard III* in a much altered auditorium, draped in black. Using the Swan's height to good effect throughout, Boyd created 'a sense of vertigo, of a society clinging desperately and ultimately in vain to a precarious vertical hierarchy' which was realized, in part, 'by some striking uses of flying'.[38] Stressing the vertical dimension and playing in the round for the *Henry VI* plays made sightlines difficult – and by the time that the *Histories* were developed in the Courtyard Theatre there was no longer an attempt to play completely in the round.

Doran's 1996 staging of Shakespeare and Fletcher's *Henry VIII* remains a vivid memory. The play affords its own challenges since it narrates a turning point in English history that is at once spectacularly public and deeply private. Robert Jones's simple yet effective set depended, nevertheless, on spectacular effects: 'Large double doors upstage, opened at intervals throughout the play . . . for its great public shows to spill onto the stage: a version of the Field of the [*sic*] Cloth of Gold at the beginning, bass drum thudding, the entire company singing "Deo Gratias", and a resplendent Henry trucked down stage astride a golden horse; the elaborate coronation procession for Anne Boleyn in her golden robe; and the christening at the end, Henry again trucked in, enthroned, more of "Deo Gratias" in chorus, lots more gold, drumbeats and pomp, and a little bundle (palpably not a baby) to prophesy over.'[39]

Such magnificent display engaged and excited the audience. Yet, as Doran explains, sometimes 'you have to shut the spectacle away' and then, in the Swan's space, 'a gesture has so much more resonance' than on a large stage.[40] The Swan worked particularly well for the trial scene, almost certainly written with performance at the intimate indoor Blackfriars theatre in mind – the Blackfriars had been the real-life location of the divorce proceedings of Henry and Katherine. Doran's production brought this intimate, emotionally-charged scene to life. In the Swan 'the trial scene was played as if the entire auditorium were the clergy and lawyers assembled at the Blackfriars and she [Jane Lapotaire as Katherine] commanded the space superbly in her impassioned self-defence, quite rightly upstaging Henry who sat on his stool centre stage staring glumly in front of him'.[41]

On the face of it, the distinctive interior of the Swan seems to limit design possibilities for the

---

36 Holland, 'Stratford Stages: Two Interviews', p. 123.

37 Michael Dobson, 'Shakespeare Performances in England, 2006', *Shakespeare Survey 60* (Cambridge, 2007), p. 293.

38 Michael Dobson, 'Shakespeare Performances in England, 2001', *Shakespeare Survey 55* (Cambridge, 2002), p. 287.

39 Robert Smallwood, 'Shakespeare Performances in England, 1997', *Shakespeare Survey 51* (Cambridge, 1998), p. 239.

40 Interview, 26 August 2010.

41 Smallwood, 'Shakespeare Performances', p. 240.

stage. It is, in Michael Reardon's phrase, 'a "theatre of the word" in which the art of the actor takes precedence over that of the scene painter'.[42] In an interview with Peter Holland in 1994 Michael Reardon explained that the brief to the architects 'was to make a strong space within which directors would work and it was Trevor Nunn's firm view that the designer would play a secondary role . . . Trevor's view was that he did not want any sets in the Swan at all: he just wanted the space for the play . . . the Swan is a space created as a framework to be decked out, not by the scene painter, but by the transformation of verbal images into visual ones'.[43]

Until its refurbishment in 2010 as part of the transformation of all the RSC's Stratford venues, the Swan had very little back-stage space. There was no concealed flying space for scenery, although the height of the room offered the possibility to experiment with the vertical plane. Director Barry Kyle's 'first impression of the new building was its height . . . what was most dynamic was the space above the stage'.[44] For Bob Crowley, designer of the Swan's opening production *The Two Noble Kinsmen*, however, there were already concerns: 'I am not sure that it's a designer's theatre . . . the problem I have with it as a designer is that it imposes itself, hugely, and no matter what you do, you design against it, at your peril.'[45] Jill Jowett, Design Assistant to the RSC, took a different if related view: 'the best designs in the Swan have been those that have used little in the way of elaborate settings . . . the intimate space in that theatre, with its stage thrust into the audience, makes it possible to achieve striking visual effects in terms of colour and costumes . . . with the minimum of scenic clutter'.[46]

It was not long before designers found innovative ways to use the invitingly bare stage, sometimes working in accord with the ambiance of the space, sometimes over-riding it. Roger Howells, who succeeded Geoff Locker as production manager in the Swan for the 1991–93 seasons, had been a keen follower of the RSC's experiments with an Elizabethan concept of staging from as early as the 'wooden O' season in the Main House in 1976,

and saw the Swan in the context of these experiments. But his expectations of simple, non-scenic staging were soon put aside. He recalls working with Adrian Noble on the *Theban Plays*: 'one of the first things that I realised was that there had been a move away from Trevor Nunn's original concept towards more complex scenic devices'.[47] Certainly the 1991-season plays in the Swan all had strong scenic elements at a time when the building had very little storage space and almost no facilities to help with large set changes between the shows. In the 1992 season, the arrival of a new designer (Kendra Ullyart) for John Caird's production of Gay's *The Beggar's Opera*, and Fotini Dimou's designs for Max Stafford-Clark's staging of Richard Brome's *A Jovial Crew*, resulted in busy settings that 'spilled into the auditorium' and involved dressing the balcony fronts – a feat achieved on a tight budget by recycling materials from earlier shows.[48]

The Swan was used to the full during the ambitious 'Complete Works Season' of 2006–07, hosting five RSC productions with multiple performances of each (*Antony and Cleopatra*, *Much Ado About Nothing*, *King John*, *Pericles* and *The Winter's Tale*) as well as two individual performances of *The Two Noble Kinsmen* and *The Rape of Lucrece*. It also proved hospitable to a further eleven productions, bringing internationally acclaimed companies to Stratford. The visitors included Janet Suzman's Baxter Theatre Centre *Hamlet* with Vaneshran

---

[42] Reardon, 'Designing the Swan Theatre', in *This Golden Round*, p. 10.

[43] Holland, 'Stratford Stages: Two Interviews', p. 118.

[44] Barry Kyle, 'The Director in the Swan', in *This Golden Round*, p. 73.

[45] Bob Crowley, 'Designing for the Swan', in *This Golden Round*, p. 85. For a detailed discussion of the Swan's opening production, see Margaret Shewring, '*The Two Noble Kinsmen* Revived: Chivalric Romance and Modern Performance Images', in *Le Roman de Chevalerie au temps de la Renaissance*, ed. M. T. Jones-Davies (Paris, 1987), pp. 107–32.

[46] Jill Jowett, 'Designing for the Swan', p. 90.

[47] Author's interview with Roger Howells, November 2010.

[48] Interview with Roger Howells, November 2010.

Arumugam as Hamlet and John Kani as Claudius. Three contrasting productions – *Hamlet*, *The Winter's Tale* and *The Merchant of Venice* – offered innovative uses of the space. For *Hamlet* the stage was 'fitted with a circular rake' from which rose 'a commanding central flat rectangle'.[49] For Dominic Cooke's production of *The Winter's Tale*, one of the RSC's own contributions, the Swan was much altered by the decking-over of all the downstairs seating at the usual height of the thrust stage. This was complemented by the construction of a horseshoe-shaped sloping ramp by which actors moved up from this newly lifted ground level to perform on the same level as those in the audience seated in the front row of the first balcony. Meanwhile the area behind the proscenium arch had been 'converted into a bandstand on which musicians in dinner suits' were playing early 1950s dance band music.[50] On arrival the audience was invited to gather as if at a party, being served champagne and encouraged to move around the promenade space. The Brooklyn-based Theatre For A New Audience made use of three giant plasma screens in their *Merchant of Venice* in a more overtly technological production.

In 1986 Sheridan Morley, writing in *Punch*, expressed his delight with the RSC's new venue: 'visually, acoustically, and theatrically this is the most exciting dramatic space to have opened up in my play-going lifetime: there is an intimacy and a resonance here which has been achieved by none of the studio spaces of the Barbican or the National' (21 May). The question is whether subsequent work in the Swan has lived up to this early promise. From an audience's point of view, the Swan has evolved into an indispensable space bound up with changes in serving the ways in which audiences across today's world see, and understand, Shakespeare's plays and those of his contemporaries. The Swan does not enjoy the novelty of a reconstruction (as Shakespeare's Globe in Southwark does), nor does it have the capacity to overwhelm a large audience with vast spectacle. Its very intimacy facilitates comedy, particularly comedy that is poignant and under-stated. It encourages the complicity of an audience in irony and satire.

The intimacy of the Swan has encouraged the inclusion of a small selection of European plays of the late-nineteenth and early-twentieth centuries, which typically focus on the interaction of complex characters at moments of crisis whether social, economic or personal. Plays by Chekhov, Turgenev and Ibsen, directed with meticulous attention to their period detail, have unfolded in close proximity to their audiences, drawing them into the characters' personal traumas, aspirations and disappointments, and making them complicit as they seemingly eavesdrop on familiar life-stories. For the most part, twentieth- and twenty-first-century plays have been chosen with care – and rarely. Edward Bond's *Restoration* (alongside the season of Restoration plays in 1988), Peter Flannery's *Singer* (in 1989), Edward Bond's *Bingo* in 1995, and Peter Barnes's *Jubilee* (in 2001), each had a particular relevance to the Elizabethan and Jacobean stage. The Swan is a space that lends itself to story-telling as was evident in the earlier repertoire, such as David Thacker's 1989 production of *Pericles* which 'exuded through every pore' dramatic invention 'entirely at the service of the story'.[51] Three twentieth-century adaptations of traditional tales also profited from the Swan's capacity for storytelling: *Tales from Ovid* (1999), *The Canterbury Tales* (in two parts, 2005) and the *Penelopiad* (2007).

Speaking in 2010, a few months before the opening of the RSC's transformed main auditorium in Stratford, Michael Boyd said quite simply that 'the DNA of the last eight years happened in the Swan'.[52] What has been crucial is the relationship between stage and auditorium that has pushed the development of the RSC's acting ensemble

---

[49] Dobson, 'Shakespeare Performances in England, 2006', p. 289.

[50] Michael Dobson, 'Shakespeare Performances in England, 2007', *Shakespeare Survey 61* (Cambridge, 2008), pp. 319–20.

[51] Peter Holland, *English Shakespeares: Shakespeare on the English Stage in the 1990s* (Cambridge, 1997), p. 66.

[52] Michael Boyd, interview, 2 September 2010.

into new challenges and possibilities. During the period of transformation, the Swan was used to fill in gaps rather than to develop a repertoire in its own right, before going dark as the major rebuilding of the main auditorium got underway. And yet the ambition remained. As early as 1986 Peter Holland had acknowledged that 'if the Swan experiment is to be fully successful it will affect every aspect of the company's work, rather than being . . . a separate and slightly odd endeavour'.[53] The sense of 'oddity' has been decisively banished. The Swan's stage configuration has formed the basis for the (much larger) stage in the temporary Courtyard Theatre which, in turn, has been used as a template for the new main auditorium. So Terry Hands's comments as Artistic Director and Chief Executive of the RSC in 1989 take on a new and altogether positive aspect: 'the Swan is timeless'; it 'resists design signature'; 'the actor is dominant'; the Swan is 'truly a place for people not things, and the audience is its architecture'. Hands concluded: 'I suspect the Swan will lead the RSC more securely into the twenty-first century than any of its other auditoria.'[54] It appears that Hands's prediction was correct.

The decision to open the Swan in 1986 with Shakespeare and Fletcher's *The Two Noble Kinsmen* immediately demonstrated the importance of the new auditorium in extending the Company's repertoire. Twenty-five years on, in 2011, Michael Boyd and Greg Doran reaffirmed the Swan's contribution by choosing as the first new RSC production to be mounted in the reopened, modestly refurbished, space a 'lost' Jacobean play by Shakespeare and Fletcher, *The History of Cardenio* billed as 'a lost play by Shakespeare re-imagined by Gregory Doran'. Doran, now Chief Associate Director, in collaboration with Antonio Alamo (a Spanish writer who runs the Lope de Vega Theatre in Seville), has devised and remade this piece, bringing together what can be ascertained about the form and content of the 'lost' play, by drawing on and rewriting Lewis Theobald's *The Double Falsehood* and Thomas Shelton's translation into English of Cervantes's *Don Quixote*.[55] The publicity for the production, in hot colours evocative of

the play's Spanish setting, threw out a challenge as uncomfortable today as in Shakespeare's time: 'Do you trust your best friend?' Doran's production has underlined the contribution of the reopened Swan to the appreciation of neo-Shakespearean drama while also continuing to explore the potential of the Swan stage to create a fitting twenty-first-century theatre experience.

APPENDIX

(The date given in each case is the press night.)

1986

8 May: John Fletcher, *The Two Noble Kinsmen* (dir. Barry Kyle, des. Bob Crowley)

21 May: Ben Jonson, *Every Man in His Humour* (dir. John Caird, des. Sue Blane)

22 June: *The Hollow Crown* (one performance)

10 July: Aphra Behn: *The Rover* (dir. John Barton, des. Louise Belson)

23 September: Thomas Heywood, *The Fair Maid of the West* (dir. Trevor Nunn, des. John Napier)

26 October: *The English in Italy* (one performance for Word-Aid Charity)

24 November: *Close Encounters of the Swan Kind* (three performances as part of RSC/W H Smith Youth Festival 24)

24 November: *French Cabaret* (one performance as part of RSC/W H Smith Youth Festival 24)

25 November: *Simply Sondheim* (two performances as part of RSC/W H Smith Youth Festival 24)

25 November: *Thereby Hangs a Tale* (one performance as part of RSC/W H Smith Youth Festival 24)

---

[53] Holland, 'Style at the Swan', p. 208.

[54] All the quotations from Terry Hands in this paragraph are from 'Towards the Future', in *This Golden Round*, pp. 159–60.

[55] Doran describes this process on the RSC's website: www.rsc.org.uk/whats-on/cardenio/qa-doran.aspx. His account was first published in the *RSC Members' News* (December, 2010).

1 December: *The Gift* (two performances as part of RSC/W H Smith Youth Festival 24)

2 December: *The Silver King* (two performances as part of RSC/W H Smith Youth Festival 24)

6 December: *Lyrics of the Hearthside* (one performance as part of RSC/W H Smith Youth Festival 24)

1987

15 April: James Shirley, *Hyde Park* (dir. Barry Kyle, des. Gerard Howland)

12 May: William Shakespeare, *Titus Andronicus* (dir. Deborah Warner, des. Isabella Bywater)

14 July: Christopher Marlowe, *The Jew of Malta* (dir. Barry Kyle, des. Bob Crowley)

10 September: Cyril Tourneur, *The Revenger's Tragedy* (dir. Di Trevis, des. Michael Levine)

10 November: Ben Jonson, *The New Inn* (dir. John Caird, des. Sue Blane)

1988

5 April: George Farquhar, *The Constant Couple* (dir. Roger Michell, des. Ultz)

27 April: William Wycherley, *The Plain Dealer* (dir. Ron Daniels, des. David Fielding)

13 July: George Etherege, *The Man of Mode* (dir. Garry Hynes, des. Ultz)

13 September: Edward Bond: *Restoration* (dir. Roger Michell, des. David Fielding)

1989

5 April: William Shakespeare, *Romeo and Juliet* (dir. Terry Hands, des. Farrah)

10 May: Christopher Marlowe, *Doctor Faustus* (dir. Barry Kyle, des. Ashley Martin-Davis)

5 July: Ben Jonson, *The Silent Woman* (dir. Danny Boyle, des. Kandis Cook)

12 September: William Shakespeare, *Pericles* (dir. David Thacker, des. Fran Thompson)

11 October: Peter Flannery, *Singer* (dir. Terry Hands, des. Sanja Jurca Avci)

5 December: John Webster, *The Duchess of Malfi* (dir. Bill Alexander, des. Fotini Dimou)

1990

5 April: Tirso de Molina and Nick Dear, *The Last Days of Don Juan* (dir. Danny Boyle, des. Kandis Cook)

26 April: William Shakespeare, *Troilus and Cressida* (dir. Sam Mendes, des. Anthony Ward)

10 July: Christopher Marlowe, *Edward II* (dir. Gerard Murphy, des. Sandy Powell)

4 September: Richard Nelson, *Two Shakespearean Actors* (dir. Roger Michell, des. Alexandra Byrne)

6 November: Anton Chekhov, *The Seagull* (dir. Terry Hands, des. Wayne Dowdeswell)

1991

28 March: Thomas Shadwell, *The Virtuoso* (dir. Phyllida Lloyd, des. Anthony Ward)

17 April: William Shakespeare, *The Two Gentlemen of Verona* (dir. David Thacker, des. Shelagh Keegan)

25 June: John Ford, *'Tis Pity She's a Whore* (Dir. David Leveaux, des. Kenny Miller)

27 August: Ben Jonson, *The Alchemist* (dir. Sam Mendes, des. Anthony Ward)

2 November: Sophocles, *Antigone* (*The Thebans*: dir. Adrian Noble, des. Ultz)

2 November: Sophocles, *Oedipus at Colonus* (*The Thebans*: dir. Adrian Noble, des. Ultz)

2 November: Sophocles, *Oedipus Tyrannos* (*The Thebans*: dir. Adrian Noble, des. Ultz)

1992

7 April: John Gay, *The Beggar's Opera* (dir. John Caird, des. Kendra Ullyart)

21 April: Richard Brome, *A Jovial Crew* (dir. Max Stafford-Clark, des. Fotini Dimou)

30 June: William Shakespeare, *All's Well That Ends Well* (dir. Peter Hall, des. John Gunter)

1 September: Christopher Marlowe, *Tamburlaine* (dir. Terry Hands, des. Johan Engels)

3 November: Thomas Middleton, *The Changeling* (dir. Michael Attenborough, des. Julian McGowan)

1993

17 January: *Cabaret* (one performance as part of the RSC Fringe Festival)

18 March: William Shakespeare, *Richard III* (dir. Sam Mendes, des. Tim Hatley)

13 May: T. S. Eliot, *Murder in the Cathedral* (dir. Steven Pimlott, des. Ashley Martin-Davis)

4 June: Carlo Goldoni, *The Venetian Twins* (dir. Michael Bogdanov, des. Kendra Ullyart)

10 August: William Wycherley, *The Country Wife* (dir. Max Stafford-Clark, des. Peter Hartwell)

26 October: David Pownall, *Elgar's Rondo* (dir. Di Trevis, des. Pamela Howard)

1994

9 January: *The Shakespeare Revue* (one performance as part of the RSC Fringe Festival)

23 March: Alan Ayckbourn *Wildest Dreams* (dir. Alan Ayckbourn, des. Roger Glossop)

4 May: Henrik Ibsen, *Peer Gynt* (translator Christopher Fry, adapter John Barton; dir. John Barton, des. Louise Belson)

24 May: William Shakespeare, *Coriolanus* (dir. David Thacker, des. Fran Thompson)

2 August: Thomas Southerne, *The Wives' Excuse* (dir. Max Stafford-Clark, des. Julian McGowan)

19 October: John Ford, *The Broken Heart* (dir. Michael Boyd, des. Tom Piper)

1995

4 April: Ben Jonson, *The Devil is an Ass* (dir. Matthew Warchus, des. Bunny Christie)

20 April: John Vanbrugh, *The Relapse* (dir. Ian Judge, des. Tim Goodchild)

4 July: Anton Chekhov, *The Cherry Orchard* (dir. Adrian Noble, des. Richard Hudson)

25 July: Edward Bond, *Bingo* (dir. David Thacker, des. Shelagh Keegan)

25 July: William Shakespeare, *The Tempest* (dir. David Thacker, des. Shelagh Keegan)

9 September: Johann Wolfgang von Goethe, *Faust, Part 1* (dir. Michael Bogdanov, des. Chris Dyer)

9 September: Johann Wolfgang von Goethe, *Faust, Part 2* (dir. Michael Bogdanov, des. Chris Dyer)

1996

18 January: *More Loose Talk with Ned Sherrin* (one performance as part of the Fringe on TOP Festival)

26 April: John Webster, *The White Devil* (dir. Gale Edwards, des. Peter J. Davison)

15 May: John Arbuthnot, *Three Hours After Marriage* (dir. Richard Cottrell, des. Tim Goodchild)

23 July: Richard Nelson, *The General from America* (dir. Howard Davies, des. William Dudley)

9 October: Anton Chekhov, *The Cherry Orchard* (dir. Adrian Noble, des. Richard Hudson)

26 November: William Shakespeare, *Henry VIII* (dir. Gregory Doran, des. Robert Jones)

18 December: Henrik Ibsen, *Little Eyolf* (dir. Adrian Noble, des. Rob Howell)

1997

7 May: Thomas Kyd, *The Spanish Tragedy* (dir. Michael Boyd, des. Tom Piper)

13 July: *Half-Time* (one performance as part of 'On the Edge')

10 September: Edmond Rostand, *Cyrano de Bergerac* (dir. Gregory Doran, des. Robert Jones)

11 December: Ben Jonson, *Bartholomew Fair* (dir. Laurence Boswell, des. Tom Piper)

16 December: *The Night Before Christmas* (eleven performances by Theatre Alibi, commissioned by the RSC)

1998

24 February: William Shakespeare, *The Two Gentlemen of Verona* (dir. Edward Hall, des. Michael Pavelka)

29 April: Stephen Poliakoff, *Talk of the City* (des. Tim Hatley)

20 July: *Baglady* (three performances in the Swan Gardens as part of the Fringe Festival)

10 December: William Shakespeare, *Troilus and Cressida* (dir. Michael Boyd, des. Tom Piper)

15 December: Ivan Turgenev, *A Month in the Country* (dir. Michael Attenborough, des. Tom Piper)

1999

24 March: Ben Jonson, *Volpone* (dir. Lindsay Posner, des. Ashley Martin-Davis)

20 April: Ted Hughes, *Tales from Ovid* (dir. Tim Supple, des. Melly Still)

16 June: T. S. Eliot, *The Family Reunion* (dir. Adrian Noble, des. Rob Howell)

1 October: Lee Hall, *Yuri Gagarin* (one performance: reading of first draft of work in progress, dir. Lucy Pitman-Wallace)

16 November: William Shakespeare, *Macbeth* (dir. Gregory Doran, des. Stephen Brimson-Lewis)

2000

30 March: Richard Sheridan, *The Rivals* (dir. Lindsay Posner, des. Ashley Martin-Davis)

19 April: William Shakespeare, *Henry IV, Part 1* (dir. Michael Attenborough, des. Tim Mitchell)

7 May: *A Shakespeare Celebration* (one performance of a celebration concert with readings)

29 June: William Shakespeare, *Henry IV, Part 2* (dir. Michael Attenborough, des. Tim Mitchell)

11 August: William Shakespeare, *Edward III* (one performance: rehearsed play reading)

18 August: Anonymous, *Thomas of Woodstock* (one performance: rehearsed play reading)

13 December: William Shakespeare, *Henry VI, Part 1* (dir. Michael Boyd, des. Tom Piper)

13 December: William Shakespeare, *Henry VI, Part 2* (dir. Michael Boyd, des. Tom Piper)

13 December: William Shakespeare, *Henry VI, Part 3* (dir. Michael Boyd, des. Tom Piper)

2001

14 February: William Shakespeare, *Richard III* (dir. Michael Boyd, des. Tom Piper)

28 March: William Shakespeare, *King John* (dir. Gregory Doran, des. Stephen Brimson-Lewis)

19 April: William Wycherley, *Love in a Wood* (dir. Tim Supple, des. Tim Supple and Sue Willmington)

19 July: Peter Barnes, *Jubilee* (dir. Gregory Doran, des. Robert Jones)

7 September, *Robin Hood* (one performance: rehearsed reading adapted by Simon Reade from the two-part play by Anthony Munday, with additional material by Ben Jonson, William Cowpland and Henry Chettle)

28 November: William Shakespeare, *The Merchant of Venice* (dir. Loveday Ingram, des. Colin Falconer)

2002

30 January: Heinrich von Kleist, *The Prince of Homburg* (dir. Neil Bartlett, des. Rae Smith: co-production between the RSC and the Lyric Theatre, Hammersmith)

The Jacobean Season

25 April: Ben Jonson, George Chapman and John Marston, *Eastward Ho!* (dir. Lucy Pitman-Wallace, des. Robert Jones)

25 April: William Shakespeare, *Edward III* (dir. Anthony Clark, des. Patrick Connellan)

30 May: Philip Massinger, *The Roman Actor* (dir. Sean Holmes, des. Anthony Lamble)

2 July: John Fletcher, *The Island Princess* (dir. Gregory Doran, des. Niki Turner)

20 August: John Marston, *The Malcontent* (dir. Dominic Cooke, des. Robert Innes Hopkins)

23 September: William Shakespeare, *King Lear* (dir. Declan Donnellan, des. Nick Ormerod: presented by the RSC Academy)

31 October: William Shakespeare, *The Merry Wives of Windsor* (dir. Rachel Kavanaugh, des. Peter McKintosh)

27 November: William Shakespeare, *Coriolanus* (dir. David Farr, des. Ti Green)

2003

20 March: William Shakespeare, *As You Like It* (dir. Gregory Thompson, des. Colin Peters)

9 April: John Fletcher, *The Tamer Tamed* (dir. Gregory Doran, des. Stephen Brimson-Lewis)

17 April: Henrik Ibsen, *Brand* (dir. Adrian Noble, des. Peter McKintosh)

6 August: William Shakespeare, *Cymbeline* (dir. Dominic Cooke, des. Rae Smith)

7 December: John Barton – Work in Progress (one performance: sonnet workshop given by John Barton)

11 December: William Shakespeare, *All's Well That Ends Well* (dir. Gregory Doran, des. Stephen Brimson-Lewis)

2004

18 February: William Shakespeare, *Othello* (dir. Gregory Doran, des. Stephen Brimson-Lewis: presented by the RSC in association with Thelma Holt and Horipro Inc.)

The Spanish Golden Age Season

2 April: Lope de Vega, *The Dog in the Manger* (dir. Laurence Boswell, des. Es Devlin)

15 June: Tirso de Molina, *Tamar's Revenge* (dir. Simon Usher, des. Es Devlin and Delia Peel)

8 July: Sōr Juana de la Cruz, *House of Desires* (dir. Nancy Meckler, des. Es Devlin and Katrina Lindsay)

9 September: Miguel Cervantes, *Pedro, the Great Pretender* (dir. Mike Alfreds, des. Rae Smith)

6 October: *Tynan* (twelve performances: part of the New Work Festival)

7 October: Zinnie Harris, *Midwinter* (dir. Zinnie Harris: seven performances as part of the New Work Festival)

8 October: Pedro Calderon de la Barca, *Daughter of the Air* (dir. Jonquil Panting: one performance as part of the New Work Festival)

14 October: Ron Hutchinson, *Head/Case* (dir. Caroline Hunt: seven performances as part of the New Work Festival)

30 November: William Shakespeare, *The Two Gentlemen of Verona* (dir. Fiona Buffini, des. Liz Ashcroft)

1 December: William Shakespeare, *Julius Caesar* (dir. David Farr, des. Ti Green)

2005

The Gunpowder Season

24 March: Thomas Middleton and William Rowley, *A New Way to Please You* (dir. Sean Holmes, des. Kandis Cook)

24 March: William Shakespeare/Anthony Munday, *Thomas More* (dir. Robert Delamere, des. Simon Higlett)

26 May: Philip Massinger, *Believe What You Will* (dir. Josie Rourke, des. Stephen Brimson-Lewis)

26 July: Ben Jonson, *Sejanus* (dir. Gregory Doran, des. Robert Jones)

29 September: Frank McGuinness, *Speaking Like Magpies* (dir. Rupert Goold, des. Matthew Wright)

17 October: Fraser Grace, *Breakfast with Mugabe* (dir. Antony Sher, des. Colin Richmond: seven performances as part of the New Work Festival)

25 October: *Sweet Charity* (devised by Daniel Kramer, des. Penny Challen: one performance as part of the New Work Festival)

28 October: Debbie Tucker Green, *Trade* (dir. Sacha Wares, des. Miriam Buether: five performances as part of the New Work Festival)

8 December: Geoffrey Chaucer, *The Canterbury Tales, 1* (adapter Mike Poulton, dir. Gregory Doran and Rebecca Gatward, des. Michael Vale)

8 December: Geoffrey Chaucer, *The Canterbury Tales, 2* (adapter Mike Poulton, dir. Gregory Doran, Rebecca Gatward and Jonathan Munby, des. Michael Vale)

2006

23 February: Thomas Middleton, *Women Beware Women* (dir. Laurence Boswell, des. Richard Hudson)

19 April: William Shakespeare, *Antony and Cleopatra* (dir. Gregory Doran, des. Stephen Brimson-Lewis)

Complete Works Festival at the Swan 2006–2007

3 March: William Shakespeare, *Hamlet* (dir. Janet Suzman, des. Peter Cazalet: Baxter Theatre Centre at the University of Cape Town, South Africa)

18 May: William Shakespeare, *Much Ado About Nothing* (dir. Marianne Elliott, des. Lez Brotherston: RSC)

21 May: William Shakespeare and John Fletcher, *The Two Noble Kinsmen* (one performance: RSC)

8 June: William Shakespeare, *A Midsummer Night's Dream* (dir. Tim Supple, des. Sumart Jayakrishnan: Dash Arts and the British Council)

11 July: William Shakespeare, *Henry IV, Part 1* (dir. Barbara Gaines, des. Neil Patel: Chicago Shakespeare Theater)

11 July: William Shakespeare, *Henry IV, Part 2* (dir. Barbara Gaines, des. Neil Patel: Chicago Shakespeare Theater)

3 August: William Shakespeare, *King John* (dir. Josie Rourke, des. Peter McKintosh: RSC)

17 August: William Shakespeare, *Love's Labour's Lost* (dir. Michael Kahn, des. Ralph Funicello: Shakespeare Theatre Company, USA)

4 September: William Shakespeare, *All's Well that Ends Well* (one performance: Young People's Shakespeare, performed by the Royal Scottish Academy of Music and Drama)

5 September: William Shakespeare, *Much Ado About Nothing* (one performance: Young People's Shakespeare, performed by the Bristol Old Vic Theatre School)

8 September: William Shakespeare, *Richard III* (one performance: Young People's Shakespeare, performed by the Royal Academy of Dramatic Arts)

10 September: William Shakespeare, *The Rape of Lucrece* (one performance: RSC)

11 September: William Shakespeare, *The Tempest* (one performance: Young People's Shakespeare, performed by the Guildhall School of Music and Drama)

13 September: William Shakespeare, *The Comedy of Errors* (one performance: Young People's Shakespeare, performed by the Royal Welsh College of Music and Drama)

21 September: William Shakespeare, *Cymbeline* (dir. Emma Rice, des. Michael Vale: Kneehigh Theatre)

15 November: William Shakespeare, *Pericles* (dir. Dominic Cooke, des. Mike Britton: RSC)

15 November: William Shakespeare, *The Winter's Tale* (dir. Dominic Cooke, des. Mike Britton: RSC)

2007

16 January: Roy Williams, *Days of Significance* (dir. Maria Alberg, des. Lizzie Clachan: RSC)

13 February: William Shakespeare, *Richard III: An Arab Tragedy* (dir. Sulayman Al-Bassam, des. George Tomlinson: The Culture Project Kuwait/Sulayman Al-Bassam Theatre)

21 February: William Shakespeare, *Macbeth* (dir. Grzegorz Bral, costume des. Christiva Gonzalez: Teatr Piesn Kozla (Song of the Goat Theatre))

28 February: William Shakespeare, *Twelfth Night* (dir. Declan Donnellan, des. Nick Ormerod: Chekhov International Theatre Festival)

6 March: William Shakespeare, *As You Like It* (dir. Samuel West, des. Katrina Lindsay: Sheffield Theatres)

15 March: William Shakespeare, *Venus and Adonis* (dir. Gregory Doran, des. Robert Jones, dir. of puppetry Steve Tiplady and Lyndie Wright: RSC)

27 March: William Shakespeare, *The Merchant of Venice* (dir. Darko Tresnjak, des. John Lee Beatty: Theatre for a New Audience)

17 April: William Shakespeare, *Macbeth* (dir. Conall Morrison, des. Tom Piper)

25 April: William Shakespeare, *A Midsummer Night's Dream* (dir. Tim Supple, Dash Arts)

25 May: Eugene Ionesco, *Macbett* (dir. Silviu Pucarete, des. Helmut Sturmer)

2 August: Margaret Atwood (dramaturg Nicola Wilson), *The Penelopiad* (dir. Josette Bushell-Mingo, des. Rosa Maggiora: in association with Canada's National Arts Centre)

PROSPERO BEHIND BARS

CURT L. TOFTELAND AND HAL COBB

I. REDEMPTION, FORGIVENESS, AND TRANSFORMATION
CURT L. TOFTELAND

Atop a five-story-cylindrical-tower . . . standing as a lone-sentinel at the corner of intersecting chain-link-fences crowned with razor-wire encircling the correctional-island . . . reside the eyes in the sky . . .

Within the tower-top . . . behind gray-rectangular-glass-plated-picture-windows . . . men . . . clad in blue-uniforms with large-black-binoculars attached to their hands and eyes . . . sweep the encircled-correctional-island . . . surveying . . . observing . . . watching . . . detailing . . . the activities of the occupants-of-this-human-zoo . . .

Down the long gray sidewalk flanked with one-story, white-washed, concrete buildings walk the nameless-inhabitants clothed in uniforms . . . some blue . . . some white . . . the majority khaki . . .

Across the expanse of the open-field at the far-end of the island, the khaki-clothed-men mark the steady march-of-time . . . playing out their physical-existence between the ticking-seconds of the clock . . . between the kicks of a rolling-soccer-ball . . . between the grunts-and-groans of the tightly-muscled-men beneath the burden of the weight-pile . . . between the leg strides of the walkers . . . joggers . . . and runners . . . repetitively-circling the earthen-track . . . between the puffs-of-smoke emitted from the conclave-of-idlers . . . standing . . . sitting . . . or reclining . . . on the fringes of incarcerated-recreational-life . . .

In building-number-one, near the entrance of the Luther Luckett Correctional Complex located in LaGrange, Kentucky, a solitary-khaki-clad-man stands at the edge of a circle-of-plastic-maroon-colored-chairs . . . his right-hand clenched in a fist, tapping lightly on his concave-chest to the rhythm of his beating-heart . . . his blue-eyes, housed in deep-sockets, filled with pools-of-reflected-anguish, fuzzy-focused on the beige-colored-tile-floor of the Luther-Luckett-Correctional-Complex-guest-visiting-room . . . his mouth sagging to the right, slightly ajar, like a one-hinged-wooden-door on a farm-outbuilding . . . his drooping-shoulders roll forward, collapsing his breast-plate on his emptying-lungs . . . on a long exhale, his body slumps down and in upon itself, mirroring the angle of his mouth . . . he breathes the words, '*No matter how hard I try . . . um . . . I can only go so deep . . .*' . . . his closed-fist opens to a flat-hand position just above his heart . . . '*Um . . . I can't get past my frozen heart . . .*' . . . his face grimaces-and-contorts, as his hand presses downward against the imagined lump-of-ice in his chest . . . '*Um . . . It's not for lack of trying . . . um . . . or the desire to go deeper . . . um . . . it's just forty-six years of secrets and suppressed feelings . . .*' . . . his open-hand returns to the clenched-fist and taps his chest with renewed vigor, as if attempting to break the imagined-ice that surrounds his heart . . . '*Heaven forbid, I should ever express my true feelings . . .*'

As childhood-memories pull him back into the 'dark-backward-and-abysm-of-time', the ice surrounding his heart spreads upward, laying claim to his face...a moment of frozen-silence...as the darkness of his interior world swallows him...a kaleidoscope of emotions play across his face...anger...guilt...regret...grief...remorse...a resounding-sadness fills his being...his life force seeps onto the floor...forming a puddle of self-pity...filling the space around him...spreading through the room...

Men, clad in drab-khaki-colored-uniforms, reside in a variety of standing-and-sitting-postures...their eyes intently-focused on the speaker...some men nod with recognition...others are silent, seeming lost in their solitude, not allowing their thoughts to surface...register...or reveal the landscape of their interior-world...as separate as they are, they share this moment, as the clock hanging on the wall above the correctional-institution-control-room-window ticks off the seconds...minutes...hours...days...weeks...years of their lives...these men dwell in obscurity on the fringe of society...they are the 'other'.

HE WHO IS UNABLE TO LIVE IN SOCIETY, OR WHO HAS NO NEED BECAUSE HE IS SUFFICIENT FOR HIMSELF, MUST BE EITHER A BEAST OR A GOD.   – ARISTOTLE

For thirteen years, I travelled back and forth to the Luther Luckett Correctional Complex in LaGrange, Kentucky where some of the worst of us are kept.

My curiosity about incarcerated men and women is not driven by sensationalist tabloid news reports of the crimes they have committed, but rather by a fundamental question: Are men and women who have committed heinous crimes against others...redeemable?

This is the question at the root of my work with correctional inmate populations. Prison is a world of alienation, a place where a humane, supportive and loving community is a foreign idea. It is here that I seek to build a community among prison inmates by using the works of William Shakespeare. His works invite self-examination, self-exploration and self-awareness. Shakespeare reveals our common humanity. He encourages us to think, but does not dictate what to think. Using Shakespeare, I created a vehicle through which convicted criminals could come to know themselves, not just for the crimes they have committed but also on the deepest level of knowing – mind, heart and soul. In this transformative process, the inmate offenders retrace the journey of their memories and experiences from early childhood through elementary school, adolescence and young adulthood, finally arriving at the point in time when they committed the crimes that brought them to prison. It is through the process of reflection that inmates are able to understand the roots of their behaviour.

More often than not, the inmate offenders are ill equipped to begin the transformative quest into their minds, hearts and souls. Their emotional/intellectual/spiritual toolboxes are bereft of the tools they need to pursue such a difficult journey. Inmate offenders who do possess some of the tools often lack the skills to use them in the transformative process.

KNOW THEN THYSELF, PRESUME NOT GOD TO SCAN; THE PROPER STUDY OF MANKIND IS MAN.
   – ALEXANDER POPE

In 1995, I founded the Shakespeare Behind Bars (SBB) program at the Luther Luckett Correctional Complex in LaGrange, Kentucky. The foundation upon which SBB is built is the belief that all human beings are born inherently good. Although a convicted criminal has too often committed heinous crimes against other human beings, this innate goodness lives deep within him and it can be called forth. The Shakespeare Behind Bars program offers inmate offenders the ability to hope and the courage to act, despite the presence of fear and in spite of the odds stacked against them.

The transformational process begins with an awakening event that comes as a discovery, insight or epiphany. It is the very moment of 'ah-ha!' It is the light of understanding illuminating the darkness of ignorance in the mind. This moment of awakening arrives through an infinite variety of ways but always shares the same inmate offender's desire . . . to become someone more than a convicted criminal. It is important to support the inmate's awakening, to encourage it, to nurture it and to have a place where it can safely manifest itself.

Through this introspective process, the inmate offender seeks to come to terms with his past, including the crimes he committed. He begins the reflective journey by examining the cause and effect of his crimes. Part of the process is to take responsibility for his crimes. He comes to understand that if it is redemption and forgiveness he seeks, then he must himself forgive those who perpetrated injustices upon him. Through this journey, the inmate offender arrives at the understanding that he need not be trapped in the shadow of his past criminal actions. He has the possibility of transforming himself into the human being he wants to be.

EDUCATING THE MIND WITHOUT EDUCATING THE HEART IS NO EDUCATION AT ALL. – ARISTOTLE

Using the healing power of the arts, the theatrical structure of producing a play over a nine-month period, and the works of William Shakespeare, I seek to create the kind of reflective journey by which an inmate offender can be transformed. Without the capability of reflection, he is doomed to repeat his previous harmful actions.

The transformational journey requires continuous, active participation and the opportunity for the inmate offender to connect to the deepest levels of his consciousness. Behaviour can be changed through a metamorphosis of the heart. This is accomplished by the structure and disciplined practice of programs like Shakespeare Behind Bars. Repatterning behaviour takes time, practice (repetition), the support of the leadership of the correctional institution, the support of peers, friends and family and, most importantly, the Shakespeare Behind Bars circle of trust.

I use theatre techniques to train the inmate offender to analyse the nuances of a fictional dramatic character's interior world that prompt the character's external behaviour. Through this process, the inmate gains insights and the skills required to apply the same process to his own life.

The journey of an actor into the depths of a character's conscious and unconscious behaviour is a multilayered journey. Like an onion, the layers are peeled away revealing the next layer, all the while working towards the inner core. With each layer revealed, emotions are discovered which were long embedded in the skin. These emotions are what drive human behaviour. The exploration of these emotional drives is the heart of 'character criticism'.

An actor's first encounter with a theatrical character is through reading the play. The actor comes to know the character by what he says (dialogue), what he does (actions), and what other characters say about him. From this superficial understanding of the character, the actor, seeking to understand the motivations behind what the character says, does, and what is said about them, uses dramatic imagination to build a character's back-story (thus, *What happened to Prospero's spouse? What happened to cause the rift between Prospero and his brother Antonio? Why was Prospero fascinated with magic?*).

While mining this rich coal bed of character analysis, the actor often identifies with the character by finding parallels in his life and the imagined life of the character. This connection develops over time, in rehearsal and in private reflection, thus deepening the relationship. In performance, the actor and the character merge to become as one. The result is a finely nuanced portrayal by a sensitive, skilled and knowledgeable actor.

The Shakespeare Behind Bars program seeks to discover the diamonds that are embedded within the coal. Through the exploration of a character's actions, the inmate actor emulates the positive and the negative aspects of human behaviour. At first, in imitation but eventually through the process, the inmate actor's understanding moves deeper. By exploring the imagined life of the character, he begins to work out his own personal issues.

The inmate actor experiences the 'ah-ha' moment; slowly a personal transformation manifests itself deep within him. With continued self-reflection, the inmate actor's heart is transformed. The inmate discovers a new way of being. He realizes that he is not the same person he was prior to beginning the transformative process.

PHILOMATH FILMS AWARD WINNING DOCUMENTARY

In 2003, I produced and directed the Shakespeare Behind Bars production of *The Tempest* by William Shakespeare. The nine-month process was the subject of a documentary by Philomath Films. The documentary began its life at the 2005 Sundance Film Festival and was selected to screen at over forty film festivals around the world, winning eleven awards.

Today, seven years after beginning its public journey, the SBB documentary continues to have life in classrooms around the world. I have travelled to more than fifty college campuses to screen the documentary, facilitate a post-screening talk-back with the audience, teach master classes and visit classrooms. In 2011, I was awarded a Fulbright Fellowship to travel to Brisbane, Queensland, Australia to bring my work to the inmates at the Borallon Correctional Centre.

The Tempest is the exploration of a character (Prospero) who has – through twelve years of development and practice of transformative powers – created a plan and prepared himself to commit a crime of revenge upon his perpetrator (his brother Antonio) and fellow conspirator (King Alonso). Inmate Hal Cobb played the role of Prospero. What follows are Hal's reflections on his journey into the character of Prospero and how playing the role affected him then and continues to affect him today.

II. MY PURSUIT OF CHARACTER
HAL COBB[1]

PROLOGUE

If looking to the future can cause trepidation, what is this uneasiness I feel in looking back? Memory has a way of playing tricks on the mind, weaving minor accomplishments into major feats, small slights to great grievances. Recollection can morph an accidental occurrence into deliberate heroism; reveal best intentions as off the mark. Painful or shameful scenes can be buried with or without conscious intent. Perspective sometimes sharpens focus, but it is often an artist's manipulation to trick the eye.

Curt L. Tofteland, Founder and Producing Director, asked me to discuss the process of developing character as part of the ongoing work in Shakespeare Behind Bars, particularly the character of Prospero in our 2002–03 production of *The Tempest*. The nine-month process is documented in the Philomath Films documentary *Shakespeare Behind Bars*. How we are remembered by ourselves, as well as by others, is largely a matter of perspective.

There is nothing either good or bad, but thinking makes it so.
                                                    – *Hamlet*

But when part of your life is irrefutably captured on film (despite director's eye and editor's cut) memory has far less free reign.

The documentary *Shakespeare Behind Bars* has been a mixed blessing. Reports that the film transforms viewers' stereotypical ideas of inmates are greatly gratifying. Conversely, seeing yourself stuck in time, stuck in a self-pitying sadness, myopically focused on forgiveness (to the detriment of not exploring Prospero's drive for revenge), seeing one's unexamined character flaws glaringly exposed while publicly declaring one's darkest deeds is unsettling. The experience is both liberating and shameful, humbling and challenging.

My pursuit of character is an ongoing activity in and out of Shakespeare Behind Bars. Each character over my fifteen years of participation in SBB has informed me, sometimes challenged my basic assumptions about myself and others, and always helped to expand my awareness and humanity.

---

[1] Awarded First Place in essay in the 2010 Pen Prison Writing Contest.

ACT ONE

Curt L. Tofteland, then the Producing Artistic Director of the Kentucky Shakespeare Festival, began volunteering at Luther Luckett Correctional Complex outside of Louisville, Kentucky in 1995 – my first year of incarceration after being convicted for the murder of my wife in 1984 – to develop a program based on the works of Shakespeare. I wasn't much of a Shakespeare fan at the time, but Curt's presence brought the only theatrical outlet I was likely to find in prison. Theatre games, monologues and scenes were used to get to know each other, slowly introduce us to the words of Shakespeare and develop trust as the program evolved into being. Initially an evening of scenes and monologues took shape to be shared with other inmates, as well as family and friends in the prison visiting room before we ventured into the full production of complete plays. Seventeen years later, we're into our sixteenth full-length play with several other evenings of scenes and monologues along the way.

Curt works with SBB differently than he works with any other company of actors. With us, he is more a facilitator than a director, a co-creator with us rather than an expert trying to impose a predetermined vision on us. The play unfolds in an organic, cooperative way. No idea is thrown out, regardless of its source, if it works and tells the story.

Curt works more like a karate sensei or Zen master whose great gift is to see into the souls of men and know how to gently nudge them to make personal discoveries. He lets us know when we are off the mark and offers questions instead of answers to facilitate our journey to the truth. And that is the bottom line for Shakespeare Behind Bars – the truth.

I am an anomaly when it comes to Shakespeare Behind Bars as one of the few participants who had theatrical experience before joining the program. Not that it makes me any better than anyone else in the program; it gives me a different baggage to deal with. More often than not, Curt spends his time defusing my actor bag of tricks, the masks that impede the truth. After requisite skits and solos

throughout elementary and Sunday school, my first full-fledged production came on the heels of the most severe beating of my childhood and a dissociative episode that forced me out of my body and locked me inside my head. Out of all the seventh grade choir boys I was selected to play Patrick in a high school production of *Mame*. I was treated like a prince in a production with 50 chorus members and a full orchestra in a state-of-the-art auditorium complete with hydraulic orchestra pit. It gave me the opportunity to be someone else, someone people liked. Acting and performing became an escape for me. It was a chance to not be the worthless piece of shit I felt I was. From that point on I threw myself into school, community and regional productions with performances and rehearsals overlapping to the point that I didn't have time to dwell on feelings.

The gift of having so many participants of SBB without prior theatrical or Shakespeare exposure is that they come to the experience clean. They have no preconceived notions of what it should or should not be. They don't get caught up in iambic pentameter or academic debates. Their reactions are pure, unbiased and visceral. Often with text memorized by rote, they can get to the gut of the matter as Curt works with them, without getting stuck in their heads.

Another gift that the process of SBB provides is the luxury (or curse) of living with the text for nine to twelve months. Most theatre companies are lucky to have a few weeks to a few months to put up a play. As one play wraps for us in May, we know what next year's play will be. Personal reading and research begins during our summer hiatus, often with group readings and study in the prison day-rooms, bullpens and recreation field. Official rehearsals begin again in the fall.

I make cheat sheets of my lines and cues, whatever character(s) I've taken on, and keep them in my pocket for the hurry-up-and-wait life-style of prison. We hurry up to get to the chow hall at the scheduled times and wait for corrections to catch up. We hurry up to get to the canteen line to pick up our once-a-week kiosk orders – a covered handrail queue like amusement parks – where the wait can be an hour or two. We hurry up to medical at the prescribed time and wait for the nurses and practitioners to catch up on over-scheduled appointments. This leaves a lot of time to memorize or ruminate on lines. It's not unusual to catch a few members with scripts running lines waiting for canteen or on smoke breaks in the bullpens or for discussions of the plays to break out in the chow hall or day-rooms.

ACT TWO

When developing any character as part of a production of Shakespeare Behind Bars, it always begins with the text. Along the way, it always returns to the text. When in doubt, what does the text say? For me, the initial private read is for general affect, my ears pricked for characters calling to me and lines resonating within me. Prospero felt like a natural fit from the get-go. The second read, often out loud, is an exploration of what characters I find interesting, to feel whose words roll most naturally off my tongue.

As we move into self-casting the play, discussion begins between members – who wants what role – and a spreadsheet is put together of each member's top three picks, so we know who's vying for each role. Egos often clash during the process and feelings get hurt during negotiations. There's an unspoken understanding that if you play a major role one year, you step back the next season and let others come to the fore. Some members are line-counters and initially pick roles based on how large a part is, while others pursue emotional connections to characters. Some want to play characters that expose the best parts of themselves, while others are drawn to what is going to challenge them to grow. And in an all-male company there's always: who's going to play the female roles? Again, there's an unspoken understanding that at some point in one's SBB career, one should take on a female role. Some swear they'll never do it, some agree kicking and screaming in protest. Those who do take on female roles discover the gift of delving into the female psyche as we strive to develop

truthful characters, not drag-show caricatures. We learn that feminine affectation is not necessary, simply tell the truth while speaking the text. I've discovered Shakespeare didn't write female roles for actresses, he wrote them for men to portray. His truthful text does the work, not actor affectation. As the cast comes together, and oftentimes well into the rehearsal process, we discover what Curt has coined as one of our mantras: 'We don't choose the roles – the roles choose us.'

I compulsively pursued the role of Prospero in the 2002–03 Shakespeare Behind Bars production of *The Tempest* for purely selfish reasons. Another prominent member of the company decided he too wanted the role of Prospero and it was on. There were private verbal knockdowns and drag-outs, and a lot of hurtful things were said on both sides of the equation, but I was determined, come hell or high water, to stand up for what I wanted. That stance was unusual and unfamiliar territory for me. I'm usually the one to run from head-to-head conflict at all costs. For undisclosed reasons, the other member backed down (not a usual stance for him either) and the role of Prospero was mine. But along with the role I held on to hurts and resentments the conflict evoked.

Prior to *The Tempest*, I attended an Impact of Crime on Victims seminar (Spring 2001) and worked with a facilitator from a Victim–Offender Reconciliation Program (VORP) through April of 2004. The VORP program included preparing for and making a video message for the survivors of my crime. Forgiveness, more specifically my desire to be forgiven, weighed heavily on me. I wanted to know why my Christian family and the Christian community from which I came could not or would not forgive me. I began extensive research on the process of forgiveness. During that research, both academic and personal, I became overwhelmed and felt myself shutting down. It reminded me of a life-long habit of avoidance, evading conflict at all costs, putting off dealing with things, repressing what I was really feeling but did not know how to identify or deal with. But I've come to understand that unconsciously choosing not to do anything is a choice. It is a choice to give into the fear of the unknown and remain in a nether land of the familiar. By choosing not to choose, I allow myself to be pushed into emotional corners unaware, which eventually caused repression to erupt into my life and the lives of others. Repressed emotion, like Glenn Close's character in *Fatal Attraction*, will not be ignored.

While working on *The Tempest* I was amazed to discover how compartmentalized my life has been. It seems for the most part, I was unaware of what was happening in different aspects of my life. It's embarrassing to acknowledge that lack of awareness. It is similar to Prospero in Milan: so focused on study of alchemy and magic, he was totally unaware of what was going on in other aspects of his life, particularly with his brother.

According to my journal in the winter of 2002–03, I was exploring writing exercises from Dr Phil's book, *Self Matters*. I was primarily exploring the ten defining moments of my life. In the midst of Dr Phil work I found buried notes from a reading of Noel Cobb's *Prospero Island: The Secret Alchemy at the Heart of The Tempest* based on a Jungian psychospiritual and metaphorical approach. I found particular interest in the assessment of Prospero's psyche when applied to Jung's 'Idea of the Four Functions of Consciousness'. There were parallels to my own psyche.

Journal Entry

The root of my desire for forgiveness began years ago, 8–9 years after I took my wife's life, a year or so before my arrest. I'd never dealt with Lisa's death. I didn't know how to wrap my mind, heart and soul around the whole concept, my responsibility for it, the pain I had caused others, the horror of the cover-up and daily denial among extended family and the church family of which I was 'a leader.' I blocked the truth out. I couldn't deal with the reality of it, or the notion that I could kill anyone, let alone the one person I'd felt had really loved me. I couldn't incorporate it into the whole of me. I was emotionally and psychically fractured. On many levels, I had shut down (and continued to be so), focused on my new 'role' of widower and single father, and looked only to the future. On the rare occasions I did look back, I blamed God for not healing me (by making me not gay), for not stopping me prior to the act of taking Lisa's life, and for not bringing her back to life immediately after the act.

After remarrying, moving to California to attend acting school, coming out, getting a divorce – things long buried began to creep to the surface. I call my first acting class 'Introduction to Therapy'. The instructor focused on Uta Hagen's *Respect for Acting* sense memory exercises. I watched younger, college-aged classmates' (I was pushing thirty at the time) walls tumbling down. I hoped tossing a few bricks over the wall would placate the instructor's demands. I couldn't go where she wanted without a complete breakdown. On the flip side, the experience with my classmates, being away from the buckle of the Bible Belt, my family, and – at least geographically – my past, finally helped me start to deal with my sexuality. But with progress of personal acceptance, my sexual acting out increased. On the surface I explained it away as simply exploring aspects of my newly acknowledged self. Beneath it all, it was a way to keep deeper emotions and reality of my past at bay. I learned to skate across the surface of emotion, and with just the slightest emotional connection manufacture the imagined pretense needed to act.

During a rehearsal for a production of Carnival at LA's Group Repertory Theater, I was required as the character of Paul to strike the ingénue, Lili. I couldn't do it. The idea of striking a woman, purposely perpetrating violence against a woman froze me. Bizarrely, I had never considered killing Lisa violent. I rationalized it as saving her from me, that God was rescuing her for eternity. The musical director kept pushing me to darken my tone – the exact opposite of the bright, hopeful gospel singer of my training. I resisted my darkness for fear of being swallowed whole. I didn't deal with my darkness, my shadow-self. I ignored it, pretended it wasn't there. I hoped it would go away. But the shadow of my past life was catching up to me.

ACT THREE

Once an SBB play is cast, the members start memorizing lines and researching character.

We're encouraged to use the text as the main source and ask the usual questions: What does the character say? What do other characters say about the character? How does your character speak? What kind of relationships does the character have? Where does your character fit into the telling of the story? Then, add Shakespeare specific questions like: are the bulk of your characters' lines written in prose or poetic form?

Curt has us work from First Folio Editions. It makes the initial read more difficult, but gives more to reap in textual clues. Contractions in the first folio can make clear the rhythms of iambic pentameter. Phonetic spellings and long vowels give clues to pronunciation. What words are capitalized (besides at the beginning of poetic line) may clue vocal emphasis. We cross reference with modern editions, use lexicons and Shakespeare encyclopedias. I find myself continually looking up words, even words I think I know, to unearth archaic, Old and Middle English definitions. I'm always amazed how Shakespeare selects words with multiple layers of meaning. The definition of the word in context is not necessarily one thing or the other, but often all of the above; or it can mean one thing in one performance and something quite different in the next.

Once I begin to know the words and phrases Shakespeare wrote, I try to go beyond mere meaning to see what images are evoked by his language. The audience doesn't have the benefit of dictionaries and encyclopedias during performance when they hear unfamiliar language. It is my job as an actor/artist to have a clear image in mind. When I know what I am saying, hold a clear image, I'm more likely to bring the audience along with me as I'm telling the story.

As we get on our feet in rehearsal, whether we've memorized the text by rote or dissected the life out of it, the major hurdle is to break out of speech patterns we developed as we learned it. Most of the initial memorization is solo work – going over the lines quietly in our heads in our cells with another inmate in a bunk two feet away, or in the hurry-up-and-wait lines of incarceration, or mumbling to oneself on endless laps around the recreational field. Some then move on to work with partners or mentors before work in a formal rehearsal. After

the initial stumble-through of saying lines out loud in front of a group of people (often a big hurdle for newbies), Curt goes about breaking us out of our unconscious vocal patterns. Calling on techniques from Peter Brook and others he'll have us repeat a passage of text hitting all the pronouns. Then we'll go back and punch all the verbs. As we place emphasis on words differently than we memorized them, we not only break vocal patterns, but also find different meanings. Focusing on what's a pronoun or verb also distracts us from the predetermined choices of what we think the line should mean or how we think it should sound. We discover the many options that are available to us in the moment if we only try them on for size. With Curt, there's always, 'An "O" is never just an "O", it comes from the gut!' Don't dare try to gloss over an 'and', 'but', 'yet', or 'or'. They demand some sort of emphasis. We inevitably feel vulnerable and stupid as the familiarity of our vocal patterns is pulled out from under us. We claim brain flatulence as we go blank while new synapses are created for the text.

Once vocal patterns break down, the next task is to bring the text out of our heads and into our bodies. As strange as that may sound, if feels even stranger to someone more comfortable in their head than in their body. You can see it in an actor when his gestures and posture don't match or support what he's saying. If he doesn't know what to do with his hands, he's in his head thinking, 'What should I do with my hands?' When the text is rooted in the body, the hands take care of themselves. In fact, every gesture, step or move is in sync and motivated by the connection of the text in the body. Curt constantly asks the infuriating question, 'Where does that live in your body?' There are times it feels like he's speaking a foreign language. 'Don't layer on an emotion, find a connection.' 'Just let it drop in.' Drop in to what? Even after years of book-learned prison yoga in an attempt to reintegrate my head with my body, heal the rift between the spirit and the physical, going within my body is not a place I go naturally. Buried emotional memory hasn't seen the light of day for years, if at all. I have to be coaxed as my heart constricts and my chest tightens in an attempt to shut down access. I try to follow my breath with techniques I learned in vocal training and meditation practice to move deeper into my body and make truthful connections. The mind tries to follow the body's lead and zone out to prevent going there. But there's safety in Curt's voice and trust in the circle of this band of bard-brothers. He will not push me farther than he sees I can go on any given day. There will be acknowledgement as he reminds the whole group, 'the nobility is in the attempt'.

Nowhere else in my life, particularly my life in corrections, am I required to reach under the surface. Nowhere else in prison am I asked to get out of my head. No one but Curt facilitates the space to process difficult truths and encourage complete responsibility for our choices and actions. The great illusion of incarceration in the United States is that warehousing and punishment requires offenders to take that responsibility and somehow miraculously rehabilitate themselves. Many inmates are stuck in the past or some imagined future, while most simply try to survive prison in the only way they know how. There are rehabilitation and educational options but they are not widespread or for the most part required and, with funds diminishing for basic services, classes and programs are the first to go. Without Curt voluntarily developing the Shakespeare Behind Bars program at no cost to the Department of Corrections, and the generous support of private patrons, hundreds of men over the past seventeen years would not have been given the opportunity to habilitate themselves. Curt makes the observation that men can't be re-habilitated if they haven't been habilitated in the first place.

One of the most powerful SBB moments I remember was not captured on film. Rehearsing the scene between Antonio (Prospero's brother and usurper) and Sebastian (King Alonzo's brother and co-conspirator against Prospero) Curt was pushing the actor portraying Antonio to dig deeper, bring the text down into his body. Antonio is trying to convince Sebastian to take advantage of the shipwreck and usurp his brother to become King of Naples. As the textual assassination plot sank in, he quietly said to himself, 'I didn't have to kill him.' The actor was the only other SBB member who had attended the Impact of Crime on Victims seminar with me. I had been privately astounded at his insistence that his crime had been justifiable homicide, killing the alleged rapist of someone close to him. He rationalized that his cultural background and military training gave him no other choice. 'I didn't have to kill him', he repeated as the room went silent. I could see the profound shift in him as Antonio's plotting and scheming took root in his personal reality. He may have never come to his conclusion and change of world-view had it not been for the Shakespeare Behind Bars experience.

We can know the text in our heads, but not fully understand it until we find a home for it in our bodies. Through Curt's insightful questions, gentle nudging and welcoming spirit, he helps to navigate the not-so-easy path to body connection. Once those connections are made, we are simply asked to let them be. They're there. We don't try to artificially drum up the connections every time, or try to recreate a moment that has come and gone. We try to make as many creative synapses as possible, build an arsenal of options that we can draw from in the moment, because the moment is always new and our only connection to what is true. The task is to learn to be totally present in the moment, trusting in your preparation, and allow it to be without judgement.

FORGIVENESS

My obsession with forgiveness kept me from consciously identifying Prospero's shadow. And as I've found out over the years, the reason we think we choose a role is often eclipsed by deeper profundity. Prospero's shadow was perhaps his obsession with all things magical and alchemical, to the exclusion of fulfilling his responsibilities as Duke of Milan and as a parent. He allowed his brother Antonio to attend to the daily demands of running the city-state, and numerous attendants to care for the infant Miranda (as revealed in Act 1, scene 2). As with many of Shakespeare's ingénues, Miranda's mother is absent – referred to in past tense, most likely deceased with no mention of how, when or why. Prospero lovingly recalls his wife as 'a piece of virtue'. Was it her loss that transformed curiosity to obsession in an attempt to drown grief in study and practice? Over-occupy his mind so he didn't have to feel his heart? Is Prospero's shadow-self his need to control? Or is Prospero's shadow his desire for revenge?

Dr Fred Luskin of Stanford University's Forgiveness Project tells us in his book *Forgive for Good*, 'Unresolved grievances are like planes on an air traffic controller's radar screen, taking up precious air space draining attention and energy, increasing stress, forcing harder work and burnout.' He posits: 'Three Core Components Underlie the Creation of Any Longstanding Grievance: (1) Exaggerated taking of personal offence; (2) Blaming the offender for how you feel; (3) Creation of a grievance story. Careful feeding and nurturing of these grievance components can keep a hurt alive forever.'

Prospero has twelve years on the island to feed and nurture his grievance story. Not only had Antonio and Alonzo deposed him and set him out to sea to die, they attempted to give his innocent daughter the same fate. While Prospero's grievance story festers, he increases his magical power and ability to such strength that when the opportunity to wreak revenge arrives through the observation of spirits he controls, he finalizes his plot by raising a tempest and forcing the wrack of the ship carrying his perpetrators. The scheme is so far-reaching that he includes his unwitting daughter in his plans to control Naples by putting a spell on her to fall in love with Ferdinand. His hurt and hatred are so great he doesn't consider the consequences of using her without consent. This is another uncomfortable aspect of Prospero's shadow-self that I did not fully explore at the time of our production. It was not a conscious choice to avoid this aspect of Prospero's psyche (and conversely mine), as much as it was something that did not or could not come to the fore at the time. Who would want to admit using a motherless infant to garner pity and a twisted sort of love and attention while deflecting reality?

But fortunately for Prospero, true love trumps his malevolent magic. I have the feeling (though no specific textual reference) that while Prospero spies on Miranda and Ferdinand's courtship their burgeoning love begins to melt his intent for revenge. He begins to see the long-term effects of his choices on Miranda and his future heirs. The 'love-seed' planted in the observation scenes comes to fruition in Act 4, scene 1 when Ariel reports the grief and suffering of Prospero's old friend and advocate Gonzalo, another innocent bystander of collateral damage in his plot for revenge. Expanded awareness of the long-term effects of his actions, coupled with Ariel's capacity for compassion with the 'were I human(e)' comment reveals to Prospero the consequences of a future without forgiveness. So drastic is this moment of discovery that Prospero abandons magic – the focus of twelve years' intense study and his means for revenge, so that he cannot return to such potential evil in the future.

The confrontation during Carnival caused a break-down/break-through that finally got me to start a twelve-step program for sexually compulsive behaviour and to seek information about therapy. I still did not know how I would handle my deepest, darkest secret, or how much I could actually discuss it with a therapist without them being legally compelled to report me to the authorities. I believed there would be little chance at personal recovery if I returned to Kentucky and turned myself in at that time. I didn't even know if I would survive facing the truth because depression and thoughts of suicide were always knocking at my door. I confided in a roommate, my twelve-step guru and friend (attending college to become a drug and alcohol counsellor) to find what a therapist's legal requirements were about reporting a crime. He was the first person I had ever admitted the truth to. I never considered the weight my admission would have on someone else, especially a person who thought he was the only one to know the truth. His fear led him to photocopy my twelve-step journal and give it to the police, opening a cold case that had long been perceived an accident. He didn't realize that I did indeed start therapy.

To make a long story short, I became aware of the investigation and secret grand jury action, which would lead to my arrest. I was so overwhelmed by the truth catching up to me before I'd had a chance to deal with it, fear of having to face those I'd hurt so deeply without knowing how and the betrayal of a friend (how's that shoe fit, Hal?) that I attempted suicide by using a friend's copy of Dr Kervorkian's book and his stash of pharmaceuticals, only to return to consciousness 36 hours later, disappointed to be alive. Still determined to disappear one way or another, I vanished within two weeks.

A NEW BEGINNING

I ended up on the Puna side of the Big Island at an off-grid spiritual retreat centre in the middle of the rain forest. They were in desperate need of kitchen help, so the son-of-a-chef, struggling actor with years of cater/waiter experience stepped up to a 30-hour workweek in exchange for room and board. Since there was no cash involved, no paperwork was required; ideal for an assumed identity with nothing to back it up. I moved into an 8 × 8-foot A-frame in the campground, spent the majority of time off meditating. My prime focus was for the well-being of the daughter I'd abandoned to my ex-wife, but the meditations began to expand out from her to include her stepparents, grandparents, her birth mother's siblings, my siblings, the members of the churches back in Lexington – everyone who had fallen under the effects of my selfish, fearful actions.

My meditation practice was an attempt to find peace, gain perspective, seek answers and effect healing. Prospero's practice of magic may have started with purer motives to satisfy curiosity, but it takes a harmful and hurtful bent when motivated by revenge. As his magical powers increase, his desire for revenge, unchecked and strengthened by his growing grievance, gives him a sense

of absolute power. Prospero believes the popular Christian/Western idea that humanity is superior to all other creatures and creation. Even before Caliban makes his misguided attempt to mate with Miranda, Prospero treats him, Ariel and all other spirits and creatures as his underlings – only there to serve his needs and do his bidding. This inherent prejudice and bigotry flares from its ugly root as he arrogantly chides both Caliban and Ariel in superior ways. While Prospero's practice brings out the worst behaviour in him, my meditation practice helps the best in me rise to the surface.

As my search for inner tranquillity continued, I began instruction with local Reiki masters. I also began participating as fire bearer in full-moon sweat lodges offered at the spiritual centre. I was hoping for understanding of my Cherokee roots, to connect with a part of me that had always been hidden from view. The facilitator taught me how to build the altar with alternating levels of wood and large lava stones to be used to produce the heat for the night's sweat. I learned to pray to the four directions, and as I was inviting participation from my ancestors, I was met with the presence of my recently deceased and long estranged half-Cherokee grandfather. In an instant I was flooded with understanding, compassion and forgiveness for whatever it was he did to my mother. Exposure to the indigenous culture of the Hawaiians and the devastating effect western culture and religion had on it helped connect me to my Cherokee culture. I felt the sense of disconnection, the cultural stripping and loss of identity my half-breed grandfather must have felt. I was not seeking to forgive my grandfather. It came upon me unexpected. With this new revelation, I began to see my situation as something much larger than my specific, fearful actions, but as a collective of unresolved multigenerational issues and events.

Similarly, Prospero's forgiveness of Antonio and Alonzo falls on him unexpectedly and unsought. He was pursuing what he believed to be a just and righteous revenge. In both Prospero's and my case, it was not so much a conscious choice in the immediate moment but rather an unconscious sense of forgiveness that washed over us. Once forgiveness came into our consciousness, the choice to embrace it or ignore it became ours. Choosing to embrace forgiveness is what Prospero refers to as 'Nobler reason'.

After six months at Kalani Honua, I moved to the other side of the Big Island to manage a Bed-n-Breakfast in Captain Cook. I leapt at the opportunity for a lighter work load, more privacy, and the time to practice meditation and Reiki, unaware that a few miles below the Samurai House was an ancient Hawaiian temple complex on Kealakakua Ba – Puu o Honua o Honaunau – The City of Refuge. Traditional Hawaiian culture had 'an eye for an eye' type of justice. If someone was killed, the family of the deceased has the right to take the life of the killer. If the killer could make it to the City of Refuge, he could not only find refuge but could seek absolution from temple priests. The priest would then negotiate a form of restorative justice and restitution with the victim's family.

I began to hitchhike down to the facility (a state park) and practice my healing meditation, hoping for forgiveness amidst the ruins of the ancient temple. After nearly a year in Hawaii, I had a shift in consciousness during a Reiki treatment from a co-initiate. My situation hadn't changed, but it felt like my head popped through the clouds, and I could see things from a higher perspective. I knew that in order to facilitate healing, I had to return to Kentucky and take personal and legal responsibility for taking Lisa's life.

In their own ways, Prospero's island and my island retreat were sanctuaries. Either fate or some guiding principle led Prospero and me to our respective islands. Initially, they were places for simple survival. They became sanctuaries for our development. While others wanted Prospero to disappear, I sought to disappear on my own. We both had to survive by our wits. As we pursued our practices, we both arrived at startling discoveries, discoveries that we weren't looking for. I found the clarity I needed to return to the mainland and own up to my wrongful actions. Prospero found the clarity to return to his kingdom. We both found the capacity to forgive.

ACT FOUR

'Live in hope, not expectation' is another Zen-like 'Curtism'. The broken little boy in me longed to be loved and accepted. I was desperate to be forgiven. The Reiki belief is that the healings are complete and simply await acceptance. Why would people choose to hold on to pain? Why would good Christian people not follow Jesus's example of forgiveness? Since I wasn't seeing the result I wanted, I became impatient with 'healing meditation'. The trial, sentencing and incarceration seemed to do nothing in terms of reconciliation and restoration.

From my perspective prison is warehousing and punishment, separation and judgement, dehumanization and abandonment. After waiting seven—eight years (okay Hal, hadn't your victims waited ten years before any sort of justice or closure?), I intellectualized the pursuit of forgiveness through study. I tried to figure out what their problem was. Even though I was intellectually aware of the concept 'you must be forgiving to receive forgiveness', I entertained many grievance stories and held on to personal pain and sense of victimization as if the grievances were a part of me. I was ignorant of the principle that as long as I held on to my grievance stories, they would define how I navigate my life. As long as I didn't forgive, I could view my perceived offenders as 'the other' and feel perfectly justified about holding on to my grudges. Just like people label me as 'the other' – convicted felon, murderer and monster. Labels and grievances dull the vision and sense that 'the other' has inherent humanity.

My grievance stories were far more petty and trivial than Prospero's. No one ever tried to depose me or abandon my daughter and me to certain death. But I hold on to my grievances as if they were the most valuable treasure. I can't seem to let go of slights from years ago. Every time I see or even think of certain people, grievances start looping my brain, indignation arises blaming the offender for what I feel instead of taking responsibility for those feelings myself. I can't seem to let go of the self-identity as 'the wronged one', and yet I expect those whom I've truly hurt to let go and forgive me.

While rehearsing Prospero other SBB members could see similarities between the character and me that I could not (or chose not to) see. Prospero was very controlling – of Caliban, of Ariel, even of his own daughter. I was not controlling, I was trying to be helpful. Could people not see that I was simply trying to be helpful? Controlling! I was offended. And blind. Not only was my desire for forgiveness rooted in my own selfish need for acceptance and love, my 'healing work' was a manipulation of the universe for my own benefit. There is an element of the greater good in my desire to facilitate healing, but my selfish attachment to outcome actually resists its good intention. Attachment to outcome is a sure sign of a control addict, no matter what helpful blanket is thrown over it. As Ariel holds up a mirror to Prospero's nature, Prospero has a flash of insight urged on by Ariel's compassionate comment in 5.1 ('I would, Sir, were I human(e)').

Prospero's control reaches its peak as he traps his offenders on the island, his 'righteous' plans for revenge come to a head but love breaks through his hard exterior. His attempts, through the use of magic, to control his daughter are not strong enough to hold back the tide of Miranda and Ferdinand's burgeoning love. It is their love that changes Prospero's worldview, showing him that his plan for revenge will have long-term effects. He begins to see the world from a higher perspective than his own grievance story. Prospero wasn't seeking to forgive Antonio and King Alonso. It came to him in a flash, unexpectedly. His head pops through the clouds of hurt and pain and he sees the bigger picture. Prospero calls it higher reason. I see it as a higher consciousness.

ACT FIVE

From Noel Cobbs's *Prospero's Island: The Secret Alchemy at the Heart of The Tempest*:

According to Jung's Idea of the Four Functions of Consciousness an individual has one superior function and its polar opposite as inferior function. [Each function can, and usually does bleed over into the next function.]

The superior function is often overdeveloped, while the inferior function is often underdeveloped, neglected, or uncultivated.

> *Thinking represses Feeling. Intuition represses Sensation.*
> *Feeling represses Thinking. Sensation represses Intuition.*

The inferior function is infuriatingly slow to develop. It is the source of many irritations and daily embarrassments. As it is extremely sensitive to criticism, it always manages to cover up and present the impression that all is well and functioning properly. In fact, most of the responses are either completely inappropriate or absent. It is only through the consistent attempt to assimilate the inferior function that it can gradually be raised to a higher level of consciousness. This is usually accomplished by a corresponding lowering of the level of the superior function – a *sacrificium intellectus*, for example, in the case of thinking as the superior function.

In Prospero's case, focusing on thinking keeps him from feeling. The study of magic and its practice give a framework for his thinking. It feeds into the masculine idea that it is better to think and do, than to feel. And it also plays into the Christian/Western idea that intelligence is what makes humans greater than other creatures. My own thinking isn't quite so focused.

Journal excerpt from winter 2002–2003
I know how to think. Thinking occupies my waking and sleeping hours. I wake up in the middle of the night with my mind racing, and quickly cannot remember what I was dreaming. I know how to think for myself but I still don't always know how to feel for myself. I can feel through characters in a book or a movie or a play, ultimately an empathetic act, but somehow still (intellectually) detached from what I'm feeling. Give me a song or a character and I can think my way to what I imagine is the appropriate feeling. Sometimes, in spite of myself there is an automatic resonance of emotion that I can't explain. I equate it with what I understand the experience of 'channeling' to be. My ego/thinking gets out of the way and a connection to something deeper and broader than I am consciously aware of appears.

On my own I don't always know what I am feeling, or how to deal with what I'm feeling. I grew up in an environment where it was appropriate to be quiet, unassuming, and appear to be happy/content. Any other emotion was deemed unacceptable.

My feelings (wants, desires, etc.) were never important; they were never honored. As a result I did not learn to identify or process deeper, particularly darker emotions. I could never be angry. Not only was it inappropriate, it was sinful.

God could be angry, adults could be angry (particularly at kids), but I could not. When my brothers and I would get into knock down drag outs when we were home alone, what I know now to be rage would often burst out — filled with hatred and a desire to hurt — that I did not understand, which in return would evoke a tremendous sense of guilt, remorse, and shame for being so sinful. But those specifics were private, never discussed, but often resulted in repeated public acts of repentance and contrition at altar call/invitation time in church. A tearful, frightened kid terrified of going to hell for such sinful acts; rededicating my life to Christ, eventually to full-time Christian service (the ultimate carrot dangled before young people at our church to prove one worthy of God's love).

Looking at Jung's Idea of the Four Functions of Consciousness' correlation to the four elements, I'm reminded of the four temperaments: choleric, sanguine, melancholic and phlegmatic. It is not lost on me that Prospero's closet relationship with an elemental creature is that with Ariel, a creature of Air. Thinking is correlated with air.

Prospero's superior function according to Cobb is the same as mine (in my own self diagnosis) — thinking. Conversely our inferior function is feeling. For me, thinking goes beyond the intellect to include the business of the mind in general, or what is called 'monkey mind' in Zen. The mind stays busy, often in a hyper-overdrive, in many cases to keep from feeling.

Prospero seems to do a better job as a parent on the island than he did as Duke of Milan. In Act 1 scene 2, Miranda remembers being attended to by many women. The attendants had primary care of parenting in the absence of her mother and Prospero's emotional distance. On the island there were no attendants; Prospero must be her primary caregiver. He prides himself, ' . . . and here / Have I thy schoolmaster, made thee more profit / Then other princes can, that have more time / For vainer hours; and tutors not so careful' (1.2.172–5). He delighted in his time 'home schooling' his daughter. Perhaps the one-on-one time makes her a well-adjusted young lady.

THE TRAP OF THINKING

There is no way to read, to study or to perform Shakespeare without thinking. I'm sure many people are drawn to Shakespeare's work primarily because of the profound thought it provokes. This by no means excludes the emotional challenges of Shakespeare and SBB. If we only intellectualize the text, we would be no more than amateur scholars. Finding a personal resonance with the text and emotional connection to character is more a part of the SBB process than intellectualization. In fact, those of us who like to intellectualize are often trapped inside our heads, much like Prospero with his magic, keeping us from feeling. Curt constantly pushes us, particularly those of us more comfortable in our heads than in our bodies, to find where the text lives, resides, resounds in our bodies. The emotional connection, emotional memory is found in our bodies, not our heads. The problem with intellectualizing the text is the trap formulating an idea, an emotional response or mood should be rather than finding an organic connection. That thought, or intellectual choice, is an imitation of life rather than a true emotional response in the moment. It plays as pretence and the audience is either unmoved or distracted by the impression of good 'acting'. Neither one is authentic or connected to the truth in the text. Connecting with real emotional memory buried in the body communicates the truth, the whole truth, and nothing but the truth. It is in the nakedness of that truth that we find emotional development and healing.

One of my favorite aspects of SBB is the lively discussion that spontaneously bursts forth during the rehearsal process. SBB participants have learned to speak their minds and are largely unafraid to voice their diverse opinions. Discussions erupt out of scholastic debate from topics of historical sources and mythological references to etymology. Many more dialogues are rooted in the personal resonances a piece of text arouses: 'This is what I feel'; 'This is what it reminds me of'; 'Oh no, I don't see it like that at all.' As Shakespeare himself says, there is nothing right or wrong but thinking makes it so. The discussions can also provide real emotional responses, from the inevitable clash of egos inherent in any group, to the reflection of personal issues that are more glaringly obvious in those around us than we wish to admit in ourselves.

Whether thinking is rooted in academic proofing or in personal experience, thinking can become a trap, a hurdle, an impediment for an actor attempting to live in the moment. Likewise, Prospero's focus on nothing but revenge becomes the trap that he must overcome.

In a production where the focus is on the moment, the text, your acting partners and the energy of the audience, thinking can trip up an actor. The skill is learning to trust all the academic and personal work of preparation and rehearsal, and letting it go. I liken it to surfing. One's preparation is the skill; the training to ride whatever wave comes your way. Curt likens it to a jazz musician who knows the structure of a melody and has the proficiency of his instrument, and then can riff on the energy present with the other musicians and audience at the time of live performance. The moment is a once in a lifetime thing that cannot be rewound and replayed, reproduced like a book or proof-tested like an academic argument.

I see it in myself and in observation of other SBB actors as we rehearse (if I see it in them, it surely must be in me), that the mind and the ego are greatly intertwined. The author Eckhart Tolle speaks of the same observation as a condition of human (un)consciousness and the fundamental flaw of Descartes's 'I think, therefore I am.' We think we are our egos, when in fact we are much more. Sometimes a personal idea is so entrenched in ego that any comment construed as criticism is taken as an attack. As actors, at times, we get so attached to an intellectual or personal choice about a character or line-reading, the ego tries to prove it is right at all costs. Supporting the decision is what seems right, and when the moment doesn't support the predetermined choice, the ego forces the issue, and it feels like failure. When one holds a choice or an idea as the ideal, and the ideal is not achieved, the effect can be devastating to the ego. The choice to defend the decision becomes the focus rather than speaking the truth, and the moment is lost. And the truth in the moment is all that really matters.

EPILOGUE

The evil that men do lives after them; / The good is oft interred with their bones.   — Antony in *Julius Caesar*

Being incarcerated often feels like being interred – dead to the world, dead to members of my family, dead to the church of my youth and former community. I imagine that if I am remembered, it is more likely for the evil I have done, eclipsing any good that may have occurred prior to or after all that surrounds the commission of my crime. There is nothing inherent in a punitive justice system that requires me to look within myself or take personal responsibility. The ongoing work of Shakespeare Behind Bars facilitates the rare occasion of personal reflection to take responsibility for my personal choices, as well as providing an opportunity to remember and encourage my goodness. It doesn't ignore my shadow-self, but holds a mirror up to it, enabling me to embrace what I'd split from or hidden. The pursuit of character within the confines of SBB opens me to all aspects of my self (SELF) and embraces them in a holistic way.

Shakespeare Behind Bars, and more particularly, the friendship and mentorship of Curt L. Tofteland, has been the most humanizing and healing experience of my incarceration. Curt does not excuse my past behaviour, nor should it be excused. He sees me as an individual of worth and potential, and even redemption – an extremely rare commodity in the warehouse wasteland of incarceration. He challenges all of us in SBB to rise above our past and current circumstance, while being totally responsible for who we were, who we are, and who we want to be. Shakespeare is the practice and Curt is the sensei who gently guides us to our own personal discoveries, self-enlightenment and healing, and helps us to develop our own healthy sense of community and family. He also reminds those of us who have taken another life, that we are not only responsible for living our own life with integrity, we have the responsibility to make up for – as best we can – the life we took. No one else in my prison experience has ever even hinted at such a concept, let alone encouraged or supported such an effort.

Shakespeare Behind Bars is a program of choice. No one is compelled to participate with a carrot of educational good-time (time reduction earned and deducted from minimum serve-out dates), fulfilment of sentencing guidelines, or parole board requirements dangled in front of our noses. We self-select this often difficult but ultimately rewarding process of soul-searching, personal responsibility and truth telling. Our greatest mantra is 'tell the truth'. As we strive to tell the truth of a character with Shakespeare's eloquent words, we must first examine our own personal truth to reflect and resound a character's truth.

Prospero is not finished with me yet, nor I with him. In 2003, it was my blindness, my overwhelming drive for control, my prejudice towards those who navigate the world differently from me, and the desire to create a better world for my daughter that were my strongest connections to Prospero. If I took on the role again today, he would be a very different man, as I myself am in a different place than I was six years ago. The moments then cannot be recreated now. As I'm encouraged to find the truth in the moment while working with Shakespeare's text, I see a spiritual dimension and correlation which I can apply to my everyday life.

The only path to reconciliation of my past and my future is in the present.

But release me from my bands / With the help of your two hands.   – Prospero

The momentary absolution of audience applause dissipates as they are escorted from the prison visiting room and I am strip-searched before returning to the yard and my cell.

As you from crimes would pardon'd be / Let your indulgence set me free.   – Prospero

There is no priest to sacramentally absolve me of my sin, remit my punishment or negotiate recompense and reconciliation. Sadness still stalks me, seeking inroads. The joy of connection with company and audience – potent human connection – fades as the reality of distance from those I hurt the most sinks in.

A student of *Shakespeare Behind Bars*, documentary producer Jilanne Spitzmiller responded to a viewing of the film in a way that makes me realize my pursuit of character is hardly over: 'The happy ending to this movie would be to find the guy that is totally free in his concrete prison.' This is the moment in which I live, and the experience of Shakespeare Behind Bars reminds me that there is a spark of goodness in me yet. I trust the work I've accomplished and continue the work. I stand in the moment of infinite possibility. And in this moment there is potential freedom.

SHAKESPEARE PERFORMANCES IN ENGLAND (AND WALES) 2011

CAROL CHILLINGTON RUTTER

January 6, 2011. I begin, in film mode, with a reverse shot. Last year's performance survey opened in long shot, with a view from a bridge. I was ankle-deep in snow on the old tramway bridge where it crosses the Avon, looking at another bridge, one distantly under construction three naked storeys up, bleak in the freezing winds that turned its exposed concrete blue. That bridge was connecting the nearly completed, newly rebuilt Royal Shakespeare Theatre to an eight-storey observation platform towering over it. A year later, my fancied camera shot reversed, I'm on the finished walkway bridge, standing behind steel and sheet glass looking down at a Narnia-esque winter townscape laid out like some children's board game devised by C. S. Lewis. From here, even in the gloom that passes for daylight in England in January, I see the shape of the Malvern Hills and, beyond them, I imagine Wales.

So, I muse. Who'd have put money on it? It's finished. Actually finished! The project that took three years and cost £112.8 million: the RST has reopened 'on time, on budget' (a phrase in the RSC's PR lexicon that keeps popping up like a yahoo window) and in time to celebrate the company's 50th anniversary.

Of course, it won't *officially* reopen until March when the Queen makes a visit (which will also remember the charter Peter Hall secured in 1961, ironically establishing, it was said at the time, that the 'royal' in the company's new name meant that the RSC 'virtually belongs to the nation'). And for most of us it won't *really* reopen until the inaugural production of the season hits the stage in

April. But in fact, the theatre's doors have been open to the public front of house since the end of November for tours and demonstrations and to run all the tests that license a building for performance (including the one involving a cast of 1000 locals simulating a full-scale evacuation of a capacity audience). Actors have been working on the stage for nearly as long. A couple of last season's productions have been put into the space for short runs to test the facilities. And to test the backstage, too. That's when actors venturing with whoops of delight onto their chic river-side balconies discover they can't get back into their dressing rooms. The glitch is fixed when two-way door locks are fitted.

Wandering around the 'transformed' RST, I'm struck by how much is familiar, like the Elizabeth Scott-designed 1932 façade; the art deco foyer; the *verde di prato* marble stairway sweeping down from the circle to end in the shallow fountain where punters are already pitching pennies; even the auditorium, with the thrust stage we've gotten used to after four seasons in the Courtyard. I'm impressed with the gloriously new, like the river side of the building, opening the frontage onto a promenade that's going to spread the theatre's arms wide to embrace the public if we get a summer. But I'm also disconcerted by architectural palimpsest, stumbling into things I know but see as strangely alienated, as though I've wandered onto the set of Julie Taymor's *Titus*. Like the foyer panelling. (Only now it's three storeys up, cladding the new roof-top restaurant.) Like the scalloped steel art deco box office. (But now it's less 'deco' than 'surreal', standing decommissioned on cartoon stilts over a foyer that no longer sells tickets, only interval drinks.) And like the battered stage floorboards, removed to the front of house and laid to cover the gap between the old theatre's shell and the new rotunda that sits inside it: so now spectators enter the stalls across boards that remember the footfall of thousands of stage entrances and exits.

The architects promised they'd leave 'scars' in the fabric, stripping back layers of subsequent building to uncover a self-referential archaeology remembering 'the theatre's "ghosts"'. And they have. On the ground floor, there are original unplastered walls that look like primed flats from the pre-1960s. And in the second circle (now the café) where the 'gods' used to be, there's a part-demolished section of the old auditorium's back wall, with a single forlorn seat fixed right at its top, showing the *backest* back row in the gallery – and how far, how very, very far the cheapest seats in the old RST were from the stage. ('Scars?', one commentator snorts. Fakes: design-produced 'self-inflicted wounds' whose tricksy 'trauma' yields a brand of 'false memory syndrome'.)

As the tartness of that remark shows, notices on the building are mixed. While the Royal Institute of British Architects shortlists it for the prestigious Stirling Prize, architectural journalists call it 'clunky'; 'graceless'; 'as standard, corporate, bland and wipe-clean as your local multiplex'; evoking 'the ennui of the business park'. The old 'jam factory' is transformed, all right, by its tower into 'Stalag-upon-Avon' with a profile that 'resembles a power station' and an interior as cheerless as 'Barnsley train station on a bad day'. While the *Guardian's* theatre reviewer chirps up from Row D in the stalls that the 'intimate' space 'works!', the company's leading actor, in his dressing room, growls, 'no, it doesn't'. The new vertical arrangement of the galleries may mean that no spectator is further than fifty feet from the action, but it also (for this actor) means that the theatre is 'appallingly undemocratic'. 'From the galleries spectators only see the tops of actors' heads, and from the sides of the thrust, only their backs.' I notice another 'democracy' gone. Remember the old RST's standing

tickets? Tickets you could queue up to buy on the day, even for sell-outs, for prices students could afford? Remember the thousands of us over the years who stood at the back of the stalls just behind the toffs and tiaras to see Brook's *Dream*, Nunn's *All's Well*, Hands's *Henry V*? The new theatre has places for only four standers – right at the top and so far around the sides that you're practically backstage. For now, though, I'll leave comment with the RSC's Artistic Director, the Hercules who's delivered this labour of vision, determination and love. For Michael Boyd, the new theatre is 'a miracle of a space that combines the epic and the intimate, the hugest metaphysics with the tiniest psychological detail'. Boyd's will be the first new production into the space. I add only, 'We'll see'.

HISTORIES

With all the Shakespeare history being made in Stratford this year, you could be forgiven for thinking there wasn't any happening anywhere else. But you'd be wrong. Indeed, the *histories*, thanks to Propeller touring the UK, appeared almost everywhere except in Stratford.

At this point I'd aimed at a neat segue: from the bridges of my opening conceit to the Bridge Project, the transatlantic collaboration between Sam Mendes and Kevin Spacey at the Old Vic, now in its third and final year, wanting to put their modern-dress *Richard III* against Propeller's dystopian, time-bending and gleefully anarchic touring production, reviewed in last year's *Survey* and arrived in London just days before the Vic's *Richard* opened. But alas, the commercial theatre management is interested only in the commercial reviewer. After the Vic's Press Office told me they'd run out of press tickets, the conversation went like this:

> 'I'll pay for a ticket.'
> 'We're sold out.'
> 'Can I buy a standing ticket?'
> 'We don't sell standing tickets to reviewers. The sightlines aren't that good.'

Better, I thought, than the sightlines I'd get standing outside the theatre on the Waterloo Road – but I stopped arguing. Readers who want the low-down on Spacey's *Richard* will need to consult the press, though I'm told that, unlike Propeller's, Spacey's was very much a one-man show and that it constantly bid for a connection between history and the contemporary, the daily reports we were getting from Tahrir Square and Benghazi. In case any spectator missed them, they were laid out in the programme where a 'Trail of tyranny' 'from the winter of discontent to the Arab spring' offered 'parallels between today's headline grabbing dictators' and the man it called 'the forerunner of them all'.

At the Tobacco Factory, Andrew Hilton and his designer, Harriet de Winton, resisted the temptation of the easy parallel. With neither space nor budget to indulge 'concept', he used the barest means to locate *Richard II* in the medieval past: a stained glass window was the council chamber's single light source; a throne was as seen in the Beauneveu portrait, and costumes as they appear in psalters. But he probed the contemporary by other means. Rotten regimes, the caterpillars they breed: these are effects. But where do regimes start going rotten? When did Mubarak's spine start to twist, Gaddafi's teeming nest of sons start making worm's meat of the body politic? Is the monster spectacular evidence of some original political sin, a found object? Or is he made, day by day, by acts that degrade, that deform the self and corrupt the men around him?

If Richard Gloucester by Spacey answered the first question, Richard Plantagenet in Hilton's production demonstrated the second, asking questions of identity, selfhood and the roles we play that I heard like a first run-through of *King Lear*: 'Who is it that can tell me who I am?' (Shakespeare, Hilton observes briefly in a programme note, is the 'greatest of all creators of roles' and 'remains one of the greatest analysts of our need to play them'.)

This production gave Richard space to run through a whole repertoire of roles and, by running out of roles, to discover his self. To begin

with, this king was the clown Bullingbrook (as this production made him) would later remember 'skipping . . . up and down / With shallow jesters and rash bavin wits'. His peers entered, heavyweights in black who stood like figures in funeral procession around the footing of a table tomb. Then from off-stage came an explosive giggle. A fluttering of feet. John Heffernan's lanky Richard dashed in, in white and gold, yanking at his slipped cloak, cramming his crown on over scarecrow red hair, covering himself with *faux* solemnity: 'Old John of Gaunt . . . !' What a lark it was to be king! You could 'do' the part in so many voices! From mock puzzlement over comically knit brows ('What does our cousin lay to Mowbray's charge?') to stentorian roaring ('We were not born to sue but to command') to witty *sententiae* to tickle the sycophants ('This we prescribe . . . ').

Retrospectively, that first image would haunt. Heffernan's was a king who had all the accoutrements, but wasn't ready; and they were already slipping away from him. This giddy (but never girly, never camp) adolescent who constantly wore the ambiguous half-smile that curls the lips of the stranger in *The Bacchae*: was he a monster? Surely not. He had no idea he was presiding over a political crisis in the opening debate – did he? By the time he got to Coventry, however, the flouncer was flirting with the despot: turning the appellants' accusations into faults, finagling with his counsellors to patch up the banishment, reaching piously for justification in the common good (so 'that our kingdom's earth should not be soiled . . . '), quashing objection. Mowbray's observation on banishment, played as flat misery by the solid, stolid Paul Currier, that he will be languageless, his 'native English' useless, his 'tongue' 'engaoled' to 'barren Ignorance', himself condemned to 'speechless death', got only a ranting Herod kick in the teeth: 'After our sentence, plaining comes too late!' – as if there'd been any pre-sentencing chance to 'plain'. But it was only when Richard confiscated his still-warm dead uncle's estate to fund his Irish adventures that the monster was out of the bag, released by that conscience-, custom- and time-dodging line, 'Think what you will, we . . . '. (You

41. *Richard II*, 1.1. Shakespeare at the Tobacco Factory, directed by Andrew Hilton. John Heffernan as Richard II.

could see Heffernan's Richard mentally dressing himself up as the medieval equivalent of young Idi Amin.)

It's one of the triumphs of this play that so much of it is about returns, about come-downs (from Ireland, from the walls of Flint castle, to London, to Pomfret), so the question that protesting York (played by a wonderfully flapping Roland Oliver as an early draft of Polonius) put to Richard at Gaunt's death – 'How art thou a king . . . ? – comes back over and over to re-interrogate and finally, in this production, to intrigue him. Heffernan was best when Richard was worst. He'd played out histrionics (throwing himself prostrate on England's 'dear earth'); self-deluding fantasies ('God for His Richard hath in heavenly pay . . . angels'); shrieking hysterics ('Where is Bagot . . . Bushy . . . Green . . . villains, vipers . . . !'); feeble self-indulgence ('let us sit': so they did). He'd wrong-footed his cousin in the

power hand-over: not just forcing him into a tug of war for the crown ('Here cousin, *seize* . . . ') but making him reflect, literally, on his actions. The mirror Richard called for he held up to catch the image of Bullingbrook before smashing it with his fist. He'd peeled back role after role to uncover, it appeared, the answer to York's interrogation with his own question, weeping real tears, his voice thick with grief: 'Subjected thus / How can you say to me I am a king?'

The answer to that question came at the end, when, alone at Pomfret, his cell furnished with a single stool, himself barefoot in coarse linen, Heffernan's Richard remade his kingdom, with himself its king, a man saved for thoughtfulness, populating space with small gestures of his hands. As far as studies of monsters go, Richard II ends where Richard III begins: talking to the audience. And Heffernan's quiet talking to us of a mind that might 'beget' 'thoughts' to 'people' his 'little world' (put that creative thinking against the spider, spinning plots in Gloucester's brain, or the frantic nightmare self-interrogation of the crook-back's ending) was a meditation that redeemed whatever waste Plantagenet accused himself of. This Richard, then, finding what he needed to know to live, the wastrel understanding what he'd wasted, died: his history, tragedy.

Flanking this king (like side panels in a triptych) was a magnetically inscrutable Bullingbrook: Matthew Thomas, playing the hand of his ambition so close to his chest you couldn't tell whether he held kings or knaves or whether what he aimed at was abdication or usurpation – until the moment, prompted by his canny cousin, when he thrust out his hand and the gesture was named: 'seize'. On the other side: Benjamin Whitrow's almost monastically dignified Gaunt, making 'This England' not a jingo-istic rabble-rouser – after all, there was only his decrepit brother York listening – but a lament for lost youth: their own, their nephew's, England's. (And making this speech a master class in verse speaking: I hope the youth in the wings were paying attention.) His scene with the Duchess of Gloucester (Julia Hills) was a study in geriatric weariness: she flexing arthritic fingers to fumble with her gown to cover her grief; he, repeating what it sounded like he no longer believed: 'God's is the quarrel'; 'Let heaven revenge'. Watching these two tired old people I thought of Edgar: 'World, world, O world!', and the 'strange mutations' that make the living long for death. What *were* the youth up to in this England?

In Shakespeare's sequel, Peter Hall's company playing the two parts of *Henry IV* at the Theatre Royal, Bath, told us. The active among them were rioting in the streets. The wasters were drinking their livers dead in pubs. Here again 'history' was set in the past, this time, a Victorian past, but there was plenty that the audience could hear needling the present: like that sour view of youth culture; like the old regime's wily advice to the new to 'Busy giddy minds / With foreign quarrels'. (Though as Bardolph would see, when it actually came to supplying soldiers on the ground, the advisers in the command room – *pace* Afghanistan –

would have to 'strategize'.) I doubt that Rumour's cynical thoughts on the 'blunt monster', the 'multitude', and the 'continual slanders' it scoffs off gossip's 'tongues' has ever sounded more nastily topical than in this summer when the News International phone-hacking scandal broke.

The world Simon Higlett designed was Dickensian: a Coketown warehouse interior, industrial architecture as monumentally self-important as a Gradgrind, with thick, twisted brick columns supporting a vaulted roof. It was a busy space: ladders led to viewing platforms; several exits left the shop floor; panels part-revealed rooms beyond. But the work done here was evidently dirty: the bricks were scarred, smoke-blackened; plaster had dropped from the walls; dereliction weighed in the air in artificial light that, when the power source surged, reached what you might call 'gloomy'. It was also a theatrical space. An arch spanned the width like a false proscenium. The move to the Boar's Head was made when it lowered, crushing the grim cathedral to capitalism into what felt like a subterranean thieves' kitchen, low roofs for low-lifers. (And a nice joke, that England's industry rested on the slackers and dissolutes sloshing around in Mistress Quickly's basement.) The place made your heart sink.

The brilliance of Higlett's design was that it didn't end there. It gave spectators the reverse shot, of epic England. Thus, in the opening sequence, the brick backwall slid away. Revealed behind was a distance-less long view through dream-like fog of a giant in military blue who took the crown he held loosely in his hand and pulled it down hard on his head before stepping forward, an icon tripped into action. Such moves between the narrow view and the panoramic would punctuate this production. In *Part 1* we'd watch Hotspur's army in silhouette cross the horizon headed for Shrewsbury followed, half a beat later, by a Monty Python parody, the halting, limping, stumbling gaggle of ragtag recruits to Falstaff's outfit: 'food for powder' on parade. In *Part 2* we'd cut from the open landscape of Shallow's orchard to a closet, the dying King in bed. The final stage picture would reprise the first: the back wall flying out, a giant in military blue stepping forward, his significant gesture not to plant the crown on his head – he was already wearing it, put there by his father – but to raise his sword. Ah! We were headed for France. For empire.

We got the picture: narrow/wide; monumental/crushed; flush/bust. This England was bi-polar. As things progressed, we saw England constituted of twins who were either split personalities or opposites of their doubles. Take David Yelland's magnificent Henry IV. Perpetually in cavalry uniform, he was the sort of nerveless military man you'd imagine single-handedly spiking the guns at Balaclava. But his original gesture was a giveaway. Nobody had crowned him. He'd had to do it himself. He'd 'snatch'd' 'honour' 'with boisterous hand'. And that knowledge was like a brain tumour, constantly chafed by the crown his son said later 'fed on the body' of his dad. Thus: two Henries. One was imperious. (Poor old Worcester – Philip Voss at his silken best, managing to be both cringing and obnoxious, a lackey in a morning suit with a poisonous line in sarcasm – didn't know what hit him when 'GET THEE GONE!' ploughed into him.) Henry's double, though, was a casualty, an invalid who, in *Part 2*, shuffled around clutching his crown to his chest like a mobile heart monitor.

Fantasizing about changelings and fairy kidnaps mixing up boys at birth, Yelland-as-father had to be struck by an excruciating irony: Hal and Hotspur looked like twins. (Were the actors cast as such? They could be future Antipholuses – or Dromios.) Same hair. Same beard. Same build. Same boots. Same habits, infuriating the king. Both rebels. But opposites: Hotspur appeared in uniform; Hal, slopping around half-dressed. Yelland's Henry twitched, listening to the youth who, having taken them in battle was taking his time explaining that he 'did deny no prisoners' (but nevertheless would keep them). Henry paced. Clenched and unclenched his fists. But didn't interrupt the dilatory, self-excusing account of the post-battle popinjay with his pouncet-box and endless chat – indeed, appeared so captivated by Ben Mansfield's virile, charismatic and plausible Hotspur that he had to pull himself up to remember

where the whole folderol had started: 'Why yet he doth deny his prisoners!' Later, when Lady Percy (Katie Lightfoot) was as exasperated trying to get a straight answer out of her husband – 'I'll break thy little finger, Harry' – Mansfield's Hotspur simply swept her up in his arms and carried her off, roaring with laughter, like Petruccio taking another Kate to bed. Did I call Matthew Thomas's Bullingbrook 'magnetic'? Mansfield's Hotspur was true north!

Cut to the Boar's Head. Cut to a rogues' gallery of bit players drawn by Cruikshank. Cut to another youth fielding awkward questions ('shall there be gallows standing in England when thou art king?'). Tom Mison's Hal was first seen in slack shirt-tails bent over a basin throwing water on his face. That was a gesture, like so much actorly detail in this production, that registered far beyond the event: I'd remember it late in the day in Hal's bombastic promise to his dad to 'scour his shame' with ablutions of blood. He'd clearly been up all night. His knees were locked in hangover mode. But he'd be ready for the day. The cold water would see to that. Held in the gesture, then, were this Hal's twin tendencies: a delinquent who knew how to use a face flannel; a bad boy with the means to clean up his act. The great pleasure of Mison's performance was that he held self-contradiction in tension throughout. Thus, when the mountainous tangle of what looked like a month's laundry piled up behind him came to life with a bovine snort and John Falstaff worked himself loose from the linen wreckage to emerge like a squinty-eyed boar from a wallow dressed like Mr Pickwick in a walrus-sized floppy red neckerchief, Mison's Hal played along with the game of imagining futures ('when thou art king'). But at the same time he poked sceptical fun at the notion of a sot clock-watching. In that first scene he was indulgent, playing straight man to Falstaff's invention. But he knew his plan, delivered it as flat reportage: 'I know you all . . .' The complexity of his relationship with Falstaff only emerged in the fall-out to the Gadshill caper, when we got the measure of Desmond Barrit's Sir John.

This was Barrit's second go at Falstaff. He played him ten years ago at the RSC. Back then he had

42. *Henry IV Part 1*, 2.4. The Peter Hall Company at the Theatre Royal, Bath, directed by Peter Hall and Cordelia Monsey. Desmond Barrit as Falstaff, Edward Harrison as Poins, Tom Mison as Prince Hal, Alex Blake as Peto, Lizzie McInnery as Mistress Quickly, Cornelius Booth as Bardolph.

both the girth and the guile for the part and made Falstaff a roistering life-force. Now, despite all his fantastically delusive claims to be 'in the vaward of our youth', this Falstaff showed the wear and tear of his debauchery, the too much sack, the too little bread, felt intimations of mortality. Liverish, lumpen, querulous, dragging around bloated obesity whose real problem was the dead weight of its spiritual avoirdupois, this proxy dad was evidently on a twin track with his double, the real dad, the king. The only roister left was a glint in the eye. He delivered his observation black: 'I am not only witty in myself, but the cause that wit is in other men.' And jokes like that felt like IOUs to keep grinning death at bay. Making laughter, this Falstaff was always the first to stop. After Gadshill, when Hal lambasted him, he could keep

up, trading insult for insult: 'bed-presser . . . horse-breaker'; 'eel-skin . . . bull's pizzle'. It was like bait to a carp shot back in torpedoes. Finally outed by the prince (triumphantly throwing down the trump, 'What trick hast thou now?'), he went silent. But only for the time it took one lip to hike, freeze, then spread from criminal snigger to broad, beatific smile, as he trumped Hal's ace high with a wild-card jack that doubled as royal flush: 'I knew ye as well as he that made ye! . . . instinct!' Mison's Hal simply collapsed. Routed.

But when they played this double act the second time, the 'Do thou stand for my father' routine produced a very different ending. When Hal-as-Henry launched into his epithets – 'a devil . . . trunk of humours . . . bolting-hutch of beastliness' – the spectators on this morality

43. *Henry IV Part 2*, 5.5. The Peter Hall Company at the Theatre Royal, Bath, directed by Peter Hall and Richard Beecham. Tom Mison as Prince Hal, Desmond Barrit as Falstaff, full company.

tale roared with laughter. And kept on roaring even when the prince's voice hardened and the names got crueller, meaner, uglier – 'bombard of sack . . . stuffed cloak-bag of guts'. Then Hal lost the plot. Started playing for real. 'Vice! . . . Iniquity! . . . Ruffian! . . . Vanity in years!' Falstaff had stopped laughing some while ago. Battered, he stood dumb. The rest fell deadly silent. A silence that felt interminable. Then the old pattermaster cranked himself up to ask, gently: 'Whom means your grace?' He tried like a music hall turn to get the laughter going again – but Hal simply wasn't biddable. 'Banish plump Jack' wasn't wheedling. It was grim. And Hal withdrew the hand Falstaff had taken. 'I do' he spoke as King. Silence. Then as Hal, he added in a voice as cold as that morning's water on his face, 'I will.' Here, Falstaff couldn't take that as an answer. 'Play out the

play!', even as the knock at the door interrupted the action, and again, 'Play out the play', eyeballing Hal, was giving the lad the chance to renege on 'I will'. In *Part 2* when we returned yet again to comic turns performing double bluffs with identity – Hal showing up at the Boar's Head disguised as a drawer then stepping forward to mock the 'withered elder', doxy perched on his knee, with (an oh, yeah, sure) 'you knew me!', Falstaff refused the bait. 'No.' The negative was leaden. This Falstaff had simply run out of scams. This Falstaff rejected Hal before Hal got round to rejecting him.

Hall's production didn't get everything right. It was a mistake to exclude the metaphysical, to play Owen Glendower (Robert East, a much better actor than allowed here) as (just) a boring old codger. After all, Glendower reads the runes right. When you're in Wales, withering bay trees are a tip-off. So he cancels his date in Shrewsbury. Hotspur, meanwhile, gets correspondence that spells things out. He gets letters *in English* telling him, straight up, to run – but daffs them aside, unread. So who's the dope? (I wish directors could find a way of pointing that moment: to see the letter York writes in 4.4 delivered in 5.2, and how all the post that flies across these two plays comes to this, when there's still time: written instructions saving Hotspur's life. That Mansfield's Hotspur could 'not read them now' rendered history as tragedy.)

It was also a mistake to cast Philip Voss as Justice Shallow. I believed in his (bigged-up) life at the Inns of Court – but he was clearly a townie who wouldn't have known a pippin from an old spot. And where was that accent from? More Ruritania than rural Gloucestershire. Still, the picture of him sitting on a bench reminiscing with the other old geezers – Silence (Robert East, much more happily parted), Falstaff (meditative, out-talked, out-fantasized) – was magic.

There were things in the production that I've never seen done better. Like the final show-down between Hal and Hotspur, choreographed electrifyingly by Kate Waters (surely the best fight arranger in the business), close combat with sabres that went on, and on, and exhaustingly on; and at the end, a ferocious Hotspur, super-human, who refused to die, whom Hal had to *keep on killing*, on his knees, on guard long after the opponent's breath blurted its last: 'And food for...' Sides heaving, Mison held the silence, couldn't speak, listened for breathing, got his own breath back, then finished the sentence: 'For worms, brave Percy'. Those thoughts on 'ill-weaved ambition' were bitter reportage: oh, the waste of it! There was no sentiment, no grief until, wearily retrieving his fallen weapon, he turned, saw Falstaff and yelped. That sound was raw anguish: 'old acquaintance!' (This lad, we'd see again in *Part 2*, found it much easier to tell his dads he loved them when they were dead.) He fell on the body, embraced it, fisted away tears, then pulled himself to attention to deliver his second eulogy of the day, this one quite consciously

rendering as comic patter couplets that rhymed 'thee' with 'vanity': a kind of Falstaffian homage-as-recuperation, the kind of eulogy Falstaff might have pronounced upon Falstaff. It was a perfectly pitched moment – that not even the old ruffian's turning up alive could wreck.

What emerged in the clear story-telling of Hall's direction (assisted by two talented lieutenants, Richard Beecham and Cordelia Monsey) was the plays' wondrous shapeliness, scene echoing scene; speech revisiting speech; a notion that England was making progress by replaying its past. Case in point: the 'do thou stand for my father' patriarchal interrogation scene. We saw various versions of it five times, the last when the Lord Chief Justice (Paul Bentall), sweating, resigned, knowing he was for the chop in the new regime – having jailed Prince Hal for contempt – still defended that action, arguing that 'in th'administration of his law' he acted in 'the person of your father'. Now he proposed that Harry 'be...the father'. Mison's Hal paused. Then became Henry. Standing for the father, imagining a future when he would 'see a son of mine / Offend you and obey you, as I did', the new king took a new dad, adopting 'Justice...as a father to my youth'. So the Father of Lies would be out of a job.

<h2 style="text-align:center">COMEDIES</h2>

I'd intended to review two *Much Ado*s, the one (much hyped) at Wyndham's opening only days after the other (less thought-of) at the Globe. But here we go again. Alas, the commercial theatre...blah, blah, blah. Sorry: no review tickets. If you want to know what David Tennant made of Benedick opposite his *Dr Who* co-star, Catherine Tate, you'll have to read the newspapers. Only I can tip you this wink: the director, Josie Rourke, set the play in 1982, the fleet on shore leave in Gibraltar, so men behaving badly had behind them the Falklands, and the women had Germaine Greer. At the Globe in his debut there, Jeremy Herrin went for something 'traditional'. (Counter-instinctively? Until then, he'd been best known for directing new plays at the Royal Court. Funny what happens to directors when they imagine Shakespeare under thatch.) Herrin shifted Messina from Spanish-ruled Sicily further south, to Morocco, with costumes that looked like Elizabethan Marrakesh and the English bodies inside them, 1970s-style hippies: when he showed up, Dogberry wore a fez. Fortunately, the set (also designed by Mike Britton) made more sense and gave actors better material to work with. The tiring house wall was handsomely panelled with dark wood grille-work cut à la morisco (that put me in mind of the Alhambra in Granada): perforated surfaces; walls you could look through; a culture architecturally designed for 'noting'. Along the balcony were trained orange branches, laden with bright fruit; and on a fore-stage extension, shallow pools of ankle-deep water. This was a hot place: of hot-headed youth, of seething revenges, of tongues that whipped themselves into a lather shooting off volleys of barbed wit. You wished the men – hot-foot from war – would take a paddle and cool down. Certainly, the over-heated notion they'd brought home from camp of 'friend'-ship as male bonding glueing 'love' to 'honour' to 'reputation' wasn't fit for domestic purpose. I'm thinking here about how Claudio's sour disappointment in 2.1 – 'Friendship is constant in all other things, / Save . . . love' – travelled to the rancid 'Give not this rotten orange to your friend' in 4.1.

Messina's was a culture built on internal contradictions: 'I am trusted with a muzzle and enfranchised with a clog', sneered Matthew Pidgeon's toxic Don John. (In the chemistry of this production, he was definitely the heavy metal, the plutonium.) Talking of himself, the terms of reconciliation with his brother, he might have been describing Messina at large. This place cultivated honour – but expected betrayal; hyped courtesy – but practised disdain; wanted truth – but went through elaborate rituals to perform lies (the masked dance, the paired over-hearing scenes, the scam at Hero's window); fetishized 'noting' – but couldn't see the nose on its own face; and in the lewd pun loaded into the homonym that makes noting/nothing slang for 'vagina', made everything and nothing of women's chastity.

44. *Much Ado About Nothing*, 3.1. Globe Theatre, directed by Jeremy Herrin. Ony Uhiara as Hero, Eve Best as Beatrice, Helen Weir as Ursula.

The juvenile leads walked through this cultural minefield like a couple of raw recruits. Philip Cumbus's Claudio ricocheted from emotional extreme to extreme, a kid with a beard, but still no man: tongue-tied, declaring his love for Hero to his Prince (Ewan Stewart); guileless, unsuspecting, *elated* that the prince should proxy woo her; bitter, betrayed, thinking he'd won her (the strings on his mask he twisted as he talked read like a metaphor for thoughts knotting his heart in arterial tangles); brutal in church; conscienceless after the fact (until he got the point of Benedick's straight-talking); desperate at Hero's tomb (though it was a mistake to bring her on for burial); saved, through tears, at the end. Ony Uhiara's Hero felt deliberately superficial or, better said, inscrutable, non-disclosing:

virginal 'fair paper' awaiting (male) inscription. That her eyes were settled on Claudio was giddily clear from her first scene. That she would accept the suitor daddy approved – 'remember what I told you'; 'you know your answer' – was equally, depressingly clear. Where duty trumped desire, where to be culturally true women had to be emotionally false, no wonder men should presume women 'inconstant'. Where Uhiara triumphed was in the wrecked wedding scene: Cumbus's Claudio didn't just accuse her; he assaulted her; the Prince, exiting, spat in her face; her father (Joseph Marcell) savaged her. And she felt every blow, took every word on the heart, both utterly dazed and hyper-responsive, a Hero who in waves of meticulously observed reactions registered the wrongs men did making women 'nothings'.

She was lucky to have her cousin Beatrice's arms around her, and, minutes later, to have Beatrice, alone with Benedick, stop dead in its tracks his habits of a life-time (and stop the show) with 'Kill Claudio'. In that imperative the honour code came home to roost. Beatrice had hit the mark – ouch! – when she'd called him 'the prince's jester', 'his gift, devising impossible slanders': how prescient, given the guys he hung out with. Now, Charles Edwards's Benedick, whose trajectory in the military had evidently been from boot-camp clown to tent-flap entertainer, had to decide for the cocks or hens, and whether he was chicken. Earlier, he'd had trouble with words. 'Hu – hu – hu – husband', he'd stuttered, his Tin-tin quiff shuddering, his pop-eyes ping-ponging. He'd used his privileged time with the audience down on the forestage in conversation or stuck up a ladder in soliloquy to endear himself across some of the best lines Shakespeare ever wrote: 'If her breath were as terrible as her terminations...'; 'he is turned orthography'; 'When I said I would die a bachelor...'; 'the world must be peopled'. His transformation from silly ass to honour killer was electrifying. And not before time.

For me, though, the star of this production was Eve Best's Beatrice. Obviously her uncle's orphan, obviously the house's poor relation, plain as a bread-and-butter pudding (and her hair evidently cut around the pudding basin), this Beatrice

was a veteran campaigner in the word-war with Benedick, and had the scars to prove it. To the gentle gibe from the Prince that 'you have lost' Benedick's 'heart', her riposte was brittle. Not lost; for he had only 'lent it... awhile'. Her damaged mirth, we glimpsed, was the lint on her wounds. But moments later, when, cued by her jokes about spinsters leading apes in hell, the Prince offered to get her a husband and asked, 'Will you have me, lady?' she was as thrown as Benedick would later be on 'Kill...' She did a double take. He was serious! Overwhelmed, her feet lost co-ordination, started away in opposite directions. The ugly duckling, realizing herself mistaken for a swan, flapped, fled.

The end of her eavesdropping scene was delicious. The scam started with women's work: laundry; a sheet hung between the stage pillars that Hero and Ursula (Helen Weir) made mischievously to slide up and down as a gigantic game of strip tease, exposing (but not quite) what they knew was hiding behind. When lapwing-Beatrice finally ducked out from under the sheet to face spectators, it momentarily draped around her. We saw a bride in a veil, a lass tucked in bed, a chastened, self-reproaching Beatrice – 'What fire is in mine ears?' – trussed up in the early modern garment of the penitent. The wry comment she'd made on her birth – about her mother who cried, the star that danced – wonderfully caught at the double impulses of a performance that was feisty and spikey, pained and rueful, outrageous and maddening, gawky, frequently graceful, very, very funny – and ultimately (at the end, with the phoney warriors' eyes glued to the stolen documents that informed against them) wonder-full.

The other main stage Shakespeare in this summer's Globe repertoire was *All's Well That Ends Well*, an interesting pairing with *Much Ado*, both comic takes on love and war and lads who need to grow up, but what either of them was doing in a season billed 'The Word is God' is anybody's guess. The set design (by Michael Taylor) was handsome enough. The tiring house wall was hung, from the heavens to the stage floor, with canvas cloths printed in black and white like ink drawings, giving trees in the foreground and, behind, a long vista ending at the vanishing point in a castle: so Rousillion was set in perspective against the Court. The late-Elizabethan costumes were sumptuous, but went for decoration, not anything logical they were saying about the characters or story. Would the Countess have shed mourning for that gorgeous embroidered gown quite so soon? Would Helena arrive at court in rich green velvet? Anyway, isn't that the wrong place to put her costume change? And Parolles: he's a walking tailor's dummy, an early modern fashionista. So I went with the high-heeled baubled boots, the orange slashed sleeves on the black velvet doublet, even the lace cuffs. But the stand-up parrot hair? The red sash wound around his temples like a sweatband on a waiter in a sushi bar? In that get-up not just La Few but Bertram must have seen through him as a 'window of lattice'.

The problem was that the actors never got near the heart of this most introverted, secret and riddling of scripts. Janie Dee's Countess was more early Ayckbourn than late Shakespeare: shallow and shrill and simply without the depth of feeling or felt memory to make sense of enigmatic speeches like 'If ever we are nature's these are ours . . . ' And what oddities: she slapped Helena across the face to stop the girl's tears on 'No more of this . . . ' and later cuffed her son, bestowing the family ring on him. Ellie Piercy, in practically her first Shakespeare job, was simply o'er-parted for Helena. She couldn't perform inwardness (a tough enough assignment for anyone, on the Globe's open platform stage). And James Garnon (Parolles), tediously hyperactive, couldn't stop mugging up outwardness.

But the worst disaster was Sam Crane's Bertram. Bertram is Shakespeare's most magnificent portrait of the graceless adolescent as churl, where he invents Holden ('all adults are phoneys') Caulfield. Looking at the play from Bertram's point of view, you've got to be on his side. He's barely out of the nursery. His study has evidently been all Malory. He just wants to 'do' heroics, 'do' dragon-bashing, do the stuff boys think makes them men. Leaving for Court, he might arrive in Camelot! But then, getting stalled there, no wonder he's irked, 'forehorse to a smock', 'Creaking [his] shoes on

the plain masonry' while the other lads are off to Italy, licensed to kill. Doomed to matrimony, what could be worse? 'O my Parolles, they have *married me*!' is as anguished, spelling the end of heroic dreams, as is Helena's ''twere all one / That I should love a bright particular star', spelling the end of romantic ones. So Dr Johnson got him right. He is 'noble without generosity, and young without truth'. He's a 'coward', a 'profligate' who, when he thinks his first wife 'dead by his unkindness, sneaks home to a second marriage, is accused by a woman he has wronged, defends himself by falsehood', and, in conclusion, 'is dismissed to happiness'.

But not 'dismissed' before he's been put through the wringer of Shakespeare's play! Not before he's seen his fatuous boy's-own heroics exposed in Parolles's Captain Spurio; seen himself humiliated, exposed as liar and cheat; felt his pretentiousness and arrogance scoured by the cool heat of Diana's mocking riddles (played here by Naomi Cranston with lovely understatedness); and has done that thing that youths do: he's grown up. He's ready for Helena. So what did the director, John Dove, do? Wrecked him! He sentimentalized Bertram: had him proleptically recuperated (because subliminally *in luuuuv*) from the off. He brought Crane into close-up with Helena in the first scene's farewell; had him fondly kiss her on the forehead, pocket her (eye-catching) green handkerchief which he'd used to dab her tears – which afterwards he always had to hand. He twisted it in the 'married me' speech; stared at it hard, as though having second thoughts, on 'She will away tonight?'; clenched it when he was made general of the duke's horse; was still running it through his hands in the final scene while he contemplated, with La Few, a second marriage. That most choked of Helena's convoluted utterances, 'Strangers and foes do sunder and not kiss', answered with Bertram's cruellest rebuff, 'Pray you stay not . . . ', she begging a kiss, he denying it, here produced a long, deep, lingering kiss and a Bertram who held out a yearning hand to protest Helena's departure. This was a Bertram Parolles had to *drag* off to the wars – and to the interval, with the apologetic ad lib 'Just give me fifteen minutes with him.' (Oh dear!) But a Bertram-in-love in Act 1 short-cuts the journey of the next four acts. He and Helena are both pilgrims in this play. And if they don't go the distance, they don't arrive at the miracles Shakespeare writes at their ending.

Two productions of *The Comedy of Errors* showed this script's tolerance to extremes of performance. Take their Lucianas as epitomes of their styles. Both were blue-stockings. Both, girls in glasses. At the Tobacco Factory, Ffion Jolly was a primly earnest Edwardian Luciana whose stockings were (also) metaphors: a Pankhurst foot-soldier with definite views on marriage (which was why she wasn't having it) who, when she wasn't preaching to her sister, spent her time reading, through thick-rimmed tortoise shell spectacles, no doubt, Wollstonecraft's *Vindication*. For Propeller on tour, David Newman's Luciana's blue stockings were outrageously actual – but fell well short of feminist politics: leggings that didn't quite reach the shocking pink socks filling the screaming peacock blue heels tied up in pretty bows. Cadillac-winged glasses by Dame Edna. Handbag by Mrs Thatcher. Hair by 'Bride of Frankenstein'. Halter dress with circle skirt, fetching 'kiss me' bows down the front, and 'unbutton me' button-up sweater on top: straight out of 1950s America. This was a Luciana as prim as Jolly's who offered marriage guidance counsel with knees glued together. But where Jolly's Luciana fended off her wooer with righteous indignation, Newman's used karate chops. At the Tobacco Factory, then, Andrew Hilton directed, and Harriet de Winton designed, *The Comedy of Errors* as drawing-room comedy; Edward Hall with Michael Pavelka made it high-camp, high-octane farce. But both of them made room for big mood swings.

Hilton's Ephesus was a serious place, populated by Phileas Foggs in linen suits and cravats. The Duke (Paul Currier) in a fez and frock coat sitting at a desk littered with court papers, inkwell and blotter, the back wall of his office the heavy studded door to the prison, listened to the Syracusan in front of him with mounting dismay. David Collins's belt-and-braces greyed Egeon told a family story ludicrous for its sequence of improbably heaped-up disasters and near-missed recoveries. (Surely this play's generic default setting is farce!) But when that story reached its heart-rending conclusion (so, maybe not farce after all), it hit the brakes into a skid of tragic irony. This weary father had reached a place where he was happy to die *if only* 'all my travels' could 'warrant me they' – his sons – '*live*'. That last word glowed like prophecy in Collins's mouth. Slap-stick death. Miraculous life. This story deserved a reprieve. Giving it, how could the Duke know the interim would be mayhem?

Several things emerged from Hilton's 'concept-lite' direction. The Edwardian design helped locate class divisions, Upstairs/Downstairs. It normalized a kind of male street-life, gents as flâneurs lunching out of the city where of course, if your lady-wife at home got the vapours, there was hospitality to be found among Lady Pliants elsewhere. Locked out of doors, Matthew Thomas's Antipholus/Ephesus was murderous – but recovered when Kate Kordel's Courtesan wafted past, the kind of vision you see in sepia vintage 'art' photographs, exotic, beddable, in oriental silk out-door kimono. It normalized, too, the Dromios' treatment as bashable drones. Gareth Kennerley (Ephesus) and Richard Neale (Syracuse), skin-headed, in waistcoats and footman's trousers, were not just visual but temperamental doubles of dogged endurance – who made you long for the violent class adjustments just around the corner, post-1918.

But what most seriously emerged was not an investigation of nostalgia, the longing for the lost twin, the lost self told in Antipholus of Syracuse's (Dan Winter) beautifully poignant but bamboozled narration of his history, searching 'like a drop of water / That in the ocean seeks another drop' (a recall of *The Symposium* where the joke-meister Aristophanes tells us we're all selves radically amputated from our other halves). The search for fraternal twins might be one thing. The tougher issue was *marital* twins – and how you put your self back together when the flesh-of-your-flesh that you thought was your other half disclaims any knowledge of you. This *Comedy* staged the tragedy of Adriana. At home, contesting gender disparity

45. *The Comedy of Errors*, 2.2. Shakespeare at the Tobacco Factory, directed by Andrew Hilton. Dorothea Myer-Bennett as Adriana, Doron Davidson as Merchant, Ffion Jolly as Luciana.

('Why should their liberty be more than ours?') Dorothea Myer-Bennett's gorgeous Adriana with flame-thrower red hair coiffed in modest Edwardian twist was a wife no husband should keep waiting. (But you could hear her souring around the gills, growing shrewish – 'None but asses will be bridled so' – and wailing self-pityingly: 'Hath homely age th'alluring beauty took / From my poor cheek?') Taking to the streets to arrest wayward Antipholus, she'd dressed to the nines, put a feather in her cap, shocked her little sister (who audibly gasped) when she launched into that language about the 'harlot brow' and the 'adulterate blot'. Back at home, supposed to be dining with the man she'd lured into some suggestive private space 'above', she sat in corset and petticoat, alone; he, across the stage diagonal, remote, ignoring her, while Dromio/Ephesus covered their sad silence with a song. She got her revenge spilling her story to the Duke (and a round from the audience: she never took breath; a tour de force). But then Antipholus/Ephesus momentarily got his when she squawked, 'I see TWO husbands.' Her life was about to improve. And so

was her sister's. The wooer who'd wooed her? He wasn't her sister's husband! 'What I told you then', began Antipholus/ Syracuse. But Luciana was already facing him – and had whipped off her glasses.

The errors Propeller's *Comedy* staged were ballsier, even farcically cartoonish. (They're an all-male company, after all, and they push gender jokes to outrageous limits.) But the mistaken identities and false encounters were immediately familiar to the audience as epitomes of frantic modern life. We recognized all the trappings. The Goldsmith (Tom Padden), in gold lamé, delivered his products in a heaped-up shopping trolley; Adriana (Robert Hands), ordering Dr Pinch (Tony Bell) to get to work on her husband, swiped her credit card through the handset he instantly produced; Antipholus/Ephesus (Sam Swainsbury), locked out of his house, screamed through the intercom before dragging it off the wall along with miles of wire and stomping on it like a demented gorilla – but still couldn't silence the damned buzzing. Carted off to cure, he and Dromio/Ephesus (Jon Trenchard) were stuffed butt first into municipal wheelie bins: Antipholus made his bounce across the stage, powered by ranting.

This *Comedy* was set in a post-consumerist present at that international schlock tourist destination (where the 'emptor' must always, *always* 'caveat'), the permanently under-construction Costa del Concrete: Dromio/Syracuse (Richard Frame) arrived with a Gap Year-sized pack on his back sprouting every bit of holiday equipment from fishing net to life preserver. Metal scaffolding stood in place of (abandoned) resort development. The litter was piled around its footings like industrial compost, the grimness made worse by the tacky strings of coloured party lights sagging through it. At the back and sides, corrugated metal sheets graffitied with spray-painted pop art looked like the security entrance to a building site. This set was pure genius. (Pavelka has to be among the smartest designers working on Shakespeare today.) Collapsible and adaptable (because its structural components had to double on tour for the abattoir world of *Richard III*), it was also brilliantly constructed for farce. It made space to stack images on top of each other. (On cue, doors above opened during Egeon's back-story monologue to show first the 'goodly twins', his sons – now grown; in identical purple cords and pink floral shirts; intent on grooming identical quiffs – then the 'mean' set of 'twins' he'd 'bought': the Dromios, 'identical' in fright wigs, smiley-face T-shirts and blue bovver-boots.) But it also made space for manic cross-traffic: Keystone Cops-style chases through opposite doors that opened and closed so fast they nearly spun on their hinges.

What we saw in Hilton's *Comedy* was bewilderment. In Hall's, we got a study of manic frustration: hyper-stressed, strung-out humans in melt-down, as if Lear's 'Does any here know me?' were reproduced as Munch's *Scream*. And it wasn't just the mistaken visitor, the cold-shouldered wife, and the unjustly thumped servants who wanted to scream. It was, too, the duped goldsmith, the dumped doxy, the set-upon quack doctor (last seen here in a parody of exorcism streaking naked through the audience, a lit firecracker protruding from his bum). It was all hilarious – but, joking apart, it was also seriously relevant to audiences who know more than a little these days about identity theft and the loss of self in systems that refuse to recognize you or consign you to that virtual limbo called 'hold'.

In the pre-set, lads hung around in local uniform – aertex sports jerseys in eye-watering primary colours, sombreros – playing 1980s numbers on guitar, accordion, maracas, while a dumpy dude with a greasy manner (Wayne Cater) papered the audience with dodgy adverts and a bandy-legged cop in leather trousers that quacked like a duck when he walked (Dominic Tighe) bullied spectators in an atrocious Spanish accent about their mobile phones. This was an Ephesus both on the skids and on the make. Momentarily, activity in the town hit the 'pause' button while John Dougall's Egeon told his story to an impassive Solinus who smoked a cigar (Richard Clothier, in red satin suit a slimline Santa would kill for) before putting a pistol to his prisoner's temple. When the reprieve came, the pace shifted into over-drive.

The boy band in their daft hats would be a constant presence – a chorus, a crowd – but we'd gradually become aware that its make-up was constantly shifting (as though under the influence of 'nimble jugglers that do deceive the eye'), lads slipping out to re-enter in a named part (male or female) then resurfacing in the ensemble. So the audience experienced this *Comedy* as a series of stand-ups, double acts and massed production numbers. The most literally disgraceful was Tony Bell's, who emerged through dry ice to perform Dr Pinch as a Pentecostal televangelist from somewhere below the Mason/Dixon line, with a full song-and-dance routine (complete with angel-winged backing group) stomping out the chorus: 'I've been SAVED!' The rectal firecracker? He deserved what he got.

Everywhere in this production actorly inventiveness rose to the occasions Shakespeare gives his players. Every time he came on stage Richard Frame's holiday-seeking Dromio/Syracuse arrived in a different virtual vehicle and parked it up. Fleeing greasy Nell he used the width of the

46. *The Comedy of Errors*, 2.1. Propeller on tour, directed by Edward Hall. David Newman as Luciana, Jon Trenchard as Dromio/Ephesus, Robert Hands as Adriana.

proscenium to gauge the breadth of her hips. At home, Robert Hands's Adriana was a zoomorphic dog's dinner of a female: bats for eye-lashes, from neck to thigh, a hornet in gold-and-black belted frock, a pair of languid boa constrictors for legs sheathed in leopard-skin spandex (that she'd lock around the man she later took for her husband). On the street, she strutted like a high fashion model on the Milan catwalk – but acted like a one-woman SWAT team. (Though it was her little sister in that top-of-wedding-cake dress who, when things got hot, calmly opened her hand-bag and pulled out its contents, a nunchuck that she used on the man she took for her brother-in-law.) Kelsey Brookfield was a pneumatically inflated Courtesan who looked like an escapee from Hugh Hefner's Bunny Club and alarmingly propositioned the front row, bass-voiced: 'Y'right?' Chris Myles's Abbess in winged coif, mini-skirt habit and flagellist's whip

suckered poor Adriana into revealing herself a shrew then, booming 'BE QUIET, PEOPLE!', flattened the hub-bubbing throng. Insisting he was 'sent for nothing but a rope' – the one he had in his hand and beat to a pulp in time with his own increasingly frustrated head-banging – Jon Trenchard's Dromio/Ephesus managed, flinging it away, to garrotte himself. And wandering innocently through this carnage of minds boggling, tempers fraying, and neighbours attempting violence on neighbours Dugald Bruce-Lockhart's wonderfully gormless Antipholus/Syracuse managed to present himself as the temperamental twin of his irascible brother. (In this production, it was Swainsbury's Antipholus/Ephesus who got the round from the audience for the tour de force speech, his breath-defying account to the Duke of the day's activity, which brought to hilarious fulfilment a two-hour-long acoustic gag on the 'ding' that had sounded every time someone mentioned the blasted gold chain.)

And did all this inventiveness serve beyond the pleasure of the belly laughter it produced in the theatre? Yes. No amount of silliness could mute the searching questions other halves were asking of their 'selves' here, like Adriana's interrogation of (the wrong) Antipholus, 'How comes it . . . husband . . . / That thou art estranged from thyself?' Her lines on the mystical incorporation of married selves were profoundly moving:

> as easy mayst thou fall
> A drop of water in the breaking gulf,
> And take unmingled thence that drop again
> Without addition or diminishing,
> As take from me thyself, and not me too.

Now there's an idea that Shakespeare's future comedy is going to ponder on!

Compared to the slam-bang-wallop of Propeller's *Comedy*, other comedy felt as lively as cold scrambled eggs. At the Rose, Kingston, Stephen Unwin's cod-period dress *As You Like It* had to negotiate the most useless set (designed by Jonathan Fensom) I saw all year: a steep mound of bare black dirt with a brown-leafed oak branch suspended over it, as though Arden were run by Stig of the Dump and the forest was in permanent winter. This production gave me plenty of time to ask awkward questions. Where did those Granny Smith windfalls that Orlando (David Sturzaker) was collecting in his first scene drop from? That bristle on Touchstone's (Michael Feast) noggin: was it a Mohawk haircut or a post-modern impression of a cockscomb? Why was Jacques (Adrian Lukis) so eupeptic: hadn't he read the malcontent's CV? How did the exiles come by those classy clean clothes: yellow boots, velvet cloaks, jauntily feathered hats? And why would any of them want to go home? Arden was full of buxom young rurals bouncing around in designer rustic ready to set up picnics and break into 'Riverdance'. (I know why all the extras. The Rose collaborates with Kingston University to give their drama post-grads stage time. But where pedagogy unbalances production, I, the pedagogue, cry, 'Cut!')

There were some delightful moments: the backward look Feast's Touchstone gave, assessing the property Celia/Aliena (Phoebe Fox) had just acquired; the horrified recoil Orlando made, realizing he'd revealed his parentage a second time in twenty-four hours, then his collapse into the Duke's (Paul Shelley) arms when the exile told him 'I . . . lov'd your father.' But there was also a lot of nonsense: silly sound effects of baa-ing sheep, a zoo-full of howling wolves, the new-flayed sheepskin Corin (Rod Arthur) worked on, as bloody-handed as Macbeth, blandly wondering, 'How like you this shepherd's life . . . ?'; the absence of material evidence: only one puny poem pinned to the overhead branch. And a bigger gap: a hole where Rosalind should have been. The Rose is not a kind theatre for actors, acoustically, and Georgina Rich didn't have the vocal technique for the space, so great lines that needed precise articulation like 'I see no more in you . . .' came out in a blur of white noise. Even the 'woo me, woo me' scene felt bogged down in a performance where the actor knew all her words – but somehow missed what the words were *doing*.

Things were somewhat better at the National Theatre. Given carte blanche to direct whatever he wanted to celebrate his eightieth birthday (and his fifty-odd years running the RSC, the NT, the Kingston Rose and his own name-branded company) Peter Hall staged a chamber-sized *Twelfth Night* in the Cottesloe with his daughter Rebecca at its centre. Anthony Ward designed an austerely elegant space that played with perspective, anticipating the optical reversals to come that have so many people in this play puzzling over what they're looking at. Along the back wall on a little shelf sat toy-sized timber-framed houses. You got the sense of Illyria as one of those Cornish villages, Mousehole, perhaps, perched on a high sea wall. Mid-stage hung a leaf-patterned sun shade, lit gold and orange, throwing autumnal shadows on the bleached wood floor. In the second scene, it fell, cut loose by the sound of a storm, to become a stretch of sand across which Viola, drenched, in petticoat and corset, struggled. For the rest, with hardly any stuff on stage, the visual effects were left to the costumes. This was a Caroline *Twelfth Night*: a style that interestingly effeminized the men, both Marton Csokas's quirky, tortured Orsino in branched velvet, high-heeled court shoes, and Heathcote Williams mane, and Rebecca Hall's languid cross-dressed Cesario, in red satin doublet and hose, Earl of Southampton hair and love knot.

But while this production was never less than competent, it was hardly ever more than that: clearly spoken, yes, and offering a workmanlike serving up of the text; but so slow! The food of love ingested on a drip-feed. And a production almost devoid of performance where, when actors got around to doing something, it almost always felt wrong: like Toby Belch leaping onto a table. (Toby – leap? No, no, no!) The space Ward's design created was rarely bridged by actors connecting across it: the detachment was palpable. Hall, her voice a two-note vibrato, got the melancholy of Cesario remembering a sister who 'loved a man', but never the pluck of Viola: 'shall I to this lady?' This part is like Rosalind. It carries sorrow like a leviathan weighing down the heart. But also, like Rosalind, it must be capable of instant Ovidian metamorphoses that make the black beast leap with joy and 'dance on sands'. Alas, here there was just a trudging through dunes.

Other parts felt solipsistic – like Simon Callow's Toby Belch. But then, Callow's natural habitat is the one-man show. Weaving in and out of 'I'm drunk' acting like some actors weave in and out of accents, he appeared to be giving a bad impression of Donald Sinden. Or maybe he always sounds like a parody. And why was Belch in such sparkling gear? Shouldn't he at least have gravy down his front and significant fraying at the cuffs? The knight's a slob, isn't he, and impecunious? Is 'celebrity glam' in Callow's contract? Where was the carnivore in this Belch? Opposite him, Aguecheek (Charles Edwards: next to be seen as the Globe's Benedick) was an over-sized Gainsborough Blue Boy, as hang-dog as a lurcher; David Ryall's Feste, a drowned spaniel in filthy motley and a cap that hung down over his face in despondent

donkey ears; and Simon Paisley Day's Malvolio, thin-faced, humourless (and not funny with it), the range of his voice as narrow as Hall's, and appearing to have no story he wanted to tell as Olivia's steward, not even in the gulling scene, Malvolio's moment in the sun. All of them were depressives – or maybe it was just that the pace of this production was so lethargic as to suggest the terminal ward.

Against this sluggishness, Amanda Drew's spirited Olivia negotiated the two wooing scenes with a waywardness that veered from giddy to frigid (as though she'd taken a leaf out of Ganymede's wooing manual), riding the rollercoaster of her lines ('he says he'll come. / How shall I feast him? What bestow on him?'). When Ben Mansfield turned up, swashbuckling, throbbingly virile, the alpha+ twin to Viola's wilted, faked masculinity (no wonder Hall would later cast Mansfield as Hotspur in *Henry IV*), the production finally got an erotic charge that kicked it into life. The wink he gave the audience answering Olivia's imploring 'come' with a full-blooded 'I will!', contained both wonder and cocky desire. (But that post-wedding acid-orange gown she wore into 5.1: what a mistake! Not just ugly and anachronistic – produced by twenty-first-century chemical dyes. But illogical. This is a woman who wants her marriage concealed!)

In an interview the octogenarian birthday-boy commented ruefully that 'he used to be known as a radical' but now, 'surprise', was being 'labelled a traditionalist'. (If Hall wanted to keep his radical street cred, however, he'd be advised against printing as his programme note something he wrote fifty years back.) Surely there's a place for the 'traditional' in the theatre, particularly where by 'traditional' we mean the radicalisms Peter Hall normalized across fifty years, including verse-speaking that honours the plays' writing and storytelling that honours the lives they contain; and more particularly where today's 'radical' – as we'll see later – is currently producing in the house that Hall built some very stupid Shakespeare that takes the audience for mugs. The problem with Hall's *Twelfth Night* wasn't that it was traditional but that it was 'deadly' (see Peter Brook in *The Empty Space*): it brought 'no challenge to the conditioned reflexes' of the director, didn't 'start . . . afresh from the void', fell back on 'repetition'. Or maybe Hall at eighty was just tuckered out from all the cakes and ale and ice-cream.

Peter Hall's wasn't the only big birthday this year. *The Tempest* turned 400. On some stages, she acted her age. On others, she came up new. Sometimes she did both. At the Theatre Royal Haymarket, directed by Trevor Nunn, we got first '*The Tempest*: The Musical' (where Inigo Jones met Andrew Lloyd Webber), then '*The Tempest* – or – Shakespeare in Love'. This production was *full of* production. The programme credited 'Director of Flying', 'Video Designer' and 'Illusionist'. (But for all the production – or perhaps because of it – oddly, there wasn't much acting.)

The designer, Stephen Brimson Lewis, masked the theatre's gilded baroque proscenium and side boxes with swathes of blacks, like ragged ship's tackle. Upstage was a brick wall; downstage, a staff, a book, a cloak. Entering from a side ramp, Prospero (Ralph Fiennes) planted an hourglass on the forestage, put on the cloak, opened the book, began mumbling. Then as he retreated way upstage, all hell broke loose. Thunder. Lightning. Rain clouds exploding (or illusions of rain). A ship's bridge lowering. Hatches opening. Lighting changes turning the world blue, brown, black. From the flies, sailors slid down rigging – then later, tangled in it, drowned. Three Shock-Headed-Peter Ariels (dressed like sea-nymphs from the chorus line of a Jonson/Jones masque) 'flamed amazement'. Flying. Vanishing. Suddenly acrobatically materializing. It was all very 'WOW!'

Later, musical under-scoring would tell you what to think. 'Full fathom five' would be produced by Tom Byam Shaw's Ariel (with Steven Butler and Charlie Hamblett, his 'Divided Selves') as a 1720s counter-tenor aria and 'You are three men of sin' as Mozart's Commedatore. 'Freedom high-day' would send Giles Terera's leather-backed Caliban (his deformity, scales and bone and a claw hand) into 1980s rock musical mode. The masque would conjure up Busby Berkeley, one stunt right out of Reinhardt's film of *A Midsummer Night's Dream*, Iris appearing to walk down a rainbow that decanted from the heavens. One brilliant effect would come right at the end of the masque, on 'Avoid!', when a lighting change (the designer, the always inventive Paul Pyant) would instantly convert the technicolour world of revels into a grey-and-black 'pageant faded', Oz into Kansas. Very, very *WOW!*

The problem was where to put the performances. Fiennes's Prospero (a beachcomber in grizzled beard and the ruins of Jacobean dress) skulked around the margins as though trying not to get trapped in the machinery, performing a kind of actorly detachment that made me rethink how unkind I'd been to Stephen Dillane's Prospero last year (*Shakespeare Survey 64*). Or is 'absent' what fathers are these days? Michael Benz – a gorgeous Silvius at the Globe in 2009 (*Shakespeare Survey 63*) – giving the same performance here, was too gormlessly 'gee shucks' for Ferdinand, even opposite a Miranda (Elisabeth Hopper) who did lots of 'I'm-just-a-kid-when-I'm-happy-I-hunch-up-my-shoulders' acting. Clive Wood was miscast as Stephano (but could give Simon Callow a masterclass in stage drunk-acting); and Nicholas Lyndhurst (who shared top billing with Fiennes, presumably because of his past life in *Only Fools and Horses*) as Trinculo didn't raise a laugh. For the actors, this production was deeply conventional. Its effect (*pace* Peter Hall) was deadly traditional.

Or that's what the carping side of my spectatorly brain observed – even as it kept being 'Shushed!' by the visuals working on my imagination. I found myself holding my breath in the delicate moment when Ariel flew down to perch, one-footed, on the palm of Prospero's up-turned hand before the 'chick' went 'free'. Earlier, Byam Shaw's delivery of 'Mine would, were I human' put no pause in the line, made it a statement of puzzlement on what it might mean to be 'human'. This Prospero, then, had to make a decision about forgiveness, which he did, dispensing it *universally*, though sometimes through clenched teeth. (Nunn's direction here produced the most resolved ending to *The Tempest* I can remember. And revealed Nunn as a shamelessly unreconstructed romantic. Earlier, he'd rearranged scenes so that the interval would come after the younglings kissed at the end of 3.1.) Antonio (Julian Wadham), forgiven, threw himself on his knees and clasped his brother around the waist. Caliban, chastened, cowered. Then he heard the word 'Pardon', held out in a long pause that saved. He stood, invested by Miranda with the fetish necklace Prospero handed over: Caliban, King of the Isle.

Alone, drowning his books, Prospero opened a hatch not seen before, into a shute, a void. He threw them in. But the splash never came. Instead, we heard the sound of a rushing up-wind, imagined the tumbling books ripped from their bindings, the pages spinning in air, redistributing all his words – Prospero's books – throughout space and time. (Happy 400th birthday, *Tempest*!) Fiennes' best moments were these at the end. He gave the epilogue with a disarming simplicity. Finished. Turned. Walked upstage through a door that opened for the first time. Into the glare of a white light. Reality. Dream over. While this wasn't a dream I'd have cried to dream again it *was* the production this year that I found the most intriguing technically, and that I'd most liked to have watched – to see its workings – from back-stage.

Nunn, in over-full production terms, delivered *The Tempest* in a hogshead; Little Angel in association with the RSC at the Swan put it in a pint pot, child-sized, in a cut version for young audiences, staged by a mixed cast of puppets and seven actors (who played all the principals, worked and voiced the puppets, and made the music). I spent as much time watching the children in the audience as the action on stage, and they were rapt. David Fielder's crabby dad Prospero in his shaggy robe and woggling eyebrows, Anneika Rose's Miranda who went everywhere cradling her rag-doll: these were people the children recognized; stories from home; stories from fairy tale. (Miranda dropped her doll when she met Ferdinand (Christopher Staines). Her dad retrieved it. A souvenir of childhood, and a poignant moment for the adults in the audience sitting next to their kids.)

The stage was set simply with a ship's sail (that would unfurl to screen the masque as shadow play) and a permanent wooden sculpture – like something fabricated by Richard Deacon – of eight receding curls or gigantic wood shavings that evoked a cresting wave, green-grey, the colour of the sea just before a storm breaks. Fielder's Prospero made the storm by rasping his staff around the wooden curve like he was striking a match.

The puppets became the (inanimate) loci of this production's violence. The wreck was a puppet ship flown in that de-structed on stage. Ariel's imprisonment by Sycorax in the pine had the puppet Ariel (worked by Jonathan Storey) literally re-membering, knotting his articulated limbs into terrible contortions. (Beaky, sloe-eyed with purple lids and lips, winged, and sometimes buzzing the mortals as irritatingly as a mosquito, he looked like a Manga comic book character.) The transformation of the dinner-serving dancing spirits into jowl-slathering hounds hunting the humans was genuinely scary: effected by the flipping over of puppet bodies. These puppets, however, managed also to contain the violence. The first entrance had several puppet seagulls flapping in, a chorus of comic clowns. And they got the last laugh at the end – returning to perch on abandoned Caliban's head.

Peter Glanville, directing, sometimes allowed performances to descend into 'schools Shakespeare' mode. The human clowns in joke-Jacobean gear (below mod-spiked hair) were an embarrassment of big bottom gags (Brett Brown/Stephano; Ruth Calkin/Trinculo). Some of the humour was inappropriate: the testicle joke on 'brave brood' that had Trinculo touching up Stephano needed cutting. More unfortunately, the company's movement work too often replaced the story they were *telling*: Fielder wonderfully narrated their life's long backstory to Miranda by moving chess pieces across a board, but then threw away 'We are such stuff...' in a rush of snarl, as though his audience wouldn't have ears for Prospero's poetry.

How wrong he was! The children – and the adults – were enchanted by Caliban, and *hung* on his 'Fear not. The island...' Admittedly, Caliban (worked by Jonathan Dixon) was the star of this show. Part toad, dinosaur, reluctant dragon,

47. *The Tempest*, 1.2. Little Angel in association with the Royal Shakespeare Company at the Swan, directed by Peter Glanville. Caliban puppet worked by Jonathan Dixon.

he was web-footed, armadillo-tailed, pot-bellied, cauliflower-eared. He had scary red eyes and sharp claws, and his skin had split over his ribs. But he was a 'monster' with a conscience. And somehow cuddly. Caught in the storm in a canvas raincoat, called 'savage' by the humans who found him, he recoiled at the word. Then cried 'No!' and flapped his ears when they accused him of roaring. Rebuked, he hunkered down like a dog, lowered his head and swung it like a bull, scratched behind his ear. He was wonderful. And I can't have been the only mom in the audience who'd have taken him home. So I was glad that the seagulls were going to adopt him. And delighted that he got the final curtain call.

At both the Swan and the Haymarket, the tempest came from without: we saw Prospero make it. In Cheek by Jowl's *Tempest*, directed by Declan Donnellan, designed by Nick Ormerod, played by the Russian side of the company, in Russian, with English surtitles, it came from within: within the mind of Prospero.

An old man with a face like a punched-in paper bag, striped shirt, braces, dilapidated trousers, down-at-heel sandals, shuffled in the half-light of the pre-set around the upstage where objects – some pails, piles of sand, lengths of rope – sat at the foot of a set that looked like a fold-up toy theatre: three flats, three doors, duckboard flooring like a seaside promenade. The shuffler – a geriatric servant out of Chekhov, a stagehand checking props – picked up a slatted wooden crate, brought it downstage, sat, stared out, hands on knees, fists clenched. Behind him, first imperceptibly, there was the sound of a whine, a whistle, humming, as the doors began gently rattling, loofing, flapping, then banging vigorously, violently in a wind that rose to gale force. (I thought of Mrs Ramsay in *To the Lighthouse*, hearing doors distant at the top of the house slamming, thinking, 'someone's left a window open', the sea wind getting in. Here, Prospero's stony face – Igor Yasulovich – never reacted.) On a huge crack of thunder, the doors in the flats left and right banged open, and spectators saw behind, framed in one doorway, a prow, the stern in the other, sailors handing ropes and passengers drenched by waves crashing over them. Between the two apertures, our brains supplied the whole length of the vessel, and saw it doomed. We heard noise: the storm, the mariners' cries, Antonio's curses.

When those doors closed, the central door crashed open. Miranda (Anya Khalilulina), a Raphael angel of a girl with the habits of a feral cat, barefoot, dirty, came screaming on (shrieks that blended with the storm and cries of drowning), attacking her father, pummelling him who fought back, dragging her violently into his past with the story of her childhood. When he handed her his handkerchief to wipe her tears, she threw it at his feet. He retrieved it, ground it into her face until it stifled her cries. This was a love based on fear and pain, a story recounting wrongs still felt as raw, open wounds. When Prospero spoke of Antonio (Evgeny Samarin) a door opened; out he stepped in sharp suit, reading; of Alonso (Mikhail Zhigalov), the other door, posturing. Miranda, on all fours, scrambled around them, gazing. He put her to sleep by smacking her in the face – then catching her falling body. When he summoned Ariel, the doors, replaying the storm, began flapping, and six spirits appeared. Ariel (Andrey Kuzichev) barefoot, bare-chested in a black suit, stared sweetly out as he told of the storm. Opening the central door to report Ferdinand's leap overboard, he showed him (Yan Ilves), framed in the doorway as if drowned, suspended swinging upside down in eerie green light.

This Prospero had no books, no magic cloak, no staff. The storm issued, it appeared, from a mind whose felt sorrows, whose felt wrongs and memories materialized, impersonated. But the storm, too, persisted, becoming an organizing trope in the way Donnellan used water throughout. Invisible (but we saw them) spirits poured water from invisible (but we saw them) watering cans that looked to the castaways like fresh streams falling from the air. An even more delicious joke: spirits dashed buckets of water in Trinculo's face (Ilya Iliin) every time he opened one of the doors to escape this haunted place. Pans of water were used as a footbath then a full body-scrub for Miranda and Ferdinand, stripped naked: ritual cleansing for a first meeting and, in new clothes, their betrothal. Because it persisted, transformed to other uses, the storm in this *Tempest* became a trope of forgiveness. And the beauty of its simplicity was profoundly moving.

Eventually, I longed to hear Shakespeare's words. On my ears (permanently ruined by Khrushchev in the 1960s), the Russian fell like the antidote to forgiveness. Besides, I knew from their laughter that the Russians in the audience were hearing a different script from the Shakespeare transcript in the surtitles. (*Why* don't we get a re-translation of the translation so we'd have some sense of what the new script is *doing*? That said, I enormously appreciated how the screen would occasionally go blank – giving us the characters' 'silent' time to think, too.)

But the absence of playtext was handsomely compensated by the abundance and inventiveness of performance: Ariel forced to remember Sycorax twisting himself into a knot; Miranda visiting blubberly, bald, stripped-to-the-waist Caliban (Alexander Feklistov), a 'monster' her father's age but with her simple habits of child-ness, making mouths at each other in the bottom of a tin washbasin used for a mirror; Miranda yanking away from the necklace – some souvenir of her mother? – that Prospero tried to clasp around her throat as though he were collaring her, and biting it, to see if it were edible; Prospero cooling Ferdinand's ardour with a bucket of cold water; Trinculo – the only Trinculo I saw this year who raised laughter; and *continuous* laughter – utterly bamboozled by the mobile water fountains (and continually suckered into opening another door). This actor spent most of the night dripping wet. And the best physical theatre of all: the log-moving scene, where Ariel played the logs, leaning back-to-back, full length onto Ferdinand's back as the prince shouldered the 'burden', carried thus across the stage, rolled off onto a 'pile', rising, circling back as Ferdinand trudged to his starting place, becoming the next log to be carried – over, and over, and over.

There was plenty of signature Cheek by Jowl here: an austerity on the retina, the design using a limited palette of colours; overlapping scenes that used freeze-framing to bleed bits of narrative into each other. 'Do you love me?'; 'Yes' was one such moment, held soundlessly, suspended, before the action continued. There was plenty of vulgarity. The duping of the clowns translated them to a politburo-only Moscow department store; gave them credit cards and mobile phones. And there was plenty of outrageousness. The masque was back-projected black-and-white footage of happy Stalin-era down-on-the-commune farming: peasant women with tree-trunk arms turning hay, strong-thewed men atop gim-crack tractors, the soundtrack an anthem to the Soviet collective, belted out to accordion accompaniment. When Prospero ended these 'revels', we all

48. *The Tempest*, 3.1. Cheek by Jowl on tour, directed by Declan Donnellan. Andrey Kuzichev as Ariel, Yan Ilves as Ferdinand.

got a shock. The theatre house-lights came up. Ferdinand confronted Prospero then stormed off stage through the auditorium. The stage manager appeared, wearing headphones. The actors left. Alone, Yasulovich's Prospero told us about the end of dreams. In the glare of the merciless white light, we had to see the theatre (any theatre) for what it was.

This desperately human Prospero found it almost impossible to forgive: violent from the first raising of the memory-proxying storm, violent to his daughter, to his slave, to her betrothed, he was still threatening violence at the end. When Ariel volunteered, 'Mine would...', the irascible old man rounded on him, making him back off, crouch, wait in the awful silence for the blow to fall. That it didn't was a miracle.

Finally, Ariel played the servant-fixer: dressing Prospero, gently wiping his face, buttoning his shirt, leaving him to sit, quietly reading a book – the first! the only! – as the mad conspirators came to their senses and recognized him. When all the wonder was distributed and the exit to Milan set in motion, the betrothed couple exiting hand in hand, Prospero was left on stage with Caliban. Ariel entered. With a suitcase. Set it at Prospero's feet. Caliban looked, recognized its meaning. And roared! Howled! Primally. With grief, in pain. The back door crashed open. Miranda flew in, grabbed Caliban – her 'baby' brother – wrapped him in her arms, rocked him as they both wailed. Ferdinand stormed in. Tackled his wife. Peeled her away. She kicked, screamed; he dragged her off, slammed the door. Prospero said his goodbyes to his adopted children. Left through the door. In the silence, Ariel gazed at huddled Caliban. Then gently took Prospero's seat on the up-turned crate. Reached out – and touched the other on the head: a touch that made them both human. This *Tempest* made that magic thing: the perfect theatrical alloy of thinking and feeling.

Outside Clwyd Theatr Cymru the poster advertising Terry Hands's *The Taming of the Shrew* teased punters with a quotation: 'Such duty as the subject owes the prince, / Even such a woman oweth to her husband.' But it finished the couplet with a question mark. Playful, mischievous, provocative: the punctuation announced a production that would question every noun and verb in the quotation – to reclaim *Shrew* for comedy.

The designer, Mark Bailey, set a free-standing timber-framed Warwickshire country inn centre stage. There was nothing English Heritage about it: the daub was falling off the wattle; birds had run off with bits of the roof. In the distance, an orange sun hung in a dark sky – or was it a hunter's moon? We heard a story begin before we saw it: the mew of a falcon in flight; then a woman, bellowing as she, a low-down-at-heels Hostess (Sara Harris-Davies) in an apron that looked like it had carried coal, turfed a staggeringly drunk and swaggeringly abusive Christopher Sly (Brendan Charleson) out on his ear into the mud. This was a place where men were unreconstructed. And women could hold their own.

When Kate and Petruccio later appeared, in a playing space that opened up the inn's façade like the front of a doll's house to show a lovingly if scruffily furnished Elizabethan interior, they were versions of this original warring couple. Bailey's design was really smart: costumes, wittily 'period' – Elizabethan fashion made up in twenty-first-century materials to produce a look that was modishly 'retro'; a set built for games. In Act 4, three chase scenes would be staged simultaneously, superimposed on each other in the depth of the stage: far upstage, Kate and Petruccio travelling home; far downstage, Grumio stood-up but still hopeful of a promised assignation; on the diagonal, streaking through mid-stage, the youngsters, eloping.

I objected, however, to Steven Meo's lazy acting choice to rationalize Petruccio's boorishness by playing him as a drunk – an homage to another Welshman, Richard Burton? There were better options he could have taken to account for Hedydd Dylan's gorgeous Kate's fascination. (She's an actor for whom the term 'flashing eyes' might have been invented.) Because fascinated she was. The wooing was a scrap between shag-haired terrier (he) and elegant greyhound (she) that reached a stand-off on her genuinely intrigued, 'Where did you study all this goodly speech?' The wedding was a horrifying insult: she, dressed like Elizabeth in the Ditchley portrait (wow! this Kate had been putting together her trousseau *for years*!); he, like a car crash. The wedding night was a let-down: in an interpolated scene, Kate appeared from the bedroom in her negligée (more trousseau!), saw Petruccio passed out on the floor, and, clearly crushed, retreated.

But the sun/moon scene worked itself into a glorious duet: Petruccio had sobered up, and Kate had stumbled upon a sense of humour. '[I]t shall be so for Katherine' erupted from her with a huge laugh; the couple fell upon each other, right there, in the road, on the way to Padua, in a heap of playfulness – that persisted when they got home. At her sister's wedding breakfast, Kate stuffed her face, then exited behind the other women to the parlour – armed with a plate *stacked* with food. But her best revelation, best 'play', came at the end of her wedding speech: here, not a capitulation but a thoughtful statement of partnership in marriage, that she finished with a flourish by (shock!) dropping her skirts, showing trousers underneath, then catching her husband who leaped into her arms (a revised replay of her exit from her own wedding, now role-reversed) and carrying him off – to BED.

Terry Hands's achievement in this production was not just to preserve the ugly, the mean, the brutal, the sting of the humiliations in the play, but to recognize the play's generosity, its wisdom, its iconoclasm ('To me she's married, not unto my clothes'; 'What, is the jay more precious than the lark...?'; 'If thou account'st it shame, lay it on me'). Ultimately, those recognitions make space for understanding the war that the *Shrew*

49. *The Taming of the Shrew*, 3,1. Clwyd Theatr Cymru, directed by Terry Hands. Steven Meo as Petruccio, Simon Holland Roberts as Grumio.

reports on as comedy. Neither was this *Shrew* just a sensational double act. It showed an ensemble working at a peak of comic performance: Simon Holland Roberts's long-suffering Grumio in his leather skullcap and Godot boots was half spaniel (listening to Petruccio's exhausting wooing palaver with his chin rested on a bench), half flying buttress (wedging his master upright); James Haggie's endearingly dim Biondello didn't have enough brainpower to light a low-watt bulb – but could still see through Lucentio's disguise, which defeated Robert Blythe's Baptista (but then, Baptista was a dad busy calculating his daughter's dowry on an abacus). Grumio's (John Cording) account of the wedding – he a doddering geriatric balanced dangerously on a couple of wobbling walking sticks, but foxy in his negotiations over Bianca – was hilarious for its sepulchral deadpanned-ness.

And the bright young things? Well, you could see in the tutor scene that the shine on Amy Morgan's dazzling Bianca was only skin-deep; Daniel Llewelyn-Williams's besotted Lucentio had a tin ear, not to hear the brass in her voice.

Hands made one cut that was bound to raise the eyebrow of any editor in the audience: Petruccio's 4.1 soliloquy, 'Now have I politicly begun my reign', arguing plausibly (or not) that the speech is a later interpolation and recognizable as such because it gives the tamer's game away. (But if an interpolation: why not another explanation? That first audiences – *women* – were so incensed at Petruccio's outrages that Burbage asked Shakespeare for a speech that would end with an appeal – finishing in a question mark – to men in the audience?) But Hands also designed one joke purely for editors in the audience. 'And what's the name of your comedy?' asked the Lord. 'The Taming of a Shrew,' answered one player. 'THE Shrew', chorused the rest.

With Hands's *Shrew*, in this 50th anniversary year of the RSC, the old RSC completed a hat-trick: three of the original directorate who established the company – Hall, Nunn, Hands – staging work that showed them all still very much worth the whistle.

TRAGEDIES

2011 was a slow year for tragedy, the work mostly running from the solidly competent to the undistinguished. Maybe theatre simply couldn't compete with the grim stuff happening in the real world: the global economic depression that had us all taking the nasty medicine by the bucketloads, with no perceptible effect; the Arts Council further depressing the cultural industries in England by making swingeing cuts of 15 per cent to its *lucky* grant recipients. (The unlucky lost funding entirely.)

At the Sheffield Crucible, directed by Daniel Evans, another celebrity pairing (see Tennant/ Tate; Spacey/Mendes) brought the (English) stars of the (US) TV series *The Wire* (Clarke Peters,

Dominic West, a local Sheffield boy) home for *Othello*. Played in Jacobean dress on a near-bare platform stage paved like the stones of a piazza against a plastered wall that evoked a Venetian palazzo, it looked striking (designer: Morgan Large). But the acoustic was dreadful: actors' voices disappeared into the roof, and it didn't help that several of them on press night were still very shaky with the script. The lighting designer (Lucy Carter) didn't appear to have *read* the script: night scenes in Venice were set with the lighting full up; in Cyprus the glaring white light that made the place swelter was sometimes on, sometimes off.

Lily James, a year out of drama school, made a lovely, dignified Desdemona, but not a Desdemona you'd suspect capable of 'treason of the blood' or knotting the bedsheets to escape out the window into the arms of her lover in a gondola; not a Desdemona who could find the oxymoronic modest impudence of the Senate scene, the anxiety-covering gamesomeness of the quayside scene, the punched-gut silence at the end of the brothel scene, the desolation of the willow scene, the child in the woman and the woman in the child that Shakespeare writes into the part. James needs another crack at the role when she has more technique under her belt. Alongside her, Alexandra Gilbreath (a veteran of plenty of Shakespeare) played Emilia (inexcusably) as a vulgar, insinuating, eye-rolling, bosom-heaving doxy who out-Bianca-ed Bianca: a 'customer' Iago'd be well advised to keep an eye on, sitting splay-legged in the afternoon heat, fanning her fanny up her skirts, behaving as though the 'general camp, / Pioneers and all' had pitched up there. Not that West's Iago appeared to care very much. His one-paced Iago was a phlegmatic northerner (but after Ian McKellen and Conrad Nelson, who both did it brilliantly, isn't the monster as bluff Hovis-man something of a cliché?). I couldn't work out whether he, the actor, was doggedly dull or he, the actor, was playing an Iago who was playing at being doggedly dull. In any case, he wasn't able to do what both McKellen and Nelson could, mark the stunning *voltes-face* – or are they only sequences of 'seeming'? – that register the voided-ness of Iago's amorality where

one minute 'Reputation' is an 'idle . . . false imposition', the next, 'Good name' is 'the immediate jewel' of men's 'souls'. What he *was* able to show, in partnership with Peters, is how *Othello* is a play of two halves. The first half is Iago's show: the flesh-fly injecting poison under the skin of the man he wants to turn into an animal, a sting here, a bite there. But in the second, he takes a back seat (and West backed off), and we watched Peters's Othello, as instinctually as a dog, worry himself senseless to dislodge a tick that was sickening him and driving him nuts. (Only where was the parasite fixed? On his skin? On his heart? His head? In the blood? The brain?) The awfulness of this *Othello* was that such a decent man as Peters's Moor could be wrecked by such a dullard as West's Iago.

Northern Broadsides' touring *Hamlet* represented a departure for the company: the first Shakespeare in Broadsides' near-twenty-year-long history to be directed by someone other than the artistic director, Barrie Rutter. Clearly, the company is looking to its future (and you've got to wonder what plans other companies are making whose creative work is so closely identified with an individual or creative team: Propeller, Cheek by Jowl, Shakespeare at the Tobacco Factory). Conrad Nelson (who has a long history with Broadsides as actor, musical director and director of new writing) set *Hamlet* in 1949, a 'time between', and made Elsinore a blue world (designed by Lis Evans) where earth, sea and sky merged: raked gangways intersected with pools of water; modernist banners tethered to the floor doubled as walls then evaporated, back lit, when memories appeared as ghosts. The opening beat gave spectators the 'just-married' wedding party at the end of the evening. An ebullient Claudius (Fine Time Fontayne) in shirt sleeves at the keyboard played a swing tune for Ophelia (Natalie Dew) at a microphone to sing the lyrics to 'St Valentine's Day' that would come back to haunt her while Becky Hindley's movie star Gertrude sashayed among the guests – and Hamlet, so far off as not to have been on, sat in the huddled pose of Rodin's Thinker, deaf to celebration.

There were some memorable moments: the Murder of Gonzago played in the style of *Brief*

Encounter, all cut-crystal accents and shot cuffs; Ophelia, mad, squatting to paddle in one of the pools, then standing, skirts streaming, a vision of her future, drowned; Hamlet, handed his paternal inheritance by the Ghost along with 'revenge', holding the sword like a cross, then raising it like a sword swallower about to choke it down – a first image of suicide. There were fine performances from Fontayne (who clearly saw *Hamlet* as the 'tragedy of Claudius, would-be king of Denmark'), Hindley (her brittle Gertrude, hysterical after the closet scene, was headed, under escort, to an asylum), Guy Lewis (Horatio, constantly staggered by goings-on in Elsinore), and Andy Cryer (simpering as Reynaldo, salaciously appreciating his mission-to-spy; then Osric, a brown-noser in a brown suit). Excellent, too, was the way the stage became the littered dumpsite of performance. 'TO BE ® NOT TO BE', chalked like graffiti on the castle's entrance ramp with arrows connecting subsequent thoughts (DIE SLEEP DREAM), remained throughout, scuffed by passing feet. The love letters Ophelia scattered in her first mad scene and the flowers she strewed in the second fluttered forgotten in corners or floated forlornly on the pool's surface.

But there were also serious directorial miscalculations. Playing the Ghost with a number of bunraku-style puppets (in fencing masks: a nudge in the ribs towards the ending) detracted from the desperate in-bodiedness of the story the Ghost tells, dead, but still so *attached* to life. But in any case, that story of the 'leperous distilment' and its effect, the 'instant tetter' that 'barked about / . . . All my smooth body', couldn't be heard because Nelson underscored it with an extra-diegetic *a capella* chorale on a balcony that drowned it out. Given Broadsides' politics of the (northern) voice, I found it incredible that while the company's signature voice was otherwise muted (fine, they've won the battle, actors don't need any longer to be pugnaciously northern), the clowns came on as joke 'raiit braad' Yorkshiremen.

The most significant casualty of directorial miscalculation was Nicholas Shaw's split-personality Hamlet. There was one Hamlet who, young, frank and charismatic, was utterly disarming speaking to the audience ('O what a rogue . . . ') and shocking, scrabbling and scribbling ('TO BE . . . '). But there was another who presented Hamlet – or was it Shaw himself? – as the kind of actor Declan Donnellan in *The Actor and the Target* diagnoses as 'blocked'. It was as though Shaw were trying to give someone else's performance – the director's, perhaps? – going through motions that were not his own, in borrowed intonations. But Shaw is a better actor than that. And as this production ultimately showed, Hamlet without Hamlet isn't much *Hamlet*. This *Hamlet*, then, was a rehearsal for one Shaw has yet to play.

The insight the Broadsides' programme note gave into a director's mind, where Nelson was interestingly confessional, hinting that directing *Hamlet* was never, quite, going to compensate for having missed the chance to play the part, can be put against what could be learned from David Thacker's note to *Romeo and Juliet* at the Bolton Octagon. For one thing, he let Richard Wilson reprint something he 'originally' wrote for Thacker's first *Romeo* '30 years ago' verbatim because, concludes Wilson, 'nothing has happened since to make me change what it says', What an admission! Nothing 'happened'? No 'change'? That's the kind of smugness that gives academic writing – and academic input into the 'now' of performance – a name that stinks like week-old cod. For his own part, Thacker used the programme to do some public 'Brainstorming' with his company: 'What is the point of doing this play?'; 'So let's list some of the ways we think Shakespeare is showing us the "form and pressure" of our time.' Should this have escaped the rehearsal room? I think not.

Clearly, though, 'the "form and pressure" of our time' is uppermost in any Thacker production: he puts Shakespeare in modern dress. Here, in the pre-set, muzak from a 'love themes' compilation tape played Chopin, Albéniz, tracks from the movies. The space (designed by Ruari Murchison) was empty, and somehow both urban and glitzy: as black as asphalt, with a floor surface as shiny as hardened lava, the only feature a narrow bridge thrusting out of the upstage wall, straddling a central exit, that would serve as the balcony. Actors in rehearsal gear appeared. A guy. A girl. They spoke the Prologue, sharing the sonnet, sailing on the iambic pentameter, making a pitch for poetry. Then yobs in cheap sports gear off the market, blue jeans and sunglasses, armed with baseball bats, and 'souf London' accents came in with prosaic street slang and trashed the place. (But why London? This was Bolton! Surely the yobs could have talked like locals!) When Romeo (David Ricardo-Pearce) showed up (from the Prologue), he was a kid who'd stayed out all night and now stretched his hoodie down over his face to muffle Benvolio's (Lloyd Gorman) good council. Juliet (Jade Anouka) (also from the Prologue) stood in her bathrobe, lithe as a leopard (and as unself-conscious) listening to her socialite mother (Paula Jennings) and chic, stiletto-heeled Nurse (Michelle Collins: no wormwood had been within a hundred miles of those nipples!) rabbit on, then, at the ball, was wooed by Paris (Tobias Beer) with a schmaltzy violin riff that her cousin, the dark and dangerous and flirtatious Tybalt (Jake Norton), captured and made over on the electric guitar: Mozart taken hostage by Jimi Hendrix. Meanwhile, the Montague boys had turned up in bad suits – and Romeo on the bridge had spotted Juliet. Ironically, her genial, conscientious dad (Rob Edwards), kicking out of the party his spoiling-for-a-fight nephew, robbed Juliet of her best protector; as soon as Tybalt was gone, Mercutio (Kieran Hill) moved in on her. Then Romeo.

The kids in Thacker's audience recognized a youth culture that had too much drink, time and testosterone on its hands. I watched them – watching, as the inevitability of the violence in the 'morning after' scene shaped up, a waiter clearing six empties off Mercutio's table before Tybalt arrived; audible groans when Romeo offered his hand – and Tybalt spat in his face. The knife fight was ugly, nasty, up close, and so impetuous as to be almost not happening. When Romeo slashed Tybalt across the back of the neck then, when he spun round, thrust the blade into his guts, Benvolio stood aghast. And so did Romeo. The line he

wailed about being 'fortune's fool' ended the first half.

That this was a play about more than hyperactivity and gang violence was largely down to Anouka's Juliet, the dark quality of her voice working over the writing to express its sound and structure as well as sense: inhabiting every image that crossed her mind with physical intensity; shifting rhetorical gears from the lyrical to the conversational to the shockingly raw, guttural; giving form, and substance and imagination, and a way of being in Romeo's world. She started the second half flat on her back, gazing up at the sun, urging Phoebus's steeds to get a lick on, to 'gallop apace' to *bring on night*. She was, then, by turns first giddy girl, then demure bride poised on Hymen's threshold. Later, when she tackled Friar Lawrence (Colin Connor, a streetwise Belfast parish priest in a roll-neck jumper), the pulse of her rising desperation produced speech like gangsta rap – speech I'd heard earlier walking through Bolton market on my way to the theatre. This was a Juliet who woke on her black joke of a marriage bed with her groom sprawled dead across her – but somehow achieved a Cleopatra moment: just a girl, but 'marble constant'. Thacker gave the ending to the youngsters: he cut the revelations and explanations that re-do the plot (and give the elders plenty of time to gaze on what they've produced in Verona, the 'tragic loading of this bed'). He had Romeo and Juliet rise to share the Prince's final speech: 'A glooming peace . . . ' But also the Prince's final instruction: 'Go hence, to have more talk of these sad things.' It was instruction – kids talking straight to kids – I could see the kids in the audience taking on board.

A single inflection cued Derek Jacobi's King Lear at the Donmar Warehouse. Christopher Oram's design put the play in a white box, a bunker or stockade, built (walls, ceiling, all) of distressed floorboards, like ship's planking or a seaside promenade scoured by sand and salt (a premonition of Dover cliffs); and in costumes that weren't exactly period but, in their cut, suggested a time 'ago'. Bucking recent theatre practice (see, for example, David Farr's *Lear* at the RSC last year, or Trevor

Nunn's in 2007, *Shakespeare Survey 61, 64*) the director Michael Grandage devised no prologue scene, no back-story to contextualize or make politically correct the family histories, the ugly cultural fissures (joked about in the everyday story of a son's bastardy) and seismic shocks (the division of the kingdom that goes wildly wrong over daughters' bodies) that Shakespeare sets to devastate the opening scene. Here, the lights came up. (And in Neil Austin's pitiless lighting plot, they mostly stayed up.) Two men stepped into the space with urgent gossip: 'I thought the King...' And we were away, tugged into the riptide of what was happening as violently as the characters themselves.

Jacobi's Lear – his white hair close-cropped; his cheeks, rubicund – entered behind his elder daughters and their husbands, arm-in-arm, whispering with his youngest child (so we saw the family first as three couples), evidently all twinkle (though interrupted by momentary geriatric tetch – 'Attend the lords...!' – had Paul Jesson's just-on-the-point-of-relaxing Gloucester barked into action). It was the tone of a later line, however, that gave this Lear's heart away. He'd done the bit about the 'darker purpose' (twinkle, joke); he'd called for the map (an ancient thing, spread out on the ground); he'd spoken about his 'constant will' to prevent 'future strife' with timely publication of some dowers. (More twinkle, more joke.) Then he got to the part about his youngest daughter's suitors, 'Great rivals in... love'. (Twinkle, twinkle; laughter.) But it was almost as if those twinkling thoughts of rivals in love triggered a near childlike need to know something. 'Tell me, my daughters', he began, 'Which of you shall we say doth love *us* most?'

That emphasis was a complete self-exposure. It contained Lear's (and *Lear's*) whole future. It achieved its effects by the simplest of theatrical means: an actor working with Shakespeare's writing. And it signalled what this production would do best: clear the space of clutter and concept, leave it open for actors to grapple with speech and turn words into performance. An actor told me that Grandage's directorial motto appears to be 'Cast high and get out of the way.' Certainly, that seemed to be the principle working here, with the likes of Ron Cook (Fool), Gina McKee (Goneril), Michael Hadley (Kent) and Jesson supporting Jacobi. This was a production with practically no props. I counted six: from the map to the stocks to a stool. De-cluttered, this was a *Lear* that was all about the acting.

Which was electrifying. McKee's Goneril, a brittle ice-maiden, given her portion of the kingdom, paused over the map, looked down her nose, committed it to memory as in one of those photographic flashes TV's *Spooks* have made chillingly familiar, passed on. This Goneril never broke sweat, killed with frostbite: later, mocking her husband's 'manhood! Mew!' she grabbed his balls, twisted, but while he writhed, her frozen face never cracked. The other half of this ugly sister act, Justine Mitchell's Regan, began as an anxious piggy-in-the-middle (checking Goneril, checking dad) flashing dazzling smiles, but turned into a bitch on heat. The blinding of Gloucester was horrifying not just for its sickening violence but for its staging: he, pinned flat up against the back wall so spectators were fixed on the huge widening of his eyes as he saw what was coming; she, coming in close to whisper into the ear that was pooling with blood his son's betrayal.

And what of Jacobi's Lear? Michael Coveney called him 'a poet and a coward'; a poet perhaps not just for the way Jacobi, the actor, handled those great Lear eruptions and meditations technically (from 'Thy truth then be thy dower' to 'Hear, Nature, hear' to 'O, reason not the need' to 'Poor naked wretches' to 'Every inch a king!' to 'forget and forgive' to 'Howl, howl, howl, howl, howl'). But a poet, too, for what Lear, the role, was doing, the way his mind constructed his encounters with his 'felt wrongs' as poetry. Lear's is a mind that stretches from the macro to the micro; takes in the centaur and the mouse, the anatomy theatre and the prison-birdcage; prays and curses and howls; is an extraordinary 'maker' of imagery: 'Dost thou squiny at me?' he challenges the man whose eyes are out. 'No, do thy worst, blind Cupid, I'll not love.' Wherever Lear, the poet, took the actor,

Jacobi went, encountering every line as if for the first time.

And what of the coward? Jacobi is too 'nice' (I mean that as a compliment) an actor for 'brave' (if that's what they are) sensationalisms like McKellen (2007) dropping his trousers to show Lear naked, his manhood 'no more' than a 'bare, forked animal', or Greg Hicks (2010) reaching into his pants to masturbate into a hand that later needed wiping because it 'smells of mortality'. What the actor, Jacobi, did bravely was to render Lear's cowardice: the moment when, battered by the latest round of the Fool's pitiless truth-as-paradox (Cook playing him as a stubby white-faced eastern European clown, eyes marked in vertical kohl lines like perpetual tears), Lear suddenly reached out a hand to clasp the Fool's hand and whisper, 'O let me not be mad.' This Lear had looked into the abyss: and he was terrified. Later, waking in clean clothes, he quailed before the daughter whose revenge he knew he deserved, and so pitched himself out of his wheelchair onto his kneels to grope towards her forgiveness. (But the self-righteous Cordelia (Pippa Bennett-Warner) of the opening scene now knew more about the need to speak love: they clung to each others' embraced forgiveness.) And perhaps the most impressive staging moment of all: Lear cowarded by the storm. Grandage produced its pitiless pelting soundlessly, silently, and therefore weirdly terrifyingly. The storm came as light strobing through the gaps in the planks that built Lear's world, as though only matchsticks stood between Lear and cataclysm, Jacobi *whispering* 'Blow winds, and crack your cheeks', making it almost a prayer carried on the storm.

For all that Gwilym Lee's Edgar gestured, at the end, at a survivors' future (he, who'd made himself a fratricide to ensure the kingdom's future), I got the feeling that the Britain of Grandage's *King Lear* would be 'Closed Until Further Notice'. Metaphoric signage – but, as it happened, literally the sign that was going up on the Everyman in Liverpool at the end of its run of *Macbeth* in July. Launched in 1964 by (among others) Terry Hands, the theatre is going to be reduced to rubble for the next two years while it undergoes a

£28 million refurbishment. Marking this valedictory moment, David Morrissey, who started his career at the Everyman in the 1980s (though most viewers know him from television's *Dr Who*), was returning to Shakespeare for the first time in twenty years to play Macbeth. His fans were thrilled. But his time away from live theatre showed.

Only a couple of degrees of dereliction marked the set off from the raked seating surrounding it on three sides. (The refurb is coming none too soon.) Francis O'Connor's brutalist design suggested an underground bunker with rising damp: a cement backwall fitted with sheet-metal that slid open for reveals; a manky stairwell to the side; doors up on rises that went nowhere; down front, shallow pools of sulfurous-looking water; hanging into them, electrical flexes that shot crackling blue currents into the dark; underscoring it, a white-noise soundscape heard as rolling tympani or a distant storm that resolved into the screams of horses and dying men when the witches entered, more Fates than Weird Sisters, muffled burkha-like, and began pushing around figures like chess pieces on what now appeared as a map of ancient Scotland. One was a withered crone and pregnant; another, a wraith who fashioned a doll-baby out of rags; the third, a child (Nathan McMullen, who'd double as young Fleance and Macduff's boy). Scotland was their gaming table.

Walking into this weird wasteland Morrissey's stolid Macbeth didn't appear to take in its strangeness. In flak jacket, his victims' blood dried black on his hands, he was the kind of monosyllabic career NCO who's wheeled in front of the microphones to talk of killing operations in those flat-toned one-liners that sound like some sort of military cypher: 'So fair and foul a day I have not seen.' This was a Macbeth who could do the leather-skinned soldier, but not the flayed consciousness that's revealed when the soldier starts thinking, starts imagining. So Morrissey's Macbeth was like a tank thudding across the landscape, but not a tank equipped with all it needed, sophisticated sighting, thermal imaging technology that would let him see through the apparitions projected on the screen the witches hauled from the

50. *Macbeth*, 1.1. The Everyman, Liverpool, directed by Gemma Bodinetz. Gillian Kearney, Nathan McMullen and Eileen O'Brien as the Witches.

fetid pool. He was a hulk who ploughed through the soliloquies.

Julia Ford, drafted in for Lady Macbeth with only days' rehearsal after first casting went missing ('for personal reasons'), was as interestingly dull as her husband; dull, like in gun metal; dull, as in completely incapable of imagining consequences; stupidly monosyllabic: 'What's done is done.' She was even dull in appearance: a woman in a brown coat. But together, they were like those electrical flexes shorting in the water. He was *fascinated* by her plan. He listened so hard it was as though he was hearing words forming in the space between them like things he could grasp. That little exchange – 'Duncan comes here tonight'; 'when . . . hence?'; 'Tomorrow . . .'; 'O never . . .' – contained the whole doing of the murder. Later, 'was the hope drunk . . .' was battering that caught him on the jaw.

Directing, Gemma Bodinetz made excellent use of limitations. The opening scene's map table rose to expose its underbelly as a grille and its feet as interrogation lamps, then lowered again for the banquet. Her thirteen-strong cast produced some wicked doubles: McMullen as child of light and dark; Richard Bremmer, a character out of Fuseli, a face like a raptor, a body like a cadaver, first as Duncan then the Porter then the Doctor (who looked like he would beat his patient to the grave). Bodinetz didn't duck the violence: even Lady Macbeth was shocked when Macbeth came out of the murder chamber with blood on his hands *for the second time*. And the drowning of Lady Macduff, head held under water interminably, was sickening.

I followed a Liverpool lass out for the interval and heard her lip-smacking her star-struck approval for Morrissey in local demotic: 'He's as fit as a butcher's dog.' By the end, the dog had wallowed in the butcher's offal trough and wasn't even fit for hanging. In a trompe l'oeil moment, back against the upstage wall, he faced Macduff (Matthew Flynn), who swung his sword. As blood splattered, the lights cut. We supplied the rest, 'saw' the decapitation. It was a fittingly theatrical darkening of a stage going dark that has staged so much memorable theatre for Liverpool.

Of course, it wasn't the end: Macduff came on to dump the head, and Malcolm (Mark Arends), to talk about the future and 'What's more to do'. It's not the end for the Everyman either: much 'more to do' there. But for locals, this *Macbeth* was a thrilling way to hang up a 'Back Soon' notice.

STOOPID SHAKESPEARE

Where do I locate the RSC's work this year, its first season in the new theatre that Michael Boyd, remember, called a 'miracle of space' combining 'the epic and the intimate'? It's early days. (And I remember the settling-in pains of the 1972 season when *Coriolanus* was almost exclusively about the theatre's new 'toy', the whizzy hydraulics that changed the stage's scene-by-scene configuration like automated 3-D architectural drawings on fast forward, and did more acting than the actors. Within a couple of seasons the 'toy' had sunk without trace.) But I have to report of this RSC season, I saw no miracles, nothing either epic or intimate. What I saw was three productions driven by directorial concepts that had to depend (at some level of the directors' consciousness) on the cynical assumption that the audience wasn't really going to 'get' the play: the 'hard' language, the 'difficult' poetic densities, stories you have to listen to to follow; that, therefore, the directors were *ad lib* to play fast and loose with Shakespeare. So 'concept' replaced Shakespeare's ambiguity, his multiplicity with the director's big idea (call it 'fixation') or series of random local thoughts; told the audience what to think by overlaying Shakespeare's writing with disconnected supplementary counter-texts that distracted, supplanted or made nonsense of the writing; gave them a visually

coercive repertoire of sights and sounds and razz-ma-tazz to frog-march their reactions this way or that; substituted busy spectacle for textual, narrative, and rhetorical complexity, and pictures for words. And simply ignored – counting on the audience not to notice? – what didn't fit 'the concept': the logical inconsistences, the narrative discontinuities, the failures of meaning. These productions didn't fall happily into *Survey*'s regular review categories. I've had to invent a new one: 'Stoopid Shakespeare'.

Take Nancy Meckler's *A Midsummer Night's Dream*. Meckler is the director who produced, at the RSC in 2006, a modern-dress Sicilian *Romeo and Juliet* built on the conceit of ritual re-enactment: that the play was a substitute for the 'grudge' and 'mutiny' that had killed the children (last year? ten generations back?); that it was got up annually by the rival peasant families to keep the truce. How did you know any of this? You had to read the programme – or decipher the choreography of the ten-minute opening dumbshow that 'told' the backstory. (But as Michael Dobson in *Survey 60* remarked, 'The merest GCSE drama student could have recognized' this 'directorial concept' as 'a non-starter before the first rehearsal' – not least because it turned the actors into functional window dressing, 'dummies' going through the concept's motions.)

This year's *Dream* was similarly fixed on a concept. And it was STOOPID. Again, there was a long pre-set dumbshow. We were in a grey industrial space: a breeze-block warehouse with lorry-sized sheet metal doors at the back, wire mesh switchback stairs in one corner, fluorescent strip lighting, a naked bulb hanging from a flex, downstage a café-style table where men in dreadlocks and sharkskin suits were drinking, playing cards, while women undressed as tarts with 1950s beehive hair-dos cruised through, like some remaindered backing group to the Supremes: leather thigh boots, bustiers, and not much else. Everything, everyone: grey, black, white. Centre stage, facing out, was one of those cheap leather-look sofas advertised going for peanuts in factory clearances. On it, a dame, gazing, bored, smoking, hatchet-faced, bare foot, unclothed to her slip; over it, a deep-pile mink coat. Underscoring this scene: rumbles like distant thunder or maybe traffic passing outside. Then there was a bang, smoke poured up from a basement; one of the poker players opened the trap as upstage there was a kerfuffle and a load of comic-book workmen hustled in, tripping each other up, carrying, dropping, heating equipment, duct pipe. They disappeared underground. (To fix the boiler? Later, when everyone had forgotten about them, they'd explode out of the basement on 'Is all our company here?', none of us spectators supposed to wonder why a weaver and a tailor were repairing the plumbing.)

Meanwhile, a hard-faced mafioso with a pony-tail appeared, the stooges snapped to, the girls lined up. He inspected what his flunkey handed him – it was clearly a passport (at least, 'clearly' from where I, the reviewer, sat, Row D in the stalls). He snapped it shut, pocketed it, addressed her on the sofa: 'Now fair Hippolyta . . . ' On 'wed thee in another key', a goon entered, carrying a diva-sized floral tribute, in screaming pink. She trashed the orchid he offered. On 'Come my Hippolyta', she spat in his face, stalked off. But not off. Actually, retreated upstage where a big faux-leather chair was turned to the wall, climbed into it, fell asleep. The rest of this *Dream*, then, was, according to Meckler, Hippolyta's dream. Only, I didn't see the crucial concept-defining move into sleep (silly me, attending to the dialogue downstage) and had to be told it afterwards. And 90 per cent of the audience *couldn't* have seen it.

So what do we have? 'Athens' as the grey transit site for a sex trafficking operation. Women held in prostitution – shoes, clothes, passports confiscated (but handed 'sweeteners': orchid, mink). Hippolyta a trafficked woman; all women, sex hostages.

But it's okay: because, as we'll see, in the morning, all that nasty history will have vanished – like a dream! While the dream itself will work like magic! In the 'woods' everything will appear as its 'pretty' double: grey chairs will hang in the air, pastel-coloured; the sofa will be a flying bower, strung with flowers. (Well, almost everything: a dark idea will take shape in the form of baby dolls – proxies for the Indian boy, fashioned like monster fetishes by the badly behaved fairies and thrown around.) Theseus's goon, Philostrate, will reappear in technicolour – Puck, wearing a dozen psychedelic neckties, making a roll-up of the 'little western flower' and smoking it. Thuggish Theseus will be changed into Oberon – a superannuated rock star in Rolling Stones mode, bare-chested, his coat tails having grown spangles, and his eyelids, glitter – and thence into cuddly 'new man'. Hippolyta in her 'dream' alter ego as Titania will have experienced (in Bottom: here, a boorish, physically repulsive yeti) degradation (kneeling to savour the Ass's crotch where a salami penis hung like red meat) worse than subjection to her big city 'John'. She'll have tripped her way into a new dress via a 'transformation dance'. And in Act 5 she'll be deliciously in luuuuuuv (and ready for some serious displacement activity: Quince's play).

Right. I'd like Meckler to try that fantastic scenario on the 1535 European women found trafficked into the 342 brothels closest to Stratford-upon-Avon in the West Midlands last year. Just go to sleep, girls; everything'll look different in the morning. STOOPID. And politically obnoxious.

The actors did their best with this farrago: among them, Jo Stone-Fewings (Theseus/Oberon), Pippa Nixon (Hippolyta/Titania) and Matti Houghton as a pierced punk Hermia in goth-black opposite a loathsomely preppy Helena (Lucy Briggs-Owen), all designer classic clothes and big eyes. (Though this actor is getting into some terrible habits of self-indulgence, milking laughs on business beside the text as she rolls those eyes and stretches a line like 'I am as ugly as a bear' into a major career statement.) Other actors seemed to have given up: Arsher Ali, absent from Puck, delivered the role in a sequence of hand signals. Felix Hayes wandered around aimlessly as Snug. (Why was his lion's head made of paintbrushes? *He's a joiner, stoopid!*) Even Stone-Fewings had lost interest by the time he got to the 'lunatic, the lover and the poet': the speech went for nothing. I notice in Meckler's company of twenty, fourteen actors were making their RSC debuts. Some of them – Marc Wootton (Bottom) – appeared to be making their debut with Shakespeare. I guess if your concept requires dummies for actors, inexperience is an advantage. Still, inexperienced or not, Snout – Chiké Okonkwo – should be contacting his agent to start proceedings against this production for acts of gross indecency against a Wall.

The concept Michael Boyd overlaid on *Macbeth* was Tudor Reformation iconoclasm, a world out of Eamon Duffy's *The Stripping of the Altars*, quoted in the programme: 'image-hating Protestantism . . . a countryside punctuated with relics of greatness defiled . . . hatchets, hammers . . . government-backed zealots . . . pious barbarism . . . the art of medieval England . . . swept into oblivion'. (Though Tom Piper, as I read his notes scribbled on the set design also reproduced in the programme as illustration, seemed to think we were a hundred years later: the 'smashed states, ripped altar cloths' in his drawing belonging to the English 'civil war'.) What he designed on the deep thrust stage was the wrecked inside of a pre-Reformation church. At stage level, along the back wall, a fresco of saints' icons was literally defaced, eyes razed away. In front of it, rubble was piled: remains of burnings, battered masonry, splintered wood. Above, along a balcony reached by metal staircases left and right, a row of stained-glass windows was partly blown out: evangelists lacked heads, arms. And a massive hole, produced as if from heavy mortar fire, had exploded through the wall, ripping out the stonework. Like Tom Piper, I thought Cromwell's Roundheads had been through. But what did any of this Englishness have to do with Duncan's Scotland – either in the time Holinshed places him or Shakespeare (post the 1605 Gunpowder Plot) writes as 'parallel' time? Or in any other time? Given the 'period' gestures, what were the high wattage film-set lamps doing there, fixed to the balcony, focused out? Why was the lighting overhead industrial, the kind of fluorescent strips you get in butchers' shops? Who were the three cellists who took up positions on the balcony? Witches? Wrong.

Months earlier, when Boyd announced he'd be launching the new RST's opening season with his production of the theatrically unluckiest play in the canon, the superstitionists gulped. It was just 'typical', wrote one arts journalist, of Boyd's 'cussedness', to pooh-pooh tradition. Though I wonder if he began having second thoughts when things started to go wrong – big time. First he lost one star actor. Kathryn Hunter, Cleopatra in his *Antony and Cleopatra*, which should have been touring to the US, then wasn't, walked out, making a very public resignation from the company – even handing back her 'Artistic Associate' badge. The press release was tightlipped: 'We have not been able to achieve together the full range of ambitions that we shared.' Among them, perhaps a decent production of *Antony and Cleopatra* (see *Shakespeare Survey 64*)? Then he lost another. (Words like 'misfortune' and 'carelessness' spring to mind. Or maybe 'curse' and 'hubris'.) In the first week of September (when I saw the show), Jonathan Slinger was off (after a nasty cycling accident). His understudy on. For the rest of the season. As Macbeth. In, bizarrely, a Bronx accent – which Aidan Kelly (whose 'real' voice is Irish) kept slipping into from his other part this season, a wise-cracking New York Solanio in *The Merchant of Venice*. So the line in *Macbeth* came out: 'Da cry is still, "Dey cum!"'

But that was the least of this production's problems. At the level of basic story-telling, this vaguely Jacobean *Macbeth* was utterly incoherent. To begin with, Boyd cut Shakespeare's opening scene (and most of the rest of the Witches' part; there was no 'Where hast thou been sister . . . '; no 'Double, double'; no 'pricking thumbs'). He started instead with a plunge into blackness then lights up on the Bloody Captain – who would turn out to be Malcolm (Howard Charles) – bleeding, traumatized, centre stage, while, from a side balcony a man in black vestments (who would turn out to be Ross – Scott Handy – who would turn out to play, also, everything from Priest to Informant) leaned down and prompted, 'Doubtful it stood. *Doubtful* it stood. *DOUBTFUL* . . . ' until Malcolm/Captain took up the line and stumbled through the speech, a trick that was repeated at the end with Ross again prompting the closing speech: 'We shall not spend . . . We SHALL NOT spend . . . ' (And the

51. *Macbeth*, 1.2. Royal Shakespeare Theatre, directed by Michael Boyd. Jonathan Slinger as Macbeth, Steve Toussaint as Banquo, Charlie Blackwood, Tallulah Markham, Anwar Ridwan as Weird Children, Elaine Ackers, Clare Spencer-Smith, Suzanne Walden as cellists.

point of this was? A world ventriloquized by troublesome priests?)

Macbeth and Banquo (Steve Toussaint, in distinctly non-period Rasta dreadlocks) climbed into the wrecked sanctuary through the mortar-blasted hole in the wall. While they were poking around, three pint-sized corpses, like Jacobean dolls, hung on meat-hooks, dropped from the flies. On 'What are *these*?' their dead toes started to wiggle. They came alive. Lowered to the floor, they spoke the witches' 'all hails' and scampered away. They'd return to hang around the rubble, observing, and to scream through the 'What hath made them drunk . . . ' scene as 'the owl' that 'shrieked'. Later, these 'weird children' (as they were called, and the team I saw were horrifyingly disturbing: Charlie Blackwood, Anwar Ridwan, Tallulah Markham)

would turn out to have been the spotlessly innocent infants of Macduff, playing at their mother's feet – then murdered. But hang on, how did becoming victims make them evil-ones? Were they 'bad', getting themselves murdered? And how did they get 'good' again, at the end, when, reanimated, they presided, pygmy triumphalists, over the death of Macbeth? This Macbeth who faced them: how could he have spent all day on the battlefield 'unseam[ing]' men from 'the nave to the chops' and appear as squeaky-clean as a bridegroom, but later kill a sleeping man and look like he'd spent the afternoon in an abattoir?

Not just incoherent, this *Macbeth* was unconscionably derivative: the children-as-witches, nicked from Penny Woolcock's film, *Macbeth on the Estate* (where, as feral orphans they made total sense). And nicked from Rupert Goold's 2007 *Macbeth*, the ghost of Banquo smashing through the rood screen into the banquet (for all the world, Jack Nicholson in *The Shining*), to 'kill' Macbeth before our eyes and before the interval, then to play the scene again, after the interval, from the top, this time with Macbeth grotesquely writhing, solo, in time to his hallucinations while Lady Macbeth (Aislín McGuckin) in her retro-pompadour hairdo laughed hysterically. But then the whole banquet scene was ludicrous: there was no table, no sitting in degrees, no representation of social order: the thrust mitigates against such staging because of the sightlines, so the 'guests' were dispersed down the voms, the effect more a buffet than a banquet. Boyd even borrowed Boyd: from *The Histories* (*Shakespeare Survey 62*), the coronation (pouring a stream of water from the flies like the sand in *Richard II*), faux-Jacobean rituals, including a pre-banquet court dance, the return of the dead (Banquo, Lady Macduff, her children conscripted to Malcolm's army). The Porter (Jamie Beamish) repeated from the histories the figure who came to preside over all the 'disappeareds' as hell-gate-guarder, in red, like him, but strapped up in dynamite, a suicide bomber. Or, given Boyd's approximate 'historicizing', Guy Fawkes? Whichever, the actor's Irish accent made this a politically tasteless decision. Even the design turned out to be self-quotation: just a bigger version of Boyd's 1998 *Troilus and Cressida* set.

And at the end, when the 'butcher' lay 'dead', we got a moment of staggeringly incoherent 'recuperation': a walk-past of the vindicated dead had them gloating over the corpse as the wooden shutters that had closed across the blown-out sanctuary windows swung open – and showed the glass miraculously whole! So this story of ruin was proleptically the retrospective effect of Macbeth's evil – and fixed by his death? STOOPID.

The tag-line for this production should have been 'Confusion now has made his masterpiece'. And the thing is, 'concept' is so slow: despite the deep cuts to this leanest of tragedies, this *Macbeth*, which will be perhaps Boyd's last production as Artistic Director, he having announced his retirement from next year, dragged its way across almost three hours. And not insignificantly, the tag-line that's been fixed (in capital letters, like 'USP' – 'Unique Selling Point') on the company's work under Boyd's regime appears to be going into retirement with him: there has been no talk this year of 'the ensemble'. Indeed, there has been nothing spectators would recognize from the work on stage as an 'ensemble'. So: a concept that has served its PR purpose and now is simply dumped?

To finish this year's RSC repertoire, there was Rupert Goold's *Merchant of Venice*. This comedy is Shakespeare's most provocative investigation of the risks we take in loving. Its discriminations, its choosings, its meditations on what we bargain for as against what drops on our undeserving heads like rain from heaven are framed around tropes of comparative religion where words like 'lottery' and 'hazard' pack a spiritual punch. It's a profound play to challenge both early modern 'profession' and contemporary Western secularism. And what did Goold produce? He might have been Old Gobbo, he was so blind to the work this play is doing.

He gave us something glitzy, cheap, superficial, consumerist: a crass morality tale set now, for a culture grown morbidly obese on capitalist consumption. A tale built on crude translations. 'Lottery' = gamble. 'Venice' = Las Vegas, 2011. 'The Rialto' = a casino decorated 1950s-retro, which licensed (but didn't) some of the ugliest of the offensiveness: when he first appeared, Morocco (Chris Jarman), a blubbery Mohammed Ali stripped to gold-lamé prize-fighter's shorts with boxing gloves hung round his neck, had bananas showered down on him by goons in the balcony making monkey noises. But then, this was a production that would manage to be sexist, misogynist, racist, homophobic, anti-Semitic – and sentimental. And somehow we were supposed to accept it as 'Shakespeare'.

The pre-show was set in the casino (designer: Tom Scutt) – plenty of gilt, flashing lights, brash colours, mobile gaming tables serviced by chits in stilettos (that covered more of their feet than their hotpants did their fannies) and thronged with milling extras recruited from Stratford's expat community. (Goold had two requirements an insider told me: they had to be Americans 'for authenticity', and they had to be fat.) The logo presiding over this gamblers' palm court (where in a church, the rose window would be) was the come-on figure of a girl car-hop, in neon, all tits and bum. At one of the tables, morose, a half-smile on his otherwise immobile face, only a finger gesturing the next ante, sat Antonio (Scott Handy), losing. (Of course it was him: he was spot lit.) Did Shylock (Patrick Stewart) own the casino? His servant, Launcelot Gobbo (Jamie Beamish) spent all his time there as Elvis impersonator (covering the opening with 'Viva Las Vegas!' belted down a microphone). When we saw Shylock in his office, toupéd, in the sharpest of sharp suits, coolly playing carpet golf while Bassanio yammered on, I thought he might be a property developer (an architect's model covered a table behind), but banked video monitors overhead showed surveillance into the casino and 24-hour news of the stock-market. (But wasn't the exchange rate all wrong? '3000 ducats' was here converted to $3000: surely loose change for today's Shylock.)

'Casino Rialto' was, then, an American melting pot made up of Jonsonian grotesques out of *The Alchemist*, naïfs and hardened hucksters looking to turn the mean dross of their lives into gold (and all speaking approximate American accents that nobody seems to have bothered to locate in terms of class, education or social standing). So Lorenzo (Daniel Percival) was an East Coast preppie (who, in the street carnival that covered their elopement, dressed as Batman to steal Jessica – who happened to have a Robin costume in her wardrobe: what a coincidence!). Solanio (Aidan Kelly) was Alf Garnett from the Bronx in Hawaiian shirt and porkpie hat; Gratiano (Howard Charles), a nasty Puerto Rican grease-ball who sounded like he was auditioning for a bit part in *Some Like It Hot* (but 'no-buddy taks like *dat*'). Richard Riddell (Bassanio) can't help it if he has a face made for gangster films – a brow so low it letter boxes his eyes. But Bassanio is the romantic lead: he has glorious speeches ('In Belmont is a lady . . .'; 'Lady, you have bereft me of all words . . .') that this Bassanio – somehow simultaneously lumpen and arrogant –

made sound like he was reading the Dow-Jones Index.

So if Venice is Vegas, what is Belmont? Answer: a TV studio, evidently Portia and Nerissa's permanent residence, where they play out continuous rounds of a reality game-show (cue: sound spike, strobes, search-lights sweeping the studio set as the title lights up): 'DESTINY!' (As in: 'Hanging and wiving go by destiny'.) Susannah Fielding's Portia was Alabama trailor trash, a saucer-eyed peroxide blonde bimbo, styled by 'Dallas': 'Aw, Nur-is-suh, ma li'l bawdy iz-a *wurry*-a this gret wur-ruld'. (Also, ostentatiously racist: when 'Morocco' sat next to her, she wiped off his black touch as though it might soil her.) Emily Plumtree's Nerissa played air-head chat-show oppo, the gosh-gee-wow!-nudge-nudge-wink-wink-voiced interviewer quizzing her on her suitor/contestant preferences; both of them simultaneously sexualized and infantilized, one in pastel pink, the other in pastel blue, gingham rah-rah dresses, ankle-socks and matching platform high-heels. Like they'd put on fake TV voices, they'd put on themed costumes to meet each of the contestants: for, as we'd have to work out retrospectively, 'Morocco' was a DESTINY! player. So was 'Arragon' (Jason Morell), a hapless janitor plucked from the casino lift and kitted out in joke sombrero. (So thinking backwards, who threw the bananas? Studio camera operators? They'd be sacked – and slapped with writs – in 2011. But clearly, Goold wasn't expecting me to be *analysing* his 'concept'.) We only learned any of this when Bassanio turned up (in the same cheap suit he wore in Venice; what had he spent Antonio's money on?) and 3.2 ('Uh praaay yuh, terry . . . ') was staged around the game show floor manager prepping him. He disappeared (into wardrobe?). 'Go – HUR-CU-LEES!' cued his return, through dry ice, dressed as – Augustus Caesar. (STOOPID: a kindergartener knows Hercules by his iconic lionskin and club.)

Won, Fielding's Portia, bizarrely, got 'real': slipped off the heels, dragged off what turned out to be a wig, stood, simply, 'Sich as uh-yam', a brunette – though with no voice-box transplant. So: a woman trapped, like a fairy princess, by a spell

52. *The Merchant of Venice*, 1.2. Royal Shakespeare Theatre, directed by Rupert Goold. Emily Plumtree as Nerissa, Susannah Fielding as Portia.

now broken? Nope. Or maybe? Who knows. The wig, shoes and bimbo 'performance' got reinstated the minute Lorenzo et al. appeared. It goes without saying that it was impossible to get the wondrous sense of Portia's wondrous 'giving herself away' speech, she having to direct it at a Neanderthal in a peplum. And in a culture built entirely on fakery, it was impossible to see where dissimulation ended, sincerity began.

It was as hard to make connected sense of Venice. Stewart's Shylock was sincere wanting to 'be friends . . . / Forget the shames that you have stained me with'. The 'bond' really was 'merry'. But all that went out the window when Jessica absconded (Caroline Martin, making Jessica a pinched girl in horn-rim glasses who read by the light of a single naked light bulb, dad clearly a miser. How Jewish!) This Shylock 'got religion' just before the interval: 'Go Tubal!' had him breaking

into ethnic dance, then as the lights cut, emitting a Hebrew howl.

At the trial, he was in kippah, talis – and the right. Antonio was in orange Guantanamo prison overalls – pulled down to his thighs as he was strung up, wrists high, chest bare, on a meat hook ('prepare his bosom for the knife'), where he hyperventilated with terror – that trope accounting for this trial being conducted in a meat-packing unit? Upstage, behind plastic abattoir curtains, hung beef carcasses [sic]. Every image, then, was sensationalist, gratuitous, disconnected. Portia-as-Lawyer (*surely* she should have been outed the instant she opened her mouth: 'Wich iz th'murrchunt . . . wich thu Jee-yew?') turned from nervous incompetent – nothing in her pre-history suggesting she could read, never mind read law – into rabid Jew-baiter, vicious, vitriolic, pursuing with vengeance; Shylock from Old Testament zealot to simpering, wheedling, shrugging convert ('I am content'). Antonio, cut down, was cured of his infatuation with Bassanio. Earlier, he'd been unable to speak the name 'P – p – p – ortia'. Now, the two of them left behind, he pushed away Bassanio's embrace, disgusted. He staggered from the courtroom alone.

So how was it that at Belmont/DESTINY! a completely different, cozily homo-erotic story was in view, husband and friend, wedging up against Portia on the game show sofa, hands touching? The final scene was ugly and cynical – no dawn but a descent into nightmare. Swivelling eyes left/right, Bassanio/Antonio, Portia leaped up. Fled. Lost one high-heel. Looked back at them. Then began a broken-gaited little dance, a Stepford wife trapped in a black fairytale for all time, as Launcelot Gobbo-as-Elvis started crooning a new theme song that he just happened to have ready, Presley's 'Are you lonesome tonight?' Blackout. STOOPID.

In a production that constantly shouted 'Don't think! Look!', there was no room for poetry, metaphor, ambiguous characterization, difficult story, or indeed anything but the director's rather low-grade stand-up comedy commentary on the play ('What about this guy Shakespeare? Huh? Am I right, guys? Huh?'). It filled me with two great sadnesses. The first, was wondering what first-time viewers of the play would make of Shakespeare's *Merchant* from this travesty. The second was watching excellent actors (Handy, Martin, Stewart, particularly Fielding) working their socks off inhabiting a director's concept that didn't need actors, only dummies.

For me, then, this RSC anniversary season was a dismal wash-out. But by coincidence and as luck would have it, this year I also had conversations with four of the RSC's founder directors. They cheered me up. They approve the new building, are optimistic of the future, are (almost all of them) awesomely generous talking about colleagues. When I moaned, they stopped me. 'The RSC had the Age of the Builders. That finished when Terry Hands left. Then the Age of the Inheritors (which hasn't worked out very well). The present climate is for self-advertisement in directors. But that will change. That won't be there forever. There's a lot of "concept" about. But it will pass, and the imagination will come back again. Heart, humility, rigour: they'll come back. Another Peter Brook will emerge, somewhere, somehow.' Hopeful, but slightly impatient, I respond: 'Bring it on.'

PROFESSIONAL SHAKESPEARE PRODUCTIONS IN THE BRITISH ISLES JANUARY–DECEMBER 2010

JAMES SHAW

Most of the productions listed are by professional companies, but some amateur productions are included. The information is taken from *Touchstone* (www.touchstone.bham.ac.uk), a Shakespeare resource maintained by the Shakespeare Institute Library. Touchstone includes a monthly list of current and forthcoming UK Shakespeare productions from listings information. The websites provided for theatre companies were accurate at the time of going to press.

ANTONY AND CLEOPATRA

Royal Shakespeare Company. Courtyard Theatre, Stratford-upon-Avon, 10 April–28 August; Theatre Royal, Newcastle, 12–16 October; Roundhouse Theatre, London, 8–30 December.
www.rsc.org.uk
Director: Michael Boyd
Antony: Darrel D'Silva
Cleopatra: Kathryn Hunter

Nuffield Theatre, Southampton, 6–22 May.
www.nuffieldtheatre.co.uk
Director: Patrick Sandford

Liverpool Everyman Theatre Company. Everyman Theatre, Liverpool, 8 October–13 November.
www.everymanplayhouse.com
Director: Janet Suzman
Antony: Jeffery Kissoon
Cleopatra: Kim Cattrall

Adaptation
TARA! Tara Studio, London, 7 October.
www.tara-arts.com
Storyteller: Jan Blake
Part of Black History Month.

AS YOU LIKE IT

Old Vic Theatre. The Old Vic, London, 1 June–21 August.
www.oldvictheatre.com
Director: Sam Mendes
Jacques: Stephen Dillane
Rosalind: Juliet Rylance

Sprite Productions. Ripley Castle, Harrogate, 22 June–11 July.
www.spriteproductions.co.uk
Director: Alex Hassell

Royal Shakespeare Company. Courtyard Theatre, Stratford-upon-Avon, 21 July–4 September; Roundhouse Theatre, London, 13 January–5 February 2011.
www.rsc.org.uk
Director: Michael Boyd
Rosalind: Katy Stephens

West Yorkshire Playhouse. Quarry Theatre, West Yorkshire Playhouse, Leeds, 17 September–16 October.
www.wyp.org.uk
Directed by Ian Brown

SHAKESPEARE PRODUCTIONS IN THE BRITISH ISLES

THE COMEDY OF ERRORS

Manchester Royal Exchange. Royal Exchange
Theatre, Manchester, 31 March–8 May.
www.royalexchangetheatre.org.uk
Director: Roxana Silbert

Shakespeare's Globe. UK tour 17 June–
4 September.
www.shakespeares-globe.org
Director: Rebecca Gatward

New Shakespeare Company. Open Air Theatre,
London, 24 June–31 July.
http://openairtheatre.org
Director: Philip Franks

Royal Shakespeare Company & Tale Told by an
Idiot. The Courtyard Theatre, Stratford-upon-
Avon, 7 August–11 September; The
Roundhouse, London, 21 December–
1 February 2011.
www.rsc.org.uk
Director: Paul Hunter

CORIOLANUS

Grayscale. Ustinov Studio, Theatre Royal, Bath,
1–3 March.
www.theatreroyal.org.uk
Director: Lorne Campbell
Three actors playing all the parts.

CYMBELINE

C Company. Bridewell Theatre, London,
1–25 June.
www.stbridefoundation.org/bridewelltheatre
Part of the Lunchbox Theatre Series.

Shakespeare at the George. The George Hotel,
Huntingdon, 22 June-3 July.
www.atthegeorge.co.uk
Director: Michael Williamson

HAMLET

Rapture Theatre. Greenwich Theatre, London,
4–13 February.

www.rapturetheatre.co.uk
Director: Michael Emans
Gangster-themed interpretation.

Crescent Theatre, Birmingham, 13–20 March.
www.crescent-theatre.co.uk

Recognition Theatre Company. Brockley Jack
Pub, London, 7–25 September.
Director: Tanith Lindon

Sheffield Crucible. Crucible Theatre, Sheffield,
16 September–23 October.
www.sheffieldtheatres.co.uk
Director: Paul Miller
Hamlet: John Simm
Gertrude: Barbara Flynn

National Theatre. Olivier Theatre, London,
30 September–9 January 2011.
www.nationaltheatre.org.uk
Director: Nicholas Hytner
Hamlet: Rory Kinnear
Gertrude: Clare Higgins

Ni Drama Theatre Skopje. Mercury Theatre,
Colchester, 29 September–2 October.
www.mercurytheatre.co.uk
Director: Dejan Projkovski
Performed in Macedonian with English surtitles.

Fluellen Theatre Company. Grand Theatre,
Swansea, 9–12 November.
www.fluellentheatre.co.uk

Adaptation
The Tragedy of Handlet
Homemade Shakespeare. Ustinov Studio, Theatre
Royal, Bath, 4–6 March.
Playwright: Nola Rae
www.nolarae.com
A version for two gloved hands. Part of
Shakespeare Unplugged Festival.

Tiny Ninja Theater. The Egg, Theatre Royal,
Bath, 7–9 March.
www.tinyninjatheater.com
Director: Dov Weinstein

Company of 100 ninja figurine puppets. Part of
　　Shakespeare Unplugged Festival.

Young People's Shakespeare Hamlet
Royal Shakespeare Company. The Courtyard
　　Theatre, Stratford-upon-Avon, 1 May–
　　11 September; Theatre Royal, Newcastle-
　　upon-Tyne, 8–9 October; The
　　Roundhouse, London, 18 December–
　　26 January 2011.
www.rsc.org.uk
Adaptor: Tarell Alvin McCraney
Director: Bijan Sheibani
Hamlet: Dharmesh Patel
Seventy-minute version aimed at younger
　　audiences. Claimed to cast the first
　　British-Asian Hamlet.

Hamlet – House of Horror!
Westminster Theatre Company. Old Red Lion,
　　London, 10–28 August.
Director: Chris Barton
Shakespeare's play in gothic vaudeville style,
　　employing mime, satire and the original music
　　of The Horror House Band.

Kupenga Kwa Hamlet
Two Gents Productions and the Watermill
　　Theatre. UK tour 13 October–6 November.
Director: Arne Pohlmeier
A performance of the First Quarto. A company of
　　two playing all the roles.

Prince of Denmark
Royal National Theatre. Cottesloe Theatre,
　　Royal National Theatre, 14–26 October.
www.nationaltheatre.org.uk
Playwright: Michael Lesslie
Director: Antony Banks
Fifty-minute prequel featuring the teenage
　　Hamlet, Ophelia and Laertes.

Hamlet the Comedy
Oddsocks. UK tour, 29 November–5 March
　　2011.
www.oddsocks.co.uk
Director/Adaptor: Andy Barrow

HENRY IV, PART 1

Shakespeare's Globe. Shakespeare's Globe Theatre,
　　London, 6 June–9 October.
www.shakespeares-globe.org
Director: Dominic Dromgoole
Falstaff: Roger Allam

Adaptation
Shakespeare's Henry IV
Oxford Triptych Theatre Company. OFS Studio
　　Theatre, Oxford, 16–20 March.
www.o-t-t.co.uk
Adaptor and Director: Simon Tavener
Conflation of Parts 1 and 2.

HENRY IV, PART 2

Shakespeare's Globe. Shakespeare's Globe Theatre,
　　London, 6 June–9 October.
www.shakespeares-globe.org
Director: Dominic Dromgoole
Falstaff: Roger Allam

Adaptation
Shakespeare's Henry IV
Oxford Triptych Theatre Company. OFS Studio
　　Theatre, Oxford, 16–20 March.
www.o-t-t.co.uk
Adaptor and Director: Simon Tavener
Conflation of Parts 1 and 2.

HENRY V

Southwark Playhouse, 24 February–20 March.
www.southwarkplayhouse.co.uk
Director: Emily Lim

Bristol Brewery, 10 September–16 October.
Director: Andy Burden
Abbreviated version with four actors.

Company Boudin. The Tobacco Factory Studio
　　Theatre, Bristol, 21 September–2 October.
Director: Andy Burden

Adaptation
Henry the Fifth

Theatre Gruene Sosse (Germany). Theatre Royal, Bath, 23–27 February.
www.theatreroyal.org.uk
Playwright: Ignace Cornelissen
Adaptation aimed at children. Part of the Shakespeare Unplugged Festival.

HENRY VI, PARTS 1–3

Adaptation
Queen Margaret
Glasgow, Botanic Gardens, 25 June–9 July.
Director and Adaptor: Jennifer Dick
Adapted from the first tetralogy.

HENRY VIII

Shakespeare's Globe. Globe Theatre, London, 15 May–21 August.
www.shakespeares-globe.org
Director: Mark Rosenblatt
Henry VIII: Dominic Rowan
Katherine: Kate Duchêne

Adaptation
Anne Boleyn
Shakespeare's Globe Theatre, London, 24 July– 21 August.
www.shakespeares-globe.org
Playwright: Howard Brenton
Director: John Dove
Played in rep with *Henry VIII*.

KING LEAR

Royal Shakespeare Company. Courtyard Theatre, Stratford-upon-Avon, 18 February–26 August; Theatre Royal, Newcastle-upon-Tyne, 5–9 October; Roundhouse Theatre, London, 21 January–4 February 2011.
www.rsc.org.uk
Director: David Farr
Lear: Greg Hicks

Company of Common Sense. Tara Studio, London, 27 February.

Storyteller: Inno Sorsy
www.tara-arts.com

Glasgow, Botanic Gardens, 25 June–9 July.
www.bardinthebotanics.co.uk
Director: Gordon Barr
King Lear: George Docherty

Adaptation
Lear and His Daughters
Spadra Bus Company. The Rosemary Branch Theatre, London, 16–24 February.
www.rosemarybranch.co.uk
Playwright: Bobby Fincher

Special Staged Reading. Theatre Royal, York, 3 October.
www.yorktheatreroyal.co.uk
Lear: Freddie Jones
A staged reading to celebrate the career of Freddie Jones.

LOVE'S LABOUR'S LOST

Guildford Shakespeare Company. Guildford Castle Grounds, 17 June–3 July.
www.guildford-shakespeare-company.co.uk
Director: Simon Usher

MACBETH

Studio Theatre of the Broadway Theatre, Catford, 27 January–20 February.
www.broadwaytheatre.org.uk
Director: Alice Lacey

Rose Theatre, London, 18 February–6 March.
www.rosetheatre.org.uk
Director: David Pearce

Cheek By Jowl. Barbican, London, 18 March– 10 April; Theatre Royal, Brighton, 11–15 May.
www.cheekbyjowl.com
Director: Declan Donnellan
Macbeth: Will Keen
Lady Macbeth: Anastasia Hille

Shakespeare's Globe. Shakespeare's Globe Theatre, London, 23 April–27 June.
www.shakespeares-globe.org
Director: Lucy Bailey

The Pantaloons. UK tour 15 May–27 August.
www.thepantaloons.co.uk
New Shakespeare Company. Open Air Theatre, London, 3–24 July.
http://openairtheatre.org
Director: Steve Marmion

Adaptation
Dunsinane
Royal Shakespeare Company. Hampstead Theatre, 17 February–6 March.
www.rsc.org.uk
Director: Roxana Silbert
Playwright: David Greig

Macbeth
Homemade Shakespeare with Nola Rae & Lasse Åkerlund, Ustinov Studio, Theatre Royal, Bath, 4–6 March.
www.nolarae.com
Part of Shakespeare Unplugged Festival. Mime adaptation.

A Season Before The Tragedy of Macbeth
British Touring Shakespeare. Camden People's Theatre, London, 4–8 August.
www.facsimileproductions.co.uk
Director: Andrew Hobbs
Playwright: Gloria Carreno
A prequel. Part of the Camden Fringe 2010.

Just Macbeth!
Bell Shakespeare. Assembly Rooms, Edinburgh, 5–29 August.
www.bellshakespeare.com.au
Playwright: Andy Griffiths
Show for children.

Theatr Piezn Koyla (Song of the Goat Theatre).
The Pit, Barbican Centre, London, 3–20 November and UK tour.
www.piesnkozla.pl

Grzegorz Bral and Anna Zubrzycki.
In Polish.

Opera
Glyndebourne Festival, East Sussex, 13 June–24 July.
www.glyndebourne.com
Composer: Giuseppe Verdi
Director: Richard Jones

MEASURE FOR MEASURE

Almeida Company. Almeida Theatre, London, 11 February–3 April.
www.almeida.co.uk
Director: Michael Attenborough
Isabella: Anna Maxwell Martin

Sherman Cymru. Provincial Theatre, Cardiff, 24 November–5 December.
Director: Amy Hodge
Isabella: Kezia Burrows
Duke: Robert Bowman

THE MERCHANT OF VENICE

Theatre Royal Bury St Edmunds. 17–27 February.
www.theatreroyal.org
Director: Abigail Anderson

Chapterhouse. UK tour 11 June–28 August.
www.chapterhouse.org

Theatre Set-up. UK tour 1 July–21 August.
www.ts-u.co.uk

Adaptation
Pascal Theatre Company. Studio 1, Arcola, London, 18–19 September.
www.arcolatheatre.com
Director: Julia Pascal
A Warsaw ghetto survivor sees a performance of *The Merchant of Venice* in modern-day Venice.

Euro-Japan Theatre Organisation & Theatre Du Sygne. Arcola Theatre, London. 18–19 November.
www.arcolatheatre.com

Director: Nicholas Barter
In Japanese with English subtitles.

THE MERRY WIVES OF WINDSOR

Stafford Festival Theatre. Stafford Castle, Stafford, 24 June–10 July.
www.staffordfestivalshakespeare.co.uk
Director: Peter Rowe

The Hazlitt Arts Centre and The Changeling Theatre Company. UK tour 3 July–8 August.
www.hazlittartscentre.co.uk
Director: Robert Forknall

Shakespeare's Globe. Shakespeare's Globe Theatre, London, 14 August–2 October and UK tour until December.
www.shakespeares-globe.org
Director: Christopher Luscombe
Falstaff: Christopher Benjamin
Mistress Ford: Sarah Woodward

A MIDSUMMER NIGHT'S DREAM

Bolton Octagon. Octagon, Bolton, 4 February–6 March.
www.octagonbolton.co.uk
Director: David Thacker

Rose Theatre, Kingston. 9 February–20 March.
www.rosetheatrekingston.org
Director: Sir Peter Hall
Titania: Judi Dench

Shakespeare at the Tobacco Factory. Tobacco Factory, Bristol, 11 February–20 March.
www.sattf.org.uk
Director: Andrew Hilton

Practical Productions. UK tour 8 March–27 April.
www.practicalproductions.co.uk
Director: Harry Denford

Shakespeare's Globe. Shakespeare's Globe Theatre, London, 3–14 May and UK tour until 28 August.
www.shakespeares-globe.org

Director: Raz Shaw

Stephen Joseph Theatre Company. The Round Auditorium, Stephen Joseph Theatre, Scarborough, 4 June–31 July.
www.sjt.uk.com
Director: Chris Monks

Chapterhouse. UK tour 10 June–30 August.
www.chapterhouse.org

Oddsocks. UK tour 12 June–26 July.
www.oddsocks.co.uk

C Company. Bridewell Theatre, London, 6–30 July.
www.stbridefoundation.org/bridewelltheatre
Part of the Lunchbox Theatre Series.

Adaptation
Midsummer
Soho Theatre, London, 14 January–6 February
Director: David Greig
Revival of 2008 Traverse production. The summer solstice brings sexual confusion for Helena and Bob.

Trestle Theatre Company and Moon Fool, UK tour 3 February–26 March.
www.trestle.org.uk
Director: Ian Morgan
Three-hander focusing on the fairy characters.

Pocket Dream
Propeller Theatre Company. UK tour July–October.
www.propeller.org.uk
Director: Edward Hall
Sixty-minute version for younger audiences.

Ill Met by Moonlight
Hijinx Theatre Company. UK tour 21 September–11 December.
www.hijinx.org.uk
Playwright: Charles Way
Director: Louise Osborn
Gwarwyn-a-throt, a descendent of Puck, causes mischief in contemporary Wales.

Shakespeare 4 Kidz. UK tour 27 September–7 April 2011.
www.shakespeare4kidz.com

Midwinter Dream
Bridge House Theatre Company. Bridge House Theatre, Warwick, 3–18 December.
www.bridgehousetheatre.co.uk
Director: Alison Sutcliffe
A Christmas show with the Mechanicals rehearsing a panto.

Opera
English Touring Opera. Sadler's Wells, London, 10 March and UK tour until May.
www.englishtouringopera.org.uk
Composer: Benjamin Britten

MUCH ADO ABOUT NOTHING

The Pantaloons. UK tour 11 June–30 August.
www.thepantaloons.co.uk

Chapterhouse. UK tour 23 June–2 September.
www.chapterhouse.org

Stamford Shakespeare. Rutland Open Air Theatre, Tolethorpe Hall, Stamford, 6 July–28 August.
www.stamfordshakespeare.co.uk

Chester, Grosvenor Park, 16 July–8 August.
Director: Edward Dick

OTHELLO

ArtsBeat. Tara Studio, London, 17–19 February.
www.tara-arts.com
Director: Filiz Ozcam
Lazarus Theatre Company. The Blue Elephant, London, 13 April–8 May.
www.lazarustheatrecompany.webs.com
Director: Ricky Dukes
Ninety-minute version.

Stamford Shakespeare. Rutland Open Air Theatre, Tolethorpe Hall, Stamford, 15 June–21 August.
www.stamfordshakespeare.co.uk

Ludlow Festival Society. Ludlow Castle, Ludlow, 26 June–10 July.
www.ludlowfestival.co.uk
Director: Ben Crocker

Adaptation
Otieno
Metta Theatre Company. Southwark Playhouse, 25 May–15 June.
www.southwarkplayhouse.co.uk
Playwright: Trevor Michael Georges
Director: Poppy Burton-Morgan
Set during Zimbabwe elections of 2008.

Tara Arts. Tara Studio, London, 6 October.
www.tara-arts.com
Storyteller: Inno Sorsy
Storytelling event for Black History Month.

PERICLES

Adaptation
Common Sense Production. Tara Studio, London, 26 February.
www.tara-arts.com
Storyteller: Jan Blake
Part of the RE-MIXED Festival.

RICHARD III

Love and Madness. Riverside Studios, London, 2 February–21 March and UK tour.
www.loveandmadness.org
Director: Ben Kidd
Richard: Carl Prekopp

Propeller. UK tour 18 November–7 May 2011.
www.propeller.org.uk
Director: Edward Hall
All-male Company.

Adaptation
Queen Margaret
Glasgow, Botanic Gardens, 25 June–9 July.
Director and Adaptor: Jennifer Dick
Adapted from the second tetralogy.

Now is the Winter
Alarum Theatre. The Vault, Edinburgh, 7–
30 August
www.alarumtheatre.co.uk
Playwright and Director: Kate Saffin
Monologue by Richard's servant.

ROMEO AND JULIET

Oddsocks. UK tour 1 January–29 January.
www.oddsocks.co.uk
Mercury Theatre Company. Mercury Theatre,
Colchester, 25 February–13 March.
www.mercurytheatre.co.uk
Director: Ed Hughes

Royal Shakespeare Company. Courtyard Theatre,
Stratford-upon-Avon, 12 March–27 August;
Theatre Royal, Newcastle, 28 September–
2 October; Roundhouse Theatre, London,
30 November–1 January 2011.
www.rsc.org.uk
Director: Rupert Goold
Juliet: Mariah Gale
Romeo: Sam Troughton

Ruby In The Dust. Basement of Leicester Square
Theatre, London, 1 June–11 July.
www.rubyinthedusttheatre.com
Director: Linnie Reedman

Miracle Theatre Company. UK tour 2 June–
30 August.
www.miracletheatre.co.uk

Illyria Theatre Company. UK tour 11 June–
24 August.
www.illyria.uk.com

Creation Theatre Company. Saïd Business
School, Oxford, 9 July–4 September.
www.creationtheatre.co.uk
Director: Charlotte Conquest

Get Over It Productions. The Lion & Unicorn
Theatre, London, 24–29 August.
www.myspace.com/getoveritproductions
All-female cast.

Pilot Theatre Company. Theatre Royal, The
Studio, York, 10–25 September and
UK tour.
www.pilot-theatre.com
Directors: Marcus Romer and Katie Posner

Royal Lyceum Theatre, Edinburgh,
17 September–16 October.
www.lyceum.org.uk
Director: Tony Cownie

Proper Job Theatre Company. UK tour
21 September–15 October
www.properjob.org.uk

Adaptation
Homemade Shakespeare with Nola Rae & Lasse
Kerlund, Ustinov Studio, Theatre Royal, Bath,
4–6 March.
Mime version, part of Shakespeare Unplugged
Festival.

Tiny Ninja Theater. The Egg, Theatre Royal,
Bath, 9–10 March.
www.tinyninjatheater.com
Director: Dov Weinstein
Company of 100 ninja figurine puppets. Part of
Shakespeare Unplugged festival.

Juliet and Her Romeo
Bristol Old Vic, Bristol, 10 March–2 May.
www.bristololdvic.org.uk
Playwright: Tom Morris
Juliet: Sian Phillips
Romeo: Michael Byrne
A match between octogenarian lovers is opposed
by their children.

People's Romeo
Ustinov Studio, Theatre Royal, Bath, 10–
13 March. Tara Studio, London, 9–10
September and UK tour.
Director: Mukul Ahmed
Part of Shakespeare Unplugged Festival. A fusion
of Shakespeare and Bengali poetry.

Ballet

Moscow City Ballet. Chichester Festival Theatre, Chichester, 5–7 January and UK tour.

Royal Ballet Company. Royal Opera House, 12 January–12 March.
www.roh.org.uk
Composer: Prokofiev
Choreography: Kenneth Macmillan

Scottish Ballet. Theatre Royal, Glasgow, 20–24 April and UK tour.
www.scottishballet.co.uk
Choreography: Kryszstof Pastor

Birmingham Royal Ballet. The Lowry, Salford, 30 June–3 July and UK tour.
www.brb.org.uk
Composer: Prokofiev
Choreography: Kenneth Macmillan

English National Ballet. Palace Theatre, Manchester, 14–17 October and UK tour.
www.ballet.org.uk
Composer: Prokofiev
Choreography: Rudolf Nureyev

THE TAMING OF THE SHREW

Principal Theatre. UK tour 24 June–6 August.
www.principaltheatrecompany.com

Adaptation
Taming
Bristol Shakespeare Company. The Brewery, Tobacco Factory, Bristol, 12–14 July.
www.bristolshakespeare.org.uk
Director: Grace Wessels
Part of the Bristol Shakespeare Festival.

THE TEMPEST

Platform4. UK tour 28 January–17 March.
www.platform4.org
Director: Simon Plumridge
Three actors focusing on the island characters and Ferdinand.

Firebird Theatre in Association with Bristol Old Vic. Bristol Old Vic, Bristol, 4–6 March.
www.firebird-theatre.com
Director: John Nicholson
A cast of disabled actors.

Shakespeare at the Tobacco Factory. Tobacco Factory, Bristol, 26 March–1 May.
www.sattf.org.uk
Director: Andrew Hilton

The Faction. Brockley Jack Pub, London, 27 April–15 May.
www.thefaction.org.uk

Unicorn Theatre Company. Unicorn Theatre, 15 May–19 June.
www.unicorntheatre.com
Director: Tony Graham
Production for younger audiences.

The Festival Players. UK tour 29 May–5 September.
www.thefestivalplayers.co.uk

Old Vic Theatre, London, 1 June–31 August.
www.oldvictheatre.com
Director: Sam Mendes
Prospero: Stephen Dillane
Ariel: Anne-Marie Duff

The Lord Chamberlain's Men. UK tour 2 June–22 August.
www.tlcm.co.uk
Director: Andrew Normington

Oxford Shakespeare Company. Wadham College, Oxford, 4 July–19 August; Hampton Court Palace, Hampton, 21–30 August.
www.osctheatre.org.uk
Director: Mick Gordon

The Rose Theatre. Rose Theatre, London, 5–30 October.
www.rosetheatre.org.uk
Director: David Pearce

Adaptation
Miranda

West Drawing Room, Assembly Rooms,
   Edinburgh, 5–29 August.
Playwright: Farouk Dhondy
A Bollywood actress joins a British touring
   production of *The Tempest*.

TITUS ANDRONICUS

Hephaestus Productions. Camden's People's
   Theatre, London, 18–21 August.
Sixty-minute version.

Action to the Word. The Space, 7–19 December.
www.actiontotheword.com
Director: Alexandra Spencer-Jones

TWELFTH NIGHT

Royal Shakespeare Company. Duke of York's
   Theatre, London, 19 December 2009–27
   February.
www.rsc.org.uk
Director: Gregory Doran
Malvolio: Richard Wilson
Viola: Nancy Carroll

Sell a Door Theatre Company. Greenwich
   Playhouse, London, 16 February–14 March.
www.selladoor.com
Director: Bryn Holding

Birmingham Stage Company. Old Rep Theatre,
   Birmingham, 16–17 March and Middle East
   tour.
www.birminghamstage.net
Director: Andrew Normington

The National Theatre. Cottesloe, London, 16–27
   February; Bristol Old Vic 27 April–1 May.
www.nationaltheatre.org.uk
Director: Carl Heap
Adapted for younger audiences.

Filter Theatre Company. Tricycle Theatre,
   London, 4–29 May and UK tour until
   November.
www.filtertheatre.com
Director: Sean Holmes

Nottingham Playhouse Theatre Company.
   Nottingham Playhouse, 24 September–16
   October.
www.nottinghamplayhouse.co.uk
Director: Paulette Randall

THE WINTER'S TALE

Royal Shakespeare Company. The Courtyard
   Theatre, Stratford-upon-Avon, 14 July–2
   September; Roundhouse Theatre, 14–30
   December.
www.rsc.org.uk
Director: David Farr
Leontes: Greg Hicks
Hermione: Kelly Hunter

POEMS AND APOCRYPHA

Precious Friends – Shakespeare's Sonnets Staged
Tabard Theatre, London, 23 March–11 April.
Adaptor: Simon Reade
Director: Mark Leipacher

Supermarket Shakespeare
Teatro Vivo. Sainsbury's supermarkets, 20 April –
   16 May.
Director: Mark Stevenson
Three 20-minute promenade pieces inspired by
   Sonnet 23. Performed during supermarket
   opening times.

The Rape of Lucrece
Grand Opera House, Belfast, 29 April and tour
   until October.
www.britishshakespearecompany.com
Adaptor and Performer: Gareth Logan

Double Falsehood
KDC Theatre. Union Theatre, London, 17–
   21 August.
www.kdctheatre.com
Director: Barrie Addenbrooke

Cardenio
Warehouse Croydon, 8–21 November.
www.bardinthebotanics.co.uk

Director: Jonathan Busby
A production of *The Second Maiden's Tragedy*, attributed by the company to Shakespeare, Fletcher and Middleton.

MISCELLANEOUS

The Animated Tales of Shakespeare

The Egg, Theatre Royal, Bath, 20 February–6 March.
www.theatreroyal.org.uk
Part of Shakespeare Unplugged Festival. Two plays brought to life by an actor and an illustrator.

Bingo
Chichester Festival Theatre. Minerva Theatre, Chichester, 15 April–22 May.
www.cft.org.uk
Playwright: Edward Bond
Director: Angus Jackson
Shakespeare: Patrick Stewart
Jonson: Richard McCabe

Gift to the Future
The Lantern Theatre, Sheffield, 13–18 September.
Playwright and Performer: Colin David Reese
John Heminges arrives at the Globe with First Folio and recounts his career with Shakespeare.

I, Elizabeth
Guy Masterson/TTI @ George Street, Edinburgh, 5–30 August.

Director: Guy Masterson
Adapted from the speeches, letters, poems and prayers of Elizabeth I.

The Man from Stratford: Being Shakespeare
Theatre Royal, Bath, 28–30 June and tour until 2 October.
Playwright: Jonathan Bate
Performer: Simon Callow

Shakespeare Inc.
Second Skin Theatre. The Rosemary Branch Theatre, London, 2–21 March.
Director: Andy McQuade
Playwright: Don Fried
Authorship controversy farce.

Shakespeare's Kings & Westminster Abbey
Royal Shakespeare Company & Westminster Abbey. Westminster Abbey, London, 13 April–11 May.
www.westminster-abbey.org
Excerpts from the history plays.

Shakespeare's Will
Clwyd Theatr Cymru, Mold. Director Emma Lucia. 18 March–3 April.
Playwright: Vern Thiessen.
www.clwyd-theatr-cymru.co.uk
Anne Hathaway recounts her life after Shakespeare's funeral.

THE YEAR'S CONTRIBUTION TO SHAKESPEARE STUDIES

1. CRITICAL STUDIES
reviewed by CHARLOTTE SCOTT

FREE THINKING

The publication of a book by Stephen Greenblatt is always a significant event and *Shakespeare's Freedom* is no exception. Opening with a claim that may surprise many, Greenblatt asserts that 'Shakespeare as a writer is the embodiment of human freedom':

Though he lived his life as the bound subject of a monarch in a strictly hierarchical society that policed expression in speech and in print, he possessed what Hamlet calls a free soul.

Addressing Shakespeare's 'free soul', here construed as a kind of capacious creativity, Greenblatt explores the contest between an 'absolutist world' and 'literary genius' and 'the ways that Shakespeare establishes and explores the boundaries that hedge about the claims of the absolute'. Drawing on his usual eclectic range of theoretical models Greenblatt interprets a selection of plays with all that was original and refreshing about new historicism – reading against the grain, historical anecdote and an acute sense of Shakespeare's interest in power on display. The book is structured around five major themes and their dramatization – absolute limits, beauty, hatred, authority and autonomy. Shakespeare is seen as a supremely creative free thinker, working within an absolutist society but with an apparently infinite capacity for imaginative investment. Thinking outside the confines of his culture, Shakespeare was able to create and destroy versions of these concepts, enabling us to recognize the depth of his achievement. Taking on morality, for example, in *Measure for Measure*, Greenblatt examines Barnadine's peculiarly comic refusal to die:

Barnadine, so unnecessary and so theatrically compelling, serves as an emblem of the freedom of the artist to remake his world. But this strange character is – by Shakespeare's careful design – a most unlikely emblem of artistic freedom; penned up, drunken, filthy, and rustling in the straw, the convicted criminal Barnadine is the embodiment of everything that is mortal, bodily and earth-bound.

It is this notion of 'artistic freedom' that drives the book and, for Greenblatt, such freedom is revolutionary. In deploying terms of beauty, for example, Shakespeare works against the 'feature-less' culture of Elizabethan form and goes some way in creating an individual aesthetic. Innogen's mole, for example, though neither ornament nor a quality of perfection, is 'a mark of all that Shakespeare found indelibly beautiful in singularity and all that we identify as indelibly singular and beautiful in his work'. For Greenblatt these moments become wholesale metaphors for Shakespeare's creative capacities.

As always, Greenblatt is capable of exquisite writing. His ability to turn a thought into a memorable construction is frequently in evidence, and he has the ability to make old ideas seem new. His essay on hate, for example, which begins by synthesizing racial tension into contemporary anxiety of radicalism, revisits the question of anti-Semitism in *The Merchant*: 'We are in effect watching the fashioning of full ethnic or religious identification, as if Shylock, by virtue of his propensity and his entrepreneurial energy, had until now held himself aloof from the communal account of what it meant to be Jewish.'

Sometimes *Shakespeare's Freedom* reads like a memoir, or even a Greenblatt reader, a summation of what Greenblatt brought to the field of Shakespeare's studies and how he articulated a new way of thinking through questions of power, history and the self. But there is also a sea change: the idea of an autonomous self (as well as the notion of genius) is fully accommodated into his writing and no longer the premise for rejection, which may please some but puzzle others who have assimilated Greenblatt's long-standing caution concerning the autonomous subject. The title sets up certain expectations on which the book does not necessarily deliver. It is not, for example, a Lockean examination of questions of free will, or free-thinking, nor does Greenblatt revisit the confrontation with autonomy that ended *Renaissance Self-Fashioning*. His interest here is in exploring the 'rich and compelling moral life' of Shakespeare's characters and to that end free-thinking becomes a proto-liberal attitude to art: 'But if some form of subjection is the inescapable human condition, Shakespeare may nonetheless have thought that radical freedom was possible for a poem or a play.' Greenblatt is ultimately interested in artistic freedom, and the book ends with an exploration of artistic apologies in which the play is either a useless, but pleasurable, diversion (*Dream*) or a potentially offensive experience (*The Tempest*): 'the shift we see from "dream" to "crime" is a measure of . . . [Shakespeare's] deepening awareness of the nature of his craft and the risks it entailed'. Whilst Greenblatt celebrates Shakespeare as thinking beyond the limits of his cultural context, many of this year's critical studies seek to reorient our understanding of that context altogether.

For Michele Marrapodi, in *Shakespeare and Renaissance Literary Theories: Anglo-Italian Transaction*, the 'nature of [t]his craft' is dominated by a comparative analysis of the plays in order to 'highlight Shakespeare's exploitation of mixed drama in the context of the period's widespread resistance to any aspects of generic virtuosity imported from abroad and from Italy in particular'. To that end, this book brings together a range of esteemed scholars to talk about Renaissance attitudes to literature that we might now call 'literary theories'. Central to these theories are competing notions of decorum, genre, style, temporality, register and rhetoric; and whilst there is a general acknowledgement of Roman tradition there is also a distrust of contemporary Italian artifice. This collection of essays re-engages with the 'presence of Italian literary theories against and alongside the background of English dramatic traditions and . . . assess[es] this influence in the emergence of Elizabethan theatrical conventions and the innovative dramatic practices under the early Stuarts'. The essays cover a wide range of topics and methodologies, including formal style, generic forms, aesthetics and representation. Even within these topics, however, there is a wide breadth: Stephen Orgel's essay on 'the suppression or subversion of memory' examines the relationship between creativity and forgetting in *King Lear* and *The Winter's Tale*; while Marrapodi's essay examines the texture of the later plays in his analysis of genre and Shakespeare's 'reworking of the third genre theorised by Giraldi Cinthio', 'a variant of pastoral satire'. All the essays in this collection emphasize the fluidity of cultural ideas and forms and the ways in which we can understand Shakespeare in a European context. Neither exclusively humanist nor historicist in its approach, this collection explores Shakespeare's drama with a 'wide net' in its commitment to 'the insistently theatrical Italianate character of much of Shakespeare's work'. Rather distractingly, however, many of these essays retain their signposts as conference papers, failing to edit out the 'talk' from the text.

The presence of Italy continues this year through Louise George Clubb's *In Pollastra and the Origins of Twelfth Night: Parthenio, commedia (1516) with an English Translation*, where she looks beyond the influence of the Sienese comedy *Gl'ingannati* on Shakespeare's play to *Parthenio*, 'as a significant site to be excavated for more knowledge about half-hidden connections in early Cinquecento culture'. Part of this excavation is to reproduce an English and Italian text of the play along with a thorough introduction to both the form of Italian comedy as well as its place within the larger context of early modern European drama. Like Marrapodi's collection, Clubb's book focuses on the ways in which Italian drama inflects the development of early modern English theatre.

Europe remains a dominant context this year and Graham Holderness shifts the focus to Venice in his book, *Shakespeare and Venice*. Holderness begins by unpicking the common critical assumption that Shakespeare's foreign geography was largely 'poetic' (a term of devaluation, which he rightly questions) or 'refracted projection[s] of London'. Tracing the conceptual problems of how we understand the past without the projections of the present, Holderness approaches Venice as geographically specific with a 'deliberately realized historical time and place'. Central to Holderness's thesis is the exploration of 'myth' as a 'false consciousness', a prevailing assumption and a linear construction of organized perceptions. Venice has multiple mythologies, which Holderness shows to be formulated and perpetuated by certain literary discourses that ritualize its representations. From the economic, romantic, ethereal, transitional, festive and political, Holderness seeks to reposition Shakespeare's Venice as a 'historical society' in which myth is 'a real and powerful form of human consciousness'. Providing new perspectives on Shakespeare's Venetian plays, this book explores the city as place of change (or 'turning'), in which fantasy and deviancy coexist: 'a place of difference; the home of strangers; the territory of the Other'.

Geography – cultural and spatial – remains of fundamental interest in Shakespeare studies (and beyond as Julie Sanders's *The Cultural Geography of Early Modern Drama, 1620–1650* testifies) and this is demonstrated by Willy Maley and Margaret Tudeau-Clayton in *This England, That Shakespeare: New Angles on Englishness and the Bard*.

Through a collection of essays on the broad theme of regional and national identities as well as the relationships that Shakespeare explores between nationalism and patriotism, Maley and Tudeau-Clayton reflect on Englishness, both modern and early modern. This is a comprehensive collection, aiming – and largely succeeding – to represent the ways in which we should engage with questions of national identity, geographical space and vernacular identities. Inevitably, conflict becomes a central concern of these essays, since it provides the point at which we can identify if not always recover a range of historical voices. Rather predictably essays on the history plays predominate, but there are also some intriguing reflections on *Pericles* and *The Merchant of Venice*. Thomas Roebuck and Laurie Maguire, for example, tackle *Pericles* through the work of Anthony Smith, in which land, cultures and institutions are the 'constituent categories of nationalism', and Margaret Tudeau-Clayton explores 'the nearest Shakespeare gets to what we call "ideology"' in *The Merchant* and *Richard II*. As Emma Smith has astutely noted elsewhere, *Richard II* has become the 'poster-boy' of Shakespeare's studies, and it is certainly all over this collection. There are some compelling arguments, however, and a concerted intellectual effort to understand 'Shakespeare not as an object so much as a collaborator in the project of collective self-understanding'. Sarah Grandage's essay traces the lexicon of Englishness through the rhetoric of public power. Beginning with Gaunt's 'sceptered isle' speech, she examines the 'cultural depth charge' of Gaunt's language as well as his ideology. Working from the moment in which Shakespeare composed *Richard II* to a local newspaper's report on Iain Duncan Smith's address to his party at the 2003 Conservative Party Conference, Grandage follows the rhetorical appropriations of Englishness as they are translated across time to form a 'shorthand' for the symbolic register of both aggression and emotion, allegiance and antipathy. Unlike much of the work on *Henry V*, however, Grandage focuses on the interrelations between island geography and elegiac fantasy.

SPECTRES OF HISTORY

The significance of context – historical or geo-graphical – continues to haunt Shakespeare studies, and it is notable that some of the most penetrat-ing books published this year are anxious to rede-fine the role of critical analysis in our pursuit of a history of the present. In *Shakespearean Genealo-gies of Power: A Whispering of Nothing in Hamlet, Richard II, Julius Caesar, Macbeth, The Merchant of Venice, and The Winter's Tale*, Anselm Haverkamp focuses on the 'latent' in his interrogation of 'literary effect and transport'. Drawing on a com-plex mix of high German idealism and mod-ernism, Haverkamp explores the question of history – what is it, when did it start, and is it always defined from a genealogy of the present? Summon-ing the work of Nietzsche and Foucault in his title, Haverkamp explores aspects of Shakespeare's plays through the critical philosophies of Hegel, Fou-cault, Schmitt, Kantorowicz and Benjamin. Like Greenblatt, Haverkamp explores the theatre as a place in which 'characters make History readable as a script, as hieroglyphics in a human form. And as we read history in these characters, it disappears in the figures in which it enters the stage: of these fig-ures of history, thus, we perceive nothing but their character as the trace of the readability of History.' In search of the readability of history, Haverkamp focuses on certain elements of his titular plays. Our first encounter with History is through the Ghost in Hamlet, a 'phantom full of lies', 'a his-tory of History' that uses vengeance and memory 'to draw what comes after into the same deceit-ful orbit of compassion'. Exploring the complex relationships between memory, paternity, history and legitimacy, Haverkamp's analysis of the play discerns a 'master trope beyond memory's rhetoric whose apparition resides in the machinery of the stage itself'. Such a 'master trope' manifests as the secularization of theology into politics, legitimized by its transition and masquerading as moder-nity: 'justice as the dire necessity and urgency of secular law is mocked by the ghost of his-tory calling for remembrance'. Subsequent chap-ters work through some of the machinations of the invidious relations between history and ideology, politics and secularization. A chapter on *Richard II* exposes how the illegitimate becomes legitimized through the king's 'two bodies' and the central-ity of theatre in the 'paradoxical performance of self-deposition'; *Julius Caesar* provides a model for a 'counter history' which asks 'for another sense of the political, which was to include a different sense of the historical to begin with'. The chapter on *Macbeth* explores the 'unlimited futurity' that 'dwells in violence', exposing the play's horrifying modernity and 'an unforeseeable political affirma-tion in the biopolitical success of blood'. In one of Haverkamp's most brilliant insights, he concludes:

The princes did not become leaders, nor the politicians villains, but they became managers of risk-politics; the Fates are no longer witches but instead go by the name of media. For the media, the blood secretly congealed into semen; for the politicians the end of the salvation-expectation was frozen into torture.

The final chapter focuses more explicitly on theatre and the 'politics of tragic humor', which leads him to Botticelli's *Primavera* and an analysis of *The Win-ter's Tale*. Although Haverkamp begins by telling his reader that 'this is not a Foucault book', it is unquestionably embedded in a tradition of philoso-phy in which all history is a history of the present. The book is highly intellectual and provocative; the material is dense and often self-reflective, but the chapters are brief, sometimes penetrat-ing to the heart of an idea only to set it down again.

In many ways, Julia Reinhard Lupton's *Thinking with Shakespeare: Essays on Politics and Life* picks up where Haverkamp left us. She begins with Shylock's 'pricked flesh' to draw our attention to the character's famous question of humanness, one which she construes as 'political' but that 'also bears on life'. The relationship between life and politics is central to Lupton's thesis and she goes on to establish her critical model through key fig-ures in political philosophy, most notably Hannah Arendt, who provides Lupton with a methodolog-ical dialogue between 'divergent forms of life', objects, space, animals and the 'biopolitical and theopolitical themes in Shakespeare'. She argues that bringing Arendt into a dialogue with Shakespeare produces 'a biopolitical critique of liberalism'. The terms of this critique are reiterated throughout the book in various different keys (from Aristotle's *bios* and *zoē* to Foucault and Giorgio Agamben) to suggest the complex interrelationships between life and living. Although occasionally tendentiously, Lupton explores moments or aspects of certain plays within the terms of this methodology: in *The Taming of the Shrew* she pursues the biopolitical 'with respect to both sexual and creaturely divisions of labour', as well as 'the copious object world' of the play: what she uncovers is 'a diagnosis of all that is unwell in states present and future'. In *Hamlet*, she explores the concept of election, returning to Schmitt's political theology and the political community of the play, and in her chapter on *All's Well That Ends Well*, she identifies that play as 'Shakespeare's anatomy of consent'. Like election or biopolitics, consent is involved in the multiple discourses of politics, ethics, sex and drama. Lupton returns to her long-standing interest in the New Testament in a chapter on *Timon of Athens* and the Book of Job, and, later in the book, St Paul. Her chapter on *The Winter's Tale* returns to Arendt within the context of the human action and how such action revolves around 'hospitable entertainment'. In *The Tempest*, Lupton explores Caliban through a Lockean idea of parental power, where the child or minor is an image for the exploration of a 'counter-patriarchal scheme', in which the 'flow of obligation arises from the right of the child to shelter and education rather than from the absolute sovereignty of the father'. Like Haverkamp, Lupton wants to re-engage with the interrelations between historicism and presentism, not as an ideal critical model but as a provocative space for 'salvaging potentialities within democratic thought for unknown futures'.

Given the ways in which Lupton foregrounds Arendt it is disappointing that she does not make it into Jonathan Gil Harris's *Shakespeare and Literary Theory*. Harris does, however, provide an up-to-date synoptic account of over two hundred years of critical methodologies. Each chapter is headed according to type, from formalism and structuralism to feminism. Harris refreshingly includes the scientific rationalism of writers like Bruno Latour, Michal Serres and Gilles Deleuze, who in their exploration of 'noise' and 'things' work against the grand epistemologies of Michel Foucault, who appears alongside Greenblatt and Sinfield in a chapter on New Historicism and Cultural Materialism. Harris makes sense of what is frequently opaque, often contradictory and occasionally perverse. His approach to what is essentially a vast body of competing social discourses is extremely skilled. He outlines the prevailing attitudes of particular theoretical positions and then explores them through Shakespeare's work. He rarely relies on abstraction or takes refuge in abstruse terminologies. He distinguishes, for example, between the competing strains within Marxist criticism which strive to elide the bourgeois individualism of Shakespeare's plays, whilst simultaneously recognizing the importance of contradiction in Shakespeare's work. Central to Harris's perception of the multivocality of Marxism is an understanding of history, and to what extent, if any, we can find 'a comforting narrative of progress'. Despite the necessary differences between these various methodologies, Harris strives for cohesion in the book, which occasionally suggests critical 'progress' but more often than not provides the reader with the comfort of control, as though bringing together all the pieces of a vast critical puzzle. Addressing Brecht's positive assimilation of radical conflict into something more like necessary 'discomfort', Harris concludes: 'Brecht not only reworks elements of Russian formalism but also anticipates certain themes in poststructuralist thought. This hint of affinity was to blossom, in subsequent decades, into a full-fledged dialogue between Marxism and poststructuralism, particularly deconstruction and Lacanian psychoanalysis.' Such a hint of affinity is foregrounded in the shrewd quotations from Shakespeare that open each chapter. Bringing together this clamorous group of social historians, radical thinkers and public intellectuals through aspects of Shakespeare's work, Harris shows why we continue to teach, read, watch and study Shakespeare, or, as he says, 'if Shakespeare is theoretical, the theory is clearly Shakespearian'.

GREAT SHAKESPEAREANS

If theory is Shakespearian then so is criticism, celebrity and textual practice; or at least, so the contributors to *Great Shakespeareans* would argue. This series presents a collection of canonical figures that have made and been shaped by the Shakespeare of our modern mind. Through a modern ambassador, each volume explores key figures in the development of a commodified Shakespeare. Volume 1 begins with Dryden and the prevailing assumptions about the eighteenth century. Simon Jarvis's essay on Pope is an elegant reminder of the extent to which we have come to rely on Pope's editing whenever we open our text. But it is also a fascinating insight into the whimsical nature of editing, its quiddities, mysteries and internal networks of meaning. As Jarvis reminds us, Pope's edition of Shakespeare 'shows us a crucial moment in the formation of the practice (which at this date by no means conforms with the theory) of the new discipline of vernacular textual criticism. It is, of course, an instructive episode in the history of literary taste, and of Pope's singular taste.' Freya Johnston's essay on Samuel Johnson carefully teases out questions of taste with wry humour and evocative anecdotes. She begins with a description of Johnson embarking, with Boswell, on his 'Grand Tour' in search of *Macbeth*'s heath. It is a lovely moment, as both writers 'spook' themselves with the eerie incantations of the witches only to later discover that they were entirely in the wrong place. This is a wonderful essay, providing glimpses into Johnson's empathy, his attitude and the ways in which he displays the 'cooperative bent' of his criticism. Such cooperation inevitably leads to arresting expressions of affinity: 'both Shakespeare and his editor emerge "not systematick and consequential, but desultory and vagrant, abounding in casual allusions and light hints"'. The 'casual allusions and light hints' are a world in themselves, as Johnston takes us through Johnson's Shakespeare who is not always perfect or complete – the 'conclusion, in which nothing is concluded' – but 'consolatory' in his capacity 'to heal a diseased imagination, to inform the understanding, and tutor the heart'. Johnston displays a similar sympathy towards her subject, resuscitating some of the great paradoxes of Shakespearian drama through the intense admiration of someone who laboured to understand as well as represent him.

Volume 2 is dedicated to the theatre and its craft. Each essay takes a renowned actor as its focus point and explores the complex relations between character, celebrity, entertainment and audience in the creation of a Shakespeare that both defines and shapes nineteenth-century theatre. As scholarship is increasingly invested in understanding the role of the theatre in early modern culture, this set of essays is commendable for drawing back the curtain on the formation of an art dependent on the personality of its performers, the flexibility of its texts and the interpretive agency of its audience. In these essays there is a more finely tuned sense of failure as well as success, peppering the creation of a celebrity culture with the seeds of personal destruction through the work and lives of Garrick, Kemble, Siddons and Kean. Peter Holland identifies Garrick as the 'most painted non-royal of the century', and explores the emerging value system that celebrates authenticity and originality in the craft of acting. Making free with the text, Garrick understood that successful theatre was about pleasing the audience. A 'Shakespearean' to the grave, he constructed his death, like his life, through appropriations of the bard. Garrick's role in the Jubilee, 'Shakespeare as virtual theme park', is testimony to what Holland calls 'economics as culture' and marks the 'apotheosis of Shakespeare as cultural symbol almost completely dissociated from the messy complexities of the works themselves'. While Holland is compelling on Garrick's immersion in a fantasy of posterity as well as identity, developing his modes of realism through a heightened performance of emotional intensity, Michael Dobson reminds us that John Philip Kemble was celebrated in his time as 'one of the best commentators on the text of Shakespeare'. In the interrelations between Kemble's performances and his 'Gothic' personal life, Dobson explores how sexual assault, fraud and misjudgement came to define the actor as well as destroy him. For Dobson, '[t]he episode of the Ireland forgeries marked a struggle for the right to pass judgement on matters Shakespearean between amateur opinion and a newly professionalized form of specialist scholarship'. From Kemble's peculiar pronunciations, his backstage behaviour to his self-fashioning as a 'Shakespearean', Dobson reveals how Kemble became a public figure of both antagonism and admiration. Shareholder, actor, celebrity and scholar Kemble made as many mistakes as he did successes. Dobson examines his extraordinary career with verve and fascination, retracing the lurid brilliance of Drury Lane.

Retaining the focus on celebrity, Russ McDonald's wonderful essay on Sarah Siddons examines the 'first great Shakespearean actress' and the ways in which Siddons carved out a unique space for Shakespeare's heroines in a conventionally male tradition: 'She imagined her character as existing in a network of other persons, actions and words, and this sort of reticulation was novel.' Siddons's attention to 'the entire text' supported her commitment to the play rather than her part within it and her defining sense of 'professional responsibility'. Peter Thomson's excavation of Kean, however, traces the 'unwelcome' illegitimate son of a jobbing actress, through the tragedies of his young adulthood to his controversial debut at Drury Lane, his renown and, ultimately, his theatrical legacy. What emerges from this portrait is a fighter, an anti-establishment, gifted man for whom 'it was pay-back time'. Kean's career was dogged by his temperament, 'a monster, drink-sodden and syphilitic', but, as Thomson powerfully argues, that did not exclude him from becoming the 'first great Romantic actor and the matchless interpreter of Shakespeare'.

Volume 3 is more thematic in structure and examines figures as diverse as Voltaire, Goethe, Schlegel and Coleridge. Exploring the emergence of Shakespeare 'criticism', it understands these authors as having created an historical (Voltaire),

empathetic (Coleridge) or 'transcendental' Shakespeare (Goethe and Schlegel). Common to all these essays is an interest in 'progress' with competing definitions of what such progress looks like. The European scope discloses interesting tensions within conceptions of national identity and how Shakespeare is appropriated or assimilated into literary traditions. Notoriously provocative, Voltaire features as a catalyst for iconoclastic debates, and Michèle Willems's essay is careful in its consideration of the complexity of this debate. Goethe, on the other hand, is understood as having used the playwright as a platform for his own art and the development of a German theatrical tradition. In contrast Schlegel assimilates Shakespeare by making him more German than English, whilst Coleridge supports the claim for Shakespeare's 'Genius'. Here, however, Reginald Foakes tackles 'the long and sterile debate about Coleridge's so-called plagiarism' and lays it to rest. His essay resituates Coleridge within a far wider context of criticism, confronting questions of theatre practice, illusion, classical legacies and the need to attack 'the basic ideas of preceding critics . . . to establish general criteria and new definitions of critical terms in commencing his lectures on Shakespeare's poems and plays'. Coleridge's Shakespeare is a 'political hero, an absolute genius providing England with a philosophical and moral superiority over Napoleon, the commanding genius who had military and political domination over Europe'.

The fourth volume explores three celebrated writers of the nineteenth century and their creation of a language of appreciation for Shakespeare that would metamorphose into 'gusto', 'passion' and, ultimately, 'genius'. Felicity James's essay on Charles Lamb examines the creation and context of the *Tales from Shakespeare* that would form such an important part of Victorian literary tradition. Behind such formative texts, however, James explores the emergence of a discernible 'Shakespeare', puffed out in biography and personality to fall in line with the later eighteenth-century investment in 'character'. *Falstaff's Letters* parodies such an interest whilst simultaneously developing it, providing as it did 'rumbustious background' stories for *The Merry Wives*, *Henry V* and the two parts of *Henry the Fourth*. Like many of his contemporaries Lamb's use of the essay form developed his sympathetic representations of the formative relationships between the stage and the page, the actor, the audience and the character. The discursive form of the essay allows it to apparently register the needs of its readers as well as its writer and – for Lamb – it became a testing ground for the 'conflict' between a developing celebrity culture of Shakespeare actors and an equally developing investment in scholarly editions.

The 'protean' qualities of Shakespeare's art to which Hazlitt responded are explored by Uttara Natarajan. In this lucid essay, Natarajan examines the complex interplay of the emotional and the intellectual through Hazlitt's theatre reviews, and most notably his responses to Kean's renditions of Shakespeare's heroes. As the idea of 'character' begins to emerge through a conflation of the 'textual and the conceptual', Hazlitt begins to construct a notion of 'genius' that became so identifiably 'Romantic'. Like a ventriloquist, Shakespeare 'throws his imagination out of himself, and makes every word appear to proceed from the very mouth of the person whose name it bears'. Centralizing terms that would become synonymous with the 'Romantics', Natarajan explores the sublime, the transcendental and the imagination as they are perceived in the Shakespearian character, on stage and page.

Philanthropist in scope, these essays approach Shakespeare through the perspectives of each great Shakespearean. The multiple attitudes, agendas and achievements here remind us of the extent to which our modern Shakespeare has been defined and sustained by the legacies of these individuals. All of these essays richly represent their subject's material, creating multi-faceted attitudes, perspectives, observations, witticism, criticisms and laconic asides. Although this collection is perhaps provocative in its reinforcement of a canonical tradition, it works hard to resurrect some of the fundamental voices that have made Shakespeare great, as well as great Shakespearians.

SHAKESPEARE IN CONTEXT

While *Great Shakespeareans* focuses on the afterlife of the plays and their role in defining a certain 'economics of culture', this year's Arden Companions shift our attention to Shakespeare's current life, and our better understanding of it. In *Shakespeare Upstart Crow to Sweet Swan*, Katherine Duncan-Jones is more interested in contemporary attitudes to Shakespeare than his legacy. Most particularly, Duncan-Jones is drawn to the conflict between the dead, 'national treasure' of Shakespeare in 1623 and the Elizabethan Shakespeare, who was prone to 'episodes of social failure and disappointment, as well as outbreaks of mockery'. In order to explore Shakespeare's passage from crow to swan, Duncan-Jones examines a range of material, including biography, contemporary accounts, Jacobean court politics, the professionalizing of public theatres, the 'Rival Poets', and the 'poets war'. Running throughout is her commitment to Shakespeare the actor. Duncan-Jones's Shakespeare is more irreverent and deeply imbedded in Elizabethan and Jacobean life than is usually suggested, and although her machinations of thought are compelling, they are not always convincing. Following the trajectory of cow/calf images with which the book opens, she examines the dense intertexts of Greene's now famous comment and weaves her narrative through the multiple threads of contemporary allusions, including Thomas Edwards, Samuel Daniel, Thomas Watson, Henry Chettle and Christopher Marlowe. She is interested in how Shakespeare shapes his own career, as well as how it is shaped by others: 'his cultural status, both among the learned and with the wider public; and his social standing, as a man who was by birth the son of a provincial glover and thus, like Daisy Ashford's Mr Salteena, "not quite a gentleman"'. Despite the chronological trajectory of the book, Shakespeare's career comes across as anything but linear: through a close exploration of the networks of contemporary relations as they became expressed in appropriation, imitation, mockery, censorship or assimilation, she reveals an Elizabethan culture in which Shakespeare played an active part. By her own admission she is often speculative but couches this in terms that are courageous rather than cavalier. Throughout the book, Duncan-Jones takes on her fellow Shakespearians (she is particularly annoyed with Schoenbaum's reluctance to speculate), and she tackles specific questions with a lively tenacity. The book presents a complex Shakespeare who was both derided and celebrated but remained resolutely embedded in the playhouse: 'He played major roles throughout his life. If the claim was excessive, there were plenty of readers in 1623 who would have been aware of it.'

Understanding Shakespeare as an actor and somebody who was actively engaged in the mechanics of early modern theatre is written deep into a number of this year's books. It seems that critical thought has accepted the significance of the theatrical space in Elizabethan culture and has now turned its attention to the specifics of that art. In *Shakespeare and Language*, Jonathan Hope approaches the mutability of language, the legacy of rhetorical form, the multiplicity of spelling and the complexities of representation within the context of a rapidly developing theatrical art. The book is structured according to various methodological approaches, including the philosophical, scientific, anthropocentric and technical. It follows a linear narrative in which the development of language is framed as a progressive journey towards its use and understanding as a vast and reasonable system of expression. Hope establishes his argument through the exploration of language theories in which he sets out the arbitrary and hierarchical nature of signs. He then moves through contemporary discourses on language, the relationship between speech and writing, theories of artifice and the complex participation of knowledge in the aetiology of signs. Hope uses a comprehensive range of material, including frontispieces, emblem books, mythologies, plays, poems and translations in his investigation of early modern attitudes to language. Chapter 3 opens with a wonderful hunt for the comedy in *The Comedy of Errors* but then deals with more hostile approaches to Shakespeare's wordplay, including the 'unfunny' and the 'arbitrary', as well as a demolition of the pun. Hope moves between the linguistic and the philological as he examines specific word use and conceptual attitudes in his exploration of syntactic effects. Hope's book understands the complex systems of language that produce and suppress meaning, as he also understands the ways in which Shakespeare develops his style – 'the use of many subordinate verbs', for example – in pursuit of the representation of interiority:

In terms of classical rhetoric, Shakespeare's style can be seen to shift towards the psychological level, as his syntax seeks ways to appeal to our emotional experience of the world, and represent the subjectivity of his characters in play in the moment-to-moment flow of speech and thought.

Shakespeare and Language is precise, informed, comprehensive and intelligent. Hope has a great skill in making complex constructions and unfamiliar attitudes clear and compelling. The final chapter considers what Hope calls the 'linguistic texture' of the plays, in which he explores the relationship between language and genre. Here Hope offers a compelling case for 'the language of genre', rather than subject, character or form. Through a study of the use of catalogue pages for the 'imposition of generic labels' he then turns to language as a means of generic identification, for which he uses a Docuscope (a highly sophisticated computer program which identifies word clusters and strings of words assigned to a predetermined set of categories). Strikingly, what this analysis reveals is that 'each of the folio genres was differentiated from the others on the basis of one or more linguistic features'. Out of this analysis come further surprises. The number of 'first-person strings', for example, which reveal the interior identification strategies between character and audience, varies between genre, the greatest number of them appearing in the Comedies rather than the Tragedies. Hope makes those rare moves between technical skill and conceptual brilliance, and in doing so he lifts the veil from the often arcane and frequently specialized art of linguistics.

Lifting a different but equally important veil is Helen Cooper in her *Shakespeare and the Medieval World*. Beginning with the assertion that 'The world in which Shakespeare lived was a medieval one', Cooper goes on to intervene in 'our patchy state of awareness'. Patchy it is, given that almost all the books reviewed here tend to occlude the medieval period despite Cooper's claim that Shakespeare 'found in fifteenth-century English history a prime way of representing *England* to itself'. Her book, however, explains that 'the medieval for Shakespeare . . . was specifically English. It connected with the contemporary nationalist movement that for the first time was insisting that English could hold its own against the best of Europe and the Classics – and a key element of Englishness was its own past, the vernacular traditions inherited from the Middle Ages'. This concept of Englishness – verbal, spatial and local – is not a national attitude but an inherited language of expression as well as representation. It is less about establishing difference than developing belonging, and it is through a complex notion of belonging that Cooper explores the 'imprint' of the medieval. Central to her methodology is a social understanding of the human capacities to learn – 'habit', 'practice', 'memory' and 'persistence' – and their roots in shared experience.

Acutely conscious of the limits of periodization, the pressures of historical time-frames to constitute literary borders and Burkhardt's legacy of the medieval veil, Cooper 'demonstrate[s] the pervasiveness of those deep structures of medieval culture in Shakespeare's work and his times'. She rightly observes: 'We often label everything we like in the Middle Ages as proto-Renaissance, and everything we don't like in the Renaissance as medieval.' What her book, shows, however, is the false value of these terms and the profoundly complex ways in which cultures oscillate between systems of thought. Despite the increasingly sceptical attitudes to literary or cultural periodization, it remains a central feature of the study of literature, as we continue to offer students historical packages of thought. Cooper, however, wants 'to adjust the baseline from which we measure the extraordinary

achievements of Shakespeare and his contemporaries and rethink the nature of their originality'.

Part of Cooper's achievement is to reveal the extent to which inherited systems of thought continue to mutate and develop over multiple institutions. One such institution is the law, which Andrew Zurcher takes up in his book, *Shakespeare and Law*. Here Zurcher focuses on 'judgement' – legal, literary and a synthesis of the two: 'the law offered Shakespeare not just an analogy for the interpretive opportunities and perils facing his own literary art, but a rich and apt language in which to posit and test these insights'. Alongside the more obvious relationships between stage and court, Zurcher posits the 'complex interactions between personal interests and legal processes'. Looking at how the language of the law affects Elizabethan and Jacobean life, Zurcher explores the practical, moral, philosophical and social implications of a system that 'helped to transform London into the congested, dynamic metropolis it had, by Shakespeare's day, become; and, probably more so than any other institution or activity, the law and legal life provided the plasma in which that congested dynamism could quicken, and flourish'. Zurcher makes a distinction between 'Shakespeare's legal thinking . . . [as] philosophically deliberate, rather than, say, practically polemical'. This distinction keeps Zurcher tuned to the moral complexities of legal diction and the ambiguities of interpretation. The first half of the book examines the historical context of Tudor law – courts and common law – acknowledging Shakespeare's biography through his father's brief role as a bailiff. The second half turns towards Shakespeare's works and provides some shrewd moments of analysis. *The Rape of Lucrece* is examined using an Augustinian model of the difference between acquiescence and resistance. The result is fascinating, as is his exploration of Hamlet's ontological aporia: 'Put simply, one cannot simultaneously both be, and know, oneself. Hamlet's problem is that of the theatre; it is also that of the law.' The relationship between theatre and law is elegantly developed, not only through the capacious use of legal diction and performative similarities but in the nature of the audience, which Zurcher identifies as 'made up of the fashionable young lawyers of Donne's *Satires*'. Zurcher also identifies fundamentally legal issues in *As You Like It* (the critical use of 'as', for example), *King Lear*, *King John* and a number of the Histories. He shows how a sonnet can 'flirt sleepily with legal language', whilst those to the lovely boy 'treat love as an ethical discourse of interest assimilated to a legal discourse of kindly self-possession', the middle sonnets 'dealing with the friend "truth" is represented recurrently as a system of legal rights and obligations', whilst those directed at the fair mistress explore 'a love grounded not upon rights, but wrongs'. The book is putatively constructed on a linear narrative in which *A Lover's Complaint* provides a culmination of 'the overall legally based scheme of the [sonnet] sequence'. But Zurcher remains a keen reader throughout and avoids anachronisms and abstractions. He writes with originality and self-possession which makes for a refreshing and enlightening read.

It has often been suggested that Shakespeare was more interested in law than religion but Alison Shell's *Shakespeare and Religion* shows us that we need to rethink the usefulness of these critical binaries in our understanding of Elizabethan drama. Like Helen Cooper, Shell paints with a broad brush because she knows the detail so well. Fully aware of the grand questions that surround such a subject, she tackles Shakespeare as 'one whose language is saturated in religious discourse and whose dramaturgy is highly attentive to religious precedent, but whose invariable practice is to subordinate religious matter to the particular aesthetic demands of the work in hand'. Like many of the authors considered here, Shell is very conscious of the relations between her subject and theatrical practice and immediately draws a common alliance through 'Shakespeare's high doctrine of audience'. Shell is not, however, drawn to simple moves between the structures of the theatre and the Church; on the contrary, she recognizes that 'while a preacher would have taxed his audience's memories for evangelistic and didactic reasons, the biblical allusions in the work of professional playwrights like Shakespeare tend to be deployed in the service of generalised moralism, or of simple ornamentation'. There is a beguiling confidence in Shell's writing: she avoids unnecessary caveats and qualifications, and acknowledges the conflicts in her arguments, but she doesn't apologize for them and highlights areas of omission. For example, 'only a few Jews and Muslims' were living in London at the time but 'notions of them had an enormous imaginative importance'. Such an approach makes a short book on a vast subject very accessible and well pitched. It is structured according to a basic chronological pattern in which Catholicism gave way to Elizabethan Protestantism and focuses on the debates that both articulated and shaped a changing culture of belief. Shell is acutely aware of the potential discrepancies between religious views and practice and takes account of the 'legal requirement' of church attendance as well as the impossibility of accounting for those who protested in more silent ways (including Shakespeare). The book presents a carefully balanced attitude, recognizing for instance that whilst Shakespeare is indebted to medieval religious drama, many of his plays 'convey a more neutral attitude to the faith than those of . . . a contemporary'. Such balance may frustrate those searching for Shakespeare's denomination, but it is part of what allows Shell to turn to the more complex questions of faith that Shakespeare's work so often invokes. Crucially, she asks 'why, when Shakespeare's drama so often turns on issues of forgiveness, so little explicit attention is given to repentance' and how do the plays explore questions of conversion or 'metanoia', the Christian endeavour of repenting and turning towards God'?

Her section on *The Winter's Tale* is especially compelling, focusing as she does on Calvinist points of repentance and damnation. Whilst always clear *Shakespeare and Religion* is never simple: Shakespeare may have turned to the Geneva Bible more than any other translation, appropriated Catholic traditions, resisted anti-popery jibes (unlike many of his contemporaries) but he is also the object of Catholic outrage as well as a reluctant moralist. Yet Shell is keen to steer her readers away from liberal complacency: 'is there, indeed, something troubling about a writer who motions his audience to a seat outside the forum or moralistic interchange, and about a critical body that has taken up this invitation to voyeurism so readily?' As ambivalence seems to have become the holy grail of critical analysis, Shell's challenge is very timely.

Gesturing us back into the forum of moralistic interchange, however, is Margaret Healy in *Shakespeare, Alchemy and the Creative Imagination: The Sonnets and A Lover's Complaint.* Following the terms and images of alchemy, Healy suggests that this practice of transformation provided profound models of expression and identification for writers of this period. One such model is that of unity, or harmony, to which, she suggests, Shakespeare is wholly committed. Healy is particularly interested in unities and transformations and how these '*conjunctios*' or marriages support new models of identification. Attempting to create a network of socio-scientific relations based on a consensual investment in 'alchemical–aesthetic interactions', Healy identifies Shakespeare as someone who 'subscribed to a powerfully transformative chemical vision in which working the mettle/metal of the mind had a strangely literal, uncanny, as well as important theosophical implications'. In pursuit of this argument, she casts a wide net, moving between continental Neoplatonism, Hermeticism, Christianity, Islam, mysticism, metallurgy, numerology, geometry and meditation to suggest that the conflagration of transformative images 'played an important part in the English Renaissance's wider ferment of creativity'. Healy is keen to show that alchemy is far more assimilated into this ferment than has previously been assumed, and, more contentiously, that for Shakespeare it is 'indicative of a self-conscious artistic stance, promoting religious toleration and unity'. In the sonnets she explores numerology and the science of number patterns not only within individual poems but the sequence as a whole, suggesting that Shakespeare created a conscious pattern of interpretation. She also examines colour and the idea of 'blackness' through the 'dark lady' and paradoxical treatments of the colour black in the period. Using Elizabeth I as a model she explores representations and

appropriations of blackness to argue that 'blackness could resonate with perfection and divinity'. In her pursuit of harmony and unity, Healy hopes to rescue Shakespeare from charges of misogyny in her reading of the dark lady. The mistress is not so much an identifiable Other but a 'projection of the speaker's inner nature – his dark soul – she/he also emerges at points as a type of church and even as Christ/Solomon'. Healy develops this attention to the inward mind throughout the book and explores friendship, divine love and creativity, in which she comes close to making Shakespeare into a figure more akin to Donne than John Crowe Ransom would have ever allowed. Her lateral readings of the sonnets reveal traces of a highly wrought, complex, sometimes logical and metaphysical conceit that Shakespeare is not usually credited with. For Healy, 'sex and the sacred were legitimately united in alchemical discourses and symbolism', a belief she believes enables us to approach the poetry with a 'heightened sceptical consciousness and a preparedness to look (and listen) from oblique perspectives, which were considered more suited in this period to discerning spiritual truths'. It is through these oblique perspectives that Healy explores *A Lover's Complaint,* a work 'with an alchemical narrative'. Alongside her 'chemical lens' and theosophical approach Healy examines whether the sonnets are a 'true' 'record of spiritual experience' and the relationship between spirituality and creativity: 'the central concern of Shakespeare's densely philosophical sonnet sequence is with creative "making" – a process inseparable from soul remaking and which is couched in the language and rhythms of alchemy'. In her final chapter, Healy returns to one of her most insistent claims: that Shakespeare is a poet of religious toleration. Identifying our especially modern suspicion of binaries and anxieties about occultism, she discusses how 'alchemy's lexicon of conjunctions and "chymistry's" refusal of binaries became charged with significance'. Sometimes this significance seems over-played and exclusive: there is little attention to Ovid's *Metamorphoses* or alternative models of transformation, and more demotic literature, the importance of distilling to both cooking and medicine, is rarely considered. However, despite Healy's claim that the languages of alchemy are not 'simply' metaphorical, her book draws attention to the extraordinary semantic scope of such kinetic processes and their identification with human action.

HUMAN NATURE

Despite the divergent interests of many of this year's books, the interpretive lens remains steadfastly focused on the representation of the human subject. Alongside action, language, objects and alchemy, however, the non-human emerges to provoke complex reflections on the status of the early modern self. Bruce Boehrer's *Animal Characters: Nonhuman Beings in Early Modern Literature* offers an exploration of the changing relations between the animal and the human in sixteenth- and seventeenth-century representations of subjectivity. Building on his work on anthropocentrism, Boehrer here explores the shifting boundaries between the human and animal worlds. At times the human world sympathetically allies itself with animal 'qualities', and at other times it fiercely guards such difference. This reveals how writers are consciously constructing networks of sympathy and identification for the benefit of 'character', which is explored through the ways in which the writers of the early modern begin to develop it – literary, human or animal. Establishing the animal as a critical or zoological form through which the human learns to both recognize and refashion itself, each chapter focuses on a different animal or bird: horses, parrots, cats, peacocks and sheep. The chapter on horses addresses the question of chivalry and mastery. Fraught with questions of dominance and submission, mobility, class, utility and aesthetics, the horse is a profoundly important body in the history of human/animal identification. In *Richard II*, for example, he looks at 'the topos of equine civil disobedience', in which 'the horse's behaviour embodies a broader failure of relationship: a fracture of the bonds of gratitude and obedience that unite culture to nature and both to God'.

The chapter on parrots, or psittacidae, is less evocative at the level of 'the character of humanity' because these birds occupy a much smaller space in our modern psyche. At a linguistic level, however, Boehrer shows how the symbolic 'language' of the parrot maps an extraordinary journey from the spiritual to the satiric, and how representations of the parrot has a particular role in the history of western aesthetics.

The chapter on cats revisits the question of cat-torturing in relation to Catholic festivals and Protestant misrule, expanding Robert Darnton's famous thesis in which he not only questions the promiscuity of cat-torturing but also their direct link to festivals. Instead such practices are seen as expressions of a variety of social responses including entertainment, superstition, anti-papist and, at times, a more endemic absorption of unquestioned and random rituals. Central to this chapter, and the entire book, is the question of animal character and when the animal is invested with something akin to an independent identity, and how this identity makes such practices of torture effective or empathetic. The cat it seems is a useful social animal – perhaps why it is now the most ubiquitous pet – in representing a vast range of cultural impulses from the brutal to the sympathetic. Boehrer ends this chapter with a reference to C. S. Lewis's *The Lion, the Witch and the Wardrobe*, in which he sees the allegory of Christ in the torture of Aslan as one in the eye for American Creationists. Separating the human and animal worlds fragments our representations of faith rather than endorses them. Boehrer explores a wide range of material which is at its most fascinating when it is at its most flippant – the off-hand remarks about sacks of screaming cats or Tyndale's linguistic slippage between parrots and preachers, or the demotion of the horse from symbolic majesty to quotidian carriage. His investment in borders means that he is very aware of the porosity of the material and the metaphoric: as he explains in his chapter on animal husbandry, in an 'effort to identify the literal, material presence of animals in early modern writing . . . [we] discover in the process that these literal animals are somehow always being reabsorbed into metaphor'.

The semantic relationship between the human and non-human is nowhere more evocatively explored, however, than in Andreas Höfele's *Stage, Stake, and Scaffold: Humans and Animals in Shakespeare's Theatre*. The book aims to expose and understand the foundational spaces of entertainment, cruelty and execution in Elizabethan culture – the stage, the stake and the scaffold. The proximity of these places as well as the 'powerful semantic exchange . . . between stage, stake, and scaffold crucially informed Shakespeare's explorations into the nature and workings of humanness as a psychological, ethical, and political category'. In order to fully understand conceptions of 'humanness', Höfele explores the complex movement between 'presence' and 'representation' and how these varying conditions of mimesis invite or exclude empathy. Looking at structures of bodily pain he examines the interchange between the theatre and the bear-pit and how the proximity of such spaces supported a blurring of boundaries between animal and human. Fundamental to this fog is the ways in which the bear is an object of pity as well as delight, an expression of human emotion and a vehicle of social revenge. The history and reception of public spectacle has a complex heritage which Höfele traces through its religious, social, penal and ritualistic imperatives. He moves effortlessly between contemporary records and critical theory, drawing on social history, anthropology, psychology and zoology as he exposes how 'the unleashing of animality is intricately bound up with the Renaissance ascendancy of "man"'. Examining the interrelations between the human and animal subject, the book demonstrates how 'Animals and animal nature provide Shakespeare not with one semantic possibility but with a whole keyboard of possibilities which he can sound singly or in various chords or discords.' The flexibility, fluidity and dynamism is traced by Höfele through a series of case studies, including *Titus Andronicus, Richard III, Hamlet, Coriolanus, Macbeth, King Lear* and *The Tempest*. Exploring 'Shakespeare's human-animal

border traffic', the violence of Shakespeare's theatre 'was enhanced by the calculated savagery of the neighbouring bear-garden, just as the pleasure of watching that savagery was enhanced by a calculated infusion of theatrical human-likeness into the struggle of the beasts'.

What emerges from this book is an exploration of the ways in which the foundational institutions of 'civilization' are entirely dependent upon our borders with the animal. Unpacking the common Renaissance assumption that man stood in the middle of a cosmic graph between god and beast, Höfele shows that definitions of the human were always in motion and that the animal was a vital form in the development of representations of human interiority as well as emotion. The book's power lies in its skilful deconstruction of critical commonplaces and of the fascinating ways in which it complicates human/animal relations rather than stratifying or allegorizing them. Focusing on the role of the public space, it also becomes a history of early modern theatre, as it analyses the ways in which 'presence' developed into 'representation' and the impact that such a development had on the human qualities of reason, emotion, pity, empathy, anticipation, etc. Höfele examines the figure of the bear as it is tormented and torn apart; sometimes the bear may be a human representative for collective anger, sometimes he is a 'character' – Hunks or Sackerson, for example – and sometimes it is the limit upon which human observers test their capacity for cruelty. The spectacular nature of this terrifying triumvirate of social power becomes a hub for semantic exchange as terms of identification or elision are traded over their borders. In *Macbeth*, for example, the stage of the public playhouse becomes 'the centrepiece of the triptych whose wings are formed by the baiting arena and the gallows. Such a triple vision generates a powerful intermediality, whose palpable effect is mutual reinforcement.' Each case study provides an in-depth analysis of how Shakespeare interrogates questions of the 'human'. In this way, Macbeth is a figure in which 'the boundary between human and in-human becomes obsessively intense' as the play presents a 'spectacle of the damned' in its 'slippage of species boundaries'; whilst Richard of Gloucester, on the other hand, is a 'single emblematic figure, the consummate actor, the beast, the traitor'. Like the bear-pit and the public stage, Höfele examines the stake or executioner's block for the codified expressions of a penal system intent on using its performative energies as part of its structural power (Foxe's *Acts and Monuments* is a central text here). Such rituals of execution are necessarily social and involve complex references to status and power: baiting and hunting, for example, become formative images in Höfele's interrogation of *Coriolanus*, in which the hero is not 'a political animal, but an animal caught up in politics'. The chapter on *King Lear* is exemplary, bringing together the powerful trafficking of human emotion through images of torture, mock justice, playing and animality: 'At its most devastating, Shakespeare's theatre does not raze the species divide; it flattens it, as Lear's howl echoes and is echoed by the creatures in the bear-garden.' Höfele is acutely aware that this is not only a book about animals, or indeed humans, but a complex semiotic system that developed through public spectacle and methods of identification. In the vast remit of his intellectual scope, Höfele considers Cartesian duality, Nietzsche's 'idea of the natural animal body', Hobbes's Leviathan monster, Montaigne's ethically superior cannibals, Pico's 'self-creative Adam', Foxe's flayed martyrs, and Bodin's commonwealth in his defining narrative of the 'plasticity of human character'. Central to this narrative is an understanding that human evolution is not a linear continuum but that 'The collusion between stage, stake, and scaffold... in Shakespeare's theatre thus draws us with renewed urgency to what it means to be an animal that considers itself human.'

Underlying much of this year's material is a tacit confrontation with Harold Bloom's assertion that Shakespeare invented the human: for Höfele, Haverkamp, Boehrer and Lupton the human is still in contention.

SHAKESPEARE'S ENVIRONMENT

Jeffrey Theis continues the interrogation of the non-human in his *Writing the Forest in Early Modern England*, in which he addresses the role of the forest in key texts of the sixteenth and seventeenth centuries. Theis attempts to expose the forest as a conflicted and dialogic space, in which, like the stage, it 'is always a multiple place that means different things to different characters'. He traces such multiplicity through competing historical representations of the forest. His project is to 'examine the ways in which writers transformed pastoral... to register and negotiate the historical and environmental anxieties the English held toward their woodland region'. The 'sylvan pastoral' is a key term for Theis and he uses it to identify 'pastoral moments set in a wood', where writers engage 'forest-related issues' and where 'literary form and tradition intermix with early modern forest history'. In texts from Shakespeare to Milton, Theis sets out to expose the forest as an ideological space in which writers could explore their histories as well as their fantasies. Through key texts such as *A Midsummer Night's Dream*, *As You Like It* and *The Merry Wives* Theis interrogates the forest as a social space for the projection, and interruption, of desires, fears and class relations. Necessarily more politicized, the last three chapters engage Evelyn, Marvell, James Howell, Gerrard Winstanley and Milton and how the forest became a site of national fantasy. Here, Theis focuses on the woodland as a resource as well as a literary construction, and the contemporary attitudes to the forest alongside allegorical constructions of refuge and trauma. It is here that Theis most directly engages with ecocriticism and notions of 'proto-environmentalism'. Nature in *Paradise Lost* is 'the focal point of questions regarding ownership, property, human agency, and protection from external threats like Satan'. Ultimately, Milton becomes the maverick of the book, working against the largely conservative strains of his predecessors and instead 'eras[ing] concepts of the nation in general, and the English nation in particular'. There is 'no sanctity' in Milton's nature. This is an ambitious book that attempts to address the interrelationships between our social and organic worlds and to that end it provides some refreshing readings and a much needed focus on the politics of early modern nature. There are a few frustrations, however: at a conceptual level there is a marked reluctance to address the complex 'cultures' of nature, and the consistent misspelling of a central scholar is annoying.

In Lynne Bruckner and Dan Brayton's collection, *Ecocritical Shakespeare*, however, there is a wider theoretical awareness of the terms of the debate. The editors make their agendas very clear: ecocriticism is not just about nature, it is also about education, 'our current environmental crisis is not merely a discourse or representational field but an urgent historical juncture that forces us to rethink the role of scholarship'. As the rather clotted foreword establishes, ecocriticism, despite its idioms, is not anachronistic, for there is 'in early modernity a sincere concern for the human impact on the biophysical environment, and its resultant effects'. Despite the variety and quality of this collection there is an overarching attempt to locate and analyse the 'environmental and ecopolitical topics in the works of Shakespeare'. The result is an assorted collection of essays, some exemplary, which range through the natural world from the organic, the meteorological, animal and experiential to the ecological. Karen Raber's essay, like Höfele's *Stage, Stake, and Scaffold*, is invested in the 'instability of the human–animal divide that underwrites the civil actions and civilised self-control upon which social interaction in the crowded city environment relies'. Similarly committed to confronting the 'category of the human', Robert Watson's sharp and lucid essay on A *Midsummer Night's Dream* offers a vivid de-construction of the idea of a composite self: 'that our insularity as individuals and as a species is a destructive illusion, an enclosure crisis of the human self'. Whilst the first section of the book offers various conceptual models for the exploration of human natures, the second focuses on matter, organic and animal. Like Raber, Paul Yachnin and J. A. Shea, in their essay on the 'well-hung shrew', observe that 'humans are also animals,

which means that the plays are about the lines of continuity among the world of creatures as much as they are about an ideal human transcendence over nature'. Vin Nardizzi's essay discusses early modern woodland in *The Merry Wives of Windsor* and how timber, as resource and organic architecture, enacts 'a fantasy of environmental destruction on crown land'. In her essay on *The Winter's Tale*, Jennifer Munroe addresses 'the practices and gendered implications of art used to alter nature in husbandry and housewifery manuals' in order to provoke 'new ways to read art/nature debate and gendered power relations in the play . . . What if it *is* all about the gillyvors?' The final section, which turns explicitly to 'presentism and pedagogy', includes an essay by Richard Kerridge on *Macbeth*'s 'ecosystem'. He suggests that the play is 'anti-dualist', 'in which a powerfully-impelled attempt to see, and manage, the world and the self in dualistic terms becomes untenable and has to give way to holistic terms'. For Kerridge, such holism strikes at the chords of 'our present environmental predicament'. Simon Estok's afterword draws the book to a close with a somewhat laconic edge, describing the collection as 'a noble project, for all of its flaws, rifts, fissures, tensions, questions, and tons of CO_2 damage it has produced'. It is rather surprising then to find further CO_2 damage in the reproduction of this same essay in Estok's *Ecocriticism and Shakespeare: Reading Ecophobia*. From the outset Estok establishes his interest in what he terms 'ecophobia', or 'how contempt for the natural world is a definable and recognizable discourse'. Within this context, Estok groups 'contempt' for the natural world alongside the bigotry of homophobia, racism, anti-Semitism and misogyny. He wants to put the politics back into nature, suggesting that we are all guilty of 'ecophobia' in any act of cultivation or 'mastery' over nature. Attempting to establish this as a theory, Estok then produces some very novel readings of Shakespeare. He argues that *2 Henry VI* 'both participates and subverts a popular radical vegetarian environmentalist ethic', whilst *Henry IV* is complicit in the 'stage marginalisation of vegetarianism'. *Coriolanus* is surprisingly accused of 'ecophobic scorn'. Estok is apparently interested in 'unpredictability' which is pursued in *King Lear*, 'vivid in its foregrounding of environmental unpredictability and its dramatisation of a fear of nature'. Examining Cordelia's 'nothing', Estok sees it as further ecophobia, 'as palpable as any of the characters on stage or meteorological assaults on the heath'. Estok's readings of the plays are unconvincing: in *The Winter's Tale* he points to the play's use of natural metaphors as offensive to nature, 'If nature is made to resemble people in the psychology that is ascribed to it, we do not see pain or suffering similarly ascribed to nature.' These often bizarre readings are not helped by lazy sentences: lists often end with 'and so on', 'things' are invoked as a catchall term for goodness-knows-what (the 'increasingly global view of things' attributed to the seventeenth century, for example) and the oddly repetitive prose is often simply banal, as when Leontes is accused of creating 'a sort of psychological no-fly zone'.

READING SHAKESPEARE

Far more useful, however, is Eugene Giddens's *How to Read a Shakespearean Play Text*. This neat, concise, clear and well-structured guide to early modern print culture is invaluable for teachers, editors, and students of bibliography and of early modern material culture. Giddens's book focuses on the material conventions of print and 'cultures of performance', guiding the reader through how to 'read' an Elizabethan play. He has assimilated a great deal of traditionally specialized material into an accessible format. This includes the physical aspects of text, theatrical acquisitions of plays, the ways in which early modern print conventions shape our reading experience and the implications of grammar, punctuation, line setting, spaces and delineation. Giddens also examines the difference between quartos and folios, offers advice on how to get the most out of EEBO and how editorial policy can affect modern editions. The book begins with the conditions that surround – and define – the relationship between playbook

and publisher. Giddens examines the 'various permutations that might affect the transmission of a play from author(s) to page', including commissioning, authorial manuscripts, record, censorship and licensing. Although Giddens carefully attends to the conditions in which plays were printed and produced he is also aware of the legacy of such conditions and the history they produce: 'For many of the period's quartos, authorship attribution is either deliberately misleading, mistaken, or incomplete, and therefore this part of the title page should always be regarded with suspicion.' Each chapter ends with a very concise list for 'further reading' and the whole book is well-judged in its attempts to engage students in the material culture of print and playing, whilst remaining alert to the conceptual interests of bibliography and the legacy of its critical history.

Equally invaluable to anyone needing to let fresh air into a stale seminar room is James Schiffer's *Twelfth Night: New Critical Essays*. The book includes fourteen original essays which work to recover early modern meanings, analyse multiple receptions of the play, examine ideological appropriations and define the role of performance in the play's critical heritage. Loosely constructed around a linear narrative of interpretation, which moves from textual detail to thematic crux, the collection opens with Patricia Parker's puzzle of the eunuch. Parker focuses on recovering some of the folio's textual ambiguities (including punctuation) in her exploration of gender instability. Alongside her brilliantly lateral and dense interrogations of the Folio text she shows how modern editions suppress the 'multiple resonances of the plays' and period's copious terms', reminding us that we are always in a process of learning 'a language that never ceases to surprise'. Bruce Smith's essay focuses on terms of 'fancy' and the synaesthesia that this word invites; or, as he puts it, the 'metamorphoses [of] the poly-sensuous into the polysemous'. His essay explores the multiple meanings of 'fancy' and its creative or transformative power: 'In meta-theatrical moments throughout his career Shakespeare calls on fancy as the faculty that takes the sights, sounds, smells, tastes, and textures of drama in performance and turns them into something that is more than the sum of these parts.' The exploration of the senses is further developed in David Schalkwyk's essay which talks about 'the affective landscape of the play': love, passion, desire, emotion and, crucially, the differences between them. Ever lively to the relationship between language and performance, Schalkwyk pursues 'the differences between love as a kind of interior state and a form of action or behavior'. In pursuit of these 'differences' he examines the various ways in which the play synthesizes 'love' with feeling, and the contemporary discourses that support, or divide, such notions, including Galen. Following on from the body's performance of love, Laurie Osborne's essay explores the relationships between amity and sexual union, suggesting that despite the 'desexualization' of the friendship between Orsino and Cesario their 'sexual union' is its 'ultimate realization', whilst Goran Stanivuković's piece examines the play's reassessment of romantic codes of masculinity, suggesting that *Twelfth Night* 'is in fact more interested in social status than sex, because the culture has started to define masculinity more according to parentage and social rank and less according to heroic achievements'. As Schiffer's introductory chapter establishes, the reciprocal relationship between performance and scholarship is always in evidence and he structures this collection to reflect that. One of the most intriguing essays, and the first to deal explicitly with performance, is Marcela Kostihová's analysis of how Czech interpretations of the play reflect anxieties about Czech national identity. Central to her notion of national identity is sexuality: 'In the social arena of Czech art, one of the prime sites of "culture", the dilemma of representing homosexuality uncovers a deep rift between what is perceived to be True, or "high" art, reportedly representative of humanity itself, and popular "low" art, supposedly bringing the sensation-hungry audiences snippets of latest Western fashions.' Examining European appropriations of the play opens up fascinating lines of national preoccupations, and Christa Jansohn's essay on twentieth century German performances (notably the

Nazis' privileging of Schlegel's translation) shows how renditions of *Twelfth Night* reflect (or suppress) the tensions between culture and politics. Within the context of place, both Nathalie Rivère de Carles and Catherine Lisak explore Illyria, the former in the context of the 'exotic' and the latter in terms of 'strangeness'. Both writers ask us to re-engage with the country as a geographically specific place with an accessible early modern history and not simply a Belmont-esque site of fantasy. Alan Powers elucidates ceremony and ritual through tokens, mourning and marriage, whilst Ivo Kamps focuses more acutely on the characters of Malvolio, Toby and Maria in his essay on the dynamics of madness, diagnosis and cure. The last two essays bring the play into the present tense, as Jennifer Vaught writes about the assimilation of the play into post civil-war American rituals and 'the extent to which popular, festival customs can be appropriated by elite groups for conservative, repressive, and violent purposes'. Cynthia Lewis's final essay serves as an epilogue to the collection retuning us the grand questions of interpretation and the ambivalence of the play's ending: 'the audience's understanding of many aspects of the play's plot is frustrated by a final proliferation of interpretation, creating an undertow to its artistic coherence'. This is a very good collection of essays that works hard to present new ideas whilst retaining a strong sense of the play's dense critical history. As a body of work, the individual essays occasionally contradict each other (the idea of Illyria, the reality of the ring, the reference to 'Good mistress Mary', for example) but this makes it all the stronger for its refusal to iron out interpretative conflicts. As Lisak says: 'As the last of the romantic and festive comedies unfolds, its spectators are made to feel foreign, estranged, or strange, for the play continually challenges their sense of what it means to be human.' What it means to be human is a question that dominates many of this year's books and it is a question that has moved further and further away from Harold Bloom's romantic formalism to something much more fragmented, mercurial and provocative.

2. SHAKESPEARE IN PERFORMANCE
reviewed by RUSSELL JACKSON

Cognition in the Globe by Evelyn B. Tribble appears in the series 'Cognitive Studies in Literature and Performance', informed by the proposition (as stated by the general editors Blakey Vermeule and Bruce McConachie) that psychology, 'now that it has undergone its empiricist revolution', can be brought to bear on the arts in a new spirit: 'scholarship in this field should be generally empirical, falsifiable, and open to correction by new evidence and better theories – as are the sciences themselves' (Preface, p. xi). Accordingly Tribble brings theories of 'distributed cognition' to bear on the kind of evidence for playhouse practices revisited recently by a number of scholars. The general tendency has been to question the preconceptions brought by Greg and others to such materials as 'plots' (or 'plats') and actors' parts. In particular, the assumption that, in early modern theatres, innovation and artistic excellence were limited by 'routine' and 'mechanical' technique has been challenged by an appeal to the notion that such 'systems' were the starting point for creativity rather than indications of its limitation. The approach adopted here is defined by Tribble, quoting the psychologist John Sutton, as 'a view that "cognition" is not a brain-bound activity, but rather is "unevenly distributed across social, technological and biological realms'" (p. 2). The significance of distributed cognition lies in the importance attached to 'the material, social and environmental surround' of playing and the reassessment of assumptions regarding the actors' ability to deliver accurate verbatim readings of the given text. This has a bearing on a number of aspects of early modern theatre and its plays, including the texture of the writing itself and the transmission of texts from author to stage, printer and, ultimately, the hands of the modern editor. The study focuses on the methods by which roles might be memorized in a repertoire with a rapid turnover of plays, and reviews the evidence for rehearsal strategies, the likely procedures of training ('enskillment') for players – particularly boy players – and the management of the traffic of the stage.

Tribble deals convincingly with the methods that can be attributed to a theatre in which custom underlay innovation, and which in retrospect has much in common with that of actors in 'weekly rep' during the first half of the twentieth century. The work would be supported by similarities in the kind of roles (the actor's line of parts) and generic kinship between situations and plotting in different plays. However, in the early modern playhouse the means of support available during performance (once the actor's study of his own parts was achieved) would not be directly comparable to those of the old 'rep' system or the contemporary professional theatre. To take one notable example, also relevant more generally to the use of documentary evidence in the historiography of theatre, Tribble points out that the surviving 'plots', while 'often maddeningly incomplete', should be understood as not designed 'to solve problems for scholars four hundred years later, but to help a company put on a play' (p. 50). In detailed discussion of Shakespearian examples, Tribble shows how the patterning of verse in early plays provides the speaker with what Sir Philip Sidney called 'seats of memory', in contrast to the irregular nature of later writing in which these have become 'musical chairs' (pp. 84–5). An analysis of the staging of the sequence of 2.2 – 2.4 in the Folio text of *King*

Lear examines the logic of exits and entrances on a stage without scenic locations but with at least two means of access. Whatever semiotic significance is attached to the lateral doors and the 'discovery space' it seems useful to recognize, as Tribble does, that the stage doors 'function something like the large levers in a power station' – preferred to the smaller buttons that would do the job just as well because they make the operators' actions more easily defined. Considered in this light, they can be seen as 'anchor points that coordinate movement across the stage', and 'a critical component in the management of the workspace on the stage, simplifying choice, perception and computation . . . for both players and playgoers' (p. 44). These are useful insights, and it is unfortunate that Tribble does not find space for further examinations along these lines of particular speeches, scenes and sequences in the Shakespeare canon.

Cognition in the Globe asserts the importance of avoiding the 'deficit model' in statements about the effectiveness and accomplishments of boy players, by which inappropriate emphasis has been placed on the degree to which they might come short of the female performer of their roles. In this, Tribble insists on the significance of apprenticeship in the training of young actors and the specifics of 'action' among the rhetorical skills to be acquired. The study reinforces our understanding of the skills of both actors and audiences, and the cognitive resources they shared. In this respect it brings a fresh perspective to the evidence for early modern performance, tending to qualify but not discount the work of earlier investigators and to support such accounts as that of John Astington in *Actors and Acting in Shakespeare's Time*, with its attention to 'the art of stage playing'. Astington provides a valuable account of attitudes to acting – what was expected of the performers – as well as the techniques they needed to acquire. His chapters on apprenticeship, and the importance of oratory in education, can be usefully complemented by Tribble's specifically cognitive approach. The connection between the traditions of oratorical training and the theatre is located by Astington in 'its inescapable stress on the living, physically present speaker as a potent means of communication' (p. 46). Essentially, the lesson to be gathered from this is that oratorical skill was a positive and prized element of the actor's art in the period, rather than some kind of throwback to a less 'realistic' (let alone 'naturalistic') method. After all, the actor who delivers Priam's speech at Hamlet's request simulates feeling in himself and elicits it from his hearers to the point where the self-professed connoisseur Polonius can take no more of it.

The subtitle of David Roberts's biography of Thomas Betterton sets out its agenda: 'the greatest actor of the Restoration stage'. Roberts is able to go further than other modern accounts by way of substantiating this accolade, and the analyses of evidence for the actor's performances are persuasive and authoritative. This calls for a skill in locating 'the individual amid the rules and the roles' (p. 23). He offers correction to the impression of Restoration acting given by Stephen Jeffries's play and the feature film based on it: the result of Betterton's studies of sculpture and painting 'was neither artificiality nor the eruption of naturalism imagined in *Stage Beauty*, but a quality Betterton was uniquely prepared for by upbringing, physique and ability to supply: craftedness, the projection of performance as a discipline, a visibly mastered skill that strove to chime with its surroundings whether they were a painted version of St James's Park or the real thing' (p. 57).

The private and public dimensions of the actor's life are vividly evoked and brought into fruitful relation with one another throughout. On a cultural-historical level, Betterton, Roberts proposes, 'lent stability to the term "gentility" by reconciling the values of royal service with the virtues of bourgeois industry' (p. 38). The transition from 'courtier-manager' to 'actor-manager' in the management and artistic policies of the theatre is identified and explored. The biography thus offers an alternative approach to Restoration theatre that complements and partially displaces the emphasis on sexual politics that has arisen from an understandable degree of attention to the figure of the actress. The evidence for a degree of continuity with the pre-Commonwealth stage is weighed, in particular the famous passage in Downes's *Roscius Anglicanus* asserting that the role of King Henry VIII 'was so right and justly done' because Betterton was 'instructed in it by Sir William [Davenant], who had it from old Mr Lowin that had his instructions from Mr Shakespeare himself'. Roberts takes issue with Joseph Roach's interpretation of this as a claim for quasi-royal descent inimical to 'true performance', insisting that the concept of authenticity meant different things to different actors 'within the context of professional discipline' (p. 95). The text of Davenant's *Macbeth* is characterized as 'baroque theatre' with due attention to its emphases, omissions and theatrical techniques, while the production's shifting scenery 'provided a new medium for expressing the play's shifting world of shadows, its oscillations between the intimate and the public, the domestic and the uncanny' (p. 111). The performance culture of the period is evoked in terms immediately intelligible to the modern reader: Drury Lane, Roberts writes, was 'the sort of place where you might hope for Mozart but get Lloyd Webber' (p. 116).

The status of *The Tempest* as a 'cultural mediator from its inception to the present' guides Virginia Mason Vaughan's volume in the Manchester University Press 'Shakespeare in Performance' series. The diverse developments in performance of the play's various dynamics – father/daughter, master/slave and king/subject – are related to their cultural and historical moments, and to the ways in which theatre manages to find out new directions while rediscovering older ones. A stable text in itself, by virtue of its existence in a Folio version unchallenged by rival contemporary witnesses, *The Tempest* has been hospitable to an extraordinary variety of innovations by the authors, actors and directors who have acquired plantation of its isle.

It would be hard to formulate a pithier description of the post-colonial turn in *Tempest* productions than Vaughan's description of post-war approaches:

In the years following World War II when most of Europe's colonial subjects gained their independence, productions restored lines that had frequently been cut and placed more emphasis on Prospero's relationships to Caliban and Ariel: Prospero's authority was diminished not simply by the exploration of his subconscious drives . . . but also by challenges to his rule and the necessity that he relinquish power to his subordinates.

(p. 98)

Vaughan points out that one consequence of Aimé Césaire's 1967 adaptation, *Une Tempête*, lay in its underscoring of 'colonial situations that were mere suggestions in Shakespeare's romance, but were to become a theatrical mainstay to the end of the twentieth century' (p. 105). In parallel with this tendency, and beginning in the 1940s, was the emergence of the play as 'the vehicle of choice for independent, avant-garde directors who saw in Shakespeare's Prospero a mirror image of their own creative powers' (p. 127). This chimes with the mid-Victorian actor-managers' appropriations, in which Macready, Phelps and Charles Kean played the magician on-stage as well as behind the scenes. The play of power in and around *The Tempest* takes on a new dimension with the advent of the female Prospero, most notably Vanessa Redgrave at Shakespeare's Globe in 2000 and Helen Mirren as the grammatically correct Prospera in Julie Taymor's 2010 film. Taymor has filled in the back-story of her maternal mage with additional lines, and the elaborate special effects effectively return the play to the Restoration theatre's inventive re-visions, characterized sympathetically by Vaughan when she describes Pepys as responding to the 1674 version 'the way we might to the contemporary effects of the Cirque du Soleil' (p. 26).

Vaughan is unafraid to ask the awkward questions raised by some of the post-war, post-colonial productions: what exactly is the impact on audiences of multicultural or intercultural performance, and do radical interventions necessarily lead to enlightenment? George C. Wolfe's 1995 production for the New York Shakespeare Festival may have been dismissed by some reviewers as a 'hodge-podge' or 'mish-mash' of techniques (Bunraku puppets, Indonesian shadow play, Caribbean carnivals and more, much more) but 'audiences thronged to the sell-out performances'. (Some credit for this goes to the appearance as Prospero of Patrick Stewart, better known to many playgoers in the mid-1990s for his appearance in *Star Trek* rather than as a Shakespearian actor.) Arguably, as one critic expressed it, Wolfe was 'making a point about the clash of cultures in the burgeoning age of colonialism' (p. 114). Whatever audiences made of the eclecticism, the central performances exuded a degree of bitterness (including the 'attitude' displayed by Miranda) that lent the play an unusual urgency and emotional charge. Was the excitement generated by the razzmatazz of styles relevant to this? Vaughan's account, with careful balancing of reviewers' responses, suggests that at least it did not obscure it. Stewart returned to the role in 2006 in a production for the RSC by Rupert Goold, set this time above the Arctic Circle, with a 'robot-like' Ariel, Caliban as (or suggesting) an Inuit native of the isle (or floe?), Prospero (angry again) as a shaman, and the performers of the masque more like the weird sisters than classical deities. My impression, seeing the show in Stratford and at the University of Michigan, was that some audience members were disturbed by what they took to be a colonization of Inuit culture; others simply failed to find any connection between these trappings and the story being told. (Were any Inuit available for comment?) Vaughan reflects that the production 'exemplified the limits of postcolonial productions in the metropolitan world, where the predominantly white audience's experience of colonial rule is conceptual rather than visceral' (p. 121).

A valuable aspect of this study is the thoughtful consideration given to the relationship between the excitements of aesthetic eclecticism and the cultural politics of productions in their own time and place, as well as their dialogue with an English seventeenth-century text. Just as it is no diminishment of the achievements of Edward Said to suggest that elements of European orientalism have not invariably worked to the Orient's disadvantage, it is surely the case that without some important appropriations – such as Artaud's reaction to Balinese performance – European theatre would be impoverished, even when (as with Artaud) the borrowed techniques have been misunderstood. Citing Dennis Kennedy's and Tetsuo Kishi's critique of Yukio Ninagawa's *Tempest* (seen in London in 1992), an 'exotic cultural cocktail', Vaughan suggests that 'twenty-first century audiences who live in a global, intercultural world served by wilfully eclectic mass media' can benefit from the combination of a translation of the original text with a mixture of Japanese and European theatrical techniques (p. 161).

In *Murder Most Foul* David Bevington begins his account of '*Hamlet* through the Ages' with magisterial chapters on the play's textual complexities, its probable staging in its own time and the likely responses of its original audiences to such aspects as revenge, the status of the ghost (and the question of Purgatory), the incestuous nature of the queen's second marriage and the likely consequences of his bloody actions for the hero in the afterlife. The insights afforded here are accompanied by an emphasis on the play's openness. Starting from the proposition that 'what we call *Hamlet* . . . will hardly stay still, even as a text', the dynamic, shifting quality of its interpretation through the centuries is celebrated, and Bevington makes sure that the reader is not allowed to relax into the notion that an appeal to evidence of attitudes held in its own time would somehow foreclose debate. Elizabethan spectators 'were given good reason to conclude, if they chose to agree, that Hamlet's story ends justly and providentially' (p. 75). This 'if' is characteristic of the presentation of the play as 'pre-eminently a play in which questions are asked but not fully answered' and supports Bevington's contention that it remains 'a more controversial play today than ever before' (p. 6). The characterization of subsequent performances (to adopt Jonathan Miller's useful concept) and literary reincarnations is both concise and comprehensive. The statement that the Hamlet of the Romantics 'possessed a delicate poetic sensitivity through which he [was] attuned to the great mystery of things' (p. 107) is characteristic of Bevington's summaries, and the division of chapters is effective and thought-provoking. The category of 'post-modern' *Hamlet* makes a serviceable though not unexamined

framework for the discussion of the play's interpreters since 1980.

The impressive energy and inclusiveness of Bevington's survey make it an appropriate introduction to the play for general readers as well as students, but like any account of a text's entire critical and performance history, there are times when it seems somewhat rushed: once the twentieth century's contending theories and practices break out and the new media begin to effloresce, the pace quickens. Even so, space is found for effective discussion of a varied range of *Hamlet* events, from the epic expansiveness of Branagh's 'full-length' film to the skilful parody of Olivier's in *The Last Action Hero* and the astringent brevity of Richard Curtis's *Skinhead Hamlet*, in which Polonius's attempt to pluck out the heart of Hamlet's mystery gets impressively short shrift: 'Oi you!' – 'Fuck off, granddad!' ('*Exit Polonius*', unsurprisingly.) In 199 pages of text and a further 12 of closely packed and useful notes, it is hardly surprising that a few points of fact are questionable. Did Irving really excel 'more as a manager than as an actor'? Is it correct to state that the costuming in Kevin Kline's modern dress *Hamlet* for New York's Public Theatre (recorded for PBS and available on DVD) was 'traditional'? But these are relatively insignificant objections. The dominant qualities of the book lie in the formidable scope, the liveliness of Bevington's writing and the impression that is given of a play open to the talents.

Courtney Lehmann's volume in Methuen's *Screen Adaptations* series, *Shakespeare's 'Romeo and Juliet'*, fulfils the brief to examine the 'relationship between text and film' by devoting its first 80 pages ('Literary contexts') to the specifics of the text, establishing the status of Shakespeare's *Romeo and Juliet* itself as an adaptation, and alerting readers to the existence of different versions of the play in its own time. This facilitates a discussion of subsequent adaptations that demonstrates the continuing life of the play rather than measuring them against a textual ideal. In this respect, Lehmann's work shares the quality of Vaughan's account of *The Tempest*'s afterlives and Bevington's approach to *Hamlet*. Appropriately, after a concise guide to the 'brief history of *Romeo and Juliet* on screen', the first film to be discussed in detail is *West Side Story*. The chapter, with impressive attention to detail, charts the musical's reorganization of the play and the dramatic effect of its musical numbers, with appropriate emphasis on the vexed question of its treatment of racial and social issues – the controversial casting of 'white' performers in Latino/Latina roles and the relationship between youth culture of the 1950s and its depiction on screen and on stage. Lehmann proceeds to an account of two other dominant film versions, directed by Franco Zeffirelli and Baz Luhrmann. Perceptive commentary on the scene-by-scene (sometimes shot-by-shot) detail is framed in a developing critical argument that deftly alerts the reader to theoretical issues and cultural contexts. Lehmann has an acute and sympathetic eye and ear for popular culture and its uses. Luhrmann embeds his retelling in the aural and visual world of a 'youth' audience, and the film calls for the kind of specificity in recognition and interpretation that is offered here. Camera and editing technique and *mise-en-scène* are analysed carefully. The identification of the film's effect in generating 'the spectator's sense of being unstuck in space and time' is impressively responsive and concise, the kind of connection between the general and the particular that characterizes the critical method of the book: it sends the reader back to the film to try out the idea for her- or himself.

There is a persuasive elegance in Lehmann's conduct of her argument. The section on *West Side Story*, after discussion of the film's final moments and the citation of Peter Conrad's comments on them, ends with the suggestion that 'the silence [of the closing moments] might be read as an act of conscientious objection, indeed, a refusal to allow music to pacify us in the face of tragedy', and that 'we, too, remain "baffled" by the reality that *West Side Story* is a show that plays not in a distant "somewhere", but, rather, everywhere, all the time, around the world – and we have yet to figure out a way to avert the tragic ending' (pp. 132–3). The open question offered here prepares the ground for the sections that follow, which cumulatively suggest that responses to the strategies of

the films are always provisional. Openness is not taken as an excuse for abdicating critical responsibility: the second element of the title *William Shakespeare's Romeo + Juliet* suggests (and invites) radical rethinking while the author's name asserts cultural authority. As Lehmann observes, rather than catalogue its aesthetic failures, a 'more productive project', which she then engages in, is that of 'calibrating the degree to which Luhrmann's film resists easy insertion into the postmodern "legend" that originality is impossible' (p. 169). Writing at this level in a 'series book' is especially valuable for the intended student audience. Lehmann's approach asserts by example that the textual questions of the play are important (and not just a section that might be skipped in the introduction to an edition); that theoretical issues have a life that is shared with the object of study rather than being an optional or avoidable extra; and that detailed reading of the film-as-text is a rewarding skill.

Patrick Cook's *Cinematic Hamlet* discusses four feature films – those of Olivier, Zeffirelli, Branagh and Almereyda – with a formidable degree of attention to the analyses of previous critics that complements the meticulousness of his readings. The 'Introduction' offers an extended justification of the methodology adopted that is useful in itself, although once the ground has been cleared for the theoretically minded, the exposition of the films' ways and means makes only infrequent reference to such matters. Watching these *Hamlets* through Cook's eyes is a stimulating and informative experience. As is inevitable in such work, there are moments of what Horatio warns against as enquiring too curiously. Does Olivier's Ophelia really 'unwittingly' justify her brother's warning about opening her 'chaste treasure' when she fondles him 'too suggestively, grabbing his phallic dagger and reaching into the purse at his waist'? (p. 32). Given Olivier's interest in Freud (O heavy burden!), which manifests itself explicitly in Hamlet's dealings with his mother, anything is possible, but sometimes a dagger is just a dagger. On the other hand, Cook's explication of Almereyda's invocation of the uncanny (in the titles on Horatio's bookshelves) is both lucid and to the point.

Another moment of possible over-interpretation, this time of a different kind, occurs in the account of the delayed first appearance of Branagh's Hamlet in the play's first court scene. Here the camera tracks to find him down a 'corridor' that 'does not exist in other shots that take in its location', an effect (Cook writes) that may 'confuse' the viewer's 'understanding of the prince's place in relation to the king and queen'. This strikes Cook as a sign that 'the disorientation of the ghost scene' has 'entered Elsinore's "clean, well-spoken place" before Hamlet learns of his father's return' (p. 113). Is this the reaction of all spectators of the film? Moreover, is the 'corridor' read as an architectural feature rather than as an undefined space? (In fact it is the gap between the bleachers on which the courtiers sit and the mirrored wall of the hall.) This is one of the few moments when Cook's careful attention to the flow of the film's unfolding sequences may be said to falter. In general the reader is guided with a sure hand through the succession of shots and scenes with exemplary attention to what is shown and may be inferred. A persuasive account is given of the overall effect of each film, the nature of its characterizations and the trajectory of its plot. It is a mark of the high quality of the writing and critical acumen that equal justice is done to the different film-making techniques of the 'conventional' versions as well as the elaborate post-modern density of Almereyda's *Hamlet*. That film's allusive richness has made it a rewarding hunting-ground for subtle and hawk-eyed commentators, but Cook is able to elicit new elements of its referential dimensions – the sense it cultivates of 'belated and retroactive understanding' in spectators and characters – while noting the sophisticated cinematic effects that operate on another, more immediately accessible level. The skill of his account can be represented by his description of Hamlet's approach to the Hotel Elsinore:

A low-angle power shot of [its] impressive metal and glass entry, its absolutist symmetry reinforced by a centrally placed doorman, is followed by a closer shot of one of its revolving doors. The spinning door both informs us that Hamlet has entered and, in its visual echo of the Denmark Corporation logo, presents one more sign of the power he will confront. (p. 166)

Like Cook's reading of the advertising signs visible in the Times Square location, and his analysis of Hamlet's approach to the making and recycling of images, this is illuminating critical writing of the first order.

Michael Dobson's *Shakespeare and Amateur Performance: A Cultural History* is 'a history of how successive groups of people have committed themselves to incorporating [the plays] into their own lives and their immediate societies' (p. 2). Outdoor Shakespeare in England, with its tendency to favour plays that depict events 'all of which might have happened on wet grass' (p. 182) takes its place alongside more exotic locations and casting decisions. These include the 1834 production of *The Merry Wives of Windsor* in St Vincent, part of 'a charade by which the soldiers and colonists alike pretended to be in Merry England, or at worst in the West End, while actually in the midst of tropical fever and incipient discontent' (p. 127) and the appearance of Ulysses S. Grant as Desdemona in a Texas military encampment preparing for action against the Mexicans in 1845. Grant, it is recorded, 'looked very like a girl, dressed up' (p. 131). The staging of plays by British prisoners of war in Nazi Germany during the Second World War raised some awkward questions, not least when the script in question was *The Merchant of Venice*. With no disrespect to the inmates of these camps or disregard for the deprivations they suffered, it could be argued that here, as in the more prominent example of the arts in occupied France, the maintaining of cultural tradition bordered on collaboration.

Closer to home (for this is predominantly an account of English amateur Shakespeare), the tendency of amateur performance to shade off into its professional counterpart – more of a continuity, perhaps, than a strict demarcation – is represented both by the shared custom of outdoor production (often calling on the reserves of good will of audience and actors alike) and the fact that

early in the twentieth century some regional repertory theatres owed their origins to amateur societies: in a number of cases the parent organization
had a say in the choice of repertoire and appointment of actors. Shakespeare takes his place in the
spectrum of pageants and pageant-like activities
celebrated in fiction by Virginia Woolf in *Between
the Acts* and E. F. Benson in *Mapp and Lucia*. Events
of this kind, as Dobson observes, 'integrate specific
places within the nostalgic vision of the nation, its
history and its culture' (p. 187). With pardonable
tartness, performances at Shakespeare's Globe in
Southwark, which opened in 1997, are characterized in terms of the amateur aesthetic. In an age of
international instantaneously available mass media,
writes Dobson, 'one thing which an enormous
international audience evidently still wants from
[Shakespeare] is a globally recognisable, incipiently
Luddite, perennially amateurish, deeply parochial
Englishness. Complete with the weather' (p. 196).
This captures a not insignificant aspect of audiences at Shakespeare's Globe, but does not adequately characterize the totality of the theatre's
work to date. It has the ring of a critic who has
suffered. Generally, though, Dobson is sympathetic
to the efforts of the genuine amateurs. In his 'Conclusion', after describing a performance celebrating the 475th anniversary of Cambridge University Press of *A Midsummer Night's Dream* (featuring
the newly discovered though silent and somewhat
disgruntled fairy Knotgrass), Dobson declares that
'there are many things to do by way of interpreting, understanding and sharing a Shakespeare play
that are completely beside the point compared to
actually living in it for a while' (p. 216).

On 17 October 1863 Charlotte Cushman
appeared in *Macbeth* – Abraham Lincoln's favourite
play – at Grover's National Theatre in Washington DC. Alexander Nemerov's *Acting in the
Night: 'Macbeth' and the Places of the Civil War*
is a feat of dense extrapolation. At a superficial
level (and for a less adventurous or unconventional
book) it would have helped if Lincoln had been
watching Shakespeare's play, rather than *Our
American Cousin*, when John Wilkes Booth shot
him on the evening of 14 April 1865. That kind

of coincidence, welcome to less abstruse enquir-
ers, would not have served Nemerov's purpose.
Invoking Wallace Stevens ('Anecdote of the Jar')
and Heidegger, his project is 'to see how a performance of the play might have shaped the world
around it' (p. 1). By the end of his introduction, the
intention has become at once better defined and
vaguer, a paradoxical effect of alternating sharp and
soft focus that recurs almost page by page:

The tale I tell here about that day is finally that of the
performance's power to shape, or not to shape, the world:
its power to say something meaningful precisely when it
failed to send a message as planned – when it showed us
instead the world of resonant emptiness and dislocation,
with here and there a shaded spark or glow that helps us
see the performance, too, as a glittering fragment of that
lost day.   (p. 6)

This seems to mean that anything goes – or perhaps not. Nevertheless, the impressive range of
materials for the quest includes diaries, newspaper reports, photographs, paintings and other
artefacts, and along the way Nemerov offers perceptive accounts of all of them, including a suggestive reading of Cushman's performance and
personality.

The result is an often perplexing blend of scholarship, historiography, fiction, poetry and meditation. At times fiction seems to be embarrassed by
history (more conventionally construed) and vice
versa, and the terms of poetic licence are extended
too far. In his account of Cushman's Lady Macbeth, Nemerov expatiates on the significance of
the statuesque in the actress's performances and in
accounts of their reception. However, the over-
reading (or reading alongside the data) soon takes
over. We are told that when Cushman's Lady Macbeth spoke her invocation to 'murdering ministers'
in the play's fifth scene, 'she probably incarnated
this world-stopping power of the aesthetic to inhale
the universe, to internalize it as a sculpturally dense
form', and that 'Like the ingredients of the witches'
brew . . . the far-flung world of randomness might
gather in the cauldron of the play's incantations,
creating an all-but-sculptural image of memorable
thickness' (p. 35). The review cited as evidence

here is hardly sufficient to support what Nemerov makes of the alleged effect, and is hardly specific to Cushman: the statement could have been written by William Winter (or other critics) about many other performances of the passage. The book abounds in such effects, amounting to sleight-of-metaphor, together with insistent uses of 'might' and 'must have' and continual assertions of possibilities and probabilities. At times the effect is one of bathos, a combination of over-reading and easy paradox: 'October 17 was an ordinary day in Washington – full of the social malfeasance and ordinary devastating unhappiness that the evening's grand performance would so earnestly try to exclude' (p. 96). Life in Washington, one gathers, was pretty depressing, an 'ordinary' sensation of desperation fitfully mitigated by artistic endeavour. When the president sees a firework display, 'to Lincoln these garish illuminations might only have shown the loneliness of the faces they lit' (p. 77). Again, they might not have: did Lincoln mention anything? After a while the reader realizes that such objections are beside the point, and that to benefit from the book's many insights one just has to entertain conjecture for a while to an extent normally not warranted in historical writing.

Points are often stretched to the limit: the presence at the performance of Alexander Dallas Bache, 'a long-time member of the Smithsonian Board of Regents and vice-president of the Sanitary Commission', may well suggest 'the goals shared by the performance and the museum' (p. 129). The pages that follow take the reader to the design of lecture auditoria, the measurement of earthquake waves – 'Like Shakespeare in the mid-nineteenth-century imagination, Bache comprehended vastness' – and lighthouses, in which Bache had a degree of professional interest. As a consequence of the last of these,

> The great burning swirl of *Macbeth* on October 17 – a wavering of existential torches beneath the glitter of a thousand gaslights – might then have struck Bache more as the epitome of progress than as a swaying above the abyss. The theater interior would glow with a concentrated light as if it held the light of the entire nation that night. (p. 133)

Is it mean-spirited to observe that passages such as this are exactly the kind of writing one spends a good deal of time and ink persuading students to eschew? Have we established what makes those torches 'existential'? Would the effect on Bache have been the same if he had been watching any other play with effects of dark and light? Nemerov's writing impresses with the plenitude of its learning, often fascinating, but frustrates by its frequent defiance of the rules of evidence accepted by those of us who are, by implication, unable to soar at his pitch. Sophisticated and persuasive readings of specific phenomena or art objects – for example, Randolph Rogers's statue *Nydia, the Blind Flower Girl of Pompeii* or Winslow Homer's painting *In Front of Yorktown* – command respect, while passages like those quoted above inspire incredulity. But if one took out the 'might have' element, in many respects the contextualization of the play in this time and place would be more persuasive. As it stands, it can be read as a series of learned meditations on aspects of art and life, a contribution to the study of American culture and a play's place in it.

North American Shakespeare performance of more recent vintage is compendiously represented by two volumes of the *Directory of Shakespeare in Performance* edited by Katherine Goodland and John O'Connor for Palgrave: volume 2 deals with Canada and the USA, from 1970 to 1990, while volume 3 continues 'since 1991'. Together, the volumes total some 2,200 pages of excerpted reviews, giving a vivid and far-ranging picture of the 'complexity and contradiction' that, as Goodland states in her introduction to volume 3, characterize the formidable quantity (and often, quality) of what is on offer. 'Veneration and nostalgia coexist with innovation and patriotism.' Patriotism? The clue to this lies in Goodland's opening paragraph, which describes 'something like a return of the native' in the final decades of the twentieth century: 'Shakespeare was nudged from his pedestal and his plays began appearing with increasing frequency in college auditoriums, tents, decaying mansions, forest and fields, their four-hundred year old poetry tripping off the tongues of Canadian and American actors no longer self-conscious about their accents and before enthusiastic, unabashedly grateful audiences' (p. xi). The 'patriotism' lies to some extent in the matter of accent, the dethroning of the 'Shakespearian' voice and the concomitant opening up of the plays to diverse regional and ethnic groups.

Like the dominant assumption that Shakespeare is for the people (and ideally by and with them), the acceptance that Shakespeare can be heard without recourse to British-sounding pronunciation is a legacy of such tireless agitators as Joseph Papp, whose work for (and by and with) the Public Theater and the New York Shakespeare Festival was celebrated in 2009 by the long-delayed appearance of *Free for All*, co-authored by Kenneth Turan, with major contributions by many of Papp's collaborators and, not least, Papp himself, billed as co-author with the assistance of Gail Merrifield Papp. The subtitle says it all: *Joe Papp, the Public and the Greatest Theatre Story Ever Told*. The 'story' is indeed some sort of epic, Papp, multi-tasking, omnipresent and endlessly combative, struggled to achieve his goals: getting Shakespeare on trucks out into the open spaces and, eventually (and under cover of darkness) into Central Park; establishing the Delacorte Theater for the free Shakespeare seasons; and building an empire of performance spaces with productions sometimes directed by him but always billed as Papp presentations. Meanwhile, across the continent, Shakespeare festivals burgeoned in the postwar years, their doings chronicled not only in the local or regional press but also in *Shakespeare Quarterly* and *Shakespeare Bulletin*, often only briefly but at least placing them on record for a wider readership. The volumes edited by O'Connor and Goddard gather together many of these productions, an excellent starting point for students and researchers trying to get to grips with their number and variety.

As for patriotism, in its more acceptable form of proper pride in local and national achievement, the card is played in the title of Paul Barry's *A Lifetime with Shakespeare: Notes from an American Director of all 38 Plays*, a work that reflects its author's industry, expertise and imagination over 60 years'

engagement with the playwright he tends to call 'Master Will'. The cards are laid out early on when the author announces 'I have always resented producers who hire British directors for American Shakespeare productions out of some misguided notion of British superiority, especially when they try to impose British dialects as "proper speech"' (p. 10). There may be other reasons for hiring particular directors, and it is to be hoped that sounding British is no longer one of them, but there is no arguing with the proposition that 'the best speech for Shakespeare is that which is most understandable to the audience', which for Barry means the use of 'American dialects or speech that is as dialect-free as possible' so as to make 'performances clear and accessible' (p. 11). Barry's productions, in particular those directed for the New Jersey Shakespeare Festival, appear to exemplify the priorities of accessibility and liveliness (in comedy) or directly experienced emotion (in tragedies) that characterize much of the North American festival scene. (Production photos from the comedies, like the one on the cover of Barry's book, seem to privilege boisterousness.) Access to non-equity extras surely informs his recommendation that 'the director must give Claudius sufficient bodyguards and keep them close at hand through all the Hamlet/Claudius scenes so that it is clear that Hamlet couldn't get within 20 feet of Claudius without being chopped down' (p. 36). (This does suggest that Hamlet need not ponder too much why, knowing this thing's to do, he doesn't seem to get anywhere with doing it.) *A Midsummer Night's Dream* is 'the perfect Shakespeare-in-the-Park show', a conclusion shared by Michael Dobson's account of amateur 'wet-grass' performances. This is pragmatic Shakespeare, with the director of *Henry IV* plays advised to 'cast these plays well and stay out of the way' (p. 151). There are some idiosyncratic observations (*The Comedy of Errors* 'can't be trusted') and more than one appeal to an engaging variant on Coleridge's phrase, 'the wilful suspension of disbelief' (a new criminal offence?).

Barry's lively and engaging descriptions of work with the plays, valuable in themselves if taken with the occasional pinch of salt, paint an attractive picture of popular, festive Shakespeare. A similar effect, from a slightly different angle, is achieved in Michael Flachmann's *Shakespeare in Performance: Inside the Creative Process*, whose subtitle refers to the work of the Utah Shakespeare Festival, and the author's labours as its dramaturg. His credits also include teaching as a university professor and working with the Oregon Shakespeare Festival, the La Jolla Playhouse and many other Shakespeare-producing companies in the USA. The chapters include programme essays, talks given on a variety of occasions about the process of production and the plays themselves, and round-table discussions. The description of the founding and – in particular – funding of the first Utah festival season in 1962 is especially valuable for the light it sheds on the difficulties faced by companies of this kind: the relationship between sponsors, artistic directors, amateur enthusiasts and professionals is complex. The greater part of Flachmann's book deals, as announced, with the production processes. This is not an author likely to advise casting and then getting out of the way as a directorial strategy. Its tone is subtler and more tentative than Barry's but the picture of available, intelligible and intelligent performances is similarly appealing.

These are works that discuss the day-to-day activities of North American theatre festivals, and along the way their authors consider the underlying issue of who is to be addressed by the plays. Once one has said 'American audiences', a start has been made, but a good many questions have been begged. Ayanna Thompson's *Passing Strange: Shakespeare, Race and Contemporary America* is an important contribution to the discussion of just that subject. Lively, acute and innovative in its engagement with the specific territory and cultures of its title, it has implications that range beyond them, with its examination of the assumptions behind 'non-traditional casting' and multicultural theatre that bears on practice and interpretation beyond the United States. The argument about 'colour-blind casting', whose classic formulation was the exchange between Robert Brustein and August Wilson in four successive issues of *American Theatre* in 1996, turns on the appropriateness of casting people of colour in roles that do not express (in one view, suppress) their ethnic identity and can thus be seen as a form of colonialism rather than a sign of progress in a multicultural society. Thompson's account of the published policies of theatre companies reveals a – perhaps unsurprising – claim to be extending their activities to ever wider audiences while allowing actors of colour access to the full range of dramatic roles. The underlying assumption has to be the definition of Shakespeare as being 'for all time' rather than an age, which takes the reader back to Thompson's experience of her students' reaction to racist elements of the plays' dialogue, characters or situations: disparaging references to Jews or 'Ethiopes' elicit an appeal to the pressure of the text's historical moment as a strategy to maintain his claim to universal relevance, making the author both 'timely' (the 'Soul of the age') and timeless. Thompson's book is characterized by an incisive and clearly articulated sense of the contradictions inherent in Shakespearian performance, balanced by generous appreciation of the work it can do as part of an intervention in society, and her analyses range from mainstream theatrical productions to 'Classroom-inspired Performance Videos on YouTube' (the title of her seventh chapter) and 'reform programmes' in prisons and hospitals. The appropriation of blackface performance by actors of colour raises questions about the complex relations between intention, practice and reception in the (re)production of texts composed for all-male actors who cross-dressed and used blackface as necessary. Responses to the effect of the language like the statement that 'Shakespeare sounds as good as a black artist, female artist, and so forth' (p. 67) have a 'destabilizing' effect that by reversing the polarity of familiar terms offers a fresh perspective on discussion of the plays as active elements of a culturally diverse society.

Thompson's book, with its clearly reasoned and open-minded discussion of complex ethical dimensions of performance and skill in addressing new kinds of Shakespearian activity in the ever-developing electronic media, is an outstanding contribution to its field. It has important messages for both practitioners and commentators, and will undoubtedly prove to be one of the year's most influential works.

WORKS REVIEWED

Astington, John, *Actors and Acting in Shakespeare's Time: The Art of Stage Playing* (Cambridge, 2010)

Barry, Paul, *A Lifetime with Shakespeare: Notes from an American Director of All 38 Plays* (Jefferson, NC and London, 2010)

Bevington, David, *Murder Most Foul: 'Hamlet' Through the Ages* (Oxford, 2011)

Cook, Patrick, *Cinematic 'Hamlet': The Films of Olivier, Zeffirelli, Branagh and Almereyda* (Athens, OH, 2011)

Dobson, Michael, *Shakespeare and Amateur Performance: A Cultural History* (Cambridge, 2011)

Flachmann, Michael, *Shakespeare in Performance: Inside the Creative Process* (Salt Lake City, 2011)

Goodland, Katherine and John O'Connor (eds.), *A Directory of Shakespeare in Performance: Volume 2, Canada and USA, from 1970 to 1990* (Houndmills and New York, 2010); *Volume 3: Canada and USA since 1991* (Houndmills and New York, 2011)

Lehmann, Courtney, *Screen Adaptations: Shakespeare's 'Romeo and Juliet': The Relationship between Text and Film* (Methuen, 2010)

Nemerov, Alexander, *Acting in the Night: 'Macbeth' and the Places of the Civil War* (Berkeley, CA and London, 2010)

Roberts, David, *Thomas Betterton: The Greatest Actor of the Restoration Stage* (Cambridge, 2010)

Thompson, Ayanna, *Passing Strange: Shakespeare, Race and Contemporary America* (New York, 2011)

Tribble, Evelyn B., *Cognition in the Globe: Attention and Memory in Shakespeare's Theatre* (Houndmills and New York, 2011)

Turan, Kenneth and Joseph Papp, with the assistance of Gail Merrifield Papp, *Free for All: Joe Papp, the Public and the Greatest Theatre Story Ever Told* (New York, 2009)

Vaughan, Virginia Mason, *Shakespeare in Performance: 'The Tempest'* (Manchester, 2011)

3. EDITIONS AND TEXTUAL STUDIES
reviewed by ERIC RASMUSSEN

When Stanley Wells first asked me to take on this review essay in 1998, I was honoured and terrified. I was then an assistant professor with two editions of Marlowe to my credit (both co-edited with David Bevington, my dissertation supervisor) but nothing resembling an international reputation and absolutely no idea how I might go about critiquing the editions and textual studies prepared by established figures in the field. However, I knew I could collate. So instead of critiquing arguments, I criticized texts. I read every new edition against its quarto or folio copy-text and often found numerous errors in the text and especially in the collations. The resulting errata have been the foundations of my reviews for the last fourteen years; and my longevity as a *Survey* reviewer (most serve only three-year stints) may be due in some part to the *schadenfreude* that readers feel when distinguished editors make howling errors.

Having often condemned the lack of attention to textual detail, I now find myself, in my final review, compelled to declare that two recent editions – Anthony B. Dawson and Paul Yachnin's Oxford *Richard II* and John Jowett's Arden 3 *Sir Thomas More* – are textually perfect (or very nearly so).

The same cannot be said, however, for John Drakakis's Arden 3 edition of *The Merchant of Venice*, which contains numerous errors of various sorts. In the text at 2.9.18 for 'so I have' read 'so have I'; at 3.2.231 for 'E'cr' read 'Ere' (that is, the contraction of 'before' rather than 'ever' in Bassanio's 'Ere I ope his letter, / I pray you tell me how my good friend doth'). The claim that the emendation at 3.1.67 SP is unique to this edition is manifestly wrong; the identical emendation was made in the Oxford Complete Works. There are two dozen errors in the collations,[1] the most serious of which occurs at 4.1.49 where the textual note records the emended reading adopted from Dyce, and gives a historical collation of readings from Pope, Johnson, Capell and Malone, but does *not* provide the reading of the quarto text that is being emended. A syllabic 'è' is omitted at 2.9.60 ('And of opposed natures. What is here?'). On page 113, for 'After 1603' read 'After 1605'. At 1.3.174, a verse line is indented too far, and there's a stray blank line in the middle of the Clown's speech at 2.5.39.

The noble aim of Drakakis's edition is 'to contribute to an understanding of the internal workings of prejudice – all prejudice – and to its eventual eradication'. Drakakis's explorations of the meaning of Venice in the Elizabethan imagination and the theological objections to usury are admirable. But the carelessness of the text and collations is evident in Drakakis's introduction as well, especially in his handling of quotations from previous scholars. (The observations that follow emerged from discussions with my longtime editor, Arthur Evenchik, to whom I am much indebted.) Take, for instance, the following passage from Albert Memmi's *Racism*, in which Memmi discusses the nature of anti-Semitism:

The claim has been made that anti-Semitism is totally different from racism. I would disagree. Although it does not resemble any other form of social exclusion, it is not any less a variety of racism for all that. *It is a racism specific to its object.* That is, anti-Semitism is racism directed against Jews. As such, it has a particular character that it acquires from its particular victims and from the original relation between them and those who attack them.[2]

In context, Memmi's sentence '*It is a racism specific to its object*' makes perfect sense. But Drakakis obscures its meaning by quoting it out of context:

What makes the *Merchant of Venice* a racist text is that the dramatic action turns upon an acknowledgment of *difference* that is, in Albert Memmi's pregnant phrase, used 'against someone to one's own advantage' (Memmi, 52),

at the same time that it fuels a judgemental laughter. Not merely that, but Memmi goes on to describe it as '*a racism specific to its object*' (67) in which the persecutor and victim exist in close proximity to each other as both 'familiar and alien'.

In the second sentence, the 'it' in 'Memmi goes on to describe it' has no clear antecedent; one must consult Memmi's book to understand that the antecedent should be 'anti-Semitism'. Moreover, readers may wrongly conclude from Drakakis's account that Memmi is commenting directly on *The Merchant of Venice*.

Drakakis has long complained about 'the modern tendency to normalise speech prefixes, resting, as it appears to, upon some stable conception of dramatic "character"'. This tendency, he once wrote, forces editors of *The Merchant of Venice* to make a choice: 'either "*Shylock*" or "*Jew*". No edition yet has been prepared to follow the instability of Q1 (1600) *and* F1 (1623) in representing *both*'.[3] It seemed clear that Drakakis was laying the groundwork for his Arden 3 edition, which one assumed would be the first to preserve the instability of the speech headings in the original texts. And, indeed, his introductory essay speaks of the necessary 'reconsideration of a group of speech prefixes

---

[1] 1.1.73 for '*Anthonio*' read '*Anthonio,*'; 1.3.7 should record that Q1 lines 'me? / Shall'; 1.3.48 for 'Shyloch' read '*Shyloch*'; 2.1.0.1 for 'Morochus' read '*Morochus*'; 2.2.9 for 'Fia' read '*fia*'; 2.4.1–3 for 'time' read 'time,'; 2.5.5 for 'apparaille' read 'apparraille'; 2.5.8–9 for 'me' read 'me,'; 2.5.26 for 'Ashwensday' read 'ashwensday'; 2.5.41 for '*Iewes*' read 'Iewes'; 2.6.46–8 for 'runaway' read 'runaway,'; 2.7.62–4 for 'scrowle' read 'scrowle'; 2.8.39 for 'Slumber' read 'slumber'; 2.9.0.1 for '*Seruitor*' read 'Seruiture'; 3.2.69 for 'bell.' read '*bell.*'; 3.2.135 for 'pleasd' read '*pleasd*'; 3.2.154–5 for 'account' read 'account,'; 3.2.216,1 for '*after* 217' read '*after* 218'; 3.4.53 for 'tranect' read 'Tranect'; 3.5.57 for '*Clown*' read '*Clowne*'; 4.1.29 Q1 reading for 'state' read 'states'.

[2] *Racism*, trans. Steve Martinot (Minneapolis, 1999), pp. 67–8.

[3] Quoted from Drakakis's 'Afterword' to *A Concise Companion to Shakespeare and the Text*, ed. Andrew Murphy (Oxford, 2007), pp. 229–30. See also '"*Jew*. Shylock is my name": Speech Prefixes as Symptoms of the Early Modern', in *Shakespeare and Modernity: Early Modern to Millennium*, ed. Hugh Grady (London, 2000). Leah Marcus's Norton Critical Edition of the play (New York, 2006) was the first to preserve the Q1 variant speech-headings in a modernized text.

that editorial tradition has hitherto sought to stabilize' and asserts that 'the present edition reinstates a tension that these variant speech prefixes disclose and that editors and commentators have long overlooked'. But, utterly surprisingly, Drakakis opts to normalize all of Shylock's speech headings to '*Jew*'.

There are sound bibliographical reasons for believing that Shakespeare used the speech heading '*Iew*' throughout his manuscript, and that the Q1 compositors only employed '*Shylock*' (or an abbreviation) when supplies of italic '*I*' ran short. Drakakis's edition deserves to be acknowledged as the first in history to emend to '*Iew*' throughout. He makes similarly motivated decisions with the speech headings '*Clown*' (rather than '*Launcelot*' or '*Lancelet*') and '*Giobbe*' (rather than '*Gobbo*'), but his discussion of the speech heading variation is muddled in places. For instance, Drakakis argues that, faced with shortages of italic '*I*', the compositor 'substituted . . . an italic capital "*G*" for "*I*" in what was in the manuscript either "*Iobbe*" or "*Gobbe*"'. But if the manuscript indeed read '*Gobbe*', then the compositor obviously did not substitute another letter; he was simply setting the spelling he found in his copy.

There's a sense of backing and filling in Drakakis's prose, in which successive sentences often begin with 'But' or 'However'. In the passage below, one is especially puzzled by the transition from the second sentence to the third, unhelpfully mediated by 'However':

The variety of performances in the USA, on the continent of Europe and as far as Australia serves to illustrate the extent to which the *Merchant of Venice*, perhaps more than most Shakespearean texts, was submitted to the forms and pressures of the time. But, as John Gross observes, within the USA between the First and Second World Wars, it was the traditional portrayal of Shylock that distinguished performances (Gross, 168ff.). However, the 1925 Old Vic production drew attention once more to the figure of Portia, with Edith Evans in the role out-acting Baliol Halloway's Shylock.

There are real difficulties with some of Drakakis's glosses, such as the note on the passage at 2.3.15–21:

Farewell, good Lancelet.
Alack, what heinous sin is it in me
To be ashamed to be my father's child!
But, though I am a daughter to his blood,
I am not to his manners. O, Lorenzo,
If thou keep promise I shall end this strife,
Become a Christian, and thy loving wife.

In glossing 'strife', Drakakis writes 'antagonism or opposition (*OED* 1), but, in Jessica's case, divided loyalties; she is the victim both of her father's antagonism, which she assumes will extend to Lorenzo but which she thinks marriage will resolve, and also of the opposition between Jew and Christian'. This is bewildering. First, how could Jessica's marriage 'resolve' her father's antagonism towards Lorenzo? Does Drakakis mean that Jessica expects Shylock to accept Lorenzo as a suitable son-in-law once he has recovered from the shock of the elopement? If this is her hope, then why does she steal from Shylock in the act of fleeing his house? The theft would certainly seem to dim the chances of an ultimate reconciliation. Second, it's unclear what Drakakis means when he says that Jessica 'is the victim . . . of her father's antagonism'. Is he saying that Shylock is antagonistic *towards* Jessica, and that she thinks this hostility 'will extend' *from her* to Lorenzo? Or is he saying that Jessica is the victim of Shylock's antagonism towards Christians, since (1) it causes him to behave in ways that she finds morally repugnant, or (2) it makes him (at least for now) hostile to the idea of her dating one? In response to the first issue, I see no way in which Jessica's marriage could resolve 'her father's antagonism' towards anyone. It can only resolve Jessica's own internal 'strife' – between shame (at being her father's child) and guilt (over her disloyalty), or between her biological relationship to Shylock ('I am a daughter to his blood') and her revulsion towards his conduct ('I am not [a daughter] to his manners').

There is another seeming misinterpretation concerning Jessica in the gloss on the Clown's speech at 3.5.1–5:

Yes, truly, for, look you, the sins of the father are to be laid upon the children; therefore, I promise you, I fear you. I was always plain with you, and so now I speak my agitation of the matter. Therefore be of good cheer, for, truly, I think you are damned.

Drakakis glosses 'be . . . damned' as 'a parody of John 16.32–3; Jessica is *damned* because she has forsaken her father'. But surely this is not a correct reading: she is damned because her father's sins will be laid upon her.

With the publication of Dawson and Yachnin's *Richard II*, the Oxford Shakespeare series of individual plays is now complete – and this glorious edition is (so to speak) a crowning achievement. With grace and elegance, Dawson and Yachnin write of the subtle changes from the first tetralogy to the second: 'a new note is audible, a more nuanced representation of the political conflicts of the English past'. Since theirs is the first major edition to appear since Paul Hammer's important reconsideration of the performance of *Richard II* commissioned by Essex's men,[4] Dawson and Yachnin seize the opportunity to set the record straight: it now seems clear that the Essex 'rebellion' did not intend to dethrone Elizabeth and put Essex in her place but 'to restore the Earl's favour with the Queen, convince her to dismiss some of her closest counsellors (men who were Essex's enemies), and pave the way for James VI of Scotland to become Elizabeth's heir'. Although Essex and his men 'clearly interpreted the play as supporting their position', it is 'very doubtful that they saw the performance as a call to arms'. Rather, they would have viewed it as portraying 'the kinds of injustices that Essex felt he was the victim of, wrongs perpetrated by an arbitrary monarch'. Dawson and Yachnin characterize the play's performance by the Lord Chamberlain's Men on 7 February 1601 as 'a local and not terribly important side event', and observe that the queen could not have been too upset with the acting company since they performed at court only a few weeks later.

But given this newly revised history, what is one to make of Queen Elizabeth's reported claim that the 'tragedy' of Richard II was 'played forty times in open streets and houses'? Dawson and Yachnin set about parsing the queen's words and conclude that 'it seems most likely that the "playing" she is referring to is that of the Earl himself, a man much given to extravagant displays, and has little to do with performances on the part of Shakespeare's, or any other company'.

Dawson and Yachnin's text is perfect until, heartbreakingly, the final word (the '*Exeunt*' at 5.6.62 does not appear in Q1, so should have been bracketed and collated).[5] There are four minor errors in the textual notes.[6] This edition seems to be of two minds regarding textual matters. On the one hand, the editors assert that they are intentionally leaving out textual minutiae or relegating them to the notes, so as not to bore general readers: 'We have tried to keep the present discussion of the text as succinct as possible, omitting or consigning to footnotes elements that might bog down our presentation.' On the other hand, they acknowledge that since many editorial decisions 'are necessarily subjective, readers interested in this aspect of the play are encouraged to pay close attention to the collation (the small print below the play text on each page)'. And since 'reading the collation, which is written in a kind of shorthand, takes some practice', they provide some sample entries as 'a brief guide to an interested but potentially confused reader'. (Dawson and Gretchen Minton did this as well in their Arden 3 edition of *Timon*; it is a wonderful idea.)

In reviewing John Jowett's edition of *Sir Thomas More* in the second edition of the Oxford Complete Works (2005), I suggested that its elaborate system of typographical markers, deployed to indicate various sorts of revision in the manuscript, might be off-putting for some readers. One has no such concerns about Jowett's new Arden 3 edition of the play, which presents the text in a manner that both

---

[4] 'Shakespeare's *Richard II*, the Play of 7 February 1601, and the Essex Rising', *Shakespeare Quarterly*, 59 (2008), 1–35.

[5] Dawson and Yachnin break ranks with other single-text Oxford editions in that 'all editorial changes or additions to the stage directions in our text are placed in square brackets'.

[6] At 2.1.0.1–2 the assertion that '*and attendants*' is '*not in* Q1' perhaps overlooks the copy-text's '*&c.*'; 2.1.186–8 for 'please.' read 'please,'; 4.1.159 for 'here' read 'heere' in the Q4 reading; 5.1.333–4 for 'daie' read 'daie.'

acknowledges and records the tangles in the heavily revised manuscript while still enabling the reader to experience the text as a play. Although one might question a few of Jowett's editorial decisions – such as using bracketed blank lines in the modernized text to mark lacunae in the manuscript, and then assigning line numbers to the blank lines (e.g. 2.40, 2.121–2, 3.76, 6.240, 7.64, 9.96, 17.48) – these are small quibbles that do not detract from his magnificent achievement.

As the first stand-alone edition of *Sir Thomas More* in a Shakespeare series, the Arden 3 marks a milestone in the play's acceptance into the canon – despite the spate in the 1990s and 2000s of what Jowett characterizes as 'a number of allusive but deeply sceptical comments as to Shakespeare's involvement in *Sir Thomas More*' which 'appeared in key Shakespeare studies commonly without reference to any specific counter-evidence'. Jowett details at some length the 'elaborate and now convincing' case for Shakespeare's authorship of the Hand D pages. He is more tentative about the identification of Henry Chettle as one of the original authors: 'There remains a strong suspicion that Munday did not write the Original Text alone' but since 'the clearest potential evidence is too conflicting for confident pronouncement to be made on the pattern or even presence of collaboration' he must 'leave the question unresolved'. However, there appears to be a disconnect between the caution of this authorship discussion and the confident pronouncement on the edition's title-page: 'Original Text by Anthony Munday and Henry Chettle'.

Given the limited critical discourse on the play and an even more limited record of theatrical performance, the fact that Jowett's edition runs to 522 pages is nothing short of amazing. His introduction provides a wealth of contextual information, reminding readers, for instance, of the central role that drama played in More's life: his sister Elizabeth was married to John Rastell, author of the early morality play *The Four Elements*; their daughter Joan married the interlude writer John Heywood. As a page in the household of Cardinal Morton, More would have interacted with the chaplain, the playwright Henry Medwall.

Jowett is especially good at guiding one through the Byzantine complexities of *The Book of Sir Thomas More* and reconstructing the possible stages in its revision, which he accurately characterizes as 'not so much an outcome as a collaborative process' in which Hand C served as 'project manager' and at least two of the 'play-doctors' were somewhat removed from the process: 'Heywood and Shakespeare worked separately, presumably in their homes, without immediate access to what was being written elsewhere.' (Jowett does not further pursue the provocative issue he raises about the physical space in which collaborating playwrights worked. Presumably, if any of the *More* authors had shared a writing 'chamber', as apparently Kyd and Marlowe did, the process of revision might have been more immediately interactive.)

Jowett's text is letter perfect. The sole error I found in the collations is utterly trivial: Jowett credits the Oxford Complete Works as the first to correctly read a bit of punctuation in Shakespeare's Hand D passage in which a superscripted full stop is followed by a normal full stop: 'straingers·.' (note 146 on p. 414). However, the Oxford transcription actually has a comma rather than a second full stop.[7]

Gabriel Egan, who has for the last decade been my counterpart as reviewer of editions and textual studies for OUP's *The Year's Work in English Studies*, reports that his new book, *The Struggle for Shakespeare's Text: Twentieth-Century Editorial Theory and Practice*, had its genesis in a negative reader's report several years ago on his proposal to prepare an edition of *All's Well that Ends Well* for the Internet Shakespeare Editions project. (I felt a bit queasy learning this: it was I, in my capacity as general textual editor for the ISE, who sent Egan that rejection letter, although I didn't write it.) In turning down the proposal, the anonymous reviewer argued that Egan was misguidedly basing his editorial principles on those of the New Bibliography,

---

[7] The cross-references are off in two places: on p. 125 for 'p. 486' read 'p. 490'; on p. 487 for 'pp. 99–102' read 'pp. 97–99'; the citations to 'Greg' on p. 346n and p. 352 must surely be to 'Jenkins²'; in the footnote on page 459 for 'Andrew Murphy' read 'John Drakakis'.

which had recently been, in the reviewer's opinion, thoroughly discredited. The reader's report spurred Egan to undertake a detailed exploration of both 'the intellectual tradition of the New Bibliography' and 'the growing influence of its detractors since the 1970s'. The result, which includes material from his annual *YWES* reviews, is one of the best histories to date of Shakespearian editing over the last century.

Coupled with this historical narrative is an extended defence of 'certain aspects and certain varieties of New Bibliography' which Egan deems 'essential to future editorial work'. He is especially critical of the 'currently fashionable dispersal of agency', which he seeks to displace by insisting upon 'authors as the main determinants of what we read'. Egan has no patience for post-structuralism but the similarity of his critiques of major textual critics may prompt his readers to lose patience with him: Paul Werstine's work is 'disabled' by the 'fashionable late 1980s postmodern caricature of authorship'; Randall McLeod's work is similarly undermined by his 'post-structuralist preference for dispersal, contradiction and multiplicity'. So, too, Stephen Orgel's work is 'weakened by overstatement of the post-structuralist insights, such as the claim that the author becomes "a curiously imprecise, intermittent and shifting figure" when Christopher Marlowe's last name is misspelled "Marklin" on a quarto title page for *Doctor Faustus*'. (Orgel's point in this instance may be weakened by the fact that the printed name on the 1616 title page in question was the abbreviation '*Mar.*' to which the '*klin*' was later added in pen and ink. But that's bibliographical oversight, not post-structural overstatement.)

This is not to say that Egan's arguments are made *ad hominem*. Quite the contrary: sometimes he gives scholars a local habitation but no name. Witness the odd discussion of Ann Thompson and Neil Taylor's Arden 3 *Hamlet* in which they do not appear:

The successor to Jenkins's Arden Shakespeare in the same series followed the Oxford editors' instinct in offering fully edited versions of Q2 and F (as well as Q1) in the shared belief that F probably contains Shakespeare's changes made when copying out fairly. However, these Arden editors treated differently . . .

The leitmotif that emerges from Egan's book is that some New Textualists 'let theory trump evidence every time'. Thus, the scholars who come in for praise here are those whose work might be characterized as less driven by theory (Jowett is 'brilliant'; Urkowitz 'passionate'; Rasmussen 'ingenious').

My dear friend Sonia Massai will be taking on the mantle of *Survey* reviewer next year, and I wish her well. This has been and continues to be an exciting time in Shakespearian textual studies, and one wonders if Egan's work might be a harbinger of a coming turn away from theory and towards renewed analytical rigour in bibliographical studies. We will be eagerly turning to Sonia's reviews to find out.

WORKS CITED

Egan, Gabriel, *The Struggle for Shakespeare's Text: Twentieth-Century Editorial Theory and Practice* (Cambridge, 2010)

Munday, Anthony, Henry Chettle, Thomas Dekker, Thomas Heywood, and William Shakespeare. *Sir Thomas More*, ed. John Jowett, Arden 3 (London, 2011)

Shakespeare, William, *The Merchant of Venice*, ed. John Drakakis, Arden 3 (London, 2010)

Richard II, ed. Anthony B. Dawson and Paul Yachnin, Oxford Shakespeare (Oxford, 2011)

INDEX

INDEX

INDEX

INDEX